Turkey

James Bainbridge
Brett Atkinson, Jean-Bernard Carillet, Steve Fallon, Joe Fullman,
Virginia Maxwell, Tom Spurling

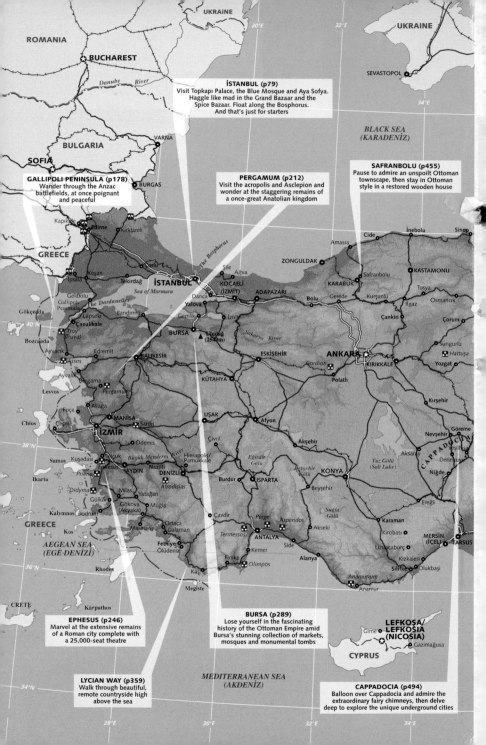

İSTANBUL (p79)
Visit Topkapı Palace, the Blue Mosque and Aya Sofya.
Haggle like mad in the Grand Bazaar and the
Spice Bazaar. Float along the Bosphorus.
And that's just for starters

SAFRANBOLU (p455)
Pause to admire an unspoilt Ottoman
townscape, then stay in Ottoman
style in a restored wooden house

GALLIPOLI PENINSULA (p178)
Wander through the Anzac
battlefields, at once poignant
and peaceful

PERGAMUM (p212)
Visit the acropolis and Asclepion and
wonder at the staggering remains of
a once-great Anatolian kingdom

EPHESUS (p246)
Marvel at the extensive remains
of a Roman city complete with
a 25,000-seat theatre

BURSA (p289)
Lose yourself in the fascinating
history of the Ottoman Empire amid
Bursa's stunning collection of markets,
mosques and monumental tombs

**LEFKOŞA/
LEFKOSIA
(NICOSIA)**

LYCIAN WAY (p359)
Walk through beautiful,
remote countryside high
above the sea

CAPPADOCIA (p494)
Balloon over Cappadocia and admire the
extraordinary fairy chimneys, then delve
deep to explore the unique underground cities

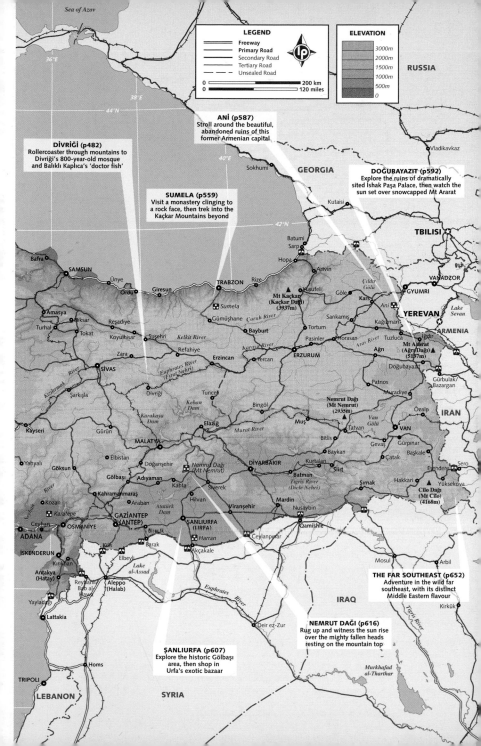

LEGEND

Freeway
Primary Road
Secondary Road
Tertiary Road
Unsealed Road

0 ———— 200 km
0 ———— 120 miles

ELEVATION

3000m
2000m
1500m
1000m
500m
0

ANİ (p587)
Stroll around the beautiful, abandoned ruins of this former Armenian capital

DİVRİĞİ (p482)
Rollercoaster through mountains to Divriği's 800-year-old mosque and Balıklı Kaplıca's 'doctor fish'

DOĞUBAYAZIT (p592)
Explore the ruins of dramatically sited İshak Paşa Palace, then watch the sun set over snowcapped Mt Ararat

SUMELA (p559)
Visit a monastery clinging to a rock face, then trek into the Kaçkar Mountains beyond

THE FAR SOUTHEAST (p652)
Adventure in the wild far southeast, with its distinct Middle Eastern flavour

NEMRUT DAĞI (p616)
Rug up and witness the sun rise over the mighty fallen heads resting on the mountain top

ŞANLIURFA (p607)
Explore the historic Gölbaşı area, then shop in Urfa's exotic bazaar

Sea of Azov

RUSSIA

GEORGIA

Vladikavkaz

Sokhumi

Kutaisi

TBILISI

VANADZOR

GYUMRI

YEREVAN

Lake Sevan

ARMENIA

Batumi
Sarp
Hopa
Artvin
Rize
TRABZON
Yusufeli
Göle
Kars
Ani
Kağızman
Çıldır Gölü

Bafra
SAMSUN
Ünye
Ordu
Giresun
Gümüşhane
Mt Kaçkar (Kaçkar Dağı) (3937m)
Sumela
Bayburt
Tortum
Sarıkamış

Amasya
Niksar
Reşadiye
Koyulhisar
Suşehri
Refahiye
Bayburt
Pasinler
Horasan
Aras River
Tuzluca
İğdır

Turhal
Tokat
Kelkit River
Çoruh River
Karasu River
Erzincan
Tercan
ERZURUM
Ağrı
Mt Ararat (Ağrı Dağı) (5137m)
Doğubayazıt

Zara
SİVAS
Euphrates River (Fırat Nehri)
Gürbulak/ Bazargan

Şarkışla
Divriği
Tunceli
Keban Dam
Bingöl
Muş
Nemrut Dağı (Mt Nemrut) (2935m)
Patnos
Muradiye

Kayseri
Gürün
MALATYA
Karakaya Dam
Elazığ
Murat River
Bitlis
Van Gölü
Tatvan
VAN
Özalp
IRAN

Yahyalı
Göksun
Elbistan
Doğanşehir
Nemrut Dağı (Mt Nemrut)
DİYARBAKIR
Kurtalan
Baykan
Gevaş
Gürpınar
Başkale
Sero

Kozan
Kahramanmaraş
Gölbaşı
Adıyaman
Kahta
Siverek
Batman
Siirt
Tigris River (Dicle Nehri)
Şırnak
Hakkari
Cilo Dağı (Mt Cilo) (4168m)
Yüksekova
Esendere

Karatepe
Araban
GAZİANTEP (ANTEP)
Hilvan
Viranşehir
Mardin
Nusaybin
Qamişhle

Ceyhan
OSMANİYE
ADANA
Atatürk Dam
ŞANLIURFA (URFA)
Birecik
Harran
Ceylanpınar
Mosul
Arbil

İSKENDERUN
Kilis
Barak
Elbeyli
Lake al-Assad
Akçakale
IRAQ
Kirkük

Kırıkhan
Antakya (Hatay)
Reyhanlı
Bab al-Hawa
Aleppo (Halab)
Euphrates River
Tigris River

Yayladağı
Lattakia
Deir ez-Zur
Murkhafad al-Tharthar

TRIPOLI
Homs

LEBANON
SYRIA

On the Road

JAMES BAINBRIDGE COORDINATING AUTHOR

Cappadocia's fairy chimneys and tuff valleys are extraordinary enough seen from the ground. Clapping eyes on them from a hot-air balloon (p510) at up to 1000m above terra firma, with snowy mountains glistening in the distance, added to the thrill. Equally amazing was gliding through the valleys, then rising to discover another balloon or a strange structure like Uçhisar Castle (p507).

JEAN-BERNARD CARILLET Here I'm standing amid the ruins of Ani (p588), a stone's throw from the Armenian border. This site is truly exceptional, but only a handful of visitors were there to enjoy it – this is why I love eastern Anatolia, it's still largely unspoiled. Ani is one of the most poignant and eerie places I've ever seen. I can feel something mystical here.

BRETT ATKINSON More than two decades after first visiting the wonderful ruins at Afrodisias (p329), I was surprised to again have the site of the ancient city almost to myself. A few hours away the centuries-old marble streets of Ephesus were bustling with hundreds of contemporary visitors, but at Afrodisias it was just myself, a few skittering lizards, and the friendly family from Seattle who took this photo.

STEVE FALLON Gallipoli (p178) is at once a peaceful and a disturbing place, the anguished cries and stench of burning flesh still palpable nigh on to a century later. I was happy to call it a day and leave Pink Farm Cemetery behind to get on with the Job. Just too many ghosts.

JOE FULLMAN Here I am, standing on the edge of a Roman theatre at the Asclepion (p214) in Bergama. Some sections of the theatre are gleaming, new and restored, while others are old and crumbling, a fitting description for this part of Turkey. Considering the quality of its ancient ruins, Bergama probably doesn't get the number of visitors it deserves, although that does allow for some easy, quiet exploring.

VIRGINIA MAXWELL My son Max and I arrived in İstanbul on the first day of the International İstanbul Tulip Festival and decided to see the famous tulip display at Hıdiv Kasrı (p123). The huge garden around this gorgeous villa was full of tulips of every possible variety and colour. Sultan Ahmet III, known for his tulipmania, would have been beside himself with excitement!

TOM SPURLING Kayaköy (p367) is much like Turkish history in a bottle, plus it's as pretty as a kid ghost. Any place fit for a good novel is worth hanging out in too, and so I did, over a few fine bottles in the Levissi Garden and Kaya Wine House.

For full author biographies see p707.

Turkey Highlights

Pristine beaches and fairy-tale Cappadocian landscapes, buzzing bazaars and laid-back Turkish ways, cosmopolitan İstanbul, remote rural villages and crumbling ruins: Turkey offers delights and attractions for all budgets and tastes. Travellers have been coming here for millennia and many have been moved to wax lyrical about the treasures they have discovered. We asked our authors, staff and readers what they love most about Turkey. Share your Turkey highlights at lonelyplanet.com/turkey.

CHRIS BEALL

1 THE TURQUOISE COAST UNDER SAIL

A group of us spent the most relaxing week of our lives aboard a *gület* which sailed from Fethiye (p354) around the Blue Lagoon, Butterfly Valley and the 12 islands. The fresh seafood we caught was the highlight! We fished and snorkelled to our heart's content. A week wasn't long enough...

Sarah Grimstone, traveller, Australia

BUYING CARPETS

It's inevitable you'll buy some sort of carpet when you're in Turkey. So why not enjoy the experience (p669). Find a shop owner you like and let them take care of you; experience real hospitality with apple tea, great chatter and Turkish delights.

Keely Sonntag, traveller, Australia

3

EOIN CLARKE

DIANA MAYFIELD

2 FAIRY CHIMNEYS

Even after an exhausting overnight bus trip, the sight of Göreme (p497) in Cappadocia is unlike any other. Its fairy chimneys and Flintstones-like setting is amazing. We extended our stay here, we enjoyed it so much. The cave pensions are a highlight, hiking through the valleys is a must, and there are many historic sites in the area.

Warren Harrower, traveller, Australia

4 ENTER A ROMAN CITY AT EPHESUS

Explore the best-preserved Roman city on the Mediterranean coast, Ephesus (p246), with its two-storey library and intact streets in a nice setting.

DALLAS STRIBLEY

Wildurb, traveller, Switzerland

DIEGO LEZAMA

5 FIRST VIEWS OF İSTANBUL

In most cities, the journey from the airport to the centre is eminently forgettable, but not in İstanbul (p79). No matter how many times I've made the trip, it never fails to excite and astound. I stumble exhausted and jet-lagged into a waiting taxi and then…the revelation. There's nothing to equal the sighting of the first grand mosque atop a hill, and then another – and another! And when you see the Golden Horn laid out before you, you know you're in a magical place.

Peter Handsaker, traveller, Australia

MARK PARKES

6 ANZAC COVE, GALLIPOLI

A tranquil sprawl of sand that runs along a coastline of the deepest blue (p178). It's hard not to feel connected to this piece of history. Let the cool water wash over you. Walk the hills and inhale the different scents of wild herbs. There is a peacefulness that transcends the notoriety of this area. Unforgettable.

cortimcdonald, traveller

SUMELA MONASTERY

Carry on up the winding road past the main track leading to Sumela (p559) and you're rewarded with beautiful views across the valley of the monastery clinging improbably to a sheer cliff face. A little further on, a less busy second track leads along a narrow ridge to Sumela. Either way, I try and get to the monastery when it opens so I've got the best chance of experiencing the haunting location by myself.

Brett Atkinson, Lonely Planet author, New Zealand

JEAN-BERNARD CARILLET

7

8

BUTTERFLY VALLEY

Drifting up by boat to untouched, idyllic Butterfly Valley (p368) will take your breath away. In a small cove set between two cliffs you'll be welcomed by beautiful waters and a pleasantly rocky shore, with plenty to explore on land. And, with a bit of luck, lots of privacy.

Karen Burrows, traveller, New Zealand

9

THE RUINS OF ANİ

Ani (p587): fabled city of a thousand churches, now a ghost city floating in a sea of grass. Ruins evoke images of a once great Armenian capital. The stunning panoramas include a distant snowcapped Mt Ararat. Could that tiny speck be Noah's ark?

natsphotos, traveller

DAWN AT NEMRUT DAĞI

Two-thousand-year-old monuments of stone heads (p616) and mythological figures along with the most breathtaking dawn – watch the sun rise while sipping traditional Turkish tea. You will not be disappointed.

Yasar, traveller

10

ANDREW BURKE

ISLAND IDYLL

Bozcaada (p200) is one of the last areas of the world unspoilt by tourism. Friendly people, no hassle, local wines and seafood, clean sandy beaches and a sea so clear. A gem.

linann, traveller

11

WILL GOURLAY

DALLAS STRIBLEY

ARCHAEOLOGICAL SURPRISES
Walk to the Lycian tombs cut into the rock above Fethiye (p352) – small versions of Jordan's Petra.
Wildurb, traveller, Switzerland

Contents

Regional Map Contents

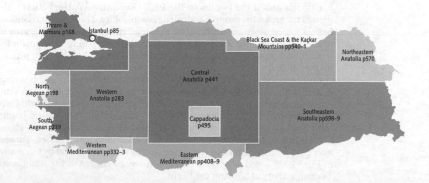

Destination Turkey

Connecting Western Europe and the Balkans to Central Asia and the Middle East, Turkey has been a kingpin in Eurasian history. Silk Rd traders, Alexander the Great, Julius Caesar and Mongolian horsemen were just a few of the folk who passed through the country, while the Ottoman sultans used İstanbul as the capital of an empire that sprawled from Budapest to Baghdad.

Given this historical prominence, it's unsurprising that Turkey conjures up strong images. There's Turkish cuisine (did someone mention kebaps?), Mediterranean and Aegean beaches, İstanbul's minaret-punctured skyline, and exotic bazaars and hamams. But the home of Troy and Ephesus also boasts more Greek and Roman ruins than Greece and Italy, and unique landscapes such as fairy chimney–dotted Cappadocia and Nemrut Dağı (Mt Nemrut), with its decapitated stone heads. This is the place to get stuck into activities ranging from kayaking over an underwater city to watching dervishes whirl.

It's also a country where modernisation is gathering momentum. The Marmaray subway line under the Bosphorus and a 1¼-hour rail link between Ankara and Konya are set to open in the coming years. Technology-loving Turks make the country the world's third-highest user of MSN Messenger, with a third of its 75 million inhabitants chatting.

None of the chat is buzzing with excitement about the EU; Turkey became a candidate for membership back in 1999 and many think 2020 will pass before it joins. Nonetheless, Prime Minister Erdoğan's AKP government is working doggedly towards accession, key issues being freedom of speech and resolution of the Cyprus dispute.

Against this broadly progressive background, 2008 was a tumultuous year. The AKP's opponents brought a dramatic closure case against the government, accusing it of 'nonsecular activities' for changing the law banning women's headscarves in schools and workplaces. Political meltdown was avoided when the Constitutional Court ruled against the closure, but many Turks remain uneasy about the government's pro-Islamic leanings.

Another event (that could have been a scene in a Turkish *Da Vinci Code*) was the indictment of conspirators in the Ergenekon plot, which aimed to oust the government by force. İstanbul was also rocked by an attack on the US consulate, in which six people died in a gun battle, and by two bombs that killed 17 and wounded 150.

Officials linked the bombs to the PKK (Kurdistan Workers Party), although the separatist group has denied responsibility. The Kurdish rebellion has simmered down in southeastern Anatolia and the mountainous area is open to travellers, but the Turkish army has been attacking PKK positions in Kurdish Iraq's Zap Valley. Some fear this will destabilise the most peaceful part of Iraq.

More positively, Turkey is improving its relationship with neighbouring Armenia. President Abdullah Gul became the first Turkish leader to visit Armenia, in a day trip that coincided with the countries' soccer World Cup qualifying match. It was an appropriate occasion for the historic jaunt; most Turks love soccer even more than technology, and the İstanbul clubs Galatasaray and Fenerbahçe have one of the world's great rivalries. Turkey won 2-0 – a better result than its disappointing semi-final defeat by Germany in Euro 2008 – and as good an excuse as any to engage in the traditional Turkish activity of blowing car horns.

'There's Turkish cuisine, Mediterranean and Aegean beaches, İstanbul's minaret-punctured skyline, and exotic bazaars and hamams.'

Getting Started

Travelling in Turkey is a breeze thanks to the laid-back charm of the locals, bus transport that's second to none, and the sheer volume of accommodation options, from friendly cheap-as-chips backpackers to immaculately groomed boutique guest houses. During the height of peak season or on public holidays you should book ahead; at other times you can generally turn up and find your first accommodation choice awaiting.

WHEN TO GO

Spring (April to May) and autumn (September to October) are the best times to visit, since the climate will be perfect for sightseeing in İstanbul and on the Aegean and Mediterranean coasts. It will be cool in central Anatolia, but not unpleasantly so. Visiting before mid-June or after August may also help you avoid mosquitoes. If your primary drive is for beach-bumming, mid-May to September is perfect for the Aegean and Mediterranean coasts, if a little steamy out of the water. The Black Sea coast is best visited between April and September – there will still be rain but not as much of it. Head to eastern Turkey from late June to September, but not before May or after mid-October unless you're prepared for snow, road closures and bone-chilling temperatures.

See Climate Charts (p658) for more information.

With the exception of İstanbul, Turkey doesn't really have a winter tourism season (see p18 for more details). Most accommodation along the Aegean, Mediterranean and Black Sea and in some parts of Cappadocia is closed from mid-October until late April. These dates are not set in stone and depend on how the season is going. High season is from May to September, and prices are at their peak; many western Mediterranean businesses double their prices during the period.

Anticipate crowds along all coastal areas from mid-June until early September. You will need to plan ahead when travelling during the four- or five-day Kurban Bayramı festival (p664), as banks shut and ATMs may run out of cash. Also, try not to visit the Gallipoli Peninsula around Anzac Day (25 April) unless it's particularly important for you to be there at that time.

COSTS & MONEY

Turkey is no longer Europe's bargain-basement destination, but it still offers good value for money. Costs are lowest in eastern Anatolia, and Cappadocia, Selçuk, Pamukkale and Olympos still offer bargain prices. Prices are highest in cities such as İstanbul, İzmir and Ankara, and in the touristy coastal cities and towns, particularly in Mediterranean regions such as between Dalaman and Antalya. In these places you can get by on as little as TL60 per day, provided you use public transport, stay in pensions, share bathrooms and eat out at a basic eatery once a day (add extra for entry to sights). Away from İstanbul and the Aegean and Mediterranean coasts, budget travellers can survive on TL40. Throughout the country for just over TL100 per day you can upgrade to midrange hotels with private bathrooms and eat most meals in restaurants. In all cases, when you come to move on, it skews your spend upwards if you are using an intercity bus; the prices are almost as high as in some parts of Europe, eg TL30 to TL35 from İstanbul to Çanakkale. With cash at your fingertips you can live like a sultan from about TL300 per day, enjoying boutique hotels, taking occasional flights, and wining and dining every day.

TOURING TURKEY IN WINTER

Unlike other Mediterranean hot spots, Turkey doesn't have a winter tourism season. However, for some travellers winter is the best time to visit İstanbul: expect snow and chilly temperatures, but you get to enjoy the sights without the tourist press, and the touts are too busy savouring the low season to bother you in earnest.

All restaurants and hotels remain open year-round in İstanbul, and in big, nontouristy cities such as Ankara and İzmir where hotels cater primarily to business travellers. It's worth booking ahead throughout the year in such cities, as accommodation can fill up with business people.

Even during a mild winter most hotels and restaurants along the Aegean and Mediterranean, and many in Cappadocia, close from mid-October to late April. Forget about choice – you may have to stay in the one place in town that's open.

Deep snow is a standard feature of the eastern Turkish winter, with mountain passes regularly closed and buses delayed. Even some airports may close because they lack radar equipment. The central and western Anatolian winter is more fickle. One year you can be picnicking in the Ihlara Valley in January, the following year subzero temperatures, deep snow and lethal ice make it impossible to venture further than the nearest shop.

If you're lucky enough to find a hotel open in winter, you'd be well advised to verify whether the heating is turned on before checking in. If the hot water comes from solar panels, beware – like pipes, the panels freeze up in winter.

We have quoted prices in Türk Lirası, or Turkish lira (TL; p666) and occasionally in euros or US dollars, depending on which currency operators quote their prices in.

TRAVELLING RESPONSIBLY

Since our inception in 1973, Lonely Planet has encouraged our readers to tread lightly, travel responsibly and enjoy the magic independent travel affords. International travel is growing at a jaw-dropping rate, and we still firmly believe in the benefits it can bring – but, as always, we encourage you to consider the impact your visit will have on both the global environment and the local economies, cultures and ecosystems.

HOW MUCH?

Short dolmuş trip TL1.50

Hürriyet Daily News
TL1.50

Old man's *şapka* (hat)
TL10

T-shirt TL10

100km by bus TL25

Getting There & Away

There are a number of low-emission ways to get to Turkey from Europe. You can catch ferries and hydrofoils from Greek islands such as Rhodes to Aegean and Mediterranean Turkish ports including Bodrum and Kaş. Ferries also link Brindisi and Ancona in Italy with Çeşme, and Sochi in Russia with Trabzon. Buses cross the borders between Turkey and most of its neighbours, but the train is more romantic. Express services (in name only) connect İstanbul with Thessaloniki (Greece), Bucharest (Romania; connected to Budapest, Hungary) via Sofia (Bulgaria; convenient for Serbia), Aleppo (Syria) and even Tehran (Iran). See p677 for more information.

Slow Travel

Although they don't receive good press compared with Turkey's efficient bus network, the country's trains are gaining popularity with slow travellers such as the Man in Seat 61 (see boxed text p690). Try an 'express' train trip like the 1900km, two-day journey from İstanbul to Lake Van (Van Gölü). Another option, popular in areas like Cappadocia where there is a lot to see in a small area, is spending longer in one place and making forays by foot, bike or dolmuş (minibus). *Gület* (wooden yacht) cruises are popular in the western Mediterranean and there are ferries from İstanbul to locations including Bandırma, where you can catch the train to İzmir, and Bodrum.

Accommodation & Food

The many package holidays available on the Mediterranean coast do little to boost the local economy, as the participating resorts are often isolated and self-contained. Fortunately, independent travel is easy in the region, and the majority of pensions are family run and fantastic value. Ecofriendly hotels and camp sites are popping up along the coast in locations such as Çıralı, Phaselis and Kabak.

The old-fashioned *ev pansiyonu* (pension in private home) is dying out, but the tradition continues in isolated pockets including Gökçeada (where locals may approach you and offer their spare room) and Safranbolu.

Desertification is a long-term threat in central Anatolia, yet Cappadocia's hotel bathrooms are crammed with jacuzzis, massage showers, even mini-hamams. You could ask for a room without such facilities.

Dining on the coast, avoid large predatory fish, such as swordfish, which are depleted in most fishing areas. Fishing is supposedly banned on the Black Sea in Thrace between June and September, but local fish still finds its way to the table. Mediterranean bluefin tuna is on the verge of extinction.

Responsible Travel Organisations

Turkey's environmental movement is still embryonic, but there are a few small organisations, such as the Alaçatı Preservation Society (see boxed text p235). Some of the Gallipoli tour agencies are committed to conserving the national park. **Greenpeace Mediterranean** (www.greenpeace.org/mediterranean) has an informative website covering coastal issues.

READING UP

Since time immemorial travellers have written about their rambles across Turkey. Herodotus, Xenophon and Strabo have all left us accounts of Anatolia before Christ. The famous march to Persia by the Greek army, immortalised in Xenophon's *Anabasis* (c 400 BC), was retraced some 2400 years later by Shane Brennan in his fabulous tale *In the Tracks of the Ten Thousand: A Journey on Foot Through Turkey, Syria and Iraq* (2005). Mary Wortley Montagu's *Turkish Embassy Letters* (1763) details the author's travels to İstanbul with her husband, the British ambassador to Turkey, in 1716. It's a surprisingly nonjudgmental account of life at the heart of the Ottoman Empire.

Edmondo De Amicis' classic *Constantinople* (1877) beautifully details İstanbul's bustle, atmosphere and cosmopolitan nature in the 19th century.

DON'T LEAVE HOME WITHOUT...

■ 'Cover-up' clothing for mosque visits. Women might want to bring a scarf, although if you don't you've got a good excuse to go shopping.

■ Slip-on shoes or sandals. Highly recommended as they are cool to wear and easy to remove before entering mosques or Turkish homes.

■ Books in English. Those available in Turkey are hard to find and can be pricey. Secondhand book exchanges plug the gaps, but you'll need to have something to swap.

■ Tampons. They can be hard to find as most Turkish women use pads.

■ Universal sink plug.

■ An appetite for kebaps.

■ First-aid kit including sunscreen, which can be expensive in Turkey.

■ Checking your government's travel warnings (see p660).

TOP PICKS

o Ankara
TURKEY
Greece
Syria
Iran

MUST-READS

Turkey's long history and vibrant culture has provided copious source material for authors old and new, local and foreign. For more on Turkey's authors and literary tradition, see p56.

- *Snow* (Orhan Pamuk) – This Kars-set fictional insight unearths Turkey's contemporary challenges.
- *Portrait of a Turkish Family* (Irfan Orga) – This page-turner is so intimate you'll feel like an honorary family member.
- *Atatürk* (Andrew Mango) – Get to know one of the 20th century's most intriguing political figures.
- *Memed, My Hawk* (Yaşar Kemal) – If this were a movie, it would rival *Gone with the Wind*.
- *Birds Without Wings* (Louis de Bernières) – Superbly written and researched historical fiction.
- *Osman's Dream* (Caroline Finkel) – The historian charts the Ottoman Empire through seven centuries.
- *Tales from the Expat Harem* (edited by Anastasia Ashman) – Stories by women who made the move to Turkey.
- *Deadly Webb* (Barbara Nadel) – Nadel won the Silver Dagger award for this yarn about a hard-drinking İstanbul detective.

FAVOURITE FESTIVALS

Turks really know how to have a good time, and a festival or event is on nearly every other day. These are a few favourites; see p662 for others.

- Camel wrestling (p242) – Bloodless bull-wrestling.
- Kırkpınar Oil Wrestling Festival (p172) – Yet more battling, but this time it's greasy buck-wrestling!
- Kiraz Festivali (p663) – Cherry-gobbling and judging, music and oil-wrestling.
- Nevruz (p662) – Ancient Middle Eastern spring knees-up.
- Aspendos Opera & Ballet Festival (p404) – Unbeatable Roman-era venue.
- Uluslararası Bursa Festival (p663) – Music from Roma bands to Portuguese *fado*.
- International İstanbul Biennial (p663) – Art, performances and contemporary culture.

NATURAL WONDERS

Turkey's diverse landscapes tell of its position at the conjunction of continents – these are some of our favourites.

- Bafa Gölü (p263) – The lake is flanked by rugged mountains and dotted with islands.
- Cappadocian valleys (p502) – Soft white rock eroded into curvy cliff faces.
- Selge (p404) – Offers a spectacular view of the Taurus Mountains.
- Dilek National Park (p259) – A slice of wilderness, wildlife, glorious scenery and great beaches on the overdeveloped south Aegean coast.
- Phrygian Valley (p303) – A surreal rocky escarpment and dramatic forests.
- Gökçeada (p192) – Check out the views of Heavenly Island's southern coast from the mountain road running west to east.
- Amasra to Sinop (p543) – A spectacular drive, taking in the rugged Black Sea coast.

Tom Brosnahan worked for the Peace Corps in 1960s' İstanbul and İzmir, and the former Lonely Planet author recounts the experience in *Turkey: Bright Sun, Strong Tea* (2004).

In *From the Holy Mountain* (1997), William Dalrymple retraces the journey of a 6th-century monk through eastern Byzantium, from Mt Athos, Greece, with stops in İstanbul and Anatolia. It's a gripping meditation on the declining Christian communities. Rory MacLean follows idealistic folk of another kind through a harshly changed world in *Magic Bus: On the Hippie Trail from Istanbul to India* (2006). Andrew Eames' *The 8.55 to Baghdad* (2004) retraces the crime queen Agatha Christie's travels on the *Orient Express*, with a chapter dedicated to Turkey.

Nicolas Bouvier's wonderful *The Way of the World* (1963), which has a short section on Turkey, recounts an artist's journey from Geneva to the Khyber Pass in a Fiat Topolino. Also researched in the 1950s, Irfan Orga's evocative *The Caravan Moves On: Three Weeks Among Turkish Nomads* (1958) mixes travelogue with insights into the lives and lore of the nomads. The disappearing Yörük, once one of Anatolia's largest nomadic tribes, have long captivated writers; another excellent example is *Bolkar: Travels with a Donkey in the Taurus Mountains* (1982), Dux Schneider's bitter-sweet account of the Yörük and Tatars today.

If you want some beach reading, *Turkish Coast: Through Writers' Eyes* (2008; edited by Rupert Scott) examines the coastline from İzmir to Antalya with the help of scribes from Plutarch to Freya Stark.

INTERNET RESOURCES

All About Turkey (www.allaboutturkey.com) Multilingual introduction to history and the main sites.

Hürriyet Daily News (www.hurriyet.com.tr/english/home/) All the latest national news.

Lonely Planet (www.lonelyplanet.com) Check out the Thorn Tree bulletin board to find the latest travellers' tips for travelling the country, especially out east.

My Merhaba (www.mymerhaba.com) Aimed at expats with lots of general information of use to visitors too (such as what's on in İstanbul).

Skylife magazine (www.thy.com/en-US/skylife) Click through to the archive of the excellent Turkish Airlines in-flight magazine, *Skylife*, with articles on all sorts of aspects of life in Turkey.

Tourism Turkey (www.tourismturkey.org) Government website with grab-bag of articles and information.

Turkey Travel Planner (www.turkeytravelplanner.com) An ever-growing site with up-to-the-minute information on all aspects of travel in Turkey.

Turkish Culture (www.turkishculture.org) Arts encyclopedia with links to sites covering cuisine and music.

Itineraries
CLASSIC ROUTES

FROM THE GOLDEN HORN TO THE SACRED WAY

One Week/
İstanbul to Ephesus

Begin this trip through the triumphs and tragedies of empires in İstanbul's Ottoman **Topkapı Palace** (p103), then obelisk-hop the ancient **Hippodrome** (p100). Having steamed away any aches in the **Çemberlitaş Hamamı** (p126), spend the evening cruising **İstiklal Caddesi** (p115), the heart of modern Turkey. Start day two at the **Blue Mosque** (p100) and the **Aya Sofya** (p98), then head underground at the **Basilica Cistern** (p101). After lunch, explore the labyrinthine **Grand Bazaar** (p109) or, weather permitting, take an afternoon or evening cruise along the **Bosphorus** (p121).

Come day three, rise early and head down to Çanakkale, so you can start touring the **Gallipoli battlefields** (p178) by early afternoon. The devastation witnessed here during WWI needs no introduction. Next morning head to famous **Troy** (p197), worth a visit even without Brad Pitt. Cross the ruin-dotted **Biga Peninsula** (p204) to beachy **Assos** (p204) and nearby **Behramkale** (p204), with its hilltop Greek village and ancient temple. You'll need another early start to bus down to **Ephesus** (p246), the best-preserved classical city in the eastern Mediterranean.

Starting in İstanbul, once the glittering heart of the Byzantine and Ottoman Empires, tick off the city's A-list sights before moseying southwest. In a week you can take in the Gallipoli battlefields and the ruins of Troy, Behramkale and Ephesus – a 1450km journey.

PALM TREES & FAIRY CHIMNEYS Three Weeks/İstanbul to Cappadocia

For the first week, follow the first itinerary. Then, from your base at Selçuk, take a day trip to the travertines and ruins of **Hierapolis** (p324) at Pamukkale. The brilliant white terraces can be dizzying in the midday sun, but swimming among submerged marble columns in the **Antique Pool** (p324) will restore your cool.

Heading back to the coast, ignore the overblown resorts of Bodrum and Marmaris and head straight for **Fethiye** (p351) and beautiful **Ölüdeniz** (p365). This is the spot to take to the air on a paraglide or lay way low on a beach towel. You're now within kicking distance of the famous **Lycian Way** (p359); hike for a day through superb countryside to overnight in heavenly **Faralya** (p368), and further inroads into the Lycian Way will definitely top your 'next time' list. Back on the coast, have a pit stop at laid-back **Kaş** (p379), its pretty harbourside square alive nightly with the hum of friendly folk enjoying the breeze, views, boutique browsing and a beer or two. You may want a few days more unwinding at the famous beach tree-house complexes at nearby **Olympos** (p388).

Antalya's old **Kaleiçi quarter** (p393) is well worth a wander against the backdrop of that jaw-dropping mountain range. Then it's time to fold your bikini into a matchbox and head inland. Catch an overnight bus north to claim your cave in **Göreme** (p497). This low-key travellers' hang-out is the best place to base yourself in Cappadocia, a surreal moonscape with phallic tuff cones, no less. For most the cones don't overshadow the more orthodox sights including the superb rock-cut frescoed churches of **Göreme Open-Air Museum** (p499) and the spooky underground cities at **Kaymaklı** (p524) and **Derinkuyu** (p524).

This is one trip you won't forget in a hurry. Pack your towel, pumps and pedometer: you're seeing the sights of Old İstanbul, the highlights of the Aegean and Mediterranean coasts and finishing off in kooky Cappadocia – a whopping 3100km of travel.

ROADS LESS TRAVELLED

EASTERN DELIGHTS   Three to Four Weeks/Trabzon to Harran

Buzzing **Trabzon** (p552) has a few sights worth a quick look, though most people head straight to nearby **Sumela Monastery** (p559), peering down on a forested valley from its precarious-looking rockface. The route from here to Kars is spectacular. First travel to **Erzurum** (p560 and p570), which is best tackled by car or taxi to appreciate the breathtaking views and ruined churches of medieval Georgia. The onward drive via **Yusufeli** (p578) is one of Turkey's most scenic, with roadways passing over dramatic mountains, through gorges frothing with white water and past crumbling castles. **Kars** (p582) is beguiling, but its star attraction is nearby **Ani** (p587). Once a thriving Armenian capital, it's now a field strewn with magnificent ruins overlooked by the border guards of modern Armenia. Head south to the raffish frontier town of **Doğubayazıt** (p592) and the outstanding **İshak Paşa Palace** (p593).

Further south is **Van** (p645), its proud drawcards the spectacular **Hoşap Castle** (p651) and the 10th-century **Akdamar church** (p643), the sole inhabitant of a teeny island in Lake Van (Van Gölü). The church's superbly preserved carvings surpass its magnificent setting with their wow factor. Heading west, don't miss **Hasankeyf** (p639), with its soaring rock-cut castle by the ancient Tigris River, and **Mardin** (p633), a gorgeous, honey-coloured town overlooking the roasting plains of Mesopotamia. Then head to **Diyarbakır** (p627), the heartland of Kurdish culture, its ancient sights ringed by even older city walls. Next, see what all the fuss is about at **Nemrut Dağı** (Mt Nemrut, p616); its gigantic stone heads are about the only image of eastern Turkey that makes it into brochures. Finish with a trip south, almost to the Syrian border, to visit **Harran** (p613), which is mentioned in Genesis and is one of the oldest continuously inhabited spots on earth.

Escape the crowds and hightail it to the Turkey rarely seen in glossy tourist brochures, the other Turkey: the wild, magnificent east. After it casts its spell you'll find western Turkey downright tame. Some 2850km and never a dull moment.

ARCHITECTURE ALLA TURCA   Two Weeks/Edirne to Erzurum

Caravanserais or *hans* (see p59), dotting the ancient trade routes, were the ancient equivalent of the roadhouse. Restored or crumbling, they evoke the nights of snorting animals tethered in the courtyard, with the rooms above abuzz with the snores of travellers and merchants.

Begin your architectural amble past these Seljuk service stations, and other relics of long-gone empires, in grand style at Edirne's **Selimiye Mosque** (p169). Its 71m-high minarets are the finest work of the great Ottoman architect Mimar Sinan (p111).

On the other side of the Sea of Marmara, Bursa's 15th-century **Yeşil Camii** (Green Mosque, p292), accompanied by the **Yeşil Türbe** (Green Tomb; p292), is the earliest mosque displaying a purely Turkish style. Continue the green theme at İznik's **Yeşil Cami** (p287), which pre-dates its Bursa counterpart by 35 years and looks considerably more Iranian.

Now zip across the top of the country for an Ottoman double bill in **Safranbolu** (p455) and **Amasya** (p469), where half-timbered mansions, hamams and *hans* jostle for attention with stunning settings.

From Amasya head southwest to Cappadocia, a region with more caravanserais than fleas on a camel. Highlights include **Ağzıkara Hanı** (p534), the superb **Sultanhanı** (p493), Turkey's largest caravanserai, and **Sultan Han** (p538), runner-up to that title. **Sarıhan** (p513) doubles as a set for whirling dervish ceremonies, and **Saruhan** (p527) is home to a fine eatery.

From Cappadocia head east to **Battalgazi** (p626), with its Ottoman caravanserai and Roman walls, before pointing your camel north to Divriği's **Ulu Cami and Darüşşifa** (p483). Sporting three incredible carved stone doorways, the 780-year-old complex is on the World Heritage list. Finally, rest up in Erzurum, beneath the tile-covered twin minarets of the magnificent Seljuk **Çifte Minare Medrese** (p480).

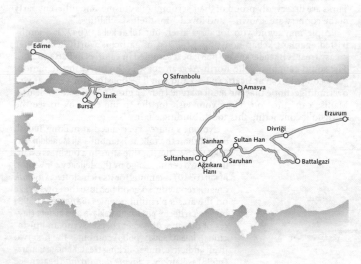

No camels and very little grunt are required on this 2415km zigzag through Turkey's lesser-known but magnificent hinterland. From the Greek border to the mountainous northeast, saddle up and hit the hans.

TAILORED TRIPS

NINE WONDERS OF TURKEY

Unesco has applied World Heritage status to nine of Turkey's sights.
Start by soaking up the treasures of **Old İstanbul** (p98), then point your
compass towards the Mediterranean and **Troy** (p197), where city has layered
upon city for 5000 years. **Pamukkale** (p322) boasts the famous dazzling-white
travertines and the ruins of Hierapolis, a city once known for the curative
powers of its warm calcium-rich waters.

Xanthos (p372) was once the glittering Lycian capital city, while nearby
Letoön (p372) was its religious sanctuary. Inland, hidden in Cappadocia's
fairy-tale landscape, **Göreme Open-Air Museum** (p499)
is a cluster of rock-hewn Byzantine churches and
monasteries. The going gets more rugged on
southeastern Anatolia's 2150m-high **Nemrut Dağı**
(p616), where the proud 'thrones of the gods' have
been standing sentinel for more than two millennia. North is the mosque complex at **Divriği** (p482),
Turkey's least-visited World Heritage site yet one
of the country's most rewarding for its out-of-the-
way location and jaw-dropping ornamentation.

West, the Hittites' magnificent capital was
Hattuşa (p465), its remote location as enthralling as
the sprawling city's remains. Head back to İstanbul
via the pristine Ottoman townscape of **Safranbolu**
(p455), where you can soak up the atmosphere in
a meticulously maintained 'Ottomansion'.

TURKEY FOR TASTEBUDS

Turks are deservedly proud of their scrumptious cuisine, and different parts
of the country are known – and loved – for their specialities.

People may avoid you for days after, but **Tokat kebap** (p477), a lamb-
basted eggplant kebap boasting a full fist of garlic, is worth it. Another
greasy treat is **İskender kebap** (p68), best sampled in eateries in **Bursa** (p298).
The squid caught off the north-Aegean coast is the finest in the nation;
get it cooked fresh at **Sığacık** (p236) and you'll be boasting for years. If you
overindulge, hope that the **mesir macunu** (power gum; p230) sold in nearby
Manisa can cure you. Time your visit for the spring equinox to see the
townsfolk concocting this tooth-binding elixir.

No one's more experienced at making **Turkish
delight** than the folk at İstanbul's **Ali Muhiddin Hacı
Bekir** (p157), the flagship store in a business established two centuries ago by the delicacy's inventor.
Afyon (p310) is famous for its rich clotted *kaymak*
cream, reputedly so good because the cows graze
on the area's plentiful poppies. **Gaziantep** (p598)
boasts a trifecta: **pistachios**, **baklava** and **künefe** (layers of dough with sweet cheese, syrup and pista-
chios). **İmam Çağdaş** (p603) combines the first two
in an addictive, finger-licking treat. **Kahramanmaraş**
(p598) is Turkey's *dövme dondurma* (beaten ice
cream) capital: served in fist-sized blocks, it's best
tackled with a knife and fork.

CLASSICAL TREASURES

If you love Greek and Roman ruins you will be thrilled to learn that Turkey has more of them than Greece or Italy.

Start at the famous ruins of **Troy** (p197), then head south to the crumbling **Acropolis** (p215) and **Asclepion** (p214) at Bergama (Pergamum) and the Byzantine remains at **Sardis** (p230). Towards the bottom of the Aegean coast, Selçuk is the best base for exploring the well-preserved classical city of **Ephesus** (p246), as well as the **Ephesus Museum** (p240). Ruin addicts will then want to detour inland to Pamukkale, to see the sprawling ruins of **Hierapolis** (p324) and **Afrodisias** (p328), which some people rate above Ephesus.

From Selçuk (or Kuşadası) you can also visit the sites at **Priene** (p261), **Miletus** (p262) and **Didyma** (p262). Continuing along the southern coast, you'll find the Unesco World Heritage–listed remains of **Letoön** (p372) and **Xanthos** (p372) and, hidden behind a gorgeous beach, the ruins of **Patara** (p373). There are more evocative sites further east at **Olympos** (p387) and at **Phaselis** (p391).

Pause in Antalya and inspect the **Antalya Museum** (p394) before nipping northwest to romantic **Termessos** (p401). Next, head east to explore the extensive ruins at **Perge** (p402), **Aspendos** (p403) and **Side** (p407). End your trip among the forgotten ruins at **Anamurium** (p416), on the Mediterranean coast just west of Anamur.

WE DARE YOU

On this trailblazing trip, explore some Turkish regions and activities unknown even to most Turks, and drop in on the country's exotic neighbours. Do your own research and make sure you check out the latest travel advice (p660) before striking out on any adventure.

Now that the troubled southeast is on the mend, former no-go zones are opening to visitors (see p652). The **upper valley of the Euphrates** (p624) is still uncharted territory, as is the wild scenery surrounding isolated **Bahçesaray** (p650), **Hakkari** (p651), and **Şırnak** (p640).

Cappadocia's claustrophobic but compelling underground cities (p524) were once havens from invading armies. Hire a guide and shine a torch on the lesser-known cities at **Özlüce** (p524), **Güzelyurt** (p531) and **Özkonak** (p514).

Head to **Saklıkent Gorge** (p371) for white-water rafting, canyoning and hiking. Walkers could also check out developments at **Cilo Dağı** (Cilo Mountains; p651), and **Mt Ararat** (p595) has long captivated the imaginations of mountaineers.

Eastern Anatolia has gnarly frontiers with **Georgia** (p582), where you can sample full-bodied red wine, and **Nakhichevan** (p678), an isolated pocket of **Azerbaijan**. Alternatively, follow the hippy trail to **Iran**, entered from Doğubayazıt (p595) or the more-intrepid Esendere-Sero crossing (p652). You can even follow the LP Turkey team's resident border-crossing junkie into **Iraq** (p635).

History

Fate has put Turkey at the junction of two continents. A land bridge, meeting point and battleground, it has seen peoples moving between Europe and Asia throughout history. That human traffic has left monuments and debris, dynasties and cultural legacies, which have contributed to the character of modern Turkey.

EARLY CULTURES, CITIES & CLASHES

Archaeological finds indicate that Anatolia (the land mass of Turkey within Asia) was first inhabited by hunter-gatherers during the Palaeolithic era. By around the 7th millennium BC some folk formed settlements. Çatalhöyük, which arose around 6500 BC, may be the first ever city. It was certainly a centre of innovation, locals developing crop irrigation, domesticating pigs and sheep, and creating distinctive pottery. Relics from this settlement can be seen at Ankara's Museum of Anatolian Civilisations (p444).

The chalcolithic age saw the rise of Hacılar, in Central Anatolia, and communities in the southeast that absorbed Mesopotamian influences, including the use of metal tools. Across Anatolia more and larger communities sprung up and interacted – not always happily: settlements were often fortified.

By 3000 BC advances in metallurgy allowed power to be concentrated, leading to the creation of various Anatolian kingdoms. One such was at Alacahöyük, in the heart of Anatolia, yet even this place showed Caucasian influence, evidence of trade beyond the Anatolian plateau.

Trade, too, was increasing on the western coast, with Troy trading with the Aegean islands and mainland Greece. Around 2000 BC the Hatti people established a capital at Kanesh (Kültepe, near Kayseri), ruling over a web of trading communities. Here for the first time Anatolian history materialises from the realm of archaeological conjecture and becomes 'real': clay tablets provide written records of dates, events and names.

No singular Anatolian civilisation had yet emerged, but the tone was set for millennia to come: cultural interaction, trade and war would become the recurring themes of Anatolian history.

AGES OF BRONZE: THE HITTITES

The Hatti were a temporary presence. As they declined, the Hittites assumed their territory. From Alacahöyük, the Hittites shifted their capital to Hattuşa (near present-day Boğazkale) some time around 1800 BC.

The Hittites' legacy consisted of their great capital, as well as their state archives (cuneiform clay tablets) and distinctive artistic styles. By 1450 BC the kingdom, having endured internal ructions, was reborn as an empire. In

Archaeologist Ian Hodder's *Catalhoyuk: The Leopard's Tale* is an account of the excavation of the site, which vividly portrays life as it was during the city's heyday.

Until the rediscovery of the ruins at Boğazkale in the 19th century, the Hittites were known only through several obscure references in the Old Testament.

TIMELINE

c 6500 BC	c 4000–3000 BC	c 2000 BC
Founding of Çatalhöyük, the world's first city. Over time 13 layers of houses were built, beehive style, interconnected and linked with ladders. It is estimated that at its peak the city housed around 8000.	Hattian culture develops at Alacahöyük during the early Bronze Age, although settlement has been continuous since the chalcolithic age, when stone tools were still in use. The Hatti develop distinctive jewellery and metalwork and weapons.	The Hittites, an Indo-European people, arrive in Anatolia and conquer the Hatti, claiming their capital at Hattuşa. The Hittites go on to carve out an immense kingdom extending to Babylon and Egypt.

creating the first Anatolian empire, the Hittites were warlike, but displayed other imperial trappings – they ruled over myriad vassal states and princelings while also displaying a sense of ethics and an occasional penchant for diplomacy. This didn't prevent them from overrunning Ramses II of Egypt in 1298 BC, but did allow them to patch things up with the crestfallen Ramses by marrying him to a Hittite princess.

The Hittite empire was harassed in later years by subject principalities, including Troy. The final straw was the invasion of the iron-smelting Greeks, generally known as the 'sea peoples'. The Hittites were landlocked – hence disadvantaged during an era of burgeoning sea trade – and lacked the latest technology: iron.

Meanwhile a new dynasty at Troy was establishing itself as a regional power. The Trojans in turn were harried by the Greeks, which led to the Trojan War in 1250 BC. This allowed the Hittites breathing space but later arrivals sped their demise. Some pockets of Hittite culture persisted in the Taurus Mountains, but the great empire was dead. Later city states created a neo-Hittite culture, which attracted Greek merchants and became the conduit for Mesopotamian religion and art forms to reach Greece.

Homer, the Greek author of the *Iliad*, which told the story of the Trojan War, is believed to have been born in Smyrna (present-day İzmir), before 700 BC.

CLASSICAL EMPIRES: GREECE & PERSIA

Post-Hittite Anatolia was a patchwork of peoples, indigenous Anatolians and recent interlopers. In the east the Urartians, descendants of Anatolian Hurrians, forged a kingdom near Lake Van (Van Gölü). By the 8th century BC the Phrygians arrived in western Anatolia. Under King Gordius, of Gordian knot (p30) fame, the Phrygians created a capital at Gordion, their power peaking later under King Midas. In 725 BC Gordion was put to the sword by horse-borne Cimmerians, a fate that even King Midas' golden touch couldn't avert.

On the southwest coast the Lycians established a confederation of independent city states extending from modern-day Fethiye to Antalya. Inland the Lydians dominated western Anatolia from their capital at Sardis and are credited with creating the first-ever coinage.

For further discussion of the highs and lows of life in ancient Lycia and detailed information on the sites of Turkey's Lycian coast, visit www .lycianturkey.com.

Meanwhile, Greek colonies were spreading along the Mediterranean coast, and Greek cultural influence was infiltrating Anatolia. Most of the peoples of the Anatolian patchwork were clearly influenced by the Greeks: Phrygia's King Midas had a Greek wife; the Lycians borrowed the legend of the Chimera; and Lydian art was an amalgam of Greek and Persian art forms. It seems that at times admiration was mutual: the Lycians were the only Anatolian people the Greeks didn't deride as 'barbarians', and the Greeks were so impressed by the wealth of the Lydian king Croesus they coined the expression 'as rich as Croesus'.

Increasing manifestations of Hellenic influence didn't go unnoticed. Cyrus, the emperor of Persia, would not countenance such temerity in his

c 1200 BC	c 1100 BC	547 BC
The destruction of Troy. For 10 years the Mycenaeans had besieged the city, which was strategically placed above the Dardanelles and was the key to Black Sea trade. The war was later immortalised in Homer's *Iliad*.	After the fall of the Hittites several neo-Hittite kingdoms arose, while the Assyrians and various Georgian groups encroached on southern Anatolia. It is thought that the Phoenicians brought the alphabet to Anatolia around this time.	Cyrus of Persia overruns Anatolia, setting the scene for a long Greco-Persian rivalry. He established a series of satrapies. Later Darius I and Xerxes further Persian influence in Anatolia and forestall the expansion of Greek colonies.

backyard. He invaded in 547 BC, initially putting paid to the Lydians, then barrelled on to extend control to the Aegean. Over a period of years under emperors Darius I and Xerxes the Persians checked the expansion of coastal Greek trading colonies. They also subdued the interior, ending the era of home-grown Anatolian kingdoms.

Ruling Anatolia through compliant local satrapies, the Persians didn't have it all their own way. They contended with periodic resistance from feisty Anatolians, such as the revolt of the Ionian city of Miletus in 494 BC. Allegedly fomented from Athens, the revolt was abruptly put down. The Persians used the connivance of Athens as a pretext to invade mainland Greece, only to be routed at Marathon.

ALEXANDER & AFTER

Persian control of Anatolia continued until 334 BC when a new force stormed across Anatolia. Alexander and his Macedonian adventurers crossed the Dardanelles initially intent on relieving Anatolia of the Persian yoke. Sweeping down the coast they rolled the Persians near Troy, then pushed down to Sardis, which willingly surrendered. After later successfully besieging Halicarnassus (modern-day Bodrum) Alexander ricocheted ever-eastwards, disposing of another Persian force on the Cilician plain.

In the former Phrygian capital of Gordion, Alexander encountered the Gordian knot. Tradition stated that whoever untied the knot would come to rule Asia. Frustrated in his attempts to untie it, Alexander dispatched it with a blow of his sword. Asia lay before him; he and his men thundered all the way across Persia to the Indus until all the known world was his dominion.

Alexander was more disposed to conquest than to nation-building. When he died in Babylon in 323 BC, leaving no successor, the enormous empire he had created was to be short-lived – perhaps he should have been more patient with that knot – and was divided in a flurry of civil wars.

However, if Alexander's intention was to cleanse Anatolia of Persian influence and bring it within the Hellenic sphere, he was monumentally successful. In the wake of Alexander's armies, steady Hellenisation occurred, a culmination of the process begun centuries earlier that had annoyed Cyrus, the Persian king. A formidable network of municipal communities – the lifeblood of which, as ever in the Hellenic tradition, was trade – spread across Anatolia. The most notable of these was Pergamum (now Bergama). The Pergamene kings were great warriors and enthusiastic patrons of the arts. Greatest of the Pergamene kings was Eumenes, who ruled from the Dardanelles to the Taurus Mountains and was responsible for much of what remains of Pergamum's acropolis. As notable as the building of Hellenic temples and aqueducts was the gradual spread of the Greek language, which extinguished the native Anatolian languages over several centuries.

According to legend, both of Alexander's parents foresaw his birth. His mother dreamed that a lightning strike had struck her womb, while his father dreamed that his wife's womb had been sealed by a lion. In great consternation they consulted a seer, who told them their child would have the character of a lion.

333 BC	133 BC	AD 45–60
Alexander the Great rolls the Persians and conquers most of Anatolia. Persian Emperor Darius, facing defeat, flees and abandons his wife, children and mother, who is so appalled she disowns him and 'adopts' Alexander.	On his deathbed Pergamene king Attalus III leaves his state to Rome. The Romans swiftly establish a capital at Ephesus, an already buzzing port, and capitalise on vigorous sea trade. The population grows to 250,000.	St Paul, originally from Antioch (modern Antakya), undertakes his long proselytising treks across Anatolia. St John and the Virgin Mary are thought to have ended up in Ephesus, which develops a sizeable Christian community.

All the while the cauldron of Anatolian cultures bubbled, throwing up various short-lived flavour-of-the-month kingdoms. In 279 BC the Celts romped in from southeastern Europe, establishing the kingdom of Galatia centred on Ancyra (Ankara). To the northeast Mithridates had earlier established the kingdom of Pontus, centred on Amasya, and the Armenians (long established in the Lake Van region, and often thought to be descendants of the earlier Urartians) re-established themselves, having been granted autonomy under Alexander.

Meanwhile, across the Aegean Sea, the increasingly powerful Romans were casting covetous eyes on the rich trade networks of Anatolia.

ROMAN RULE & THE RISE OF CHRISTIANITY

Ironically, Pergamum, the greatest of the post-Alexandrian cities, became the mechanism that allowed the Romans to control Anatolia. The Roman legions had defeated the armies of a Seleucid king at Magnesia (Manisa) in 190 BC, but Pergamum became the beachhead for the Roman embrace of Anatolia when King Attalus III died in 133 BC, bequeathing the city to Rome. In 129 BC Ephesus was nominated capital of the Roman province of Asia and within 60 years the Romans had overcome spirited resistance from Mithridates of Pontus and extended their reach to Armenia, on the Persian border.

The reign of Emperor Augustus was a period of relative peace and prosperity for Anatolia. In this milieu the fledgling religion of Christianity was able to spread, albeit clandestinely and subject to intermittently rigorous persecution. Tradition has it that St John retired to Ephesus to write the fourth Gospel, bringing Mary with him. John was buried on top of a hill in what is now Selçuk; the great Basilica of St John (p240) marks the site. Mary is said to be buried at Meryemana (p250) nearby. The indefatigable St Paul capitalised on the Roman road system, his sprightly step taking him across Anatolia spreading the word.

As Christianity quietly spread, the Roman Empire grew cumbersome. In the late 3rd century Diocletian tried to steady the Empire by splitting it into eastern and western administrative units, simultaneously attempting to wipe out Christianity. Both endeavours failed. Diocletian's reforms resulted in a civil war out of which Constantine emerged victorious. An earlier convert to Christianity, Constantine was said to have been guided by angels in choosing to build a 'New Rome' on the ancient Greek town of Byzantium. The city came to be known as Constantinople (now İstanbul). On his deathbed Constantine was baptised and by the end of the century Christianity had become the official religion of the Empire.

ROME FALLS, BYZANTIUM ARISES

Even with a new capital at Constantinople, the Roman Empire proved no less unwieldy. Once the steadying hand of Theodosius (379–95) was gone, the

Julius Caesar made his famous 'Veni, vidi, vici' ('I came, I saw, I conquered') speech about a military victory at Zile, near Tokat, in 47 BC.

To get the background on the search for, discovery of and ensuing controversy of Mary's final resting place, read Donald Carroll's Mary's House.

330	395	412
Constantine declares his 'New Rome', later Constantinople, as the capital of the eastern Roman Empire (Byzantium). He had earlier (in 313) converted to Christianity and in 325 hosted the Council of Nicaea, a pivotal event in Christian history.	Under Theodosius the Roman Empire becomes Christian, with paganism being forbidden and Greek influence becoming more pervasive. Upon his death the Empire is formally split along the line Diocletian had set a century earlier.	Theodosius II builds the land walls of Constantinople to protect the riches of his capital. They prove extremely effective, withstanding sieges from Avars, Arabs and Bulgars, and are only to be breached once: by Mehmet in 1453.

impact of Diocletian's reforms became unstoppable: the Empire split. The western – Roman – half of the Empire eventually succumbed to decadence and sundry 'barbarians'; the eastern half – Byzantium – prospered, gradually adopting the Greek language and with Christianity its defining feature.

Under Justinian (527–65), Byzantium took up the mantle of imperialism that had once been Rome's. Historians note Justinian as responsible for the Aya Sofya (p98) and codifying Roman law, but he also pushed the boundaries of the Empire to envelop southern Spain, North Africa and Italy. It was at this stage that Byzantium came to be an entity distinct from Rome, although sentimental attachment to the idea of Rome remained: the Greek-speaking Byzantines still referred to themselves as Romans, and in subsequent centuries the Turks would refer to them as 'Rum'. However, Justinian's exuberance and ambition overstretched the Empire. Plague and the encroachment of Avars and Slavic tribes north of the Danube curtailed further expansion.

In 1054 the line along which the Empire had split in 395 became the separating line between Catholicism and Orthodox Christianity, a fault line that persists to this day.

Later a drawn-out struggle with their age-old rivals the Persians further weakened the Byzantines, leaving the eastern provinces of Anatolia easy prey for the Arab armies exploding out of Arabia. The Arabs took Ankara in 654 and by 669 had besieged Constantinople. Here were a new people, bringing a new language, a new civilisation and, most crucially, a new religion: Islam.

THE BYZANTINES, THE ARABS... & THE RENAISSANCE

Fully 780 years before Constantinople fell to the Ottomans, a Muslim army laid siege to the Byzantine capital. Newly converted, the armies of Islam marched out of Arabia, swept through Anatolia and by 669 arrived at Constantinople's walls. The early Arab incursions into Byzantine territory so worried Emperor Constantine III that he withdrew to Sicily in 660. His son, Constantine IV, succeeded him in 668 and endured five Arabic assaults on Constantinople in 10 years.

The meeting of the Byzantines and Arabs wasn't all acrimonious, however: there was considerable cultural cross-pollination. The Islamic ban on portraying human beings in pictures was adopted by Emperor Leo in 726, thus ushering in the Iconoclastic period. More happily, domes were an innovation unknown to Arabs until they saw Byzantine churches. Thereafter the dome entered the repertoire of Muslim architects, and gradually the voluptuous skylines of Islamic cities – İstanbul not least among them – were born. And in meeting the Byzantines the Arabs also encountered the scientific and philosophical works of the classical Greeks. The Arabic translations of these works eventually made their way to Western Europe, via Islamic Spain, thus sparking off the Renaissance.

To Ottoman believers, a relic of the Arab sieges of Constantinople became the fourth most holy site in Islam: the place where the Prophet Mohammed's friend and standard bearer, Ayoub al-Ansari (Eyüp Ensari in Turkish), was buried. The site of his grave was lost during the reign of the Byzantines, but once Mehmet's soldiers took the city in 1453 it was 'miraculously' rediscovered (see p125). Thereafter it became a pilgrimage site for Ottoman sultans on ascending the throne.

527–65	600s	654–76
During the reign of Justinian, Byzantium enjoys a golden age. Justinian's military conquests include much of North Africa and Spain. He also pursues reform within the core of the Empire, while also embarking on building programs.	The Sassanid Persians, age-old rivals of the Greeks, invade, sweeping across Anatolia and then pushing into Byzantine territory in Egypt. This brings about an economic collapse in the realm and weakens the Byzantine Empire.	Muslim Arab armies invade Anatolia, capturing Ankara and besieging Constantinople. Arab incursions in the west are temporary but the eastern and southern fringes (Syria and Egypt) of the Byzantine domain are lost to the Arabs.

On the western front, Goths and Lombards impinged as well, so that by the 8th century Byzantium was pushed back into the Balkans and Anatolia. The Empire hunkered down until the emergence of the Macedonian emperors. Basil assumed the throne in 867 and the Empire's fortunes were on the up, as Basil chalked up victories against Islamic Egypt, the Bulgars and Russia. Basil II (976–1025) earned the moniker the 'Bulgar Slayer' after putting out the eyes of 14,000 Bulgarian prisoners of war. When Basil died the Empire lacked anyone of his leadership skills – or ferocity, perhaps – and the era of Byzantine expansion was comprehensively over.

For insight into the battle and aftershocks of the Seljuk's first military triumph over the Byzantines grab the scholarly Turkish Myth and Muslim Symbol: The Battle of Manzikert by Carole Hillenbrand. It sheds light on this little-known but pivotal historical event.

THE FIRST TURKIC EMPIRE: THE SELJUKS

During centuries of Byzantine waxing and waning, a nomadic people, the Turks, had moved ever-westward out of Central Asia. En route the Turks encountered the Arabs and converted to Islam. Vigorous and martial by nature, the Turks assumed control of parts of the moribund Abbasid empire, and built an empire of their own centred on Persia. Tuğrul, of the Turkish Seljuk clan, took the title of sultan in Baghdad, and from there the Seljuks began raiding Byzantine territory. In 1071 Tuğrul's son Alp Arslan faced down the might of the Byzantine army at Manzikert north of Lake Van. Although vastly outnumbered, the nimble Turkish cavalry won the day, laying all Anatolia open to wandering Turkic bands and beginning the final demise of the Byzantine Empire.

Not everything went the Seljuks' way, however. The 12th and 13th centuries saw incursions by Crusaders, who established short-lived statelets at Antioch (modern-day Antakya) and Edessa (now Şanlıurfa). In a sideshow to the Seljuk saga, an unruly army of Crusaders sacked Constantinople, the capital of the Christian Byzantines, ostensibly the allies of the Crusaders. Meanwhile the Seljuks were riven by power struggles and their vast empire fragmented.

John Julius Norwich's concise A Short History of Byzantium – a distillation of three volumes on the Byzantines – does a fantastic job of cramming 1123 eventful years of history into fewer than 500 pages.

The Seljuk legacy persisted in Anatolia in the Sultanate of Rum, centred on Konya. Although ethnically Turkish, the Seljuks were purveyors of Persian culture and art. It was the Seljuks who introduced knotted woollen rugs to Anatolia, and they endowed the countryside with remarkable architecture – still visible at Erzurum, Divriği, Amasya and Sivas. These buildings were the first truly Islamic art forms in Anatolia, and were to become the prototypes on which Ottoman art would later be modelled. Celaleddin Rumi (p485), the Sufi mystic who founded the Mevlevi, or whirling dervish, order, was an exemplar of the cultural and artistic heights reached in Konya.

In the meantime, the Mongol descendants of Genghis Khan rumbled through Anatolia defeating a Seljuk army at Köse Dağ in 1243. At the Mongol onslaught, Anatolia fractured into a mosaic of Turkish *beyliks* (principalities) and Mongol fiefdoms. But by 1300 a single Turkish *bey* (tribal leader), Osman, established the Ottoman dynasty that would eventually end the Byzantine line.

976–1014	1071	1204
Under Basil II (the Bulgar Slayer), Byzantium reaches its high-tide mark. Basil overcomes internal crises, pushes the frontiers of the Empire to Armenia in the east, retakes Italy and inflicts major defeats on the Bulgarians.	New arrivals, the Seljuk Turks take on and defeat a much larger Byzantine force at Manzikert. The Seljuks don't immediately follow on their success but it is a body blow for the Byzantines, who retreat to Constantinople.	The rabble of the Fourth Crusade sack Constantinople, an indication of the contempt with which the Western Christian powers of the time regard the Eastern Orthodox church. The Byzantines don't regain control of their city until 1261.

THE FLEDGLING OTTOMAN STATE

Byzantium: The Surprising Life of a Medieval Empire by Judith Herrin takes a thematic approach to life in the Byzantine realm and in so doing reveals the secrets of the little-understood empire.

Osman's bands flitted with impunity around the borderlands between Byzantine and formerly Seljuk territory, but once galvanised they moved with zeal. In an era marked by destruction and dissolution they provided an ideal that attracted legions of followers and they quickly established an administrative and military model that allowed them to expand with alacrity. From the outset they embraced all the cultures of Anatolia – as many Anatolian civilisations before them had done – and their traditions became an amalgam of Greek and Turkish, Islamic and Christian elements, particularly in the janissary corps, which were drawn from the Christian populations of their territories.

Vigorous and seemingly invincible, the Ottomans forged westward, establishing a first capital at Bursa, then crossing into Europe and taking Adrianople (now Edirne) in 1362. By 1371 they had reached the Adriatic and in 1389 they met and vanquished the Serbs at Kosovo Polje, effectively taking control of the Balkans.

Exuberantly told and bubbling with *bon mots*, Jason Goodwin's *Lords of the Horizons* is an energetic tilt through Ottoman history.

In the Balkans the Ottomans encountered a resolute Christian community, yet they absorbed them neatly into the state in the creation of the *millet* system, by which minority communities were officially recognised and allowed to govern their own affairs. However, neither Christian insolence nor military bravado were countenanced: Sultan Beyazıt trounced the armies of the last Crusade at Nicopolis in Bulgaria in 1396. Beyazıt perhaps took military victories for granted thereafter. Later it was he who was insolent, when he taunted the Tatar warlord Tamerlane. Beyazıt was captured, his army defeated and the burgeoning Ottoman Empire abruptly halted as Tamerlane lurched through Anatolia and out again.

THE OTTOMANS ASCENDANT: CONSTANTINOPLE & BEYOND

It took a decade for the dust to settle after Tamerlane departed, dragging a no-doubt chastened Beyazıt with him. Beyazıt's sons wrestled for control until finally a worthy sultan emerged. With Mehmet I at the helm the Ottomans got back to the job at hand: expansion. With a momentum born of reprieve they scooped up the rest of Anatolia, rolled through Greece, made a first attempt at Constantinople and beat the Serbs for a second time in 1448.

Concise, yet covering the vast sweep of Ottoman history, *Osman's Dream* by Caroline Finkel is rich in telling detail and investigates the goings on of the sultans over six centuries.

The Ottomans had regained their momentum when Mehmet II became sultan in 1451. Constantinople, the last redoubt of the beleaguered Byzantines, was encircled by Ottoman territory. Mehmet, as an untested sultan, had no choice but to claim it. He built a fortress on the Bosphorus, imposed a naval blockade and amassed his army. The Byzantines appealed forlornly and in vain to Europe for help. After seven weeks of siege the city fell on 29 May 1453. Christendom shuddered at the seemingly unstoppable Ottomans and fawning diplomats likened Mehmet to Alexander the Great, declaring him to be a worthy successor to great Roman and Byzantine emperors.

1243	1300	1349
The Mongols rumble out of Central Asia taking Erzurum and defeating the Seljuks at Köse Dağ. The Seljuk empire limps on and the Mongols depart leaving only some minor states. There is no dominant power remaining in Anatolia.	Near Eskişehir on the marches between the moribund Byzantines and the shell-shocked Seljuks, Osman comes to prominence. He takes on the Byzantine army and wins minor skirmishes, slowly attracting followers and gaining momentum.	As allies of the Byzantines, the Ottomans, under Osman's son, Orhan, make their first foray into Europe. Orhan had earlier consolidated Islam as the religion of the Ottomans; soon they are making conquests in their own right.

The Ottoman war machine rolled on, alternating campaigns between eastern and western borders of the Empire. Ottoman society was fully geared for war. The janissary system, by which subject Christian youths were converted and trained for the military, meant that the Ottomans had the only standing army in Europe. They were agile, highly organised and motivated. Successive sultans expanded the realm, Selim the Grim capturing the Hejaz in 1517, and with it Mecca and Medina, thus claiming for the Ottomans' status as the guardians of Islam's holiest places. It wasn't all mindless militarism, however: Sultan Beyazıt II demonstrated the multicultural nature of the Empire when he invited the Jews expelled by the Spanish Inquisition to İstanbul in 1492.

The Ottoman golden age came during the reign of Sultan Süleyman (1520–66). A remarkable figure, Süleyman was noted as much for codifying Ottoman law as for his military prowess. Under Süleyman, the Ottomans enjoyed victories over the Hungarians and absorbed the Mediterranean coast of Algeria and Tunisia; Süleyman's legal code was a visionary amalgam of secular and Islamic law, and his patronage of the arts saw the Ottomans reach their cultural zenith.

Süleyman was also notable as the first Ottoman sultan to marry. Where previously sultans had enjoyed the comforts of concubines, Süleyman fell in love and married Roxelana (see the boxed text, below). Sadly, monogamy did not make for domestic bliss: palace intrigues brought about the death of his first two sons. A wearied Süleyman died campaigning on the Danube in 1566, and his body was spirited back to İstanbul.

Wild Europe: The Balkans in the Gaze of Western Travellers by Bozidar Jezernik is a fascinating record of travellers' observations of the Balkans under Ottoman rule.

THE SULTANATE OF WOMEN

The Ottoman Empire may have been the mightiest Islamic Empire, but for a time women commanded great influence in the machinations of the empire. More than ever before or after, from the reign of Süleyman the Magnificent until the mid-17th century, some women of the Ottoman court assumed and wielded considerable political clout.

This period, sometimes referred to as the 'sultanate of women', began with Lady Hürrem, known to the West as Roxelana. A concubine in the harem of Süleyman, she quickly became his favourite consort, and when his mother died Roxelana became the most powerful woman in the harem. She then proceeded to shore up her own position, persuading Süleyman to marry her – something no concubine had done before.

A master of palace intrigue, she manoeuvred the sultan into doing away with Mustafa, his son from an earlier coupling, and İbrahim, his grand vizier. This left the way open for Roxelana's son, Selim, to succeed Süleyman as sultan.

Such conniving had a lasting legacy on the fortunes of the Empire. Selim proved to be an inept and inebriated leader, and some claim that the precedent of behind-the-scenes manipulation, set by Roxelana, contributed to the increasing incompetence and eventual downfall of the Ottoman aristocracy.

1396	1402	1421–51
The Crusade of Nicopolis, a hastily cobbled together conglomeration of Eastern and Western European forces, aim to forestall the Turks who are marching into Europe with impunity. Ottoman forces abruptly defeat them, and Europe is left unguarded.	Beyazıt, victor over the knights of the Crusade of Nicopolis, turns his focus to the ultimate prize, Constantinople. Ever cocky, Beyazıt takes on the forces of Tatar warlord Tamerlane. Beyazıt's army is crushed and he is enslaved.	Murat II restores Ottoman fortunes after the Tamerlane setback. He takes Greece and retires to his palace in Manisa twice, but both times is forced to reassume the throne in order to see off insurgencies in Bulgaria.

THE OTTOMAN JUGGERNAUT FALTERS

Determining exactly when or why the Ottoman rot set in is tricky, but some historians pinpoint the death of Süleyman as critical. Süleyman's failure to take Malta in 1565 was a harbinger of what was to come, and the earlier unsuccessful tilts in the Indian Ocean aimed at circumventing Portuguese influence were evidence of growing European military might.

With hindsight it is easy to say that the remarkable line of Ottoman sovereigns – from Osman to Süleyman, inspirational leaders and mighty generals all – could not continue indefinitely. The Ottoman family tree was bound to throw up some duds eventually. And so it did.

The sultans following Süleyman were not up to the task. Süleyman's son by Roxelana, Selim, known disparagingly as 'the Sot', lasted only briefly as sultan, overseeing the naval catastrophe at Lepanto, which spelled the definitive end of Ottoman supremacy in the Mediterranean. The intrigues and power broking that occurred during the 'sultanate of women' (p35) contributed to the general befuddlement of later sultans, but other vested interests, putting personal advancement ahead of that of the Empire, also played a role.

Furthermore, Süleyman was the last sultan to lead his army into the field. Those who came after him were coddled and sequestered in the fineries of the palace, having minimal experience of everyday life and little inclination to administer the Empire. This, coupled with the inertia that was inevitable after 250 years of unfettered expansion, meant that the Ottoman military might, once famously referred to by Martin Luther as irresistible, was on the wane.

THE SICK MAN OF EUROPE

The siege of Vienna in 1683 was effectively the Ottomans' last tilt at expanding further into Europe. It failed. Thereafter it was a downward spiral. The Empire was still vast and powerful, but it had lost its momentum and was rapidly falling behind the West on many levels: social, military and scientific. Napoleon's swashbuckling campaign through Egypt in 1799 indicated that an emboldened Europe was willing to take the battle right up to the Ottomans, and was the first example of industrialised Europe meddling in the affairs of the Middle East.

It wasn't just Napoleon who was hovering. The Habsburgs in central Europe and the Russians were increasingly assertive, while Western Europe had grown rich after centuries of colonising and exploiting the 'New World' – something the Ottomans had missed out on. Meanwhile, the Ottomans remained moribund, inward looking and unaware of the advances happening in Europe. An earlier clear indication of this was the Ottoman clergy's refusal to allow the use of the printing press until the 18th century – a century and a half after it had been introduced into Europe.

But it was another idea imported from the West that was to speed the dissolution of the Empire: nationalism. For centuries manifold ethnic groups had coexisted relatively harmoniously in the Ottoman Empire, but the creation

Miguel Cervantes was wounded fighting against the Ottomans at the battle of Lepanto. It is said that his experiences served as inspiration for some scenes in *Don Quixote*.

Anatolia is so named for the Greek word *anatolē* meaning 'rising of the sun'. The Turkish *anadolu* translates, very roughly, as 'mother lode'.

1453	1512–16	1520–66
Mehmet lays siege to Constantinople, coinciding with a lunar eclipse. The defending Byzantines interpret this as a fatal omen, presaging the doom of Christendom. Sure enough, the Turks are victorious within a week of the eclipse.	Selim the Grim defeats the Persians at Çaldiran and massacres Shiites in Anatolia. He proceeds to take Syria and Egypt, assuming the mantle of Caliph, then captures the holy cities of Mecca and Medina.	The reign of Süleyman the Magnificent, the zenith of the Ottoman Empire. Süleyman leads his forces to take Budapest, Belgrade and Rhodes, doubling the size of the Empire; he is also a patron of the arts.

of nation states in Western Europe sparked a desire in the Empire's subject peoples to throw off the Ottoman 'yoke' and determine their own destinies. So it was that pieces of the Ottoman jigsaw wriggled free: Greece attained its freedom in 1830. In 1878 Romania, Montenegro, Serbia and Bosnia went their own ways, while at the same time Russia was encroaching on Kars.

As the Empire shrunk there were various attempts at reform, but it was too little, too late. In 1829 Mahmut II abolished the janissaries, and in doing so slaughtered them, but he did succeed in modernising the armed forces. In 1876 Abdülhamid allowed the creation of an Ottoman constitution and the first ever Ottoman parliament. But he used the events of 1878 as an excuse for doing away with the constitution. His reign henceforth grew increasingly authoritarian.

But it wasn't just subject peoples who were restless: educated Turks, too, looked for ways to improve their lot. In Macedonia the Committee for Union and Progress (CUP) was created. Reform minded and Western looking, the CUP, who came to be known as the 'Young Turks', forced Abdülhamid in 1908 to abdicate and reinstate the constitution. Any rejoicing proved short-lived. The First Balkan War saw Bulgaria and Macedonia removed from the Ottoman map, with Bulgarian, Greek and Serbian troops advancing rapidly on İstanbul.

The Ottoman regime, once feared and respected, was now condescendingly known as the 'sick man of Europe'. European diplomats and politicians bombastically pondered the 'eastern question' and plotted how to cherry-pick the Empire's choicest parts.

WWI & ITS AFTERMATH

The military crisis saw a triumvirate of ambitious, nationalistic and brutish CUP *paşas* (generals) stage a coup and take de facto control of the ever-shrinking empire. They managed to push back the unlikely alliance of Balkan armies and save İstanbul and Edirne, but there the good they did ended. Their next move was to choose the wrong side in the looming world war. As a consequence the Ottomans had to fend off the Western powers on multiple fronts during WWI: Greece in Thrace, Russia in northeast Anatolia, Britain in Arabia (where Lawrence led the Arabs to victory) and a multinational force at Gallipoli. It was during this time of turmoil that the Armenian scenario unfolded (see p38).

It was only at Gallipoli that the Ottomans held their own. This was due partially to the inept British high command but also to the brilliance of Turkish commander Mustafa Kemal. Iron-willed, he inspired his men to hold their lines, while also inflicting shocking casualties on the invading British and Anzac (Australian and New Zealand Army Corps) forces. Unbeknown to anyone at the time, two enduring legends of nationhood were born on the blood-spattered sands of Gallipoli: Australians see that brutal campaign as

Before WWI Mustafa Kemal had served in the army in Sofia, Bulgaria, a legacy of his disagreements with the CUP revolutionaries, whom he had helped seize power in 1908.

1571	1595–1603	1683
The Ottoman navy is destroyed at Lepanto by resurgent European powers who are now in control of the lucrative Atlantic and Indian Ocean trades and who are experiencing the intellectual and scientific advances of the Renaissance.	Stay-at-home sultan Mehmet has his 19 brothers strangled to protect his throne. His successor Ahmet I institutes the Cage, in order to keep potential claimants to the throne distracted with concubines and confections.	Sultan Mehmet IV besieges Vienna, ending in the rout of the Ottoman army. By century's end, the Ottomans have sued for peace for the first time at Karlowitz and have lost the Peloponnese, Hungary and Transylvania.

THE FATE OF ANATOLIA'S ARMENIANS?

The final years of the Ottoman Empire saw human misery on an epic scale, but nothing has proved as enduringly melancholy and controversial as the fate of Anatolia's Armenians. The tale begins with eyewitness accounts, in spring 1915, of Ottoman army units marching Armenian populations towards the Syrian desert. It ends with an Anatolian hinterland virtually devoid of Armenians. What happened in between remains mired in conjecture, obfuscation and outright propaganda.

Armenians maintain that they were subject to the 20th century's first orchestrated 'genocide', that over a million Armenians were summarily executed or killed on death marches and that Ottoman authorities issued a deportation order intending to remove the Armenian presence from Anatolia. They allege that Ottoman archives relating to this event were deliberately destroyed. To this day, Armenians demand an acknowledgment of this 'genocide'.

Turkey, though, refutes that any such 'genocide' occurred. It admits that thousands of Armenians died but claim the Ottoman order had been to 'relocate' Armenians without intending to eradicate them. The deaths, according to Turkish officials, were the result of disease and starvation, direct consequences of the chaos during a time of war. A few even claim that it was the Turks who were subjected to 'genocide', at the hand of Armenian guerrillas.

Almost a century after the events the issue is unresolved. In 2005 Prime Minister Erdoğan encouraged the creation of a joint Turkish-Armenian commission to investigate the events; Orhan Pamuk, Turkey's most famous novelist and 2006 Nobel Prize Laureate, speaking in Germany, claimed that a million Armenians had been killed and that Turkey should be prepared to discuss it; and academics convened in İstanbul to discuss the issue. All three initiatives failed: Armenia flatly refused Erdoğan's offer, Pamuk was pursued by the courts for impugning the Turkish national identity (see p52) and the conference attracted vehement protests from Turkish nationalists.

The murder of outspoken Turkish–Armenian journalist Hrant Dink in early 2007 at the hand of Turkish ultranationalists appeared to confirm that rapprochement is impossible. But what happened? Thousands of Turks marched in protest and in solidarity with the slain journalist bearing placards saying 'We are all Armenians'. Is the problem solvable? We hope so.

the birth of their independence, while the Turks regard the defence of their homeland as the birth of their national consciousness.

The end of WWI saw the Turks largely in disarray. The French occupied southeast Anatolia; the Italians controlled the western Mediterranean; the Greeks occupied İzmir; and Armenians, with Russian support, controlled parts of northeast Anatolia. The Treaty of Sèvres in 1920 ensured the dismembering of the Empire, with only a sliver of dun steppe to be left to the Turks. European haughtiness did not count on a Turkish backlash. But backlash there was. A slowly building Turkish nationalist movement was created, motivated by the humiliation of Sèvres. At the head of this movement was Mustafa Kemal, the victorious leader at Gallipoli. He secured the support of the Bektaşi dervishes, began organising Turkish resistance and

1720	1760–90s	1826
Ahmet III is an extravagant sultan, spending vast amounts on follies on the Bosphorus. His rule is marked by nepotism and corruption. The Austrian Habsburgs and Russia emerge as major rivals to the Ottomans.	Despite attempts at modernisation and military training from France, Ottomans lose territory in the Black Sea and Caucasus to the Russians under Catherine the Great, who grandiosely anoints herself as protector of the Ottomans Orthodox subjects.	Major attempts at reform under Mahmut II. He reforms and centralises the Empire's administration and modernises the army, resulting in the 'Auspicious Event' where the unruly janissaries are bloodily put to the sword.

established a national assembly in Ankara, far from opposing armies and meddling diplomats.

In the meantime, a Greek expeditionary force pushed out from İzmir. The Greeks (who, since attaining independence in 1830, had dreamed of recreating the Byzantine Empire) saw this opportunity to realise their *megali idea* (great idea). Capitalising on Turkish disorder, the Greeks took Bursa and Edirne and pushed towards Ankara. This was just the provocation that Mustafa Kemal needed to galvanise Turkish support. After an initial skirmish at İnönü, the Greeks pressed on for Ankara seeking to crush the Turks. But stubborn Turkish resistance stalled them at the Battle of Sakarya. The two armies faced off again at Dumlupınar. Here the Turks savaged the Greeks, sending them in panicked retreat towards İzmir, where they were expelled from Anatolia amid stricken Greek refugees, pillage and looting.

Mustafa Kemal emerged as the hero of the Turkish people. Macedonian-born himself, he had realised the dream of the 'Young Turks' of years past: to create a modern, Turkish nation state. The Treaty of Lausanne in 1923 undid the humiliations of Sèvres and saw foreign powers leave Turkey. The borders of the modern Turkish state were set and the Ottoman Empire was no more, although its legacy lives on in manifold nation states, from Albania to Yemen.

A Peace to End All Peace: Creating the Modern Middle East, 1914-1922 by David Fromkin is an intriguing account of how the map of the modern Middle East was drawn arbitrarily by European colonial governments in the wake of the demise of the Ottoman Empire.

ATATÜRK: REFORM & THE REPUBLIC

The Turks consolidated Ankara as their capital and abolished the sultanate. Mustafa Kemal assumed the newly created presidency of the secular republic at the head of the CHP (Republican People's Party). Later he would take on the name Atatürk (literally 'Father Turk'). Thereupon the Turks set to work: they had a job ahead of them. But Mustafa Kemal's energy was apparently limitless; his vision was to see Turkey take its place among the modern, developed countries of Europe.

At the time, the country was impoverished and devastated after years of war, so a firm hand was needed. The Atatürk era was one of enlightened despotism. Atatürk set up the institutions of democracy while never allowing any opposition sufficient oxygen to impede him. He brooked little dissent and indulged an occasional authoritarian streak, yet his ultimate motivation was the betterment of his people. One aspect of his vision, however, was to have ongoing consequences for the country: his insistence that the state be solely Turkish. Encouraging national unity made sense considering the nationalist separatist movements that had bedevilled the Ottoman Empire, but in doing so a cultural existence was denied the Kurds, many of whom had fought valiantly during the independence struggle. Sure enough, within a few years a Kurdish revolt erupted in southeast Anatolia, the first of several such ructions to recur throughout the 20th century (see p47).

1839	**1876**	**1908**
Reform continues with the Tanzimat, a charter of legal and political rights, the underlying principle of which was the equality of the Empire's Muslim and non-Muslim subjects. The first newspapers, banks and secular schools are established.	Abdül Hamit II takes the throne. The National Assembly meets for the first time and a constitution is created but Serbia and Montenegro, urged by Russia and emboldened by the pan-Slavic movement, fight for independence.	The Young Turks of the Committee for Union and Progress (CUP), based in Salonika, demand the reintroduction of the constitution. In the ensuing elections the CUP wins a convincing majority, espousing fraternity within the Empire.

FATHER OF THE MOTHERLAND

To Westerners unused to venerating figures of authority, the Turks' devotion to Atatürk may seem unusual. In response the Turks simply remark that the Turkish state is a result of his energy and vision; that without him there would be no Turkey. From an era that threw up Stalin, Hitler and Mussolini, Atatürk stands as a beacon of statesmanship and proves that radical reform, deftly handled, can be hugely successful.

The Turks' gratitude to Atatürk manifests itself throughout the country. He appears on stamps, banknotes, statues – often in martial pose astride a horse – in town squares across the country. His name is affixed to bridges, airports and highways too many to mention. And seemingly every house where he spent a night from the southern Aegean to the Black Sea is now a museum.

Turkish schoolchildren are well versed in Atatürk's life and achievements – they learn them by rote and can dutifully recite them. But it may be that the history-book image of Atatürk is more simplistic than the reality. An avowed champion of Turkish culture, he preferred opera to Turkish music. Though calling himself 'Father Turk', he had no offspring and a single short and troubled marriage.

Atatürk died relatively young (aged 57) in 1938. No doubt years as a military man, reformer and public figure took their toll. His friend and successor as president, İsmet İnönü, ensured that he was to be lauded by his countrymen. The praise continues to this day. Indeed, any perceived insult to Atatürk is considered not only highly offensive but is also illegal. Cynicism about politicians may be well and good at home, but it is a no-no in Turkey as regards Atatürk.

There are two outstanding biographies of the great man. Patrick Kinross' *Atatürk: Rebirth of a Nation* is engagingly written and sticks closely to the official Turkish view, while Andrew Mango's *Atatürk* is a detached, objective and highly detailed look at a remarkable life.

Bruce Clark's *Twice a Stranger* is an investigation of the Greek–Turkish population exchanges of the 1920s. Analysing background events and interviewing Greeks and Turks who were transported, Clark recreates the trauma of the exchanges and shines new light on the fraught relationship of the two countries.

The desire to create unified nation states on the Aegean also prompted population exchanges between Greece and Turkey, whereby whole communities were uprooted: Greek-speaking peoples of Anatolia were shipped to Greece, while Muslim residents of Greece were transferred to Turkey. These exchanges brought great disruption and the creation of ghost villages, vacated but never reoccupied, such as Kayaköy. It was a pragmatic move aimed at forestalling ethnic violence, but it became one of the more melancholy episodes of the early years of the republic and, importantly, hobbled the development of the new state. Turkey found itself without much of its Ottoman-educated classes, many of whom had not been Turkish-speakers, and in their stead Turkey accepted impoverished Muslim peasants from the Balkans.

Atatürk's zeal for modernisation was unwavering, giving the Turkish state a makeover on micro and macro levels. Everything from headgear to spoken language was scrutinised and where necessary reformed. Throughout the 1920s and '30s Turkey adopted the Gregorian calendar (bringing it in line with the West, rather than the Middle East), reformed its alphabet (adopting the Roman alphabet and abandoning Arabic script) and standardised the Turkish language, outlawed the fez (seen as a reminder of the Ottoman era,

1912–13	1915–18	1919–22
The First and Second Balkan Wars. An alliance of Serbian, Greek and Bulgarian forces take Salonika, previously the second city of the Ottoman Empire, and Edirne. Edirne is reclaimed by the Turks when the alliance turns on itself.	Turkish involvement in WWI sees them fighting on the side of the Central Powers. Encroached on on four fronts, the Turks repel invaders only at Gallipoli. At war's end a British fleet is positioned off the coast of İstanbul.	The Turkish War of Independence. The humiliating terms of Treaty of Sèvres (1920) reduced Turkey to a strip of Anatolian territory but the Turks, led by Mustafa Kemal, fight off the Greeks and eject the Great Powers.

hence backward), instituted universal suffrage, and decreed that Turks should take surnames, something they had previously got by without. By the time of his death in November 1938, Atatürk had, to a greater or lesser degree, lived up to his name, having been the pre-eminent figure in the creation of the nation state and dragging it into the modern era through inspiration and sheer weight of personality.

DEMOCRATISATION & THE COUPS

Though reform had proceeded apace in Turkey, the country remained economically and military weak and Atatürk's successor, İsmet İnönü, stepped carefully to avoid involvement in WWII. The war over, Turkey found itself allied to the USA. A bulwark against the Soviets (the Armenian border then marked the edge of the Soviet bloc), Turkey was of great strategic importance and received significant US aid. The new friendship was cemented when Turkish troops fought in Korea, and Turkey was made a member of NATO.

Meanwhile, the democratic process gained momentum. In 1950 the Democratic Party swept to power. Ruling for a decade, the Democrats had raised the hackles of the Kemalists by reinstituting the call to prayer in Arabic (something Atatürk had outlawed), but when, as their tenure proceeded, they failed to live up to their name and became increasingly autocratic, the army stepped in during 1960 and removed them. Army rule lasted only briefly, and resulted in the liberalisation of the constitution, but it set the tone for years to come. The military considered themselves the guardians of Atatürk's vision – pro-Western and secular – and felt obliged and empowered to step in when necessary to ensure the republic maintained the right trajectory.

The 1960s and '70s saw the creation of political parties of all stripes, from left-leaning to fascist-nationalist to pro-Islamic, but the profusion did not necessarily make for a more vibrant democracy. The late 1960s were characterised by left-wing activism and political violence that prompted a move to the right by centrist parties. The army stepped in again in 1971 to restore order, before swiftly handing power back in late 1973. Several months later the military was ordered into Cyprus by President Bulent Ecevit to protect the Turkish minority, in response to a Cypriot Greek extremist organisation that had seized power and was espousing union with Greece. The invasion divided the island into two political entities – one of which is only recognised by Turkey – a situation that persists.

Political and economic chaos reigned for the rest of the '70s so the military seized power again to re-establish order in 1980. This they did through the creation of the highly feared National Security Council, but they allowed elections in 1983. Here, for the first time in decades, was a happy result for Turkey. Turgut Özal, leader of the Motherland Party (ANAP), won a majority and, unhindered by unruly coalition partners, was able to set Turkey back on course. An astute economist and pro-Islamic, Özal made vital economic and

European observers referred to Anatolia as 'Turchia' as early as the 12th century. The Turks themselves didn't do this until the 1920s.

1923	1945	1960
The Treaty of Lausanne, signed by the steadfast İsmet İnönü, undoes the wrongs of Sèvres. The Republic of Turkey is unanimously supported by the members of the national assembly and the process of modernisation begins.	After WWII, which the Turks have avoided, the Truman Doctrine brings aid to Turkey on the condition of increased democratisation. By 1950 the Democratic Party is in power. Turkey becomes a key Cold War ally of the US.	A military coup deposes Democrat leader Adnan Menderes, who is later hanged. A new, more liberal constitution is drafted. The next 20 years are politically turbulent, with the military stepping in twice more to oust the government.

legal reforms that brought Turkey in line with the international community and sowed the seeds of its current vitality.

The late 1980s, however, were notable for two aspects – corruption and Kurdish separatism (see p47) – that were to have an impact long beyond Özal's tenure.

THE 1990S: MODERNISATION & SEPARATISM

The first Gulf War kick-started the 1990s with a bang. Turkey played a prominent role in the allied invasion of Iraq, with Özal supporting sanctions and allowing air strikes from bases in southern Anatolia. In so doing, Turkey, after decades in the wilderness, affirmed its place in the international community, while also becoming a more important US ally. At the end of the Gulf War millions of Iraqi Kurds, fearing reprisals from Saddam, fled north into southeastern Anatolia. The exodus caught the attention of the international media, bringing the Kurdish issue into the spotlight, and resulted in the establishment of a Kurdish safe haven in northern Iraq. This in turn emboldened the Kurdistan Workers' Party (PKK), who stepped up their campaign, thus provoking more drastic and iron-fisted responses from the Turkish military, such that the southeast was effectively enduring a civil war.

Voices from the Front: Turkish Soldiers on the War with the Kurds by Nadire Mater offers sometimes harrowing first-hand accounts of the Kurdish insurgency during the 1990s.

Meanwhile, Turgut Özal died suddenly in 1993, creating a power vacuum. Various weak coalition governments followed throughout the 1990s, with a cast of figures flitting across the political stage. Tansu Çiller served briefly as Turkey's first female prime minister, but her much-vaunted feminine touch and economic expertise did not find a solution to the Kurdish issue nor cure the ailing economy. In fact, her husband's name was aired in various fraud investigations at a time when links between organised crime, big business and politicians were becoming increasingly apparent.

In December 1995 the religious Refah (Welfare) Party managed to form a government led by veteran politician Necmettin Erbakan. Heady with power, Refah politicians made Islamist statements that raised the ire of the military. In 1997 the National Security Council declared that Refah had flouted the constitutional ban on religion in politics. Faced with what some dubbed a 'postmodern coup', the government resigned and Refah was disbanded.

TOWARDS EUROPE

The capture of PKK leader Abdullah Öcalan in early 1999 may have seemed like a good omen after the torrid '90s. His capture offered an opportunity – still largely unrealised – to settle the Kurdish question. Later that year the disastrous earthquakes centred on İzmit put paid to any premillennial false hopes. The government's handling of the crisis was inadequate; however, the global outpouring of aid and sympathy – not least from traditional foes, the Greeks – did much to reassure Turks they were valued members of the world community.

1983	1985–99	2001
In elections after the coup of 1980, the Özal era begins. A populist and pragmatic leader, Özal embarks on economic reform, encouraging foreign investment. Turkey opens to the West and the tourism industry takes off.	Abdullah Öcalan establishes the Kurdistan Workers Party (PKK), a Marxist-inspired terror group calling for a Kurdish state. Escalation of PKK violence leads to a long, bloody, low-intensity war in southeast Anatolia, until Öcalan's capture in 1999.	The economy collapses, and the Turkish lira plummets. With an unwieldy coalition in political deadlock, massive foreign debt and after Kurdish problems and human rights violations of the 1990s, Turkey is at a low ebb.

An economic collapse in early 2001 (see p45) seemed to compound the country's woes, but despite the government securing IMF loans the long-suffering Turks were understandably jaded with their lot.

Things changed dramatically in late 2002 when the Justice and Development Party (AKP) swept to power in such convincing fashion that most old parties and several political perennials were confined to oblivion. The electorate held its collective breath to see if the military would intervene to prevent the pro-Islamic AKP from assuming government but the generals respected the will of the electorate. The AKP's leader, Recep Tayyıp Erdoğan, was initially banned from sitting in parliament due to an earlier conviction for 'inciting religious violence', but some deft sidestepping ensued, and he was allowed into parliament and into the prime ministership.

Pundits were concerned as to which direction Erdoğan would lead. Initial misgivings were swiftly cast aside. Clearly intent on gaining EU entry for Turkey, Erdoğan proved a skilful and inspiring leader, amending the constitution to scrap the death penalty, granting greater rights to the Kurds and cracking down on human rights violations. By the end of 2002 the EU was making approving noises and the economy was largely back on track. Turkey was as self-confident as it had been for years, steadfastly refusing American demands that the country be used as a base for attacking northern Iraq in 2003, then later the same year enduring terrorist bombings in İstanbul with resilience and solidarity. By January 2005 the economy was considered robust enough to introduce the new Turkish lira (Yeni Türk Lirası) and do away with six zeroes on each and every banknote. In 2009 the Yeni Türk Lirası was renamed the Türk Lirası (TL).

The flirtatious EU finally started accession talks with Turkey in October 2005 after many years of come-ons had come to nothing, but the road ahead still proved bumpy. Resistance from some EU member states towards Turkish membership, and the reforms that EU candidacy has imposed on Turkey, mean that the initial ardour for membership has cooled somewhat. Nonetheless Turkey continues to exhibit more self-confidence on the world stage, playing a pivotal role in ongoing peace negotiations between Syria and Israel, while also hosting Pope Benedict, Queen Elizabeth and Greek PM Costas Karamanlis between late 2006 and 2008.

Meanwhile, the political scene has been characteristically volatile. Following the AKP's triumphant re-election in mid-2007, the tussle between 'secularists' and 'Islamists' grew more heated. A legal case to close the AKP on the grounds that it was pursuing an antisecular agenda brought tensions to boiling point. This was exacerbated in mid-2008 when the police arrested scores of people associated with the ultranationalist Ergenekon movement, alleging they were fomenting a coup against the AKP government, and a series of terrorist bombs exploded in İstanbul. Everyone drew a sigh of relief when the Constitutional Court voted not to close the AKP, but the ongoing political scene is sure to be captivating viewing.

Former BBC Turkey correspondent Chris Morris ponders the rhythms and cadences of modern Turkish life in *The New Turkey: The Quiet Revolution on the Edge of Europe.*

The Turkic Speaking Peoples edited by Ergün Çağatay and Doğan Kuban is a monumental doorstop of a volume investigating, in full colour, the traditions and cultures of Turkic-speaking groups from the Balkans to the western deserts of China.

2002	2005	2008
Recep Tayyip Erdoğan's Justice and Development Party (AKP) wins a landslide election victory, a reflection of the Turkish public's disgruntlement with the established parties. Erdoğan is an astute economic manager and the economy recovers.	The EU finally begins accession talks with Turkey. Reforms to the economy and legal systems, as demanded by the EU, begin to be implemented. Resistance to Turkish membership by some EU states leads to a decrease in approval by some Turks.	After a resounding election victory in mid-2007 the AKP is threatened with closure on the grounds that it is undermining the secular nature of the Turkish nation. The court votes against closure. Political tension is alleviated.

The Culture

THE NATIONAL PSYCHE

Legion are the travellers who return from a holiday in Turkey remarking on the friendliness of the Turks. Tales abound of travellers being offered cups of çay (tea), having meals paid for, of hitchhikers being ferried vast distances out of the driver's way, of expats constantly being invited to peoples' homes for meals or picnics. The Turks are an innately gregarious people and their tradition of hospitality – perhaps linked to their Islamic faith – runs deep. Cheerful and sociable, the Turks' fascination with visitors and pride in their country mean they are keen to act as ambassadors to everyone who comes to Turkey.

It's not uncommon for picnicking Turks to welcome passers-by with cries of 'buyrun', an untranslatable term that means something like 'come and join us', and while carpet-shop touts or restaurant spruikers in resorts may be ultimately interested in your Western currency, they generally engage with you with a degree of light-heartedness and a lack of rancour.

The Turks also display an admirable joie de vivre and ability to live for the moment. The pace of modern life may be picking up but there is still always time to chat with friends and neighbours, to stop for a cup of çay or just to watch the comings and goings of the passing world. The Victorian travel writer AW Kinglake described the Turks as having an 'Asiatic contentment', perhaps not the most politically correct term but still an accurate portrayal of the Turkish ability to shoot the breeze and remain untroubled by workaday events.

Turks are also fiercely proud of Turkey. At times this may manifest itself as defensiveness or chauvinism. They may grumble about aspects of the country but they don't welcome outsiders doing the same thing. And it's surprising how many well-educated Turks subscribe to conspiracy theories about ill-defined outside forces planning to dismember Turkey.

However, with rising affluence and a degree of liberalism entering the political process, the Turks are increasingly self-confident and, despite innate conservatism, open to new ideas. The default position for most Turks is to be warm-hearted and generous, something that most visitors realise very quickly.

LIFESTYLE

Inevitably among a population of over 70 million there is no single way of life, but one common thread through all of Turkey is the importance of family. The chosen path for the majority of Turks is to marry and raise a family. Children are adored and indulged. Family gatherings occur regularly – they are long, joyous and involve a lot of food – and are perhaps the most common manifestation of the Turks' sense of community.

In fact, Turkish life tends to be lived communally. Rare is the Turkish couch potato: far preferable is convening in teahouses, parks or playgrounds, discussing the issues of the day and chewing on sunflower seeds. And on hot nights, families will sit on their balconies calling through the darkness to their neighbours and sharing jokes with passers-by.

Due to economic conditions, however, there are stark differences in lifestyles that exist side by side in Turkey. In İstanbul, İzmir, Ankara and other major cities, people live their lives much as is done in the West. Both men and women march off to jobs in offices and shops, men and women socialise together, and in their homes people sit down to dinner at tables

---

Turks claim to be able to detect someone's political affiliations from the shape of their moustache. Civil servants are given instructions on how much hair can adorn their upper lip. University students are forbidden to grow beards.

Turkey has the youngest population in Europe; some 22 million (32% of the population) are under 15 years old.

and use 'modern' (ie pedestal) toilets. But move even a short distance from the cities, or into the poorer neighbourhoods of those cities themselves, and you will find a far more traditional lifestyle. Here, men and women rarely sit (let alone socialise) together, women stay at home to look after children (or work the fields), everyone sits on the floor to eat, and toilets are of the knees-by-your-ears squat variety.

This picture has been complicated by mass emigration of villagers seeking economic opportunities in the cities in the west of the country, which means that alongside the Westernised neighbourhoods there are also pockets of traditionalism. Women in headscarves may be a rarity along İstanbul's İstiklal Caddesi, but they're the norm in the backstreets of Sultanahmet. Although people are generally becoming wealthier, with a declining number of people living under the poverty line (currently a quarter of the population), the gap between those at the top and bottom of the income pile is wide and growing wider.

Meanwhile, Turkish society appears to be adopting more liberal social mores. Part of this may be due to the influence of tourism: the first Western tourists who wore bikinis in the 1970s caused scandals in some seaside villages, but today such taboos are breaking down and young Turks in the cities behave in much the same way as young people anywhere. No doubt a more liberal approach is also a consequence of increased exposure to the West, and the forces of globalisation, in general. But here again, there can be a stark difference between what is acceptable behaviour and dress in a beach resort and what is acceptable in a rural village or conservative neighbourhood. This can cause confusion for tourists who, assuming anything goes these days, are shocked when offence is taken or reception frosty. If in doubt about how to behave, always err on the side of caution, especially in rural areas.

> A survey carried out in eastern and southeastern Turkey discovered that one in 10 women was living in a polygamous marriage, even though these became illegal in 1926.

ECONOMY

Turkey is infamous for a galloping inflation rate that tipped 77.5% in the 1990s, with so many zeros regularly added to the currency that having a 1,000,000 lira cup of tea was a bad joke come true. An economic collapse in 2001 compounded the country's woes. Inflation skyrocketed and the value of the Turkish lira further plummeted. Kemal Derviş, a newly appointed Minister of the Economy, succeeded in sweet-talking the IMF for loans and made much-needed economic reforms, thus avoiding a potentially disastrous downward spiral.

> According to a Durex Global Sex Survey in 2007, Turkey is the world's 'most virile nation'. Turkish respondents to the survey reported an average of 14 sexual partners in a lifetime, higher, even, than the Italians...

By January 2005, under the direction of the Justice and Development Party (AKP), the economy was robust enough to introduce the new Turkish lira (Yeni Türk Lirası) and finally do away with all those zeroes – something that had been promised for years. For a year or so the yeni lira looked fairly stable, but in early 2006 a global downturn saw an exodus of international money and the currency lost some 18% of its value. Investors were left feeling shaky, sadly reminded of Turkey's vulnerability due to its high debt and current-account deficit. During the final crises of 2008 the Turkish economy was affected but it did not appear to suffer as much devastation as some European economies, and Turkish investors tended to maintain an optimistic outlook. In January 2009, the Yeni Türk Lirası was renamed the Türk Lirası (Turkish lira; TL).

POPULATION

Turkey has a population of approximately 70 million, the great majority of whom are Turks. Kurds form the largest minority, and there are also small groups of Laz and Hemşin people along the Black Sea coast, and Yörüks and Tahtacıs along the eastern Mediterranean coast.

THE PLEASURES OF THE TURKISH BATH

The hamam (steam bath) was an institution that passed from the Romans to the Byzantines, and thence to the Turks. It was a much-anticipated weekly outing, for women especially, an opportunity to gossip, groom and pamper, and for mothers to size up potential matches for their sons. Although modern bathrooms have reduced the need for public bathing, the tradition of the leisurely soak is still alive, albeit on a much reduced scale. Unfortunately some of the finest old baths have raised prices for tourists, putting them out of reach for most locals, while also reducing the quality of their service on the assumption that tourists don't know what to expect and won't be coming back anyway.

Many people feel anxious the first time they go to a hamam. So what should you expect when you cross the threshold? First up, you usually need to choose and pay at the door for the service you'd like. Then you enter the *camekan,* where you'll be shown to a cubicle where you can undress, store your clothes, lock up your valuables and wrap around yourself the *peştimal* (cloth) that's provided. You'll be given a pair of *nalın* (wooden clogs), which you'll need to attempt to wear to prevent slipping on the marble floors. Then an attendant will lead you through the *soğukluk* (cold room, though it's usually warm) to the *hararet* (steam room) where you sit and sweat for a while.

It's cheapest to wash yourself (bring soap, shampoo and towel). The steam room will be ringed with individual *kurna* (basins) that you fill from the taps above. When sluicing the water over yourself try not to get soap into the water in the basin. Also, avoid splashing your neighbours, especially on a Friday when someone who has completed their ritual wash would have to start over again if soaked by a non-Muslim. But washing yourself is missing the fun. It's far more enjoyable to let an attendant do it, dousing you with warm water and then scrubbing you with a *kese* (a coarse cloth mitten), loosening dirt you never suspected you had. Afterwards you'll be lathered with a sudsy swab, rinsed off and shampooed.

When all this is complete you can have a massage, an experience certainly worth indulging in once during your trip. Some massages are carried out on the floor or a table, but usually you'll be spread out on the marble slab called the *göbektaşı* (belly stone) beneath the central dome. Take note that the *göbektaşı* can be hot. In touristy areas the massage is likely to be pretty cursory, unless you're prepared to pay the extra for an 'oil massage'. Elsewhere, however, a Turkish massage can be an unforgettable and invigorating experience.

Bath etiquette dictates that men should keep the *peştimal* on at all times. In the women's section, the amount of modesty expected varies considerably: in some baths total nudity is fine, in others it would be a blunder to remove your knickers; play safe by keeping your underwear on under your *peştimal* until inside the hot room where you can decide what is appropriate. It's worth bringing a dry change of underwear to put on after your hamam. If you want to shave your legs or armpits, do this in the *camekan* rather than in the bath.

Traditional hamams have separate sections for men and women or admit men and women at separate times. Opening hours for women are almost invariably more restricted than for men. In tourist areas some hamams are more than happy for foreign men and women to bathe together, and charge a premium price for the privilege. In traditional hamams, women are washed and massaged by other women – no Turkish woman would let a male masseur anywhere near her. Women who accept a massage from a male masseur should have their massage within view of companions and protest loudly at the first sign of impropriety.

Since the 1950s there has been a steady movement of people away from the countryside and into the towns, so that today some 66% of Turks live in cities. This process was accelerated by the years of fighting in the southeast when villagers were either forcibly relocated or decided for themselves that the grass was greener elsewhere (predominantly in Turkey's largest cities of İstanbul, Ankara, Bursa and Adana, but also in eastern towns such as Gaziantep and Malatya). The result is that cities such as İstanbul have turned into pervasive sprawls, their historic hearts encircled by rings of largely unplanned new neighbourhoods inhabited by economic emigrants from across the country.

Turks

That the Turks speak Turkish is a given, but what is not perhaps so widely known is that Turkic languages are spoken by a much larger group of people of similar ancestry who can be found spread in pockets throughout much of Eurasia: west of Turkey in Macedonia, Greece and Bulgaria; north in Ukraine and parts of Russia; and east through Azerbaijan and Iran to the nations of Central Asia and the western corner of China, Xinjiang. This is because the modern Turks are the descendants of a string of Central Asian tribal groupings, the most recognisable of which are the Huns, the Seljuks and the Ottomans. Although academics believe the Turkic languages may have been spoken as early as 600 BC, the Turks definitively first appeared in medieval Chinese sources as the Tujue (or Turks) in 6th-century Mongolia and Siberia.

As they moved westward the predecessors of the modern Turks encountered the Arabs and converted to Islam. The Seljuks established the Middle East's first Turkic empire (see p33). The Seljuks' defeat of the Byzantines in battle in 1071 opened up all of Anatolia to wandering Turkish groups, thus speeding up the westward drift the Turks had been pursuing for hundreds of years. Over the following centuries, Anatolia became the heartland of the Ottoman Empire and the core of the modern Turkish Republic.

In recent years the Turks have been more willing to acknowledge the links with their Turkic brethren and have played champion for the Turkish minority in Bulgaria, while also attempting to establish business and cultural links with the Turkic-speaking Central Asian states.

Various (not exactly academically rigorous) theories state that the Turks are descendants of Japheth, the grandson of Noah. The Ottomans themselves claimed that Osman could trace his genealogy back through 52 generations to Noah.

Kurds

Turkey has a significant Kurdish minority estimated at 14 million. The sparsely populated eastern and southeastern regions are home to perhaps seven million Kurds, while seven million more Kurds live elsewhere in the country, more or less integrated into mainstream Turkish society. Virtually all Turkish Kurds are Sunni Muslims. Kurds look physically similar to the Turks, but have a distinct culture, family traditions and language (an Indo-European tongue related to Persian) and live spread across the border regions of Turkey, Iran, Iraq and Syria.

The ongoing struggle between Kurds and Turks has been well documented. The Ottoman Empire's inclusivity meant that Kurds and Turks fought together during the struggle for independence in the 1920s, but the situation changed after the formation of the republic. Unlike the Greeks, Jews and Armenians, the Kurds were not guaranteed rights as a minority group under the terms of the 1923 Treaty of Lausanne (see p39). The Turkish state was decreed to be unitary, ie inhabited solely by Turks, hence the Kurds were denied a cultural existence. After the fragmentation along ethnic lines of the former domains of the Ottoman Empire, such an approach for the modern state was understandable and may have seemed prudent, but as the Kurds were so numerous it was perhaps inevitable that problems would arise.

As early as 1925 the Kurds rebelled against restrictions placed on their identity. Indeed, until relatively recently the Turkish government refused to even recognise the existence of the Kurds, insisting they were 'Mountain Turks'. Even today the census form does not allow anyone to identify themselves as Kurdish, nor can they be identified as Kurdish on their identity cards. This is in spite of the fact that many people in the east, particularly

The Kurds: A People in Search of Their Homeland by Kevin McKiernan recounts travels among the Kurds of Turkey, Iran and Iraq and discusses their current plight in light of their history and the geopolitics of the region.

Istanbul: Poetry of Place, edited by Ateş Orga, is a collection of star-struck poets, from Sultan Süleyman to WB Yeats, painting portraits of the great city.

IN THE FAMILY WAY

Perhaps exhibiting a vestige of their nomadic, tribal origins, the Turks seem to retain a strong sense of family within their community. Indeed, one of the more endearing Turkish habits is to use familial titles to embrace friends, acquaintances and even strangers into the extended family. A teacher may refer to his student as *'çocuğum'* (my child); a passer-by will address an old man on a street corner as *'dede'* (literally, 'grandfather'); and the old woman on the bus would not bat an eyelid if a stranger called her *'teyze'* (auntie).

It is also common for children to refer to family friends as *'amca'* (uncle) and for males of all ages to address slightly older men as *'ağabey'* (pronounced 'abi', and roughly analogous to English men saying 'guv'nor'). You will also hear small children referring to their teenage sisters as *'abla'*, equivalent to 'big sister', which may sound obvious but which is rather charming in its simplicity.

These terms are a sign of deference and respect but also of affection and inclusiveness. And perhaps this intimacy explains how some of the sense of community found in rural villages persists amid the tower blocks of sprawling cities where the majority of Turks now live.

women, speak the Kurmancı dialect of Kurdish as their first language (see boxed text, p645) and may have a limited grasp of Turkish.

In 1984 Abdullah Öcalan formed the Kurdistan Workers Party (PKK), which proved to be the most enduring – and bloodthirsty – Kurdish organisation that Turkey had seen. The PKK was and remains an outlawed organisation. Many Kurds, while not necessarily supporting the early demands of the PKK for a separate state, wanted to be able to read newspapers in their own language, have their children taught in their own language and watch Kurdish TV. The Turkish government reacted to the PKK's violent tactics and territorial demands by branding any call for Kurdish rights as 'separatism'. Strife escalated until much of southeastern Anatolia was in a permanent state of emergency. After 15 years of fighting, forced relocations, suffering and the deaths of over 30,000 people, Abdullah Öcalan was captured in Kenya in 1999. The 21st century started on a more promising note when Öcalan urged his followers to lay down their weapons and a ceasefire was called.

The best hope for change in Turkish–Kurdish relations may lie in Turkey's eagerness to join the EU, which demands the rights of cultural and ethnic minorities be protected. And an increasingly pragmatic and reasoned approach on the part of both the military and government has borne some fruit. In 2002 the Turkish government approved broadcasts in Kurdish and the go-ahead was given for Kurdish to be taught in language schools. Emergency rule was lifted in the southeast. The government started compensating villagers displaced in the troubles. Life for Kurds in the southeast has become considerably easier: harsh military rule and censorship have largely been lifted, and optimism has been fuelled by the possibility of joining the EU, and the guarantee of democratic rights that will come with it. In the general election of 2007, 20 Kurdish independents (including seven women) were elected in the national assembly. Many Kurds have been delighted with the development of the quasi-independent Kurdish state over the border in northern Iraq, but prefer to see their future with a country tied to the EU.

However, despite progress, some Kurdish activists maintain that reforms are inadequate, and bureaucratic hurdles are placed in the path of Kurds seeking to teach, publish or broadcast in their own language. Pundits also suggest that an amnesty for PKK militants would go a long way to ending ongoing military flare-ups. The ceasefire that followed the arrest of Öcalan has long since been broken and sporadic fighting continues in the southeast, with the Turkish army regularly entering Kurdish territory in northern Iraq in pursuit

According to the UN, Turkic languages are among the world's most widely used, spoken in one form or another by around 150 million people from the former Yugoslavia to northwestern China.

of the PKK. A group believed to be a front for the PKK, the TAK (Kurdistan Freedom Falcons), claims responsibility for the unrest and sporadic bombings throughout the country. When several bombs were exploded in İstanbul in summer 2008 many observers immediately blamed the PKK.

Laz

The 250,000-odd Laz people mainly inhabit the valleys between Trabzon and Rize. East of Trabzon you can hardly miss the women in their vivid red- and maroon-striped shawls. Laz men are less conspicuous, although they were once among the most feared of Turkish warriors: for years black-clad Laz warriors were Atatürk's personal bodyguards.

Once Christian but now Muslim, the Laz are a Caucasian people who speak a language related to Georgian. Just as speaking Kurdish was forbidden until 1991, so was speaking Lazuri, a language that until recently had not been written down. However, the German Wolfgang Feuerstein and the Kaçkar Working Group drew up a Lazuri alphabet (combining Latin and Georgian characters) and dictionary, and there are small signs of a growing sense of Laz nationalism.

The Laz are renowned for their sense of humour and business acumen, with many involved in the Turkish shipping industry and construction.

Hemşin

The Hemşin people mainly come from the far eastern end of the Black Sea coast, although perhaps no more than 15,000 of them still live there; most have long since migrated to the cities where they earn a tasty living as bread and pastry cooks.

The Hemşin may have arrived in Turkey from parts of what is now Armenia. Like the Laz, they were originally Christian – their relatively recent conversion could explain why they seem to wear their Islam so lightly. For example, you won't see women in veils or chadors in Ayder, although the local women wear leopard-print scarves (even more eye-catching than those worn by Laz women) twisted into elaborate headdresses.

Other

Some Turks like to say that their nation is made up of 40 tribes. Indeed, there is a multitude of minority communities throughout Turkey.

About 70,000 Armenians still live in Turkey, mainly in İstanbul, and in isolated pockets in Anatolia. The controversy surrounding the Armenians in the final years of the Ottoman Empire ensures that relations between Turks and Armenians in Turkey and abroad remain predominantly sour (see boxed text, p38). Happily, there are signs of rapprochement. In early 2007 the Armenian church on Akdamar Island (see p643) was refurbished by the Turkish Culture Ministry and reopened amid hopes that relations would improve. Turkish voters, later the same year, gave the Armenian entry in the Eurovision song contest the maximum number of votes, a move interpreted by some as a gesture of reconciliation. Throughout 2008 Ankara made several requests to the Armenian government to be able to meet face to face – something that has never happened – to start a dialogue on the issues that bedevil relations. Meanwhile, brisk Turkish–Armenian trade is ongoing, despite their mutual border being closed. Turkish manufacturers send Turkish goods to Armenia on a circuitous route through neighbouring Georgia, surely proof positive that Turks and Armenians have much in common and much to gain if they can bury their mutual distrust.

Turkey's other significant minority is the Greeks. Large Greek populations once lived throughout the Ottoman realm, but after the population exchanges

A magnificent collection of images collected over decades, *Nomads in Anatolia* by Harald Böhmer and Josephine Powell looks at the lost traditions and handicrafts of Anatolia. Difficult to find but a hugely rewarding book.

The Turkish Coast Through Writers' Eyes, edited by Rupert Scott, collects a diverse range of musings on the landscape, archaeology and way of life of this beguiling stretch where the land plunges into the blue sea.

of the early republic era (p40) and acrimonious events in the 1950s, these were reduced to a small pocket still living in İstanbul and a few Pontic Greeks in the remote valleys of the eastern Black Sea. Recent years, however, have seen a warming of relations between Greece and Turkey and the return of some Greek young professionals and students to İstanbul.

The hard-to-find *Farewell Anatolia* by Greek author Dido Sotiriou recounts the experiences of Greek villagers during the 1920s. Beloved by both Greek and Turkish readers.

There are also small communities of Circassians, Assyrians, Tatars, Bosniaks, Albanians, Arabs, Roma and Jews, as well as large – and growing – expat communities.

SPORT

Far and away the most important sport in Turkey is football (see below), but in recent years basketball has taken off. The Turkish Basketball League is now 40 years old, boasts 16 teams and attracts players from the US and elsewhere, while some Turkish players have achieved great successes in the American NBA. Turkish women's volleyball teams have been very successful in Europe, too.

Turkey is also a small but significant presence in the sport of weightlifting. The diminutive Naim Süleymanoğlu won gold at the Seoul and Barcelona Olympics, aside from setting various world records and winning world titles, while his protégé Halil Mutlu won gold medals at the Atlanta, Sydney and Athens Olympics.

In 2005 Turkey hosted its first Formula One Grand Prix. A more traditional sport is *cirit* (pronounced 'jirit'), which involves horse-borne riders hurling wooden javelins at opposing teams. Requiring a great deal of skill and horsemanship, it is thought to have evolved as a training routine for Ottoman cavalries and has recently undergone a revival in various Anatolian towns.

Football

Turks are simply mad about football (soccer). Every city has a football stadium that heaves with fans on match days. Pre- and post-match, the streets are aflutter with team flags, and the bars and tea gardens buzz with talk of nothing else.

The Turks' love affair with football began in the mid-19th century, after they were introduced to the game by English tobacco merchants. First matches saw English and Greek teams face off, but soon Turkish students from the Galata high school ran onto the field as the Galatasaray club. Fenerbahçe, Beşiktaş and Galatasaray are the top three teams, all of which are based in İstanbul and have fanatical national followings. Choose a team at your peril.

Since the 1990s Turkish teams and players have been enjoying greater success and increasingly higher profiles. In 2003, the national team made it to the semi-finals of the World Cup; Turks even outdid themselves when it came to partying hard. Summer 2008 saw the country in a high state of excitement as the national team, against expectations, made it to the semi-finals of the European Cup, only to lose to Germany.

The best place to see a game is in İstanbul (p154).

Oil Wrestling

Turkey's national sport is *yağlı güreş* (oil wrestling). The most important wrestling tournament has been taking place near Edirne since 1361 (see boxed text, p172). Every June, hundreds of amateur wrestlers from all over Turkey gather there to show off their strength.

The wrestlers are organised into classes, from *teşvik* (encouragement) to *baş güreş* (head wrestlers), with the winner in each class being designated a başpehlivan, or master wrestler. Clad only in leather shorts, they coat themselves with olive oil, utter a traditional chant and start going through a warm-up routine consisting of exaggerated arm-swinging steps and gestures. Then they get down to the nitty-gritty of battling each other to the ground, a business that involves some interesting hand techniques to say the least.

On the last day of the festival, the başpehlivans wrestle for the top prize. Finally only two are left to compete for the coveted gold belt.

Camel Wrestling

Another purely Turkish spectacle is the camel-wrestling matches held in the south Aegean town of Selçuk in late January. Huge male camels are brought together to grapple with each other, which sounds like a frightfully unfair infringement of animal rights. Actually, it all seems rather harmless, with teams of men on hand with ropes like tug-of-war teams to pull the beasts apart at the first sign of anything seriously threatening. It's an amazingly colourful sport, and the picnicking spectators love it. For more information see boxed text, p245.

MULTICULTURALISM

The Ottoman Empire was the quintessential multicultural state, a sprawling geographic realm encompassing countless ethnic communities living side by side. Ottoman policy was to allow people to live their lives in peace provided they paid the requisite taxes and obeyed the law. However, the fragmentation of the Empire into ethnically based nation states in the late 19th century, followed by the events of WWI and the Turkish War of Independence, meant that republican Turkey strived to achieve a unitary state and looked upon non-Turkish nationalism within Turkey as a threat (p39). Turkey has been slow to shake off this mindset.

Multiculturalism as it is understood in Western Europe, North America, Australia, and countries that have absorbed migrants in search of economic opportunities, is not a concept that has a lot of currency in Turkey. Because Turkey itself was reforming and establishing its economic and democratic institutions during the post-WWII era it did not attract economic migrants or refugees from elsewhere. As such, it has not needed to set up the mechanisms of modern multiculturalism. Foreigners wanting to move to Turkey often have trouble persuading officials to let them keep their own names on their ID cards, or to be allowed to register themselves as Christians or Jews.

Modern Turks will assure you that theirs is a very cosmopolitan country, but notwithstanding its various minorities (see p45), the population is almost uniformly Caucasian and Muslim. And while Turkey is a resolutely secular country, there remain lingering doubts about non-Muslim interest groups within. Indeed, avowedly secular ultranationalists are thought responsible for the gruesome murders of three Christian convert 'missionaries' in Malatya in 2007. Even the St Paul Trail (see p359) came under scrutiny for fear that volunteers waymarking the trek were really missionaries in disguise.

While Turkey didn't receive post-WWII migrants and refugees, it is now acting as a conduit and having to absorb waves of people afoot as a repercussion of globalisation. In recent years the number of asylum-seekers reaching Turkey has grown, and Turkey's position on the doorstop of Europe has made it one of the major centres for human trafficking in the world. It is estimated that more than 100,000 people annually risk their lives hidden in ships or cross the long, rugged mountain passes on Turkey's southeastern borders in the hope of continuing their journey by boat to Italy or Greece,

Louis de Bernières, of *Captain Corelli's Mandolin* fame, wrote *Birds Without Wings*, another blockbusting page-turner inspired by Kayaköy near Fethiye. It exposes the human side of the intermingling of religions and culture during the Ottoman era, war and the population exchange.

FREEDOM TO SPEAK

Although Turkey has been implementing a wide range of reforms for its EU membership bid, the country's penal code still retains the infamous Article 301, which originally prohibited people from 'insulting Turkishness', but after a lengthy political debate was amended in 2008 to prohibit 'insulting the Turkish nation'. This Article has been the basis for ongoing high-profile prosecutions of journalists, writers and artists, all of which are indicative of Turkey's tight limits on freedom of speech.

The most famous case to hit the headlines was Turkey's internationally acclaimed novelist, Orhan Pamuk, who was tried after he mentioned the killing of Armenians by Ottoman Turks at the beginning of the 20th century (see boxed text, p38). Charges were dropped in early 2006, but Pamuk had become a reluctant political symbol and a target for nationalists, and international attention was drawn to the state of affairs in Turkey.

Lesser-known but just as important cases have followed. Journalist and author Perihan Mağden was tried for 'turning people against military service' after she wrote an article in the *Yeni Akteul* newspaper entitled 'Conscientious objection is a human right'. During her case, heard in the Sultanahmet law courts in mid-2006, she was heckled by ultranationalists, whom, critics claim, security forces did little to quell. Subsequently, internationally recognised author Elif Şafak was also set to stand trial for comments made by the Armenian characters in her *The Bastard of İstanbul* before the prosecution stumbled.

Even internet phenomenon YouTube.com has been banned in Turkey several times, most recently when a video allegedly insulting Atatürk was discovered in its videologs. Some allege that the video was posted by Greek nationalists. Meanwhile, Prime Minister Erdoğan has been wont to take artists to court – and win – when he has felt he hasn't been portrayed in a flattering light.

It remains to be seen whether continuing pressure and international exposure from the increasing number of cases will eventually force the government into acting on its declared commitment to freedom of expression.

or by land into Greece. Many get stuck in İstanbul and stay as long as it takes for asylum visa applications to be processed or to earn enough money to fund the next leg of their trip.

Turkey has a large diaspora, with the largest community (some 2.6 million first- and second-generation Turks) living in Germany. Turks arrived in Germany in the 1960s as 'guest workers' at the invitation of the German government. However, the Kohl government's 1983 *Voluntary Repatriation Encouragement Act*, offering Turks financial incentives to return home, indicates that while guest workers were welcome as an economic stimulus it was not anticipated that they would stay for such long periods. There are also significant remnant Turkish populations in Bulgaria, Macedonia and Greece, and large expat communities in France, the Netherlands, UK, USA, Austria and Australia.

MEDIA

Although from the way the Turks slag their governments off in print it may look as if there's little censorship, certain subjects (the 'Armenian genocide', the 'Kurdish problem', negative portrayal of Atatürk, the army etc) still cause problems. Since editors and journalists know the likely penalties of stepping out of line, self-censorship is the order of the day. Still, some 200 journalists, artists and writers have been tried over the last two decades under Article 301, and in response, a freedom-of-speech movement has gained momentum over the last few years (see boxed text, above).

Although controls over TV have loosened, the public broadcaster, Turkish Radio and TV (TRT), still receives a certain amount of censorship from the government of the day.

RELIGION

The Turkish population is 98% Muslim, mostly of the Sunni creed, with about 20% Alevis and a small group of Shiites (around Kars and Iğdır). İstanbul, İzmir and the coastal resorts have small Christian populations. There are also small communities of Nestorian and Assyrian Orthodox Christians in and around Diyarbakır, Mardin and the Tür Abdin plateau. Turkey has had a Jewish community since the Roman era. It significantly increased in 1492 when Sultan Beyazit II welcomed the Jews expelled by the Spanish Inquisition. Today there are some 24,000 Jews in İstanbul, with smaller numbers in cities such as Ankara, Bursa and İzmir.

Turkey is a predominantly Muslim country with a secular constitution. Some 75% of Turks support the separation of state and religion, but nevertheless tensions between state and religion remain high. The urban-elite secularists, who see themselves as defenders of Turkey's republican foundations, fear the country will become an Islamic state (like its neighbour, Iran) if the fiercely guarded secular principles of the constitution are chipped away. Others say the doggedly secular laws repress basic human rights, including religious expression and duty. The headscarf has become a symbol of ongoing state-versus-religion tensions – see boxed text, below.

Biblical Sites in Turkey by Everett C Blake and Anna G Edmonds provides detailed coverage of the country's many Christian and Jewish holy places as well as the Muslim ones.

Islam

Many Turks take a fairly relaxed approach to their Muslim religious duties and practices. Fasting during Ramazan (Ramadan in many Islamic countries) is widespread and Islam's holy days and festivals are treated with due respect, but for many the holy day, Friday, and Islamic holidays are the only times they'll visit a mosque. You can also tell by the many bars and *meyhanes* (taverns) throughout the country that Turks like a drink or two. If you've travelled in other Muslim countries where the five-times-a-day prayers are strictly followed, you'll find the practice of Islam in Turkey quite different.

Like Christians, Muslims believe that Allah (God) created the world and everything in it, pretty much according to the biblical account. They

---

'ISLAMISTS' VS THE STATE: THE HEADSCARF CONTROVERSY

Who would have thought a square of cloth could cause such controversy? The issue flared up in 1998 when elected MP Merve Kavakçı tried to take the oath of office while wearing a scarf, only to be jeered at and slow hand-clapped by her fellow MPs.

Since then the headscarf *(türban* or *eşarp)* has been the issue over which secular and religiously minded Turks have tussled. Secularists argue that the headscarf is a banner for 'Islamists' and that to allow headscarf-wearing women into schools or to work in government offices would be to undermine the secular nature of the Turkish Republic. The law supports this argument. Religiously minded Turks argue that to ban women wearing headscarfs from educational facilities and government work opportunities is to unfairly deprive them of the right to an education and employment. They argue that to wear a headscarf is to be observant of religion and is indicative of a more conservative approach to life in which a woman's modesty is of heightened importance but is not an indication of 'Islamism'.

As the law stands, it's not uncommon for government ministers to be denied invitations to presidential receptions if their wives wear headscarves.

After its decisive election victory in mid-2007, the AKP amended the law. Women wearing headscarves duly turned up at universities in early 2008, but many were prevented from entering. The AKP's move was a prime catalyst for a closure case brought against the party in mid-2008 on the grounds that it was seeking to undermine the secular nature of the state. The case was overturned, but tensions remain and a solution seems elusive.

also believe that Adam (Adem), Noah (Nuh), Abraham (İbrahim), Moses (Musa) and Jesus (İsa) were prophets, although they don't believe that Jesus was divine. Muslims call Jews and Christians 'People of the Book', meaning those with a revealed religion (in the Torah and Bible) that preceded Islam.

Where Islam diverges from Christianity and Judaism is in the belief that Islam is the 'perfection' of these earlier traditions. Although Moses and Jesus were prophets, Mohammed was the greatest and last: *the* Prophet (Peygamber) to whom Allah communicated his final revelation, entrusting him to communicate it to the world.

Accordingly, Muslims do not worship Mohammed, only Allah. In fact, Muslim in Arabic means 'one who has submitted'. The *ezan* called from the minaret five times a day and said at the beginning of Muslim prayers says: 'Allah is great! There is no god but Allah, and Mohammed is his Prophet.' Allah's revelations to Mohammed are contained in the Kur'an-i Kerim, the Quran (Kuran in Turkish).

Muslims are expected to observe the following five 'pillars' of Islam:

- Say, understand and believe: 'There is no god but Allah, and Mohammed is his Prophet.'
- Pray five times daily: at dawn, noon, midafternoon, dusk and after dark.
- Give alms to the poor.
- Keep the fast of Ramazan.
- Make a pilgrimage to Mecca, if capable of doing so.

Muslim prayers are set rituals. Before praying, Muslims must wash their hands and arms, feet and ankles, and head and neck in running water. Then they must cover their head, face Mecca and perform a precise series of gestures and genuflections. If they deviate from the pattern, they must begin again.

A Muslim must not touch or eat pork, nor drink wine (interpreted as any alcoholic beverage), and must refrain from fraud, usury, slander and gambling. No sort of image of any being with an immortal soul (ie human or animal) can be revered or worshipped.

While the Ottoman Empire was a Muslim entity, its rulers weren't a particularly pious lot. No Ottoman sultan performed the Haj except Selim I – when he conquered Mecca.

The Alevis in Turkey: The Emergence of a Secular Islamic Tradition by David Shankland, based on anthropological studies in central Anatolia, sheds light on the relatively unknown traditions of the Alevis.

MOSQUE ETIQUETTE

Many Turkish mosques are breathtaking architectural and artistic creations, and, while visitors are welcome, it's important to remember that mosques are places of worship, first and foremost.

- It's best to avoid visiting while prayers are under way (ie at the call to prayer – dawn, noon, midafternoon, dusk and evening). This is particularly the case for noon prayers on Fridays, which is the Muslim holy day.
- Before entering, remove your shoes (if there is an attendant you may want to tip him when you retrieve your shoes).
- Both men and women should dress modestly and conservatively; shorts or sleeveless tops are inappropriate.
- Women should wear a scarf or head covering and a skirt or trousers that covers their knees; many of the regularly visited mosques will be able to provide a strip of material for a head covering should you not have one.
- Loud and extroverted behaviour is not appropriate, nor are displays of affection.
- Try not to disturb anyone who is praying; don't take flash photos and certainly don't walk directly in front of them.
- It will be appreciated if you drop some money into the donations box as you leave.

THE ALEVIS

An estimated 20% of the Turkish population are Alevis – Muslims whose traditions differ markedly from those of the majority Sunnis; they have more in common with Shiites. The origins of these differences lie in the quarrels that broke out in 656 between the followers and relatives of the Prophet Mohammed following his death.

The religious practices of Sunnis and Alevis differ significantly. Many Alevi beliefs correspond with those of Hacı Bektaş Veli, the 13th-century Muslim mystic whose tomb is in Hacıbektaş (see boxed text, p516) in Cappadocia. Alevism contains many aspects of Anatolian folk culture; it is a lot less rigid in its traditions – for instance men and women assemble together in a *cemevi* (assembly hall), unlike strictly segregated Sunnis – and it includes aspects of universalism and humanism.

Antipathy between the Sunnis and the Alevis has continued into modern times, with some Turks denying that Alevis are true Muslims. The left-leaning and liberal ways of the Alevis are regarded suspiciously by more-conservative Sunnis. Alevis want their religion included in textbooks (currently only the Sunni faith is covered), their rights recognised and their *cemevis* recognised as places of worship.

One of the nastiest manifestations of this antipathy is known as the Madımak tragedy (p481), where, in July 1993, a mob attacked an Alevi cultural festival, resulting in 37 deaths.

Islam has been split into many factions and sects since the time of Mohammed, and Islamic theology has become very elaborate and complex. However, these tenets are the basic ones shared by the entire Muslim community (or *umma*).

WOMEN IN TURKEY

Many women in İstanbul and other big coastal cities live a life not unlike women in the West, free to come and go pretty much as they choose, to go out to work and to dress as they wish. But for many Turkish women, especially those in villages, no such freedom exists and their lives are ruled by the need to maintain their modesty and the honour of their family for fear of retribution.

Honour killings are an ongoing headache for the country. A European Parliament investigation into women's rights in Turkey found that since 2003 the number of women allegedly murdered for 'honour' has increased. In most honour killings the 'dishonoured' family chooses a male family member to murder the woman accused of dishonouring the family, usually by having a child outside marriage or an extramarital affair. Traditionally the murderers have received reduced sentences due to pleas of provocation, but the government's recent law amendments have increased penalties. Indeed, a Turkish parliamentary commission into honour killings found some 37% of respondents thought women who commit adultery should be killed. Ongoing 'suicide epidemics' of young women out east, as described in Orhan Pamuk's novel *Snow,* is an ongoing interrelated issue. Activists think the clampdown on honour killings may be partly responsible for encouraging families to push 'dishonourable' women in the family to dispose of themselves.

Despite the country granting key rights such as the right to vote and be elected to parliament in the 1930s, long before some Western countries did so, women still don't enjoy gender equality. Studies show women earn an average 40% less than their male equivalents, that women make up only 4.4% of parliamentary representatives, and that 45% of men think they have a right to beat their wives. In 2007 the women's support group KA-DER highlighted this issue with a highly successful 'moustache protest' media campaign, whereby women sported false moustaches while asking whether it was necessary to be a man to enter parliament.

Turkey's answer to England's King Henry VIII, Sultan İbrahim (r 1640–48) had his entire harem of 280 women tied in sacks and thrown into the Bosphorus when he tired of them.

However, around one-third of all lawyers and academics in the country are female, and there's a growing pool of talented women taking executive roles in the marketing, banking and retail sectors. The AKP government has begun overhauling laws with a view to joining the EU. As of January 2003 Turkish women are technically the equal of their menfolk. The new Turkish Civil Code abolished the clause decreeing that men were the heads of every household and ruled that henceforth women will be entitled to half their household's wealth in the event of a divorce. Rape in marriage and sexual harassment are now recognised as crimes.

ARTS

Turkey's artistic traditions are rich and diverse, and here we offer an introduction to some of them.

Literature

Historically, the Turkish literary tradition consisted of epic poetry passed down orally. During the Ottoman era, highly ritualised and formal divan poetry grew popular. It is only in the last century that Turkey has developed a tradition of novel writing.

NOVELS

The notion of writer as social commentator took off in Turkey in the early 20th century, in the fertile grounds of WWI, the Russian Revolution, the demise of the Ottoman Empire and the blossoming Turkish Republic era. Yaşar Kemal was the first major internationally recognisable Turkish novelist. His *Memed, My Hawk* is a gut-wrenching insight into the desperate lives of villagers battling land-grabbing feudal lords. Of Kurdish extraction and leftist bent, Kemal has been nominated for the Nobel Prize for Literature on several occasions, and jailed a number of times for supposed pro-separatist sympathies.

Following in the footsteps of the grand old man of Turkish literature is internationally acclaimed author and 2006 Nobel Prize Laureate, Orhan Pamuk. While Kemal's work focuses on the early decades of the republic and village life in Anatolia, Pamuk tends to wrestle with the weighty issues confronting contemporary Turkey. In the course of several novels he attracted a growing audience, but he shot to international prominence in 2005 for mentioning the dreaded Armenian tragedy (see boxed text, p38). Pamuk is an inventive prose stylist, sometimes compared to Calvino and Borges. His *Black Book* is an existential whodunit set in İstanbul and told through a series of florid newspaper columns; while *My Name is Red,* set in the Ottoman era, is a murder mystery which also delves into eastern and Western concepts of art. In *İstanbul, Memoirs and the City* Pamuk ruminates on his complex relationship with the beguiling city.

For some time, the Turkish-French writer Elif Şafak has been attracting an international audience. Her novel, *The Flea Palace,* is a dense and wordy story of an elegant İstanbul apartment building fallen on hard times. The follow-up, *The Bastard of Istanbul,* is a coming-of-age saga bristling with eccentric family members and fell foul of Article 301 (see boxed text, p52). Buket Uzuner is another well-regarded female author. Her prize-winning novel *Mediterranean Waltz* is an unrequited love story set against the backdrop of civil war. Better yet is her *Long White Cloud, Gallipoli,* describing the fallout after a New Zealand woman claims a soldier revered as a war hero in Turkey is actually her great-grandfather. Meanwhile, *Dear Shameless Death* by Latife Tekin is a heady whirl of Anatolian folklore and magic realism.

Irfan Orga's autobiographical *Portrait of a Turkish Family,* set during the late Ottoman/early republican era, describes the collapse of his well-to-

Tales from the Expat Harem is a compilation of stories, sometimes funny, sometimes insightful, dealing with life in Turkey by expatriate women.

For more background reading on Turkish arts see the US-based Turkish Culture Foundation's website: www.turkish culture.org.

Orhan Pamuk's latest book, *Other Colours,* is a collection of nonfiction pieces he has written over the years. It's a lively and enquiring collection of meditations, criticism, observation and snatches from his notebooks.

do İstanbullu family and its struggle to rebuild (beautifully mirroring the times). It offers a peep into the culture of the hamam, the life of leisure in the Bosphorus *yalıs* (summer houses) and much more. Another autobiographical novel is *Young Turk*, an elegant tale related in 13 linked stories, by Jewish-Turkish writer Moris Farhi.

There is a growing trend for foreign writers – expat or otherwise – to set their tales in Turkey. Barbara Nadel writes gripping whodunits, usually set in İstanbul, featuring the chain-smoking, stubbled Inspector Çetin İkmen. *Belshazzar's Daughter*, her first, is one of the best, but the award-winning *Dance with Death* is an easy and enjoyable read, too. Alan Drew's first novel, *Gardens of Water*, looks at contemporary Turkey in the aftermath of the earthquakes of 1999. And long-term Turkophile Jason Goodwin's mysteries, *The Janissary Tree, The Snake Stone* and *The Bellini Card*, feature one of modern literatures more unlikely heroes, an Ottoman eunuch named Yashim.

See p19 for more reading recommendations.

The literary online magazine, *Turkish Book Review* (www.planb .com.tr/tbr/02), published twice a year, includes reviews and articles on movements in Turkish literature and stories by upcoming writers.

POETRY

Turkey's two most famous poets lived roughly seven centuries apart: the mystic poet Yunus Emre lived in the 13th century and Nazım Hıkmet in the 20th century.

Nazım Hikmet is not only Turkey's greatest poet but also one of the world's best. Although his work is firmly embedded in Turkey and strongly patriotic, he was also a Communist exiled for his beliefs. His poems written while incarcerated are some of his best. He died and is buried in Russia, and sadly his works are still not allowed to be taught in Turkish schools. The best introduction to his work is *Poems of Nazım Hıkmet*.

Carpets

The oldest-known carpet woven in the Turkish double-knotted Gördes style dates from between the 4th and 1st centuries BC, but it is thought that hand-woven carpet techniques were introduced to Anatolia by the Seljuks in the 12th century. Thus it's not surprising that Konya, the Seljuk capital, was mentioned by Marco Polo as a centre of carpet production in the 13th century.

Traditionally, village women wove carpets for their own family's use, or for their dowry. The general pattern and colour schemes were influenced by local traditions and the availability of certain types of wool and dyes. Patterns were memorised, and women usually worked with no more than 45cm of the carpet visible. Each artist imbued her work with her own personality, choosing a motif or a colour based on her own artistic preferences, and even events and emotions in her daily life. Knowing they would be judged on their efforts, the women took great care over their handiwork, hand-spinning and dyeing the wool.

In the 19th century, the European rage for Turkish carpets spurred the development of carpet companies. The companies, run by men, would deal with the customers, take orders, purchase and dye the wool according to the customers' preferences, and contract local women to produce the finished product. The designs might be left to the women, but were more often provided by the company based on their customers' tastes. Although well made, these carpets lacked some of the spirit and originality of the older work.

These days, many carpets are made to the dictates of the market. Weavers in eastern Turkey might make carpets in popular styles native to western Turkey, or long-settled villagers might duplicate the wilder, hairier and more naive *yörük* (nomad) carpets. Many carpets still incorporate traditional patterns and symbols, such as the commonly used 'eye' and 'tree' patterns. At a glance two carpets might look identical, but closer examination will reveal the subtle differences that give each Turkish carpet its individuality and charm.

Village women still weave carpets but usually work to fixed contracts for specific shops. Generally they work to a pattern and are paid for their final effort rather than for each hour of work. A carpet made to a fixed contract may still be of great value to its purchaser. However, the selling price should be lower than for a one-off piece.

Other carpets are the product of a division of labour, with different individuals responsible for dyeing and weaving. What such pieces lose in individuality and rarity is often more than made up for in quality control. Most silk Hereke carpets are mass-produced but to standards that make them some of the most sought-after of all Turkish carpets.

Fearing the loss of the old carpet-making methods, the Ministry of Culture has sponsored several projects to revive traditional weaving and dyeing methods in western Turkey. One such scheme is the Natural Dye Research and Development Project (Doğal Boya Arıştırma ve Geliştirme Projesi; Dobag); see p207 for more details. Some shops keep stocks of these 'project carpets', which are usually of high quality.

For advice about buying carpets, see p668.

Jon Thompson's beautifully illustrated and very readable *Carpets: From the Tents, Cottages and Workshops of Asia* is an excellent introduction that may well tempt you into parting with your money.

Architecture

The history of architecture in Turkey encompasses everything from Hittite stonework and grand Graeco-Roman temples to the most modern tower-blocks in İstanbul, but perhaps the most distinctively Turkish styles were those developed by the Seljuks and Ottomans.

SELJUK ARCHITECTURE

The Seljuks endowed Turkey with a legacy of magnificent mosques and *medreses* (seminaries), distinguished by their elaborate entrances; you can see the best of them in Konya and Sivas. They also built a string of caravanserais along the route of the 13th-century Silk Road through Anatolia (see boxed text, opposite).

OTTOMAN ARCHITECTURE

The Ottomans also left many magnificent mosques and *medreses,* as well as many fine wood-and-stone houses.

Before Ottoman times, the most common form of mosque was a large square or rectangular space sheltered by a series of small domes resting on pillars, as in Edirne's Eski Cami (p171). But when the Ottomans took Bursa and İznik in the early 14th century they were exposed to Byzantine architecture, particularly ecclesiastical architecture. Ottoman architects absorbed these influences and blended them with the styles of Sassanid Persia to develop a completely new style: the T-shape plan. The Üç Şerefeli Cami in Edirne (p169) became the model for other mosques not only because it was one of the first forays into this T-plan, but also because it was the first Ottoman mosque to have a wide dome and a forecourt with an ablutions fountain.

Each imperial mosque had a *külliye,* or collection of charitable institutions, clustered around it. These might include a hospital, asylum for the insane, orphanage, *imaret* (soup kitchen), hospice for travellers, *medrese,* library, baths and a cemetery in which the mosque's imperial patron, his or her family and other notables could be buried. Over time, many of these buildings were demolished or altered, but İstanbul's Süleymaniye mosque complex (p110) still has much of its *külliye* intact.

The design, perfected by the Ottoman's most revered architect Mimar Sinan (see boxed text, p111) during the reign of Süleyman the Magnificent,

THE ORIGINAL ROADHOUSE

The Seljuks built a string of caravanserais (caravan palaces) along the route of the 13th-century Silk Rd through Anatolia. These camel-caravan staging posts were built roughly a day's travel (about 15km to 30km) apart to provide food and lodging and to facilitate trade. Expenses for construction and maintenance of the caravanserais were borne by the sultan, and paid for by the taxes levied on the rich trade in goods.

The Ottomans were not keen builders of caravanserais like the Seljuks. Instead they built thousands of *hans*, urban equivalents of caravanserais, where goods could be loaded and unloaded near the point of sale. Ottoman *hans* were simpler in design than the caravanserais – just two-storey buildings, usually square, surrounding an open court with a fountain or raised *mescit* at its centre. On the upper level, behind an arcaded gallery, were offices and rooms for lodging and dining.

The most beautiful *hans* are the early Ottoman ones in Bursa – the Koza Han and Emir Han – but in fact every Anatolian town has at least a few *hans* in its market district. İstanbul's vast Grand Bazaar is surrounded by *hans* that are still used by traders and artisans.

For the sake of ease, this book does not really differentiate between caravanserais and *hans*. See p25 for a *han-/caravanserai*-hopping guide to the country.

---

proved so durable that it is still being used, with variations, for modern mosques all over Turkey.

For information about Ottoman houses, see boxed text, p458.

TURKISH BAROQUE

From the mid-18th century, rococo and baroque influences hit Turkey, resulting in a pastiche of hammed-up curves, frills, scrolls, murals and fruity excesses, sometimes described as 'Turkish baroque'. The period's best – or some say worst – archetype is the extravagant Dolmabahçe Palace (p117). Although building mosques was passé, the Ottomans still adored kiosks where they could enjoy the outdoors; the Küçüksu Kasrı (p122) in İstanbul is a good example.

NEOCLASSICISM

In the 19th and early 20th centuries, foreign or foreign-trained architects began to unfold a neoclassical blend: European architecture mixed in with Turkish baroque and some concessions to classic Ottoman style. Many lavish embassies were built in Pera (Beyoğlu) as vehicles for the colonial powers to cajole the Sublime Porte into trade and territorial concessions. The in-vogue Swiss Fossati brothers were responsible for the Netherlands and Russian consulates-general along İstiklal Caddesi in İstanbul.

Also in the capital, Vedat Tek, a Turkish architect who had studied in Paris, built the central post office (p84), a melange of Ottoman elements such as arches and tile work, and European symmetry. Sirkeci Train Station (p160), by the German architect Jachmund, is another example of this eclectic neoclassicism.

MODERN ARCHITECTURE

There's little worth mentioning as far as modern architecture goes. The most interesting movement in the last few decades is that Turks have begun to reclaim their architectural heritage, especially those parts of it that can be turned into dollars via the tourism industry. These days, restorations and new buildings being built in Sultanahmet and other parts of İstanbul – and even Göreme, in Cappadocia – are most likely to be in classic Ottoman style.

For magnificent mosques and minarets seen from an angle you're unlikely to be able to manage yourself, Yann Arthur-Bertrand's gorgeous *Turkey from the Air* provides a bird's-eye view of Turkey's stunning cityscapes and countryside.

STOLEN TREASURES

'Every flower is beautiful in its own garden. Every antique is beautiful in its own country.' So reads the sign in the lobby of the Ephesus Museum. It surely has a point. And yet everywhere you go in Turkey you will come across archaeological sites that have been stripped of their finest artefacts, even of their most important structures, by Western countries that now display them proudly in their own museums.

The Sphinx column from Xanthos, the altar from Pergamum, the statue from Hadrian's Library at Ephesus, Schliemann's treasure from Troy: these are just some of the more prominent monuments that you must look for in museums in Britain, Germany, Italy and Russia rather than in Turkey.

Most Western countries justify retention of such treasures by arguing that they acquired them 'legitimately'. Or they claim that we all gain by being able to see a wide range of artefacts in museums worldwide. Finally, they claim that they are better equipped to care for the artefacts than the Turks. And while these arguments had started to wear thin, and several important collections had been returned to Turkey, recent scandals of theft from archaeological museums in the country have ensured that Western governments will keep holding onto their Turkish treasures for a while yet.

In 1993 the 2500-year-old Karun Treasure was repatriated to the Uşak museum (p309) after New York's Metropolitan Museum of Art lost a costly legal battle with the Turkish government. Some 13 years later, in the midst of a scandal about a number of thefts in Turkish museums, news broke that the famed golden-winged seahorse brooch, one of the most valuable pieces in the collection, had been replicated and stolen. Investigations fingered the museum's director and nine others with embezzlement and artefact smuggling. The government promptly ordered investigations into 32 other museums, and the minister admitted he wouldn't be surprised if there were thefts from every one of them. With the museums chronically understaffed, underfunded and mismanaged – and the Karun scandal attracting international headlines – it will be a long time before Turkey's archaeological museums have any chance of winning back any more of their treasures.

Music

POP, ROCK, ELECTRONIC, HIP HOP & RAP

Turkey's home-grown pop industry is one of its big success stories. Turkish pop finally won worldwide recognition in 2003 when Sertab Erener won the Eurovision Song Contest with her hit song 'Every Way that I Can'.

Sezen Aksu is widely regarded as the queen of Turkish pop music, but it is Tarkan, the pretty-boy pop star, who has achieved most international recognition. His '94 album, *A-acayıpsin*, sold over two million copies in Turkey and almost a million in Europe, establishing him as Turkey's biggest-selling pop sensation. 'Şımarık', released in 1999, and since covered by Holly Valance (as 'Kiss Kiss'), became his first European number one. After several Europe-wide tours, he released the long-awaited *Come Closer*, sung entirely in English. It flopped, leaving fans distraught, but Tarkan's metrosexual hip-swivelling will guarantee him more hits to come.

Burhan Öçal (www.burhanocal.com) is one of the country's finest percussionists. His seminal work, *New Dream*, is a funky take on classical Turkish music, but we daren't define him by this production: he has garnered critical acclaim experimenting with diverse types of Turkish and foreign music. His recent work with the Trakya All-Stars is a Roma-Balkan investigation of the music of his native Thrace.

Turkish rock has long aped that of the West, but it's finally offering something distinctly Turkish. Look out for Duman, Replikas, 110 (electronica) and most definitely Yakup, a blend of East-meets-West oriental-indie-grunge rock. Try to catch them live if you're passing through İstanbul.

On a more electronic jazzy theme is Orient Expressions, mixing Alevi and folk with jazzed-up Turkish melodies. In a similar vein, albeit more

The Turkish bathing tradition is in fact Roman. When the Turks ventured into Anatolia they encountered the bathhouses of the Byzantines, who in turn had inherited the tradition from the Romans. The Turks so took to the steamy ablutions that they became part of the Turkish way of life.

ALL THE EMPTY HOUSES

You won't have been in Turkey five minutes before you notice the extraordinary number of half-built apartment blocks, houses and multistorey car parks littering the landscape. The reason behind this ugliness is usually housing cooperatives, whereby a group of people get together to pay for an apartment in a new development. Since they cannot pay all the money upfront (bank loans are prohibitively expensive), they can take several years to be finished – so at least some of the houses will one day be completed.

Unfortunately a lot can happen between the first breaking of the earth and the completion of the complex. The members of the cooperative may run out of money or the builder may go bankrupt. Worse still, builders have been known to disappear with the money, leaving the work to stand incomplete in perpetuity.

Even that cannot completely account for the sheer quantity of half-built blocks. Of course, some are probably entirely speculative projects, begun in the hope of tax breaks or some such reason, and abandoned just as soon as it suits the builder to pull out.

---

given to performance 'events', Baba Zula create a fusion of traditional Turkish instruments, reggae, electronic, pop and belly-dancing music – and it works!

There is a thriving rap/hip-hop scene alive in the streets of İstanbul. Ceza (www.cezafan.com) is the king – he's literally mobbed by fans. All albums in Turkey need pre-release approval by the government, which means swearing is a no-no for Turkish rappers – unless they go underground or swear in English, that is. This ends up being a bonus for travellers, as it means most artists perform in English.

ARABESK

The equally popular style of music known as *arabesk* (which, as its name implies, puts an Arabic spin on home-grown Turkish traditions) started in the 1980s. Playing to *arabesk's* traditional audience is the hugely successful Kurdish singer İbrahim Tatlıses, a burly, moustachioed, former construction worker from Şanlıurfa who pops up on TV as often as he does on radio. Orhan Gencebay is, however, the king of *arabesk,* a prolific artist and also an actor. Start with his *Akma Gözlerimden.*

CLASSICAL & RELIGIOUS

Traditional Ottoman classical and religious (particularly Mevlevi) music may sound ponderous and lugubrious to the uninitiated. These musical forms use a system of *makams,* an exotic-sounding series of tones similar in function to Western scales. In addition to the familiar Western whole- and half-tone intervals, Turkish music often uses quarter-tones, unfamiliar to foreign ears and perceived as 'flat' until the ear becomes accustomed to them.

After the banning of the Mevlevi at the beginning of the republic, it wasn't until the early '90s that a group called Mevlana Kültür ve Sanat Vakfı Sanatçıları was set up to promote the Sufi musical tradition. Mercan Dede (www.mercandede.com) has taken this music to another level altogether, fusing it with electronic, techno and classic beats.

FOLK, TÜRKÜ, FASIL & GYPSY

Turkish folk music is more immediately appealing to Western ears. Instruments and lyrics reflect the life of the musicians and village, so they will be slightly different from village to village. Kurdish big names worth looking out for include Ferhat Tunç, who has produced an album

Lovers of art nouveau architecture will be able to feast their eyes on several beautiful examples of the style in Eminönü and along İstiklal Caddesi. It was introduced to İstanbul by the Italian architect Raimondo D'Aronco.

The documentary *Crossing The Bridge: The Story of Music in İstanbul* by Fatih Akin follows the trail of musos, giving you a superb peep into the vibrant and diverse contemporary music scene in İstanbul.

A BEGINNERS' GUIDE TO TURKISH MUSIC

These are our top picks to start your collection:

- *Turkish Groove* (compilation). A must-have two-disc introduction to Turkish music with everyone from Sezen Aksu to Burhan Öçal and from pop and Sufi to drum 'n' bass.
- *Işık Doğdan Yükselir* by Sezen Aksu (contemporary folk). A stunning and diverse collection drawing on the traditions of regional Turkish folk music.
- *Su* by Mercan Dede (Sufi-electronic-techno fusion). Mercan Dede is a growing name in world music circles in İstanbul and abroad.
- *Keçe Kurdan* by Aynur (Kurdish folk). Aynur's impassioned *Kurdish Girl* album, sung entirely in Kurdish, was her excellent debut on the international scene.
- *Rapstar Ceza* by Ceza (rap). You won't understand a word (unless you speak Turkish), but you don't need to. The energy and passion are palpable.
- *Duble Oryantal* by Baba Zulu (fusion). Baba Zulu's classic, 'Belly Double', was mixed by the British dub master Mad Professor.
- *Şunu Bunu* by Yakup (rock). A Turkish version of various UK indie pop styles, with chiming guitars and shuffling drums.
- *Gipsy Rum* by Burhan Öçal and İstanbul Oriental Ensemble (gypsy). This 1998 production is an excellent, thigh-slapping introduction to Turkey's gypsy music, played by instrumental masters.
- *Avaz* by Replikas (Turkish rock). Guitar-based rock with touches of Sonic Youth, occasional jazzy touches and the ring of the *saz* (long-necked lute).
- *Konser* by Duman (Turkish rock). A live album featuring all the big hits of Turkey's answer to Fugazi.

annually since 1987, and Aynur Doğan (www.aynurdogan.net). Aynur, as she is simply known, has started touring internationally and is set for stardom. Both produce enjoyable Kurdish folk.

Türkü, a sort of halfway house between folk and pop, directly reflects experiences common to Turks. It became very popular in the 1990s.

Fasıl has been likened to a nightclub or lightweight version of Ottoman classical. This is the music you hear at *meyhanes*, usually played by gypsies. The music is played with clarinet, *kanun* (zither), *darbuka* (a drum shaped like an hourglass) and often an *ud* (a six-stringed Arabic lute), *keman* (violin) and a *cumbus* (similar to a banjo). It's usually hard to distinguish between *fasıl* and gypsy music.

Until the 1960s and '70s it was still possible to hear Turkish *aşıklar* (troubadours) in action. Although radio, TV, video and CDs have effectively killed off their art, the songs of the great troubadours – Yunus Emre (13th century), Pir Sultan Abdal (16th century) and Aşık Veysel (1894–1973) – remain popular.

A thorough investigation of the Turkish film industry, *Turkish Cinema: Identity, Distance and Belonging* by Gönül Dönmez-Colin, sheds lights on the themes and identities for an English-speaking audience.

If you're lucky you may spot wandering minstrels playing the *zurna* (pipe) and *davul* (drum). They perform at wedding and circumcision parties, and also congregate in bus stations on call-up day to see off the latest band of conscripts in style.

Cinema

The first screening of a foreign film in Turkey took place at the Yıldız Palace in İstanbul in 1896. In 1914 Turkey showed its first homemade documentary and by the end of WWI several Turkish feature films had appeared. The War of Independence inspired actor Muhsin Ertuğrul to establish a film company to make patriotic films. Comedies and documentaries followed, and within a decade Turkish films were winning international competitions. During the 1960s and '70s films with a political edge were being made alongside innumerable lightweight Bollywood-style movies usually lumped together and labelled *Yeşilcam* movies. A string of cinemas opened along İstanbul's İstiklal Caddesi, only to close again in the 1980s (or turn into porn-movie houses) as TV siphoned off their audiences. The 1990s was an exciting decade for national cinema, with films being critically acclaimed both in Turkey and abroad.

Several Turkish directors have won worldwide recognition, most notably the late Yılmaz Güney. Joint winner of the best film award at Cannes in 1982, *Yol* explored the dilemmas of a group of men on weekend-release from prison, a tale that manages to be gripping and tragic at the same time, and which Turks were forbidden to watch until 2000. His last film, *Duvar* (The Wall), made before his untimely death at only 46, was a wrist-slashing prison drama.

Following in Güney's footsteps, many Turkish directors continue to make political films. *Güneşe Yolculuk* (Journey to the Sun), by Yeşim Ustaoğlu, is about a Turk who migrates to İstanbul and is so dark-skinned he's mistaken for a Kurd and treated appallingly. Nuri Bilge Ceylan's excellent *Uzak* (Distant) is also a bleak meditation on the lives of migrants in Turkey – it won the Jury Prize at Cannes. His next, *İklimler* (Climates), which he also starred in, looks at relationships between men and women in Turkey. His latest *Üç Maymun* (Three Monkeys) won him the gong for Best Director at Cannes in 2008.

It's not all politics, though. Ferzan Özpetek received international acclaim for *Hamam* (Turkish Bath), which skilfully explores cultural nuances after a Turk living in Italy reluctantly travels to İstanbul after he inherits a hamam. It's also noteworthy for addressing the hitherto hidden issue of homosexuality in Turkish society. His *Harem Suare* (Evening Performance in the Harem) was set in the Ottoman harem, while his most recent offering, *Karşı Pencere* (The Window Opposite), ponders issues of homosexuality and marriage.

The new name to watch, Fatih Akin, produced the widely acclaimed *Duvara Karsi* (Head On), a gripping and often violent spotlight on the Turkish immigrant's life in Germany (Fatih is himself a Turkish-German). His documentary, *Crossing the Bridge: The Story of Music in İstanbul*, is also worth seeking out and his latest, *Edge of Heaven*, again ponders the Turkish experience in Germany.

Visual Arts

Until 1923 and the founding of the Turkish Republic, all mainstream artistic expression conformed to the laws of Islam, which forbid representation of any being with an immortal soul (ie animal or human). Sculpture and painting as known in the West did not exist, with the notable exception of Turkish miniature painting, which was for the upper classes only.

By the late 19th century, educated Ottomans were influenced by European-style painting. Atatürk encouraged this artistic expression, and the government opened official painting and sculpture academies, encouraging this 'modern' secular art in place of the religious art of the past.

By the 1930s many Turkish artists were studying abroad, with some becoming expatriates. Fikret Mualla is one of Turkey's most famous contemporary artists; he lived most of his life in Paris. Once again, the best place to see what modern artists are up to is İstanbul. İstanbul Modern (p115) and Santralİstanbul (p125) are the country's best modern art galleries, but

37 Uses for a Dead Sheep (dir Ben Hopkins) is a colourful documentary focusing on a group of Kirghiz exiles who sought refuge in Turkey, fleeing the Communist regime in their home in Central Asia. Insightful and entertaining, with moments of true comedy.

Osman Hamdi (1842–1910), whose Orientalist paintings are very much in vogue, was also the man responsible for establishing the İstanbul Archaeological Museums (p108).

the small private art galleries along İstiklal Caddesi are well worth checking out as well.

Dance

Although it is dying out in the towns, folk dance is still a vibrant tradition in Turkish villages, as you will realise if you attend a traditional wedding.

Folk dance can be divided into several broad categories, including the *bar* from the Erzurum/Bayburt area, the *horon* from the Black Sea and the *zeybek* from the west. Although originally a dance of central, southern and southeastern Anatolia, the *halay*, led by a dancer waving a handkerchief (or paper tissue), can be seen all over the country, especially at weddings and in *meyhanes* in İstanbul when everyone has downed one rakı (aniseed-flavoured grape brandy) too many. But it may well be the *horon* that you most remember, since it involves the men getting down and indulging in all manner of dramatic kicking, Cossack-style.

The *sema* (dervish ceremony) of the whirling dervishes is not unique to Turkey, but it's here that you are most likely to see it performed; see boxed text, p116.

Belly dancing may not have originated in Turkey, but Turks have mastered the art. Although belly dancers are frequently seen at weddings and, incredibly, at many end-of-year company parties, your best chance of seeing a decent belly dancer is at a folk show in İstanbul. If you're interested in teaching your belly to dance, see p659.

For hard-to-find Turkish music, books and paraphernalia you can't go past US-based online Turkish shopping emporium, Tulumba.com (www.tulumba.com), shipping right to your door; and you can hear music samples.

Food & Drink

Mention Turkish cuisine and many people conjure up images of greasy, pre-hangover döner kebaps and an array of supermarket-purchased dips. Somewhat oily and bland stuffed vine leaves can leap to mind, along with memories of chewy shish kebaps incinerated on backyard barbecues. Fortunately, the reality on the ground couldn't be more different.

Here, kebaps are swooningly succulent, *yaprak dolması* (stuffed vine leaves) are filled with subtly spiced rice and meze dishes such as dips are made daily with the best seasonal ingredients. Freshly caught fish is expertly cooked over coals and served unadorned, accompanied by field-fresh salads and Turkey's famous aniseed-flavoured drink, rakı. Strong çay (tea) served in delicate glasses accompanies honey-drenched baklava studded with plump pistachios from Gaziantep.

Food here is not merely belly fuel – it's a celebration of community and life. Meals are joyful, boisterous and almost always communal. Food is used to celebrate milestones, cement friendships and add cohesion to family life. When you get here you'll quickly realise that for Turks, the idea of eating in front of a TV or from a freezer is absolute anathema – this is a cuisine proud of being social, slow and seasonal.

The basics of Turkish cooking may have evolved on the steppes of Central Asia, but as the Ottoman Empire grew it swallowed up the ingredients of Greece, Persia, Arabia and the Balkans, creating a deliciously diverse cuisine. Each region has specialities and signature ingredients, meaning that travel through the country truly tantalises the taste buds. As the Turks say, *Afiyet olsun!* (Good appetite!).

STAPLES & SPECIALITIES

Turkey is one of the few countries that can feed itself from its own produce and have leftovers. This means that produce makes its way from ground to table quickly, ensuring freshness and flavour. Here, being a 'locavore' is taken for granted.

The common Turkish *kahvaltı* (breakfast) consists of fresh-from-the-oven white *ekmek* (bread), jam or honey, black olives, slices of cucumber and juicy tomatoes, a hard-boiled egg, and a block of *beyaz peynir* (salty white cheese made from ewe's or goat's milk), and innumerable glasses of sweetened black çay. Expect this feast at every hotel. Other breakfast dishes to look out for are menemen (eggs scrambled with tomatoes, onions, peppers and white cheese), and bread served with flowery honey and rich *kaymak* (clotted cream).

There's not always a lot to choose between what's on offer for lunch and dinner, but both meals frequently start with *çorba* (soup). The most common soups are *ezo gelin* (red lentil and rice) and *domates* (tomato), but you may also meet *balık çorbası* (fish soup), *sebze çorbası* (vegetable soup) and *yayla çorbası* (yoghurt soup with mint). Workers who don't have time for a leisurely breakfast at home will often pop into a cheap restaurant for a *mercimek çorbası* (lentil soup) on the way to work.

Many locals eat their lunch in a *lokanta*. These cheap and cheerful spots serve *hazır yemek* (ready food) kept warm in bain-maries. The etiquette is to check out what's in the bain-marie and tell the waiter or cook behind the counter what you would like to eat. You can order a full *porsiyon* (portion), a *yarım* (half) *porsiyon* or a plate with a few different choices – you'll be charged by the *porsiyon*. After taking a seat, you'll then be served your chosen plate of food by a waiter.

In the 17th century 1300 people slaved away in the kitchens of Topkapı Palace, where feasts for up to 15,000 people could be cooked.

The Complete Book of Turkish Cooking by Ayla Esen Algar is widely regarded as the best Turkish cookery book (in English) available.

The Ottomans were masters of the evocative culinary description, inventing such delights as 'Ladies' Thighs', 'The Sultan's Delight', 'Harem Navel' and 'Nightingale Nests'.

A night fuelled by rakı and meze (see boxed text, below) often ends up being a cherished holiday memory. In İstanbul's famous Beyoğlu *meyhanes* (taverns; see boxed text, p139), waiters heave around enormous trays full of cold meze dishes that customers can choose from – hot meze dishes are chosen from the menu.

In a *meyhane*, the meze course is usually followed by fish; a *kebapçı* (kebap restaurant) is where you should go if you're keen on sampling kebaps and a *köfteci* is the equivalent for *köfte* (meatballs; see boxed text, p68). The *ocakbaşı* (fireside) versions of the *kebapçı* are the most fun, with patrons sitting around the sides of a grill and watching their meat being prepared and cooked. *Restorans* (restaurants) often serve a mixture of kebap and *köfte* dishes, as well as fish.

Overall, the Turks are huge meat eaters, which can be a bit of a problem if you are a vegetarian (see p70). Beef, lamb, mutton and chicken are prepared in a number of ways. The most famous of these is the kebap – şiş and döner – but *köfte, saç kavurma* (stir-fried cubed meat dishes) and *güveç* (meat and vegetable stews cooked in a terracotta pot) are just as common. In Cappadocia, many restaurants serve *testı kebapı*, kebap in a mushroom and onion sauce that is slow cooked (ideally over coals) in a sealed terracotta pot that is then theatrically broken open at the table. The most popular sausage in Turkey is the spicy beef *sucuk*, and garlicky *pastırma* (pressed beef preserved in spices) is regularly used as an accompaniment to egg

MARVELLOUS MEZE

Meze isn't just a type of dish, it's a whole eating experience. If you eat in a local household, your host may put out a few lovingly prepared dishes for guests to nibble on before the main course is served. If you choose to spend a few hours in a city *meyhane* (tavern), beckoning the waiter over so that you can choose 'just a few more' inevitably means that the meze dishes will comprise most of your meal.

Turks credit Süleyman the Magnificent with introducing meze into the country. During one of his Persian campaigns, Süleyman learned from the cunning Persian rulers that food tasters were a particularly good idea for every sultan who wanted to ensure his safety. Once he was back home, Süleyman decreed that *çesnici* (taste) slaves be given small portions of his meals before he sat down to the table. These portions became known as meze, the Persian word for pleasant, enjoyable taste.

Mezes are usually vegetable-based, though seafood dishes can also feature. You will probably encounter the following dishes while eating your way around the country:

Ançüz Pickled anchovy.
Barbunya pilaki Red-bean salad.
Beyaz peynir White ewe's- or goat's-milk cheese.
Cacik Yoghurt with cucumber and mint.
Çerkez tavuğu Circassian chicken, made with chicken, bread, walnuts, salt and garlic.
Enginar Cooked artichoke.
Ezme salatası Spicy tomato dip.
Fava salatası Mashed broad-bean paste.
Haydari Yoghurt with roasted eggplant (aubergine) and garlic.
Kalamares Fried calamari, usually served with a garlic sauce.
Lakerda Sliced and salted tuna fish.
Patlıcan kızartması Salad of fried eggplant with tomato.
Patlıcan salatası Fried eggplant with tomatoes.
Semizotu Green purslane with yoghurt and garlic.
Sigara böreği Deep-fried cigar-shaped pastries, often stuffed with *peynir* (cheese).
Yaprak sarma or dolması Vine leaves stuffed with rice, herbs and pine nuts.

TRAVEL YOUR TASTE BUDS

Like most countries, Turkey has some dishes that only a local could love. Top of the confrontational stakes for most visitors is *kokoreç*, seasoned lamb intestines wrapped around a skewer and grilled over charcoal.

İşkembe (tripe) soup reputedly wards off a hangover; it's even more popular than *kelle paça* (sheep's trotter) soup.

Locals in need of extra reserves of sexual stamina swear by spicy *koç yumurtası* (ram's 'eggs').

When these don't do the trick they often resort to *boza*, a mucous-coloured beverage made from water, sugar and fermented grain.

---

dishes; it's occasionally served with warm hummus (chickpea, tahini and lemon dip) as a meze.

Fish is wonderful here, but can be pricey. In a *balık restoran* (fish restaurant) you should always try to do as the locals do and choose your own fish from the display. This is important, as the occasional dodgy restaurant may try to serve you old fish. The eyes should be clear and the flesh under the gill slits near the eyes should be bright red, not burgundy. After your fish has been given the all clear, ask the approximate price. The fish will be weighed, and the price computed at the day's per-kilogram rate. *Kalkan* (turbot) and *uskumru* (mackerel) are best consumed between March and June. Mid-July to August is the best time to feast on *levrek* (sea bass), *lüfer* (bluefish), *barbunya* (red mullet) and *istravrit* (horse mackerel), while winter means tasty and slightly oily *hamsı* (fresh anchovy).

Turks love vegetables, eating them fresh in summer and pickling them for winter (pickled vegetables are called *turşu*). There are two particularly Turkish ways of preparing vegetables: the first is known as *zeytinyağlı* (sautéed in olive oil) and the second *dolma* (stuffed with rice or meat). *Patlıcan* (eggplant/aubergine) is the sultan of all vegetables, cooked in every conceivable manner and loved by Turks with a passion.

Simplicity is the key to Turkish *salata* (salads), with crunchy fresh ingredients being caressed by a shake of oil and vinegar at the table and eaten with gusto as a meze or as an accompaniment to a meat or fish main course. The most popular summer salad is *çoban salatası* (shepherd's salad), a colourful mix of chopped tomatoes, cucumber, onion and pepper.

When travelling through central Anatolia, you will often encounter *mantı* (Turkish ravioli stuffed with beef mince and topped with yoghurt, garlic tomato and butter). It's perfect in winter but can be overly rich and heavy in hot weather.

At İstanbul's famous Çlya Sofrası (p121), owner/ chef Musa Dağdeviren serves over one thousand different dishes every year, rarely repeating the same dish twice.

Quick Eats

The nation's favourite fast food is undoubtedly döner kebap – lamb slow-cooked on an upright revolving skewer and then shaved off before being stuffed into bread or pide. Soggy cold French fries and green chillies are sometimes included, at other times garlicky yoghurt, salad and a sprinkling of slightly sour sumac are the accompaniments.

Coming a close second is in the popularity stakes is pide, the Turkish version of pizza. It has a canoe-shaped base topped with *peynir* (cheese), *yumurtalı* (egg) or *kıymalı* (minced meat). A *karaşık* pide has a mixture of toppings. You can sit down to eat these in a *pideci* (Turkish pizza parlour) or ask for your pide *paket* (wrapped to go).

Börek (filled pastries) are distinguished by their filling, cooking method and shape. They come in square, cigar or snail shapes and are filled with *peynirli*, *ıspanaklı* (spinach), *patates* (potatoes) or *kıymalı*. Bun-shaped

KEBAPS & KÖFTE

Kebaps are undoubtedly the national dish, closely followed by *köfte* (meatballs). These meat dishes come in many forms, and are often named after their place of origin. The most popular are:

Adana kebap Spicy *köfte* wrapped around a flat skewer and barbecued, then served with onions, paprika, parsley and pide (bread).

Çiğ köfte Raw ground lamb mixed with pounded bulgur, onion, clove, cinnamon, salt and hot black pepper.

Döner kebap Compressed meat (usually lamb) cooked on a revolving upright skewer over coals, then thinly sliced.

Fıstıklı kebap Minced suckling lamb studded with pistachios.

İçli köfte Ground lamb and onion with a bulgur coating, often served as a hot meze.

İskender (Bursa) kebap Döner lamb served on a bed of crumbled pide and yoghurt, then topped with tomato and burnt butter sauces.

Karışık İzgara Mixed grilled lamb.

Patlıcan kebap Cubed or minced meat grilled with eggplant (aubergine).

Şiş kebap Small pieces of lamb grilled on a skewer and usually served with a side of bulgur and char-grilled peppers. *Çöp şiş* is served rolled in a thin pide with onions and parsley.

Şiş köfte Wrapped around a flat skewer and barbecued.

Tavuk şiş Chicken pieces grilled on a skewer.

Tekirdağ köftesi Served with rice and peppers.

Tokat kebap Lamb cubes grilled with potato, tomato, eggplant and garlic.

Urfa kebap A mild version of the Adana kebap served with lots of onion and black pepper.

---

poğaca are glazed with sugar or stuffed with cheese and olives. *Su böreği*, a melt-in-the-mouth lasagne-like layered pastry laced with white cheese and parsley, is the most popular of all *börek* styles – you're sure to be instantly infatuated.

Gözleme (thin savoury crepes cooked with cheese, spinach or potato) are also great quick snacks.

Forget the Golden Arches – Turkey's favourite fast-food chain is Simit Sarayı, which sells the country's much-loved *simit* (sesame-encrusted bread ring) to thousands of happy customers every day.

Prices

Most places will have a printed menu with fixed prices. The exception to this rule is the *balık restoran* (p67), where fish is priced according to the kilo.

Restaurant prices usually include taxes but not service, although a service charge may be added to the bill automatically in some tourist areas. It's worth checking the bill and questioning unexpected additions such as hitherto unmentioned *kuver* (cover) charges. For advice on tipping, see p667.

DRINKS
Alcoholic Drinks

In tourist-heavy destinations along the coast virtually every restaurant serves alcohol. The same applies to more-expensive restaurants in the big cities. In smaller towns, there's usually at least one restaurant where alcohol is served, although in religiously conservative places such as Konya you may have to hunt hard to find one. Although Turks have a fairly relaxed attitude towards alcohol, public drunkenness is a definite no-no.

Turkey's most beloved tipple is rakı, a grape spirit infused with aniseed. Similar to Greek ouzo, it's served in long thin glasses and is drunk neat or with water, which turns the clear liquid chalky white; if you want to add ice, do so after adding water, as dropping ice straight into rakı kills its flavour.

Bira (beer) is also popular. The local drop, Efes, is a perky pilsener that comes in bottles, cans and on tap.

Turkey grows and bottles its own *şarap* (wine), which has greatly improved in quality over the past decade. Head to Ürgüp (p518) in Cappadocia or to the idyllic Aegean island of Bozcaada (p203) to taste-test. If you want red wine ask for *kırmızı şarap;* for white ask for *beyaz şarap.* Decent tipples include Sarafin chardonnay, fumé blanc, sauvignon blanc, cabernet sauvignon and cabernet merlot; Karma cabernet sauvignon; Duluca Özel Kav (Special Reserve) red, white and *lal* (rosé); Antik red and white; and Çankaya white.

Nonalcoholic Drinks

Drinking çay is the national pastime, and the country's cup of choice is made with leaves from the Black Sea region. Sugar cubes are the only accompaniment and you'll find these are needed to counter the effects of long brewing, although you can always try asking for it *açık* (weaker). The wholly chemical *elma çay* (apple tea) is caffeine-free and only for tourists – locals wouldn't be seen dead drinking the stuff.

Surprisingly, *Türk kahve* (Turkish coffee) isn't widely consumed. A thick and powerful brew, it's drunk in a couple of short sips. If you order a cup, you will be asked how sweet you like it – *çok şekerli* means 'very sweet', *orta şekerli* 'middling', *az şekerli* 'slightly sweet' and *sade* 'not at all'. Your coffee will be accompanied by a glass of water, which is to clear the palate before you sample the delights of the coffee.

Freshly squeezed juice is popular and cheap. *Taze portakal suyu* (fresh orange juice) is everywhere, and delicious *nar suyu* (pomegranate juice) can be ordered in season.

Ayran is a refreshing drink made by whipping yoghurt with water and salt; it's the traditional accompaniment to kebaps.

Sahlep is a hot milky drink that takes off the winter chill. Made from wild orchid bulbs, it's reputed to be an aphrodisiac. You might also want to try *şalgam* (see boxed text, p430) – the first gulp is a revolting salty shock, but persevere and you may find this turnip-and-carrot concoction becomes an essential accompaniment to rakı binges.

CELEBRATIONS

In Turkey, every celebration has an associated sweet. Some say this can be attributed to the Quranic verse 'To enjoy sweets is a sign of faith'. The good news is that even though these sweets are a focus during celebrations and festivities, many of them can also be enjoyed year-round in a *muhallebici* (milk pudding shop), *pastane* (cake shop) or *baklavacı* (baklava shop).

Baklava (pastry sheets soaked in sugar syrup or honey and sometimes stuffed with nuts) is traditionally reserved for festive occasions such as Şeker Bayramı (Sweets Holiday; p664), the three-day holiday at the end of Ramazan (p664), but is also popular for engagements and weddings, proving sugary stamina for the rollicking hours of party-making ahead and the couple's wedding night (wink, wink). Other sweets such as *helva* (sweet prepared with sesame oil, cereals and honey or syrup) and *lokum* (Turkish delight; see boxed text, p157) are commonly part of more-reflective occasions such as deaths and *kandil* days (the five holy evenings in the Muslim calendar). A bereaved family will make *irmik helvası* (semolina *helva*) for visiting friends and relatives, and *helva* is shared with guests at circumcision feasts.

Aşure (Noah's Ark pudding) is a sacred pudding traditionally made with 40 different dried fruits, nuts and pulses, supposedly first baked from the leftovers on Noah's Ark when food provisions ran low. These days *aşure* is traditionally made after the 10th day of Muharram (the first month of the Islamic calendar), and distributed to neighbours and friends.

Savoury dishes are integral to celebrations in Turkey, too. *Kavurma* is a simple lamb dish cooked with the sacrificial lamb or mutton of the Kurban

Grumbly tummy? Ask for an *ihlamur* çay (linden tea). Turks always have it on hand for upset stomachs.

Don't drink the grounds when you try *Türk kahve* (Turkish coffee). Instead, go to the 'Turkish Coffee'/'Fortune Telling' section of www .mehmetefendi.com/eng, Turkey's most famous coffee purveyor, for a guide to reading your fortune in them.

Look out for the wonderfully symbolic *perde pilavı,* often served at weddings and sometimes appearing on restaurant and *lokanta* menus. It's made from chicken and rooster meat (symbolising the bride and groom) cooked with rice (for blessing) and almonds (for children) and encased in pastry sheets (symbolising the home).

Bayramı (Feast of Sacrifice; see p664). The meat is cubed, fried with onions and baked slowly in its juices. During Ramazan a special round flat pide is baked in the afternoon and collected in time for *iftar* (the break-of-fast feast).

VEGETARIANS & VEGANS

Though it's normal for Turks to eat a vegetarian meal, the concept of vegetarianism is quite foreign. Say you're a vegan and Turks will either look mystified or assume that you're 'fessing up to some strain of socially aberrant behaviour.

The meze spread is usually dominated by vegetable dishes, and meat-free salads, soups, pastas, omelettes, pides and *böreks*, as well as hearty vegetable dishes, are all readily available. Ask *'etsiz yemek var mı?'* ('is there something to eat that has no meat?') to see what's on offer.

The main source of inadvertent meat eating is *et suyu* (meat stock), which is often used to make otherwise vegetarian *pilav* (a rice dish), soup and vegetable dishes. Your hosts may not even consider *et suyu* to be meat, so they will reassure you that the dish is vegetarian; ask *'et suyu var mı?'* ('is there meat stock in it?') to check.

> Legend has it that in society Ottoman-era houses chefs made baklava with over one hundred pastry-sheet layers per tray. The master of the house would test the thickness with a gold coin: if it fell to the bottom of the tray the chef kept the coin.

HABITS & CUSTOMS

In rural Turkey locals usually eat two meals a day, the first at around 11am and the second in the early evening. In the cities three meals a day is the norm. In urban areas people sit down to meals at tables and chairs, but in villages it is still usual to sit on the floor around a *tepsi* (low round table) with a cloth spread over one's knees to catch the crumbs. These days people mostly eat from individual plates, although sometimes there will be communal dishes. Most Turks eat with spoons and forks (rarely with knives).

In restaurants, it's not considered very important that everyone eats the same courses at the same pace, so the kitchen will deliver dishes as they are ready: it's quite normal for all the chicken dishes to arrive and then, five minutes later, all the lamb. You don't have to wait for everyone's food to arrive to begin eating.

Turkish waiters have a habit of snatching plates away before the diner has finished. Saying *'kalsın'* ('let it stay') may slow them down. When you have finished, put your knife and fork together to indicate that the waiter

---

DOS AND DON'TS FOR VISITORS TO A TRADITIONAL TURKISH HOME

Do

- Take a small gift, such as a box of baklava or *lokum* (Turkish delight)
- Eat only the food nearest to you from a communal dish
- Eat everything on your plate, but don't overeat. Note the Turkish proverb: 'Eat a little be an angel; eat much and perish'!
- Say *'Afiyet olsun'* ('May it be good for your health') before starting to eat. After the meal say *'Elinize sağlık'* ('Health to your hands') to compliment your hostess on her cooking (it will always be a hostess who cooks!)

Don't

- Eat anything directly from a bowl with your left hand
- Sit down beside someone of the opposite sex unless your host(ess) suggests it

can take the plate. If this has no effect (or you don't have a knife), say *'biti, alabilirsin'* ('finished, you can take it') to the waiter.

Toothpicking should be done behind your hands, but you don't need to be particularly discreet. Try to avoid blowing your nose in public; sniff or excuse yourself if you need to do this.

COOKING COURSES

Turkey has a handful of operators offering foreign-language cookery courses (p658). There are two highly regarded courses run by foreigners in İstanbul (see p128), as well as a four-day residential course at Ula, 135km from Bodrum, run by well-known Turkish cooking writer and broadcaster **Engin Akin** (☎ 0532-241 7163; www.enginakin.com).

EAT YOUR WORDS

Want to know a *köfte* from a kebap? Get behind the cuisine scene by getting to know the language. For pronunciation guidelines, see p698.

The most famous of all patlıcan (eggplant) dishes is imam bayıldı (the imam fainted), a simple dish of eggplant slow-cooked in olive oil with tomatoes, onion and garlic. Legend has it that an imam fainted with pleasure on first sampling it – after tasting a well-prepared version you'll understand why.

Useful Phrases

EATING OUT

I'd like (a/the) ..., please.
... *istiyorum lütfen.*   ... ees·*tee*·yo·room *lewt*·fen
  menu
  Menüyü   me·new·*yew*
  menu in English
  İngilizce menü   een·gee·*leez*·je me·*new*

I'd like the local speciality
  Bu yöreye özgü bir yemek İstiyorum.   boo yer·re·*ye* **erz**·*gew* beer ye·*mek* ees·*tee*·yo·room

Enjoy your meal/Bon appétit!
  Afiyet olsun!   *a*·fee·yet ol·soon

This is ...
Bu ...   boo ...
  (too) cold
  (çok) soğuk   (chok) so·*ook*
  (too) spicy
  (çok) acı   (chok) a·*juh*
  superb
  enfes   en·*fes*

The bill please.
  Hesap lütfen.   he·*sap lewt*·fen

VEGETARIAN & SPECIAL MEALS

Do you have any dishes without meat?
  Etsiz yemek var mı?   et·*seez* ye·mek·var muh

I'm allergic to ...
... *alerjim var.*   ... a·ler·*zheem* var
  dairy produce
  Süt ürünlerine   sewt ew·rewn·le·ree·*ne*
  eggs
  Yumurtaya   yoo·moor·ta·*ya*
  nuts
  Çerezlere   che·rez·le·*re*

DRINKS
(cup/glass of) tea ...
... (bir fincan/bardak) çay   *... (beer feen·jan/bar·dak) chai*
(cup of) coffee ...
... (bir fincan) kahve   *... (beer feen·jan) kah·ve*
with milk
sütlü   sewt·*lew*
with a little sugar
az şekerli   az she·ker·*lee*
without sugar
şekersiz   she-ker-*seez*
Cheers!
Şerefe!   she·re·*fe*

Food Glossary
STAPLES

bal	bal	honey
ciğer	jee·*er*	liver
çorba	chor·*ba*	soup
ekmek	ek·*mek*	bread
hamsi	ham·*see*	anchovy
kalamares	ka·la·ma·*res*	calamari
kaşar	ka·*shar*	cheddarlike yellow cheese
lahmacun	la·ma·*joon*	pizza with a thin, crispy base topped with chopped lamb, onion and tomato
lavaş	la·*vash*	thin crispy bread
midye	meed·*ye*	mussels
peynir	pay·*neer*	cheese
piliç/tavuk	pee·*leech*/ta·*vook*	chicken
pirinç/pilav	pee·*reench*/pee·*lav*	rice
tulum peyniri	too·*loom* pay·nee·*ree*	dry, crumbly goats cheese cured in a *tulum* (goatskin bag)
yoğurt	yo·*oort*	yoghurt
yumurta	yoo·moor·*ta*	egg

CONDIMENTS

kara biber	ka·*ra* bee·*ber*	black pepper
şeker	she·*ker*	sugar
tuz	tooz	salt

COOKING TERMS

ızgara	uhz·ga·*ra*	grilled
tava	ta·*va*	fried

FRUIT (MEYVE) & VEGETABLES (SEBZE)

biber	bee·*ber*	capsicum/bell pepper
domates	do·ma·*tes*	tomato
elma	el·*ma*	apple
havuç	ha·*vooch*	carrot
ıspanak	uhs·pa·*nak*	spinach
karpuz	kar·*pooz*	watermelon
kavun	ka·*voon*	cantaloupe melon
kayısı	ka·yuh·*suh*	apricot
kuru fasulye	koo·*roo* fa·*sool*·ye	white beans
muz	mooz	banana

patates	pa·ta·*tes*	potato
portakal	por·ta·*kal*	orange
salatalık	sa·la·ta·*luhk*	cucumber
şeftali	shef·ta·*lee*	peach
soğan	so·*an*	onion
taze fasulye	ta·ze fa·*sool*·ye	green beans
üzüm	ew·*zewm*	grape
zeytin	zay·*teen*	olive

DESSERT (TATLI)

aşure	a·shoo·*re*	'Noah's Ark' pudding made from 40 different fruits, nuts and pulses
baklava	bak·la·*va*	layered filo pastry with honey or sugar syrup, sometimes stuffed with nuts
dondurma	don·door·*ma*	ice cream
fırın sütlac	*fuh*·ruhn *sewt*·lach	rice pudding
kadayıf	ka·da·*yuhf*	dough soaked in syrup; often topped with a layer of *kaymak* (clotted cream)
künefe	kew·*ne*·fe	layers of *kadayıf* cemented together with sweet cheese, doused in syrup and served with a sprinkling of pistachio
lokum	lo·*koom*	Turkish delight
tavuk göğsü	ta·*vook* ger·*sew*	a decidedly strange burnt chicken-breast
kazandibi	ka·*zan*·dee·bee	pudding

DRINKS

çay	chal	tea
bira	bee·*ra*	beer
buz	booz	ice
maden suyu	ma·*den* soo·*yoo*	mineral water
meyve suyu	may·*ve* soo·*yoo*	fruit juice
rakı	*ra*·ku	grape spirit infused with aniseed
şarap	sha·rap	wine
su	soo	water
süt	sewt	milk

Environment

THE LAND

Turkey has one foot in Europe and another in Asia, its two parts separated by the famous Dardanelles, the placid Sea of Marmara and the hectic Bosphorus. Eastern Thrace (European Turkey) makes up a mere 3% of Turkey's 779,452 sq km land area. The remaining 97% is Anatolia (Asian Turkey).

Boasting 8300km of coastline, snowcapped mountains, rolling steppes, vast lakes and broad rivers, Turkey is stupendously geographically diverse. The Aegean coast is lined with coves and beaches, with the Aegean islands (most of them belonging to Greece) dotted never more than a few kilometres offshore. Inland, western Anatolia has two vast lake districts and the soaring Uludağ (Great Mountain), at 2543m one of Turkey's highest mountains and increasingly popular with ski buffs.

The Mediterranean coast is backed by the jagged Taurus Mountains. East of Antalya, however, it opens up into a fertile plain as far as Alanya, before the mountains close in again. Central Anatolia consists of a vast high plateau of rolling steppe broken by mountain ranges, and Cappadocia, a region of fantastical landscapes created by the action of wind and water on tuff thrown for miles around by volcanic eruptions in prehistory.

Like the Mediterranean, the Black Sea is often hemmed in by mountains, and at the eastern end they drop right down into the sea. At 3937m, Mt Kaçkar (Kaçkar Dağı) is the highest point of the popular Kaçkar trekking and mountaineering area at the far eastern end of the Black Sea. There, *yaylas* (high plateau pastures) come ringed with peaks and glaciers.

Mountainous and somewhat forbidding, northeastern Anatolia is also wildly beautiful, especially around Yusufeli and in the Doğubayazıt area, where snowcapped Mt Ararat (Ağrı Dağı; 5137m) dominates the landscape for miles around. Southeastern Anatolia offers windswept rolling steppe, jagged outcrops of rock, and Lake Van (Van Gölü), an extraordinary alkaline lake.

The bad news? Turkey lies on at least three active earthquake fault lines: the North Anatolian, the East Anatolian and the Aegean. Most of Turkey lies south of the North Anatolian fault line, which runs roughly parallel with the Black Sea coast. As the Arabian and African plates to the south push northward, the Anatolian plate is shoved into the Eurasian plate and squeezed west towards Greece. Thirteen major quakes in Turkey have been recorded since 1939; the latest in August 1999 hit İzmit (Kocaeli) and Adapazarı (Sakarya) in northwestern Anatolia, killing more than 18,000. Some scientists predict that much of İstanbul would be devastated by any earthquake over 7 magnitude, due to unlicensed, jerry-built construction. Locals remain half panicked, half fatalistic – but no one doubts it's coming.

WILDLIFE
Animals

In theory, you could see bears, deer, jackals, caracal, wild boars and wolves in Turkey. In practice you're unlikely to see any wild animals at all unless you're trekking.

Instead you can look out for Kangal dogs, which are named after a small town near Sivas. Kangals were originally bred to protect sheep flocks from wolves and bears on mountain pastures. People wandering off the beaten track, especially in eastern Turkey, are often alarmed at the sight of these huge, yellow-coated, black-headed animals, especially as they often wear

---

Turkey is one of only seven countries in the world that is wholly self-sufficient in agriculture.

The pigeon houses dotting Cappadocia's fairy chimneys and valleys, which once served to harvest the bird's droppings for use as fertiliser, are increasingly disused as traditional agricultural practices die out.

For more information on Turkey's wildlife, contact Doğal Hayatı Koruma Derneği (Foundation for the Protection of Nature; ☎ 0212-231 5514; www.dhkd.org, in Turkish) or WWF-Turkey (☎ 0212-528 2030; www.wwf.org.tr, in Turkish).

ferocious spiked collars to protect them against wolves. Their mongrel descendants live on the streets in Turkey's towns, villages and cities.

Some 400 species of bird are found in Turkey, with about 250 of these passing through on migration from Africa to Europe. It's particularly easy to see eagles, storks, (beige) hoopoes, (blue) rollers and (green) bee-eaters. Enthusiastic birdwatchers should head east to Birecik (p606), one of the last known nesting places in the world of the eastern bald ibis (*Geronticus eremita*). Also well off the beaten trail is Çıldır Gölü (Çıldır Lake; p590), north of Kars in northeastern Anatolia. It's an important breeding ground for various species of birds. More readily accessible is the Göksu Delta (p421), near Silifke, where some 332 species have been recorded – including the rare purple gallinule – and Pamucak (see p251), home to flamingos from February to March.

Walking and Birdwatching in Southwest Turkey, by Paul Hope, is an introduction to some of Turkey's best birdwatching spots. Also recommended is Jeremy James' *The Byerley Turk: The True Story of the First Thoroughbred*, a fictionalised biography of the Ottoman horse, whose descendants are the world's finest racing horses today.

> Regarded as harbingers of spring, storks migrate to Turkey around March. Their lofty nests can be seen along the west coast and in cities such as İstanbul, Konya and Ankara (often atop the Column of Julian). Some communities repair the nests to encourage the birds to return.

ENDANGERED SPECIES

Anatolia's lions, beavers and Caspian tigers are now extinct, and its lynx, striped hyena and Anatolian leopard have all but disappeared. The last officially recorded sighting of the distinctive leopard was in 1974, when one was shot for attacking a village woman outside Beypazarı.

Rare loggerhead turtles still nest on various beaches in Turkey, including İztuzu Beach at Dalyan, the Göksu Delta and Patara Beach (see boxed text, p348). A few Mediterranean monk seals are just about hanging on around Foça (p220), but you would be very lucky to see them.

Mediterranean bluefin tuna, used in sushi, is facing extinction and there have been clashes between Turkish tuna fishermen and Greenpeace protestors.

The beautiful, pure-white Van cat, with one blue and one green eye, has also become endangered in its native Turkey. Happily, the Anatolian wild sheep, unique to the Konya region, is making a comeback.

> Van cats are said to be able to swim the waters of Lake Van – not that their owners would let these valuable pets out of their sight to do so.

Plants

Turkey's location at the junction between Asia and Europe and its varied geology have made it one of the most biodiverse temperate-zone countries in the world. Not only do its fertile soils produce an incredible range of fruit and vegetables, they are blessed with an exceptionally rich flora of over 9000 species, 1200 of them endemic. Some sources report that a new species of flora in Turkey is discovered every five days. The most common trees and plants you will see as you travel the country are pine, cypress, myrtle, laurel, rosemary, lavender and thyme.

Turkey is one of the last remaining sources of frankincense trees (*Liquidambar orientalis*), which grow in stands along the southwest coast of the Mediterranean, especially around Köyceğiz (p344). The Egyptians used the trees' resin during the embalming process. Today, it is exported for use in perfume and incense. Also on this coast is the endemic Datça palm (*Phoenix theophrastii*), found on the Datça Peninsula and near Kumluca. These are the last remaining populations of these trees in the world.

Other notable plants include purple bougainvillea on the coast, introduced from South America. Olive trees, synonymous with the Mediterranean, originated in the Turkish part of the region and spread

> Tulips are commonly associated with the Netherlands, but the flower originated in Turkey and grew popular during the Ottoman Empire, when it was exported to Europe. Sultan Ahmed III's peaceful 18th-century reign is known as the 'Tulip Era'.

TAKE ONLY PHOTOS, LEAVE ONLY FOOTPRINTS

Tourism is not the only thing that has had a damaging impact on the Turkish environment, but it is certainly one of them. So what can you do to help?

■ Never drop litter anywhere (although, to be fair, tourists are not the worst offenders when it comes to abandoned rubbish).

■ Don't buy coral or seashells, no matter how lovely they look in a necklace.

■ It goes without saying that you should try to do without plastic bags, even though some bags in Turkey are made from recycled material.

■ Complain to the captain if you think your excursion boat is discharging sewage into the sea or if it's dropping its anchor in an environmentally sensitive area. Even better, complain to **Greenpeace Mediterranean** (☎ 0212-292 7619; www.greenpeace.org/mediterranean).

■ Consider staying in pensions and hotels that have been designed with some thought for their surroundings.

■ Refrain from purchasing water in plastic bottles wherever possible. Water in glass bottles is served in many Turkish restaurants, and you can buy water filtration systems from home before your departure. The very least you can do is to buy the 5L plastic water bottles, which you can keep in your hotel room and use to fill up a reusable smaller bottle to carry with you during the day.

west during the Roman era. Turkey also introduced cherries to Italy, thence the world, via Giresun on the Black Sea coast.

The Most Beautiful Wild Flowers of Turkey by Erdoğan Tekin is the best field guide on the market, with some 700 photos and detailed charts on each flower.

NATIONAL PARKS & RESERVES

In the last few years, thanks to EU aspirations, Turkey has stepped up its environmental protection practices. It's now a signatory to various international conventions including Ramsar and Cites (International Trade of Endangered Species). The growing number of protected areas includes 33 *milli parkı* (national parks), 16 nature parks and 35 nature reserves. It also includes 58 curiously named 'nature monuments', which are mostly protected trees, some as old as 1500 years. (For more information see www.turizm.gov.tr.) In the parks and reserves the environment is supposedly protected and hunting controlled. Sometimes the regulations are carefully enforced, but at other times a blind eye is turned to such problems as litter-dropping picnickers.

Tourism to national parks is not well developed in Turkey, and they are rarely set up with facilities for visitors. It is not even the norm for footpaths to be clearly marked, and camping spots are rarely available. Most of the well-frequented national parks are as popular for their historic monuments as they are for the surrounding natural environment.

The following national parks are among the most popular with foreign visitors to Turkey:

Gallipoli Historic National Park (p178) Historic battlefield sites on a gloriously unspoilt peninsula surrounded by coves.

Göreme National Park (p502) An extraordinary landscape of gorges and cones ('fairy chimneys') spread over a wide area.

Kaçkar Dağları National Park (Kaçkar Mountain National Park; p563) Stunning high mountain ranges popular with trekkers.

Köprülü Kanyon National Park (p404) Dramatic canyon with spectacular scenery and facilities for white-water rafting.

A surprising 26.7% of Turkey is covered in forest, 28% is pasture and 2% is wetlands.

Nemrut Dağı National Park (Mt Nemrut National Park; p616) Huge historic heads surmounting a man-made mound with wonderful views.
Saklıkent National Park (p371) Famous for its 18km-long gorge.

ENVIRONMENTAL ISSUES

Turkey faces the unenviable challenge of balancing environmental management with rapid economic growth and urbanisation, and to date it's done a pretty sloppy job. Hopeless enforcement of environmental laws, lack of finances and poor education have placed the environment so far down the list of priorities that it would pack up and leave if it could. But there are some glimmers of improvement, largely due to the country's desire to join the EU – see boxed text, p78.

The Isparta area is one of the world's leading producers of attar of roses, a valuable oil extracted from rose petals and used in perfumes and cosmetics. See p313 to find out how you can see the harvest in late spring.

One of the biggest environmental challenges facing Turkey is the threat from maritime traffic along the Bosphorus. The 1936 Montreux Convention decreed that, although Turkey has sovereignty over the Bosphorus strait, it must permit the free passage of shipping through it. At that time, perhaps a few hundred ships a year passed along the strait, but this has risen to over 45,000 vessels annually (around 10% are tankers), with some estimates suggesting traffic will grow by a further 40% in the near future.

Many of these ships are tankers or are carrying other dangerous loads. There have already been serious accidents, such as the 1979 *Independenta* collision with another vessel, which killed 43 people and spilt and burnt some 95,000 tonnes of oil (2½ times the amount spilt by the famous *Exxon Valdez*). An oil pipeline running between Azerbaijan and the Turkish eastern Mediterranean port of Ceyhan, opened in 2005, relieves some of the burden. Other pipelines are on the drawing board, but in the meantime toxic substances and most oil continues to be carried along the Bosphorus.

The oil pipeline running from Baku, Azerbaijan to Ceyhan, Turkey via Tbilisi, Georgia is the world's second longest; it takes oil a month to travel from one end to the other.

Building development is taking a terrible toll on the environment, especially along the Aegean and Mediterranean coasts. Once pleasant fishing villages, Kuşadası and Marmaris have been near swamped by tacky urban spread and are in danger of losing all appeal. Local environmentalists battling development around Bodrum say the number of secluded valleys the famed Blue Voyage (p354) cruises visit has decreased from 45 to 11 in the last few years. Worse still, much of the development is only used during the warmer months, placing intensive strains on the infrastructure.

NUCLEAR TURKEY

One of the biggest challenges facing Turkey's environmentalists is the current government's plan to build three nuclear power plants by 2015. These plants propose to provide up to 20% of Turkey's projected energy needs for the next two decades. The first nuclear reactors are planned for Mersin, on the Mediterranean coast, and the Black Sea town of Sinop (see p545). One of the Black Sea scheme's most vocal opponents is **Sinop is Ours** (www.sinopbizim.org), a community-run initiative.

Turkey's government says the country's rising dependence on energy from other countries is the main catalyst for its push for nuclear energy. Turkey currently imports some 75% of its oil and natural gas, and when it was hit, like Ukraine was in 2005, by gas cuts by Russia, internal energy security went firmly on the agenda. Experts also claim that Iran's nuclear program, and its alleged push to develop nuclear weapons, makes it an untenable potential threat on Turkey's doorstep, pushing Turkey to have some nuclear capacity. Environmentalists say reports have shown that Turkey's existing energy infrastructure is outdated, poorly maintained and should be improved, and policies should be enforced to better harvest the current energy demands before looking to implement nuclear energy. They also state that the country's seismic vulnerabilities make any nuclear reactors an unacceptable risk.

TOWARDS THE EU

Turkey's intended accession to the EU (p43) is thankfully forcing it to lift its environmental standards. The country has started to overhaul environmental practices and laws, and even given indications that it might ratify international conventions such as the Kyoto Protocol (don't hold your breath; one government quango estimated it would lower the country's Gross Domestic Product by 37%).

The government aims to harmonise all environmental legislation with the EU by 2010. Initial cost estimates put this ambitious project at some €70.5 billion; €150 million was received from the World Bank to kick-start 'green' energy developments in 2004.

While Turkish prime minister Recep Tayyip Erdoğan has displayed an ambivalent attitude to environmentalists, his Environment and Forestry Minister, Veysel Eroğlu, must be having sleepless nights trying to work out which challenge to start with. Analysts say improving food safety is a major priority, and some fear it will be hard for Turkey to meet EU-set targets in this area. Currently Turkey isn't authorised to export animal products and most nuts to the EU. The other major priorities are wastewater disposal and water treatment facilities.

Short of water and electricity, Turkey is one of the world's main builders of dams. Wherever you go you see signs to a new *baraj* (dam) construction, and it doesn't take long to hear about the problems they are causing. Furthermore, recent studies have shown Turkey's soil erosion problems are shortening the dams' life spans considerably anyway. The gigantic Southeast Anatolia Project (p607), known as GAP, is one of Turkey's major construction efforts. Harnessing the headwaters of the Tigris and Euphrates Rivers, it's creating a potential political time bomb with the countries downstream that also depend on this water.

In 2008, Hasankeyf (p640) was on the World Monuments Watch list of the planet's 100 most endangered sites (alongside four other Turkish sites including İstanbul's historic walls and Güzelyurt's Red Church), thanks to the Ilisu Dam Project's plans to drown the historic southeastern town. The Ilisu consortium plans to move the architectural remains of the town, which was historically a Silk Rd commercial centre on the border of Anatolia and Mesopotamia, but the ruins' atmospheric setting on the Tigris River among cliffs and caves would be lost. The project, which could displace 50,000-plus people and affect almost 200 settlements, is set to be completed by 2013. On the other side of Turkey, the Yortanlı Dam poses a similar threat. Already built, the dam will bring water to an arid region but flood the ruins of a 1st-century Roman spa at Allianoi (p218), near Bergama.

Disposal and treatment of industrial waste is a major headache for the government; reports suggest that up to 75% of industrial waste is discharged without any treatment whatsoever and only 12% of the population is connected to sewage treatment facilities. Turkey is adopting the EU's 'polluters pay' policy by increasing fines and improving legislation and policing. In early 2006 fines for dumping toxic waste increased from a maximum of €4500 to €1.5 million. However, locals feel this is akin to shutting the gate after the horse has bolted, as these legislative changes were announced only after barrels of toxic waste were discovered in empty lots throughout İstanbul. One of the worst-hit suburbs was Dilovası, with deaths from cancer in the area nearly three times the world average and a report saying Dilovası should be evacuated and labelled a medical disaster area (neither happened).

To end on a happy note, Turkey is doing well when it comes to beach cleanliness, with 258 beaches and 13 marinas qualifying for Blue Flag status; go to www.blueflag.org for the complete list.

Dolphins live in İstanbul's Bosphorus strait – marine biologists have likened them to street children for the hardy lives they lead.

İstanbul

In his memoir *Istanbul: Memories of a City*, Nobel Laureate Orhan Pamuk describes İstanbul as 'an archipelago of neighbourhoods' within which live people whose lives – like the history of this extraordinary city – are reflected in the city views that flow before their eyes, 'like memories plucked from dreams'. These populous neighbourhoods, some dating from the Byzantine era, some from the golden age of the Ottoman sultans and some from recent, less affluent times, make the city what it is – a dilapidated but ultimately cohesive mosaic of buildings, suburbs and people with distinctly different but equally fascinating histories and personalities.

Here, you can retrace the steps of the Byzantine emperors when visiting Sultanahmet's extraordinary monuments and museums; marvel at the magnificent mosques built by the Ottoman sultans on the city's seven hills; and wander the cobbled streets of ancient Jewish, Greek and Armenian neighbourhoods in the Western Districts. Centuries of urban sprawl unfurl before your eyes on ferry trips up the Bosphorus or Golden Horn. You can even cross between religiously conservative suburbs in Asia to hedonistic entertainment hot spots along the European shore in a matter of minutes.

The city's overwhelming feeling of decrepitude and *hüzün* (melancholy) that Pamuk deconstructs so masterfully in his memoir is being relegated to the past, replaced with a sense of energy, innovation and optimism not seen since the days of Süleyman the Magnificent. Monument building is back in fashion, with a slew of stunning contemporary art galleries opening around the city, and the strong possibility of a European-flavoured future is being wholeheartedly embraced in the glamorous rooftop bars of Beyoğlu and the powerful boardrooms of Levent. There has never been a better time to visit.

HIGHLIGHTS

■ Uncover the secrets of opulent **Topkapı Palace** (p103)

■ Marvel at one of the world's great skylines from a fashionable **rooftop bar** (p151)

■ Kick up your heels at one of İstanbul's down-to-earth **meyhanes** (tavern; p139)

■ Admire the extraordinary Byzantine mosaics and frescoes at the **Chora Church** (p113)

■ Take a ferry trip along the mighty **Bosphorus** or up the fascinating **Golden Horn** (p121)

■ Join the crush and lose yourself in the labyrinthine **Grand Bazaar** (p109)

■ Contemplate the cutting edge at one of the city's new **contemporary art galleries** (p117)

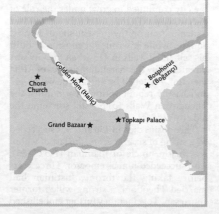

HISTORY

Byzantium

The first historically significant settlement here was founded by a Megarian colonist named Byzas. Before leaving Greece, he asked the Delphic oracle where to locate his new colony and received the enigmatic answer: 'Opposite the blind'. When Byzas and his fellow colonists sailed up the Bosphorus in 657 BC, they noticed a small colony on the Asian shore at Chalcedon (modern-day Kadıköy). Looking left, they saw the superb natural harbour of the Golden Horn on the European shore. Thinking, 'Those people in Chalcedon must be blind', they settled on the opposite shore, on the site of Lygos, and named their new city Byzantium.

Byzantium submitted willingly to Rome and fought its battles for centuries. But it finally got caught out supporting the wrong side in a civil war. The winner, Septimius Severus, razed the city walls and took away its privileges in AD 196. When he relented and rebuilt the city, he named it Augusta Antonina.

Constantinople

Another struggle for control of the Roman Empire determined the city's fate for the next 1000 years. Emperor Constantine pursued his rival Licinius to Augusta Antonina, then across the Bosphorus to Chrysopolis (Üsküdar). Defeating his rival in 324, Constantine solidified his control and declared the city the 'New Rome'. He laid out a vast new city to serve as capital of his empire and inaugurated it with much pomp in 330.

Constantine died in 337, just seven years after the dedication of his new capital, but the city continued to grow under the rule of the emperors. Theodosius I ('the Great') had a forum built on the present site of Beyazıt Square, while his son Theodosius II built his self-titled walls in 413 when the city was threatened by the marauding armies of Attila the Hun. Flattened by an earthquake in 447 and hastily rebuilt within two months, the Theodosian Walls (p114) still surround the old city today.

Theodosius died in 450 and was succeeded by a string of six emperors, the last of whom was Justin, uncle of Justinian (r 527–65), who succeeded him as emperor. Three years before taking the throne, Justinian had married Theodora, a strong-willed former courtesan. Together they further embellished Constantinople with great buildings, including the famous Aya Sofya (p98), built in 537. Justinian's ambitious building projects and constant wars of reconquest exhausted his treasury and his empire. Following his reign, the Byzantine Empire would never again be as large, powerful or rich.

Much of ancient Constantinople's building stock remains, including churches, palaces, cisterns and the Hippodrome. In fact, there's more left than most people realise. Any excavation reveals ancient streets, mosaics, tunnels, water and sewer systems, houses and public buildings buried beneath the modern city centre.

THE CONQUEST

The Ottoman sultan Mehmet II, who became known as Fatih (the Conqueror), came to power in 1451 and immediately departed his capital in Edirne, aiming to conquer the once-great Byzantine city.

In four short months, Mehmet oversaw the building of Rumeli Hisarı (p122), the great fortress on the European side of the Bosphorus; and also repaired Anadolu Hisarı, built half a century earlier by his great-grandfather Beyazıt I. Together these fortresses controlled the strait's narrowest point.

The Byzantines had closed the mouth of the Golden Horn with a heavy chain to prevent Ottoman boats from sailing in and attacking the city walls on the northern side. Not to be thwarted, Mehmet marshalled his boats at a cove (where the Dolmabahçe Palace now stands) and had them transported overland by night on rollers, up the valley (present site of the Hilton Hotel) and down the other side into the Golden Horn at Kasımpaşa. Catching the Byzantine defenders by surprise, he soon had the Golden Horn under control.

The last great obstacle was provided by the city's mighty walls on the western side. No matter how heavily Mehmet's cannons battered them, the Byzantines rebuilt the walls by night and, come daybreak, the impetuous young sultan would find himself back where he'd started. Finally, he received a proposal from a Hungarian cannon founder called Urban who had come to help the Byzantine emperor defend Christendom against the infidels. Finding that the Byzantine emperor had no money, Urban instead offered to make Mehmet the most enormous cannon ever seen. Mehmet gladly accepted and the mighty cannon breached the walls, allowing the Ottomans into the city. On 28 May 1453 the final attack began and by the evening of the 29th the Turks were in complete control of the city. The last Byzantine emperor, Constantine XI Dragases, died fighting on the walls.

İstanbul

THE OTTOMAN CENTURIES

Seeing himself as the successor to great emperors such as Constantine and Justinian, Mehmet the Conqueror at once began to rebuild and repopulate the city. He chose the conspicuous promontory of Seraglio Point as the location for his ostentatious palace, Topkapı, and he also repaired and fortified Theodosius' walls. İstanbul was soon the administrative, commercial and cultural heart of his growing empire.

The building boom Mehmet kicked off was continued by his successors, with Süleyman the Magnificent and his architect Mimar Sinan (p111) being responsible for more construction than any other sultan. The city was endowed with buildings commissioned by the sultan and his family, court and grand viziers; these include the city's largest and grandest mosque, the Süleymaniye (1550). Later sultans also added mosques and in the 19th century numerous palaces were built along the Bosphorus, among them Dolmabahçe (p117).

As the Ottoman Empire grew to encompass the Middle East and North Africa as well as half of Eastern Europe, İstanbul became a fabulous melting pot of nationalities. On its streets people spoke Turkish, Greek, Armenian, Ladino, Russian, Arabic, Bulgarian, Romanian, Albanian, Italian, French, German, English and Maltese.

However, what had been the most civilised city on earth in the time of Süleyman eventually declined along with the Ottoman Empire, and by the 19th century İstanbul had lost much of its former glory. Nevertheless, it continued to be the 'Paris of the East' and, to affirm this, the first great international luxury express train, the famous *Orient Express,* connected İstanbul and the French capital in 1883.

TURKISH REPUBLIC & RECENT EVENTS

Mustafa Kemal (Atatürk)'s post-WWI campaign for national salvation and independence was directed from Ankara. In founding the Turkish Republic, Atatürk decided to leave behind the imperial memories of İstanbul and set up his new government in Ankara, a city that could not be threatened by gunboats. Robbed of its status as the capital of a vast empire, İstanbul lost much of its wealth and glitter. The city's streets and neighbourhoods decayed, its infrastructure was neither maintained nor improved and virtually no economic development occurred.

The city stayed this way until the 1990s, when a renaissance occurred. Since this time, public transport has been upgraded, work on a cross-Bosphorus tunnel is well under way, suburbs have been reinvigorated and parklands now line the waterways. When İstanbul won the right to become the European Capital of Culture in 2010 other ambitious projects were excitedly placed on the drawing board, and the city is currently awash with restoration and remodelling projects.

İstanbul's cultural transformation is just as marked. The seedy dives of Beyoğlu have been replaced by funky cafés, bars and studios, transforming the suburb into a bohemian hub. Galleries such as İstanbul Modern, Santralİstanbul, the Pera Museum and the Sakıp Sabancı Müzesi have opened, showcasing Turkey's contemporary art to the world. The live-music scene in the city has exploded, making İstanbul a buzzword for creative, energetic music with a unique East–West twist. And a new generation of artisans is refining and repositioning the city's traditional crafts industries – making for shopping experiences that are as exciting as they can be unexpected.

In short, Turkey's bid to join the EU is underpinned by the fact that these days its beloved İstanbul is a cosmopolitan and sophisticated megalopolis that has reclaimed its status as one of the world's truly great cities.

ORIENTATION

The Bosphorus strait, between the Black and Marmara Seas, divides Europe from Asia/Anatolia. On its western shore, European İstanbul is further divided by the Golden Horn (Haliç) into Old İstanbul in the south and Beyoğlu in the north.

Sultanahmet is the heart of Old İstanbul and it's here that you'll find most of the city's famous sites, including the Blue Mosque, Aya Sofya and Topkapı Palace. The adjoining area, with hotels to suit all budgets, is actually called

İSTANBUL IN...

Two Days

Start the day by marvelling at the **Blue Mosque** (p100) and its venerable neighbour, **Aya Sofya** (p98). Next, investigate the watery depths of the **Basilica Cistern** (p101). By this stage you'll be in need of a rest, so make your way up Divan Yolu towards the **Grand Bazaar** (p109) and have lunch at **Sefa Restaurant** (p135), **Havuzlu** (p136) or **Fez Cafe** (p137 Shopping is next on the agenda – if you can't find something fabulous to take home you're just not trying hard enough! Mission accomplished, wander north through the bustling mercantile area of Tahtakale to the **Spice Bazaar** (p111) by the water at Eminönü. After taste-testing your way through this historic market, finish the day by sampling the national dish and admiring the panoramic views at **Hamdi Et Lokantası** (p136) or **Zinhan Kebap House at Storks** (p137). After dinner return to the Blue Mosque, grab a seat at **Café Meşale** (p149) and sit back and enjoy a nargileh (traditional water pipe).

Day two should be devoted to **Topkapı Palace** (p103) and the **İstanbul Archaeological Museums** (p108). Start at the palace and plan on spending at least four hours exploring. Enjoy a simple lunch or cup of tea at **Caferağa Medresesi** (p136) before making your way down the hill to the museums to marvel at their collections. For dinner, you should make your way across the Galata Bridge to cosmopolitan Beyoğlu, promenade down **İstiklal Caddesi** (p115), have a drink at a **rooftop bar** (p151) and end the night by enjoying meze and rakı with the locals at a **meyhane** (p139) on Nevizade or Sofyalı Sokaks.

Four Days

Follow the two-day itinerary, then on your third day hop onto a **ferry** (p121) at Eminönü and explore the Bosphorus or Golden Horn. In the late afternoon, pamper yourself at a **hamam** (p126) – try Cağaloğlu or Çemberlitaş for maximum Ottoman ambience. Kick on to a restaurant in **Beyoğlu** (p138) for dinner and then make your way to one of the Bosphorus superclubs on the **Golden Mile** (p152). Day four should see you heading towards the Western Districts of Old İstanbul to contemplate the extraordinarily beautiful Byzantine mosaics and frescoes at the **Chora Church** (p113) before lunch at elegant **Asitane** (p137) or at the atmospheric **Şehzade Mehmed Sofrası** (p136). In the afternoon, make your way back to Sultanahmet and check out the impressive **Museum of Turkish & Islamic Arts** (p101), before strolling along the **Arasta Bazaar** (p100) to the **Great Palace Mosaic Museum** (p100). Wind down over a delicious dinner with the city's power brokers at **Balıkçı Sabahattin** (p135) or overlooking Aya Sofya and the Blue Mosque at **Teras Restaurant** (p135).

One Week

Follow the itineraries above for your first four days. By day five, you could head over to Beyoğlu, spending the morning in **İstanbul Modern** (p115) and/or the **Pera Museum** (p116). Eat lunch in Beyoğlu and then spend the afternoon shopping (p154) or at **Dolmabahçe Palace** (p117). Stay over this side for dinner, maybe kicking onto a jazz club (p153) afterwards. On day six the water beckons again and a ferry to the **Princes' Islands** (p164) is in order. Your last day in the city could start at one of the city's most revered buildings, the magnificent **Süleymaniye Camii** (p110) and move over to **Kadıköy** (p121) in Asia, with a delectable lunch at **Çiya** (p121), a walk around the produce market and a drink in one of the hip bars on Kadife Sokak.

Cankurtaran *(jan-kur-tar-an)*, although if you say 'Sultanahmet' most people will understand where you mean.

Up the famous Divan Yolu boulevard from Sultanahmet you'll find the Grand Bazaar. To its north is the Süleymaniye Camii, which graces the top of one of the old city's seven hills. Down from the bazaar is the Golden Horn, home to the bustling transport hub of Eminönü.

Over the Galata Bridge from Eminönü is Beyoğlu, on the northern side of the Golden Horn. This is where you'll find some of the best restaurants, shops, bars and nightclubs in the city. It's also home to Taksim Sq, the heart of 'modern' İstanbul.

The city's glamour suburbs include Nişantaşı, and Teşvikiye, north of Taksim Sq, and the suburbs lining the Bosphorus, especially those on the European side. However, many locals prefer to live on the Asian side, citing cheaper rents and a better standard of living. Üsküdar and Kadıköy are the two Asian hubs, reachable by a short ferry ride from Eminönü or a drive over the Bosphorus Bridge.

İstanbul's otogar (bus station) is at Esenler, about 10km west of the city centre. The city's main airport, Atatürk International Airport, is in Yeşilköy, 23km west of Sultanahmet; a smaller airport, Sabiha Gökçen International Airport, is 50km southeast. The two main train stations are currently Haydarpaşa station near Kadıköy on the Asian side and Sirkeci station at Eminönü. See p160 and p160 for details about getting to and from these transport hubs.

Maps

A free sheet map of İstanbul is available from tourist-information offices, and while it's only of average quality, it's as good as any sheet map on sale locally. For more-detailed guidance, including all minor streets, look for MepMedya's two-volume *İlçe İlçe A'dan Z'ye İstanbul* (*İstanbul city plan and map*; TL75). You can find it at **Türkiye Diyanet Vakfı** (Map pp92-3; ☎ 0212-511 4432; Babıali Caddesi 40, Cağaloğlu; ☺ 9am-7pm Mon-Sat) or in **İstanbul Kıtapçısı** (see right).

INFORMATION
Bookshops

Bibliophiles will want to head towards the **Old Book Bazaar** (Map pp90 1; Sahaflar Çarşısı, Beyazıt), in a shady little courtyard west of the Grand Bazaar. It dates from Byzantine times. In Beyoğlu, you could spend years foraging through the stacks of secondhand books (some in English) on the two floors at **Aslıhan Pasaji** (Map pp94-5; Balık Pazar, Galatasaray).

İstanbul's best range of bookshops is along or just off İstiklal Caddesi in Beyoğlu, but there are one or two in other locations. Those useful for travellers include:

Galeri Kayseri (Map pp92-3; ☎ 0212-512 0456; Divan Yolu 11 & 58, Sultanahmet; ☺ 9am-9pm) Has some English-language fiction and glossy books set in or about İstanbul; the other shop over the road – same owner – holds near-identical stock.

Homer Kitabevi (Map pp94-5; ☎ 0212-249 5902; Yeni Çarşı Caddesi 28, Galatasaray, Beyoğlu; ☺ 10am-7.30pm Mon-Sat, 12.30-7.30pm Sun) Come here for Homer's unrivalled range of Turkish fiction, plus its enviable collection of nonfiction covering everything from Sufism and Islam to Kurdish and Armenian issues.

İstanbul Kitapçısı (Map pp94-5; ☎ 0212-292 7692; İstiklal Caddesi 379, Beyoğlu; ☺ 10am-6.45pm Mon-Sat, noon-6.45pm Sun) This government-run bookshop has English-language books on İstanbul, plus a great selection of maps, prints, postcards and music.

Linda's Book Exchange (Map pp94-5; ground fl, Şehbender Sokak 18, Tünel, Beyoğlu; ☺ 5-7pm Mon-Fri) Note the limited opening hours of this cosy den of long-term expat Linda. Unsigned, it's the first door in the building on the left.

Pandora (Map pp94-5; ☎ 0212-243 3503; Büyükparmakkapı Sokak 8b; ☺ 10am-8pm Mon-Wed, 10am-9pm Thu-Sat, 1-8pm Sun) This long-standing independent bookshop has recently opened a new store dedicated solely to English-language books. It has great crime fiction and travel sections, as well as loads of books about Turkey.

Robinson Crusoe (Map pp94-5; ☎ 0212-293 6968; İstiklal Caddesi 389, Beyoğlu; ☺ 9am-9.30pm Mon-Sat, 10am-9.30pm Sun) Wide range of English-language novels and books about İstanbul, plus travel guides and a good range of art magazines.

Emergency
Ambulance (☎ 112)
Fire (☎ 110)
Police (☎ 155)
Tourist police (Map pp92-3; ☎ 0212-527 4503; Yerebatan Caddesi 6, Sultanahmet) Across the street from the Basilica Cistern.

Internet Access

Most hotels and hostels provide a computer terminal with free internet access for their guests; many also provide free wi-fi. If this isn't the case, there are internet cafés all over the city, including:

Café Turka Internet Café (Map pp92-3; 2nd fl, Divan Yolu Caddesi 22, Sultanahmet; per hr TL2.50; ☺ 9am-midnight) Always full of backpackers and Sultanahmet locals, who come to check their email and drink tea while lolling on the beanbag chairs.

Robin Hood Internet Café (Map pp94-5; 4th fl, Yeni Çarşı Caddesi 8, Galatasaray; per hr TL2; ☺ 9am-11.30pm) Opposite the Galatasaray Lycée, this is a friendly place up a steep flight of stairs. There's wi-fi access on the balcony.

There's wi-fi access at Atatürk International and Sabiha Gökçen International Airports, at Java Studio (p136), in Sultanahmet, at

Kahvedan (p138) in Cihangir and at branches of Kahve Dünyası, Starbucks, Ozsüt and Gloria Jean's. See the website www.ttnet.net .tr for other locations throughout the city.

Laundry

It can cost up to TL20 to have a small load of clothes washed and dried in a laundry – hostels will usually charge half this. Self-service launderettes are almost unknown, so you can either seek out a local laundry and drop your load off to be done, or ask your hotel or hostel to organise this for you.

Media

The monthly English edition of *Time Out İstanbul* (TL4) has a large listings section and is the best source for details about upcoming events – you can pick it up at the airport or at newspaper booths in Sultanahmet.

Published three times per year, the glossy *Cornucopia* magazine (TL20) features many İstanbul-specific articles, including excellent restaurant and exhibition reviews. It's impossible to find in Sultanahmet, but you can buy it in most of the bookshops along İstiklal Caddesi in Beyoğlu or at airport newsagencies.

Medical Services

Although they are expensive, it's probably best to visit one of the private hospitals listed here if you need medical care when in İstanbul. The standard of care at these places is excellent and you will have little trouble finding staff who speak English. Both accept credit-card payments and charge around TL160 for a standard consultation.

Alman Hastanesi (German Hospital; Map pp94-5; ☎ 0212-293 2150; Sıraselviler Caddesi 119, Taksim; ☽ 8.30am-6pm Mon-Fri, 8.30am-5pm Sat) A few hundred metres south of Taksim Sq on the left-hand side, this hospital has eye and dental clinics and English-speaking staff.

Amerikan Hastanesi (American Hospital; Map pp86-7; ☎ 0212-444 3777; Güzelbahçe Sokak 20, Nişantaşı; ☽ 24hr emergency department) About 2km northeast of Taksim Sq, this hospital has English-speaking staff and a dental clinic.

Money

ATMs are everywhere in İstanbul and include those conveniently located next to Aya Sofya Meydanı in Sultanahmet (Map pp92-3) and all along İstiklal Caddesi in Beyoğlu.

The 24-hour *döviz bürosu* (exchange bureau) in the arrivals hall at Atatürk International Airport offers rates comparable to those offered by city bureaux. Other exchange bureaux can be found on Divan Yolu in Sultanahmet, near the Grand Bazaar and around Sirkeci station in Eminönü.

Post

İstanbul's central PTT (post office; Map pp92-3) is a couple of blocks southwest of Sirkeci Train Station. You can make phone calls, buy stamps and send and receive faxes 24 hours a day. All post-restante mail (p667) should be sent here.

There's a convenient PTT booth (Map pp92-3) on Aya Sofya Meydanı in Sultanahmet and there are PTT branches in the basement of the law courts (Map pp92-3) on İmran Öktem Caddesi in Sultanahmet; on İstiklal Caddesi near Galatasaray Sq (Map pp94-5); near the Galata Bridge in Karaköy (Map pp94-5); and in the southwestern corner of the Grand Bazaar (Map p109).

You can send parcels at the central post office, or parcels less than 2kg at other PTT branches (but not the booth in Sultanahmet). PTTs offer an express post service as well or you could try a carrier such as **DHL**, which has offices in **Sultanahmet** (Map pp92-3; ☎ 0212-512 5452; Yerebatan Caddesi 15; ☽ 10am-6.15pm Mon-Sat) and **Taksim** (Map pp86-7; ☎ 0212-444 0040; Cumhuriyet Caddesi 20; ☽ 10am-5.30pm Mon-Fri, 10am-5pm Sat).

Telephone

If you are in European İstanbul and wish to call a number in Asian İstanbul, you must dial ☎ 0216 then the number. If you are in Asian İstanbul and wish to call a number in European İstanbul dial ☎ 0212 then the number. Don't use the area codes if you are calling a number on the same shore.

For international calls pick up an IPC phonecard from one of the booths along Divan Yolu in Sultanahmet, or İstiklal Caddesi in Beyoğlu.

Tourist Information

The **Ministry of Culture & Tourism** (www.tourismturkey .org, www.turizm.gov.tr) runs the following tourist information offices:

Atatürk International Airport (☽ 24hr) Booth in international arrivals area.

Beyazıt Sq (Hürriyet Meydanı; Map pp90-1; ☎ 0212-522 4902; ☽ 9am-5pm) Note that there was talk of closing this booth when we researched this book.

(Continued on p98)

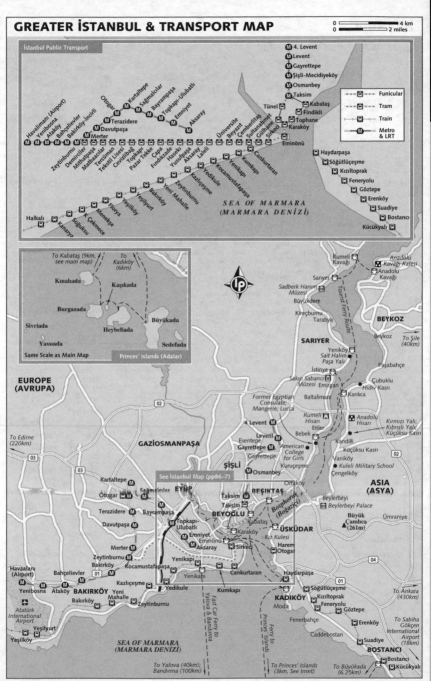

GREATER İSTANBUL & TRANSPORT MAP

İSTANBUL

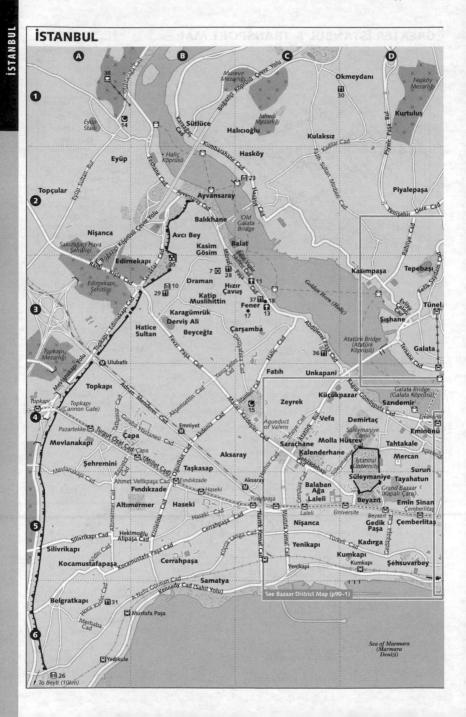

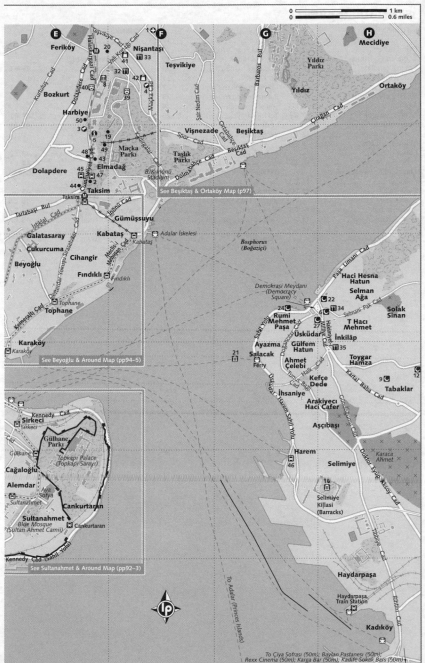

0 _____ 1 km
0 _____ 0.6 miles

Feriköy
Mecidiye
Nişantaşı
Teşvikiye
Yıldız Parkı
Ortaköy
Bozkurt
Yıldız
Harbiye
Vişnezade   Beşiktaş
Maçka Parkı
Dolapdere
Taşlık Parkı
Elmadağ
BJK İnönü Stadium
Taksim
See Beşiktaş & Ortaköy Map (p97)
Taksim
Gümüşsuyu
Galatasaray   Kabataş
Bosphorus (Boğaziçi)
Çukurcuma   Cihangir
Kabataş
Adalar İskelesi
Beyoğlu
Fındıklı
Fındıklı
Demokraşi Meydanı (Democracy Square)
Haci Hesna Hatun
Selman Ağa
Solak Sinan
Rumi Mehmet Paşa
Tophane
Tophane
T Hacı Mehmet
Üsküdar
İnkilâp
Ayazma
Gülfem Hatun
Karaköy
Karaköy
See Beyoğlu & Around Map (pp94–5)
Salacak
Ferry
Ahmet Çelebi
Toygar Hamza
İhsaniye
Kefçe Dede
Tabaklar
Arakiyecı Haci Cafer
Aşçıbaşı
Sirkeci
Sirkeci
Gülhane Parkı
Harem
Selimiye
Karaca Ahmet
Gülhane
Topkapı Palace (Topkapı Sarayı)
Cağaloğlu
Alemdar
Aya Sofya
Selimiye Kışlası (Barracks)
Sultanahmet
Cankurtaran
Cankurtaran
Sultanahmet
Blue Mosque (Sultan Ahmet Camii)
Haydarpaşa
See Sultanahmet & Around Map (pp92–3)
Haydarpaşa Train Station
Kennedy Cad (Sahil Yolu)
Kadıköy
To Adalar (Princes Islands)
To Çiya Sofrası (50m); Baylan Pastanesi (50m); Rexx Cinema (50m); Karga Bar (50m); Kadife Sokak Bars (50m)

İSTANBUL sidebar tab

İSTANBUL (pp86–7)

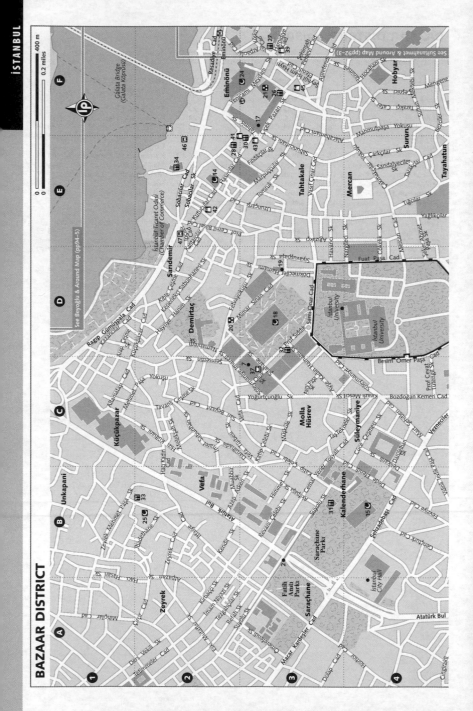

BAZAAR DISTRICT

İSTANBUL

SULTANAHMET & AROUND

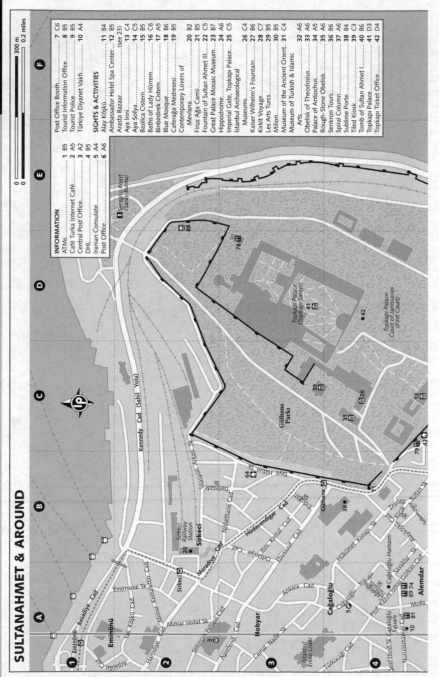

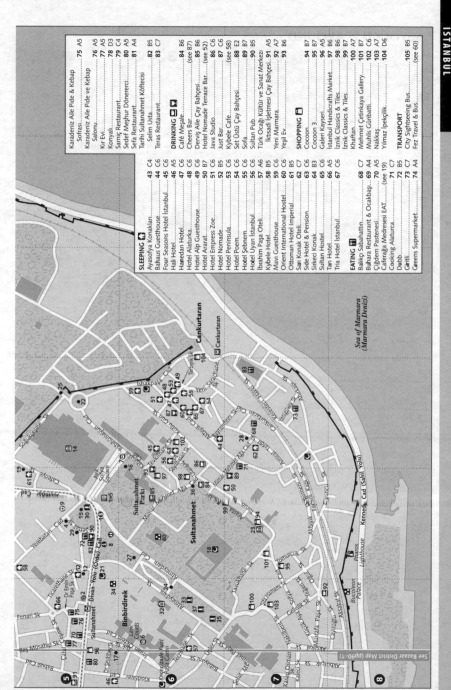

SLEEPING 🏠
Ayasofya Konakları	43 C4
Bahaus Guesthouse	44 C6
Four Seasons Hotel İstanbul	45 C6
Hali Hotel	46 A5
Hanedan Hotel	47 C6
Hotel Alaturka	48 C6
Hotel Alp Guesthouse	49 C6
Hotel Ararat	50 B7
Hotel Empress Zoe	51 C6
Hotel Nomade	52 B5
Hotel Peninsula	53 C6
Hotel Poem	54 C6
Hotel Şebnem	55 C6
Hotel Uyan İstanbul	56 C6
İbrahim Paşa Oteli	57 A6
Kybele Hotel	58 B5
Mavi Guesthouse	59 C6
Orient International Hostel	60 C6
Ottoman Hotel Imperial	61 B5
San Konak Oteli	62 C7
Side Hotel & Pension	63 C6
Sirkeci Konak	64 B3
Sultan Hostel	65 C6
Tan Hotel	66 A5
Tria Hotel İstanbul	67 C6

EATING 🍴
Balıkçı Sabahattin	68 C7
Buhara Restaurant & Ocakbaşı	69 A4
Çiğdem Pastenesi	70 A5
Caferağa Medresesi EAT	(see 19)
Cooking Alaturca	71 C7
Dababb	72 B5
Giritli	73 C7
Geens Supermarket	74 A4

Karadeniz Aile Pide & Kebap Sofrası	75 A5
Karadeniz Aile Pide ve Kebap Salonu	76 A5
Kır Evi	77 A5
Konyalı	78 D3
Sarnıç Restaurant	79 C4
Sedef Meşhur Dönercisi	80 A5
Sefa Restaurant	81 A4
Tarihi Sultanahmet Köftecisi Selim Usta	82 B5
Teras Restaurant	83 C7

DRINKING 🍸 🍷
Café Meşale	84 B6
Cheers Bar	(see 87)
Derviş Aile Çay Bahçesi	85 B6
Hotel Nomade Terrace Bar	(see 52)
Java Studio	86 C6
Just Bar	87 C6
Kybele Cafe	(see 58)
Set Üstü Çay Bahçesi	88 E2
Sofa	89 B7
Sultan Pub	90 B5
Türk Ocağı Kültür ve Sanat Merkezi	91 A5
İktisadi İşletmesi Çay Bahçesi	92 A7
Yeni Marmara	93 B6
Yeşil Ev	

SHOPPING 🛍
Cocoon	94 B7
Cocoon 3	95 B7
Galeri Kayseri	96 A5
İstanbul Handicrafts Market	97 B6
İznik Classics & Tiles	98 B6
İznik Classics & Tiles	99 B7
Khaftan	100 A7
Mehmet Çetinkaya Gallery	101 B7
Muhlis Günbatti	102 C6
Nakkaş	103 A7
Yılmaz İpekçilik	104 D6

TRANSPORT
City Sightseeing Bus	105 B5
Fez Travel & Bus	(see 60)

Sea of Marmara
(*Marmara Denizi*)

Cankurtaran

🚉 Cankurtaran

See Bazaar District Map (pp90–1)

BEYOĞLU & AROUND

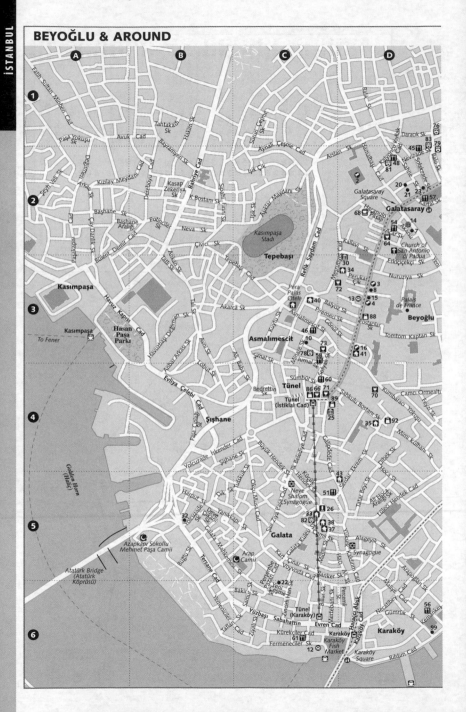

BEYOĞLU & AROUND (pp44–5)

BEŞİKTAŞ & ORTAKÖY

(Continued from p84)

Elmadağ (Map pp86-7; ☎ 0212-233 0592; ☺ 9am-5pm Mon-Sat) In the arcade in front of the İstanbul Hilton Hotel, just off Cumhuriyet Caddesi about a 10-minute walk north of Taksim Sq.

Sultanahmet (Map pp92-3; ☎ 0212-518 8754; ☺ 9am-5pm) At the northeast end of the Hippodrome.

DANGERS & ANNOYANCES

İstanbul is no more nor less safe a city than any large metropolis, but there are a few dangers worth highlighting. Some İstanbullus drive like rally drivers, and there is no such thing as a generally acknowledged right of way for pedestrians. As a pedestrian, give way to cars, motorcycles and trucks in all situations, even if you have to jump out of the way. Bag-snatching is also a slight problem, especially on Galipdede Sokak in Tünel and on İstiklal Caddesi's side streets. Lastly – and probably most importantly – you should be aware of the long-standing scam concerning men, bars and women. What could possibly go wrong you ask? See p660 for the low-down.

SIGHTS
Sultanahmet & Around

It's not surprising that many visitors to İstanbul never make it out of Sultanahmet – after all, few cities have such a concentration of sights, shops, hotels and eateries within easy walking distance. This is 'Old İstanbul', a Unesco-designated World Heritage site packed with so many wonderful things to see that you could spend several weeks here and still only scratch the surface.

AYA SOFYA

Called Sancta Sophia in Latin, Haghia Sofia in Greek and the Church of the Divine Wisdom in English, **Aya Sofya** (Map pp92-3; ☎ 0212-522 0989; Aya Sofya Meydanı, Sultanahmet; adult/under 6yr TL20/free, official guide (45 min) TL50; ☺ 9am-5pm Tue-Sun Nov-Apr, to 7.30pm May-Oct; upper gallery closes 15-30 min earlier) is İstanbul's most famous monument. Arrive early to avoid peak-season crowds.

Emperor Justinian (r 527–65) had the Aya Sofya built as part of his effort to restore the greatness of the Roman Empire. It was completed in 537 and reigned as the greatest church in Christendom until the Conquest in 1453. Mehmet the Conqueror had it converted into a mosque and so it remained until 1935, when Atatürk proclaimed it a museum.

Ongoing restoration work (partly Unesco funded) means that the dome is always filled with scaffolding, but not even this can detract from the experience of visiting one of the world's truly great buildings.

On entering his great creation for the first time almost 1500 years ago, Justinian exclaimed, 'Glory to God that I have been judged worthy of such a work. Oh Solomon! I have outdone you!' Entering the building today, it is easy to excuse Justinian's self-congratulatory tone. The interior, with its magnificent domed ceiling soaring heavenward, is so sublimely beautiful that many seeing it for the first time are quite literally stunned into silence.

As you walk into the **inner narthex**, look up to see a brilliant mosaic of Christ as Pantocrator (Ruler of All) above the third and largest door (the Imperial Door). Once through this door the magnificent main dome soars above you. Supported by 40 massive ribs, it was constructed of special hollow bricks made in Rhodes from a unique light, porous clay; these rest on huge pillars concealed in the interior walls, which creates an impression that the dome hovers unsupported. (Compare the Blue Mosque's four huge interior 'elephant's feet' pillars and you will appreciate the genius of Aya Sofya's design.)

The curious elevated kiosk screened from public view is the **Sultan's loge**. Ahmet III (r 1703–30) had it built so he could come in, pray and leave again unseen, thus preserving the imperial mystique. The ornate **library**, on the west wall, was built by Sultan Mahmut I in 1739.

In the side aisle to the northeast of the Imperial Door is the **weeping column**, with a worn copper facing pierced by a hole. Legend has it that putting one's finger in the hole can lead to ailments being healed if the finger emerges moist.

The large 19th-century **medallions** inscribed with gilt Arabic letters are the work of master calligrapher Mustafa İzzet Efendi, and give the names of God (Allah), Mohammed and the early caliphs Ali and Abu Bakr.

Mosaics

From the floor of Aya Sofya, 9th-century mosaic portraits of St Ignatius the Younger (c 800), St John Chrysostom (c 400) and St Ignatius Theodorus of Antioch are visible high up at the base of the northern tympanum (semicircle) beneath the dome. Next to these

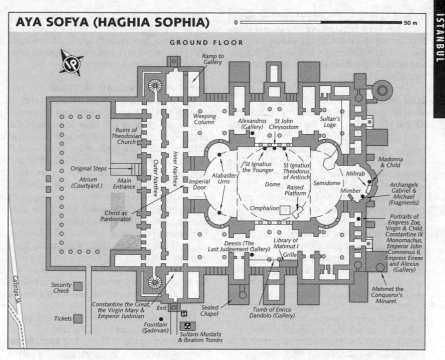

AYA SOFYA (HAGHIA SOPHIA)

0 ———————————— 50 m

GROUND FLOOR

Ramp to Gallery

Weeping Column

Alexandros (Gallery)

St John Chrysostom

Sultan's Loge

Madonna & Child

Ruins of Theodosian Church

St Ignatius the Younger

St Ignatius Theodorus of Antioch

Mihrab

Archangels Gabriel & Michael (Fragments)

Original Steps

Imperial Door

Alabaster Urns

Dome

Raised Platform

Semidome

Mimber

Atrium (Courtyard)

Main Entrance

Inner Narthex

Outer Narthex

Christ as Pantocrator

Omphalion

Portraits of Empress Zoe, Virgin & Child, Constantine IX Monomachus, Emperor John Comnenus II, Empress Eirene and Alexius (Gallery)

Deesis (The Last Judgement Gallery)

Library of Mahmut I

Grille

Security Check

Mehmet the Conqueror's Minaret

Constantine the Great, the Virgin Mary & Emperor Justinian

Exit

Sealed Chapel

Tomb of Enrico Dandolo (Gallery)

Tickets

Fountain (Şadırvan)

Sultans Mustafa & İbrahim Tombs

Caferiye Sk

three, and seen only from the upstairs east gallery, is a portrait of Emperor Alexandros. In the apse is a wonderful mosaic of the Madonna and Child; nearby mosaics depict the archangels Gabriel and Michael, although only fragments of Michael remain.

The upstairs galleries house the most impressive of Aya Sofya's mosaics and mustn't be missed. They can be reached via a switchback ramp at the northern end of the inner narthex. The magnificent *Deesis Mosaic (The Last Judgment)* in the south gallery dates from the early 14th century. Christ is at the centre, with the Virgin Mary on the left and John the Baptist on the right.

At the apse end of the southern gallery is the famous mosaic portrait of the Empress Zoe (r 1028–50), who had three husbands and changed this mosaic portrait with each one. The portrait of the third Mr Zoe, Constantine IX Monomachus, survives because he outlived the empress.

To the right of Zoe and Constantine is another mosaic depicting characters with less-saucy histories: in this scene Mary holds the Christ child, centre, with Emperor John

(Johannes) Comnenus II (the Good) to the left and Empress Eirene (known for her charitable works) to the right. Their son Alexius, who died soon after this portrait was made, is depicted next to Eirene.

As you leave the museum from the narthex, make sure you turn and look up above the door to see one of the church's finest late 10th-century mosaics. This shows Constantine the Great, on the right, offering Mary, who holds the Christ child, the city of Constantinople; Emperor Justinian, on the left, is offering her Aya Sofya.

BATHS OF LADY HÜRREM

Traditionally, every mosque had a hamam included in or around its complex of buildings. Aya Sofya was no exception and this elegant symmetrical building known as the Haseki Hürrem Hamamı or **Baths of Lady Hürrem** (Map pp92-3; Aya Sofya Meydanı 4, Sultanahmet), designed by Sinan in 1556–57, was built just across the road from the great mosque by Süleyman in the name of his wife Hürrem Sultan, known to history as Roxelana. The hamam was one of 32 designed by Sinan and is widely thought to be his best. It operated until 1910 and in recent years has been functioning as a carpet shop. It is currently closed to the public pending discussions between the Ministry of Culture and private operators about it reopening as a functioning hamam.

BLUE MOSQUE

With his eponymously named mosque, Sultan Ahmet I (r 1603–17) set out to build a monument that would rival and even surpass the nearby Aya Sofya in grandeur and beauty. Today it's more widely known as the **Blue Mosque** (Sultan Ahmet Camii; Map pp92–3; Hippodrome, Sultanahmet; ☪ closed during prayer times).

The mosque's architect, Mehmet Ağa, managed to orchestrate the sort of visual whambam effect with the mosque's exterior that Aya Sofya achieved with its interior. Its curves are voluptuous, it has six minarets and the courtyard is the biggest of all of the Ottoman mosques. The interior is conceived on a similarly grand scale: the blue tiles that give the building its unofficial name number in the tens of thousands, there are 260 windows and the central prayer space is huge.

To appreciate the mosque's design, approach it via the Hippodrome rather than straight from Sultanahmet Park through the crowds. Once inside the courtyard, which is the same size as the mosque's interior, you'll appreciate the building's perfect proportions. The mosque is such a popular attraction that admission is controlled so as to preserve its sacred atmosphere. Only worshippers are admitted through the main door; tourists must use the south door.

Inside, the stained-glass windows and İznik tiles lining the walls immediately attract attention. Although the windows are replacements, they still create the luminous effects of the originals, which came from Venice. You will also see immediately why the Blue Mosque, constructed between 1606 and 1616, more than a millennium after Aya Sofya, is not as daring as its venerable neighbour: four huge 'elephant's feet' pillars hold up the dome, a less elegant but sturdier solution to the problem of support.

The tile-encrusted **Tomb of Sultan Ahmet I** (Map pp92–3; donation expected; ☪ 9.30am-4.30pm), the Blue Mosque's great patron, is in a separate building on the north side facing Sultanahmet Park. Ahmet, who had ascended to the imperial throne aged 13, died

one year after the mosque was constructed, aged only 27. He rests here with a dozen or so children, powerful evidence that wealth and privilege didn't make the imperial family immune from tragedy.

GREAT PALACE MOSAIC MUSEUM

When archaeologists from the University of Ankara and Scotland's St Andrews University dug at the back of the Blue Mosque in the mid-1950s, they found a mosaic pavement dating from early Byzantine times (c AD 500). Covered with wonderful hunting and mythological scenes and emperors' portraits, the pavement was part of a triumphal way that led from the Byzantine emperor's Great Palace (which stood where the Blue Mosque now stands) down to the harbour of Bucoleon to the south. It is now displayed *in situ* in the **Great Palace Mosaic Museum** (Büyüksaray Mozaik Müzesi; Map pp92–3; ☎ 0212-518 1205; Torun Sokak, Sultanahmet; admission TL8; ☪ 9am-4.30pm Tue-Sun Nov-May, to 6.30pm Jun-Oct), where there are informative panels documenting the floor's rescue and renovation.

Other 5th-century mosaics were saved when Sultan Ahmet I had an *arasta* (row of shops) built on top of them. The **Arasta Bazaar** (Map pp92–3) now houses numerous carpet and ceramic shops that provide rental revenue for the upkeep of the Blue Mosque.

Enter the Great Palace Mosaic Museum from Torun Sokak behind the mosque and the Arasta Bazaar.

HIPPODROME

The Byzantine emperors loved nothing more than an afternoon at the chariot races, and the **Hippodrome** (Atmeydanı; Map pp92–3) was their venue of choice. In its heyday, the rectangular arena consisted of two levels of galleries, a central spine, starting boxes and the semicircular end known as the sphendone.

The Hippodrome was the centre of Byzantine life for 1200 years and of Ottoman life for another 400-odd years. The Byzantines supported the rival chariot teams of 'Greens' and 'Blues', which had separate political connections. Support for a team was akin to membership of a political party and a team victory had important effects on policy. A Byzantine emperor might lose his throne as the result of a post-match riot.

Ottoman sultans also kept an eye on activities in the Hippodrome. If things were going badly in the Empire, a surly crowd gathering here could signal the start of a disturbance, then a riot, then a revolution. In 1826 the slaughter of the corrupt janissary corps (the sultan's personal bodyguards) was carried out here by the reformer Sultan Mahmut II. And in 1909 there were riots here that caused the downfall of Abdül Hamit II and the rewriting of the Ottoman constitution.

Despite the fact that the Hippodrome could end up being the scene of their downfall, Byzantine emperors and Ottoman sultans outdid one another in beautifying it, adorning it with statues from the far reaches of the empire. Unfortunately, only a handful of these statues remain. Chief among the thieves responsible for their disappearance were the soldiers of the Fourth Crusade, who sacked Constantinople, supposedly a Christian ally city, in 1204.

Near the northern end of the Hippodrome, the little gazebo in beautiful stonework is actually **Kaiser Wilhelm's Fountain**. The German emperor paid a state visit to Abdül Hamit II in 1901, and presented this fountain to the sultan and his people as a token of friendship.

The immaculately preserved pink granite **Obelisk of Theodosius**, the oldest monument in İstanbul, was carved in Egypt during the reign of Thutmose III (r 1549–1503 BC) and erected in the Amon-Re temple at Karnak. Emperor Theodosius had it brought from Egypt to Constantinople in AD 390. The original obelisk was cut down for transit – the top segment was placed on the ceremonial marble base Theodosius had made. Look for the carvings of Theodosius, his wife, sons, state officials and bodyguards watching the chariot action from the *kathisma* (imperial box).

South of the obelisk is a strange column rising out of a hole in the ground. Known as the **Spiral Column**, it was once part of a golden basin supported by three entwined serpents cast to commemorate the victory of the Hellenic confederation over the Persians at Plataea. It stood in front of the temple of Apollo at Delphi from 478 BC until Constantine the Great had it brought to his new capital city around AD 330. Historians suspect the bronze serpents' heads were stolen during the Fourth Crusade.

Little is known about the 4th-century **Rough-Stone Obelisk**, except that in 869 an earthquake toppled the bronze pine cone from its top, and that it was clad with sheets of gilded bronze by Constantine VII Porphyrogenitus

(r 913–59), something commemorated in the inscription in its base. Its bronze plates were ripped off during the Fourth Crusade, but you can still see the boltholes where they would have been attached.

Note the original ground level of the Hippodrome at the base of the obelisks and column, some 2.5m below ground.

MUSEUM OF TURKISH & ISLAMIC ARTS

This impressive **museum** (Türk ve İslam Eserleri Müzesi; Map pp92–3; ☎ 0212-518 1805; At Meydanı 46, Sultanahmet; admission TL10; ⊙ 9am-4.30pm Tue-Sun) is housed in the palace of İbrahim Paşa, built in 1520 on the western side of the Hippodrome.

İbrahim Paşa was Süleyman the Magnificent's close friend and brother-in-law. Captured by Turks as a child in Greece, he had been sold as a slave into the imperial household in İstanbul and worked as a page in Topkapı, where he became friendly with Süleyman, who was the same age. When his friend became sultan, İbrahim was in turn made chief falconer, chief of the royal bedchamber and grand vizier. This palace was bestowed on him by Süleyman the year before he was given the hand of Süleyman's sister, Hadice, in marriage. Alas, the fairy tale was not to last. İbrahim's wealth, power and influence on the monarch became so great that others wishing to influence the sultan became envious, chief among them Süleyman's wife, Roxelana. After a rival accused İbrahim of disloyalty, she convinced her husband that İbrahim was a threat and Süleyman had him strangled in 1536.

Inside, you'll be wowed by one of the world's best collection of antique carpets and some equally impressive manuscripts and miniatures. Labels are in both Turkish and English.

The coffee shop in the lovely green courtyard of the museum is a welcome refuge from the press of crowds and touts in the area.

BASILICA CISTERN

When those Byzantine emperors built something, they certainly did it properly! This extraordinary **cistern** (Yerebatan Sarnıçı; Map pp92–3; ☎ 0212-522 1259; www.yerebatan.com; Yerebatan Caddesi 13, Sultanahmet; admission TL10; ⊙ 9am-6.30pm Apr-Sep, to 5.30pm Oct-Mar), built by Justinian in AD 532, is a great place to while away half an hour, especially during summer when its cavernous depths stay wonderfully cool.

GREAT PALACE OF BYZANTIUM

Constantine the Great built the Great Palace soon after he founded Constantinople in AD 324. Successive Byzantine leaders left their mark by adding to it, and the complex eventually consisted of hundreds of buildings enclosed by walls and set in terraced parklands stretching from the Hippodrome over to Haghia Sofia (Aya Sofya) and down the slope, ending at the sea walls and the Bucoleon Palace. The palace was finally abandoned after the Fourth Crusade sacked the city in 1204, and its ruins were pillaged and filled in after the Conquest, becoming mere foundations for much of Sultanahmet and Cankurtaran.

Various pieces of the Great Palace have been uncovered – many by budding hotelier 'archaeologists' – and an evocative stroll exploring the Byzantine substructure is a great way to spend an afternoon. The mosaics in the **Great Palace Mosaic Museum** (p100) once graced the floor of the complex; excavations at the Sultanahmet Archaeological Park in Babıhümayun Caddesi, southeast of Aya Sofya, have been ongoing since 1998 and were poised to open to the public as this book went to print. Controversially, some of these excavations are being subsumed into a new extension of the neighbouring luxury Four Seasons Hotel. You can also visit the Bucoleon Palace (Kennedy Caddesi) by the sea walls.

For more information, check out www.byzantium1200.com, which has 3-D images that bring ancient Byzantium to life, or purchase a copy of the lavishly illustrated guidebook *Walking Through Byzantium: Great Palace Region*, which was also produced as part of the Byzantium 1200 project. You'll find it in shops around Sultanahmet. Also of interest is the project's exhibition in the Byzantine **Binbirdirek Cistern** (Binbirdirek Sarnıcı, Philoxenos Cistern; Map pp92-3; ☎ 0212-518 1001; www.binbirdirek.com; İmran Öktem Sokak 4, Binbirdirek; admission TL10; ☺ 9am-7pm summer, 9am-6pm winter).

Like most sites in İstanbul, the cistern has a colourful history. Known in Byzantium as the Basilica Cistern because it lay underneath the Stoa Basilica, one of the great squares on the first hill, it was used to store water for the Great Palace and surrounding buildings. Eventually closed, it seems to have been forgotten by the city authorities some time before the Conquest. Enter scholar Petrus Gyllius, who was researching Byzantine antiquities in 1545 and was told by locals that they could obtain water miraculously by lowering buckets in their basement floors. Some were even catching fish this way. Intrigued, Gyllius explored the neighbourhood and discovered a house through whose basement he accessed the cistern. Even after his discovery, the Ottomans (who referred to the cistern as Yerebatan Sarayı) didn't treat the underground palace with the respect it deserved and it became a dumping ground for all sorts of junk, as well as corpses. It has been restored at least three times.

The cistern is 65m wide and 143m long, and its roof is supported by 336 columns arranged in 12 rows. It once held 80,000 cubic metres of water, pumped and delivered through nearly 20km of aqueducts.

Constructed using columns, capitals and plinths from ruined buildings, the cistern's symmetry and sheer grandeur of conception is quite extraordinary. Don't miss the two columns in the northwestern corner supported by upside-down Medusa heads or the column towards the centre featuring a teardrop design.

Walking on the raised wooden platforms, you'll feel water dripping from the vaulted ceiling and may catch a glimpse of ghostly carp patrolling the water. Lighting is atmospheric and the small café near the exit is certainly an unusual spot to enjoy a cup of çay (tea).

KÜÇÜK AYA SOFYA CAMİİ

Justinian and Theodora built this **church** (Little Aya Sofya, SS Sergius & Bacchus Church; Map p109; Küçük Aya Sofya Caddesi; donation requested) some time between 527 and 536, just before Justinian built Aya Sofya. It was named after the two patron saints of Christians in the Roman army. Its dome is architecturally noteworthy and its plan – that of an irregular octagon – unusual. Like Aya Sofya, its interior was originally decorated with gold mosaics and featured columns made from fine green and red marble. The mosaics are long gone, but the impressive columns remain. The church was converted into a mosque by the chief white eunuch Hüseyin Ağa around 1500; his tomb is to the north of the building.

After being listed on the World Monuments Fund (www.wmf.org) register of endangered buildings, this gorgeous example of Byzantine architecture has recently been restored and is looking terrific. There's a tranquil *çay bahçesi* (tea garden) in the forecourt.

After visiting Küçük Aya Sofya, go north up Şehit Mehmet Paşa Sokak and back up the hill to see the diminutive but truly beautiful **Sokollu Mehmet Paşa Camii** (Map pp90–1), designed by Sinan in 1571.

TOPKAPI PALACE

Opulent **Topkapı Palace** (Topkapı Sarayı; Map pp92-3; ☎ 0212-512 0480; www.topkapisarayi.gov.tr/eng; Babıhümayun Caddesi; admission palace TL20, Harem TL15; ⊗ 9am-7pm Wed-Mon summer, 9am-5pm winter) is the subject of more colourful stories than most of the world's royal residences put together. It was home to Selim the Sot, who drowned after drinking too much champagne; İbrahim the Mad, who lost his reason after being imprisoned for 22 years by his brother Murat IV; and the malevolent Roxelana (p35), a former concubine who became the powerful consort of Süleyman the Magnificent. And they're just three among a long progression of mad, sad and downright bad Ottomans who lived here between 1453 and 1839.

Mehmet the Conqueror started work on the palace shortly after the Conquest in 1453 and lived here until his death in 1481. Subsequent sultans lived in this rarefied environment until the 19th century, when they moved to ostentatious European-style palaces such as Dolmabahçe, Çırağan and Yıldız that they built on the shores of the Bosphorus. Mahmut II (r 1808–39) was the last sultan to live in Topkapı.

Seeing Topkapı requires at least half a day but preferably more. If you are short on time see the Harem, Treasury and the rooms around the İftariye Baldachin. Buy your ticket to the palace at the main ticket office just outside the gate to the second court; tickets to the Harem are available at the ticket box outside the Harem itself. Guides to the palace congregate next to the main ticket office. A one-hour tour will cost you TL20 per person (minimum three people or TL60). Alternatively, an audioguide costs TL5. These and maps of the palace are available at the booth just inside the turnstile entrance to the second court.

Before you enter the Imperial Gate (Bab-ı Hümayun) of Topkapı, take a look at the ornate structure in the cobbled square near the gate. This is the **Fountain of Sultan Ahmet III** (Map pp92–3), built in 1728 by the sultan who loved and promoted tulips so much that his reign was dubbed the 'Tulip Era'.

First Court

Topkapı grew and changed with the centuries, but the palace's basic four-courtyard plan remained the same. The Ottomans followed the Byzantine practice of secluding the monarch from the people: the first court was open to all; the second only to people on imperial business; the third only to the imperial family, VIPs and palace staff; while the fourth was the 'family quarters'.

As you pass through the great Imperial Gate behind the Aya Sofya, you enter the First Court, the Court of the Janissaries. On your left is the Byzantine **Aya İrini** (Hagia Eirene, Church of the Divine Peace; Map pp92–3), commissioned in the 540s by Justinian to replace an earlier church that had occupied this site. The building here is almost exactly as old as Aya Sofya. Unfortunately, it's only usually opened for concerts during the International İstanbul Music Festival (p129). Also on the left is the gate to the Imperial Mint (Darphane-I Amire), where temporary exhibitions are sometimes held.

Second Court

The **Middle Gate** (Ortakapı or Bab-üs Selâm) led to the palace's Second Court, which was used for the business of running the empire. Only the sultan and the *valide sultan* (mother of the reigning sultan) were allowed through the Middle Gate on horseback. Everyone else, including the grand vizier, had to dismount. The gate was constructed by Süleyman the Magnificent in 1524.

To the right after you enter are models and a map of the palace. Beyond them, in a nearby building, you'll find a collection of imperial carriages.

The Second Court has a beautiful, park-like setting. Topkapı is not based on a typical European palace plan – one large building with outlying gardens – but instead is a series of pavilions, kitchens, barracks, audience chambers, kiosks and sleeping quarters built around a central enclosure.

The great **Palace Kitchens**, on your right, hold a small portion of Topkapı's vast collection of

İSTANBUL

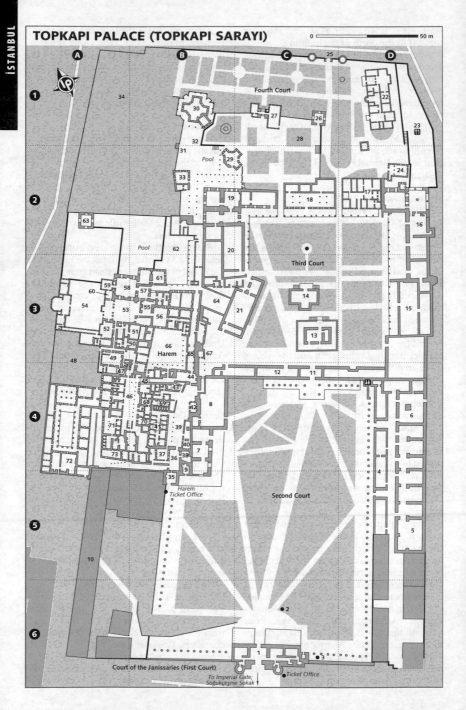

Chinese celadon porcelain. In a building close by are the collections of silverware and glassware. The last of the kitchens, the Helvahane, in which the palace sweets were made, has a display of some of the huge pots and pans that were used in the palace's heyday.

On the left (west) side of the second court is the ornate **Imperial Council Chamber**, also called the Divan Salonu. The Imperial Divan (council) met in the Imperial Council Chamber to discuss matters of state while the sultan eavesdropped through a grille high on the wall at the base of the **Tower of Justice** (Adalet Kulesi) in the Harem. North of the Imperial Council Chamber is the **Inner Treasury**, which today exhibits arms and armour, including a massive sword that belonged to Mehmet the Conqueror.

The entrance to the palace's most famous sight, the **Harem**, is beneath the Tower of Justice.

Harem

If you decide to tour the Harem – and we highly recommend that you do so – you'll need to purchase a dedicated ticket; these are available from the ticket office outside the Harem's entrance.

As popular belief would have it, the Harem was a place where the sultan could engage in debauchery at will (and Murat III did, after all, have 112 children!). In reality, these were the imperial family quarters, and every detail of Harem life was governed by tradition, obligation and ceremony. The word 'harem' literally means 'private'.

The women of Topkapı's Harem had to be foreigners, as Islam forbade enslaving Muslims. Girls were bought as slaves (often having been sold by their parents at a good price) or were received as gifts from nobles and potentates.

On entering the Harem, the girls would be schooled in Islam and Turkish culture and language, as well as the arts of make-up, dress, comportment, music, reading and writing, embroidery and dancing. They then entered a meritocracy, first as ladies-in-waiting to the sultan's concubines and children, then to the sultan's mother and finally – if they showed sufficient aptitude and were beautiful enough – to the sultan himself.

Ruling the Harem was the *valide sultan*. She often owned large landed estates in her own name and controlled them through black eunuch servants. Able to give orders directly to the grand vizier, her influence on the sultan, on the selection of his wives and concubines and on matters of state was often profound.

The sultan was allowed by Islamic law to have four legitimate wives, who received the title of *kadın* (wife). He could have as many concubines as he could support – some had up to 300, although they were not all in the Harem at the same time. If a sultan's wife bore him a son she was called *haseki sultan; haseki kadın* if it was a daughter. The Ottoman dynasty did not observe primogeniture (the right of the first-born son to the throne), so in principle the throne was available to any imperial son. Each lady of the Harem struggled to have her son proclaimed heir to the throne, which would assure her own role as the new *valide sultan*.

Although the Harem is built into a hillside and has six levels, the standard tour takes you through or past only a few dozen of the most splendid rooms on one level. Interpretive panels in Turkish and English have been placed throughout the building.

Highlights of the tour include the narrow **Courtyard of the Black Eunuchs** (map key 39), **Sultan Ahmet's Kiosk** (47), the **Courtyard of the Concubines & the Sultan's Consorts** (46), the **Quarters of the Valide Sultan** (49), the ornate **Privy Chamber of Murat III** (58) and the **Double Kiosk/ Apartments of the Crown Prince** (61).

Third Court

If you enter the Third Court after visiting the Harem you should head for the main gate into the court and enter again to truly appreciate the grandeur of the approach to the heart of the palace. This main gate, known as the **Gate of Felicity** or Gate of the White Eunuchs, was the entrance into the sultan's private domain.

Just inside the Gate of Felicity is the **Audience Chamber**, constructed in the 16th century but refurbished in the 18th century. Important officials and foreign ambassadors were brought to this kiosk to conduct the high business of state. Seated on divans whose cushions were embroidered with over 15,000 seed pearls, the sultan inspected the ambassadors' gifts and offerings as they were passed through the small doorway on the left.

Right behind the Audience Chamber is the pretty **Library of Ahmet III**, built in 1719.

To the right of the Audience Chamber (ie on the opposite side of the Harem exit) are the rooms of the **Dormitory of the Expeditionary Force**, which now house rich collections of imperial robes, kaftans and uniforms worked in silver and gold thread. Next to the Dormitory of the Expeditionary Force is the **Treasury**. See below for details of its collection.

Opposite the Treasury on the other side of the Third Court is another set of wonders: the holy relics in the Suite of the Felicitous Cloak, nowadays called the **Sacred Safekeeping Rooms**. These rooms, sumptuously decorated with İznik tiles, constitute a holy of holies within the palace. Only the chosen few could enter the Third Court, but entry into the Suite of the Felicitous Cloak was for the chosen of the chosen, and then only on ceremonial occasions.

In the entry room, notice the carved door from the Kaaba in Mecca and the gilded rain gutters from the same place. To the right a room contains a hair of Prophet Mohammed's beard, his footprint in clay, his sword, tooth and more. The 'felicitous cloak' itself resides in a golden casket in a small adjoining room.

Also in the Third Court are the **Quarters of Pages in Charge of the Sacred Safekeeping Rooms**, where the palace school for pages and janissaries was located. These days the building features exhibits of Turkish miniature paintings, calligraphy and portraits of the sultans.

Treasury

The Treasury, with its incredible collection of precious objects and simply breathtaking views, is a highlight of a visit to the palace. The building itself was constructed by Mehmet the Conqueror in 1460 and has always been used to store works of art and treasure. In the first room, look for the jewel-encrusted **sword of Süleyman the Magnificent** and the **Throne of Ahmet I**, inlaid with mother-of-pearl and designed by Mehmet Ağa, architect of the Blue Mosque. In the second room, the tiny **Indian figures**, mainly made from seed pearls, are well worth seeking out.

After passing through the third room and having a gawk at the enormous gold and diamond **candlesticks** you come to a fourth room and the Treasury's most famous exhibit – the **Topkapı Dagger**. The object of the criminal quest in the 1964 movie *Topkapı*, it features three enormous emeralds on the hilt and a watch set into the pommel. Also here is the **Spoonmaker's Diamond** (Kaşıkçı'nın Elması), a teardrop-shaped 86-carat rock surrounded by several dozen smaller stones. First worn by Mehmet IV at his accession to the throne in 1648, it is the world's fifth-largest diamond. It is called the Spoonmaker's Diamond because it was originally found in a rubbish dump in Eğrıkapı and purchased by a street pedlar for three spoons.

Fourth Court

Pleasure pavilions occupy the northeastern part of the palace, sometimes called the Tulip Garden or Fourth Court. A late addition to Topkapı, the **Mecidiye Köşkü** was built by Abdül Mecit (r 1839–61). Beneath it is Topkapı's only eatery, Konyalı restaurant; if you plan to eat here, try to arrive before noon or after 2pm to be sure of a table on the terrace.

Up the stairs at the end of the Tulip Garden are three of the most enchanting buildings in the palace, joined by a marble terrace with a beautiful pool. Murat IV (r 1623–40) built the **Revan Kiosk** in 1636 after reclaiming the city of Yerevan (now in Armenia) from Persia. In 1639 he constructed the **Baghdad Kiosk**, one of the last examples of classical palace architecture, to commemorate his victory over that city. Notice the superb İznik tiles, the mother-of-pearl and tortoiseshell inlay, and the woodwork.

Jutting out from the terrace is the golden roof of the **İftariye Baldachin**, the most popular happy-snap spot in the palace grounds. İbrahim the Mad built this small structure in 1640 as a picturesque place to break the daily Ramazan fast.

At the west end of the terrace is the **Circumcision Room** (Sünnet Odası), used for the ritual that admits Muslim boys to manhood. Built by İbrahim in 1641, the outer walls of the chamber are graced by particularly beautiful tile panels.

SOĞUKÇEŞME SOKAK

Soğukçeşme Sokak, or Street of the Cold Fountain, runs between the Topkapı Palace walls and Aya Sofya. In the 1980s the Turkish Touring & Automobile Association (TTAA) acquired all of the buildings on the street and decided to demolish most of them to build nine re-creations of the prim Ottoman-style houses that had occupied the site in the previous two centuries. A vitriolic battle played out on the pages of İstanbul's newspapers ensued, with some experts arguing that the

city would be left with a Disney-style architectural theme park rather than a legitimate exercise in conservation architecture. The TTAA eventually got the go-ahead (after the intervention of no less than Turkey's president) and in time opened all of the re-created buildings as Ayasofya Konakları (p132), one of the first boutique heritage hotels in the city. Conservation theory aside, the colourful buildings and cobbled street are particularly picturesque and worth wandering past.

CAFERAĞA MEDRESESİ

This lovely little **medrese** (☎ 0212-513 360; Caferiye Sokak; admission free; ☽ 8.30am-7pm), which is tucked away in the shadows of Aya Sofya, was designed by Sinan on the orders of Cafer Ağa, Süleyman the Magnificent's chief black eunuch. Built in 1560 as a school for Islamic and secular education, today it is home to the Turkish Cultural Service Foundation (p128), which runs workshops in traditional Ottoman arts such as calligraphy, *ebru* (traditional Turkish marbling) and miniature painting. Some of the arts and crafts produced here are for sale and there's a pleasant *lokanta* (eatery serving ready-made food) in the courtyard (see p136).

GÜLHANE PARKI

Once the park of the Topkapı Palace, shady Gülhane Parkı (Map pp92–3) is now a popular relaxation spot for locals rather than the sultans. It's particularly pretty in late March and early April, when the thousands of tulip bulbs planted to celebrate the International İstanbul Tulip Festival (see p129) come into bloom. Make sure you head to the north end of the park and enjoy a pot of tea at the **Set İstü Çay Bahçesi** (see p149), which has superb views over the Bosphorus.

To the left of the south exit is a bulbous kiosk built into the park wall. Known as the **Alay Köşkü** (Parade Kiosk), this is where the sultan would sit and watch the periodic parades of troops and trade guilds commemorating great holidays and military victories.

Across the street from the Alay Köşkü (not quite visible from the Gülhane gate) is an outrageously curvaceous rococo gate leading into the precincts of what was once the grand vizierate, or Ottoman prime ministry, known in the West as the **Sublime Porte**. Today the buildings beyond the gate hold various government offices.

İSTANBUL

İSTANBUL ARCHAEOLOGICAL MUSEUMS

It may not pull the number of visitors that flock to nearby Topkapı, but this superb **museum complex** (Arkeoloji Müzeleri; Map pp92-3; ☎ 0212-520 7740; Osman Hamdi Bey Yokuşu, Gülhane; admission TL10; ♥ 9am-5pm Tue-Sun) shouldn't be missed. It can be reached easily by walking down the slope from Topkapı's First Court, or by trudging up the hill from the main gate of Gülhane Park. Allow at least two hours for your visit.

The complex is divided into three buildings: the Archaeology Museum (Arkeoloji Müzesi), the Museum of the Ancient Orient (Eski Şark Eserler Müzesi) and the Tiled Kiosk (Çinili Köşk). These museums house the palace collections, formed during the 19th century by archaeologist and artist Osman Hamdi Bey (1842–1910) and added to greatly since the republic was proclaimed. Excellent interpretive panels are in both Turkish and English.

The first building on your left as you enter is the **Museum of the Ancient Orient**. Overlooking the park, it was designed by Alexander Vallaury and built in 1883 to house the Academy of Fine Arts. It displays Anatolian pieces from Hittite empires and pre-Islamic items collected from the Ottoman Empire.

A Roman statue of the god **Bes** greets you as you enter the **Archaeology Museum** on the opposite side of the courtyard. Turn left and walk into the dimly lit rooms beyond, where the museum's major treasures – sarcophagi from the **Royal Necropolis of Sidon** – are displayed. Osman Hamdi Bey unearthed these sarcophagi in Sidon (Side in modern-day Lebanon) in 1887 and in 1891 persuaded the sultan to build this museum to house them.

In the first room you will see a sarcophagus that is Egyptian in origin, but which was later reused by **King Tabnit of Sidon**; his mummy lies close by. Also here is a beautifully preserved **Lycian Sarcophagus** made from Paros marble and dating from the end of the 5th century. Note its beautifully rendered horses, centaurs and human figures. Next to this is the **Satrap Sarcophagus**, with its everyday scenes featuring a provincial governor.

After admiring these, pass into the next room to see the famous marble **Alexander Sarcophagus**, one of the most accomplished of all classical artworks. It's known as the Alexander Sarcophagus because it depicts the Macedonian general and his army battling the Persians. (It was actually sculpted for King Abdalonymos of Sidon, not Alexander,

though.) Truly exquisite, it is carved out of Pentelic marble and dates from the last quarter of the 4th century BC. One side shows the Persians (long pants, material headwear) battling with the Greeks. Alexander, on horseback, sports a Nemean Lion's head, the symbol of Hercules, as a headdress. The other side depicts the violent thrill of a lion hunt. Remarkably, the sculpture has remnants of its original red-and-yellow paintwork.

At the end of this room the **Mourning Women Sarcophagus** also bears traces of its original paintwork. Its depiction of the women is stark and very moving.

The rooms beyond house an impressive collection of ancient grave cult sarcophagi from Syria, Lebanon, Thessalonica, Ephesus and other parts of Anatolia.

After seeing these, turn back and walk past Bes to room 4, the first of six **galleries of statues**. Look for the Ephebos of Tralles in room 8 and the exquisite head of a child from Pergamum in room 9.

The annexe behind the main ground-floor gallery is home to a **Children's Museum**. While children will be bored stiff with the naff dioramas of early Anatolian life, they will no doubt be impressed by the large-scale model of the Trojan Horse, which they can climb into. Beside the Children's Museum is a fascinating exhibition entitled '**In the Light of Day**', which focuses on the archaeological finds that have resulted from the city's huge Marmaray transport project (p163).

If you have even a passing interest in İstanbul's rich archaeology, don't miss the mezzanine level above showcasing '**İstanbul Through the Ages**'. After seeing the displays here you can appreciate how much of the ancient city remains covered.

The last of the complex's museum buildings is the gorgeous **Tiled Kiosk** of Sultan Mehmet the Conqueror. Thought to be the oldest surviving nonreligious Turkish building in İstanbul, it was built in 1472 as an outer pavilion of Topkapı Palace and was used for watching sporting events. It now houses an impressive collection of Seljuk, Anatolian and Ottoman tiles and ceramics.

Bazaar District

Crowned by the city's first and most evocative shopping mall – the famous Grand Bazaar (Kapalı Çarşı) – the bazaar district

GRAND BAZAAR (KAPALI ÇARŞI)

0 ———————— 50 m

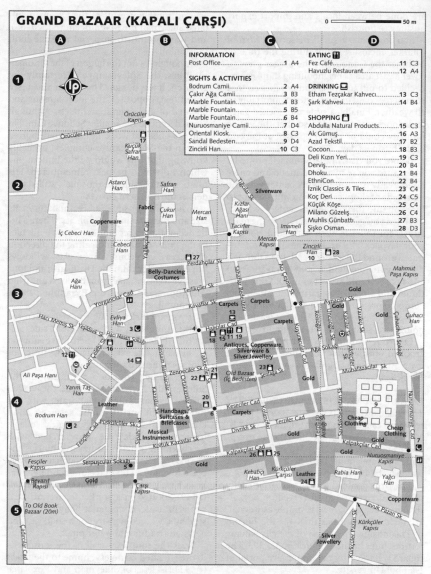

INFORMATION	
Post Office	1 A4

SIGHTS & ACTIVITIES	
Bodrum Camii	2 A4
Çakır Ağa Camii	3 B3
Marble Fountain	4 B3
Marble Fountain	5 B5
Marble Fountain	6 B4
Nuruosmaniye Camii	7 D4
Oriental Kiosk	8 C3
Sandal Bedesten	9 D4
Zincirli Han	10 C3

EATING 🍴	
Fez Café	11 C3
Havuzlu Restaurant	12 A4

DRINKING 🍷	
Etham Tezçakar Kahveci	13 C3
Şark Kahvesi	14 B4

SHOPPING 🛍	
Abdulla Natural Products	15 C3
Ak Gümüş	16 A3
Azad Tekstil	17 B2
Cocoon	18 B3
Deli Kızın Yeri	19 C3
Derviş	20 B4
Dhoku	21 B4
EthniCon	22 B4
İznik Classics & Tiles	23 C4
Koç Deri	24 C5
Küçük Köşe	25 C4
Milano Güzeliş	26 C4
Muhlis Günbattı	27 B3
Şişko Osman	28 D3

is also home to two of the grandest of all Ottoman buildings, the Süleymaniye and Beyazıt Camiis.

GRAND BAZAAR

The labyrinthine and chaotic **Grand Bazaar** (Kapalı Çarşı, Covered Market; Map pp90-1; ⏱ 9am-7pm Mon-Sat) is the heart of the old city and has

been for centuries. No visit to İstanbul would be complete without a stop here.

With over 4000 shops and several kilometres of lanes, as well as mosques, banks, police stations, restaurants and workshops, the bazaar is a covered world. Although there's no doubt that it's a tourist trap par excellence, it's also a place where business deals are done between locals and import/export businesses flourish.

Starting from a small masonry *bedesten* (market enclosure) built during the time of Mehmet the Conqueror, the bazaar grew to cover a vast area as neighbouring shopkeepers decided to put up roofs and porches so that commerce could be conducted comfortably in all weather. Finally, a system of locked gates and doors was provided so that the entire minicity could be closed up tight at the end of the business day.

Before you visit, prepare yourself properly. Make sure you're in a good mood and energised, ready to swap friendly banter with the hundreds of shopkeepers who will attempt to lure you into their establishments.

When you get to the bazaar, leave the main streets for tourists, tuck your guidebook in your daypack, and explore the alleys concentrated around the western end. Peep through doorways to find hidden *hans* (caravanserais) and take every side street to dig out tiny boutiques and workshops. Drink too much çay, compare price after price and try your hand at the art of bargaining. Allow at least three hours here; some travellers spend three days!

On your wanderings you may pass the crooked **Oriental Kiosk**, and, just north from it up Acı Çeşme Sokak, the gorgeous pink **Zincirli Han**.

BEYAZIT SQUARE & İSTANBUL UNIVERSITY

The Sahaflar Çarşısı (Old Book Bazaar) is next to **Beyazıt Camii** (Mosque of Sultan Beyazıt II; Map pp90–1). Beyazıt specified that an exceptional amount of marble, porphyry, verd-antique and rare granite be used in this mosque, which he had built between 1501 and 1506.

The large cobbled square here is officially called Hürriyet Meydanı (Freedom Sq), although everyone knows it simply as Beyazıt. Under the Byzantines this was the Forum of Theodosius, the largest of the city's many forums, built by the emperor in AD 393. The square is backed by the impressive portal of İstanbul University.

SÜLEYMANIYE CAMİİ

The **Süleymaniye Camii** (Mosque of Sultan Süleyman the Magnificent; Map pp90–1; Prof Sıddık Sami Onar Caddesi; donation requested) crowns one of the seven hills dominating the Golden Horn and provides a magnificent landmark for the entire city. It was commissioned by the greatest, richest and most powerful of the Ottoman sultans, Süleyman the Magnificent (r 1520–66), and was the fourth imperial mosque built in İstanbul.

Although it's not the largest of the Ottoman mosques, the Süleymaniye is certainly the grandest. It was designed by Mimar Sinan (see boxed text, opposite), the most famous and talented of all imperial architects. Although Sinan described the smaller Selimiye Camii in Edirne as his best work, he chose to be buried here in the Süleymaniye complex, probably knowing that this would be the building by which he would be best remembered. His tomb is just outside the mosque's walled garden in the northern corner.

Inside, the mosque is breathtaking in its size and pleasing in its simplicity. There's little decoration except for some fine İznik tiles in the *mihrab* (niche indicating the direction of Mecca); gorgeous stained-glass windows done by one İbrahim the Drunkard; and four massive columns, one from Baalbek, one from Alexandria and two from Byzantine palaces in İstanbul.

If you are lucky enough to visit when the stairs to the gallery on the northeast side (facing the Golden Horn) are open, make sure you go upstairs to the balcony. The views from this vantage point are spectacular.

The *külliye* (mosque complex) of the Süleymaniye, which is outside the walled garden, is particularly elaborate, with the full complement of public services: soup kitchen, hostel, hospital, theological college, hamam etc. Today the soup kitchen, with its charming garden courtyard, houses the Darüzziyafe Restaurant. Although it's a lovely place to enjoy a cup of tea, the food here has been barely edible on our visits. **Lale Bahçesi** (p149), located in a sunken courtyard next to Darüzziyafe, is a popular hang-out for uni students, who come here for a chat, çay and nargileh (traditional water pipe).

Near the southeast wall of the mosque is its well-tended cemetery, home to the **tombs** (☉ 9.30am-4.30pm) of Süleyman and Roxelana. The tile work in both is superb.

ŞEHZADE MEHMET CAMİİ

Süleyman the Magnificent commissioned Sinan to design the **Şehzade Mehmet Camii** (Mosque of the Prince; Şehzadebaşı Caddesi, Kalenderhane; donation requested) in memory of his son Mehmet, who died of smallpox at the age of 22. It was

THE GREAT SİNAN

Sultan Süleyman the Magnificent's reign is known as the golden age of the Ottoman Empire, but it wasn't only his codification of Ottoman law and military prowess that earned him respect. Süleyman's penchant for embellishing İstanbul with architectural wonders had a lot to do with it. And Süleyman couldn't have done this without Mimar Sinan, Turkey's best-known and greatest architect. Together they perfected the design of the classic Ottoman mosque.

Born in 1497, Sinan was a recruit to the *devşirme*, the annual intake of Christian youths into the janissaries (Ottoman army), becoming a Muslim (as all such recruits did) and eventually taking up a post as a military engineer in the corps. Süleyman the Magnificent appointed him the chief of the imperial architects in 1538. He designed a total of 321 buildings, 85 of which are still standing in İstanbul.

Most Sinan-designed mosques have a large forecourt with a central *şadırvan* (ablutions fountain) and domed arcades on three sides. On the fourth side stands the mosque, with a two-storey porch. The main prayer hall is covered by a large central dome rising much higher than the two-storey facade, and surrounded by smaller domes and semidomes.

İstanbul's superb **Süleymaniye Camii** (opposite) is the grandest and most visited work of Sinan's, so if you only have time to visit one of Sinan's masterpieces make it this one. The **Atik Valide Camii** (p120) in Üsküdar is similar to the Süleymaniye in many ways, most notably in the extent of its *külliye* (mosque outbuildings, often including hamam, theological school, hospital, cemetery and soup kitchen). The much smaller, tile-encrusted **Rüstem Paşa Camii** (below) and **Sokollu Mehmet Paşa Camii** (Map pp92–3) are both exquisite, well rewarding anyone who makes the effort to see them.

Sinan didn't only design and construct mosques. The **Çemberlitaş Hamamı** (p126) is also one of his works, giving you a perfect excuse to blend your architectural studies with a pampering session. He also designed the **Baths of Lady Hürrem** (p99) and the **Caferağa Medresesi** (p107).

Sinan's works survive in other towns of the Ottoman heartland, particularly Edirne (p168), the one-time capital of the Empire.

completed in 1548 and is noteworthy for its delicate minarets and attractive garden setting. You can also enjoy a meal or glass of tea at **Şehzade Mehmed Sofrası** (p136), in the charming *külliye* building behind the mosque.

RÜSTEM PAŞA CAMİİ

Plonked in the middle of the busy Tahtakale district to the west of the Spice Bazaar, the little-visited **Rüstem Paşa Camii** (Mosque of Rüstem Paşa; Map pp90-1; Hasırcılar Caddesi; donation requested) is an absolute gem. Built in 1560 by Sinan for the son-in-law and grand vizier of Süleyman the Magnificent, it is a showpiece of the best Ottoman architecture and tile work, albeit on a small scale.

At the top of both sets of entry steps, there's a terrace and the mosque's colonnaded porch. You'll immediately notice the panels of İznik tiles set into the mosque's facade. The interior is covered in similarly gorgeous tiles and features a lovely dome, supported by four tiled pillars.

The preponderance of tiles was Rüstem Paşa's way of signalling his wealth and in-

fluence to the world, İznik tiles being particularly expensive and desirable. It may not have assisted his passage into the higher realm, though, because by all accounts he was a loathsome character. His contemporaries dubbed him Kehle-i-Ikbal ('Louse of Fortune') because even though he was found to be infected with lice before his marriage to Mihrimah, Süleyman's favourite daughter, this did not prevent his marriage or his subsequent rise to great fame and fortune. He is best remembered for plotting with Roxelana to turn Süleyman against his favourite son, Mustafa. They were successful and Mustafa was strangled in 1553 on his father's orders.

The mosque is easy to miss because it's not at street level. Look for the stairs on Hasırcılar Caddesi, or to the left of the ablutions block on the side street.

SPICE BAZAAR

Need a herbal love potion or some natural Turkish Viagra? İstanbul's **Spice Bazaar** (Mısır Çarşısı, Egyptian Market; Map pp90-1; 8.30am-6.30pm Mon-Sat) is the place to find them, although we wouldn't vouch for the efficacy of either! The market was constructed in the 1660s as part of the Yeni Camii complex, the rents from the shops going to support the upkeep of the mosque and its charitable activities. It was called the Egyptian Market because it was famous for selling goods shipped in from Cairo.

As well as *baharat* (spices), nuts, honeycomb and olive-oil soaps, the bustling spice bazaar sells truckloads of *incir* (figs), *lokum* (Turkish delight) and fruit pressed into sheets and *pestil* (dried) – try the highly regarded **Malatya Pazari** (shop 44) if you want to take home some dried fruit or nuts. Although the number of shops selling tourist trinkets increases annually, this is still a great place to stock up on edible souvenirs, share a few jokes with the vendors and marvel at the well-preserved building. Make sure you visit shop number 41, the atmospheric **Mehmet Kalmaz Baharatçi**, which specialises in henna, potions, lotions and the sultan's very own aphrodisiac. Most of the shops offer vacuum packaging, which makes getting souvenirs home easy.

The bazaar is also home to one of the city's most atmospheric restaurants, Pandeli. Its mosaic-clad interior is gorgeous, but the food has been dreadful on our recent visits – try going before or after lunch for a tea instead. If you're keen to eat somewhere in the bazaar, **Bab-ı Hayat** (p136) is your best bet.

On the western side of the market there are outdoor produce stalls selling fresh foodstuffs from all over Anatolia. Also here is Hasırcılar Caddesi, a narrow street selling spices and other goods that are often a fraction of the price of equivalent products in the Spice Bazaar. Look out for the flagship store of the most famous coffee purveyor in Turkey, **Kurukahveci Mehmet Efendi** (Map pp90–1), which is on the corner nearest to the bazaar.

YENİ CAMİİ

Only in İstanbul would a 400-year-old mosque be called 'New'. The **Yeni Camii** (New Mosque; Map pp90-1; Yenicami Meydanı Sokak, Eminönü; donation requested) was begun in 1597, commissioned by Valide Sultan Safiye, mother of Sultan Mehmet III (r 1595–1603). Safiye lost her august position (and disposable income) when her son the sultan died, and the mosque was completed six sultans later in 1663 by Turhan Hadice, mother of Sultan Mehmet IV (r 1648–87).

In plan, the Yeni Camii is much like the Blue Mosque and the Süleymaniye Camii, with a large forecourt and square sanctuary surmounted by a series of semidomes crowned by a grand dome. The interior is richly decorated with gold, coloured İznik tiles and carved marble, and has an impressive *mihrab*.

In the courtyard near the Spice Bazaar is the **tomb of Valide Sultan Turhan Hadice** (Map pp90–1). Buried with her are no fewer than six sultans, including her son Mehmet IV.

GALATA BRIDGE

Nothing is quite as evocative as walking across the Galata Bridge (Map pp92–3). At sunset, when the **Galata Tower** (p115) is surrounded by the silhouettes of shrieking seagulls and the mosques atop the seven hills of the city are thrown into relief against a soft red-pink sky, the surrounds are spectacularly beautiful. During the day, the bridge carries a constant flow of İstanbullus crossing between Beyoğlu and Eminönü, a handful or two of hopeful anglers trailing their lines into the waters below, and a constantly changing procession of street vendors hawking everything from fresh-baked *simit* (sesame-coated bread rings) to Rolex rip-offs.

Underneath the bridge, fish restaurants and cafés on its lower level serve drinks and food all day. Come here to inhale the evocative scent of apple tobacco wisping out from the nargileh cafés and to watch the passing parade of ferry traffic plying the waters. The eateries below the bridge are much of a muchness (and that's not much at all), but the cafés are wonderful spots to enjoy a tea or late-afternoon beer.

This bridge was built in 1994 to replace an iron structure dating from around 1910, which in turn had replaced three earlier structures. The 1910 bridge was famous for its seedy fish restaurants, teahouses and nargileh joints that occupied the dark recesses beneath its roadway, but it had a major flaw: it floated on pontoons that blocked the natural flow of water and kept the Golden Horn from flushing out pollution. In 1992 the iron bridge was damaged by fire and dragged up the Golden Horn to RIP; you pass it on the ferry trip to Eyüp.

Western Districts

Broadly described as the district between the city walls and Sultanahmet, this old part of

İstanbul was once dotted with the churches of Byzantium. While most of the churches have been converted to mosques, and many of the houses are tumbledown or have been razed for ugly apartment blocks, a few hours' exploration in this area will give you a taste of workaday İstanbul. There are several sights worth visiting if you have the time, and the Chora Church is an absolute must-see for all visitors to İstanbul.

AQUEDUCT OF VALENS

Rising majestically over the traffic on busy Atatürk Bulvarı, this limestone **aqueduct** (Map pp90–1) is one of the city's most distinctive landmarks. Commissioned by Emperor Valens in AD 373, it was part of an elaborate system linking over 400km of water channels, some 30 bridges and over 100 cisterns within the city walls, making it one of the greatest hydraulic engineering achievements of ancient times.

ZEYREK CAMİİ

Originally part of an important Byzantine sanctuary comprising two churches, a chapel and a monastery, **Zeyrek Camii** (Church of the Pantocrator; Map pp90–1; İbadethane Sokak) is now in a deplorable state of disrepair, which has led to it being listed on the World Monument Fund's register of endangered buildings. The monastery is long gone and the northernmost church is derelict, but the southern church, built by Empress Eirene before her death in AD 1124 (she features in a mosaic at Aya Sofya with Emperor John Comnenus II) was saved by being converted into a mosque and still has some features intact, including a magnificent mosaic floor. The mosque and the crumbling but charming houses in the surrounding streets are Unesco World Heritage listed – it's a great spot for a wander.

The Ottoman building to the east houses the upmarket **Zeyrekhane** restaurant (p137), which has a terrace with glorious Golden Horn and Old City views.

After you've visited Zeyrek, a pleasant 15-minute walk can take you along a length of the Aqueduct of Valens northwest to Fatih Camii.

FATIH CAMII

This **mosque** (Mosque of the Conqueror; Map pp86–7; Fevzi Paşa Caddesi, Fatih), 750m northwest of the historic Aqueduct of Valens, was the first great imperial mosque to be built in İstanbul. Set in extensive grounds, the mosque complex was enormous and included 15 charitable establishments – religious schools, a hospice for travellers, a caravanserai and more. The mosque was finished in 1470 but was destroyed by an earthquake; after being rebuilt it burned down in 1782. What you see today dates from the reign of Abdül Hamit I (r 1774–89).

The much-visited **tomb of the Conqueror** (☾ 9.30am-4.30pm Tue-Sun) is in the cemetery behind the mosque, though Mehmet is actually buried under the *mimber* (pulpit) in the mosque itself.

On Wednesday both the courtyard and the surrounding streets host a huge market selling fresh produce and clothing. This is the best time to visit; at other times you may find the 18th-century mosque relatively unimpressive.

CHORA CHURCH

İstanbul has more than its fair share of Byzantine monuments, but few are as drop-dead gorgeous as the **Chora Church** (Kariye Müzesi; Map pp86–7; ☎ 0212-631 9241; Kariye Camii Sokak, Edirnekapı; admission TL15; ☾ 9am-5pm Thu-Tue). The fact that it's tucked away in the little-visited Western Districts of the city means that many visitors overlook it, but we counsel you not to do the same.

The church was originally known as the Church of the Holy Saviour Outside the Walls, but what you see today is not the first church-outside-the-walls on this site. This one was built in the late 11th century, and underwent repairs, restructuring and conversion to a mosque in the succeeding centuries. Virtually all of the interior decoration dates from 1312 and was funded by Theodore Metochites, a poet and man of letters who was auditor of the treasury under Emperor Andronikos II (r 1282–1328). One of the museum's most wonderful mosaics, found above the door to the nave in the inner narthex, depicts Theodore offering the church to Christ.

The mosaics, which depict the lives of Christ and Mary, are simply stunning. Look out for the Deesis, which shows Christ and Mary with two donors: Prince Isaac Komnenos and Melane, daughter of Mikhael Palaiologos VIII. This is under the right dome in the inner narthex. On the dome itself is a wonderful depiction of Jesus and his ancestors (*Genealogy of Christ)*. On the narthex's left dome is a serenely beautiful mosaic of Mary and the Child Jesus surrounded by her ancestors.

In the nave are three mosaics: of Christ; of Mary and the child Jesus; and of the Dormition (Assumption) of the Blessed Virgin – turn around to see this as it's over the main door you just entered. The 'infant' being held by Jesus is actually Mary's soul.

To the right of the nave is the Parecclesion, a side chapel built to hold the tombs of the church's founder and his relatives, close friends and associates. It is decorated with frescoes that equal the mosaics in quality and depict Old Testament scenes.

The Chora is one of the city's best museums and deserves an extended visit. On leaving, we highly recommend sampling the unusual Ottoman menu at the Asitane restaurant (p137), which is in the basement of the next-door Kariye Oteli. Alternatively, a simple *peynirli tost* (toasted cheese sandwich) and glass of tea can be enjoyed at the Kariye Pembe Köşk in the plaza overlooking the museum.

Finally, a plea: despite signs clearly prohibiting the use of flashes in the museum, many visitors wilfully ignore this rule. Please don't do the same – the future of these exquisite and delicate mosaics and frescoes is at stake.

To get here, catch bus 31E, 32, 36KE or 37E from Eminönü or bus 87 from Taksim Sq to Edirnekapı. A taxi from Sultanahmet should cost around TL10, from Taksim TL15.

YEDİKULE & THE CITY WALLS

Yedikule Hisarı (Fortress of the Seven Towers; Map pp86-7; ☎ 0212-585 8933; Kule Meydanı 4, Yedikule; admission TL5; ☯ 9am-6.30pm), looming over the old city's southern approaches, has a history as impressive as its massive structure.

In the late 4th century Theodosius I built a triumphal arch here. When the next Theodosius (r 408–50) built his great land walls, he incorporated the arch into it. Four of the fortress' seven towers were built as part of Theodosius II's walls; the other three, which are inside the walls, were added by Mehmet the Conqueror. Under the Byzantines, the great arch became known as the **Golden Gate** and was used for triumphal state processions into and out of the city. For a time, its gates were indeed plated with gold.

In Ottoman times the fortress was used for defence, and as a repository for the imperial

treasury, a prison and a place of execution. After the republic, Yedikule was neglected, becoming an overgrown green oasis, complete with goat herd. Recent renovations have got rid of the goats and grass and replaced them with gravel, somewhat destroying the atmosphere, but the views from the battlements are still amazing. Note that those who suffer from vertigo or who are travelling with small children should steer clear, because the stone steps are very steep and have no safety barriers.

It's possible to spend a day walking on top of or beside the walls all the way from Yedikule to Ayvansaray on the Golden Horn (6.5km), wandering past the late-13th-century **Tekfur Sarayı** (Palace of the Sovereign, Palace of Constantine Porphyrogenetus; Map pp86-7; Hocaçakır Caddesi; admission TL3; ☯ vary) on the way. Be warned, though, that the walls are in a bad condition in many spots and go through some less-than-salubrious neighbourhoods. Don't do this walk by yourself.

Yedikule is a long way from most other İstanbul sights and involves a special trip. Situated where the great city walls meet the Sea of Marmara, it's easily accessible by train from Sirkeci or Cankurtaran (the closest stop to Sultanahmet). Hop off the train at Yedikule (15 minutes), turn left as you come out of the station and walk about 500m to the entrance of the fortress.

You can also take bus 80 or 81 from Eminönü, bus 80B from Beyazıt or bus 80T from Taksim. The bus stop is across from the small park in front of the castle.

Beyoğlu & Around

The suburb of Beyoğlu (*bey*-oh-loo) rises from the shoreline north of the Galata Bridge, and incorporates both Taksim Sq and the grand boulevard, İstiklal Caddesi. In the mid-19th century it was known as Pera and acknowledged as the 'European' quarter of town. Diplomats and international traders lived and worked here, and the streets were showcases for the latest European fashions and fads. European-style patisseries, restaurants, boutiques and embassies were all built following the European architectural styles of the day. It even had telephones, electric lights and the one of the first electric tramways in the world, the Tünel.

However, all this changed in the decades after the republic. Embassies moved to the country's new capital, Ankara, the glamorous shops and restaurants closed, the grand buildings crumbled and Beyoğlu took on a decidedly sleazy air. Fortunately the '90s brought about a rebirth and Beyoğlu is once again the heart of modern İstanbul, ground zero for galleries, cafés and boutiques. Here, hip new restaurants and bars open almost nightly, and the streets showcase cosmopolitan Turkey at its best. Put simply, if you miss Beyoğlu, you haven't seen İstanbul.

The best way to get a feel for this side of town is to spend an afternoon or day exploring by foot. If you're based in Sultanahmet, catch the tram to Kabataş and the connecting funicular up to Taksim Sq. Then work your way down İstiklal Caddesi, exploring its many side streets along the way. At the foot of the boulevard is Tünel Sq; follow Galipdede Caddesi downhill and you will be able to explore the historic neighbourhood of Galata before walking across the Galata Bridge to Eminönü, from where you can catch a tram or walk back up to Sultanahmet. All up it's a walk of at least two hours – but dedicating a full day will be more rewarding.

GALATA TOWER

The **Galata Tower** (Galata Kulesi; Map pp94–5; Galata Meydanı, Karaköy; admission TL10; ☮ 9am-8pm), originally constructed in 1348, was the highest point in the Genoese fortifications of Galata and has been rebuilt many times. It has survived several earthquakes, as well as the demolition of the rest of the Genoese walls in the mid-19th century. Though the view from its vertiginous panorama balcony is spectacular, we suggest enjoying this over a drink on the terrace of the Anemon Galata hotel (p134) opposite, rather than paying the inflated entry fee here.

GALATA MEVLEVİHANESİ

This **complex** (Map pp94–5; ☎ 0212-245 4141; Galipdede Caddesi 15, Tünel; admission TL5) is home to one of the few remaining *tekkes* (dervish lodges) in İstanbul. When this book went to print, the *tekke* was undergoing a major renovation; when it reopens it may host a weekly *sema* (whirling ceremony). Check the board outside for details.

Inside the main gates there is a garden courtyard and a graveyard with graceful Ottoman tombs. The shapes atop the stones reflect the headgear of the deceased, each hat

denoting a different religious rank. The tomb of Galip Dede, the 17th-century Sufi poet who gave his name to the street, lies here.

İSTANBUL MODERN

Opened in 2004, **İstanbul Modern** (İstanbul Modern Sanat Müzesi; Map pp94–5; ☎ 0212-334 7300; www.istanbulmodern.org; Meclis-i Mebusan Caddesi, Tophane; admission adult/student/under 12yr TL7/3/free, admission free Thu; ☮ 10am-6pm Tue, Wed & Fri-Sun, 10am-8pm Thu) is the big daddy of a slew of newish, privately funded art galleries in the city. Its stunning location on the shores of the Bosphorus and its extensive collection of Turkish 20th-century art make it well worth a visit. Icing on the cake is provided by a constantly changing and uniformly excellent program of exhibitions by local and international artists in the temporary galleries on the ground floor.

There's also a well-stocked gift shop, a cinema that shows art-house films and a stylish café-restaurant with superb views of the Bosphorus.

İSTİKLAL CADDESI

In the late 19th century **İstiklal Caddesi** (Independence Ave; Map pp94–5) was known as the Grande Rue de Pera, and it carried the life of the modern city up and down its lively promenade. It's still the centre of İstanbullu life, and a stroll along its length is a must. Come between 4pm and 8pm daily – especially on Friday and Saturday – and you'll see İstiklal at its busiest best.

About half-way along İstiklal Caddesi is the **Galatasaray Lycée** (Map pp94–5), founded in 1868 by Sultan Abdülaziz as a school where students were taught in French as well as Turkish. Today it's a prestigious public school.

Close by is the Cité de Pera building, home to the famous **Çiçek Pasajı** (Flower Passage; Map pp94–5). When the *Orient Express* rolled into Old İstanbul and promenading down İstiklal Caddesi was all the rage, the Cité de Pera building was the most glamorous address in town. Built in 1876 and decorated in Second Empire style, it housed a shopping arcade as well as apartments. As Pera declined, so too did the building, its stylish shops giving way to florists and then *meyhanes* (Turkish taverns) where enthusiastic revellers caroused the night away. In the late 1970s parts of the building collapsed; once rebuilt, the passage was 'beautified' and its raffish charm was lost. These days locals bypass the touts and the mediocre food on offer here and make their way behind the passage to one of İstanbul's most colourful and popular eating precincts, **Nevizade Sokak** (see boxed text, p139). Next to the Çiçek Pasajı you'll find Şahne Sokak and Beyoğlu's **Balık Pazar** (Fish Market), with stalls selling fruit, vegetables, pickles and other produce. Leading off the Balık Pazar you'll find the neoclassical **Avrupa Pasajı** (European Passage), a small gallery with marble paving and shops selling tourist wares and some antique goods; as well as the **Aslıhan Pasajı**, a two-storey arcade bursting at the seams with secondhand books.

PERA MUSEUM

If, like many travellers, you've seen reproductions of the famous Osman Hamdi Bey painting *The Tortoise Trainer* and fallen in love with it, the **Pera Museum** (Map pp94-5; ☎ 0212-334 9900; www.pm.org.tr; Meşrutiyet Caddesi 141, Tepebaşı; adult/student/under 12yr TL7/3/free; ☺ 10am-7pm Tue-Sat, noon-6pm Sun) is the place to view the real thing. It's part of the museum's wonderful collection of Orientalist paintings, which occupies the third floor. Other floors host permanent exhibitions of Kütahya tiles and ceramics, Anatolian weights and measures and top-notch temporary exhibitions.

TAKSİM SQUARE

The symbolic heart of modern İstanbul, this busy **square** (Map pp94-5) is named after the stone *taksim* (reservoir) on its western side, once part of the city's old water-conduit system. The main water line from the Belgrade Forest, north of the city, was laid to this point in 1732 by Sultan Mahmut I (r 1730–54). Branch lines then led from the *taksim* to other parts of the city.

The square is in no way a triumph of urban design – in fact, it's a chaotic mess. At its western end, the İstiklal Caddesi tram circumnavigates the **Cumhuriyet Anıtı** (Republic Monument), created by an Italian architect-sculptor team in 1928. It features Atatürk, his assistant and successor İsmet İnönü, and other revolutionary leaders.

SEEING THE DERVISHES WHIRL

The brotherhood called the Mevlevi, or whirling dervishes, follows a mystical form of Islam that uses allegorical language to describe a love for God, and is famous for its meditative *sema*, a whirling ceremony that represents a union with God.

The Mevlevi are guided by the teachings of Celaleddin Rumi, known as Mevlâna (Our Guide). Born in 1207, Rumi was a brilliant student of Islamic theology who became profoundly influenced by Şemsi Tebrizi, a Sufi (Islamic mystic) disciple.

The Mevlevi order was outlawed by Atatürk in the 1920s as part of his reforms, but in the early 1950s the Turkish government recognised the tourist potential for 'whirling' and the Konya Mevlâna Festival (p488) was born. The whirling dervish 'performance' is a growing drawcard for visitors to Turkey, but the Mevlevi order is still technically outlawed in the country.

You can see the dervishes whirl in a number of spots around İstanbul, but frankly most of them are little more than tourist shows. The best place to see an authentic *sema* is in one of the few practising *tekkes* left in İstanbul, at Fatih, some 4km west of Sultanahmet. The *sema* is usually only held on Monday nights and it's best to come here with a local escort. You could ask at your hotel, or go with **Les Arts Turcs** (see p128), which takes travellers to the ceremony from its studio, after giving them a one-hour information session about Sufism and the *sema* (€25).

The second-best option is usually to go to the Galata Mevlevihanesi (see p115), where *semas* have been held for centuries (in recent years mainly for the benefit of tourists). When this book went to print the museum was closed for restoration – check the boards outside for updates. There is also a performance by the **Contemporary Lovers of Mevlana** (Map pp92-3; ☎ 0212-449 9081; www .whirlingdervishistanbul.com; tickets adult/student TL30/20; ☺ 7.30pm Tue & Sat) in the atmospheric exhibition hall on platform 1 at Sirkeci station in Sultanahmet. Tickets here go on sale from 5pm on the day of the performance. Note that works associated with the Marmaray project (p163) may lead to the relocation of this performance.

Remember that the ceremony is a religious one – by whirling the adherents believe that they are attaining a higher union with God – so don't talk, leave your seat or take flash photographs while the dervishes are spinning. For more information on the whirling dervishes, see p489.

İSTANBUL

CONTEMPLATE THE CUTTING EDGE

We reckon the recent trend for İstanbul's family business dynasties to endow private art galleries is the best thing to hit the city since the tulip bulb arrived. Suddenly, İstanbul has a clutch of world-class contemporary art museums to add to its already impressive portfolio of major tourist attractions. No wonder it's been named a European Capital of Culture for 2010.

The first cab off the rank was the **Proje4L/Elgiz Museum of Modern Art** (Elgiz Çağdaş Sanat Müzesi, İstanbul; ☎ 0212-281 5150; www.elgizmuseum.org; Harman Sokak, Harmancı Giz Plaza; ☻ 10am-6pm Wed-Fri, 10am-4pm Sat) in Levent, closely followed by **İstanbul Modern** (p115) in Tophane and the **Pera Museum** (opposite) in Beyoğlu. And let's not forget the privately endowed universities, which are joining the fray with style and loads of substance – the **Sakip Sabancı Müzesi** (p123) and **Santralİstanbul** (p125) are the two most prominent, but there are others as well. Many have become venues for the **International İstanbul Biennial** (www.istfest.org), held between September and early November in odd-numbered years.

All of this is great news for the visitor, who can see world-class exhibitions in drop-dead-gorgeous surrounds complete with stylish gift shops and quality cafés. Some are even free – and you gotta love that.

On the square's north side is a hectic bus terminus; on its east side is the **Atatürk Cultural Centre** and on the west is the Marmara Hotel. In the middle is the entrance to the metro running up to Levent 4 and the funicular tram running down to Kabataş.

ASKERI MÜZE (MILITARY MUSEUM)

For a rousing experience, present yourself at the splendid **Military Museum** (Map pp86-7; ☎ 0212-233 2720; Vali Konağı Caddesi, Harbiye; adult/student TL3/1; ☻ 9am-5pm Wed-Sun), 1km north of Taksim.

The museum is spread over two very large floors. On the ground floor are displays of medieval weapons and armour, military uniforms, and glass cases holding battle standards, both Turkish and captured. There's also a huge diorama of the Conquest, complete with sound effects. The upper floor has displays on WWI and the War of Independence, including a Çannakale (aka Gallipoli) diorama.

The easiest way to get to the museum is to walk up Cumhuriyet Caddesi from Taksim Sq. This will take around 20 minutes. Alternatively, take any bus heading up Cumhuriyet Caddesi from Taksim Sq. Try to visit in the afternoon so that you can enjoy the concert given by the Mehter, the medieval Ottoman Military Band, which takes place between 3pm and 4pm most days.

Beşiktaş & Ortaköy

DOLMABAHÇE PALACE

These days it's fashionable for critics influenced by the less-is-more aesthetic of the Bauhaus masters to sneer at buildings such as **Dolmabahçe Palace** (Dolmabahçe Sarayı; Map p97; ☎ 0212-236 9000; www.millisaraylar.gov.tr; Dolmabahçe Caddesi, Beşiktaş; admission Selamlık only TL15, Harem-Cariyeler only TL10; Selamlık & Harem-Cariyeler TL20, Crystal Palace & Clock Museum TL4; ☻ 9am-4pm Tue-Wed & Fri-Sun summer, 9am-3pm winter). Enthusiasts of Ottoman architecture also decry this flourish of the imperial dynasty, finding that it shares more in common with the Paris Opera than Topkapı Palace. But whatever the critics may say, this 19th-century imperial residence is a clear crowd favourite.

Less is more was certainly *not* the philosophy of Sultan Abdül Mecit, who, deciding that it was time to give lie to talk of Ottoman military and financial decline, decided to move from Topkapı to a lavish new palace on the shores of the Bosphorus. For a site he chose the *dolma bahçe* (filled-in garden) where one of his predecessors, Sultan Ahmet I (r 1607–17), had built an imperial pleasure kiosk surrounded by gardens. In 1843 Abdül Mecit commissioned architects Nikoğos and Garabed Balyan to construct an Ottoman-European palace that would impress everyone who set eyes on it. Construction was completed in 1856. Traditional Ottoman palace architecture was rejected in favour of a European-style building with neo-baroque and neoclassical decoration. Eschewing pavilions, the building turns in on itself and ignores its splendid Bosphorus views.

The palace, which is set in well-tended gardens and entered through an ornate gate, is divided into two sections: the over-the-top

Selamlık (ceremonial suites) and the slightly more restrained **Harem-Cariyeler** (Harem and concubines' quarters). You must take a guided tour to see either section (Selamlık half-hour tour, Harem-Cariyeler one hour tour). If you only have enough time for one tour, be sure to make it the Selamlık. Tours are in English and Turkish.

At the end of your tour, make sure you visit the **Crystal Palace**, with its fairy-tale-like conservatory featuring etched-glass windows, crystal fountain and myriad chandeliers. There's even a crystal piano and chair. It's next to the aviary on the street side of the palace.

Finally, don't set your watch by any of the palace clocks, as all of them stopped at 9.05am, the moment at which Atatürk died in Dolmabahçe on 10 November 1938. When touring the Harem you will be shown the quarters he used when he spent time here.

The tourist entrance to the palace is near the ornate **clock tower** built by Sultan Abdül Hamit II in 1890–94. There's an outdoor café near here with premium Bosphorus views.

İSTANBUL DENİZ MÜZESİ

Landlubbers and sea dogs alike will enjoy a visit to this **museum** (Naval Museum; Map p97; ☎ 0212-261 0040; www.dzkk.tsk.mil.tr; cnr Cezayir & Beşiktaş Caddesis, Beşiktaş; adult/student €2/1; ◷ 9am-12.30pm & 1.30-5pm Wed-Sun), which celebrates Ottoman maritime history. Exhibits focus on two great Turkish sailors: the 16th-century sailor and cartographer Piri Reis; and the admiral of Süleyman the Magnificent's fleet, Barbaros Heyrettin Paşa. Highlights include a coloured 1461 map of the Mediterranean drawn on antelope skin, and part of the huge iron chain that the Byzantines stretched across the Golden Horn to block Mehmet the Conqueror's ships.

Those with a particular interest in things military may also be pleased to know that if they come out of the museum and walk straight down to the shore they'll find a line of dolmuşes (minibuses) waiting to run them straight to the Military Museum in Harbiye.

To get here, catch the tram from Sultanahmet to Kabataş and then bus 22E, 22, 22RE or 25E to Beşiktaş.

YILDIZ PARKI

A pretty, leafy oasis alive with birds, picnickers and couples indulging in a bit of hanky-panky in the bushes, **Yıldız Parkı** (Map p97; Çırağan Caddesi; admission free) is a pleasant spot to while away a few hours. Once the imperial gardens of nearby Çırağan Palace, this is where Sultan Abdül Hamit II built an Ottoman-European palace, Yıldız Şale, where foreign dignitaries could stay and two ornate pavilions where he, his family and said visiting foreign dignitaries could relax. One of these, the **Çadır Köşkü**, built beside the Yildiz lake between 1865 and 1870, now functions intermittently as a café.

If you enter from the main entrance at Çırağan Caddesi, walk 10 minutes up the steep main road to the T-intersection at the top and then turn right, you will see the entrance to **Yıldız Sarayı Müzesi** (Yıldız Şale, Yıldız Chalet Museum; Map p97; ☎ 0212-259 4570; admission TL5; ◷ 9.30am-5pm Tue-Wed & Fri-Sun Apr-Oct, to 4pm Nov-May). Though he managed to avoid the building frenzy embraced by many of his predecessors, Abdül Hamit II (r 1876–1909) dallied at least once with architects and builders. He built this fancy guest house–palace here in 1882, and expanded it in both 1889 and 1898 for state visits by Kaiser Wilhelm II of Germany. When the Kaiser left, the sultan decided he liked the place so much that he moved in himself, deserting the much larger and more ornate Dolmabahçe in the process. As you enter, a guide will approach and give you a half-hour tour in Turkish. Although the chalet isn't as plush as Dolmabahçe, it's a lot less crowded and has many of the same features, albeit on a more modest scale.

Around 500m past the turn-off to Yıldız Şale you'll come to the **Malta Köşkü** (Map p97; ☎ 0212-258 9453; ◷ 9am-10.30pm). Built in 1870, this was where Abdül Hamit imprisoned the deposed Murat V and his family. With its views of the Bosphorus, the terrace café here is a great place for a tea or light lunch.

If you come to the park by taxi, have it take you up the steep slope to Yıldız Şale; you can visit the other kiosks on the walk down. A taxi from Taksim Sq to the top of the hill should cost around TL8.

ORTAKÖY CAMİİ

Ortaköy (Middle Village; Map p97) is a charming waterside suburb embracing a jumble of Ottoman buildings renovated as stylish boutiques, bars and eateries. On balmy nights the restaurants, bars and cafés on and around the teeny cobbled square by the water overflow with locals enjoying a drink or meal while indulging in some of the city's best people-watching.

Right on the water's edge, the decorative **Ortaköy Camii** (Büyük Mecidiye Camii) is the work of Nikoğos Balyan, one of the architects of Dolmabahçe Palace. A strange mix of baroque and neoclassical influences, it was designed and built for Sultan Abdül Mecit III in 1853–55. With the modern Bosphorus Bridge looming behind it, the mosque provides the classic photo opportunity for those wanting to illustrate İstanbul's 'old-meets-new' character.

Try to time your visit for Sunday, when the bustling street market fills the cobbled lanes. Do as the locals do and come for brunch, then pick through the market's beaded jewellery, hats and other trinkets before heading home to avoid the late-afternoon traffic crush. See p140 for our favourite eating picks.

To get here from Sultanahmet, catch the tram to Kabataş and then bus 22, 22RE, 25E or 30D; from Taksim Sq, catch bus DT2, 40, 40T or 42T (get off at the Kabataş Lisesi bus stop). Be warned that traffic along Çırağan Caddesi is almost always congested, so bus and taxi trips here can be excruciatingly slow.

Asian Shore

Although most of İstanbul's noteworthy sights, shops, bars and eateries are on the European side of town, many locals prefer to live on the Asian (aka Anatolian) shore, citing cheaper rents and a better standard of living. For others, the best thing about living in or visiting this side of town is the scenic ferry ride between the continents.

ÜSKÜDAR

Üsküdar (öö-skoo-dar) is the Turkish form of the name Scutari. The first colonists lived in Chalcedon (now Kadıköy), to the south, and Chrysopolis (now Üsküdar) became its first major offshoot; both towns existed about two decades before Byzantium was founded. It soon became clear that the harbour at Chrysopolis was superior to Chalcedon and, as Byzantium blossomed, Chrysopolis outgrew Chalcedon to become the largest suburb on the Asian shore. Unwalled and therefore vulnerable, it became part of the Ottoman Empire at least 100 years before the Conquest.

Today Üsküdar is a bustling working-class suburb with a handful of important Ottoman mosques that attract visitors. If you're here for lunch, choices include **Kanaat Lokantası** (Map pp86-7; ☎ 0216-553 3791; Selmanı Pak Caddesi 25; mains TL6-11; ☽ 11am-9pm), one of the city's most famous *lokantas*. It offers traditional dishes such as *paça çorba* (sheep's-trotter soup, TL3.30) as well as a host of less confrontational alternatives. You'll find it in the street behind the Ağa Camii. Another good option is the Üsküdar branch of **Niyazibey** (Map pp86-7; ☎ 0216-310 4821; Ahmediye Meydanı; mains TL4-18; ☽ 11am-9pm), the local branch of a popular chain of kebap restaurants. This serves a delicious and dirt-cheap *perde pılavı* (chicken and almond pie, TL6). It's on the road to the Atik Valide Camii.

If coming to Üsküdar from Sultanahmet, catch the ferry from Eminönü. This runs every 15 to 30 minutes (depending on the time of day) between 6.35am and 11pm. Ferry services also operate between Beşiktaş (from beside the Deniz Müzesi) and Üsküdar. Ferries start at 6.45am and run every 20 to 30 minutes until 9pm.

Kız Kulesi

İstanbul is a maritime city, so it's appropriate that the **Kız Kulesi** (Maiden's Tower; Map pp86-7; ☎ 0216-342 4747; www.kizkulesi.com.tr; ☽ 9am-11pm), one of its most distinctive landmarks, is on the water. Arriving at Üsküdar by ferry, you'll notice the squat tower on a tiny island to the right (south), just off the Asian mainland. In ancient times a predecessor of the current 18th-century structure functioned as a toll-booth and defence point; the Bosphorus could be closed off by means of a chain stretching from here to Seraglio Point. Some think its ancient pedigree goes back even further, referring to it as Leander's Tower after the tragic youth who drowned after attempting to swim across a strait to Europe to visit his lover, Hero – a story more usually and believably associated with the Gallipoli Peninsula. More recently, the tower featured in the 1999 Bond film *The World is Not Enough*. Though it's possible to visit the tower (which now functions as a lacklustre restaurant and café) by boat, we don't recommend wasting the TL6 charged for the trip.

Mosques

Judging that Scutari was the closest point in İstanbul to Mecca, many powerful Ottoman figures built mosques here to assist their

İSTANBUL

passage to Paradise. Every year a big caravan set out from here en route to Mecca and Medina for the Haj, further emphasising the suburb's reputation for piety.

As you leave Üsküdar dock, the main square, Demokrasi Meydanı (currently being redeveloped as part of the Marmaray project, p163), is right in front of you. Its northeastern corner is dominated by the **Mihrimah Sultan Camii** (Map pp86–7), sometimes referred to as the İskele (ferry dock) Camii. This mosque was designed by Sinan for Süleyman the Magnificent's daughter in 1547–48.

South of the square is the **Yeni Valide Camii** (New Sultan's Mother Mosque; Map pp86–7). Featuring a wrought-iron 'birdcage' tomb in its overgrown garden, it was built by Sultan Ahmet III in 1708–10 for his mother Gülnuş Emetullah. East of the square is the **Ağa Camii** (Map pp94–5).

West of the square, overlooking the harbour, is the charming **Şemsi Paşa Camii** (Map pp86–7). Designed by Sinan and built in 1580 for Grand Vizier Şemsi Paşa, its modest size and decoration reflect the fact that its benefactor occupied the position of grand vizier for only a couple of months under Süleyman the Magnificent. Its *medrese* (seminary) has been converted into a library and there's a popular *çay bahçesi* on its southern side.

The **Atik Valide Camii** (Map pp86–7; Çinili Camii Sokak) is another of Sinan's works, and is considered by many experts to be among his best designs. It was built for Valide Sultan Nurbanu, wife of Selim II (The Sot) and mother of Murat III, in 1583. Nurbanu was captured by Turks on the Aegean island of Paros when she was 12 years old, and went on to be a successful player in the Ottoman court. Murat adored his mother and on her death commissioned Sinan to build this monument to her on Üsküdar's highest hill.

The nearby **Çinili Camii** (Tiled Mosque; Map pp86–7; Çinili Camii Sokak) is unprepossessing from the outside, but has an interior made brilliant with İznik tiles, the bequest of Mahpeyker Kösem (1640), wife of Sultan Ahmet I (r 1603–17) and mother of sultans Murat IV (r 1623–40) and İbrahim (r 1640–48).

To find the Atik Valide Camii and Çinili Camii, walk up Hakimiyet-i Milliye Caddesi until you get to the traffic circle. Continue up Dr Fahri Atabey Caddesi for about 1km until you get to little Sarı Mehmet Sokak, on your left. From here you'll spot the minarets

of Atik Valide Camii. To get to Çinili Camii from Atik Valide Camii, walk east along Çinili Camii Sokak for about 300m, after which it turns north and runs uphill. Çinili Camii is about 200m further on. All up it's about a 25-minute walk to the Çinili Camii from the main square.

HAREM
Florence Nightingale Museum

The experience of visiting the Selimiye Kızlarsı (Army Barracks), where this modest **museum** (Map pp86-7; ☎ 0216-556 8161; fax 0216-310 7929; Nci Ordu Komutanliği 1; admission free; ☾ 9am-5pm Mon-Fri) is housed, is even better than the museum itself. The barracks, built by Mahmut II in 1828 on the site of a barracks originally built by Selim III in 1799 and extended by Abdül Mecit I in 1842 and 1853, is the headquarters of the Turkish First Army, the largest division in the country. It's an extremely handsome building, with 2.5km of corridors, 300 rooms and 300 windows. During the Crimean War (1853–56) the barracks became a military hospital where the famous lady with the lamp and 38 nursing students worked. It was here that Nightingale put in practice the innovative nursing methods that history remembers her for. Although they seem commonsensical from a modern perspective, it is hard to overstate how radical they seemed at the time; it's really amazing to hear that before she arrived here, the mortality rate was 70% of patients but that by the time she left it had dropped to 5% (though other factors also contributed to this decrease).

The museum is on three levels in the northwest tower of the barracks. Downstairs there is a display charting the history of the First Army and concentrating on the Crimean War. On the two upstairs levels you see Nightingale's personal quarters, including her surgery room with original furnishings (including two lamps) and her living room, with great views across to Old İstanbul.

To be allowed into the barracks, you need to fax a letter requesting to visit the museum and nominating a time. Include a photocopy of your passport photo page. Do this 48 hours before you wish to visit and make sure you include your İstanbul phone number so that someone can respond to your request.

The museum is about halfway between Üsküdar and Kadıköy, near the fairy-tale-like clock towers of the TC Marmara University. To get here, catch the Harem car ferry from

Sirkeci, next to Eminönü (it also transports passengers). This leaves every 30 minutes from 7am to 9.30pm. After alighting from the ferry, walk south (right) along the main road for approximately 10 minutes until you reach the Selimiye Kızlarsı Harem Kapısı (the barracks' Harem Gate).

KADIKÖY

If you've got a spare few hours, you may want to explore Kadıköy, the site of the city's first colony. Although there's nothing to show of its historic beginnings and no headline sights, Kadıköy has a youthful, modern vibe that can be a welcome respite from conservative Old İstanbul. There's a fantastic fresh produce market south of the ferry dock, in the middle of which is **Çiya Sofrası** (☎ 0216-330 3190; www.ciya .com.tr; Güneslibahçe Sokak 43; mains TL8-12 ☉ 11.30am-10pm), one of the city's best *lokantas*. After sampling its magnificent food, head to the authentically retro **Baylan Pastanesi** (☎ 0216-336 2881; Muvakkithane Caddesi 19; ☉ 10am-10pm) for an excellent coffee. Then make your way to Kadife Sokak to check out its independent cinema, grunge boutiques and hugely popular bars, the most popular of which is **Karga Bar** (☎ 0216-449 1725; Kadife Sokak 16; ☉ 11am-2am).

To the north of Kadıköy is the neoclassical **Haydarpaşa Train Station**, resembling a German castle. In the early 20th century when Kaiser Wilhelm of Germany was trying to charm the sultan into economic and military cooperation, he presented the station as a small token of his respect. Today there's talk of turning it and its surrounds into a controversial recreation and trade precinct, boasting seven highrise towers. Most ferries travelling between Kadıköy and Eminönü or Karaköy make a quick stop here.

To get to Kadıköy from Sultanahmet, hop on the ferry from Eminönü, which runs every 15 to 20 minutes (depending on the time of day) between 7.30am and 8.35pm. The last ferry back to Eminönü is at 8pm.

From the ferry terminal at Karaköy (the Beyoğlu side of the Galata Bridge) services run from 6.10am every 10 to 30 minutes (depending on the time of day) until 11pm. The last ferry back to Karaköy is at 11pm.

A ferry service also operates from Beşiktaş (catch it from beside the Deniz Müzesi), starting at 7.15am and running every half-hour until 9.15pm. The last ferry back to Beşiktaş is at 8.45pm.

ACTIVITIES
Ferry Cruises

During the 18th and 19th centuries the Bosphorus and Golden Horn were alive with caiques (long, thin rowboats), their oars dipping rhythmically into the currents as they carried the sultan and his courtiers from palace to pavilion, and from Europe to Asia. The *caïques* are long gone, but in their place are the sleek speedboats of the moneyed elite and the much-loved public ferries used by the rest of İstanbul's population. Few experiences are as evocative of place as a trip on an İstanbul ferry – whether it be the short return trip to Kadıköy or Üsküdar (p119), on which you cross from Europe to Asia and back again, or one of the longer trips detailed below.

BOSPHORUS CRUISE

Divan Yolu and İstiklal Caddesi are always awash with people, but neither is the major thoroughfare in İstanbul. That honour goes to the mighty Bosphorus strait, which runs from the Sea of Marmara (Marmara Denizi) to the Black Sea (Karadeniz), located 32km north of the city centre. In modern Turkish, the strait is known as the Boğaziçi or İstanbul Boğazı (from *boğaz*, meaning throat or strait). On one side is Asia, on the other is Europe.

Departure Point: Eminönü

Hop onto the boat at the Boğaz Iskelesi (Bosphorus Public Excursion Ferry Dock) on the Eminönü quay. It's always a good idea to arrive 30 to 45 minutes or so before the scheduled departure time so as to be sure of getting a seat with a view. The Asian shore is to the right side of the ferry as it sails down the Bosphorus, Europe is to the left. As you start your trip up the Bosphorus, you'll see the small island and tower of **Kız Kulesi** (p119), on the Asian side, near Üsküdar. On the European shore, you'll pass grandiose **Dolmabahçe Palace** (p117). In his travelogue *Constantinople in 1890*, French writer Pierre Loti described this and the neighbouring **Çırağan Palace** as 'a line of palaces white as snow, placed at the edge of the sea on marble docks', a description that remains as accurate as it is evocative.

Beşiktaş to Kanlıca

After a brief stop at Beşiktaş the ferry sails past Çırağan Palace (now the Çırağan Palace Hotel Kempınski) and Ortaköy Meydanı (Ortaköy Sq), known for its pretty mosque (p118) and outdoor eateries. Towering over the mosque's minarets is the huge Bosphorus Bridge (Boğaziçi Köprüsü), opened in 1973 on the 50th anniversary of the founding of the Turkish Republic. Just after the bridge, on the Asian side, is **Beylerbeyi Palace** (Beylerbeyi Sarayı; ☎ 0216-321 9320; Abdullah Ağa Caddesi, Beylerbeyi; admission TL8; ☼ 9.30am-5pm Tue, Wed & Fri-Sun Apr-Oct, 9.30am-4pm Tue, Wed & Fri-Sun Nov-Mar). Every sultan needed a little place to escape to, and this 30-room palace was the place for Abdül Aziz (r 1861–76). Look for its two whimsical marble bathing pavilions on the shore, one of which was for men, the other for the women of the Harem. The ferry doesn't stop here, but you can visit another time by catching bus 15 from Üsküdar and getting off at the Çayırbaşı stop.

Past the suburb of Çengelköy on the Asian side is the imposing **Kuleli Military School**, built in 1860 and immortalised in Irfan Orga's wonderful memoir *Portrait of a Turkish Family*. Look for its two 'witch-hat' towers.

Almost opposite Kuleli on the European shore is **Arnavutköy**, a suburb boasting a number of well-preserved, frilly Ottoman-era wooden houses, including numerous *yalıs*. The word *yalı* derives from the Greek word for 'coast', and is used to describe the wooden summer residences that were built along the Bosphorus shore by the Ottoman aristocracy and foreign ambassadors in the 17th, 18th and 19th centuries. All are now protected by the country's heritage laws.

On the hill above Arnavutköy are buildings formerly occupied by the **American College for Girls**. Its most famous alumna was Halide Edib Adıvar, who wrote about the school in her 1926 autobiography *Memoir of Halide Edib*.

Arnavutköy runs straight into the glamorous suburb of **Bebek**, famous for chic cafés such as **Mangerie** (☎ 0212-263 5199; 3rd fl, Cevdet Paşa Caddesi 69; ☼ 8am-midnight) and **Lucca** (☎ 0212-257 1255; Cevdet Paşa Caddesi 51b; ☼ noon-2am Mon, 10am-2am Tue-Sun). As the ferry passes, look out for the mansard roof of the **former Egyptian consulate**, an art nouveau minipalace built by the last khedive of Egypt, Abbas Hilmi II. It's just south of the waterside park.

Opposite Bebek is **Kandilli**, the 'Place of Lamps', named after the lamps that were lit here to warn ships of the particularly treacherous currents at the headland. Among the many *yalıs* here is the small **Kırmızı Yalı** (Red Yalı), constructed in 1790; a little further on is the long, white **Kıbrıslı Mustafa Emin Paşa Yalı**.

Next to the Kıbrıslı Yalı are the Büyük Göksu Deresi (Great Heavenly Stream) and Küçük Göksu Deresi (Small Heavenly Stream), two brooks that descend from the Asian hills into the Bosphorus. Between them is a grassy, shady delta, which the Ottoman elite thought just perfect for picnics. Foreign residents, who referred to the place as 'the sweet waters of Asia', would often join them. If the weather was good, the sultan joined the party – and did so in style. Sultan Abdül Mecit's version of a picnic blanket was the rococo **Küçüksu Kasrı** (☎ 0216-332 3303; Küçüksu Caddesi; admission adult/ student TL4/1; ☼ 9.30am-5pm Tue, Wed & Fri-Sun Apr-Oct, 9.30am-4pm Tue, Wed & Fri-Sun Nov-Mar), constructed in 1856–57. You'll see its ornate cast-iron fence, boat dock and wedding-cake exterior from the ferry. To visit, get off the ferry at Kanlıca and catch bus 11H or 15F.

On the European side, just before the **Fatih Bridge** (Fatih Köprüsü), the majestic structure of **Rumeli Hisarı** (Fortress of Europe; ☎ 0212-263 5305; Yahya Kemal Caddesi 42; admission TL3; ☼ 9am-4.30pm Thu-Tue) looms over a pretty village of the same name. Mehmet the Conqueror had Rumeli Hisarı built in a mere four months during 1452 in preparation for his planned siege of Constantinople. For its location he chose the narrowest point of the Bosphorus, opposite Anadolu Hisarı (Fortress of Asia), which had been built by Sultan Beyazıt I in 1391. By doing so, he was able to control all traffic on the strait, thereby cutting the city off from resupply by sea. Just next to the fortress is a clutch of cafés and restaurants, the most popular of which is **Sade Kahve** (☎ 212-358 2324; Yahya Kemal Caddesi 36; breakfast plates TL14; ☼ 8am-10pm), a favourite weekend brunch spot for İstanbullus. To get to Rumeli Hisarı, get off the ferry at Yeniköy or Sariyer (see opposite) and catch bus 25E back towards town. This bus stops at Emirgan (see opposite) as well as here at Rumeli Hisarı before terminating at Kabataş.

Almost directly under the Fatih Bridge on the Asian side is the **Köprülü Amcazade Hüseyin Paşa Yalı**. Built right on the water in 1698, it's the oldest *yalı* on the Bosphorus.

Kanlıca to Yeniköy

Past the bridge, still on the Asian side, is the charming suburb of **Kanlıca**, famous for its rich and delicious yoghurt, which can be sampled at the two cafés in front of the ferry stop or on the boat itself. This is the ferry's third stop, and if you so choose, you can stop and explore before reboarding the boat on its return trip. From here you can also catch a ferry across to Emirgan or Bebek on the European side and return to town by bus.

High on a promontory above Kanlıca is **Hıdiv Kasrı** (Khedive's Villa; ☎ 0216-258 9453; Hıdiv Yolu 32, Kanlıca; ☺ 8am-11pm), an exquisite art nouveau villa built by the last khedive of Egypt as a summer residence. Restored after decades of neglect, it now functions as a **restaurant** (mains TL8-16) and **garden café** (tosts TL3.50-4, sandwiches TL5-6.50). The villa is a gem, and the extensive garden is superb, particularly during the International İstanbul Tulip Festival (see p129) in April. To get here from the ferry stop, turn left into Halide Edip Adivar Caddesi and then turn right into narrow Kafadar Sokak. Walk all the way up steep Hacı Muhittin Sokağı until you see a sign for Hadiv Kasrı Caddesi – the villa is on the left.

Opposite Kanlıca on the European shore is the wealthy suburb of **Emirgan**. It's well worth visiting for the impressive **Sakıp Sabancı Müzesi** (☎ 0212-277 2200; http://muze.sabanciuniv.edu; Sakip Sabanci Caddesi 42; adult/student/under 14yr TL10/3/ free; ☺ 10am-6pm Tue, Thu & Fri-Sun, 10am-10pm Wed, 10am-7pm Sat), which hosts world-class travelling exhibitions. The museum is also home to one of the city's most glamorous eateries, **Müzedechanga** (☎ 0212-323 0901; mains TL21-49; ☺ 10.30am-1am Tue-Sun).

Yeniköy to Sarıyer

North of Emirgan is **Yeniköy**, on a point jutting out from the European shore. This is the ferry's next stop. First settled in classical times, Yeniköy later became a favourite summer resort, as indicated by **Sait Halim Paşa Yalı**, the lavish 19th-century Ottoman *yalı* of the one-time grand vizier. Look for its two small stone lions on the quay. On the opposite shore is the suburb of **Paşabahçe**, famous for its glassware factory.

Originally called Therapeia for its healthy climate, the little cove of **Tarabya** to the north of Yeniköy on the European shore has been a favourite summer watering place for İstanbul's well-to-do for centuries, although modern development has sullied some of its charm. For an account of Therapeia in its heyday, read Harold Nicholson's 1921 novel *Sweet Waters*.

North of the village are some of the old summer embassies of foreign powers. When the heat and fear of disease increased in the warm months, foreign ambassadors and their staff would retire to these palatial residences, complete with lush gardens. Such residences extended north to the village of **Büyükdere**, which is also notable for its churches and for the **Sadberk Hanım Müzesi** (☎ 0212-242 3813; www .sadberkhanimmuzesi.org.tr; Piyasa Caddesi 25-9, Büyükdere; admission TL7; ☺ 10am-5pm Thu-Tue), named after the wife of the late Vehbi Koç, founder of Turkey's foremost commercial empire. There's an eclectic collection here, including beautiful İznik and Kütahya ceramics, Ottoman silk textiles, and Roman coins and jewellery. The museum is a 10-minute walk from the next ferry stop, at Sariyer.

Sarıyer to Anadolu Kavağı

After stopping at Sariyer, the ferry sails on to **Rumeli Kavağı**, known for its fish restaurants. After a short stop here it then crosses the strait to finish the journey at **Anadolu Kavağı**. Surrounded by countryside, this is a pleasant spot in which to wander and have a seafood lunch, though it's somewhat blighted by the presence of pushy restaurant touts. Perched above the village are the ruins of **Anadolu Kavağı Kalesi** (Yoros Kalesi), a medieval castle that originally had eight massive towers in its walls. First built by the Byzantines, it was restored and reinforced by the Genoese in 1350 and later by the Ottomans. To get there, it's a 25-minute walk up steep Caferbaba Sokağı.

If you decide to travel back to town by bus rather than ferry, catch bus 15A to Beykoz or Kanlıca from the main square and then transfer to bus 15 to Üsküdar or E-2 to Taksim.

Getting There & Away

There are numerous ways to explore the Bosphorus. Most people take the public Bosphorus Excursion Ferry (one way/return TL10/17.50), which leaves Eminönü at 10.35am year-round. There are usually extra services at noon and 1.35pm from mid-April to October. These ferries depart from the Boğaz İskelesi at Eminönü and stop at Beşiktaş, Kanlıca, Yeniköy, Sarıyer, Rumeli Kavağı and Anadolu Kavağı. The journey takes 90 minutes each way; return services leave Anadolu Kavağı at 3pm (year-round) and at 4.15pm and 5pm (6pm on Saturday) from mid-April to October. Options for returning to town by bus or exploring by bus along the way are mentioned in the text above. When this book went to print, a 'Moonlight

Service' was being trialled from mid-June to the end of August, leaving at 7pm and returning from Anadolu Kavağı at 10pm (weekdays only, TL20). Check www.ido.com.tr for an update.

Another, less attractive, option is to buy a ticket on a private excursion boat. These only take you as far as Rumeli Hisarı (without stopping), although the fact that the boats are smaller means that you travel closer to the shoreline. The whole trip takes about three hours – one hour of travel each way and an hour at Rumeli Hisarı, which is just long enough to have lunch or to see the castle, but certainly not long enough to do both. Touts selling tickets for these trips are always around the Eminönü docks; they sell the tickets for TL20 to TL25, but it's always worth bargaining. These boats leave every 1½ to two hours from 11am, with the last one at 8pm from June to September (4pm at other times). Note that these departure times aren't fixed – boats don't usually leave until they fill up.

Bus tickets cost TL1.40 per leg.

GOLDEN HORN CRUISE

Most visitors to İstanbul know about the Bosphorus cruise, but not too many have heard about the Haliç (Golden Horn) trip. Until recently, this stretch of water to the north of the Galata Bridge was heavily polluted and its suburbs offered little to tempt the traveller. All that's changing these days, though. The waters have been cleaned up, beautification works are under way along the shores, and impressive museums and galleries are opening in the Haliç suburbs. Spending a day hopping on and off the ferry and exploring will give you an insight into a very different – and far less touristy – İstanbul.

Departure Point: Eminönü

These ferries start in Üskudar on the Asian side, and stop at Karaköy before taking on most of their passengers at the Haliç Iskelesi (Golden Horn Ferry Dock) on the far side of the Galata Bridge at Eminönü. The *iskelesi* is behind a car park next to the Storks jewellery store. The ferry then sails underneath the Atatürk Bridge and stops at Kasımpaşa on the opposite side of the Golden Horn. This area is where the Ottoman imperial naval yards were located, and some of the original building stock is still evident.

Fener

The next stop is on the opposite shore, at Fener. This area is the traditional home of the city's Greek population, and although few Greeks are resident these days, a number of important Greek Orthodox sites are located here. The prominent red-brick building on the hill is the **Greek Lycée of the Fener** (Megali School or Great School; Map pp86–7), the oldest house of learning in İstanbul. The school has been housed in Fener since before the Conquest – the present building dates from 1881.

Closer to the shore, to the left of the ferry stop and across Abdülezel Paşa Caddesi, is the **Ecumenical Orthodox Patriarchate** (Map pp86-7; ☎ 0212-531 9670; www.ec-patr.org; Sadrazam Ali Paşa Caddesi, Fener; donation requested; 🕑 9am-5pm). The compound is built around the historic Church of St George, which dates from 1730. Every Sunday morning, busloads of Greek Orthodox pilgrims come here for the Divine Liturgy.

To the right of the ferry stop, in the waterside park, is the attractive Gothic Revival **Church of St Stephen of the Bulgars** (Sveti Stefan Church; Mürsel Paşa Caddesi 85, Fener). This cast-iron church was constructed in Vienna, then shipped down the Danube and assembled here in 1871. It's not normally open to visitors, but sometimes functions as a venue for the International İstanbul Music Festival (p129).

If you're hungry, Fener is home to the most famous *iskembecisi* (tripe soup shop) in the city: **Tarıhı Halıç İşkembecısı** (Map pp86-7; ☎ 0212-534 9414; Abdülezel Paşa Caddesi 315, Fener; 🕑 24hr). Locals swear by the hangover-fighting properties of *işkembe* and often make late-night pilgrimages here. It's on the main road opposite the ferry stop.

Those wanting a less confrontational meal should make their way to **Ottoman** (Map pp86-7; ☎ 0212-631 7567; www.halicottoman.com; Kadir Has Caddesi 9; mains TL12-20; 🕑 noon-1am; ✗), which has a roof terrace and top-floor dining room overlooking the Golden Horn. The menu features regional specialities from Turkey's east as well as Ottoman dishes – everything is remarkably well priced and quite delicious. It's a 15-minute walk back towards Eminönü from the Fener *iskelesi*.

Balat

Staying on the western side of the Golden Horn, the ferry's next stop is usually Balat, once home to a large proportion of İstanbul's Jewish population and now crowded with migrants from the east of the country. (Please note: when this book went to print the Balat *iskelesi* was being restored and the ferry wasn't stopping here). The oldest synagogue in İstanbul, **Ahrida Sinagogu** (Vodina Caddesi 9, Balat), is located in Balat. Built by Macedonian Jews more than half a century ago, it was renovated in the early 1990s and can be visited on weekday mornings. To visit you'll need to email or fax the **Chief Rabbinate** (fax 0212-244 1980; info@ musevicemaati.com) a few days ahead of time.

If you're in Balat at lunchtime, consider making a brief stop at the tiny, unsigned **Arnavut Köftesi** (Map pp86-7; ☎ 0212-531 6652; Mürsel Paşa Caddesi 155, Balat; ☼ 8am-4pm), which is justly famous for its *köfte* (meatballs) and *piyaz* (white-bean salad). It's to the left of the ferry stop on the opposite side of the main road.

Hasköy to Sütlüce

Passing the derelict remains of the original Galata Bridge on its journey, the ferry crosses to the opposite shore and stops next at Hasköy, home to the fascinating **Rahmi M Koç Müzesi** (Map pp86-7; ☎ 0212-369 6600; www .rmk-museum.org.tr; Hasköy Caddesi 27, Hasköy; adult/child & student TL8/4, submarine adult/child & student TL4.50/3; ☼ 10am-5pm Tue-Fri, 10am-7pm Sat & Sun). Founded by the head of the Koç industrial group to exhibit artefacts from İstanbul's industrial past, this museum is as popular with children as it is with adults and is well worth a visit. It's directly to the left of the ferry stop.

After stopping at Ayvansaray on the opposite shore, the ferry crosses back to Sütlüce. Art-lovers should consider getting off at Sütlüce and catching bus 36T, 47, 47Ç or 47E to Bilgi Üniverstesi, home to the cutting-edge **Santralİstanbul** (☎ 0212-444 0428; www .santralistanbul.org; Kazım Karabekir Caddesi 1, Eyüp; admission free; ☼ 10am-8pm Tue-Sun). Housed in a converted power station, it's one of the best contemporary art galleries in the city. Check the website for what's on. If you're keen to make your way back to Taksim from here, the gallery provides a free shuttle bus leaving every 20 minutes from mid-morning to 8pm.

Eyüp

The ferry's last stop is across the water in Eyüp. This conservative suburb is built around the **Eyüp Sultan Camii & Türbe** (Camii Kebir Sokak, Eyüp; ☼ tombs 9.30am-4.30pm), one of the most important religious sites in Turkey. The tomb supposedly houses the remains of Ayoub al-Ansari (Eyüp

Ensari in Turkish), a friend of the Prophet's and a revered member of Islam's early leadership. Eyüp fell in battle outside the walls of Constantinople while carrying the banner of Islam during the Arab assault and siege of the city from 674 to 678. The mosque built next to his tomb was where the Ottoman princes came for their coronations – it was levelled by an earthquake in 1766 and the present mosque was built in its place. It's a popular place for boys to visit on the day of their circumcision and is always busy on Fridays and on religious holidays. To get here, cross the road from the ferry stop and walk up İskele Caddesi, the main shopping street, until you reach the mosque.

After visiting the mosque and tomb, many visitors head north up the hill to enjoy a glass of tea and the wonderful views on offer at the **Pierre Loti Café** (☎ 0212-581 2696; Gümüşsuyu Balmumcu Sokak 1, Eyüp; ☼ 8pm-midnight), where the famous French novelist is said to have come for inspiration. To get here, walk out of the mosque's main gate and turn right. Walk around the complex (keeping it to your right) until you see a set of stairs and a steep cobbled path winding uphill through the Eyüp Sultan Mezarlığı (Cemetery of the Great Eyüp), burial ground to many important Ottoman figures. Alternatively, a cable car (TL1.40 each way, Akbil accepted) travels from the waterfront to the top of the hill.

Getting There & Away

Haliç ferries leave Eminönü every hour from 7.50am to 8.10pm; the last ferry returns to Eminönü from Eyüp at 7.45pm. The ferry trip takes 35 minutes and costs TL1.40 per leg (slightly cheaper if you use Akbil). Check www.ido.com.tr for timetable and fare updates.

If you wish to return by bus rather than ferry, then 36E, 44B, 99 and 399B travel from outside the ferry stop at Eyüp via Balat and Fener to Eminönü. Buses 39 and 39B travel via Edirnekapı to Beyazıt, allowing you to stop and visit the Chora Church (see p113) on your way back.

To return to Taksim from Hasköy or Sütlüce by bus, catch the 36T or 54HT. For Eminönü, catch bus 47, 47Ç or 47E.

Bus tickets cost TL1.40 per leg.

Hamams

A visit to a hamam is a quintessential Turkish experience, and İstanbul's hamams are famous throughout the country. If you're only going to visit one or two while in town, we suggest you choose the 'Big Two' – Cağaloğlu and Çemberlitaş. While these touristy hamams are pricey, they're worth it for their gorgeous historic surrounds and their squeaky-clean maintenance. And as most of their clients are tourists having their first hamam experience, you won't feel out of place. Allow at least an hour. For more information about bath etiquette see boxed text, p46.

Built over three centuries ago, **Cağaloğlu Hamamı** (Map pp92-3; ☎ 0212-522 2424; www.cagaloglu hamami.com.tr; Yerebatan Caddesi 34; bath services TL30-100; 8am-10pm men, 8am-8pm women) is the city's most beautiful hamam. The surroundings are simply exquisite. Separate baths each have a large *camekan* (reception area) with private, lockable cubicles where it's possible to have a nap or a tea at the end of your bath. There's a pleasant café as well as a shop selling quality olive-oil soap and other hamam accessories. Be warned that the attendants here can be both inventive and persistent when it comes to soliciting for tips.

The **Çemberlitaş Hamamı** (Map pp92-3; ☎ 0212-522 7974; www.cemberlitashamami.com.tr; Vezir Hanı Caddesi 8, Çemberlitaş; bath services TL29-79; 6am-midnight) was designed by Sinan in 1584 and is also gorgeous. Like Cağaloğlu, it's a double hamam (separate baths for men and women); it has a splendid original *camekan* in the men's section and a recently restored/rebuilt one in the women's section. As well as an array of bath treatments, it offers facials and oil massages. Tips are included in the prices and there's a discount for ISIC holders.

The **Ambassador Hotel Spa Center** (Map pp92-3; ☎ 0212-512 0002; www.hotelambassador.com; Ticarethane Sokak 19, Sultanahmet; Turkish bath with soap & oil massage TL82, remedial & aromatherapy massages TL20-50; noon-11pm Mon-Fri, noon-midnight Sat & Sun), in a shabby modern hotel just off Divan Yolu, might lack atmosphere but its bath and massage packages are excellent and you get the pretty (but small) hamam all to yourself. The 75-minute Turkish massage treatment gives you the same package that you get in the big hamams (bath, scrub and soap massage), but adds a 30-minute oil massage after the bath. You can also book the hamam for private use (TL37 per person per hour).

Yeşıldirek Hamamı (Map pp94-5; Tersane Caddesi 74, Azapkapi; bath TL20, with massage TL30; 6am-9pm), located at the base of the Atatürk Bridge, is the city's best gay hamam (men only). It's spacious, well-maintained and has all the traditional trappings. Be discreet.

Swimming

Swimming in the Bosphorus is only an option for those who have a death wish. Those with a hankering for the water can head to the beaches at Yeşilköy and Florya (you can get to these by train from Sirkeci and Cankurtaran stations) – but only to paddle. The water around the Princes' Islands is relatively clean, though the tiny beaches are crammed bottom-to-bottom in summer. The best option, if you really want to go to the beach, is to visit Kilyos or Şile on the Black Sea coast; both are day trips from İstanbul by bus.

Most of İstanbul's pool facilities are privately owned and open to members only. However, it's possible to organise a day pass to use the leisure facilities at many of the city's luxury hotels, most of which are located on or overlooking the Bosphorus. Be warned, though: this will set you back a hefty TL100 to TL200 per day (weekdays are usually cheaper than weekends). The best pools are at the **Swissôtel İstanbul the Bosphorus** (Map p97; ☎ 0212-326 1100; Bayıldım Caddesi 2, Maçka; 8am-7pm), the **İstanbul Hilton** (Map pp86-7; ☎ 0212-315 6000; Cumhuriyet Caddesi, Harbiye; 8am-8pm), **Hotel Les Ottomans** (☎ 0212-359 1500; Muallim Naci Caddesi 68, Kureçeşme; 9am-7pm) and the **Çırağan Palace Hotel Kempinski** (Map p97; ☎ 0212-326 4646; Çırağan Caddesi 32, Beşiktaş; 7am-11pm).

WALKING TOUR

Divan Yolu, the main thoroughfare of the old city, was laid out by Roman engineers to connect the city with Roman roads heading west. This tour will have you following in their footsteps.

Start your walk at the **Milion (1)**, at the south side of the park near the Basilica Cistern. Now sad and sorry looking, this was the marble milestone from which all distances in Byzantium were measured. The tower beside it was once part of the Aqueduct of Valens (p113), delivering water to the Basilica Cistern. Head west along Divan Yolu to the little **Firuz Ağa Camii (2)**, built in 1491 during the reign of Beyazıt II (r 1481–1512). Just behind it are the ruins of the 5th-century **Palace of Antiochus (3)**. Continue along Divan Yolu and turn left into İmran Öktem Caddesi to find the 4th-century **Binbirdirek Cistern** (**4**; p102).

WALKING TOUR

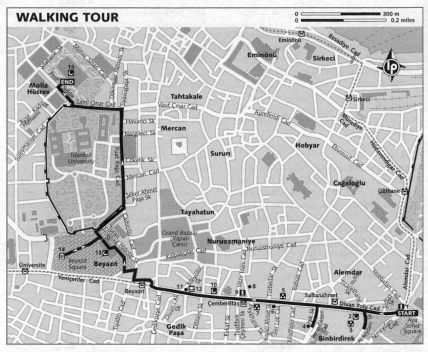

WALK FACTS

Start Milion, near Basilica Cistern
Finish Süleymaniye Camii
Distance 1.5km
Duration two hours

Back on Divan Yolu, you'll see an impressive enclosure at the corner of Babıali Caddesi, which is a cemetery housing the **tombs (5)** of the Ottoman high and mighty. There's a pleasant *çay bahçesi* (p149) here.

Exit the cemetery and cross the road to find the tiny stone **Köprülü library (6)** built by the Köprülü family in 1661. Stroll a bit further along Divan Yolu and into the Çemberlitaş district where Divan Yolu changes name to Yeniçeriler Caddesi. On the left are some more buildings from the Köprülü *külliyesi*. The **tomb (7)** is that of Köprülü Mehmet Paşa (1575–1661), and the octagonal mosque on the corner was a lecture and study room. Across the street, that strange building with a row of street-front shops is actually an ancient Turkish bathhouse, the **Çemberlitaş Hamamı (8**; opposite).

The column in the small plaza in front of the hamam entrance is the **Çemberlitaş (9)**, also known as the Banded Stone or Burnt Column. It was erected by Constantine in 330 to celebrate the dedication of Constantinople as capital of the Roman Empire and has been covered with hoardings and awaiting renovation for years. A bit further on is the **Atik Ali Camii (10)**, built in 1496 by a eunuch who was a grand vizier of Beyazıt II. Beyond Atik Ali Camii on the right (north) side is the **Koca Sinan Paşa Medresesi (11)**, resting place of Grand Vizier Koca Sinan Paşa. After you've seen the tomb here, head past the cemetery and to the right, where you'll find the quiet gardens of the **İlesam Lokalı (12**; p149), a great place to enjoy a tea break and nargileh.

Continue along Yeniçeriler Caddesi until you see the **Beyazıt Camii (13**; p110). Its *medrese* houses the **Museum of Turkish Calligraphic Art (14)**, which was closed for renovation when this book was being researched. After visiting the mosque, head towards the right of the grandiose main entrance of İstanbul University. Following the university's walls along Fuat Paşa Caddesi, turn left up Prof Sıddık Sami

Onar Caddesi and you will come to one of the most majestic of all Ottoman mosques and the last stop on this tour, the **Süleymaniye Camii** (**15**; p110). Reward your efforts with a tea at Lale Bahçesi (p149) or a quick, tasty bite to eat at Tarihi Süleymani Yeli Kuru Fasulyeci (p137).

COURSES

Note that prices for courses are usually set in euros rather than TL.

Cooking

Cooking Alaturca (Map pp92-3; ☎ 0212-458 5919; www.cookingalaturka.com; Akbiyik Caddesi 72a, Sultanahmet) Owner Eveline Zoutendijk runs excellent, hands-on Turkish cooking classes (€60 per person) from her restaurant-cum-cooking school in Sultanahmet. The delicious results are enjoyed over a five-course lunch with drinks.

İstanbul Food Workshop (Map pp86-7; ☎ 0212-534 4788; www.istanbulfoodworkshop.com; Yıldırım Caddesi 111, Fener) A well-respected outfit running walking tours for foodies as well as cooking classes focusing on both Turkish and Ottoman cuisine.

Handicrafts

Caferağa Medresesi (Map pp92-3; ☎ 0212-513 3601; www.tkhv.org; Caferiye Sokak, Sultanahmet) This gorgeous building is the home of the Turkish Cultural Services Foundation, which runs courses for locals and travellers in techniques such as calligraphy, miniature painting, *ebru* (traditional Turkish marbling), binding and glass painting. Courses are organised into 2½-hour sessions one day per week over three months and cost TL360. It also occasionally organises day courses costing TL36.

Language

Taksim Dilmer (Map pp94-5; ☎ 0212-292 9696; www .dilmer.com; Tarık Zafer Tunaya Sokak 18, Taksim) This is probably the best-known of the city's Turkish language schools. On offer are eight-week courses (96 hours total) costing €384; four-week courses (80 hours total) costing €320; 12-week weekend courses (72 hours) costing €288; and eight-week evening courses (72 hours) costing €288. Classes have a maximum of 14 students.

İSTANBUL FOR CHILDREN

Children of all ages will enjoy the **Rahmi M Koç Müzesi** (p125). The spooky **Basilica Cistern** (p101), with its upside-down heads on columns, is always a hit, as is the ferry trip down the Bosphorus, particularly if it's combined with a visit to the fortress of **Rumeli Hisarı** (p122) – but beware of the steep stairs here, which have no barriers. On **Büyükada** (p165)

and **Heybeliada** (p165), two of the Princes' Islands, you can hire bikes or circle the island in a *fayton* (horse-drawn carriage), which is lots of fun. The Mehter band playing at the **Askeri Müzesi** (p117) is usually a winner, too.

If you're staying in Sultanahmet, there are two small playgrounds near the Cankurtaran train station, and a bigger, busier one in Kadırga Park close by. If you're staying in Beyoğlu, the limited options are at least better quality: there's one in Tophane, a better one at Cihangir Park and one at the Fındıklı station of the tramline, right by the water's edge – very scenic!

If you need to resort to bribery to ensure good behaviour, there's a toyshop area in Eminönü. The biggest and best shop here is **Ekincioğlu Toys & Gifts** (Map pp90-1; ☎ 0212-522 6220; Kalçın Sokak 5; Eminönü; ♥ 9am-7pm). And there's a small shop in Beyoğlu: **İyigün Oyuncak** (Map pp94-5; ☎ 0212-243 8910; İstiklal Caddesi 415; ♥ 9am-9pm).

TOURS

Note that tour companies in İstanbul set their charges in euros rather than TL.

City Tours

İstanbul Vision/City Sightseeing bus (☎ 0212-234 7777; www.plantours.com; one-day ticket adult/student & 7-12yr/under 7yr €20/15/free) This is a naff hop-on-hop-off double-decker bus service with multi-language recorded commentary. Ticket booths are opposite Aya Sofya and in Taksim Sq or you can purchase tickets on the bus. The full circuit takes 90 minutes or you can get on and off the bus at any of the 60 stops around town, but buses only run a few times a day. Departure times change regularly so double-check ahead of time. Expect traffic congestion on the Beyoğlu section.

İstanboul Insolite (Map pp86-7; ☎ 0212-241 2846; www.istanbulguide.net/insolite; Bahtiyar Sokak 6, Nişantaşı; full-day tours per person €50-150) This small agency runs a variety of offbeat tours including the intriguing 'superstitious İstanbul', a caravanserais tour, a walk through Fener and Balat, and a 'forgotten churches' tour. English, German and French are spoken.

Kirkit Voyage (Map pp92-3; ☎ 0212-518 2282; www .kirkit.com; Amiral Tafdil Sokak 12, Sultanahmet; half- & full-day tours €23-50) This small agency specialises in small-group walking tours of the must-see sights as well as 'İstanbul the Unusual Way' and 'Asian İstanbul and its markets' tours. English and French are spoken.

Les Arts Turcs (Map pp92-3; ☎ 0212-458 1318; www .lesartsturcs.com; 3rd fl, İncili Çavuş Sokak 37, Sultanahmet; ♥ 10am-8pm) If you've ever wanted to learn *ebru*, belly dance like a gypsy or become a calligrapher, Les Arts

Turcs can make it happen. This isn't a standard tour operator, it's a collective of artists, writers and historians who come and go from a welcoming studio in Sultanahmet. Some of the courses and tours on offer include observing a dervish *sema* at a *tekke* in Fatih (€25), taking private Turkish lessons (€100 to €150 for a 2- to 3-hour crash course), and joining walking tours of the city's historic neighbourhoods (€50 to €85). It has a second office at İshakpaşa Caddesi 6, Cankurtaran, next to the entrance to Topkapı Palace.

Senkron Travel Agency (Map pp92-3; ☎ 0212-638 8340; www.senkrontours.com; Arasta Bazaar 51, Sultanahmet; full-day tours €25-60 per person; ⊗ 8am-9pm) This professional outfit offers 10 different tours, including a day tour of the Bosphorus and Dolmabahçe Palace and one of the Christian highlights of the city.

FESTIVALS & EVENTS

During the warmer months İstanbul is buzzing with arts and music events, giving the visitor plenty of options when it comes to entertainment. Most of the big-name arts festivals are organised by the **İstanbul Foundation for Culture & Arts** (☎ 0212-334 0700; www.istfest.org). Tickets to most events are available from Biletix (see p151). Headline events include the following:

April
International İstanbul Film Festival (www.iksv .org/film) Held early in the month, the program includes retrospectives and recent releases from Turkey and abroad.
International İstanbul Tulip Festival The city's parks and gardens are resplendent with tulips from late March to early April each year.

June
Efes Pilsen One Love (www.pozitif-ist.com) This two-day music festival held at Santralİstanbul (p125) features international headline acts playing everything from punk to pop, electronica to disco.
International İstanbul Music Festival (www.iksv .org/muzik) The city's most famous arts festival.

July
International İstanbul Jazz Festival (www.iksv .org/caz) The number-one jazz festival in town is an intriguing hybrid of conventional jazz, electronica, world music and rock.

August
Electronica Festival İstanbul (www.electronicafest .com, in Turkish) This popular two-day festival at Park Orman features international DJs and live electronica acts duelling it out on open-air stages.

September
International İstanbul Biennial (www.istfest.org) The city's major visual-arts shindig takes place from early September to early November in odd-numbered years.

October
Akbank Jazz Festival (www.akbanksanat.com) This boutique event features traditional and avant-garde jazz, as well as Middle Eastern fusions and a program of young jazz.

November
Efes Pilsen Blues Festival (www.pozitif-ist.com) This long-running event tours nationally and stops for a two-day program in İstanbul.

SLEEPING

Every accommodation style is available in İstanbul. You can live like a sultan in a world-class luxury hotel, doss in a friendly hostel dorm, or relax in a well-priced boutique establishment.

Hotels reviewed here have rooms with private bathroom and include breakfast, usually of the Turkish variety, in the room price. Exceptions are noted in the reviews. All prices given are for high season and include the 8% value-added tax (*katma değer vergisi*, KDV). During low season (October to April, but not around Christmas or Easter) you should be able to negotiate a discount of at least 20% on the price. Before you confirm any booking, ask if the hotel will give you a discount for cash payment (usually 10% but can be higher), whether a pick-up from the airport is included (it often is if you stay more than three nights) and whether there are discounts for extended stays. Book ahead from May to September.

Note that all hotels in İstanbul set their prices in euros, and we have listed them as such here.

For more accommodation reviews by Lonely Planet authors for İstanbul, check out the online booking service at www.lonely planet.com/hotels.

Sultanahmet & Around

The Sultan Ahmet Camii (Blue Mosque), gives its name to the quarter surrounding it. This is the heart of Old İstanbul and is the city's premier sightseeing area, so the hotels here, and in the adjoining neighbourhoods to the east (Cankurtaran), west (Küçük Aya Sofya) and north (Binbirdirek and Çemberlitaş) are supremely convenient. The area's only drawbacks are the number of carpet touts around and the lack of decent bars and restaurants.

BUDGET

Mavi Guesthouse (Map pp92-3; ☎ 0212-517 7287; www .maviguesthouse.com; Kutlugün Sokak 3, Sultanahmet; rooftop mattress/dm/d €8/12/36; 💻) The management at Mavi is very friendly, which is just as well since some rooms at this tiny place are cramped and windowless, and all have extremely uncomfortable beds. Die-hard backpackers might want to claim one of the 24 mattresses that are squeezed onto the decrepit rooftop and share one shower and toilet. Breakfast is served downstairs or at streetside tables, and there's a kitchen for communal use. Avoid the double rooms – they're ridiculously overpriced.

Bahaus Guesthouse (Map pp92-3; ☎ 0212-638 6534; www.travelinistanbul.com; Kutlugün Sokak 3, Cankurtaran; dm €15, d with/without bathroom €50/40; ✖ 💻) When it comes to hostels, word of mouth is the most reliable gauge of quality. And this place generates great word of mouth. Friendly and knowledgeable staff run a professional operation that's miles away from the institutional feel of some of its nearby and much larger competitors. Dorms have bunks with good mattresses and curtains to provide a skerrick of privacy; some have their own bathroom and all have ceiling fans. There's one shared bathroom for every seven beds and a constant supply of lukewarm water. Top marks go to the rooftop terrace bar.

Sultan Hostel (Map pp92-3; ☎ 0212-516 9260; www .sultanhostel.com; Akbıyık Sokak 21, Cankurtaran; dm €14, d with/without bathroom €44/38; ✖ 💻) Next door to – and clearly in hot competition with – the Orient, this place has recently undergone a renovation. As a result, it offers accommodation that is far more comfortable than that provided by its raffish neighbour. The freshly painted dorms have new bunk beds and good mattresses; linen is clean and crisp and towels are provided. Shared bathrooms are very clean and there are female-only dorms for those gals who want to steer clear of smelly socks. The pick of the rooms on offer is number 48, a double with lovely Sea of Marmara views and its own cubicle bathroom. Views from the terrace bar aren't as impressive as those at the Orient, but its set-up is much more relaxed and stylish. There's a 10% discount for HI cardholders.

Orient International Hostel (Map pp92-3; ☎ 0212-518 0789; www.orienthostel.com; Akbıyık Caddesi 13, Cankurtaran; dm €14, s without bathroom €30, d with bathroom €70; ✖ 💻) Always packed to the rafters with backpackers, the Orient should only be considered if you're young, don't care about creature comforts and are ready to party. There's a shower for every 12 guests, and an array of dorms, some of which are light and relatively quiet and others that are unpleasantly dark and have the most uncomfortable mattresses that we've ever encountered (and considering our job, that's really saying something). The cheapest option is a barracks-style 30-bed dorm. The rooftop terrace bar has fabulous views and is a good place to relax, unlike the noisy cafeteria and internet area (they're great meeting places, though). Private rooms are ludicrously overpriced for what they offer.

our pick **Hotel Peninsula** (Map pp92-3; ☎ 0212-458 6850; www.hotelpeninsula.com; Adliye Sokak 6, Cankurtaran; s/d €35/45; ✖ ❖) The management of this unassuming hotel could quite possibly be the friendliest we've ever encountered. And we're talking friendly in a good, nonpushy, we-really-like-meeting-people type of way, not the hi-I'm-your-new-best-friend-please-visit-my-carpet-shop kind of way. There are 12 comfortable rooms with private bathroom here, as well as a lovely terrace with sea views and comfortable hammocks. The breakfast room has traditional low stools and brass tables, and the owner's mum makes cakes, jam and yoghurt for everyone's breakfast. Great value.

Side Hotel & Pension (Map pp92-3; ☎ 0212-517 2282; www.sidehotel.com; Utangaç Sokak 20, Cankurtaran; hotel s/d €50/70, pension s/d without bathroom €30/40, pension s/d with bathroom €40/50, 2-/4-person apt €85-110; ✖ ❖ 💻) This sprawling place offers rooms that are clean and comfortable, but lack atmosphere. Those in the hotel have satellite TVs and basic bathrooms; the pension alternatives (some of which are noisy) come with either shared or private facilities. There are also fully equipped but dark apartments sleeping one to six people. Meagre breakfasts are served at the pleasant rooftop garden-lounge. Note that air-con costs an extra €10 per room per night.

MIDRANGE

Hanedan Hotel (Map pp92-3; ☎ 0212-516 4869; www .hanedanhotel.com; Adliye Sokak 3, Cankurtaran; s €40, d €60-65; ✖ ❖) Pale lemon walls and polished wooden floors give the Hanedan's rooms a light and elegant feel, as do the white marble bathrooms and firm beds covered with crisp white linen. A pleasant roof terrace overlooks the sea and Aya Sofya.

Hotel Alp Guesthouse (Map pp92-3; ☎ 0212-517 7067; www.alpguesthouse.com; Adliye Sokak 4, Cankurtaran; s/d €45/65; ✗ ✗) The Alp lives up to its location in Sultanahmet's premier small-hotel enclave, offering a range of attractive and well-equipped rooms at remarkably reasonable prices. Rooms have four-poster beds with white linen and gold hangings, wooden floorboards scattered with rugs, and extras such as satellite TV and work desks. The spacious front rooms are the pick of the bunch. The roof terrace is lovely, with great sea views and comfortable indoor and outdoor set-ups.

Hali Hotel (Map pp92-3; ☎ 0212-516 2170; www.halihotel.com; Klodfarer Caddesi 20, Çemberlitaş; s/d €45/75; ✗) All the rugs in Turkey couldn't hide this hotel's institutional feel. That said, it's worth considering because of the amazing views from the roof terrace, the huge bathrooms and its very quiet position. Third and fourth-floor rooms have views of the Sea of Marmara and Aya Sofya.

Hotel Alaturka (Map pp92-3; ☎ 0212-458 7900; www.hotelalaturka.com; Akbıyık Caddesi 5, Cankurtaran; s €70, d €85-105; ✗ ✗) Large rooms with mod cons such as minibars and satellite TVs are the hallmarks of this immaculately maintained hotel. The decor is conservative, but pleasantly so, and the roof terrace has one of the best views in the area.

Hotel Şebnem (Map pp92-3; ☎ 0212-517 6623; www.sebnemhotel.net; Adliye Sokak 1, Cankurtaran; s €70, d €90-100; ✗ ✗) Simplicity is the rule at the Şebnem, and it works a treat. Rooms have wooden floors, recently renovated bathrooms and comfortable beds. Framed Ottoman prints provide a touch of class. The large terrace upstairs has views over the Sea of Marmara (as do the more expensive double rooms), and downstairs rooms face onto a pretty private courtyard garden. Breakfast is good here, too.

Hotel Ararat (Map pp92-3; ☎ 0212-516 0411; www.ararathotel.com; Torun Sokak 3, Cankurtaran; r €75-110; ✗ ✗ ✗) The Ararat is tiny, but its charming host Haydar Sarigul and cosy rooftop terrace-bar in the shadow of the Blue Mosque make it a popular choice. Dark wooden floors, textile bedspreads and clever space-enhancing mirrors are the decorative hallmarks; quality linen and homemade *börek* (savoury pastry) for breakfast are quality touches. It's not worth paying the extra euros for a room with a view, particularly as the two terrace rooms are the smallest in the hotel.

Hotel Poem (Map pp92-3; ☎ 0212-638 9744; www.hotelpoem.com; Terbıyık Sokak 12; s €55, d €80-150; ✗ ✗ ✗) Many guests end up waxing lyrical about their stays in this cute hotel. Rooms are named after poems by well-known Turkish poets, and the tranquil rear garden is a perfect spot to linger over an anthology and a glass of tea. Some rooms are on the small side and lack style; others have huge beds, balconies and sea views. All are clean and have amenities such as satellite TV and hairdryer.

Hotel Uyan İstanbul (Map pp92-3; ☎ 0212-518 9255; www.uyanhotel.com; Utangaç Sokak 25, Cankurtaran; s €50, d standard/deluxe €99/150; ✗ ✗ ✗) The Uyan offers comfortable and attractive rooms with a good range of amenities. The elegant decor nods towards the Ottoman style, but never goes over the top – everyone will feel comfortable here. The view from the spacious roof terrace is one of the best in the area and the breakfast buffet is generous.

Tan Hotel (Map pp92-3; ☎ 0212-520 9130; www.tanhotel.com; Dr Emin Paşa Sokak 20, Alemdar; s/d €85/100; ✗ ✗ ✗) This well-run hotel off Divan Yolu is a showcase of understated modern style and high-level service. Everything here is brand spanking new; rooms are generously sized and bathrooms are excellent (all have Jacuzzis). There's even a terrace bar sporting excellent views of the Blue Mosque, Aya Sofya and the Sea of Marmara. We love the lavish breakfast buffet, too.

Hotel Nomade (Map pp92-3; ☎ 0212-513 8172; www.hotelnomade.com; Ticarethane Sokak 15, Alemdar; s €75, d €90-105; ✗ ✗) Mega style and budget pricing don't often go together, but the Nomade bucks the trend. Just a few steps off busy Divan Yolu, the hotel's 16 small rooms and three suites have great bathrooms, stylish bedlinen and satellite TV. With one of the best roof-terrace bars in town (smack-bang in front of Aya Sofya) and a Philippe Starck feel, this place is about as hip as Sultanahmet gets.

Sari Konak Oteli (Map pp92-3; ☎ 0212-638 6258; www.istanbulhotelsarikonak.com; Mimar Mehmet Ağa Caddesi 42-46, Cankurtaran; r standard/deluxe €99/129, ste €199; ✗ ✗ ✗) The Sarı Konak is a truly classy joint. Its spacious deluxe rooms are beautifully decorated with soothing colour schemes, top-notch linens and attractive prints, embroideries and etchings on the walls; the standard rooms are considerably smaller, but are just as attractive; and the suites are total knockouts – perfect for families. Guests enjoy relaxing on the roof terrace with its Sea of Marmara and Blue Mosque views, but seem to be equally partial to hanging out in the downstairs lounge and courtyard.

our pick **Hotel Empress Zoe** (Map pp92-3; ☎ 0212-518 2504; www.emzoe.com; Adliye Sokak 10, Cankurtaran; s €75, d €110-135, ste €120-240; ✗ 🔀 🖳) Named after the feisty Byzantine empress whose portrait adorns the gallery at Aya Sofya, this fabulous place is owned and managed by American Ann Nevens and her sister Cristina, who really know their stuff when it comes to running a boutique hotel. All rooms and suites are individually and charmingly decorated, and although some rooms in the main building are tiny, these are available at discounted rates (single/double €55/65). There's a gorgeous flower-filled garden where breakfast is served and a rooftop lounge-terrace with excellent views.

Ottoman Hotel Imperial (Map pp92-3; ☎ 0212-513 6150/1; www.ottomanhotelimperial.com; Caferiye Sokak 6/1; standard s/d €100/120, superior s/d €200/240; ✗ 🔀 🖳) This four-star choice is in a wonderful location just outside the Topkapı Palace walls. Once the city's main youth hostel, the building has been extensively renovated and features large rooms decorated with Ottoman-style ceramics, textiles and *ebru*. Comfort and amenity levels are high, and some rooms have Aya Sofya views. No roof terrace, but there's a lovely rear garden with restaurant and bar instead.

Kybele Hotel (Map pp92-3; ☎ 0212-511 7766; www.kybelehotel.com; Yerebatan Caddesi 35, Alemdar; s €80, d €110-140; 🔀 🖳) The gilded exterior of this small hotel reflects the decor inside, which features hundreds of coloured lights, wooden floors covered in rugs, and antique furniture and curios. Run by three brothers in a personable and professional style, it's got bucketloads of charm and lots of added extras, including a great café/bar, a charming rear garden patio and a library for guests. Rooms, which feature cute marble bathrooms, are smallish but comfortable.

Ayasofya Konakları (Map pp92-3; ☎ 0212-513 3660; www.ayasofyakonaklari.com; Soğukçeşme Sokak; s €120-140, d €170-200; 🔀 🖳) If you're keen to play out Ottoman fantasies, come here. Picturesque Ayasofya Konakları is set in a row of 19th-century wooden houses occupying an entire cobbled street abutting Topkapı Palace. Choose from a total of 63 rooms, all of which are comfortable and charmingly decorated.

Breakfast is served in a glass conservatory complete with chandeliers.

İbrahim Paşa Oteli (Map pp92-3; ☎ 0212-518 0394; www.ibrahimpasha.com; Terzihane Sokak 5, Binbirdirek; r standard/deluxe €125/175; ✗ 🔀 🖳) No doubt Ibrahim Paşa would have given the nod to this mod Ottoman renovation borrowing his name. Successfully combining Ottoman style with contemporary decor, this boutique hotel has been keeping guests happy for a number of years now and looks as if it will increase its popularity now that its new, purpose-built extension with impressive terrace bar has opened.

TOP END

Sirkeci Konak (Map pp92-3; ☎ 0212-528 4344; Taya Hatun Sokak 5, Sirkeci; r €190-320; ✗ 🔀 🖳) This terrific hotel overlooking Gülhane Parkı opened in 2007. The owners run other hotels in the Sirkeci neighbourhood and know what keeps guests happy – rooms are all large and well equipped, with extras such as tea- and coffee-making equipment, satellite TV, quality toiletries and luxe linen. There's also a wellness centre with pool, gym and hamam in the basement – a rarity on this side of town. Top marks go to the complimentary afternoon teas and Anatolian cooking lessons.

Tria Hotel İstanbul (Map pp92-3; ☎ 0212-518 4518; www.triahotelistanbul.com; Turbıyık Sokak 7, Cankurtaran; s €180, d standard/ superior €218/280; ✗ 🔀 🖳) The old adage that handsome is as handsome does certainly applies to the Tria. Extremely comfortable and quiet rooms offer tea-and-coffee making equipment, flat-screen TV, work desk and large bed; all are attractively decorated with polished floorboards, silk curtains, embroidered bedspreads and objets d'art. There's a comfortable lounge on the ground floor and a roof terrace with great views. Prices plummet in low season.

Four Seasons Hotel İstanbul (Map pp92-3; ☎ 0212-638 8200; www.fourseasons.com; Tevkifhane Sokak 1, Sultanahmet; r €280-500; ✗ 🔀 🖳) What used to be the infamous Sultanahmet prison (remember *Midnight Express*?) is now one of İstanbul's swankiest hotels. Known for its service (extraordinary), history (deliciously disreputable), location (right in the heart of Old İstanbul) and rooms (wow), it's the king of the city's hotels. Its new sister establishment on the Bosphorus at Beşiktaş might be one of the only İstanbul hotels capable of knocking it off its long-held throne.

Beyoğlu & Around

Most travellers to İstanbul stay in Sultanahmet, but Beyoğlu is becoming a popular alternative. Stay here to avoid the touts in the old city, and because buzzing, bohemian Beyoğlu has the best wining, dining and shopping in the city. Unfortunately there isn't the range or quality of accommodation options here that you'll find in Sultanahmet – the exception being an ever-increasing number of stylish apartment hotels and apartment rentals. These often command spectacular Bosphorus and Golden Horn views – something you pay for by having to climb six or seven floors of stairs.

Getting to/from the historical sights of Old İstanbul from Beyoğlu is easy: you can either walk across the Galata Bridge (approximately 45 minutes), or catch the Taksim Sq–Kabataş funicular and tram.

BUDGET

World House Hostel (Map pp94–5; ☎ 0212-293 5520; www.worldhouseistanbul.com; Galipdede Caddesi 117, Galata; dm €10-13, d €38; ✕ ▯) Hostels in İstanbul are usually impersonal hulks with jungle-like atmospheres, but World House is small, friendly and calm. Best of all is the fact that it's close to Beyoğlu's restaurant, bar and club scene, but not *too* close – meaning that it's possible to grab a decent night's kip here. The eight-bed dorms are clean and light, with good mattresses and decent linen. Bathrooms are in plentiful supply and there's a cheerful café on the ground floor.

International House (Map pp94–5; ☎ 212-244 3773; www.ihouseistanbul.com; 5 Zambak Sokak, Beyoğlu; dm €8.50-13, d €39; ✕ ▯) The young and enthusiastic owners of World House Hostel also run a second hostel, just off İstiklal Caddesi. This one is right in the thick of the action, so steer clear if you're a light sleeper.

MIDRANGE

Büyük Londra Oteli (Map pp94–5; ☎ 0212-245 0670; www.londrahotel.net; Meşrutiyet Caddesi 117, Tepebaşı; unrenovated s €35-60, d €50-80, renovated s/d €75/85; ▧) The highlight of the 1892 Büyük Londra is its wonderfully preserved lounge, which has barely been touched since it hosted well-heeled passengers fresh off the *Orient Express*. We love the ruffled curtains dangling with tassels, the decorated mouldings, the deep maroon carpets and the bar. The gilded staircase, complete with mammoth Bohemian crystal chandelier, leads up to the rooms…and this, folks, is where our enthusiasm falters. Some of the rooms are musty and worn (very *Addams Family*). Book one that's been recently renovated – these have air-con and are comfortable.

Vardar Palace Hotel (Map pp94–5; ☎ 0212-252 2888; www.vardarhotel.com; Sıraselviler Caddesi 16, Taksim; s €46-69, d €85-96; ▧ ▯) This hotel just off Taksim Sq offers excellent value for money and so is well worth considering. Rooms at the rear are darkish and quiet, front rooms are light but face onto a noisy nightclub strip – all are very clean and come with cable TV. There's a roof terrace with great views.

Eklektik Guest House (Map pp94–5; ☎ 0212-243 7446; www.eklektikgalata.com; Kadrıbey Çıkmazi 4, Galata; r €95-115; ✕ ▧ ▯) Advertising itself as offering 'the first and only gay accommodation in İstanbul', this gay-owned-and-managed place offers seven individually decorated rooms with satellite TV. You can enact fantasies in the Pasha Room, chill out after a big night in the Zen Room or just feel funky in the Retro Room. Think about booking one of the more expensive rooms, as these have the best bathrooms. The staff here are both friendly and helpful.

Manzara İstanbul (☎ 0212-252 4660; www.manzara-istanbul.com/en; office 2nd fl, Galata Kulesi Sokak 3; apt per night €65-160) Turkish/German architect and artist Erdoğan Altindiş has stylishly renovated 14 residential apartments around Galata, Cihangir and Kabataş that he rents out to holiday makers. Sleeping between one and six people, these offer well-priced alternatives to hotels in the area. A number of the apartments have extraordinary Bosphorus views, some have wi-fi and a couple have air-con.

İstanbul Holiday Apartments (☎ 0212-251 8530; www.istanbulholidayapartments.com; apt per night €115-260; minimum stay 3 or 7 nights; ▧ ▯) Saying that holiday apartments in İstanbul are easy to find is like saying the sultans were celibate, which is why the ever-expanding portfolio of apartments run by American Ann Taboroff Uysel is as unique as it is welcome. Now in locations as diverse as Galata, Cihangir, Taksim, Şişli and Beşiktaş, these handsome apartments sleeping between one and seven people are perfect for city sojourns of three days or more. All are fitted out with washer/drier, good kitchens, CD players and satellite TVs; some have air-con and/or dishwashers and some have knock-'em-dead views over the Golden Horn and Bosphorus.

İSTANBUL

TOP END

Anemon Galata (Map pp94-5; ☎ 0212-293 2343; www
.anemonhotels.com; cnr Galata Meydanı & Büyükhendek
Caddesi, Galata; s/d €120/140; ☒ ☒ ☐) Located on
the attractive square that's been built around
Galata Tower, this wooden building dates
from 1842 but has been almost completely rebuilt inside. Individually decorated rooms are
extremely elegant, featuring ornate painted
ceilings, king-sized beds and antique-style
desks. Large bathrooms have baths and marble basins. Best of all is the restaurant, which
boasts one of the best views in the city. Book
well ahead and request a room with a view.

our pick **Istanbul Suites** (Map pp94-5; ☎ 0212-393
7900; www.wittistanbul.com; Defterdar Yokuşu 26, Cihangir;
ste per night €150-290; ☒) Opened in 2008, this
stylish apartment hotel is a real find. Just up
the hill from the Tophane tram stop in the
trendy suburb of Cihangir, it has 15 suites
with fully equipped marble kitchenettes, seating areas with flat-screen satellite TVs, CD/
DVD players, king-sized beds and huge bathrooms (Molton Brown toiletries). Some suites
look over to the old city and the top-floor
gym has a panoramic view of the Bosphorus.
There's a café and 24-hour reception; weekly
and long-term rates are available.

Richmond Hotel (Map pp94-5; ☎ 0212-252 5460;
www.richmondhotels.com.tr; İstiklal Caddesi 445, Tünel; s
€149-175, d €159-199, ste €279; ☒ ☐ ☒) Next to the
palatial Russian consulate, the Richmond has
a fabulous location right on the city's major
boulevard. Behind its 19th-century facade,
the place is modern, quite comfortable and
well run. Standard rooms are comfortable
and well set up, and the suites are knock-outs,
with modernist decor, excellent views, great
workstation, Jacuzzi and plasma TV. Best of all
is the fact that one of the best bars in the city
(Leb-i Derya Richmond) is on the top floor,
meaning that your bed will only be a short
stagger away. A mainly business clientele
keeps the place busy, so book ahead.

Marmara Pera (Map pp94-5; ☎ 0212-251 4646; www
.themarmarahotels.com; Meşrutiyet Caddesi 1, Tepebaşı; standard s/d €140/160, superior s/d €210/240; ☒ ☒ ☐ ☒ ☒)
This funky little sister of the landmark hotel
in Taksim Sq opened in 2004 and has been a
popular choice with glam globetrotters ever
since. Rooms are smallish but extremely well
appointed, featuring quality touches such as
a magazine selection, pillow menu and stylish white linen. Stand-out amenities include
one of the best restaurants in the city (Mikla,

see p139), a rooftop pool bar with spectacular
views, and a 24-hour fitness centre. It's worth
paying extra for a room on a higher floor with
sea view. Breakfast costs an extra €20.

Beşiktaş & Ortaköy
TOP END

Radisson SAS Bosphorus Hotel (Map p97; ☎ 0212-310
1500; www.radissonsas.com; Çırağan Caddesi 46, Ortaköy;
r standard/superior €220/255, ste €510; ☒ ☒ ☐ ☒)
Stay here if you're in town to party at the
Bosphorus superclubs. Prominently located
on the Golden Mile, it offers 120 well-sized
and very comfortable rooms, some of which
have Bosphorus views and all of which share
the modern style that the Radisson chain is
known for. There's a spa and wellness centre
on site (no pool, though), as well as a branch
of the London-based Japanese restaurant,
Zuma. Breakfast costs an extra €20.

W İstanbul (Map p97; ☎ 0212-381 2121; www
.whotels.com/istanbul; Suleyman Seba Caddesi 22, Akaretler; r
€300-432, ste €560-10,590; ☒ ☒) Opened in 2008,
this uberstylish 'design hotel' is located between the glam shopping district of Nişantaşi
and the party precinct along the Bosphorus.
Though the setting is historic (the 1890s
building housed domestic staff working at
Dolmabahçe Palace), the renovation here is
unrelentingly modern and highly theatrical.
Rooms have good work desks, comfortable
beds and fabulous bathrooms with hamam-
influenced showers. There's an Estee Lauder
day spa, a fitness centre and a branch of New
York's Spice Market restaurant. Breakfast
costs an extra €12 to €24.

EATING
İstanbul is a food-lover's paradise. Teeming
with affordable fast-food joints, cafés and
restaurants, it leaves visitors spoiled for
choice when it comes to choosing a venue.
Unfortunately, Sultanahmet has the least
impressive range of eating options in the
city. Rather than eating here at night, we
recommend crossing the Galata Bridge and
joining the locals in Beyoğlu, Ortaköy and
the Bosphorus suburbs. Absolutely nothing
can beat the enjoyment of spending a night
in a *meyhane* on Nevizade Sokak or in the
Asmalımescit quarter (both in Beyoğlu), or
dining at one of the swish restaurants on the
Bosphorus. There are other pockets of town
worth investigating – Eminönü has the enjoyable Hamdi Et Lokantası and Zinhan Kebap

House, Samatya is home to the best kebaps in town at Develi, and Edirnekapı has the excellent Asitane – but on the whole you will be well served by making your way across the Galata Bridge every night.

If you are planning to take a ferry trip to Üsküdar, Kadıköy, the upper reaches of the Bosphorus or the Golden Horn, we have listed dining recommendations in the Asian Shore (p119) and Ferry Cruises (p121) sections.

Close to Sultanahmet there are a number of small supermarkets. The best is **Greens** (Map pp92-3; Nuriosmaniye Sokak 1, Cağaloğlu; ⊙ 7am-8.30pm). Beyoğlu also has many small supermarkets (including Gima) open daily; most are along Sıraselviler Caddesi, running off Taksim Sq.

Sultanahmet & Around
RESTAURANTS
Sefa Restaurant (Map pp92-3; ☎ 0212-520 0670; Nuruosmaniye Caddesi 17, Cağaloğlu; mains TL6.50-16; ⊙ 7am-5pm) Locals rate this place on the way to the Grand Bazaar highly, and after sampling the simple dishes on offer you'll understand why. You can order from an English-language menu or choose from the bain-marie. Try to arrive early for lunch because many of the dishes run out by 1.30pm.

Buhara Restaurant & Ocakbaşı (Map pp92-3; ☎ 0212-527 5133; Nuruosmaniye Caddesi 7a, Cağaloğlu; kebaps TL10-17; ⊙ 11am-10pm) If you're craving a kebap and haven't the time or inclination to walk down the hill to Eminönü's Hamdi Et Lokantası (p136) or Zinhan (p137), this unassuming eatery might be the solution. Management can be gruff and the servings are on the small side, but the quality of the meat is consistently good.

Kİr Evi (Map pp92-3; ☎ 0212-512 6042; Hoca Rüstem Sokak 9; mains TL16.50-21; ⊙ 10.30am-2.30am) We were in two minds as to whether we should include this place, but the infectious exuberance of its management and the enormous amount of fun that customers were having when we visited ruled in its favour. Meals are worthy of comment for their size and reasonable price rather than their quality, but the biggest draw is the entertainment. The owner and waiters serenade guests with everything from Donna Summer disco anthems to emotional Turkish arabesk numbers, and everyone joins in (well, they do after the second and third bottle of wine has been opened at their table). Not the place for a romantic dinner.

Dubb (Map pp92-3; ☎ 0212-513 7308; İncili Çavuş Sokak, Alemdar; mains TL12-24; ⊙ noon-3pm & 6-10.30pm) One of İstanbul's few Indian restaurants, Dubb specialises in mild tandoori dishes, but also serves a large range of fragrant curries, including vegetarian options. Its outdoor terrace on the 4th floor offers fabulous views of Aya Sofya.

Cooking Alaturca (Map pp92-3; ☎ 0212-458 5919; www.cookingalaturka.com; Akbıyık Caddesi 72a, Sultanahmet; set lunch TL40; ⊙ lunch only; ✗) This great little restaurant is run by Dutch-born foodie Eveline Zoutendijk, who both knows and loves Anatolian food. She serves a set four-course menu that changes daily according to what produce is in season and what's best at the local markets. Eveline says that she aims to create a little haven in the midst of carpet-selling frenzy and she has indeed done this. She also sells unusual and authentic produce such as homemade jams, pomegranate vinegar and *pekmez* (grape molasses), as well as cook books and Turkish cooking utensils.

Sarnıç (Map pp92-3; ☎ 0212-512 4291; Soğukçeşme Sokak; mains TL20-30; ⊙ 7-11pm) It's not every day you get to dine in a wonderfully atmospheric candle-lit Byzantine cistern, so we're listing Sarnıç despite the fact that its food can be somewhat disappointing. Book ahead.

Teras Restaurant (Map pp92-3; ☎ 0212-638 1370; Hotel Armada, Ahırkapı Sokak, Cankurtaran; mains TL20-34; ⊙ 7-11pm) The chef at this upmarket hotel restaurant came up with an inspired idea when he devised his Turkish degustation menu (TL58). Six sampling courses of 'İstanbul cuisine' feature and are complemented by an excellent and affordable wine list. You can also order from the à la carte menu – the fish is particularly good. Book a terrace table with a Blue Mosque view.

Balıkçı Sabahattin (Map pp92-3; ☎ 0212-458 1824; Seyit Hasan Koyu Sokak 1, Cankurtaran; mains TL25-60; ⊙ noon-midnight; ✗) The limos outside Balıkçı Sabahattın pay testament to its enduring popularity with the city's establishment, who join hoards of cashed-up tourists in enjoying its limited menu of meze and fish. The food here is excellent, though the service can be harried. You'll dine in a wooden Ottoman house or under a leafy canopy in the garden. It's wise to book.

Giritli (Map pp92-3; ☎ 0212-458 2270; Keresteci Hakkı Sokak, Cankurtaran; set menus TL75; ⊙ 11am-11pm) Bring a big appetite to enjoy Giritli's set banquet menu, which offers over 10 types of hot and cold meze, octopus, fish and more. Alcohol is included in the price, but don't expect the quality of the tipple to match that of the excellent Cretan fare it accompanies. Summer dining is in a courtyard; in winter, patrons dine in a rickety wooden house.

CAFÉS

Çiğdem Pastanesi (Map pp92-3; ☎ 0212-526 8859; Divan Yolu Caddesi 62a; ☯ 8am-11pm) Çiğdem Pastanesi has been serving locals since 1961 and it's still going strong. The *ay çöreği* (pastry with a walnut, sultana and spice filling) is the perfect accompaniment to a cappuccino and the *su böreği* (soft cheese *börek*) goes wonderfully well with a cup of tea or fresh juice.

Hafız Mustafa Şekerlemeleri (Map p109; ☎ 0212-526 5627; Hamidiye Caddesi 84-86, Eminönü; ☯ 11am-7pm Mon-Sat) Choosing between the delicious baklava, tasty *börek* or indulgent *meshur tekirdağ peyniri helvası* (a cheese-based sweet prepared with sesame oil, cereals and honey or syrup) is the challenge that confronts customers at this popular place in Eminönü. You can enjoy your choice with a glass of tea in the upstairs café.

Java Studio (Map pp92-3; ☎ 0212-517 2378; Dalbastı Sokak 13; ☯ 7am-11pm) Celebrating the 'fine art of coffee', this laid-back café in the shadow of the Blue Mosque offers an extensive list of coffees, teas, milkshakes and lassis, accompanied by freshly baked cakes. There's comfortable seating, chess and backgammon, free wi-fi and a book exchange.

QUICK EATS

Nominating the best take-away döner kebap in Sultanahmet is a hard ask; all we'll say is that many locals are keen on the *döner* (TL4 to TL9) served at **Sedef Meşhur Dönerci** (Map pp92-3), just up from the McDonald's on Divan Yolu. It's only open during the day.

Caferağa Medresesi (Map pp92-3; ☎ 0212-513 3601; Cafariye Sokak; soup TL3, köfte TL10; ☯ 8.30am-6pm) In Sultanahmet, it's rare to nosh in stylish surrounds without paying through the nose for the privilege. That's why this teensy *lokanta* in the gorgeous courtyard of this Sinan-designed *medrese* near Topkapı Palace is such a find. The food isn't anything to write home about, but it's fresh and keenly priced.

Tarihi Sultanahmet Köftecisi Selim Usta (Map pp92-3; ☎ 0212-520 0566; Divan Yolu Caddesi 12; ☯ 11am-11pm) Don't get this place confused with the other *köfte* (meatball) places along this strip

purporting to be the *meşhur* (famous) *köfte* restaurant – No 12 is the real McCoy. Locals flock here to eat the signature *köfte* (TL7) served with white beans (TL4), pickled chillies and salad (TL4).

Karadeniz Aile Pide ve Kebap Salonu (Map pp92-3; ☎ 0212-528 6290; Hacı Tahsın Bey Sokak 1; pide TL7-8.50, kebaps TL7-11; ☯ 11am-11pm) This long-timer off Divan Yolu serves a delicious *mercimek* (lentil soup) and is also a favourite for its pide (Turkish pizza). You can claim a table in the utilitarian interior, but most people prefer those on the cobbled lane.

Karadeniz Aile Pide & Kebap Sofrası (☎ 0212-526 7202; Dr Emin Paşa Sokak 16; ☯ 11am-11pm) Opposite and equally welcoming.

Bazaar District

RESTAURANTS

Havuzlu Restaurant (Map p109; ☎ 0212-527 3346; Gani Çelebi Sokak 3, Grand Bazaar; mains TL9-12; ☯ 11.30am-5pm Mon-Sat) There are few more pleasant experiences than parking one's shopping bags and enjoying a meal at the Grand Bazaar's best eatery. A lovely space with vaulted ceiling and ornate central light-fitting, Havuzlu serves up tasty and reliable fare to hungry hordes of tourists and shopkeepers. It also has a clean toilet, something quite rare in the bazaar.

Bab-ı Hayat (Map pp90-1; ☎ 0212-520 7878; Mısır Çarşısı 47, Eminönü (Spice Bazaar); pides TL6.50-7.50, kebaps TL8-12.50; ☯ 7.30am-7.30pm Mon-Sat) It took seven months for a team headed by one of the conservation architects from Topkapı Palace to restore and decorate this vaulted space over the eastern entrance to the Spice Bazaar. The result is an atmospheric setting in which to enjoy well-priced, unadorned Anatolian dishes. Enter through the Serhadoğlu fast-food shop.

Hamdi Et Lokantası (Hamdi Restaurant; Map pp90-1; ☎ 0212-528 0390; www.hamdirestorant.com.tr; Kalçın Sokak 17, Eminönü; kebaps TL13-18; ☯ noon-11pm) A favourite İstanbullu haunt since 1970, Hamdi's phenomenal views overlooking the Golden Horn and Galata are matched by great kebaps, professional service and a bustling atmosphere. Book online as far ahead of your meal as possible and request a spot on the terrace.

Şehzade Mehmed Sofrası (Map pp90-1; ☎ 0212-526 2668; www.sehzademehmed.com.tr; Şehzadebaşı Caddesi, Fatih; pides TL8-10, grills TL10-19; ☯ 9am-11pm) Located in the magnificent *külliye* of the historic Şehzade Mehmed Sofrası Camii, this welcoming restaurant and *çay bahçesi* serves

---

KEBAP KINGS

If Turkey has a signature dish, it has to be the kebap. Turks will tuck into anything cooked on a stick with gusto, and if asked where they would like to celebrate a special event, they will inevitably nominate one of the city's two most-famous *kebapçis*: Develı and Beyti.

■ **Develi** (Map pp86-7; ☎ 0212-529 0833; Gümüşyüzük Sokak 7, Samatya; mains TL12-25; ☯ noon-midnight) opened its first restaurant in Kuruluş in 1912, but its most popular outlet is at Samatya, in the shadow of Theodosius' Great Wall. The succulent kebaps here come in many guises and often reflect the season – the *keme kebabi* (truffle kebap) is only served for a few weeks each year, for instance. Prices here are extremely reasonable for the quality of food that is on offer, and the service is exemplary. Catch the train from Sirkeci or Cankurtaran and get off at Koca Mustafa Paşa station.

■ **Beyti** (Map pp86-7; ☎ 0212-663 2990; Orman Sokak 8, Florya: mains TL27-34; ☯ noon-midnight Tue-Sun) is located in an affluent suburb way out near the airport, but serious meat lovers know that it's worth the trip. Mr Beyti's famous *kuzu şiş* (skewered lamb kebap) and other meat dishes are extraordinarily good and worth every *kuruş* (cent) of their relatively hefty price tags. Catch the train from Sirkeci or Cankurtaran and get off at Florya station.

---

simple but tasty meals (no alcohol). There's live Turkish music most evenings at 7pm and you're welcome to come just for a tea and nargileh if you so choose.

Zeyrekhane (Map pp90-1; ☎ 0212-532 2778; www .zeyrekhane.com; İbedethane Arkası Sokak 10, Zeyrek; mains TL22-30; ☯ 9am-10pm Tue-Sun) This fine-dining establishment in the restored former *medrese* of Zeyrek Camii (p113) also has an outdoor garden and terrace with magnificent views of the Golden Horn and back to the Süleymaniye mosque. It serves beautifully presented and well-executed Ottoman-influenced food in extremely attractive surrounds.

Zinhan Kebap House at Storks (Map pp90-1; ☎ 0212-512 4275; rezervasyon@zinhan-kebap-house.com; Ragıpgümüşpala Caddesi 2-5, Eminönü; kebaps TL12.50-21; ☯ noon-11pm Mon-Sat) Zinhan's regal position next to the Galata Bridge (p112) is one of the best in the city. Its top floor roof terrace offers sensational views and is an excellent place to enjoy a tasty kebap and salad meal served in elegant and extremely comfortable surrounds. Book ahead and request a table with a view.

CAFÉS

Fez Cafe (Map p109; ☎ 0212-527 3684; Halıcılar Caddesi 62, Grand Bazaar; ☯ 11.30am-5pm Mon-Sat) Set in a rough-stone den, the popular Fez is one of the only Western-style cafés in the Grand Bazaar. The flower-adorned tables are perfect spots to people-watch while having a drink and bite to eat (sandwiches are the speciality and the coffee is excellent).

QUICK EATS

İmren Lokantası (Map pp90-1; ☎ 0212-638 1196; Kadırga Meydanı 143, Kadırga; mains TL3.50-7; ☯ 7am-10.30pm) A tiny neighbourhood *lokanta* with extremely friendly staff, İmren is well off the tourist trail but is worth the walk. It serves excellent, dirt-cheap dishes such as peppery lamb *guveç* (stew) or *musakka* (baked aubergine and mincemeat). Go for lunch rather than dinner.

Namli (Map pp90-1; ☎ 0212-511 6393; Hasırcılar Caddesi 14, Eminönü; ☯ 7am-7pm Mon-Sat) Namli's mouth-watering selection of cheeses, *pastırma* (air-dried beef) and meze are known throughout the city. Fight your way to the counter and order a tasty fried *pastırma* roll or a takeaway container of meze. In-the-know customers eat what they've bought upstairs in the cafeteria, where you can also grab a tasty light lunch. There's another branch on Rıhtım Caddesi in Karaköy (Map pp94–5; open 7am to 10pm).

Tarihi Süleymani Yeli Kuru Fasulyeci (Map pp90-1; ☎ 0212-513 6219; Prof Sıddık Sami Onar Caddesi 11, Süleymaniye; fasulye & pilav TL6.50; ☯ 11am-4pm Mon-Sat) Join the crowds of hungry locals at this long-time institution in the former *kütüphanesi medrese* (theological-school library) of the Süleymaniye Camii. It has been dishing up its spicy signature *fasulye* (broad bean) dish for more than 80 years. Try it with *ayran* (yoghurt drink).

Western Districts

Asitane (Map pp86-7; ☎ 0212-534 8414; www.asitane restaurant.com; Kariye Camii Sokak 6, Edirnekapı; mains TL24-32; ☯ 11am-midnight) This elegant restaurant next to

THE FISH SANDWICH – AN İSTANBUL INSTITUTION

The cheapest way to enjoy fresh fish from the waters around İstanbul is to buy a fish sandwich from a boatman. Go to the Eminönü end of the Galata Bridge and you'll see food stands next to the quay selling fried fresh fish crammed into a quarter loaf. In each boat, men tend to a cooker loaded with fish fillets. The quick-cooked fish is crammed into a quarter loaf of fresh bread and served with some salad. It will set you back a mere TL3.50 or so. Delicious!

the Chora Church serves the most authentic Ottoman cuisine in town. The chefs here have tracked down recipes from the imperial kitchens of the Topkapı, Edirne and Dolmabahçe palaces, which they prepare using original ingredients and cooking methods. Lunch here is as delicious as it is unique.

Beyoğlu & Around
RESTAURANTS

Refik (Map pp94-5; ☎ 0212-243 2834; Sofyalı Sokak 10, Tünel; mezes TL4-8, mains TL10-16; ⊙ 11am-1am, closed lunch Sun) Refik is the original *meyhane* in the happening Asmalımescit precinct, and it's always full of liquored-up locals enjoying well-cooked Black Sea fish and decent meze. Join them and you're bound to have a good time.

Boncuk Restaurant (Map pp94-5; ☎ 0212-243 1219; Nevizade Sokak 19; mezes TL4-8, mains TL10-16; ⊙ 11am-1am) Armenian specialities differentiate Boncuk from its Nevizade Sokak neighbours. Try the excellent, superfresh *topik* (meze made from chickpeas, pistachios, onion, flour, currants, cumin and salt). Arrive early and book ahead to get a table on the street, which is where all the action occurs.

ourpick Sofyalı 9 (Map pp94-5; ☎ 0212-245 0362; Sofyalı Sokak 9, Tünel; mezes TL4-8, mains TL10-16; ⊙ 11am-1am Mon-Sat) Tables here are hot property on Friday and Saturday night, and no wonder. This gem of a place serves up some of the city's best *meyhane* food, and does so in surroundings as welcoming as they are attractive. Regulars swear by the *Arnavut ciğeri* (Albanian fried liver), fried fish and exceptionally fine meze.

Kahvedan (Map pp94-5; ☎ 0212-292 4030; Akarsu Caddesi 50, Cihangir; www.kahvedan.com; breakfast plates TL7-12, soups TL5-6, wraps TL9-14, mains TL13-21; ⊙ 9am-

2am Mon-Fri, 9am-4am Sat & Sun) This expat haven serves dishes such as bacon and eggs, French toast, *mee goreng* and falafel wraps. Owner Shellie Corman is a traveller at heart, and knows the importance of things such as free wi-fi, decent wine by the glass, keen prices and good music.

Kiva Han (Map pp94-5; ☎ 0212-292 9898; www.galatakivahan.com; Galata Kulesi Meydanı 4, Galata; mains TL6-10; ⊙ 7.30am-8pm) In the shadow of Galata Tower, this simple but stylish *lokanta* specialises in seasonal dishes from the different regions of Turkey. Inspect the dishes on display or peruse the menu – the food is as excellent as it is unusual. No alcohol, but the filtered coffee served in individual plungers (TL5) is a great way to end the meal.

Tarihi Karaköy Balik Lokantası (Map pp94-5; ☎ 0212-251 1371; Kardeşim Sokak 30, off Tersane Caddesi, Karaköy; fish soup TL6, mains TL18-25; ⊙ 11.30am-3.30pm Mon-Sat) Walk through the run-down quarter behind the Karaköy Fish Market and you'll come across this unassuming treasure, one of the few old-style fish restaurants remaining on the Golden Horn. Everything is so fresh it's almost writhing – the fish baked in paper is a taste sensation and the dirt-cheap fish soup is the best in town. No alcohol.

ourpick Gani Gani Şark Sofrası (Map pp94-5; ☎ 0212-244 8401; www.naumpasakonagi.com; Taksim Kuyu Sokak 11; pides TL7-9.50, kebaps TL7.50-10; ⊙ 10am-11pm) Young Turkish couples love lolling on the traditional Anatolian seating at this cheap and friendly eatery. If you'd prefer to keep your shoes on, you can claim a table and chair on the first floor to enjoy excellent kebaps, rich *mantı* (Turkish ravioli topped with yoghurt, tomato and butter, TL7) and piping-hot pide. No alcohol.

ourpick Hacı Abdullah (Map pp94-5; ☎ 0212-293 8561; Sakızağacı Caddesi 9a; www.haciabdullah.com.tr; mains TL9-18; ⊙ 11am-11pm; ✗) Just thinking about Hacı Abdullah's sensational *imam bayıldı* (eggplant stuffed with tomatoes, onions and garlic and slow cooked in olive oil) makes our taste buds go into overdrive. This İstanbul institution (it was established in 1888) is one of the city's best *lokantas*, and is one of the essential gastronomic stops you should make when in town. No alcohol.

Zencefil (Map pp94-5; ☎ 0212-243 8234; Kurabiye Sokak 8; mains TL10-12; ⊙ 11am-11pm Tue-Sun) This popular vegetarian café is comfortable and quietly stylish. Try the daily and weekly specials to get crunchy-fresh produce (all organic) and guilt-free desserts. The slabs of homemade bread are a highlight.

Doğa Balik (Map pp94-5; ☎ 0212-293 9144; info@ dogabalik.com; 7th fl, Villa Zurich Hotel, Akarsu Yokuşu Caddesi 36, Cihangir; mezes TL10-20, mains TL25-60; ☽ noon-midnight) There's something awfully fishy about this place – and the locals love it. On the top floor of a modest hotel in Cihangir, Doğa Balik serves fabulously fresh fish in a dining space with wonderful views across to the old city. It also has a lavish serve-your-own meze buffet.

Kafe Ara (Map pp94-5; ☎ 0212-245 4104; Tosbağ Sokak 8a; mains TL13-18; ☽ 8am-midnight) In the Beyoğlu popularity stakes this café stands head and shoulders above the rest. A funky converted garage with tables and chairs spilling out into a wide laneway opposite the Galatasaray Lycée, it's a casual and welcoming setting in which to enjoy well-priced paninis, salads and pastas. No alcohol.

White Mill (Map pp94-5; ☎ 0212-292 2895; www .whitemillcafe.com; Susam Sokak 13, Cihangir; breakfast plate TL17-19, mains TL15-23; ☽ 9.30am-1.30am) White Mill serves up tasty (often organic) food in industrial-chic surrounds. In fine weather, the huge and shady rear garden is a wonderful spot in which to enjoy a leisurely weekend breakfast. It's also a great bar.

Hünkar Lokantası (Map pp86-7; ☎ 0212-225 4665; Mim Kemal Öke Caddesi 21, Nişantaşı; mains TL15-20; ☽ noon-midnight) After a morning spent abusing your credit card in the upmarket shops around here, you'll be ready to claim a table at this highly regarded *lokanta* and enjoy a relaxed lunch and glass of wine. The chefs take enormous pride in cooking and presenting traditional foods supremely well – everything is delicious. It's a 20-minute walk from Taksim Sq.

It's a Joke (Map pp86-7; ☎ 0212-373 2300; 5th fl, City's Nişantaşı Mall, Teşvikiye Caddesi 162, Teşvikiye; mains TL15-27; ☽ noon-midnight) This restaurant/bar in the City Nişantaşı shopping mall was so full when we last visited that people were literally swinging from the ceiling (clutching mirror balls). If it stays this hot, we fear that it and its rich-young-thing clientele may self-combust. Food is of the pizza and burger variety. To get here catch a metro to Osmanbey from Taksim and then walk down Rumeli Caddesi.

Cezayır (Map pp94-5; ☎ 0212-245 9980; Hayriye Caddesi 16, Galatasaray; mains TL15-25; ☽ noon-11.30pm) Housed in an attractive building that was once home to an Italian school, Cezayir is heavy on charm and relatively light on the wallet. The food is Mod Med with Turkish influences and the crowd is upmarket boho. In summer, the courtyard is always packed with happy diners.

our pick Mikla (Map pp94-5; ☎ 0212-293 5656; mikla@ istanbulyi.com; Marmara Pera Hotel, Meşrutiyet Caddesi 15, Tepebaşı; mains TL36-46.25; ☽ noon-3pm & 7pm-1am Mon-Fri, 7pm-1am Sat) This is the city's best restaurant – bar none. Local celebrity chef Mehmet Gürs is a master of perfectly executed Mediterranean

---

MEYHANE – THE BIGGEST PARTY IN TOWN

If you only have one night out on the town when you're in İstanbul, make sure you spend it at a *meyhane* (Turkish tavern). On every night of the week, *meyhanes* such as **Refik** (opposite), **Boncuk** (opposite) and **Sofyalı 9** (opposite) are full of groups of chattering locals choosing from the dizzying array of meze and fish dishes on offer, washed down with a never-ending supply of rakı (aniseed brandy). On Friday and Saturday nights, *meyhane* precincts such as Nevizade and Sofyalı Sokaks literally heave with people and are enormously enjoyable places to be.

Traditional *meyhanes* often host musicians playing *fasıl*, a lively local form of gypsy music. The best of these *meyhanes* is **Despina** (Map pp86-7; ☎ 0212-247 3357; Açıkyol Sokak 9, Kurtuluş; meze TL4-6, mains TL10; ☽ noon-12.30am Mon-Sat, music 8.30pm-midnight most nights), which was established back in 1946 and is known for its excellent music. It's way off the well-beaten tourist track and is hard to find – so ask your hotel to organise a taxi. Other options include **Cumhuriyet** (Map pp94-5; ☎ 0212-293 1977; Sahne Sokak 4; mezes TL5-7, mains TL10-25; ☽ 9am-2am, music 8.30pm-midnight most nights) in Beyoğlu's Balık Pazar (Fish Market); and **Andon** (Map pp94-5; ☎ 0212-251 0222; Sıraselviler Caddesi 51, Taksim; set menus incl alcohol TL60; ☽ 2pm-4am Mon-Sat, live music 9pm-2am most nights) situated just off Taksim Sq.

If you eat at a *meyhane* where there's live music make sure you tip the musicians when they play at your table, as they work for tips rather than salary. Between TL5 to TL10 for each person at the table is about right.

cuisine, and the Turkish accents he employs make his food truly memorable. Extraordinary views, luxe surrounds and exemplary service complete the experience.

CAFÉS

İnci (Map pp94-5; ☎ 0212-243 2412; İstiklal Caddesi 124, Beyoğlu; 🕙 9am-9pm) İstanbullus' naughty secret is to sidestep into vintage İnci for a sinful fix of the city's best profiteroles (TL5), and then to reappear on İstiklal as if nothing ever happened.

our pick **Karaköy Güllüoğlu** (Map pp94-5; ☎ 0212-293 0910; Rıhtım Caddesi, Katlı Otopark Altı, Karaköy; porsiyons TL2.75-4.50; 🕙 8am-7pm Mon-Sat) The Güllü family opened its first baklava shop in Karaköy in 1949, and it has been making customers deliriously happy and dentists obscenely rich ever since. Go to the register and pay for a glass of tea and *porsiyon* (portion) of whatever baklava takes your fancy (*fıstıklı* is pistachio, *cevizli* is walnut and *sade* is plain). You then queue to receive a plate with between two or three pieces, depending on the type you order. The *börek* (TL4 to TL4.50) here is also exceptionally fine.

Saray Muhallebicisi (Map pp94-5; ☎ 0212-292 3434; İstiklal Caddesi 173, Beyoğlu; 🕙 7.30am-10pm) This *muhallebici* (milk-pudding shop) is owned by İstanbul's mayor, no less. It's been dishing up puddings since 1935 and is always packed with locals scratching their heads over which of the 35-odd varieties of sweets they want to try this time. Try the *fırın sutlaç* (rice pudding), *aşure* (dried fruit, nut and pulse pudding) or *kazandibi* (slightly burnt chicken-breast pudding).

QUICK EATS

Canim Ciğerim İlhan Usta (Map pp94-5; ☎ 0212-252 6060; Minare Sokak 1, Asmalimescıt; set meal TL10; 🕙 10am-midnight) The name means 'my soul, my liver', and this small place behind the Ali Hoca Türbesi specialises in a set meal of grilled liver served with herbs, *ezme* (spicy tomato sauce) and grilled vegetables. If you can't bring yourself to eat offal, fear not – you can substitute liver with beef if you so choose. No alcohol.

Güney Restaurant (Map pp94-5; ☎ 0212-249 0393; Kuledibi Şah Kapısı 6, Tünel; soups TL3, mains TL3.50-18; 🕙 Mon-Sat) You'll be lucky if you can fight your way through the crowds of hungry locals to claim a lunchtime table at this bustling *lokanta* opposite Galata Tower. The food is nothing special, but the friendly and efficient service compensates.

Konak (Map pp94-5; ☎ 0212-252 0684; www.konak kebap.com; İstiklal Caddesi 259, Galatasaray; pides TL6.50-7.50, kebaps TL8-15; 🕙 7.30am-11.30pm) Eateries on İstiklal are often dreadful, but this long-time favourite bucks the trend. It serves excellent kebaps and pides; try the delectable İskender kebap and follow up with a serving of Turkey's famous but hard-to-find Maraş ice cream and you'll be both happy and replete. There's another branch near Tünel, but this one is much better.

Beşiktaş & Ortaköy

Eateries on and around the Golden Mile can get pricey, and if you're on a tight budget you should probably limit yourself to brunch – like most young locals do. On weekends the stands behind the Ortaköy Camii do brisk business selling *gözleme* (savoury pancakes) and *kumpir* (baked potatoes filled with your choice of sour cream, olive paste, cheese, chilli or bulgur).

Aşşk Kahve (Map p97; ☎ 0212-265 4734; Muallim Naci Caddesi 64b, Kuruçeşme; 🕙 9am-10pm, closed Mon in winter) The city's glamour set loves this garden café to bits, and its weekend brunches are an institution. Go early to snaffle a table right at the water's edge. It's accessed via the stairs behind the Macrocenter. To get here from Sultanahmet catch the tram to Kabataş and then bus 22 or 25E to Kuruçeşme.

House Café (Map p97; ☎ 0212-261 5818; İskele Sq 42, Ortaköy; breakfast platters TL24, sandwiches TL17.50-23.50, pizzas TL16.50-28.50; 🕙 noon-2am) This casually chic café is one of the best spots in town for Sunday brunch. A huge space right on the waterfront, it offers a good-quality buffet spread for TL45 between 9am and 2pm. Food at other times can be disappointing, though that doesn't deter the locals, who flock here every weekend.

Banyan (Map p97; ☎ 0212-259 9060; www.banyan restaurant.com; 3rd fl, Salhane Sokak 3, Ortaköy; mains TL24-39; 🕙 11am-midnight) The excellent Asian food served at this stylish eatery is nearly as impressive as its view of the Bosphorus Bridge and Ortaköy Mosque. The terrace is a wonderful place to enjoy a romantic dinner or a well-priced three-course fixed-menu lunch (TL40).

DRINKING

It may be the biggest city in a predominantly Islamic country, but let us assure you that İstanbul's population likes nothing more than a drink or three. If the rakı-soaked atmosphere

(Continued on page 149)

EXPERIENCE TURKEY

Turkey is famously associated with sizzling kebaps and steamy hamams, but travel its 780,000 sq km and you will develop your own favourite Turkish experiences. These might include locking eyes with a hard-bargaining carpet salesman in the bazaar, lounging on the beach or wandering among Cappadocia's fairy chimneys. With the country's landscapes ranging from statue-dotted Nemrut Dağı (Mt Nemrut) to Olympos' tree-house-lined beach, and its cuisine from İstanbullu fish sandwiches to Antakya's beloved Atom shake, there's no telling which aspect of Turkey will lodge itself in your imagination.

Beaches

Sun-seekers will find themselves swimming in options when deciding where to recline by the 'wine-dark sea' (in the words of Homer). Turkey is surrounded by the Mediterranean, the Aegean, the Black Sea and the Sea of Marmara. This being a country lathered in history, sunbathers can contemplate the Greek myths that took place on the Turkish coast.

❶ Pamucak

Close to the busy southern Aegean hot spots of Kuşadası and Selçuk, but significantly less developed, Pamucak's wide expanse of delta river sand (p251) is one of the region's best.

❷ Gökçeada

The southern coast of one of just a pair of remote Turkish islands in the northern Aegean offers something you'll never find in Turkey's more popular and built-up areas: isolation (p192).

❸ Patara

The Mediterranean melting pot of villagers and eccentric expats once drew visitors to the temple and oracle of Apollo, but today sun-seekers and nesting sea turtles prefer its 20km of white sand (p372).

❹ Kıyıköy

It may be called the Black Sea, but the pond to the north of Turkey looks all blue from the sandy expanses at Kıyıköy (p194), also home to a rock-cut monastery and a 6th-century castle.

❺ Badavut

The beach here (p209) is sandy, quiet and rather windswept, like a low-key, and much more pleasant, version of the nearby Aegean package hot spot of Sarımsaklı.

❻ Kabak

This Mediterranean idyll (p369) is a community as much as a beach, and a few days under its relaxing influence could see you re-evaluate where you came from – 3km up a very steep cliff!

Bazaars

Centuries ago, Seljuk and Ottoman traders travelled the Silk Road, stopping at caravanserais to do business. The tradition is alive and haggling in Turkey's bazaars, where locals and tourists converge in labyrinthine alleys to buy gear ranging from kilims (pileless woven rugs) to mosque alarm clocks. Go in a good mood and you might emerge from the scrum with a bargain!

❶

❶ Grand Bazaar, İstanbul

Hone your bargaining skills over çay (tea) and chatter in the city's original and best shopping mall, the Grand Bazaar (p109), a covered world with more than 4000 shops.

❷ Kemeraltı Bazaar, İzmir

Despite all the shiny new development that's taken place in İzmir over the past decade, the old bazaar (p224) remains its noisy, crowded, haggling heart. Leather goods are a speciality.

❸ Urfa Bazaar

With its narrow alleyways and its unique ambience, Urfa's bazaar (p610) has a Middle Eastern flavour, courtesy of its proximity to Syria. Backgammon-playing gents in shady courtyards might invite you to share a cuppa.

❹ Wait a Minute, We're Supposed to Haggle!

True to the scene in Monty Python's *Life of Brian,* bagging a carpet can be an entertaining, theatrical process. The technique and etiquette involved in haggling (p669) entail repeat visits and gallons of çay.

❺ Kapalı Çarşı, Bursa

Explore the silk and gold shops in the heritage labyrinth of Bursa's bazaar (p293), an old-world mall that will effortlessly alleviate any disappointments you have after visiting more-touristy markets.

❻ Spice Bazaar, İstanbul

Colourful pyramids of spices and ornate displays of jewel-like *lokum* (Turkish delight) provide eye candy at the fragrant Spice Bazaar (or Egyptian Market; p111), once famous for selling goods imported from Cairo.

Culinary Treats

Turkey may have introduced the world to the döner kebap (and, less famously, the cherry), but the country offers a variety of epicurean experiences:
from the reassuring smell of bread wafting from an İstanbullu bakery to the
sumptuous treat of an evening of meze and rakı (aniseed brandy) on a Cappadocian terrace.

2

❶ Fish Sandwich, İstanbul

For food with a tasty view, grab İstanbul's favourite fast food, a fresh fish sandwich (p138), from a bobbing boat moored at the chaotic but picturesque Eminönü ferry docks.

❷ Pistachio Baklava, Gaziantep

Sweet tooths, you'll lose all self-control in the pistachio baklava (p603) capital of the world, with more than 180 pastry shops serving these damned little squishy things. If you can resist, you're not human.

❸ İskender Kebap, Bursa

Combining pide, yoghurt and melted butter, an İskender kebap (p289) probably wouldn't be recommended as a daily choice by your friendly health professional. But you have to try Bursa's most famous culinary creation at least once.

❹ Atom Shake, Eastern Mediterranean

This delicious energy booster (p438) is found mostly between Mersin and Antakya. Usually consisting of banana, apricot, sultanas, honey, pistachio and milk, it's available in street stalls for a few well-spent lira.

❺ Ayvalık Oil

Although its name translates as 'quince orchard', the Aegean town of Ayvalık (p207) owes its economic fortunes to another crop, olives. The oil produced here is generally regarded as some of the finest going.

❻ Edirne Ciğeri

Start the feast right on the border in Edirne (p173), which has many local specialities. Its dish of choice is thinly sliced calf's liver, deep-fried and eaten with crispy fried red chillies and strained yoghurt.

Hamams

Hamams are also known as Turkish baths, a name coined by the Europeans who were introduced to their steamy pleasures by the Ottomans. With their domed roofs, they combine elements of Roman and Byzantine baths. Go for a massage or just soak in the calming atmosphere.

❶ Çemberlitaş Hamamı, İstanbul

Bare all at the recently refurbished Çember-litaş Hamamı (p126), where patrons have been getting soapy and steamy since 1584. Bath treatments, facials and oil massages are on offer.

❷ Sefa Hamam, Antalya

Retaining many of its Seljuk features, this recently restored 13th-century Seljuk beauty (p394) is found between Ottoman houses and the Roman harbour in Kaleiçi (Old Antalya). Go all out with 'the works'.

❸ Yıldırım Beyazıt Hamam, Mudurnu

Mudurnu is fast developing a reputation as an Ottoman revival town, and leading the restoration focus is the exquisitely resurrected Yıldırım Beyazıt hamam (p284). A steam sans scrub and massage costs just peanuts.

(Continued from page 140)

in the city's *meyhanes* isn't a clear enough indicator (p139), a foray into the thriving bar scene around Beyoğlu will confirm it.

Alternatively, you can check out the alcohol-free, atmosphere-rich *çay bahçesi* or *kahvehanes* (coffeehouses) dotted around the old city. These are great places to relax and sample that great Turkish institution, the nargileh, accompanied by a cup of *Türk kahvesi* (Turkish coffee) or çay. This will cost around TL1.50 for a tea and TL8 to TL13 for a nargileh at all of the places listed here.

Tea Gardens & Coffeehouses
SULTANAHMET & AROUND
Set Üstü Çay Bahçesı (Map pp92-3; Gülhane Parkı, Sultanahmet; 10am-11pm) Locals adore this terraced tea garden and every weekend they can be seen parading arm-in-arm through Gülhane Parkı to get here. Follow their example and you can enjoy a pot of tea and a *tost* (toasted sandwich) while enjoying spectacular water views. No nargileh.

Yeni Marmara (Map pp92-3; 0212-516 9013; Çayıroğlu Sokak, Küçük Ayasofya; 8am-midnight) This cavernous teahouse is always packed with locals playing backgammon, sipping çay and puffing on nargilehs. The place has bags of character, featuring rugs, wall hangings and low brass tables. In winter a wood stove keeps the place cosy; in summer patrons sit on the rear terrace and look out over the Sea of Marmara.

Derviş Aile Çay Bahçesi (Map pp92-3; Mimar Mehmet Ağa Caddesi; 9am-11pm Apr-Oct) Locations don't come any better than this. Directly opposite the Blue Mosque, the Derviş' comfortable cane chairs and shady trees beckon patrons in need of a respite from the tourist queues.

Café Meşale (Map pp92-3; 0212-518 9562; Arasta Bazaar, Utangaç Sokak, Cankurtaran; 24hr) Generations of backpackers have joined locals in claiming a stool and enjoying a çay and nargileh here. In the summer months there's live Turkish music at night. You'll find it in the sunken courtyard behind the Blue Mosque and next to the Arasta Bazaar.

Türk Ocağı Kültür ve Sanat Merkezi İktisadi İşletmesi Çay Bahçesi (cnr Divan Yolu & Babıali Caddesis, Çemberlitaş; 8am-midnight, later in summer) Tucked into the rear right-hand corner of a shady Ottoman cemetery, this popular tea garden is a perfect place to escape the crowds and relax over a tea and nargileh.

BAZAAR DISTRICT
Erenler Çay Bahçesi (Map pp90-1; 0212-528 3785; Yeniçeriler Caddesi 36/28; 9am-midnight, later in summer) Packed to the rafters with students from nearby İstanbul University doing their best to live up to their genetic heritage and develop a major tobacco addiction, this nargileh place is set in the leafy courtyard of the Çorlulu Ali Paşa Medrese.

Etham Tezçakar Kahveci (Map p109; Halıcılar Caddesi, Grand Bazaar; 8.30am-7pm Mon-Sat) This teeny tea and coffee stop is smack-bang in the middle of Halıcılar Caddesi. Its traditional brass-tray tables and wooden stools stand in stark contrast to the funky Fez Café opposite. No nargileh.

İlesam Lokalı (Map pp90-1; 0212-511 2618; Yeniçeriler Caddesi 84; 8am-midnight, later in summer) This club in the courtyard of the Koca Sinan Paşa Medrese was formed by the enigmatically named Professional Union of Owners of the Works of Science and Literature. Fortunately, members seem happy for strangers to infiltrate their ranks. After entering the gate to Koca Sinan Paşa's tomb, go past the cemetery – it's the second teahouse to the right.

Lale Bahçesi (Map pp90-1; Sifahane Sokak, Süleymaniye; 9am-11pm) In a sunken courtyard that was once part of the Süleymaniye *külliye*, this charming tea garden is always full of students from the nearby İstanbul University, who come here to spend a lazy hour or two on cushioned seats alongside a pretty fountain. In winter the students huddle inside the atmospheric kilim-clad *medrese*.

Şark Kahvesi (Map p109; 0212-512 1144; Yağlıkçılar Caddesi 134, Grand Bazaar; 8.30am-7pm Mon-Sat) The Şark has had a long pedigree as a popular spot for stall-holders to come and enjoy a tea break. These days they have to fight for space with tourists, who love the quirky 'flying dervish' murals, old photographs on the walls and cheap çay. No nargileh.

BEYOĞLU & AROUND

Haco Pulo (Map pp94-5; ☎ 0212-244 4210; Passage ZD Hazzopulo, İstiklal Caddesi; ☯ 9am-midnight) There aren't nearly as many traditional teahouses in Beyoğlu as there are in atmospheric Old İstanbul, so this one is treasured by the locals. Set in a delightfully picturesque cobbled courtyard, it's stool-to-stool 20- to 30-somethings on summer evenings. Walking from İstiklal Caddesi through the skinny arcade crowded with offbeat shops adds to the experience.

Kahve Dünyasi (Map pp94-5; ☎ 0212-293 1206; Meclis-i Mebusan Caddesi, Tütün Han 167, Tophane; ☯ 7.30am-9.30pm; ☒) The name means 'coffee world', and this new coffee chain has the local world at its feet. The secret of its success lies with the huge coffee menu, decent snacks, reasonable prices, delicious chocolate spoons (yes, you read that correctly), comfortable seating and free wi-fi. The filter coffee is better than its espresso-based alternatives. It's near the Kabataş tram. There's another branch in Nuruosmaniye Caddesi in Cağaloğlu, near the Grand Bazaar. Neither offers nargileh.

our pick **Tophane Nargileh** (Map pp94-5; off Necatibet Caddesi, Tophane; ☯ 24hr) This atmospheric row of nargileh cafés behind the Nusretiye Mosque and opposite the Tophane tram stop is always packed with trendy teetotallers. Follow your nose to find it – the smell of apple tobacco is incredibly enticing.

Bars

SULTANAHMET

Put simply, there isn't a bar scene in Sultanahmet. Most of the drinking spots worth considering are in hotels.

Just Bar (Map pp92-3; ☎ 0532-409 6369; Akbıyık Caddesi 18, Cankurtaran; ☯ 10am-2am) Slap-bang in the middle of backpacker central, this Sultanahmet fixture offers chilled streetside drinking and a late-night knees-up if there are plenty of travellers in town. Cheers Bar, next door, offers more of the same.

Sofa (Map pp92-3; ☎ 0212-458 3630; Mimar Mehmet Ağa Caddesi 32, Cankurtaran; ☯ 11am-11pm) Ten candlelit tables beckon patrons into this friendly café/bar just off Akbıyık Caddesi. There's a happy

hour between 5pm and 6.30pm each day, and a decidedly laid-back feel. The food's adequate rather than inspired, but if you're only after something cheapish to soak up the alcohol you'll be happy enough with what's on offer.

Sultan Pub (Map pp92-3; ☎ 0212-511 5638; Divan Yolu Caddesi 2; ☯ 9.30pm-1am) This local version of Ye Olde English Pub has been around for yonks. The 30-to-40ish crowds come for spectacular sunsets on the rooftop terrace or peerless people-watching from the sun-drenched streetside tables.

Kybele Cafe (Map pp92-3; ☎ 0212-511 7766; Yerebatan Caddesi 35, Alemdar; ☯ 3pm-1am) The lounge bar at this charming but vaguely eccentric hotel is chock-full of antique furniture, richly coloured rugs and old etchings and prints, but its signature style comes courtesy of the hundreds of colourful glass lights hanging from the ceiling.

Hotel Nomade Terrace Bar (Map pp92-3; ☎ 0212-513 8172; Ticarethane Sokak 15, Alemdar; ☯ noon-11pm) The intimate terrace of this boutique hotel overlooks Aya Sofya and the Blue Mosque. Settle down in a comfortable chair to enjoy a glass of wine, beer or freshly squeezed fruit juice. The only music that will disturb your evening's reverie is the old city's signature sound of the call to prayer.

Yeşil Ev (Map pp92-3; ☎ 0212-517 6785; Kabasakal Caddesi; ☯ noon-10.30pm) The elegant rear courtyard of this Ottoman hotel is a true oasis for those wanting to enjoy a quiet drink. In spring, flowers and blossom fill every corner; in summer the fountain and trees keep the temperature down. It's pricey, though.

BEYOĞLU & AROUND

The most popular bar precincts are on or around Balo Sokak and Sofyalı Sokak, but there are also a number of sleek bars on roof terraces on both sides of İstiklal – these have fantastic views and prices to match.

Pasific House (Map pp94-5; Sofyalı Sokak, Asmalımescit; ☯ noon-2am) There are loads of bars in Beyoğlu, but not many that are both cheap and well located. This casual place on one of the city's most happening streets is a welcome exception.

Badehane (Map pp94-5; ☎ 0212-249 0550; General Yazgan Sokak 5, Tünel; ☯ 9am-2am) This tiny unsigned watering hole is a favourite with locals because of its cheap beer. On a balmy evening the laneway is crammed with chattering, chain-smoking artsy types sipping

ROOFTOP REVELRY

The prohibitively expensive superclubs along the Bosphorus are where the city's bronzed, Botoxed and blinged set glams up and gets down. Fortunately, there's an equally glamorous, but much more affordable, entertainment alternative that we can recommend: investigating the city's vibrant rooftop bar scene.

İstanbul's sensational skyline and wonderful waterways provide the perfect backdrop for a rapidly growing number of rooftop bars in Beyoğlu. Most offer spectacular views; some also provide live music, morphing into dance clubs after midnight. They rarely levy cover charges and their dress codes are relatively relaxed, though you should don the best your suitcase has to offer. Drinks average between TL15 to TL20.

The best of a rapidly growing crop include **360** (below), **5 Kat** (below), **Leb-i Derya** and **Leb-i Derya Richmond** (below), and **Nu Teras** (below).

a beer or three; when it's cold they squeeze inside. Dress down and come ready to enjoy an attitude-free evening.

Leyla (Map pp94-5; ☎ 0212-245 4028; Tünel Sq 186a, Tünel; ⏰ 7am-2am) After dominating Beyoğlu's bar scene from a location in Cihangir, ultra-popular Leyla has migrated to the other end of İstiklal and brought most of its trendy clientele along for the ride. A great location opposite the Tünel entrance means that it's a popular meeting place.

KeVe (Map pp94-5; ☎ 212-251 4338; Tünel Geçidi 10, Tünel; ⏰ 8.30am-2am) Located in a plant-filled belle-époque arcade, atmospheric KeVe is invariably full of 30- to 40-somethings enjoying a drink before kicking on to an exhibition opening along İstiklal.

5 Kat (Map pp94-5; ☎ 0212-293 3774; www.5kat.com; 5th fl, Soğancı Sokak 7, Cihangir; ⏰ 10am-1.30am) This İstanbul institution is a great alternative for those who can't stomach the style overload at 360 and the like. In winter, drinks are served in the boudoir-style bar; in summer, action moves to the outdoor terrace. Both have great Bosphorus views.

our pick 360 (Map pp94-5; ☎ 0212-251 1042; www.360istanbul.com; 8th fl, İstiklal Caddesi 311, Galatasaray; ⏰ noon-2am Mon-Thu & Sun, 3pm-4am Fri & Sat) İstanbul's most famous bar, and deservedly so. If you can score one of the bar stools on the terrace you'll be happy indeed – the view is truly extraordinary. The place morphs into a club after midnight on Fridays and Saturdays.

Club 17 (Map pp94-5; Zambak Sokak 17; cover charge TL10 Fri & Sat only, incl 1 drink; ⏰ 11pm-4am Sun-Thu, 11pm-5.30am Fri & Sat) Aggressive techno music and a jam-packed interior are the hallmarks of this popular gay bar. At closing time, there's a veritable meat rack outside.

Leb-i Derya (Map pp94-5; ☎ 0212-244 1886; www.lebiderya.com; 7th fl, Kumbaracı Yokuşu 115, Tünel; ⏰ 11am-2am Mon-Fri, 8.30am-3am Sat & Sun) Ask many İstanbulites to name their favourite watering hole and they're likely to nominate this unpretentious place. On the top floor of a dishevelled building off İstiklal, it has wonderful views across to the old city and down the Bosphorus, meaning that seats on the small outdoor terrace or at the bar are highly prized. There's another, more upmarket branch in the Richmond Hotel on İstiklal Caddesi that has even better views.

Nu Teras (Map pp94-5; ☎ 0212-245 6070; www.istanbulyi.com; 6th fl, Meşrutiyet Caddesi 149, Tepebaşı; ⏰ 6.30pm-2am Mon-Thu & Sun, 6.30pm-4am Fri & Sat Jun-Oct) This summer-only terrace bar is a great place for a sunset drink. Its view is unusual in that it focuses on the Golden Horn, but it's no less spectacular for that. It also functions as a restaurant.

ENTERTAINMENT

There's an entertainment option for everyone in İstanbul. With its array of cinemas and almost religious devotion to all forms of music, it's rare to have a week go by when there's not a special event, festival or performance scheduled. In fact, the only thing that you can't do in this town is be bored.

For an overview of what's on in town make sure you pick up a copy of *Time Out İstanbul* (see p84) and check out **Biletix** (Map pp94-5; ☎ 0216-556 9800; www.biletix.com). You can buy tickets for most events either at the venue's box office or through Biletix. Biletix outlets are found in many spots throughout the city, but the most convenient for travellers is at the **İstiklal Kitabevi** (Map pp94-5; İstiklal Caddesi 55, Beyoğlu; ⏰ 10am-10pm). Alternatively, it's easy to buy

GAY & LESBIAN İSTANBUL

In the past the gay scene in İstanbul has been characterised as homely rather than raunchy; 'all about boys going out in trousers neatly pressed by their mothers who have no idea that they are gay', is how one aficionado summed it up. The scene is changing though, and becoming more dynamic and accepted every day. Check www.istanbulgay.com for a general guide.

There seems to be a hot new gay bar or club opening in Beyoğlu every week, mainly around the Taksim Sq end of İstiklal Caddesi. Check our listings on p150 and below for a few recommendations, and see the Gay & Lesbian section in the monthly *Time Out İstanbul* to get updates.

There is an excellent gay-owned-and-run hotel in Beyoğlu (Eklektik Guest House, see p133), and a friendly and efficient tour company specialising in gay travel in Sultanahmet, **Pride Travel Agency** (☎ 0212-527 0671; www.turkey-gay-travel.com; 2nd fl, Ateş Pasaji, İncili Cavuş Sokak 33, Sultanahmet; 10am-6pm Mon-Sat).

Hamams are a gay fave, but the scene here is very discreet. The best-known gay hamams (men only) are **Ağa Hamamı** (Map pp94-5; ☎ 0212-249 5027; Turnacıbaşı Sokak 66, Beyoğlu; bath TL20, with massage TL30; 5pm-5am), **Çeşme Hamamı** (Map pp94-5; ☎ 0212-552 3441; Yeni Çeşme Sokak 9, Karaköy; bath TL15, with massage TL25; 8am-7pm) and **Yeşildirek Hamamı** (p126). There's also a popular gay sauna, **Aquarius** (Map pp94-5; ☎ 0212-251 8925; Sadri Alisik Sokak 29, Beyoğlu; admission TL30, massage per hr TL50; 24hr).

your ticket by credit card on Biletix's website and collect the tickets from either Biletix outlets or the venue before the performance.

A night out carousing to *fasil* music is a must while you're in İstanbul. The best place to do this is at a *meyhane* – see p139.

Nightclubs

İstanbul has a killer nightlife, and the best nightclubs are clustered in what is known as the 'Golden Mile' between Ortaköy and Kuruçeşme on the Bosphorus. This sybaritic strip is where world-famous clubs such as Reina and Sortie are located, and it's also where the city's live jazz scene has recently started to gravitate.

To visit any of the Golden Mile venues, you'll need to dress to kill and be prepared to outlay loads of lira – drinks start at TL20 for a beer and climb into the stratosphere for imported spirits or cocktails. Booking for the restaurants at these venues is a good idea, because it's usually the only way to get past the door staff – otherwise you'll be looking at a lucky break or a tip of at least TL100 to get the nod. Venues are busiest on Friday and – especially – Saturday nights, and the action doesn't really kick off until 1am or 2am.

The Beyoğlu clubs are cheaper, and relatively attitude free. They don't have the same wow factor, though.

BEYOĞLU & AROUND

Araf (Map pp94-5; ☎ 0212-244 8301; 5th fl, Balo Sokak 32; no cover charge; 5pm-4am) Grungy fun central

for English teachers and Turkish-language students, who shake their booties to the in-house gypsy band and swill the cheapest club beer in town.

Cahide Caberet (Map pp86-7; ☎ 0212-219 6530; Kadırgalar Caddesi, Maçka Parkı; www.cahidecabaret.com; tickets through Biletix or by emailing info@cahidecabaret.com, cover charge TL65 incl 1 drink; 11pm-late Apr-early Oct) Drag queens, divas and daddy's darlings all adore Cahide. It's kitsch, decadently enjoyable and ruinously expensive – consider yourself warned.

Ghetto (Map pp94-5; ☎ 0538-230 1500; www.ghettoist.com; Kalyoncu Kulluk Caddesi 10; cover charge varies; 8pm-4am) This three-storey club behind the Çiçek Pasajı (p115) has a bold postmodern decor and an interesting musical program featuring local and international acts. At Ghetto Teras (reached via a back staircase), techno and house music rule, presided over by DJs who really know their stuff.

Love Dance Point (Map pp86-7; ☎ 0212-296 3357; www.lovedancepoint.com; Cumhuriyet Caddesi 349/1, Harbiye; cover charge TL30 incl 1 drink; 11.30pm-4am Wed, 11.30pm-5am Fri & Sat) The major player in the city's gay club scene, Love is now in its eighth year and shows absolutely no sign of having its star wane. Here, gay anthems meet hard-hitting techno and Turkish pop, making for one hell of a party. Straights can occasionally be spotted on the dance floor.

ORTAKÖY & KURUÇEŞME

Angelique (Map p97; ☎ 0212-237 2844; www.istanbuldoors.com; Salhane Sokak 10, Ortaköy; no cover charge;

6pm-4am May-Oct) The cleverly positioned angled mirrors make the most of Angelique's location right on the waterfront, ensuring that the few corners of the club without views of the Bosphorus Bridge and Ortaköy Mosque still bathe in their reflections. This is glam with a capital G – wear your Blahniks and make sure you make a reservation.

Blackk (Map p97; ☎ 0212-236 7256; www.blackk .net; Muallim Naci Caddesi 71, Kuruçeşme; no cover charge; 7.30pm-4am Fri & Sat) This ultrafashionable supper club is divided into three areas – club, resto-lounge and Levendiz Greek tavern. The club relies on its giant mirror ball for the wow factor, but both the resto-lounge and *meyhane* have great Bosphorus views.

Crystal (Map p97; ☎ 0212-229 7152; www.club crystal.org; Muallim Naci Caddesi 65, Kuruçeşme; adult/student TL35/25 includes one drink; midnight-5.30am Fri & Sat) Crystal is home to the city's techno aficionados, who come to appreciate sets put together by some of the best DJs from Turkey and the rest of Europe. There's a great sound system, a crowded dance floor and a lovely covered garden. Best of all is the fact that there's less attitude evident here than at the rest of the Golden Mile clubs.

ourpick Reina (Map p97; ☎ 0212-259 5919; www .reina.com.tr; Muallim Naci Caddesi 44, Kuruçeşme; cover charge TL50 on weekends, free on weekdays) This is İstanbul's most famous nightclub. It's where Turkey's C-list celebrities congregate, the city's nouveaux riches cavort and an occasional tourist gets past the doorman to ogle the spectacle and the magnificent Bosphorus view. Nearby Sortie (Map p97; www.sortie. com.tr) offers more of the same. You are highly unlikely to get into either without a dinner reservation.

Live Music

Babylon (Map pp94-5; ☎ 0212-292 7368; www.ba bylon.com.tr; Şehbender Sokak 3, Tünel; cover charge varies; 9.30pm-2am Tue-Thu, 10pm-3am Fri & Sat) Babylon devotes itself almost exclusively to live performances, and the eclectic program often features big-name international acts. DJ chill-out sessions are in the restaurant/lounge behind the concert hall. Buy tickets at the box office (open 10am-6pm) opposite the venue.

Balans Music Hall (Map pp94-5; ☎ 0212-251 7020; www.balansmusichall.com in Turkish; Balo Sokak 22; admission varies; closed summer, from 10pm Wed-Sat in winter) This three-level space has one of the best sound systems in town, and regularly hosts big- and small-name local rock bands. It's a friendly, mixed crowd; join the crush up front to make friends fast. On the top floor is Tonique (www.balanstonique.com), a part open-air duplex where memorable electronic and house music plays and local scenesters congregate.

Nayah Cafe Bar (Map pp94-5; ☎ 0212-244 1183; Balo Sokak 14A, Galatasaray; cover charge varies; 10am-2am) This vibrant place is one of the few bars – if not the only bar – in İstanbul headlining reggae and world music. It's a second home to some of the city's African migrants and many other expats. Enter off Nevizade Sokak.

Roxy (Map pp94-5; ☎ 0212-249 1283; www.roxy .com.tr; Arslan Yatağı Sokak 7; cover charge varies; 9pm-3am Wed & Thu, 10pm-4am Fri & Sat) It's been going since 1994, but bright young things still flock to this dance-and-performance space off Taksim Sq. Expect anything from retro to rap, hip hop to jazz fusion and electronica to anthems.

Jazz

İstanbul Jazz Center (Map p97; ☎ 0212-323 5050; www .istanbuljazz.com; Salhane Sokak 10, Ortaköy; cover charge varies; from 7pm, live performances 9.30pm & 12.30am Mon-Sat) Affectionately known as JC's, this is the city's best-known jazz club. Big-name international acts regularly perform on Friday and Saturday nights – check the website for details. There's a set dinner menu costing TL60, or you can order à la carte.

Nardis Jazz Club (Map pp94-5; ☎ 0212-244 6327; www. nardisjazz.com; Galata Kulesi Sokak 14, Galata; cover charge varies; 8pm-1am Mon-Thu with sets at 9.30pm & 12.30am, 8pm-2am Fri & Sat with sets at 10.30pm & 1.30am) Just downhill from the Galata Tower, this venue run by jazz guitarist Önder Focan and his wife Zuhal is where real jazz aficionados go. It's small, so you'll need to book if you want a decent table.

Cinemas

İstiklal Caddesi, between Taksim and Galatasaray, is the heart of İstanbul's *sinema* (cinema) district, so you can simply cinema-hop until you find something you like. The only cinema close to Sultanahmet is the Şafak Sinemaları at Çemberlitaş. Foreign films are mostly shown in English with Turkish subtitles, but double-check at the box office in case the film has *Türkçe* (Turkish) dubbing, which sometimes happens with blockbusters and children's films.

When possible, buy your tickets a few hours in advance. Tickets cost TL12 at most venues – many places offer reduced rates on Wednesday.

Decent cinemas include:

AFM Fitaş (Map pp94-5; ☎ 0212-251 2020; İstiklal Caddesi 24-26, Beyoğlu)

Citylife Cinema (Map pp86-7; ☎ 0212-373 3535; www.citylifecinema.com; 6th fl, City's Nişantaşı Mall, Teşvikiye Caddesi 162, Teşvikiye)

Emek (Map pp94-5; ☎ 0212-293 8439; Yeşilçam Sokak 5, Beyoğlu)

Rexx (Map pp86-7; ☎ 0216-336 0112; Sakızgülü Sokak 20-22, Kadıköy)

Şafak Sinemaları (Map pp92-3; ☎ 0212-516 2660; Divan Yolu 134, Çemberlitaş)

Sport

There's only one spectator sport that really matters to Turks: football. Eighteen teams from all over Turkey compete from August to May, and three of the top teams – Fenerbahçe, Galatasaray and Beşiktaş – are based in İstanbul. Each season three teams move up from the second division into the first and three get demoted. The top team of the first division plays in the European Cup.

Matches are usually held on weekends, normally on a Saturday night. Almost any Turkish male will be able to tell you which is the best match to see. Tickets are sold at the clubhouses at the *stadyum* (stadium) or at **Biletix** (☎ 0216-556 9800; www.biletix.com) and usually go on sale between Tuesday and Thursday for a weekend game. Open seating is affordable; covered seating – which has the best views – can be expensive. If you miss out on the tickets you can get them at the door of the stadium, but they are usually outrageously overpriced.

SHOPPING

If you love shopping you've come to the right place. Despite İstanbul's big-ticket historic sights, many travellers come here and find the highlight of their visit was searching and bantering for treasures in the magnificent

Grand Bazaar (p109). Come here for jewellery, leather, textiles, ceramics and trinkets. And if you're still standing after a serious session in the Grand Bazaar, you may want to visit the **Arasta Bazaar** (p100) behind the Blue Mosque in Sultanahmet, which is home to an excellent range of carpet, textile and ceramic shops.

Tahtakale, the area between the Grand Bazaar and Eminönü, is the best place to fossick for good-value haberdashery, manchester, kitchen goods, and especially dried fruits, spices and lotions in the Spice Bazaar – locals say if you can't find it in Tahtakale it doesn't exist. Over in Beyoğlu, **İstiklal Caddesi** (p115) is lined with book and music shops. A few steps away is **Çukurcuma**, with some good antique shops.

Come energised, come with maximum overdraft, come with an empty suitcase.

Art, Antiques & Jewellery

Khaftan (Map pp92-3; ☎ 0212-458 5425; www.khaftan .com; Nakilbent Sokak 33; ☽ 9am-8pm) Owner Adnan Cakariz sells antique Kütahya and İznik ceramics to collectors and museums here and overseas, so you can be sure that the pieces he sells in his own establishment are top-notch. Gleaming Russian icons, delicate calligraphy (old and new), ceramics, Karagöz puppets and contemporary paintings are all on show in this gorgeous shop.

Sofa (Map pp90-1; ☎ 0212-520 2850; Nuruosmaniye Caddesi 85, Cağaloğlu; ☽ 9.30am-7pm Mon-Sat) As well as its eclectic range of prints, ceramics, calligraphy and Ottoman and Byzantine curios, Sofa sells contemporary Turkish art and books. The range of jewellery made out of antique Ottoman coins and 24-carat gold is extraordinarily beautiful.

Design Zone (Map pp90-1; ☎ 0212-527 9285; www .designzone.com.tr; Alibaba Türbe Sokak 21, Nuruosmaniye; ☽ 9am-6pm Mon-Sat) Contemporary Turkish designers show and sell their work in this attractive boutique. Look out for the superstylish jewellery created by owner Özlem Tuna and unique collectables such as the hand-crafted hamam-bowl sets. The varied stock caters to all budgets.

Milano Güzeliş (Map p109; ☎ 0212-527 6648; Kalpakçılar Caddesi 103, Grand Bazaar; ☽ 9am-7pm Mon-Sat) When this family-run business started trading here in 1957, it was one of only 10 or so jewellery shops in the Grand Bazaar. The Güzeliş' have been making jewellery to order using every gold grade and every

MAKING A LIVING IN THE GRAND BAZAAR

İlhan Güzeliş is the owner and chief designer at Milano Güzeliş, a well-known jewellery store in the Grand Bazaar. The family-owned business was established by his great-grandfather in Mardin, in Turkey's southeast, and his father moved it to İstanbul in 1957. At that time there were fewer than 10 jewellery stores in the bazaar – these days 1500 of the bazaar's 4000 shops sell jewellery and the surrounding streets are littered with jewellery workshops. İlhan began learning his trade from his father when he was seven years old, but he fears that his own sons won't be following in his footsteps – it's hard to make a good living from individually designed and hand-crafted jewellery these days due to competition from glitzy megastores and malls, which sell relatively inexpensive mass-produced jewellery. He fears that the days of jewellers and their customers interacting over individual pieces are about to end.

One aspect of the bazaar that İlhan likes to discuss is its cultural and religious diversity. He points out that Muslims and Christians have always worked together harmoniously here, and that most of the diamonds the jewellers use are supplied by Jewish diamond traders. İlhan himself is a member of the Assyrian Orthodox Church – in İstanbul, half of the church's 15,000 members are involved in the jewellery business. Like many of the bazaar's shopkeepers he speaks a number of languages (in his case Turkish, English, German, French, Italian, Spanish, Portuguese and Arabic), but he and around 50% of his fellow Assyrian Christians can also speak Aramaic, one of the world's oldest languages.

İlhan will stay on in the bazaar for as long as he can keep on making a good livelihood and paying his rent. This is calculated separately for each store according to how much space the store occupies and where it is – all of the stores on Kalpakçılar Caddesi, where Milano Güzeliş is located, pay hefty rents because their street is perhaps the busiest in the bazaar. The rent is paid in gold (which seems particularly appropriate for jeweller tenants!), and can cost anywhere between half a kilogram to eight kilograms of the precious metal per year.

conceivable gem ever since, and have built a trusted reputation in the process. See also boxed text (above).

Artrium (Map pp94-5; ☎ 0212-251 4302; Tünel Geçidi 7, Tünel; ⏱ 9am-7pm Mon-Sat) This Aladdin's cave is crammed with antique ceramics, Ottoman miniatures, maps, prints and jewellery.

Carpets & Textiles

our pick **Cocoon** (Map pp92-3; ☎ 0212-638 6271; www .cocoontr.com; Küçük Aya Sofya Caddesi 13, Sultanahmet; ⏱ 8.30am-7.30pm) There are so many rug and textile shops in İstanbul that choosing individual shops to recommend is incredibly difficult. We had no problem whatsoever in singling this one out, though. Felt hats, antique costumes and textiles from Central Asia are artfully displayed in one store, while rugs from Persia, Central Asia, the Caucasus and Anatolia adorn the other. There's a third shop in the Arasta Bazaar and a small shop selling felt objects in the Grand Bazaar.

Mehmet Çetinkaya Gallery (Map pp92-3; ☎ 0212-517 6808; www.cetinkayagallery.com; Tavukhane Sokak 7; ⏱ 9.30am-8.30pm) When rug experts throughout the country meet for their annual shindig, this is one of the places where they come to check out the good stuff. There's a second shop in the Arasta Bazaar.

Yılmaz İpekçilik (Map pp92-3; ☎ 0212-638 4579; Ishakpaşa Caddesi 36; ⏱ 9am-9pm Mon-Sat, 3-9pm Sun) Hand-loomed textiles made in a family-run factory in Antakya are on sale in this out-of-the-way shop. Good-quality silk, cotton and linen items at reasonable prices make it worth the short trek.

Dhoku (Map p109; ☎ 0212-527 6841; Takkeciler Sokak 58-60, Grand Bazaar; ⏱ 9am-7pm Mon-Sat) One of a new generation of rug stores in the Bazaar, Dhoku (meaning texture) designs and sells contemporary kilims featuring attractive modernist designs. The same people run EthniCon (www.ethnicon.com) opposite.

Muhlis Günbattı (Map pp92-3; ☎ 0212-511 6562; Perdahçılar Sokak 48, Grand Bazaar; ⏱ 9am-7pm Mon-Sat) One of the most famous stores in the Grand Bazaar, Muhlis Günbattı specialises in *suzani* (needlework) fabrics from Uzbekistan. These spectacularly beautiful bedspreads and wall hangings are made from fine cotton embroidered with silk. There's another store opposite the Four Seasons Hotel in Sultanahmet.

Şişko Osman (Fatty Osman; Map p109; ☎ 0212-528 3548; www.siskoosman.com; Zincirli Han 15, Grand Bazaar;

İSTANBUL

9am-6pm Mon-Sat) The Osmans have been in the rug business for four generations and their popularity has seen their original shop triple its size. The range and customer service here are certainly hard to beat.

Handicrafts & Ceramics

İstanbul Handicrafts Market (İstanbul Sanatlar Çarşısı; Map pp92-3; ☎ 0212-517 6782; Kabasakal Caddesi, Sultanahmet; 9am-6.30pm) Set in the small rooms surrounding the quiet, leafy courtyard of the 18th-century Cedid Mehmed Efendi Medresesi, this handicrafts centre is unusual in that local artisans work here and don't mind visitors watching them. It's a hassle-free place to purchase calligraphy, embroidery, glassware, miniature paintings, ceramics and costumed dolls.

İznik Classics & Tiles (Map pp92-3; ☎ 0212-517 1705; Arasta Bazaar 67 & 73, Sultanahmet; 9am-8pm) İznik Classics is one of the best places in town to source hand-painted collector-item ceramics made with real quartz and using metal oxides for pigments. Admire the range in the two shops and gallery in the Arasta Bazaar, in its Grand Bazaar store or in the newish outlet at 17 Utangaç Sokak.

Nakkaş (Map pp92-3; ☎ 0212-458 4702; Mimar Mehmet Ağa Caddesi 39; 9am-7pm) As well as pricey rugs and jewellery, Nakkaş stocks an extensive range of ceramics made by the well-regarded İznik Foundation. One of the reasons the place is so beloved of tour groups is the beautifully restored Byzantine cistern that's in the basement – make sure you have a peek.

Ak Gümüş (Map p109; ☎ 0212-526 0987; Gani Çelebi Sokak 8, Grand Bazaar; 9am-7pm Mon-Sat) Specialising in Central Asian tribal arts, this delightful store stocks an array of felt toys and hats, as well as jewellery and other objects made using coins and beads.

Deli Kızın Yeri (Map p109; ☎ 0212-511 1914; Halıcılar Caddesi 42, Grand Bazaar; 9am-7pm Mon-Sat) Don't let the name – the Crazy Lady's Place – put you off. With a cute line of handmade Turkish teddies, dolls and puppets on offer, this is a great place to pick up gifts for the little ones in your life.

Güven Tıcaret (Map pp90-1; ☎ 0212-526 0307; Kutucular Caddesi 26, Rüstempaşa; 6am-6pm Mon-Sat, 8am-6pm Sun) Cheap hamam bowls, cooking pans and coffee pots are sold at this simple shop at the end of Hasırcılar Caddesi near the Spice Bazaar. You'll pay approximately a quarter of the price of their Grand Bazaar equivalents.

SIR (Map pp94-5; ☎ 0212-293 3661; www.sircini.com; Serdar Ekrem Sokak 66, Galata; 11am-7pm Mon-Sat) Ceramics produced in İstanbul can be prohibitively pricey, but the attractive hand-painted plates, platters, bowls and tiles sold at this small atelier are exceptions to the rule.

Homewares & Clothing

Abdulla Natural Products (Map p109; ☎ 0212-522 9078; Halıcılar Caddesi 62, Grand Bazaar; 9am-7pm Mon-Sat) Be sure to keep your luggage allowance in mind when entering this stylish shop. It sells handmade woollen throws from eastern Turkey, top-quality cotton bed and bath linen, and beautifully packaged olive-oil soap.

Azad Tekstil (Map p109; ☎ 0212-512 4202; Yağlıkçılar Caddesi 16, Grand Bazaar; 9am-7pm Mon-Sat) If you're after well-priced cotton bedspreads, tablecloths or peştemals (cloth wraps used in bathhouses), this place is definitely worth checking out.

Derviş (Map p109; ☎ 0212-514 4525; www.dervis.com; Keseciler Caddesi 33-35, Grand Bazaar; 9am-7pm Mon-Sat) Gorgeous raw cotton and silk peştemals share shelf space here with traditional Turkish dowry vests and engagement dresses. If these don't take your fancy, the pure olive-oil soaps and old hamam bowls are sure to step into the breach. There's another store at Halıcılar Caddesi 51.

Vakko İndirim (Map pp90-1; ☎ 0212-522 8941; Yenicamii Caddesi 1/13, Eminönü; 9.30am-6pm Mon-Sat) This remainder outlet of İstanbul's most glamorous department store should be on the itinerary of all bargain hunters. Top-quality men's and women's clothing is sold here for a fraction of its original price.

ANTIQUES, ANYONE?

Those seeking out authentic Ottoman souvenirs should visit the **Horhor Antikacılar Çarşısı** (Horhor Antique Market, Horhor Bitpazarı; Map pp86-7; vary according to shop), where the city's serious collectors congregate. This decrepit building in Aksaray is home to five floors of shops selling antiques, curios and bric-a-brac of every possible description, quality and condition. To get here, catch the tram to Aksaray, walk up Horhor Caddesi, and turn right into Kırma Tulumba Sokak; the market is on the right-hand side of the street.

TURKISH DELIGHT

Ali Muhiddin Hacı Bekir was the most famous of all Ottoman confectioners. He came to İstanbul from the mountain town of Kastamonu in 1777 and opened a shop in the old city where he concocted delicious boiled sweets and the translucent jellied jewels known to Turks as *lokum* and to the rest of the world as Turkish Delight. His products became so famous throughout the city that his sweetshop empire grew, and his name became inextricably linked in the minds of İstanbullus with authentic and delicious *lokum*. Today, locals still buy their *lokum* from branches of the business he began over two centuries ago.

The flagship store of **Ali Muhiddin Hacı Bekir** (www.hacibekir.com.tr/eng) is located at Hamidiye Caddesi 83, Eminönü (Map pp90–1), near the Spice Bazaar. There are also stores on İstiklal Caddesi (Map pp94–5) and in the produce market at Kadıköy.

As well as enjoying *sade* (plain) *lokum*, you can buy it made with *cevizli* (walnut) or *şam fıstıklı* (pistachio), or flavoured with *portakkallı* (orange), *bademli* (almond) or *roze* (rose water). Ask for a *çeşitli* (assortment) to sample the various types.

Gönül Paksoy (Map pp86-7; ☎ 0212-261 9081; Atiye Sokak 6/A & 1/3, Teşvikiye; ☷ 10am-7pm Mon-Sat) Paksoy creates and sells pieces that transcend fashion and step into art. These two shops showcase her distinctive clothing, which is made using naturally dyed fabrics and is often decorated with vintage beads.

Berrin Akyüz (Map pp94-5; ☎ 0212-251 4125; www.berrinakyuz.com; Havyar Sokak 26, Cihangir; ☷ 10.30am-7pm Mon-Sat) Local lasses love the reworked vintage clothing on offer at this Cihangir boutique, and no wonder. It's well priced and extremely stylish.

Mariposa (Map pp94-5; ☎ 0212-249 0483; Şimşirci Sokak 11a, Cihangir; ☷ 10am-8.30pm Mon-Fri, 11am-8.30pm Sat & Sun) The Mariposa atelier turns out a particularly fetching line in floral frocks. Fashionistas will adore the fact that as well as selling ready-to-wear, it also makes to order, and designs and tailors unique ensembles. As well as the dresses, coats and jackets on the racks, it sells pretty bedspreads and pillowslips.

Leather

Koç Deri (Map p109; ☎ 0212-527 5553; Kürkçüler Çarşısı 22-46, Grand Bazaar; ☷ 9am-7pm Mon-Sat) Fancy a leather jacket or coat? Koç is bound to have something that suits. It's one of the bazaar's busiest and longest-running stores.

Küçük Köşe (Little Corner; Map p109; ☎ 0212-513 0335; Kalpakçılar Caddesi 89-91, Grand Bazaar; ☷ 9am-7pm Mon-Sat) If you've always wanted a Kelly or Birkin but can't afford Hermès, this is the place for you. Its copies of the work of the big-gun designers are good quality and a lot more affordable.

Derimod (Map pp86-7; ☎ 0212-247 7481; Vali Konağı Caddesi 103-116, Nişantaşı; ☷ 10am-7pm Mon-Sat) If

you're looking for top-quality leather goods, make your way to this branch of Derimod. It sells clothes for both men and women, as well as a large range of shoes and bags.

Music

A good range of Turkish musical instruments can be found in the shops along Galipdede Caddesi (Map pp94–5), which runs between Tünel Sq and the Galata Tower.

Lale Plak (Map pp94-5; ☎ 0212-293 7739; Galipdede Caddesi 1, Tünel; ☷ 9am-7pm Mon-Sat) This long-standing magnet for music aficionados is crammed with CDs in every genre, including jazz, Western and Turkish classical, Turkish folk and electronica.

Mephisto (Map pp94-5; ☎ 0212-249 0687; İstiklal Caddesi 197, Beyoğlu; ☷ 9am-midnight) This is the spot to pick up Turkish pop, rap and hip hop.

GETTING THERE & AWAY

İstanbul is the country's foremost transport hub.

Air

İstanbul's main international airport is **Atatürk International Airport** (IST; Atatürk Hava Limanı; ☎ 0212-465 5555; www.ataturkairport.com), 23km west of Sultanahmet. The international (*dış hatlar*) and domestic terminals (*iç hatlar*) are side by side. Check the website for flight arrivals and departure times.

There are car-hire desks, money-exchange offices, a pharmacy, ATMs and a PTT in the international arrivals hall and a 24-hour supermarket on the walkway to the metro. There's also a **tourist information desk** (☷ daily) that supplies a very limited range of maps and advice.

The **left-luggage service** (per suitcase per 24hr TL12-15; ⊗ 24hr) is to your right as you exit customs.

For domestic flights it's a good idea to arrive at least an hour before your departure time, especially on weekends and during public holidays, as check-in and security queues can be long.

One of the few annoying things about Atatürk International Airport is that travellers must pay to use a baggage trolley. You can pay in Turkish liras (TL1), euros (€1) or US dollars (US$1); fortunately, attendants give change. You get the money back when you return the trolley.

İstanbul also has a smaller airport, **Sabiha Gökçen International Airport** (SAW; ☎ 0216-585 5000; www.sgairport.com), some 50km east of Sultanahmet, on the Asian side of the city. It's increasingly popular for cheap flights from Europe, particularly Germany. There's a bank, minimarket and PTT here and use of trolleys is free of charge.

Many of the city's airline offices are along Cumhuriyet Caddesi between Taksim Sq and Harbiye, but Turkish Airlines has offices around the city. Travel agencies can also sell tickets and make reservations for most airlines.

For details of international flights to and from İstanbul, see p676. For information on flights from İstanbul to other Turkish cities, see p684.

Boat
KARAKÖY
Cruise ships arrive at the **Karaköy International Maritime Passenger Terminal** (Map pp94-5; ☎ 0212-249 5776) just near the Galata Bridge.

YENİKAPI
Yenikapı (Map p90-1) is the dock for the **İDO** (İstanbul Deniz Otobüsleri; www.ido.com.tr) fast ferries across the Sea of Marmara to Yalova and Bandırma (from where you can catch a train to İzmir). These carry both passengers and cars. For more details on services to Yalova see p283 and for Bandırma, see p197.

Bus
BUS STATIONS
The **International İstanbul Bus Station** (Uluslararası İstanbul Otogarı; Map p85; ☎ 0212-658 0505) is the city's main bus station for both intercity and international routes. Called simply the 'otogar', it's in the western district of Esenler, about

10km northwest of Sultanahmet. There's an ATM here, a few cafés and unspeakably filthy toilets.

The easiest way to get to the otogar is to catch the tram from Sultanahmet to Aksaray and then connect with the Light Rail Transit (LRT) service, which stops at the otogar on its way to the airport – all up a half-hour trip costing only TL2.60 (cheaper if you use Akbil). If you're coming from Taksim or Beyoğlu, bus 830 leaves about every 20 minutes from around 6.30am to 8.40pm from Taksim Sq, taking about an hour to reach the centre of the otogar (TL1.40). Many bus companies run a free *servis* (shuttle bus) between the otogar and Taksim Sq or Sultanahmet. Ask if there's a *servis* when you buy your ticket or when you arrive at the otogar. A taxi from Sultanahmet to the otogar will cost around TL22 (20 minutes); from Taksim Sq around TL30 (30 minutes).

The otogar is a monster of a place, with over 150 ticket offices all touting for business. Buses leave from here for virtually everywhere in Turkey and for countries including Azerbaijan, Armenia, Bulgaria, Georgia, Greece, Iran, Romania and Syria. For details of international bus services, see p677 to p682.

Excluding holiday periods, you can usually come to the otogar, spend 30 minutes comparing prices and departure times and be on your way within the hour. There's no easy way to find the best fare; you have to go from one office to another asking prices and inspecting the buses parked around the back. If you plan to leave sooner rather than later, make sure you ask about departure times as well as fares. Touts will be happy to sell you a cheap fare on a bus leaving in four hours' time, but in the meantime several buses from other companies offering similar rates could have seen you on your way.

There is a much smaller bus station on the Asian shore of the Bosphorus at **Harem** (Map p86-7; ☎ 0216-333 3763), south of Üsküdar and north of Haydarpaşa Train Station. If you're arriving in İstanbul by bus from anywhere in Anatolia (the Asian side of Turkey) it's always quicker to get out at Harem and take the car ferry to Sirkeci/Eminönü (ferry from 7am, then every half-hour until 9.30pm daily; TL1.40). If you stay on the bus until the otogar, you'll add at least an hour to your journey (and then you'll still have to travel into town).

INTERNATIONAL AIRLINE OFFICES

Most of the offices below are open from Monday to Friday between 9am and 5.30pm.

Aeroflot (Map pp86-7; ☎ 0212-296 6725; Cumhuriyet Caddesi 26b, Elmadağ)

Air France Taksim (Map pp94-5; ☎ 0212-310 1919; 14th fl, Emirhan Caddesi 145, Dikilitaş); Atatürk International Airport (☎ 0212-465 5491)

Azerbaijan Airlines Taksim (Map pp86-7; ☎ 0212-296 3733; 4th fl, Cumhuriyet Caddesi 163, Elmadağ); Atatürk International Airport (☎ 212-465 3000)

British Airways 4 Levent (☎ 0212-317 6600; 17th fl, Büyükdere Caddesi 209, Tekfen Tower); Atatürk International Airport (☎ 0212-465 5682)

Corendon Airlines (☎ 0216-585 5954; Sabiha Gökçen Airport)

Emirates Airlines Şişli (☎ 0212-315 4545; Şişli Plaza, 19 Mayis Caddesi 57, 8th fl, A Blok); Atatürk International Airport (☎ 0212-663 0708)

German Wings (☎ 0212-354 6666 call centre only)

Iran Air (Map pp86-7; ☎ 0212-225 0255-7; Vali Konağı Caddesi 17, Harbiye)

JAL (Japan Airlines) (Map pp86-7; ☎ 0212-233 0840; 2nd fl, Cumhuriyet Caddesi 107, Elmadağ)

KTHY Cyprus Turkish Airlines Mecidiyeköy (☎ 0212-274 6932; Büyükdere Caddesi 56b) Atatürk International Airport (☎ 0212-465 3597)

Lufthansa (☎ 0212-315 3400; Büyükdere Caddesi 122, 5th fl, Özsezen Is Merkezi C Block, Zincirlikuyu)

Olympic Airways Elmadağ (Map pp86-7; ☎ 0212-296 7575; Cumhuriyet Caddesi 171a); Atatürk International Airport (☎ 0212-465 3388)

Onur Air (☎ 0212-663 2300; Çatal Sokak 3, Florya)

Pegasus Airlines Call Centre (☎ 0212-444 0737); Sabiha Gökçen Airport (☎ 216-588 0160)

Singapore Airlines Yeşilköy (☎ 0212-463 1800; GSA Turizm ve Havacilik Ltd, EGS Business Park Plaza, 8th fl, 278, Block B2); Atatürk International Airport (☎ 0212-465 3473)

Swiss International Air Lines (☎ 0212-354 9919; Büyükdere Caddesi 122, 5th fl, Özsezen Is Merkezi C Block, Zincirlikuyu)

Turkish Airlines Taksim (Map pp86-7; ☎ 0212-252 1106; Cumhuriyet Caddesi 7, Elmadağ); Atatürk International Airport (☎ 212-463 6363) The Elmadağ office is also open on weekends.

BUS COMPANIES

The top national lines, offering premium service at marginally higher prices, are:

Kamil Koç Otogar (☎ 444 0562 country-wide; www .kamilkoc.com.tr in Turkish; ticket office No 144-6); Beyoğlu ticket office (Map pp94-5; ☎ 0212-252 7223; İnönü Caddesi 31)

Ulusoy Otogar (☎ 444 1888 country-wide; www.ulusoy .com.tr; ticket office No 128), Beyoğlu ticket office (Map pp94-5; ☎ 0212-244 6375; İnönü Caddesi 59)

Varan Turizm Otogar (☎ 444 8999 country-wide; www .varan.com.tr; ticket office No 16); Beyoğlu ticket office (Map pp94-5; ☎ 0212-251 7474; İnönü Caddesi 19b)

Car & Motorcycle

The E80 Trans-European Motorway (TEM) from Europe passes about 10km north of Atatürk International Airport, then as Hwy 02 takes the Fatih Bridge across the Bosphorus to Asia, passing some 1.5km north of Sabiha Gökçen International Airport. This will be your main route for getting to and from İstanbul, but try to avoid rush hours (7am to 10am and 3pm to 7pm Monday to Saturday) as the traffic is nightmarish and the Bosphorus bridges come to a standstill.

Don't plan to use your car in İstanbul; park it for the duration of your stay (p163). If you want to hire a car for your travels, we recommend you hire it from either of the airports on your way *out* of İstanbul. This will mean lugging your baggage by taxi or public transport to the airport, but it won't mean navigating İstanbul's manic roads in an unfamiliar vehicle – you'll be comfortably on your way out of the city before you even get behind the wheel. Alternatively, you could catch public transport to your next destination, and then rent.

Reliable car rental agencies:

Avis Taksim (Map pp86-7; ☎ 0212-297 9610; www .avis.com.tr; Abdülhak Hamit Caddesi 72a; ☯ 9am-7pm); Atatürk International Airport (☎ 0212-465 3455-6; ☯ 24hr); Sabiha Gökçen International Airport (☎ 0216-585 5154; ☯ 7am-11pm)

Hertz Taksim (Map pp86-7; ☎ 0212-225 6404; www .hertz.com.tr, in Turkish; Yedikuyular Caddesi 4); Atatürk International Airport (☎ 0212-465 5999; ☯ 24hr); Sabiha Gökçen International Airport (☎ 0216-588 0141; ☯ 9am-7pm)

İSTANBUL

SERVICES FROM İSTANBUL'S OTOGAR

Destination	Fare (TL)	Duration (hr)	Distance (km)
Alanya	50	16	860
Ankara	25-44	6	450
Antakya	40	18	1115
Antalya	40-45	12½	740
Bodrum	50	12½	860
Bursa	17	4	230
Çanakkale	30-35	6	340
Denizli (for Pamukkale)	40	12	665
Edirne	17-20	2½	235
Fethiye	50	12	820
Göreme	40	11	725
İzmir	30-49	8	575
Kaş	60	12	1090
Konya	40	10	660
Kuşadası	45	9	555
Marmaris	50	12½	805
Trabzon	60	24	970

National Taksim (☎ 0212-254 7719; www.national car.com; Şehit Muhtar Mahallesi, Aydede Sokak 1/2; ⏱ 8.30am-7pm); Atatürk International Airport (☎ 0212-465 3546; ⏱ noon-midnight)

Train

At the time of writing, all trains from Europe were terminating at **Sirkeci Train Station** (Map pp92-3; ☎ 0212-527 0051). Outside the station's main door there's a convenient tram that runs up the hill to Sultanahmet or the other way over the Golden Horn to Kabataş, from where you can travel by funicular rail up to Taksim Sq. Note that after the Marmaray project (p163) is finished, trains will terminate at Yenikapı.

Trains from the Asian side of Turkey and from countries east and south currently terminate at **Haydarpaşa Train Station** (Map pp86-7; ☎ 0216-336 4470), on the Asian shore close to Kadıköy. Ignore anyone who suggests you should take a taxi to or from Haydarpaşa. The ferry between Eminönü and Haydarpaşa/Kadıköy is cheap and speedy; taxis across the Bosphorus always get stuck in traffic. Haydarpaşa has an *emanet* (left-luggage room), a restaurant, numerous snack shops, ATMs and a small PTT. Tickets for trains leaving from Haydarpaşa Train Station can also be purchased from Sirkeci Train Station. Note that as part of the Marmaray project, Haydarpaşa Train Station is scheduled to close and services will move to a new station currently being built in Söğütlüçeşme, near Üsküdar.

Major domestic train services departing from Haydarpaşa include:
4 Eylül Mavi (Malatya via Ankara, Kayseri & Sivas)
Doğu Ekspresi (Kars via Ankara, Kayseri, Sivas, Erzurum)
Güney Ekspresi (Kurtalan via Ankara, Kayseri, Sivas, Malatya & Diyarbakır)
İç Anadolu Mavi (Adana via Konya)
Meram Ekspresi (Konya)
Pamukkale Ekspresi (Denizli via Eğirdir)
Toros Ekspresi (Gaziantep via Konya & Adana)
Vangölü Ekspresi (Tatvan via Ankara, Kayseri & Malatya)

There are six services between İstanbul and Ankara: the Baskent, Cumhuriyet, Fatih, Boğaziçi, Anadolu and Ankara Expresses. Fares on these range from TL8.75 to TL71.

GETTING AROUND

Moving some 16 million people around İstanbul is a challenge (understatement of the year), but in the last few years the government has begun to implement the ambitious Marmaray project (see p163), which aims to ease the city's horrendous traffic problems. Thankfully most of the major sights you're likely to visit on a short visit to the city are within walking distance or a short tram or bus ride away.

To/From the Airport
ATATÜRK INTERNATIONAL AIRPORT

Getting from the airport to Sultanahmet by public transport is cheap and easy. There

INTERNATIONAL TRAIN SERVICES TO/FROM İSTANBUL

For timetable and fare updates, and to check details of when these services depart European destinations on their return trips, go to www.tcdd.gov.tr.

From Sirkeci Train Station

All the following services are express trains. The fares quoted are for a seat (cheapest) to a single couchette (most expensive). All seats on the Dostlu/Filia Ekspres are couchettes, so we have listed 1st- and 2nd-class fares.

Destination	Train	Fare (TL)	Frequency	Departs	Arrives	Duration (hr)
Belgrade, Serbia	Bosfor/Balkan Ekspresi	92.40-252.60	daily	10pm	8.12pm	22
Bucharest, Romania	Bosfor Ekspresi	81.10-283.50	daily	10pm	5.09pm	19
Thessaloniki, Greece	Dostlu/ Filia Ekspresi	101.30-178.20	daily	8.30am & 9pm	10.02pm & 8.30am	11½
Sofia, Bulgaria	Bosfor Ekspresi	37.80-98.30	daily	10pm	12.40pm	15

From Haydarpaşa Train Station

The fares quoted are for a 1st-class couchette (the only option available).

Destination	Train	Fare (TL)	Frequency	Departs	Arrives	Duration (hr)
Aleppo, Syria	Toros Ekspresi	101.20	Sun	8.55am	3pm	30 (via Adana, Konya, Eskişehir)
Tabriz, Iran	Trans-Asya Ekspresi	111.20	Wed	10.55pm	6.35pm	66½ (via Ankara, Kayseri, Van)

are a couple of options, but the most convenient and quickest is to take the Light Rail Transport (LRT) service from the airport six stops to Zeytinburnu (TL1.40), from where you connect with the tram (TL1.40) that takes you directly to Sultanahmet – the whole trip takes about 50 minutes. The airport station is on the lower ground floor beneath the international arrivals hall – follow the 'Hafif Metro – Light Rail System' signs down the escalators and right to the station. Services depart every 10 minutes or so from 5.40am until 1.40am.

Hostels and some of the smaller hotels in Sultanahmet can book minibus transport from the hostel to the airport for around TL10 per person. Unfortunately, this option only works if you're going *from* town to the airport and not the other way around, and there are only six or so services per day. Reserve your seat in advance and allow lots of time for the trip as the minibus may spend up to an hour collecting all its passengers before finally heading out to the airport (30 to 45 minutes).

If you are staying near Taksim Sq, the **Havaş airport bus** (Map pp86-7; ☎ 0212-244 0487; www.havas .com.tr; one way TL9 6am-midnight, TL11.25 midnight-6am)

is the easiest option. Buses leave the airport every 15 to 30 minutes from 4am until 1am; from Taksim Sq, buses depart every 15 to 30 minutes from 4am to 1am.

Alternatively, you could take the LRT all the way to Aksaray (TL1.40), and then catch a bus from the nearby Pertevniyal V Sultan stop to Taksim Sq. Loads of buses from here go to Taksim – look for any number preceded by a 'T'.

A taxi between the Atatürk International Airport and Sultanahmet or Taksim Sq should cost around TL35, more between midnight and 6am or if there's heavy traffic.

SABIHA GÖKÇEN INTERNATIONAL AIRPORT

Some 50km east of Sultanahmet and Taksim Sq, **Sabiha Gökçen International Airport** is a

---

İETT

İstanbul Elektrik Tramvay ve Tünel (İETT) is responsible for running the public bus, tram, LRT and metro systems in the city. Its excellent website (www.iett.gov.tr) has useful timetable and route information in Turkish and English.

lot less convenient to get to than Atatürk International Airport – no matter which mode of transport you take, it's at least an hour-long trip.

The **Havaş airport bus** (☎ 0212-444 0487; www .havas.com.tr; one way TL10) travels between the airport and Taksim Sq. These depart the airport 25 minutes after planes land. They leave the Havaş office at Taksim every hour or so between 4am and 1am.

İETT buses travel between the airport and the Levent 4 metro station (TL1.40), where you can connect with the metro to Taksim Sq (TL1.40), and then the funicular (TL1.40) and tram (TL1.40) to Sultanahmet. These depart between 5am to 7.50pm Monday to Saturday and 2am to 1am Sunday.

There is also an İETT bus service to Kadıköy (TL1.40), from where you can catch a ferry to Eminönü (TL1.40) and then a tram (TL1.40) up to Sultanahmet. These depart between 6am and 10.30pm weekdays, 6.30am to 10.30pm Saturday and 7am to 9.30pm Sunday.

Most hotels and hostels in Sultanahmet can book minibus transport from your accommodation to Sabiha Gökçen for around TL30 per head.

A taxi from Sabiha Gökçen International Airport and Sultanahmet costs at least TL80; to Taksim it will be at least TL60.

Boat

The most enjoyable and efficient way to get around town is by ferry. **İstanbul Deniz Otobüsleri** (☎ 0212-444 4436; www.ido.com.tr) has timetable information or you can pick up a printed timetable at any of the ferry docks. *Jetons* (transport tokens) cost TL1.40 and

it's possible to use Akbil (see below) on all routes.

The main ferry docks are at the mouth of the Golden Horn (Eminönü, Sirkeci and Karaköy) and at Beşiktaş, a few kilometres northeast of the Galata Bridge, near Dolmabahçe Palace. There are also busy docks at Kadıköy and Üsküdar on the Asian (Anatolian) side. Ferries travel many routes around the city, but the routes commonly used by travellers include:

Beşiktaş–Üsküdar (every 20 to 30 minutes from 6.45am to 9pm)

Beşiktaş–Kadıköy (every 30 minutes from 7.15am to 9.15pm)Eminönü–Anadolu Kavağı (Boğaziçi Özel Gezi; Bosphorus Excursions Ferry; between one and three services per day)

Eminönü–Haydarpaşa–Kadıköy (approximately every 20 minutes from 7am-8pm)

Eminönü–Kadıköy (approximately every 15 to 20 minutes from 7.30am to 8.35pm)

Eminönü–Üsküdar (approximately every 20 minutes from 6.35am to 11pm)

Kabataş–Kadıköy–Kınalıada–Burgazada–Heybeliada–Büyükada (Princes' Islands ferry; at least eight ferries per day)

Karaköy–Kadıköy–Haydarpaşa (approximately every 20 minutes from 6.10am-11pm)

Sirkeci–Harem (daily car ferry from 7am, then every half-hour until 9.30pm)

Üsküdar–Karaköy–Eminönü–Kasımpaşa–Fener–Balat–Hasköy–Ayvansaray–Sütlüce–Eyüp (approximately every hour, from 7.30am to 7.50pm)

Car & Motorcycle

Driving in İstanbul is a nightmare: constant traffic jams, careless drivers, traffic lanes habitually ignored, thin streets choked with parked cars – and you're expected to be

---

AKBIL

An Akbil is a computerised debit fare tag that will save you time and money when hopping on and off trams, trains, the LRT, ferries and buses all around the city. Akbil tags are available at the Akbil Gişesi booths at the Sultanahmet tram stop or the Sirkeci, Eminönü, Aksaray or Taksim Sq bus stands for a TL6 deposit. Unfortunately, you cannot purchase them at either of İstanbul's airports. When you have your tag, you can charge it unlimited times with TL5, TL10, TL20 or TL50 at any Akbil booth or at machines at the Tünel or metro stations (using TL50 notes in the machines can be problematic, so we suggest only doing this at the manned booths). You can also purchase daily (*günlük*), weekly (*haftalık*), 15-day (*15 günlük*) and monthly (*aylık*) tags. Press the tag or card's metal button into the fare machine on a bus, ferry, LRT, train, metro, tram or funicular and – beep – the fare is automatically deducted from your line of credit. It's perfectly acceptable if one person in a group buys an Akbil and presses it the appropriate number of times when everyone boards together. Akbil fares are 10% lower than cash or ticket fares. You'll get your deposit back when you return the tag.

THREE CHEERS FOR MARMARAY

Marmaray (www.tcdd.gov.tr/tcdding/marmaray_ing.htm) is an ambitious public transport project aimed to relieve İstanbul's woeful traffic congestion. Its name comes from combining the name of the Sea of Marmara, which lies just south of the project site, with *ray*, the Turkish word for rail. Plans show the Sirkeci–Halkali rail line, which presently follows the coast to Yeşilköy near the airport, going underground at Yedikule and travelling to underground stations at Yenikapı and Sirkeci. From Sirkeci it will travel some 5km in a new tunnel being built under the Bosphorus to another underground station on the Asian side at Üsküdar. From there it will come to ground level at Söğütlüçeşme, some 2km east of Kadıköy, where it will connect with the Gebze Anatolian rail line.

The project was slated to be completed by 2010, but the deadline has been extended to 2012 and may take even longer. Old İstanbul is built on layers upon layers of history. No sooner had workmen commenced digging when they found an ancient port and bazaar in Üsküdar, and a 4th-century Byzantine harbour in Yenikapı. Diggers were replaced by brushes, and archaeologists got to work. The works, which are still under way, have been documented in the excellent 'Light of Day' exhibition on show at the İstanbul Archaeological Museums (p108).

---

able to turn on a postage stamp. Put simply, we recommend you park your car and use İstanbul's cheap and efficient public transport system instead.

Most top-end hotels offer undercover parking for guests, and many midrange options have a streetside park or two that is nominally theirs to use. Organise this with the hotel ahead of your arrival.

There are few undercover long-term car parks in the city. Instead, car parking is dotted all over the city in empty blocks overseen by a caretaker; there's an hourly fee to pay in these. There is also roadside parking, free of charge. There is no fixed system: one street can be free; turn the corner and a fee collector will be waiting. There are also no street signs to tell you where parking lots are. Your best bet is to ring your accommodation and, upon arrival, ask them to point out the nearest and/or cheapest parking option. Negotiate a rate for the duration of your stay. Expect to pay TL10 to TL15 for a 24-hour period.

If you baulk at the thought of even driving into the city to park, consider parking at Atatürk International Airport, and catching public transport or a taxi into the city to your accommodation. Parking costs TL59 for four days, or TL96 per week. See www.ataturk airport.com for more information.

Dolmuş

İstanbul dolmuşes are privately run minibuses working defined routes. As a short-term visitor to the city, you won't have much, if any, cause to use them.

Public Transport

BUS

İstanbul's bus system is extremely efficient. The major bus stations are at Taksim Sq, Beşiktaş, Aksaray, Rüstempaşa-Eminönü, Kadıköy and Üsküdar. Most services run between 6.30am and 11.30pm. Destinations and main stops on city bus routes are shown on a sign on the kerbside of the *otobus* (bus) or on the electronic display at its front.

İETT (www.iett.gov.tr) buses are run by the city and you must have a ticket (TL1.40) before boarding. You can buy tickets from the white booths near major stops or from some nearby shops for a small mark-up (look for 'İETT *otobüs bileti satılır*' signs). Think about stocking up a supply to last throughout your stay in the city or buying an Akbil (see opposite). Blue private buses regulated by the city called Özel Halk Otobüsü run the same routes; these accept cash (pay the conductor) and Akbil.

FUNICULAR RAILWAY

The Tünel was built in the late 19th century to save passengers the steep walk from Karaköy up the hill to İstiklal Caddesi in Beyoğlu. The three-minute service still runs today from 7am to 9pm Monday to Friday (from 7.30am on weekends), every five or 10 minutes and the fare is TL1.40.

A new funicular railway runs through a tunnel from the Bosphorus shore at Kabataş, where it connects with the tram, up the hill to the metro station at Taksim Sq. The three-minute service runs around every three minutes and cost TL1.40.

LIGHT RAIL TRANSIT (LRT)

An LRT service connects Aksaray with the airport, stopping at 15 stations including the otogar along the way. Services depart every 10 minutes or so from 5.40am until 1.40am and cost TL1.40, no matter how many stops you travel. There are plans to eventually extend this service to Yenikapı.

METRO

İstanbul's underground metro system runs north from Taksim Sq, stopping at Osmanbey, Şişli-Mecidiyeköy, Gayrettepe, Levent and Levent 4. Plans are on the drawing board to extend this north to Ayazağa. Services run every five minutes or so from 6.30am to 12.20am (TL1.40).

TRAIN

İstanbul has two *banliyö treni* (suburban train lines). The first rattles along the Sea of Marmara shore from Sirkeci Train Station, around Seraglio Point to Cankurtaran (Sultanahmet), Kumkapı, Yenikapı and a number of stations before terminating past Atatürk International Airport at Halkala. The second runs from Haydarpaşa Train Station to Gebze via Bostancı. Though decrepit, the trains are reliable (nearly every half-hour) and cheap (TL1.40).

TRAM

An excellent tramway *(tramvay)* service runs from Zeytinburnu (where it connects with the airport LRT) to Sultanahmet and Eminönü, and then across the Galata Bridge to Karaköy (to connect with the funicular to Tünel) and Kabataş (to connect with the funicular to Taksim Sq). Trams run every five minutes or so from 6am to midnight. Tickets cost TL1.40.

A quaint antique tram rattles its way up and down İstiklal Caddesi in Beyoğlu every day, beginning its 15-minute journey just outside the Tünel station and travelling to Taksim Sq, stopping in front of the Galatasaray Lycée (p115) en route. Tickets aren't available on board – you must use an Akbil or purchase a ticket (TL1.40) from the Tünel station.

Taxi

İstanbul is full of yellow taxis. A base rate is levied during the *gündüz* (daytime); the *gece* (night-time) rate, from midnight to 6am, is 50% higher. Meters, with LCD displays, flash '*gündüz*' or '*gece*' when they're started.

Occasionally, drivers try to put the *gece* rate on during the day, so watch out.

Taxi rates are very reasonable – from Sultanahmet to Taksim Sq should cost around TL10; ignore taxi drivers who insist on a fixed rate as these are much higher than you'd pay using the meter. Double-check the money you give the driver too: drivers have been known to insist they were given a TL5 note for payment, when they were really given TL20.

Few of the city's taxis have seatbelts. If you catch a taxi over either of the Bosphorus bridges it is your responsibility to cover the toll. The driver will add this to your fare.

As far as tipping goes, locals usually round up the fare to the nearest 0.5TL.

AROUND İSTANBUL

If you're staying in İstanbul for a while you may want to consider taking a day trip to the Princes' Islands, a peaceful antidote to the hustle and bustle of the big city.

PRINCES' ISLANDS
☎ 0216

Most İstanbullus refer to the Princes' Islands as 'The Islands' (Adalar). They lie about 20km southeast of the city in the Sea of Marmara and make a great destination for a day's escape.

In Byzantine times, refractory princes, deposed monarchs and others who had outlived their roles were interned on the islands (rather like Abdullah Öcalan, the ex-PKK leader, marooned today on Imrali Island in the Sea of Marmara). A ferry service from İstanbul was started in the mid-19th century and the islands became popular summer resorts with Pera's Greek, Jewish and Armenian business communities. Many of the fine Victorian villas built by these wealthy merchants survive today.

You'll realise after landing that there are no cars on the islands, something that comes as a welcome relief after the traffic mayhem of the city. Except for the necessary police, fire and sanitation vehicles, transport is by bicycle, horse-drawn carriage and foot, as in centuries past.

All of the islands are extremely busy in summer, particularly on weekends, so we recommend avoiding a Sunday visit. If you wish to stay overnight during the summer months it is imperative that you book ahead. Many of the hotels are closed during the winter.

There are nine islands in the Princes' Islands group, five of them populated. The ferry stops at four of these; the fifth, Sedef, has only recently attracted a resident population. There are 15,000 permanent residents scattered across the five, but numbers swell to 100,000 during the summer months when İstanbullus – many of whom have holiday homes here – come here to escape the city heat.

The ferry's first stop is **Kınalıada** (a favourite holiday spot for İstanbul's Armenian population), which is sprinkled with low-rise apartments, all sporting red tiled roofs and oriented towards the water. The island has a few pebble beaches, a modernist mosque and an Armenian church to the left of the ferry station. The second stop, **Burgazada**, has always been favoured by İstanbullus of Greek heritage. Sights include a hilltop chapel, mosques, a synagogue, a handful of restaurants and the home of the late writer Sait Faik, now a modest **museum**. Frankly, neither island offers much reward for the trouble of getting off the ferry.

In contrast, the charming island of **Heybeliada** (Heybeli for short) has much to offer the visitor. It's home to the Turkish Naval Academy, which was founded in 1773 and is seen to the left of the ferry dock as you arrive. It also has several restaurants and a thriving shopping strip with bakeries and delicatessens selling picnic provisions to day trippers, who come here on weekends to walk in the pine groves and swim from the tiny (but crowded) beaches. The island's major landmark is the hilltop **Haghia Triada Monastery** (☎ 0216-351 8563). Perched above a picturesque line of poplar trees in a spot that has been occupied by a Greek monastery since Byzantine times, this building dates from 1894 and has an internationally renowned library. The monastery functioned as a Greek Orthodox school of theology where priests were trained until 1971, when it was closed on the government's orders. The Ecumenical Orthodox Patriarchate (p124) in Fener has applied for permission to reopen the school. You may be able to visit if you call ahead.

Heybeliada has a couple of hotels, including the Merit Halki Palace (p166), which is perched at the top of Rafah Şehitleri Caddesi and commands wonderful views over the water. The delightful walk up to this hotel passes an antique shop and a host of large wooden villas set in lovingly tended gardens. There are many lanes and streets leading to picnic spots and lookout points off the upper reaches of this street. To do this walk, turn right as you leave the ferry and make your way past the waterfront restaurants and cafés to the plaza with the Atatürk statue. From here walk up İşgüzar Sokak, veering right until you hit Rafah Şehitleri Caddesi.

If you don't feel like a walk (this one's uphill but not too steep), you can hire a bicycle from one of the shops in the main street (TL2 to TL3.50 per hour) or a *fayton* (horse-drawn carriage) to take you on a tour of the island. A 25-minute tour *(küçük tur)* costs TL20, a one-hour tour *(büyük tur)* TL30. Some visitors choose to spend the day by the **pool** (weekdays/weekends TL50/60) at the Merit Halki Palace, but most locals swim at the beaches around the island, though it pays to check the cleanliness of the water before you join them.

The largest island in the group, **Büyükada** ('Great Island'), shows an impressive face to visitors arriving on the ferry, with gingerbread villas climbing up the slopes of the hill and the bulbous twin cupolas of the Splendid Otel (p166) providing an unmistakable landmark.

The **ferry terminal** is a lovely building in the Ottoman kiosk style dating from 1899. Inside there's a pleasant café with an outdoor terrace. There are eateries serving fresh fish to the left of the ferry terminal, next to an ATM.

The island's main tourist attraction is the Greek **Monastery of St George**, in the saddle between Büyükada's two highest hills. To get here, walk from the ferry straight ahead to the clock tower in İskele Meydanı (Dock Sq). The shopping district (with cheap eateries) is to the left along Recep Koç Sokak. Bear right onto 23 Nisan Caddesi, then head along Çankaya Caddesi up the hill to the monastery; when you come to a fork in the road, veer right. The enjoyable walk, which takes at least one hour, takes you past a long progression of impressive wooden villas set in gardens. About a quarter of the way up on the left is the **Büyükada Kültür Evi**, a charming spot where you can enjoy a tea or coffee in a garden setting. The house itself dates from 1878 and was restored in 1998. After 40 minutes or so you will reach a reserve called 'Luna Park' by the locals. The monastery is a 25-minute walk up an extremely steep hill from here; some visitors prefer to hire a donkey to take them up the hill and back down again (TL10). As you ascend you will see pieces of cloth tied onto the branches of trees along the path – each represents a prayer, mostly offered by female supplicants who are visiting the monastery to pray for a child.

When you reach the monastery, there's not a lot to see. A small and gaudy church is the only building of note, but there are fabulous panoramic views from the terrace, as well as a small restaurant (see right). From here it's possible to see all the way to İstanbul, as well as over to the nearby islands of Yassıada and Sivriada.

Bicycles are available for rent in town, and shops on the market street can provide picnic supplies, although food is cheaper on the mainland.

Just off the clock tower square and opposite the Splendid Otel you'll find a *fayton* stand. Hire one for a long tour of town, the hills and shore (one hour, TL45) or a shorter tour of the town only (TL35). It costs TL16 to be taken to 'Luna Park'. A shop just near the *fayton* stand hires out bicycles for TL2.50 to TL3 per hour.

Sleeping & Eating

There's not really much of an argument for staying here overnight – it's much more sensible to spend a day here and then return to the city, where the sleeping and eating options are better and less expensive.

HEYBELIADA

Merit Halki Palace (☎ 0216-351 0025; www.halki palacehotel.com; Rafah Şehitleri Caddesi 94; s/d Sun-Thu €65/85, s/d Fri & Sat €85/135; 🐾) This comfortable hotel is a popular weekend-break destination for İstanbullus. Its pool area is particularly impressive, and its restaurant serves meals and drinks on the poolside terrace.

Mavi Restaurant (☎ 0216-351 0128; Yali Caddesi 29; mains TL12-20; 🕙 24hr) This fish restaurant on the main waterfront promenade is popular with locals and has loads of outdoor seating.

BÜYÜKADA

Splendid Otel (☎ 0216-382 6950; www.splendidhotel.net; Nisan Caddesi 23; s TL105, d TL150-175; 🐾) This landmark building is indeed splendid. Rooms aren't quite as impressive as the exterior or the common rooms, but are comfortable enough. It's well worth forking out the extra TL24 for the front rooms with small balconies and sea views (not available for singles).

Hotel Princess Büyükada (☎ 0216-382 1628; www .buyukadaprincess.com; İskele Meydanı 2; r Sun-Fri TL150-180, Sat TL230-260; 🐾 🚇) This recently refurbished hotel is right in the heart of things on the clock tower square. Rooms are large and pleasant enough. Sea-view rooms are worth the €10 extra.

Yücetepe Kır Gazinosu restaurant (Monastery of St George; mains YT7-8; 🕙 daily Apr-Oct, weekends only Nov-Mar) Simple but appetising food is served at the outdoor tables here.

Getting There & Away

At least nine daily ferries run to the islands every day between 6.50am and 7.40pm, departing from the Adalar İskelesi ferry dock at Kabataş, opposite the tram stop. The most useful departure times for day trippers are 8.30am, 9.20am, 10.10am and 11.35am on weekdays and 8.30am, 9am, 9.30am, 10am, 11am and noon on weekends, but timetables change, so check www.ido.com.tr beforehand. The ferry returns from Büyükada at times including 3.15pm, 4pm and 5.45pm on weekdays and 3.15pm, 4.30pm 5.05pm and 5.45pm on weekends, stopping at Heybeliada en route to Kabataş. The last ferry of the day leaves Büyükada at 10pm (9.45pm on weekends). The trip costs TL2.80 to the islands, and the same for each leg between the islands and for the return trip. The cheapest and easiest way to pay is to use your Akbil (see p162). Note that the ferries seem dangerously overcrowded on summer weekends; time your trip for weekdays or make sure you board the vessel and grab a seat at least half an hour before departure unless you want to stand the whole way.

The ferry steams away from Kabataş and after 20 minutes makes a quick stop at Kadıköy on the Asian side before making its way to the first island, Kınalıada. It's not uncommon to see dolphins on this leg of the trip (25 minutes). After this, it's another 10 minutes to Burgazada, another 15 minutes again to Heybeliada and another 10 minutes to Büyükada.

Many day trippers stay on the ferry until Heybeliada, stop there for an hour or so and hop on a ferry to Büyükada, where they have lunch and spend the rest of the afternoon.

You can also take a fast catamaran from Eminönü or Kabataş to Bostancı on the Asian shore, then another from Bostancı to Heybeliada and Büyükada, but you save little time and the cost is much higher.

Thrace & Marmara

You could almost call this Turkey's forgotten corner. Despite its easy access to İstanbul, the northwest is not a very common stop on the tourist circuit. Of course there are reasons for this, well, oversight.

Thrace (Trakya), the Roman province shared with Greece and Bulgaria and the country's only foothold in Europe, covers just a fraction of the nation's total land mass and is Turkey at its most Balkan, without the well-known draws of the south and east. Marmara, the Asian mainland around the eponymous sea, may be just a hop, skip and a jump from İstanbul but it's built-up and heavily industrialised along its southern shores. And there really aren't any big cities here with 'household' names.

Ah, but the things you'll miss if you don't make it here. Thrace has an embarrassment of Ottoman architecture, with mosques and civic buildings equal to those in the capital. It can also boast Turkey's finest rakı (aniseed barndy), the world's oldest sporting event after the Olympic Games and delightfully unspoiled fishing villages on its Black Sea coast. Marmara, meanwhile, is littered with beaches, claims one of Turkey's two inhabited Aegean islands and, in the west, where it straddles the Dardanelles, preserves the memory of one of WWI's fiercest and most costly battles on the Gallipoli Peninsula.

What's more, you don't even have to go through İstanbul to see the sights. Northwest Turkey is an easy gateway to and from Greece and Eastern Europe via Bulgaria (not to mention Aegean Turkey). If you've just arrived overland from elsewhere in Europe, this is the perfect introduction to Turkey and the Turks.

HIGHLIGHTS

- Marvel at the floating dome in master architect Mimar Sinan's masterpiece, the **Selimiye Camii** (p169) in Edirne
- Get down and slippery at the annual oil wrestling festival in late June at the **Kırkpınar** (p172) near Edirne
- Walk through the blood-soaked past and peaceful present of the **Gallipoli battlefields** (p178)
- Enjoy the rugged landscape and the eerily out-of-time Greek atmosphere of some villages on the remote island of **Gökçeada** (p192)
- Cool off in the gin-clear waters of the Black Sea at the delightfully unspoiled fishing village of **Kıyıköy** (p194)

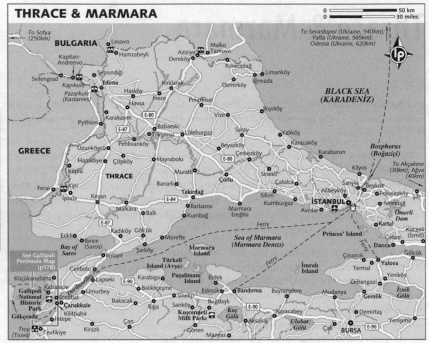

EDİRNE

☎ 0284 / pop 136,000

The largest settlement in European Turkey outside İstanbul, Edirne is largely disregarded by all but a handful of travellers who come to enjoy its stunning architecture. Edirne was briefly the capital of the Ottoman Empire and many of its key buildings are still in excellent shape. You'll find none of the razzamatazz or crowds of the Aegean or Mediterranean coasts here, but Edirne is hardly a backwater. With the Greek and Bulgarian frontiers a half-hour's drive away, Edirne is a bustling border town and the streets are crowded with foreigners, locals and off-duty soldiers from the central garrison.

History

Emperor Hadrian made Hadrianopolis (later Adrianople) the main centre of Roman Thrace in the early 2nd century AD. The settlement was an important stop on the Via Ignatia linking Rome with İstanbul. In the mid-14th century the nascent Ottoman state began to grow in size and power. In 1363 its army crossed the Dardanelles, skirted Constantinople and captured Adrianople, which the Ottomans made their capital.

For a century, Edirne was the city from which the Ottoman sultan launched campaigns in Europe and Asia. When the time was ripe for the final conquest of the Byzantine Empire, Mehmet the Conqueror (Mehmet Fatih) set out for Constantinople from here.

When the Ottoman Empire collapsed after WWI, the Allies handed Thrace to the Greeks and declared Constantinople (now İstanbul) an international city. In the summer of 1920 Greek armies occupied Edirne, only to be driven back by forces under the command of Mustafa Kemal (Atatürk). The Treaty of Lausanne (1923) ceded Edirne and eastern Thrace to the Turks.

Orientation

The centre of town is Hürriyet Meydanı, at the intersection of the two main streets, Saraçlar Caddesi (and its continuation Hükümet Caddesi) and Talat Paşa Caddesi.

The otogar (bus station) is 9km east of the city centre on the access road to the Trans-European Motorway (TEM).

South of the centre, two graceful Ottoman bridges lead across the Tunca and Meriç Rivers to a cluster of inviting restaurants. To the northeast, another Ottoman bridge leads to Sarayiçi and the Kırkpınar stadium, where the annual oil-wrestling contests are held (p172).

Information

Araz Döviz (Ali Paşa Bazaar, Talat Paşa Caddesi; ⏰ 9am-7pm Mon-Sat) Changes cash and travellers cheques; you'll find a half-dozen commercial banks opposite.

Aşkin Net (Orhaniye Caddesi; per hr TL1; ⏰ 8am-2am) Internet access in Kaleiçi.

Post office (PTT; Saraçlar Caddesi)

Tourist office (☎ 213 9208; Talat Paşa Caddesi; ⏰ 9am-6pm) Very helpful, with English-language brochures and city map.

Sights

SELİMİYE CAMİİ

Edirne's grandest house of worship, the **Selimiye Mosque** (1569–75), was designed by the great Ottoman architect Mimar Sinan (p111) for Sultan Selim II (r 1566–74). The mosque is smaller but more elegant than Sinan's Süleymaniye Camii in İstanbul, and it is said that the master considered this to be his finest work.

Enter the mosque though the courtyard to the west, as the architect intended, rather than through the terraced park and the subterranean row of shops to the south. The complex lit up at night is a spectacular sight.

The broad, lofty dome – at 31.3m marginally wider than that of İstanbul's Aya Sofya – is supported by eight unobtrusive pillars, arches and external buttresses, creating a surprisingly spacious interior. As they only bear a portion of the dome's weight, the walls are sound enough to hold dozens of windows, the light from which brings out the colourful calligraphic decorations of the interior.

The delicately carved marble *mimber* (pulpit) with its conical roof of İznik tiles and the *şadırvan* (ablutions fountain) beneath the central prayer-reader's platform are particularly exquisite. The best views of the interior are from the mezzanine-level *mahfel* (gallery).

Part of the Selimiye's striking effect comes from its four 71m-high minarets, which Sinan fluted to emphasise their height. Each tower also has three *şerefes* (balconies), Sinan's respectful nod, perhaps, to his predecessor, the architect of the Üç Şerefeli Cami (right).

A *medrese* (seminary) in the southeast corner of the complex houses the **Turkish & Islamic Arts Museum** (Türk İslam Eserleri Müzesi; ☎ 225 1120; admission TL3; ⏰ 8am-5pm Tue-Sun), whose 15 rooms and central courtyard contain a variety of stone inscriptions and early Ottoman artefacts, plus displays on oil wrestling and dervishes.

EDİRNE ARCHAEOLOGY & ETHNOGRAPHY MUSEUM

This **museum** (Edirne Arkeoloji ve Etnografya Müzesi; ☎ 225 1120; admission TL5; ⏰ 9am-noon & 1-5pm Tue-Sun) east of the Selimiye Camii faces a garden of janissary gravestones. The museum grounds contain all kinds of jars, sculptures, a dolmen, menhirs (standing stones) and a Roman family tomb from the 2nd century AD. Inside, the displays focus on local history and traditional products (p174), embroidery, textiles, calligraphy and coffee ware. There are several reconstructions of rooms in old houses, including bridal and circumcision rooms. The archaeological section runs from prehistory through to the classical period of Hadrianopolis and displays finds from recent digs around the Macedonian Tower (p171) and the rich Taşlıcabayır tumulus near Kırklareli to the east. The terracotta sarcophagi (6th century BC) from Enez (Aenus) in southwest Thrace are exquisite.

EDİRNE URBAN HISTORY MUSEUM

Housed in the restored Hafızağa Mansion, a particularly fine 19th-century Ottoman villa, this small **museum** (Edirne Kent Tarihi Müzesi; ☎ 214 4026; Arif Paşa Caddesi; admission TL2; ⏰ 8.30am-noon & 1-6pm) has poster displays on Edirne's historic buildings, old maps and postcards. As there are no English captions, it's not an essential stop, but the house itself is lovely and offers great views onto the west side of the Selimiye Mosque. There's a great shop selling traditional Edirne products here.

ÜÇ ŞEREFELİ CAMİ

The **Three-Balcony Mosque**, with its four strikingly different minarets, dominates Hürriyet Meydanı. The name refers to the three balconies on the tallest minaret. The second highest has only two.

It was built between 1438 and 1447 in a design halfway between the Seljuk Turkish-style mosques of Konya and Bursa and the truly Ottoman style, which would later

EDİRNE

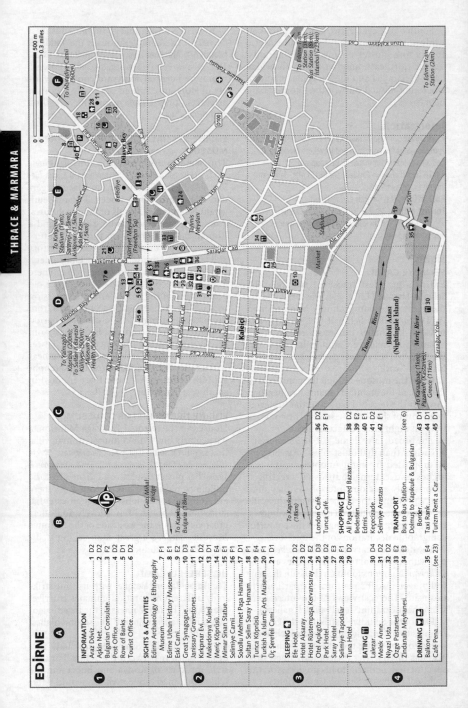

reach its pinnacle in İstanbul. In the Seljuk style, smaller domes are mounted on square rooms, whereas here the 24m-wide dome is mounted on a hexagonal drum and supported by two walls and two massive hexagonal pillars. The covered courtyard, with its central *şadırvan*, was another innovation that came to be standard.

Across the street from the mosque is the atmospheric **Sokollu Mehmet Paşa Hamam** (wash & massage TL20; 8am-10pm for men, 10am-6pm for women), designed by Mimar Sinan for Grand Vizier Sokollu Mehmet Paşa in the 16th century.

MAKEDONYA KULESİ
Southwest of the hamam stands the restored **Macedonian Tower**, part of the city fortifications dating back to Roman times. Around its base, excavations carried out in 2002 and 2003 have uncovered parts of the old city wall, a necropolis and the remains of a Byzantine church. Artefacts and smaller finds, including the Cemetery Stele with three figures and an angel, can be seen in the Edirne Archaeology and Ethnography Museum (p169).

ESKİ CAMİ
West of Hürriyet Meydanı is the **Old Mosque** (1403–14), which exemplifies one of the two classic mosque styles used by the Ottomans in their earlier capital, Bursa. Like Bursa's great Ulu Cami, the Eski Cami has rows of arches and pillars supporting a series of small domes. Inside, there is a marvellous *mimber* and striking red, white and black geometric patterns on the dome; huge calligraphic inscriptions cover the walls. The columns at the front of the mosque were recycled from a Roman building.

KALEİÇİ
The Kaleiçi area, framed by Saraçlar Caddesi, Talat Paşa Caddesi, the railway line and the Tunca River, was the original medieval town, with narrow streets laid out on a grid plan. Exploring at will is easy, but you could start by walking south from the tourist office along Maarif Caddesi, which takes you past some fine examples of ornate wooden houses with attractive Edirnekâri woodwork and finishes at Edirne's derelict **Great Synagogue** (Büyük Sinagog; 1906). Cumhuriyet Caddesi, running perpendicular to Maarif Caddesi, is another interesting street.

MURADİYE CAMİİ
A 15-minute walk northeast of the Selimiye Mosque along Mimar Sinan Caddesi brings you to the **Muradiye Mosque**, built for Sultan Murat II and topped with an unusual cupola. Note the massive calligraphy on the exterior. Built between 1426 and 1436, it once housed a Mevlevi whirling dervish lodge. The mosque's T-shaped plan, with twin *eyvans* (domed side chambers) and fine İznik tiles, is reminiscent of Ottoman work in Bursa.

The small cemetery on the east side contains the grave of Şeyhülislâm Musa Kâzım Efendi, the Ottoman Empire's last chief Islamic judge, who fled the British occupation of İstanbul after WWI and died here in 1920.

SULTAN II BAYEZİD KÜLLİYESİ
This **mosque complex** was built by the Ottoman architect Hayreddin for Sultan Bayezid II (r 1481–1512) between 1484 and 1488. Today it stands in splendid isolation to the north of Edirne. In style, the mosque lies midway between the Üç Şerefeli and Selimiye models: its large prayer hall has one large dome, similar to the Selimiye, but it also has a courtyard and fountain, like the earlier Üç Şerefeli. The interior has a rough, almost unfinished feel to it.

The complex is extensive and includes a *tabhane* (travellers hostel), bakery, *imaret* (soup kitchen), *tımarhane* (asylum), *medrese* and *darüşşifa* (hospital). The last two, to the west of the mosque, have been converted into the innovative and award-winning **Museum of Health** (Sağlık Müzesi; 212 0922; www.trakya.edu.tr/kulliye; admission TL10; 9am-7pm).

The seminary consists of a dozen rooms on three sides of a courtyard and traces medical education under the Ottomans, with recreated classrooms, students' quarters, a library and surgical operations in progress. The first two courtyards of the hospital, traditionally reserved for outpatients and the hospital administration, have 10 rooms examining in great detail aspects of Ottoman medicine – from pharmaceuticals to gynaecological disorders. The best part is the hexagonal structure at the end called the *şifahane* (healing room) where resident patients stayed. The winter and summer rooms are filled with mock-ups of patients with various maladies (psychosis, neurosis, depression, epilepsy etc) being treated in surprisingly 'New Age' ways: soothing music, water bubbling from a central fountain, aromatherapy and, yes, even

THRACE & MARMARA

THRACE & MARMARA

SLIP-SLIDING AWAY IN EDİRNE

One of the world's oldest and most bizarre sporting events, in which muscular men naked except for a pair of heavy leather shorts coat themselves with olive oil and throw each around, takes place annually in late June/early July at Sarayiçi in northern Edirne. It's called the **Tarihi Kırkpınar Yağlı Güreş Festivali** (Historic Kırkpınar Oil Wrestling Festival).

The origins of this oleaginous contest go back almost six-and-a-half centuries to the early days of the Ottoman Empire. Before the conquest of Edirne in 1361, sultan Orhan Gazi sent his brother Süleyman Paşa with 40 men to conquer the Byzantine fortress at Domuz in Rumelia, the part of the Ottoman Empire in Europe. The two-score soldiers were all keen wrestlers and after their victory challenged each other to bouts. Two of them were so evenly matched that they fought for days without any clear result, until both of them finally dropped dead. When the bodies were buried under a nearby fig tree, a spring mysteriously appeared. The site was given the name Kırkpınar, or '40 Springs', in the wrestlers' honour.

The original Kırkpınar is now the village of Samona just over the border in Greece; the annual three-day contest has been held here since the birth of the republic. Wrestlers, who are classed not by weight but by height, age and experience, compete in 13 categories – from *minik* (toddler) to *baş* (first class) – with dozens of matches taking place simultaneously in the large Sarayiçi stadium. Bouts are now capped at 30 or 40 minutes, after which they enter 'sudden death' one fall–wins overtime. When all the fights are decided, prizes are awarded for gentlemanly conduct and best entry technique, as well as the coveted and hotly contested *başpehlivan* (head wrestler) title.

For more information visit **Kırkpınar Evi** (Kırkpınar House; ☎ 212 8622; www.kirkpinar.com; ☉ 10am-noon & 2-6pm) with displays in Edirne or check out its website. For better videos and links, visit www.turkishwrestling.com.

---

basket-weaving and what looks suspiciously like macramé.

Approach the complex via the Ottoman **Yalnızgöz Köprüsü** (Lone Eye Bridge; 1570) crossing the Tunca River.

SARAYİÇİ

The **Inner Palace** is actually a scrub-covered island that was once the private hunting reserve of the Ottoman sultans. Today it's the site of the famous Kırkpınar oil-wrestling matches (above).

Near the modern stadium, which is flanked by uberbutch *başpehlivan* (champions) in bronze, stands the **Adalet Kasrı** (Justice Hall; 1561), a stone tower with a conical roof that dates from the time of Süleyman the Magnificent. In front of it are two square columns: on the Seng-i Hürmet (Stone of Respect) to the right people would place petitions to the sultan, while the Seng-i İbret (Stone of Warning) on the left displayed the heads of high-court officers who had managed to dis the sultan.

Behind the Justice Hall is the small **Fatih Köprüsü** (Conqueror Bridge; 1452). Cross it and on your right you'll see a sombre **Balkan Wars memorial** and graves. Straight ahead and to the left are the scattered ruins of **Edirne Sarayı**

(Edirne Palace). Begun by Sultan Bayezid II in 1450, this palace once rivalled İstanbul's Topkapı Palace in size and luxury, though you'd be hard-pressed even to visualise the palace nowadays.

To get here walk north along Hükümet Caddesi and cross the Tunca River via the **Saray Köprüsü** (Palace Bridge; 1560). Alternatively, it's a scenic 1km walk along the river embankment from the Sultan Bayezid II complex.

SOUTH OF THE CENTRE

To reach the quiet south from the busy town centre, simply follow Saraçlar Caddesi under the railway line and cross the **Tunca Köprüsü**, an Ottoman stone humpback bridge dating to 1615, and the much newer **Meriç Köprüsü** (1847). The area around the bridges is packed with restaurants, tea gardens and bars, all great places to come for a drink or a meal in warm weather. The best ones are those on the southern side of the Meriç River, which offer perfect sunset river vistas and great views of the illuminated Selimiye Camii.

Sleeping

Most of Edirne's budget and midrange hotels are along Maarif Caddesi running parallel to Saraçlar Caddesi.

BUDGET

Hotel Aksaray (☎ 212 6035; fax 225 6806; Alipaşa Ortakapı Caddesi; s/d/tr without bathroom TL30/55/70, s/d/tr/q TL35/65/80/100; ❉) The cheapest option in town, the 'White Palace' has 12 basic rooms in a charmingly decrepit old building, and bathroom cubicles rammed into impossibly small spaces. The ceiling fresco in ground-floor room 103 is an unexpected bonus.

Saray Hotel (☎ 212 1457; www.edirnesarayhotel.com in Turkish; Eski İstanbul Caddesi 28; s/d/tr TL35/60/75; ❉ 🖳) It may look like a smart business-class option from the outside, but inside this place is nothing more than a modern and very clean 44-room budget hotel. It's a bit away from the action.

Otel Açıkgöz (☎ 213 1944; www.acikgoz.com in Turkish; Tüfekçiler Çarşısı 54; s/d/tr TL40/60/80; ❉ 🖳) One of two hotels run by the 'Open Eye', a company specialising in bathrooms and kitchens, enjoys a quiet location in Kaleiçi. The 35 rooms are bare-bones but clean.

Tuna Hotel (☎ 214 3340; fax 214 33 23; Maarif Caddesi 17; s/d/tr/q TL50/70/90/100; ❉ 🖳) This 18-room hotel at the quieter southern end of Maarif Caddesi is an excellent choice for the price. Room 106 overlooks a neat little courtyard and a back annexe with triples and quads.

MIDRANGE

Park Hotel (☎ 225 4610; parkotel@superonline.com; Maarif Caddesi 7; s/d/tr/ste €40/57/75/100; ❉ 🖳) There's nothing spectacular about the Park's 60 rooms, but the facilities go a long way to make it an attractive option, with a restaurant and café-bar and a big lounge with bright Picasso prints and a fireplace.

Efe Hotel (☎ 213 6166; www.efehotel.com; Maarif Caddesi 13; s/d TL85/125; ❉ 🖳) A personal favourite, the Efe is a very stylish place, especially the lobby, which is filled with antiques and curios. The 22 rooms, especially the second-floor doubles, are big and bright and have fridges and even electric kettles. The hotel's flashy English Pub opens from September to May.

Hotel Rüstempaşa Kervansaray (☎ 212 6119; kervansarayhotel@mynet.com; İki Kapılı Han Caddesi 57; s/d/tr €47/85/110; ❉ 🖳) Just south of the Eski Cami, this *han* (caravanserai) was built for Süleyman the Magnificent's grand vizier Rüstempaşa in about 1550 and turned into a hotel in 1972. Its inner courtyard offers a romantic setting for breakfast but the 75 guestrooms, though of a good size, are distinctly underwhelming and airless. Reach them via 21 narrow stone steps.

TOP END

our pick Selimiye Taşodalar (☎ 212 3529; www.tasodalar.com; Taşodalar Sokak 3; r €80-135, ste €200; ❌ ❉ 🖳) Edirne's first boutique hotel, the 'Stone Rooms' could not be in a choicer spot: a series of rebuilt Ottoman-era cells in a garden overlooking Selimiye Mosque and the ruined Sultan Selim Saray Hamam. The nine rooms, whose prices are negotiable, are of different sizes and each bears the name of a sultan. The decor might be a little too Ottoman for some tastes and the plastic flowers and factory-made carpets are naff, but the rooms are bright and airy, the furniture of lovely Turkish cedar and the welcome warm. Choose double room 106 or family room 108, both of which face the mosque. The hotel has an in-house restaurant and a pleasant outdoor tea garden.

Eating
RESTAURANTS

There's a wide assortment of eateries along Saraçlar Caddesi. The riverside restaurants south of the centre are more atmospheric, but most open only in summer and are often booked solid at weekends for wedding and circumcision parties.

The city's dish of choice is *Edirne ciğeri*, thinly sliced calf's liver deep-fried and eaten with crispy fried red chillies and yoghurt.

Özge Pastanesi (☎ 212 2333; Murat Turgu Caddesi; dishes from TL2) Upstairs seating and a good selection of cakes and fast food have kept the Özge's popularity up. It's right behind the main PTT.

Melek Anne (☎ 213 3263; Maarif Caddesi 18; dishes from TL2; ⏱ 8am-8pm) A whitewashed old house provides the setting for 'Mama Angel's' good home cooking including *mantı* (Turkish ravioli; TL4.50) and *gözleme* (savoury pancake). There's a vegetarian menu.

Zindanaltı Meyhanesi (☎ 212 2149; Saraçlar Caddesi 127; dishes from TL4; ⏱ 10am-midnight) A three-storey *meyhane* (tavern) with above-average mezes and grills (eg *pirzola*, or flattened lamb chop, TL8). The rooftop seating and 'seaside' fountain are worth the climb.

Niyazi Usta (☎ 213 3372; Alipaşa Ortakapı Caddesi 5; dishes from TL6; ⏱ 11am-9.30pm) If you're ready to try Edirne-style calf's liver, this bright, modern and spotlessly clean eatery opposite the Hotel Aksaray is the place. The pictures on the walls show the chef meeting with the crew from CNN Türkiye.

Lalezar (☎ 213 0600; Karaağaç Yolu; mains TL8-15; ⏱ 11am-11pm) The best riverside option in Karaağaç, Lalezar has a bilingual menu offering *güveç* (stew cooked in an earthenware pot), grills and fish. The grounds are a delight, and some choice tables are set on raised platforms among the trees

Drinking & Entertainment

Tunca Café (☎ 212 4816; Hurriyet Meydanı; ⏱ 8am-midnight) This very leafy tea garden is set around a duck pond facing Zübeyde Hanım Kadın Kakları Parkı, a 'Women's Rights Park' named after Atatürk's mother.

Café Pena (☎ 225 6969; Alipaşa Ortakapı Caddesi 6; ⏱ 9.30am-midnight) This modern-style café in a restored wooden building next to the Hotel Aksaray serves a full menu of fancy coffees and attracts a lively, young crowd. Need a friend? Come here.

London Café (☎ 213 8052; Saraçlar Caddesi 74; ⏱ 9am-midnight) This unexpected pleasure palace on two floors serves non-Turkish staples such as pasta and sandwiches but its raison d'être is the dispensing of booze.

Balkon (☎ 214 9454; Karaağaç Yolu 22; ⏱ 6pm-3am) This ambitious two-storey bar-club with live music nightly and a huge covered balcony is the best of a string of drinking spots on the spit of land between the Tunca and Meriç Bridges known as Bülbül Adası (Nightingale Island). Love the leopard-skin bar stools.

Shopping

The atmospheric **Ali Paşa Covered Bazaar** off Saraçlar Caddesi was designed by Mimar Sinan in 1569, while the **Bedesten**, across the road from the Eski Cami, dates from 1418. Each morning the merchants in the **Selimiye Arastası** (Selimiye Arcade), also known as Kavaflar Arastası (Cobblers' Arcade) below Selimiye Mosque, promise to do business honestly.

Traditional Edirne souvenirs include fruit-shaped soaps (*meyve sabunu*) scented with attar of roses, and marzipan (*badem ezmesi*). Buy the former at **Edmis** (☎ 214 12 71; Arif Paşa Caddesi), a shop next to the Edirne Urban History Museum, and the latter at the branch of **Keçecizade** (☎ 212 1261; Saraçlar Caddesi 50) across from the post office. You'll also find these as well as *aynalı süpürge*, miniature brooms decorated with mirrors and embroidery, and given to young girls for their dowry, at the gift shop of the Edirne Urban History Museum.

Getting There & Around
BUS & DOLMUŞ

Edirne's otogar is 9km east of the centre on the access road to the TEM. There are frequent buses for İstanbul (TL20, 2½ hours) and at least five daily buses to Çanakkale (TL25, four hours). City bus 5 (TL0.50) and frequent minibuses (TL0.50) run to the otogar from in front of the tourist office on Talat Paşa Caddesi.

If you're heading for the Bulgarian border crossing at Kapıkule, catch a dolmuş (minibus; TL5, 25 minutes) from opposite the tourist office on Talat Paşa Caddesi.

Pazarkule, the nearest Greek border post, is 13km south of Edirne, but there are no direct dolmuşes to take you there. You could catch a dolmuş to Karaağac and then take a taxi, but it's easier just to pick up a taxi all the way from the centre (TL20, 10 to 15 minutes).

For more information on all Bulgarian and Greek border crossings in this area, see p678.

CAR

The old highway D100 runs east from Edirne across the rolling, steppe-like terrain of eastern Thrace, following the ancient Via Ignatia, which once linked Rome with Constantinople. However, the E80 (or TEM) offers a far quicker route to İstanbul, and is used by most of the bus companies. The toll from Edirne to İstanbul is under TL10.

You can hire a car from **Turizm Rent A Car** (☎ 214 8478, 0535-724 8440; www.turizmrentacar.com; Talat Paşa Caddesi 32). Prices start at around TL60 per day (TL50 a day for more than a week) for a small sedan.

TRAIN

Edirne train station is 4km southeast of the Eski Cami. Bus 3 comes right here but any dolmuş or city bus along Talat Paşa Caddesi can drop you on the road 200m away. A taxi will cost around TL10.

The *Edirne Ekspresi* connects Edirne and İstanbul (TL13), leaving Edirne at 7.30am and returning from Sirkeci station at 3.50pm. It makes 31 stops and takes five hours. There's a second return journey from Edirne at 4.05pm. The *Bosfor Ekspresi* to Sofia and Bucharest passes through Edirne at 2.35am.

UZUNKÖPRÜ
☎ 0284 / pop 39,100

About 63km southeast of Edirne on the E87/ D550, the farming town of Uzunköprü (Long

Bridge) sits on the banks of the Ergene River. Amazingly, the 1392m-long Ottoman bridge (1426–43), after which the town is named, is still standing with all of its 174 arches intact. It remains the town's main access road from the north, an impressive feat after nearly six centuries of continuous use. If approaching from the south, you'll find it at the end of Hayrabolu Caddesi.

GETTING THERE & AWAY

Uzunköprü is the border crossing on the rail line connecting İstanbul with Greece; the *Dostluk-Filia Ekspresi* passes through at midnight, heading back to Sirkeci at 3.50am. The *Uzunköprü Ekspresi* offers a more convenient trip to İstanbul at 4.40pm (TL11.50, four hours). The station is 4km north of town – get a bus to Edirne (TL5, one hour) from the station by the bridge to drop you off, or take a taxi for TL7.

TEKİRDAĞ

☎ 0282 / pop 134,000

Famous both for its grapes – used to produce some decent wines and even better rakı (p176) – and cherries, Tekirdağ is perched in the hills above an attractive bay on the northern shore of the Sea of Marmara. Since most travellers pass through on their way to or from Greece, Tekirdağ is often no more than a pit stop. That's a shame, as the city once known as Rodosto has interesting architecture, including some lovely wooden *yalı* (seafront mansions), excellent museums and unusual mosques. And you certainly won't go hungry here; Tekirdağ boasts its very own spicy variety of *köfte* (meatballs).

Sights

The **waterfront** is the city's focal point, with a long promenade running round the bay and punctuated by cafés, restaurants, parks, playgrounds and a small **tourist office** (☎ 261 1698; ☼ 9am-6pm Mon-Fri year-round, 10am-7pm Sat & Sun Jun-Sep).

One of the most unusual museums in Turkey, the **Rakoczi Museum** (Rakoczi Müzesi; ☎ 263 8577; Macar Sokak 21 & Barbaros Caddesi 32; admission TL2; ☼ 9am-noon & 1-5pm Tue-Sun) is devoted to the life and times of Transylvanian Prince Ferenc (Francis) II Rákóczi (1676–1735), the courageous leader of the first Hungarian uprising against the Habsburgs between 1703 and 1711. Forced into exile, Rákóczi eventually turned up in Turkey and was given asylum by Sultan

Ahmet III; he settled in Tekirdağ in 1720 and lived here until his death. In 1906 the prince's remains were returned to Kassa in Hungary (now Košice in Slovakia), along with the interior fittings from the house. Between 1981 and 1982, however, these were painstakingly reproduced and put on display in a surprisingly informative museum that is something of a pilgrimage site for visiting Magyars. The 10 rooms on three floors contain portraits, weapons, contemporary kitchen equipment and ceramics and even an 18th-century Turkish-style toilet. The finest room is the 2nd-floor reception, with stained-glass windows, walls painted with Hungarian folk motifs and a chair made by the good prince himself. Worth seeing are the lovely watercolours of old Tekirdağ by Aladar Edivi Illes (1870–1958) on the 1st floor. To get here, walk west along the waterfront for about 1km until you see the large wooden Namık Kemal Kütüphane (library) above you to the right. The museum is up the small slope on the left.

From the Rakoczi Museum, walk east along Barbaros Caddesi, which counts a number of ramshackle wooden mansions facing the sea, until you come to the **Tekirdağ Museum** (☎ 261 2082; Barbaros Caddesi 1; admission TL3; ☼ 9am-5pm Tue-Sun), housed in a fine late-Ottoman building. Here you can see the finds from several local tumuli (burial mounds) and from a site at Perinthos (Marmara Ereğlisi). The most striking exhibits are the marble chairs and the table set with bronze bowls from the Naip tumulus dating to the early 5th century BC; and a wonderful pottery brazier in the form of a mother goddess from the Taptepe tumulus (4300 BC). Most interesting are the poignant inscriptions from a number of Roman gravestones translated into English. Read them and weep; they are timeless.

Further east and downhill, past the early-Ottoman **Eski Cami** at No 17 and the brown stone **Orta Camii** (1855) at No 3, you'll find the gingerbread-like wooden **Namık Kemal House** (Namık Kemal Evi; Namık Kemal Caddesi 9; admission free; ☼ 9.30am-5pm Mon-Sat), a small ethnographical museum dedicated to Tekirdağ's most famous son, who was born nearby. A nationalist poet, journalist and social reformer, Kemal (1840–88) had a strong influence on Atatürk, who called him 'the father of my ideas'. The two-storey house is beautifully restored; don't miss the music room, the kitchen with its Turkish utensils, and the beautiful coffered ceilings.

THREE CHEERS FOR RAKI

The unofficial national drink of Turkey is rakı (pronounced 'rah-kuh'), an aniseed-flavoured distillation not unlike French pastis. Like the latter, it is drunk with lashings of ice and water. But unlike the French tipple, which is an appetiser, rakı is often consumed with food. Turkey is the world's third-largest producer of grapes, a high percentage of which are grown around Tekirdağ. About a third of these grapes are consumed fresh but much of the rest goes into the making of rakı. It's a long and very complicated process, involving fresh grapes or well-preserved raisins that are mashed, shredded, mixed with water and steamed. Anise is then added and the product goes through a double-distillation process. After that it is watered down to an alcoholic strength of about 45% and aged for between 60 and 75 days. The most common brand is Yeni Rakı (New Rakı) but arguably the best is Tekirdağ Rakısı, said to have a very distinctive flavour because of the artesian water it uses from Çorlu, a town to the northeast of Tekirdağ. Turks drink what they call aslan sütü (or 'lion's milk', possibly because of the milky-white it turns when water is added) with anything, but it's best with cold meze, white cheese and melon, and with fish.

To get back to the waterfront, cross over to Mimar Sinan Caddesi and head downhill past the small, square **Rüstem Paşa Külliyesi** (Mimar Sinan Caddesi 19) on the right, designed in 1546 by the great Mimar Sinan. At the bottom of the hill there's a **statue** commemorating another famous Tekirdağan, the great oil wrestler Hüseyin Pehlivan (1908–82).

Festivals & Events
The red-letter event of the year here is the **Kiraz Festivali** (Cherry Festival), a week-long orgy in mid-June of cherry-gobbling and judging as well as music concerts and oil-wrestling matches.

Sleeping & Eating
Golden Yat Hotel (☎ 261 1054; www.goldenyat.com, in Turkish; Yalı Caddesi 42; s/d/ste TL65/120/170; ✕ ▢) Not remotely yacht-like, this 54-room hotel has had a major facelift in recent years and is now *the* place to stay by the harbour. Upper floors are brighter and have balconies; room 403 is a corker and you won't forget the views from the eyrie-like 5th-floor breakfast room in a hurry.

Rodosto Hotel (☎ 263 3701; www.rodostohotel.com, in Turkish; İskele Caddesi 34; s TL45-70, d/ste TL100/150; ✕ ▢) The 30-room Rodosto, the only other accommodation on the waterfront, seems to have been left in the wake of its upgraded neighbour. Rooms are tired and in need of a refit, especially the boxy 'economy' single (TL45). At the other end of the scale, two 'suites' (large guestrooms, really) come with jacuzzis.

Buses to Greece often pause for lunch in Tekirdağ, pulling up at the row of *köfte* res-taurants opposite the promenade serving the celebrated *Tekirdağ köftesi*, a spicy version of the ubiquitous meatball eaten with rice and peppers. Head for **Meşhur Köfteci Ali Usta** (☎ 261 1621; Yalı Caddesi; dishes from TL4; ✹ 8am-midnight), the 'Famous Master Ali Köfte Restaurant', which has been at it since 1966. Another option is the **Liman Lokantası** (☎ 261 4984; Yalı Caddesi 38; mains TL5-12; ✹ 8am-midnight), which also has a terrace café opposite on the harbour.

Getting There & Away
Buses for İstanbul (TL10, two hours), Edirne (TL10, two hours), Eceabat (TL20, three hours) and Çanakkale (TL25, 3½ hours) drop off and pick up along the waterfront.

GELİBOLU
☎ 0286 / pop 31, 200
The pretty little harbour town of Gelibolu is not the same as Gallipoli. It's just the largest town on the peninsula and happens to have the same name, though it is almost 50km from the main battlefield sites. If you do fall victim to such confusion and get off at the wrong stop, you'll find Gelibolu to be a very pleasant stop. Hotels, restaurants, a post office, banks and internet cafés – just about everything you'll need – are clustered around the harbour, which is also where the ferry to Lapseki across the Dardanelles docks.

Sights
On the entrance road into town is the award-winning **Gallipoli War Museum** (Gelibolu Savaş Müzesi; ☎ 566 1272; www.gelibolusavasmuzesi.com, in Turkish; Sahil Yolu; TL2.50; ✹ 9.30am-7pm Tue-Sun), which, though it lacks any English-language signage, gets top

marks for presentation; artefacts – weapons, mess kits, spent shells, fob watches, Bovril jars – are before, above and even below you under glass. Unlike most such collections, most of the 7000-odd pieces come from just one area of the peninsula.

The **Piri Reis Museum** (☎ 566 1011; donation requested; ☒ 8.30am-noon & 1-5pm Fri-Wed) is housed in a stone tower overlooking the harbour walls, all that is left of the Greek settlement of Callipolis, which gave the present town and peninsula their name. The museum honours the swashbuckling admiral and cartographer Piri Reis (1470–1554), whose statue stands in the harbour on the way to the ferry pier. He is celebrated for his *Kitab-i-Bahriye* (Book of the Sea), which contains detailed information on navigation and very accurate charts of ports in the Mediterranean. But the fruit of his life's work, dating back to 1513, was the first known map to show the Americas in their entirety. Inside there's a large, shallow well and an upstairs chamber displaying copies of pages from Reis' famous map.

The road from the museum veers uphill, passing several military buildings. After about 800m you'll come to the pretty shrine of **Ahmed-i Bican Efendi**, above the road in a minipark to the left. Across the road is the much grander tomb of **Mehmed-i Bican Efendi**, author of a commentary on the Quran called the *Muhammadiye*.

Return to the south road and walk to the landmark **Hallac-ı Mansur Türbesi**, which looks more like a mosque than a tomb. Just before it, turn right onto Fener Yolu (Lighthouse St) and begin walking out to the headland, the site of what was once the 14th-century **Gelibolu Fort**. A short distance on the left you'll see flag-draped steps leading down to the **Bayraklı Baba Türbesi** (Flag Father Tomb). It contains the mortal remains of one Karaca Bey, an Ottoman standard bearer who, in 1410, ate the flag in his keeping piece by piece rather than let it be captured by the enemy. When his comrades asked where the flag was; he told them but they refused to believe him. Karaca duly split open his stomach to prove his actions and a legend was born. The tomb is decked out with hundreds of Turkish flags; the attendant will sell you one to add to the collection.

At the edge of the headland, about 50m west of the tea garden, is the unusual **Azebler Namazgah**, a vaguely Mogul-looking outdoor

mosque built in 1407 complete with white marble *mihrab* (niche indicating the direction of Mecca) and *mimber*. On the beach below the headland is the small outdoor **Deniz Kuvvetleri Kulturpark** (Sea Forces Culture Park) full of spent torpedoes, mines and even a tiny submarine.

Return to the main road and continue downhill; on the left a tall modern bell tower marks a **French Cemetery** from the Crimean War (1853–56), what the French call the Guerre d'Orient, which also houses an ossuary containing the bones of 11 Senegalese soldiers who died in the Gallipoli campaign and were buried here between 1919 and 1923. Next door is the **Saruca Paşa Türbesi**, the tomb of a late 14th-century Ottoman military hero. The road continues down to **Hamzakoy**, the resort part of town, which has a thin strip of rough sandy beach.

Sleeping

Yılmaz Hotel (☎ 566 1256; fax 566 3598; Liman Mevki 8; s/d TL25/50) The 20-room Yılmaz is convenient and friendly, if not the smartest or quietest place in town, and rates may be negotiable.

Oya Hotel (☎ 566 0392; fax 566 4863; Miralay Şefik Aker Caddesi 7; s TL30, d TL50-60, tr TL70) This is a better and even more central choice than Yılmaz, with something of a nautical theme. All rooms have digital TV and some have small bathtubs.

Otel Hamzakoy (☎ 566 8080; www.hamzakoy.8m.com, in Turkish; s/d TL50/70; ▢) This pink-tinged block overlooking the bay about a kilometre north of the centre is Gelibolu's premier resort hotel. The 50 rooms are full of light and are spacious, with modern furnishings and balconies. There is a licensed restaurant on site and a café-bar right on the beach just opposite.

Eating

Have dinner at one of the harbourside restaurants, where you can tuck into local *sardalya* (sardines) cooked in a clay dish. One of the most reliable places is **İlhan Restaurant** (☎ 566 1124; Balikhane Sokak 2; mains TL7-15; ☒ 10am-midnight) right on the pier, with both sea and harbour views. The menu is also that bit more adventurous, with such delicacies as small-scaled scorpion fish. Yum.

Getting There & Away

The otogar is 500m southwest of the harbour on Kore Kahramanları Caddesi, the main road to Eceabat, and served by buses to İstanbul (TL27, 4½ hours) and Edirne (TL20, three hours). You can pick up minibuses to Eceabat (TL5, 35 minutes) and Çanakkale (TL7, one hour via Lapseki) from here or beside the harbour.

The Gelibolu–Lapseki ferry (TL2, bicycles and scooters TL5, cars TL23, 30 minutes) runs every hour on the hour in either direction between 9am and midnight, with six departures each way between 1am and 8am.

GALLIPOLI (GELİBOLU) PENINSULA
☎ 0286

For a millennium the slender peninsula that forms the northwestern side of the Dardanelles strait across the water from Çanakkale has been the key to İstanbul: any navy that could break through the strait had a good chance of capturing the capital of the Eastern European world. Many fleets have tried to force open the strait, but most, including the mighty Allied fleet mustered in WWI, have failed.

Antipodeans and many Britons won't need an introduction to Gallipoli; it is the backbone of the 'Anzac legend' in which an Allied campaign in 1915 to knock Turkey out of the war and open a relief route to Russia turned into one of the greatest fiascos of WWI. By the end of the campaign 130,000 men were dead, a third from Allied forces and the rest Turkish.

Today the Gallipoli battlefields are peaceful places, covered in brush and pine forests. But the battles fought here nearly a century ago are still alive in many memories, both Turkish and foreign, especially Australians and New Zealanders, who view the peninsula as a place of pilgrimage. The Turkish officer responsible for the defence of Gallipoli was none other than Mustafa Kemal – the future Atatürk – and his victory is commemorated in Turkey on 18 March. The big draw for foreigners, though, is Anzac Day (25 April), when a dawn service marks the anniversary of the Allied landings, attracting ever-increasing numbers of travellers from Down Under and beyond (p185).

The most convenient base for visiting the Gallipoli battlefields is Eceabat on the western shore of the Dardanelles, although Çanakkale, on the eastern shore, has a wider range of accommodation and restaurants and more vibrant nightlife. Despite its name, Gelibolu, 42km northeast of Eceabat, is not really an option.

The southern third of the peninsula is given over to a national park. Even if you're not well

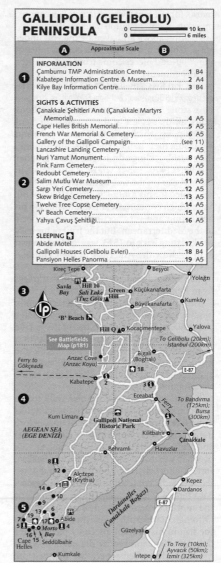

up on the history, it's still worth visiting for the rugged natural beauty of the area.

History

Not even 1500 metres wide at its narrowest point, the Strait of Çanakkale (Çanakkale Boğazı), better known as the Dardanelles or the Hellespont in English, has always offered the best opportunity for travellers – and armies – to cross between Europe and Asia Minor.

King Xerxes I of Persia forded the strait with a bridge of boats in 481 BC, as did Alexander the Great a century and a half later. In Byzantine times it was the first line of defence for Constantinople, but by 1402 the strait was under the control of Sultan Bayezid I, which allowed his armies to conquer the Balkans. Mehmet the Conqueror fortified the strait as part of his grand plan to conquer Constantinople (1453), building eight separate fortresses. As the Ottoman Empire declined during the 19th century, Great Britain and France competed with Russia for influence over this strategic sea passage.

In a bid to seize the Ottoman capital, then First Lord of the Admiralty Winston Churchill organised a naval assault on the strait early in 1915. In March a strong Franco-British fleet tried to force them without success. Then, on 25 April, British, Australian, New Zealand and Indian troops landed on Gallipoli, and French troops near Çanakkale. Both Turkish and Allied troops fought desperately, devastating one another. After nine months of ferocious combat but little headway gain, the Allied forces withdrew.

The outcome at Gallipoli was partly due to bad luck and leadership on the Allied side, and partly due to reinforcements to the Turkish side brought in by General Liman von Sanders. But a crucial element in the defeat was that the Allied troops landed in a sector where they faced then Lieutenant Colonel Mustafa Kemal.

A relatively minor officer, Kemal had managed to guess the Allied battle plan correctly when his commanders did not, and he stalled the invasion in spite of bitter fighting that wiped out his regiment (p184). Although suffering from malaria, Kemal commanded in full view of his troops throughout the campaign, miraculously escaping death several times. At one point a piece of shrapnel hit him in the chest, but was stopped by his pocket watch. His brilliant performance made him a folk hero and paved the way for his promotion to *paşa* (general).

The Gallipoli campaign lasted until January 1916, and resulted in a total of more than half a million casualties, of which 130,000 were deaths. The British Empire saw the loss of some 36,000 lives, including 8700 Australians

and 2700 New Zealanders. French casualties of 47,000 made up over half the entire French contingent; 8800 Frenchmen died. Half the 500,000 Ottoman troops became casualties, with almost 86,700 killed. Despite the carnage, the battles here are often considered the last true instance of a 'gentleman's war', with both sides displaying respect towards their enemy.

Orientation

The Gallipoli Peninsula is a fairly large area to tour, especially without your own transport; it's over 35km as the crow flies from the northernmost battlefield to the southern tip of the peninsula.

There are currently three dozen Allied war cemeteries in the national park, with about another 20 Turkish ones. The principal battles took place on its western shore, near Anzac Cove and Arıburnu, and in the hills just east. Anzac Cove is about 12km northwest of Eceabat and 19km from Kilitbahir. If time is tight or you're touring by public transport, head for Anzac Cove and Arıburnu first.

Information

KİLYE BAY INFORMATION CENTRE

Opened in 2005, this **centre** (Kilye Koyu Ana Tanıtım Merkezi; Map p178; admission free, parking TL3; ☉ 9am-noon & 1-5pm) is the main information point for all visitors to the battlefields but focuses on assisting Turkish travellers. The complex includes the information centre, several exhibition areas, a cinema, library and café. It's about 2km north of Eceabat, some 100m off the İstanbul highway.

KABATEPE INFORMATION CENTRE & MUSEUM

This older **centre** (Kabatepe Müzesi ve Tanıtma Merkezi; Map p178), roughly 1km east of the village of Kabatepe, contains a small museum with old blood-stained uniforms, rusty weapons, cartridge cases all welded together and other battlefield finds, including the skull of a luckless Turkish soldier with a bullet lodged in the forehead. Perhaps the most touching exhibit is a letter from a young officer who had left law school in Constantinople to volunteer in the Gallipoli campaign. He wrote to his mother in poetic terms about the beauty of the landscape and of his love for life. Two days later he died in battle. Another soldier wrote rather timelessly to his mother: 'You are proud to have given birth to four soldiers... I have enough money. I don't want underwear.'

Be aware that during the winter of 2007–08, damage to the centre's roof forced the information centre and collection to move to the **Çamburnu TMP Administration Centre** (Çamburnu TMP İdari Merkezi; Map p178; ☎ 814 1128; adult/student TL2.50/1; ☎ 8am-7pm), about 1.5km south of Eceabat. It might still be there when you visit; make sure to phone ahead.

The excellent bilingual (and most historically accurate) reference is *Gallipoli Battlefield Guide* (*Çanakkale Muharebe Alanları Gezi Rehberi*; TL25) by Gürsel Göncü and Şahin Doğan, available at certain bookshops in Çanakkale and Eceabat. Also worthwhile is *Gallipoli: A Battlefield Guide* by Australians Pam Cupper and Phil Taylor. The very detailed *Gallipoli Peninsula National Historic Park Guide Map* (*Gelibolu Yarımadası Tarihi Milli Parkı Kılavuz Harita*; TL5) can be bought at the park information centres.

You can also find plenty of history and practical information on the internet, including the **Visit Gallipoli** (www.anzacsite.gov.au) and **Gallipoli Association** (www.gallipoli-association.org) websites. While Peter Weir's 1981 film *Gallipoli* is an easy way to get an overview of the campaign, more factual is the documentary *Gallipoli* (*Gelibolu*; 2005) by Tolga Örnek. The documentary *Gallipoli: The Fatal Shore* (1987) by Harvey Broadbent is now quite dated, but it includes invaluable footage of interviews with veterans of the campaign. Most hotels and guest houses in Çanakkale and Eceabat screen at least one of these every night.

Tours

Many people visit Gallipoli on a guided tour, which is the best way to see a lot in a short amount of time. Also, the usually very well-informed guides can explain the battles as you go along, answer question and even help you locate a specific gravesites. The five- or six-hour tour includes transport by car or minibus, guide, picnic lunch and a swim from a beach on the western shore.

The best agencies in Çanakkale and Eceabat are listed here:

Crowded House Tours (☎ 814 1565, 0535-416 6473; www.crowdedhousegallipoli.com; TL50) Based at the Hotel Crowded House in Eceabat; afternoon tours led by the indefatigable Bülent 'Bill' Korkmaz (p183) are among the most informative and popular on the peninsula. You can combine a battleship tour with a morning of snorkelling

(TL25, including transportation and equipment) in Suvla Bay, north of Anzac Cove, where there are more than 200 shipwrecks from the campaign.
Hassle Free Travel Agency (☎ 213 5969; www.hasslefreetour.com; TL45-55) Operates tours out of the Anzac House Hostel (p189) in Çanakkale, with a branch in Eceabat (☎ 814 2431; Yahya Çavuş Sokak 3a). Hassle Free also runs tours out of İstanbul to Gallipoli for €89, inclusive of one night's stay at Anzac House before visiting the ruins at Troy and either travelling on to Selçuk or Kuşadası and back to İstanbul. Visiting the battlefields straight after a five-hour bus ride can be exhausting; it might be better to take the tour from Çanakkale.
TJs Tours (☎ 814 3121; www.anzacgallipolitours.com; TL45) Based at TJs Hotel (p186) in Eceabat, this agency comes highly recommended from readers. İlhami 'TJ' Gezici marries historical knowledge with genuine enthusiasm. A private two-person tour can cover the less-visited sites at Cape Helles and around Suvla Bay for around €130.
Trooper Tours (☎ 217 3343; www.troopertours.com; TL55) Run by Fez Travel, the people behind the Fez Bus and based at the Yellow Rose Pension (p190) in Çanakkale, this outfit also has tours of Troy for TL50, including transport and entrance fee.

Battlefield Sites

Gallipoli National Historic Park (Gelibolu Yarımadası Tarihi Milli Parkı) encompasses 33,000 hectares of the peninsula and all of the significant battle sites. There are several different signage systems in use: normal Turkish highway signs; national park administration ones; and wooden signs posted by the Commonwealth War Graves Commission. This can lead to confusion because the foreign troops and the Turks used different names for the battlefields, and the park signs don't necessarily agree with the ones erected by the highway department. We've used both English and Turkish names in the text and on the Gallipoli Battlefields map.

NORTHERN PENINSULA

About 3km north of Eceabat a road marked for Kabatepe and Kemalyeri heads west into the park. We describe the sites in the order most walkers and motorists are likely to visit them.

Kabatepe Village (Kabatepe Köyü)

The small harbour here (Map p178) was probably the object of the Allied landing on 25 April 1915. In the predawn dark it is possible that uncharted currents swept the Allies' landing craft northwards to the steep cliffs of

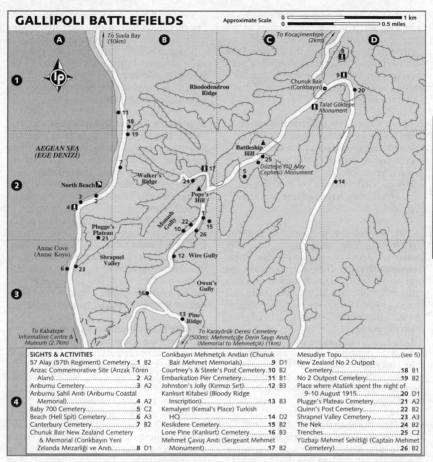

GALLIPOLI BATTLEFIELDS

Approximate Scale

Arıburnu – a bit of bad luck that may have sealed the campaign's fate from the start. Today there's little in Kabatepe except for a camping ground, café and dock for ferries that go to the island of Gökçeada (p192).

The road uphill to Lone Pine (Kanlısırt) and Chunuk Bair begins 750m northwest of the Kabatepe Information Centre and Museum (see p179). Anzac Cove is another three kilometres or so to the north.

Anzac Cove (Anzac Koyu)

Heading northwest from the information centre, it's 3km to **Beach (Hell Spit) Cemetery** (Map p181). Almost opposite, a dirt track cuts inland to **Shrapnel Valley Cemetery** and, further north, to **Plugge's Plateau Cemetery**.

Following the coastal road for another 400m from the turn-off will take you to Anzac Cove, beneath and just south of the Arıburnu cliffs, where the ill-fated Allied landing was made on 25 April 1915. Ordered to advance inland, the Allied forces at first gained some ground but later in the day met with fierce resistance from the Ottoman forces under the leadership of Mustafa Kemal, who had foreseen where they would land and disobeyed an order to send his troops further south to Cape Helles. After this failed endeavour, the Anzacs concentrated on consolidating and expanding the beachhead while awaiting reinforcements.

In August of the same year a major offensive was staged in an attempt to advance beyond the beach up to the ridges of Chunuk

Bair and Sarı Bair. It resulted in the battles at Lone Pine and The Nek, the bloodiest of the campaign, but little progress was made.

Another 300m along is the **Arıburnu Sahil Anıtı** (Arıburnu Coastal Memorial), a very moving Turkish monument with Atatürk's famous words of peace and reconciliation spoken in 1934:

To us there is no difference between the Johnnies and the Mehmets…You, the mothers, who sent your sons from faraway countries, wipe away your tears; your sons are now lying in our bosom…After having lost their lives in this land, they have become our sons as well.

Just beyond the memorial is **Arıburnu Cemetery** and, 750m further north, **Canterbury Cemetery**. Between them is the **Anzac Commemorative Site**, where dawn services are held on Anzac Day. Look up and you can easily make out the image in the sandy cliff face nicknamed the Sphinx by young 'diggers' (Aussie infantrymen) who had arrived from Australia via Egypt.

Less than 1km further along the seaside road on the right-hand side are the cemeteries at **No 2 Outpost**, set back inland from the road, and **New Zealand No 2 Outpost**. The **Embarkation Pier Cemetery** is 200m beyond the New Zealand No 2 Outpost on the left.

Lone Pine (Kanlısırt)

Return to the Kabatepe Information Centre and Museum and follow the signs just under 3km up the hill for **Lone Pine** (Kanlısırt; Map p181), perhaps the most moving of all the Anzac cemeteries. It's another 3km uphill to the New Zealand Memorial at Chunuk Bair.

The first monument, **Mehmetçiğe Derin Saygı Anıtı**, on the right-hand side of the road about 1km from the junction, is dedicated to 'Mehmetçik' (Little Mehmet), the Turkish 'tommy' or 'digger'. Another 1200m brings you to the **Kanlısırt Kitabesi** (Bloody Ridge Inscription), which describes the battle of Lone Pine from the Turkish viewpoint.

At Lone Pine itself, 400m uphill, Australian forces captured the Turkish positions on the afternoon of 6 August. Within just a few days of the assault, 4000 men died here. The trees that shaded the cemetery were swept away by a fire in 1994, leaving only one: a lone pine

planted years ago from the seed of the original tree that stood here during the battle. Today reforestation is once again under way.

The tombstones carry touching epitaphs and the cemetery includes the grave of the youngest soldier to die here, a boy of just 14. The remains of trenches can be seen just behind the parking area.

Johnston's Jolly to Quinn's Post

Progressing up the hill from Lone Pine, the ferocity of the battles becomes much more apparent; at some points the trenches are only a few metres apart. The order to attack meant certain death to those who followed it, and virtually all did as they were ordered on both sides.

At **Johnston's Jolly** (Kırmızı Sırt; Map p181), 200m on the right beyond Lone Pine, at **Courtney's & Steele's Post**, another 300m along, and especially at **Quinn's Post**, 100m uphill, the trenches were separated only by the width of the modern road. On the eastern side, almost opposite Quinn's Post, is the **Yüzbaşı Mehmet Şehitliği** (Captain Mehmet Cemetery).

57 Alay (57th Regiment) Cemetery

Just over 1km uphill from Lone Pine on the eastern side of the road is the cemetery and monument for officers and soldiers of the Ottoman 57th Regiment, led by Mustafa Kemal, and which he sacrificed to halt the first Anzac assaults. The **cemetery** (Map p181) has a surprising amount of religious symbolism for a Turkish army site, as historically the republican army has been steadfastly secular. The statue of an old man showing his granddaughter the battle sites is that of Hüseyin Kaçmaz, who fought in the Balkan Wars, the Gallipoli campaign and at the fateful Battle of Dumlupınar during the War of Independence. He died in 1994, aged 110, the last of the Turkish survivors of Gallipoli.

Down some steps from here, the **Kesikdere Cemetery** contains the remains of another 1115 Turkish soldiers from the 57th and other regiments.

Sergeant Mehmet Monument (Mehmet Çavuş Anıtı) & The Nek

About 100m uphill past the 57th Regiment Cemetery, a road goes west to the **Sergeant Mehmet Monument** (Mehmet Çavuş Anıtı; Map p181), dedicated to the Turkish sergeant who fought with rocks and his fists after he ran

THRACE & MARMARA

BÜLENT 'BILL' YILMAZ KORKMAZ

How's things in Oz? I don't know. I've never been to Australia. In fact, I've never been outside Turkey.

But, your accent... I've been working as a tour guide on the peninsula for a dozen years. I'd say 90% of the visitors are from Australia and New Zealand. I guess the accent comes with the territory.

Fair dinkum, so your people are fully appraised of the Anzac legend then. Oh, sure. They've learned all about the Gallipoli campaign in school and are usually well informed. I'd say more than 80% have a very good idea of what's what.

Ever get any know-it-alls? That's not a problem but the British army sometimes sends over groups of historians or medical people or logisticians for three or four days. That's intensive and they can ask some pretty difficult questions.

Is it difficult escorting the former enemy around? I like giving both sides of the story and I think they like hearing it. With a military group, though, I'll take the Turkish side.

Are there any battlefields or cemeteries that people are particularly keen to visit or spots that especially move them? The Australians want to see Lone Pine and, of course, Anzac Cove. The New Zealanders are keen to get to Chunuk Bair. Everyone knows about The Nek – it's the last part of the *Gallipoli* movie. And everyone seems moved by Atatürk's message of reconciliation on the Arıburnu monument.

Has all this time hoofing around battlefields affected the way you view war and peace? When I'm exploring on my own time, I think a lot about a whole generation of young men who were lost simply because a bunch of politicians said go and fight.

On your own time? War and peace, love and marriage... Sounds like you're married to your job. I guess I am. In winter you'll find me roaming the peninsula, following old maps, exploring trenches, reading headstones. And I'm getting married this summer but we've had to postpone the honeymoon till the end of the year.

Which – let me guess – will be somewhere along the Somme, right? It hasn't been decided but one thing's for sure – the place won't include any war sites.

Bülent 'Bill' Yılmaz Korkmaz (bulentbill@yahoo.com) is a certified tour guide who leads groups around the battlefields, cemeteries and other sights of the Gallipoli Peninsula.

---

out of ammunition, and **The Nek**. It was here on the morning of 7 August 1915 that the 8th (Victorian) and 10th (Western Australian) Regiments of the third Light Horse Brigade vaulted out of their trenches into withering fire and were cut down before they reached the enemy line, an episode immortalised in Peter Weir's film *Gallipoli*.

Baby 700 Cemetery & Mesudiye Topu

About 300m uphill on the right from the access road to The Nek is the **Baby 700 Cemetery** (Map p181) and the Ottoman cannon called the Mesudiye Topu. Baby 700 was the limit of the initial attack, and the graves here are mostly dated 25 April.

Düztepe & Talat Göktepe Monuments

Another 1.5km uphill brings you to a monument (Map p181) marking the spot where the Ottoman 10th Regiment held the line. The views of the strait and the surrounding countryside are superb. About 1km further along from Düztepe is a monument (Map p181) to a more recent casualty of Gallipoli: Talat Göktepe, chief director of the Çanakkale Forestry District, who died fighting the devastating forest fire of 1994.

Chunuk Bair (Conkbayırı)

At the top of the hill, 600m past the Talat Göktepe Monument, is a T-intersection. A right turn takes you east to the **Suyatağı Anıtı** (Watercourse Monument; Map p181) where, having stayed awake for four days and nights, Mustafa Kemal spent the night of 9–10 August directing part of the counterattack to the August offensive. Further south is **Kemalyeri**, 'Kemal's Place' at Scrubby Knoll, his command post, and the road back to the Kabatepe Information Centre and Museum.

A left turn leads to **Chunuk Bair** (Map p181), the first objective of the Allied landing in April 1915, and now the site of the **New Zealand**

Cemetery and Memorial on the western side of the road

As the Anzac troops made their way up the scrub-covered slopes on 25 April, Mustafa Kemal, the divisional commander, brought up the 57th Infantry Regiment and gave them his famous order: 'I am not ordering you to attack, I am ordering you to die. In the time it takes us to die, other troops and commanders will arrive to take our places'. The 57th was wiped out but held the line and inflicted equally heavy casualties on Anzac forces below.

Chunuk Bair was also at the heart of the struggle for the peninsula from 6 to 9 August 1915, when 28,000 men died on this ridge. The peaceful pine grove of today makes it difficult to imagine that blasted wasteland, when bullets, bombs and shrapnel mowed down men as the fighting went on day and night. The Anzac attack on 6 to 7 August, which included the New Zealand Mounted Rifle Brigade and a Maori contingent, was deadly, but the attack on the following day was of a ferocity which, according to Mustafa Kemal, 'could scarcely be described'.

To the east a side road leads to the Turkish **Chunuk Bair Mehmet Memorials** (Conkbayırı Mehmetçik Anitları) (Map p181), five giant tablets with Turkish inscriptions describing the battle.

SOUTHERN PENINSULA

Far fewer people visit the sites of the **southern peninsula** (Map p178), which makes it a good place to come to escape the traffic and tour groups, at least during the low season.

From Kabatepe it's about 12km to the village of **Alçıtepe**, formerly known as Krithia. Close to the village's main intersection is the privately run **Salim Mutlu War Museum** (admission free; 8am-5pm), which houses shells, camp equipment and other finds from the northern and southern battlefields. Nearby, the much more ambitious **Gallery of the Gallipoli Campaign** (admission TL2; 8am-noon & 1.30-5pm) takes a more illustrative approach to events; its 12 rooms are filled with mock-ups, dioramas and sound effects. In the village, signs point southwest to the **Twelve Tree Copse** and **Pink Farm Cemeteries**, and north to the Turkish **Sargı Yeri Cemetery** with its enormous statue of 'Mehmet' and the solid **Nuri Yamut Monument**.

Heading south, the road passes the **Redoubt Cemetery** on the right. About 5.5km south of

Alçıtepe, just after the **Skew Bridge Cemetery**, the road divides, the right fork heading for the village of Seddülbahir and several Allied memorials. **Seddülbahir**, around 2km from the intersection, is a sleepy farming village with a few pensions, a post office and the ruins of an Ottoman/Byzantine fortress overlooking a small harbour.

Follow the signs for the **Yahya Çavuş Şehitliği** (Sergeant Yahya Cemetery) to reach the **Cape Helles British Memorial**, 1km beyond Seddülbahir. The initial Allied attack was two-pronged, with the southern landing at the tip of the peninsula on 'V' Beach. Sergeant Yahya was the Turkish officer who led the first resistance to the Allied landing on 25 April 1915, causing heavy casualties. **'V' Beach Cemetery** is visible a half-kilometre downhill. The **Lancashire Landing Cemetery** is off to the northwest of the Cape Helles British Memorial.

From the Cape Helles British Memorial return to where the road divides and then head east following signs for Abide or Çanakkale Şehitleri Anıtı (Çanakkale Martyrs Memorial) at Morto Bay. Along the way you'll pass the **French War Memorial and Cemetery**. French troops, including a regiment of Africans, attacked Kumkale on the Asian shore in March 1915 with complete success, then re-embarked and landed in support of their British comrades-in-arms at Cape Helles, where they were virtually wiped out. The French cemetery is rarely visited but quite moving, with rows of metal crosses and five white concrete ossuaries each containing the bones of 3000 soldiers.

The **Çanakkale Şehitleri Anıtı** (Çanakkale Martyrs Memorial), also known as the Abide monument, is a gigantic four-legged stone table almost 42m high that commemorates all the Turkish soldiers who fought and died at Gallipoli. It's surrounded by landscaped grounds, including a rose garden planted to commemorate the 80th anniversary of the conflict in 1995.

Sleeping

There are some excellent accommodation options inside the park itself, including some well-equipped camp sites. But most are around Seddülbahir and can be tricky to get to without your own transport.

Pansiyon Helles Panorama (862 0035; www .hellespanorama.com; s/d without bathroom TL30/60) Just west of the centre of Seddülbahir, this welcoming guesthouse has seven rooms and a

GALLIPOLI UNDER THREAT

It's a world away from the early 1980s in Gallipoli when Australian film director Peter Weir spent two days scampering over the hills of the peninsula and saw not a living soul. The numbers of visitors have grown by leaps and bounds since then and they're not just foreigners. Since 2004, when 81 students from the 81 provinces in Turkey made the patriotic pilgrimage to where national hero Mustafa Kemal led their nation to victory, *belediye* (town and city councils) from Edirne to Van have been sending their citizens in by the busload. According to Turkish official sources, domestic visitors numbered two million in 2007, up from between 400,000 and 500,000 five years before.

This increased popularity has made site conservation of the national park here particularly challenging, and many people feel that the local government and park administration don't always handle the situation effectively. In recent years the flow of bus and coach traffic has become extremely heavy, particularly around the most-visited Turkish cemeteries and monuments. Supposed 'improvements' such as car parks and road-widening schemes have caused considerable damage to some areas, most shockingly at Anzac Cove. The beach there is now little more than a narrow strip of sand.

Still, nothing compares with the crowds that turn up at the dawn Anzac Day memorial service, one of the most popular events in Turkey for foreign visitors and almost a rite of passage for young Australians in particular. In 2005 more than 20,000 people came to mark the 90th anniversary of the Gallipoli landings, overwhelming the peninsula's modest infrastructure. Since then totals have been between 7000 and 10,000 people, including such high-ranking officials as the defence minister of Australia, and New Zealand's foreign minister. Traffic reaches all-day jam proportions the day before, and some people coming in from as close as Çanakkale don't always make it in time.

In 2008 a Victoria University academic made the 'blasphemous' suggestion that Australians stop swamping the peninsula on Anzac Day and mark the occasion on their own shores instead. Indeed, it's easier to appreciate Gallipoli's poignancy and beauty at almost any other time, and many visitors find their emotional experience completely different if they take the time to explore at leisure away from the crowds. Perhaps the only way to save Gallipoli is to do the 'unpatriotic' thing and stay away, at least on 25 April.

lovely garden. The 'panorama' part of the name refers to the view of the dramatic Çanakkale Şehitleri Anıtı (opposite). Some rooms have mansard ceilings.

Abide Motel (☎ 862 0010; s/d full board TL55/110) This reasonably priced establishment is in a great location at Morto – or Corpse – Bay, northwest of Seddülbahir near the Abide monument and the French Cemetery. The food is highly rated, and the owner, who worked for years at an American military base in the eastern part of the country, speaks excellent English.

ourpick Gallipoli Houses (Gelibolu Evleri; ☎ 814 2650; www.gallipoli.com.tr; Kocadere Köyü; s/d half-board €65/80; ☒ ☒ ☐ ☒) As welcome an addition to the park as reinforcements on 25 April 1915 is this newly built guest house, with three rooms in the main stone house and seven more in equally attractive annexes. The rooms are stylishly decorated and fully equipped, with fridges and coffee- and tea-making fa-

cilities. The food is innovative and copious (four courses is the norm at dinner), and the wine served are from the region. We love the views of the battlefields and sights (Chunuk Bair, Kemalyeri) as well as the stars from the rooftop terrace. The Belgian owner is a history buff and can answer just about any question you may have on the campaign.

Getting There & Around

With your own transport, you can easily tour the battlefields to the north in a day. Trying to do both the northern and southern parts of the peninsula is possible, provided you get an early start. Touring by public transport is tricky; dolmuşes serve only a few sites and villages. The most important group of monuments and cemeteries, from Lone Pine uphill to Chunuk Bair in the northern peninsula, can be toured on foot.

Ferries run from Çanakkale on the eastern side of the Dardanelles to Eceabat

THRACE & MARMARA

and Kilitbahir on the peninsula; see p191 for details.

Taxi drivers in Eceabat will run you around the main sites for around TL100, but they take only two to 2½ hours and few of them speak English well enough to provide a decent commentary. An organised tour (p180) is probably a better idea.

ECEABAT
☎ 0286 / pop 5500

Just over the Dardanelles strait from Çanakkale, Eceabat (Maydos) is a small, easy-going waterfront town with the best access to the main Gallipoli battlefields of any main centre. It's especially attractive to those who don't fancy the hustle and bustle of Çanakkale. Ferries dock by the main square, Cumhuriyet Meydanı, which has hotels, restaurants, ATMs, post office, bus company offices, and dolmuş and taxi stands.

Like most of the peninsula, Eceabat is swamped with groups of students and Turkish tour groups from afar over weekends from April through to mid-June and again in late September.

Sleeping

Hotel Boss I (☎ 814 1464; www.heyboss.com; Cumhuriyet Meydanı 14; s/d/tr TL20/40/60; 🔀) A small, narrow budget hotel right on the main square, this 12-room place with a clapboard facade is as cheap and basic as you'll find in Eceabat. Opt for a corner room or one facing the water (eg room 1) to get a bit more space. Only some rooms are air-conditioned.

Hotel Boss II (☎ 814 2311; Mehmet Akif Sokak 48; 🔀) Charges the same rates as but is bigger than Hotel Boss I, with more accommodation options, including dormitory beds (TL15) and some pleasant wooden bungalows. It's a 15-minute walk southwest from the town centre.

TJs Hotel (☎ 814 2458; www.anzacgallipolitours.com; Cumhuriyet Meydanı 2a; dm/s/d TL15/50/70; 🔀 🖵) Making the most of its commanding central position, what was until recently known as the Eceabat Hotel has rooms to suit every budget, from the basic hostel bunk rooms on the 2nd floor to the smarter hotel rooms with air-con balconies on the 3rd and 4th floors. The roof bar with its Ottoman-style decor and regular live events is fabulous.

Aqua Boss Hotel (☎ 814 2864; www.heyboss.com; İstiklal Caddesi; s/d/tr/q TL45/70/105/120; 🔀 🖵) The third part of the Boss trinity, this cavernous,

castle-like building (once a tomato-canning factory – note the glass jars used as lamps) on the waterfront has a touch of quirky style in its 40 rooms and terraced restaurant, though the headache-making carpets are a bit frayed.

our pick Hotel Crowded House (☎ 814 1565; www.crowdedhousegallipoli.com; Huseyin Avni Sokak 4; dm/s/d/t TL20/35/50/69; 🔀 🔀 🖵) Eceabat's newest caravanserai – named after the Antipodean band and not the state of the accommodation – is housed in a spanking-new four-storey building just a hop, skip and a stumble from the ferry. The 24 rooms and three dormitories (each with six bunks) are basic but spick-and-span, with ultramodern bathrooms and nonallergenic parquet floors. There's a laundry service (TL10), book exchange and a wonderful café-bar on the ground and mezzanine floors. Best of all is the welcome and the atmosphere, both warm and chilled.

Eating

Hanımeli (☎ 814 2345; Zübeyde Hanım Meydanı 21; mains TL4-10; 🕑 6am-10pm) This simple little café on the waterfront southwest of the centre serves up breakfast and some of the best home-cooked traditional dishes (eg *mantı*) in town.

Gül Restaurant (☎ 814 3040; Zübeyde Hanım Zübeyde Meydanı 5; mains TL4-13) Just up from the Hanımeli, the 'Rose' is a typical kebap and *pide* (Turkish pizza) canteen, in the middle of the row of shops and cafeterias, and family-friendly.

Liman Restaurant (☎ 814 2755; İstiklal Caddesi 67; mains TL6-15; 🕑 10am-12.30am) At the southern end of the waterfront, the 'Harbour' is generally considered to be the best restaurant for fish in Eceabat and the covered terrace is a delight in all weather. Service is excellent here.

Drinking

Kafe'e (☎ 814 1636; Cumhuriyet Caddesi 72; 🕑 9am-10pm) This new kid on the block, housed in the Eceabat Cultural Centre where Atatürk himself once laid his head, north of the centre, serves breakfast, snacks and light meals but is most notably a lovely glassed-in café with sweeping views of the Dardanelles.

Boomerang Bar (☎ 814 2144; Cumhuriyet Caddesi 102; 🕑 5pm-late) This dive at the far northern end of town near the start of the road to İstanbul is the only option for a late-night drink if you can't be bothered with the ferry-hop to Çanakkale. It's aimed mainly at thirsty young Antipodeans.

Getting There & Away

Long-distance buses pass through Eceabat on the way from Çanakkale to İstanbul (TL30, five hours).

The Çanakkale–Eceabat ferries (TL2, bicycles TL2, cars TL22.50, 25 minutes) run on the hour every hour from 7am to midnight (every 30 minutes in summer), with three services between 2am and 6am from Eceabat to Çanakkale. From Çanakkale to Eceabat the overnight sailings are at 1am, 3am and 5am.

Hourly buses or minibuses run to Gelibolu (TL3.50, one hour). In summer there are several dolmuşes daily to the ferry dock at Kabatepe (TL2, 15 minutes) on the western shore of the peninsula. These can drop you at the Kabatepe Information Centre and Museum, or at the base of the road up to Lone Pine and Chunuk Bair.

Dolmuşes also run down the coast to Kilitbahir (TL1.50, 10 minutes).

KİLİTBAHİR

Just across the Narrows from Çanakkale and easily accessible by small ferry (p191), Kilitbahir (Lock of the Sea) is a tiny fishing harbour dominated by a massive **fortress** (admission TL3; 8am-noon & 1-7pm Tue-Sun) built by Mehmet the Conqueror in 1452 and given a grand seven-storey interior tower a century later by Süleyman the Magnificent. It's well worth a quick look around – and up the railless staircase onto the walls if your nerves will stand it (people suffering from heart disease, hypertension and vertigo are warned not to do so and you'll soon see why). Check out the **Namazgah Tabyası** (Namazgah Redoubt), a mazelike series of defensive bunkers behind the castle built in 1893–94.

From the ferry, dolmuşes and taxis run to Eceabat and Gelibolu as well as to the Turkish war memorial at Abide, although you may have to wait for them to fill up.

ÇANAKKALE

☎ 0286 / pop 86,600

The liveliest settlement on the Dardanelles, this sprawling harbour town would be worth a visit for its sights, nightlife and overall vibe even if it didn't lie opposite the Gallipoli Peninsula. An added bonus is the sweeping waterfront promenade that heaves in the summer months.

Çanakkale is also a popular base for visiting the ruins at Troy (p197) and has become a very popular destination for weekending Turks. If possible plan your visit for midweek.

Orientation

Çanakkale is centred on its harbour, with a PTT booth, half-a-dozen ATM machines and public phones right by the docks, and hotels, restaurants, banks and bus offices all within a few hundred metres. The otogar is about 1km inland beside a large Carrefour supermarket. Dolmuşes to Troy and the seaside resort town of Güzelyalı, 14km south of Çanakkale, leave from a lot 500m to the south at the foot of the bridge over the Sarı River.

Information

Maxi Internet (☎ 217 7240; Fetvane Sokak 51; per hr TL1.50; 10am-1am) Internet access in the centre.
Tourist office (☎ 217 1187; Cumhuriyet Meydanı; 8am-noon & 1-7pm Jun-Sep, to 5pm Oct-May) Some 150m from the ferry pier.

Sights

MILITARY MUSEUM

A park in the military zone at the southern end of the quay houses the **Military Museum** (Askeri Müze; ☎ 213 1730; Çimenlik Sokak; admission TL3; 9am-noon & 1.30-5pm Tue, Wed & Fri-Sun) and all sorts of military paraphernalia. Confusingly, it is also called the Dardanelles Straits Naval Command Museum (Çanakkale Boğaz Komutanliği Deniz Müzesi).

A sea-facing late-Ottoman building contains informative exhibits on the Gallipoli battles and some artfully displayed war relics, including fused bullets that hit each other in mid-air. Apparently the chances of this happening are something like 160 million to one, which gives a chilling idea of just how much ammunition was being fired.

Nearby is a replica of the **Nusrat minelayer** (Nusrat Mayin Gemisi), which played a heroic role in the sea campaign. The day before the Allied fleet tried to force the straits, Allied minesweepers proclaimed the water cleared. At night the *Nusrat* went out and picked up and relaid loose mines. Three Allied ships struck the *Nusrat*'s mines and were sunk or crippled.

Mehmet the Conqueror built the impressive **Çimenlik Kalesi** (Meadow Castle) in 1452. The cannons surrounding the stone walls are from French, English and German foundries. Inside are some fine paintings of the battles of Gallipoli.

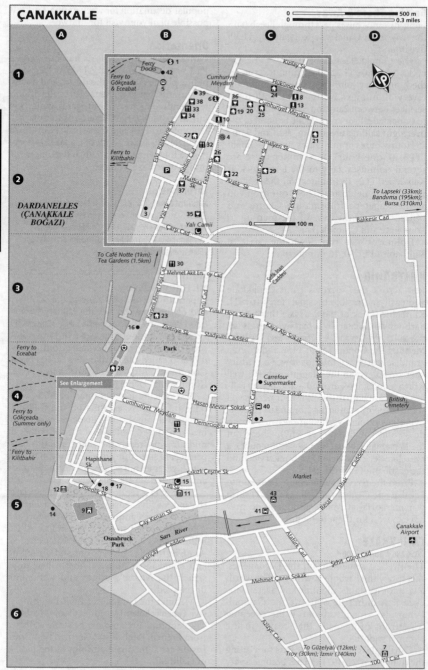

ARCHAEOLOGY MUSEUM

Just over 1.5km south of the otogar on the road to Troy is the **Archaeology Museum** (Arkeoloji Müzesi; ☎ 217 6565; 100-Yıl Caddesi; admission TL5; ⏰ 8am-5pm), also called the Çanakkale Museum (Çanakkale Müzesi).

The best exhibits here are those from Troy (p197) and Assos (p204), although the finds from the tumulus at Dardanos, an ancient town some 10km southwest of Çanakkale, are also noteworthy. There's quite a bit on display in the small garden.

Dolmuşes heading down Atatürk Caddesi towards Güzelyalı or Troy will drop you off near the museum for TL1.

OTHER ATTRACTIONS

The landmark five-storey Ottoman **clock tower** (*saat kulesi*) near the harbour was built in 1897. It was paid for by an Italian consul and Çanakkale merchant who left the town 100,000 gold francs in his will for the purpose when he died.

Housed in a 19th-century former school in the old town, the **Korfmann Library** (Korfmann Kütüphanesi; ☎ 213 7212; Tifli Sokak; admission free; ⏰ 10am-6pm), just south of the Tifli Mosque in Çarşı Caddesi, was the bequest of the late Manfred Osman Korfmann (1945–2005), archaeological director at Troy from 1988 to 2003. It contains 6000 volumes on history, culture, art and archaeology.

At the **Yalı Hamam** (Çarşı Caddesi 5; ⏰ 6am-11.30pm for men, 8am-5pm for women), the full works costs TL25. The women's entrance is round the corner on Hapishane Sokak.

In Cumhuriyet Meydanı stands a **monument** of old WWI cannons. The inscription

reads: 'Mehmets (Turkish soldiers) used these cannons on 18 March 1915 to ensure the impassability of the Çanakkale Strait'. Behind it is an oversized copy of a **Çanakkale pot** – a rather kitsch 19th-century style that is slowly gaining popularity.

Along the waterfront promenade north of the main ferry pier don't be surprised to see a much larger-than-life model of a **Trojan Horse**, as seen in the movie *Troy* (2004). The model of the ancient city and information displays beneath it are better than anything you'll find at Troy.

Festivals & Events

The Turks celebrate what they call the **Çanakkale Naval Victory** (Çanakkale Deniz Zaferi), when Ottoman cannons and mines succeeded in keeping the Allied fleet from passing through the Dardanelles, on 18 March. Australians and New Zealanders come to mark **Anzac Day** (25 April), the anniversary of the Allied landings on the peninsula in 1915. A dawn service near Anzac Cove begins a day of commemorative events. This is when Çanakkale is at its most unbearably overcrowded (see p185).

Sleeping

Çanakkale has hotels to suit all budgets, except on Anzac Day, when rip-offs and price-jacking abound. If you do intend to be in town around 25 April, book well in advance and check prices carefully.

BUDGET

Anzac House Hostel (☎ 213 5969; www.anzachouse .com; Cumhuriyet Meydanı 59-61; dm TL16, s/d/tr without bathroom TL28/40/54; 🖳) Not to be confused with the three-star Anzac Hotel (below), Anzac House is the first place most backpackers head for – it's central, cheap and the base for Hassle Free Travel Agency (see p180). Its 15 rooms are quite small and the dorms have up to 14 beds each, but there are fans, three showers per floor and computers to check your emails.

Efes Hotel (☎ 217 3256; www.efeshotelcanakkale .com; Aralık Sokak 5; s/d TL30/50; ✗ ✗) Near Çanakkale's choicest hotel, the Kervansaray (see below), the Efes is an excellent budget choice, with cheery decor and a very welcoming owner. The largest of the 20 rooms are nicer than the standard singles, with their open showers, and even boast orthopaedic mattresses. The breakfasts are great, and there's a flower-filled little garden with a fountain in back.

Yellow Rose Pension (☎ 217 3343; www.yellow rose.4mg.com; Aslan Abla Sokak 5; dm/s/d/tr TL17/30/55/60; ✗ 🖳) This bright, attractive guest house with 18 rooms has a quiet though still central location and lots of extras, from laundry service (TL15), fully equipped kitchen and back garden to book exchange and video library. It's also the local agent for Trooper Tours (see p180) and Fez Travel.

MIDRANGE

Anzac Hotel (☎ 217 7777; www.anzachotel.com; Saat Kulesi Meydanı 8; s/d/tr €30/40/50; ✗ 🖳 ♿) Recent (and very thorough) renovations have added another star to this very central 27-room hotel. The attention to detail here is legendary, from the nonallergenic parquet floors to the Gallipoli campaign mirror images in the mezzanine café. Choose room 401 or 402; they're big and face the sea.

Hotel Helen (☎ 212 1818; www.helenhotel.com; Cumhuriyet Meydanı 57; s/d/tr €25/50/65; ✗ 🖳) Just next to Anzac House Hostel, the Helen aims for the classical in its marble foyer – that's the Trojan lady herself in the lobby. The 44 rooms may never launch a thousand ships, but they have everything you need for a break on your own personal odyssey. It's a very friendly place too.

our pick Hotel Kervansaray (☎ 217 8192; www .otelkervansaray.com; Fetvane Sokak 13; s/d/tr €35/50/60; ✗ ✗ 🖳) Çanakkale's first and only boutique hotel is as lovely as you could hope for, laying on plenty of Ottoman touches in keeping with the restored house it occupies, once owned by

an early 20th-century *hakim* (judge). The 19 rooms have a dash of character without being overdone. The ones with showers are in the main historical building and the rest (with bathtubs) in a new back annexe sympathetic to the red-brick original. Choose room 103 or 206 overlooking the inviting courtyard and garden.

Otel Anafartalar (☎ 217 4454; otelanafartalar@hot mail.com; İskele Meydanı; s/d/tr €40/55/65; ✗ ✗ 🖳) A big pinkish block with 71 rooms in a prime location near the ferry docks, the Anafartalar has fine views of the strait if you can bag a front room with balcony. The bathrooms and the blue and red wavy carpet could do with an upgrade, though.

Çanak Hotel (☎ 214 1582; www.canakhotel.com; Dibek Sokak 1; s/d €35/60; ✗ ✗ 🖳) This is an excellent midrange option tucked just off Cumhuriyet Meydanı, with a stunning roof bar and games room, and a skylit atrium connecting the floors. Some of the 52 smart but low-key rooms have balconies; room 508 is a corner room with wonderful views.

Hotel Artur (☎ 213 2000; www.hotelartur.com; Cumhuriyet Meydanı 28; s/d/tr €45/60/75; ✗ 🖳) This upper-end hotel with 32 rooms has a nicely designed lobby with bar-restaurant and spacious modern rooms. Rooms 501 and 502 lead on to a roof terrace with stunning views but be aware that the lift stops at the 4th floor.

TOP END

Maydos Hotel (☎ 213 5970; www.maydos.com.tr; Yalı Caddesi 12; s/d/tr €50/70/90/110; ✗ 🖳) This relatively swish hotel with almost half of its 36 rooms facing the harbour looks a world away from the cramped budget lodgings at its cousin, the Anzac House Hostel. If you must, accept a room overlooking the street (there's double-glazing) but note the ugly internal light shaft. We love the breezy waterfront bar-restaurant.

Hotel Akol (☎ 217 9456; www.hotelakol.com.tr; Kayserili Ahmet Paşa Caddesi; s/d/tr/ste €65/85/105/155; ✗ 🖳 ✗) Near the start of the *kordon* (waterfront promenade), this balcony-studded grey concrete tower is much easier on the eyes from the inside, where you can catch the strait views and admire the slightly overblown classical-themed lobby. Its 135 rooms are mainly occupied by tour groups, so expect the Akol to have plenty of high-capacity facilities to feed and water.

Eating

The whole waterfront is lined with licensed restaurants; for something on the hoof, browse the street stalls along the *kordon* offering corn on the cob, mussels and other simple items. A speciality of the region is *peynir helvaş*, made with soft white village cheese, flour, butter and sugar and served natural or baked.

Köy Evi (☎ 213 4687; Yalı Caddesi 13; menus TL5; ☿ 8am-midnight) Proper home cooking rules in this tiny eatery, where local women make *mantı*, *börek* (filled pastry) and filling *gözleme* (TL1.50).

Doyum (☎ 217 1866; Cumhuriyet Meydanı 13; dishes TL4.50-10) Generally acknowledged to be the best kebap and pide joint in town – a visit to Doyum is worth it for the good cheer alone.

Rıhtım Restaurant (☎ 217 1770; Eski Balıkhane Sokak 9a; mains TL5-12; ☿ 11am-midnight) One of many waterfront restaurants south of the harbour, the 'Pier' is tried and true and has a varied menu of Turkish and Western cuisine along with dependable fish dishes.

Café Notte (☎ 214 9112; Kayserili Ahmet Paşa Caddesi 40; mains TL4.50-16.50; ☿ 8am-11.30pm) In the heart of the trendier northern waterfront strip, this smart bar-bistro has a cosmopolitan menu and some competent cocktails (TL5 to TL8.50). It also does simpler things like pizzas and sandwiches (TL4 to TL10).

Drinking & Entertainment

Çanakkale has an unusually frenetic bar and club scene, catering to a local student crowd and, in season, marauding young Aussies and Kiwis. Many venues have regular live music, and most of the busiest places are clustered around Fetvane Sokak and Matbaa Sokak running off it. Any admission charge usually includes a drink.

Benzin (☎ 212 2237; Eski Balıkhane Sokak 11; ☿ 8.30am-1am) This waterfront café-bar done out in 1960s decor is a relaxing spot for a drink and a bite (pizzas TL8 to TL12.50) but gets very packed at the weekend.

Han Bar (Fetvane Sokak 26; admission free-TL5; ☿ 9.30pm-4am) Upstairs in the old Yalı Han, this is a very popular music venue where the bands may play anything from Turkish rock to Madonna. The outside gallery overlooks an equally popular courtyard tea garden.

Hayal Kahvesi (☎ 217 0470; Saat Kulesi Meydanı 6; admission free-TL5; ☿ noon-1am) Facing the clock tower, this dual-identity café-bar (also called TNT Bar) is the most popular bar for live rock music. There's courtyard seating in back and happy hour is from 4pm to 9pm.

Hedon Club (☎ 212 0552; Yalı Caddesi 41; ☿ 2pm-late) This big venue attempts a spot of lounge sophistication up front (jazz), until you get to the barn-like dance floor, where everything from rock to salsa goes. Admission depends on the night; it's usually around TL10 when there's a band on.

Şişe (Eski Balıkhane Sokak 7a; ☿ 5pm-2am) The 'Bottle', with three distinctly different bars on as many floors (head for the top) is as chilled a spot as you'll find in Çanakkale.

Getting There & Away

AIR
You can fly between Çanakkale and İstanbul on **Atlasjet** (www.atlasjet.com) daily except Saturday from İstanbul and except Sunday from Çanakkale for under TL100. A shuttle bus (TL2) links **Çanakkale airport** (☎ 213 1021; Şehit Gürol Caddesi), 2km to the southeast, with the centre.

BUS & DOLMUŞ
Çanakkale's otogar is 1km east of the ferry docks but most buses pick up and drop off at the bus company offices near the harbour. There are regular services to Ankara (TL40, 11 hours), Ayvalık (TL20, 3½ hours), Bandırma (TL17, 2¼ hours), Bursa (TL25, 4½ hours), Edirne (TL25, 4½ hours), İstanbul (TL30, six hours) and İzmir (TL30, 5½ hours).

Dolmuşes to Troy (TL4, 35 minutes) and Güzelyalı (TL2.50, 20 minutes) leave from a separate dolmuş station at the northern end of the bridge over the Sarı River.

To get to Gelibolu take a bus or minibus from the otogar to Lapseki (TL4, 45 minutes) then the ferry across the Dardanelles. Alternatively, take the ferry to Eceabat or Kilitbahir and then a minibus.

If you're heading for Çanakkale from İstanbul, the quickest way is to hop on a ferry from Yenikapı to Bandırma then take a bus to Çanakkale (TL17, three hours). It's easier than trekking out to İstanbul's otogar for a direct bus.

BOAT
Two car ferries cross the Dardanelles from Çanakkale to the Gallipoli Peninsula. A privately run one goes to Kilitbahir, the public one to Eceabat.

The smaller Çanakkale–Kilitbahir ferry (TL1.50, cars TL17.50, 15 to 20 minutes) can carry only a few cars and waits until it is full before departing. For information about ferries between Çanakkale and Eceabat, see p187.

For information about getting to Gökçeada island from Çanakkale, see p194.

GÖKÇEADA

☎ 0286 / pop 8600

Just north of the entrance to the Dardanelles, rugged, sparsely populated Gökçeada (Heavenly Island) is one of only two inhabited Aegean islands belonging to Turkey. Measuring 13km from north to south and just under 30km from east to west, it is by far the nation's largest island. Gökçeada is a fascinating place, with some dramatic scenery packed into a small area, and a Greek feel to it throughout. It's a great place to escape to after visiting Gallipoli.

Gökçeada was once a predominantly Greek island called Imbros. During WWI it was an important base for the Gallipoli campaign; indeed, Allied commander General Ian Hamilton stationed himself at the village of Aydıncık (then Kefalos) on the island's southeast coast. Along with its smaller island neighbour to the south, Bozcaada (p200), Gökçeada was retained by the new Turkish Republic in 1923 but was exempted from the population exchange. However, in the 1960s when the Cyprus conflict flared up the Turkish government put pressure on local Greeks, who numbered about 7000, to leave; today only a few hundred pensioners remain.

Gökçeada's inhabitants mostly earn a living through fishing, sheep- and cattle-rearing, farming the narrow belt of fertile land around Gökçeada town, and tourism. Apart from some semideserted Greek villages, olive groves and pine forests, the island boasts fine beaches and craggy hills. It is a rare example of an Aegean island that hasn't been overtaken by mass tourism and, because it is heavily militarised, will no doubt stay that way.

Information

The ferry docks at Kuzulimanı but most things of a practical nature are to be found inland at Gökçeada town, where just under 85% of the island's population lives. These include ATMs, taxis, internet cafés and, in season, a helpful **tourist office** (☎ 887 2800; Cumhuriyet Meydanı; ⏰ 10am-8pm Jun-Sep) housed in a kiosk on the main square. The island's official website is www.gokceada17.net but you may find the private www.gokceada.com more useful.

The island's only petrol station is 2km from the town centre on the road to Kuzulimanı.

Sights

Gökçeada town itself is useful but not particularly inspiring. Most people head straight for **Kaleköy** (formerly Kastro), which has a tiny public beach – the military and the unsightly Gökçeada Resort Hotel take the lion's share of it – a hillside old quarter, a lovely whitewashed former Greek church and the remains of an Ottoman-era castle. But its harbour setting has been blighted by a large yacht marina, which opened in early 2008. The coastline between Kaleköy and Kuzulimanı forms a **national marine park** (sualtı milli parkı).

Along the stunningly picturesque southern coast of the island, **Aydıncık** is said to have the best beach on the island and is adjacent to **Tuz Gölü** (Salt Lake), where you can go for some self-administered mud treatments. There are smaller beaches at **Kapıkaya**, **Yuvalı** and **Uğurlu**.

Heading west from the centre you'll skirt the Greek villages of **Zeytinli** (Aya Theodoros), 3km from Gökçeada town, **Tepeköy** (Agridia), another 7km on, and **Dereköy** (Shinudy), another 5km west. All of them were built on hillsides overlooking the island's central valley to avoid pirate raids. Nowadays, many of the houses are deserted and falling into disrepair, particularly at Dereköy, which is reminiscent of the ghost town of Kayaköy (p367) near Fethiye. However, Tepeköy and Zeytinli are both discovering the benefits of small-scale tourism thanks to a couple of inspired accommodation options, and both are worth a visit. Tepeköy is absolutely gorgeous, surrounded by green-grey scree-covered hills, with views over valleys and a large reservoir, plus a dash of Greek heritage in its main square and taverna. The Greek church and its iconostasis is impressive; apparently this is the only settlement in all of Turkey that does not have a mosque.

Festivals & Events

During the **Yumurta Panayırı** (Egg Festival) in the first week of July many former Greek inhabitants, including the current Orthodox Patriarch of İstanbul, return to the island.

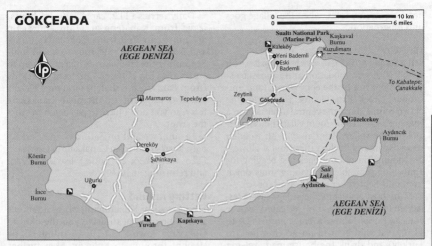

GÖKÇEADA

Sleeping & Eating

The old-fashioned *ev pansiyonu* (pension in a private home), which has virtually died out elsewhere, is still alive and kicking on Gökçeada. It's not unusual for locals to approach and offer you a spare room in their house, usually for around TL10 a head including breakfast. A two-room house with kitchen costs from TL50 per couple. Note that single rooms are in short supply, especially in July and August.

GÖKÇEADA TOWN

Otel Taşkın (☎ 887 3266; www.taksinotel.com; Zeytinli Caddesi 3; s/d/tr TL35/60/75; 🖥) Pick of the crop of Gökçeada town's handful of central hotels, this establishment has a blue-tiled exterior (including mosaic of a *gület*, a wooden yacht) and 20 spacious, good-value rooms with TV, balcony and lots of light. Rooms 106 and 107 open on to what could only be described as a farm.

Places to eat on or just off the main square include the marvellous **Gökçeadalıçakır'in Yeri** (☎ 887 2393; Atatürk Caddesi 26; mains TL5-20; 🕑 8.30am-2am), a vine-covered restaurant/café/pub/shop with local honey, jams, herbal soaps and wine, run by 'Gökçeada Blue Eyes' Rifat. Try his five-herb tea and a vegetarian dish. More predictable is **Taylan Aile Lokantası** (☎ 887 2451; Atatürk Caddesi 39; mains TL2-9; 🕑 6am-midnight, to 9pm Oct-May), a 'family restaurant' next to the Pegasus Otel, with a menu of Turkish staples. For excellent snacks and shop-made desserts the **Meydanı Café** (☎ 887 4420; Atatürk Caddesi 35; 🕑 6am-midnight) is big and airy, and attracts a young crowd.

KALEKÖY

Yakamoz Motel (☎ 887 2057; www.gokceadayakamoz .com, in Turkish; s/d/tr TL40/70/90; 🖥) Perched on the hill overlooking the harbour in Yukarı Kaleköy (Upper Kaleköy), the multiterraced 'Phosphorescence' has 18 bare-bones rooms and – our favourite spot on the island – a pleasant terrace restaurant with million-dollar views over the bay and hills.

Gökçe Motel (☎ 887 2726; www.gokceadarehberi .com/asp/konaklama/kalekoy/motel/kalekoym.htm; r per person TL30) At the foot of the road going up to Yukarı Kaleköy, this quirky place is less a motel than *'mini tatil köyü'* (mini holiday village) with neat little huts (total 15 rooms) around a garden, with solar-powered lights, bright linen and a small kitchen.

Kale Motel (☎ 887 4404; www.kalemotel.com; Barbaros Caddesi 34; r per person TL30-40; 😺 🖥) Arguably the best of the half-dozen hotel-restaurants lining the harbour, the Kale has a wide range of rooms (a total of 25), cool marble corridors and broad shared balconies (eg room 101), some of which are shaded by vines.

ZEYTİNLİ

Zeytindali Hotel (☎ 887 3707; www.zeytindalihotel .com; Zeytinli 168; s €50-60, d €60-70; 😺) A narrow cobbled street (leave the car behind!) wends its way up through the village to this delightfully stylish 16-room hotel inside a restored stone building. Rooms are imaginatively decorated in a style that mixes old and new, and there's a restaurant on the ground floor. The hotel closes in winter, when the village goes into hibernation.

TEPEKÖY

Barba Yorgo (☎ 887 4247; www.barbayorgo.com; r per person TL30) Accommodation at this unique establishment run by the eponymous (and gregarious) Greek 'Papa George' is either in one of two rooms above the central taverna or in a lovingly restored four-room village house overlooking the valley 200m away, with wooden floors, sparrows in the rafters and a glowering mountain right out back just begging for a morning scramble. Everything shuts down from mid-September to mid-April (or so).

Mine host also runs the village **tavern restaurant** (mains TL9-15), a film-set eatery where you can sample above-average meze (TL4 to TL10), eat wild boar (a no-no elsewhere in Turkey) and drink the house-made retsina wine (TL17 to TL19 a bottle).

UĞURLU

Mavi Su Resort (☎ 897 6090; www.mavisuresort.com; s/d €45/65; ⌗ ▯) If you really want to get away from it all, the 'Blue Water' with 35 rooms and suites, is for you. It's in Uğurlu, which is about as far as you can get from anything in Gökçeada. Rooms are large, bright and airy (corner room 108 is choice), and the lovely long garden stretches virtually into the sea.

Shopping

Gökçeada is committed to becoming the first community in Turkey to produce only organic foodstuffs; at present its 120,000 trees produce an annual 2000 tonnes of oil, most of which is organic. At the forefront of this endeavour is **Elta-Ada** (☎ 887 4581; www.elta-ada.com.tr), a farm that produces organic olive oil, dairy products (soft white cheeses, yoghurt and butter) and assorted fruits and vegetables. In summer it sells its produce from a **kiosk** (Cumhuriyet Meydanı; ❧ 8am-9pm) opposite the Pegasus Otel. If you happen to visit Gökçeada in June, experience its organic black cherries. You'll think you've died and gone to heaven.

Getting There & Away

There are two boat services to Gökçeada: the main one from Kabatepe on the western side of the Gallipoli Peninsula and a very limited one from Çanakkale on the eastern side of the Dardanelles that runs at weekends in summer only.

Daily ferries (TL2, cars TL20, 1½ hours) leave from Kabatepe at 11am and again at 7pm, returning from Gökçeada at 7am and 5.30pm. From mid-June to about mid-September the frequencies increase to up to six ferries a day between 7am from Gökçeada (from 8am from Kabatepe) to 9pm. Tickets are also valid for the Eceabat–Çanakkale ferry, so you don't have to pay again to cross the strait.

In summer and on Saturday and Sunday only, a ferry runs from Çanakkale to Gökçeada (TL5, cars TL25, 2½ hours), leaving at 7am and returning at 10.30pm.

Getting Around

Ferries dock at Kuzulimanı, where dolmuşes should be waiting to drive you the 6km to Gökçeada town (TL1.50, 15 minutes), or straight through to Kaleköy, 5km further north (TL2.50, 30 minutes). A bus service runs between Kaleköy, Gökçeada and Kuzulimanı roughly every two hours, though it doesn't always stick to the timetable.

Otherwise, the island is tricky to get around without your own transport. Taxis in Gökçeada charge TL7 to Kaleköy or Zeytinli, TL10 to Kuzulimanı, TL13 to Tepeköy and TL25 to Uğurlu.

KIYIKÖY

☎ 0288 / pop 2500

One of European Turkey's handful of settlements on the Black Sea, Kıyıköy (formerly Salmidesos) is a popular breakaway for İstanbullus but can be just as easily reached from mainland Thrace. Come here for the long sandy **beaches** on the Black (and very blue) Sea; the 6th-century **Monastery of St Nicholas** (Aya Nikola Manastırı) hewn from solid rock and straight out of an Indiana Jones film; the remains of **Kıyıköy Castle** (Kıyıköy Kalesı) dating from the same period; and the bustling local **market** on Tuesday.

Budget accommodation (TL25 to TL45 for a double) is in pensions scattered throughout the village, including the **Ender Pansiyon** (☎ 388 6057; Nolu Sokak 1) on a side street just after the castle's South Gate; and the motel-like **Midye Pansiyon** (☎ 388 6472; Cumhuriyet Caddesi), with 12 rooms just east of the main square.

ourpick **Hotel Endorfina** (☎ 388 6364; www.hotel endorfina.com; Manastır Üstü; r per person TL100-120; ▯), a boutique hotel on a bluff above the monastery overlooking the sea and just 500m southwest of the castle's West Gate, is *the* place to stay in these parts – a destination in its own right. It has oodles of charm (ask for corner room 10 or 20), two of the best managers this side of Harvard Business School and an excellent restaurant, where fish, especially *kalkan* (turbot) from the Black Sea, is the speciality. If you're nice, owner/manager Mehmet will take you down to the harbour at night to buy the daily catch from the village fishermen.

Other reliable restaurants include **Yakamoz** (☎ 388 6159; Yakamoz Sokak), in a shed-like building on a cliff high above the sea northwest of the main square, and **Kösk** (☎ 0535-358 2010; Güneş Sokak), with good meze as well as grills and fish. **Kartal** (☎ 0542-634 9956; Sur Sokak), a garden café

near the West Gate, is a wonderful place to recharge the batteries. **Marina** (☎ 388 6058; Akşam Sefası Sokak), perched high above the harbour east of the centre, serves food but is notably a place for the perfect sundowner.

There's one direct bus a day from Istanbul (TL15, three hours) at 4pm year-round, with an additional departure in the morning in summer. They return at 8am and 8pm, respectively. More reliable is the service between İstanbul and Saray (TL11, 2½ hours), 30km to the southwest, which departs every half-hour. In Saray catch one of the minibuses to Kıyıköy (TL4, half-hour) that run every two hours or, if you've booked ahead, call Hotel Endorfina and someone will come and fetch you.

THRACE & MARMARA

North Aegean

If the south Aegean is Turkey's younger wayward child – a noisy, boisterous show-off, desperate for attention – then the north Aegean is the older, quieter, more serious and, in truth, less popular sibling. Though it boasts a similar topography with plenty of fine beaches and dramatic cliff-top scenery, there are no dedicated resort towns of the scale and intensity of Bodrum or Kuşadası. North Aegean resorts tend to be quieter, more refined affairs, like Assos, Foça and Alaçatı, aimed more at vacationing Turks than the package hordes from Europe.

That's not to say that the north Aegean doesn't have its own urban sprawl. İzmir is Turkey's third-largest city, and just as noisy, congested and confusing as either İstanbul or Ankara. Still, if you can overlook the stupefyingly ugly suburbs and relentless, honking traffic, you'll find much to entice you, including a buzzing bazaar, a vibrant nightlife and one of the Aegean's most pleasant waterfronts.

İzmir aside, much of the region is rural. Life is arranged around the patterns of the growing, not the tourist, seasons. Indeed, such is the air of bucolic calm that it can be difficult to believe this region was once the setting for some of the bloodiest confrontations in history. Ancient ruins litter the landscape, including Troy, the most famed of all – even if the remains are far from legendary. Spectacular Pergamum does a better job of living up to its billing.

The north Aegean also boasts its own island, pretty little Bozcaada, which, with its vine-covered hills, picturesque town of old stone houses and quiet beaches, perhaps offers the finest distillation of the region's charms.

HIGHLIGHTS

- Explore the ruins of the Roman Empire at **Pergamum** (Bergama; p212), one of the country's finest ancient sites

- Windsurf by day, and fine-dine by night at **Alaçatı** (p234), the region's favourite boutique bolt hole

- Relax on the beach and sample the local vino on the idyllic, laid-back island of **Bozcaada** (p200)

- Hunt for bargains in **İzmir**'s (p221) chaotic bazaar before retiring to the waterfront for an elegant sunset drink

- Tour the crumbling, atmospheric backstreets of **Ayvalık**'s (p207) old town

- Clamber up the dusty slopes to Behramkale's amazing **Temple of Athena** (p205) with its glorious sea views

BANDIRMA

☎ 0266 / pop 110,250

An undistinguished 20th-century *betonville* (concrete city), the port town of Bandırma marks the junction between İzmir-bound trains and the Bandırma–İstanbul ferry line, so you may well need to pass through it.

The otogar (bus station) is 1.8km southeast of the centre, out on the main highway and served by *servis* (shuttle buses) from the centre.

Getting There & Away

At least two daily **İstanbul Deniz Otobüsleri fast ferries** (İDO; ☎ 444 4436; www.ido.com.tr; per car/pedestrian/passenger TL115/30/25) connect Bandırma with İstanbul's Yenikapı docks (1¾ hours). It's a comfortable service, with assigned seats, trolley-dollies selling fresh orange juice and sandwiches, a business-class lounge and a lift for disabled passengers.

In theory, the ferry connects with the morning train from İzmir. However, in reality it does so only from mid-July until August. The rest of the year you'll have to cool your heels in Bandırma for a couple of hours.

The *Alti Eylül Ekspresi* train departs year-round from Bandırma Gar (the main station) at 9.45am daily, arriving at İzmir's Basmane station at 3.20pm. Between April and October a second service, the *Onyedi Eylül Ekspresi,* leaves at 5.45pm, arriving in İzmir at 9.30pm (TL16, 6½ hours, 342km).

Bandırma is midway on the bus run between Bursa (TL15, two hours, 115km) and Çanakkale (TL17, 2¾ hours, 195km).

TROY (TRUVA) & TEVFİKİYE

☎ 0286

It has to be said, if it wasn't for the name – and its legendary associations – almost nobody would visit this place. Of all the breathtaking ancient sites in Turkey, the remains of what you would hope to be the most wondrous of all, the great city of Troy, are in fact among the least impressive. To get the best out of a trip here you'll have to use your imagination, and reconstruct almost all of the city's former splendour inside your head. Still, for any history buff, it's an important site to tick off the list.

History

The first people lived here during the early Bronze Age. The cities called Troy I to Troy V (3000–1700 BC) had a similar culture, but Troy VI (1700–1250 BC) took on a different Mycenae-influenced character, doubling in size and trading prosperously with the region's Greek colonies. Archaeologists argue over whether Troy VI or Troy VII was the city of King Priam who engaged in the Trojan War. Most believe it was Troy VI, arguing that the earthquake that brought down the walls in 1250 BC hastened the Achaean victory.

Troy VII lasted from 1250 to 1000 BC. An invading Balkan people moved in around 1190 BC, and Troy sank into a torpor for four centuries. It was revived as a Greek city (Troy VIII, 700–85 BC), then as a Roman one (Novum Ilion; Troy IX, 85 BC to AD 500). Before eventually settling on Byzantium, Constantine the Great toyed with the idea of building the capital of the eastern Roman Empire here. As a Byzantine town, Troy didn't amount to much.

The Fourth Crusaders sometimes claimed that their brutal behaviour in Turkey was justified as vengeance for Troy, and when Mehmet the Conqueror visited the site in 1462 he, in turn, claimed to be laying those ghosts to rest. After that, the town simply disappeared from the records.

Sights

The ticket booth for the **ruins of Troy** (☎ 283 0536; per person/car TL10/3; 🕒 8.30am-7pm May-15 Sep, to 5pm 16 Sep-end Apr) is 500m before the site.

Guides are available for tours (€50, 1½ hours); inquire at the ticket booth or restaurants, or email in advance to Mustafa Askin (thetroyguide@hotmail.com). Illustrated guidebooks (TL10 to TL60) and maps (TL5) are sold at the souvenir shops.

The first thing you see as you approach the ruins is a huge replica of the city's most potent symbol – and the means of its legendary demise – a wooden horse, built by the Ministry of Tourism and Culture. You can climb up inside and admire the views through windows in the horses' sides (which presumably didn't feature in the original Greek design).

The **Excavations House**, to the right of the path, was used by earlier archaeological teams, and today holds models and superimposed pictures to give an idea of what Troy looked like at different points in its history, as well as information on the importance of the Troy myth in Western history. Opposite is the small **Pithos Garden**, with a collection of outsize storage jars and drainage pipes.

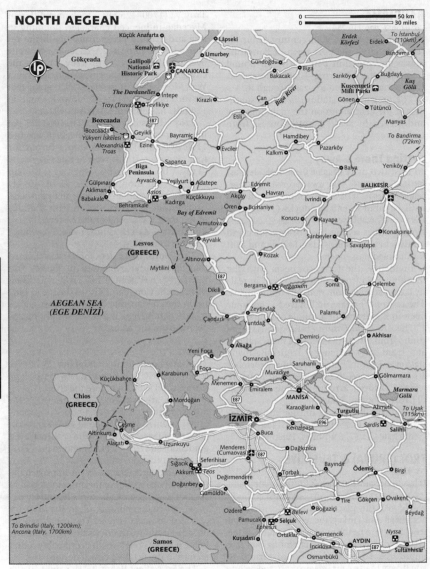

NORTH AEGEAN

Although the site is still fairly confusing, the circular path around the ruins has signboards to help you understand what you're seeing.

As you approach the ruins, take the stone steps up on the right. These bring you out on top of what was the **outer wall of Troy VIII/IX**, from where you can gaze on the fortifications of the **east wall gate** and **tower of Troy VI**.

Descend the stairs and follow the path round the walls to the right, and then up a knoll from where you can look at some original (as well as some reconstructed) red-brick **walls of Troy II/III**. Immediately above them was the site of a Graeco-Roman **Temple of Athena**, of which only traces of the altar remain today.

DISCOVERING TROY

Until the 19th century, many historians doubted whether Troy was a real place at all. One man who was convinced of its existence – to an almost obsessive level – was the German businessman Heinrich Schliemann (1822–90), who in 1871 received permission from the Ottoman government to excavate a hill near the village of Hisarlık, which archaeologists had previously identified as a possible site for the city. This was to be no slow, forensic excavation, however. Schliemann was more of an eager treasure hunter than a methodical archaeologist and quickly tore open the site, uncovering the remains of a ruined city, which he confidently identified as the Troy of Homeric legend, and a great cache of gold artefacts, which he named, with typical understatement, 'Priam's Treasure'. These discoveries brought Schliemann world fame, but also greater scrutiny of his rather slapdash methods, prompting no little criticism and revealing that not all of his findings were quite as he presented them.

In his haste, Schliemann had failed to appreciate that Troy was not a single city, but rather a series of settlements built successively one on top of the other over the course of about two-and-a-half thousand years. Subsequent archaeologists have identified the remains of nine separate Troys, large sections of which had been damaged during Schliemann's hot-headed pursuit of glory. Furthermore, it was soon established that his precious treasures were not from the time of Homer's Troy (Troy VI), but were from the much earlier Troy II.

Schliemann's dubious attitude towards archaeological standards continued after the excavation when he smuggled part of 'Priam's Treasure' out of the Ottoman Empire. Much of it was displayed in Berlin, where it was seized by invading Soviet troops at the end of World War II. Following decades of denials about their whereabouts, the treasures were eventually found hidden away in the Pushkin Museum in Moscow, where they remain while international wrangles over their true ownership continue.

Note that Troy is a popular destination for weekending school parties. Do yourself a favour and visit midweek.

Continue following the path, past traces of the **wall of Early/Middle Troy (Troy I Gate)**. Opposite are remains of the **houses of Troy II**, inhabited by a literal 'upper class' while the poor huddled on the plains.

The path then sweeps past **Schliemann's original trial trench**, which was cut straight through all the layers of the city. Signs point out the nine city strata in the trench's 15m-high sides.

Just round the corner is a stretch of wall from what is believed to have been the two-storey-high Troy VI **Palace Complex** and then, to the right, traces of an ancient **sanctuary** to unknown deities. Later, a new sanctuary was built on the same site, apparently honouring the deities of Samothrace. Nearby are remains of the **Skaean Gate** in front of which Achilles and Hector supposedly fought their duel. Eventually, the path passes in front of the Roman **Odeon**, where concerts were held, and the **Bouleuterion** (Council Chamber), bringing you back to where you started.

Sleeping & Eating
Most visitors stay in Çanakkale (p189) and visit Troy in passing. However, the atmosphere of the nearby village of Tevfikiye makes a pleasant change from the hassle of Çanakkale.

Varol Pansiyon (☎ 283 0828; s/d TL40/55) The Varol, right in the heart of the village, is clean, lovingly cared for and homely. Rooms are of a decent size, and guests can also use the kitchen.

Hotel Hisarlık (☎ 283 0026; thetroyguide@hotmail .com; s/d €25/35) This hotel is run by the family of the local guide Mustafa Askin. It's opposite the gate to the ruins and has comfortable rooms emblazoned with the names of characters from Greek myths. The restaurant (open 8am to 11pm) serves good Turkish home cooking. Try the hearty *güveç* (beef stew).

Getting There & Away
From Çanakkale, dolmuşes (minibuses) to Troy (TL2, 35 minutes, 30km) leave every hour on the half-hour from 9.30am to 5.30pm from a station under the bridge over the Sarı, and drop you right by the ticket booth.

From Troy to Çanakkale, dolmuşes leave every hour on the hour 7am to 5pm in high season and 7am to 3pm in low season.

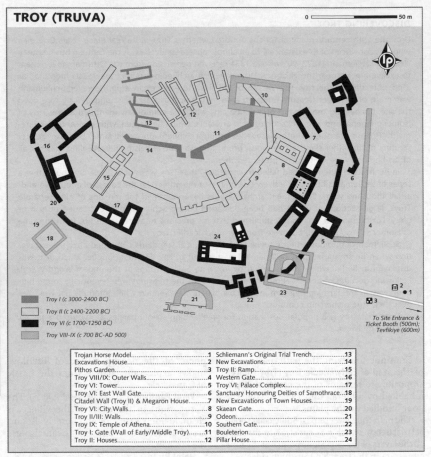

TROY (TRUVA)

0 ————— 50 m

Troy I (c 3000-2400 BC)
Troy II (c 2400-2200 BC)
Troy VI (c 1700-1250 BC)
Troy VIII-IX (c 700 BC-AD 500)

To Site Entrance &
Ticket Booth (500m);
Tevfikiye (600m)

Trojan Horse Model.................................1	Schliemann's Original Trial Trench..............13	
Excavations House....................................2	New Excavations....................................14	
Pithos Garden..3	Troy II: Ramp...15	
Troy VIII/IX: Outer Walls..........................4	Western Gate...16	
Troy VI: Tower...5	Troy VI: Palace Complex...........................17	
Troy VI: East Wall Gate............................6	Sanctuary Honouring Deities of Samothrace...18	
Citadel Wall (Troy II) & Megaron House.........7	New Excavations of Town Houses..................19	
Troy VI: City Walls...................................8	Skaean Gate..20	
Troy II/III: Walls......................................9	Odeon..21	
Troy IX: Temple of Athena.......................10	Southern Gate..22	
Troy I: Gate (Wall of Early/Middle Troy).......11	Bouleterion..23	
Troy II: Houses......................................12	Pillar House...24	

The travel agencies offering tours to the Gallipoli (Gelibolu) battlefields also offer tours to Troy (around €25 per person). This is worth considering if you want a guided tour of both sites at an affordable rate. For details of the various tour companies, see p180.

BOZCAADA
☎ 0286 / pop 2700
Beautiful little Bozcaada. The second of Turkey's two inhabited Aegean islands (the other is Gökçeada), it's the sort of place where you arrive planning to spend a night and wind up wishing you could stay forever. A trip here also makes a good break from the usual tourist trail.

Windswept Bozcaada (formerly Tenedos) has always been known to Anatolian oenophiles for its wines, and vineyards still blanket its sunny slopes (see boxed text, p203). As in Bodrum (p267), a huge medieval fortress towers over the harbour. In its wake huddles one of Turkey's least-spoilt small towns, a warren of picturesque vine-draped old houses and cobbled streets.

The island is small (about 5km to 6km across) and easy to explore. Lovely unspoilt sandy beaches line the coast road to the south.

Be warned that outside the school-holiday period (mid-June to mid-September) you may find cafés and the like closed, except at weekends and on Wednesdays, when a market fills the main square.

Information

There is no tourist office, but you can pick up a rough map from some of the hotels, pensions and cafés, including the Ada Café.

There's a Ziraat Bankası ATM in Bozcaada town, right beside the PTT, although as it doesn't have agreements with every international bank, you'll need to bring sufficient cash with you. The **Captain Internet Kafe** (☎ 697 8507; Trüya Sokak; per hr €1.10; ⏰ 9am-midnight) is nearby.

Sights

Bozcaada is a place for hanging out, rather than doing anything specific. The one official tourist attraction is the impressive **fortress** (☎ 0543-551 8211; admission TL1; ⏰ 10am-1pm & 2-7pm May-Nov), in Bozcaada town, which dates back to Byzantine times, although most of what you see are later Venetian, Genoese and Ottoman additions. Inside the double walls you will find traces of a mosque, several ammunition dumps, a barracks and an infirmary.

The **church**, in the old Greek neighbourhood directly behind the castle, is sadly rarely open.

The **Bozcaada Local History Museum** (Bozcaada Yerel Tarih Müzesi; www.bozcaadamuzesi.com; Lale Sokak 7; adult/child TL5/3; ⏰ 10am-8pm mid-Apr–Sep) is a treasure trove of lovingly collected island curios – maps, prints, photographs, seashells and day-to-day artefacts. It's a fascinating place where you can fossick through the island's history.

The best **beaches** – Ayana, Ayazma and Habbele – straggle along the south coast, although Tuzburnu to the east and Sulubahçe to the west are also passable. Ayazma is by far the most popular and best equipped, boasting several cafes (offering the usual Turkish fare) as well as a small, abandoned **Greek monastery** uphill.

Sleeping

BUDGET

Prices can rise dramatically in summer, although from 2009 onwards room rates are to be regulated by the municipality.

Güler Pansiyon (☎ 697 8454; Tuzburnu Yolu Üzeri; r per person TL40) Though simple, the 120-year-old farmhouse has an authentic island feel and a beautiful setting amid vineyards. There's a quiet beach 100m away with tables, sunloungers and a shower. It lies about 2.5km from town on the Tuzburnu road.

Kibele Konukevi (☎ 697 0576; www.kibelekonukevi .com; Çınar Çarşı Caddesi 90; r per person TL70-80; ⏰) An affordable option in the fast-gentrifying Greek neighbourhood. This restored stone house boasts seven rather simple rooms done out in a striking pink, green and yellow colour scheme. There's also a pleasant central courtyard where breakfast is served.

Apart Akarsu Otel (☎ 697 8435; Gürsel Sokak 36; r per person incl breakfast TL50; ⏰) With four spotless, spacious one-bedroom apartments with full kitchens, this place also boasts a fabulous rooftop terrace with views over the fortress. Reserve at least two weeks in advance.

Kale Pansiyon (☎ 697 8617; www.kalepansiyon.net; s/ d TL60/80) Uphill behind the Otel Ege Bozcaada, the Kale has simple but fastidiously clean rooms and an open-buffet breakfast (on a terrace with lovely views) that gets top marks from travellers. Pakize, the owner, is keen to please and makes delicious jam.

MIDRANGE

Otel Ege Bozcaada (☎ 697 8189; www.egehotel.com; Bozkaada Kale Arkası; s/d TL75/150; ⏰ 10 Apr-15 Nov; ⏰ 💻) A 19th-century primary school now turned into a cavernous hotel with 35 attractively furnished rooms, each with the name of a poet, and an extract of their verse, engraved on the door. Six rooms have balconies with views over the fort.

Hotel Katına (☎ 236 2421; www.katinaas.com; Eylül Caddesi 20; r per person TL75; ⏰ 💻) Terribly 'boutique', this renovated 150-year-old house has seven very stylish rooms – wooden floors and uplighting – equipped with LCD TV screens, large beds and swish bathrooms. Here and there some of the original stonework has been left exposed to add some nice rustic touches. Breakfast is served at the hotel's smart café.

Otel Kaikias (☎ 697 0250; www.kaikias.com, in Turkish; per person TL80; ⏰) Though built in 2001, the building has been artfully decorated to appear aged with antique Greek furniture, paintings and photos. Rooms boast wooden floors, four-poster beds (draped with white muslin) and marble bathrooms. Four rooms have fort views.

Rengigül (☎ 697 8171; www.rengigul.net; Atatürk Caddesi 31; s/d TL80/120) This character-filled 138-year-old Greek house has six tastefully decorated, antique-strewn rooms (Özcan, the owner, also runs an art gallery and clearly has a good eye), a cosy lounge and library area, and a large, peaceful, walled garden.

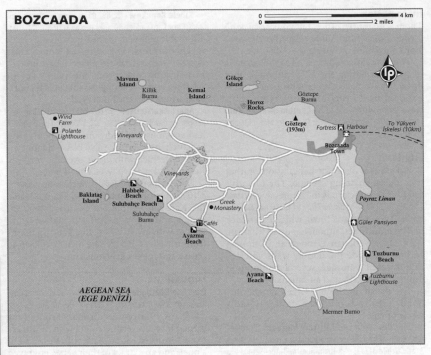

BOZCAADA

NORTH AEGEAN

Eating

Always check the price of fish before ordering. There have been complaints from some travellers about the exorbitant prices in some restaurants.

Café at Lisa's (☎ 697 0182; Liman Sokak; 8.30am-midnight; 🖳) At the southern end of the harbour 200m from the disembarkation point, this charming café is run by Lisa, an Australian who also runs the local rag (so is very au fait with all the island goings-on!). It's a great place for breakfast (TL4 to TL10) – Lisa's omelettes are legendary – cake (TL3 to TL5), soup (TL5) or salad (TL6 to TL8).

Koreli (☎ 697 8098; Yali Caddesi 12; noon-midnight) In business now for three generations, this charming place by the harbour clearly knows what it's doing, and roars with regulars who come for the *köftes* (meatballs; TL6) or fresh seafood such as *kalamar tava* (fried squid; TL12).

Sandal Restaurant (☎ 668 1025; Alsancak Sokak 31; 9am-2am) With its strict blue-and-white colour scheme (which even includes the boat stuck to the outside wall), there's no mistaking the Greek influence here. It's renowned for its fish dishes and stews, and the *kalamar tava* (TL10) are finger-lickin' good.

Boruzan (☎ 697 0352; Liman Sokak 10; fish mains TL10-15; 9am-2am) A buzzing harbourside place, Boruzan is particularly good for mezes, which feature produce from the restaurant's own vegetable patch, and simple seafood dishes, such as *kalamar tava* (TL10) and octopus meatballs (TL8). A second branch opens in summer at Ayazma Beach.

Güverte (☎ 668 9582; İstiklal Sokak 7; 8am-midnight) Diagonally opposite Sandal, this is a cosy little choice with vine-shaded tables and a wide selection of mezes, including *cevizli kabak* (zucchini with walnuts and yoghurt; TL5), and plenty of good fish and seafood (TL10 to TL15).

Ada Café (☎ 697 8795; www.bozcaada.info; Çınar Çeşme Sokak 4; köfte TL7, meals TL10-15, beer TL4; 8am-noon May-Sep) The İstanbul-born owners, Melih and Semra, have thrown themselves wholeheartedly into island life, running this popular café, which serves good snacks (such as pilchards wrapped in vine leaves), and becoming an unofficial tourist information point for visitors. The red poppy cordial (TL15 for a bottle) is a speciality.

FINE WINE

Bozcaada has been one of the country's great wine-growing regions since ancient times when enormous quantities of wine were used to fuel the debauchery at festivals for Dionysus, the Greek god of wine. Nobody is quite sure why, but some magical alchemy of the island's climate, topography and soil make-up just seems to suit the growing of grapes. There are four winemakers on the island: Ataol, Corvus, Talay and Yunatçılar. **Talay** (☎ 0286-697 8080; www .talay.com.tr; Lale Sokak 5; ☼ 8.30am-6pm), one block west of the *belediye* (town hall) in Bozcaada town, allows visits to its premises. You can tour the bottling unit and fermentation tanks and also taste and buy wines (TL7 to TL35) at the little shop opposite. It has plans to open a wine museum in the future.

If travelling in June, try to coincide with the annual Wine Festival, which offers free tastings, tours of the wine houses and lectures on the processes of viticulture.

Battı Balık (☎ 697 881; Alsancak Sokak; mains TL10-18; ☼ 9.30am-12.30am) A recent arrival to the restaurant scene; the former grocery store has been transformed into a rather elegant dining space with an outside seating area illuminated by paper lanterns. As the name suggests, fish and seafood dominate the menu, although it also does a mean line in cheeses.

Around 50m from the Sandal restaurant, **Bozcaada Tüketim Market** (☎ 697 8046; Alsancak Sokak 20; ☼ 8am-1am high season, 9am-9pm low season), with fresh bread and fruit, cheeses and meats, is great for getting up a picnic.

Drinking

Polente (☎ 697 8605; Yali Sokak 41; ☼ 8pm-2am) Polente, off the main square, plays an eclectic mix of music, including Latin and jazz, and attracts an equally eclectic mix of locals and visitors (mostly 20- and 30-somethings). Waterside bonfires keep out the chill in winter.

Salhane Bar (Liman Sokak 4; ☼ 9am-3am high season) Bozcaada's hippest – and certainly most striking – hot spot, housed in a converted slaughterhouse on the waterfront. It's a good place for a drink and a dance; it really starts rocking after midnight.

Bar Ali (☎ 697 8001; Çınar Çarşı Caddesi 12; ☼ 8am-4am high season) The waterfront seating area overlooks the fortress, and is, festooned with cushions, beanbags and deckchairs, is the place to wind down at the end of the day. Inside there's a more formal area where you can tuck into wines and cheese, plus a mezzanine with comfy leather chairs.

Getting There & Away

Ferries depart from Yükyeri İskelesi (Yükyeri harbour) 4km west of Geyikli, south of Troy. Dolmuşes from Çanakkale otogar run to Geyikli (55km) about every 45 minutes during the day (TL5.5, one hour); tell the driver to drop you off at the harbour. Coming back from Bozcaada, minibuses from the harbour go to Çanakkale, Geyikli and Ezine.

In low season, boats leave Yükyeri İskelesi daily at 11am, 3pm and 7pm. In high season, there's an extra daily service at 9pm, and on Friday to Sunday at midnight. From Bozcaada to Yükyeri İskelesi, boats leave at 7.30am, noon and 6pm in low season. In high season, there are extra daily services at 10am, 2pm, 4pm, 8pm and, from Friday to Sunday, 11pm. Return tickets per person/car cost TL3/23 and the journey takes 35 minutes.

For confirmation of ferry departures and times, phone **Geyikli ticket office** (☎ 632 0263) or **Bozcaada ticket office** (☎ 697 8185).

If you're coming to Yükyeri İskelesi with public transport from the south, go first to Ezine, where dolmuşes usually connect with the ferries. In high season many intercity buses connect with the first boat, so go straight to the port.

Getting to Behramkale/Assos by public transport is not straightforward. You may have to take a bus from Yükyeri İskelesi to Ezine otogar (TL0.75, 30 minutes), then walk out to the main Çanakkale–Ayvacık highway and flag down an Ayvacık minibus (TL1.50, 30 minutes). In Ayvacık you'll have to get a third minibus on to Behramkale (TL1.50, 30 minutes).

Getting Around

Frequent dolmuşes connect Bozcaada town with the Ayazma, Sulubahçe, Habbele and Mermer Burno beaches in high season (TL1.50, 15 minutes). To walk from Bozcaada town to Ayazma takes about 1½ hours.

BİGA PENINSULA
☎ 0286

With your own transport you may want to visit the isolated Biga Peninsula and its assorted, all-but-forgotten ruins along the way. You can go by public transport too, but be prepared for lots of waiting along exposed roadsides.

Alexandria Troas

Ten kilometres south of Geyikli lie the ruins of **Alexandria Troas** (admission TL5), scattered around the village of Dalyan.

After the collapse of Alexander the Great's empire, Antigonus, one of his generals, took control of this land, founding the city of Antigoneia in 310 BC. Later, he was defeated in battle by Lysimachus, another of Alexander's generals, who took the city and renamed it in honour of his late commander. After a period of Roman occupation, an earthquake eventually destroyed much of the city.

The site is undeniably atmospheric, with its great grass-strewn ruins, but also rather confusing, with little in the way of clear signage. Much of the site remains buried and excavations are ongoing. So far archaeologists have identified a theatre, palace, temple, agora (marketplace), necropolis, harbour, city walls and what is believed to be the largest Roman bathing complex in Anatolia.

Infrequent dolmuşes run between Ezine and Dalyan, or you can get here by bus from Çanakkale otogar.

Gülpınar

Gülpınar is a one-street farming town south of Geyikli with few services beyond a petrol station. However, it was once the ancient city of **Khrysa**, famous for its 2nd-century-BC Ionic temple to Apollo and its mice. An oracle had told Cretan colonists to settle where 'the sons of the earth' attacked them. Awaking to find mice chewing their equipment, they decided to settle here and built a temple to Smintheion (Lord of the Mice). The cult statue of the god, now lost, once had marble mice carved at its feet.

The remains of the **Apollon Smintheion** (admission incl museum TL5; ✆ 8am-5pm) lie 300m down a side road off the main road (look for the sign 100m after the post office if coming from Babakale). The wonderful reliefs with illustrated scenes from the *Iliad* found amid the ruins are kept in the site's **museum** (✆ Jul-end Aug).

Buses to Gülpınar run from Çanakkale and Ezine. From Gülpınar there are buses to Babakale (TL1.25, 15 minutes) and onwards to Behramkale (TL2, one hour).

Babakale (Lekton)

From Gülpınar a road heads 9km west through a line of coastal developments to Babakale, the westernmost point of mainland Turkey. It's a small, sleepy fishing village that seems almost overawed by the vast, restored Ottoman **fortress** overlooking its attractive small harbour.

The fort was built to combat pirates and is notable for being the last Ottoman castle built in present-day Turkey. There's not much else to look at, beyond views of Lesvos and Bozcaada over the water, but it's a pleasant place to unwind for a day or two.

The **Uran Hotel** (☎ 747 0218; s/d €14/28; 🗷) on the seafront has simple but sea-breeze-fresh rooms of a reasonable size. Three have harbour views. There's also a large terrace overlooking the fortress and harbour and a good and very reasonably priced **fish restaurant** (☎ 747 0218; ✆ 7.30am-midnight). Try the speciality, *kalamar* (TL8).

Buses from Gülpınar (TL1.25, 15 minutes) to Behramkale (TL1.75, one hour) stop at Babakale.

BEHRAMKALE & ASSOS
☎ 0286

Behramkale and Assos are the names of two separate parts of the same settlement: an old hilltop Greek village spread out around the ruins of an ancient temple to Athena (Behramkale); and, at the bottom of the hill, a former working harbour, with a small pebbly beach, which over the past two decades has seen its old stone buildings and warehouses transformed into boutique hotels and restaurants (Assos). They make a fine combination, although, if you can, try to avoid visiting on weekends and public holidays from the beginning of April to the end of August, when tourists pour in by the coach load.

History

The Mysian city of Assos was founded in the 8th century BC by colonists from Lesvos, who later built its great temple to Athena in 530 BC. The city enjoyed considerable prosperity under the rule of Hermeias, a one-time student of Plato who also ruled the Troad and

Lesvos. Hermeias encouraged philosophers to live in Assos, and Aristotle himself lived here from 348 to 345 BC, and ended up marrying Hermeias' niece, Pythia. Assos' glory days came to an abrupt end with the arrival of the Persians, who crucified Hermeias and forced Plato to flee.

Alexander the Great drove the Persians out, but Assos' importance was challenged by the ascendancy of Alexandria Troas to the north. From 241 to 133 BC the city was ruled by the kings of Pergamum.

St Paul visited Assos briefly during his third missionary journey, walking here from Alexandria Troas to meet St Luke before taking a boat to Lesvos.

In late-Byzantine times the city dwindled to a village. Turkish settlers arrived and called the village Behramkale. Only the coming of tourism revived its fortunes.

Orientation & Information

Approaching the village from Ayvacık, look out for the 14th-century Hüdavendigar Bridge, to the left of the road. At the crossroads, the road left leads to the scruffy beach at Kadırga (4km), the road right to Babakale and Gülpınar. Go straight ahead until you reach a fork in the road, then left (uphill) along the rough road for the old village, or straight on (downhill) to the harbour. Both roads are very steep.

The village road winds up through a small square, with a teahouse and a bust of Atatürk, to the peak of the hill, which offers a spectacular view towards the Greek island of Lesvos (Mytilini or Midilli in Turkish).

Note that there's no bank, ATM, post office, petrol station, tourist office or pharmacy in Behramkale or Assos.

Sights & Activities

Right on top of the hill in Behramkale village is the 6th-century Ionic **Temple of Athena** (admission TL5; ☽ 8am-dusk). The short tapered columns with plain capitals are hardly elegant, and the concrete reconstruction hurts more than helps, but the site and the view out to Lesvos are spectacular and well worth the admission fee.

Beside the entrance to the ruins, the 14th-century **Hüdavendigar Camii** is a simply constructed Ottoman mosque – a dome on squinches set on top of a square room – built before the Turks had conquered Constantinople and assimilated the lessons

of Sancta Sophia. It's one of just two remaining Ottoman mosques of its kind in Turkey (the other is in Bursa).

Villagers set up stalls all the way up the hill to the temple, touting herbs, woollen socks and locally made kilims (woven rugs).

Ringing the hill are stretches of the **city walls** of medieval Assos, which are among the most impressive medieval fortifications in Turkey. Scramble down the hillside to find the **necropolis**. Assos' sarcophagi (from the Greek, 'flesh-eaters') were famous. According to Pliny the Elder, the stone was caustic and 'ate' the flesh off the deceased in 40 days. There are also remains of a late-2nd-century-BC **theatre** and **basilica**.

Sleeping

Where you sleep depends on whether you prefer the picturesque and lively Assos harbour (even if the interiors of the lovely stone houses are often something of a letdown), or the more peaceful and atmospheric Behramkale village.

In high season, virtually all the hotels around the harbour insist on *yarım pansiyon* (half-board), though you could try negotiating.

ASSOS

Çakır Pansiyon (☎ 721 7048; www.assoscakirpansiyon .com; camp site per person TL8, s/d incl breakfast TL40/60, half-board TL60/80; ✸) Around 100m east along the seafront from the town entrance, this pension has simple but clean rooms in wooden bungalows, and a small camping site. It boasts its own floating platform where breakfast is served, while dinner is provided in a delightful lantern-lit restaurant.

Yıldız Saray Hotel (☎ 721 7025; www.yildizsaray -hotels.com; r incl breakfast TL180; ✸) Though rooms are on the small side, they're traditionally furnished, attractive and good value. All eight have direct sea views overlooking the harbour, and three have access to a small terrace. The brasserie-style restaurant has a good reputation. The owners also operate another hotel, just east along the coast at Kadırga.

Hotel Behram (☎ 721 7044; www.behram-hotel.com; s/d with half-board TL120/180; ✸) On the front, by the town entrance, this has smallish rooms, although they are enlivened by some nice bright decor and are well equipped. There's also a good open-air restaurant right on the water, and a range of tours (to Bergama, Babakale, Troy etc) is offered.

BEHRAMKALE

Old Bridge House (☎ 721 7426; www.assos.de/obh; camp sites TL10, dm/d TL20/100; ☼ Mar-Nov; ✂ 🖳) Near the Ottoman bridge at the entrance to town, the Old Bridge House is a long-time travellers' favourite, offering four large double rooms, a six-bed dorm and three garden-set cabins. The helpful and hospitable owner, Diana, is a mine of information about the area.

Dolunay Pansiyon (☎ 721 7172; s/d TL25/50) Right in the centre of the village by the dolmuş stop, the Dolunay is a homely affair with six spotless, simple rooms set around a pleasant courtyard. There's also a pretty terrace with sea views where you can have a scenic breakfast.

Timur Pansiyon (☎ /fax 721 7449; timurpansiyon@ yahoo.com; s/d TL35/60; ☼ Apr–mid-Sep) The 200-year-old Timur, remote, rustic and rather ramshackle, is not unlike a shepherd's croft. Its characterful rooms may prove a bit basic for some, but the fabulous setting above the village right beside the temple more than compensates.

Eris Pansiyon (☎ 721 7080; www.erispansiyon.com; Behramkale Köyü 6; s/d TL90/130; ☼ Apr-Nov) Set in a stone house with pretty gardens at the far end of the village, this pension has fairly ordinary (for the price) but pleasant and peaceful rooms. Afternoon tea is served on a terrace with spectacular views over the hills. It also has a library and book exchange, and Clinton, the retired American owner, needs only the smallest excuse to tell you all about the area's history.

our pick **Biber Evi** (☎ 721 7410; www.biberevi.com; s/d incl breakfast TL150/200, half-board TL170/240; ✂) A real delight – this old stone house boasts a peaceful garden, a small terrace with lovely views, and a gourmet restaurant. Rooms are Ottoman-rustic in style complete with *gusulhane* – washing facilities hidden in a cupboard! – and under-floor heating. Bookings need to be for a minimum of two nights.

Eating & Drinking

In contravention of the way these things usually work, the settlement at the bottom of the hill is actually the 'posh' part of town where prices, if not standards, are higher than at the top. Be sure to check the cost of fish and bottles of wine before ordering.

ASSOS

Uzunev (☎ 721 7007; mains TL10-16; ☼ 10am-midnight) Uzunev is considered the best fish restaurant in town, and has pleasant tables on the terrace and seafront. Try the succulent speciality, sea bass à l'Aristotle (steamed in a special stock), or the delicious seafood meze (TL10 to TL12). In high season after 10pm, it metamorphoses into a disco-bar.

Grand Assos (☎ 721 7723; mezes TL14, fish TL14-20; ☼ 11am-midnight) In the same block as the Hotel Behram, and serving a good selection of fresh fish (including sea bass and red snapper) and lobster (choose your favourite from the tank outside) in an attractive waterfront dining area.

BEHRAMKALE

Aile Çay Bahçesi (☎ 721 7221; tea TL1.10, soft drinks TL1.50; ☼ 7am-midnight) For a coffee or Coke on the main square, this place has a pleasant shaded terrace offering attractive views. It serves *gözleme* (savoury pancakes; TL3) good enough to gobble, and drinks.

Assos Kale Restaurant (☎ 721 7430; ☼ 8am-1am Apr-Oct) On the road leading up to the temple, the Kale has a pleasant shaded terrace and is a great place for a quick eat, offering good home cooking at reasonable prices. Try the delicious *mantı* (Turkish ravioli; TL4) or homemade creamy *ayran* (yoghurt drink).

Assos Restaurant (☎ 721 7050; Main Sq; köfte & kebaps TL6-9; ☼ 7am-midnight) The diminutive but endearing Assos provides excellent home cooking at pleasing prices and is highly recommended. It offers no less than 25 dishes including veggie options. Take a table on the tiny terrace overlooking the main square.

Biber Evi Restaurant (☎ 721 7410; Biber Evi Hotel; mezes TL8-14, mains TL16-28; ☼ 7.30am-10pm) The 'Chilli House' serves superb Turkish cuisine made from ingredients fresh from its kitchen gardens. It even smokes its own fish. The charming owner, Lütei (an ex-actor and theatre director), also boasts a famous collection of malt whiskies.

Getting There & Away

Regular buses run from Çanakkale (TL7.50, 1½ hours) to Ayvacık, where you can pick up a dolmuş (which leaves when full) to Behramkale (TL3, 20 minutes). Some dolmuşes make a second stop down in Assos, but some don't, obliging you to switch to the shuttle service.

Alternatively, you can get to Behramkale from Gülpınar (TL3, one hour) or Küçükkuyu (TL4, one hour).

In low season, dolmuşes run much less frequently and you can have trouble getting away from Behramkale. If you do visit then try to get to Ayvacık as early in the day as you can to catch a dolmuş to Behramkale. If you miss the last one, Ayvacık has a couple of hotels, or a taxi will cost around €25 to €30.

Driving is not permitted in the centre of either Behramkale or Assos. You'll have to park and walk up or down.

Getting Around

In summer, there's a regular shuttle service throughout the day between Behramkale and Assos (TL1), which also connects with buses from Assos to Ayvacık. When there's demand, an extra dolmuş is put into service; it leaves when it's full. In winter, workers shuttle back and forth and you can normally jump on one of their buses.

AYVACIK

☎ 0286 / pop 7610

Heading to or from Behramkale you may have to transit Ayvacık, which has a big **Friday market** where women from the surrounding villages sell fruit, vegetables and baskets. Those in long satiny overcoats or brightly coloured headscarves are the descendants of Turkmen nomads who settled in this area.

Two kilometres out of Ayvacık on the Çanakkale road you can also visit the **Doğal Boya Arıştırma ve Geliştirme Projesi** (Dobag; Natural Dye Research & Development Project; ☎ 712 1274; fax 712 1705; ☥ 9am-6pm), which was set up in 1981 to encourage villagers to return to weaving carpets from naturally dyed wool. At about €245 per sq metre, the rugs in the upstairs exhibition hall are certainly not cheap (about five times the cost of those in the Ayvacık carpet cooperative) and the great majority are exported, but the prices are hardly extravagant considering what goes into the process, with every stage – shearing, carding, spinning, weaving, knotting and dyeing – done by hand. Unfortunately the women weavers themselves are paid little and their working conditions aren't great. Still, the project has achieved some good things for the community.

Getting There & Away

Regular buses run to/from Çanakkale (TL7.50, 1½ hours). There are also regular buses to Ayvacık from Ezine, Behramkale and Küçükkuyu.

BAY OF EDREMİT

☎ 0286

From Behramkale a four-lane highway heads east along the shores of the Bay of Edremit. There are several camping grounds out here and several hotels right on the lengthy beach at **Kadırga**, 4km east of Behramkale (firmly package-holiday territory).

The road continues east to rejoin the main coastal highway at **Küçükkuyu**, where you could pause to inspect the **Adatepe Zeytinyağı Museum** (admission free; ☥ 9am-5pm), housed in an old olive-oil factory and explaining the process of making olive oil.

From Küçükkuyu, head 4km northeast up into the hills to visit the pretty village of **Adatepe**, a cluster of old stone houses, many of them restored as second homes for wealthy İstanbullus. Here you'll find the blissfully tranquil **Hünnap Han** (☎ 752 6581; www.hunnaphan.com; s/d half-board TL175/225), a restored house with large, traditionally decorated rooms, a lovely garden and stone courtyard.

Alternatively, you could travel 4km northwest into the hills to **Yeşilyurt**, which has not been quite so sensitively restored but where the **Öngen Country Hotel** (☎ 752 2434; www.ongencountry.com; s/d half-board TL120/240) offers rooms with attractive modern decor and spectacular views over the wooded hillside.

In high season, four or five buses a day run back and forth between Behramkale and Küçükkuyu, passing through Kadırga. To get to Adatepe and Yeşilyurt from Küçükkuyu you'll need to take a taxi (around TL12 return to either).

The road continues east along the Bay of Edremit, passing a depressing sprawl of holiday villages, hotels and second-home developments aimed at the domestic tourist market.

At Edremit, the road turns south towards Ayvalık. **Edremit** is little more than an important local transport hub. Coming from Ayvacık to Ayvalık, or from Bandırma via Balıkesir, you may well have to change in Edremit. South of Edremit there's a fine, 5km-long beach with sulphur springs at **Akçay**, while the beach at **Ören** stretches for 9km, making either of them possible places to break your journey.

AYVALIK

☎ 0266 / pop 34,650

At first glance, there would appear to be little remarkable about the seaside resort and

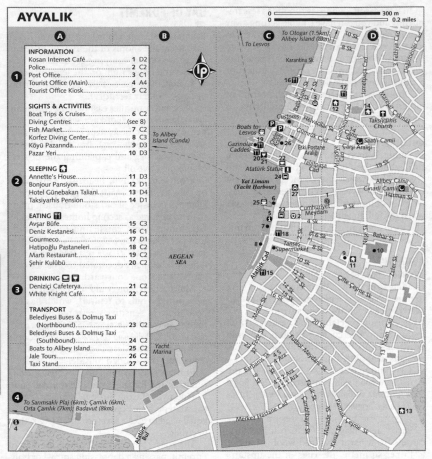

AYVALIK

INFORMATION	
Kosan Internet Café................	1 D2
Police...............................	2 C2
Post Office........................	3 C1
Tourist Office (Main).............	4 A4
Tourist Office Kiosk..............	5 C2

SIGHTS & ACTIVITIES	
Boat Trips & Cruises..............	6 C2
Diving Centres......................	(see 8)
Fish Market........................	7 C2
Korfez Diving Center.............	8 C3
Köyü Pazarında....................	9 D3
Pazar Yeri.........................	10 D3

SLEEPING	
Annette's House...................	11 D3
Bonjour Pansiyon.................	12 D1
Hotel Günebakan Taliani.........	13 D4
Taksiyarhis Pension..............	14 D1

EATING	
Avşar Büfe........................	15 C3
Deniz Kestanesi...................	16 C1
Gourmeco..........................	17 D1
Hatipoğlu Pastaneleri............	18 D1
Martı Restaurant..................	19 C2
Şehir Kulübü......................	20 C2

DRINKING	
Deniziçi Cafeterya...............	21 C2
White Knight Café................	22 C2

TRANSPORT	
Belediyesi Buses & Dolmuş Taxi (Northbound)...................	23 C2
Belediyesi Buses & Dolmuş Taxi (Southbound)...................	24 C2
Boats to Alibey Island............	25 C2
Jale Tours.........................	26 C2
Taxi Stand.........................	27 C2

fishing town of Ayvalık (the name means Quince Orchard). Though pleasant enough, its seafront is a facsimile of a number of others along this stretch of coast, with a harbour filled with excursion boats, a palm-tree-lined waterfront and plenty of tourist-oriented fish restaurants. Back from the front, however, it's a different story. Here, a charmingly crumbly old Greek village provides, in the words of local hotel owner Annette Steinhoff, a 'wonderful outdoor museum'. Horses and carts clatter down narrow streets lined with picturesque shuttered houses – some restored, many more ignored and left to decay. The whole place has an appealingly tumbledown feel to it, with life proceeding at torpor pace amid the shadows – headscarf-wearing women hold

court from their doorsteps while dogs sleep at the roadside and cats prowl the bins.

Olive-oil production is the traditional business around here, and is still thriving with lots of shops selling the end product (the broken chimney next to the Tansaş supermarket in the centre of town belongs to a now abandoned olive-oil factory), although these days the town is perhaps better known as a gateway to local islands, including Alibey, just offshore, and the Greek island of Lesvos.

Orientation & Information

Ayvalık is small and manageable by foot, although the otogar is 1.5km north of the town centre and the tourist office 1.5km to the south. A road lined with grand mansions leads a few kilometres south of Ayvalık to Çamlık and Orta Çamlık, which have a scattering of pensions and camping areas popular with holidaying Turks. The heaving package-resort of Sarımsaklı Plaj (Garlic Beach), also called Küçükköy, is 6km south of the centre.

Kosan Internet Café (Cumhuriyet Meydanı; per hr TL2; ⏰ 8am-1am) A few blocks inland from the front.

Post office (İnönü Caddesi) At the northern end of town just off the main street.

Tourist office Main branch (☎ 312 2122; Yat Limanı Karşısı); Kiosk (Yat Limanı; ⏰ Jun-Sep) The main tourist office is beyond the yacht marina, but in high season you can get information, including decent maps, from the kiosk on the waterfront south of the main square, Cumhuriyet Meydanı.

Sights & Activities

There are few specific sights but Ayvalık's old town is a joy to wander around, with its mazy tangle of cobbled streets lined with wonderfully worn-looking Greek houses. Thursday plays host to one of the region's largest and most vibrant **markets**, when stalls seem to fill the whole town. There are two main parts: the **köyü pazarında** (the villagers market) and the **pazar yeri** (bazaar). A daily **fish market** also takes place on the front next to the terminal for the ferry to Alibey (p211).

Otherwise, most of the major activities tend to be out of town. There are a number of good, sandy **beaches** a few kilometres to the south. Sarımsaklı is the most famed and will inevitably be the most crowded, as this is hard-core, package-holiday country. Stay on the bus a bit longer till you reach Badavut to the west, and you'll find some much more deserted stretches.

The offshore waters have a number of good dive sites (see boxed text, p210) and in the summer there are daily ferries to Lesvos, as well as **cruises** (per person incl meal TL10-12) around the bay's islands, stopping here and there for some sunbathing and swimming. They usually depart at 11am and return at 6pm. Excursions to more far-flung destinations, such as Assos, can also be arranged.

Sleeping

Taksiyarhis Pension (☎ 312 1494; www.taksiyarhispension .com; r without bathroom per person TL28) Rooms of all shapes and sizes fill a pair of 120-year-old Greek houses behind the eponymous church. It has a lot of character, with exposed

---

GHOSTS FROM THE PAST

Walking the quiet backstreets of Ayvalık, it can be difficult now to appreciate that you are passing the relics and remains of one of the most traumatic events in the country's history – the great population exchange that took place soon after the creation of the Turkish state (see p39).

The early 1920s hold mixed memories for the town. Pride over its role in the Turkish War of Independence – it was here that the first shots were fired – is tempered by what happened afterwards when the Ottoman Greeks who made up the majority of the population were forced to abandon the land of their birth and relocate to the Greek island of Lesvos, while the Turks from that island were, in turn, compelled to start new lives in Ayvalık. Despite the enormous distress this must have caused, the Ayvalık–Lesvos exchange is nonetheless regarded today as one of the least damaging episodes of the period. The reasons why the exchange caused, in the words of journalist Fatih Turkmenoglu, 'less pain' than many others had much to do with the proximity of the two communities, which enabled people from both sides to continue visiting their former homes – mixed though their emotions must have been during those trips. Furthermore, both communities were involved in the production of olive oil and so would have found much that was familiar in the other.

Today, whispers from the past are everywhere. Some of the locals still speak – and a few of the restaurants still have their menus in – Greek. Many of the town's former Greek Orthodox churches remain standing, albeit now converted into mosques. The Ayios Ioannis has become the Saatlı Camii (Clock Mosque, so named for its clock tower), while the former Ayios Yioryios is today the Çınarlı Camii, named after the *çınar* (plane trees) that presumably once grew here, although, in a rather poignant analogy for the town itself, none now remain. One of the grandest of all the old Greek churches, the Taksiyarhis, was never converted. However, it no longer functions as a church either, but rather sits empty and forlorn, waiting to be 'transformed into a museum' at some unspecified future date.

NORTH AEGEAN

DIVING OFF AYVALIK

The waters around Ayvalık are famed among divers for their red coral. However, as most of it grows at depths of between 30m and 42m, reaching it is not an activity for beginners. There are various dive companies in Ayvalık that can organise trips to see the coral and its attendant marine life, including moray eels, grouper, octopus and sea horses. One of the best is the **Korfez Diving Center** (☎ 0286-312 4996; www.korfezdiving.com; ☺ Mar-Nov), whose boat is moored by the fish market. A day's diving (including two dives, lunch, all equipment hire and insurance) costs €50 per person. The company also runs various PADI courses, including a two-day open-water course for €290.

---

wooden beams and a jumbly assortment of cushions, rugs and handicrafts. Travellers are well catered for with a communal kitchen, a book exchange and bicycles for hire. For an extra TL7 you can enjoy breakfast on a vine-shaded terrace.

Bonjour Pansiyon (☎ 312 8085; www.bonjourpansiyon.com; Fevzi Çakmak Caddesi, Çeşme Sokak 5; s/d without bathroom TL30/60; ✷) In a fine-looking house that once belonged to an ambassador to the sultan, this has a musty, faded grandeur to it with aged furniture and antique knick-knacks filling every corner. The 12 rooms are immaculately presented and you receive a terrific welcome from the owners, Hatice and Yalcin. Just two rooms have bathrooms. Breakfast is available for TL8.

ourpick Annette's House (☎ 312 5971; www.annetteshouse.com; Neşe Sokak 12; s/d incl breakfast €21/42) On a quiet square (Thursdays excepted when it's the site of the villagers market), this is an oasis of calm and comfort. Nothing is too much trouble for the efficient Annette, a retired German teacher, who presides over a charming collection of large, clean, well-decorated rooms (in order to keep things clean, guests are asked to remove their shoes) and a pleasantly shady breakfast garden.

Hotel Günebakan Taliani (☎ 312 8484; www.talianihotel.com; 13 Nisan Caddesi 33; r incl breakfast €65, apt €80; ☺ Apr-Dec) A lovely hotel set in lush gardens and occupying a hillside location perched above the town. Its five rooms and five apartments are beautifully decorated (the apartments have balconies overlooking the seafront). The delightful owner, Meliha, a retired teacher from Ankara, oversees the lavish breakfasts of cheeses, biscuits, jams and olives (the hotel produces its own olive oil) served on a flower-filled terrace.

Eating
RESTAURANTS
Şehir Kulübü (☎ 312 1088; Yat Limanı; fish per 500g TL15; ☺ 10am-2am) Jutting right over the water, the 'city club' has long been the top choice for reasonably priced fish. There's no menu. Instead, you choose your fish (bass, bream, sole etc) from the giant freezer, and the accompanying mezes (TL4 to TL7) from the pick-and-point counter.

Martı Restaurant (☎ 312 6899; Gazinolar Caddesi 9; mains TL14-22; ☺ 7.30am-midnight) A good choice if the Şehir Kulübü is full, this has an excellent reputation. It specialises in Ayvalık and regional specialities as well as fish.

Deniz Kestanesi (☎ 312 3662; Karantina Sokak 9; mains TL14-28; ☺ 11am-midnight) Perhaps the smartest and certainly the most expensive restaurant in town, the 'sea urchin' is a very stylish indoor/outdoor affair right on the waterfront, with wooden floors, high ceilings, leather chairs and great views of the twinkling lights of Alibey. Fish and seafood dishes are both expertly prepared and, something of a rarity, elegantly presented.

CAFÉS & QUICK EATS
Hatipoğlu Pastaneleri (☎ 312 2913; Atatürk Caddesi 12; tea/coffee TL1.10/1.50; ☺ 6.30am-midnight; ✷) With a great selection of traditional Turkish puds, pastries and cakes, this popular patisserie makes a terrific breakfast or tea stop. Try the Ayvalık speciality, *lok* (sponge oozing honey; TL3).

Gourmeco (☎ 312 3312; Ismetpasa Mahallesi Cumhuriyet Caddesi 54; ☺ 8am-10pm Mon-Sat, 8am-6pm Sun) This mellow, traditional coffeehouse serves a wide range of flavoured Turkish coffees and herbal teas (TL2 to TL3), as well as food fashioned from local ingredients, including sandwiches, crêpes and salads (TL5 to TL7).

Drinking & Entertainment
Deniziçi Cafeterya (☎ 312 1537; Gazinolar Caddesi 1; beer TL3; ☺ 7.30am-12.30am) Occupying the southwest corner of the quay, in among the fish restaurants, is this perfect spot for a sundowner. It

also serves light meals and snacks, including pizzas (TL6.50 to TL9.50) and Ayvalık *tost* (TL3; see boxed text below).

White Knight Café (☎ 312 3682; Cumhuriyet Meydanı 3; beer TL3; ☺ noon-midnight) Popular café by the statue of Atatürk, overseen by the ever-welcoming Ahmet and his British wife, Anthea. The vibe is mellow and chilled, except when major soccer matches are shown, and it sells previous-day European newspapers as well as the *Hürriyet Daily News*.

Getting There & Away
BOAT
From June to September, at least one boat sails daily to Lesvos, Greece (passenger one way/return €40/50, car €60/70, 1½ hours). From October to May, boats sail twice a week (Wednesday and Thursday), returning from Lesvos to Ayvalık on Thursday and Friday. Note that you *must* make a reservation (in person or by telephone) 24 hours before. When you pick up your tickets, bring your passport.

For information and tickets, contact **Jale Tours** (☎ 312 2740; Gümrük Caddesi 24).

BUS
Coming from Çanakkale (TL12, 3¼ hours, 200km) or Edremit (TL6, one hour, 56km) some buses will drop you on the main highway, from where you'll have to hitch to the centre. Çanakkale/Truva and Metro bus companies, however, have a *servis*.

There are frequent buses from İzmir to Ayvalık (TL7.50, three hours, 150km), and it is also possible to make a day trip to Bergama from Ayvalık (TL6, 1¾ hours, 45km). Hourly Bergama buses leave from the main terminal and drive slowly south through town so you can pick them up in the main square.

If driving, you might want to opt for the slightly slower, more scenic route to Bergama

via Kozak, which winds through idyllic pine-clad hills.

Getting Around
The town centre is served by dolmuş taxis (white with red stripes running around them) that stop to put down and pick up passengers along a series of short set routes. You can catch them heading in either direction at the main square. Destinations include Armutçuk, 1km to the north of town, and across the causeway to Alibey Island. All journeys cost TL1.50.

Heading further afield, Ayvalık *belediyesi* (town) buses (TL2 to TL3) run right through town from the otogar to the main square, then south to the tourist office and onto Çamlık, Orta Çamlık and the beaches of Sarımsaklı.

Minibuses (TL1.50 to TL2) also depart for the beaches from beside the Tansaş supermarket sign south of the main square.

A taxi from the otogar to the town centre costs TL5; to Alibey Island from the town centre costs TL10.

Driving through the fiendishly narrow one-way streets of Ayvalık's old town can be a very stressful experience. You'd be better off parking at one of the car parks along the waterfront. They generally cost TL6/9 per day/night.

ALİBEY ISLAND
Named after a hero of the Turkish War of Independence, Alibey Island, known to the locals as Cunda, lies just offshore, facing Ayvalık across the water. It's linked to the mainland by a causeway and is generally regarded as a quieter extension of Ayvalık itself, with residents of both communities regularly shuttling back and forth between the two. Accessible both by dolmuş taxi and the more pleasant option of the ferry, the island makes for a fine day trip from Ayvalık.

The ferry will drop you at a small quay, in front of which is a long line of fish restaurants.

FAST FOOD – AYVALIK STYLE
Ayvalık may have made its name as an olive-oil producer, but these days it's better known throughout Turkey for a rather less refined culinary offering – *Ayvalık tost* (Ayvalık 'toast'). The town's take on fast food consists of a large baked roll into which is stuffed all manner of ingredients, including cheese, *sucuk* (spicy veal sausage), salami, pickles and tomatoes. The whole thing is then covered (unless you specifically request otherwise) in lashings of ketchup and mayonnaise. It's available at cafés and stalls throughout town. **Avşar Büfe** (☎ 0266-716 6611; Atatürk Caddesi 67; ☺ 24hr high season, 8am-2am low season) is probably the most famous purveyor. *Tost* costs TL1 to TL3 depending on the size, but take note – a large one will keep you going for an entire day.

Behind these sits a small, distinguished-looking town made up of old (and in parts rather dilapidated) Greek stone houses. As with Ayvalık, the people here were compelled into a population exchange in the early 1920s; in this instance with Muslims from Crete.

To the north of the ferry stop is the town's main square, where there's a large public map pointing out the island's main historic sites. There is no tourist office, but the branches in Ayvalık should be able to provide you with all the relevant information, including maps. Behind the square is a small tourist market with stalls selling jewellery and various other trinkets.

One of the most famous relics of the town's Greek past, the **Taksiyarhis church** (not to be confused with the church of the same name in Ayvalık), sits perched on a hill, just inland from the town. Though it avoided being turned into a mosque, the church suffered severe damage during an earthquake in 1944, and today stands in picturesque decrepitude. Inside are some faded and rather forlorn-looking frescoes.

The nicest parts of the island are to the west, where there are good beaches for sunbathing and swimming, and to the north, much of which is taken up by the **Patriça Nature Reserve**, which has a number of good walking routes, and from where you can see the ruins of the Greek **Ayışığı Manastırı** (Moonlight Monastery) on an offshore island.

Sleeping & Eating

Alibey has some decent places to stay, though most are over the restaurants and likely to be noisy.

Ada Camp (☎ 327 1211; www.adacamping.com; Alibey Adası; camp sites per person/car TL15/12, per tent TL3-8, r in caravan/bungalow TL50/70; Ⓨ Apr-Nov) The island's largest and best-equipped camping ground lies 3km to the west of town. The air-conditioned bungalows are simple but spotless, although the grounds are a little worn-looking. The site boasts its own beach and restaurant. Guests can also use the kitchen.

Zehra Teyze'nin Evi (☎ 327 2285; www.cundaevi.com; Namık Kemal Mahallesi 7; s/d TL60/80; Ⓧ) Occupying a 136-year-old house right beside the Taksiyarhis church, this pension has attractive, traditionally decorated rooms.

Bay Nihat (Lale Restaurant; ☎ 327 1063; seafood mezes TL10-14; Ⓨ noon-midnight) A very attractive 150-year-old Greek house, with a neat

seafront dining area, this has a huge range of excellent and often highly unusual mezes (squid eggs, clams in whisky, octopus and pomegranate etc), which have won several pan-Turkey awards.

Papalina Restaurant (☎ 327 1041; Sahil Boyu 7; mezes TL6, fish mains TL18-24) Named after the *papalina balık,* a local fish speciality (one portion TL6), this has a lovely position right next to the fishing boats and has a cheery, bustling atmosphere, with waiters gliding through the chequered tables.

Drinking & Entertainment

Delikedi Café (☎ 327 1412; Belediye Sokak 16; beer TL4; Ⓨ noon-1am) In a restored old stone house, its walls adorned with brightly coloured modern art, this is a great place to while away the evening with comfy leather seats and an easygoing atmosphere. The music, a mixture of Western and Turkish beats, gets louder and steadily more intense as the night progresses.

Taş Kahve (☎ 327 1166; Sahil Boyu 20; coffee TL1.10; Ⓨ 7am-midnight) A local institution – smoky, cavernous and very atmospheric, all the town tittle-tattle takes place here. It's also good for a cheap Turkish breakfast (TL5).

Getting There & Around

Boats to Alibey Island (June to August; TL2, 15 minutes) leave from a quay behind the tourist kiosk just off the main square in Ayvalık. Alternatively, you can take a dolmuş taxi from the other side of the road, which will get you there slightly more slowly (around 20 minutes) and slightly more cheaply (TL1.50). Dolmuşes drop off at the eastern end of the esplanade.

BERGAMA (PERGAMUM)
☎ 0232 / pop 58,210

As Selçuk is to Ephesus, so Bergama is to Pergamum, a small, workaday market town that's become a major stop on the tourist trail because of its proximity to some most remarkable ruins – in this instance Pergamum, site of the Asclepion, the pre-eminent medical centre of Ancient Rome. It's less of a one-note town than Selçuk, but then it doesn't attract nearly the same volume of visitors, giving it a more laid-back, friendly feel than its southern rival. As a result, many visitors end up falling for Bergama.

There has been a town here since Trojan times, but Pergamum's heyday was during the period between Alexander the Great and the Roman domination of all Asia Minor when it was one of the Middle East's richest and most powerful small kingdoms.

History

Pergamum owes its prosperity to Lysimachus, one of Alexander the Great's generals, who took control of much of the Aegean region when Alexander's far-flung empire fell apart after his death in 323 BC. In the battles over the spoils Lysimachus captured a great treasure, estimated at over 9000 gold talents, which he entrusted to his commander in Pergamum, Philetarus, before going off to fight Seleucus for control of Asia Minor. But Lysimachus lost

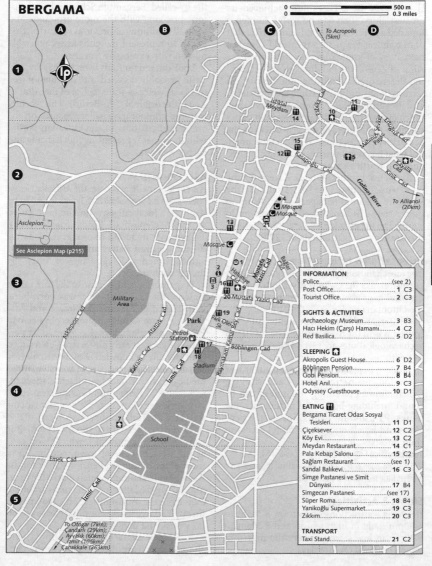

BERGAMA

NORTH AEGEAN

the battle and was killed in 281 BC, where-upon Philetarus set himself up as governor.

Philetarus, a eunuch, was succeeded by his nephew Eumenes I (263–241 BC), who was in turn followed by his adopted son, Attalus I (241–197 BC). Attalus declared himself king, expanding his power and forging an alliance with Rome.

During the reign of Attalus' son, Eumenes II (197–159 BC), Pergamum achieved its greatest glory. Rich and powerful, Eumenes founded a library that would in time rival that of Alexandria, Egypt, then the world's greatest repository of knowledge. He also added the Altar of Zeus to the buildings already crowning the acropolis, built the 'middle city' on terraces halfway down the hill, and expanded and beautified the Asclepion. Inevitably, much of what the Pergamese kings built hasn't survived the ravages of the centuries (or the acquisitive enthusiasm of Western museums), but what has is impressive, dramatically sited and well worth visiting.

Eumenes' brother Attalus II kept up the good work but under his son, Attalus III, the kingdom began to fall apart again. With no heir, Attalus III bequeathed his kingdom to Rome, and the kingdom of Pergamum became the Roman province of Asia in 129 BC.

Orientation & Information

The most handsome, if rather tumbledown, part of town flanks the Galinos River to the north: the Muslim neighbourhood is on the west bank, the Ottoman Greek one on the east.

Of Bergama's four main sights, only the museum is in the town centre. The two main archaeological sites are several kilometres out of town.

Modern Bergama lies spread out either side of one long main street, İzmir Caddesi, along which almost everything you'll need can be found, including hotels and restaurants, the banks, PTT and museum. Most of the pensions and hotels offer free internet access to their guests.

Tourist office (☎ 631 2851; İzmir Caddesi 54; ☽ 8.30am-noon & 1-5.30pm) Just north of the museum, it offers little more than a sketch map.

Sights & Activities

Bergama's attractions open from 8.30am to 6.30pm daily in high season and 8.30am to 5.30pm in low season (except the museum, which is closed on Monday).

ARCHAEOLOGY MUSEUM

Right in the centre of town, the **Archaeology Museum** (Arkeoloji Müzesi; ☎ 632 9860; İzmir Caddesi; admission TL2) boasts a small but substantial collection of artefacts, including a wealth of coins (Greek, Roman and Byzantine) and the obligatory abundance of pottery. Most interestingly, it also features a collection of statues from the 4th century BC that formed part of the so-called 'Pergamum School' when sculptors, breaking with the more grotesque and stylised traditions of previous centuries, first began to represent the gods as recognisably human with expressive features.

Look out too for finds from the nearby, and quite probably doomed, site of Allianoi (see p218), as well as a scale replica of the Altar of Zeus (the original is in Berlin). The recently restored ethnography gallery focuses on the crafts and customs of the Ottoman period with dioramas representing folk dancing and carpet weaving.

ASCLEPION

An ancient medical centre, the **Asclepion** (Temple of Asclepios; admission/parking TL10/3) was founded by Archias, a local citizen who had been cured at the Asclepion of Epidaurus (Greece). Treatments included massage, mud baths, drinking sacred waters and the use of herbs and ointments. Diagnosis was often by dream analysis.

Pergamum's centre came to the fore under Galen (AD 131–210), who was born here, and studied in Alexandria, Greece and Asia Minor, before setting up shop as physician to Pergamum's gladiators. Recognised as perhaps the greatest early physician, Galen added considerably to knowledge of the circulatory and nervous systems, and also systematised medical theory. Under his influence, the medical school at Pergamum became renowned. His work was the basis for Western medicine well into the 16th century.

Two roads head up to the Asclepion. One runs from the centre of town. The other is at the western edge of town, cutting up in front of the Böblingen Pension – look for the Asklepion Restaurant, which marks the turning. Taking the latter road, the ruins are about 3km from the tourist office. This road passes through a large Turkish military base; be off it by dusk and don't take photos.

A Roman **bazaar street**, once lined with shops, leads from the car park to the cen-

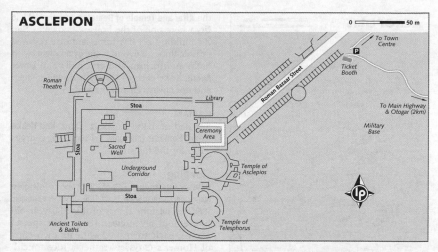

ASCLEPION

0 — 50 m

Roman Theatre

Library

Stoa

Roman Bazaar Street

To Town Centre

P

Ticket Booth

To Main Highway & Otogar (2km)

Military Base

Stoa

Sacred Well

Ceremony Area

Underground Corridor

Temple of Asclepios

Stoa

Ancient Toilets & Baths

Temple of Telesphorus

tre where you'll see the base of a column carved with snakes, the symbol of Asclepios (Aesculapius), god of medicine. Just as the snake sheds its skin and gains a 'new life', so the patients at the Asclepion were supposed to 'shed' their illnesses. Signs mark a circular **Temple of Asclepios**, a **library** and a **Roman theatre**.

You can take a drink from the **Sacred Well**, although the plastic tube out of which the water flows doesn't look particularly inviting, and pass along the vaulted underground corridor to the **Temple of Telesphorus**, another god of medicine. Patients slept in the temple hoping that Telesphorus would send a cure or diagnosis in a dream. The names of Telesphorus' two daughters, Hygeia and Panacea, have passed into medical terminology.

Soft drinks are available from the glut of stalls by the Asclepion entrance, albeit at a hefty premium.

RED BASILICA

The cathedral-sized **Red Basilica** (Kinik Caddesi; admission TL5) was originally a giant temple to the Egyptian gods Serapis, Isis and Harpocrates built in the 2nd century AD. It's still an imposing-looking place, though rather scattered and battered-looking these days with bits of modern piping and corrugated iron lying amid all the antique clutter – a testament to the site's ongoing funding difficulties. Be careful as you make you way around as several sections of the basilica's high walls are severely damaged.

During its pagan pomp, this must have been an awe-inspiring place. In his Revelation, St John the Divine wrote that this was one of the seven churches of the Apocalypse, singling it out as the throne of the devil. Look for a hole in the podium in the centre, which allowed a priest to hide and appear to speak through the 10m-high cult statue. The building is so big that the Christians didn't convert it into a church but built a basilica inside it. One tower now houses the small Kurtuluş Camii, which is currently closed for restoration.

The curious red flat-brick walls of the large, roofless structure are visible from midway down the road to the acropolis. You can easily walk to the Red Basilica, or stop your taxi there on your way to or from the acropolis.

ACROPOLIS

The road up to the **acropolis** (admission TL10; ⏰ 8.30am-5.30pm) winds 5km from the Red Basilica, around the northern and eastern sides of the hill, to a car park (TL3) at the top. Next to the car park are some souvenir and refreshment stands. If you're planning to walk to the site, take plenty of water as you won't be able to stock up on the way.

A line of rather faded (and in some places completely obliterated) blue dots marks a suggested route around the main structures, which include the **library** as well as the marble-columned **Temple of Trajan**, built during the reigns of the emperors Trajan and Hadrian and used to worship them as well as Zeus. It's the only Roman structure surviving on

ACROPOLIS

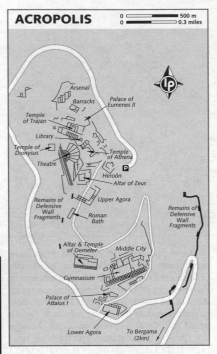

0 _____ 500 m
0 _____ 0.3 miles

Arsenal
Barracks
Palace of Eumenes II
Temple of Trajan
Library
Temple of Dionysus
Theatre
Temple of Athena
Heroön
Altar of Zeus
Remains of Defensive Wall Fragments
Upper Agora
Roman Bath
Remains of Defensive Wall Fragments
Altar & Temple of Demeter
Middle City
Gymnasium
Palace of Attalus I
Lower Agora
To Bergama (2km)

the acropolis, and its foundations were used as cisterns during the Middle Ages.

The vertigo-inducing, 10,000-seat **theatre** is impressive and unusual. Its builders decided to take advantage of the spectacular view and conserve precious building space on top of the hill by building the theatre into the hillside. In general, Hellenistic theatres are wider and rounder than this, but at Pergamum the hillside location made rounding impossible and so it was increased in height instead.

Below the stage is the ruined **Temple of Dionysus**, while above the theatre is the **Altar of Zeus**, which originally was covered with magnificent friezes depicting the battle between the Olympian gods and their subterranean foes. However 19th-century German excavators were allowed to remove most of this famous building to Berlin, leaving only the base behind.

Piles of rubble on top of the acropolis are marked as the **Palaces of Attalus I** and **Eumenes II**, and there's an **Upper Agora**, as well as fragments of the once-magnificent defensive **walls**.

To see everything, walk down the hill behind the Altar of Zeus, passing the **Roman bath**,

the **Altar and Temple of Demeter** and the **Middle City** where one of the houses, known as Bau Z ('Building Z') has some fantastic restored mosaic floors. Beyond is the **gymnasium** (with bath, auditorium and cult hall) and **Lower Agora**. Take care as the path down is steep and not always clearly marked.

HAMAM

Situated near the Kulaksız Cami, **Hacı Hekim (Çarşı) Hamamı** (men only; ⏱ 8am-11pm) charges TL25 for the full works.

Sleeping

Odyssey Guesthouse (☎ 653 9189; www.odysseyguesthouse.com; Abacıhan Sokak 13; dm TL10, s/d without bathroom TL20/35) The four floors of this 180-year-old house hold seven clean (but rather sparse) rooms, each furnished with its own copy of Homer's *Odyssey* (rather a nice touch). There's a trading library for guests, and Ersin, the friendly proprietor, oversees the breakfasts served on the rooftop terrace, from where there are views of the Red Basilica.

Gobi Pension (☎ 633 2518; www.gobipension.com; Atatürk Bulvarı 18; s/d without bathroom €14/22, with bathroom €20/32; 🖥) On the main road behind a shady terrace draped in greenery, this is a great family-run place with bright, cheery rooms, most of which have brand-new private bathrooms (with 24-hour hot water, another recent innovation). Five have air-con and four have balconies with garden views. It's well set up for travellers, with a communal kitchen, laundry service and free wi-fi.

Böblingen Pension (☎ 633 2153; dincer-altin@hotmail.com; Asklepion Caddesi 2; s/d TL35/55; 🖥 🖥) This pension run by the friendly Altın family is spotless, although some of the rooms are a little musty and the bathrooms are rather basic. Still, it has a cosy sitting area, as well as a book exchange and laundry service. To find it, look for the sign to the Asclepion off the main road.

our pick **Akropolis Guest House** (☎ 631 2621; www.akropolisguesthouse.com; Kayalık Caddesi 5; s/d €20/49; 🖥 🖥) This 150-year-old stone house is the closest Bergama gets to boutique. Eight attractively decorated rooms surround a peaceful pool and garden. There's also a restaurant set in a lovely old barn and a terrace at the top of a small tower with views of the acropolis. It's a gem, and good value, too.

Hotel Anıl (☎ 631 1830; www.anilhotelbergama.com; Hatuniye Caddesi 4; s/d incl breakfast €37/50; 🖥) The

NORTH AEGEAN

Anıl's main attraction is its central location. The rooms have everything you need, including fairly decent bathrooms, wi-fi and TVs, but somewhat insipid decor, in contrast to the alarming pink colour of the exterior. The covered roof terrace has great panoramic views. The four-course set menu is €10.

Eating

RESTAURANTS

Bergama Ticaret Odası Sosyal Tesisleri (☎ 632 9641; Ulucamii Mahallesi; mezes TL5, mains TL6-8; ☏ 10.30am-11pm) A new restaurant set up and run by Bergama municipality in a beautifully restored 200-year-old Greek house 100m north of the Ulu Camii. Here, you can eat great food in great surroundings at great prices (kept low by the municipality).

Meydan Restaurant (☎ 633 1793; İstiklal Meydanı 4; mains TL6-9; ☏ 7am-midnight) One of three branches of this Bergama institution serving simple regional food at fair prices. It also has tables outside. Try the Bergama speciality, *lahmacun* (wheat cakes with minced meat).

Sağlam Restaurant (☎ 632 8897; Cumhuriyet Meydanı 47; mains TL6-11; ☏ 8am-11pm) This large, simple place is well known in town for its high-quality home cooking. It does a good selection of mezes, which change daily, and specialises in delicious kebaps.

Sandal Balıkevi (☎ 631 6116; Hatuniye Caddesi 6; fixed menus TL10; ☏ 8am-midnight) Well-run, popular fish restaurant next to the Hotel Anıl with tables inside and out. Fish is fresh and prices are reasonable. There's live music on some evenings.

QUICK EATS

Süper Roma (İzmir Caddesi, Sitat Dükkarleri 19; 2 scoops TL1.50; ☏ 8am-1am Apr-Aug) Head here on a hot summer's day for ice cream.

Zıkkım (İzmir Caddesi 39; pides TL2-4; ☏ 7am-midnight) With shady garden seating just off the main road, this makes a welcome mid-town pit stop, serving cheap and tasty kebap sandwiches (chicken TL4, lamb TL6) and salads (white-bean salad TL3).

Pala Kebap Salonu (☎ 633 1559; Kasapoğlu Caddesi 4; kebaps €2.20; ☏ 8am-11pm Mon-Sat) Though small and simple, this place is terrifically popular in Bergama and the food is delicious. Try the spicy Bergama *köfte* (TL6).

Çiçeksever (☎ 633 3822; Banklar Caddesi 71; ☏ 7.30am-10.30pm) Just a few doors down from, and similar to, the Pala.

CAFÉS

Köy Evi (Village House; ☎ 632 4816; Galinos Caddesi 12; ☏ 7.30am-9pm) This is a fabulous family-run place with cosy seating inside or out in the courtyard. Menus change daily, but regular specialities include *gözleme* (TL2) and *mantı*.

For a coffee and a cake in between the sightseeing, **Simge Pastanesi ve Simit Dünyasi** (☎ 631 1034; İzmir Caddesi 19; 2 pastries TL1, ice cream TL0.75; ☏ 7am-midnight) and, next door, **Simgecan Pastanesi** (☎ 631 1034; Böblingen Caddesi 4; ☏ 7.30am-1am) are considered the best patisseries in town and are run by two brothers. There's a good selection of pastries, cakes and Turkish puddings.

SELF-CATERING

Bergama has a bustling Monday **market** (☏ 8am-6pm), which stretches for about 3km from the otogar to the Red Basilica. It's great for fresh fruit and veg. Böblingen Caddesi and the area around the old bus station are good for picnic-hunting. Cheese, olives, fresh bread and dried fruit are all sold. Also near here is **Yanikoğlu Supermarket** (☎ 632 7942; Merkez Çamipark Karşısı Karş 21, İzmir Caddesi; ☏ 8am-midnight).

Getting There & Away

Buses run to İzmir (TL10, two hours, 110km) every 45 minutes, to Ayvalık (TL7.50, 1¼ hours, 60km) at least every hour, and to Ankara (TL50, eight to nine hours, 916km). For İstanbul, there are nightly (daily too in high season) buses, but it's cheaper and quicker, surprisingly, to go to İzmir first and take an express bus from there. For Bursa, take the Ayvalık bus.

Bergama's new otogar lies 7km from the centre at the junction of the highway and the main road into town. From here a dolmuş service shuttles into town (TL2). A taxi should cost around TL15 during the day, TL20 at night. Dolmuşes to Dikili, Ayvalık and Çandarlı also leave from here at least every half-hour.

Getting Around

Bergama's sights are so spread out that it's hard to walk round them all in one day. The Red Basilica is over 1km from the tourist office, the Asclepion is 3km away and the acropolis is over 5km away. A more convenient option is to book a taxi for a 'City Tour'. From the centre to the acropolis, basilica, Asclepion and museum, it should cost around TL50 to

TL60 in high season, TL40 to TL50 in low season. Taxis wait near some of the mosques and around the otogar.

AROUND BERGAMA
Allianoi

In 1998 local farmers made an exciting discovery in the Valley of Kaikos at Allianoi, 20km east of Bergama – the remains of a Roman spa and asclepion, among the oldest and best preserved yet found. A fine statue of Aphrodite on display in the Bergama museum (p214) came from Allianoi.

Unfortunately, the archaeological site is now a centre of controversy. The Valley of Kaikos is the proposed site of the new Yortanlı Dam – already built, although not yet open – which will bring vital water reserves to the region, but also submerge the archaeological site under 17m of water. The archaeologists in charge of the site have started a petition to save it, which has attracted over 30,000 signatures, but it looks to be a losing battle. Although 90% of the site remains unexcavated, the government took the decision in late 2007 to open the dam, albeit not before the site has been surrounded by a wall and covered with a layer of (hopefully) protective clay – essentially re-burying the site (and the problem) in the hope that future generations might be able to come up with a solution.

At the time of writing, the floodwaters had still not arrived, but the bulldozers (employed to cover the site in 'protective' clay) have, and, according to the *Hürriyet Daily News*, have already caused significant damage to the site. Turkish archaeologists and students are working feverishly at the site to uncover and rescue what they can. For more information on Allianoi, visit www.europanostra.org/save_allianoi.html.

There is no bus service, but you could try taking the infrequent bus from Bergama to Paşakoy (TL5, 45 minutes), which can drop you at the turn-off to Paşaka, and then walk the 1km to Allianoi. Returning to Bergama is tricky. You can only try hailing a passing bus. A taxi here from Bergama costs TL50 to TL60.

ÇANDARLI
☎ 0232

The small and tranquil resort town of Çandarlı (ancient Pitane) sits on a peninsula jutting into the Aegean, 33km south of Bergama. It's dominated by a small but stately 14th-century restored Genoese **castle** (admission free; 24hr Jul & Aug), which has sporadic opening hours outside high season, and has a sandier beach than some of its neighbours. It makes a good base for a couple of days off.

Local tourism fills most of the pensions in high summer. From late October to April/May it's pretty much a ghost town.

Most of the shops, internet cafés and the PTT are within spitting distance of the bus stop. The castle, the restaurants and the pensions line the seashore. Market day is Friday.

Sleeping

Most of the hotels and pensions lie west of the castle, facing a thin strip of coarse sand.

Hotel Samyeli (☎ 673 3428; www.otelsamyeli.com; Sahil Plaj Caddesi 18; s/d TL35/55;) In the middle of the bay, Hotel Samyeli has simple, spotless and cheerful rooms (20 have little balconies, 14 with sea views) and a seafront fish restaurant. Reserve in advance (a week in summer).

Hotel Emirgan (☎ 673 2500; www.otelsamyeli .com; Talat Emmi Caddesi 1; s/d half-board TL45/90;) Operated by the same owners as the Hotel Samyeli, the Emirgan is 150m to the west and right on the beach. It's tranquil and quiet and all rooms have direct sea views.

Eating

For fresh fruit, the daily *çarşı* (market), in the shadow of the town mosque, is a good place to replenish.

Kalender (☎ 673 3490; Çarıçı 14; 10am-midnight, 24hr high season) One of the cheaper options along the seafront. Tuck into a couple of mezes and a grilled catch-of-the-day for around TL20 – although be sure to check prices first.

Samyeli Restaurant (☎ 673 3428; Sahil Plaj Caddesi 18; small portion fish & seafood TL10-15; 8am-midnight) Belonging to the hotel of the same name, but with a good reputation for fish, the restaurant has tables right on the seafront.

Drinking & Entertainment

Pitaneou Cafe-Bar (☎ 673 3916; Sahil Plaj Caddesi 27; beer TL4; 11am-midnight, to 3am high season) A trendy hang-out with pleasant tables under vines on the seafront, it claims to play 'the best music in Turkey'. Snacks are available.

Musti Bar (☎ 673 3991; Sahil Plaj Caddesi 38a; beer TL4; 11am-3am) On the seafront one block west of the castle, this is currently Çandarlı's one and only dancing 'hot spot'.

Getting There & Away

Frequent buses run between Çandarlı and İzmir (TL7.50, 1½ hours) via Dikili (TL2, 15 minutes). At least six minibuses run daily to and from Bergama (TL3, 30 minutes).

YENİ FOÇA

☎ 0232 / pop 3470

This delightful small resort set around a harbour boasts a strip of coarse beach and an unusually large number of crumbling Ottoman mansions and old Greek stone houses. Long discovered by second-home hunters, Yeni Foça now has its fair share of modern monstrosities alongside the aged marvels. Nevertheless, it's a pleasant place to laze away a day or two. There are some more secluded beaches to the south towards Foça (Eski Foça).

The traditionally styled **Otel Naz** (☎ 814 6619; Sahil Caddesi 113; s/d €17/33) is at the far, western end of the bay about 500m from the harbour. It has large, quite attractively decorated rooms, seven with sea views and three with balconies. It's good value, and there's a café-bar out front.

On the far eastern side of the bay, the endearing little **Tan-say Restaurant** (☎ 814 5599; Kordon Caddesi 11; mains TL8-16; 🕙 9am-10pm) looks like a kind of Turkish bistro. There are a couple of tables on the seafront, and the food and prices are impressive. Try the *karides* (shrimps; TL10).

Buses leave every half-hour to İzmir (TL5.50, 1¾ hours) and every two hours to Foça (TL2). Taxis to Foça cost around TL25.

FOÇA

☎ 0232 / pop 13,260

If Çandarlı is a bit too quiet and Kuşadası (south Aegean) too noisy, Foça could be just the ticket. Sometimes called Eski Foça (Old Foça) to distinguish it from its newer, smaller neighbour (Yeni Foça) over the hill, Foça hugs twin bays and a small harbour. Graceful old Ottoman-Greek houses line a shoreline crowded with fishing boats and overlooked by a string of restaurants and pensions.

Eski Foça, the ancient Phocaea, was founded before 600 BC and flourished during the 5th century BC. During their golden age, the Phocaeans were great mariners, sending swift vessels powered by 50 oars into the Aegean, Mediterranean and Black Seas. They were also keen colonists, founding Samsun

on the Black Sea, as well as towns in Italy, Corsica, France and Spain.

More recently, this was an Ottoman-Greek fishing and trading town. It's now a prosperous, middle-class Turkish resort with holiday villas gathering on the outskirts.

Orientation & Information

Foça's seafront is divided into two bays by a peninsula, at the end of which sits an old and much restored Byzantine castle. To the north is the Küçük Deniz (Small Sea), which is the most picturesque part of town, comprising a harbour filled with small fishing vessels, a long esplanade (where people fish) and a line of restaurants and pensions. There's also a thin, dusty beach and a number of swimming platforms.

The Büyük Deniz (Big Sea) to the south is a more no-nonsense sort of place with just a couple of restaurants. This is where the town's excursion boats and big fishing vessels moor.

The otogar, on the edge of the Büyük Deniz, is just east of the main square. Walk west past the taxi rank to your left, turn right (north) and you'll be on the main drag, such as it is. A stroll up its pedestrianised confines will take you past the tourist office, the PTT and several banks until you reach, after around 350m, the harbour. Continue along the right-hand (eastern) side to find the pensions.

Captain Net (☎ 812 3411; Fevzi Paşa Mahallesi 210 Sokak 26a; per hr €0.85; 🕙 9am-1am) Running parallel to the east of the main street in a narrow alley.

Tourist office (☎ /fax 812 1222; Cumhuriyet Meydanı; 🕙 8.30am-noon & 1-5.30pm Mon-Fri, 10am-7pm Sat)

Sights & Activities

Little remains of **ancient Phocaea**: a ruined theatre, remains of an aqueduct near the otogar, an *anıt mezarı* (monumental tomb), 7km east of town on the way to the İzmir highway, and traces of two shrines to the goddess Cybele.

In recent years, the townsfolk made an exciting new discovery near Foça high school. Known as the **Temple of Athena**, the site was found to contain, among other things, a beautiful griffin and a horse's head believed to date to the 5th century BC. Excavations are undertaken there every summer.

If you continue past the outdoor sanctuary of Cybele you'll come to a partially rebuilt fortress called **Beşkapılar** (Five Gates), which was built by the Byzantines and repaired by the Genoese and the Ottomans in 1538–39,

NORTH AEGEAN

FOÇA'S SEALS

Foça's offshore islands provide some of the last remaining homes to the endangered Mediterranean monk seal, once common throughout the region. There are thought to be fewer than 400 left in the world, so you shouldn't bank on seeing one. Thankfully, much of Foça's offshore area is now a protected zone, the extent of which was extended in 2007. For more information on the Mediterranean monk seal, contact **SAD-AFAG** (Underwater Research Society-Mediterranean Monk Seal Research Group; ☎ 0312-440 3520; www.sadafag.org), which is based in Ankara but oversees protection programs in Foça, Karaburun and Bozyazi.

The seals' habit of basking on rocks and their wailing plaintive cries are believed to have been the inspiration for the legend of the Sirens, as featured in Homer's *Odyssey*.

Living on rocky islands, the sirens were strange creatures, half-bird, half-woman, who used their beautiful, irresistible singing voices to lure sailors towards them, where their ships would be dashed against the rocks, and the sailors killed. Odysseus supposedly only managed to resist their entreaties by having himself lashed to his ship's mast.

Appropriately enough, one of the seals' favourite modern basking spots is the Siren Kayalıkları (Siren Rocks), a collection of small islets, just off Foça's shore, although these days it is the seals' lives, rather than those of local sailors, that are in danger.

---

and clearly much restored since. Another fortress, the **Dışkale** (External Fortress), guards the town's approaches from the end of the peninsula that shapes the southwestern arc of the bay. It's best seen from the water (on a boat trip) as it's inside a military zone.

BOAT TRIPS

In summer (May to September) boats leave daily between 10.30am to 11.30am from both the Küçük Deniz and Büyük Deniz for day trips around the outlying islands with various swim stops en route. Trips cost TL15 to TL20 (but negotiate prices) and include lunch and water.

Sleeping

Foça has plenty of budget sleeping places but few midrange or top-end options.

Siren Pansiyon (☎ 812 2660; www.sirenpansiyon.com; 161 Sokak 13; s/d TL35/50) The Siren is a short walk from the seafront, very quiet, and a spotless, pleasant and good-value choice. Seven rooms have balconies, and there's a roof terrace. Guests have use of the kitchen.

Hotel Villa Dedem (☎ 812 2838; www.villadedemhotel .com; Sahil Caddesi 66; s/d from TL35/60; 🐾) It enjoys a central quayside location, but you might struggle to claim a room in summer, as it tends to welcome the same (Turkish) families back year after year, and specialises in long-term rentals. Still, if you get lucky, try to bag one of the eight rooms with sea views.

Hotel Grand Amphora (☎ 812 3930; İsmetpaşa Mahallesi 206 Sokak; s/d €35/45; 🐾 📶) Not quite

as grand as the name would suggest, this is nonetheless the only hotel in town with a pool (albeit small), and it's good for sun-soaking on the sunloungers. Rooms are small but comfortable. It's just beyond Foça hospital on the seafront.

our pick Foçantique Boutique Hotel (☎ 812 4313; www.focantiquehotel.com; Sahil Caddesi 154; d incl breakfast €130-168) The town's top choice for comfort and style, lying at the far, quiet end of Küçük Deniz. The beautiful old Greek stone house has been lovingly restored and features beautifully decorated rooms, of varying sizes, filled with Turkish antiques and modern conveniences: satellite TV, coffee-makers, DVD players etc. The set menu at the restaurant is TL35 and there's also an apartment for longer stays (three-day minimum from €163).

Eating

Foça has a decent Tuesday market, which is a good place to stock up for a picnic. There are also various grocery stores.

Sedef (☎ 812 2233; Atatürk Mahallesi 53; mezes TL3.50; 🕙 9am-midnight) On the harbourside square, Sedef's meat-heavy menu makes a welcome change from the fishy norm. Enjoy a decent kebap (TL8 to TL11) and watch town life pass by.

Celep (☎ 812 1495; Sahil Caddesi 48; mezes TL4-5, fish TL20-28 🕙 9am-midnight) In among a glut of seemingly identical establishments, all with tables lined up along the front, Celep nonetheless maintains its reputation as the town's finest purveyor of fish, which you select yourself from the giant freezer (sole, sea bass, bream and turbot are usually available) and then send it off to be prepared according to your fancy.

Ridvan Ustanın Yeri (☎ 812 6867; İş Bankası; stews TL4-6; ⏰ 24hr) The perennially popular chain, this one opposite the tourist office, serves good staple cooking at pleasing prices at outdoor tables just off the main square.

Fokai Restaurant (☎ 812 2186; Sahil Caddesi 11; ⏰ 10am-midnight) On the waterside, this is a fish restaurant in the Celep mould, but a touch cheaper. Specialities include fish slow-cooked in yoghurt and garlic (TL12).

Drinking

Neco Café & Bar (☎ 812 5020; Sahil Caddesi 10; tea TL1, beer TL4; ⏰ 24hr) Consisting of little more than a few tables under an awning, this café and bar is much loved by locals, for whom it is a favourite daytime tea stop. It's a little more boisterous in the evening.

Keyif Café & Bar (☎ 812 2313; Sahil Caddesi 42a; beer €2.25; ⏰ 9am-4am) Slightly funkier than the nearby Neco – it's got a glitter ball – Keyif plays predominantly Western music and has an inside bar where dancing has been known to occasionally take place.

Getting There & Away

Frequent buses connect Foça with İzmir (TL5.50, 1½ hours, 86km), passing through Menemen (for connections to Manisa). To get to Bergama, go to Menemen, wait on the highway and flag down any bus heading north.

Three to five city buses run daily from Foça to Yeni Foça (TL2, 30 minutes, 25km); the timetable is in the otogar. These buses also pass the pretty, small coves, beaches and camping grounds north of Foça.

If you're staying in the area for a few days you might want to hire a car from **Foça Rent-a-Car** (☎ 812 2496; Favzi Paşa Mahallesi 191/7), near the harbour.

İZMİR

☎ 0232 / pop 2.6 million

Though you may eventually fall for its charms – its hectic nightlife, great shopping and top-notch museums – İzmir can take some getting used to. Certainly nowhere else in the region can prepare you for the sheer size, sprawl and intensity of the place.

It may be Turkey's third-largest city in terms of population, but in the congestion stakes İzmir has to be challenging for top honours. Great, choking highways flow around and through its confines – whichever your direction of approach, you'll be gobbled up by a hungry ribbon of tarmac and sucked past a seemingly endless succession of suburbs, before eventually being spat out somewhere near the seafront.

So far, so unpleasant, but at the water's edge İzmir really comes into its own. Here the relentless rule of the car has been beaten back; İzmir owes a huge debt to its late mayor Ahmet Piristina, who managed to overturn a remarkably ill-conceived plan to build yet another highway right along the water's edge. Snatched from development's claws, the seafront is now one of the city's main attractions, the wide, pleasant esplanade of Birinci Kordon providing countless eating, drinking and sunset-watching opportunities.

Inland, things are a little more hectic. Traffic flows ceaselessly through the streets, forming a great unbroken snake of honking urgency. It's a similarly crowded story on the pavements, where your progress will be by degrees as you stop, start and side-step your way around the hurrying hordes. Persevere, however, and you'll find a commendable selection of attractions to while away your days, including a buzzing, labyrinthine bazaar, plenty of interesting ruins and a newly restored Jewish quarter.

History

İzmir was once Smyrna, a city founded by colonists from Greece some time in the early part of the 1st millennium BC. Over the next 1000 years it would grow in importance as it came under the influence of successive regional powers: first Lydia, then Greece, and finally Rome. By the 2nd century AD it was, along with Ephesus and Pergamum, one of the three most important cities in the Roman province of Asia. Under Byzantine rule, however, its fortunes declined as the focus of government turned north to Constantinople. Things only began to look up again when the Ottomans took control in 1415, after which Smyrna rapidly became Turkey's most sophisticated commercial city.

After the collapse of the Ottoman Empire at the end of WWI, the Greeks invaded, but were eventually expelled following fierce fighting, which, along with a subsequent fire, destroyed most of the old city. The day that

İZMİR

0 ————— 500 m
0 ————— 0.3 miles

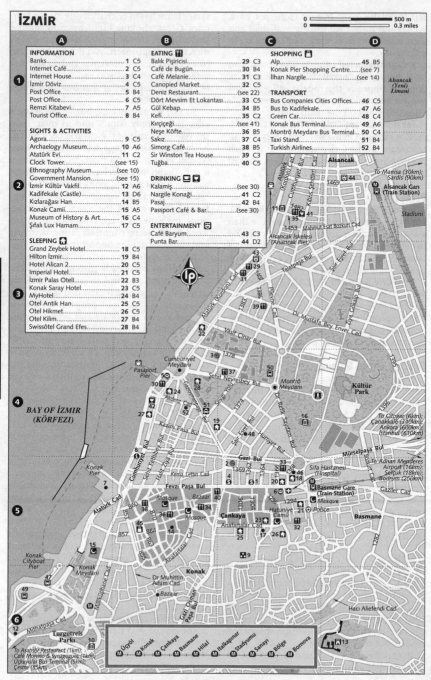

INFORMATION

Banks...................................	**1** C5
Internet Café.....................	**2** C5
Internet House...................	**3** C4
İzmir Döviz.........................	**4** C5
Post Office.........................	**5** B4
Post Office.........................	**6** C5
Remzi Kitabevi...................	**7** A5
Tourist Office.....................	**8** B4

SIGHTS & ACTIVITIES

Agora..................................	**9** C5
Archaelogy Museum............	**10** A6
Atatürk Evi..........................	**11** C2
Clock Tower.....................(see 15)
Ethnography Museum........(see 10)
Government Mansion.........(see 15)
İzmir Kültür Vakfi...............	**12** A6
Kadifekale (Castle)............	**13** D6
Kızlarağası Han...................	**14** B5
Konak Camii......................	**15** A5
Museum of History & Art...	**16** C4
Şifalı Lux Hamam................	**17** C5

SLEEPING

Grand Zeybek Hotel............	**18** C5
Hilton İzmir........................	**19** B4
Hotel Alican 2....................	**20** C5
Imperial Hotel....................	**21** C5
İzmir Palas Otell................	**22** B3
Konak Saray Hotel..............	**23** C5
MyHotel..............................	**24** B4
Otel Antik Han...................	**25** C5
Otel Hikmet.......................	**26** C5
Otel Kilim..........................	**27** B4
Swissôtel Grand Efes..........	**28** B4

EATING

Balık Pişiricisi.....................	**29** C3
Café de Bugün...................	**30** B4
Café Melanie......................	**31** C3
Canopied Market................	**32** C5
Deniz Restaurant...............(see 22)
Dört Mevsim Et Lokantası...	**33** C5
Gül Kebap..........................	**34** B5
Kefi....................................	**35** C2
Kırçiçeği...........................(see 41)
Neşe Köfte.........................	**36** B5
Sakız..................................	**37** C4
Simorg Café.......................	**38** B5
Sir Winston Tea House........	**39** C3
Tuğba................................	**40** C5

DRINKING

Kalamiş...........................(see 30)
Nargile Konaği...................	**41** C2
Pasaj..................................	**42** B4
Passport Café & Bar.........(see 30)

ENTERTAINMENT

Café Baryum......................	**43** C3
Punta Bar..........................	**44** D2

SHOPPING

Alp.....................................	**45** B5
Konak Pier Shopping Centre......(see 7)
İlhan Nargile....................(see 14)

TRANSPORT

Bus Companies Cities Offices....	**46** C5
Bus to Kadifekale...............	**47** A6
Green Car..........................	**48** C4
Konak Bus Terminal...........	**49** A6
Montrö Meydanı Bus Terminal...	**50** C4
Taxi Stand..........................	**51** B4
Turkish Airlines..................	**52** B4

Atatürk recaptured Smyrna (9 September 1922) marked the moment of victory in the Turkish War of Independence, and it is now the biggest local holiday. The events of 1922 are commemorated in the rather top-heavy monument gracing the waterfront.

Orientation

İzmir's two main avenues run parallel to the waterfront. The waterfront street is officially Atatürk Caddesi (Birinci Kordon or First Cordon), but locals just call it the Kordon. A block inland is Cumhuriyet Bulvarı, the İkinci Kordon (Second Cordon). The city's two main squares – Konak Meydanı (Government House Sq) to the south, and Cumhuriyet Meydanı – are along these two parallel avenues.

Konak opens onto the bazaar. The bazaar's main street, Anafartalar Caddesi, winds all the way to the train station, Basmane Garı, which is also linked to Konak by the metro. The Basmane/Çankaya area is home to dozens of small and midrange hotels, restaurants and bus ticket offices.

İzmir's shopping, restaurant and nightclub district of Alsancak is to the north, while the UFO-like otogar stands in splendid isolation, 6.5km northeast of the centre.

Information

There are branches of the PTT on Cumhuriyet Meydanı and on Fevzi Paşa Bulvarı. Banks with ATMs can be found on Fevzi Paşa Bulvarı in Basmane and around Cumhuriyet Meydanı.

Internet Café (1369 Sokak 9; per hr €0.83; ☑ 8am-1am) Friendly and helpful.

Internet House (☎ 464 1078; 1378 Sokak 26; per hr TL1.50; ☑ 9am-midnight) One of the fastest connections in town, and as a consequence usually packed full of gamers.

İzmir Döviz (☎ 441 8882; Fevzi Paşa Bulvarı 75, Çankaya; ☑ 7am-7pm Mon-Sat) Moneychanger where no commission is charged.

Remzi Kitabevi (☎ 489 5325; Konak Pier, Atatürk Caddesi) Large branch of the nationwide bookshop chain in the air-conditioned confines of the Konak mall. Large selection of English-language books, both for adults and children.

Tourist office (☎ 483 5117; fax 483 4270; Akdeniz Mahallesi 1344 Sokak 2) Inside the ornately stuccoed İl Kültür ve Turizm Müdürlüğü building just off Atatürk Caddesi. Has English-, German- and French-speaking staff.

Dangers & Annoyances

Like any big city, İzmir has its fair share of crime. However, the main tourist routes are fairly safe, with the possible exceptions of the Kadifekale neighbourhood and the area around Basmane station, which is something of a red-light district – lone women should take special care. In the bazaar, be alert to pickpockets and thieves.

Sights & Activities

KORDON & ALSANCAK

Very much the symbol of the new İzmir, this long boulevard has over the past decade been transformed into as fine a waterfront area as you'll find on this coast. The Kordon's (largely) pedestrianised confines are now home to a great selection of bars and restaurants that attract droves of people at the end of the day to watch the picture-perfect sunsets. Reminders of what might have been, however, lie to the north, by the Alsancak docks, where huge concrete struts mark the foundations of a waterfront motorway that was, thankfully, never built. Inland, the Alsancak district has also undergone much restoration in recent years and is now the focus of the city's nightlife scene.

During İzmir's 19th-century heyday the Kordon was lined with stately offices and the fine houses of the wealthy. Most of these have long since vanished, although in Alsancak the preserved wooden **Atatürk Evi** (admission free; ☑ 8.30am-noon & 1-5pm) gives an idea of what the homes of the wealthy would have looked like. Atatürk stayed here between 1930 and 1934 whenever he visited the city.

KONAK MEYDANİ

On a pedestrianised stretch of İkinci Kordon (Cumhuriyet Bulvarı), this wide plaza, named after the Ottoman **government mansion** (hükümet konağı), pretty much marks the heart of the city – signs pointing to the centre simply say 'Konak' – and is now linked to the waterfront by two wooden bridges spanning Atatürk Caddesi, one to the south opposite the Konak Cityboat Pier, and the other to the north in front of Konak Pier. It's the site of a late Ottoman **clock tower** (saat kulesi) given to the city in 1901 by Sultan Abdül Hamit II. Its ornate Orientalist style may have been meant to atone for 'infidel Smyrna's' European ambience. Beside it the pretty **Konak Camii**, dating from 1748, is covered in Kütahya tiles.

At its southern end, the traffic returns with a vengeance in the form of the wide multilane Halil Rifat Paşa Caddesi, across from which is Turgetreis Parkı and, on the hill above (but not signposted), İzmir's archaeology and ethnography museums.

The **Archaeology Museum** (Arkeoloji Müzesi; ☎ 489 0796; Arkeoloji Müzesi Caddesi; admission TL5; ☼ 8am-5pm Tue-Sun) is a little dry in places, but contains a fine collection of remnants from the city's various pasts: Bronze Age pottery, Greek statuary, Roman mosaics. Look out in particular for the beautifully decorated sarcophagi and the impressive frieze depicting the funeral games from the mausoleum at Belevi (250 BC).

More interesting is the **Ethnography Museum** (Etnografya Müzesi; ☎ 489 0796; admission TL2; ☼ 8am-5pm Tue-Sun), next door. Originally built in 1831 as the St Roche Hospital, this lovely old four-storey stone building houses colourful displays (including dioramas, photos and information panels) demonstrating local arts, crafts and customs. You'll learn about everything from camel wrestling, pottery and tin-plating to felt-making, embroidery and the art of making those curious little blue-and-white 'evil eye' beads (see also boxed text, p228). Other displays include weaponry, jewellery and beautiful illustrated manuscripts.

AGORA

The ancient **Agora** (Agora Caddesi; admission TL2; ☼ 8am-5pm), built for Alexander the Great, was ruined in an earthquake in AD 178, but rebuilt soon after by the Roman emperor Marcus Aurelius. Colonnades of reconstructed Corinthian columns, vaulted chambers and arches give you a good idea of what a Roman bazaar must have looked like. Later, a Muslim cemetery was built on the site and many of the old tombstones can be seen around the perimeter of the Agora. Ask for the free brochure, which gives a good introduction. The entrance to the site is just off Gazi Osman Paşa Bulvarı, just southeast of the main bazaar area.

If bathing facilities at your hotel are rudimentary, you can patronise the **Şifalı Lux Hamam** (bath & massage full works €20; ☼ 7am-11pm for men, 8am-6pm for women), just to the north on Anafartalar Caddesi. It's clean, with a lovely domed and marble interior.

KEMERALTI BAZAAR

İzmir's version of a Turkish **bazaar** (☼ 9.30am-9pm Mon-Sat high season, to 5pm low season) may be disappointingly unexotic if you've never visited one before. Much of what goes on sale here is aimed squarely at the domestic audience – pots and pans, socks, wedding dresses, clocks etc, albeit enlivened here and there with more-intriguing items, such as water pipes, beads and plenty of leather goods (a speciality of the city). The architecture is no great shakes either, with the exception of the restored **Kızlarağası Han** (☼ 9.30am-9pm Mon-Sat high season, to 5pm low season), a covered market built in 1744 and rather like a (much) smaller, calmer version of İstanbul's famous Covered Bazaar.

What the bazaar most certainly does have, however, is atmosphere. It can, to put it mildly, get rather busy. The streets are narrow and the people are many. It's a great place to lose yourself for a couple of hours – and with alleys intertwining here, there and everywhere, that is pretty much a guarantee. When it all gets too much, revive yourself with a shot of coffee at one of the numerous cafés. To help find your bearings, try to enter along Anafartalar Caddesi, which rings the main bazaar area and is its principal thoroughfare.

KÜLTÜR PARK

Much of the inland centre of town, between Alsancak and Basmane, an area that was heavily damaged in the 1922 fire, is taken up by the Kültür Park, a rather bland attempt to inject a little greenery into the city's concrete and tarmac expanses. Still, it's popular enough, attracting strolling couples and joggers – who have their own dedicated track. Specific attractions include a 50m parachute tower, an open-air theatre, exhibition halls for the yearly İzmir festival (see opposite) and, pick of the bunch, the city's **Museum of History & Art** (Tarih ve Sanat Müzesi; ☎ 489 7586; admission €2.75; ☼ 8am-5pm Tue-Sun). Containing three separate departments (Sculpture, Ceramics, and Precious Artefacts), it gives a good overview of the region's artistic heritage. Look out in particular for the 2nd-century-AD high relief of Poseidon and Demeter and the large hunting mosaic from Kadifekale. It also has a small but quite well-stocked bookshop with publications on Turkish art, cooking and culture.

KADİFEKALE

Following its sacking by Lydia in the 6th century BC, Smyrna would have to wait another couple of centuries before being refounded, by Alexander the Great. He chose a secure site on Kadifekale (Mt Pagus) in the centre of the modern city, erecting the fortifications

---

İZMİR'S SYNAGOGUES

İzmir still has a sizeable Jewish population – although not nearly as large as it was in Ottoman times – and it is possible to take a tour of some of the city's beautiful old **synagogues** (guided tours €25-35). The tours usually take in some of the restored synagogues of the Old Jewish Quarter, including the **Bet Israel**, which has a museum on its upper floor, and lies next to the **Asansör**, a 19th-century elevator (TL0.25) that links the Karataş and Halil Rifat Paşa areas of town – the alternative is 155 steps. Other highlights include the three Ottoman-style synagogues on Havra Sokak in the bazaar, the remainder of nine that used to stand here. To arrange a tour, call the tourist office (p223).

---

that still crown the hill. It's well worth taking a bus up to the 'Velvet Fortress' to see the view, especially just before sunset. During the day you can watch women migrants from Mardin in southeastern Anatolia hard at work on horizontal carpet looms, though this is an increasingly rare sight.

Bus 33 from Konak will carry you up the hill and you can easily walk some of the way back down again. However, the surrounding neighbourhood is pretty rough – don't walk back alone after dark.

Festivals & Events
From mid-June to mid-July the annual **International İzmir Festival** offers performances of music and dance in Çeşme and Ephesus as well as İzmir (in the Kültür Park). Call the **İzmir Kültür Vakfı** (İzmir Culture Foundation; ☎ 463 0300; www.izmirfair.com.tr; Mithatpaşa Caddesi 50/4) south of town to find out what's on where.

Sleeping
İzmir's waterfront is dominated by large high-end business hotels, which fill up quickly during the summer trade shows, while inland are plenty of budget and midrange places, particularly in the area close to the Basmane train station. 1294 Sokak and 1296 Sokak, just southwest of the station, boast a number of hotels occupying restored Ottoman houses; be aware that, although the facades are often very pretty, the interiors can be rather grungy and uninviting. Here and there, you'll also find a few 'boutique' (or *butik*) offerings, this modern trend having reached İzmir in the past few years.

BUDGET
Otel Hikmet (☎ 484 2672; 945 Sokak 26; s with/without shower TL20/15, d TL45/35) The sign outside says 'Hotel very good' and it's not wrong. Tucked away on cobbled streets off a nargileh (water

pipe)-café-lined square, this simple, family-run three-storey house is chock-full of character. Though longing for a lick of paint, the rooms are spotless.

Imperial Hotel (☎ 425 6883; fax 489 4688; 1294 Sokak 54; s/d TL20/45; 🖳) One of the best among a glut of similar offerings. The grandiose entrance columns, marble floors and carpets promise great things, but the rooms are much more modest. But they're still a decent size, spotless and terrific value.

MIDRANGE & TOP END
Hotel Alican 2 (☎ 425 2912; alicanotel@hotmail.com; 1367 Sokak; s/d incl breakfast €19/35; 🖳) One of the safer choices in the station area (there's a 24-hour reception), this has 13 decent-sized, well-maintained rooms with good, modern bathrooms.

Grand Zeybek Hotel (☎ 441 9590; www.grandzeybekhotels.com; Fevzi Paşa Bulvarı 1368 Sokak 5-7, Basmane; s/d €30/50; 🖳) Despite the name, this isn't grand at all, but a perfectly acceptable two-star – the trouble is, it's billed as a three-star. Still, the owners operate another three properties, so it's a good option if other places are full.

our pick Konak Saray Hotel (☎ 483 7755; www.konaksarayhotel.com; Anafartalar Caddesi 635; s/d €35/50; 🖳 🖳) One of the nicest and best-value options in town, the Konak Saray occupies a beautifully restored old Ottoman house that's been transformed into a superior boutique hotel. Rooms are stylish and modern – lots of wood and marble – if a touch small, and soundproofed to keep the bazaar noise out. There's also a great top-floor restaurant and free wi-fi.

Otel Kilim (☎ 484 5340; www.kilimotel.com.tr, in Turkish; Atatürk Caddesi, Çankaya; s/d €45/60; 🖳 🖳) There are better options along the seafront, but they tend to cost more. If you want views without the price, this is a pretty good choice, with a decent fish restaurant. The rooms were decorated a few years ago and are blandly comfortable, but only 12 have sea views so book at least one week in advance to avoid disappointment.

Otel Antik Han (☎ 489 2750; www.otelantikhan.com; Anafartalar Caddesi 600; s/d €45/65; 🖳) Once belonging to Atatürk's father, this is one of İzmir's very few historic hotels, with pleasant (if in places a little threadbare) rooms set around a tranquil courtyard, a world away from the hustle and bustle of the bazaar outside. The hotel also has six charming little 'flats' (in fact rooms with a mezzanine floor) that cost the same price as rooms.

İzmir Palas Oteli (☎ 465 0030; www.izmirpalas .com.tr; Atatürk Caddesi 2, Çankaya; s/d €65/85; ✕ 🔅) Established in 1927, the Palas is İzmir's oldest hotel, although, as it was rebuilt in 1972, don't expect any architectural wonders. It's rather boxy on the outside, and businesslike and bland within, but very comfortable with all the conveniences you'd expect for the price, and a reasonable restaurant. Its biggest boon is the location; most of its 138 rooms have balconies overlooking the bay.

MyHotel (☎ 445 3837; www.myhotel.com.tr; Cumhuriyet Bulvarı 132; s/d incl breakfast €65/90; 🔅 🖳) A sort of business/boutique affair, MyHotel is new and very stylish with glass floors, 30 clean minimalist (if a touch dark) rooms and plenty of designer furniture. It's near the seafront but doesn't have sea views.

Hilton İzmir (☎ 497 6060; www.hilton.com; Gaziosmanpaşa Bulvarı 7; s/d €95/130; ✕ 🔅 🖳 🍸) Reputedly the tallest building on Turkey's Aegean coast, the Hilton literally stands above the competition. The public rooms luxuriate in grey marble, and there are fabulous views from its well-appointed bedrooms, restaurants and bars, as well good facilities, including health club, pool, tennis and squash courts.

Swissôtel Grand Efes (☎ 414 0000; www.swissotel .com.tr; Gaziosmanpaşa Bulvarı 1; r €135-360; ✕ 🔅 🖳 🍸) The new five-star luxury-business Grand Efes is perhaps the biggest player in town right now, occupying a prime location in the centre of Cumhuriyet Meydanı overlooking the water. The rooms are as generically luxurious as you'd expect, with flat-screen TVs, large beds and elegant leather and steel furniture, although you might have to look out of the window (or take a trip up to the Sky Bar) to remind yourself which city you're in. Also boasts an excellent restaurant and spa.

Eating

For fresh fruit, veg or freshly baked bread and delicious savoury pastries (€0.13), head for the canopied market, just off Anafartalar Caddesi.

RESTAURANTS

The place to be seen on a romantic summer's evening is the sea-facing Kordon. Though you pay for the location – most restaurants have streetside tables with views of the bay – some serve excellent food as well. In Alsancak, you lose the sunset views but gain on atmosphere. Try in particular 1453 Sokak (Gazi Kadinlar Sokağı).

Sakız (☎ 484 1103; Şehit Nevresbey Bulvarı 9a; mains TL8-12; 🕙 11am-midnight) It must have been a bold move opening a vegetarian café in the mainly carnivorous confines of İzmir, but it seems to have paid off. The food is traditional Turkish, just removed of its meat and fish elements, made with fresh local ingredients. Good wine list.

Kefi (☎ 422 6045; 1453 Sokak 17; mezes TL5, mains TL14; 🕙 11am-midnight) Alsancak's restaurant scene is booming but volatile, with new places opening and closing all the time. Kefi, however, seems to have stood the test of time with its superb cooking and elegant dining room set in a restored Ottoman house. Fish and seafood take up most of the menu but it also does some mean meat dishes – try the lamb with fennel.

Balık Pişiricisi (☎ 464 2705; Atatürk Caddesi 212a; mains TL10-16; 🕙 noon-11.30pm) The queues of diners on the street and waiters galloping from table to table tell much about this fish restaurant. Though simple and modern, it has a reputation for good seafood at reasonable prices. Try the speciality, *dil şiş* (grilled sole).

Asansör (☎ 261 2626; Dario Moreno Sokağı; mains TL10-18; 🕙 8am-midnight) Housed at the top of a 40m 19th-century elevator, the location is İzmir's best. In addition to the stunning panoramic views, it makes a cool refuge in summer, well away from the main tourist trail. If you can't afford to eat at the main restaurant, try the smaller Café Moreno opposite (mains TL8 to TL14, open same hours) or come for a beer (from €3). It's about 2km from the town centre.

Café Melanie (☎ 482 4158; Atatürk Caddesi 206a; mains TL10-20; 🕙 11am-2am) Unashamedly glam and aimed squarely at the smart set who like to be seen, Melanie offers pretty much the archetypal Kordon experience, with a cool dining room and smart, seafront seating. The menu is European and very good (particularly the shrimp casserole) and there's regular live music. Not as expensive as you might think.

our pick **Deniz Restaurant** (☎ 464 4499; Atatürk Caddesi 188b; mains TL10-22; ⏱ 11am-11pm) Founded by a father and run by his three sons, the family has firmly held onto Deniz' ranking as İzmir's premier fish restaurant. Try the house speciality, *tuzda balık* (fish baked in a block of salt that's dramatically broken at your table) or the sumptuous seafood. Expect your fellow diners to be in their best party frocks.

QUICK EATS

Tuğba (☎ 441 9622; Gazi Osman Paşa Bulvarı 56, Çankaya; ⏱ 8.30am-11pm) For dried fruit, nuts, baklava, Turkish delight and all things nice.

Gül Kebap (☎ 425 0126; Anafartalar Caddesi 415, Kemeraltı; meals TL3-5; ⏱ 6.30am-5pm Mon-Sat) For a fuel stop in the bazaar, head for this perennially popular place, feeding the good people of İzmir since 1949.

Neşe Köfte (☎ 445 3868; 906 Sokak 28; meals TL6; ⏱ 11am-6pm Mon-Sat) At the other end of the bazaar, this place claims İzmir's 'best-*köfte*-in-town' crown. Try also the *piyas* (white beans and onion in olive oil and lemon juice), an Aegean speciality. Later, have a coffee at one of the pretty cafés nearby.

Kırçiçeği (☎ 464 3090; Kıbrıs Şehitleri Caddesi 83; kebaps TL8-10; ⏱ 24hr) Simple but spotless and with exemplary service. This is the place in Alsancak to come for good Turkish food at great prices. The pick-and-point menu may help new arrivals or those keen to try out other dishes.

Dört Mevsim Et Lokantası (☎ 489 8991; 1369 Sokak 51a; meals TL10-16; ⏱ 9.30am-midnight) Famous as far afield as Ankara and İstanbul, this award-winning *lokanta* (eatery serving ready-made food) dishes up excellent food at reasonable prices. From the open ocakbaşı (grill), try the delicious chargrilled-melted cheese, stuffed aubergine kebap, or *köfte* with chilli (the house specialities).

CAFÉS & PATISSERIES

Sir Winston Tea House (☎ 421 8861; Dr Mustafa Bey Enver Caddesi 20c; tea TL0.75-2; ⏱ 8am-8pm Mon-Sat) On a street known for its quality tea- and coffee-houses this is one of the best, serving over 60 types of tea (green, herbal, fruit etc) and good pastries. There's shady seating outside.

Café de Bugün (☎ 425 8118; Atatürk Caddesi 162 1-2; sandwiches TL6, coffee TL4; ⏱ 8am-11pm) Along the seafront and in complete contrast to the little cafés and patisseries in the bazaar is the posh Café de Bugün, which rather resembles a French Regency salon.

Simorg Café (☎ 445 7449; 895 Sokak 2a; meals TL4-5, tea TL0.20; ⏱ 8am-9.30pm Mon-Sat) With its Orientalist interior (complete with carpets, old maps and portraits of sultans and their harems), this café makes a great place to recline and rest after a run around the bazaar. The 'coffee made in cup' is a speciality of the area. There's live Turkish music on Wednesday, Friday, Saturday and Sunday from 7pm to 9.30pm.

Drinking

Nargile Konaği (☎ 463 4050; 1482 Sokak 12; ⏱ 8am-1am) Enjoy one of the city's most traditional pleasures, toting on a nargileh (€2), in its liveliest and most fashionable district. Surrounded by other bars and cafés, this is small and cosy with little tables on the street.

Kalamiş (☎ 425 3901; Atatürk Caddesi 144, Konak; nargilehs €3; ⏱ 24hr) For a nargileh over a game of backgammon or *okey* (a kind of Turkish dominoes) head for this atmospheric institution. Old men line the yellowed interior, but students (of both sexes) occupy the 1st floor.

Passport Café & Bar (☎ 489 9299; Atatürk Caddesi 140; beer €1.65; ⏱ 8am-2am) More modern and more central is this new and funky place with tables on the seafront.

Pasaj (☎ 425 9445; Atatürk Caddesi 132; beer TL5; ⏱ 10am-2am) Unlike many of the other sunset bars along this strip, where the focus is primarily on the waterfront seating, this also has a nice, high-ceilinged wooden interior where you can while away the evening once the sun has dropped over the horizon. Popular and lively.

Entertainment

The locals start their evening's entertainment with a stroll along the Kordon, which is also good for a sundowner on the seafront. Things get steadily trendier and livelier the further north you go. The row of bars around the Balık Pişiricisi Restaurant is particularly popular. Alsancak plays host to the city's hottest nightlife, particularly in the clubs and bars of Sokaks 1452, 1453 and 1487.

Punta Bar (☎ 463 1504; 1469 Sokak 26; admission free; beer TL3-5; ⏱ 9pm-4am Wed-Sat) One of the most popular Alsancak venues, this stages regular live music (mostly rock, but then most live music in Alsancak is) and attracts intense, happy crowds.

THE EVIL ALL-SEEING EYE

However short your trip to Turkey, you can't fail to notice the famous 'evil eye' watching you wherever you go. This age-old superstition is still remarkably persistent throughout Turkey today, and the beads, pendants and other artefacts emblazoned with the eye are made just as much for the local market as they are for the tourists.

In a nutshell, certain people are thought to carry within them a malevolent force that can be transmitted to others via their eyes. Charms, resembling eyes, known as *nazar boncuk,* are used to reflect the evil look back to the originator.

The majority of the evil-eye production takes place in the Aegean region, and İzmir is a great place to buy them (see below).

Café Baryum (☎ 463 4902; Atatürk Caddesi 230a; beer inside/outside €2.25/2.75; ☼ 8am-2am) The lively and popular Baryum plays live music from 9pm to 2am nightly.

Shopping

These days İzmir's shopping scene spans all sections of the market. On the one hand, there's the bazaar with its crowded intensity, its haggling and its old-world commercial exuberance, and on the other there's the Konak Pier shopping centre, a bright, shiny, modern mall jutting out over the water and filled with big-name chains – Tommy Hilfiger, Lacoste etc. The former offers atmosphere and plenty of (sometimes unwanted) human interaction, the latter air-conditioned sterility and hands-off deference – take your pick.

İlhan Nargile (☎ 441 7404; Kızlarağası Han; ☼ 8am-6pm) The city's oldest manufacturers of water pipes operate two shops and a factory in the heart of the bazaar and stock all manner of colourful, convoluted contraptions.

Alp (☎ 445 9017; 856 Sokak 51, Kemeraltı; ☼ 8am-6pm Mon-Sat) This amazing shop specialises in the famous evil-eye beads (see boxed text, above) in all shapes, sizes and settings – pendants, jewellery, pictures etc.

Getting There & Away

AIR

Since the opening of the new international terminal at İzmir's **Adnan Menderes Airport** (☎ 455 0000; www.adnanmenderesairport.com) in late 2006, flights to the city from European destinations have greatly increased. See p684 for more details.

Turkish Airlines (☎ 484 1220; www.thy.com; Halit Ziya Bulvarı 65, Çankaya) offers nonstop flights to İstanbul (from TL109, 50 minutes) and Ankara (from TL59, one hour and 15 minutes) with connections to other destinations. Other airlines flying to İzmir:

Atlasjet (www.atlastjet.com)
Fly Air (www.flyair.com.tr)
Izair (www.izair.com.tr)
Onur Air (www.onurair.com.tr)
Sun Express Airlines (www.sunexpress.com.tr)

BUS

İzmir's mammoth otogar lies 6.5km northeast of the city centre. For travel to coastal towns on Friday or Saturday, buy your ticket a day in advance; in the high season, two days in advance. Tickets can also be bought from the bus company offices in the city centre.

Long-distance buses and their ticket offices are found on the lower level; regional buses (Selçuk, Bergama, Manisa, Sardis etc) and their ticket offices are on the upper level. City buses and dolmuşes leave from a courtyard in front of the lower level.

From İzmir there are frequent local buses to Bergama (TL10, two hours, 110km), Çeşme (TL10, 1½ hours, 116km), Foça (TL5.50, 1½ hours, 86km), Kuşadası (TL10.50, 1¼ hours, 95km), Manisa (TL5, 50 minutes, 45km), Salihli (for Sardis; TL7.50, 1½ hours, 80km) and Selçuk (TL6, one hour, 80km).

Short-distance buses (eg to the Çeşme Peninsula) leave from a smaller local bus terminal in Üçkuyular, 6.5km southwest of Konak. Recently short-distance buses started picking up and dropping off at the otogar also.

Details of daily long-distance bus services to important destinations are listed in the table, opposite.

TRAIN

Though İzmir has two train stations, **Alsancak Garı** (☎ 464 7795) and **Basmane Garı** (☎ information 484 8638, reservations 484 5353), most intercity trains as well as the airport train arrive at the latter.

The *Alti Eylül Ekspresi* train to Bandırma (TL16, 6½ hours) departs year-round from İzmir Basmane at 9am and arrives in Bandırma Gar (main station) at 2.50pm. Between April and October, a second service,

SERVICES FROM İZMİR'S OTOGAR

Destination	Fare (TL)	Duration (hr)	Distance (km)	Frequency (per day)
Ankara	48	8	550	every hour
Antalya	40	7	450	at least hourly
Bodrum	25	3¼	286	every 30min in high season
Bursa	24	5	300	every hour
Çanakkale	38	6	340	at least hourly
Denizli	18	3¼	250	every 30min
İstanbul	50	9	575	at least every hour
Konya	40	8	575	every 1 to 2 hours
Marmaris	35	4	320	hourly

the *Onyedi Eylül Ekspresi,* leaves at 2.15pm, arriving at 8.10pm. From Bandırma, you can catch a ferry (p197) across the Sea of Marmara to İstanbul.

Express trains also run to Ankara (sleeper TL26.50, 13 to 15 hours) daily at 5.30pm, 6.15pm and 7.30pm via Manisa (TL3, 1¾ hours), Kütahya (TL15, eight hours) and Eskişehir (sleeper TL17.25, 11½ to 13½ hours). For İstanbul, change at Eskişehir.

Further express services are available to Denizli (for Pamukkale; TL11, five hours) three times daily at 9am, 3.15pm and 6.30pm; Selçuk (TL3.50, 1½ hours) at 9am, noon, 3.15pm, 6.30pm and 9.30pm; Nazilli (for Afrodisias; TL7.25, four hours) at 9am, noon, 3.15pm, 6.30pm and 9.30pm; Isparta (TL17, 10 hours) at 9.30pm; and Burdur (TL14, nine hours) at 9.30pm; Kutahya trains are at 5.30pm, 6.15pm and 7.30pm and cost Tl15 to TL18.

For trains to northern or eastern Turkey, change at Ankara.

Getting Around
TO/FROM THE AIRPORT
The airport is 18km south of the city near Cumaovası on the road to Ephesus and Kuşadası. Frequent Havaş airport buses (TL10, 30 minutes) leave from Gaziosmanpaşa Bulvarı, north of the Hilton, and from the airport (where they meet flights).

More-or-less hourly suburban trains (TL2.50, 30 minutes) connect the airport with Basmane Garı (TL2.50), but a taxi (€20 to €30, 30 minutes) is likely to be faster and more dependable.

TO/FROM THE BUS STATIONS
If you've arrived at the main otogar on an intercity bus operated by one of the larger bus companies, a free shuttle *servis* is provided to Dokuz Eylül Meydanı in Basmane. If you arrive on a local bus, you can catch a dolmuş (TL1.75, 25 minutes) that runs every 15 minutes between the otogar and both Konak and Basmane Garı, or you can take buses 54 and 191 (every 20 minutes), bus 64 (every hour) to Basmane (TL2) or bus 505 to Bornova (TL2). Tickets can be bought either on board the bus or at the white booth beside the bus stop.

To get to the otogar, the easiest way is to buy a ticket on an intercity bus at Dokuz Eylül Meydanı and then take the bus company's *servis.* However, if you need to take a local bus from the otogar (eg to Salihli), you'll need to take a dolmuş or bus from Basmane or Bornova.

To get to the bus station at Üçkuyular, catch bus 11 (TL2) from the Konak bus terminal. Soon, you will also be able to take the metro (see p230).

BOAT
The nicest way to get about İzmir is by **ferry** (🕓 6.30am–1am). Frequent timetabled services link the piers at Konak, Pasaport, Alsancak and Karşiyaka. *Jetons* (transport tokens) cost TL4 each.

BUS
City buses lumber along the major thoroughfares, but the one-way system and lack of numbering on the bus stops makes them hard for outsiders to use. Two major terminal or transfer points are Montrö Meydanı, by the Kültür Park, and Konak, beside the Atatürk Evi. You can buy a ticket (TL2) from a white kiosk in advance or on board from the driver.

CAR
The large international car-hire franchises and many smaller companies all have desks

(open 24 hours) at the airport, and many have a desk in town.

Avis (☎ 274 1790; www.avis.com.tr)
Europcar (☎ 274 2163; www.europcar.com.tr)
Green Car (☎ 446 9131; www.greenautorent.com; Şair Eşref Bulvarı 18a, Çankaya) A good local company and the largest in the Aegean region.

METRO

İzmir's **metro** (⏰ 6.30am-11.30pm; jeton TL1) is clean and quick. There are currently 10 stations running from Üçyol to Bornova via Konak (you're most likely to travel from Basmane station to Konak or Bornova), although there are plans to expand the system throughout much of the city, extending the current line and adding another two.

TAXI

You can either hail a taxi or pick one up from a taxi stand or from outside one of the big hotels. Fares start at TL1.50 and depend on distance; prices are 50% more at night. Make sure the meter is switched on.

AROUND İZMIR

If you are staying in İzmir for a few days, a number of destinations make good day or half-day excursions. Local buses leave from the upper level of İzmir otogar.

Manisa

☎ 0236 / pop 281,890

Backed by mountains, the modern town of Manisa was once the ancient town of Magnesia ad Sipylus. The early Ottoman sultans left Manisa many fine mosques, but retreating Greek soldiers wreaked terrible destruction during the War of Independence. The main reasons to visit are to inspect the mosques and the finds from Sardis in the museum or to take in the Mesir Şenlikleri festival.

SIGHTS & ACTIVITIES

Of Manisa's many old mosques, the **Muradiye Camii** (1585), the last work of the famous architect Sinan, has the most impressive tile work. The adjoining building, originally constructed as a soup kitchen, is now **Manisa Museum** (admission TL2; ⏰ 9am-noon & 1-5pm Tue-Sun), which houses some fine mosaics from Sardis (right).

More or less facing the Muradiye, the **Sultan Camii** (1522) features some gaudy paintings. The **hamam** (admission TL15; ⏰ 10am-9pm) next door has separate entrances for men and women.

Perched on the hillside above the town centre is the **Ulu Cami** (1366), ravaged by the ages and not as impressive as the view from the teahouse next to it.

FESTIVALS & EVENTS

Should you be able to visit during the four days around the spring equinox, you would catch the **Mesir Şenlikleri**, a festival in celebration of *mesir macunu* (power gum).

According to legend, over 450 years ago a local pharmacist named Müslihiddin Celebi Merkez Efendi concocted a potion to cure Hafza Sultan, mother of Sultan Süleyman the Magnificent, of a mysterious ailment. Delighted with her swift recovery, the queen mother paid for the amazing elixir to be distributed to the local people.

These days townsfolk in period costumes re-enact the mixing of the potion from sugar and 40 spices and other ingredients, then toss it from the dome of the Sultan Camii. Locals credit *mesir* with calming the nerves, stimulating the hormones and immunising against poisonous stings.

GETTING THERE & AROUND

It's easiest to get to Manisa by hourly bus from İzmir (TL5, 45 minutes, 30km). You can continue direct from Manisa to Salihli (TL3.50, 1½ hours) to see the ruins at Sardis.

To get to Manisa's historic mosques, take dolmuş 5 from in front of the otogar (TL0.75) and hop off at Ulu Parkı.

Sardis (Sart)

Sardis was once the capital of the wealthy Lydian kingdom that dominated much of the Aegean before the Persians came along. Its ruins, 90km east of İzmir, make a particularly worthwhile excursion destination.

Sardis was near the Pactolus River, which carried specks of gold that the Lydians collected with fleece sieves. Croesus (560–546 BC) was a king of Lydia, and the Greeks presumably thought him abnormally rich because he could store so much wealth in his seemingly bottomless pockets rather than in the form of vast estates and livestock. Coinage seems to have been invented here, hence the phrase 'rich as Croesus'. Sardis became a great trading centre partly because its coinage facilitated commerce.

The then Persian town was sacked during a revolt in 499 BC. After the Persians,

Alexander the Great took the city in 334 BC and embellished it even more. An earthquake brought down its fine buildings in AD 17, but it was rebuilt by Tiberius and developed into a thriving Roman town. The end for Sardis happened soon after Tamerlane visited in 1401 in his usual belligerent mood.

The ruins of Sardis are scattered around the village of Sart (Sartmustafa) in a valley overshadowed by a strikingly craggy mountain range.

SIGHTS

The most extensive **ruins** (admission TL2; 🕓 8am-5pm, to 7pm high season) lie at the eastern end of Sart village, immediately north of the road. Information panels dot the site.

You enter the site along a **Roman road**, past a well-preserved **Byzantine latrine** and rows of **Byzantine shops** backing onto a synagogue, which belonged to Jewish merchants and artisans. Some of the buildings have been identified from inscriptions and include a restaurant, Jacob's Paint Shop, an office, a hardware shop, and shops belonging to Sabbatios and Jacob, an elder of the synagogue.

Turn left from the Roman road to enter the **havra** (synagogue), impressive because of its size and beautiful decoration: fine geometric mosaic paving and coloured stone on the walls.

Beside the synagogue is the grassy expanse of what was once the hamam and gymnasium. This complex was probably built in the 2nd century AD and abandoned after a Sassanian invasion in 616.

Right at the end is a striking two-storey building called the **Marble Court of the Hall of the Imperial Cult**, which, though heavily restored (and somewhat hideous), gives an idea of the former grandeur of the building. Behind it you'll find an ancient **swimming pool** and rest area. Look out also for the Roman altar with two Roman eagles on either side and lions back-to-back.

Across the road from the enclosed site continuing excavations have uncovered a stretch of the **Lydian city wall** and a **Roman house** with painted walls right on top of an earlier Lydian residence.

Temple of Artemis

A sign points south down the road beside the teahouses to the **Temple of Artemis** (admission TL3; 🕓 8am-5pm), just over 1km away. Today,

only a few columns of a once-magnificent but never completed building still stand. Nevertheless, the temple's plan is clearly visible and very impressive. Next to it is an **altar** used since ancient times, refurbished by Alexander the Great and later by the Romans. Clinging to the southeastern corner of the temple is a small brick **Byzantine church**.

As you head back to İzmir, look to the north of the highway and you'll see a series of softly rounded **tumuli**, the burial mounds of the Lydian kings.

GETTING THERE & AWAY

Buses for Salihli (TL6.75, 1½ hours, 90km) leave from İzmir otogar at least every 30 minutes. You must then take an onward dolmuş to Sart (TL0.75, 15 minutes, 9km) from the back of Salihli otogar.

Buses also run between Salihli and Manisa (TL3.50, 1½ hours), making it possible to visit both places in the same day.

ÇEŞME PENINSULA

The Çeşme Peninsula is İzmir's summer playground, which means that it can get very busy with Turkish tourists at weekends and during the school holidays. The main places to visit are Çeşme itself, a family-oriented resort and transit point for getting to the Greek island of Chios, and Alaçatı, a much more upmarket affair whose central core of old Greek stone houses now holds a multitude of boutique hotels and high-end restaurants, the majority opened in the past five years. The nearby beach has become a windsurfing mecca in recent years.

ÇEŞME
☎ 0232 / pop 21,300

Çeşme, 85km due west of İzmir, has perked up considerably in recent years and now makes a good base for a few days' holiday, especially when travelling to and from Chios, 8km away across the water. Inevitably, it's popular with weekending İzmiris and can get busy during the school holidays, when prices rise accordingly.

Orientation & Information

To the north of the main square is the waterfront esplanade, which is largely pedestrianised and lined with fish restaurants and excursion boats. At its far northern end is

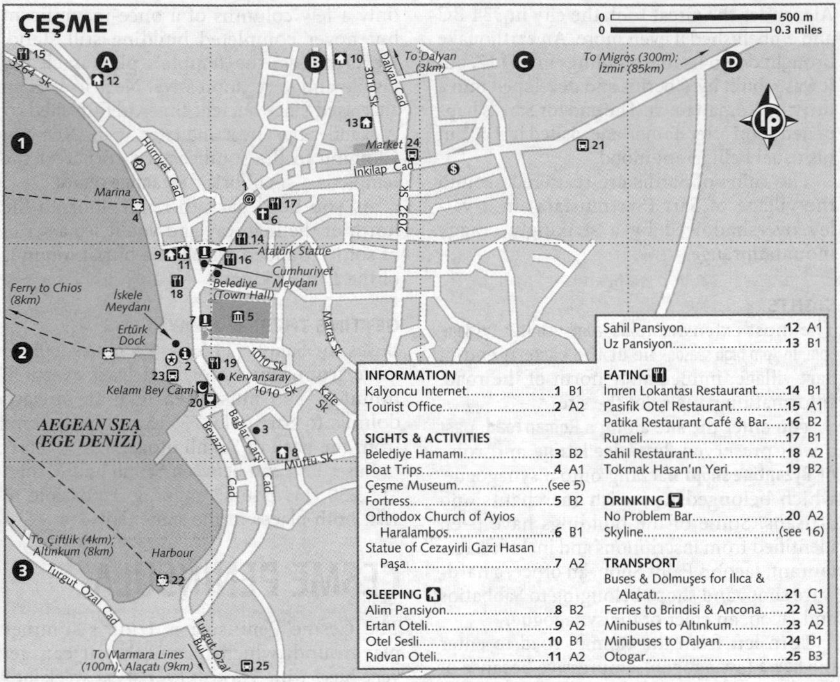
ÇEŞME
0 500 m
0 0.3 miles
A
B
C
D
1
2
3
3264 Sk
Hürriyet Cad
Marina
To Dalyan (3km)
3010 Sk
Dalyan Cad
To Migros (300m); İzmir (85km)
Market
İnkilap Cad
2032 Sk
Atatürk Statue
Cumhuriyet Meydanı
Belediye (Town Hall)
Ferry to Chios (8km)
İskele Meydanı
Ertürk Dock
Kervansaray
1010 Sk
Maraş Sk
Kale Sk
Kelamı Bey Cami
AEGEAN SEA (EGE DENİZİ)
Bağlar Çarşı Cad
Beyazıt Cad
Müftü Sk
To Çiftlik (4km); Altınkum (8km)
Harbour
Turgut Özal Cad
Turgut Özal Bul
To Marmara Lines (100m); Alaçatı (9km)
INFORMATION
Kalyoncu Internet....1 B1
Tourist Office....2 A2
SIGHTS & ACTIVITIES
Belediye Hamamı....3 B2
Boat Trips....4 A1
Çeşme Museum....(see 5)
Fortress....5 B2
Orthodox Church of Ayios Haralambos....6 B1
Statue of Cezayirli Gazi Hasan Paşa....7 A2
SLEEPING
Alim Pansiyon....8 B2
Ertan Oteli....9 A2
Otel Sesli....10 B1
Rıdvan Oteli....11 A2
Sahil Pansiyon....12 A1
Uz Pansiyon....13 B1
EATING
İmren Lokantası Restaurant....14 B1
Pasifik Otel Restaurant....15 A1
Patika Restaurant Café & Bar....16 B2
Rumeli....17 B1
Sahil Restaurant....18 A2
Tokmak Hasan'ın Yeri....19 B2
DRINKING
No Problem Bar....20 A2
Skyline....(see 16)
TRANSPORT
Buses & Dolmuşes for Ilıca & Alaçatı....21 C1
Ferries to Brindisi & Ancona....22 A3
Minibuses to Altınkum....23 A2
Minibuses to Dalyan....24 B1
Otogar....25 B3

a small, sandy beach. The otogar is almost 1km south of Cumhuriyet Meydanı, although you can just as easily pick up transport to İzmir, Ilıca or Alaçatı from the western end of İnkilap Caddesi.

The **tourist office** (☎/fax 712 6653; İskele Meydanı 6; 🕑 8.30am-noon & 1-5.30pm Mon-Fri), ferry and bus ticket offices, banks with ATMs, restaurants and hotels are all within two blocks of Cumhuriyet Meydanı, the main square near the waterfront with the inevitable statue of Atatürk.

The main shopping drag, İnkilap Caddesi, curves gently uphill to the northeast. Around 200m on the left is **Kalyoncu Internet** (3042 Sokak 18a; per hr TL3; 🕑 10am-1am).

Sights

The Genoese **fortress**, whose dramatic walls dominate the town centre, was built in the 16th century and repaired by Sultan Beyazıt, son of Sultan Mehmet the Conqueror (Mehmet Fatih), to defend the coast from attack by pirates. Later the Knights of St John of Jerusalem based on Rhodes also made use of it. The battlements offer excellent views of Çeşme but otherwise the interior is disappointingly empty. The one exception is the north tower, which houses the **Çeşme Museum** (Çeşme Müzesi; admission TL2; 🕑 8am-5pm), displaying some archaeological finds from nearby Erythrae.

Facing İskele Meydanı, with its back to the fortress, is a **statue of Cezayirli Gazi Hasan Paşa** (1714–90), who was sold into slavery but became a grand vizier. He is shown accompanied by a lion.

To the north, the imposing but redundant 19th-century **Orthodox Church of Ayios Haralambos** (İnkilap Caddesi) is used for temporary exhibitions of arts and crafts during the summer months.

Past the Çeşme Kervansaray Hotel on Bağlar Çarşı Caddesi is Çeşme's restored 18th-century **Belediye hamamı** (☎ 712 5386; wash & massage TL43; 🕑 8am-11pm). With its dome and marble interior, it's an attractive place. Bathing is mixed (though *peştemals* – hamam bath towels – are used).

Activities

From June to September, *gülets* (traditional Turkish wooden yachts) offer one-day **boat**

trips (incl lunch TL25) to the nearby islands of Wind Bay, Black Island and Donkey Island, where you can swim and snorkel. Browse the waterfront to compare prices and negotiate. Boats usually leave around 10am and return around 5pm.

Sleeping

BUDGET

Alim Pansiyon (☎ 712 6971; tamerakpinar@hotmail.com; 1021 Sokak 3; s/d TL30/40) The friendly and quiet Alim lies south of the centre and has simple, cheerily decorated rooms, all with TVs (some with balconies).

Uz Pansiyon (☎ 712 6579; uzpansiyon@gmail.com; 3010 Sokak 7; s/d TL35/55; ▨) Close to the bus station and 450m from the centre, this is one of Çeşme's cheapest. It's spotless and terrific value, with a communal kitchen and free wi-fi available.

Otel Sesli (☎ 712 8845; www.otelsesli.com; 3025 Sokak 35; s/d €20/40; ▨ ▨) Set on a hill well above the seafront, and recently renovated, this place offers 20 rather bare rooms arranged around a pleasant central pool area adorned with potted plants. It's a 10-minute walk to the centre.

Sahil Pansiyon (☎ 712 6934; www.cesmesahilpansiyon .com; 3265 Sokak 3; d from €40; ▨) Up the stairs near the northern waterfront, this is a peaceful place set in a rambling house and garden. The immaculate rooms have small balconies, some with sea views (ask for room 9). The family's very accommodating and keen to please.

MIDRANGE

Ertan Oteli (☎ 712 6795; www.ertanotel.com.tr.tc; Hürriyet Caddesi 12; d €55; ▨) In the same block as the Rıdvan, the Ertan enjoys the better location, right on the seafront. Though by no means a good-looking hotel, the staff are helpful, the restaurant reasonable and the rooms are a decent size and have balconies – a choice of sea or square views.

Rıdvan Oteli (☎ 712 6336; www.ridvanotel.com; Cumhuriyet Meydanı 11; s/d €40/55; ▨) Slightly more well-to-do than its neighbour, this boasts 36 balconied rooms, some with castle views, some with side views of the sea. There's a branch of Özüt on the ground floor with seating on the square.

Eating

The most touristy restaurants are all along the waterfront and specialise mainly in fish and seafood – and have their menus printed in a wide variety of languages. For cheaper, more locally oriented places, head to İnkilap Caddesi.

Rumeli (☎ 712 6759; İnkilap Caddesi; ⏰ 8am-8pm) Great ice cream (TL0.75 per scoop) served from the side window of this *pastane* (patisserie), which specialises in all manner of jams, pickles and preserves.

Tokmak Hasan'in Yeri (☎ 712 0519; Çarşı Caddesi 11; mains TL4-8; ⏰ 7am-8pm Mon-Sat) Rather hidden away, this simple place serves terrific home cooking at low prices. There's a cool, quiet garden at the back.

İmren Lokantası Restaurant (☎ 712 7620; İnkilap Caddesi; mezes TL4.50, mains TL9-17.50; ⏰ noon-9pm) Çeşme's first restaurant opened way back in 1960 and is set in a bamboo-roofed atrium with fountain and plants. It's famous locally for its traditional, high-quality Turkish food, including excellent stews (TL7).

Patika Restaurant Café & Bar (☎ 712 6357; Cumhuriyet Meydanı; mains TL10-16; ⏰ 3pm-midnight) Set above a souvenir shop on the main square, this is the place for fish at affordable prices. Alcohol is not served. Between 9pm and 1am daily there's live Turkish music and sometimes belly dancing.

Pasifik Otel Restaurant (☎ 712 7465; 3264 Sokak; mains TL10-16; ⏰ noon-9pm) If you fancy a walk and some fish, head here, to the far northern end of the seafront, where you can enjoy a great fish casserole (TL14) on seating overlooking the beach.

Sahil Restaurant (☎ 712 8294; Cumhuriyet Meydanı 12; soup TL4, mains TL12-18; ⏰ 8am-midnight) Right on the waterfront, this Mediterranean-style place is known for its fish, though its meat dishes are also good. But make sure you ask the fish prices in advance; for some travellers, the bill's been a nasty surprise. *Barbun* (red mullet, €20) is the house speciality.

Drinking & Entertainment

Skyline (☎ 712 7567; Cumhuriyet Meydanı; beer €2.75; ⏰ 10am-3am, later in high season) It may call itself a 'dance-bar', but this tiny rooftop place (above the Patika Restaurant Café & Bar) is perhaps better described as Çeşme's best wind-down bar, offering good views and enjoying cooling breezes.

No Problem Bar (☎ 712 9411; Çarşı Caddesi 14; beer TL5; ⏰ 7.30am-3am high season only) This unashamedly traveller-trapping place opposite the old Kervansaray offers beer at competitive prices and bacon butties (TL7) to boot!

NORTH AEGEAN

Getting There & Away

BUS

You have to transit İzmir to get to Çeşme (and from Çeşme to most other places) as there's no longer any onward public transport from Urla to Çeşme.

Buses from Çeşme's otogar run at least every 45 minutes to İzmir's main otogar (TL8, two hours) and its smaller, western Üçkuyular terminal (TL7.50, 1¼ hours, 85km).

There are daily direct buses to İstanbul (TL55, nine hours) and to Ankara (€45, seven hours).

Dolmuşes for Ilıca and Alaçatı leave from a spot 200m northeast of the town centre, and minibuses to Dalyan from near the Hükümet Konağı (Government Building) on Dalyan Caddesi. Minibuses to Altınkum leave from near the tourist office.

FERRY

Many travellers visit Çeşme on their way to or from the nearby Greek island of Chios. Ferries sail between Çeşme and Chios (one way €40, return €65, car €140 to €180 return, 1½ hours) at least five times weekly in high season and twice a week in low season (usually Tuesday and Saturday), generally leaving Çeşme at 9am and returning from Chios at 4pm. You don't need to buy your ticket in advance unless you have a car.

During the summer (and sporadically throughout the rest of the year) ferries also leave at least once a week to the Italian ports of Ancona and Brindisi (low season from €50, high season from €70, car from €150, 36 to 40 hours). As times (and destinations) change every year, check the current timetables. Note that the ferries to Italy do not currently stop off in Greece.

Ferry tickets can be bought direct from **Marmara Lines** (☎ 712 2223; www.marmaralines.com; Turgut Özal Bulvarı).

AROUND ÇEŞME

Altınkum

Southwest of Çeşme, the increasingly built-up resort of Altınkum boasts a series of delightful sandy coves easily reachable by regular dolmuşes that leave from behind Çeşme tourist office (TL2.50, 15 minutes, 9km).

A few places offer rental equipment for water sports, especially windsurfing (boards from €40/140 per day/week). **Tursite** (☎ 722 1221; per tent/caravan €10/15), 8.5km from Çeşme and

500m before Altınkum, is pleasant and clean, with a nice beach and camping ground.

Alaçatı

☎ 0232

A few kilometres southeast of Çeşme, on the other side of the peninsula, lies Alaçatı, which, until the early part of this century, was a largely forgotten backwater of old, tumbledown Greek stone houses. In 2001, however, someone had the bright idea of restoring one of these houses and turning it into an upmarket boutique hotel. It was a huge success, soon spawning a host of imitators (now up to 36 and counting). Over the past few years Alaçatı has become a veritable restoration bubble, with something like a thousand new holiday homes having been constructed on its outskirts, and seemingly every house in its historic centre now taken up by a hotel, a high-end restaurant or an art gallery. Whether development can continue at such a pace without having an adverse effect on the character of the place remains to be seen. All eyes are currently on the town's beach, 4km away, which seems to be on the cusp of a similarly dramatic expansion (see boxed text, opposite).

Well-heeled İstanbullus and İzmiris pour into town in summer (and fill the motorway back to İzmir come nightfall), giving its main street, Kemalpaşa Caddesi, a lively, buzzing feel. It's a great place to wander, even if there are no sights as such, just a general feeling of contented well-to-do-ness.

SLEEPING

Most hotels (and restaurants) open only from mid-May to mid-October and for Christmas and New Year. Some restaurants open at weekends in low season. Reservations are essential in the high season.

our pick Alaçatı Taş Otel (☎ 716 7772; www.tasotel .com; Kemalpaşa Caddesi 132; s/d from TL180/240; ❇ ▣) The acorn from which the mighty oak has grown, the Taş, at the far eastern end of town, was the city's first boutique hotel. Under the dynamic direction of its owner, Zeynep Ozis, it's still setting the standard with gorgeous rooms overlooking a lovely walled garden with a large swimming pool. Lavish breakfasts of local produce (the hotel has its own olive grove) are served on a peaceful shaded terrace. Open year-round.

Sailors Medan Otel (☎ 716 8765; www.sailorsotel .com; Kemalpaşa Caddesi 66; r TL190-260; ❇) There

WINDSURFING & HIGH LIFE IN ALAÇATI

Alaçatı beach, which occupies a small bay 4km from the town, is being pulled in two different directions. Until recently a fairly deserted place, what appeal it had lay not so much in its small beach and rather bleak landscape, but in its flat waters and, more importantly, its strong, consistent northerly winds – blowing at a steady 16 to 17 knots – which have made it a big hit with the windsurfing community. It is now generally recognised as one of the prime destinations outside Europe for the sport.

However, the beach's proximity to Alaçatı town, which, from a standing start has over the past decade turned itself into one of the region's most exclusive bolt holes, has the developers circling. A large waterside complex, the Alaçatı Beach Resort, comprising a hotel, several restaurants and a beach club, recently opened, and a new development, 'Port Alaçatı', is under construction. When finished, it will comprise a 250-berth marina, several hotels, waterfront housing and an 18-hole golf course. So far just one hotel, the Port Hotel Alaçatı, is open.

Some locals have expressed reservations about the projects. Zeynep Ozis, owner of the town's first boutique hotel, is concerned 'not just because of the possible negative effect they could have on windsurfing – houses blocking the wind, pollution of the water, motorboats hurtling through surfers – but because of the damage that may be done to the ecology of the coastline', something for which there has been no proper scientific evaluation. To raise awareness of the issues, she has founded a campaign group, the Alaçatı Preservation Society, whose remit is to 'set the standards for the town' and to prevent the increase of 'self-destructing development' that has blighted so much of Turkey's coast. For their part, the people behind their developments maintain that the projects are being done in an environmentally sensitive way and will have no impact on windsurfing, which they see as one of the primary draws for the developments.

For now, windsurfing continues largely unhindered, with the main season running from mid-May to the beginning of November. Around a dozen windsurfing clubs, plus a few hotels, now cater for the sport. Note that in high season, equipment and lessons should be booked at least one week in advance. Recommended:

Alaçatı Windsurf Okolu (☎ 0232-716 6161; www.alacatiwindsurf.com) Part of the mammoth Alaçatı Beach Resort, this offers two-hour windsurfing lessons for €90, six-hour lessons for €130 and 10-hour lessons for €180, plus board rental for €60 per day.

ASPC (Alaçatı Surf Paradise Club; ☎ 0232-716 6611; www.alacatı.de; Liman Yolu; boards per day €30-60, wetsuits per day €10; ⏱ 15 Mar-Oct) The largest windsurfing club in Turkey, this German-run operation is professionally managed, offering good courses and high-quality equipment. A three-hour starter course is €75, a 10-hour one €130. Kite-surfing instruction is also offered for €162 for six hours.

are two Sailors Hotels: this one on the main square, which has a buzzing streetside café, is a slightly quieter, more expensive choice, a couple of minutes from the main road. It's decorated in a refined-rustic style. The friendly owners also operate Café Agrilia.

Değirmen Otel (☎ 716 6714; www.alacatidegirmen .com; Değirmen Sokak 3; d €120) Taking fancy to a whole new level, this boutique hotel occupies three converted windmills set on a small hill near the main entrance to town. Rustic in feel but beautifully decorated – right down to old telephones and original stone hearths – with a great open terrace restaurant. It's a gorgeous place.

O Ev Hotel (☎ 716 6150; www.o-ev.com, in Turkish; Kemalpaşa Caddesi; d TL310-340; 🐾) In a restored olive-oil warehouse, this beautiful boutique

hotel rather resembles a small Moorish palace. There's a small pool set in pretty walled gardens and the gourmet restaurant has an excellent reputation. Breakfast is an extra TL25.

EATING

There are few better places to eat in the whole north Aegean than Alaçatı, although you will have to pay for the privilege. Of the 30-plus restaurants to have opened in the past decade, the vast majority are gourmet affairs aimed at the smart set, with mains typically starting at around TL18. The style of service offered in Alaçatı's restaurants is also a change from the tourist norm. Far from being accosted by zealous waiters eager to grab your custom and sit you down, you're more likely to be met with a cold, appraising stare. In Alaçatı, the restaurateurs expect their customers to beg for attention, not the other way round.

Rasim (☎ 716 8420; Kemalpaşa Caddesi 44; meals with salad TL8-12; ☻ 8am-11pm) Established in 1962, this simple but cheerful restaurant (the town's first) is still serving hearty Turkish fare at excellent prices. There's also a point-and-pick counter.

Yusuf Usta Ev Yemekleri (☎ 716 8823; Zeytinci Is Merkezi 1; mains from TL8; ☻ 11am-1am) With most of the town's restaurants specialising in 'modern Turkish' and various 'fusion' cuisines, it's nice to go somewhere where the cuisine (and prices) remain traditional. It serves excellent, cheap home-cooked fare – soups, kebaps, pide etc.

Cafe Agrilia (☎ 716 8594; Kemalpaşa Caddesi 75; mains TL16-30; ☻ 9am-midnight) One of the town's oldest 'new' restaurants (it's been open over a decade) and still considered one of the best, enjoying a lovely cool dining room, set in a former tobacco warehouse and serving a top-notch Italian-inspired menu.

Lavanta (☎ 716 6891; Kemalpaşa Caddesi 99; mains TL16-35; ☻ 9am-midnight) If you're tired of Turkish, this Mediterranean bistro-style place serves good Italian- and French-inspired dishes. There are also tables outside.

Kalamata (☎ 716 6357; Seydi Reis Sokak 4; mezes TL7-9, mains TL18-35) A very Alaçatı sort of affair: superb 'modern Turkish' food, a picturesque alley setting and jazz tinkling in the background. To find it look for the sign giving distances to various European capitals.

GETTING THERE & AWAY

Frequent dolmuşes run from Çeşme to Alaçatı (TL2, 10 minutes, 9km), and from İzmir to Çeşme via Alaçatı (TL10, one hour, 75km).

SIĞACIK
☎ 0232

More remote and much less spoilt than many coastal towns, Sığacık is a pretty port village, tucked inside crumbling medieval walls. With no beach (which deters the crowds), there's not much to do here except stroll the picturesque waterfront, take a boat trip and watch the fishermen returning with their catch. Tranquil and peaceful, it's a lovely place to relax.

Sığacık is also famous for its fish, particularly *barbun*, and *kalamar*. If you haven't yet indulged in Turkey's wonderful fresh fish, now might be the time.

Sleeping & Eating

Sığacık's hotels are situated on the waterfront. To find them head towards the harbour then follow the waterfront promenade to the right beside the city walls.

With a nice family feel and well-maintained, attractive rooms, **Teos Pansiyon** (☎ 745 7463; www.teospension.com; 126 Sokak 14; s/d TL30/60; ☒) is great value. Four rooms have sea views, six are like little suites. You can also buy fresh fish from the market and ask the obliging family to cook it for you.

Around 60m beyond the Teos at the far end of the bay, **Sahil Pansiyon** (☎ 745 7199; fax 745 7741; 127 Sokak 48; d small/large €22/28) has 10 simple but cheerful rooms, five with gorgeous Aegean views.

Dominating the harbour, the **Yeni Buṛ Restaurant** (☎ 745 7305; Liman Meydanı 17; ☻ 8am-1am) and **Liman** (☎ 745 7011; Liman Meydanı 19; ☻ 9am-11pm) are slightly soulless and touristy. They're not cheap (TL15 to TL25 for 500g of fish), but the fish is fresh and the seafront views are good.

For cheaper eats, cut inland behind the Burg Pansiyon to find **Çerkezağa** (☎ 745 7421; Sığacık Çarşı İçi 7; kebaps €3.35-3.80; ☻ 8.30am-midnight) next to the teahouse, with tables in a delightful courtyard around an old drinking fountain.

Getting There & Away

To get to Sığacık from İzmir you must first take a bus to Seferihisar from the Üçkuyular otogar (p228; TL4.50, 50 minutes); buses leave every 20 minutes. From Seferihisar there are regular dolmuşes and buses to Sığacık (TL1.25, 10 minutes, 5km).

Coming from Çeşme you will have to travel via İzmir; no dolmuşes run along the coast road from Çeşme to Urla.

AKKUM & TEOS
☎ 0232

Two kilometres over the hills from Sığacık is the turn-off west to **Akkum**. A protected cove, it used to attract windsurfers in their thousands in summer but has recently been rather eclipsed by Alaçatı (see boxed text, p235). Because of this, it's quieter and cheaper than Alaçatı and has larger waves.

Of its two smooth, sandy beaches, Büyük Akkum has the better facilities, but Küçük Akkum is likely to be quieter.

A few kilometres past Akkum are the scattered **ruins** at Teos, primarily a few picturesque fluted columns re-erected amid grass and olive groves left over from a temple to Dionysus. Teos was once a vast Ionian city, and you can roam the fields in search of other remnants (including a theatre and an *odeon*, used for musical performances). It's a good place to come for a picnic.

To get here, follow the road from Sığacık, turn left off the main road where signposted, then keep left all the way to the bottom of the hill (around 5km from Sığacık).

Sleeping & Eating

Club Resort Atlantis (☎ 745 7455; www.clubresort atlantis.com; s/d from €68/90; 🏊) With two pools, a PADI dive centre, windsurfing school, mountain biking, water-sports facilities, fitness centre, beach volleyball, basketball and tennis courts, the resort is a great place for an activity holiday. Windsurfing board hire is €20/50 per hour/day. Sailing, snorkelling and fishing trips are also available.

From Akkum, head up to the main road and turn right to the **Teos Orman İçi Dinlenme Yeri**, a pine-shaded forestry department picnic grove about 1km east of the turn-off. Here you can buy snacks and cold drinks to enjoy beneath shady pine trees overlooking the sea.

Getting There & Away

In summer, frequent dolmuşes and city buses run to Akkum from Seferihisar (TL2.50, 20 minutes) via Sığacık.

Taking a taxi to Teos (3km) shouldn't cost more than TL30 including waiting time (but negotiate).

NORTH AEGEAN

South Aegean

With its coast home to some of the country's largest and most popular resorts and its interior seemingly filled with the faded wonders of lost civilizations, the south Aegean would seem the perfect place to experience the best of both modern and ancient Turkey. True, the region has its critics – its swarming, package-orientated holiday towns are not to everyone's taste and there are too many examples of once-idyllic hillsides having been submerged beneath gluts of ugly, hastily erected hotels and holiday apartments – but the good points easily outweigh the bad.

Development has extended its tentacles inland, but its embrace is by no means complete. Unspoilt, undeveloped pockets remain at places like Pamucak and the Dilek National Park, a glorious wilderness and wildlife haven. So rich is the area's history that it sometimes seems that for every modern high-rise there are another three ancient ruins. These include the grand-daddy of them all, Ephesus, one of the Mediterranean's best-preserved classical cities, even if it is today as big a tourist trap as any of the coastal towns, and often just as crowded. Priene, Labranda and Iasos receive far fewer visitors, and as such perhaps offer more pointed evocations of the faded past, their ancient stones now overgrown with weeds and home to scuttling lizards.

But you can only deny the area's true nature for so long. For all its aesthetic and historic wonders, there's no denying that the south Aegean is primarily visited for its party towns: Kuşadası, bloated, ugly and almost entirely artificial, but possessing a fine and surprisingly varied nightlife; and classier Bodrum, with its winning summer combination of cool cafés and a thumping, pumping, laser-strobing club scene.

HIGHLIGHTS

- Come see how the Romans lived, worked and played at **Ephesus** (p246), the best-preserved classical city in the eastern Mediterranean

- Explore the fragrant world of fruit wine at the charming hillside village of **Şirince** (p251), set amid blooming orchards

- Dive intensely, dine stylishly and dance wildly in **Bodrum** (p267), the region's premiere party town

- Try tracking down the rare Anatolian panther, then cool off with a swim in a secluded cove in the wonderful wilderness of **Dilek National Park** (p259)

- Be overwhelmed by natural splendour at **Bafa Gölü** (p263), a glorious lake fringed by olive-clad hills

- Roam the remarkable but less-visited ruins of **Priene** (p261), **Miletus** (p262) and **Didyma** (p262)

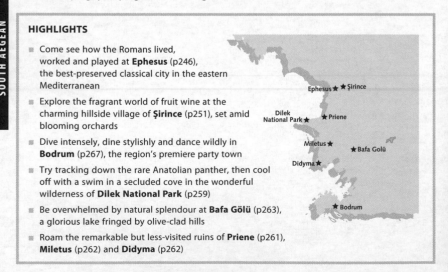

Ephesus ★ ★ Şirince

Dilek National Park ★ ★ Priene

Miletus ★ ★ Bafa Gölü

Didyma ★

★ Bodrum

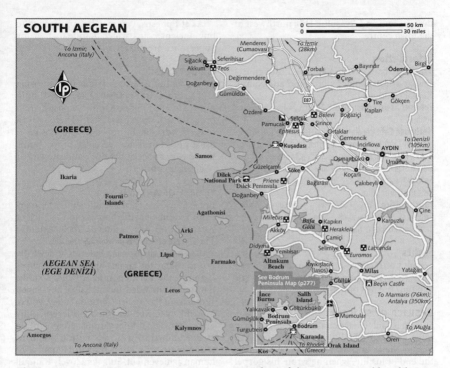

SOUTH AEGEAN

History

The Mycenaean and Hittite civilisations were the earliest recorded along the south Aegean. From 1200 BC, Ionians fleeing Greece established themselves in the area along the coast and founded important cities at Ephesus, Priene and Miletus. South of Ionia was mountainous Caria where the great King Mausolus' tomb, the Mausoleum of Halicarnassus, became one of the Seven Wonders of the Ancient World. Caria was also home to Herodotus, the 'Father of History'. Roman Ephesus prospered with rich trade and commerce, becoming the capital of Asia Minor. The city also attracted a sizeable Christian population. St John settled here with the Virgin Mary, where he is said to have written his gospel. In the 15th century the Knights of St John briefly captured the area now called Bodrum before the Ottoman forces took over.

SELÇUK

☎ 0232 / pop 27,280

For such a major tourist destination, visitors might expect Selçuk to be a bit more than it is. After all, it's the site of one of the Seven

Wonders of the Ancient World and boasts an excellent museum, a fine old basilica and mosque, a stork nest–studded aqueduct and, of course, the ruins of Ephesus right on its doorstep. However, compared to the vast tourism factory of nearby Kuşadası, Selçuk's tourism industry is more of a small scale, workshop-sized affair. It's not exactly a provincial backwater, but it's not too far removed either, with a collection of pleasant, low-key pensions that cater mainly to independent travellers on budgets.

Orientation

Selçuk otogar (bus station) lies just east of the İzmir–Aydın road (Atatürk Caddesi), with the town centre and some pensions immediately north of it. Three pedestrianised shopping streets – Namık Kemal, Cengiz Topel and Siegburg Caddesis – run east from a round fountain on the main road, north of the otogar, through to the train station.

On the western side of the main road a park spreads out in front of one wing of the famous Ephesus Museum. Many more small pensions can be found in the quiet, hilly streets between

SOUTH AEGEAN

the museum and Ayasuluk Hill, northwest of the town centre.

Information
There are banks with ATMs and foreign exchange offices along Cengiz Topel and Namık Kemal Caddesis.

Ephesus Assistance (☎ 892 2500) A 24-hour medical hotline.

Nethouse Café (Siegburg Caddesi 4/B; per hr TL1.50; ⏱ 8am-1am) Just around the corner from the town hall.

Post office (☎ 892 6480; Cengiz Topel Caddesi) Will also change cash, travellers cheques and Eurocheques.

Selçuk Hospital (☎ 892 7036; Dr Sabri Yayla Bulvarı) Near the tourist office.

Tourist office (☎ 892 6945; www.selcuk.gov.tr; Agora Caddesi 35; ⏱ 8am-noon & 1-5pm Mon-Fri winter, daily in summer) Opposite the museum.

Sights
Selçuk's attractions open from 8am to 7pm May to September and 8am to 5pm (or 5.30pm) the rest of the year.

BASILICA OF ST JOHN
St John is said to have come to Ephesus twice: once between AD 37 and AD 48 with the Virgin Mary, and again in AD 95 towards the end of his life, when he wrote his gospel on Ayasuluk Hill. A 4th-century tomb was believed to house his remains, so in the 6th century Emperor Justinian (527–65) erected a magnificent church, the **Basilica of St John** (St Jean Caddesi; admission TL5), on top of the tomb.

Earthquakes and building-material scavengers left it as a heap of rubble until a century ago when restoration began; virtually all of what you see now is restored. Nevertheless, it's still a very impressive building. In its day it was considered a near-marvel and attracted thousands of medieval pilgrims and still draws busloads of 'holy site' tourists during the season. Look out for the information panel with a plan and drawing, which gives a very good idea of the building's once-vast size – as do the old marble steps and monumental gate. It's well worth a wander.

Ayasuluk Hill offers fine views of the surrounding sites. The hilltop **citadel** to the north was constructed by the Byzantines in the 6th century, rebuilt by the Seljuks and restored in modern times. It remains closed since part of the wall collapsed. Restoration work is under way and it should eventually reopen, though lack of funding seems to be holding it up.

As at Ephesus, you may be approached to buy 'ancient' coins, which despite their grimy appearance are modern.

İSA BEY CAMİİ
At the foot of Ayasuluk Hill is the imposing and beautiful **İsa Bey Camii** (St Jean Caddesi), built in 1375 by the Emir of Aydın in a post-Seljuk/pre-Ottoman transitional style. There's a bust of İsa Bey diagonally opposite. The mosque is usually open to visitors except at prayer times. Leave your shoes at the door and remember to cover up properly.

TEMPLE OF ARTEMIS
Ephesus used to earn sizeable sums of money from pilgrims paying homage to the ancient Anatolian fertility goddess Cybele/Artemis. The **Temple of Artemis** (Artemis Tapınağı; admission free; ⏱ 8.30am-5.30pm), between Ephesus and Selçuk, was in its day the largest in the world, eclipsing even the Parthenon at Athens, a status that got it included in the list of the Seven Wonders of the Ancient World. Today, you're more likely to wonder where it all went. Only one of its original 127 columns remains, often as not topped by a stork's nest, a poignant testament to the often transitory nature of human achievement. Still, it's a lovely tranquil place, the enormous pillar giving you some indication of the vast size of the temple.

EPHESUS MUSEUM
This excellent **museum** (☎ 892 6010; Uğur Mumcu Sevgi Yolu Caddesi; admission TL5) houses a striking collection of artefacts recovered from the ancient city. The first gallery you come to is dedicated to finds from the Terrace Houses of Ephesus – scales, jewellery, cosmetic boxes etc. This is also where you'll find the famous effigy of Priapus, the Phallic God, as seen plastered on every postcard from İstanbul to Antakya. No doubt to avoid offending delicate sensibilities, it's displayed inside a darkened case. Press the light to see him illuminated in all his rampant glory.

The other display areas, which include an outdoor courtyard, hold, among other things, collections of coins, grave goods and plenty of statuary, ranging from hand-sized representations of Eros to an enormous, and slightly creepy looking, head and arm of the Emperor Domitian, which once formed part of a 7m-high statue. Look out as well for the exquisitely carved multi-breasted marble

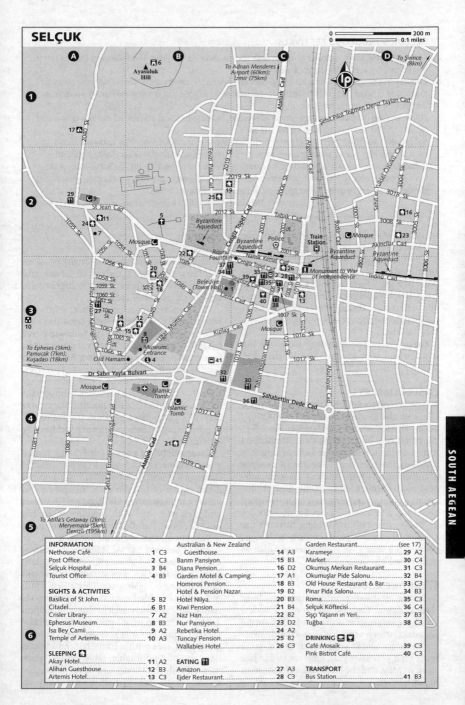

SELÇUK

SOUTH AEGEAN

SELÇUK'S FABULOUS FESTIVALS

For such a tiny town, Selçuk has more than its fair share of festivals. The following lists its finest. If you can, try and coincide your visit with one.

Camel Wrestling (Third Sunday in January) From all across Turkey, camel owners marshal their male camels for the big fight in Selçuk. The eve of the festival is celebrated with much feasting, drinking and dancing. For more on the wrestling itself, see the boxed text, p245.

Oil Wrestling (First Sunday in May) Famous oil wrestlers, known in Turkish as *pehlivan*, rub themselves from head to foot with olive oil then grapple each other until one gives up.

Selçuk/Efes Festival (First week of September) This showcase of traditional dance from Turkey and around the world sees each country's representatives stage an energetic demonstration of their homeland's highlights. During the festival, Turkish folk and pop music concerts are also held throughout the city. The bazaar is one of the festival's main venues, with the erection of a stage for musicians and dancers, as well as a craft village where potters, glassmakers, carvers, furniture makers and carpet weavers demonstrate their skills.

With thanks to Osman Bölük for help compiling this information

---

statues of Cybele/Artemis, which have become icons of the city.

The final room, near the entrance, holds an interesting exhibition based on the excavations of a gladiators' cemetery discovered in 1993. Displays describe the gladiators' weapons, detail their training regimes and cheerfully catalogue the various gruesome injuries they suffered.

Go early in the morning to avoid the schools and tour groups, and ideally after seeing Ephesus.

CRISLER LIBRARY

A new arrival to Selçuk, **Crisler Library** (☎ 892 8317; www.crislerlibraryephesos.com; Prof Anton Kallinger Caddesi 40; admission free; ⊙ 10am-5pm Mon-Fri) is the result of a bequest from a distinguished American biblical scholar and archaeologist, B Cobbey Crisler. Proving to be a terrific source of information on the ancient, classical, biblical and Islamic history of the area, it also boasts a full lecture program, a well-stocked bookshop and a coffee shop. Set up in order to 'build cross-cultural bridges through the medium of education and scholarly exchange', it's worth a visit – for neophytes as much as hard-core Ephesus fanatics.

BYZANTINE AQUEDUCT

Running east–west intermittently along Namık Kemal Caddesi and İnönü Caddesi stand the impressive remains of a Byzantine aqueduct, which serve today as a handy nesting place for storks who return to the same spots on it year after year. Eggs are laid in late April or May, and the birds stay right through to September.

Sleeping

BUDGET

Competition between Selçuk's many pensions is intense, and the standard of service and value offered by these places is higher here than perhaps anywhere else.

Pension and hotel prices are set by the municipality, so proprietors tend to compete on extras. Most offer the following: free breakfast, home-cooked meals at good prices, free transport to Ephesus and Meryemana (and sometimes Şirince), free use of bicycles, good-value excursions and free internet access. If any of these are particularly important to you, check first. Many hotels charge extra (say TL2 per person per day) for use of air-conditioning or fans in summer and heating in winter.

Garden Motel & Camping (☎ 892 6165; info@galleriaselciukidi.com; Kale Altı 5; camp sites per person/tent/car/campervan TL10/5/5/10, tent hire for TL12; ⬜) Located 200m north of the mosque, this green and grassy camping ground is large, well designed and well provided with facilities including kitchen, pool, laundry facilities, a very good restaurant and amusements for children.

Atilla's Getaway (☎ 892 3847; www.atillasgetaway .com; dm €8, bungalows without bathroom €8, r with bathroom €16; ⬜ ⬜) This is an attractively laid-out camping and bungalow complex 2.5km south of Selçuk. Presided over by the eponymous Atilla, an extremely welcoming and helpful Turkish-Australian, it's packed with facilities and has a fun, buzzing atmosphere. There's a great pool area with a lively bar, and guests have use of a pool table, table tennis equipment, a volleyball court and travel office. The rooms are simple but nicely done and airy, although you can get air-con for an extra €4.50. Half-board is an extra €5.

Western Selçuk
Australia & New Zealand Guesthouse (☎ 892 6050; www.anzguesthouse.com; 1064 Sokak 12; dm TL12.50, d with/without bathroom TL45/30; ✖ 🖳) The rules posted in each room, 'don't smoke, don't be loud, don't eat your own, don't leave late, don't lose your key', suggest that this is a less welcoming place than is actually the case. Lots of comfortable clutter – sofas, cushions, rugs etc – adorn its central courtyard; the rooms are small and simple, and there's a great covered roof terrace where barbecue dinners are served for TL12. Movie nights are also occasionally organised up here. Bike hire is free or you can hire a motor-scooter for TL35 a day. Air-con is an extra TL9.50 a day, breakfast TL3.

Barım Pansiyon (☎ 892 6923; barim_pansiyon@hotmail.com; 1045 Sokak 34; r per person TL25; 🖳) This has a more staid vibe than some of the town's other more party-orientated pensions and is a good choice for anyone wanting simple accommodation, friendly, helpful (but not intrusive) staff and a bit of peace and quiet. The rooms in this attractive 140-year-old stone house (its hideous exterior notwithstanding) are comfortable and filled with the wrought-iron work of Adnan, the owner. There's also a pleasant courtyard.

Alihan Guesthouse (☎ 892 9496; alihanguesthouse@yahoo.com; 1045 Sokak 34; r with shower per person TL25; ✖) All spick and span with gleaming wood following a recent renovation, this is a cheery little place, just up the hill from the park, presided over by the keen-to-please Isa, his wife Melissa, and Sheila the dog. It's a mishmash of styles but is friendly, informal and cheap.

Homeros Pension (☎ 892 3995; www.homerospension.com; 1050 Sokak 3; s/d TL25/50; ✖) On a quiet alley, the Homeros has rooms spread over two houses, all imprinted with the quirky character of the welcoming owner, Derviş. A carpenter, he is responsible for most of the traditional-style furniture, which gives the rooms a real lift, lacking in some of the more basically decorated competitors. Both buildings have roof terraces with good views.

Hotel & Pension Nazar (☎ 892 2222; www.nazarhotel.com; 2019 Sokak 14; s/d TL35/50; ✖ ✖ 🖳) Completely overhauled a few years ago, the Nazar now offers a superior standard of pension accommodation. The 13 rooms are big, clean and comfortable. Air-con is a rather steep €10 a day, although this is offset by superb home-cooked meals served on the roof terrace for a very reasonable €7. There's also a pool set in a courtyard-garden and an ever-friendly welcome from the owner, Osman.

Tuncay Pension (☎ 892 6260; www.tuncaypension.com.tr; 2019 Sokak 1; d with/without air-con €50/35; ✖) It's a touch expensive for a pension, but a good choice, nonetheless, with very friendly owners. There's a cool courtyard area with a fountain where generous breakfasts are served, and the rooms are a good size and nicely decorated.

Also recommended if the above are full is the **Akay Hotel** (☎ 892 7249; www.hotelakay.com; 1054 Sokak 7; s €14-25, d €28-33; ✖ 🖳). The hotel's main asset is its small pool set in a peaceful garden full of birdsong. The large roof terrace also has good views.

Eastern Selçuk
Kiwi Pension (Alison's Place; ☎ 892 4892; www.kiwipension.com; 1038 Sokak 26; dm TL12, s/d without bathroom TL20/32, s/d with bathroom TL25/40; 🖳) Presided over by the energetic Alison, an English woman, the Kiwi Pension is well run, friendly and receives glowing reports from travellers. Rooms are simple but spotless and bright (complete with fresh daisies in a bedside glass), and a few have balconies. Guests can use the pool table, kitchen and laundry facilities and have access to a large and lovely private pool set 1km away in a mandarin orchard.

Diana Pension (☎ 892 1265; brothers_place@mynet.com; 3004 Sokak 30; s/d without bathroom TL20/30, s/d with bathroom TL25/40; ✖ 🖳) If you're counting your Turkish lira, the Diana is cheap and cheerful with a pretty courtyard and terrace. It's quite close to the train station.

Artemis Hotel (☎ 892 6191; www.artemisguesthouse.net; 1012 Sokak 2; s/d €25/40; ✖) Following its recent renovation the Artemis, close to the train station, is still pretty good value. All rooms have large, new beds, fresh linen and decent bathrooms. There's also a courtyard and a carpeted lounge area with nargileh pipes (traditional water pipe for smoking).

Nur Pansiyon (☎ 892 6595; www.nurpension.com; 3004 Sokak 16; s/d TL28/44; ✖ 🖳) Past the train station in a part of town that can seem quite spooky and dark at night – but is generally pretty safe – the Nur is competitively priced, offering accommodation that is probably one class up from the Diana. The bedrooms are comfortable, but the bathrooms are rather small. The owners can help arrange tours.

If the above are full, try **Wallabies Hotel** (☎ 892 3204; www.wallabieshotel.com; Cengız Topel Caddesi 2; s/d €11/22; ✺ 🖳) where some rooms have aqueduct views.

MIDRANGE
Naz Han (☎ 892 8731; nazhanhotel@gmail.com; 1044 Sokak 2; r €50-70; ✺ 🖳) Living up to its name, which means 'coy', the Naz Han is hidden away behind high walls. This 100-year-old Greek house has five simple but comfortable rooms arranged around a charming little courtyard filled with trinkets, artefacts and antiques. A small roof terrace grants views over Selçuk's scenic surrounds.

Hotel Nilya (☎ 892 9081; www.nilya.com; 1051 Sokak 7; s/d TL75/115; ✺) The courtyard of the Nilya, set behind a high wall, is a lovely, calm place with shady trees, lanterns and a tinkling fountain. The traditionally decorated rooms, though perfectly reasonable, don't quite come up to the same standard, being a little dark with small (and not particularly new) bathrooms. Still, it makes a relaxing choice. Meals can be arranged on request.

Rebetika Hotel (☎ 892 8078; www.rebetikahotel.com; 1054 Sokak 2; s/d TL80/120; ✺ ✺ 🖳) The town's first avowedly 'boutique' offering, the Rebetika has a nice, fresh, newly-minted feel to it, especially as (another town first) it's completely non-smoking. It does conform to local type with its roof terrace, but this is nicely done and the rooms have wooden floors and large wrought iron beds, although the decorations are perhaps more suggestive of 'upmarket *pansiyon*' than true boutique.

Eating
RESTAURANTS
Ejder Restaurant (☎ 892 3296; Cengiz Topel Caddesi 9/E; pide TL4, kebap TL7; ✷ 8.30am-11pm) A firm favourite with travellers, this simple little place has seating on a café-lined square with views of the aqueduct. It's run by a welcoming husband-and-wife team: Mehmet does the meat, his wife the veg – she can put together a mean vegetable kebap, but then all the food is pretty tasty.

Okumuş Mercan Restaurant (☎ 892 6196; 1006 Sokak 44; mezes TL4-5, mains TL7-9; ✷ 7am-11pm) Set in a courtyard beside a fountain in the shade of a 100-year-old mulberry tree, this place is loved locally for its traditional home fare at good prices.

Garden Restaurant (☎ 892 6165; Garden Motel, Kale Altı 5; mezes TL5.50, mains TL7-11; ✷ 8am-11pm) About

as organic an experience as you'll find in town, the restaurant enjoys a great bucolic setting amid plots where the majority of the produce that finds its way onto your plate is grown. And to keep things totally fresh, there's also a pick-and-point trout pond. The selection of mezes, which includes some tasty stuffed vine leaves, is particularly good.

Selçuk Köftecisi (☎ 892 6696; Şahabettin Dede Caddesi; köfte TL6, mains TL6-9; ✷ 8am-9pm winter, 8am-midnight summer) Established way back in 1959, and rather monopolised by tour groups these days, this family-run place opposite the market nonetheless churns out some superb home cooking at decent prices. If you want a table outside in the shade, come early or late.

Old House Restaurant & Bar (Eski Ev; ☎ 892 9357; 1005 Sokak 1/A; mains TL6-9; ✷ 8am-midnight) With tables set in a little courtyard amid grapefruit and pomegranate trees, and decorated with lanterns, bird cages and wicker chairs, this is a pretty, cool and intimate place that does tasty Turkish dishes. Try the appetising speciality 'Old House Kebap' (TL9) served sizzling on a platter.

Amazon (☎ 892 3879; Prof Anton Kallinger Caddesi 22; mains TL10-18; ✷ 10am-midnight) It's certainly one of the best-looking restaurants with a cool modern interior – stools around the bar and paintings by local artists on the walls. The menu is a bit of a hotchpotch of international dishes, some pretty good, some not so. The outside seating, just across the road, has views of one of the Seven Wonders of the Ancient World (and it's not every restaurant that can say that).

CAFÉS & QUICK EATS
Roma (☎ 892 6436; Siegburg Caddesi 21; 1 scoop TL1; ✷ 8am-midnight Apr-Dec) Having learnt the art of making ice cream from his father, Feridun, the owner, now produces some heavenly homemade flavours. His particular recommendations are: walnut, black mulberry and mixed chocolate.

Okumuşlar Pide Salonu (☎ 892 6906; Şahabettin Dede Caddesi 2; pide TL4; ✷ 10am-11pm) Next door to the bus station (and one of several branches), this busy place does fabulous pides (including veggie ones).

Pınar Pide Salonu (☎ 892 9913; Siegburg Caddesi 3; pide TL4; ✷ 9am-midnight) Some travellers claim that this little place serves the best pide anywhere. That may be stretching it a bit, but it definitely does what it does very well. Pide

---

CAMEL WRESTLING

Though camel wrestling exists throughout Turkey, it's primarily found along the Western Mediterranean and particularly Aegean coasts. Selçuk holds an annual festival (see the boxed text, p242), which is a great place to witness this ancient sport.

Wrestling camels known as *tülüs* are bred by crossing two distinct breeds. During winter, the camels come into season, which gets them interested in doing two things: finding a female to mate with, and fighting off any potential male rivals. Harnessing the latter behaviour is where the festival comes in, as the locals bring the aggressive, sexually-charged males together to 'wrestle'.

Though the camels' desire to fight is natural, ancient rules and practices govern the sport. First and foremost, camels must use accepted 'techniques' for wrestling. A board of judges and referees presides over the match and 14 *urgancı* (ropers) are close at hand to step in and separate the camels if required. The camel's mouths are also bound tightly with string so that they cannot bite one another. Instead, the camels must use their heads, necks and bodies to overcome their opponents. For a camel to be declared a winner, he must either force his opponent to flee the ring or force him to fall on to his side.

If you get the chance to watch a wrestle, do so: it's a colourful event. The venue used to be the stadium at Ephesus – what a spectacle that must have been – but was changed to a field near Pamucak a few years ago for fear of what an angry ungulate might do to the ancient ruins. Town criers publicise the event, then the *tülüs* – decked out in all their finery – are proudly paraded through the streets by their owners, accompanied by drummers and musicians, before the wrestling begins. There's no official seating, rather spectators watch from a 'natural grandstand' formed by a dip in the field. Tickets are around TL5.

---

are the mainstay, but it also does some pretty good kebaps and salads.

Sişçı Yaşar ın Yeri (☎ 892 3487; Atatürk Caddesi; ☣ 9am-10pm winter, 10am-midnight summer) This small stall on the main road is hugely popular with those in-the-know for its delicious *köfte* (meatballs) and kebaps (all TL6). Although rather hidden away, there's a small, shaded seating area around the back with a few tables.

Karameşe (☎ 892 0466; St Jean Cadessi 18; meals about TL10; ☣ 9am-midnight) Perhaps the town's most idyllic café, Karameşe lies away from the central hurly-burly, amid cool, rambling gardens adorned with statues and artefacts. It's a great place for a cuppa, a *gözleme* (savoury crepe, TL4) or even a snooze.

SELF-CATERING

Tuğba (☎ 892 1773; 1006 Sokak; ☣ 9am-midnight) This well-known chain sells Turkish delight in all colours, flavours and forms, as well as dried nuts, seeds and fruit (great for long bus journeys). They also gift-wrap if you want to cart a year's supply home.

Every Saturday, Selçuk holds a fantastic **market** (Şahabettin Dede Caddesi; ☣ 9am-5pm winter, 8am-7pm summer) behind the bus station. With its fresh fruit, veg, cheese and olives, it's a great place to stock up for a picnic.

Drinking

Pink Bistro Café (☎ 892 9801; Siegburg Caddesi 24; beer big/small TL5/2.50; ☣ 10am-2am winter, 10am-4am summer) The oldest drinking establishment in Selçuk, it's called a café, looks like a pub, but functions as a bar-cum-nightclub. Ask Mesut, the bartender, to demonstrate some magic tricks.

Café Mosaik (☎ 892 6508; 1005 Sokak 6/B; beer/nargileh €1.65/2.75; ☣ 10pm-1am winter, 9.30pm-3am summer) Kind of like an open-ended den, Café Mosaik is carpet-clad and cushioned and decorated very much *à la Turquie*. It's a fun place for beer or a nargileh with a good mix of European, Turkish and Arabic music.

Getting There & Around
BUS & DOLMUŞ

Selçuk's otogar is across the road from the tourist office. While it's easy enough to get to Selçuk direct from İzmir (TL6, one hour, 80km), coming from the south or east you generally have to change at Aydın, from where buses leave almost hourly to other destinations (such as Bodrum, Marmaris, Fethiye, Denizli and Antalya). Dolmuşes (minibuses) to Aydın (TL5, one hour) leave every 40 minutes from Selçuk.

There are direct buses from Selçuk nightly for İstanbul (TL45, 11 hours) via Bursa, and in summer at least one bus daily to Denizli (TL19).

Dolmuşes run to Kuşadası every 20 minutes (TL4, 30 minutes) and Pamucak (TL2.50, 10 minutes). There are no buses or dolmuşes to Söke; either change at Kuşadası or take a train (below).

If you're going to Priene, Mila or Didyma, the easiest way is to go to Söke and get one of the many buses from there.

TAXI
Taxi rides around town usually cost TL5 and to İzmir airport €80 to €100 (though many pensions can organise it for less). You can usually find taxis around the bus station.

TRAIN
Six trains run daily from **Selçuk train station** (☎ 892 6006) to İzmir (TL3.25, two hours), the first at 6.25am and the last at 7pm year-round. Trains also leave every evening to Söke (one hour) – the first at 7am, the last at 6pm – and five leave daily to Denizli (four hours): the first at 9.39am, the last at 11.05pm.

EPHESUS (EFES)
The best-preserved classical city in the eastern Mediterranean, **Ephesus** (☎ 892 6010; admission/parking TL20/3; ☺ 8am-5pm Oct-Apr, 8am-7pm May-Sep) is *the* place to get a feel for what life was like in Roman times. For information on the two different entrance gates, see p250.

Ancient Ephesus was a great trading city and a centre for the cult of Cybele, the Anatolian fertility goddess. Under the influence of the Ionians, Cybele became Artemis, the virgin goddess of the hunt and the moon, and a fabulous temple was built in her honour. When the Romans took over and made this part of the province of Asia, Artemis became Diana and Ephesus became the Roman provincial capital.

To avoid the heat of the day – which can get extremely intense, the sun reflecting harshly off the stones – come early in the morning or in the late afternoon. In the height of summer Ephesus can be a very crowded place, with busloads of visitors pouring in. But, in a way, all those people do at least make it easier for you to visualise it as a proper, working metropolis. The city load of people it welcomes every day has the effect of making Ephesus seem quite city-like – noisy, congested and, at times, rather frustrating. To avoid the very

worst (but by no means all) of the crowds, the advice is again to get here either early or late. And, if possible, try to avoid public holidays altogether. Note that the terrace houses cost an extra TL15 (and take about an hour) to visit.

You can hire one of the Ephesus guides (two hours for two to 20 people for €40) who hang around the ticket barriers. Consider bringing water with you as drinks at the site are expensive.

There are also (and quite good) one-hour **audio guides** (adult TL5) available. Note that only Turkish lira are accepted for the admission fee. An exchange office operates opposite the ticket office if you need to change money.

History
EARLIEST TIMES
According to legend, Androclus, son of King Codrus of Athens, consulted an oracle about where to found a settlement in Ionia. The oracle answered in typically cryptic style: 'Choose the site indicated by the fish and the boar'.

Androclus sat down with some fishermen near the mouth of the Cayster River and Mt Pion (Panayır Dağı), the hill into which Ephesus' Great Theatre was later built. As they grilled some fish for lunch, one of the fish leapt out of the brazier, taking with it a hot coal, which ignited some shavings, which in turn ignited the nearby brush. A wild boar hiding in the brush ran in alarm from the fire and the spot at which the fishermen killed it became the site of Ephesus' Temple of Artemis (p240).

Despite modern tourist brochures' description of Ephesus as the place 'where history and sea meet', the two actually parted company a long time ago. In ancient times the sea came much further inland than it does today, almost as far as Selçuk, allowing early settlers to found a harbour, which by around 600 BC had become a prosperous city. The nearby sanctuary of Cybele/Artemis had been a place of pilgrimage since at least 800 BC.

CROESUS & THE PERSIANS
Ephesus prospered so much that it aroused the envy of King Croesus of Lydia, who attacked it around 600 BC. The Ephesians, who had neglected to build defensive walls, stretched a rope from the Temple of Artemis to the town, a distance of 1200m, hoping to win the

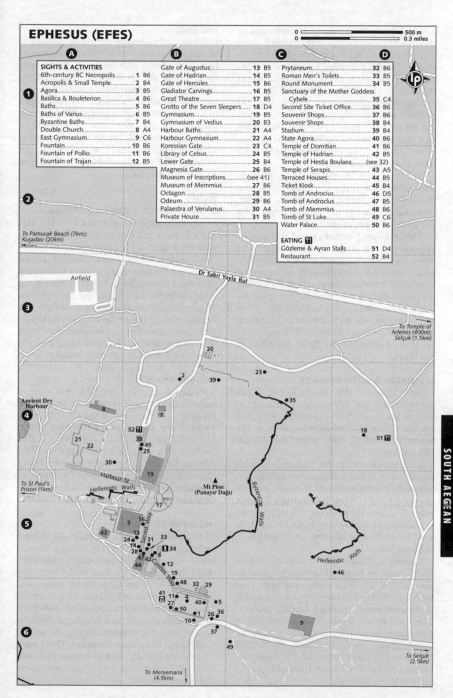

EPHESUS (EFES)

0 ————————————— 500 m
0 ————————————— 0.3 miles

SIGHTS & ACTIVITIES
6th-century BC Necropolis.......... 1 B6
Acropolis & Small Temple........... 2 B4
Agora.................................... 3 B5
Basilica & Bouleterion............... 4 B6
Baths.................................... 5 B6
Baths of Varius....................... 6 B5
Byzantine Baths....................... 7 B4
Double Church......................... 8 A4
East Gymnasium....................... 9 C6
Fountain................................ 10 B6
Fountain of Pollio.................... 11 B6
Fountain of Trajan................... 12 B5

Gate of Augustus...................... 13 B5
Gate of Hadrian....................... 14 B5
Gate of Hercules...................... 15 B6
Gladiator Carvings.................... 16 B5
Great Theatre.......................... 17 B5
Grotto of the Seven Sleepers.... 18 D4
Gymnasium............................. 19 B5
Gymnasium of Vedius............... 20 B3
Harbour Baths......................... 21 A4
Harbour Gymnasium................. 22 A4
Koressian Gate........................ 23 C4
Library of Celsus...................... 24 B5
Lower Gate............................. 25 B4
Magnesia Gate........................ 26 B6
Museum of Inscriptions..........(see 41)
Museum of Memmius............... 27 B6
Octagon................................. 28 B5
Odeum................................... 29 B6
Palaestra of Verulanus............. 30 A4
Private House.......................... 31 B5

Prytaneum.............................. 32 B6
Roman Men's Toilets................. 33 B5
Round Monument..................... 34 B5
Sanctuary of the Mother Goddess
  Cybele................................ 35 C4
Second Site Ticket Office........... 36 B6
Souvenir Shops........................ 37 B6
Souvenir Shops........................ 38 B4
Stadium................................. 39 B4
State Agora............................. 40 B6
Temple of Domitian.................. 41 B6
Temple of Hadrian.................... 42 B5
Temple of Hestia Boulaea........(see 32)
Temple of Serapis.................... 43 A5
Terraced Houses....................... 44 B5
Ticket Kiosk............................ 45 B4
Tomb of Androcius................... 46 D5
Tomb of Androclus................... 47 B5
Tomb of Memmius.................... 48 B6
Tomb of St Luke....................... 49 C6
Water Palace........................... 50 B6

EATING
Gözleme & Ayran Stalls............. 51 D4
Restaurant.............................. 52 B4

To Pamucak Beach (7km);
Kuşadası (20km)

Airfield

Dr Sabri Yayla Bul

To Temple of
Artemis (400m);
Selçuk (1.5km)

Ancient Dry
Harbour

8

7

52

38
45
25

21
22

30

19

2

39

23

35

18

51

Harbour St

To St Paul's
Prison (1km)

Hellenistic Walls

17

Mt Pion
(Panayır Dağı)

Byzantine Walls

43

3
16
13

24
14
28
47 42
44

33

34
6
12
15
48 32 29
41
11
27 4 40
50 1
10 26 36
37

Sacred Way

Curetes Way

Hellenistic Walls

46

5

9

49

To Meryemana
(4.5km)

To Selçuk
(2.5km)

SOUTH AEGEAN

goddess' protection. Croesus responded to this quaint defensive measure by giving some of his famous wealth for the completion of the temple. But he destroyed Ephesus and relocated its citizens inland to the southern side of the temple, where they built a new city.

Neglecting again (or perhaps forbidden) to build walls, the Ephesians were forced to pay tribute to Croesus' Lydia and, later, to the new regional masters, the Persians. They then joined the Athenian confederacy, but later fell back under Persian control.

In 356 BC the Temple of Cybele/Artemis was destroyed in a fire set by Herostratus, who claimed to have done it to get famous, proving that modern society has no monopoly on a perverted sense of celebrity.

The Ephesians planned a grand new temple, the construction of which was well under way when Alexander the Great arrived in 334 BC. Much impressed, Alexander offered to pay for the cost of construction in return for having the temple dedicated to himself. The Ephesians declined his offer, saying tactfully that it was not fitting for one god to make a dedication to another. When finished, the temple was recognised as one of the Seven Wonders of the World.

LYSIMACHUS & THE ROMANS

After Alexander the Great's death, Ionia came under the control of Lysimachus, one of his generals. As the harbour silted up, the Ephesians moved reluctantly to the western side of Mt Pion, where the Roman city remains.

Little survives of Lysimachus' city, although at one time it had a defensive wall almost 10km long, long stretches of which survive on top of Bülbül Dağı (Mt Coressos), the high ridge of hills on the southern side of Ephesus. A prominent square tower, nicknamed 'St Paul's Prison', also survives on a low hill to the west.

Roman Ephesus was the capital of Asia Minor and its population rapidly grew to around 250,000. Successive emperors vied with one another to beautify the city and it drew immigrants from all around the empire. Despite the fame of the cult of Diana, Ephesus soon acquired a sizeable Christian congregation. St John supposedly settled here with the Virgin Mary, and St Paul lived in the city for three years (probably in the AD 60s).

THE END

Unfortunately, despite efforts by Attalus II of Pergamum, who rebuilt the harbour, and Nero's proconsul, who dredged it, the harbour continued to silt up. Emperor Hadrian tried diverting the Cayster, but eventually the sea was forced back to Pamucak. Ephesus began to decline. It was still an important enough place for the Third Ecumenical Council to be held here in AD 431, but by the 6th century, when the Emperor Justinian was looking for a site to build a basilica for St John, he chose Ayasuluk Hill in Selçuk.

Sights

GYMNASIUM OF VEDIUS & STADIUM

As you walk along the side road from Dr Sabri Yayla Bulvarı, the first ruin you will pass on your left was once the Gymnasium of Vedius (2nd century AD), with exercise fields, baths, toilets, covered exercise rooms, a swimming pool and a ceremonial hall. A bit further along is the Stadium, dating from the same period. The Byzantines removed most of its finely cut stones to build the castle on Ayasuluk Hill. This 'quarrying' of pre-cut building stone from older, often earthquake-ruined structures was a constant feature of Ephesian history.

DOUBLE CHURCH

Just past the car park, which is ringed with çay bahçesis (teahouses), restaurants and souvenir shops, are the ruins of the Church of the Virgin Mary, also called the Double Church. The original building was a museum, a Hall of the Muses – a place for lectures, teaching and debates. Destroyed by fire, it was rebuilt as a church in the 4th century. Over the centuries several other churches were built here, somewhat obscuring the original layout.

HARBOUR ST

As you walk down into the main site along a path bordered by evergreen trees, a few colossal remains of the **harbour gymnasium** are off to the right. At the end of the path you reach marble-paved Harbour St, which was the grandest street in Ephesus, a legacy of the Byzantine emperor, Arcadius (r AD 395–408). In its heyday, water and sewerage channels ran beneath the marble flagstones and 50 street lights lit up its colonnades. There were shops along its sides, and the **harbour baths** and triumphal columns at the harbour end. It was and is a grand sight.

GREAT THEATRE

At the eastern end of Harbour St is the Great Theatre, reconstructed by the Romans between AD 41 and AD 117. The first theatre on the site dated from the Hellenistic city of Lysimachus, and many features of the original building were incorporated into the Roman structure, including the ingenious design of the *cavea* (seating area), capable of holding 25,000 people: each successive range of seating up from the stage is pitched more steeply than the one below, thereby improving the view and acoustics for spectators in the upper seats. It is still (sometimes controversially) used for performances.

Behind the Great Theatre, Mt Panayır rears up, with a few traces of the ruined **city walls** of Lysimachus.

SACRED WAY

From the theatre, walk south along marble-paved Sacred (or Marble) Way, noting the remains of the elaborate water and sewerage systems beneath the paving stones, and the ruts made by wheeled vehicles (which were not allowed to drive down Harbour St). The large open space to the right of the street was the 110-sq-metre **agora** (marketplace), heart of Ephesus' business life. It would have been surrounded by a colonnade and shops selling food and craft items. Note the fine carvings of gladiators that survive along the Sacred Way.

On the left as you approach the end of the street is an elaborate building, which used to be called a brothel but is now believed to have been a **private house**. Either way, its main hall contains a fine mosaic of the *Four Seasons*.

The Sacred Way ends at the Embolos, with the Library of Celsus and the monumental Gate of Augustus to the right, and Curetes Way heading east up the slope.

LIBRARY OF CELSUS

Celsus Polemaeanus was the Roman governor of Asia Minor early in the 2nd century AD. According to an inscription in Latin and Greek on the side of the front staircase his son, Consul Tiberius Julius Aquila, erected this library in his father's honour after the governor's death in 114. Celsus was buried under the western side of the library.

The library held 12,000 scrolls in niches around its walls. A 1m gap between the inner and outer walls protected the valuable books from extremes of temperature and humidity. The library was originally built as part of a complex, and architectural sleight of hand was used to make it look bigger than it actually is: the base of the facade is convex, adding height to the central elements; and the central columns and capitals are larger than those at the ends.

Niches on the facade hold statues representing the Virtues: Arete (Goodness), Ennoia (Thought), Episteme (Knowledge) and Sophia (Wisdom). The library was restored with the aid of the Austrian Archaeological Institute and the originals of the statues are in Vienna's Ephesus Museum.

As you leave the library, the **Gate of Augustus** on the left leads into the *agora*. This monumental gateway was apparently a favourite place for Roman ne'er-do-wells to relieve themselves, as a bit of ancient graffiti curses 'those who piss here'.

CURETES WAY

As you head up Curetes Way, a passage on the left leads to the famous communal **Roman men's toilets**. The much-copied statuette of Priapus was found in the nearby **well**. It's now in the Ephesus Museum in Selçuk.

You can't miss the impressive Corinthian-style **Temple of Hadrian**, on the left, with beautiful friezes in the porch and a head of Medusa to keep out evil spirits. It was dedicated to Hadrian, Artemis and the people of Ephesus in AD 118 but greatly reconstructed in the 5th century. Across the street a row of shops from the same period are fronted by an elaborate 5th-century mosaic.

Across from the Temple of Hadrian are the magnificent **Yamaç Evleri** (Terraced Houses; admission TL15; 9am-4.30pm). It's a crying shame that the off-putting admission fee will deter most people from visiting a site that offers the next best chance after Pompeii (Italy) to appreciate the luxury in which the elite of the Roman world lived. In places, the Terraced Houses still stand to two storeys; their walls are covered in frescoes and their floors in elaborate mosaics. To add insult to injury, parts of the terraces regularly close, with no advance warning. Some small finds from the houses are on display in the Ephesus Museum (p240) in Selçuk.

Further up Curetes Way on the left is the **Fountain of Trajan**. Of the huge statue of the emperor (AD 98–117) that used to tower above the pool, only one foot now remains.

EPHESUS FROM THE AIR

If you fancy getting an elevated perspective on the famous ruins **Sky and Sea Adventures** (☎ 892 2262; www.skyltd.com .tr; flights €50) offer trips in a two-seater microlight out of Selçuk Airport, just east of Ephesus. Your journey will take you up above Selçuk taking in all of its principal sites, before heading out to the coast for a sky-high gawp at the more modern attractions of Kuşadası. To soothe any understandable nerves, the operator assures his clients that, even if the motor cuts out 'the aircraft will remain airborne' – although how comforting it is to know that there's a chance of engine failure is open to debate.

UPPER EPHESUS

Curetes Way ends at the two-storey **Gate of Hercules**, constructed in the 4th century AD, with reliefs of Hercules on both main pillars. To the right a side street leads to a colossal **temple** dedicated to the emperor Domitian (r AD 81–96), part of which serves as a rarely accessible **Museum of Inscriptions**.

Up the hill on the left are the very ruined remains of the **Prytaneum** (a municipal hall) and the **Temple of Hestia Boulaea**, in which a perpetually burning flame was guarded. Finally, you reach the **Odeum**, a small theatre dating from AD 150 and used for musical performances and meetings of the town council. The marble seats at the bottom suggest the magnificence of the original.

To the east of the Odeum are more **baths** and, further east, the **East Gymnasium**. There is a second site ticket office across from the slight remains of the **Magnesia Gate**.

Festivals & Events

During the International İzmir Festival (see p225) in mid-June to early July many events take place at Ephesus. The world-class acts – opera, ballet and music – are certainly worth getting tickets for. Tickets are sold at the Ephesus Museum. See also the boxed text, p242.

Getting There & Away

Many pensions in Selçuk offer free lifts to Ephesus. Note that there are two entry points roughly 3km apart. You may prefer to be dropped off at the upper entrance (the southern gates or *güney kapısı*) so that you can walk back downhill through the ruins and out through the lower main entrance. It's a 30- to 45-minute walk from the tourist office in Selçuk to the main admission gate. The first 20 minutes are easy enough, along a tree-shaded road, but the next uphill section is much harder work with no pavement and little shade (not to mention constant attention from taxi drivers).

Frequent Pamucak and Kuşadası minibuses pass the Ephesus turn-off (TL4, five minutes, 3km), leaving you with a 20-minute walk to the main ticket office.

A taxi from Selçuk to the main entrance should cost about TL12. One good plan is to take a taxi to Meryemana for a short visit, then have it drop you at the southern entrance to Ephesus (about TL40). You can then spend as long as you like at Ephesus, before walking the 3km back to Selçuk.

AROUND SELÇUK
Meryemana (Mary's House)

Believers say that the Virgin Mary came to Ephesus with St John towards the end of her life (AD 37–45). In the 19th century, nun Catherina Emmerich of Germany had visions of Mary at Ephesus, although she had never visited the place herself. Using her descriptions, clergy from İzmir discovered the foundations of an old house on the wooded slope of Bülbül Dağı (Mt Coressos), not far from Ephesus, which have been dated to around the 6th century AD, albeit with some earlier elements, possibly from the 1st century. Pope Paul VI 'unofficially' authenticated the site on a visit in 1967 and it quickly became a place of pilgrimage. A service to honour Mary's Assumption is held in the chapel every 15 August. Mass is held at 7.15am Monday to Saturday (evening service at 6.30pm), and at 10.30am on Sunday. Note that 'appropriate dress' is required to enter.

The tiny **chapel** (☎ 894 1012; admission per person/car TL10/3; ☉ 8am-7pm) is usually mobbed by coach parties. There are information panels in various languages, but if you are interested in why over a million people visit here each year, we recommend *Mary's House* by Donald Carroll, which traces the extraordinary history of the site over 2000 years. A small shop also sells brochures (TL3.50 to TL6).

To Muslims, Mary is Meryemana, Mother Mary, who bore İsa Peygamber, the Prophet

Jesus. Below the chapel a wall is covered in rags: Turks tie the bits of cloth (or paper or plastic – in fact anything at hand) to a frame and make a wish.

If you want refreshments, head for **Café Turca** (☎ 894 1010; Meryemana Evi; coffee/breakfast TL2/6; ✆ 7.30am-7pm). Otherwise, the site is a great spot for a picnic – it's cool, verdant and full of birdsong.

The site lies 7km from Ephesus' Lower (northern) Gate and 5.5km from the Upper (southern) Gate. There's no dolmuş service so you'll have to hire a taxi (around TL40 return from the otogar) or take a tour.

Grotto of the Seven Sleepers

If you're driving from Meryemana to Ephesus you'll pass the road leading to the Grotto of the Seven Sleepers. According to legend, seven persecuted Christians fled from Ephesus in the 3rd century AD and took refuge in a cave on the northeastern side of Mt Pion. Agents of their persecutor, Emperor Decius, found the cave and sealed it. Two centuries later an earthquake brought down the wall, awakening the sleepers who ambled into town for a meal. Finding all their old friends long dead, they concluded that they had undergone some sort of resurrection. When they died they were buried in the cave and a cult following developed.

The grotto is actually a Byzantine-era **necropolis** (admission free; ✆ 24hr) with scores of tombs cut into the rock. It lies around 200m from the car park (1.5km from Ephesus); follow the well-trodden path up the hill.

It's probably not worth a special trip, as there's not a great deal to see, but the shady and kilim-covered *ayran* (yoghurt drink) and *gözleme* places by the junction make great places for a spot of R&R after Ephesus. The *gözleme* are famous.

Çamlık Steam Locomotive Museum

Trainspotters will delight in this open-air **museum** (☎ 894 8116; Köyü Selçuk; admission TL2; ✆ 8am-5pm Oct-Apr, 8am-6pm May-Sep), 10km from Selçuk on the Aydın road. The attractively landscaped site has over 30 steam locomotives, some as old as the 1887 C-N2 from the UK, and all of which you are free to climb on. Atatürk had his headquarters here and kept his special white train at this station during Aegean manoeuvres. A restaurant operates here but it's open to tour groups only.

Pamucak

☎ 0232

If you fancy seeing what Kuşadası looked like before tourism bloated it to its current extreme proportions, come to Pamucak beach, a few kilometres north along the coast and about 7km west of Selçuk. Although there are a few buildings and hotels here, particularly at the southern end where the great Richmond Grand Ephesus rises above the terrain like a land-locked ocean liner, much of this stretch of coast is undeveloped and all the more pleasant for it. The beach is sandy and very wide, which means that it doesn't feel crowded even on summer weekends when Turkish families descend en masse. Out of season, you may even get it entirely to yourself. However, be warned, there are no lifeguards and the waters here can get very choppy – swimming should only be undertaken with the utmost caution.

Without teams of hotel staff to mop up the daily detritus, parts of the beach do get a little litter-strewn at times, but this is by no means a dirty beach. From February to March, the estuary wetlands (a 15-minute walk from the beach) attract flamingos.

Minibuses run every half-hour from Selçuk (TL2.50, 10 minutes, 7km) in summer and every hour in winter. To/from Kuşadası, go to Selçuk first.

ŞİRİNCE

☎ 0232 / pop 960

Nine kilometres east of Selçuk, at the end of a long narrow road that winds its way up into the hills passing by grapevines and peach and apple orchards, sits Şirince, a perfect collection of stone-and-stucco houses with red-tiled roofs. It was probably originally settled when Ephesus was abandoned but what you see today mostly dates from the 19th century. The story goes that a group of freed Greek slaves settled here in the 15th century and called the village Çirkince (Ugliness) to deter others from following them. In 1926 a governor of İzmir decreed that its name be changed to the more honest Şirince (Pleasantness).

A century ago a much larger and more prosperous Şirince was mainly inhabited by Ottoman Greeks and acted as the economic focus for seven monasteries in the hills around. The villagers, who moved here from Salonica and its vicinity during an exchange of populations in 1924, are ardent fruit farmers who also make interesting fruit wines (TL8 to

TL20), including raspberry, peach melon and black mulberry varieties. Some are very nice – light and refreshing – while others require a good deal of chilling to be made palatable.

It is an idyllic place, but in recent years the cruise ships with their 'Authentic Turkish Village' day trips have all but turned it into a parody with high prices and souvenir shops cheek-by-jowl the entire length of the main street, which means incessant attention and entreaties as you make your way round. Of course, if you ignore this and stay the night (at a stiff premium of course) you'll be well rewarded with the chance to see the real village after the tour buses have gone.

The minibus from Selçuk drops you at the centre of the village near the restaurants.

Sights & Activities

Although you may want to drop into the ruined **Church of St John the Baptist** and examine its fast-fading frescoes, the real pleasure of a visit to Şirince lies in wandering its backstreets and looking at the lovely old houses.

The town is also a good, if not particularly cheap, place to shop. Pretty much every third house seems to be a wine shop, and plenty of places offer free tastings (accompanied by the inevitable intense sales pitch). Other shops and stalls sell jewellery, carvings, leather goods and locally produced olive oil and olive soap. Incidentally, if a local woman invites you to inspect her 'antique house', you should assume she'll have lace for sale.

Sleeping

Şirince is a captive market and prices, with a few exceptions, can be ludicrously inflated for what you get. Prices here are for rooms with bathroom and breakfast included.

Dionysos Pension (☎ 898 3130; www.dionysospension .com; s/d TL70/90) A tiny but delightful old village house, the Dionysos has four large rooms that have retained some of their original features and have a charming antiquey feel. It's not great value, but the pension has tonnes of character and a little garden-terrace outside with views over the valley. Follow the signs from the village centre and look out for the two churches – it lies in-between.

Giritli Pansiyon (☎ 898 3029; www.sirincelejardin.com; r €40-60) In the centre of the main street, this is a homey, slightly noisy choice. The bedrooms are nice and big, with colourful quilts, rugs and dark wood furniture and there's an apart-

ment with a fully equipped kitchen, complete with washing machine. The hotel restaurant, Le Jardin, just up the hill towards the town entrance, is very good.

Kırkınca Pansiyon (☎ 898 3133; www .kirkinca.com; s/d €50/70) Just up the hill opposite the bazaar, the Kırkınca is a sort of 'butik' complex comprising a pension, with 15 rooms, and another four 'apart houses'. They've all been very elegantly done and furnished with a mixture of quality bespoke modern pieces and antiques. Some of the rooms have four-poster beds and one even has its own mini-hamam. The main building has a shaded roof terrace with views of the town and countryside.

Nişanyan Evleri (☎ 898 3208; www.nisanyan.com; s/d from TL120/180; 🖳) There are several choices here. The main inn, set in a 19th-century renovated stone house, is probably Şirince's smartest place, although you will have to brave the fairly steep 250m climb to the top of the village. Its five rooms are individually decorated à l'Ottoman, and there's a library, a good restaurant and a pretty terrace with views. The owners also operate a budget alternative, the Kilisealtı near the village entrance, which offers a more basic, cheaper version of the same (single/double TL60/90). Three restored village houses can also be rented out nearby (TL185/260 for one/two people per night).

Eating

Le Jardin (☎ 898 3029; meze TL5-7, mains TL8-15; 🕑 9am-11pm) Around 100m past the town entrance, the Jardin is a pretty place with tables set on a greenery-filled terrace with good views of the town and valley beyond. The menu features plenty of snacks – such as *gözleme* for TL4 – and grilled meats, as well as a few international offerings for the cruise hordes (hamburgers, 'spag bol' etc).

Artemis Şirince Şarapevi Restaurant (☎ 898 3240; mains TL11-15; 🕑 8am-midnight) This former Greek school is set right by the entrance overlooking the valley and has perhaps the best views of any restaurant. The interior has old stoves and darkened floorboards, while outside there's a large terrace. It looks very grand and expensive but isn't (although check the price of wine before ordering), and the food is good (try the vermicelli with walnuts and cheese for TL5.50). You can also come here just for a drink.

By the bazaar, overlooking the main square where the buses stop, with a pleasant shaded terrace and serving both mains and snacks at good prices is **Köy Restaurant** (☎ 898 3120; snacks TL4-6, mains TL8-14; ⓧ 8am-11pm).

Getting There & Away

Minibuses (TL2.50) leave from Selçuk to Şirince every 15 minutes in summer, and every half-hour in winter.

TİRE, KAPLAN, ÖDEMİŞ & BİRGİ

Pleasant as Selçuk is, no one could call it un-discovered. However, it's possible to make a straightforward day trip into the Aegean hinterland, which will give you a fascinating insight into less-touristy Turkey. You can do this by dolmuş, but it really works best if you hire a car.

Tire, at the base of the Bozdağlar Mountains and surrounded by farmland, hosts a very popular Tuesday market, which has become a frequent stop for tour groups in recent years. As a consequence, the town is now not quite as unfamiliar (and inquisitive) of tourists as was once the case, although you should prepare yourself for a bit of careful scrutiny.

Head uphill to find the Tahtakale neigh-bourhood where it's possible to inspect *hans* (caravanserai) dating back to the 15th cen-tury and still in use as shopping centres. Poke around the backstreets and you will be able to watch felt-makers hard at work at a craft that has all but died out elsewhere in Turkey.

Tire is also known throughout the region for the religious intensity of its inhabitants, which no doubt accounts for the plethora of Ottoman mosques (over 30) clustered in its limited confines. The pick is the 15th-century **Yeşil Imaret Camii**, which was built during the reign of Murat II.

The market is a great place to stock up on lunch supplies for a relaxing picnic, or if you want something more formal, take the road to **Kaplan**, a tiny village perched high in the hills, and enjoy a meal and the sensational views from **Kaplan Restaurant** (☎ 512 6652; meals TL12; ⓧ 8am-10pm).

Ödemiş is less interesting except on Saturday when there's a lively market. But from Ödemiş you can take a dolmuş or drive on to **Birgi**, an undeveloped village that's home to the gor-geous **Çakıroğlu Konağı** (admission TL2; ⓧ 8.30am-noon & 1-5.30pm Tue-Sun), one of the finest historical houses open to the public in Turkey. The three-storey wooden house, completely cov-ered in frescoes, was probably built in 1761

for Şerif Aliağa, a tradesman who owned the local tanning yards and had two wives, from İstanbul and İzmir. To keep them happy he had vistas of their home towns painted on the upstairs walls. Next door, **Konak** (☎ 531 6069; Çakırağa Sokak 6) is a café in a restored house.

Birgi also has a fine **Ulu Cami** (1311) with carved doors and windows and an old stone lion incorporated into the stonework, and the **Birgivi**, a shrine on the outskirts of town that is popular with devout Muslims.

Getting There & Away

There are hourly minibuses to Tire from Selçuk (TL3.25) and hourly onward buses from Tire to Ödemiş (TL2, 34km). Dolmuşes leave for Birgi from Ödemiş otogar (€1.50, 20 minutes, 8km).

KUŞADASI

☎ 0256 / pop 54,660

It's easy to sneer at Kuşadası, 22km southwest of Selçuk. With its package hotels, fast food restaurants, in-your-face bazaar, karaoke bars, tattoo parlours and larger holiday crowds, it doesn't always show its best face to the world. But there are many locals who are very proud of the place, who see it as exemplifying a sort of can-do, make-the-best-of-yourself spirit, and see those who revile it as little more than snobs. After all, as one local bar owner put it, 'what's wrong with having a good time?' It all depends on your definition of 'good time'.

What you won't get in Kuşadası is much in the way of Turkish culture (although there is some, if you're prepared to seek it out). What you will get is a decent, if very crowded, beach and some of the coast's row-diest, headiest nightlife – think Irish pubs, happy hours, sing a longs, tribute acts and drunken, swaying discos. Now, if that sounds all too ghastly for words, then you'd be better off basing yourself in the quieter confines of nearby Selçuk.

But if you want to let your hair down for a night or two of guilt-free Esperanto hedonism before heading back onto the cultural trail, then Kuşadası is your place.

And even if you don't like what it does, you still have to admit that it does it well. It's like a vast tourism machine – accommodat-ing, feeding, entertaining and replacing an endless stream of visitors, who arrive from all points of the compass by charter plane, by bus and, more and more frequently, by cruise

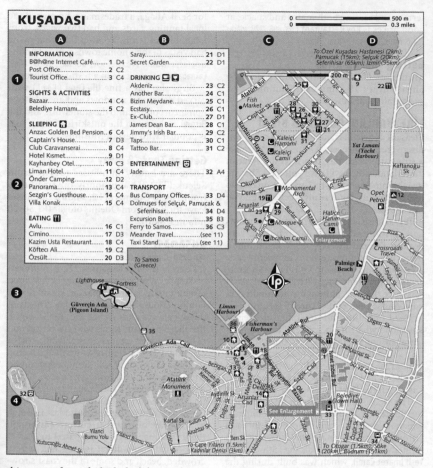

KUŞADASI

INFORMATION
B@h@ne Internet Café......... 1 D4
Post Office............................ 2 C2
Tourist Office....................... 3 C4

SIGHTS & ACTIVITIES
Bazaar.................................. 4 C4
Belediye Hamamı.................. 5 C2

SLEEPING
Anzac Golden Bed Pension.. 6 C4
Captain's House.................... 7 D3
Club Caravanserai................ 8 C4
Hotel Kismet........................ 9 D1
Kayhanbey Otel.................. 10 C3
Liman Hotel........................ 11 C4
Önder Camping................... 12 D2
Panorama............................ 13 C4
Sezgin's Guesthouse............ 14 C4
Villa Konak......................... 15 C4

EATING
Avlu.................................... 16 C1
Cimino................................ 17 D3
Kazim Usta Restaurant........ 18 C4
Köftecı Ali........................... 19 C2
Özsült................................. 20 D3

Saray.................................. 21 D1
Secret Garden..................... 22 D1

DRINKING
Akdeniz.............................. 23 C2
Another Bar........................ 24 C1
Bizim Meydane.................... 25 C1
Ecstasy............................... 26 C1
Ex-Club.............................. 27 D1
James Dean Bar.................. 28 C1
Jimmy's Irish Bar................ 29 C1
Taps................................... 30 C1
Tattoo Bar.......................... 31 C2

ENTERTAINMENT
Jade................................... 32 A4

TRANSPORT
Bus Company Offices.......... 33 D4
Dolmuşes for Selçuk, Pamucak &
    Seferihisar...................... 34 D4
Excursion Boats................... 35 B3
Ferry to Samos.................... 36 C3
Meander Travel.............(see 11)
Taxi Stand.....................(see 11)

To Özel Kuşadası Hastanesi (2km);
Pamucak (15km); Selçuk (20km);
Seferihisar (65km); İzmir (95km)

ship, up to four of which dock here a day in high season.

Orientation

Kuşadası's central landmark is the Öküz Mehmet Paşa Kervansarayı, an Ottoman caravanserai that is now a hotel, known as Club Caravanserai. It lies 100m inland from the cruise-ship docks, at the intersection of the waterfront boulevard, Atatürk Bulvarı, and the town's main street, the pedestrianised Barbaros Hayrettin Bulvarı, which cuts inland.

Just beyond the PTT on the northern side of Barbaros Hayrettin Bulvarı, a passage leads to the old Kaleiçi neighbourhood (part of old Kuşadası) of narrow streets packed with restaurants and bars.

Turn right off Barbaros Hayrettin Bulvarı to find raucous Barlar Sokak (Bar St) and the hillside pensions overlooking Kuşadası's harbour.

The most useful dolmuş stand is 1.5km inland on Adnan Menderes Bulvarı. The otogar is right out on the bypass road.

Information

INTERNET ACCESS

B@h@ane Internet Café (Öge Sokak 4/A; per hr TL1.50; 8.30am-midnight) You can take drinks up here from the downstairs café.

MEDICAL SERVICES

Özel Kuşadası Hastanesi (613 1616; Anıt Sokak, Turkmen Mahallesi) Kuşadası's excellent private hospital is 3km north of the centre on the Selçuk road, and has English-speaking doctors.

MONEY

There are several banks with ATMs on Barbaros Hayrettin Bulvarı.

POST

Post office (☎ 612 3311; Barbaros Hayrettin Bulvarı 23-25; ⏰ 8.30am-12.30pm & 1.30-5.30pm Mon-Sat winter, 8am-midnight daily summer)

TOURIST INFORMATION

Tourist office (☎ 614 1103; fax 614 6295; İskele Meydanı, Liman Caddesi; ⏰ 8am-noon & 1-5pm Mon-Fri) Near the wharf where the cruise ships dock, about 60m west of the caravanserai. They don't have a lot of information, although they can provide up-to-date maps.

Sights & Activities

Kuşadası's town has a small artificial beach, but the area's most famous stretch of sand, and the primary focus for the majority of its package holiday visitors, is **Kadınlar Denizi** (Ladies Beach), 2.5km south of town and served by dolmuşes running along the coastal road. It's nice enough but crowded with big hotels and woefully inadequate for the high summer crowds. The coast south of Kadınlar Denizi has several small beaches, each backed by big hotels.

In town, the main formal attraction is the minor stone **fortress** that occupies most of Güvercin Ada (Pigeon Island), a small island connected to the mainland by a causeway. Its main hall hosts exhibitions of handicrafts and there are a few coops on stilts for the eponymous pigeons, but the fortress' main appeal is as a strolling route – it's particularly popular with local courting couples who secrete themselves among the battlements and canoodle.

East of the island are the cruise ship docks and, handily situated immediately to the south, the main **bazaar** area. This is a strictly tourist-oriented place – cheap leather jackets, knock-off designer bags, carpets, jewellery etc – and used to be a byword for extreme hassle, with vendors leaping en masse to present their pitches to the waves of cruise visitors. A crackdown by the authorities, however, which even saw a couple of the businesses shut down for a couple of days, seems to have reigned in the more persistent offenders.

Kuşadası's hamams are of the 'un-Turkish type', where there's mixed bathing (albeit with

towels). The **Belediye Hamamı** (☎ 614 1219; Yildirim Caddesi 2; admission €15; ⏰ 9am-7.30pm Apr-Oct) is up the hill from Bar St. It's a restored hamam (the original dates back 600 years) and is atmospheric and clean.

It's possible to use Kuşadası as a base for exploring much of the region. The town has numerous tour operators and travel agents offering trips to all the major local attractions, including Ephesus (full day with lunch from €45), 'PMD' (Priene, Miletus, Didyma, from €30) and Tire Market (from €30), as well as further afield to Pamukkale (from €40) and even İstanbul (two days from €200). Try **Crossroads Travel** (☎ 618 3326; www.crossroadstravel .com; Atatürk Bulvarı 70; ⏰ 8am-8pm).

Sleeping

Kuşadası is chock-a-block with hotels and more are being erected all the time. The main budget places line the steep narrow streets just southwest of the bazaar. Only a few places stay open from November to March.

BUDGET

Camping

Önder Camping (☎ 618 1690; www.onderotel.com; Atatürk Bulvarı 84; camp sites per person/tent/caravan/car TL5/3/5/3; ▣) Despite its location on the main road opposite the Opet garage, this is a peaceful, almost bucolic camping ground with plenty of facilities, including a tennis court, swimming pool, laundry facilities and a decent restaurant. Plots are shaded by pine trees and olives.

Pensions

Beware the pension touts at the otogar and harbour (who are paid commission – your hotel hasn't shut down). Decide where you're heading before arrival and stand your ground.

Panorama (☎ 614 6619; www.otelpanorama.com; Kıbrıs Caddesi 14; s/d €20/28, ▨ ▣) Just a few steps from the bazaar, this used to be Sammy's Palace, a backpacker favourite of legendary long standing. It's now been taken over by Sammy's cousins, Ali and Murat, who are keeping up the good work and will offer you a warm welcome (and probably try to sell you a few tours and a belly dancing evening) when you arrive. The rooms are rather spartan and dog-eared, but exactly what you'd expect for the price and there's a rooftop terrace for the breakfasts and optional dinners.

ourpick Sezgin's Guesthouse (☎ 614 4225; www.sezginhotel.com; Arsanlar Caddesi 68; s/d €20/24;

GETTING WET IN KUŞADASI

Culture is all very well and the ruins of Ephesus and the like undeniably impressive and evocative, but sometimes you just want to slide down a big tube filled with water. The opportunity for a bit of wet and wild adventure is provided at **Adaland** (☎ 618 1252; www.adaland.com; Çamlimanı Mevkii; adult/child €20/12; ⏱ 10am-6pm 5 May-5 Oct), Europe's largest waterpark with dozens of chutes, slides, river rides and pools, as well as a newly opened seapark, home to a variety of marine life.

For something a little more worthy, you can learn to scuba-dive – or if you've already learnt, just go for a dive – with the **Aquaventure Diving Center** (☎ 612 7845; www.aquaventure.com.tr; Miracle Beach Club, Kadınlar Denizi; ⏱ 8am-6pm), by Ladies' Beach, which offers PADI open water courses for €250 and reef dives from €30. Staff can arrange pick-up from most of the major hotels.

⊠ 🖳 🖳) Perhaps the top budget choice, you really do get a good deal for your money: large, almost Swiss-style wood panelled rooms, comfortable beds, armchairs, TVs, fridges and small balconies overlooking a compact garden and pool. The owner, Sezgin, is friendly and helpful and organises regular special events, including Turkish-style barbecues and belly dancing.

Liman Hotel (Mr Happy's; ☎ 614 7770; www.liman hotel.com; Kıbrıs Caddesi, Buyral Sokak 4; s/d €24/35; ⊠ 🖳) Presided over by the appropriately named 'Mr Happy' (AKA the more mundane Hasan Degirmenci), this is a stalwart of the budget scene. It occupies one of the best positions of any pension, right on the seafront. Some of the 17 clean, well-maintained rooms have sea views and there's a great terrace where breakfast (included), dinner (optional extra) and the obligatory belly dancing evenings are laid on. Extras include a library and free maps.

Captain's House (☎ 614 4754; www.captainshouse pansiyon.com; İstiklal Caddesi 66; s/d TL25/50; ⊠) Everything is clean and shipshape in the Captain, which occupies a prime position on the seafront, opposite the beach in among the fish restaurants. The interiors of the 18 rooms aren't particularly inspiring, but are nice enough with pictures of seascapes on the walls and items of nautical paraphernalia here and there. Four rooms have large balconies with side sea views. The next-door restaurant/café is a popular nightspot.

Anzac Golden Bed Pension (☎ 614 8708; www .kusadasihotels.com/goldenbed; off Arsanlar Caddesi, Uğurlu 1 Çıkmazı 4; r with/without bathroom TL65/35; ⊠ 🖳) Rather tucked away on a hillside cul-de-sac, the Golden Bay is worth seeking out. The rooms are, as the Australian proprietor Sandra admits, 'simply furnished', but bright and spotless and there's a host of extras to attract travellers: airport pick-up, book ex-

change, free Ephesus transfers etc. Up top is a nice terrace where you can have breakfast while admiring the views over town.

MIDRANGE & TOP END

Villa Konak (☎ 612 2170; www.villakonakhotel.com; Yıldırım Caddesi 55; s/d €40/50; ⊠ 🖳) Hidden away from the hubbub in the old quarter of town is the Villa Konak, a restored 140-year-old stone house. The recently updated rooms have been attractively done with the odd Orientalist flourish and are arranged around a large and rambling courtyard-garden complete with pool, ancient well and citrus and magnolia trees. It's peaceful and cool and there's a bar, restaurant and library.

Club Caravanserai (☎ 614 4115; www.kusadasiho tels.com/caravanserail; Atatürk Bulvarı; s/d €50/75; ⏱ 1 Mar-15 Nov; ⊠) It's one of the town's unmistakeable sites, a grand 17th-century caravanserai, which at night has its battlements illuminated by yards of neon. It's a similar historic/cheesy story inside where the attractive courtyard plays host to gloriously kitschy 'Turkish nights' on summer weekends (very popular with cruise guests; €40 with dinner, €30 without). The rooms are very attractively done and the restaurant isn't bad.

Hotel Kısmet (☎ 618 1290; www.kismet.com.tr; Atatürk Bulvarı 1; s/d €90/130; ⏱ 15 Mar-15 Nov; ⊠ 🖳) About as big a contrast to the town's core constituency as you can get, the Kısmet is a very grand affair. Located at the northern end of town, the hotel occupies a building created by a descendant of the last sultan with lovely manicured gardens and very large, very well-equipped, but slightly blandly decorated rooms. All have balconies, either looking out to sea, or over the town. From up here everything looks serene and calm. There are several bars and restaurants and entertainment is provided by cruise-style crooners.

If the above are full, try the **Kayhanbey Otel** (☎ 614 1190; www.kayhanbey.com; Güvercin Ada Caddesi; s/d €60/80; 🐾 🖳 🍴), just west of the cruise dock, with 72 comfortable (albeit anodyne) rooms with balconies with lovely sea views. There's also a hamam, and an outdoor pool on the roof terrace.

Eating

The town's prime dining location is down by the picturesque marina but competition keeps bills down. Always ask in advance the price of seafood and wine.

For the cheapest options, it's simple: head inland. The Kaleiçi, the old part of Kuşadası behind the PTT, has some atmospheric dining rooms as well as a few cheap and cheerful joints.

RESTAURANTS

Avlu (☎ 614 7995; Cephane Sokak 15; mains TL5-8; 🕑 8am-midnight) In the old town, this offers first-class home cooking in a clean and cheerful environment at unbeatable prices. A long-standing local fave, in recent times it's been discovered by the more daring cruise-ships tourists too. There's a great pick-and-point counter for those unsure what to order. It's a good choice for veggies too, as well as for sampling delectable Turkish puds.

Secret Garden (☎ 618 1178; Setur Marina; meze TL5-7; fish per 500g TL15-22; 🕑 9am-1am) Right at the far end of town, this place enjoys a very pleasant setting overlooking the marina. It's great for a splurge and for generally feeling a bit posh, with a wide range of fish (typically including bass, bream and turbot), and some excellent seafood specials.

Saray (☎ 612 0528; Bozkurt Sokak 25; mains TL10-18; 🕑 9am-2am) Enjoying a dedicated following among both locals and expats, the Saray shows two different faces to the world. Outside is a rather refined courtyard, all shady trees, candlelight and linen, while inside, particularly later in the evening, it can be a bit more happy hour and sing-along. The menu is a typical Kuşadası calling-all-ports affair – Chinese, Indian, Mexican, fish and chips etc – but with some decent Turkish choices, and several vegetarian options.

Kazim Usta Restaurant (☎ 614 1226; Liman Caddesi 4; meze TL5-12, mains TL15-30; 🕑 6am-midnight) Opposite the tourist office, this venerable establishment founded way back in 1950 is considered the top fish restaurant in town, though it's not cheap. The sumptuous fish soup (TL15) is a speciality. If you want a table on the waterfront, reserve at least a day in advance.

CAFÉS & QUICK EATS

Köftecı Ali (Arsanlar Caddesi 14; 🕑 9am-midnight winter, summer 24 hr) Situated near the entrance of Bar St, ready to hoover up the early morning post-club traffic, this simple street booth does some terrific spicy wrapped pide kebaps for TL5. The chances are you'll be served by Ali himself who sleeps just four hours a night in the season.

Özsüt (☎ 612 0650; İsmet İnönü Bulvarı 30; 🕑 9.30am-midnight; 🐾) This well-known İzmiri chain has the usual delicious selection of traditional Turkish puds served up in smart surrounds, as well as great coffee and ice cream (TL1.25 per scoop).

Cimino (☎ 614 6409; Atatürk Bulvarı 56/B; 🕑 10am-midnight) A place to meet-and-eat locally, this mellow bistro-cum-café serves good cappuccino (TL4) and mainly Italian-style fare (TL5 to TL16). It's opposite the seafront and plays good jazz music.

Drinking & Entertainment

The centre of the town's tourist nightlife is the infamous Barlar Sokak (Bar St), which should probably be renamed Irish St as pretty much every bar is now themed on the Emerald Isle: Paddy's, Temple Bar etc. It's all incredibly full-on, like a sort of never-ending stag/hen party. The bartenders are employed to get everything started, leading the crowd in sing-alongs and dance routines, and, in a slightly queasy touch, all wear name tags with Anglicised names, so Yasser becomes Charlie, and so forth. From October to March, the scene shrinks to pretty much nothing.

Akdeniz (☎ 612 1120; Arsanlar Caddesi 1; beer TL4; 🕑 8am-2am Apr-Oct) With its elevated position overlooking the entrance to Bar St, this is a perfect spot to watch the dolled up crowds emerge for the evening's raucousness. The bar itself is shaded by a tall tree and rather peaceful. There's also an attached restaurant (not bad) and apart-hotel.

Jimmy's Irish Bar (☎ 612 1318; Barlar Sokak 8; beer TL5; 🕑 8pm-4am Apr-Nov) Still the biggest name in town, partly because it has the handiest position at the entrance to the street. For all its mass-market, karaoke, 'hey, where you from?' faults, this can be a good place to meet other travellers (so long as you can hear what

BEACH CLUBS

Kuşadası's nightlife is still overwhelmingly mass-market, but here and there the shoots of something more cultured are beginning to grow. The prime examples are the beach clubs of **Cape Yılancı** (Yılancı Burnu), the peninsula that lies less than 1.5km west of the town centre. Like giant entertainment complexes, they boast a wealth of facilities, including restaurants, volleyball parks, kids' playgrounds, tennis courts and four-poster sun-lounges for daytime fun. At night the attention turns to the elegantly furnished bars, dance platforms and stages set right over the water, where live bands perform – typically jazz, Latin and funk – and al fresco discos go on till the early hours. Aimed at a high-end clientele – as the champagne holders built into each table will testify – the best is currently **Jade** (☎ 612 7220; Yılancı Burnu; admission weekday TL20, weekend with drink incl TL30, beer from TL7; ⊙ 10am-7pm & 8pm-midnight end May-end Sep).

To get here, take a dolmuş towards Kadınlar Denizi (Ladies Beach; €0.55). It can drop you at the roundabout from where it's a short walk.

they're saying, it's very loud). The giant satellite dish on the roof beams in the compulsory football matches.

There is another nightlife scene in Kuşadası, based largely in the old town where a number of old houses and courtyards have been turned into a collection of fabulously swanky bar-cum-nightclubs patronised largely (but not exclusively) by locals. In contravention of the way things normally work, these tend to be much more expensive than the tourist-oriented places, with beers costing around TL10. Most are open 10pm to 4am May to September, and a few sporadically open at weekends in winter.

Another Bar (☎ 614 7552; Tuna Sokak 10) Converted from an old citrus orchard, tables and stools are dotted among the remaining trees and a large, central palm. There's also a large screen and a dance floor.

Ex-Club (☎ 614 7550; Tuna Sokak 13) It's more of a club than a bar, although there's no designated dance area, so everyone just sort of cavorts between the tables. It can get very crowded.

James Dean Bar (☎ 614 3827; Sakarya Sokak 14) Set in a 200-year-old building, this recently refurbished club is open-air amid orange trees and beautiful bars draped with beautiful people.

Ecstasy (☎ 612 2208; Sakarya Sokak 10) bar is similar. Known to be gay-friendly are **Tattoo Bar** (☎ 612 7693; Tuna Sokak 7) and the British pub-style **Taps** (☎ 612 1371; Tuna Sokak 4).

MEYHANES

Kaleiçi (the old part of Kuşadası) is home to several *meyhanes* (taverns) where meze and rakı (aniseed brandy) are served up accompanied by live music.

Bizim Meyhane (☎ 614 4152; Kişla Sokak; beer/rakı €2.75/2.20; ⊙ 8.30pm-4am) Low-beamed and covered with musical instruments on the old stone walls, this place looks more barn than bar. Run by a sister and brother who sing and play instruments, it's atmospheric, infectious and fun. Join the locals tossing back the rakı.

Getting There & Away
BOAT

All Kuşadası travel agents sell tickets to the Greek island of Samos.

From 1 April to 31 October, boats depart daily from Kuşadası to Samos at 8.30am. From 1 May, there's an additional boat at 5pm. Note that ferries do not operate in winter. Tickets cost €30 for a single, €35 for a same-day return and €50 for an open return.

If you stay the night you will be landed with a €9 tax for leaving Greece and another €9 tax for coming back into Turkey. Some pensions discount these tickets, so ask, and flash your student card. You must be at the harbour 45 minutes before sailing time for immigration formalities.

The boats are operated by **Meander Travel** (☎ 612 3859; www.meandertravel.com; Kıbrıs Caddesi 1; ⊙ 9am-7pm winter, 9am-9pm summer), which has its office right by the dock and also offers a range of other domestic tours.

BUS

Kuşadası's otogar is at the southern end of Kahramanlar Caddesi on the bypass highway. Several companies have ticket offices on İsmet İnönü Bulvarı and offer *servis* (shuttle minibuses) to save you the trek out there. Note that dolmuşes leave from the centrally located Adnan Menderes Bulvarı.

DOLMUŞ SERVICES FROM SÖKE'S OTOGAR

Destination	Fare (TL)	Distance (km)	Frequency (per day)
Aydın	6.50	59	every 20 min
Bafa	6.50	30	every 20 min
Balat (for Miletus)	5	35	every 30 min
Didyma	5.50	56	every 20 min
Güllübahçe (for Priene)	3.25	17	every 20 min
Güzelçamlı	4.50	22	every 20 min
Kuşadası	4	20	every 20 min
Milas	7.50	82	every 20 min

In summer, three buses run daily to Bodrum (TL20, two to 2½ hours, 151km); in winter, take a dolmuş to Söke (TL4, at least every 30 minutes all year). For Didyma, Priene and Miletus, change also at Söke. For more information about getting to the 'PMD' ruins, see p260.

For Selçuk (TL4, 25 minutes), dolmuşes run every 15 minutes. For Pamucak or Ephesus, take the Selçuk dolmuş (which can drop you off there). For Seherihisar (TL6.50, 70 minutes), dolmuşes leave every 45 minutes all year.

Getting Around

You can't get a bus direct from Kuşadası to İzmir's Adnan Menderes airport, but will have to take the much more long-winded route of taking a bus to İzmir otogar (TL15, 1¼ hours, 80km), take the free shuttle service to the centre, then take a bus (see p229) or a taxi (€40).

Şehiriçi minibuses (TL1.25) run every few minutes in summer (every 15 to 20 in winter) from Kuşadası otogar to the town centre, and up and down the coast. Kadınlar Denizi minibuses speed along the coast road south to the beach. You can pick up a mini bus heading north along the coast to Kuştur (TL4) at the junction of İstiklal Sokak and Atatürk Bulvarı.

SÖKE

☎ 0256 / pop 66,160

Söke is a modern town that's enlivened only by Wednesday and Sunday markets. However, it's the main transport hub for this part of the region and you may be forced to come here to change buses as you travel around the coast.

You can also base yourself here for visiting the Dilek Peninsula or Priene, Miletus and Didyma, cutting out the transport time from Selçuk or Kuşadası.

Buses run to İzmir (TL10 to TL15, usually every 15 minutes), to Denizli (for Pamukkale; TL15 to TL20, four times daily) and Bodrum (TL15 every hour). For dolmuş services see the table (above). For Selçuk, go to Kuşadası and change.

DILEK PENINSULA

About 26km south of Kuşadası, the Dilek Peninsula juts westwards into the Aegean, almost touching the Greek island of Samos. West of the village of Güzelçamlı is **Dilek National Park** (Dilek Milli Parkı; admission per person/car TL5/10; ⊙ 8am-7pm summer, 8am-5pm winter), a peaceful, mountainous nature reserve with some fine walking and horse-riding areas, and unspoilt coves for swimming.

Just outside the park entrance, look out for a brown sign with 'Zeus Mağarası' written on it, which indicates the location of a cave where you can swim in water that's icy-cool in summer and warm in winter.

National park dolmuşes drop you off at the cliff top above **İçmeler Koyu**, a protected cove about 1km past the entrance. It's a steep walk down to the sandy beach, which is very popular locally (and inevitably rather cigarette butt-strewn) and has lounge chairs and umbrellas. A paved road runs along the cliff-top, beside which are a number of purpose-built viewing points, where you can take in the lovely views out to sea. About 3km beyond İçmeler Koyu an unpaved turn-off heads 1km downhill on the right to **Aydınlık Beach**, a quieter pebble-and-sand strand about 800m long with surf and backed by pines.

Less than 1km further along is a *jandarma* (police) post. Shortly afterwards a turn on the left is signposted **Kanyon**. If you follow this path all the way it will eventually bring you back to Güzelçamlı, after about six hours' stiff walking through beautiful, peaceful pine forest. Alternatively, you can just take a turn up and down the hill and then return to the main road.

After another 500m you reach the turn-off for **Kavaklı Burun** (also known as Kalamaki Beach and the last dolmuş stop), a sand-and-pebble surf beach. As at Aydınlık, there's a second entrance to the beach at the far end, another 1km along.

A final rather scrubby and pebbly beach, **Karasu Koyou**, is a further kilometre on. Just beyond this the park becomes a military zone to which members of the public are not admitted – slightly frustratingly as this is where the park's most exciting wildlife (including, reputedly, the extremely rare Anatolian panther) resides. It's 9.5km back to the park entrance.

Sleeping & Eating

Ecer Pension (☎ 646 2737; www.turkeypension.com; s/d €12.50/25) Though you'd be forgiven for mistaking it for a ramshackle farmhouse, the pension's rooms are simple, tidy and clean. Run by a charming Turkish-German couple, Anneliese and Necip, you can sip their homemade wine in their rambling garden. It lies 200m east of the bus station on the main road.

The owners' son can also arrange horses and guides (€15 to €30 per person for one to five hours) or take you on a trek (from one hour to eight hours) in the park. The scenery is beautiful and you may see ruined Byzantine monasteries and wildlife including wild horses and boar.

Although camping is not allowed in the national park, there are several sites near the gate at Güzelçamlı.

Outside the park are several, similar fish restaurants perched right on the water; choose the most popular when you visit. The beaches in the park have small cafés selling cold drinks and simple meals, as well as picnicking facilities.

Getting There & Away

Minibuses from Söke travel as far as İçmeler Koyu (TL4, 35 to 40 minutes); minibuses from Kuşadası continue right down the peninsula to Kavaklı Burun (TL4.5). You pay the park entrance fee while on the bus. Minibuses generally run from 7am to midnight in summer and 7am to 6.45pm in winter, but the later dolmuşes fill up quickly, especially at weekends.

You can walk the 2km from Güzelçamlı to İçmeler Koyu in 30 minutes.

PRİENE, MİLETUS & DİDYMA
☎ 0256

Ephesus may be the crème de la crème of the Aegean archaeological sites, but south of Kuşadası lie the ruins of three other, much-less-frequently visited (but still important) ancient settlements. Priene occupies a dramatic position overlooking the plain of the Büyük Menderes (Meander) River; Miletus preserves a spectacular theatre; and Didyma has a Temple of Apollo vaguely reminiscent of the great temples at Karnak in Egypt.

Beyond Didyma lies **Altınkum Beach**, one of Turkey's finest and busiest beaches, its swathe of 'golden sand' popular with the English package-holiday brigade for whom innumerable British-style cafés dish up the tastes of home. If you end your tour of the ruins at Didyma, you might want to take a quick dip in the sea at the beach before returning to base.

GETTING THERE & AROUND
If you start early in the morning from Kuşadası or Selçuk, it's just about possible to get to Priene, Miletus, Didyma and Altınkum Beach in the same day using public transport. However, it can be awkward and time-consuming as dolmuş services are patchy and you may have to keep backtracking to Söke.

If you do want to do it yourself, start out by catching a dolmuş from Kuşadası (TL4, 20km) to Söke and then another (TL3.25, 17km) to Güllübahçe (for Priene). When you've finished at Priene, wait for a passing dolmuş heading for Miletus or Söke, hitch the 22km across the flood plain to Miletus, or return to Söke and set out again. For more information on the dangers of hitching see p689.

Getting from Miletus to Didyma can be tricky. Dolmuşes do run from Miletus to Didyma (TL4) but if there's no sign of a dolmuş from Miletus to Akköy, you will either have to try hitching or return to Söke and start out all over again. From Akköy, there are dolmuşes every 20 minutes to Didyma (TL3) and Altınkum.

Lost already? If so it's easy to pick up an organised 'PMD' tour, as they're known (around €30 per person) from Selçuk otogar, or any of the tour operators in Selçuk or Kuşadası. Your hotel in either town will probably be able to take care of the arrangements. Minibuses usually leave around 9am, and spend one hour at Priene, 1½ hours at Miletus, 2½ hours at Didyma and 1½ hours at Altınkum Beach, before returning to Selçuk at about 6pm.

In high summer, tours run daily and you may need to book in advance. At other times, however, they may only operate when enough people have expressed an interest. In winter, note that there are fewer direct dolmuşes and you have to change more frequently from town to town.

Without a doubt, hiring a car is the easiest way to visit these places, allowing you to do them in reverse order, saving Priene, which enjoys the most splendid setting, till last. Ask at your hotel. Most international agencies rent out cars for around €50 a day, while a host of smaller travel agencies do it for about half that. Shop around.

Priene (Güllübahçe)

Priene is one of the most atmospheric of all of Turkey's ancient sites. Perched high on the craggy slopes of Mt Mykale, it enjoys an isolated, windswept aesthetic in stark contrast to the crowds and commerce of Ephesus.

Outside of the official tours that arrive each day from Selçuk and Kuşadası, the site may be pretty sparsely populated when you visit – you may even get it completely to yourself. The emptiness can give it an almost eerie vibe, with the only sounds the wind, the high-pitched whirring of cicadas, and the soft scuttle of the lizards scampering around the stones.

Though an important city in around 300 BC when the League of Ionian Cities held congresses and festivals here, **Priene** (☎ 547 1165; admission TL3; ⏱ 8.30am-6.30pm May-Sep, 8.30am-5.30pm Oct Apr) was smaller and less important than nearby Miletus. As such, its Hellenistic buildings did not vanish beneath newer Roman ones.

Of the numerous buildings that remain, the most impressive are those of the **Temple of Athena**, which enjoys commanding views of the plain below. Designed by Pythius of Halicarnassus, it is regarded as the epitome of an Ionian temple. Five columns have been re-erected and all around lie the sections of other columns, like giant stone wheels, all in seemingly good condition and arranged so neatly as to look like the careful preparations for something new, rather than the aftermath of something very old. So many remain that

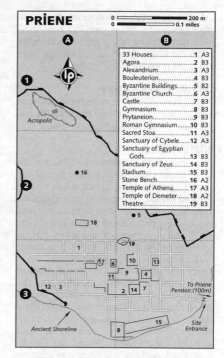

PRIENE

33 Houses	1 A3
Agora	2 B3
Alexandrium	3 A3
Bouleuterion	4 B3
Byzantine Buildings	5 B2
Byzantine Church	6 A3
Castle	7 B3
Gymnasium	8 B3
Prytaneion	9 B3
Roman Gymnasium	10 B3
Sacred Stoa	11 A3
Sanctuary of Cybele	12 A3
Sanctuary of Egyptian Gods	13 B3
Sanctuary of Zeus	14 B3
Stadium	15 B3
Stone Bench	16 A2
Temple of Athena	17 A3
Temple of Demeter	18 A2
Theatre	19 B3

the temple's former reality seems tantalisingly close. As one American tourist asked, vocalising the unspoken thoughts of many, 'why don't they just put it back together again?'.

Elsewhere, the **theatre** is one of the best-preserved examples from the Hellenistic period. It had a capacity to seat 6500 people; look out for the finely carved front seats for VIPs. Also worth seeking out are the remains of the **bouleuterion** (council chamber), a **Byzantine church**, the **gymnasium** and the **stadium**.

SLEEPING & EATING

All of the following are on or just off the main road, Atatürk Caddesi.

Priene Pension (☎ 542 1725; fax 547 1565; camping per person TL8, s/d TL40/60) Currently the only hotel in town, the Priene boasts a beautifully kept garden. Rooms are simple but quite spacious and clean.

Around 30m beyond the Priene, where the dolmuş stops is the **Şelale Restaurant** (☎ 547 1009; ⏱ 8am-11pm). Attractively positioned in the shadow of a ruined Byzantine aqueduct, it has a pool home to trout (which you can eat; TL8) and ducks (which you can't). Next door is the **Villa Sultan Café Bar Restaurant** (☎ 547 1204; köfte TL6, kebap TL7-9; ⏱ 8am-11pm) in a converted kilim factory. The tables are set in a lovely courtyard with a fountain and orange trees and it offers excellent traditional fare.

GETTING THERE & AWAY
Dolmuşes run every 15 minutes between Priene (Güllübahçe; TL3.25, 17km) and Söke; the last one back to Söke leaves Priene at 7pm.

Miletus (Milet)
The ancient town of **Miletus** (☎ 875 5562; admission TL3; ⏱ 8.30am-6.30pm May-Jun, 8.30am-7.30pm Jul-Aug, 8.30am-5.30pm Oct-Apr) lies 22km south of Priene. Its **Great Theatre**, rising up as you approach from the south, is the most significant – and impressive – reminder of a once-grand city, which was a commercial and governmental centre from about 700 BC to AD 700. Later, the harbour filled with silt and Miletus' commerce dwindled. The 15,000-seat theatre was originally a Hellenistic building, but the Romans reconstructed it extensively during the 1st century AD. Though nearly 2000 years old, it's in good condition and has many features, including covered walkways around each tier of seating, still used in today's stadiums, which really help to bring it to life.

It's well worth climbing to the top of the theatre where the ramparts of a later Byzantine castle provide a viewing platform for several other groups of ruins. Look left and you'll see what remains of the **harbour**, called Lion Bay after the stone statues of lions that guarded it. Look right and you'll see the **stadium**; the northern, western and southern **agoras**; the vast **Baths of Faustina**, constructed for Emperor Marcus Aurelius' wife; and a **bouleuterion** between the northern and southern agoras.

South of the main ruins stands the fascinating **İlyas Bey Camii** (1404), dating from a period after the Seljuks but before the Ottomans, when this region was ruled by the Turkish emirs of Menteşe. The doorway and *mihrab* (niche indicating the direction of Mecca) are exquisite, and you'll probably have them to yourself.

Across the road from the Great Theatre, there are a couple of **cafés** (⏱ 7am-6pm) serving reasonably priced snacks including delicious *gözleme* (TL3) and salads (TL5).

GETTING THERE & AWAY
From Söke take a dolmuş (TL2.50) to Balat and ask to be dropped at the Miletus turn-

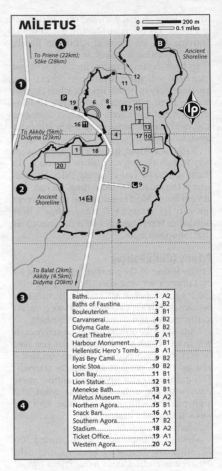

MİLETUS

Baths.....................................1	A2
Baths of Faustina.....................2	B2
Bouleuterion............................3	B1
Carvanserai.............................4	B2
Didyma Gate...........................5	B2
Great Theatre..........................6	A1
Harbour Monument..................7	B1
Hellenistic Hero's Tomb.............8	A1
İlyas Bey Camii.........................9	B2
Ionic Stoa..............................10	B2
Lion Bay................................11	B1
Lion Statue.............................12	B1
Menekse Bath........................13	B1
Miletus Museum.....................14	A2
Northern Agora......................15	B1
Snack Bars.............................16	A2
Southern Agora......................17	B2
Stadium.................................18	A2
Ticket Office...........................19	A1
Western Agora.......................20	A2

off, from where it is about a 1km walk. From Miletus there are no dolmuşes so you'll have to re-trace your steps to the main road. If there's not much traffic about, it may be quicker to return to Söke (TL2.50) and start out again for Didyma. For current information on local timetables (which change regularly), ask at the ticket office at Miletus. If you get stuck, the staff can sometimes call the Balat dolmuş station and request a pick-up.

Didyma (Didim)
Ah, what might have been. Just a few more columns and Didyma's **Temple of Apollo** (☎ 811 0035; admission TL3; ⏱ 8.30am-7.30pm 15 Apr-Sep, 9am-5.30pm Oct-14 Apr) might have been one of the Seven Wonders of the Ancient World. But its

122 columns made it only the second-largest temple in the world, and with 127, the Temple of Artemis (see p240) near Ephesus took the slot instead.

It was still a very important site in its day, home to an oracle whose influence was second only to the one in Delphi (there's a bit of a pattern emerging here). But ancient Didyma was never a real town; only the priests who specialised in oracular temple management lived here. There's a town here now, all right, with the ruins of the temple crowded in on all sides by pensions, carpet stalls and restaurants.

It may be of little comfort now, but the ruins of the temple are much more impressive than those of Artemis. Significant sections of the thick, imposing walls remain standing and three columns have been reconstructed, showing their richly carved bases. Behind the temple porch is a great doorway where oracular poems were written and presented to petitioners. Covered ramps on both sides of the porch lead down to the *cella* (inner room), where the oracle sat and prophesied after drinking from the sacred spring. All around the ground are scattered fragments, including a photogenic head of Medusa (she of the snake hairdo). There used to be a road lined with statues that led to a small harbour, but after standing unmoved for 23 centuries the statues were taken to the British Museum in 1858.

Lovely Altınkum Beach (p260) is nearby.

SLEEPING & EATING

Medusa House (☎ 811 0063; www.medusahouse.com; s/d €30/55) Just around the corner from the temple on the Altınkum road is this restored 150-year-old stone house with five pleasantly decorated rooms set in a very attractive garden (complete with original Greek urns and shaded terraces).

Oracle Pension (☎ 811 0270; s/d €35/55) Next door to Medusa House, the Oracle has simple, rather weary-looking rooms, but this is more than made up for by the stunning views over the temple just next door from the shaded terrace.

Apollon Café & Bar (☎ 811 6050; snacks TL5-6, mains TL7-112; ⏰ 8pm-midnight) Across from the temple entrance, the Apollon is located in a traditional stone house and has seating either in the cool interior or on the pleasant terrace overlooking the temple. The menu is extensive (it's aimed mainly at tour groups) and prices reasonable.

GETTING THERE & AWAY

Dolmuşes run frequently between Söke and Didim (TL7.50, one hour) and Altınkum (TL7.50, 1½ hours). There are also frequent dolmuşes from Didim to Akköy (TL3.25, 30 minutes) from where you may be able to hitch to Miletus.

HERAKLEİA (LATMOS)
☎ 0252

About 30km south of Söke, the highway skirts the southern shore of the huge Bafa Gölü (Lake Bafa), once a gulf of the Aegean but left behind as a lake as the sea retreated. At the southeastern end of the lake is a village called Çamiçi (Bafa), from which a paved road is signposted 10km north for Kapıkırı (for Herakleia). Watch carefully for the sign, which is easily missed.

At the end of a twisting, rock-dominated road, you'll come to the ruins of Herakleia ad Latmos in and around the village of Kapıkırı, which enjoys a dramatic lakeside setting.

Above the village looms dramatic **Beşparmak Dağı** (Five-Fingered Mountain; 1500m), the ancient Mt Latmos that featured in Greek mythology as the place where the hunky shepherd boy Endymion happened to fall asleep. While he was napping, the moon goddess Selene glanced down and fell in love with him. Endymion had asked Zeus to grant him eternal youth and beauty in exchange for staying asleep for eternity. The unfortunate Selene could only gaze down at him night after night, as the moon is forever fated to look down on us mere mortals.

Bafa is an area where Christian hermits took refuge during the 8th-century Arab invasions (note the many ruined churches and monasteries in the vicinity). The monks reputedly considered Endymion a saint for his powers of self-denial.

Herakleia is a fascinating place where the urban and the rural co-exist in such proximity that it almost seems as if a village has been built in the middle of a farm. Fields dotted with beehives close in on all sides, chickens and donkeys stroll the roadsides and there are probably more cowsheds than houses. Remnants of ancient sites are strewn throughout the town, popping up here and there as you make your way around. In a way, the whole village is the attraction, which is why the ticket booth has been set up at its entrance (TL8 if the ticket attendant is around).

SOUTH AEGEAN

Note that there's only one small shop and no bank or ATM in the village.

Tourism has brought much needed revenue to an otherwise rather impoverished community. However, there is still a good deal of poverty and you can pretty much guarantee that when you arrive, you will attract the attention of the town's women (and it will be the women) who may latch on to you as impromptu guides. All carry trays of goods – tablecloths, jewellery, lace etc – wrapped beneath a scarf on their backs, which they will offer to you in hope of a purchase. You will probably get in a lot of refusing practise.

Sights & Activities

The main draw is the glorious lake itself, with the village enjoying wonderful views over its silvery expanses. To get to its edge, head down the road past the **Temple of Endymion**, partly built into the rock, until you reach the ruins of a **Byzantine castle**, which looks down on the city's **necropolis** – a series of rectangular tombs cut directly into the rock.

At the lakeside, near the ruins of a **Byzantine church**, there's a small beach of white coarse sand. The island just offshore can sometimes be reached on foot as the lake's water level falls. Around its base can be seen the foundations of several ancient buildings.

The Agora Pension, among others, offers boat trips around the lake to see the birds and the ruins and to swim. Half-day tours cost €30 and full-day tours €50. The restaurants by the lake also offer tours.

Elsewhere, a path behind the Agora car park leads westwards to the large **Temple of Athena**, on a promontory overlooking the lake. Though only three walls remain, the large and beautifully cut building blocks (put together without cement) are impressive. Other signposted paths lead eastwards to the **agora**, the **bouleuterion** and, several hundred metres through stone-walled pastures and across a valley, to the unrestored and oddly sited **theatre**; its most interesting features are the rows of seats and flights of steps cut into the rock. Stretches of **city wall** dating from around 300 BC are also dotted about the village.

Sleeping & Eating

Pensions offer half-board, but you can normally request bed and breakfast if you wish.

Haus Yasemin Pension (☎ 543 5598; s/d €22/45) Further up the hill, past the *agora*, this place has a welcoming feel, its grounds filled with family clutter. The traditionally styled rooms are simple but spotless and there's a nice terrace with views over the village. It's better value than most.

Agora Pansiyon (☎ 543 5445; www.agora.pansiyon.de; s/d with shower & half-board €40/50; ❄ 🖳) Though the rooms are attractively decorated, the hotel's setting is its biggest asset, with flower-filled gardens and a peaceful outlook. There's also a *hamam* and shaded terrace with hammocks. Mithat, the son of the owner, can act as guide to the area and take you hiking (seven-day hiking programs, with half-board accommodation from €460).

Pelikan Restaurant (☎ 543 5158; meze TL5, fish mains TL12-18; ⏰ 7am-midnight) With great views from its terrace out over the lake, this restaurant offers a simple menu made from local ingredients – pine honey, olives, cheese, eggs and, of course, fish. There's also a slightly gloomy attached pension and the owner, Murat, offers boat tours of the lake.

Kaya Restaurant & Pansiyon (☎ 543 5380; meals €5.55; ⏰ 8am-midnight) This is another good restaurant with a great position down by the waterfront. To get to it, take the road that forks left down to the water just before the ticket booth if entering the village.

If you don't fancy staying in the village, there are other lakeside accommodation options. One of the best is the **Club Natura Oliva** (☎ 519 1072; www.clubnatura.com; Pıarcık Köyü; s/d with half-board €35/53; ❄ 🖳), around 10km north of Herakleia turn-off, a lovely 30-room hotel set in an olive plantation (it makes its own olive oil using a traditional stone mill) with awe-inspiring views over the water and offering a wide program of nature walks.

Getting There & Away

Minibuses from Bodrum (TL6.25), Milas (TL3.50, 45 minutes) or Söke (TL5, one hour) will drop you at Bafa. Unfortunately dolmuşes no longer run from Bafa to Herakleia, but you can get a taxi (TL12), or if you've decided where to stay, you can call the pensions for a free pick-up. From Bafa, dolmuşes run to Milas and Söke only.

MİLAS

☎ 0252 / pop 48,890

As Mylasa, Milas was capital of the Kingdom of Caria, except during the period when Mausolus ruled the kingdom from Halicarnassus (present-day Bodrum). Today, it's a fairly sleepy but still sizeable agricultural town. Don't be put off by what you see from the otogar – the town is fairly attractive and makes a pleasant break from the bright lights of the coastal resorts. On Tuesday there's an excellent local market, which has become an attraction in its own right, welcoming weekly tour parties in summer from Bodrum.

Since Milas is actually closer to Bodrum's international airport than Bodrum itself, you could stay the night in Milas if you arrive late in the day during high season when Bodrum is likely to be full.

Orientation

Approaching Milas from Söke, you pass the otogar 1km before reaching the road to Labranda on the left. To the right, İnönü Caddesi is marked for 'Şehir Merkezi' (city centre). It's another 1km to the centre of town at the Milas Belediye Parkı.

Sights & Activities

Coming into town along İnönü Caddesi, watch for signs pointing to the right for the *belediye*; opposite the *belediye* turn left for the **Baltalı Kapı** (Gate with an Axe). Cross a small bridge and look left to see the well-preserved Roman gate, which has marble posts and lintel, plus Corinthian capitals. The eponymous double-headed axe is carved into the keystone on the northern side.

Return to the road until you reach the shady Milas Belediye Parkı. Turn right at the traffic roundabout, in the centre of which is a model of the Gümüşkesen monumental tomb.

Continue to the end of the road and turn right, then left at Gümüşkesen Caddesi (by the Ambar Cafe), from where, following a steep 600m walk to the top of the hill, you'll find the **Gümüşkesen** ('That Which Cuts Silver' or 'Silver Purse'; admission free), a Roman tomb dating from the 2nd century AD and thought to have been modelled on the Mausoleum at Halicarnassus (albeit on a much smaller scale). As in the mausoleum, Corinthian columns support a pyramidal roof, beneath which is a tomb chamber with fine carvings on the ceiling. A hole in the platform floor allowed devotees to pour libations into the tomb to quench the dead souls' thirst. The small surrounding park is popular with local families.

Return to the roundabout and continue straight across, until you reach the end of

the road. Turn left and, around 100m further on, you'll find the city's small archaeological collection, the **Milas Müzesi** (Şair Ülvi Akgün Caddesi; admission TL3; 🕑 8.30am-noon & 1-5.30pm), which houses various finds from the local region, including Bronze Age tools, gold pieces from Stratonikeia, one of the most important towns in ancient Caria, and various fragments of Roman statuary and buildings, many of which are displayed in the garden outside.

You might also want to see some of Milas' fine mosques, especially the **Ulu Cami** (1378) and **Orhan Bey Camii** (1330), built when Milas was capital of the Turkish principality of Menteşe. The larger, more impressive **Firuz Bey Camii** (1394) was built shortly after Menteşe was incorporated into the new and growing Ottoman Empire.

Milas has kept some of its older houses and there is some very impressive Ottoman and early-20th-century architecture, especially along Atatürk Bulvarı and behind the *belediye*.

Sleeping & Eating

Yazar Otel (🕿 512 4203; Kadıağa Caddesi 70; s/d TL35/50; 🔀) Conveniently located for the Tuesday bazaar (which starts at its steps), this hotel is small but cheerful, comfortable and clean. Rooms have TV and minibar. It lies right next door to the Halk Bank.

Milashan Otel (🕿 513 7901; www.milashanotel.com; Cumhuriyet Caddesi; s/d with bathroom & air-con €50/65; 🔀) Handy for the airport, the Milashan is on the opposite side of town to the Yazar, opposite the Ören road. It's big, pink and businessy, but the rooms are comfortable and there's a reasonable restaurant. A good overnight pit-stop.

Dilek Pastaneleri (🕿 512 4140; Kadıağa Caddesi 32; coffee from TL1.20, ice cream TL0.75; 🕑 7.30am-midnight) On the same street as Yazar Otel, this is a pleasant place for breakfast, snacks or coffee and cake.

Other decent stop-offs include **Pamukkale** (🕿 512 1919; Menteşe Caddesi; 🕑 7.30am-1am), just around the corner from the Yazar Otel where you can get a good kebap in pide for TL4 and the **Park Café** (Milas Belediye Parkı; 🕑 8am-7.30pm), where you can enjoy a tea (TL0.50) under shady trees while you plan your next move.

Getting There & Away

The otogar is on the main Bodrum to Söke road, 1km from the centre, although dolmuşes from Bodrum (TL6.50, one hour) drop off in town as well. There are also frequent dolmuş services from Söke (TL7.50, 82km).

A small **dolmuş station** (☎ 512 4014; Köy Tabakhane Garaji) in the town centre offers timetabled minibus services to Ören (TL4) and Iasos (TL4.25).

AROUND MİLAS
Beçin Castle
Just over 1km along the road from Milas to Ören (watch for the brown sign immediately after a corner), a road on the right leads to **Beçin Kalesi** (Beçin Castle; admission TL3; ◷ 8am-dusk), a Byzantine fortress on a rocky outcrop that was largely remodelled by the Turkish emirs of Menteşe who used Beçin as their capital in the 14th century.

The castle walls are striking, perched on high with a giant Turkish flag flapping in the breeze, and offer great views of Milas down below. Be careful when exploring as the drops from the unfenced sides are sheer and steep. Don' let anyone tell you to 'go back a bit' for a photo.

There's not a lot to see inside. Atop the adjacent hill, some 500m away, are other remnants of the 14th-century Menteşe settlement, including the **Kızılhan** (Red Caravanserai), **Orhan Bey Camii**, the **Ahmet Gazi tomb** and, the highlight, a newly restored **medrese** (seminary).

Labranda
Set into a steep hillside in an area that once supplied the ancient city of Mylasa with its water, the site of ancient Labranda is surrounded by fragrant pine forests peopled by beekeepers. Late in the season (October) you can see their tents pitched in the groves as they go about their business of extracting the honey and rendering the wax from the honeycombs. It's a beautiful place to visit that's well worth seeking out, not least because so few people make it up here.

Labranda (admission TL8; ◷ 8am-5pm) was a holy place, where worship of a local god was going on by the 6th century BC and perhaps long before. Later it became a sanctuary to Zeus, controlled for a long time by Milas. The great **Temple of Zeus** honours the god's warlike aspect (Stratius, or Labrayndus, which means 'Axe-Bearing'). There may have been an oracle here; certainly festivals and Olympic games were held at the time.

Two men's banqueting halls, the **First Andron** and **Second Andron**, are in surprisingly good condition, as is a fine 4th-century **tomb** and other buildings. Excavated by a Swedish team in the early 20th century, the ruins are interesting enough but it's the site itself, with its spectacular views over the valley, which is most impressive.

Labranda seems to have been abandoned around AD 1000. Today, a caretaker will show you around; he speaks only Turkish (with a few words of English), but the site is well labelled.

GETTING THERE & AWAY
The junction for the road to Labranda is just northwest of Milas on the road to Söke. It's 14km to the site. The road passes through the village of Kargıcak, 8km along, but even if you could find a dolmuş going as far as that you'd still have a long walk ahead of you. Do be careful as there's a quarry up past the site, and lorries roar up and down the narrow road all day long. Hitching is possible but not always reliable.

A taxi from Milas shouldn't cost more than TL30 – the drivers near the Otel Arı seem more willing to negotiate than those near the Ören dolmuş station. Be sure to agree on a price that includes at least an hour's waiting time.

Euromos
The ancient city of Euromos once stood on a site about 12km northwest of Milas and 1km from the village of Selimiye. Today, almost all that remains of it is the picturesque, and partly restored, **Temple of Zeus** (admission TL8; ◷ 8.30am-5.30pm Oct-Apr, to 7pm May-Sep) with some unfluted columns, which suggest it was never completed.

First settled in the 6th century BC, Euromos originally held a sanctuary to a local deity. With the coming of Greek (then Roman) culture, the local god's place was taken by Zeus. Euromos reached the height of its prosperity between 200 BC and AD 200. Emperor Hadrian, who built so many monuments in Anatolia, is thought to have also built the temple here.

If you're interested in ruins, you can clamber up the slopes to find other bits of the town. Climb up through the olive groves past the toilets, past part of a fortification wall and you'll find yourself on flat ground that was once the stage of the ancient **theatre**. It's badly ruined, with olive trees poking up from the few remaining rows of seats. The town's **agora** is down by the highway, with only a few toppled column drums to mark it.

GETTING THERE & AWAY

To get here, take the Milas to Söke bus or dolmuş and ask to get out at the ruins. They're around 200m from the highway. Alternatively, take a dolmuş from Milas to Kıyıkışlacık, get out at the road junction for Iasos and walk the short distance north along the highway until you see the Euromos ruins on the right.

Kıyıkışlacık (Iasos)

☎ 0252

About 2km southwest of Euromos (10km northwest of Milas) is a sign for Kıyıkışlacık (Iasos). From here a road heads coastward for around 20km, winding high up into the hills, and offering great views of the river plain, until it reaches Iasos, a sleepy Aegean fishing village set amid the tumbled ruins of the ancient city.

The small harbour is crowded with fishing boats. A handful of small pensions and restaurants cater for travellers who want to get away from it all for a few days.

SIGHTS

About 100m before your reach Iasos proper, the road forks. Bear right along the gravel road where the large yellow sign reads 'Balık Pazari Açik Hava Müsei', and you should come to the **Balıkpazarı Açıkhava Müzesi** (Iasos Museum; admission TL3; ⏰ 8.30am-5.30pm Tue-Sun) and, opposite it, a small cabin (the ticket office). Housed in the old fish market, the museum holds the village's most interesting ruin, a monumental Roman tomb (as well as various other classical fragments).

If, instead, you bear left, the road continues to the port, then up over the hill and along the coast. The hill above the port is covered with ruins, including a walled **acropolis-fortress** (admission TL2; ⏰ 8.30am-5.30pm Tue-Sun). Excavations have also revealed the city's *bouleuterion* and *agora*, a gymnasium, a basilica, a Roman temple of Artemis Astias (AD 190) and numerous other buildings.

SLEEPING & EATING

Climb the hill behind the restaurants to find the delightful **Cengiz** (☎ 537 7181; cengiz1955@gmail .com; s/d TL25/40), the **Zeytin** (☎ 537 7008; s/d TL25/40; ⏰ Apr-20 Oct) and **Kaya Pension** (☎ 537 7439; www

.iasos.de; s/d €15/29; ▨). All have simple, spotless rooms and lovely terraces with gorgeous views. The rooms of the Cengiz and Zeytin have balconies (some with sea views – ask for rooms 1, 2 or 6 at the Cengiz), but the Kaya has a nice pool. All places lie on Kıyıkışlacık Köyü, the main road, on the hill above the harbour.

If you haven't yet feasted on Turkish fish, here's your chance. Restaurants offer delicious fresh fish at feasible prices. The **Dilek Restaurant** (☎ 537 7307; ⏰ 9am-midnight May-Sep) at the far end of the harbour has a great, open meze buffet (with around 20 different types of meze) for TL15, and fish (such as sea bream) for around TL10 to TL18. **Iasos Deniz Restaurant** (☎ 537 7066; ⏰ 10am-midnight) also serves fish (from TL10), and has a terrace right over the water where you can watch little fish dart in and out of the seaweed.

GETTING THERE & AWAY

In theory, during summer and on Thursdays during the rest of the year (for the Güllük market), municipality boats sail from Güllük to Iasos (TL6, 15 minutes) and back. In practice, they often don't, so check. You can also hire a fishing boat yourself (TL20 one way, 20 minutes) if you want to.

Between Iasos and Milas (TL4), dolmuşes run every hour in summer (every 1½ hours in winter).

BODRUM

☎ 0252 / pop 28,580

Some people will tell you that Bodrum is an unsophisticated low-end resort town. These people obviously haven't been to Kuşadası. In fact, while Bodrum certainly welcomes the hordes during the summer months, it manages to do so without diluting its essential character or charm – not an easy trick to pull off.

With laws in place restricting the height of the town's buildings, it has nice architectural uniformity to it. Out of season, its whitewashed houses and subtropical gardens can appear almost idyllic. And even when its seafront bars are spilling over with people and its clubs are pumping, there's still something rather refined about the place. Despite its full-on reputation, tourism is by no means restricted to packagers and budget travellers, although they are very well catered for. Rather, Bodrum operates a sort of two-tier form of tourism with plenty of happy-hour bars and cheap excursion boats for

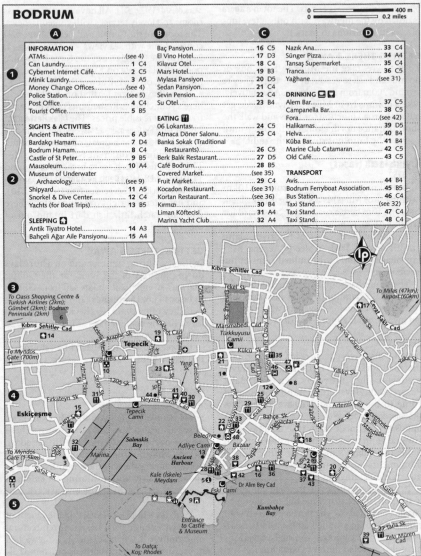

BODRUM

INFORMATION		
ATMs..(see 4)		
Can Laundry.................................. **1** C4		
Cybernet Internet Café.................. **2** C5		
Minik Laundry.............................. **3** A5		
Money Change Offices..............(see 4)		
Police Station...........................(see 5)		
Post Office.................................. **4** C4		
Tourist Office.............................. **5** B5		

SIGHTS & ACTIVITIES		
Ancient Theatre............................ **6** A3		
Bardakçı Hamam........................... **7** D4		
Bodrum Hamam............................ **8** C4		
Castle of St Peter......................... **9** B5		
Mausoleum................................. **10** A4		
Museum of Underwater		
Archaeology...........................(see 9)		
Shipyard..................................... **11** A5		
Snorkel & Dive Center................. **12** C4		
Yachts (for Boat Trips)................. **13** B5		

SLEEPING		
Antik Tiyatro Hotel..................... **14** A3		
Bahçeli Ağar Aile Pansiyonu.......... **15** A4		

Baç Pansiyon.............................. **16** C5
El Vino Hotel............................. **17** D3
Kilavuz Otel............................... **18** C4
Mars Hotel................................. **19** B3
Mylasa Pansiyon......................... **20** D5
Sedan Pansiyon.......................... **21** C4
Sevin Pension............................ **22** C4
Su Otel..................................... **23** B4

EATING		
06 Lokantası.............................. **24** C5		
Atmaca Döner Salonu.................. **25** C4		
Banka Sokak (Traditional		
Restaurants)............................ **26** C5		
Berk Balık Restaurant.................. **27** D5		
Café Bodrum.............................. **28** B5		
Covered Market.......................(see 35)		
Fruit Market............................... **29** C4		
Kocadon Restaurant.................(see 31)		
Kortan Restaurant....................(see 36)		
Kırmızı...................................... **30** B4		
Liman Köftecisi........................... **31** A4		
Marina Yacht Club....................... **32** A4		

Nazık Ana................................. **33** C4
Sünger Pizza............................. **34** A4
Tansaş Supermarket.................... **35** C5
Tranca..................................... **36** C5
Yağhane.................................(see 31)

DRINKING		
Alem Bar................................... **37** C5		
Campanella Bar.......................... **38** C5		
Fora.......................................(see 42)		
Halikarnas................................. **39** D5		
Helva....................................... **40** B4		
Küba Bar................................... **41** B4		
Marine Club Catamaran............... **42** C5		
Old Café................................... **43** C5		

TRANSPORT		
Avis.. **44** B4		
Bodrum Ferryboat Association....... **45** B5		
Bus Station................................ **46** C4		
Taxi Stand.............................(see 32)		
Taxi Stand................................ **47** C4		
Taxi Stand................................ **48** C4		

the fun-and-sun seekers from Europe, along-side a marina filled with multi-million dollar yachts and a collection of high-end restaurants aimed at wealthy Turks.

Sunbathing, dining and nightlife aside, Bodrum does boast a few worthwhile at-tractions, chief among them the outstand-ing Museum of Underwater Archaeology,

located in the Castle of St Peter, the town's defining landmark.

History

Aeons ago Bodrum rose to fame on the back of the Mausoleum, the spectacular tomb of the Carian King Mausolus that Roman his-torian Pliny the Elder designated one of the

BODRUM'S BIG BLUE

With high visibility, clean water, and pleasant and steady temperatures, Bodrum is a good place for diving or snorkelling. Marine life that can potentially be spotted in its waters include octopus, turtle, barracuda, jack fish and parrot fish, although sadly not much coral. Diving clubs also have access to 'two old navy hulks' and are pushing to be given permission to dive some of the hundreds of incredible wrecks lying just off Bodrum's coast, which if granted would probably make it one of the best wreck diving sites in the world.

The **Snorkel & Dive Center** (☎ 313 6017; Cevat Şakir Caddesi 5; ☘ 10am-6pm winter, 9am-midnight summer) sells and rents snorkelling and diving equipment, and organises dives (full day's diving with two dives, boat, all equipment, insurance, hotel transfers and lunch per person €45). All-day snorkelling trips cost €20 per person. A four-day PADI Open Water course costs €350 per person.

Seven Wonders of the World. Sadly, not much remains to be seen today. Most visitors will be more impressed by the Castle of St Peter, standing sentinel over the town's twin bays.

Herodotus (c 485–425 BC), the 'Father of History', was Bodrum's most famous son. Between the two World Wars, writer Cevat Şakir Kabaağaç lived in political exile here and wrote an account of idyllic voyages along the Carian and Lycian coasts, then completely untouched by tourism. The 'Fisherman of Halicarnassus' called his most famous book *Mavi Yolculuk* (Blue Voyage), a name since co-opted for all cruises along these shores. More recently the late singer Zeki Muran settled in Bodrum, putting it on the map for gay travellers.

Orientation

The road to Bodrum winds through pine forests before cresting a hill to reveal a panorama of the town dominated by its striking Crusader castle, which sits atop a promontory neatly dividing the town into two roughly equal-sized bays. The main road into town is Cevat Şakir Caddesi, which takes you down past the otogar (around 400m inland) and then down along the front of the Salmakis Bay, where it turns into Neyzen Teyfik Caddesi.

From the otogar, walk south towards the sea, past the fruit market, and you'll come to a small white mosque, the Adliye Camii (Courthouse Mosque), which pretty much marks the centre of town. Just ahead of you is the covered bazaar and beyond that a small square where you'll find the tourist office. Continue south and you'll reach the castle entrance and ferry pier.

Bodrum's two bays have very different characters. Salmakis Bay, which runs from the castle promontory to the marina, is the more self-consciously upmarket side of town, its waters filled with expensive yachts backed by a row of mostly high-end restaurants and clubs. Kumbahçe Bay, on the other hand, is very much the budget side of town, its services geared mainly towards European visitors. It's here that you'll find the town's narrow and rather ugly beach – although that doesn't stop it from being packed with sun-loungers in summer. Running behind it is the pedestrianised Dr Alim Bey Caddesi, packed with shops, bars and restaurants, and its continuation, Cumhuriyet Caddesi, whose long line of bars stretches all the way down to famed Halıkarnas, which marks the end of the bay. Past the club is another small curve of beach and a cruise ship pier.

Information

There are many ATMs and currency exchanges along Dr Alim Bey Caddesi and Cevat Şakir Caddesi.

Can Laundry (☎ 316 4089; Türkkuyusu Caddesi 99; per 5kg load TL4; ☘ 8.30am-9pm Mon-Sat, 10am-9pm Sun)
Cybernet Internet Café (☎ 316 3167; Üçkuyular Caddesi 7; per hr TL2; ☘ 24hr)
Minik Laundry (☎ 316 7904; Neyzen Tevfik Caddesi 236; 4kg wash & dry TL7.50)
Post office (☎ 316 2760; Cevat Şakir Caddesi; ☘ post office 8.30am-5pm, telephone exchange 8am-midnight)
Tourist office (☎ 316 1091; Kale Meydanı; ☘ 9am-6pm Mon-Fri, daily in summer) There is also a small tourist information booth next to the otogar entrance.

Sights & Activities
CASTLE OF ST PETER

When Tamerlane invaded Anatolia in 1402, throwing the nascent Ottoman Empire temporarily off balance, the Knights Hospitaller based in Rhodes took the opportunity to capture Bodrum. By 1437 they had erected the Castle of St Peter, which they continued to augment with new defensive features – including moats, walls and water cisterns – over the ensuing decades. However, in 1522, when Süleyman the Magnificent captured the Knights' headquarters in Rhodes, the Bodrum contingent was forced to abandon the castle without having ever truly tested its fearsome defensive capabilities. The castle fell into decline during the succeeding centuries and suffered some shell damage during WWI. Reconstruction didn't begin in earnest until the 1960s, when it was used as an informal storage space for the booty collected during underwater archaeology missions, before becoming, in 1986, Bodrum's **Museum of Underwater Archaeology** (☎ 316 2516; www.bodrum -museum.com; admission TL10; ☸ 9am-noon & 1-7pm Tue-Sun summer, 8am-noon & 1-5pm winter).

It's an excellent museum and arguably the most important of its kind in the world with imaginatively displayed well-lit items, accompanied by plenty of information panels, maps, models, reconstructions, drawings, murals, dioramas and videos.

The views of the town from the battalions are spectacular and worth the entry price alone. As the museum is spread throughout the castle, you need two hours to do it justice. Arrows suggest routes around it (red for long; green for short), but guides are not available.

As you head up the stone ramp into the castle past a **Crusader coats of arms** carved in marble and mounted on the stone walls, keep an eye out for bits of marble filched from the ancient Mausoleum. The ramp leads to the castle's main court, centred on an ancient mulberry tree. To the left is a long display of **amphorae** – the castle owns one of the largest collections in the world – with examples from the 14th century BC to the present day, all recovered from the waters of southwest Turkey. The adjoining courtyard café, adorned with Greek and Roman statuary, provides a shady resting place, and there's a small glass-blowing workshop where you can watch glass bottles and jewellery being created (similar to those recovered from coastal wrecks).

The chapel here contains both a one tenth-size complete model and a full-sized reconstruction of the stern of a 7th-century eastern **Roman ship** discovered off Yassıada. Visitors can walk the decks, stand at the helm, look below decks at the cargo of wine and peek into the galley.

Follow the path to the left of the chapel to ascend to the towers. Up the ramp is the **Glass-Shipwreck exhibit** (admission TL5; ☸ 10-noon & 2-4pm Tue-Fri). As you enter, look for the castle-shaped dovecote on the castle wall. Discovered by a sponge diver in 1973 and excavated by the American Professor George Bass and a team of marine archaeologists, the 16m-long, 5m-wide ship sank in AD 1025 while carrying 3 tonnes of mainly broken glass between Fatimid Syria and the Black Sea.

Next up is a small **Glass Hall** where glass finds from the 15th century BC to the 14th century AD are displayed. The assorted Mycenean beads, Roman glass bottles and Islamic weights are kept in near darkness with each piece backlit individually so as to better reveal its delicate structure. Next door is a small exhibition of coins, including numerous examples from Ancient Caria.

Beyond, the **French Tower** has finds taken from the *Tektaş Burnu*, the only ancient Greek shipwreck (thought to date from around 480 BC to 400 BC) from the Classical period to be fully excavated. Displays include numerous amphorae, talismanic marble discs, kitchen utensils, as well as photographs of the excavation itself, which took place off the coast of the Çesme Peninsula in 2001.

Next door, the **Carian Princess Hall** (admission €2.75; ☸ 10am-noon & 2-4pm Tue-Fri) holds the remains and effects of a high status woman, discovered by Turkish archaeologists in 1989. Though popularly said to belong to Queen Ada, the last Carian queen, who was brought back from exile and installed as monarch by Alexander the Great following his conquest of Halicarnassus in 334 BC, there is no concrete evidence for this. Buried with a gold crown, necklace, bracelets, rings and an exquisite wreath of gold myrtle leaves, her identity doesn't lessen the incredible value of the find.

Guarding the castle's southeast corner, the **English Tower** was built during the reign of King Henry IV of England (whose coat of arms is displayed above the entrance to the uppermost hall) and is now fitted out as a medieval refectory with a long central dining table surrounded by suits of armour, stag horns and the standards of the Grand Masters of the Knights Hospitaller and their Turkish adversaries. Piped medieval music plays in the background giving the place the feel of a Crusader Knights theme restaurant. Look out for the Latin graffiti carved into the stone window ledges by Crusaders.

Just to the north is the extraordinary gallery of **Bronze Age shipwrecks**. Its principal exhibit is the 14th-century BC *Uluburun*, the oldest excavated shipwreck in the world. There are full size replicas of the ship's interior and the wreck site on the seabed. The aptly named Treasure Room holds a wealth of finds, including Canaanite gold jewellery, bronze daggers, ivory cosmetic boxes, wooden writing boards and the gold scarab of Queen Nefertiti of Egypt.

Further north, descend the **Gatineau Tower** to the dungeons beneath. Over the inner gate is the inscription 'Inde Deus abest' (Where God does not exist). The dungeon was used as a place of confinement and torture by the Knights from 1513 to 1523. A sign warns that the exhibits of torture implements might not be suitable for children, but most video-game–hardened visitors will find the display dummies and the taped groans more laughable than disturbing.

MAUSOLEUM

Founded some time in the 11th century BC, the ancient kingdom of Caria, which encompassed modern day Bodrum, became absorbed into the Persian Empire, although it continued to exercise a degree of autonomy until the arrival of Alexander two centuries later. During that time its most famous leader (or satrap) was Mausolus (c 376–353 BC), an admirer of Greek culture, who moved the capital from Mylasa to Halicarnassus. After his death, his wife, Artemesia, undertook the construction of a monumental tomb, as planned by Mausolus himself and designed in a Hellenic-style by Pytheos, the man behind the Temple of Athena at Priene. The Mausoleum, an enormous white-marble tomb topped by a stepped pyramids became one of the Seven Wonders of the Ancient World and stood relatively intact for almost 19 centuries, until it was broken up by the Crusaders in 1522 and the pieces used as building material. The most impressive remains, including friezes incorporated into the walls of the Castle of St Peter, and statues of Mausolus and Artemesia discovered at the site, were shipped off to the British Museum in London in the 19th century, where they remain.

In light of its almost utter obliteration, you may consider giving the **Mausoleum** (Turgutreis Caddesi; admission TL8; ⏲ 8.30am-5.30pm Tue-Sun) a miss. In fact, the site is still worth visiting. It has pleasant gardens, with the excavations to the right and a covered arcade to the left. The arcade contains a copy of the famous frieze now in the British Museum. The four original fragments on display were discovered more recently. Models, drawings and documents give an idea of why this tomb made Pliny's list of Wonders. Other exhibits include a model of Halicarnassus at the time of King Mausolus, and a model of the Mausoleum and its precincts.

A description written in 1581, supposedly taken from a 1522 eyewitness account, describes how the Knights Hospitaller discovered the buried Mausoleum, uncovered it, admired it and returned to the castle for the night. That night, pirates broke in and stole the treasures, which had been safe as long as they had been buried. The next day the knights returned and broke the tomb to pieces for use as building stone. In reality, research suggests that tomb robbers had already beaten the knights to the treasure and that earthquakes had shattered it long before they ever set foot in Turkey.

Don't hold your breath in expectation over the actual site. Of the remains, only a few pre-Mausolean stairways and tomb chambers, the Mausolean drainage system, the entry to Mausolus' tomb chamber, a few bits of precinct wall and some large fluted marble column drums survive.

OTHER RUINS

A restored **ancient theatre** (Kıbrıs Şehitler Caddesi; admission TL8; ⏲ 8am-5pm Sat-Thu), which could originally seat 13,000 people, is cut into the rock of the hillside behind town on the busy main road to Gümbet. Recently, tombs dating to before the theatre were discovered here.

Just beyond the marina are the recently restored remains of the **shipyard** (Şafak Sokak; ⏲ 9am-6pm). In 1770 the entire Ottoman fleet was destroyed by the Russians at Çeşme and had to be rebuilt from scratch in boatyards like this. The shipyard was fortified as a defence against pirates in the 19th century. Its tower occasionally hosts art exhibitions, while the rest of the site is mainly used as a children's playground and is principally memorable for the views from the top, where there are several old tombstones dating from the period when the Latin alphabet was replacing Arabic.

BOATING IN BODRUM

Boats are the big thing in Bodrum, according to Chris Drum Berkaya, Editor of the *Bodrum Observer*, a newspaper aimed at the peninsula's expat community. 'The influx of the wealthy with their boats makes everyone think sailing/boating is out of reach, but I still think the best experience in Bodrum is to take a day boat trip out. Choose your boat, there are noisy ones, or quiet ones, some with good food, but they all drop anchor in a few bays over the day where you can swim and enjoy a five-star life for the day.'

Most of the excursion boats are moored along Neyzen Tevfik Caddesi and depart daily, either at 10am returning at 5pm, or noon returning at 7pm, and cost around €12, including lunch and afternoon tea.

The itineraries tend to change daily, but nearly always take in **Karaada** (Black Island), where hot springs gush out of a cave and swimmers rub the orange mud from the springs onto their skin, as well as a few of the area's other more idyllic beaches and swim spots. You can book the trips directly at the boats, through most of the town's hotels or at one of the numerous tour operators on Cevat Şakir Caddesi who can also arrange trips to more far-flung destinations, including the Milas Tuesday market (€8), Dalyan (€30), Ephesus (€30) and Pamukkale (€30). Try **Botur** (☎ 313 1922; botur@usa.net; Cevat Şakir Caddesi 24), just south of the otogar.

At the far western end of Turgutreis Caddesi are the restored remains of the **Myndos Kapısı** (Myndos Gate), the only surviving gate from the original 7km-long walls, which were probably built by King Mausolus in the 4th century BC. In front of the twin-towered gate are the remains of a moat in which many of Alexander the Great's soldiers drowned in 334 BC.

HAMAMS

Across from the otogar, **Bodrum Hamam** (☎ 313 4129; www.bodrumhamami.com.tr; Cevat Şakir Caddesi, Fabrika Sokak 42; full massage TL35; ☉ 6am-midnight) is convenient and clean with separate sections for men and women. Though the exterior looks unpromising, the **Bardakçı Hamam** (☎ 313 8114; Kumbahçe Mahallesi Dere Sokak 22; bath/massage TL15/30; ☉ 7am-midnight), founded in 1749, has a lovely marble-clad interior and great atmosphere. Bathing is mixed.

Festivals & Events

For two weeks in August each year, the Castle of St Peter hosts national and international ballet stars at the **International Ballet Festival** (☎ 313 7649), which showcases classical, modern and experimental dance. Check out www .biletix.com for information on tickets. In the first week of October, there is a colourful international **Yacht Festival**.

Sleeping

Bodrum's accommodation options fall into three main categories: package, budget and boutique. Most of the former types of hotel

are located well outside town and cater mainly to large groups arriving en masse by charter plane. Still, if you're planning to stay a week or so, it's worth checking with the relevant agencies to see if you can pick up some kind of cheap deal.

There are plenty of budget hotels and pensions, particularly in the centre and along Kumbahçe Bay, although be aware that the closer you are to the front the less chance you'll have of getting a good night's sleep – action at the clubs rarely kicks off before midnight and usually goes on until past 4am. Thankfully there are also a number of quieter inland choices.

Upmarket boutique hotels are a recent and fast-growing addition to the holiday scene. A number line the coast just east of Kumbahçe Bay.

In high summer, especially at weekends, Bodrum fills up quickly, so try to arrive early in the day. More places stay open in winter than in previous years, although the majority do close.

BUDGET

There are various camping grounds on the Bodrum Peninsula's northern shore. Check with the tourist office for information and bookings.

Sedan Pansiyon (☎ 316 0355; off Türkkuyusu Caddesi 121; s/d without bathroom €10/16, s/d with bathroom €12/24) Very much at the basic end of the spectrum with rooms of varying sizes and states of repair arranged around a ramshackle but peaceful courtyard, tucked away off the street. It's friendly and good value, and guests can use the kitchen.

Sevin Pension (☎ 316 7682; www.sevinpension.com; Türkkuyusu Caddesi 5; dm €13, s €18-22, d €25-36; ☒ ▣) Be under no illusions, it's basic – think cracked floor tiles, grimy taps and furniture made level with folded cigarette packets. But for the price it offers a lot: a prime (albeit very noisy) location, TV, free wi-fi, good breakfasts and friendly, helpful staff. Its 37 rooms vary in size considerably, so check what you're getting.

Mylasa Pansiyon (☎ 316 1846; www.mylasapansiyon .com; Cumhuriyet Caddesi Dere Sokak 2; s/d €25/35; ☒) The archetypal Bodrum pension. Just back from the beach but very much at the heart of the party scene. The rooms are small with TVs, but none too modern looking. But then, that's hardly the point. The café-restaurant is lively (and operates the obligatory happy hour discounts) and there are great panoramic views from the rooftop terrace. Don't expect to get much sleep.

Bahçeli Ağar Aile Pansiyonu (☎ 316 1648; 1402 Sokak 4; s/d €20/36) This endearing little pension is in a passageway off Neyzen Tevik Caddesi, opposite the marina. Run by İbrahim and family, and with a little courtyard overhung by vines, it has an intimate feel, and guests have use of the kitchen. Rooms are small and simple, but spotless, quiet and peaceful; all have balconies.

Kilavuz Otel (☎ 316 3892; www.kilavuzotel.com; Atatürk Caddesi Adliye Sokak 17; s/d €35/40; ☒ ▣) Striking a good balance between proximity to the front and the need for a bit of peace and quiet, this family-run place offers 15 simply-furnished, clean rooms, a moderately sized pool, good meals at its adjoining restaurant and, its biggest asset, great friendly service.

Baç Pansiyon (☎ 316 2497; bacpansiyon@turk.net; Cumhuriyet Caddesi 14; s €28-33, d €45-65; ☒) Small but stylish and all in marble, wood and wrought iron, this centrally situated hotel also boasts about the best hotel views in Bodrum. A gem amid the market maelstrom, it sits right above the water and four of its 10 comfortable rooms have delightful balconies over the water.

Mars Otel (☎ 316 6559; www.marsotel.com; Imbat Çıkmazı 29; s/d €34/45; ☒ ▣) Set a good five-minute-walk from the front, the Mars is quiet, peaceful and good value. It's a bit of an exercise in miniaturisation with compact rooms – all clean and tidy with TVs – a small pool and a two-person bar, but Murat, the owner, is keen to please and there are free bus station transfers.

MIDRANGE

Su Otel (☎ 316 6906; www.suhotel.net; Turgutreis Caddesi, 1201 Sokak; s €55-65, d €65-85; ☒ ▣) Follow the blue mosaic snake down the alley to find this cheery number, whose bright multicoloured decor makes it look a bit like a giant children's climbing frame. All of the large, clean rooms have balconies, some overlooking the large central pool. If you're in Bodrum for more than a week, the Su also has a couple of lovely old cottages near the mausoleum (from €80 for up to three people) for rent.

El Vino Hotel (☎ 313 8770; www.elvinobodrum.com; Pamili Sokak; s/d €80/120; ☒ ▣) The dark back-street location doesn't look that promising, but behind the stone wall is one of the town's loveliest hotels. Rooms are large and well appointed with wooden floors, large beds, TVs and writing desks. The best have views of the central pool and garden area (where breakfast is served) or the town. Even better views are available from the rooftop restaurant.

TOP END

Antik Tiyatro Hotel (☎ 316 6053; www.antiquetheatre hotel.com; Kıbrıs Şehitler Caddesi 243; d/ste from €120/225; ☒ ▣) Rooms, arranged around a lovely pool set on the edge of a terraced hillside, have stunning views over the castle and sea, and are stylishly decorated with original art work and antiques. Double glazing keeps out most of the noise of the busy nearby road and there's a great poolside restaurant.

Eating

Bodrum's finest and most expensive restaurants are all located along the western bay; its worst in the eastern. In between, on Cevat Şakir Caddesi and in the bazaar are the best value options. Here you'll find a collection of Turkish restaurants and *bufes* (snack bars), where you can pick up a döner wrapped in pide for TL4.

Restaurants open and close all the time. Those described here have proved more long-standing and dependable.

SALMAKIS BAY

In July and August prices in Bodrum's gastronomic heartland can exceed even those of İstanbul, although there are some notable cut-price exceptions. As elsewhere, check prices before ordering fish.

Liman Köftecisi (☎ 316 5060; Neyzen Tevfik Caddesi 172; meze TL4; ☼ 8am-midnight) Despite being nationally famous, the Liman serves delicious food at very decent prices. *Köfte* are the speciality. Of the six types (TL7 to TL12.50), the TL10 *Liman köfte* – served with yoghurt, tomato sauce and butter – is the house speciality. The service is also exemplary.

Kırmızı (☎ 316 4918; Neyzen Tevik Caddesi 44; meze TL5-8, mains TL10-14; ☯ 11.30am-midnight) Serving Mediterranean food made from the freshest local ingredients, the Kırmızı is a characterful place with three floors and a garden terrace. The walls are used to exhibit the works of local artists, and Duygu, the charming owner, will accord you a warm welcome. The three-course fixed lunch for only TL6 is astonishing value.

Sünger Pizza (☎ 316 0854; Neyzen Tevfik Caddesi 218; salads TL5-7.50; ☯ 8am-midnight) Named after the owner's grandfather who was a *sünger* (sponge) diver, this place is generally packed with locals. The 'best pizza in Bodrum' comes in four sizes: small, medium, large and jumbo (TL14/24/32/38 respectively for the 'special'). Grab a table on the rooftop if you can.

Marina Yacht Club (☎ 316 1228; Neyzen Tevfik Caddesi 5; beer €2.75, pizzas TL9-17, mains TL15-30; ☯ 8am-2am) Despite the rather grand entrance and chichi yachting surrounds, the food and prices are quite reasonable at this three-restaurant complex and there's live music every night from 9pm to 1am. It serves either traditional Turkish food or Italian food in the Café Vela.

Kocadon Restaurant (☎ 316 3705; Saray Sokak 1; meals €15-25; ☯ dinner May-Oct) Expensive but worth it, this attractive dining space set in the cobbled courtyard of a very attractive 200-year-old stone house serves some of the town's very finest food. The three-course set menu (for lunch or dinner, TL40), which includes an open buffet of 10 meze, a fish dish and seasonal fruits is excellent. Otherwise mains from the à la carte menu start at TL25. Dig into your wallet and enjoy some fine cuisine alongside Bodrum's high flyers.

Yağhane (☎ 313 4747; Neyzen Tevfik Caddesi 170; mains TL16-28; ☯ 10.30am-midnight) Housed in an old olive mill built in 1894, this is an attractive and atmospheric place, with the walls hung with the works of local artists. The menu, which specialises in old Ottoman dishes, is very imaginative. Try the delicious regional speciality *çökertme* kebap – grilled meat with garlic yoghurt, grated potatoes and butter (€11). The wine list is also impressive.

CENTRE

At the very southern end of the bazaar, Banka Sokak (locally known as Meyhaneler Sokak or Tavern St) is a lovely and strangely quiet alleyway, shaded by foliage and filled with attractive, traditional Turkish restaurants and *köfteci* (*köfte* restaurants) where many locals come for their lunch.

Nazik Ana (☎ 313 1891; Eski Hukumet Sokak 7; meat mains TL4-5, veg mains TL2-3; ☯ 9am-10pm, closed Sun in winter) Rather hidden away down a narrow alley but definitely worth hunting out, this simple but atmospheric place is a huge hit locally, particularly with the police officers from next door. With its point-and-pick counter, it's a great place to sample different Turkish dishes. If you don't like something, it's so incredibly cheap it doesn't really matter. It lies off Cevat Şakir Caddesi.

Atmaca Döner Salonu (☎ 313 4150; Cevat Şakir Caddesi 39; beer €1.10; ☯ 11am-10pm) Very popular locally for its delicious kebaps (pide sandwich TL4, döner with rice TL9, İskender kebap TL13) at dirt-cheap prices, this place also has a secret, shaded garden behind the stall front. It's clean and cool and the food's delicious.

Café Bodrum (☎ 316 6163; Iskele Meydanı 10; mains TL22-28; ☯ 10.30am-midnight) In a 200-year-old building next to the excursion boats, this café serves a pretty decent selection of fish, seafood and grilled meat choices – the sea bass with spicy sauce is particularly good – but the real draw is the rooftop terrace overlooking the harbour. From up here everything seems idyllic and serene.

KUMBAHÇE BAY

Dr Alim Bey Caddesi and Cumhuriyet Caddesi are packed with bars and restaurants, most with seating over the water or by the beach. Here, at the sunbathing and dancing end of town, prices and standards are generally lower than in the western bay, although costs can shoot up in summer when tables are at a premium. The food is a mixture of Turkish and the national cuisines of the major package nations: roast beef (with 'real gravy sauce'), schnitzel, pizza, 'Irish breakfasts' etc.

06 Lokantası (☎ 316 6863; Cumhuriyet Caddesi 115; meze TL5, mains TL8-11; ☯ 9am-3am winter, 24hr summer) Though simple, the Lokantası is well-run, reasonably priced and much loved locally; its prices are unbeatable. Grilled meats and kebaps are the menu mainstays, although fresh fish is also served as are good veggie options.

Berk Balık Restaurant (☎ 313 6878; Cumhuriyet Caddesi 167; meze TL5-7, all fish per 500g TL12; ☾ noon-1am) Run by a group of friends, this restaurant specialises in fish and seafood, served on a terrific upstairs terrace that buzzes like a village tavern. It's absolutely packed with locals tossing down octopus in garlic and butter or excellent fresh fish at pleasing prices.

Tranca (☎ 316 6610; Cumhuriyet Caddesi 36; meze TL8-10, mains TL12-24; ☾ 11am-midnight) Jutting out into the bay, the family-run Tranca probably boasts about the best views of anywhere. Its specialities are *tuzda balık* (fish baked in salt) and *testi kebabı* (casserole served in a clay pot that's broken at your table), both cost TL40 to TL50 with a minimum of two people. Reserve a seafront table if you can.

Kortan Restaurant (☎ 316 1300; Cumhuriyet Caddesi 32; ☾ 9am-1am Apr-Sep) Worth a visit just to see the interior of this lovely, 350-year-old former tavern, the Kortan also boasts five tables on a pretty terrace (phone to reserve one). The speciality is grilled fish (sea bass, red snapper and bream for TL12, swordfish TL26 for 500g).

SELF-CATERING
The large covered market about 250m north of the bus station is a great place for picnic-hunting, selling very fresh fruit and veg as well as Turkish sweets and nuts. And if you can't find everything on your list, there's a large adjoining **Tansaş supermarket** (☎ 313 4932; Garaj Üstü; ☾ 8.30am-10pm).

There's also a fruit market on Cevat Şakir Caddesi just south of the main crossroads, and a small collection of butchers and wet fish shops, just behind it on Çarşı Sokak.

Drinking & Entertainment
As with accommodation and eating out, there's a simple rule of thumb: for cheap and cheerful head to the eastern bay, for expensive and classy, think western bay. Dr Alim Bey Caddesi and Cumhuriyet Caddesi are teh town's main evening promenading routes, offering a long line of loud, largely interchangeable waterfront bar-clubs. Expect happy hours, big-screen TVs showing major football matches, bartenders performing synchronised dance routines and a largely (but not exclusively) foreign clientele. In all these places local beer, rakı and spirits will be much cheaper than imported liquor.

Over on the western bay you'll find a collection of more sophisticated alternatives: elegantly designed open-air places patronised largely by Turks and charging upwards of TL10 for a beer.

Halıkarnas (The Club; ☎ 316 8000; www.halikarnas.com.tr; Cumhuriyet Caddesi; admission weekday/weekend TL30/35; beer & spirits from TL10; ☾ 10pm-5am mid-May–Oct) Since 1979 the open-air Halıkarnas has been a clubbers' institution. With its kitschy Roman temple styling and top-quality sound and light equipment, it's an extraordinary experience, particularly when at capacity (5000 people). Internationally known DJs regularly play. Women go half-price on Sunday's 'Ladies' Nights'. Note that it doesn't get going much before 1am. Guests are asked to 'dress for the occasion' but it's unlikely you'll be refused entry.

Marine Club Catamaran (☎ 313 3600; www.club bodrum.com; Hilmi Uran Meydanı 14; admission weekday/weekend TL30/35, beer TL10; ☾ 10pm-5am mid-May–Sep) This floating nightclub sets sail at midnight for five hours of frenzied fun. Its transparent dance floor can pack in no fewer than 1500 clubbers plus attendant DJs. A free shuttle operates every 15 minutes back to the eastern bay. It lies on Hilmi Uran Meydanı (square) on Dr Alim Bey Caddesi.

Helva (☎ 313 2274; Neyzen Tevfik Caddesi 44; ☾ noon-4am) Quieter and a bit less super-fashionable than Küba down the road, this is nonetheless aimed at the Turkish smart set. Despite its exhortations to 'express yourself in dance' this is more of a sit-down bar at which dancing sporadically breaks out rather than a proper disco. It's stylish, lively and (inevitably) expensive.

Fora (☎ 316 2244; www.forabar.com; Hilmi Uran Meydanı 10; ☾ 10am-4am May-Oct; ☾) If you want to dance the night way and don't fancy paying for the privilege, this is the place to do it. Set above the water, with modern minimalist decor, it boasts great views of the castles. It's cool and peaceful during the day when it serves a simple bar menu (club sandwich TL6) and fast and fun during the night. Happy 'hour' is between 9pm and 11pm daily.

Küba Bar (☎ 313 4450; Neyzen Tevfik Caddesi 62; beer €8.35, meals €25; ☾ 9am-4am summer, 9am-2am winter, Wed-Sat only Dec & Feb) With its chic black and marble counters, this place is popular with İzmiri socialites and fashionistas tempted out from their peninsula summer homes to drink and dance. It's fun but rather expensive.

SERVICES FROM BODRUM'S OTOGAR

Destination	Fare (TL)	Duration (hr)	Distance (km)	Frequency (per day)
Ankara	50	12	689	1 nightly
Antalya	35	8	496	2
Denizli	25	5	250	1
Fethiye	25	6	265	2
İstanbul	70	12	851	2 nightly
İzmir	25	4	286	3
Konya	45	12	626	6
Kuşadası	20	2½	151	2
Marmaris	20	3	165	hourly
Milas	15	1	45	hourly
Muğla	15	2	149	hourly
Söke	15	2	130	4

Campanella Bar (☎ 316 5302; Cumhuriyet Caddesi; ⊙ noon–4am) Though small, this Orientalist-style bar, adorned with flower boxes set above a shop on a small alley, is full of atmosphere and usually has live music playing.

If you fancy a puff on a nargileh, the **Old Café** (☎ 316 1928; Cumhuriyet Caddesi 110; nargileh TL10, beer TL5; ⊙ 10am–midnight winter, 24hr summer) has comfortable seats in either the Ottoman-style salon or on the beach outside. Water-pipe smoking is also on offer at the **Alem Bar** (☎ 316 4084; Cumhuriyet Caddesi; nargileh TL10, beer TL4; ⊙ 10am–midnight winter, 24hr summer), which stages live Turkish music between 10pm and 4am every night in summer.

The castle and the antique theatre are often used for cultural events such as opera and ballet performances. Check out www.biletix.com to see if anything is on while you're in town.

Getting There & Away

AIR

The **Bodrum international airport** (☎ 523 0080), 60km away, is nearer to Milas than Bodrum. Check the charter-flight brochures for bargains, especially at the start and end of the season, but prepare to be disappointed as there are fewer flights than you might expect. **Turkish Airlines** (THY; ☎ 317 1203; www.thy.com; Kıbrıs Şehitler Caddesi) is in the Oasis Shopping Centre, about 2km out of town off the Gümbet road. To get here, take a dolmuş (TL1.25) from the otogar asking for 'Oasis'.

To get to the airport, you can take the Havaş (airport) **bus** (☎ 523 0040; €3) run in conjunction with Turkish Airlines, which leaves two hours before all Turkish Airlines departures from the Turkish Airlines office. It also meets flights and drops passengers at the otogar. If you're not flying with Turkish Airlines, an expensive taxi (€45 from the centre) is really your only option.

BOAT

If you want to visit İstanbul, and don't mind taking your time, **Deniz Cruise & Ferry Lines** (☎ 444 3369; www.denizeline.com.tr) operates a twice weekly service from Bodrum from July to September. The journey takes 24 hours.

Ferries for Datça and the Greek islands of Kos and Rhodes leave from the western bay. For information and tickets contact the **Bodrum Ferryboat Association** (☎ 316 0882; www.bodrumferryboat.com; Kale Caddesi Cümrük Alanı 22), on the dock past the western entrance to the castle. Check times as they can change.

For Kos, ferries (one way or same-day return €25, open return €50) leave Bodrum daily throughout the year (weather permitting) at 9.30am, returning at 4.30pm. The hydrofoil service (one way €30, same-day return €35, open return €60, 20 minutes) operates from Monday to Saturday between May and October, departing at 9.30am and returning at 5pm.

For Rhodes, hydrofoils (one way €50, same-day return €60, open-day return €100, 2¼ hours) leave Bodrum from June to September at 8.30am on Monday and Saturday and return at 5pm the same day.

For Datça, ferries (single/return/car/passenger TL20/30/50/5, two hours) leave Bodrum at 9am or 5pm from April to May, and twice a day at 9am and 5pm from June to October. No same-day returns are available. The ferry docks at Körmen on the peninsula's northern coast, and the onward bus journey to Datça (15 minutes) is included in your fare.

You don't need to book in advance unless you have a car (on the ferries only).

BUS

Bodrum has bus services to more or less anywhere you could wish to go. The table lists some useful summer daily services. For Gökova, change at Muğla. For Pamukkale, change at Denizli and go from there (TL6, 10 minutes, 14km).

CAR

Major car-rental agencies can be found on Neyzen Tevfik Caddesi. **Avis** (☎ 316 2333; www .avis.com; Neyzen Tevfik Caddesi 92/A) rents compact cars without air-conditioning from TL100 per day.

Getting Around

Short hops around town in a dolmuş cost TL1.25. Note, if driving, that most of Bodrum's roads follow a strict clockwise one-way system. Miss your turning and you'll probably have to go all the way out of town and do the whole thing again.

BODRUM PENINSULA

☎ 0252

Once upon a time the Bodrum Peninsula must have been a pretty idyllic place. You can get some idea of its former glories on the road between Torba and Gölköy, a still relatively pristine stretch of coast where pine-clad hills overlook serene bays. Much of the rest of the peninsula, however, has been given over to tourism, some of it fairly grim, with patches of Legoland-like housing eroding the hillsides, and some of it rather fancy. Though there's little to do beyond swim, drink and eat, several of the beach villages make for enjoyable day trips from Bodrum, boasting boutique hotels whose style and luxury are unrivalled along the coast.

GETTING AROUND

Dolmuşes from Bodrum's otogar ply back and forth to most places on the peninsula. The furthest journey, to Gümüşlük, will cost TL3.50. In low season, you need to watch out for the departure times of the last minibuses back to Bodrum. Alternatively, you can hire a scooter and ride around the peninsula, although the

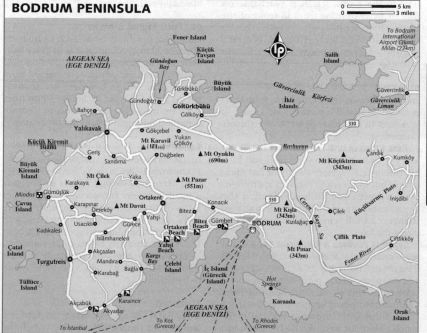

BODRUM PENINSULA

main road from Bodrum to Turgutreis is basically a highway.

Slightly bizarrely, there's no dolmuş from Gümüşlük to Yalıkavak and no dolmuş service from Yalıkavak to Gölköy, so you'll have to keep returning to Bodrum to proceed along the northern coast.

Gümüşlük

About 18km from Bodrum is Gümüşlük, a hamlet on the shore of a fine natural harbour protected by high headlands. New building work is prohibited, ensuring that the actual village retains its quiet charm. However, that hasn't been enough to protect the views. Ranks of half-built villas massing on the hillside opposite illustrate the difficulty of shielding anywhere on the coast from developers.

SIGHTS & ACTIVITIES

Gümüşlük makes the best day trip from Bodrum. Come here to swim or climb the headlands and to take lunch on the shore; or come for an afternoon swim and stay for a sunset dinner.

Little remains of ancient **Mindos** apart from slight ruins on Tavşan Island, the rocky islet to the north, which is reachable on foot or by swimming from in front of the Fenerci Restaurant.

The **beach** to the south is long and generally uncrowded. Though weedy in places, the sea is fine for swimming.

SLEEPING

In the low season (mid-October to mid-May) most of Gümüşlük's pensions are closed. If you want to visit early or late in the season, phone first.

Hera Pansiyon (☎ 394 3065; fax 394 4021; Yalı Mevkii 89; apt for 2/4 people €44/55) Well-run by a charming family, Hera Pansiyon has eight simple but spotless and pleasant apartments set in a garden near the beach. There is also a reasonably priced restaurant and a shaded lounging area. It is located just over halfway along the bay.

Sysyphos Pansiyon & Restaurant (☎ 394 3016; www.sysyphos-gumusluk.net; Yalı Mevkii 97; s/d TL60/90, 2-bedroom apt TL110; ☾ May-Oct) At the quiet southern end of the beach, perched almost on the waterfront, this 80-year-old, bougainvillea-clad pension has a large, rambling garden that's filled with birdsong, making it the perfect place for some R&R. The 20 rooms

boast delightful balconies, some directly overlooking the sea.

Liman Motel (☎ 394 3747; fax 394 3463; s/d €45/60; ☾ May-Oct) By the harbour, the newly opened Liman is the town's first 'boutique' choice. The seven rooms, five with sea views, are large and tasteful with TVs and minibars and there's a decent restaurant by the water.

EATING & DRINKING

Batı Restaurant (☎ 394 3079; mains TL18-30; ☾ 8am-3am May-Oct) An old travellers' favourite, this is a great place for both eating and drinking. A 120-year-old fig tree leans on the restaurant and provides shade for its customers. There's also a fun, cushion-clad chilling area in one corner. The friendly owner is a mine of information about the town and his *güveç* (casseroles; TL10 to TL14) are well worth sampling.

For a mellow drink watching the sunset under giant, grass-roofed parasols, try the **Gusta Restaurant Café Bar** (☎ 394 4228; Yalı Mevkii 95; beer TL2; ☾ 8.30am-2am summer only) or **Club Gümüşlük** (☎ 394 3401; beer TL2; ☾ 6.30am-2am) at the northern end of the bay, which is a popular haunt for younger locals (and is open all year).

GETTING THERE & AWAY

Dolmuşes run from Gümüşlük to Bodrum (TL3.50, 30 to 40 minutes) at least every half-hour and to Turgutreis (TL1, 15 minutes) every 20 minutes. Vehicles are banned from entering the village, but there is a municipal car park (TL3 per 12 hours) 300m from the waterfront. The last dolmuş to Bodrum departs at midnight (10pm out of season).

Yalıkavak

In the northwestern corner of the peninsula, 18km from Bodrum, is Yalıkavak. As Datça is to Marmaris, so Yalıkavak is to Bodrum: a smaller, quieter version with the constant threat of similar development looming over it. In the meantime it's remarkably pleasant, with no high-rise buildings to spoil the harbour and several attractive hotels and restaurants.

Yalıkavak's *köfte* are rightfully famous throughout Turkey; there's no better place to try them.

SLEEPING

Miray Hotel (☎ 385 4920; www.e-mirayhotel.com; Begonvil Sokak 17; s/d €32/45; ☷ ☖) This hotel

---

PENINSULA PECULIARITIES

As you potter around the peninsula, look out for some interesting architectural anomalies. The odd-looking igloo-shaped buildings are *gümbets* (stone cisterns), once used to store fresh water for times of need. On many hilltops, old windmills still stand, though most are redundant, making way for modern living. More unusual are the *kule evleri* (stone tower houses), similar to those seen on the Mani Peninsula in Greece. In Ortakent, you can find two fine 17th-century examples – on the older stone house, look out for the turned-up corners of the roof. It's an architectural effect that can be traced to Minoan Greece. The 'horns' are said to hark back to the cult of the Minoan bull and were probably put on the houses to ward off the evil eye.

---

lies in the centre of town, just a minute from the seafront and has 15 comfortable rooms, a swimming pool, a bar-restaurant and a nargileh garden.

Adahan (☎ 385 4759; www.adahanotel.com; Seyhulislan Ömer Lütfü Caddesi 55; s/d €75/95; ☼ Apr-Oct; ❂ ❑) Designed to look like an old caravanserai with pointed arches and imposing wooden doors, the Adahan has spacious and comfortable rooms arranged around an arcaded courtyard containing a lovely pool. Anatolian antiques furnish the corners and from the kitchen come scintillating smells – the charming owners also run a gourmet restaurant. It lies around 80m from the new yacht harbour on the road to Gümüşlük.

Taskule Hotel (☎ 385 4935; www.taskulehotel.com; Plaj Caddesi; d €75-100, ste €100-225; ❂ ❑) Right by the beach the 'boutique' Taskule has been thoroughly renovated in the past few years and now has 15 bright, modern-looking rooms, all with wooden floors, large beds and wi-fi. There's also a pool and a good little restaurant (mains TL18 to TL22) for watching the sunset.

4 Reasons Hotel (☎ 385 3212; www.4reasonshotel .com; Bakan Caddesi 2; d €165, 3-4 person apt €165-200; ❂ ❑) One of the peninsula's top hotels – as featured in dozens of lifestyle magazines – this place enjoys an idyllic position (and views) on a hill 2km from Yalıkavak. There's a nice pool, a great poolside restaurant (live jazz on summer weekends) and the rooms are large and designery, with TVs, minibars and fireplaces, and come in three options: 'passionate' (with balcony), functional (twin bedrooms) and casual (no sitting area). In case you're wondering the 'four reasons' are serenity, design, attitude and quality.

EATING & DRINKING
All of the following are found at the northern end of the bay.

Kavaklı Köfteci (☎ 385 4748; Merkez Çarşı İçi; meatballs TL6-7; ☼ 7.30am-midnight) Around 50m inland, this place is famous for its Yalıkavak meatballs served up on simple wooden tables with garlic bread. Smoky-flavoured, slightly spiced and succulent, they're gorgeous! Fight for a table if you have to.

Cumbalı (☎ 385 4995; İskele Meydanı 126; 400g fish TL18-20; ☼ 8.30am-midnight) A favourite for fish, Cumbalı does delicious dishes at pleasing prices 'to attract locals as well as tourists' as the owner puts it. The seafood meze (TL5 to TL7), which you can eat right on the seafront, are sumptuous.

Ali Baba (☎ 385 3139; İskele Meydanı 166; 400g fish TL18-22; ☼ 11am-1am) On the edge of the harbour with seafront seating, the Ali Baba does a fine line in fish and seafood, including grilled sea-bass, octopus casserole and pan-friend jumbo prawns, although, if you really want to get everyone's attention, order the amphora kebap, which your waiter will smash open at your table.

Dede (☎ 385 5257; Plaj Caddesi 6/A; cocktail TL5-8, ☼ 11am-1am) With cushions and sun-loungers, Dede, by the town's small beach, is the place to hang out with a cocktail at the end of the day. It also offers a decent menu of casseroles, kebaps, steak and fish (TL17 to TL24.50).

GETTING THERE & AWAY
Dolmuşes go to Bodrum (TL3, 25 minutes) every half-hour in summer (but only when full in winter). Surprisingly, although the road is good, there's no dolmuş to Göltürkbükü. You'll have to take a taxi for around TL30 to TL40 daytime and TL40 to TL50 at night, or return to Bodrum and catch another dolmuş (TL2, every 45 minutes) from there.

Göltürkbükü
About 18km northwest of Bodrum lies Göltürkbükü, the self-styled 'Turkish St Tropez'.

The name is a portmanteau amalgamation of two separate villages, Gölköy and Türkbükü, which lie either end of a small bay and today represent the peninsula's most upmarket tourist destinations (www.golturkbuku.com).

GÖLKÖY

Long seen as the lesser of the two villages, Gölköy is currently trying to push itself in a more upmarket direction with new hotels – all studiously boutique – opening almost monthly, most boasting beach clubs with large wooden platforms, laden with cushions and sun-loungers, erected over the sea. The beach, however, is narrow, pebbly and poor.

Made up of a series of modern buildings decorated in a traditional style, **Sultan Hotel** (☎ 357 7260; www.sultangolturkubuku.com; Sahil Sokak 3; s/d €45/75; ☒ Apr-Nov; ☒) is set in a peaceful garden. Rooms are simple but spotless and have little balconies from where you can hear the water lap. There's also a good seafront restaurant that's open to the public and offers three courses for a very reasonable TL14.

Set on the waterfront at the southern end of town, the **Villa Kilic Hotel** (☎ 357 8118; www.villakilic .com; Sahil Sokak 22; s/d €120/165; ☒) is a new and very luxurious addition to the accommodation scene with 33 lavish, designer rooms – think flat-screens, hardwoods and marble – and suites (which have hot tubs), a large pool, a conservatory restaurant and the largest bathing platform in town (300 sq metres) where DJs play in summer.

Nearby, the restaurant of the **Orkide Hotel** (☎ 357 7626; snacks TL7-12; ☒ 8am-midnight May-Oct) is shaded by greenery and makes a welcome spot for a drink or a light snack.

TÜRKBÜKÜ

About 1.5km north of Gölköy along a twisting, turning road is Türkbükü, the summer playground for many of Turkey's rich and infamous. It boasts a small harbour backed by a long beach made up of a mixture of pebbles and sand, although most of the swimming and sunbathing is done from the hotels' purpose-built wooden platforms, and a long esplanade of fancy boutiques and restaurants (plus a few cheaper souvenir and trinket stalls to provide a bit of balance). At the northern end of town is a collection of terribly luxurious hotels and beach clubs where A-listers descend en masse in summer. It's a great place to people-watch.

SLEEPING & EATING

Maki Hotel (☎ 377 6105; www.makihotel.com.tr; Kelesharimi Mevkii; d from €200; ☒ ☒) Much beloved by the fashionable, the rich and the beautiful, Maki Hotel is right at the northern end of the seafront and offers comfort *and* style. There's a gorgeous pool set just above the sea, a restaurant with a fine Italian chef, hyper-hip rooms (check out the chrome and orange–painted balconies) and a large and very stylish bathing platform, complete with bar.

Ada Hotel (☎ 377 5915; www.adahotel.com; Tepecik Caddesi 128; d €245-290, ste €575-900; ☒ Apr-Oct; ☒ ☒) Designed to resemble an old stone house, the most basic room category here is deluxe, which should give you some idea of prices. It boasts a hamam, a health centre and two restaurants, while room adornments include antiques, candles and CD players.

Divan Hotel (☎ 377 5601; Keleşharım Caddesi 6; meze TL10-28, fish mains TL22-40; ☒ 11.30am-1am) Famous throughout Turkey, the restaurant here is considered by many as the top table in town. With an İstanbullu chef with a reputation for creativity, the dishes are superb.

Fidèle (☎ 377 5081; beer TL8; ☒ 11.30am-1am) Nearby Fidèle is a great spot for an evening drink. Try the house speciality – spicy vodka.

Ship Ahoy (☎ 377 5070; meze €4-12, fish mains €10-14; ☒ 8am-6am May-Aug) The perennially popular Ship Ahoy is a pretty place on the seafront. It serves up superb fish and meze and turns into a nightclub from 11pm in summer.

Another place worth seeking out, right at the southern end of the front, is **Iasos** (☎ 377 5141; Atatürk Caddesi 31; meze TL5, fish mains TL15-30; ☒ 11.30am-2am May-Sep), a popular fish restaurant whose prices are a bit lower than the town norm.

ÖREN
☎ 0252

A relatively low-key seaside resort patronised mainly by Turkish families. Ören has a trim and tidy seafront with a long pebbly **beach** lined with sun-loungers and bordered by neat flowerbeds, behind which sits a row of largely interchangeable fish restaurants. Inland, it's a slightly less tranquil story. The original village of old Ottoman houses, 1.5km inland, surrounded by the ruins of the ancient city of **Keramos**, has had numerous litters. New developments now sprawl into the surrounding fields in all directions.

Hamile Dağı (Pregnant Woman Mountain) soars above the village. With a bit of imagination the jagged western hump becomes the face, the swollen middle hump the belly, and the long ridge closest to town the legs of the woman. Paragliders launch from the 'knees', now sprouting radio towers.

Bring funds with you unless you want to have to trek about 4km back along the road to Milas to use the ATM machines outside the gates of the Kemerköy power station.

Sleeping & Eating

Ören has a handful of pensions and hotels near the waterfront.

Hotel Keramos (☎ 532 2250; www.hotelkeramos.com; Atatürk Bulvarı 30; s/d TL35/55; ☒ May-Oct; ☒) Just back from the front, the modern neoclassical-style Keramos has small but sparkling rooms with nice balconies overlooking gardens.

Hotel Kardelen (☎ 532 2678; www.orenkardelen.com; Yalı Mevkii Milas; s/d TL35/60; ☒) Across from the minibus stop, the Kardelen has simple and rather stark but spacious rooms, as well as a large rooftop terrace.

Hotel Alnata (☎ 532 2813; www.alnatahotel.com; per person with half-/full board €25/35; ☒ ☒) Ören's top hotel, the three-star Alnata enjoys a striking green and yellow colour scheme and is comfortable and well run. All rooms have balconies, some with direct sea views. There's a nice pool as well as a pebble beach with sunloungers. Various water activities are offered, along with boat trips.

In summer, there's a mass of places along the seafront selling pide, kebabs and fish. You're best advised to browse and pick the most popular: places change fast in Ören.

Güverte Restaurant (☎ 532 3319; Yalı Mahallesi Sahil Yolu; meze TL3-7, fish per 500g TL10-15; ☒ 8.30am-midnight summer) Operated by the same people as the Hotel Keramos, this is a good waterfront dining option serving a wide rage of fish and seafood as well as decent kebabs for TL10.

Getting There & Away

Minibuses run from Milas to Ören village and beach and back (TL4.50, one hour), every hour. To Bodrum (TL7.50) and Muğla (TL6.25) three minibuses leave daily.

Western Anatolia

For many travellers the diverse highlights of western Anatolia roll past in a cinematic scroll as they traverse the region a little *too* quickly heading from İstanbul to Pamukkale, or further south to Antalya's Mediterranean vibe. From Cappadocia west to Ephesus it's a similar story, with just a stop to explore the distinct calcium-enriched landscapes of Pamukkale and the sprawling ruins of Hierapolis. But western Anatolia offers much more than that particular natural and historical combo.

The peaks and river canyons of Turkey's Lake District provide a rugged backdrop for walking, mountain biking and skiing, with the St Paul Trail a well-marked opportunity to follow in the footsteps of the Apostle. Expect an ever-changing backdrop of natural hues with shimmering poppy fields and gleaming lakes reflecting stark rocky landscapes. After all that exertion, retire to one of western Anatolia's thermal resorts to recharge in a relaxing mineral bath.

The architectural and design heritage of the Ottoman Empire is showcased in bustling Bursa and sleepy İznik, and Bursa also offers a modern big city buzz. Earlier eras are brought to life at the ancient cities of Sagalassos and Afrodisias, and if a dearth of other travellers makes you think you're a pioneer, the even older civilisation of the Phrygian Valley will remind you that people have occupied these lands since very early times.

While other parts of Turkey may seem more instantly memorable, in western Anatolia you'll discover an essentially Turkish heart and soul of this country.

HIGHLIGHTS

- Discover the proud architectural heritage of the Ottoman Empire in bustling **Bursa** (p289)
- Share a lakefront sunset with relaxed local families in sleepy **İznik** (p285)
- Spend a night in a restored Ottoman mansion in up and coming **Mudurnu** (p284)
- Uncover the surprising influence of a little-known culture amid the rocky bluffs of the **Phrygian Valley** (p303)
- Negotiate Pamukkale's travertine pools to explore the expansive and poignant ruins of **Hierapolis** (p324)
- Come face to face with civilisation's shared history at the ancient cities of **Afrodisias** (p328) and **Sagalassos** (p313)
- Kick back with dinner at a waterfront restaurant after getting active around **Eğirdir Gölü** (Lake Eğirdir; p315)

WESTERN ANATOLIA

YALOVA
☎ 0226 / pop 87,400

Yalova is the primary terminal for the fast ferries traversing the Sea of Marmara, the quickest and easiest route between Bursa and İstanbul. Yalova was badly damaged in the earthquake of 1999, but this key transport hub now has a bustling and vibrant waterfront area.

Getting There & Away
BOAT

The dock for **İDO fast ferries** (☎ 444 4436; www .ido.com.tr) to İstanbul is near Yalova's main square. Ferries leave roughly every two hours between 7.30am and 11.30pm for Yenikapı docks (TL12, TL60 for a car and driver, TL10 for additional passengers, one hour). A second service runs every 1¼ hours for the port at Pendik (TL5, TL50 for a car and driver, TL4 for additional passengers, 45 minutes), south of Bostancı. This still leaves a 100km drive or three more pedestrian ferry hops into İstanbul itself.

BUS

At the time of writing Yalova was building a new otogar (bus station) 3km south of the ferry port. Arriving by ferry from İstanbul, frequent dolmuşes (shuttle minibuses) will shuttle you to the otogar. From the otogar there are frequent buses or dolmuşes to Termal (TL2, 30 minutes), İznik (TL7.50, one hour) and Bursa (TL9, 1¼ hours).

TERMAL

☎ 0226 / pop 2200

About 12km southwest of Yalova, off the road to Çınarcık, Termal combines a lovely spa resort and a ho-hum village dotted with cheap pensions favoured by visitors from the Gulf States.

First exploited by the Romans but developed further by the Ottomans and finally by Atatürk, the baths harness hot, mineral-rich waters gushing from the earth. Set in a beautiful tree-lined valley, there is also an arboretum built by Atatürk, and pleasant walking trails to provide a balance of rigour and relaxation.

Sights & Activities

The main spa complex, the **Kurşunlu Banyo** (☎ 675 7400; ⏱ 7am-10.30pm Mon-Wed & Fri & Sat, 7am-8pm Sun, 7am-noon Thu), features an open-air pool for TL12, an enclosed pool and sauna for TL10, and small private cubicles for TL10 to TL15. At the **Valide Banyo** (admission TL5) men and women bathe separately in indoor pools, while at the **Sultan Banyo** (1/2 people TL15/20) you can rent a private bath by the hour. The **Sira Banyo** offers more spacious family pools.

Sleeping & Eating

The **Çinar and Çamlik hotels** (☎ 675 7400; www.yalova termal.com; s/d from TL70/120) are run by the same company, Yalova Termal Kaplıca Tesisleri. Rooms at the Çamlık are more expensive but both are quiet and inviting, if slightly old-fashioned. Rates include use of the baths. The Çamlık's own marketing spiel – 'Who doesn't want to awaken in a green valley full of bird tweets?' – sums up nicely the low-key appeal of Termal. The Çınar has a tree-shaded courtyard café while the Çamlık plumps for a proper restaurant.

Getting There & Away

There are frequent buses and dolmuşes (TL2.50, 30 minutes) from Yalova. The İDO fast ferry (p283) makes it possible to visit Termal as a day trip from İstanbul.

MUDURNU

Another 25km southwest of Abant Gölü (see boxed text below) is the lovely small town of Mudurnu. It's not on the standard north–south route of western Anatolia, but east towards the Black Sea Coast, and definitely worth a detour for fans of Ottoman architecture.

The town used to be famous only for its 'Mupi' brand chicken, but it is now being lauded as an Ottoman revival town. It doesn't rival Safranbolu (p455) yet, but slowly and carefully the old houses are being restored and repurposed to attract visitors. And with a current profile only with domestic Turkish visitors, it's a sleepily authentic place without the touristy buzz of Safranbolu.

There's a lively bazaar area and the beautifully restored **Yıldırım Beyazıt hamam** (Büyükcami Caddesi; ⏱ 8am-7pm; Mon, Wed, Sat for women) is a real find, charging just TL3 if you forego the scrub and massage (not available to women anyway).

Around 500m southwest of Mudurnu's subdued main square, a canal-side walk begins at the **Kancini Sultan Sülemaniye Camii**, a rustic timber and stone mosque. Bookended by two wooden bridges, the path explores quiet neighbourhoods filled with wooden Ottoman houses in various states of repair

---

LAKEFRONT & MOUNTAINSIDE: DETOURS FROM THE HIGHWAY

For many travellers, western Anatolia is just the area they speed through from İstanbul to Ankara. Nestling in lush, green countryside, the lake district around **Bolu** is a handy detour midway between the two cities.

The town of Bolu itself is not especially exciting, but 30km southwest is **Abant Gölü**, a gorgeous spot for a picnic. It's a 5km walk round the shores of the lake which is dotted with a campsite and two five-star hotels. On weekends and public holidays the lakefront comes alive with families, and waterfront restaurants are essential afternoon distractions.

Even if you don't divert to Abant Gölü you should stop on the slopes of **Bolu Dağı** (Mt Bolu), with restaurants and panoramic views. Keen skiers should investigate the resort at **Kartalkaya**, which has good powder from December to March.

This area is definitely best explored with your own wheels, but on summer weekends you can usually find a direct dolmuş (TL5) from Bolu otogar to Abant Gölü. Regular buses link Bolu to İstanbul (TL25) and Ankara (TL17).

and disrepair. It ends near **Keyvanlar Konaği**, a restored family mansion now housing a hotel and restaurant.

Orientation & Information

Mudurnu occupies a narrow valley, with the compact otogar 400m east on the edge of town. The tourist information booth, 200m north of the main square, doubles as a craft shop. It's often locked, but assistance usually comes from the grocery stall across the road. A couple of internet cafés are near the main square.

Sleeping & Eating

Prices at Mudurnu hotels increase at weekends when advance booking is also recommended.

Hacı Abdullahlar Konağı (☎ 421 2284; Belediye Yanı 3; s/d TL40/80) Just off the main square, this hotel has gorgeous Ottoman-style rooms (some without bathroom) in a restored house. There's an inviting upstairs sitting area and a small garden.

Yarışkaşı Konağı (☎ 421 3604; www.yariskasi.com, in Turkish; s/d TL40/80) On the edge of town coming from Bolu, this hotel is in the old style but newly built, with mod cons including wi-fi. Rooms are comfortable if simple, and there are great forest views from private balconies.

Keyvanlar Konaği (☎ 421 3750; Kardelen Sokak 3; r TL80) This restored family home is crammed with poignant personal mementos from several centuries. The nine rooms are both comfortable and traditional, and excellent meals are served in the garden filled with well-established trees probably even older than the house. Follow the signs west across the canal from the town centre.

Değirmenyeri Konaklari (☎ 421 2677; www.degir menyeri.com.tr; Kilözü Köyü, Dağ Mevkii; TL100-140) On the Bolu road 8km northeast of Mudurnu, this cluster of five mountain cabins provides rustic and isolated splendour on the site of an old mill.

Mupi (mains TL6-10) Chicken every which way is on offer at the official 'Mupi' restaurant just off Mudurnu's main square. That means terrific kebaps and güveç (casserole). There are good vegetarian options too.

Tucked behind Mupi is a delightful tree-lined tea garden.

Getting There & Away

There are regular buses from Bolu to Mudurnu (TL5, 1½ hours). Bolu can be reached by bus from İstanbul (TL25) and Ankara (TL17).

İZNİK

☎ 0224 / pop 22,200

Given İznik's long history and its legacy of making the beautiful tiles incorporated into the finest of Ottoman architecture, the town's rural streetlife comes as a surprise. Farmers hanging out in teahouses and tractors waiting at traffic lights reinforce the town's focus on producing olives and stone fruit from the farms studding the hilly rustic surrounds. The whole place has a sleepy, laid-back atmosphere, especially in the restaurants and tea gardens along the sprawling lakefront.

Badly damaged in the War of Independence (1919–22), İznik's traditional farming economy is now being boosted as a favourite weekend retreat for İstanbul folk, and through the resurrection of the town's proud tile-making heritage.

History

İznik was founded around 1000 BC, and grew in significance under one of Alexander the Great's generals in 316 BC. A rival general, Lysimachus, captured it in 301 BC and named it after his wife, Nikaea. Nicaea became the capital city of the province of Bithynia extending along the Sea of Marmara. By 74 BC the entire area was incorporated into the Roman Empire, but invasions by the Goths and the Persians ruined the flourishing city by AD 300.

Under Constantinople, Nicaea once again acquired importance. In 325 the first Ecumenical Council took place and produced the Nicene Creed, outlining the basic principles of Christianity. Four centuries later, the seventh Ecumenical Council was held in Nicaea's Aya Sofya (Hagia Sofia) church.

During the reign of Justinian I (527–65), Nicaea was refurbished with buildings and defences that provided security when the Arabs invaded. Like Constantinople, Nicaea never fell to its Arab besiegers, but did eventually fall to the Crusaders.

In 1331 Sultan Orhan conquered İznik and established the first Ottoman theological school. In 1514 Sultan Selim I captured the Persian city of Tabriz and despatched its artisans to İznik. The Persian craftsmen were skilled at making coloured tiles, and soon İznik's kilns were turning out faience (tin-glazed earthenware) unequalled even today.

In a new century İznik tile making is undergoing a resurrection through the excellent

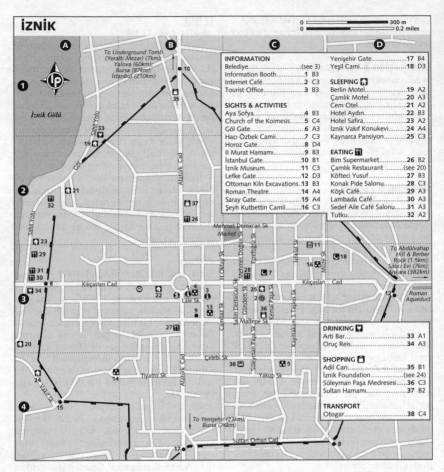

İznik

INFORMATION
Belediye..............................(see 3)
Information Booth....................1 B3
Internet Café........................2 C3
Tourist Office.......................3 B3

SIGHTS & ACTIVITIES
Aya Sofya............................4 B3
Church of the Koimesis...............5 C4
Göl Gate.............................6 A3
Hacı Özbek Camii.....................7 C3
Horoz Gate...........................8 D4
Il Murat Hamamı......................9 B3
İstanbul Gate.......................10 B1
İznik Museum........................11 C3
Lefke Gate..........................12 D3
Ottoman Kiln Excavations............13 B3
Roman Theatre.......................14 A4
Saray Gate..........................15 A4
Şeyh Kutbettin Camii................16 C3

Yenişehir Gate......................17 B4
Yeşil Cami..........................18 D3

SLEEPING
Berlin Motel........................19 A2
Çamlık Motel........................20 A3
Cem Otel............................21 A2
Hotel Aydın.........................22 B3
Hotel Safira........................23 A2
İznik Vakıf Konukevi................24 A4
Kaynarca Pansiyon...................25 C3

EATING
Bim Supermarket.....................26 B2
Çamlık Restaurant ....(see 20)
Köfteci Yusuf.......................27 B3
Konak Pide Salonu...................28 C3
Köşk Café...........................29 A3
Lambada Café........................30 A3
Sedef Aile Café Salonu..............31 A3
Tutku...............................32 A2

DRINKING
Arti Bar............................33 A1
Oruç Reis...........................34 A3

SHOPPING
Adil Can............................35 B1
İznik Foundation.................(see 24)
Süleyman Paşa Medresesi.............36 C3
Sultan Hamamı.......................37 B2

TRANSPORT
Otogar..............................38 C4

---

work done by the İznik Foundation (see boxed text, opposite).

Orientation & Information

Historic İznik is still enclosed within its crumbling city walls. With the exception of a few hotels and restaurants on the lake-facing side of town, everything you'll need is inside the walls. In the town centre, the ruins of the Aya Sofya stand at the intersection of the two main boulevards, Atatürk Caddesi and Kılıçaslan Caddesi. These two roads lead to the four principal *kapılar* (gates) in the city walls.

The otogar is a few blocks southeast of the Aya Sofya.

The **tourist office** (☎ 757 1454; www.iznik.bel.tr; 130 Kılıçaslan Caddesi; ☼ 9am-noon & 1-5pm Mon-Fri) is

in the *belediye* (town hall) building. There is also an infrequently-staffed **information booth** near the Aya Sofya.

There is an **internet café** (☼ 9am-11pm) beside the Kaynarca Pansiyon (p288) and wi-fi at Oruç Reis (p289) near the lakefront.

Sights & Activities
AYA SOFYA

What was once the **Aya Sofya** (Church of the Divine Wisdom; admission TL3; ☼ 9am-noon & 1-6pm Tue-Sun) is now a crumbling ruin slumbering in an attractively landscaped rose garden. The one building actually encompasses the ruins of three completely different structures. A mosaic floor and a mural of Jesus with Mary and John the Baptist survive from the original

---

RESURRECTING AN ESSENTIAL PAST

Crafted from the 15th to 17th centuries, İznik tiles were an artistic high point of the Ottoman Empire. Following the end of the Ottoman era, the demand for significant public works evaporated and the tile makers' skills were buried in the mists of history. In 1993 the İznik Foundation was founded to revive this lost art. The foundation's journey has involved scouring 15th-century manuscripts, working with university laboratories and training craftspeople from across Turkey.

Made from 85% quartz from the hills surrounding İznik, the tiles' unique thermal properties keep buildings warm in winter and cool in summer. Reflected sound waves create perfect acoustic qualities; all reasons why İznik tiles were so popular for decorating the interiors of mosques in Ottoman times.

In a sunny atelier above the foundation's kilns that fire the tiles to 900°C, a team of designers meticulously detail floral designs onto pristine white tiles. True to tradition, only cross-sections of flowers are painted and, in a modern twist, all the designers are women. Apparently 'only women have the patience' to spend up to 70 days on one of the foundation's larger works; examples of which now grace structures as diverse as İstanbul's metro system and the World Bank in Ankara.

---

church. Built during the reign of Justinian and destroyed by an earthquake in 1065, it was later rebuilt with the mosaics set into the walls. After the Ottoman conquest the church became a mosque, but a fire in the 16th century again destroyed everything. Reconstruction was supervised by the great architect Mimar Sinan, who added İznik tiles to the decoration. At the time of writing, significant restoration work was being undertaken with the church scheduled to re-open in 2009.

YEŞİL CAMİ
Built between 1378 and 1387 under Sultan Murat I, the Yeşil Cami (Green Mosque) has Seljuk Turkish proportions influenced more by Iran (the Seljuk homeland) than by İstanbul. The green- and blue-glazed zigzag tiles of the minaret foreshadowed the famous industry that arose here a few decades later.

İZNİK MUSEUM
Opposite the Yeşil Camii is **İznik Museum** (İznik Müzesi; ☎ 757 1027; Müze Sokak; admission TL3; ☉ 8amnoon & 1-5pm Tue-Sun), housed in the old soup kitchen that Sultan Murat I had built for his mother, Nilüfer Hatun, in 1388. Born a Byzantine princess, Nilüfer married Sultan Orhan to cement a diplomatic alliance.

The museum's grounds are filled with marble statuary. Inside, the lofty whitewashed halls contain examples of original İznik tiles, with their milky bluish-white and rich 'İznik red' hues. Other displays include 8000-year-old finds from a nearby *tumulus* (burial mound) at Ilıpınar, believed to show links with Neolithic Balkan culture.

Across the road is the restored **Şeyh Kutbettin Camii** (1492).

CITY WALLS & GATES
With some imagination it's still possible to recreate İznik's imposing walls, which were first erected in Roman times, then rebuilt and strengthened under the Byzantines. Four main gates – İstanbul Kapısı, Yenişehir Kapısı, Lefke Kapısı and Göl Kapısı – still transect the walls, and the crumbling remains of another 12 minor gates and 114 towers are also evident. In places, the walls still rise to a height of 10m to 13m.

The **Lefke Gate** to the east actually comprises three gateways dating from Byzantine times. Climb to the top of the walls here for a good vantage point of the surrounding area.

The **İstanbul Gate** is similarly imposing, with huge stone carvings of heads facing outwards. However, little remains of the **Göl (Lake) Gate**. To the southwest are the remains of the more minor **Saray (Palace) Gate** – Sultan Orhan (1326–61) had a palace near here in the 14th century. Inside the walls nearby are the ruins of a 15,000-seat **Roman theatre**.

The walls between the **Yenişehir Gate** and the Lefke Gate still stand at a considerable height. Follow the footpath beside them for the best indication of the scale.

Diverting back inside the walls from the ruins of the minor **Horoz (Rooster) Gate** are the sparse ruins of the **Church of the Koimesis** (c AD 800) on the western side of Kaymakam S Taşkın Sokak. Only some foundations remain, but the church was the burial place of the Byzantine emperor Theodore I (Lascaris).

When the Crusaders took Constantinople in 1204, Lascaris fled to Nicaea and established his court here. It was Lascaris who built Nicaea's outer walls, supported by over 100 towers and protected by a wide moat – no doubt he didn't trust the Crusaders, having already lost one city to them. In a bittersweet final twist, the church was dynamited after the War of Independence.

OTHER SIGHTS

Southeast of Aya Sofya, the brick-built **İl Murat Hamamı** (☎ 757 1459; wash & massage from TL12; ☼ 6am-midnight for men, 1-5pm Mon, Thu & Sat for women) was constructed during the reign of Sultan Murat II in the first half of the 15th century.

Across the road are the overgrown remains of the 15th- to 17th-century **Ottoman kilns**. The finds are in the İznik Museum.

In the centre of town on Kılıçaslan Caddesi, **Hacı Özbek Camii**, dating from 1332, is one of İznik's oldest mosques.

Outside the Lefke Gate around **Abdülvahap Hill** are the remains of a Roman aqueduct, an Arab *namazgah* (open-air mosque), several tombs and a shady cemetery. Head out an hour before sunset to explore these features.

Climb the hill for great views of **Berber Rock**, a shattered monumental mausoleum carved from a single rock, and the tomb of Abdülvahap Sancaktari, the Turkish-Arab flag bearer who gave his name to the hill after dying during an 8th-century siege.

Sleeping

Advance booking on busy summer weekends is recommended. Bursa has more hotels and restaurants, providing a good base for a day trip to İznik. Note you'll be heading back to Bursa just as the İznik lakefront is at its bustling best and is crowded with holidaying Turks and strolling locals.

BUDGET

Kaynarca Pansiyon (☎ 757 1753; www.kaynarca .s5.com; Kılıçaslan Caddesi, Gündem Sokak 1; dm TL20, s/d/tr TL30/50/75; ☒ ☐) Ali Bulmuş's cheerful and central pension is a budget traveller's dream. It's pathologically clean, BBC World is on the telly, and there's a spacious rooftop terrace for leisurely breakfasts (TL5). No advance reservations are taken, but if it's full, the effusive Ali will hunt down a nearby alternative.

Cem Otel (☎ 757 1687; www.cemotel.com; Göl Sahil Yolu 34; s/d TL30/70; ☒) Close to the lake and

the city walls the Cem Otel is great value, with TV and plenty of space, especially in the family-friendly suites. If you can't land a lakefront room, score a seat downstairs in the terrace restaurant.

Berlin Motel (☎ 757 3355; www.berlinmotel.com.tr; Göl Sahil Yolu 36; s/d/tr TL35/70/105; ☒) Turkish-owned but run with Teutonic efficiency, the Berlin's boxy four-storey lakefront facade conceals good value rooms, and the biggest big screen TV this side of the Sea of Marmara.

MIDRANGE

Hotel Aydın (☎ 757 7650; www.iznikhotelaydin.com; Kılıçaslan Caddesi 64; s/d/tr TL50/80/100) The Aydın is best known locally for its excellent on-site *pastanes* (patisserie/bakery), which also serves breakfasts on the front terrace. The smallish rooms come with TV, phone, balcony and overly chintzy bedspreads.

Çamlık Motel (☎ 757 1631; www.iznik-camlikmotel. com; Göl Sahil Yolu; s/d TL60/100; ☒) At the southern end of the lakefront, this modern Western-style motel has spacious rooms and a restaurant with water views. It's a favourite with tour groups so you might want to book ahead on summer weekends. Say hi to the friendly dogs playing in the garden.

Hotel Safira (☎ 757 1700; www.izniksafira.com; Göl Sahil Yolu; s/d TL60/100; ☒ ☐ ☒) This slightly characterless luxury spot is redeemed with very comfortable rooms with warm decor. Swim in the pool or across the road in the lake, and don't forget to make serious noises about a midweek discount.

İznik Vakıf Konukevi (☎ 757 6025; info@iznik.com; Vakıf Sokak 13; per person TL70) A charming guesthouse set in a delightful rose and lavender trimmed garden just inland from the lake. The rooms are managed by the İznik Foundation (p287) and are as classy and downright cool as you might expect. Booking ahead is highly recommended as the nine rooms are sometimes booked by groups of artists or musicians.

Eating

İznik is known for its lake fish with tasty variations from deep-fried to kebaps. Grab a table at sunset and you're sorted.

Konak Pide Salonu (Kılıçaslan Caddesi; meals TL4-6) This busy main drag eatery does a brisk trade in pide (Turkish-style pizza) and *lahmacun* (Arabic-style meat pizza). It was spring cleaning when we dropped by, but the place was already spotless.

WESTERN ANATOLIA

Köfteci Yusuf (☎ 757 3597; Atatürk Caddesi 75; mains from TL5) A favourite lunchtime spot for locals ordering juicy *köfte* (meatballs) and other grills with chunky bread and hot green peppers. Leave room for the gorgeously sweet desserts (even if you need a lie down afterwards).

Tutku (Göl Sahil Yolu; meals from TL8; ☷ 11am-11pm) This open-sided pavilion combines friendly service, a wide array of creamy mezes, smartly prepared fish, and the essential lure of big glasses of ice-cold draught Tuborg beer.

Çamlık Restaurant (☎ 757 1631; Göl Sahil Yolu; mains from TL8; ☷ 11am-11pm) Recommended by proud locals as İznik's best spot to enjoy fish, the Çamlık Restaurant is adjoined to the Çamlık Motel. That means a spacious garden and lakefront location to enjoy the sunset. Our recommendation is the winning combination of a fish kebap and a chilled Efes beer.

On the lakefront the Kösk Café, Sedef Aile Café Salonu and Lambada Café are all good for a (non-alcoholic) drink and simple snacks.

Self-catering central is the **Bim supermarket** (☎ 411 2216; Atatürk Caddesi; ☷ 8.30am-9.30pm Mon-Sat, 9am-9pm Sun).

Drinking

Arti Bar (Göl Sahil Yolu; ☷ noon-11pm) Shaded by weeping willows this simple garden bar is not particularly arty, but it's still a prime spot for a beer and sunset combo.

Oruç Reis (Göl Sahil Yolu; ☷ 2-11pm) Ostensibly an off-license selling cold beer and soft drinks, this lakefront spot with echoes of a Caribbean cabana has a few simple tables if you're looking to linger. Wi-fi is another reason to stick around if you're toting a laptop.

Shopping

The revival of tile making in İznik has seen many shops selling local tiles and ceramics. Some of the work is tourist tat (fridge magnets and key rings anyone?) but there are also more carefully-crafted examples on offer. Good places to start exploring are the small workshops along Salim Demircan Sokak, and the workshop belonging to the **İznik Foundation** (☎ 757 6025; www.iznik.com; Vakıf Sokak 13) – see boxed text, p287.

The **Süleyman Paşa Medresesi**, founded by Sultan Orhan shortly after he captured Nicaea, now houses half a dozen ceramic and craft workshops.

North of the roundabout on Atatürk Caddesi, the **Sultan Hamamı** is another restored building filled with craft shops and an art gallery.

At **Adil Can** (☎ 757 6529; Atatürk Caddesi) browse a superb range of local ceramic tableware – medium-sized bowls cost around TL75 – and other ceramics from all over Anatolia.

Getting There & Away

There are hourly buses to Bursa (TL7.50, 1½ hours) until about 7pm or 8pm, plus frequent buses to Yalova (TL7.50, one hour).

BURSA

☎ 0224 / pop 1.8 million

Because of its proximity to İstanbul's metropolitan sprawl, Bursa is overlooked and bypassed by most travellers to Turkey. But those who do detour to this modern city beneath the slopes of Uludağ (Great Mountain) rarely leave disappointed. First glance reveals an energetic and cosmopolitan 21st-century city, but a closer look reveals the stately and beautiful architectural achievements that are reminders of Bursa's esteemed 14th-century history as the first capital of the Ottoman Empire.

If you've come from İstanbul, you'll love the big city buzz without the constant tourist tout interruptions, and if you've arrived from the wide open and often dusty spaces of Anatolia, the green parks of Bursa are a welcome respite.

Just a short cable car ride away is the crisp mountain air of Uludağ. After walking on the mountain's tree-clad slopes retire to the old spa suburb of Çekirge and be rejuvenated in thermal baths that have provided restorative healing for visitors for centuries.

Bursa is also renowned in Turkey for the Dursu, or İskender, kebap. You'll find it all over Turkey, but here you can go direct to the source. Look forward to döner kebap on a bed of fresh pide bread, topped with tomato sauce, yoghurt and melted butter. Time for another mountain stroll perhaps?

History

Bursa dates back to at least 200 BC. According to legend, it was founded by Prusias, the King of Bithynia, but soon came under the sway of Eumenes II of Pergamum and thereafter under Roman rule.

Bursa first grew to importance in the early centuries of Christianity, when the thermal baths at Çekirge (p295) were developed.

WESTERN ANATOLIA

BURSA

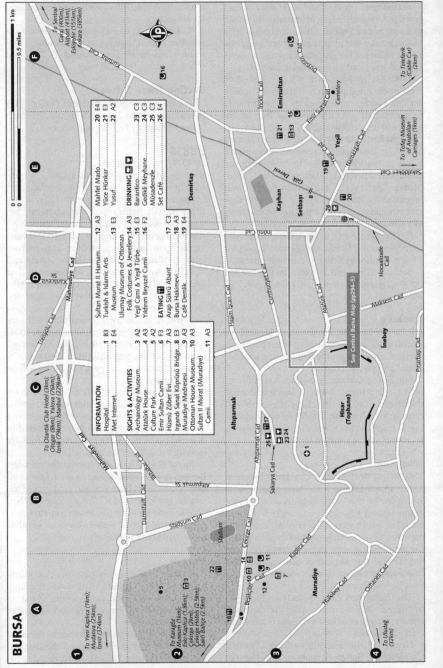

INFORMATION	
Hospital..................................1	B3
Met Internet............................2	E4

SIGHTS & ACTIVITIES	
Archaeology Museum..............3	A2
Atatürk House.........................4	A3
Culture Park...........................5	A2
Emir Sultan Camii...................6	F3
Hüsnü Züber Evi.....................7	A3
Irgandi Sanat Köprüsü Bridge...8	E3
Muradiye Medresesi................9	A3
Ottoman House Museum........10	A3
Sultan II Murat (Muradiye)	
Camii...................................11	A3
Sultan Murat II Hamam..........12	A3
Turkish & Islamic Arts	
Museum..............................13	E3
Ulumay Museum of Ottoman	
Folk Costumes & Jewellery...14	A3
Yeşil Cami & Yeşil Türbe........15	E3
Yildirim Beyazit Camii...........16	F2

EATING 🍴	
Arap Şükrü Abant..................17	C3
Bursa Hakimevi.....................18	A3
Café Demlik..........................19	E4
Mahfel Mado.........................20	E4
Yüce Hünkar.........................21	E3
Yusuf...................................22	A2

DRINKING 🍷 🍸	
Barantico..............................23	C3
Gedikli Meyhane....................24	C3
Müsadenizle..........................25	C3
Set Café...............................26	E4

To Yeni Kaplica (1km);
Mudanya (25km);
İzmir (374km)

To Karagöz Museum (1km);
Eski Kaplica (1.8km);
Çekirge (2km);
Çekirge Hotels (2.5km);
Saklı Bahçe (2.5km)

To Otantik Club Hotel (3km);
Otogar (8km); Yalova (76km);
İznik (79km); İstanbul (229km)

To Sentral
Garaj (400m);
Airport (41km);
Eskişehir (151km);
Ankara (385km)

To Uludağ (32km)

To Tofaş Museum of Anatolian Carriages (1km)

To Teleferik (Cable Car) (2km)

See Central Bursa Map (pp294–5)

However, it was Justinian I (r AD 527–65) who really put Bursa on the map.

With the decline of the Byzantine Empire, Bursa's location near Constantinople attracted the interest of would-be conquerors, including Arabs and Seljuk Turks. Having rolled through much of Anatolia by 1075, the Seljuks took Bursa (then Prusa) with ease. But 22 years later the First Crusade arrived, and the city entered a cycle of conquest and reconquest, changing hands periodically for the next 100 years.

With ongoing Turkish migrations into Anatolia during the 12th and 13th centuries, small principalities arose around individual Turkish warlords. The warlord Ertuğrul Gazi formed a small state near Bursa, and in 1317 the city was first besieged by his son Osman, who established the Ottoman line. He finally starved Bursa into submission in 1326 and made it his capital. Osman was succeeded by Orhan Gazi (r 1326–59), who expanded the fledgling Ottoman Empire to encircle the Byzantine capital at Constantinople (see p34).

Orhan took the title of sultan, struck the first Ottoman coinage and, near the end of his reign, was able to dictate to the Byzantine emperors, one of whom, John VI Cantacuzene, became his close ally and father-in-law.

Although the Ottoman capital moved to Edirne in 1402, Bursa remained an important city. Both Osman and Orhan were buried there; their tombs are still important monuments (p293).

With the founding of the Turkish Republic, Bursa developed as an industrial centre. In the 1960s and '70s boom times arrived as Fiat (Tofaş) and Renault established factories here, and today it's still a major commercial centre. The upcoming opportunity is Bursa's campaign to hold the 2018 Winter Olympics at nearby Uludağ (p300).

Orientation

Bursa's main square is Cumhuriyet Alanı (Republic Sq), known as Heykel (Statue) because of its large Atatürk monument. Atatürk Caddesi runs west from Heykel through the commercial centre to the Ulu Cami (Great Mosque). Further west stands the striking blue-glass pyramid of the Zafer Plaza shopping centre, a handy landmark as you approach the city centre.

Heading northwest, Atatürk Caddesi becomes Cemal Nadir Caddesi, then Altıparmak

Caddesi, and finally Çekirge Caddesi, which leads to the spa suburb of Çekirge, a 10-minute bus ride away. Çekirge is where the spa hotels are located.

East of Heykel, at Setbaşı, Namazgah Caddesi crosses the Gök Deresi (Gök Stream), which tumbles through a dramatic gorge. Just after the stream, Yeşil Caddesi veers left to the Yeşil Camii and Yeşil Türbe, after which it changes names to become Emir Sultan Caddesi.

From Heykel, Setbaşı and Atatürk Caddesi you can catch dolmuşes and buses to all parts of the city.

Information

There's a post office and numerous ATMs on Atatürk Caddesi (Map pp294–5), and plenty of exchange offices in the Kapalı Çarşı (Covered Market; Map pp294–5).

Discover Internet Centre (Map pp294-5; Taşkapı Caddesi; per hr TL1.25; ☾ 9am-midnight)

FiMa Bookshop (Map pp294-5; Atatürk Caddesi) Sells European newspapers.

Met Internet (Map p290; Yılmazsoy İşhanı 6, Hocaalizade Caddesi; per hr TL1.25; ☾ 9am-midnight)

Tourist Office (Map pp294-5; ☎ 220 1848; ☾ 8am-12.30pm & 1.30-5.30pm Mon-Fri, 9am-12.30pm & 1.30-6pm Sat & Sun) Beneath Atatürk Caddesi, in the row of shops at the north entrance to Orhan Gazi Alt Geçidi. Expect a friendly welcome.

Dangers & Annoyances

Heavy traffic makes it almost impossible to cross Atatürk Caddesi, so use the *alt geçidi* (pedestrian underpasses). The Atatürk Alt Geçidi (the one nearest to Heykel) has a lift for disabled people; the nearby florist has the key to operate it.

Sights & Activities

EMİR SULTAN CAMİİ

Rebuilt by Selim III in 1805 and restored in the early 1990s, the Emir Sultan Camii (Map p290) echoes the romantic decadence of Ottoman rococo style, rich in wood, curves and painted arches on the outside. The interior is surprisingly plain, but the setting, next to a tree-filled hillside cemetery overlooking the city and valley, is very pleasant.

Take a dolmuş heading for Emirsultan or any bus with 'Emirsultan' in its name. Walking from Yeşil Camii and Yeşil Türbe, you'll pass a cemetery containing the **grave of İskender Usta**, the kebap maestro himself.

YEŞİL CAMİİ & YEŞİL TÜRBE

A few minutes' walk uphill from Setbaşı, the **Yeşil Camii** (Green Mosque; Map p290), built for Mehmet I between 1419 and 1424, is a beautiful building representing a turning point in Turkish architectural style. Before this, Turkish mosques echoed the Persian style of the Seljuks, but in the Yeşil Camii a purely Turkish style emerged, and its influence is visible in Ottoman architecture across the country. Note the harmonious facade and the beautiful carved marble work around the central doorway. Look closely and you'll see the calligraphy around the niches framing the main door is all different and in some cases unfinished, the legacy of construction petering out three years after the death of Mehmet I in 1421.

As you enter, you pass beneath the sultan's private apartments into a domed central hall with a 15m-high *mihrab* (niche indicating the direction of Mecca). The greenish-blue tiles on the interior walls gave the mosque its name, and there are also fragments of a few original frescoes.

Inside the main entrance a narrow staircase leads to the sumptuously tiled *hünkar mahfili* (sultan's private box) above the main door. This was the sultan's living quarters when he chose to stay here, with his harem and household staff in less plush digs on either side.

In a small cypress-trimmed park surrounding the mosque is the **Yeşil Türbe** (Green Tomb; Map p290; admission free; 8am-noon & 1-5pm). The mosque is not actually green, with the blue exterior tiles from Kütahya (p305) added following the Bursa earthquake of 1855. However, this relatively recent makeover doesn't distract from the sublime, simple beauty of the structure, and the original interior tiles still provide an authentic and poignant touch.

Walk round the outside to see the tiled calligraphy above several windows. Inside, the most prominent tomb is that of the Yeşil Cami's founder, Mehmet I (Çelebi), surrounded by those of his children. There's also an impressive tiled *mihrab*.

At the time of writing the Yeşil Türbe was closed for restoration, but was scheduled to re-open in 2009.

Nearby the Yeşil Camii is its *medrese* (seminary), which now houses the **Turkish & Islamic Arts Museum** (Map p290; admission TL3; 8am-noon & 1-5pm). The collection includes pre-Ottoman İznik ceramics, the original door and *mihrab* curtains from the Yeşil Camii, jewellery, embroidery, calligraphy and dervish artefacts.

YILDIRIM BEYAZIT CAMİİ

Across the valley from the Emir Sultan Camii are the twin domes of the Yıldırım Beyazıt Camii (Mosque of Beyazıt the Thunderbolt, 1391; Map p290), which was built earlier than the Yeşil Camii but forms part of the same architectural evolution.

Next to the mosque is its *medrese*, once a theological seminary, now a public health centre. Here are the tombs of the mosque's founder, Sultan Beyazıt I, and his son İsa.

IRGANDI SANAT KÖPRÜSÜ

Crossing the river north of the Setbaşı road bridge, the Irgandı Sanat Köprüsü (Irgandı Bridge; Map p290) has been restored in Ottoman style as a charming arcade of tiny shops. Relaxed cafés and an array of artisans' workshops – with a definite emphasis on 'shops' – make it an interesting, if slightly touristy, spot to while away a lazy Bursa afternoon.

TOFAŞ MUSEUM OF ANATOLIAN CARRIAGES

A short uphill walk south from Setbaşı, along Sakaldöken Caddesi, brings you to a small **museum** (☎ 329 3941; Kapıcı Caddesi, Yıldırım; 10am-5pm Tue-Sun) exhibiting old cars and even older horse-drawn carts. If the kids are all mosqued-out, bring along a few picnic goodies to throw together in the lovely Ottoman gardens. The museum used to be a silk factory.

BURSA CITY MUSEUM

Bursa's modern **City Museum** (Bursa Kent Müzesi; Map pp294-5; ☎ 220 2486; www.bursakentmuzesi.gov.tr; admission TL1.50; 9.30am-5.30pm) is housed in the city's former courthouse. Ground-floor exhibits zip through the history of the city, with information on the various ruling sultans. Especially interesting is the display on the War of Independence. Most labelling is in Turkish, so ask for the handy booklet with English translations. Upstairs the cultural and ethnographical collections need little explanation, and down in the basement are reconstructions of old shops with films showing old-fashioned artisans at work. Don't miss the multimedia touch screens that allow visitors to explore the gloriously retro musical and acting careers of a few of Bursa's luminaries from last century.

MARKETS

Behind the Ulu Cami, Bursa's sprawling **Kapalı Çarşı** (Covered Market; Map pp294–5) is proudly local, especially if you find İstanbul's Grand Bazaar too touristy. At its centre the *bedesten* (vaulted, fireproof enclosure for valuable goods) was built in the late 14th century by Yıldırım Beyazıt, although it was reconstructed after an earthquake in 1855.

As you wander around, look for the **Eski Aynalı Çarşı** (Old Mirrored Market), which was originally the Orhangazi Hamam (1335) – the bath house of the Orhan Camii Külliyesi – as indicated by the domed ceiling with its skylights. This is a good place to shop for Karagöz shadow puppets and other traditional items.

The Kapalı Çarşı tumbles out into the surrounding streets, but at some point you'll find the gateway into the **Koza Han** (Cocoon Caravanserai), built in 1490. Unsurprisingly, the building is full of expensive *ipek* (silk) shops. In the courtyard is a small mosque constructed for Yıldırım Beyazıt in 1491.

Beside the Ulu Cami is the **Emir Han**, used by many of Bursa's silk brokers. Camels from the silk caravans were corralled here and goods stored in the ground-floor rooms. Drovers and merchants slept and conducted business in the rooms above. It has a lovely fountain in its courtyard tea garden.

ULU CAMİ

Prominently positioned on Atatürk Caddesi is the huge Ulu Cami (Map pp294–5), which is completely Seljuk in style and easily the most imposing of Bursa's mosques. Yıldırım Beyazıt funded the monumental building in 1396. His original pledge following victory over the Crusaders in the Battle of Nicopolis was to build 20 new mosques. His grandiose plans eventually got watered down to one mosque with 20 small domes, but despite the design trade off, Ulu Cami is still a bold architectural statement. A minaret of daunting girth augments the 20 domes of the exterior, while inside the 'bigger is better' theme continues with immense portals and a forest of square pillars. Notice the fine wooden carvings on the *mimber* (pulpit) and the preacher's chair, as well as the calligraphy on the walls. The *mimber* and the central fountain – originally open to the vagaries of Bursa's weather – were both being restored at the time of writing. According to legend, the tradition of Karagöz shadow puppet theatre (see p296) began when the Ulu Cami was constructed.

TOMBS OF SULTANS OSMAN & ORHAN

A steep cliff riddled with archaeological workings overlooks Cemal Nadir Caddesi. This oldest section of Bursa was once enclosed by stone ramparts and walls, parts of which still survive. From the Ulu Cami, walk west and up Orhan Gazi (Yiğitler) Caddesi, a ramplike street that leads to the section known as Hisar (Fortress) or Tophane.

In a park on the summit are the **Tombs of Sultans Osman and Orhan** (Osman Gazi ve Orhan Gazi Türbeleri; Map pp294–5; admission by donation), founders of the Ottoman Empire. The original structures were destroyed in the earthquake of 1855 and rebuilt in Ottoman baroque style by Sultan Abdül Aziz in 1868. Osman Gazi's tomb is the more richly decorated of the two. Remove your shoes before entering either tomb.

A six-storey **clock tower** is the last of four that originally doubled as fire alarms. Beside the clock tower is a delightful **tea garden** with fine views over the valley. Look for the bloke renting binoculars to give you a close-up view of the Bursa vista before you and the peak of Uludağ behind you. You won't need ocular assistance to spy the twin cooling towers on the horizon that have caused local *Simpsons* fans to dub Bursa 'Springfield'.

MURADİYE COMPLEX

Combining a shady park and a quiet cemetery, the **Sultan II Murat (Muradiye) Camii** (Map p290) is a peaceful oasis in busy Bursa. The mosque dates from 1426 and imitates the style of the Yeşil Cami, with painted decorations and a very intricate *mihrab*. Around the mosque the Ottoman houses lining the quiet backstreets of Muradiye are slowly being restored.

Beside the mosque are 12 **tombs** (☯ 8.30am-noon & 1-5pm) that date from the 15th and 16th centuries, including that of Sultan Murat II (r 1421–51) himself. Like other Islamic dynasties, the Ottoman one was not based on primogeniture, so any son of a sultan could claim the throne upon his father's death. As a result the designated heir (or strongest son) would often have his brothers put to death rather than risk civil war. Many of the occupants of the Muradiye tombs, including all the *şehzades* (imperial sons), were killed by close relatives.

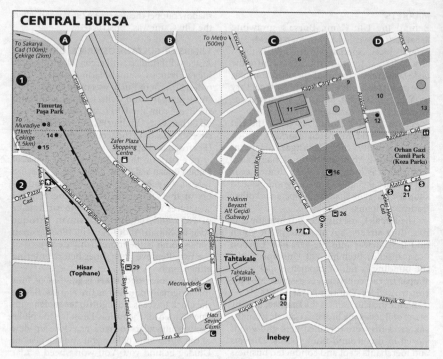

CENTRAL BURSA

The tombs are opened on a rotational basis and many are trimmed with beautiful İznik tiles. Other tombs are simple and stark with the final resting place of the ascetic, part-time dervish Murat II being unadorned and austere.

Across the park from the mosque is the **Ottoman House Museum** (Osmanlı Evi Müzesi; Map p290; admission TL2; 10am-noon & 1-5pm Tue-Sun), though you'll be lucky if anyone is around to open the doors. On the western side of the tombs is the 15th-century **Muradiye Medresesi**, a theological seminary restored in 1951 as a tuberculosis clinic.

Also nearby is the **Ulumay Museum of Ottoman Folk Costumes & Jewellery** (Osmanlı Halk Kıyafetleri ve Takıları Müzesi; Map p290; İkincimurat Caddesi; admission TL6; 9am-7pm), an impressive private collection opened in the restored 1475 Sair Ahmet Paşa *medrese* in 2004. The heritage building now houses around 70 costumes and more than 350 different pieces of jewellery.

On a short walk uphill behind the Sultan Murat II Hamam (Map p290), follow the signs to the Ottoman **Hüsnü Züber Evi** (Map p290; Uzunyol Sokak 3; admission TL3; 10am-noon & 1-5pm

Tue-Sun). Like the Ottoman House it's sporadically staffed, but worth a knock on the door if you're in the area. Nearby, winding alleys, local shops and crumbling Ottoman houses definitely reward map-free exploration.

Catch a Heykel bus or dolmuş to Muradiye. Some buses from Çekirge to Heykel also pass this way.

KÜLTÜR PARKI

The Culture Park (Map p290) lies north of the Muradiye complex but some way down the hill. The whole park was relandscaped in 2006, and the lawns, trees and shrubs are now doing very well, thank you. If you've arrived in Bursa from dusty Anatolia, the grassy expanses will be a welcome change. Visit at dusk to share the twilight with scores of local families. As well as tea gardens, playgrounds and a couple of licensed restaurants, the park also houses the **Archaeology Museum** (Arkeoloji Müzesi; Map p290; admission TL5; 8.30am-12.30pm & 1.30-5pm Tue-Sun), a predominantly classical collection of finds from local sites with a frustrating lack of English signage.

A few hundred metres west and across the busy road to Çekirge, **Atatürk House** (Atatürk Evi;

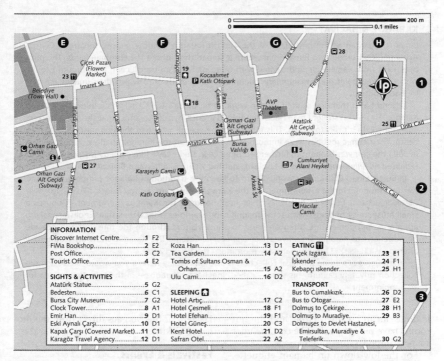

INFORMATION		
Discover Internet Centre	1	F2
FiMa Bookshop	2	E2
Post Office	3	C2
Tourist Office	4	E2
SIGHTS & ACTIVITIES		
Atatürk Statue	5	G2
Bedesten	6	C1
Bursa City Museum	7	G2
Clock Tower	8	A1
Emir Han	9	D1
Eski Aynalı Çarşı	10	D1
Kapalı Çarşı (Covered Market)	11	C1
Karagöz Travel Agency	12	D1

Koza Han	13	D1
Tea Garden	14	A2
Tombs of Sultans Osman &		
Orhan	15	A2
Ulu Cami	16	D2
SLEEPING		
Hotel Artıç	17	C2
Hotel Çeşmeli	18	F1
Hotel Efehan	19	F1
Hotel Güneş	20	C3
Kent Hotel	21	D2
Safran Otel	22	A2

EATING		
Çiçek Izgara	23	E1
İskender	24	F1
Kebapçı İskender	25	H1
TRANSPORT		
Bus to Cumalıkızık	26	D2
Bus to Otogar	27	E2
Dolmuş to Çekirge	28	H1
Dolmuş to Muradiye	29	B3
Dolmuşes to Devlet Hastanesi,		
Emirsultan, Muradiye &		
Teleferik	30	G2

Map p290; admission free; 8.30am-12.30pm & 1.30-5pm Tue-Sun) is a swish 1895 chalet in a pretty garden framed by statuesque pine trees. The restored rooms are set up as they would have been during the Father of Turkey's occasional visits. We're not sure how authentic the stuffed dog is.

Reach the Kültür Parkı and Atatürk House from Heykel by any bus or dolmuş going to Altıparmak, Sigorta or Çekirge.

ÇEKIRGE

An old suburb west of the city centre, Çekirge is Bursa's spa centre. The warm mineral-rich waters that spring from the slopes of Uludağ have been famous for their curative powers since ancient times, and even today the ailing and infirm stay for several weeks to soak and recuperate. Most people stay in hotels with their own mineral baths, and there are also several independent *kaplıcalar* (thermal baths).

The **Yeni Kaplıca** (236 6955; Mudanya Caddesi 10; 6am-11pm), on the northwestern side of the Kültür Parkı, was renovated in 1522 by Sultan Süleyman the Magnificent's grand vizier, Rüstem Paşa, on the site of a much

older bath built by Justinian. Besides the Yeni (New) bath itself, you'll also find the Kaynarca (Boiling) baths, limited to women; and the Karamustafa baths, with facilities for family bathing. Last admission is at 10pm; the full massage costs TL25 per half-hour.

Perhaps the most attractive bath is the beautifully restored **Eski Kaplıca** (233 9300; admission men/women TL55/50; 7am-10.30pm) on Çekirge's eastern outskirts, managed by the Kervansaray Termal Hotel next door. The bath

THE SILK TRADE

Silkworm-raising is a local cottage industry, with a history almost as long as the city itself. Each April villagers buy silkworms from the cooperatives, take them home and feed them on mulberry leaves. Once the worms have spun their cocoons they are brought to the Koza Han to be sold. If you visit in June or September, you may see some of the 14,000 villagers who engage in the trade haggling over huge sacks of precious white cocoons.

KARAGÖZ & HACIVAT

Bursa is regarded as the birthplace of the Turkish Karagöz shadow puppet theatre, a Central Asian tradition brought to Bursa, from where it spread throughout the Ottoman lands. The puppets – cut from camel hide and treated with oil to make them translucent, then brought to life with coloured paint – are manipulated behind a white cloth onto which their images are cast by back-lighting.

Legend has it that one of the foremen working on Bursa's Ulu Camii was a hunchback called Karagöz. He and his straight man Hacivat indulged in such humorous antics that the other workers abandoned their tasks to watch. This infuriated the sultan, who had the two miscreants put to death. Their comic routines were immortalised, however, in the Karagöz shadow puppet shows. In 2006 the pair was brought to further prominence in Ezel Akay's film comedy *Hacivat & Karagöz* (released as *Killing the Shadows* in English), starring Haluk Bilginer and Beyazit Öztürk.

In Bursa, Şinasi Çelikkol has worked hard to keep the tradition of Karagöz puppetry alive and was instrumental in the establishment of the **Karagöz Museum** (Karagöz Müzesi; ☎ 232 3360; www .karagozmuzesi.com; Çekirge Caddesi 59; admission free), opposite the Karagöz monument. It houses a small museum of puppetry with some magnificent examples from Uzbekistan. English-speaking apprentice puppeteers are often on hand to show visitors through the museum and provide introductions to Karagöz's quirky cast of characters. Catch a live Karagöz show on Wednesday afternoons (TL4; 🕑 11am) or Saturday mornings (TL1.50; 🕑 2pm).

Şinasi Çelikkol's ethnographical collection is also on display here. If you would like to see the collection privately call into his shop – called, inevitably, Karagöz – in the Eski Aynalı Çarşı for an appointment.

---

is done out in creamy marble and the hot rooms have plunge pools. The cost includes soap, shampoo, sauna and massage.

For the low-down on hamam etiquette, see p46.

Çekirge's other main feature is the unusual **I Murat (Hüdavendigar) Camii**, behind the Ada Palas Oteli. Its basic design is the early-Ottoman inverted 'T' plan, which first appeared in the Nilüfer Hatun *imareti* (soup kitchen) in İznik (p287). Here, however, the 'T' wings are barrel-vaulted rather than dome-topped. On the ground floor at the front are the rooms of a *zaviye* (dervish hostel). The 2nd-floor gallery on the facade, built as a *medrese*, is not evident from within except for the sultan's loge (box) in the middle at the back of the mosque. From the outside it almost looks like a Christian edifice.

The huge **sarcophagus of Sultan Murat I** (r 1359–89), who died at Kosovo quelling a rebellion by his Albanian, Bosnian, Bulgarian, Hungarian and Serbian subjects, can be viewed in the tomb across the street. Nearby is a tea garden with great city views that is popular with local families at the end of the day.

Çekirge's main street is I Murat Caddesi (Birinci Murat Caddesi). To get here, take a bus or dolmuş (both TL1.50) from Heykel or Atatürk Caddesi to Çekirge or SSK Hastanesi. Bus 96 goes direct from the otogar to Çekirge.

Festivals & Events

The **Uluslararasi Bursa Festival** (www.bursafestivali .org), Bursa's long-standing music and dance festival, runs for three weeks in June and July. Expect a diverse program featuring gems like Roma bands from Eastern Europe, *fado* music from Portugal, and the occasional dubious pleasure like Julio Iglesias. It's very affordable and tickets for the top acts are only around TL20. In July the **Golden Karagöz Dance Festival** draws international groups.

Every November the **Karagöz Festival** attracts Karagöz shadow puppeteers (above), Western puppeteers and marionette performers for five days of festivities and performances.

Tours

Karagöz Travel Agency (Map pp294-5; ☎ 221 8727; www .karagoztravel.com; Kapalıçarşı, Eski Aynalı Çarşı 4) offers interesting local tours, including city excursions and trips to Cumalıkızık (p301).

Sleeping

Though slightly more expensive, the hillside suburb of Çekirge (3km west of Central Bursa) offers the most attractive sleeping options in Bursa. Most hotels have their own bathing facilities, often with private or public bathing rooms in the basement. Baths are usually included in the room price. Eating options are limited in Çekirge, but it's just a short hop down the hill by dolmuş to central Bursa.

ÇEKIRGE & SOĞANLI

Mutlu Hotel (☎ 233 2829; mutluhotel@mynet.com; Murat Caddesi 19; s/d/tr TL50/78/90; ⊠) A reliable and friendly choice, the Mutlu combines a rustic wooden exterior with spacious thermal baths decked out in marble. The decor of the rooms struggles to get past 1973, but the ambience in the relaxed café outside is slightly more modern.

Hotel Ada Palas (☎ 233 3990; www.adapalas.com; Murat Caddesi 21; s/d/tr TL55/90/130; ⊠ 🖳) The flash reception isn't matched by some slightly tatty rooms in need of a paint job, but the accommodation is spacious, albeit with pokey bathrooms. Breakfast is a diverse spread, adding further to the good value equation at the Ada Palas. Every floor has a thermal bath.

Termal Hotel Gold 2 (☎ 235 6030; www.hotelgold .com.tr; I Murat Cami Aralığı; s/d TL60/90; ⊠ 🖳) This restored 1878 house next to the I Murat Camii is a great choice in a quiet location, decked out in full wooden interiors, 'period' furniture and deep red drapery. Baths and parking are included and the roof terrace is a bonus.

Atlas Termal Hotel (☎ 234 4100; www.atlasotel .com.tr; Hamamlar Caddesi 29; s/d/tr TL80/130/150; ⊠ 🖳) Another restored building blending modern and traditional style, with pine fittings, a sunny internal courtyard and a rooftop terrace with views of Bursa. Prices include use of the private thermal baths.

Huzur Termal Otel (☎ 234 5250; www.huzurotel .com.tr; Murat Caddesi 31; s/d/tr TL100/150/180; ⊠ 🖳) In a town where chintzy is respected as a legitimate decorating style, the Huzur has comfortable rooms just like your favourite auntie's place. Satellite TV, minibars and a billiard room provide a more masculine balance, and thermal baths and an external garden come as standard. It's overpriced so ask for a discount.

Otantik Club Hotel (☎ 211 3280; www.otantikclub hotel.com; Soğanlı; d TL200, ste TL300; ⊠ 🖳 🖭) One of Bursa's best hotels, tucked away in a botanic garden in the suburb of Soğanlı, north of the centre. All the rooms are gorgeous, but the suites, with the sun streaming through their stained-glass windows onto Ottoman-

style fabrics, are exquisite. Two great restaurants and a cosy bar provide the essential finishing touches.

our pick **Hotel Gönlüferah** (☎ 233 9210; www.gon luferah.com; Murat Caddesi 22; s/d €105/150; ⊠ 🖳 🖭) This is more like it. Dating from 1890, the hilltop Gönlüferah is a perfect blend of heritage charm and modern convenience. Rooms are swathed in delicate silk and feature beautifully restored wooden floors. The in-house spa treatments get two very relaxed ticks. Ask about a discount and you're getting a splurge-worthy bargain.

CENTRAL BURSA

Hotel Güneş (Map pp294–5; ☎ 222 1404; İnebey Caddesi 75; s/d/tr/q without bathroom TL26/46/54/68) In a restored Ottoman house, the friendly family-run Güneş is Bursa's best budget pension. The small, neat rooms have Ezy-Kleen laminate floors and the walls are trimmed with inspirational tourist-board photos of Turkey. In season look forward to a welcome bowl of cherries or watermelon.

Hotel Artıç (Map pp294–5; ☎ 224 5505; www.artichotel .com; Ulu Camii Karşısı 95; s/d/tr TL60/90/100; ⊠ 🖳) A decent option towards the western end of Atatürk Caddesi. Rooms are light and fairly spacious with wi-fi and a minibar. From the breakfast salon there are good views of Ulu Camii. Posted rates are overpriced so ask for a discount.

Hotel Çeşmeli (Map pp294–5; ☎ 224 1511; Gümüşçeken Caddesi 6; s/d/tr TL65/100/130) In close proximity to Bursa's bustling market, the Çeşmeli is friendly, clean, and features an all-female staff, making it an excellent choice for women travellers. The buffet breakfast is excellent with the old school decor complemented by gracious old school service at reception,

Safran Otel (Map pp294–5; ☎ 224 7216; safran_otel@ yahoo.com; Arka Sokak 4, Tophane; s/d TL70/130; ⊠) Opposite the Osman and Orhan tombs, the Safran is housed in a characterful restored house in a historic neighbourhood high above the city. The Ottoman trappings don't extend to the rooms, but it's an inviting place with a good restaurant next door.

Hotel Efehan (Map pp294–5; ☎ 225 2260; www.efe han.com.tr; Gümüşçeken Caddesi 34; s/d/tr TL85/130/170; ⊠ 🖳) Revelling in a veneer of modern style trimmed with plenty of marble, the Efehan is solid three-star value with a central location. Wi-fi and friendly, (usually) English-speaking staff at reception come as standard, and it's definitely worth asking for a discount. What's with the model ships in reception though?

Kent Hotel (Map pp294-5; ☎ 223 5420; www.kentotel .com.tr; Atatürk Caddesi 69; s/d/tr €70/90/120; ✂ ▢) Solid and central business-oriented option with a good location opposite the Ulu Camii. A relatively recent modern makeover is balanced with interesting black-and-white pics of Ye Olde Bursa in the lobby.

Eating

As well as the legendary İskender kebap, Bursa is well known for İnegöl *köftesi*, a rich grilled meatball named after nearby İnegöl. Other culinary specialities include fresh fruit (especially *şeftali* – peaches – in season) and *kestane şekeri* (candied chestnuts).

RESTAURANTS

Expect to pay more for İskender kebap in Bursa compared to the rest of Turkey. The buttery yoghurt sauce is incredibly rich and tasty in this town, so the premium is largely justified. Prices start around TL12 for *bir porsyon* (one serving) or TL18 if you dive in and order *bir buçuk porsyon* (1½ portions). Note that for legal reasons most places advertise İskender kebap as Bursa kebap.

Çiçek Izgara (Map pp294-5; ☎ 221 6526; Belediye Caddesi 15; mains TL9-12; ✆ 11am-9.30pm) One block from Koza Parkı behind the half-timbered *belediye*, the Çiçek grill house is bright and modern (good for solo women travellers), with a 1st-floor salon to catch the flower-market action below.

our pick Yusuf (Map p290; Kültür Parkı; mezes TL4-10; ✆ 11am-11pm) 'Joe's Place' features a meze-and grill-laden terrace set among established trees providing shade. The service is so good it's the only time we've seen middle-aged waiters actually break out into a brisk trot. We can also personally recommend Yusuf for celebrating a birthday a long way from home. Just be warned it's the kind of place you'll want to fly your friends and family in for a big night. Come along at dusk and share the moment instead with scores of loyal locals over a beer or glass of rakı (aniseed brandy). You'll find Yusuf around 300m from the stadium and around 150m from Çekirge Caddesi.

Bursa Hakimevi (Map p290; ☎ 233 4900; Çekirge Caddesi 10; mains TL8-15; ✆ noon-10pm) This restored Ottoman house on the edge of the Kültür Parkı is now a tastefully low-key restau-

rant doing a fine line in mezes. Friday and Saturday nights are very popular so make a booking to ensure a spot on the verdant outdoor terrace.

Kebapçı İskender (Map pp294-5; ☎ 221 4615; Ünlü Caddesi 7; mains TL15-22.50; ✆ 10am-10pm) This legendary kebap shop dates back to 1867 and its owners claim to be descendants of İskender Usta himself. However, at TL15 a portion you're paying a *lot* for a taste of history. Pictures of good old Izzy himself line the walls of the faux-heritage building. (Think KFC's Colonel Sanders without the goatee…)

İskender (Map pp294-5; Atatürk Caddesi 60; mains TL14.75; ✆ 10am-10pm) Same, same but different at this central spot which also makes a competing claim to be the original home of the İskender kebap. Leave the legal machinations to the lawyers and tuck into the slightly cheaper, but equally tasty, kebaps at this main drag spot housed in a cosy wooden abode.

Yüce Hünkar (Map p290; ☎ 327 8910; Yeşil Cami Yanı 17-19; meals TL15-25; ✆ 11am-10pm) The Hünkar has a wonderful location overlooking the valley in front of the Yeşil Cami, which (almost) offsets the tourist-trap prices. Maybe just have a slice of baklava (dessert) and coffee and save your dosh for the seafood restaurants of Sakarya Caddesi.

Formerly part of Bursa's Jewish quarter, **Sakarya Caddesi** (Map pp294–5) acquired new fame from one Arap Şükrü, who returned home after the War of Independence and opened a seafood restaurant. It was so successful that his descendants followed him into the business and the street now has several restaurants of the same name. The whole upper end of the narrow lane is crammed with tables, so wander along and check the buzz before making your choice. Fish and seafood are the speciality, starting around TL12 per portion, but meat and mezes are also available.

Arap Şükrü Abant (Map p290; ☎ 221 1453; Sakarya Caddesi 27; mezes TL4-12; ✆ 11am-11pm) is run by his sons and does a great *karides güveç* (shrimp casserole) and excellent octopus in olive oil. Sakarya Caddesi is also a good spot for a quiet beer or rakı.

Sakarya Cadessi is on the northern side of the Hisar district, just south of Altıparmak Caddesi. It's about 10 minutes' walk from the Ulu Cami, or you can take a Çekirge-bound bus or dolmuş (TL1.25) from Heykel to the Çatal Fırın stop, opposite the Sabahettin Paşa Camii.

CAFÉS & QUICK EATS

Café Demlik (Map p290; ☎ 326 4483; Yeşil Caddesi 25; dishes from TL3; ☽ 11am-9pm) This charming old house has been converted into an Ottoman-style eatery where you can sit on floor cushions and get stuck into *gözleme* (savoury pancakes).

Set Café (Map p290; ☎ 225 1162; Köprü Üstü; dishes from TL3) Across the stream from the Mahfel Mado, this multi-terraced venue has live music and an entertainingly confusing layout. Entry is to the left of the ice-cream spot that hovers above.

ourpick **Sakli Bahçe** (Çekirge Caddesi 2; mains TL4-8; ☽ 11am-11pm) The perfect place to watch the sunset if you're staying in Çekirge, this chilled-out hilltop tea garden features low slung tables, scatter cushions and complimentary fleece wraps for when the sun goes down. It's the preferred meeting place for Bursa's bright young things, lured by excellent pizza and kebaps, and wi-fi access with a view.

Mahfel Mado (Map p290; ☎ 326 8888; Namazgah Caddesi 2; mains TL5-10; ☽ 8am-11pm) Bursa's oldest café is open from breakfast to dessert. It also has live music on its riverside terrace and an art gallery in the basement. What more do you really need?

SELF-CATERING

Self-caterers should visit **Tahtakale Çarsısı** (Tahtakale Market; Map pp294–5) near Hotel Güneş, for fresh fruit, vegetables and cheeses.

Drinking & Entertainment

After eating in Sakarya Caddesi you'll find a few places nearby to kick on. Alternatively Yusuf restaurant (opposite) in Kültür Parkı is a good place for a few beers and mezes.

Barantlco (Map p290; ☎ 222 4049; Sakarya Caddesi 55; drinks from TL3; ☽ 11am-10pm) Tucked away in a courtyard, this place features a vaguely New Age vibe with the added attraction of occasional live music.

Müsadenizle (Map p290; ☎ 220 9428; Altıparmak Caddesi 9/D) Funky chocolate brown and orange decor and classic tunes (think Bob Marley and the Rolling Stones) make this Bursa's best approximation of what you're probably used to in a bar. Jugs of beer and a good cocktail list keeps everyone happy. Just be warned: it charges like a wounded bull for bowls of peanuts – we found out the hard way.

Gedikli Meyhane (Map p290; ☎ 224 4313; Sakarya Caddesi 47) Trimmed with maritime memorabilia, the Gedliki is as much restaurant as bar. With a good selection of beers and excellent mezes and bar snacks, it's the perfect spot to while away a few increasingly pleasant hours.

Getting There & Away

AIR

Turkish Airlines (☎ 444 0849; www.thy.com) flies twice a week to Diyarbakır, Erzurum and Trabzon. During summer months **SunExpress** (☎ 444 0797; www.sunexpress.com.tr) flies from Bursa to Antalya, Trabzon, İzmir, Diyarbakır and Erzurum.

BUS

Bursa's otogar is 10km north of the centre on the Yalova road. See below for information on getting from the otogar to the city centre and Çekirge. Information on some major bus routes and fares is provided in the table, p300.

The fastest way to İstanbul (TL20, 2½ to three hours) is to take a bus to Yalova, then the **IDO fast ferry** (☎ 444 4436; www.ido.com.tr) to İstanbul's Yenikapı docks. Get a bus that departs Bursa's bus terminal at least 90 minutes before the scheduled boat departure.

Karayolu ile (by road) buses to İstanbul drag you all around the Bay of İzmit and take four to five hours. Those designated *feribot ile* (by ferry) take you to Topçular, east of Yalova, and then by ferry to Eskihisar, a much quicker and more pleasant way to go.

The table (p300) lists daily services on selected routes from Bursa.

Getting Around

TO/FROM THE BUS STATION

City bus 38 crawls the 10km between the otogar and the city centre (TL1.50, 45 minutes). Returning to the otogar, it leaves from stop 4 on Atatürk Caddesi. Bus 96 from the otogar goes direct to Çekirge (TL1.50, 40 minutes).

A taxi from the otogar to the city centre costs around TL20, to Çekirge about TL22.

BUS

Bursa's city buses (BOİ; TL1.50) have their destinations and stops marked on the front and kerb side. A major set of yellow bus stops is lined up opposite Koza Parkı on Atatürk Caddesi. Catch a bus from stop 1 for Emirsultan and Teleferik (Uludağ cable car); from stop 2 for Muradiye; and from stop 4 for

SERVICES FROM BURSA'S OTOGAR

Destination	Fare (TL)	Duration (hr)	Distance (km)	Frequency (per day)
Afyon	27	5	290	8
Ankara	30	6	400	hourly
Bandırma	14	2	115	12
Çanakkale	30	5	310	12
Denizli	40	9	532	several
Eskişehir	15	2½	155	hourly
İstanbul	20	3	230	frequent
İzmir	25	5½	375	hourly
İznik	10	1½	82	hourly
Kütahya	17	3	190	several
Yalova	9	1¼	76	every 30 min

Altıparmak and the Kültür Parkı. You can also pick up buses to the Botanik Parkı (15) and Cumalıkızık (22) from here.

These days, all city buses run on a pre-pay system; you can buy tickets from kiosks or shops near most bus stops (keep an eye out for the BuKART sign). If you're staying for a few days there are various multitrip options available.

DOLMUŞ

In Bursa, cars and minibuses operate as dolmuşes. The destination is indicated by an illuminated sign on the roof. The minimum fare is TL1.25. Dolmuşes are usually as cheap as buses and definitely faster and more frequent, especially linking central Bursa with Çekirge.

Dolmuşes go to Çekirge via the Kültür Parkı, Eski Kaplıca and I Murat Camii from a major dolmuş terminal immediately south of Heykel. Other dolmuşes wait in front of Koza Parkı.

METRO

Bursa has a modern metro system, but as it serves only the outskirts of town it is seldom used by visitors.

TAXI

A ride from Heykel to Muradiye costs about TL5, to Çekirge about TL10.

AROUND BURSA
Uludağ
☎ 0224

With its proximity to İstanbul, Bursa and Ankara, Uludağ (Great Mountain; 2543m), on the outskirts of Bursa, is Turkey's most popular ski resort. A *teleferik* (cable car) runs up to Sarıalan, 7km from the town of Uludağ and the main hotel area (called 'Oteller' naturally). The cluster of accommodation and ski hire joints springs to life during the ski season from December to early April, and slumbers quietly in the off-season. Even if you don't plan to go skiing or do the three-hour hike to the summit, it's still a worthwhile trip year-round to take advantage of the view and the cool, clear air of Uludağ National Park. With pine forests and the occasional snowy peak, the scenery is slightly reminiscent of New Zealand's South Island or western North America.

At the cable-car terminus at Sarıalan there are a few snack and refreshment stands and a basic national park camp site that's usually full. You're best to treat the 'Great Mountain' as a day trip in summer, or check out www.uludaghotels.com for accommodation options during the ski season.

GETTING THERE & AWAY
Cable Car

Take a Bursa city bus from stop 1 or a dolmuş marked 'Teleferik' (TL1.50) from behind the city museum to the lower terminus of the cable car, a 15-minute ride from Heykel. The cable cars (TL8 return, 30 minutes) depart every 40 minutes between 8am and 10pm in summer and between 10am and 5pm in winter, wind and weather permitting. At busy times they'll leave whenever there are 30 people on board.

The cable car stops first at Kadıyayla, then continues upwards to the terminus at Sarıalan (1635m). Stand at the rear of the car for the best views of Bursa as you go up.

Dolmuş

Dolmuşes from central Bursa to Uludağ (TL7) and Sarıalan (TL10) run several times daily in summer and more frequently in winter.

At the 11km marker you must stop and pay an admission fee for the **national park** (per car TL5). The hotel zone is 11km up from the entrance.

The return ride can be difficult in summer, with little public transport on offer. In winter dolmuşes and taxis are usually eager to get at least some money for the trip downhill, so bargain hard.

Cumalıkızık

☎ 0224 / pop 700

This unique slice of Turkeyana on the slopes of Uludağ, about 16km east of Bursa, was settled 700 years ago by the Turcoman Kızıks and is full of wonderfully preserved early Ottoman rural architecture. Wander around to enjoy the peaceful atmosphere, with brightly painted traditional houses sitting proudly adjacent to crumbling unrestored structures.

Across recent years TV tourism has dulled some of Cumalıkızık's bucolic hush. From 2000 to 2005 the village was the location for the popular series *Kınalı Kar (Henna in the Snow)*, and souvenir shops sprung up to lure star-struck visitors. A few years on the village's star status is receding and the biggest game in town is the regular Sunday morning market. Cumalıkızık is a preferred destination of Bursa folk for a leisurely weekend brunch in an array of rustic garden restaurants, or as a convenient spot to pick up fresh fruit, local honey and village handicrafts. Come during the week though, and it could be just you and a few relaxed locals in the narrow uphill lanes that do their utmost to redefine the words 'quaint' and 'heritage'.

SLEEPING & EATING

There are only two accommodation options in the village, both of which serve food. Other small cafés and informal *gözleme* joints provide alternative eating.

Konak Pansiyon (☎ 372 4869; d TL70) Take the right fork up into the village to reach this beautifully restored guest house, which has just eight rooms ranging from Ottoman-style floor mattresses to some *huge* double beds. The restaurant opposite offers standard kebaps, salads, mezes, and *gözleme* for lunch.

Mavi Boncuk (☎ 373 0955; www.cumalikizik-mavi boncuk.com; Saldede Sokak; d TL70) Veering left instead

of right, signs lead to another old house, also well restored and swamped in appealing gardens. The six rooms are simple but inviting, with plenty of places to relax inside and out. The food is superb with a steady stream of Bursa locals enjoying brunches of *menemen* (Turkish scrambled eggs) and Turkish bread toasted on an open fire. It's the kind of relaxed eatery you wish your own hometown had.

GETTING THERE & AWAY

From Bursa take bus 22 (TL3, 50 minutes) from stop 3 on Atatürk Caddesi. Buses leave roughly every 90 minutes between 7.30am and 9pm. The last bus back to Bursa usually leaves at 8.30pm. More frequent dolmuşes (TL2.50) also run to and from the Sentral Garaj, which is connected to Atatürk Caddesi by other dolmuşes and buses.

ESKİŞEHİR

☎ 0222 / pop 517,000

Ironically, Eskişehir (Old City) is a thoroughly modern town, built over the scant remnants of the Greco-Roman city of Dorylaeum. A small Ottoman district still survives, but most of the city is newly built and has a bustling student-enlivened atmosphere.

The area is rich in mineral springs, there are many hamams, and several hotels offering thermal water in their bathrooms.

Orientation & Information

Pedestrianised Hamamyolu Caddesi runs north–south between Yunus Emre and İki Eylül Caddesis. Odunpazarı, the Ottoman old-town district, is just beyond the southern end of the street.

Eskişehir's **tourist office** (☎ 230 1752) is in the Valiliği (regional government) building on the southwest side of İki Eylül Caddesis. It's a handy spot to pick up information on the Phrygian Valley (p303).

The train station is northwest of the centre, the otogar 3km east of the centre. Trams and buses run from the otogar to Köprübaşı, the central district just north of Hamamyolu Caddesi.

Internet cafés and ATMs are at the southern end of Hamamyolu Caddesi.

Sights & Activities

Eskişehir is famous for its 'white gold': **meerschaum** *(luletaşı)*, a light, porous white stone, which is mined in local villages and then shaped into pipes and other artefacts. Visit the Yunus Emre Kültür Sarayı, next to the post office, which contains the **Lületaşı Museum** (İki Eylül Caddesi). This informal collection includes fine old and new meerschaum pipes and photos of the mining process.

Head south past the imposing yellow **Anadolu Üniversitesi Cumhuriyet Müzesi** (admission free; ☽ 8.30am-6pm Mon-Fri, 9am-5pm Sat), a sepia-heavy collection of Atatürk memorabilia, to find *eski* Eskişehir, the old Ottoman quarter. At its centre, the large **Kurşunlu Camii** (1525) retains most of its *külliye* (mosque complex), including an *aşevi* (cookhouse) bristling with chimneys and an *okuma odası* (reading room) with pillars that incorporate capitals from ancient Dorylaeum.

The surrounding streets are lined with old Ottoman houses, many being restored in an ongoing rejuvenation project. The **Beylerbeyi Konağı** (Kurşunlu Camii Sokak 28; ☽ 10am-noon) is supposedly open to the public, although you'll be lucky to find it unlocked. The infrequently staffed **İsmail Alkılıçgil Fotograf Evi** (Belediye Caddesi 16; admission free; ☽ 10am-4pm) has a worthwhile collection of sepia-tinged prints of old Eskişehir.

Further west, the **Archaeological Museum** (Arkeoloji Müzesi; Hasan Polatkan Bulvarı 86; admission TL3; ☽ 8.30am-noon & 1.30-5pm Mon-Fri) contains finds from Dorylaeum, including several crude mosaic floors and Roman statuettes of Cybele, Hecate and Mithras.

Take a dip in the thermal baths around the north end of Hamamyolu Caddesi. Most of them are men-only, but the **Kadinlar Kaplıca** (admission TL8; ☽ 5.30am-10pm), near the Has Termal Hotel, is open to women.

Sleeping

The best places to stay are the hotels with thermal baths around Hamamyolu Caddesi.

Termal Otel Sultan (☎ 231 8371; Hamamyolu Caddesi 1; s/d/tr TL45/65/80) The Sultan may be a little worn around the edges, but the bathrooms are clean and it is comfortable enough. Wi-fi access is a welcome concession to the 21st century.

Uysal Otel (☎ 221 4353; www.uysalotel.com; Asarcıklı Caddesi 7; s/d TL80/140) Caution: must like red. The designers have had a field day in the reception at this uber-chintzy spot just off Hamamyolu Caddesi. Upstairs the rooms are slightly simpler in crimson and scarlet, but relatively spacious and come with mod cons like wi-fi access. Thankfully the attached thermal baths are clean and classic in neutral marble tones.

Eating

Eskişehir has a wealth of good value kebap and grill places, and a couple of other well-frequented spots for lunch or dinner. The pedestrianised part of Hamamyolu Caddesi features cafés and tea gardens.

Şomine Et Lokantası (☎ 220 8585; Köprübaşı Caddesi 18; mains TL4-12; ☽ 9am-10pm) With an open-sided 1st-floor salon, this is the pick of Eskişehir's cafeteria restaurants. A diverse crowd from students to business folk crowds in for a gargantuan menu of Turkish dishes. Check out the trays downstairs – it's all good.

Osmanlı Evi (☎ 221 5460; Yeşil Efendi Sokak 22; mains TL6-20; ☽ 11.30am-9pm) The Ottoman House was one of the first in Odunpazarı to be restored, and now functions as a fine café-restaurant. It's up a side street behind the Kurşunlu Camii.

At the time of writing a couple of characterful teahouses and cafés were opening in the nearby streets of the old Ottoman quarter. Good luck exploring.

Shopping

Eskişehir is the place to buy meerschaum pipes, cigarette-holders, prayer beads and other items made out of *luletaşı*. Some hotels sell meerschaum but the shopping is better in local shops.

Eskişehir also has many sweet shops. Go local with rolls of *med helvası* or chunks of *nuga helvası* (two types of nougat).

Getting There & Away

All official city transport runs on a prepay system – buy tickets (TL1.50) from a booth or kiosk. Trams, city buses and dolmuşes serve the vast otogar; look for signs saying 'Terminal' or 'Yeni Otogar'. A taxi from Köprübaşı costs around TL8.

From the otogar there are regular buses to Afyon (TL13, three hours), Ankara (TL15, 3¼ hours), Bursa (TL15, 2½ hours), İstanbul (TL25, six hours), İznik (TL18, three hours) and Kütahya (TL8, 1½ hours).

Eskişehir **train station** (☎ 255 5555) is an important railway terminus, and there are various services from İstanbul (four to six hours) and Ankara (2½ to four hours) day and night.

AROUND ESKİŞEHİR
Seyitgazi
☎ 0222 / pop 3200

This small town 43km southeast of Eskişehir is dominated by the hilltop 13th-century **Battalgazi mosque complex** (admission TL5). Combining Seljuk and Ottoman architecture, the complex also contains pieces of marble presumably taken from the ruins of the Romano-Byzantine town of Nacolea. The mosque commemorates Seyit/Seyyid Battal Gazi, a warrior who fought for the Arabs against the Byzantines and was killed in 740. His wildly elongated tomb sits in a side chamber off the main mosque.

Features of the *külliye* include an *aşevi* (kitchen) with eight skyline-piercing chimneys, a *semahane* (dance hall) where dervishes would have gathered, and a *medrese* containing several grim *çilehanes*, or 'places of suffering' – cells in which the devout lived (and died) like hermits with only their Qurans for company. Numerous calligraphic inscriptions singing the praises of Battal Gazi dot the walls. At the time of writing the complex was part building site and part bombsite. Once restoration is complete in 2009, it's worth a detour.

GETTING THERE & AWAY
Seyitgazi Belediyesi buses run from Eskişehir to Seyitgazi (TL5, 45 minutes). Some buses from Eskişehir to Afyon also pass through.

PHRYGIAN VALLEY
The rock-hewn monuments in the so-called Phrygian Valley (Frig Vadisi) between Eskişehir and Afyon are the most impressive relics to survive from Phrygian times. You really need a car to explore the area fully. Hitching is not recommended because traffic is very light.

Even if you're not interested in the Phrygians, the valley is a beautiful part of Turkey, virtually untouched by tourism. Craggy escarpments dotted with fir trees conceal the forgotten ruins of the Phrygian culture and the spectacular scenery is almost more diverse than Cappadocia. Visit in early June, when delicate opium poppies bloom in white and purple patches amid a rugged green-grey-brown backdrop.

Orientation
The Phrygian Valley separates neatly into two sections, the northern area near Eskişehir and Seyitgazi, and the southern sector around Afyon.

Most sites are along dirt tracks and some can be hard to find, even when you're right beside them. Navigation is slowly getting better in the southern Afyon section, where local authorities have designated a 'Turizm Kuşağı Yolu' (Tourism Zone Route) and embarked on a program of road improvements along its 170km length. Despite this, expect to get pleasantly lost a few times and just keep exploring.

The following outlines the sights of the Phrygian Valley, starting from Eskişehir and Seyitgazi and ending nearer Afyon.

Sights
YAZILIKAYA VALLEY
Heading from Seyitgazi to Afyon, after around 3km turn south (left) into a road

---

THE PHRYGIANS

Emigrants from Thrace to central Anatolia around 2000 BC, the Phrygians spoke an Indo-European language, used an alphabet similar to Greek, and established a kingdom with its capital at Gordion (p454), 106km west of Ankara. The empire flourished under its most famous king, Midas (c 725–675 BC), one of many Phrygian monarchs to have that name, until it was overrun by the Cimmerians (676–585 BC).

Considering they lived in rock dwellings, the Phrygians were a sophisticated people with a dedication to the arts. Phrygian culture was based on Greek culture, but with strong Neo-Hittite and Urartian influences. They're credited with inventing the frieze, embroidery and numerous musical instruments, including cymbals, double clarinet, flute, lyre, syrinx (Pan pipes) and triangle. Not bad for cave dwellers and just maybe the original rock music.

Phrygian civilisation was at its most vigorous around 585 to 550 BC, when the rock-cut monuments at Midas Şehri – the most impressive Phrygian stonework still in existence – were carved. Phrygian relics can be seen in many Anatolian museums, providing fascinating insights into a culture that bridged the gap between 'primitive' and 'advanced' amid the scrub and rocks of central Turkey.

marked with a brown sign pointing to Midas Şehri. Further along this rough road a sign leads right 2km to the **Doğankale** (Falcon Castle) and **Deveboyukale** (Camel-Height Castle), both of them plugs of rock riddled with formerly inhabited caves.

Further south another rough track to the right leads 1km to the **Mezar Anıtı** (Monumental Tomb), where a restored tomb is cut into the rock.

Continuing south is another temple-like tomb, called the **Küçük Yazılıkaya** (Little Inscribed Stone).

MIDAS ŞEHRI

A few kilometres on from Küçük Yazılıkaya is what archaeologists call Midas Şehri (Midas City). It is actually the village of **Yazılıkaya** (Inscribed Rock), 32km south of Seyitgazi.

The sights at Yazılıkaya are clustered around a huge rock. Tickets (TL3) are sold at the library in front of the steps leading up to the site. The friendly local custodian will meet you and give you the excellent 'Highlands of Phrygia' brochure (he usually keeps them in the back of his car). A second 'Eskişehir' brochure has good maps of the entire Phrygian Valley, and an essential guide to exploring Yazılıkaya.

Carved into the soft tufa, the so-called **Midas Tomb** is a 17m-high relief covered in geometric patterns and resembling the facade of a temple. At the bottom is a niche where an effigy of Cybele would be displayed during festivals. Inscriptions in the Phrygian alphabet – one bearing Midas' name – circle the tomb.

Opposite the inscribed rock is another huge rock riddled with caves that once contained a **monastery**.

Behind the Midas Tomb a path leads down to a tunnel, then passes a second **smaller tomb**, unfinished and high up in the rock. The path continues upwards to the top of the rock, which was an **acropolis**. Here you will find a stepped stone, labelled an **altar**, which may have been used for sacrifices, and traces of walls and roads. Even with a map following the paths can be confusing, but the main features are easy to spot. Heading down from the acropolis notice a portion of the **ancient road**, identifiable from the wagon-wheel ruts worn into the rock.

Note there are several ancient water cisterns on the backside of the rock – some unmarked – so take care when walking.

KÜMBET

Heading 15km west from Midas Şehri is the village of Kümbet, which boasts a Seljuk *kümbet* (tomb) with old Byzantine marble carvings reused around its doorway. Near the *kümbet* is a rocky outcrop with several magnificent **rock fireplaces**. Also nearby is the **Arslanlı Mezarı** (Lion Tomb), another rock-cut Phrygian tomb with lions carved into its pedimental facade.

OTHER SITES

The following sites are to the southwest of Kümbet.

The small village of Doğer boasts a *han* (caravanserai) dating back to 1434. Unfortunately it's usually locked. From here, dirt tracks go to lily-covered **Emre Gölü** (Lake Emre), a perfect picnic place overlooked by a small stone building once used by dervishes; and a rock formation with a rough staircase called the Kirkmerdiven Kayalıkları (Rocky Place with 40 Stairs). The dirt track then runs on to **Bayramaliler** and Üçlerkayası with rock formations called *peribacalar* (fairy chimneys), just like Cappadocia.

After Bayramaliler is **Göynüş Vadisi** (Göynüş Valley), with fine Phrygian rock tombs decorated with lions (*aslantaş*) and snakes (*yılantaş*). This valley is a 2km walk from the main Eskişehir to Afyon road.

At **Ayazini** village there was once a rock settlement called Metropolis. Look out for a huge church with its apse and dome cut clear out of the rock face, and a series of rock-cut tombs with carvings of lions, suns and moons.

Around the village of Alanyurt are more caves at **Selimiye** and fairy chimneys at **Kurtyurdu**. Another concentration is around Karakaya, Seydiler and İscehisar, including the bunker-like rock **Seydiler Castle** (Seydiler Kalesi).

Getting There & Around

You need a car to explore this area properly. The usual starting points are Afyon and Eskişehir, or you can head east from Kütahya. Brown signs indicate many sites but they're not always clear so expect to get occasionally lost.

You could also hire a taxi from any fair-sized town in the region; Seyitgazi and İhsaniye are good bets and conveniently located. Rates start around TL60 for a short tour, but are entirely negotiable depending on your plans.

KÜTAHYA

☎ 0274 / pop 211,000

Like İznik, Kütahya upholds the Turkish tradition of coloured tiles (*çini*) and pottery. And while İznik resurrects its pedigree in the handmade and high-end sector, Kütahya's factories take pride in the prosaic with local tiles decorating everywhere from fountains to bus stations.

Kütahya is a university town with trendy cafés and bars lining the straight-as-an-arrow tree-lined avenues. But venture a few hundred metres from Kütahya's boulevards to discover the bustling ambience of the labyrinthine market area. Carry on exploring into winding lanes dotted with crumbling Ottoman-era mansions.

Standing sentinel above Kütahya's energetic melding of old and new is an imposing fortress, and huddled at the base of the citadel, excellent museums showcase Kütahya's kiln-fired past. Visit in July to see the city's creative future on display at the annual Dumlupınar Fair (Fuarı), Turkey's pre-eminent handicrafts fair.

History

Kütahya's earliest known inhabitants were Phrygians. In 546 BC it was captured by the Persians, and then had a succession of rulers including Alexander the Great, the kings of Bithynia, and the emperors of Rome and Byzantium, who called the town Cotiaeum.

The first Turks to arrive were the Seljuks in 1182. Ousted by the Crusaders, they returned to found the Emirate of Germiyan (1302–1428), with Kütahya as its capital. The emirs cooperated with the Ottomans in nearby Bursa, and when the last emir died his lands were incorporated in the growing Ottoman Empire. Tamerlane swept in at the beginning of the 15th century, made Kütahya his temporary headquarters and then returned to Central Asia.

After Selim I took Tabriz in 1514, he brought all of its ceramic artisans to Kütahya and İznik. Since then the two towns have rivalled one another in the quality of their tilework.

Orientation

A huge vase-shaped fountain marks Zafer (Belediye) Meydanı, the town's main square, which is overlooked by the *vilayet* (provincial government building) and *belediye*. The otogar, Kütahya Çinigar (Tile Station

– you'll see why), is 1km northeast of Zafer Meydanı, along Atatürk Bulvarı. Hotels, restaurants, ATMs and tile shops cluster around the square.

The town's main commercial street is Cumhuriyet Caddesi, running southwest from the *vilayet*, past the PTT and on to the Ulu Cami. Check out the use of local tiles on everything from shopfronts to street furniture.

Information

Anatolia Internet Café (Belediye Caddesi 9; per hr TL1; ☉ 9am-midnight)

Hayalet Internet (Atatürk Bulvarı; per hr TL1; ☉ 9am-midnight)

Tourist information kiosk (☎ 223 6213; Zafer Meydanı; ☉ 9am-1pm & 2-6pm) Little English spoken but good maps.

Sights & Activities

The turreted **Ulu Cami**, at the far end of Cumhuriyet Caddesi, has been restored several times since construction in 1410. Fine marble panels are incorporated into its ablutions fountain and there is lovely sunburst woodwork above the side door.

The **Archaeology Museum** (Arkeoloji Müzesi; ☎ 224 0785; admission TL3; ☉ 9am-1pm & 2-5.45pm Tue-Sun) is next door to the Ulu Cami in the Vacidiye Medresesi, which was built by Umur bin Savcı of the Germiyan family in 1314. The centrepiece of the collection is a Roman sarcophagus from Aizanoi's Temple of Zeus (p308), carved with scenes of battling Amazons. There are also finds from the Phrygian Valley and interesting Roman votive stellae.

The **Tile Museum** (Çini Müzesi; ☎ 223 6990; admission TL3; ☉ 9am-1pm & 2-5.45pm Tue-Sun) is housed in the İmaret Camii on the opposite side of the Ulu Cami, beneath a magnificent dome. Most of the collection is Kütahya pottery, including work by the master craftsman Hacı Hafız Mehmet Emin Efendi, who worked on İstanbul's Haydarpaşa station. In deference to the town's main rival, there are also some wonderful İznik tiles and a lot of beautiful embroidery. To one side is the 14th-century, blue-tiled tomb of one Yakup Bey.

Nearby is the **Dönenler Cami**, which was built in the 14th century and later served as a *mevlevihane*, or home to a group of Mevlevi dervishes. Inside it has a wonderful, galleried *semahane* with paintings of tall Mevlevi hats on the columns.

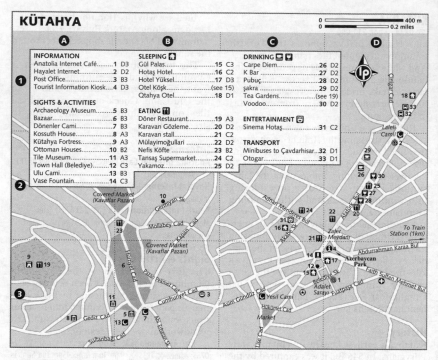

KÜTAHYA

INFORMATION	
Anatolia Internet Café	1 D3
Hayalet Internet	2 D2
Post Office	3 B3
Tourist Information Kiosk	4 D3

SIGHTS & ACTIVITIES	
Archaeology Museum	5 B3
Bazaar	6 B3
Dönenler Cami	7 B3
Kossuth House	8 A3
Kütahya Fortress	9 A3
Ottoman Houses	10 B2
Tile Museum	11 A3
Town Hall (Belediye)	12 C3
Ulu Cami	13 B3
Vase Fountain	14 C3

SLEEPING	
Gül Palas	15 C3
Hotaş Hotel	16 C2
Hotel Yüksel	17 D3
Otel Köşk	(see 15)
Qtahya Otel	18 D1

EATING	
Döner Restaurant	19 A3
Karavan Gözleme	20 D2
Karavan stall	21 C2
Mülayimoğullari	22 D2
Nefis Köfte	23 B2
Tansaş Supermarket	24 C2
Yakamoz	25 D2

DRINKING	
Carpe Diem	26 D2
K Bar	27 D2
Pubuç	28 D2
şakra	29 D2
Tea Gardens	(see 19)
Voodoo	30 D2

ENTERTAINMENT	
Sinema Hotaş	31 C2

TRANSPORT	
Minibuses to Çavdarhisar	32 D1
Otogar	33 D1

Northeast of the Ulu Cami is a sprawling **bazaar** area and, tucked away nearby, Germiyan Sokak, where restored **Ottoman houses** rub shoulders with their crumbling neighbours. To find the bazaar head north up Hürriyet Caddesi.

Follow the signs behind the Ulu Cami to **Kossuth House** (Kossuth Evi; ☎ 223 6214; admission TL3; 9am-1pm & 2-5.45pm Tue-Sun), also called Macar Evi (Hungarian House). It's roughly 250m straight on up the hill; look for the wood-and-stone house on the left, marked by plaques in Turkish and Hungarian.

Lajos Kossuth (1802–94) was a prominent member of the Hungarian parliament. In 1848, chafing at Hapsburg rule from Vienna, he and others rose in revolt, declaring Hungary an independent republic in 1849. When Russian troops intervened on behalf of the Austrians he was forced to flee. The Ottomans offered him a refuge and he lived in Kütahya from 1850 to 1851.

A stately whitewashed exterior conceals various rooms that provide poignant insights into the life of upper-class Kütahyans in the mid-19th century. The 1st-floor veranda,

overlooking a rose garden with a statue of Kossuth, offers lovely views of the encircling hills. A large map details Kossuth's international travels from 1849 to 1861. He certainly got around.

Looming above the town, **Kütahya fortress** was built in two stages by the Byzantines, then restored and used by the Seljuks, the Germiyan emirs and the Ottomans. The latest building work seems to have taken place in the 15th century, the most recent restoration in the 1990s. One look at the remains of dozens of round towers makes it clear what a formidable obstacle this would have been to any army. It's a long walk up to the fortress so you might want to take a taxi (around TL8). Afterwards you can descend along a steep, scree-covered path that ends near the Ulu Cami.

Sleeping

Kütahya isn't overrun with accommodation options, but there are some OK places to stay.

Hotel Yüksel (☎ 212 0111; Afyon Caddesi 2; s/d/tr TL20/30/40) Neat rooms and bright linen distinguish this fairly friendly hotel opposite the clock tower. Breakfast isn't included, but prices are flexible and there's a bakery next door or the Karavan *gözleme* booth just across the road.

Otel Köşk (☎ 216 2024; Lise Caddesi 1; s/d/tr TL30/40/50) Despite the tiled reception and spacious rooms, the Köşk suffers the triple whammy of slightly dodgy showers, plywood beds and pink walls. Breakfast is included, but the dining room is so dim you'll probably want to pop around to the bakery near the Yüksel.

Hotaş Hotel (☎ 224 8990; Menderes Caddesi 5; s/d/tr TL37/56/69) Finally the promise of a flash lobby is fulfilled with comfortable (if exceedingly floral) rooms, satellite TV and wi-fi access. Once you've got your money's worth from the rooms there's a souvenir shop and Turkish bath to explore. Ask at reception about the six-room Ottoman-style Şeker Konaği ('Sugar House') with rooms in nearby Germiyan Sokak.

Qtahya Otel (☎ 226 2010; www.q-tahya.com; Atatürk Bulvarı 56; s/d/tr TL50/80/110) Flat screen TVs and leather couches feature in reception, and the rooms above are equally comfortable and modern in this convenient spot opposite the otogar. Wi-fi access and a good rooftop restaurant top things off nicely.

Gül Palas (☎ 216 2325; www.gulpalas.com; Zafer Meydanı; s/d/tr TL55/85/110) The tiled facade can't compete with the *belediye* opposite, but the Gül Palas definitely takes old school design honours over any hotel in town. Who couldn't love a tile-trimmed lobby with chandeliers and a rock garden? The rooms and facilities are equally high quality and also feature wi-fi access.

Eating

Kütahya's a university town so there's lots of cheap eats. A basic kebap can start at TL1.25, with a set meal with drink, salad, side order and dessert around TL5. Happy döner discovery along Atatürk Bulvarı.

RESTAURANTS

Karavan Gözleme (☎ 226 4045; Atatürk Bulvarı 12/A; meals TL2-8) It may serve 15 types of *gözleme*, from *haşhaşlı* (poppy-seed) to chocolate, but the Karavan is more than just a pancake place, and also does great pide and *lahmacun*. Pop upstairs to find a small terrace with a mini-jungle and an inviting nargileh lounge with

wi-fi internet. There's another handy Karavan stall nearby for *gözleme* on the go.

Nefis Köfte (☎ 223 0926; Hurriyet Caddesi 43; mains TL4-5; ☽ 11am-11pm) This crazily popular *köfte* joint at the edge of the covered market has been dishing up great Turkish meatballs since 1942. Leave room for dessert from the adjoining baklava bar.

Mülayimoğllari (☎ 224 9203; Atatürk Bulvarı 11; mains TL4-8) The restaurant with the longest name in town has an even longer menu of all your Anatolian favourites, with kebaps, *köfte* and pide served up in flash surroundings trimmed with the best of local Kütahya ceramics.

Yakamoz (☎ 223 0926; Atatürk Bulvarı; mains from TL5; ☽ 11am-11pm) This vast café-restaurant, with indoor and outdoor tables, is extremely popular with young Kütahyalıs. Its extensive menu covers everything from pizzas to Turkish puddings.

Döner Restaurant (☎ 226 2176; mains TL6-12; ☽ 11am-9pm) Inside the ruins of the fortress, the Döner used to be a revolving nightclub (no, really), but is now a hilltop restaurant-meets-tea garden. Run by the Karavan chain, the food is decent if a little expensive. The addition of a children's playground – sorry kids – has dulled a previous bohemian vibe, but it's still worth the trek by foot or taxi. After dark, candles produce a softly romantic ambience.

SELF-CATERING

For fresh fruit and vegetables, browse the open-air **market** up the hill on Lise Caddesi. It's at its liveliest on Saturday. Alternatively, there's a **Tansaş supermarket** (Adnan Menderes Bulvarı; ☽ 9am-10pm).

Drinking & Entertainment

Atatürk Bulvarı is Kütahya's main drinking strip, with venues crammed around Yakamoz. On busy nights it stays open until after midnight.

Voodoo (☎ 226 4146; Atatürk Bulvarı 26) The most pub-like of the bars, complete with wooden beams, a relaxed student vibe, and 0.7L beers to dull the dustiest of bus and dolmuş combos. The music's usually pretty good too. How does Nick Cave and Johnny Cash sound?

K Bar (Atatürk Bulvarı) A cosmopolitan spot with outdoor tables and a cool and compact private bar tucked away in the corner. Blur your eyes a little (actually maybe a little more…), and you could almost be in Melbourne or Manhattan.

Pubuç (Atatürk Bulvarı) Kütahya's prime spot for 'public drink and dance' (their words, not ours), also advertises itself as 'Exclusive Pub and Club'. Don't worry, it's not that flash. You should be fine in your cleanest dirty shirt.

Carpe Diem (Kambur Sokak; ☺ 11am-11pm) Cool music (vintage reggae when we visited), coffee and tea are combined with mismatched furniture from your first student flat at this laid-back spot. Wi-fi, scrabble and backgammon all come as standard.

Across the lane **şakra** (Kambur Sokak; ☺ 11am-11pm) is same, same but different with a minimalist and arty vibe.

There are good **tea gardens** around Zafer Meydanı and Azerbaycan Parkı, and good views from the outdoor cafés inside Kütahya fortress.

Sinema Hotaş (☎ 216 6767; admission TL9) is opposite the Hotaş Hotel.

Shopping
You can find Kütahya pottery in most Turkish souvenir shops, but it's also good to browse the small stores around Zafer Meydanı. Shops have fine, midrange pieces in a variety of designs, and often a few masterworks for connoisseurs.

Getting There & Away
Kütahya is a provincial capital with regular services to Afyon (TL9, 1½ hours), Ankara (TL20, five hours), Bursa (TL17, three hours), Denizli (TL25, five hours), Eskişehir (TL8, 1½ hours), İstanbul (TL30, six hours) and İzmir (TL25, six hours).

Minibuses to Çavdarhisar, for Aizanoi (TL6, one hour), leave from the local bus stand next to the otogar.

AİZANOİ (ÇAVDARHİSAR)
☎ 0274 / pop 2400
The subdued farming village of Çavdarhisar, about 60km southwest of Kütahya, is home to Aizanoi, one of Anatolia's best-preserved Roman temples. Long after the Romans had vanished, a group of Çavdar Tartars used the site as a citadel, giving the village its present name: 'Castle of the Çavdars'.

A couple of hours is enough to see all the ruins, and there's a basic restaurant opposite the entrance.

Sights
TEMPLE OF ZEUS
The great **Temple of Zeus** (admission TL3; ☺ 8am-5.30pm) dates from the reign of Hadrian (r AD 117–138), and was dedicated to the worship of Zeus (Jupiter) and the Anatolian fertility goddess Cybele.

The temple stands deserted but proud in a quiet meadow, founded on a broad terrace created to serve as its precinct. Like the abandoned set of a Hollywood epic, the north and west faces of the temple have their double rows of Ionic and Corinthian columns intact, but the south and east rows have fallen into a picturesque jumble. The three columns at the northeastern corner were toppled by the disastrous Gediz earthquake of 1970, but have since been re-erected. The cella (inner room) walls are intact enough to give a good impression of the imposing whole. An enclosure beside the ticket office holds some of the best pieces of sculpture found here, and dotted around the site are good explanations in Turkish, English and German.

If the ticket office is empty, the custodian will find you to sell you a ticket. Ask him to show you the cryptlike sanctuary of Cybele beneath the temple. Most days the site is deserted, and it will just be you alone with a team of darting lizards, delicate birdsong and the rumble of passing tractors.

OTHER RUINS
After the temple, turn left then right along a path into the fields opposite the temple. Here are the remnants of a 2nd-century AD **Roman bath** and the more substantial ruins of a **theatre** and **stadium**. The stones have crumbled badly and now provide a home for birds and a posse of skittish cats. Approaching the stadium, on the right is an ancient sporting Hall of Fame, with an isolated stretch of wall inscribed with medallions featuring the names of Olympic victors.

Çavdarhisar village is also dotted with chunks of fallen Roman masonry. Black-on-yellow signs also lead to a **Roman bridge** over a small stream (much of the stonework dates back to Hadrian's reign). Follow the signs into the village and the remains of a 2nd-century AD **bath complex**. The shed contains a fine mosaic pavement, mostly covered with geometric patterns but also with a picture of a satyr and maenad. It's kept locked so ask around to find the temple custodian. He'll

WESTERN ANATOLIA

throw some water on the mosaic to bring out the colours, an activity which should not be encouraged.

Another sign points to what's called a colonnaded street, but is probably the remains of the Roman **forum**, or marketplace, with fine columns and a marble pavement. Nearby is a **circular market building** with a little turret reconstructed beside it, which dates back to 301 AD, during the reign of Diocletian. On the walls you'll see fixed prices for market goods inscribed in Roman numerals, an attempt to combat inflation. One of these prices reads 'two horses for a strong slave, three slaves for a horse, both equalling 30,000 dinars'. This is one of the earliest known buildings of its type, and nearly two millennia later it's easy to conjure up the hustle and bustle of daily commerce in the Roman era.

Getting There & Away

Çavdarhisar is on the Kütahya–Gediz road. There are minibuses to Çavdarhisar from Kütahya otogar (TL6, one hour) or you can take a Gediz or Emet bus, which passes through Çavdarhisar. Tell the driver you're going to Aizanoi and they'll usually drop you right at the site.

UŞAK

☎ 0276 / pop 173,000

Few visitors stop in Uşak, but there are two treats best appreciated on an overnight stay.

Lydian art, gold and silver treasures feature in the **Archaeology Museum** (Doğan Sokak; admission TL2; ☒ 8.30am-1pm & 2-5.45pm Tue-Sun), just off the main square. The beautiful silver bowls, incense burners, jugs and vases were discovered in *tumuli* around the Gediz river valley and date back to the second half of the 6th century BC. Even more evocative are the eerily Egyptian-style wall paintings from the tombs. Thefts from the museum made world headlines in 2006 and 2007 (see boxed text below).

At the far end of the town centre, past the 1406 Ulu Camii, is the **Otel Dülgeroğlu** (☎ 227 3773; www.dulgeroglu.com.tr; Cumhuriyet Meydanı 1; s/d TL90/135, ste TL170; ☒ ☐). Housed in a *han* designed by a 19th-century French architect, the hotel has very comfortable rooms overlooking a light-filled atrium courtyard with a cosy adjoining bar. Rooms fill up with business travellers midweek, but are empty and discount-friendly on weekends. Highly recommended.

Getting There & Away

Frequent minibuses connect Uşak with Afyon (TL10, 1½ hours), and there are periodic buses from İzmir (TL20, 2½ hours). If you get dropped on the highway (Dörtyöl) follow the signs for the *şehir merkezi* (city centre); it's about 1.5km to the Otel Dülgeroğlu. From the otogar, a taxi should cost around TL8.

UŞAK MUSEUM THEFTS

In 2006 Turkey's cultural establishment was shaken when an inspection of the Uşak museum's Lydian Hoard collection revealed that certain priceless items had been removed and replaced with copies. Nine people (including the director of the museum) were arrested in connection with the theft that included easily concealed items like a tiny winged seahorse. Uşak wasn't the only place to suffer, and subsequent checks revealed similar occurrences at Topkapı Palace in İstanbul, and the Erzurum and Kahramanmaraş museums. Another check of the Uşak museum in June 2007 revealed that a further 38 gold items were missing, but investigators were unsure if this was a result of the 2006 heist.

The Turkish Ministry of Culture and Tourism has since embarked on a dual strategy of installing sophisticated security systems, and the massive project of checking the authenticity and inventories of all items in Turkish museums. At the time of writing in 2008, the court case against the 'Uşak Nine' was ongoing, but none of the items discovered to be missing in 2006 had been recovered. Prosecutors were still pressing for 25-year jail sentences.

Ironically this isn't the first time these objects were 'stolen'. The original 1960s American excavators removed them from *tumuli* in the valley of the Gediz River and promptly spirited them back to the United States. In 1993 a landmark court ruling decreed they should be returned to their country of origin. It's ironic that Turkey should put so much effort into retrieving its lost treasures, only to lose them from its own museums.

AFYON

☎ 0272 / pop 129,000

Modern Afyon is a provincial capital lounging in the shadow of its ancient and supremely spectacular castle. Once your gaze has tired of this mighty citadel – warning: this might take a while – Afyon has a fine museum, magnificent mosques, and some gloriously ramshackle Ottoman houses.

History

Afyon's history started around 3000 years ago. After occupation by the Hittites, Phrygians, Lydians and Persians, it was settled by the Romans and the Byzantines. Following the Seljuk victory at Manzikert in 1071, Afyon was governed by the Seljuk Turks. The important Seljuk vizier Sahip Ata took direct control of the town and it was called Karahisar-i Sahip through Ottoman times (1428–1923).

During the War of Independence, Greek forces occupied the town on their push towards Ankara. During the Battle of Sakarya, in late August 1921, the republican armies under Mustafa Kemal (Atatürk) stopped the invading force within earshot of Ankara in one of history's longest pitched battles. The Greek forces retreated and dug in for the winter near Eskişehir and Afyon.

On 26 August 1922 the Turks began their counteroffensive along an 80km front, advancing rapidly on the Greek army. Within days Atatürk had set up his headquarters in Afyon's *belediye* building and had half the Greek army surrounded at Dumlupınar, 40km to the west. This decisive battle destroyed the Greek army as a fighting force and sent its survivors fleeing towards İzmir. Like Gallipoli, the battlefields are now protected, forming the Başkomutan National Historical Park.

In 2004 the official name of the town was amended from Afyon ('Opium') to Afyonkarahisar ('Black Fortress of Opium'), a reference to the region's historical role as an opium growing region and the imposing citadel hovering above the town (see boxed text below).

Orientation

The main square, called Hükümet Meydanı and marked by an imposing statue commemorating the Turkish victory over the Greek army in 1922, is northeast of the citadel, at the intersection of Ordu Bulvarı and Milli Egemenlik (Bankalar) Caddesi. About 250m to the southeast another traffic roundabout marks the starting point for Kadınana Caddesi, which runs 2km northeast to the old otogar.

The PTT, ATMs, and hotels and restaurants all lie between the two traffic roundabouts.

The train station is 2km from the centre, at the northeastern end of Ordu Bulvarı. At the time of writing a new otogar was under construction around 3km northwest of the centre on the road to Kütahya.

Information

AVM Kadinana Internet (Bankalar Caddesi 19; per hr TL1; ☽ 9.30am-11pm) On the 4th floor of Afyon's central department store.

Tourist office (☎ 213 5447; Hükümet Meydanı; ☽ 8am-noon & 1.30-5.30pm Mon-Fri) Of debatable value to English-speaking travellers, but at least it offers an ex-

---

OPIATE OF THE PEOPLE

Afyon's proper name, Afyonkarahisar, actually means Black Fortress of Opium, a tag that not only characterises the castle's appearance but also reflects the area's main cash crop. The peaceful countryside around Afyon produces more than a third of the world's legally grown pharmacy-grade opium, and for two weeks in mid-June the fields shimmer with white and mauve *haşhaşlı çiçekleri* (hash or opium poppies).

The trade is strictly regulated and Afyon is one of only 12 provinces permitted to cultivate the poppies. Most growers are small-scale farmers who use the flowers as a convenient spring crop to bridge the gap between autumn grain harvests. It's not easy money though and it takes a labourer 72 hours to pick and process enough poppies to produce 1kg of opium. The end product is then bought by the government to manufacture morphine.

Afyon is also renowned for its *kaymak* (thick cream). Reputedly it's so good because the local cows graze on the magic poppies.

So if you find yourself standing in uptown Afyon waiting for your man to deal you some primo dairy produce, now you know why…

cellent map. For information on the Phrygian Valley (p303) you're better off seeking information in Eskişehir (p301).

Sights & Activities

CITADEL

Soaring from the plains, the craggy rock with the *kale* or *hisar* (citadel) hovers imposingly above the town. For a closer look find the lane across the street from the Ulu Cami, and follow the green and brown signs. Around 700 steps lead to the summit, passing through a series of guard towers. It's a good workout and unfortunately there is no easier way up. Around the halfway mark, don't be surprised if you start questioning the wisdom of the people that managed, voluntarily, to build such a large fortress somewhere so inaccessible.

Blame the Hittite king Mursilis II for building the first castle around 1350 BC. Every subsequent conqueror since has added their own features. Despite its eventful history there's little to see inside, and contemporary restorations broke clumsily with the original *kara hisar* (black citadel) look by using white stones.

The views from the summit (226m) are spectacular, and it's worth coming up at prayer time for the surround sound of the muezzins from Afyon's many mosques. Note that the castle isn't lit at night which can make it tricky coming down after dusk.

For the best photos of the castle from below, head to the **Kültür ve Semt Evi** (Zaviye Türbe Caddesi), a restored hamam with unobstructed views from its raised terrace.

ARCHAEOLOGICAL MUSEUM

Take a dolmuş along Kurtuluş Caddesi, the continuation of Bankalar Caddesi, to Afyon's **Archaeological Museum** (Arkeoloji Müzesi; admission TL3; 9am-1pm & 2-5.45pm), near the intersection with İsmet İnönü Caddesi. Externally there's not much to distinguish this museum from other local collections, but inside the collection features interesting Hittite, Phrygian, Lydian and Roman discoveries. There are lots of marble statues, reflecting that the nearby quarries at Dokimeon (now İscehisar) were (and still are) an important source of the lustrous rock.

OTHER SIGHTS

The **İmaret Camii**, Afyon's major mosque, is just south of the traffic roundabout at the southern end of Bankalar Caddesi. Built for Gedik Ahmet Paşa in 1472, its design shows the transition from the Seljuk to the Ottoman style, with the spiral-fluted minaret decorated, Seljuk-style, with blue tiles. The entrance on the eastern side is like an *eyvan* (vaulted hall) and leads to a main sanctuary topped by two domes, front and back, a design also seen in the early Ottoman capitals of Bursa and Edirne. The shady park beside it provides a peaceful refuge from bustling Bankalar Caddesi.

Next door, the **İmaret hamamı** (5am-midnight for men, 8am-8pm for women), housed in a former church, is still well patronised and retains some of the precious old stone basins.

The **Mevlevihane Camii** was once a dervish meeting place and dates back to Seljuk times (13th century), when Sultan Veled, son of dervish founder Celaleddin Rumi, established Afyon as the empire's second-most important Mevlevi centre after Konya. The present mosque, with twin domes and twin pyramidal roofs above its courtyard, dates from only 1908, when it was built for Sultan Abdül Hamit II.

Afyon's **Ulu Cami** (1273) is one of the most important surviving Seljuk mosques, so it's a shame that it's usually locked outside prayer times. If you do manage to get inside you'll find 40 soaring wooden columns with stalactite capitals and a flat-beamed roof. Note the green tiles on the minaret.

The area around the Ulu Cami has many old **Ottoman wooden houses**. Safranbolu (p455) may be in better repair, but Afyon showcases an interesting variety of styles, and still teems with everyday life.

Just along from the tourist office, the **Zafer Müzesi** (Victory Museum; Hükümet Meydanı; admission TL1; 9am-1pm & 2-5.45pm Tue-Sun) was the first building Atatürk stayed in after liberating Afyon in 1922, and has photos, battle plans and military relics from the battlefields.

Sleeping

Otel Hocaoğlu (213 8182; Kadinana Caddesi, Ambaryolu 12; s/d/tr TL30/45/55) Five storeys of surprisingly bright accommodation near the İmaret Camii. English is (usually) spoken at this spot, just off the main drag, with a tiny lift but a friendly attitude. Rates don't include breakfast.

Hotel Soydan (215 2323; Turan Emeksiz Caddesi 2; s/d/tr TL35/60/70) Behind the calming green facade this nominal two-star is good value with spacious rooms, wi-fi access, and just maybe Afyon's best fruit and veg shop downstairs.

Çakmak Marble Otel (☎ 214 3300; www.cakmak marblehotel.com; Süleyman Gönçer Caddesi 2; s/d/tr TL77/130/165, ste TL280; ☒ ▣ ☒) One block east of Hükümet Meydanı, the Çakmak is the best in town with real deal four-star standards, spacious rooms and marble bathrooms. The carpet's a bit tatty, but excellent service, a swimming pool and Jacuzzi in the basement, and a great breakfast buffet provide positive balance. The Çakmak's 'American Bar' is more faux-Parisian than American, but is one of the only places in town to get a cold beer.

Eating & Drinking

Nazar Döner (cnr Bankalar Caddesi & Uzunçarşı Caddesi; mains TL2-4; ☯ 11am-11pm) A redoubtable and popular choice for good value kebaps, the Nazar dominates this street corner with a beautifully restored bronze antique sign.

AVM Kadinana (☎ 214 7900; Bankalar Caddesi 19; mains TL6-9; ☯ 9.30am-11pm; ▣) The top two floors of this department store cater for a multitude of whims, incorporating a restaurant, *pastanes*, big-screen TV lounge and rooftop café-nargileh terrace with live music. It's hugely popular, and not just for the great views.

İkbal Lokantası (☎ 215 1205; Uzunçarşı Caddesi 21; mains TL6-12; ☯ 9am-10pm) Southwest of Hükümet Meydanı, the İkbal first opened its art deco-tinged doors in 1922 and still holds its own against the competition. There's a good choice of kebaps, stews and desserts, but we just wish the formal waitstaff would lighten up a tad.

Hancıoğlu (Turan Emeksiz Caddesi) Underneath the Hotel Soydan is this superb fruit shop with fresher-than-fresh produce.

Scores of shops around town are draped with necklaces of locally made *sucuk* (sausage) and padded out with pillows of cheese. Grab a loaf of crisp Turkish bread and that's lunch sorted.

Don't forget to pop into one of the local *şekerleme* (sweet shops) for a taste of Afyon's famous *lokum* (Turkish delight).

There are pleasant **çay bahçesi** (tea gardens) in Anıt Parkı, overlooking Hükümet Meydanı. For something stronger head to the **American Bar** at the Çakmak Marble Hotel.

Getting There & Away

Afyon is on the inland routes connecting İstanbul with Antalya and Konya, and İzmir with Ankara and the east. There are regular buses to Ankara (TL20, four hours), Antalya (TL20, five hours), Denizli/Pamukkale (TL18, four hours), Eskişehir (TL13, three

hours), Isparta (TL13, three hours), İstanbul (TL35, eight hours), İzmir (TL20, 5½ hours), Konya (TL25, 3¾ hours) and Kütahya (TL10, 1½ hours).

The **train station** (☎ 213 7919) is 2km north of the town centre. Three or four express trains a day run to İstanbul Haydarpaşa (TL18.25, nine hours), mostly at night; a sleeping compartment costs from TL90. There are also daily services to Eskişehir (TL7, three hours) via Kütahya (TL5.50, two hours), Konya (TL11, five hours) and Denizli (for Pamukkale TL11, five hours).

To get to the centre from the new otogar look for dolmuşes marked 'Çarşı' (TL2); a taxi costs about TL8. To get to the otogar look for a dolmuş marked 'Yeni Otogar' in Gazlıgöl Caddesi, near the tourist information kiosk.

LAKE DISTRICT

Travelling in often dusty Anatolia, you don't need to head to Turkey's southern or western coasts for a few relaxing days beside the water. The Anatolian Lake District comprises three main lakes (*göller*) – Burdur, Eğirdir and Beyşehir – and is a handy substitute forgoing a long bus ride.

The town of Eğirdir is a popular lakeside holiday haven ringed with mountains. Good value pensions provide tours to nearby attractions and lakefront restaurants specialise in local fish. Further south, Beyşehir is worth a visit for its wonderful 13th-century lakeside mosque and old town.

Classics buffs should definitely detour to the ancient cities at Antiocheia-in-Pisidia and Sagalassos; while outdoor enthusiasts can trek or ski in the nearby mountains, visit Çandır Kanyon in the Yazılı Nature Park or Lake Kovada National Park, and follow in the footsteps of an apostle along the St Paul Trail.

The best time to visit this lush and verdant region is spring. In April the apple trees blossom, and from mid-May to mid-June the annual rose harvest takes place. Around a month later, the lakes become the favourite summer escape for Turkish families drawn to this relaxing 'coastline' many kilometres inland from the Aegean, Mediterranean or Black Seas.

ISPARTA

☎ 0246 / pop 180,000

Famous for its attar of roses (see boxed text, opposite), Isparta is an important junction east to Eğirdir. Turkey's ninth president

ROSE TOURS

Every May and June the fields around Isparta come into flower. Rose petals plucked carefully at daybreak are made into attar of roses, a valuable oil used in making perfume. The petals are placed in copper vats with steam passed over them. This steam is drawn off and condensed, leaving a thin layer of oil on the surface of the water to be skimmed off and bottled. A hundred kilos of petals produces just 25g of attar of roses, leaving a vast amount of rosewater to be sold locally.

To see the process in action, the Lale Pension (p318) in Eğirdir organises factory tours for TL40 per person, or you may be able to arrange something direct with a manufacturer. **Gülbirlik** (☎ 218 1288; www.gulbirlik.com) is the world's biggest source of rose oil with four processing plants handling 320 *tonnes* of petals every day. Tours usually take place from mid-May to mid-June each year at the height of the rose season.

(1993–2000), Süleyman Demirel, was a local boy, and there's a quirky statue of him in the town centre.

The **Ulu Cami** (1417) and the **Firdevs Bey Camii** (1561) with its neighbouring **bedesten** (covered market) are both worth a look, with the latter two buildings attributed to the great Mimar Sinan (see boxed text, p111). Also wander into the huge **Halı Saray** (Carpet Palace; Mimar Sinan Caddesi). Four days a week, from 8am to 10am, fine Isparta carpets are auctioned to dealers.

Getting There & Away

The most frequent services to Eğirdir leave from the Çarşı terminal (also called the *köy garaj*) in the town centre, as do dolmuşes for Ağlasun (for Sagalassos). Coming north from Antalya you may find yourself dropped on the outskirts of Isparta and ferried to the otogar in a *servis* (minivan).

To get to Eğirdir (TL4, 30 minutes) from the otogar, take any Konya-bound bus. Direct minibuses from the Çarşı terminal run every 30 minutes (TL4).

There are regular services from Isparta otogar to Afyon (TL13, three hours), Antalya (TL11, two hours), Burdur (TL5, 45 minutes), Denizli (TL13, three hours), İzmir (TL27, six hours) and Konya (TL27, five hours).

To get to the Çarşı terminal catch a Çarşı city bus from in front of the otogar. Note that the hourly minibus service to Burdur leaves from the otogar, not from the Çarşı terminal.

SAGALASSOS

Dramatically sited on the terraced slopes of Ak Dağ (White Mountain), **Sagalassos** (admission TL5; ⏲ 7.30am-6pm) is a ruined ancient city backed by sheer rock. Since 1990 Belgian archaeologists have been excavating the city,

one of the largest archaeological projects in the Mediterranean region. It's envisaged Sagalassos may one day rival Ephesus or Pergamum in splendour. The researchers are also reconstructing buildings, made possible because Sagalassos was never pillaged. Surrounded on three sides by mountains, the spectacular backdrop and valley views are unforgettable. Unfortunately the rugged terrain means some ruins are inaccessible to visitors.

Sagalassos dates back to at least 1200 BC, when it was founded by a warlike tribe of 'Peoples from the Sea'. Later it became an important Pisidian city, second only to Antiocheia-in-Pisidia near Yalvaç. The Pisidians built their cities high on easily defended mountains; Termessos (p401) is another example. Sagalassos's oldest ruins date from Hellenistic times, although most surviving structures are Roman. The Roman period was the city's most prosperous, but plague and earthquakes blighted its later history, and Sagalassos was largely abandoned after a massive 7th-century tremor.

The ticket office sells an informative map guide (TL4). From the entrance a path leads to the **lower agora**, with massive reconstructed Roman **baths** dating from AD 180. A flight of steps lead down from the lower agora to a paved street and the **Temple of Antoninus Pius**, built to honour the cult of the Roman emperors. Heading back to the lower *agora,* climb a slope to the **upper agora**. Facing the *agora* is a huge **fountain complex**, while to the right lies the **bouleuterion** (council meeting-place), with some of its seating intact. The **heroon** (hero's shrine) used to be decorated with carvings of dancing girls. Copies are slowly being reinstated at the site while the originals are gradually being rehoused in Burdur Museum

WESTERN ANATOLIA

(right). The *heroon* reputedly once housed a statue of Alexander the Great, who captured the city in 333 BC.

Sagalassos's biggest structure is the 9000-seat **Roman theatre**, one of the most complete in Turkey. Earthquakes have tumbled the rows of seats but otherwise it is intact. Scramble around the rear of the complex to see the tunnels where performers and contestants entered the arena.

Nearby is the late-Hellenistic **fountain house** and the Roman **Neon library** with a fine mosaic floor. Both have been rebuilt, and the fountain house is again functioning using the original water supply. It's an exceptional structure, providing cool and serene sanctuary from the unforgiving surroundings outside. The pavilion housing the Neon library is usually locked, but a good view of the beautiful mosaic floor is possible from the viewing platform.

The cliffs above Sagalassos are dotted with tombs. Except during the summer months when the archaeologists are at work, you're likely to share the site with only a few hardy birds and even hardier lizards. Striding uphill along the ancient trails, the exceptional defensive qualities of Sagalassos soon become apparent.

It's treeless and exposed, so aim for an early start to avoid the midday sun. The ticket office sells drinks. Walking the entire site via the 'scenic' route takes up to 3½ hours, or you can see the most significant structures near the ticket office in about an hour. Signage is excellent with detailed and colourful representations of how various structures looked in Sagalassos' halcyon days. A visit to Sagalassos should be teamed with a trip to Burdur's excellent museum (right).

Getting There & Away

Take a dolmuş south from Isparta's Çarşı terminal to Ağlasun (TL4, one hour, hourly from 6am to 5pm). The last dolmuş from Ağlasun to Isparta leaves at 8pm in summer.

From Ağlasun a signposted turn-off points 7km up the mountain. If you're fit, you could walk up, but it's probably easier to pay the dolmuş driver an extra TL20 to drive you there, wait for an hour and bring you back down again. To get the driver to wait longer you will probably have to agree on a higher fee.

The most straightforward alternative is to join an organised trip from Eğirdir for around TL40 (see p317).

BURDUR

☎ 0248 / pop 63,400

Despite its proximity to saltwater Burdur Gölü (Lake Burdur), Burdur is a modern town enlivened only by an excellent museum and two wonderfully preserved Ottoman houses. Buses from Isparta drop you on the eastern outskirts. From the otogar, turn right and walk along Gazi Caddesi for 15 minutes to the town centre, or catch a city bus from just outside.

To find the **Burdur Museum** (Burdur Müzesi; admission TL5; ☉ 9am-6pm Tue-Sun), turn right opposite the Hacı Mahmut Bey Camii in Gazi Caddesi. The most impressive exhibits are ceramics, and Hellenistic and Roman statues from Kremna and Sagalassos. But there are also Neolithic finds from the nearby Hacılar and Kuruçay mounds; a 2nd-century bronze torso of an athlete; and several exquisitely carved 'man and wife' sarcophagi. The terrace teahouse in the front is great for a post-museum snack.

Burdur's dusty, modern 'burbs also conceal two of Anatolia's best preserved Ottoman houses. **Taş Konaği** (cnr Mehmet Akif Caddesi & Veyis Sokak; admission free; ☉ 10am-5pm Tue-Sun) houses the Tasoda Ethnographic Museum and dates from the 17th century. With a spacious private courtyard, the ground floor of the house was originally the stables for livestock. On the 1st floor is the *başoda* (main room), an ornate confection with a beautifully carved roof, trimmed with delicate gold and silver. This was where the owner of the house conducted business and received his guests. To find the Taş Konaği from the museum, head south across busy Gazi Caddesi and climb the hill to Ulu Camii. From the mosque head downhill southeast on Ozdemir Sokak. Veyis Sokak is the first street on your right, leading east to the river.

The second of Burdur's museum houses is **Bakibey Konaği** (Divan Baba Caddesi; admission free; ☉ 10am-5pm Tue-Sun). From Taş Konaği walk southwest up the river to the third bridge along. Cross the river to Divan Baba Caddesi, and Bakibey Konaği is located behind the local Tourism and Cultural Centre. The helpful team there will open the house up for you. The highlight of Bakibey Konaği is an exquisitely carved *eyvan* (balcony). Inside the shady *başoda* is lined with colourful red- and blue-painted wooden panels, some restored, but others with the gloriously faded patina of old age.

Hourly minibuses run to Burdur from the Isparta otogar (TL5, 45 minutes).

DAVRAZ DAĞI (MT DAVRAZ)

The skiing season on Mt Davraz (2635m) runs from mid-December to March. Both Nordic and downhill skiing are possible and there's one 1.2km-long chairlift. A day's skiing, with equipment hire and lift pass, costs around €40; summit treks and paragliding are also possible.

Accommodation is available at the main ski centre and the five-star Sirene Davraz Mountain Resort, but it's really as easy (and cheaper) to stay in Isparta or Eğirdir.

In season there are regular dolmuşes from Isparta (TL8, 40 minutes) and less frequent ones from Eğirdir (TL5, 30 minutes) on weekends. A taxi should cost around TL50.

EĞİRDİR

☎ 0246 / pop 20,400

Sitting peacefully at the southern tip of Eğirdir Gölü (Lake Eğirdir), Eğirdir (pronounced eh-*yeer*-deer) is a pretty spot to recharge during your travels. It's conveniently located on the road from Konya to Antalya and the Aegean, or if you're heading west from Cappadocia to Pamukkale and Ephesus. It's always been a popular stopover and in Lydian times it straddled the Royal Rd, the main route between Ephesus and Babylon.

Overlooked by Davraz Dağı (Mt Davraz; 2635m), Eğirdir is increasingly important as a trekking and climbing base for people exploring Sivri Dağı (Mt Sivri), negotiating Yazılı Kanyon, or trekking part of the St Paul Trail (see p359). Mountain biking, windsurfing and donkey trekking are alternative ways to work off too many meze and fish dinners. In winter it's a cosy base for skiing on Mt Davraz.

Fishing on Lake Eğirdir used to be big business, but at the end of 2000 a four-year ban on professional fishing was put in place to give the fish population a chance to grow.

History

Founded by the Hittites, Eğirdir was taken by the Phrygians (c 1200 BC) and then the Lydians, captured by the Persians and conquered by Alexander the Great. Alexander was followed by the Romans, who called the town Prostanna. Contemporary documents suggest that it was large and prosperous, but no excavations have been done at the site, which lies within a large military enclave.

In Byzantine times, as Akrotiri (Steep Mountain), it was the seat of a bishopric.

Later, it became a Seljuk city (c 1080–1280) and then the capital of a small principality ruled by the Hamidoğulları tribe (1280–1381). The Ottomans took control in 1417, but the population of Yeşilada remained mostly Greek Orthodox until the 1920s.

Under the Turks Akrotiri became Eğridir, meaning 'crooked' or 'bent'. In the 1980s, this was changed to Eğirdir, which means 'she is spinning' – the new name was intended to remove the negative connotations of the old one (and stop the constant jokes), but is also supposedly a reference to an old folk tale about a queen who sat at home spinning, unaware that her son had just died.

Orientation & Information

Eğirdir stretches for several kilometres along the shore of Eğirdir Gölü. Its centre is at the base of a promontory jutting into the lake, marked by an Atatürk statue and a small otogar.

A few hundred metres northeast of the centre, the castle walls rise up at the beginning of the causeway that leads to Canada, (*jahn*-ah-da, or 'Soul Island') and Yeşilada ('Green Island'). Most of the town's best pensions are on Yeşilada or around these walls. A taxi from the otogar to Yeşilada is around TL7 and a dolmuş makes the 1.5km journey (TL1) around 10 times daily.

The **tourist information office** (☎ 311 4388; 2 Sahilyolu 13; ☼ 8am-noon, 1-5pm Mon-Fri) is on the main road coming into town. Right beside the otogar there is an infrequently staffed tourist information booth that hands out decent maps.

Head to **Kl@s Internet** (Belediye Caddesi; per hr TL1; ☼ 10am-10pm) to check your email. There is a huddle of ATMs near the Hotel Eğirdir.

Sights & Activities

Eğirdir's sights include the **Hızır Bey Camii**, built as a Seljuk warehouse in 1237, but turned into a mosque in 1308 by the Hamidoğulları emir Hızır Bey. The mosque is quite simple, with a clerestory (row of windows) above the central hall and new tiles around the *mihrab*. Note the finely carved wooden doors and the blue tile trim on the minaret.

Opposite the mosque, the **Dündar Bey Medresesi** was built as a caravanserai by the Seljuk sultan Alaeddin Keykubat in 1218 but converted into a *medrese* in 1285 for the Hamidoğulları emir, Felekeddin Dündar Bey. Now it's a bazaar filled with shops selling tacky

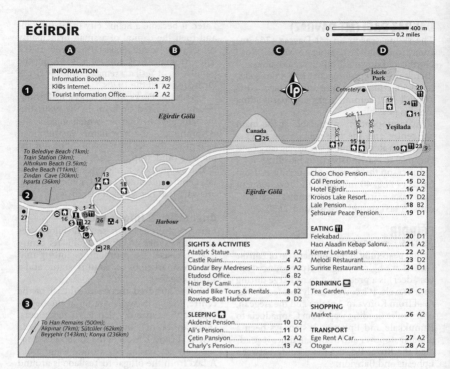

EĞİRDİR

INFORMATION	
Information Booth	(see 28)
KI@s Internet	1 A2
Tourist Information Office	2 A2

To Belediye Beach (1km);
Train Station (3km);
Altınkum Beach (3.5km);
Bedre Beach (11km);
Zindan Cave (30km);
Isparta (36km)

To Han Remains (500m);
Akpınar (7km); Sütçüler (62km);
Beyşehir (143km); Konya (236km)

SIGHTS & ACTIVITIES	
Atatürk Statue	3 A2
Castle Ruins	4 A2
Dündar Bey Medresesi	5 A2
Etudosd Office	6 B2
Hızır Bey Camii	7 A2
Nomad Bike Tours & Rentals	8 B2
Rowing-Boat Harbour	9 D2

SLEEPING	
Akdeniz Pension	10 D2
Ali's Pension	11 D1
Çetin Pansiyon	12 A2
Charly's Pension	13 A2

Choo Choo Pension	14 D2
Göl Pension	15 D2
Hotel Eğirdir	16 A2
Kroisos Lake Resort	17 D2
Lale Pension	18 B2
Şehsuvar Peace Pension	19 D1

EATING	
Felekabad	20 D1
Hacı Alaadin Kebap Salonu	21 A2
Kemer Lokantasi	22 A2
Melodi Restaurant	23 D2
Sunrise Restaurant	24 D1

DRINKING	
Tea Garden	25 C1

SHOPPING	
Market	26 A2

TRANSPORT	
Ege Rent A Car	27 A2
Otogar	28 A2

stuff you didn't know you needed. An unusual walk-through minaret with an arch in its base connects the complex to the mosque.

A few hundred metres towards Yeşilada stand the massive walls of the ruined **castle**. Its foundations were probably laid during the reign of Croesus, the 5th-century BC king of Lydia, but it was continually added to by subsequent conquerors.

Out of town towards Konya is a crumbling old **han**.

The local mountain club, **Etudosd** (☎ 311 6356), has its office on the road to Yeşilada and can advise on treks to Mt Davraz, the Barla massif and other good spots. Alternatively, discuss the possibilities and rent tents and sleeping bags from Ibrahim at Lale Pension (p318).

MARKETS

Eğirdir's normal weekly market takes place every Thursday, but for the 10 Sundays between August and October the Yörük people from the mountain villages come to Eğirdir to sell their apples, goats and yoghurt, and to buy winter supplies. It's an opportunity for people from different villages to meet, and was traditionally the focus for inter-village dating.

On the Saturday before the last Sunday market, when trading was nearly completed, there used to be a market attended only by women. On that day, mothers with sons of marriageable age approached the mothers of acceptable potential daughters-in-law and offered them a handkerchief. If the handkerchief was accepted, introductions between the families and the prospective bride and groom could begin. If all went well, the marriage took place in the spring of the following year.

BEACHES

Yeşilada has no real beaches, although there's nothing to stop you swimming off the rocks around the island. The small cove opposite Ali's Pension is relatively sheltered and clean, but you might want to keep your flip-flops on to battle the awkwardly-shaped pebbles. To sunbathe you'll need to find a more isolated stretch of beach to the northwest of the island.

The following local beaches have changing cabins and food stands or restaurants.

The free, sandy **Belediye Beach** is at Yazla, less than 1km from the centre on the Isparta road.

Pebbly **Altınkum Beach** (admission TL2.50) is several kilometres further north. In summer, dolmuşes run here every 15 minutes (TL1) from in front of the otogar. A taxi is around TL10. With a good licensed restaurant, it's a fine place to take your foot off the travel accelerator for an afternoon.

Further north, 11km on the road to Barla, **Bedre Beach** has 1.5km of pristine sand. Cycle here or catch a taxi (around TL12 each way).

Tours

Most pensions offer **boat trips**, or you'll be offered one by the guys near the harbour. Some trips are free with accommodation, though usually you'll pay up to TL25 per person.

Other **day trips** are to Sagalassos, Lake Kovada National Park or Yazılı Canyon Nature Park. Expect to pay around TL30 to TL40 per person, although this can be higher for small groups. During the peak season there should be enough travellers around to score a good deal.

Nomad Bike Tours & Rentals (☎ 3116688; www.nomad biketours.com; Ata Yolu Üzeri) can suggest itineraries and organise custom tours as well as hiring out mountain bikes at TL15/20 per half-day/full day. Fully guided trips including a day-long descent of Mt Davraz cost around US$40. At the time of writing, Nomad's friendly owner Kadir Can was planning two- to five- day donkey treks and renting out kayaks and windsurfers. At the very least it's worth popping in for some of Eğirdir's best coffee.

For information on local rose tours see boxed text, p313.

Another option is to go exploring with a rental car. **Ege Rent A Car** (☎ 311 4983; Sahil Yolu 2; per day TL130) has a small fleet of Sagalassos-ready sedans.

Sleeping

Choose between staying on Yeşilada at the end of the promontory, or in the mainland part of town. Yellow signs point the way to most pensions.

If you arrive at the start or end of the season, remember that nights can be cold, so look for a pension with central heating. Most places have hot water, although you may need to ask your host to turn it on.

In high season (from mid-June to mid-September), Eğirdir pension owners, especially on Yeşilada, are sometimes reluctant to take single travellers. Even if you offer to pay the double rate, they may still turn you down because they won't be able to sell two meals.

YEŞİLADA

Yeşilada has a dozen or so family-run pensions and restaurants. Most of the pensions are fairly similar and none is in a particularly inspiring building, but the island is small enough to walk around in 15 minutes so it's easy to make a quick circuit before choosing. Remember it's a 1.5km walk back to town across the causeway, but there is enough variety with the eateries on Yeşilada for at least a couple of nights.

Şehsuvar Peace Pension (☎ 311 2433; www.peace pension.com; s/d TL35/50) Spacious rooms and a quiet, shaded terrace trimmed with grapevines feature in this low-key family-run pension that's a few hundred metres inland near the island's sleepy *meydan* (main square). Rowboats and bicycles are available for rent, and the restaurant does a fine line in fish and lobster.

Akdeniz Pension (☎ 311 2432; s/d TL35/50) This pension is run by an elderly couple who don't speak much English, but offer lots in the way of gentle homespun hospitality. It has four simple but spotless balcony rooms and a vine-shaded terrace.

Choo Choo Pension (☎ 319 4926; huseyinp01@hotmail. com; s/d/tr TL35/55/65) The mock-castle exterior is a bit odd, but inside the spacious rooms are well kept and clean, and there's the convenient bonus of the Halikarnas lakefront restaurant a few metres away.

our pick **Ali's Pension** (☎ 311 2547; www.alispension .com; s/d/tr TL35/55/65; 💻) A flash new sunset-friendly balcony and rustic wooden floors feature at this nine-room pension on the far side of the island. Excellent English is spoken and hostess Birsen and her family redefine the boundaries of genuine hospitality. Yeşilada's best breakfasts regularly break the mould of the same old bread, cheese and cucumber combo, and we challenge you to find fresher and tastier *çigara börek* (deep-fried savoury pastries) anywhere in Turkey. Ali's is open year-round to cater to ski and snowboard types heading for Mt Davraz.

Göl Pension (☎ 311 2370; ahmetdavras@hotmail .com; r TL60-70; 💻) Run by a trio of sisters, the welcome at Göl can be more stand-offish and business-like than the warm, family welcomes at other pensions around town, but the rooms are spacious and well-maintained. Downstairs features shared bathrooms, while upstairs are two rooms with separate bathrooms and a private terrace. An OK backup.

Kroisos Lake Resort (☎ 311 5006; www.kroisoshotel .com; s/d/tr TL50/90/110) Caution: must like green. This conventional hotel, with some rooms resembling Kermit's abode, lacks the personal family atmosphere of the better pensions. On the plus side, facilities include ski and bike hire, a lounge with piano and occasional live music in the restaurant.

MAINLAND

Charly's Pension (☎ 311 4611; www.charlyspension.com; Kale Mahallesi; dm TL12, s/d/tr TL20/35/45) This new opening from the team at Lale Pension is in a heritage (1890) lakeside house with crazily sloping wooden floors and chill-out areas looking onto a private beach. Dorm rooms with shared bathrooms are simple, but with cool beats and wi-fi access don't be surprised if you stay longer than you'd originally planned. A couple of other rooms feature private bathrooms. Breakfast is TL6.

Çetin Pansiyon (☎ 311 2154; Kale Mahallesi; s/d/tr TL30/50/60) A friendly family run this welcoming spot with six airy and bright rooms on the quieter side of the castle. A shared upstairs lounge has excellent views across the lake to Mt Barla. Breakfast is an additional TL6.

Lale Pension (☎ 311 2406; www.lalehostel.com; Kale Mahallesi 5 Sokak 2; s/d/tr/q TL35/55/65/80; 🍴 🖳) Up behind the castle, the Lale Pension has neat air-con rooms with private bathrooms and a quiet, family atmosphere. There are great lake views from a rooftop lounge that's also crammed with information on tours and treks. Bike hire is TL20 per day, boat tours and canyon trips TL40 per person, and breakfast TL6. In a separate building nearby, the Lale Hostel has rooms with shared bathroom (TL20 to TL45) as well as backpacker-friendly dorm beds (TL12). At the time of writing the go-ahead team at Lale were also planning to open a boutique hotel. Ask at Lale Pension for the latest.

Hotel Eğirdir (☎ 311 3961; www.hotelegirdir.com; 2 Sahil Yolu 2; s/d/tr TL45/70/90) The main port of call for tour groups, this big three-star block has an impressive lobby and modest but adequate rooms with appealing linen and small balconies overlooking the lake. The bar's a good place to celebrate another day on the road.

Eating

Virtually every pension and hotel has a restaurant attached; these often provide the best-value meals, but there are other dining options if you want a bit of variety. Local *istakoz* (crayfish) is in season in July–August, but before you order check if the restaurant is serving the local delicacy fully-grown and mature.

Hacı Alaadin Kebap Salonu (☎ 311 4154; Belediye Caddesi 17; mains TL2-7; 🕑 9am-10pm) Tucked amid shops in the town centre, this reliable spot gets the woodfires burning early in the day to provide excellent kebaps, pide and *lahmacun*. Try that strange Eğirdir speciality, *şekerli* pide (cheese pide sprinkled with sugar). It's only TL2 so where's the risk?

Kemer Lokantasi (☎ 311 4247; Sahil Yolu 20; mains TL6-8; 🕑 11am-10pm) Very popular value eatery with lots of veg options. If your inner carnivore demands attention, Eğirdir's best kebap stalls are lurking a few metres away in a pedestrian square with loads of outdoor tables.

Felekabad (☎ 311 5881; Yeşilada; mains TL6-10; 🕑 11am-10pm) A simple restaurant with a conservatory section and lakefront seating enjoying a faint garden ambience. It's alcohol free and has a playground, so it's popular with local families.

Sunrise Restaurant (☎ 311 5852; Yeşilada; mains TL6-12; 🕑 11am-10pm) Next to the Felekabad, the Sunrise is popular with Turkish visitors from the city. And yes, you can get a cold beer to go with your meze or fresh fish.

Melodi Restaurant (☎ 311 4816; Yeşilada; mains TL8-14; 🕑 11am-10pm) Excellent meze, caught-this-morning fish and an absolute lakefront location add up to the eatery widely regarded as the best in town. The food's certainly very good, but the occasional bout of inattentive service sometimes lets the side down.

The popular *çay bahçesi* on Canada makes a fine place to stop for a drink or a snack; it also has a children's playground.

Getting There & Away

If there's no bus leaving straightaway for your destination, hop on a minibus to Isparta (TL5, 30 minutes) and catch one from there (see p313).

TRAIN

At the time of writing train services to Eğirdir had been suspended. Even trains nominally to Isparta usually involve being offloaded at

BUS SERVICES FROM EĞİRDİR'S OTOGAR

Destination	Fare (TL)	Duration (hr)	Frequency (per day)
Ankara	29	7	3 morning & evening
Antalya	13	2½	3 morning & afternoon
Denizli	15	3	3 morning & evening
İstanbul	42	11	1 evening only
İzmir	27	7	3 morning & evening
Konya	25	4	3 morning & afternoon
Nevşehir	30	8	2 morning & evening
Sütçüler	10	1½	frequent
Yalvaç	8	1	frequent

the town of Dinar to complete the journey to Isparta by bus. Getting to and from Eğirdir is most straightforward by bus.

AROUND EĞİRDİR
Sivri Dağı (Mt Sivri) & Akpınar

Sivri Dağı ('Sharp Mountain'; 1749m) dominates views southwest of Eğirdir. High up on its steep slopes, the tiny village of Akpınar clings with a winning combo of apple orchards and photogenic lake views. To get there, head 3km south of Eğirdir along the lakeshore road to the suburb of Yeni Mahalle, where a road winds 4km up the mountain to the village. It's a steep walk, which should take about two hours if you're in reasonable shape. A taxi there and back from Eğirdir costs around TL15.

The village has a ramshackle collection of mismatched chairs and tables masquerading as a teahouse. Expect zingy homemade *ayran* (yoghurt drink) and freshly made *gözleme*. The terrific views of Eğirdir reinforce how downright fragile the slim causeway to Yeşilada looks from this high.

Serious hikers can continue to the top of the mountain, but some of the rocks are unstable and there have been fatalities in the past – seek local advice before setting out and take great care. Don't try climbing from the commando base (north) side, as chances are the boys in green won't appreciate it.

Kovada Gölü National Park, Yazılı Canyon Nature Park & Çandır Kanyon

Noted for its flora and fauna, **Lake Kovada National Park** (Kovada Gölü Milli Parkı) surrounds a small lake connected to Lake Eğirdir by a channel. It's a pleasant place for a hike and a picnic. The St Paul Trail (see p359 for details) passes nearby. Close by is the **Kasnak**

Forest, visited by botanical enthusiasts for its rare orchids.

About 73km south of Eğirdir, the **Yazılı Canyon Nature Park** (Yazılı Kanyon Tabiat Parkı; admission TL1, car TL2) protects a forested gorge deep in the mountains separating the Lake District (ancient Pisidia) and the Antalya region (Pamphylia). After paying the admission fee at the car park, follow a path 1km upstream through the glorious **Çandır Kanyon** to some shady bathing spots; the water is icy cold even in late spring. In July and August the canyon heaves with sunbathing Turkish families, but at other times you could be all alone. The canyon is also part of the St Paul Trail with signs marking it's another eight extremely scenic hours walking to the hilltop town of Sütçüler.

The park takes its name from the inscriptions carved in the rocks lining the gorge (*yazılı* means 'written'); they are still clearly visible, although most have unfortunately been vandalised.

The **Yazılı Kanyon Restaurant and Kamping Alanı** (2-person tent TL25), in the car park at the entrance, offers meals of fresh trout, salad and a drink for TL8. We especially like the restaurant tables half-submerged in the crystalline waters of the babbling brook. Imagine that after walking eight hours on the St Paul Trail.

GETTING THERE & AWAY

The easiest way to get to Kovada Gölü and the Çandır Kanyon is to sign up with a tour from one of the pensions in Eğirdir (around TL25). Out-of-season taxi tours, including a three-hour wait, will cost around TL60 to the lake, or TL100 to the lake and the canyon. You could also try hitching on a summer Sunday when locals head out for picnics.

Zından Mağarası (Zından Cave)

Another possible excursion is to Zından Mağarası, which lies 30km southeast of Eğirdir and 1km north of the village of Aksu, across a fine Roman bridge. The kilometre-long cave has Byzantine ruins at its mouth, lots of stalactites and stalagmites, and a curious room dubbed the Hamam. There's a pleasant walk along the river if caves aren't really your thing.

Pensions organise tours to the cave in summer (around TL25), or taxis charge about TL60 per carload.

Sütçüler

☎ 0246 / pop 3700

The area around Eğirdir is increasingly popular with walkers, particularly now the well-waymarked St Paul Trail (see p359) passes through the area. Easily accessible from Eğirdir, Sütçüler is a fairly unremarkable small town spread out along a winding mountain road. The views effortlessly whet the appetite for a good trek though, and the location is a good base for a few days' walking.

As well as the walking possibilities, buses from Eğirdir pass within 1km of the romantically deserted ruins of the Roman town of **Adada**, where recognisable remnants include a dramatic Roman road entrance, a 1000-seat *agora* and the temple of Trajan.

Sütçüler only has one accommodation option, **Otel Karacan** (☎ 351 2411; www.karacanotel.com; Atatürk Caddesi 53; half-board TL40; 🖳), which has 25 spacious rooms, some without bathroom. The garden terrace and the indoor restaurant (which has big windows) look out to the green vistas below; and a well-worn guitar and a row of nargilehs hint at fun nights after a long day's walking. Meals at this family hotel are prepared with organic produce and the owners are thoroughly helpful, with some English spoken. A short walk down the hill from the Karacan is Sütçüler's compact village square which has a good selection of outdoor cafés. During the peak walking season (in July and August) Otel Karacan is popular with groups and booking in advance is recommended.

GETTING THERE & AWAY

Seven daily buses run between Isparta and Sütçüler (TL12, 1½ hours), passing through Eğirdir (TL10).

YALVAÇ & ANTİOCHEİA-İN-PİSİDİA

☎ 0246 / pop 28,900

You might want to pause in the market town of Yalvaç to visit the extensive ruins of Antiocheia-in-Pisidia, located on a stark mountainside to the northeast. The town is easily reached as a day trip from Eğirdir.

Antiocheia-in-Pisidia

About 2km from Yalvaç centre lies the site of **Antiocheia-in-Pisidia** (admission TL3; 🕑 9am-6pm), an ancient city that was abandoned in the 8th century after Arab attacks.

From the gate, a Roman road leads uphill past the foundations of a triumphal archway, then turns right to the **theatre**. Further uphill, on a flat area surrounded by a semicircular wall of rock, is the city's main **shrine**. This was originally dedicated to the Anatolian mother goddess Cybele, then later to the moon god Men, but in Roman times it featured an imperial cult temple dedicated to Augustus. A path heads left to the **nymphaeum**, once a permanent spring but now dry.

Several arches of the city's **aqueduct** are visible across the fields. Downhill from the nymphaeum are the ruins of the **Roman baths**. Several large chambers have been excavated and much of the original ceiling is intact. On the way back to the entrance you pass the foundations of **St Paul's Basilica**, built on the site of the synagogue. The itinerant tent-maker and apostle's preaching here provoked such a strong reaction that he and St Barnabas were expelled from the city.

After exploring the site drop into the excellent **Yalvaç Museum** (Yalvaç Müzesi; admission TL3; 🕑 8.30am-5.30pm Tue-Sun). Housed in a wonderfully restored heritage building in the town centre, a plan of the ruins and a modest collection of finds from the site will complete your visit. The museum's ethnography section has a fine recreation of the Ottoman-era living room of a wealthy household.

Getting There & Away

Regular buses link Yalvaç with Eğirdir (TL10, one hour).

BEYŞEHİR

☎ 0332 / pop 41,700

The main town on this region's third major lake, fast-growing Beyşehir has preserved its Ottoman heart against the waves of modernity, and is home to one of Anatolia's best medieval mosques. Founded around the 6th century BC, Beyşehir has changed hands innumerable times in the course of history (including 20 times between just 1374 and 1467!), but was most favoured under the 13th-century Seljuks, who considered it a second capital.

In 1296 Şeyheddin Süleyman Bey was responsible for creating the **Eşrefoğlu Camii**, which, with its 42 soaring wooden pillars, coloured mosaics and beautiful blue-tiled *mihrab*, is second only in architectural importance to Afyon's Ulu Cami. Originally it was open to the skies and used only on Friday; nowadays, however, the roof has been covered over. Süleyman Bey is buried beside the mosque. Other key old-town buildings are nearby, including the many-domed **Dokumacılar Hanı** *bedesten* (Cloth Hall; storage chamber), the **Çifte Hamamı** and the **İsmail Ağa Medrese**.

The mosque is right on the lakeshore, reached from the town centre by crossing the impressive arched 1908 railway bridge and following the waterline. Evening boat tours are also on offer with **Eşrefoğlu Yat** (☎ 0542 841 8784; tour TL5), which lets you see the lake-facing side mosque while nibbling some cheap-as-chips *köfte* (TL3).

There are a couple of accommodation options in town if you need to stay over; the **Beyaz Park Motel** (☎ 512 4535; s TL22, d TL50-55), by the bridge, has a great terrace café-restaurant.

Getting There & Away

There are regular buses to Eğirdir (TL12, two hours) and Konya (TL10, one hour). City buses (TL1) serve the otogar twice hourly, passing near the mosque.

PAMUKKALE REGION

Pamukkale is the biggest tourist drawcard in western Anatolia, with one million visitors annually drawn by posters – quite possibly manipulated in PhotoShop – of happy travellers frolicking in gleaming white travertines.

Sadly the hype was too effective in past decades, and the state of the pools spiralled into pollution and overuse. Since being granted World Heritage status in 1988, access to the travertines is carefully controlled; and a Unesco-authorised strategy (see boxed text, p324) is trying to undo the damage and prevent any further degradation of this unique site. The poignant and extensive ruins of the Roman spa town of Hierapolis also make Pamukkale worth a visit. In summer just be prepared to share the vistas with scores of visitors deposited by tour buses.

NYSSA (NYSA)

East of Aydın, you're in the fertile country of the Büyük Menderes River valley. Cotton fields fill the horizon, and during the late October harvest the highways are jammed with tractors hauling trailers laden with the white puffy stuff. Other important crops include pomegranates, pears, citrus fruits, apples, olives and tobacco.

About 31km east of Aydın stands the town of Sultanhisar. A 3km uphill walk to the north brings you to ancient **Nyssa** (admission TL3; ☉ during daylight), set on a hilltop amid olive groves. A custodian will show you around the **theatre**, and there's also a 115m-long **tunnel** beneath the road and parking area that was once the ancient city's main square. Walk another five minutes up the hill, along the road and through a field, and you'll come to the **bouleuterion**, with some attractive sculpture fragments. Other highlights include a **library** and a portico-lined **agora**. Compared to Ephesus, you'll need a greater sense of imagination to bring this ancient city to life, but you'll definitely be rewarded by the hilltop location that's usually devoid of other visitors.

Getting There & Away

İzmir–Denizli trains stop in town, and many east–west buses run along the highway. Dolmuşes run to Sultanhisar from Nazilli every 15 minutes (TL1.50).

DENİZLİ

☎ 0258 / pop 323,000

The prosperous town of Denizli is famous for its textiles, and lining the road to Pamukkale you'll see many outlet centres selling cheap but good quality towels and bed linen. For most travellers though, it's just a place to hop off a bus or train and onto a bus or dolmuş heading north to Pamukkale.

Getting There & Away
AIR
Turkish Airlines (www.thy.com) has daily flights to Denizli from İstanbul at 6.55am and 5.55pm. From the airport a Turkish Airlines shuttle

WESTERN ANATOLIA

SERVICES FROM DENİZLİ'S OTOGAR

Destination	Fare (TL)	Duration (hr)	Distance (km)	Frequency (per day)
Afyon	18	4	240	8
Ankara	35	7	480	frequent
Antalya	25	5	300	several
Bodrum	25	4	290	several
Bursa	40	9	532	several
Fethiye	20	5	280	several
Isparta	13.50	3	175	several
İstanbul	45	12	665	frequent
İzmir	20	4	250	frequent
Konya	30	6	440	several
Marmaris	20	3	185	several
Nevşehir	35	11	674	at least 1 nightly
Selçuk	18	3	195	several, or change at Aydın

bus (TL12) drops passengers at the Denizli otogar on request. A taxi from the airport to Denizli is around TL40 and around TL75 to Pamukkale.

On departure there is no public transport from Denizli to the airport. Catch a dolmuş to the otogar (TL2), a taxi to the Turkish Airlines office (TL10) and then the Turkish Airlines shuttle (TL12) to the airport. The shuttle bus leaves the Turkish Airlines office around two hours before flight time. For Turkish Airlines' 8.40am departure to İstanbul you'll need to catch a taxi direct to the Turkish Airlines office as dolmuşes do not run early enough.

BUS

There are frequent buses between İzmir and Denizli via Aydın and Nazilli. The Denizli otogar has an *emanetçi* (left-luggage office) next to the PTT.

Denizli is a key transport hub for all of Turkey. Some daily services are listed in the table above.

The local bus service to Pamukkale leaves from inside the otogar and runs every 15 minutes, with no waiting about for it to fill up. Touts taking commissions from hotels may try to get you to take the dolmuşes that wait beside the otogar instead of the bus. In summer these fill up quickly, but at other times you could be waiting around. Buses and dolmuşes to Pamukkale cost exactly the same (TL2).

TRAIN

The train station is on the main highway, across the road from the otogar and a short distance from the Üçgen roundabout.

On arrival at the train station, walk out of the front door, cross the highway, turn left and walk one block to the otogar to catch a dolmuş or bus to Pamukkale.

The nightly *Pamukkale Ekspresi* (seat TL25, couchette TL34, sleeper TL64 to Tl104, 15½ hours) travels between Denizli and İstanbul via Afyon (TL20, six hours). It leaves from İstanbul (Haydarpaşa) at 5.30pm and from Denizli at 5pm. At the time of writing track work was making the journey longer than normal, but this was scheduled to be completed in late 2008.

Many people enjoy the relatively short run from Denizli to Selçuk (TL10, two hours), which passes through attractive countryside and leaves/arrives during sensible daylight hours.

At the time of writing the Denizli to İzmir train (TL12, 4½ to 5½ hours) via Afyon was suspended for track work.

PAMUKKALE
☎ 0258 / pop 2500

The restorative qualities of the calcium-rich waters of the town of Pamukkale ('Cotton Castle') have a centuries-old reputation. The unique travertine (calcium carbonate) shelves and pools above the town were created when warm mineral water cooled and deposited calcium as it cascaded over the cliff edge. The Romans built a large spa city, Hierapolis, to take advantage of the water's curative powers.

Centuries later the visitors are still coming, many now staying only a few hours, before being whisked to Ephesus or for a night in tawdry Karahayıt a few kilometres west of Pamukkale.

WESTERN ANATOLIA

Pamukkale village has some excellent and good-value hotels and pensions, and if you steer clear of the touristy ambience of the main road beneath the travertines, the settlement's sleepy village charm is still largely intact. Several other attractions are within easy reach, including Afrodisias (p328), one of Turkey's most absorbing archaeological sites, and Laodicea (p328), one of the Biblical 'Seven Churches of Asia'.

Orientation & Information

Pamukkale and Hierapolis form a national park, with main entrances to the north and south. Cars can reach the southern entrance (güney girişi) via Pamukkale village (1km), or the northern entrance (kuzey girişi) via Karahayıt. It's a 500m walk from the southern entrance to the centre of the site, and 2.5km from the northern entrance. These two entrances are mainly used by tour buses.

Independent travellers usually use a third entry point via a ticket kiosk opposite Pamukkale's main road, Mehmet Akif Ersoy Bulvarı. From there it is a 250m walk uphill through the travertines to the plateau where Hierapolis is located.

Pamukkale **tourist office** (☎ 272-2077; www .pamukkale.gov.tr; ☼ 8am-noon & 1-5.30pm Mon-Sat) is on the plateau above the travertines, along with a PTT, ATM, and first-aid post. There is another ATM and police post at the base of the travertines near the ticket kiosk; and a third ATM, another PTT and internet cafés are located in Pamukkale village. Most pensions also provide internet access. The nearest banks are in Denizli.

Pamukkale now receives over one million visitors per year, and the recent increase in entrance fee is funding the landscaping of the area below the travertines and improved facilities on the plateau.

For a sky high view of Hierapolis and the travertines try **Blue Sky Microlights** (☎ 461 2432; www.fly-blue-sky.com; 12-min flight US$70, 17-min flight US$95; ☼ daylight only). You'll find it at the northern entrance of the travertines.

Sights

TRAVERTINES

Most people come to Pamukkale to see its famous **travertines** (admission TL20; ☼ during daylight). Walking around them – you'll need to take

PAMUKKALE

0 ——————————— 100 m

To North Entrance (3km); Karahayıt (7km);

To Travertine Pools & Blue Sky Microlights (250m); Tourist Office (250m); Hierapolis (350m)

To South Entrance (900m)

Stad Cad

Cumhuriyet Square; Belediye

Atatürk Cad

Stream

Çoşkun Cad

To Denizli (18km); Ak Han (6km); Kaklik Cave (30km)

INFORMATION		
ATM	1	B2
ATM	2	C1
Police Post	3	C1
Post Office	4	B2

SIGHTS & ACTIVITIES		
Public Swimming Pools	5	B1
Ticket Kiosk	6	C1

SLEEPING		
Artemis Yörük Hotel	7	B2
Aspawa Pension	8	B2
Beyaz Kale Pension	9	B2
Hotel Dört Mevsim	10	B3
Hotel Hal-Tur	11	B1
Kervansaray Pension	12	B2
Melrose Hotel	13	B3
Venüs Hotel	14	B3

EATING		
Konak Sade Restaurant	15	B1
Mustafa's	16	C2

DRINKING		
Kayaş Restaurant & Bar	17	B1
Tropical Bar	18	B1

TRANSPORT		
Bus Company Offices	19	B2
Dolmus Stop for Denizli	20	C1

WESTERN ANATOLIA

ENSURING A FUTURE FOR PAMUKKALE

You may be disappointed by the state of the travertines, especially if you've seen older photographs of Pamukkale in tourist offices around Turkey. But since Unesco World Heritage protection was granted in 1988, significant steps have been taken to ensure the future of the site. Hotels on the plateau were demolished and a road that went through the heart of the travertines removed.

And despite the hearsay, it's not the swimming pools of the pensions in the village below causing the pools to be bereft of water. A managed process authorised by Unesco actually drains and fills the pools of water on a rotating basis. The aim is to reduce pollution and algae in the pools and to allow the sun to bleach the pools a glistening white, only possible when the pools are empty of water.

With over a million visitors each year, Pamukkale continues to be under significant environmental pressure, but unlike 30 years ago the future of the site is now under more careful and considered protection.

---

your shoes off – is enjoyable, but there are only certain areas with unrestricted access. If you're whistled at by a strident uniformed security guard, don't be too surprised. You'll also notice an influx of day trippers – mainly Russians – who regard it as appropriate to wander around the travertines and the ancient wonders of Hierapolis wearing skimpy bathing attire. Personally we'd like to see Pamukkale's whistling security personnel also adopt a wider brief as fashion police. Note that the TL20 admission fee is only applicable for one day, and we've also heard reports of travellers being refused re-entry when they returned for a second visit later in the day. It's best to treat your entry on a once-only basis.

From the ticket kiosk it's a 250m barefoot walk to the plateau along a calcium path through the travertines themselves. Tiny ridges of calcium make this tough on tender feet. The best time to visit is morning and late afternoon to avoid the massive influx of tour buses.

Swim in the Antique Pool (see right) in Hierapolis, or the **public swimming pools** with travertine views on the main road past Pamukkale village.

HİERAPOLİS

The ruins of Hierapolis brilliantly evoke life in the early centuries of the modern era. Here pagan, Roman, Jewish and early Christian elements evolved into a distinctly Anatolian whole. To inspect the sprawling ruins carefully could take a day, but most visitors settle for a couple of hours.

Founded around 190 BC by Eumenes II, king of Pergamum, Hierapolis was a cure centre that prospered under the Romans and even

more under the Byzantines, when it gained a large Jewish community and an early Christian congregation. Sadly, recurrent earthquakes regularly brought disaster and after a major tremor in 1334 the city was abandoned.

The centre of Hierapolis may originally have been the sacred pool, which is now the swimming pool in the courtyard of the **Antique Pool** (adult/child TL18/9; ☺ 9am-7pm) spa. You can still bathe in it amid submerged sections of original fluted marble columns. The water temperature is a languid 36°C. There are lockers for your gear, and the pool is surrounded by a number of café-bar kiosks. In the peak season from around 11am to 4pm, the pool is a busy watery scrum of day trippers, but it generally empties out later in the afternoon.

Near the Hierapolis Archaeology Museum stand a ruined **Byzantine church** and the foundations of a **Temple of Apollo**. As at Didyma and Delphi, the temple had an oracle tended by eunuch priests. The source of inspiration was an adjoining spring called the Plutonium, dedicated to Pluto, god of the underworld. To confirm its direct line to Hades, the spring released toxic vapours, lethal to all but the priests, who would demonstrate its potent powers by tossing small animals and birds in to watch them die.

To find the spring, walk up towards the Roman theatre, enter the first gate in the fence on the right, then follow the path down to the right. To the left, in front of the big, block-like temple, is a small subterranean entrance closed by a rusted grate and marked by a sign reading 'Tehlikelidir Zehirli Gaz' (Dangerous Poisonous Gas). Listen and you will hear the gas bubbling up from the waters below. Note that it is still deadly poisonous, and before the grate was installed there were several fatalities among those with more curiosity than sense.

The spectacular **Roman theatre**, capable of seating more than 12,000 spectators, was built in two stages by the emperors Hadrian and Septimius Severus. Much of the stage survives, along with some of the decorative panels and the front-row 'box' seats for VIPs. It was restored by Italian stonecutters in the 1970s (see boxed text below). The new wooden rails are intended to stop people toppling down the tiers.

From the theatre, rough tracks lead uphill to the extraordinary octagonal **Martyrium of St Philip the Apostle**, built on the site where it's believed that St Philip was martyred. The arches of the eight individual chapels are all marked with crosses. The views are wonderful and few of the tours bring visitors this far.

Across the hillside in a westerly direction is the completely ruined **Hellenistic theatre**. Looking down you'll see the 2nd-century **agora**, one of the largest ever discovered. Marble porticoes with Ionic columns surrounded it on three sides, while a basilica closed off the fourth.

Walk down the hill and through the *agora*, and you'll re-emerge on the main road along the top of the ridge. Turn right towards the northern exit and you'll come to the marvellous colonnaded **Frontinus Street**, with some of its paving and columns still intact. Once the city's main north–south commercial axis, this street was bounded at both ends by monumental archways. The ruins of the **Arch of Domitian**, with its twin towers, are at the northern end, but just before them don't miss the surprisingly large **latrine** building, with two channels cut into its floor, one to carry away sewage, the other for fresh water.

Beyond the Arch of Domitian are the ruins of the **Roman baths**, then the Appian Way of Hierapolis, an extraordinary **necropolis** (cemetery), extending several kilometres to the north. Look out for a cluster of circular tombs, supposedly topped with phallic symbols in antiquity. In ancient times Hierapolis was a place where the sick came for a miracle cure, but the scale of the necropolis suggests the local healers had mixed results.

UNEARTHING AN ESSENTIAL PAST

How long were you involved in the excavations of Hierapolis? I'm retired now, but I worked with Paolo Verzone and the Italian Archaeological Mission for 29 years from 1975. There were also Germans and Argentineans involved in the excavation of Hierapolis. Germany and Argentina both also provided sponsorship.

How did you get the job? In the 1970s up to 90% of Pamukkale village was working at Hierapolis. In those days, Pamukkale was still called Ecirli. It was just a matter of chance to get assigned to be a winch operator. I only had a couple of weeks training and then I began working in the Roman theatre. When I first began I was very nervous, and we'd have up to six people working together on stones weighing up to 4 tonnes. I was always scared the rope would break. We'd take one block at a time very, very carefully. One day the winch moved and the block of stone just stayed put. Another time the rope actually did break. It was pretty dangerous work.

How have the excavations changed over the years? In the early days we had no electric motors and everything was done by hand. It was very slow and painstaking work. There were more than 200 people involved in the excavations in the 1970s. Now there are only 80 or 90 people involved. They've still got lots to do though. It's estimated only 5% of the entire site has been excavated.

How have the excavations changed Pamukkale over the years? These days tourism is more important. Some of my kids are working in a silver shop, but one of my sons is still working at Hierapolis. He's a çavuş (foreman).

What's your favourite memory of the excavations? It has to be the Italian music concert that was held in the Roman theatre in 2007 for the 50th anniversary of the excavations. It was very emotional to see the theatre full of people and to hear the music, especially after all the hard work my workmates and I had done over the years.

Hasan Özel is a retired winch operator in Pamukkale

WESTERN ANATOLIA

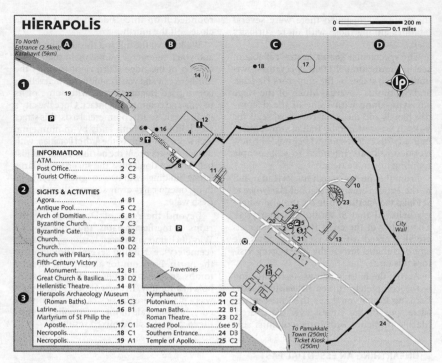

HİERAPOLİS

To North Entrance (2.5km); Karahayıt (5km)

INFORMATION
ATM....................................1 C2
Post Office........................2 C2
Tourist Office...................3 C3

SIGHTS & ACTIVITIES
Agora.................................4 B1
Antique Pool.....................5 C2
Arch of Domitian..............6 B1
Byzantine Church.............7 C3
Byzantine Gate.................8 B2
Church...............................9 B2
Church.............................10 D2
Church with Pillars.........11 B2
Fifth-Century Victory
  Monument......................12 B1
Great Church & Basilica..13 D2
Hellenistic Theatre.........14 B1
Hierapolis Archaeology Museum
  (Roman Baths)..............15 C3
Latrine............................16 B1
Martyrium of St Philip the
  Apostle...........................17 C1
Necropolis.......................18 C1
Necropolis.......................19 A1

Nymphaeum....................20 C2
Plutonium........................21 C2
Roman Baths....................22 B1
Roman Theatre................23 D2
Sacred Pool...............(see 5)
Southern Entrance..........24 D3
Temple of Apollo............25 C2

Travertines

City Wall

To Pamukkale Town (250m); Ticket Kiosk (250m)

Hierapolis Archaeology Museum

Housed in what were once the Roman baths, this excellent **museum** (admission TL3; ☉ 9am-12.30pm & 1.30-7.15pm Tue-Sun) has three separate sections, one housing spectacular sarcophagi, another small finds from Hierapolis and Afrodisias, and the third friezes and Roman-era statuary from the Afrodisias school. Those depicting Attis, lover of the goddess Cybele, and a priestess of the Egyptian goddess Isis, are especially fine.

Festivals & Events

In early June the annual **Turkish-Greek Friendship Festival** (Türk-Yunan Dostluk Festivali), takes place. Pamukkale is twinned with Samos in Greece, and a series of talks, concerts and performances are held in both locations over several days, often using the travertines and Hierapolis as venues.

Sleeping

Prices vary seasonally, peaking in July and August. Competition ensures excellent value for money, with services such as internet access, book exchanges, multilingual TV,

in-house catering and swimming pools all commonplace. Pension owners will crowd around your bus and flood you with offers, and anyone with rooms still available after this initial onslaught will intercept you on the street. If you've booked in advance or know where you want to stay, give the accommodation a call and someone will often collect you from Denizli otogar for free.

CAMPING

There are several **camp sites** (camp site per person about TL7) set around swimming pools beside the highway as you come into Pamukkale from Denizli. Some pensions also allow camping on their grounds.

PENSIONS & HOTELS

Several welcoming, family-run pensions are clustered at the junction of İnönü and Menderes Caddesis.

  Hotel Dört Mevsim (☎ 272 2009; www.hoteldort mevsim.com; Hasan Tahsin Caddesi 19; dm TL10, s/d TL20/35; ☒ ▣ ☒) The 'Four Seasons' is quite different to its top-end namesakes, but has simple and clean family-run rooms in a quiet lane. Expect

WESTERN ANATOLIA

excellent home-cooked food, lots of bright decor and an even brighter welcome. A camp site is TL10 for two people and there's free wi-fi and a pool. Breakfast is an extra TL5.

Artemis Yoruk Hotel (☎ 272 2073; www.artemis yorukhotel.com; Atatürk Caddesi; dm €7, s/d/tr/q €15/19/25/32; 🞫 🖳 🕱) With a super-central location, this sprawling edifice has a wide range of rooms from four-bed backpacker dorms through to single, double, triple and five-bed family rooms. It's a popular choice for small groups, so the bar offering 'bloody cold beer' can get pleasingly raucous.

Aspawa Pension (☎ 272 2094; www.aspawapen-sion.com; Turgut Özal Caddesi 28; s/d €13/22; 🞫 🖳 🕱) Another centrally located pension, the Aspawa ticks all the requisite boxes for good value Pamukkale: pool, aircon, wi-fi and good food in a family atmosphere. A worthwhile backup.

Melrose Hotel (☎ 272 2767; www.allgauhotel.com; Hasan Tahsin Caddesi; s/d TL35/50; 🞫 🖳 🕱) Recent renovations have installed an outdoor dining area at this friendly, family-run spot with clean-as-a-whistle rooms and a deserved reputation for excellent home-cooked food. There are also flasher rooms (TL70-80) with bijou balconies and kitschly romantic circular beds. There are also two swimming pools. Decisions, decisions.

Beyaz Kale Pension (☎ 272 2064; www.beyazkale pension.com; Menderes Caddesi; s/d €15/25; 🞫 🖳 🕱) The 'White Castle' is handy to the centre of the village and has spotless aircon rooms arrayed around a pool. Welcoming family hostess Haçer is a whiz in the kitchen, especially when it comes to vegetarian food. Larger rooms sleeping up to six are also available.

Kervansaray Pension (☎ 272 2209; www.kervansaray pension.com; İnönü Caddesi; s/d €15/25; 🞫 🖳 🕱) This honeysuckle-scented place has comfortable and clean rooms and a breezy terrace with excellent views of the travertines, especially when the spotlights are switched on after dark. Downstairs is a compact pool that's probably best enjoyed during daylight hours.

Venüs Hotel (☎ 272 2152; www.venushotel.net; Hasan Tahsin Caddesi; s/d/tr/q €20/28/38/41; 🞩 🞫 🖳 🕱) One of Pamukkale's best, the Venüs combines spotless rooms – some recently built – with an airy poolside restaurant and a wonderful kilim-lined social area. Right down to two friendly dogs, Çilek (Strawberry) and Findik (Hazelnut), the Durmuş family couldn't be more welcoming. Excellent food and wi-fi

access make choosing the Venüs a straightforward decision. Rates include breakfast.

Hotel Hal-Tur (☎ 272 2723; www.haltur.net; Mehmet Akif Ersoy Bulvarı 71; s/d €40/60; 🞫 🖳 🕱) With unencumbered views of the travertines and arguably Pamukkale's best swimming pool, the Hal-Tur is a step up from most other places around town. Sauna, massage, free wi-fi and… er…table tennis cover all mod cons but it's still worth asking for a discount.

Eating & Drinking

Pensions and group travel dominate the Pamukkale market and conventional restaurants have struggled to hold their own. There are a couple worth trying, but the home-cooked food at your pension is bound to be good.

Mustafa's (Atatürk Caddesi 22 mains TL8-13; 🕑 9am-10pm) Scatter cushions and rustic tables overlooking the street are a top location for wood-fired pizzas and good value falafel wraps (TL5).

Konak Sade Restaurant (☎ 272 2002; Ataturk Caddesi 23; mains TL8-14; 🕑 9am-10pm) Attached to the hotel of the same name, travertine views and garden water features add a little flavour to more of the usual dishes.

Kayaş Restaurant & Bar (☎ 272 2267; Atatürk Caddesi 3; mains TL8-15; 🕑 from noon) As well as a diverse menu, the Kayaş' terrace offers plenty of scope for a big night out, with cocktails, a nargileh corner and satellite TV coverage of big football matches.

Tropical Bar (☎ 272 2267; Atatürk Caddesi 17; 🕑 from noon) This rustic bolthole with Kilims-R-Us decor offers five different beers and a good array of spirits. Make a night of it in the nargileh area that lingers casually out front.

Getting There & Away
BUS

In summer Pamukkale has direct buses to Selçuk, but it's best to assume for most destinations you'll have to change in Denizli. Check when you book your ticket.

Pamukkale has no proper otogar. Buses drop you at the Denizli dolmuş stop. Ticket offices are on the main street. We've had reports of travellers buying tickets to Pamukkale, but being offloaded in Denizli. Insist you're reimbursed the additional TL2 you'll need to catch a bus or dolmuş on to Pamukkale.

Buses run between Denizli and Pamukkale every 15 minutes or so, more frequently on

Saturday and Sunday (TL2, 30 minutes). The last bus runs at 10pm for most of the year, but check before leaving it late.

In summer dolmuşes (TL2) run more frequently, but see p322 for a warning on pension touts and delays.

TAXI
A taxi between Denizli and Pamukkale costs about TL40, but don't take one until you're *sure* the bus and dolmuş services have stopped for the day, as drivers will try to take you to a hotel where they can claim commission.

AROUND PAMUKKALE
Laodicea (Laodikya)
Once a prosperous commercial city at the junction of two major trade routes, Laodicea was famed for its black wool, banking and medicines. It had a large Jewish community and a prominent Christian congregation, and was one of the Seven Churches of Asia mentioned in the New Testament Book of Revelation. Cicero lived here for a few years before being put to death at the behest of Mark Antony.

Although the spread-out **ruins** (admission TL5; 8.30am-5pm Tue-Sun) suggest a city of considerable size, there's not much of interest left for the casual visitor. The outline of the **stadium** is visible, although most of the stones were purloined to construct the railway. One of the two **theatres** is in better shape, with most of the upper tiers of seats remaining. More striking are the remains of the **agora**, with the ruins of the **basilica church** mentioned in the Bible right beside it.

Heading from Pamukkale to Denizli by bus, a sign in the village of Korucuk leads to Laodicea. From the sign it's a 1km walk to the site. Alternatively, you might want to sign up for a tour from Pamukkale that also takes in other local sites.

Kaklık Mağarasi (Kaklık Cave) & Ak Han
Hidden away beneath a field, **Kaklık Mağarasi** (admission TL2) is like an underground Pamukkale. Calcium-rich water flows from near the surface into a large sinkhole, creating a bright, white pyramid with warm travertine pools at the bottom. Guides claim that the deposits became white only after the local earthquake of the mid-1990s. Outside there is a pool for bathing. Surrounded by concrete it looks just like a pool at Sea World; cavort in the shal-

lows for long enough and someone might throw you a fish.

En route to the cave, pause to inspect the **Ak Han** (White Caravanserai; admission free; daylight hr), a Seljuk *han* 1km past the Pamukkale turn-off on the main Denizli–Isparta highway. With a beautifully carved gateway, its excellent condition belies its construction in 1251.

Getting to the cave by public transport is time-consuming and it's easiest to take a tour from Pamukkale. To visit independently, catch a bus or dolmuş (TL4) going west from Denizli to Afyon, Isparta or Burdur. In the village of Kaklık a huge sign points left (north) to the cave. Grab a ride on a farm vehicle, or walk 4km to the cave.

Afrodisias
Sprawling and well-preserved, Afrodisias is where visitors can most easily conjure up the grandeur of a lost classical city. And with fewer visiting tour buses, you could be exploring the city's exalted stadium and theatre without constant chatter in several modern languages. While there are finer individual ruins in Ephesus and elsewhere in Turkey, Afrodisias is where the scale of an ancient city can be best appreciated. Come in May or June and you'll find the rambling ruins awash with blazing red poppies.

HISTORY
Excavations have proved that the Afrodisias acropolis is a prehistoric mound built up by successive settlements from around 5000 BC. From the 6th century BC its famous temple was a popular pilgrimage site, but it wasn't until the 2nd or 1st century BC that the village grew into a town that steadily prospered. By the 3rd century AD Afrodisias was the capital of the Roman province of Caria, with a population of 15,000 at its peak. However, under the Byzantines the city changed substantially: the steamy Temple of Aphrodite was transformed into a chaste Christian church and ancient buildings were pulled down to provide stone for defensive walls (c AD 350).

During the Middle Ages Afrodisias continued as a cathedral town, but it was abandoned in the 12th century. The village of Geyre sprang up on the site some time later. In 1956 an earthquake devastated the village, which was rebuilt in its present westerly location, allowing easier excavation of the site.

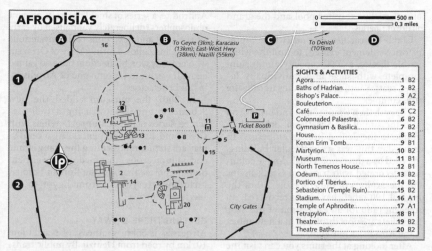

AFRODISIAS

SIGHTS & ACTIVITIES	
Agora.................................1	B2
Baths of Hadrian.......................2	B2
Bishop's Palace........................3	A2
Bouleuterion..........................4	B2
Café................................5	C2
Colonnaded Palaestra...................6	B2
Gymnasium & Basilica...................7	B2
House...............................8	B2
Kenan Erim Tomb......................9	B1
Martyrion..........................10	B2
Museum............................11	B1
North Temenos House..................12	B1
Odeum.............................13	B2
Portico of Tiberius....................14	B2
Sebasteion (Temple Ruin)..............15	B2
Stadium............................16	A1
Temple of Aphrodite...................17	A1
Tetrapylon.........................18	B1
Theatre............................19	B2
Theatre Baths.......................20	B2

The pleasant plaza in front of the museum was the main square of pre-1956 Geyre.

Although other archaeologists worked on the site before him, Afrodisias will always be associated with the work of Professor Kenan T Erim of New York University, who directed work at the site from 1961 to 1990. His book *Afrodisias: City of Venus Aphrodite* (1986) tells the story. After his death, Professor Erim was buried at the site that he had done so much to reveal.

SIGHTS

Most ruins at **Afrodisias** (admission TL8; ☺ 9am-7pm May-Sep, 9am-5pm Oct-Apr) date back to at least the 2nd century AD. The site is well laid out, with excellent signage in English and Turkish, and a suggested route marked by yellow-and-black arrows. Follow the route we outline to go against the flow of the tour groups, which usually arrive around 11am. A tractor and train combo transports visitors from the main highway 500m down the hill to the entrance. If you arrive by private car expect to pay an additional TL5 for the privilege of parking.

Turn right beside the museum and on the left you'll see the site of a grand **house** with Ionic and Corinthian pillars. Further along on the left is the magnificently elaborate **tetrapylon** (monumental gateway), which once greeted pilgrims as they approached the Temple of Aphrodite and has been reconstructed using 85% of the original blocks. The tomb of Professor Erim is on the lawn nearby.

Follow the footpath until you come to a right turn that leads across the fields to the 270m-long **stadium**, one of the biggest and best preserved in the classical world. The stadium has a slightly ovoid shape to give spectators a better view of events. Most of its 30,000 seats are overgrown but still in usable condition, and you can easily imagine a big event taking place with thousands of cheering locals. Some seats were reserved for individuals or guilds. The eastern end of the stadium was converted into an arena for gladiatorial combats and you can still see the tunnels where the fighters made their menacing entrances.

Return to the main path and continue to the once-famous **Temple of Aphrodite**, completely rebuilt when it was converted into a basilica (c AD 500). Its cella was removed, its columns shifted to form a nave and an apse added at the eastern end, making it hard to imagine how it must have been in the years when orgies in celebration of Aphrodite were held here. Near the temple-church is the **Bishop's Palace**, a grand house that may have accommodated the Roman governor long before any bishops turned up.

Just after the Bishop's Palace, a path leads east to the beautiful marble **bouleuterion**, preserved almost undamaged for 1000 years in a bath of mud.

South of the odeum was the **north agora**, once enclosed by Ionic porticoes but now little more than a grassy field. The path then leads through the early 2nd-century AD **Hadrianic Baths** to the **southern agora**, with a long, partially excavated pool, and the grand **Portico of Tiberius**.

Climb the earthen mound (where a prehistoric settlement existed) to find the white marble **theatre**, a 7000-capacity auditorium complete with stage and individually labelled seats. South of it stood the large **theatre baths** complex.

The path then wraps round and brings you onto the site of the **Sebasteion**, originally a temple to the deified Roman emperors. In its heyday this was a spectacular building, preceded by a three-storey-high double colonnade decorated with friezes of Greek myths and the exploits of the emperors; 70 of the original 190 reliefs have been recovered, an excellent ratio for an excavation of this size. The reliefs are now displayed in a new annex in the Afrodisias museum.

After looking at the ruins you can visit the **museum** (admission incl in Afrodisias ticket). During Roman times, Afrodisias was home to a famous school for sculptors attracted by high-grade marble 2km away at the foot of Babadağ (Mt Baba). The museum collection reflects the excellence of their work. Noteworthy works include a 2nd-century cult statue of Aphrodite, a series of shield portraits of great philosophers (deliberately vandalised by early Christians), and depictions of the mysterious Caius Julius Zoilos, a former slave of Octavian who not only won his freedom but also gained enough wealth to become one of Afrodisias' major benefactors.

In 2007 the museum added the new Sebasteion annex showcasing a well-preserved series of 1st-century AD reliefs with Greek and Roman influences. Also on display are statues representing the many ethnic and cultural groups that made up the ancient human mosaic that was the Roman Empire, including everywhere from Egypt to the Iberian peninsula.

GETTING THERE & AWAY

Afrodisias is 55km southeast of Nazilli and 101km by road from Denizli. By public transport, catch a bus from Denizli to Nazilli, another bus to Karacasu and finally a dolmuş to Afrodisias. It's more sensible to arrange a tour (TL30) from Pamukkale. Tours leave with a minimum of four people, which is usually not a problem to arrange in summer. You'll have around 2½ hours at the site.

Western Mediterranean

The Turquoise Coast is a glistening stretch of clear blue sea where gods once played in sublime pebble coves and now spectacular ruins abound. It's here too – in villages too pretty to postcard – that sun-kissed locals smile at travellers' never-ending quest for the 'Med Life'. The trick is deciding what to do; covering it all can prove exhausting, indeed detrimental to your olive oil glow. Yet by far the most dramatic way to see this stretch of coastline is by skimming through the crystal waters aboard a *gület* (traditional wooden yacht) where you can party till it's every man and woman overboard, or plain relax with the salt between your toes. Alternatively, you can negotiate the Lycian Way on foot high above Akdeniz.

However you go, it's the region's seamless mix of history and holiday that will inspire and enchant. At places like Patara, Phaselis and Olympos, your hand-packed sandcastles are humbled by vine-covered Corinthian temples and Lycian tombs. If you prefer to interact with your surroundings a little more, the western Mediterranean has plenty of 'X' factor. Scuba diving at Kaş, paragliding off Baba Dağ, kayaking atop the Sunken City in Kekova, and canyoning at Saklıkent are only a few of the options. Those preferring a slower pace can fine dine in hip Kalkan, get feral in Kabak, or wander the Ottoman houses of Antalya, an increasingly sophisticated neo-European city with a sparkling old town. Listening to the strains of European opera at nearby Aspendos – a fully functional Roman theatre – is another surreal travel moment. But travel here is not a well-kept secret. In towns like Marmaris, the swirling beast of package tourism roars deep into the night. Luckily the crowds are fenced in by concrete and convenience, and the creative traveller can still find the Turkey before the travel brochure – you can still find the gods' own playground.

HIGHLIGHTS

- Hire a scooter and hit the high roads and hidden coves of the **Hisarönü Peninsula** (p341)
- Dine exquisitely daily in **Kalkan** (p376), an epi-(curean)-centre of Mediterranean cooking
- Centre yourself while camping at **Kabak** (p369)
- Bargain for a boat and take a trip around the islands off **Fethiye** (p353) or **Kaş** (p379)
- Sample a section of the Lycian Way from the cliffs above **Ölüdeniz** (p365)
- Potter around the ruins of **Patara** (p372) before plunging into the sea on its beautiful beach
- Sea-kayak over the stunning sunken city of **Üçağız** (Kekova; p384
- Sample the Ottoman splendour of **Kaleiçi** (p393) – the old quarter of Antalya – and wander through a world-class museum

WESTERN MEDITERRANEAN

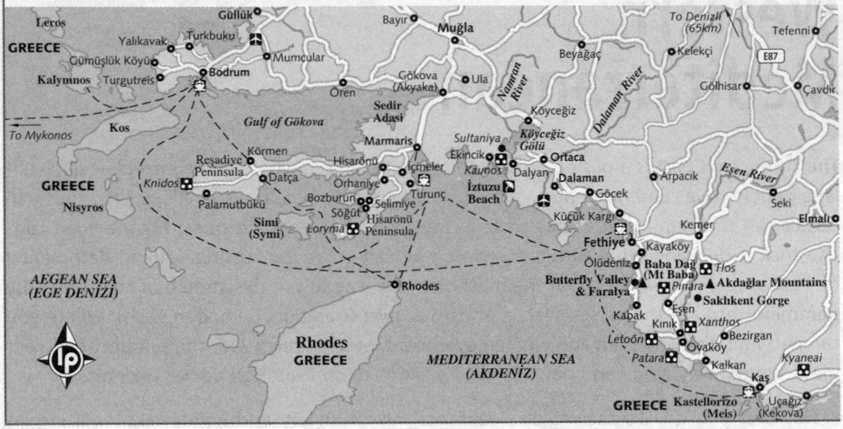

MUĞLA

☎ 0252 / pop 49,000

Muğla can make a pleasant re-introduction to Turkish life after the heady times of nearby Marmaris or Bodrum. It boasts a fine historic quarter, well-preserved, whitewashed Ottoman neighbourhoods and an array of excellent *çay bahçesi* (tea gardens) filled with urgent, friendly student banter.

The town is rare for a Turkish provincial capital; compact, tree-lined and invariably relaxed. Set in a rich agricultural valley, Muğla also prides itself on having appointed Turkey's first female *vali* (governor).

Orientation & Information

Muğla is easy on foot. The centre of town is Cumhuriyet Meydanı, the traffic roundabout with the statue of Atatürk. The otogar (bus station) is 1km downhill (south), and the bazaar and historic quarter 500m uphill (due north) along İsmet İnönü Caddesi.

The excellent **tourist office** (☎ 214 1261; fax 214 1244; Marmaris Bulvarı 24/1) is 100m past the Hotel Petek and across the road in İl Turizm Müdürlüğü (Provincial Tourism Directorate), on the main road running east (on the right as you face uphill) from Cumhuriyet Meydanı. It has a useful map of the town centre (free).

Sights & Activities

Go north along İsmet İnönü Caddesi from Cumhuriyet Meydanı to the **Kurşunlu Cami**, which was built in 1494, repaired in 1853 and had a minaret and courtyard added in 1900. Nearby is the **Ulu Cami** (1344), dating from the time of the Menteşe emirs, although repairs made in the 19th century have rendered its pre-Ottoman design almost unrecognisable.

Continue walking north into the **bazaar**, its narrow lanes jammed with artisans' shops and small local restaurants. Giant plane trees add shade. Proceed up the hill to see Muğla's **Ottoman houses**, many of them in good condition. The winding alleys between whitewashed walls give it a classic Mediterranean ambience.

Muğla's **museum** (☎ 214 4933; Eski Postahane Caddesi; admission TL3; ⏲ 8am-noon & 1-5pm) is close to the *belediye* (town hall) and contains a small collection of Greek and Roman antiquities (with captions and information panels in English) displayed in rooms around a courtyard. There's also a room containing traditional arts and crafts, and another for various fossils. The museum faces the beautiful **Konakaltı İskender Alper Kültür Merkezi**, which houses a community centre.

The **Vakıflar Hamam** (☎ 214 2067; Mustafa Muğlalı Caddesi 1; bath/massage TL8/25; ⏲ 6am-midnight), built in 1344, has mixed bathing, though there's a separate women's area too.

Sleeping & Eating

Otel Tuncer (☎ 214 8251; Saatlı Kule Altı, Kütüphane Sokak 1; d TL40) A long block northeast of the Kurşunlu Cami (follow the signs), the hotel is clean and spacious, with friendly management; ask for a balcony.

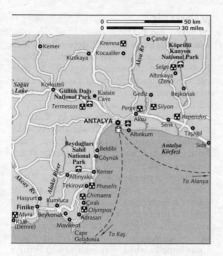

Hotel Petek (☎ 214 1897; fax 214 3135; Marmaris Bulvarı 27; s/d TL50/80) Though the three-star Petek's a bit characterless, it's comfortable and professionally run.

Muğla Konakları (☎ 213 0608; Süeymanbey Sokak 10; s/d TL50/100) This is a charming revamped Ottoman boutique hotel in the old centre of town. There's a certain cottage feel to the place, and the rooms are cute and spacious.

Muğla Lokantası (☎ 212 3121; İsmet İnönü Caddesi 51; mains TL3-6; ☾ 6.30am-10pm) With a great pick-and-point counter containing a delicious selection of traditional Muğla dishes at rock-bottom prices, this place is permanently packed.

Doyum 98 (☎ 214 2234; Cumhuriyet Caddesi 22; mains TL4-12; ☾ 9am-11pm) Next door to the tourist office, this place has become a favourite locally for its delicious pides (TL4 to TL6) and *köfte* (grilled meatballs, TL7). It has a few tables outside.

Muğla Belediyesi Kültür Evi (Muğla Culture House; ☎ 212 8668; İsmet İnönü Caddesi 106; breakfast TL5, coffee TL1.25; ☾ 8am-8.30pm) This 200-year-old house is a lovely place to come for breakfast or coffee. Peaceful and tranquil, it's popular with the locals who read or play backgammon here. Prices are kept low by the municipality which restored the place to its current glory.

Sanat Evi (☎ 213 0220; Hekimbaşı Sokak 9; breakfast €2.75, mains TL5-6, beer TL4; ☾ 7am-2am) In a 150-year-old Ottoman house, this café is great for a drink or a bite to eat. At the back there's a delightful shaded terrace beside a small pool that resonates with birdsong or the strains of classical Turkish music. The chef serves

different Muğla dishes daily. It's next door to a theatre celebrating the works of the iconic poet Nazım Hikmet.

Ardore (☎ 213 0681; Simdi Keyif Zamani; mains TL6-12) A crowd-pleasing menu of pizzas and sandwiches at this medium-paced place near the cinema. The baked potatoes (TL3) are plump.

Getting There & Away
Muğla's busy otogar runs services to all major destinations in the region. If you're heading east along the coast, change in Marmaris. Buses leave every half-hour (hourly in low season) to both Marmaris (TL6, one hour, 55km) and Bodrum (TL13, 2½ hours).

GÖKOVA (AKYAKA)
☎ 0252
Backed by pine-clad mountains, Akyaka village lies tucked away on a little grey sand beach where the river meets the sea. Here day trippers mix with summer residents in attractive summer houses with pantile roofs and intricate wooden balconies draped in bougainvillea.

If you're coming from the north, the road from Muğla comes over the Sakar Geçidi (Sakar Pass; 670m) to reveal breathtaking views of the Gulf of Gökova. It then switches back down into a fertile valley. At the base of the hill, signs point the way to Akyaka, often called Gökova.

Every Saturday there is a busy **market** in the centre of town. The local boat cooperative runs tours of beaches along the gulf, which make a nice day trip for around TL40.

Çinar beach, 1km out of town, is the best spot to swim. To get there, turn right at the primary school as you head towards the marina – then take the high road veering right.

Yücelen Hotel Sports Club (☎ 243 5434; www.gokovaruzgar.com) offers windsurfers, sea kayaks, canoes, pedalos, sailing boats and mountain bikes for rent, as well as tuition and courses. Canyoning and paint-balling is also possible.

Sleeping & Eating
Otel Terzioğlu (☎ 243 5437; www.terziogluturizm.com; Lütfiye Sakıcı Caddesi; s/d TL30/60; ☒ ☒) This high-season hang-out around the corner from the Golden Roof (p334) is cheap and quite cheerful, but the views only reach to the car park. Rooms are compact; all include TV and fridge.

Susam Otel (☎ 243 5863; www.mepartours.com; Lütfiye Sakıcı Caddesi; s/d TL40/80; ☒ ☒) On the same road as Şirin Lokanta, the Susam has immaculate and pleasant rooms – most with balconies – as well as a small garden with a pretty pool.

Otel Yücelen (☎ 243 5108; www.yucelen.com.tr; s/d TL80/140; 🅿 🖭) What you'd expect from the multi-faceted Yücelen group: large, well managed and well designed. Facilities include two pools, a fitness centre and hamam (bathhouse). Avoid the weekends if possible; it's packed with Muğla students.

Sezgin Apart (☎ 243 5959; www.sezginapart.com; Lütfiye Sakıcı Caddesi; 3-bedroom apart TL150; 🅿 🖳 🖭) A good alternative, particularly if you plan to stay a few extra nights, is to rent a holiday apartment. There are numerous options, including this one. Otherwise, ask at the Golden Roof.

Şirin Lokanta (Lütfiye Sakıcı Caddesi 45; mains TL4-5; 🕑 8am-2am) Around 25m from the Golden Roof, this place does great home cooking. Dishes change daily.

Golden Roof Restaurant (☎ 408 9898; Lütfiye Sakıcı Caddesi 43; meze TL2, mains TL9-15; 🕑 8am-1am Apr–mid-Nov) On the prime corner in town, this family-run affair does good pizza and pasta, as well as home-cooked Turkish fare. The affable young host knows all the town gossip.

Maydanoz (☎ 243 5587; Lütfiye Sakıcı Caddesi; set menu TL24) A big open place near the beach with loads of outdoor tables, generous happy hours and an appealing seafood set menu.

About 750m beyond the village is the picnic and camp ground of **Gökova Orman İci Dinlenme Yeri** (☎ 243 4398; admission per person/car TL1/6, camp site per tent/car TL8/10, bungalow up to 6 people TL150).

Another 500m beyond that is the port hamlet of İskele, with a few basic restaurants serving the tiny beach at the end of the small cove. **Club Çobantur** (☎ 243 4550; www .asuhancobantur.com; Eski İskele Mevkii; s/d TL90/140 depending on room & season; 🅿 🖭) is housed in an old seamen's lodging and set on the seafront amid gardens, a cool mountain stream and a pool. Rooms are comfortable and 13 have sea views.

Getting There & Away

Minibuses run from Gökova to Muğla (TL3, 30 minutes, 26km) every half-hour, and to Marmaris (TL3.50, 30 minutes) twice a day in high season only. Minibuses coming from Marmaris can drop you at the highway junction 2.5km from the beach. You can either walk or wait for a minibus.

MARMARİS
☎ 0252 / pop 35,160

Marmaris is heaven or hell, depending which way your boat floats. An unashamedly brash harbour town that swells to over 200,000 people during summer, Marmaris is a classic case of what you see is what you get; all the time, all-inclusive, Euro-disco 3000.

Marmaris also sports one of Turkey's swankiest marinas (with suitably swanky yachts), and a stunning natural harbour where Lord Nelson organised his fleet for the attack on the French at Abukir in 1798.

Whatever your opinion of Marmaris, if it's a last night out, a *gület* cruise along the coast, or a ferry to Greece you're after, then this tourist haven is pretty much the full package. Bar St is unparalleled Med Coast decadence, while on the rejuvenated promenade, charter-boat touts happily whisk you eastward to Fethiye and beyond.

If it is a quieter, more peaceful Turkish experience you're after, then head for the rugged coastline around Marmaris. Only 10km from the bright lights and banging techno of the city, the deeply indented Reşadiye and Hisarönü peninsulas hide bays of azure backed by pine-covered mountains and gorgeous fishing villages that still find time to sleep.

Orientation

The otogar is about 3km north of the town centre, near the turn-off to Fethiye. From there, dolmuşes (minibuses) run down the wide Ulusal Egemenlik Bulvarı and deposit arrivals at the Tansaş Shopping Centre and at the Siteler dolmuş stop.

At the Atatürk statue, Yeni Kordon Caddesi veers left along the waterfront for 300m to the İskele Meydanı, the harbour-side plaza with the tourist office. The conservation area behind, above and south of the office has some of Marmaris' few remaining old buildings, including its small castle (now a museum). Three kilometres to the right (west) is a marginally more mellow offshoot of tourist utopia, Uzunyalı.

Inland from İskele Meydanı stretches the çarşı (bazaar) district, much of it a pedestrianised covered area. Also known as Bar St, 39 Sokak runs from the bazaar to a canal from where a bridge leads over to the marina. The bazaar can be difficult to negotiate post–Bar St (Hacı Mustafa Sokak).

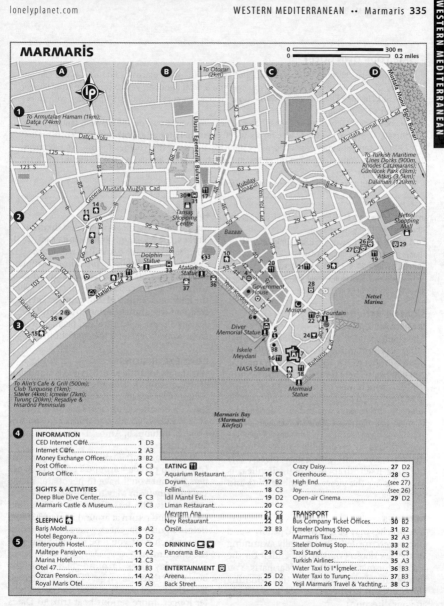

MARMARİS

Şirinyer is about 5km southwest of İskele Meydanı; and İçmeler, another beach resort area, is 8km southwest.

About 1km southeast of town is the harbour for ferries to Rhodes; 3.5km southeast of the centre is Günlücek Park, a forest park reserve; and just beyond it is Aktaş, a seaside village with several hotels and camping grounds.

Information

Getting online is easy here – the alley beside the PTT is a sure bet. There are plenty of banks with ATMs and money-exchange offices on Ulusal Egemenlik Bulvarı and Yeni Kordon Caddesi.
CED Internet C@fé (☎ 413 0193; 28 Sokak 63B; per hr TL3; ⏰ 10am-midnight low season, to 2am high season) A fast, friendly choice. You can buy drinks from the café below.

SAIL YOUR OWN GÜLET

If you want to charter a boat, Marmaris and Fethiye are good places to find one. If you can get a party of up to 16 people together, you can hire a *gület* (wooden yacht) complete with skipper and cook. In May chartering the whole boat is likely to cost around €450 per day, with prices rising to €700 in August.

Experienced sailors can opt for a bareboat charter where you do the crewing (and cooking) yourself. To hire a bareboat sleeping six to 11 passengers for one week in spring costs around €2300. In high summer expect to pay €3000 for a week. Extra charges for one-way journeys, employing a skipper, cleaning up at the end of the voyage and so on can bump up the price even more.

The boxed text, p354, describes other *gület* cruises.

Internet C@fe (☎ 412 0799; Atatürk Caddesi, Huzur Apt 30; per 30 min TL2; ☉ 10am-1am).
Post office (PTT; 51 Sokak; ☉ 8.30am-midnight) Phones are accessible 24 hours a day.
Tourist office (☎ 412 1035; İskele Meydanı 2; ☉ 8am-noon, 1-5pm Mon-Fri mid-Sep–May, daily Jun–mid-Sep) It's right near the castle.

Sights & Activities

MARMARIS CASTLE

The small castle on the hill behind the tourist office was built during the reign of Süleyman the Magnificent. In 1522 the sultan massed 200,000 troops here for the attack and siege of Rhodes, which was defended by the Knights of St John. He'd have a fair fight on his hands keeping the masses out today. The fortress is now the **Marmaris Museum** (Marmaris Müzesi; ☎ 412 7420; admission TL3; ☉ 8am-noon & 1-5pm Tue-Sun). Exhibits are predictably nautical, though there are some interesting glass pieces. The building itself, draped in bougainvillea, is lovely, as are the views over the marina and out to sea.

BEACHES

The beaches may be narrow and pebbly – and often overcrowded – but actually swimming in the sea doesn't appear to be high on the agenda for many travellers to Marmaris. You can often splash about alone (not counting the hordes of bright red sun-bathers staring in your direction).

The beaches at İçmeler and Turunç (p339) can be reached by dolmuşes from outside the Tansaş Shopping Centre, and water taxis from Yeni Kordon Caddesi southeast of the Atatürk statue. The beach at Günlücek Park is also accessible by dolmuş from outside Tansaş. Dolmuşes to İçmeler cost TL1.50, to Turunç TL5.

HAMAM

Supposedly the second-biggest hamam in Turkey, the enormous **Armutalan Hamam** (☎ 417 5375; 136 Sokak 1; bath & scrub TL20, with massage TL35; ☉ 9am-10pm May-Oct) lies behind the government hospital just off Datça Caddesi, about 2km from the town centre. Go after 6pm when the hamam is empty of tour groups. There's a frequent free shuttle service from outside the Tansaş Shopping Centre and back, as well as from some hotels and the tourist office.

BOAT EXCURSIONS

If it stands for little else, Marmaris stands for cruising around in yachts. An array of companies offer excellent day tours of Marmaris Bay, its beaches and islands. You'll usually visit Paradise Island, Aquarium, Phosphoros Cave, Kumlubuku, Amos, Turunç, Green Sea and İçmeler.

It costs around TL350 to TL450 per boat (up to four people – around TL50 to TL80 per person), but you'll have to negotiate. Yachts sail roughly from May to October.

Boats usually leave between 9.30am and 10.30am and return at around 5pm to 5.30pm. Before signing up, check where the excursion goes, which boat you'll be on and what's on the lunch menu.

Two-day trips (around TL800 for the boat) and three-day trips (TL1000) often go to Dalyan and Kaunos. You can also charter longer, more serious boat trips to Datça and Knidos, west of Marmaris, or along the Hisarönü Peninsula to Bozburun. Finally, there's the ever-popular Blue Voyages (see p354) to Fethiye and further adrift.

DIVING

Several centres offer scuba diving excursions and courses from April to October. The **Deep**

Blue Dive Center (☎ 412 4438; Yeni Kordon Caddesi) charges €340 for a PADI open water course over two to four days. Day excursions cost €35 including two dives, all equipment, a divemaster and lunch. **Professional Diving Centre** (☎ 456 5888; Yeni Kordon Caddesi) charges €30.

Sleeping

Marmaris has hundreds of good-value sleeping options, especially for self-caterers, so try to check out a few. The following listings include high season prices – in the off-season, expect serious discounts.

Interyouth Hostel (☎ 412 3687; interyouth@turk.net; 42 Sokak 45; dm or s without bathroom with/without ISIC card TL10/15, d without bathroom TL30; ⌨) Located inside the covered bazaar, this hostel is efficiently run and a great source of travel information. Rooms, though smallish and rather spartan, are spotless and well maintained. There's a laundry service, café, small bookshop and book exchange. From June to September there's a free pasta night on the rooftop. Scooters can be hired (TL30 per day), and boat tickets to Rhodes and for *gület* cruises (see boxed text, p354) are sold here.

Maltepe Pansiyon (☎ 412 1629; 66 Sokak 9; s/d TL30/50; ✖ ⌨) The shady garden is the main attraction of this long-standing budget choice. Rooms are small but spotless, internet access is free and the friendly manager Memo goes out of his way to help. Call ahead.

Özcan Pension (☎ 412 7761; 66 Sokak 17; s/d TL35/60) Looks like an old apartment block from the outside, but this surprisingly spic 'n' span pension is a good-value place. A few rooms have balconies and there's a pleasant garden terrace. It's near the Barış.

Hotel Begonya (☎ 412 4095; fax 412 1518; 39 Sokak 101; d TL60; 🅝) With seven cosy rooms set around a shaded courtyard, this place is beguilingly peaceful. But set slap-bang in the middle of Bar St, it's for party-goers only, as the owner freely admits! Do as they do and snatch a siesta during the day.

Barış Motel (☎ 413 0652; barismotel@hotmail.com; 66 Sokak 10; s/d TL40/60; ✖) This sleepy place is about as close as you get to old-fashioned family values in Marmaris. The amiable young manager is proud of his clean and quite spacious rooms, most with balconies.

Club Turquoise (☎ 417 2790; www.clubturquoise .com; Yunus Nadi Caddesi; s/d/apt TL50/80/100; ✖ ⛲) If you can ignore the poolside shenanigans and group tour romps, then this place to

the west of the centre – in the less manic pocket of Uzunyalı – has cheap, enormous apartments that suit longer stays. It's well managed, too.

Marina Hotel (☎ 412 0010; www.marmarismarina hotel.com; Barbaros Caddesi 39; s/d TL60/80; ✖ ⛲) Don't be put off by the castle-cut-out entrance. The rooms, canary-yellow with frilly curtains and doilies in the bathroom, are homely and comfy. The biggest boon is what the hotel claims is the 'best terrace in Marmaris' with wonderful panoramic views over the marina and castle. There's even a fixed telescope for serial boat-spotters.

Otel 47 (☎ 412 4747; www.hotel47.com; Atatürk Caddesi 10; s/d TL60/90; ✖ ⌨) Amid the bright lights and swaying palm trees of Atatürk Caddesi, there's a certain Miami Beach vibe going on at 47. Regulars return for the prime location and white terrace overlooking the traffic. Rooms are small but smart, with brown-tiled floors.

Royal Maris Otel (☎ 412 8383; www.royalmaris otel.com; Atatürk Caddesi 34; s/d TL100/150; ✖ ⛲) Two pools, a private beach, a hamam and a fitness centre, spacious balconies with stunning views, but remarkably affordable. Standing aboard the roof terrace shaped like a ship's deck is a kookishly Marmaris experience.

Eating
RESTAURANTS

For something cheap and cheerful, try the bazaar area between the post office and the mosque; the old town area around the castle where there's a host of small Turkish restaurants; and along 39 Sokak (Bar St), where stalls cater to the ravenous late-night revellers.

Meryem Ana (☎ 412 7855; 35 Sokak 62; mains TL5-6) Simple and understated, this place serves terrific traditional home cooking. A firm family affair, you can see the mother and aunt hard at work in the kitchen stuffing vine leaves. It has an excellent reputation locally and is a good choice for veggies too (a large mixed plate costs TL10).

Ney Restaurant (☎ 412 0217; 26 Sokak 24; mezes TL4, mains TL10-15) Tucked away off the street up some steps is this tiny but delightful restaurant set in a 250-year-old Greek house. Decorated with seashells and wind chimes, it's run by the charming Birgül, owner and cook, who offers delicious home cooking at pleasing prices. Try the *mantı böreği* (Turkish ravioli).

Liman Restaurant (☎ 412 6336; 40 Sokak 38; mains TL10-20) While something of an institution and well known for its mezes (TL5 to TL15), this lively restaurant inside the bazaar is not the cheapest of places. But the fish soup (TL10) is famous, and the *buğlama* (steamed fish, TL40 for 500g) a sumptuous speciality.

Fellini (☎ 413 0826; Barboras Caddesi 61; meals TL20; ◷ 9am-midnight) Perennially popular with both locals and visitors in the know, this attractively set waterfront restaurant does great thin-crust pizzas (TL15 to TL20) and also has pasta (TL10 to TL20).

Aquarium Restaurant (☎ 413 1522; Barboras Caddesi; meals TL20; ◷ 9am-midnight) Run by a friendly Turkish-Kiwi couple, this loud and proud port-side restaurant serves large grills and steaks to a jovial crowd of Turks and tourists. Slightly overpriced, but it's got the location covered.

CAFÉS & QUICK EATS

Özsüt (☎ 413 4708; Atatürk Caddesi 4; ice cream per scoop TL1.50, puddings TL3-4) This ever-popular chain, with tables set on the seafront, is the perfect place to tuck into a Turkish pud or two. Try the delightfully named *aşure* (Noah's pudding).

Doyum (☎ 413 4977; Ulusal Egemenlik Bulvarı 17; mains TL4-12; ◷ 24 hr) The Doyum is all-too-rare in Marmaris: dirt cheap and high quality local food. Perhaps that's why it's packed with appreciative locals. Clean, friendly and always open, it's a good place for an early breakfast (TL5), and also serves an array of tasty veggie dishes (TL4 to TL5).

Alin's Cafe & Grill (☎ 413 0826; Barboras Caddesi 61; meals TL12) It might be just another chicken chain joint on the outside, but on the inside it's packed full of young Turkish families feasting on healthy grills and kebaps.

İdil Mantıl Evi (☎ 413 9771; 39 Sokak 140; mezes TL5-6, mains TL8-20; ◷ 4pm-4am) Conveniently located in Bar St, this is a great place for the night-nibbles. With simple wooden tables around a traditional oven, it's a delightful and atmospheric place. Guests leave little messages or their names on the wooden panels of the interior. Veggie dishes (TL8 to TL14) are available. The *gözleme* (crêpes, TL6 to TL10) make a great snack.

Drinking & Entertainment

Marmaris is a party town. The aptly named 'Bar Street' (39 Sokak, also known as Hacı Mustafa Sokak) has a string of places that are wildly popular in summer.

Unless stated otherwise, the following bars open from 7pm to 4am daily. Beers cost TL8, spirits TL12 and there are regular foam parties, as well as dance and laser shows.

Keeping up with the hottest clubs is hard work, but we rate **Joy** (☎ 412 6572; 39 Sokak) at the top for sheer loose behaviour. **High End** (☎ 412 3728; 39 Sokak) is an old techno banger that relocated from around the corner on Long Beach, and clearly hasn't skipped a beat. The ever-popular **Back Street** (☎ 412 4048; 39 Sokak 93) and **Areena** (☎ 412 2906; 39 Sokak 54), with its bar elevated above a large dance floor, are also worth a nudge. If you still need a proper rinse out, try **Crazy Daisy** (☎ 412 4048; 39 Sokak 121) with its raised terraces (good for dancing on), as well as the cavernous **Greenhouse** (☎ 412 8792; 39 Sokak).

The **Panorama Bar** (☎ 413 4835; Hacı İmam Sokağı 40; beer TL6; ◷ 9am-midnight mid-Apr-Oct), off 30 Sokak, is more of a permanent fixture and less of a club. Its terrace, though not large, more than justifies the bar's name – it probably boasts the best views in Marmaris. To find it, follow the signs from left of the museum and castle.

At the eastern end of Bar St, near the Netsel Marina, there is also an **open-air cinema** (tickets TL8; ◷ Jun-Sep) behind the Keyif Bar. All movies are English-language releases and are screened at sunset.

Getting There & Away

AIR

The region's principal airport is at Dalaman, 120km east of Marmaris. Turkish Airlines runs an airport bus (known as the Havaş bus; TL6) for its passengers from the Turkish Airlines office in Marmaris, departing about 3½ hours before each Turkish Airlines flight. Otherwise, take one of Marmaris Coop's buses to Dalaman (TL8) from Marmaris otogar, and take a short but quite expensive taxi ride (TL25) from there. TL100 will score you a ride in a brand new four-person shuttle.

Turkish Airlines (☎ 412 3751; Atatürk Caddesi 26-B) has an office about 400m west of the Atatürk statue on the waterfront. See p350 for info on flights.

BOAT

Catamarans sail daily to Rhodes Town in Greece (one way/same-day return/open return €50/50/75 including port tax, 50 minutes) from 15 April to 1 November, leaving at 9am. They return from Rhodes at 4.30pm. Cars cost €150/180/250 for a one-way/same-day return/open-return ticket.

Greek catamarans also sail during the same period from Rhodes to Marmaris (one way/same-day return/open return €60/60/90) at 8am daily, returning from Marmaris at 4.30pm. Cars cost €110/135/190 for a one-way/same-day return/open return.

Turkish cargo boats (carrying up to 78 passengers) also sail once a week in high season to Rhodes (same prices as the catamarans, two hours, departures usually 12.30pm), and two to three times a week in low season, depending on weather (departures usually 9am). They either return the same day or stay in Rhodes for a period of two or three days.

Note that catamarans do not operate from November to mid-April, and there are no Greek cargo boats. Also note that the Sunday morning service runs only sporadically in June and July.

Tickets can be bought from any travel agency including **Yeşil Marmaris Travel & Yachting** (☎ 412 2290; www.yesilmarmaris.com; Barbados Caddesi 13; ☽ 7am-midnight Mon-Sat high season, 8.30am-6.30pm low season).

Book tickets at least one day in advance (more if you have a car) and bring your passport. You need to be at the ferry dock one hour before departure. Some agencies provide a free pick-up service from hotels in the town centre. Note that when you return from Rhodes (even if you've just been for a day trip) you'll still need to buy a new Turkish visa from the immigration authorities in front of customs in Rhodes.

BUS
Marmaris' otogar lies 3km north of the centre of town. Dolmuşes run to and from the otogar along Ulusal Egemenlik Bulvarı every few minutes in high season. Bus companies have ticket offices around the Tansaş Shopping Centre.

Buses run to Bodrum (TL18, 3½ hours, 165km) every one to two hours in high season, every three hours in low season. All year round, buses run to İstanbul (TL55, 13 hours, 805km) four times a day, to İzmir (TL30, 4¼ hours, 320km) every hour, to Fethiye (TL14, three hours, 170km) every half-hour and to Antalya (TL35, six hours, 590km) twice a day. Buses go hourly to Muğla (TL6, one hour, 55km).

For Datça (TL9, 1¾ hours) dolmuşes run every hour in high season and every 1½ hours in low season. For Köyceğız (TL11, 40 minutes) take the Fethiye bus. For Dalyan, take the Fethiye bus and change at Ortaca (TL7, 1½ hours) then take the dolmuş. Finally, the dolmuş for Selimiye and Bozburun (TL7, 55 minutes) runs six times a day.

Getting Around
Frequent dolmuşes run around the bay, beginning and ending at the Tansaş Shopping Centre on Ulusal Egemenlik Bulvarı. They have been colour-coded to denote different routes: the green dolmuşes go to Uzunyalı (TL1, 3km) and Turban-Siteler (TL1.80, 6km), and the orange ones to İçmeler (TL2.50, 11km).

AROUND MARMARİS
Eight kilometres southwest from Marmaris is the miniature package colony of **İçmeler** However, its beach is relatively clean and the decibel count is markedly lower.

Turunç is the next beach resort, but its isolated position at the bottom of a steep mountain has protected it from massive over-development. Dolmuşes make the trip from Marmaris every 40 minutes (TL6). It's also an excellent place for commencing scenic drives through the peninsula.

From May to the end of October, water taxis run from various points on the waterfront between the tourist office and the Atatürk statue to İçmeler (TL8, 30 minutes, every 30 minutes) and Turunç (TL10, 50 minutes, every hour).

REŞADİYE & HİSARÖNÜ PENINSULAS
Two largely undiscovered slivers of land, known in ancient times as the Peraea, trickle west from Marmaris for 100km into the Aegean Sea. The western stretch is called the Reşadiye or Datça Peninsula; its southern branch is known as the Hisarönü or Daraçya Peninsula, with the ruins of the ancient city of Loryma at its tip.

This is spectacular, raw Turkish coastline, whether seeing it from bus, bike or boat. Aside from the joy of sailing near the peninsula's pine-clad coasts and anchoring in some of its hundreds of secluded coves, visitors come to explore fishing villages, mountain towns, wee hamlets and epic ruins. At Knidos there are ferry connections to Rhodes and the neighbouring Greek island of Simi (Symi).

Selimiye
☎ 0252

The stark beauty of this traditional boat-builders' village belies its proximity to mass tourism. Selimiye is unremarkable at first, but its charm will grab you soon enough. Here you can get real solitude by the seaside, or find yourself among a particularly laid-back yachting set. The town itself – a tiny stretch of promenade still graced by the odd goat – lies on a calm bay beneath a few toppled ruins.

To get here, take the Bozburun road about 9km south of Orhaniye and follow the signs.

SLEEPING & EATING

Hotel Begovina (☎ 446 4292; fax 446 4181; s/d TL30/60) Run by Zeki, a retired shoemaker, this hotel offers good-sized, spotless rooms with direct sea views (some with large balconies). All have fridges and a few have kitchenettes. It's just metres from the shingle beach and represents excellent value.

Jenny's House (☎ 446 4289; s/d TL40/70; ✂ ⌨) Across the road from the harbour, this charming bed and breakfast is surrounded by banana trees and a blooming summer garden. The friendly owner cordially hosts many return visitors to the seven pretty bungalows that maintain a rural English air.

Nane Limon Pansiyon (☎ 446 4146; s/d TL40/70; ✂ ⌨) Nejdet pops down from İstanbul for six months each year to oversee his blue-and-white striped guesthouse of ultimate relaxation. A garden path leads to a large house set back from the water where rooms are bright and stylish, many with balconies. It's next door to the Aurora Restaurant.

Bahçe Pansiyon (☎ 446 4235; s/d/apt TL40/80/100; ✂ ⌨) A fairly inconspicuous pension made up of three sparse, clean rooms literally 10 steps from the water's edge and a few larger apartments. Three quiet brothers do a fine job of running the place.

Sardunya Bungalows (☎ 446 4003; s/d with half-board TL50/100; ✂ ⌨) An impressive makeover has made this popular complex even more highly sought after. The 10 fully-decked stone bungalows circle a pretty, cool garden. It's an ideal choice for families.

Café Çeri (Selimiye Köyu; coffee TL2, baklava TL3) Delicious patisserie near the marina.

Falcon Restaurant (☎ 446 4105; Selimiye Köyu; mains TL12-18) Offering similar fare to the Aurora, this family-run restaurant is about 100m from the town centre and 40m from the sea.

Sardunya Restaurant (☎ 446 4003; mains around TL15) The service and menu are equally marvellous at this popular organic restaurant. The *kalamar* (squid) stuffed or fried (TL18) is famous. Try also the delicious *buğulama* (fish casserole, TL30).

Aurora Restaurant (☎ 446 4097; Bahçeıçı; mains TL15-20; ☽ Apr-Oct) The Aurora is very prettily set in a 200-year-old stone house with a shaded terrace as well as tables on the seafront. Fish is its speciality; the mezes are mouth-watering too. Out the back is a primo cocktail bar.

GETTING THERE & AWAY

Dolmuşes run to and from Marmaris (TL6.25) every two hours. For Bozburun, you can hop on the Bozburun to Marmaris bus (which passes through Selimiye) if there's space.

Bozburun
☎ 0252

Lying 12km further down the peninsula on Sömbeki Körfezi (Sömbeki Bay) is the charming village of Bozburun. This is another major boat-building port, but you'd hardly guess it from the unhurried pace of life. Fishing and farming still distract most villagers, although the modest flow of tourists keeps some folk gainfully employed.

If you want to swim, walk around the harbour to the left as you face out to sea – here you can dip into the startlingly blue water from the rocks. This is also a great place to charter private vessels to explore the surrounding bays. For those with wobbly sea legs, there are interesting walks in the nearby countryside.

SLEEPING

Yilmaz Pansiyon (☎ 456 2167; www.yilmazpansion.com; İskele Mahallesi 391; s/d TL40/80) Try to nab a balcony room in this friendly little pension with simple, cheerful rooms. The vine-covered terrace is metres from the sea where the hotel does a good breakfast spread. It's around 100m from the centre.

Pembe Yunus (Pink Dolphin; ☎ 456 2154; www.pembe yunus.net; Kargı Mahallesi 37; s/d TL40/80; ✂ ⌨) This delightful pension feels like a Turkish ladies' club in fluffy lavender blue. Rooms are decked out in rustic-style furniture, and some have stunning sea views. Fatma, the mother, cooks famously – set-menu dinners cost TL25. It's 700m from the dolmuş station (though you can ask to be dropped here).

HISARÖNÜ PENINSULA BY SCOOTER

The mountainous, deeply indented Hisarönü Peninsula is the perfect place to escape the madness of Marmaris.

It's a rugged place with remarkably varied landscapes; lush pine forests on a high plateau inland from Turunç give way to steep, bare rocky hillsides as you approach Bozburun. You can go via the main road to Bozburun but it's more fun to do a loop, heading down on village roads and coming back on the main road.

Setting off from Marmaris, head for İçmeler along Atatürk Caddesi. In İçmeler the main road branches; take the right-hand road, which leads around the back of the town and begins a steep, winding ascent towards Turunç. Take the unpaved road to the right through the pine forest before you get there. The road narrows and gets steeper, slowly winding down to the inland village of **Bayır**. There couldn't be a sharper contrast between the concrete houses of Marmaris and İçmeler and rustic Bayır. The village square is at the foot of an ancient plane tree and has pleasant restaurants with terraces overlooking the valley. After Bayır the landscape becomes much drier, and the land falls steeply away into inaccessible coves. From tiny Söğüt the road is relatively level on the way to **Bozburun**, which has several good cafés for lunch.

From Bozburun a good road leads back along the western side of the peninsula, past the idyllic bays of Selimiye and Hisarönü, before rejoining the main Datça–Marmaris road.

The whole circuit of the peninsula is about 120km, and takes about six hours with rests, swims and photo stops. Many places in Marmaris rent scooters by the day, most for around TL30 to TL40. The roads are steep and winding, so speed is hardly an asset. Just bear in mind that Turkey has one of the highest road traffic accident rates in the world; it's necessary to wear a helmet, and appropriate clothing is advisable to protect against road rash if you come off.

The only petrol stations on the peninsula are at Bozburun and Turunç, so it's best to fill up in Marmaris before setting out.

Dolphin Pansiyon (☎ 456 2408; www.dolphin pension.com; Kargı Mahallesi 51; s/d with half-board TL80/160) As good a reason as any to visit Bozburun, this four-year labour of love was built stone by Bozburun stone by Yılmaz (son of the indefatigable Fatma from Pembe Yunus). The 10 good-sized and pleasantly decorated rooms have balconies and sensational sea views. You can practically drop off the front porch into the Aegean, or take a daily boat excursion.

Sabrinas Haus (☎ 456 2045; www.sabrinashaus .com; d €200-300, extra bed €50) Only reachable by boat or a 20-minute walk from the Dolphin Pansiyon, Sabrinas Haus is the ultimate getaway-from-it-all place. There are 20 simple but well-designed rooms in three buildings hidden in a beautiful garden filled with mature trees, hibiscus and bougainvillea. The accommodating German owner offers kayak trips to the many deserted inlets nearby, as well as trekking trips.

EATING & DRINKING
Kandil Restaurant (☎ 456 2227; İskele Mahallesi 3; mezes TL4) On the southern corner of the town square, this local favourite serves excellent fresh fish, especially red mullet. The delicious *kalamar tava* (fried squid, TL14) is also worth a try.

Fishermen House (☎ 456 2730; İskele Mahallesi 391; mezes TL4, seafood mezes TL8, fish TL20-25 per 500g) Run by the same guy as Yilmaz Pansiyon, a local fisherman, this place offers fresh fish at the same prices. There are tables on the waterfront.

Sabrinas Haus (☎ 456 2045; İskele Mahallesi) Serving traditional Turkish Mediterranean cuisine in a lovely setting, the restaurant (in the hotel of the same name) has a refined reputation. The set menu costs TL40. Note that you can eat here as long as the restaurant's not filled with hotel guests. Call to check and for a boat to pick you up from town.

Marin Cafe Bar (☎ 456 2181; Ataturk Caddesi 56) Very chilled daytime bar with old radio, comfy couches, backgammon and sleeping dog. Drink a bottle of Efeş for TL4 and sing shanties in the early evening sun.

GETTING THERE & AWAY
Minibuses run between Bozburun and Marmaris (TL5, 55 minutes) six times a day via Selimiye year-round.

Datça

☎ 0252 / pop 10,600

The new highway winding west from Marmaris, through the Reşadiye Peninsula, dips down into the delightful harbour town of Datça. Despite being also accessible by a daily ferry from Bodrum and a weekly hydrofoil from Rhodes, Datça seems to have floated away from the big resorts. It has some good beaches and an easy-going mix of salt-stained Europeans and trendy İstanbul expats. For the short-term visitor, it's the closest town to the wind-swept ruins of Knidos, a series of undiscovered coves and the finely aged town of Eski Datça (Old Datça).

ORIENTATION

The main street, İskele Caddesi, runs downhill from the highway to a small roundabout with a big tree. Immediately before the roundabout, Buxerolles Sokak on the right has several small pensions.

After the roundabout İskele Caddesi forks left and runs to Cumhuriyet Meydanı, the main square with a market and otogar. From there it continues to the harbour, with a cluster of small pensions on the left, finally running out at the end of a short peninsula, once an island called Esenada, which features an open-air **cinema** (☼ Jun–Sep).

Datça has three small beaches: Kumluk Plajı (Sandy Beach), tucked away behind the shops on İskele Caddesi; Taşlık Plajı (Stony Beach), running west from the end of the harbour; and Hastane Altı (Hospital Beach), Datça's biggest beach.

SLEEPING

Ilıca Camping (☎ 712 3400; www.ilicacamping.com; Taşlik Plaji; per person/campervan TL25/50, 3-bed bungalow with/without bathroom TL60/40) Dusted clean and meticulously run camping ground on the eastern bay and right on the seafront. It's well shaded by eucalyptus trees, under which resident ducks waddle. It's also great for swimming in summer.

Tunç Pansiyon (☎ 712 3036; Buxerolles Caddesi; s/d TL25/50, apt for up to 5 people TL80) Terrific town pension found down the second street on the right after the *hükümet* (government) building. It's colourful and friendly, featuring sunny and spotless rooms. The owner also runs one-day car excursions to Knidos and surrounds, charging just for the petrol (TL25 for one to three people).

Villa Tokur (☎ 712 8728; www.hoteltokur.com; r TL80, 1-bedroom apt for up to 4 people TL150; ❄ ▯ ◈) A lovely elevated position, quality rooms and furnishings, and a luxurious swimming pool make this the preferred choice for tourists. Karina from Germany lives here with her Turkish husband. It's about a five- to 10-minute walk uphill from Taşlık Plajı

Villa Carla (☎ 712 3541; Kargı Koyu Yolu; s/d TL80/150; ❄ ▯ ◈) The views are the real star at this fastidious hotel a few kilometres to the west, high above town. All rooms have direct sea views and most have balconies too. At 5pm tea and Turkish pastries are served. To get here, follow the road that branches right off the main road at the foot of the mosque. Keep going for roughly 3km till you see a sign.

EATING

Zekeriya Sofrası (☎ 712 4303; İskele Caddesi 60; Turkish breakfast TL6, köfte TL7) The best home-cooked food in town, run by its namesake, the friendly Zekeriya. The servings are plentiful and the vegetable dishes are savoury sweet. It's a good place for breakfast and also does a mean *inegöl köfte* (mixed meat and lamb meatballs) to Zekeriya's own secret recipe.

Papatya Restaurant & Bar (☎ 712 2860; Kargı Yolu Caddesi 4; köfte TL10) A smart alternative to the marina haunts is this pretty old stone house, with a chic vine-covered terrace. It's about 60m up the hill from the mosque. Try the *karides güveç şarapli fırında* – shrimps oven-baked in wine.

Emek Restaurant (☎ 712 3375; Yat Limanı; mains TL12-25) There are various operators side by side above the harbour, but Emek is Datça's oldest and most reliable. The owner's son is a fisherman, which guarantees fresh fish at pleasing prices. Service is relaxed but attentive.

Fevzinın Yeri (☎ 712 9746; Ambarcı Caddesi 13/A; meals around TL15) Specialising only in fish, the theme is marine museum nautical and guests leave their comments too, but on the walls! The fish has an excellent reputation and the prices are unbeatable.

Culinarium (☎ 712 9770; Yat Limanı) The close second to Emek is the more refined Culinarium, just a couple of doors down. The tantalising three-course set menu is exquisite value at only TL35 a head. The wine list is also rather fetching.

DRINKING

Datça's nightlife centres around bars on the harbour, including:

Bolero (☎ 712 9865; Yalı Caddesi 16; beer TL4; ☼ 8am-2am) Ever popular.

Mojo Bar (☎ 712 9742; Yat Limani; beer TL4; ☼ 10am-3am) At the start – or finish – of the relaxed bar strip. The high padded stools are great for toasting the street traffic.

Nurs Gallus Garden (☎ 712 9865; admission incl drink TL10, beer TL6; ☼ 11am-4am Jun-Sep) On the hill about 150m from the beach. Shares the pleasant poolside bar and bay views with the Sound Dance Club.

Sound Dance Club (admission incl drink TL10, beer TL6; ☼ 11am-4am Jun-Sep) Next door to Nurs Gallus, it sometimes stages live music.

GETTING THERE & AWAY

Dolmuşes run to Marmaris (TL9, 1½ hours, 60km) every hour in high season, five times a day in low season. Change here for buses to other destinations. The bus companies have offices along İskele Caddesi between Buxerolles Caddesi and Kargı Yolu.

Despite what touts in Marmaris might tell you, from May to September hydrofoils sail to Rhodes (single/return TL90/180, 45 minutes) and Simi (single/return TL60/120, 15 minutes) on Saturdays, normally at 4pm. There's also a weekly ferry to Simi (one hour) leaving at the same time as the hydrofoil and for the same price.

A *gület* sails two to three times a week from Datça to Simi (TL120, 70 minutes) at 9am. If there are fewer than eight people it doesn't sail, though in high season it almost always does.

Knidos Yachting (☎ 712 9464; Yalı Caddesi 17) at the marina sells tickets for the hydrofoils, ferries and *gülets*. For Rhodes and Simi, come at 11am on the Saturday of your departure with your passport; for the *gület*, reserve by telephone. Diving trips can also be organised (TL70/110 for one/two dives per day).

From mid-June to mid-November regular ferries run daily between Bodrum and Körmen (the name of Karaköy's harbour which is about 5km from Datça on the Gulf of Gökova). From June to September, ferries leave daily for Bodrum (passenger single/return TL25/40, car and driver TL65, extra passengers TL5). In May they leave on Monday, Wednesday and Friday at 9am, and on Tuesday, Thursday, Saturday and Sunday at 5pm. In April and October they run on Monday, Wednesday and Friday and return the same days. The trip takes about two hours. From Bodrum they return on Tuesday, Thursday, Saturday and Sunday at 9am, and the rest of the week at 5pm. Tickets are sold in the **Bodrum Ferryboat Association** (☎ 712 2143;

fax 712 4239; Turgut Özal Meydanı) next to the town mosque, and there's a free bus shuttle that takes you from Datça to Karaköy.

Boat excursions to Datça often leave from Marmaris and you can sometimes buy a one-way ticket on these. Otherwise, if you can muster a group, you can hire a boat for one day (TL450 per day, maximum 10 people) or more.

Eski Datça
☎ 0252

Eski Datça (Old Datça) was once the capital of a district stretching all the way to Greece. Today it's a picturesque hamlet of cobbled streets and old stone houses, most of them lovingly restored. If you choose not to stay here, be sure to at least visit the ex-governor's house, now an upmarket hotel.

Doğa Pansiyon (☎ 712 2178; www.dogapansiyon.com; Datça Mahallesi 9; TL40/80) Has simple but spotless rooms with fridge and a little kitchenette that share a veranda overlooking the yard.

Yağhane Pansiyon (☎ 712 2287; www.dedepansiyon.com; Can Yücel Sokak; s/d TL60/100; ☒ ☲) Also known as Surya Yoga, this blissful retreat caters mostly to the chakra-centred crowd. The compact rooms are inviting and the outdoor yoga studio is an airy design coup.

Dede Pansiyon (☎ 712 3951; www.dedepansiyon.com; Can Yücel Sokak; s/d TL60/100; ☒ ☲) This 150-year-old stone house with a pool is set in a gorgeous walled garden. The six rooms have individual characters and their own little kitchen.

Mehmet Ali Ağa Konağı (☎ 712 9257; www.kocaev.com; r €190 Stone Room, €400 Mansion Room; ☒ ☐ ☲) This stunning hotel was the home of the Tuhfezade family, who were politically influential in the region for over 200 years. Their traditional Anatolian landed-gentry mansion was largely derelict when purchased in recent years by Mehmet Pir. Traces of the original mansion remain – most notably in the €700 per night Mansion Suite – and the remainder has been kept faithful in its restoration as an elite 'museum hotel'. The attention to detail is inspiring, such as the baroque fresco ornamentation of the Main Room, the scented pine throughout, and the French and Viennese antiques. The giant citrus grove is splendid and the famed restaurant, Elakı, presents rare Ottoman dishes finished by the herb garden.

With tables under a vine-clad pergola, **Datça Sofrası** (☎ 712 4188; Hurma Sokak 16; mains TL3.85-5.55) is a picturesque place for lunch or dinner.

It specialises in barbecued fish and meat. Occasionally one of the owners, Mehmet, gets out his *ney* (Turkish clarinet) for a tune or two. Cheaper is the **Karya Restoran** (☎ 712 2253; Datça Mahallesi; mains TL5-6) on the main square, with tables inside and outside.

GETTING THERE & AWAY

From Datça to Eski Datça (TL2), minibuses run every hour on the hour from May to October. From Eski Datça to Datça, they run every half-hour on the hour. In low season, they run every two hours. From June to August hourly buses run into the village from Datça.

Knidos

The **ruins of Knidos** (admission TL8; ☒ 9am-6pm), the once prosperous Dorian port city of 400 BC, are scattered along 3km at the end of a peninsula occupied only by goatherds, their flocks and the occasional wild boar. The setting is dramatic: steep hillsides terraced and planted with groves of olive, almond and fruit trees rise above two picture-perfect bays in which a handful of yachts rest at anchor.

The winds change as one rounds the peninsula and ships in ancient times often had to wait at Knidos for favourable winds, giving it a hefty business in ship repairs, hospitality and trading. The ship taking St Paul to Rome for trial was one of the many that had to hole up a while in Knidos.

Few of the ancient buildings are easily recognisable, but you can certainly appreciate the importance of the town by exploring the site. Don't miss the **temple of Aphrodite** and the **theatre**, the 4th-century BC **sundial** and the fine carvings in what was once a Byzantine church. The guardian will show you around for a small tip.

The ruins aside, Knidos consists of a tiny *jandarma* (police) post with a phone for emergencies, a couple of places to eat and a repository for artefacts found on the site. Overnight stays in the village are not allowed, so there are no facilities. You can swim in the bays from wooden piers, but the beaches are several kilometres out of town.

GETTING THERE & AWAY

Knidos Taxi, near Cumhuriyet Meydanı in Datça, will take up to three people from Datça to Knidos and return, with up to two hours' waiting time, for TL100.

Ask in Datça harbour about excursions to Knidos. Boats tend to leave around 9am or 9.30am and return in the early evening, and cost about TL25 per person.

KÖYCEĞİZ

☎ 0252 / pop 7,550

The star attraction here is the beautiful and serene Lake Köyceğiz. As it's so tough to rival the Med, this farming town attracts only modest tourism, and still depends mostly on citrus fruits, olives, honey and cotton for its livelihood. This region is also famous for its liquidambar trees (frankincense trees), source of precious amber gum. Despite its sleepiness, the surrounding Köyceğiz-Dalyan Nature Reserve has a growing reputation among outdoor types for its excellent hiking and cycling. Köyceğiz town can also be reached by an easy boat trip across the lake from Dalyan.

Orientation & Information

The otogar is near the highway turn-off, about 2.5km from the waterfront. The main street, Atatürk Bulvarı, runs from the highway past the police station to the main square. When you reach Kordon Boyu, the road skirting the lake, turn right (west) to find several pensions and restaurants, and some fine mature eucalyptus trees. The local market is held every Monday near the police station.

The **tourist office** (☎ 262 4703; ☒ 8.30am-7pm Mon-Fri), next to Köyceğiz Öğretmenevi (Teacher's Lodge) on the main square's eastern edge, stocks a simple map. Nobody speaks English.

Sights & Activities

This is a town for strolling. Hit the lakeshore promenade and walk past the pleasant town park, shady tea gardens and several restaurants. You can rent out bicycles from most pensions, so take a ride out to the surrounding orchards and farmland. The road along the western shore of the lake to the Sultaniye mud baths (p350) and Ekincik (opposite) offers superb views of the lake. It's 35km by road to the mud baths or, if you can take a boat excursion from the promenade, it's eight nautical miles away on the lake's southern shore.

There's a small **waterfall** about 7km west of town, where locals go for a spot of bathing. Take any minibus heading west towards Marmaris and Muğla and tell the driver you want to get off at the *şelale* (waterfall). It's near the 'Arboretum' sign if they miss it. The waterfall is about 800m from the highway.

You can take **boat trips** to Dalyan and the Kaunos ruins for TL20 to TL30 per person including lunch; the vessels line up on the waterfront.

Sleeping

Most of the accommodation lies west of the mosque.

Fulya Pension (☎ 262 2301; fulyapension@mynet.com; Ali İhsan Kalamaz Caddesi 100; s/d TL20/40; ✄ ▢) The bubbly young owner keeps Fulya safe as a brilliant budget option. Rooms are clean and cheap, all have balconies and there's a large roof terrace. Bikes are available free of charge, and boat trips (TL15) to the local attractions, including lunch, are a bargain.

Flora Hotel (☎ 262 4976; www.florahotel.info; Kordon Boyu 96; s/d/apt TL20/40/60; ✄ ▢) The foyer is filled with flags in tribute to the foreign guests who often come for arranged walks into the nearby Gölgeli Mountains. The rooms here have only side views of the lake, however, while apartments sleep two adults and two children.

Tango Pansiyon (☎ 262 2501; www.tangopension.com; Ali İhsan Kalmaz Caddesi 112; dm/s/d per person TL15/30/50; ✄ ▢) Managed by the local school sports teacher, this place is big on activities including day and night boat trips (TL20), trekking (TL25) and rafting (YT45). Prices include lunch and transfers. Rooms are bright, cheerful and well maintained, and there's a pleasant garden. It's next door to Fulya, and you may need to book.

Alila Hotel (☎ 262 1150; Emeksiz Caddesi 13; s/d high season TL40/70; ✄ ▣) By far the most character-filled hotel in town, 12 of the Alila's rooms also boast direct views of the water. The friendly owner Ömer, who built the hotel, runs the place professionally and attends to every detail (right down to the swan-folded towels).

Panorama Plaza (☎ 262 3773; www.panorama-plaza .net; Cengiz Topel Caddesi 69; s/d TL60/90; ✄ ▣) The Panorama is an ugly building with an outdated, cheesy lobby, but the rooms here are spiffy and well priced, while the swimming pool is five-star. Plus there's free sailing for guests. The only downside is the location 1km west of town.

Eating

There are lots of cheap and cheerful restaurants off the main square.

Mutlu Kardeşler (☎ 262 2480; Tören Alanı 52; soup TL3, köfte TL5, kebap TL6, pide TL2-3; ✄ 7am-1am) Funky in a rural kind of way, this simple place off the main square is much loved locally and has tables on a little green and shaded terrace out the back.

Colıba (☎ 262 2987; Cengiz Topel Caddesi 64; köfte TL6; ✄ 10am-1am) In the 'sweet little house', cool-headed staff serve delicious *ordövr* (mixed meze platter) to young couples and businessmen. The house speciality is *alabalık* (trout, TL15), though the grills (TL9) are a bargain. Whitewashed and wooden, it has a shaded terrace with views of the lake front. It's about 100m from the Alila Hotel.

Pembe Restaurant (☎ 262 2983; Cengiz Topel Caddesi 70; meals around TL8-10) Next door to Colıba is the Pembe, housed in a pink and purple building and does cheap seafood and meat dishes.

Thera Fish Restaurant (☎ 262 3514; Cengiz Topel Caddesi 1; fish per 350g TL14-25; ✄ 9am-midnight) Pick your fish from the large tank at the counter (don't order the owners' pets!) of this long-time local favourite. The red mullet fillets (TL8) are excellent value, likewise the bream (TL9). The Thera also has a waterfront terrace.

Getting There & Away

Most buses will drop you at the Köyceğiz otogar on the outskirts of town, 2.5km from the lake. Dolmuşes (TL1) run every 15 minutes between the otogar and town.

Dolmuşes also run to Dalaman (TL4, 30 minutes, 34km), Marmaris (TL5, one hour, 60km) and Ortaca (TL2.50, 25 minutes, 20km) every half-hour. Buses run to Fethiye (TL8, 1¾ hour, 95km) every half-hour.

EKİNCİK

☎ 0252 / pop 860

Ekincik is a beautiful lakeside village 36km south of Köyceğiz that offers genuine peace and quiet. It's surrounded by high pine-clad hills pitching down to a long, crescent-shaped gravel beach. It's a lovely place – isolation is its strength.

Sights & Activities

Outside the Lycian Way, Ekincik is arguably the best base for **trekking** on the western Med. Ahmed at Hotel Akdeniz is the go-to-guy for information.

You can also hire boats from the **Ekincik Boat Cooperation** (☎ 266 0192; ✄ 9am-7pm May-Oct) on the southern side of the beachfront. Trips are for three hours (to Kaunos, TL200 for up to 12 people), six hours (Kaunos and Dalyan, TL240) and a full day (Kaunos, hot springs, turtle beach etc, TL300). For swimming, try the municipality-run **Köyceğiz Belediyesi Restaurant ve Halk Plaji** (☎ 266 0001; Ekincik Köyü Bulvarı; meals TL5-15; ⊙ mid-Apr–mid-Sep) which has showers, sun lounges and tables, as well as cheap drinks and meals.

Sleeping & Eating

Ekincik Pansiyon (☎ 266 0179; fax 266 0003; s/d half-board TL40/60; ❄) A real bargain set 350m from the beach, this spotless, family-run pension has neat rooms and a pleasant shaded area outside under trees, with tables and hammocks. It's just to the right of the main road.

Hotel Akdeniz (☎ 266 0255; www.akdenizotel .com; s/d TL20/40, half-board TL40/80; ❄) A real bargain, the Akdeniz has cool, clean and light-filled rooms with tiled floors and balconies. Ahmed, the friendly owner, can guide you on treks in the mountain pine forests or organise picnics. There's also a roof terrace with sweeping views of the sea and surrounding landscape. It's just uphill from the Ekincik Pansiyon,

Ekincik Hotel (☎ 266 0203; www.hotelekincik .com; Ekincik Köyü; per person TL80-100; ❄) Recently renovated, this waterfront *butik* hotel is well designed and features a much-loved garden. All rooms have balconies and nine have direct sea views.

Ship A Hoy (☎ 266 0045; Ekincik Köyü; mezes from TL5, mains TL20-25; ⊙ 8am-midnight Apr-Oct) A fairly fancy restaurant serving freshly caught fish (TL15 to TL20 per 500g) under giant white parasols and grass-roofed huts. It's next to the Ekincik Pansiyon right on the beach.

For cheap eats, there are plenty of cafés and stalls selling snacks and *tost* (toasted sandwiches, TL2) along the seafront in summer.

Getting There & Away

Ekincik is tricky to get to without a car. During the school holidays (mid-June to early September), a bus leaves the Köyceğiz main square (not the otogar) at 9.30am daily (TL4, one hour). It returns from Ekincik at 6pm.

DALYAN

☎ 0252

Dalyan is a laid-back river-mouth community with a strong farming pedigree and a growing penchant for tourism. It makes

an entertaining base for exploring the surrounding fertile waterways, in particular the popular turtle nesting grounds of Iztuzu Beach and Lake Köyceğiz. Dalyan's most famous feature is the impressive cliff-side ruins of ancient Kaunos, which peer down on the pretty willow trees and bougainvillea that wilt on hot, windless days. Dalyan is just resisting the lure of package tourism, although on summer afternoons as the cruise boats shuttle through the reed beds, raising both volume and prices, you get the feeling the Dalyan folk won't dally on the fringe for much longer.

Orientation

It's about 10km from the highway at Ortaca to Dalyan's Cumhuriyet Meydanı (main square) between the mosque and the PTT. Minibuses stop behind the square, near the large Atatürk statue and pair of concrete turtles.

The river runs along the west side of town. The preferred stretch of hotels is found along Maraş Caddesi, a 1km southbound road that ends at a sharp bend in the river.

Information

There's an ATM on the southeastern side of the PTT building in the centre.

Tourist office (☎ 284 4235; Maraş Caddesi 2/C; ⊙ 8am-noon & 1-5pm Mon-Fri winter, 8am-7pm summer) Seeking new premises at the time of writing.

Ünsal Internet Café (Karakol Sokak 23/A; per hr TL2; ⊙ 8.30am-midnight) East of Maraş Caddesi, near the police station.

Sights & Activities

KAUNOS

Founded around the 9th century BC, **Kaunos** (admission TL8; ⊙ 8.30am-5.30pm) became an important Carian city by 400 BC. Right on the border with the Kingdom of Lycia, its culture reflected aspects of both kingdoms. The **tombs**, for instance, are in Lycian style (you'll see many more of them at Fethiye, Kaş and other points east). If you don't take a boat, walk south from town along Maraş Caddesi for about 15 minutes to get a good view of the tombs.

When Mausolus of Halicarnassus was ruler of Caria, his Hellenising influence reached the Kaunians, who eagerly adopted that culture. Kaunos suffered from endemic malaria; according to Herodotus, its people were famous for their yellowish skin and eyes. The

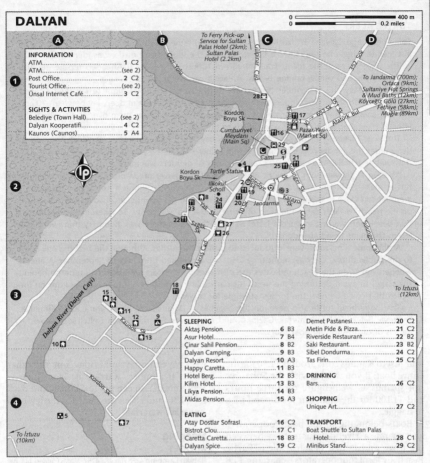

DALYAN

Kaunians' prosperity was also threatened by the silting of their harbour. The Mediterranean Sea, which once surrounded the hill on which the archaeological site stands, has now retreated 5km to the south, pushed back by silt from the Dalyan River.

Apart from the tombs, the **theatre** is very well preserved; nearby there are parts of an **acropolis** and other structures, such as baths, a basilica and defensive walls. The curious wooden structures in the river are *dalyanlar* (fishing weirs).

Two-hour guided boat trips cost around TL15. Alternatively, you might snag a willing rowboat for around TL10. Either way, your boat will arrive at the western bank; then it's a five-minute walk to the site.

BOAT TRIPS

You can save yourself a lot of money – and ensure your lira are spread evenly around town – by taking boats run by the local cooperative, **Dalyan Kooperatifi** (☎ 284 7843) located near the turtle statue. It's a fairly self-explanatory process, but if you need help, ask for Eddy.

Every day in summer, boats leave the quayside at 10am to cruise to Köyceğiz Gölü and the Sultaniye hot springs and mud baths (p350), the ruins of Kaunos (opposite) and İztuzu Beach (p350) on the Mediterranean coast. These excellent tours, including lunch, should cost around TL20 per person.

If you can drum up a team of like-minded folk, perhaps hire an entire passenger boat that holds from eight to 12 people. A two-hour

WESTERN MEDITERRANEAN

TURTLE ALERT

Some years ago Dalyan's İztuzu Beach shot to world fame when a serious threat to one of the last Mediterranean nesting sites of *Caretta caretta,* the loggerhead turtle, was identified.

The loggerhead turtle (*deniz kaplumbağa* in Turkish) is a large flat-headed reptile, reddish brown on top and yellow-orange below. An adult can weigh up to 130kg.

Between May and September the female turtles come ashore at night to lay their eggs in the sand. Using their back flippers they scoop out a nest about 40cm deep, lay between 70 and 120 soft-shelled white eggs the size of ping-pong balls, then cover them over. If disturbed, the females may abandon the nests and return to the sea.

The eggs incubate in the sand for 50 to 65 days and the temperature at which they do so determines the gender of the ensuing young: below 30°C all the young will be male; above 30°C they will be female. At a steady 30°C an even mix of genders will hatch.

As soon as they're born (at night when it's cool and fewer predators are about), the young turtles make their way towards the sea, drawn by the reflected light. If hotels and restaurants are built too close to the beach, their lights can confuse the youngsters, leading them to move up the beach towards danger instead of down to the sea and safety. So when it was discovered that developers wanted to build a hotel right on the beach there was an outcry that eventually led to the plans being abandoned.

At the same time, rules were introduced to protect the turtles. Although the beach is still open to the public during the day, night-time visits are prohibited from May to September. A line of wooden stakes on the beach indicates the nest sites and visitors are asked to sunbathe behind the stakes to avoid disturbing the nests. It's particularly important not to leave any litter on the beach that could hamper the turtles' struggle for survival.

The loggerhead turtle also nests on the beaches at Dalaman, Fethiye, Patara, Kale, Kumluca, Tekirova, Belek, Kızılot, Demirtaş, Gazipaşa and Anamur and in the Göksu Delta. See below for details of turtle-spotting boat tours.

tour just to Kaunos costs around TL50 for the entire boat; if you want to visit the Sultaniye hot springs as well, figure on three hours and TL100 for the boat, but it's a good idea to haggle.

Boats belonging to the boat cooperative also operate a 'river dolmuş' service between the town and İztuzu Beach (called 'Turtle Beach' by local tour operators), charging TL8 for the return trip. In high summer boats head out around every 20 minutes from 10am to 2pm and return between 1pm and 6pm. (In high summer minibuses make the 13km run to İztuzu by land as well and drop you at the other, less crowded end of the beach.) There are multiple kebap stands on the beach.

The boat cooperative also offers a two-hour early morning turtle-spotting tour, which leaves at 6.30am every day (TL20). Dolmuş boats also go to Kaunos three times a day (TL15 return), and to the mud baths in the early evening (TL15). The cooperatives will reluctantly pick you up from your hotel if it's on the water.

Evening sunset cruises (TL25 per person including dinner) are also offered twice a

week (Wednesday and Friday, but also other nights if numbers warrant it) from June to September. You can get to Ekincik and back for TL30, and about the same for the icy-cold Yuvarlak waterfall.

Sleeping
BUDGET

Dalyan Camping (☎ /fax 284 4157; Maraş Caddesi 144; per tent/caravan TL15/25, 2-/3-/4-person bungalows TL20/40/60; ⊙ Apr-Oct) This compact, well-shaded site is centrally located by the river opposite the tombs. The eight pinewood bungalows are simple, clean and quite attractive.

Çınar Sahil Pension (☎ 284 2402; www.cinarsahilpan siyon.com; Yalı Sokak 14; s/d TL30/50) A revelation right in the heart of town, this savvy pension has impeccably clean rooms and a terrace with possibly the best views in Dalyan. The lobby restaurant and chill-out area is first class. Ask for one of the four rooms with balconies and river views. BBQs are organised in season and a boat is rented out for TL60 per day (for up to four people).

Aktaş Pansiyon (☎ 284 2042; aktaspension@hotmail .com; Maraş Caddesi 116; s/d TL30/60; ⊠) Popular with both international and domestic tourists, Aktaş is a fine budget choice with timber rooms and a top-notch restaurant. Though the rooms are simple and small (with even smaller bathrooms), seven have river views and there's a terrace right on the riverbank.

Likya Pension (☎ 284 2233; www.likyapansion.com; Kaunos Sokak 32; s/d TL50/60; 🌐) One of the oldest pensions in Dalyan is also one of the best. Tucked down the end of Kaunos Sokak, this self-described 'peaceful and pleasant' lodging is pretty much a sure thing. The pokey rooms have recently been renovated, and there's a genuine park life vibe.

Midas Pension (☎ 284 2195; www.midasdalyan.com; Kaunos Sokak 32; s/d TL50/60; 🌐) Selçuk and Saadet Nur are wonderful hosts of this riverside pension raised on stilts. The 10 rooms are smartly decked out, with private bathrooms attached. Free pick-ups from Dalaman airport are happily arranged.

Dalyan Resort (☎ 284 5499; www.dalyanresort.com; Kaunos Sokak 50; s/d TL50/60, ste TL200; 🌐) This elegant new hotel is a short hike from the town centre. The discreet service is typically five-star, and an evening by the pool is all class. The suites, however, are a touch brochure-like.

MIDRANGE & TOP END

Kilim Hotel (☎ 284 2253; www.kilimhotel.com; Kaunos Sokak 7; s/d TL35/70; 🌐 Apr-Nov; 🌐 🌐) The active English owner Becky presides over this buzzing midrange hotel that features a pool and seating area set in a terrace shaded by old palms. Guests seem particularly at home in the spacious rooms containing king-size beds. There's a ramp for wheelchair access, complimentary use of bicycles, and daily yoga and aerobic workouts for TL5.

Asur Hotel (☎ 284 3232; www.asurotel.com; d €00-80, 🌐 May-Oct; 🌐 🌐) Award-winning architect Nail Çakırhan landed this peculiar hotel on the near-desert fringes, and it's a pretty cool place to stay. The 32 octagonal bungalows are rather Oriental-looking but are beautifully finished and each has a little veranda. There are also good-value apartments (€100) – set just around the corner – which have an equally lovely swimming pool.

Hotel Berg (☎ 284 5359; www.dalyanberghotel.com; Kaunos Sokak 20; s/d TL80/120, 🌐 🌐) Despite having an entrance like a real estate agency, the Berg is a great new addition to Dalyan. The corridor, which leads through to the open garden and waterfront, is sleek white, with

tasteful furnishings throughout, and the guest rooms are similarly chic.

Happy Caretta (☎ 284 2109; www.happycaretta.com; Kaunos Sokak 26; s/d TL80/150) National Geographic staff stay here, and so might you after a few minutes in the magical garden of cypress trees and grounded birds. Rooms are simple and smallish but stylishly decorated with natural materials. Munir, the owner, makes her own jams from her fruit trees and lays on a good breakfast.

Sultan Palas Hotel (☎ 284 2103; www.sultanpalas dalyan.co.uk; Horozlar Mevkii; s/d with half-board TL60 per person; 🌐 May–mid-Oct; 🌐 🌐) Staying at Sultan Palas is worth it for the ferry ride alone. Guests here seek solitude and slow-cooked, home-style hosting courtesy of Nil, the becalmed manager. The suite rooms are satisfyingly restrained; each with its own veranda. The food is market fresh and the swimming pool is long enough to keep restlessness at bay. To get here, either catch one of the five scheduled daily boat shuttles from town or, outside hours, call the hotel for a ferry pick-up service from a spot on the riverbank 2km north of town.

Eating & Drinking

Dalyan's restaurant scene swings between high quality and lousy value, so be selective where you eat. For a drink, keep your ears pricked along Maraş Caddesi.

RESTAURANTS

Atay Dostlar Sofrası (☎ 284 2156; Camı Karşısı 69; mains TL5-6; 🌐 6.30am-midnight) Here you'll find great staff and unbeatable prices at the local workers' restaurant where visitors are greeted warmly. There's a point-and-pick counter and dishes are fresh daily. It's opposite the mosque.

Metin Pide & Pizza (☎ 284 2877; Julariyer Sokak 3/B; pide TL2-4, pizzas TL6-10; 🌐 8.30am-midnight) This is the busiest eatery in Dalyan, thanks to its freshly made pide and pizza. There are tables in a shaded garden opposite the restaurant.

Caretta Caretta (☎ 284 3039; Maraş Caddesi 124; mezes TL5, mains incl fish TL10-20; 🌐 8am-1am Mar-Nov) Lots of wagons and wooden platforms and Nail Çakırhan designs in this larger than average signature riverbank restaurant. The *bonfile ve tavuk cığerli börek* (beef fillet with chicken livers baked in puff pastry) is still leading the impressive menu. It's a great place also for a beer (TL4).

Saki Restaurant (☎ 284 5212; Yalı Sokak; mezes TL4-8; 🌐 10am-11pm) A brilliant new location in the town centre has only enhanced the offerings of this wholesome Turkish restaurant. There's no menu; just a glass cabinet of homemade goodness care of some very proud women.

Bistrot Clou (☎ 284 3452; Pazar Yeri Sokak; mezes TL4-6; ♥ 9am-midnight Apr–mid-Oct) A familial dining experience just off Market Sq where pretty much everything is made from scratch, including the crocheted tablecloths and gourd lamps. A fine wine list accompanies a range of juicy *güveç* (casseroles, TL12 to TL20). There's jazz and traditional music most nights.

Riverside Restaurant (☎ 284 3166; Sağlık Sokak 7; mezes TL5-15, fish per 450g TL9-11; ♥ 8.30am-midnight) Considered Dalyan's best fish restaurant, the Riverside also boasts a gorgeous and breezy terrace where you can dine under mulberry trees while admiring the Lycian tombs and listening to the quack of ducks. The owner, an ex–head chef who still does his own cooking, offers exquisite seafood and fish accompanied by his own special sauces. The stuffed fish is a speciality.

CAFÉS & QUICK EATS

Tas Fırın (☎ 284 3839; Sulunger Sokak 2) Diagonally opposite the Metin, it sells good fresh bread.

Demet Pastanesi (☎ 284 4124; Maraş Caddesi 39; coffee TL2; ♥ 7.30am-midnight) With priceless pastries and tantalising Turkish puds (TL3.50), it's a great place for brekkie or for picnic preparations. The hazelnut and walnut tart (TL4) is to die for.

Dalyan Spice (☎ 284 4397; Maraş Caddesi 37; ♥ 8.30am-midnight Apr-Oct) Sells gorgeous Turkish delight (box TL8 to TL15), as well as local spices and honey. For ice cream, head for **Sibel Dondurma** (☎ 284 4363; Maraş Caddesi 43/A; 1 scoop TL1; ♥ 7am-midnight May-Oct), which sells 20 flavours, all locally made.

Shopping

Unique Art (☎ 284 4426; www.theuniqueart.com; Maraş Caddesi 42) Handmade semi-precious jewellery and ceramics, without an evil eye in sight.

Getting There & Away

There are no direct minibuses from here to Dalaman. First take a minibus to Ortaca (TL1.50, every 30 minutes in high season, every hour in low season) and change there. At Ortaca otogar buses go to Köyceğiz (TL2.50, 25 minutes, 20km) and Dalaman (TL1, 15 minutes, 5km). Dalyan's minibuses leave from the stop behind the mosque.

AROUND DALYAN
Sultaniye Hot Springs & Mud Baths

For good, dirty fun, head for **Sultaniye Hot Springs** (Sultaniye Kaplıcaları; admission TL5), southwest of Köyceğiz Gölü. These bubbling hot mud pools (temperatures can push 40°C) contain mildly radioactive mineral waters that are rich in calcium, sulphur, iron, nitrates, potassium and other mineral salts, and are said to be good for skin complaints and rheumatism. At the smaller baths just before Dalyan River joins the lake, pamper yourself with a restorative body-pack of mud in a steaming sulphur pool. It's quite an experience as strangers stand around chatting while their beauty treatments dry, before being power-showered shiny and new.

To get here, you can get a 'dolmuş boat' (TL5, 30 minutes), which leaves when full (around every half-hour in summer, every hour outside the high season).

İztuzu Beach

This 4.5km sandbar is a victory for conservationists worldwide. An excellent swimming beach accessed from the Dalyan River, İztuzu Beach has long been the target of greedy hotel developers. Fortunately, the commercial activity is limited to a few snack bars and countless sun beds. More importantly, İztuzu is one of the last nesting sites in the Mediterranean of the loggerhead turtle (see boxed text, p348) and special rules to protect the turtles are strictly enforced. To get here on your own, minibuses (TL5, 15 minutes) run from Dalyan every half-hour in high season.

DALAMAN
☎ 0252 / pop 19,600

Little has changed in this agricultural town since the regional airport was built on the neighbouring river delta. Most visitors pass straight through and bus connections are good.

It's 5.5km from the airport to the town, and another 5.5km from the town to the east–west highway. Besides seasonal flights to many European cities, there are about five daily flights from Dalaman to İstanbul year-round, costing around TL150 one way. In high season, several bus companies pick up passengers outside the airport. At other times you may need to get a taxi into Dalaman for roughly TL15.

From Dalaman's otogar, near the junction of Kenan Evren Bulvarı and Atatürk Caddesi, you can bus it to Antalya (TL15, 5½ hours, 272km), Köyceğiz (TL3, 45 minutes, 34km) and Marmaris (TL9, two hours, 120km). All routes north and east pass through either Muğla or Fethiye.

GÖCEK
☎ 0252

Göcek was once the holiday retreat of Turgut Özal, Turkey's go-getting 1980s prime minister-cum-president. Today, the village has matured into a high-end yacht spot – pop star Rod Stewart often moors here – and the attractive bay makes a relaxing alternative to Fethiye if you want to pick up the 12-island cruise (see p353). Otherwise, the steep, dry mountain backdrop adds a touch of drama to an otherwise regulation seaside lullaby. For those desperate and boat-less among us, there's a fairly scrappy swimming **beach** at the western end of the quay.

Buses drop you at a petrol station on the main road, from where it's a 1km walk to the centre. Minibuses drive down to the main square, which has a bust of Atatürk, a collection of small restaurants, a PTT and ATMs. If you're driving from Marmaris, take the new toll road (3TL) heading straight through the tunnel.

Sleeping
CAMPING
About 10km east of Göcek, **Küçük Kargı Orman İçi Dinlenme Yeri** (per tent €2.75) has camping facilities in woodland overlooking a lovely bay. About 2km further east, at Katrancı, there's another picnic and camping ground with a small restaurant on a beautiful little cove with a beach.

PENSIONS & HOTELS
Tufan Pansiyon (☎ 645 1334; Marina; s/d TL30/60) Just 25m from the sea, the family-run Tufan has small but spotless and rather sweet rooms, four of which have a shared balcony with sea views.

Başak Pansiyon (☎ 645 1024; fax 645 1862; Skopea Marina; s/d TL40/60) At the western end of the harbour, it has simple but spotless rooms with a nice veranda.

Dım Pansiyon (☎ 645 1294; www.dimhotel.com; Sokak 14; s/d TL60/100; ✿ ✉) With simple but well-furnished rooms and a pleasant terrace, medium-

sized pool and a location 30m from the beach, this is great value.

A&B Home Hotel (☎ 645 1820; www.abhomehotel .com; Turgut Özal Caddesi; s/d high season TL120/160; ✿ ✉) The smallish rooms are dolled up a bit with wallpaper and furnishings, but the real boon is the medium-sized pool on the attractive terrace. A good breakfast buffet is served.

Eating & Drinking
Can Restaurant (☎ 645 1507; Skopea Marina; mezes €1.75, seafood mezes €3-8; ✹ 7am-midnight) Set back from the seafront but with a lovely terrace shaded by an old yucca tree, this is an old local favourite that serves a great selection of mezes. The speciality is *tuzda balık* (fish baked in salt, €42 for two to three people).

West Café & Bar (☎ 645 2794; Turgut Özal Caddesi; breakfast TL10, mains TL9-15; ✹ 9am-midnight low season, to 12.30am high season) Well-named, it's Western in cuisine and Western in feel with wireless internet connection, bacon for breakfast and tarts for tea. If you're kebaped-out it's good for a change, but it's not cheap.

Anatolia (☎ 645 6941; Marina; mezes TL5-15; mains TL20-30; ✹ 7am-midnight) Has a pleasant terrace at the back of its cavernous interior and specialises in Anatolian dishes.

Dice Cafe (☎ 620 8514; Safı Villalar Önü) This snappy new bar on the marina has good mojitos (TL10) and free wireless internet.

Del Mar Cafe (☎ 620 2181; Skopea Marina) is a trendy poolside bar popular with yachties and fashionistas.

Getting There & Away
Minibuses depart every half-hour to Fethiye (TL3.50, 30 minutes, 30km). For Dalyan, change at Otacer (TL3, 25 minutes, 25km, every hour) first.

FETHİYE
☎ 0252 / pop 56,000

In 1958 an earthquake levelled the old harbour city of Fethiye, sparing only the ancient remains of Telmessos (400 BC) from its wrath. Fifty years on and Fethiye is once again a prosperous and proud hub of the western Mediterranean. It's also an incredibly low-key place for its size, due mostly to the high-rise building restrictions and the transitory nature of the *gület* gangs.

Fethiye's natural harbour, tucked away in the southern reaches of a broad bay scattered with pretty islands, in particular Şövalye

WESTERN MEDITERRANEAN

FETHİYE

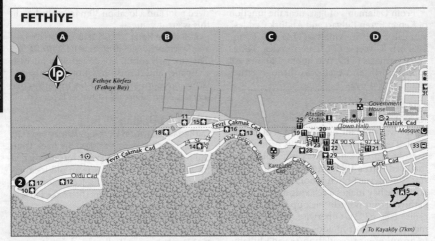

Adası, is perhaps the region's finest. About 15km south is Ölüdeniz (p365), one of Turkey's seaside hot spots, and the surrounding countryside has many interesting sites to explore, including the ghost town of Kayaköy (Karmylassos, p367), waiting in silence just over the hill.

Orientation
Fethiye's busy otogar is 2.5km east of the town centre, with a separate station for minibuses 1km east of the centre. The bulk of accommodation options are either up the hill or west of the marina. Dolmuşes run along the main street, Atatürk Caddesi. The town's Tuesday market takes place along the canal between Atatürk Caddesi and the stadium (Pürşabey Caddesi). Yachting agencies are clustered around the marina.

Information
Atatürk Caddesi has banks with ATMs and foreign exchange offices.

Tourist office (☎ 614 1527; İskele Meydanı; ❀ 10am-noon & 1-5.30pm daily May-Sep, Mon-Sat Oct-Apr) Opposite the marina, just past the Roman theatre. Open Sunday if the marina is busy enough.

Sights & Activities
ANCIENT TELMESSOS
The **Tomb of Amyntas** (admission TL5; ❀ 8am-7pm) is an Ionic temple facade carved into the sheer rock face in 350 BC. Located behind the town, it gets crowded at sunset in summer, the most pleasant time to visit. Other, smaller tombs lie about 500m to the east. Throughout the town you will notice curious Lycian stone **sarcophagi** dating from around 450 BC. There's one north of the

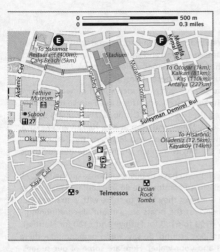

belediye and others in the middle of streets or in private gardens – the town was built around them. All were broken into by tomb robbers centuries ago.

On the hillside behind the town, just north of the road to Kayaköy, notice the ruined tower of a **Crusader fortress** built by the Knights of St John on earlier foundations dating back to perhaps 400 BC.

Behind the harbour you'll see the excavated remains of a **theatre** dating from Roman times.

FETHİYE MUSEUM

Among its most interesting exhibits, **Fethiye Museum** (Fethiye Müzesi; 505 Sokak; admission TL5; ☺ 8.30am-5pm Tue-Sun) has some small statues and votive stones (the Stelae of Graves and Stelae of Promise) and the trilingual stele (Lycian•Greek•Aramaic) from Letoön (see p372), which was used to decipher the Lycian language. It describes how King Kaunos gave money to do some good work in honour of the gods. The museum was closed for renovations at the time of research, but should reopen in 2009.

WATER SPORTS

Next to the tourist office, the friendly **Ocean Turizm & Travel Agency** (☎ 612 4807; www.ocean travelagency.com; İskele Meydanı 1; ☺ 9am-9pm) sells boat tickets, diving trips (per person including two dives, all equipment and lunch TL100) and parasailing (per person for 30 minutes including all equipment TL150).

About 5km northeast of the centre is **Çalış**, a narrow stretch of gravel beach lined with mass-produced hotels and British retirees. Dolmuşes depart for Çalış (TL1.50, 10 minutes) from the minibus station every five to 10 minutes throughout the day.

Tours

Many travellers to Fethiye not partaking in a longer cruise instead opt for the **12-Island Tour** (per person incl lunch TL25; ☺ 9am-6.30pm, mid-Apr-Oct), a boat trip around Fethiye Bay (Fethiye Körfezi). The boats usually stop at six islands and cruise by the rest, but either way it's idyllic (though be sure to check beforehand if it's booze-cruise-style). Hotels and agencies sell tickets or you can negotiate a price with the boat companies at the marina.

The normal tour (Fethiye Körfezi) visits **Yassıcalar** (Flat Island) for a stop and a swim, then **Tersane Island** for a dip in the turquoise waters and a visit to the ruins, followed by **Akvaryum** (Aquarium) for lunch, a swim and a snorkel. **Cennet Köü** (Paradise Bay) is next for a dip, followed by **Klopatra Hamamı** (Cleopatra's Bath), and finally **Kızıl Ada** (Red Island) with its beach and mud baths.

If there are too many boats at an island at the same time, itineraries may change and you may visit some of the other islands.

If you have another day or so, excellent boat tours go to or include **Butterfly Valley** (per person TL20; ☺ 9.30am-6.30pm mid-Apr–Oct) via Ölüdeniz and allow you to walk, swim and visit ruins; as well as the **Saklıkent Gorge Tour** (per person TL40; ☺ 9am-6.30pm), which includes the ruins at Tlos and walking, trout tickling and a trout lunch; and the **Dalyan Tour** (per person TL40; ☺ 9am-6.30pm), which includes a shuttle to Dalyan, a tour of the lake, Sultaniye mud baths, Dalyan, the tombs at Kaunos and beach at İztusu.

Sleeping

Fethiye has some good value midrange digs, but not much at the deluxe end.

BUDGET

Most budget places will pick you up from the bus station if you give them a call on arrival. Otherwise, regular dolmuşes marked 'Karagözler' run along Fevzi Çakmak Caddesi towards the pensions.

Ideal Pension (☎ 614 1981; www.idealpension.net; 26 Sokak 1; dm/s/d from TL20/35/40; 🖈 💻) For the past two decades Ideal Pension has provided

BLUE VOYAGES

Between the wars, writer and painter Cevat Şakir Kabaağaç lived in Bodrum and wrote an account of his idyllic sailing excursions along Turkey's southern Aegean and western Mediterranean coasts, an area completely untouched by tourism at the time. Kabaağaç called his book *Mavi Yolculuk* (Blue Voyage), a name now coopted for any cruise along these shores.

For many travellers a four-day, three-night cruise on a *gület* (wooden yacht) between Fethiye and Kale (Demre) is the highlight of their trip to Turkey. Usually advertised as a Fethiye to Olympos voyage, the boats actually start or stop at Kale and the trip to/from Olympos (1¼ hours) is by bus. From Fethiye, boats call in at Ölüdeniz and Butterfly Valley and stop at Kaş, Kalkan and Kekova, with the final night at Gökkaya Bay. A less common route is between Marmaris and Fethiye, also taking four days and three nights. Aficionados say this is a much prettier route but for some reason it's not as popular.

Food and water is usually included in the price, but you have to buy your booze on the boat. All boats are equipped with showers, toilets and smallish but comfortable double cabins (usually six to eight of them). This might make a single person uneasy if they have to share with a stranger, but in practice most people sleep on mattresses on deck as the boats are without air-conditioning.

Depending on the season the price is usually €100 to €180 for Fethiye and €180 for Marmaris per person, not at all cheap, so it makes sense to look around. Be savvy and demanding – there are many shoddy operators working the waters and your wallet. Here are some of our suggestions to avoid getting fleeced:

- Ask for recommendations from other travellers.
- Bargain, but don't necessarily go for the cheapest option because the crew will skimp on food and alcohol.
- Check out your boat (if you are in Fethiye) and ask to see the guest list.
- Ask whether your captain and crew speak English.
- Don't pay until the day you leave, just in case the weather turns foul.
- Don't go for gimmicks such as free water sports. They often prove to be empty promises and boats rarely have insurance for them in case of accidents.
- Confirm whether the boat actually uses the sails, rather than relying on a noisy diesel engine.
- Don't buy your ticket in İstanbul, as pensions and commission agents take a healthy cut.
- Trust your gut (especially if your gills turn green) – if instinct tells you that three days at sea in this boat sounds horrible, then trust yourself!
- Don't take a boat just because it is leaving today.
- Book well ahead for July and August in order to be sure of getting on a cruise.

We recommend the owner-operated outfits because they run a much tighter ship. Boats come and go just about every day of the week between late April and October (the Marmaris boats usually run twice a week from mid-May to the end of September). Competition is stiff between the following:

Almila Boat Cruise (☎ 0535-636 0076; www.beforelunch.com) Run by a Turkish-Australian couple who own two superior boats and offer the popular 12-Islands Cruise (see p353). Numbers are limited to 10 people and the food has garnered good reports.

Big Backpackers (☎ 0252-614 9312; www.bluecruisefethiye.com) A newish venture run from Ideal Pension in Fethiye and offering the Fethiye–Kale cruise.

Interyouth Hostel (☎ 0252-412 3687; interyouth@turk.net) In Marmaris, organises high-quality cruises on its own boat to Fethiye, stopping at the Dalyan mud baths and visiting the 12 islands. Numbers are limited to 12 people.

Olympos Yachting (☎ 0242-892 1145; www.olymposyachting.com) Offers a four-day/three-night cruise direct from Olympos beach to Kaş, run in conjunction with Türkmen's at Olympos (p389).

Yeşil Marmaris Travel & Yachting (☎ 412 2290; www.yesilmarmaris.com) In Marmaris, ask for the helpful Tolunay Bükülmez.

high quality, cheap beds to weary travellers. Aside from the clean (albeit small) rooms, a large terrace with bay views and a generous choice of breakfast, the owner, a retired teacher, offers various services and free boat trips for long-stays.

Tan Pansiyon (☎ 614 1584; fax 614 1676; 30 Sokak 43; s/d TL30/50) If the backpacker grind wears thin, try this traditional Turkish pension run by a charming elderly couple. Rooms are small (the bathrooms smaller), but it's sparkling clean and quiet. It's good also for self-caters, who can enjoy their creations on the fabulous terrace.

Ferah Pension (Monica's Place; ☎ 614 2816; www.ferahpension.com; 2 Ordu Caddesi 21; dm/s/d TL20/30/50; ✗ ☐) A reputation for cleanliness and expert local knowledge has long made the Ferah one of Fethiye's best. A stunning glass-enclosed terrace turns the dormitory experience into something quite special, while the greenery is reminiscent of a more rural, even tropical, escape. Also known as Monica's Place, the sizeable, tidy rooms have a real mother's touch. Call to arrange a shuttle from the otogar.

Duygu Pension (☎ 614 3563; www.duygupension.com; Ordu Caddesi 54; s/d TL30/50; ✗ ☎) This is another appealing budget option at the west end of the harbour. Colourful mosaics and carpets brighten up these small, spiffy rooms. It also boasts a roof top with blinding bay views and a small pool.

Horizon Hotel (☎ 612 3153; Abdi İpekçi Caddesi 1; dm TL20, s TL40, d TL60 depending on season; ✗ ☎) Fresh renovations should help match the Horizon to its lofty position high above Fethiye. The new management has responded to bad reports by completely refitting the 17 rooms and terrace restaurant, though the jury is still out on the service. The views, needless to say, are amazing.

MIDRANGE & TOP END

İrem Hotel (☎ 614 3006; tutantur@yahoo.com; Fevzi Çakmak Caddesi 38; s/d high season TL40/80; ✗ ☎) Quieter and more private than many, this hotel is good value and has a well-maintained medium-sized pool. Three rooms have balconies overlooking the bay.

Villa Daffodil (☎ 614 9595; www.villadaffodil.com; Fevzi Çakmak Caddesi 115; s/d TL50/90; ✗ ☎) This large Ottoman-designed guest house is one of the few older buildings to survive. The rooms have slanted ceilings and a homely feel; the best have sea views and anterooms.

The dining terrace and decent-sized pool light up in the evening, with a somewhat older travel set. Hussein, a retired colonel, is a genial manager.

Yacht Plaza Hotel (☎ 612 5067; Karagozler 1; s/d TL80/120) The large pool terrace just a fence hop from the harbour is the most pleasing aspect of this efficient and friendly large hotel. Regulars return (always a good sign), and nostalgia for the locale may overwhelm the dim corridors and somewhat gloomy rooms.

Ece Saray Marina & Resort (☎ 612 5005; www.ecesaray.net; Karagözler Mevkii 1; s €100-165, d €125-195 depending on season; ✗ ☐ ☎) Despite lacking much character, the Ece boasts good facilities including well-furnished rooms, a large pool, fitness centre, large landscaped gardens, a brilliant hamam (available for nonguests, TL80), its own supermarket, and a Wellness Centre.

Eating
RESTAURANTS

Tas Fırın (Atatürk Caddesi 150; meals TL8-12) Opposite the school, the 'Furnace' is a hit with locals who gorge on cheap grilled fish and kebaps.

Duck Pond (☎ 614 4040; Lika Sokak 15; meals TL15-20) This lively place is surrounded by a pond replete with tepid waterfall. The Turkish food is straightforward and wholesome, such as the Adana kebap (TL15), served with piles of rice and potato.

Hilmi et Balık Restaurant (☎ 612 6242; Hal ve Pazar Yeri 53; mezes TL5, fish per 400g TL15-20; ☺ 10am-midnight) Set inside the fish market building, this place does meat dishes as well as fish (its speciality) and is a firm favourite locally. You can also bring-your-own (see boxed text, p356).

Yakamoz Restaurant (☎ 612 4226; Yeni Kordon Dolgu Sahası; meals TL20-25) Huge portions of somewhat pricey fish are dished up at this atmospheric restaurant on the promenade. The traditional Turkish menu will grab some; the sunset cocktails on the big cushions will grab others. It's 1km east of the centre.

Meğri Restaurant (☎ 614 4040; Lika Sokak 8-9; meals TL20-30; ☺ 9am-midnight) The Meğri is spread throughout a leafy covered bazaar decorated with traditional artefacts. The enormous menu is a little inconsistent (though the Italian dishes are a nice change), but the service is flash and friendly. Nearby shops open late for mid-meal browsing.

Kizilada Lighthouse Hotel (☎ 686 4686; www.kizilada.com; ☺ 9am-midnight) The historic lighthouse on Red Island has just been restored and

BYOF – BRING YOUR OWN FISH

One way to taste Fethiye's fabulous fish without losing too many Turkish lira is to bring your own! Follow fishy smells to find the market, browse what's on offer, check the day's prices chalked up on the boards, then take your time choosing. Next, ferry the fish to one of the rows of restaurants that surround the market – pick the most popular – and ask them to cook it. A nominal cover charge of just €2.75 is levied, but this will procure you a green salad, bread with garlic butter, a sauce to accompany the fish, and fruit and coffee; it's a bargain fit for a king.

reopened as a restaurant. This is a wonderfully romantic place. You can arrange a pick-up from Ece Say Marina Resort.

CAFÉS
Café Oley (☎ 612 9532; 38 Sokak 4; breakfast €3.35-6, meals TL8-10; ☺ 8am-midnight; ▣) The superstar Atilla is famed for her smoothies, Vegemite and pancakes (served separately!). There are also good salads and sandwiches. Customers have free internet access and there's a book exchange.

Özsüt (☎ 612 9989; Atatürk Caddesi; ☺ 8am-1am) Serving the usual tantalising Turkish puds and pastries, this excellent chain also sells good ice cream (TL1 per scoop).

QUICK EATS
Nefis Pide (☎ 614 5504; Eski Cami Sokak 9; meals TL5; ☺ 9am-midnight) Stark and simple but sparkling clean, this popular place does delicious pides (TL3 to TL6). It's right next to the mosque – and doesn't sell alcohol!

Paşa Kebab (☎ 614 9807; Çarşı Caddesi 42; mezes TL3-4, pide TL2-6, pizza TL8-10; ☺ 9am-midnight) Considered locally to offer the 'best kebaps in town', this honest and unpretentious place has a well-priced menu (with useful little photos of dishes!). Try the Paşa special (TL10) – a delicious oven-baked beef, tomato and cheese concoction.

Meğri Lokantasi (☎ 614 4047; Çarşı Caddesi 26; mains TL14-25; ☺ 8am-2am low season, 8am-4am high season) Packed with locals who spill onto the streets, the Meğri does excellent and hearty home-style cooking at very palatable prices. The *güveç* (casseroles, TL12 to TL20) are something of a speciality.

Drinking & Entertainment
Fethiye's bars and nightclubs are mostly cheek-by-jowl on one little street, Hamam Sokak, just off İskele Meydanı.

Ottoman Dancing Bar (☎ 612 9491; beer TL5; ☺ noon-4am) Decorated to the extreme *à l'Ottoman*, this is a long-time favourite with both locals and travellers who come to drink or smoke a nargileh (water pipe, TL12) on the comfy outdoor seating.

Car Cemetery (☎ 612 7872; Haman Sokak 25; beer TL4; ☺ 10am-3am) British-pub-meets-club, this place is particularly popular with locals and rarely reports a dull night.

Val's Bar (☎ 612 2363; Müge Sokak; beer TL4; ☺ 9am-1am) English Val has been keeping the local expat community well informed and happily quenched for 18 years. Her cute little bar stocks a mean selection of poison and suitably strong coffee. It's near the new Cultural Centre.

M & M Bar (Haman Sokak 30; beer TL5; ☺ noon-3am) More straight-up Euro-techno for your jumping up and down pleasure in this fun establishment next to Car Cemetery.

Club Bananas (☎ 612 8441; beer TL5; ☺ 10pm-5am) Any venue where staff set fire to the bar then dance on it is hard to overlook on a big night out. Bananas is Fethiye's premier party joint – expect foam parties, random remixes and TL10 cover charge on the busiest nights. It's housed one block north of Hamam Sokak.

Shopping
Unique Exclusive (☎ 612 9515; 37 Sokak 4; ☺ 9am-8pm) The Unique emporium, popping up throughout the arcade, includes separate stores dedicated to silver, art, fashion, bric-a-brac and even real estate. The Exclusive store is a carpet specialist, with a stunning selection of quilts and tapestries. Like everywhere, bargain hard.

Getting There & Away
Fethiye is hemmed in by mountains, so for northbound buses, you must change at Antalya or Muğla. Buses from the otogar to Antalya (TL20, 7½ hours, 295km) head east along the coast at least every hour in high season, stopping at Kalkan (TL7, 1½ hours, 81km), Kaş (TL8, 2½ hours, 110km) and

(Continued on page 365)

Turkey's Outdoors

Test your rafting skills on the Çoruh River rapids (p578)

Need a break from monuments and historic sites? You've come to the right place. Turkey offers a wide array of activities, from the hair-raising to the serene: you want to shoot down a river in a raft? Swim over archaeological remains? Tackle challenging summits? Explore the countryside on horseback? No problem, it's all here. If we still haven't piqued your interest, fear not as Turkey's outdoor pursuits don't stop here. Whether you're an aspiring kayaker or a dedicated skier, you'll find superb playgrounds. And of course, let's not forget about Cappadocia's legendary hot-air balloon trips. If you want to customise your itinerary around the outdoors, the best outdoor-friendly areas in Turkey are Cappadocia, the western Med, eastern Anatolia and, for water sports, the south Aegean. Good safety standards can be expected whatever activity you choose, provided you stick to reputable operators who employ qualified, English-speaking staff.

The good thing with Turkey is that epicurean indulgences are never far away. After all that exertion, few things could be better than gobbling up a baklava (or two) or relaxing in the nearest hamam. The thrill of the outdoors, good food and well-being: what a great combination.

WALKING & TREKKING

Walking in Turkey is increasingly popular among both Turks and foreigners, and a growing number of specialist firms in Europe offer walking holidays here. The country is blessed with many mountain ranges, from the Taurus ranges to the Kaçkars in the Pontic Alps, among others, which all provide fabulous hiking opportunities. Hiking is also the best way to visit those places and villages that are rarely seen by holidaymakers and it will give you a taste of life in rural Turkey.

Mt Ararat (p595) offers amazing views and fantastic landscapes

IZZET KERIB

Snow-covered, beautiful Cappadocia
DALLAS STRIBLEY

SADDLE UP!

Cappadocia (p512) is *the* top spot in Turkey for horse riding. Numerous good riding tracks criss-cross the region's marvellous landscapes, and a number of reputable outfits are ready to take you on a guided ride ranging from one-hour jaunts to week-long, fully catered treks. The best thing about horse riding in Cappadocia is that you can access terrain you can't get to otherwise – a wise (and ecofriendly) way to escape the crowds.

Hiking options range from challenging multiday hikes, such as Mt Ararat, Turkey's highest summit, to gentle afternoon strolls, such as in Cappadocia. There is something for all tastes and abilities.

A word of warning: bar a couple of well-known and well-maintained trails, most trails are not signposted and it's recommended to hire a guide. Be aware that weather conditions can fluctuate quickly between extremes, so come prepared and check out the local conditions before setting off.

For more information, click on www.trekkinginturkey.com.

Day Walks

For half- or full-day walks, Cappadocia is unbeatable, with a dozen valleys that are easily negotiated on foot, around Göreme (p502) and Ihlara (p528). What about the Love Valley (p502), darling? Walking is the best way to do the region's surreal landscapes and sights justice and discover areas that travellers usually don't touch. And there aren't many places in the world where can you take a walk along a string of ancient, rock-cut churches set in a lunar-like landscape. These walks, all two to four hours in length, with minor gradients, are perfectly suited to casual walkers and even families.

Waymarked Trails

Turkey has two iconic long-distance trekking routes, the Lycian Way and the St Paul Trail. Both trails are waymarked and described in detail in two walking guides, *Lycian Way,* by Kate Clow, and *St Paul Trail,* by Kate Clow and Terry Richardson. Also check out www.lycianway.com.

Chosen by the *Sunday Times* as one of the world's 10 best walks, the Lycian Way is about 500km long and extends between Fethiye and Antalya, partly inland, partly along the coast of ancient Lycia, via Patara, Kalkan, Kaş, Finike, Olympos and Tekirova. Highlights include stunning coastal views, pine and cedar forests, laid-back villages, ruins of ancient cities, Mt Olympos and the Baba Dağ.

The St Paul Trail is also 500km long, from Perge, 10km east of Antalya, to Yalvaç, northeast of Lake Eğirdir. It partly follows the route walked by St Paul on his first missionary journey in Asia Minor. It's a bit more challenging than the Lycian Way, with more ascents. Along the way you'll pass canyons, waterfalls, forests, a medieval paved road, Lake Eğirdir, a Roman aqueduct (p320) and road, and numerous quaint villages.

You don't have to walk these trails in their entirety; it's easy to bite off just a small chunk. Both routes are best done in spring or autumn.

Enjoy the Kaçkars' (p563) short hiking season
JEAN-BERNARD CARILLET

HIKER'S DILEMMA: ARARAT OR KAÇKARS

Zafer Onay is a trekking guide based in Doğubayazıt. He guides hikers in the Kaçkars and on Mt Ararat. 'Mt Ararat is a great climb, but landscapes in the Kaçkars are more scenic; they form a range, which means you can expect more diversity. It's more colourful, you can watch flowers and, if you're lucky, you can spot bears and ibex. Birdwatching is also an option in the Kaçkars.'

Mountain Walks

Turkey is home to some seriously good mountain walking. Turkey's highest mountain, the majestic and challenging Mt Ararat (5137m; p596), near the Armenian border, is one of the continent's top climbs and can be tackled in three days (but preferably four). You'll need to be cashed up and patient with all the bureaucracy (a permit is mandatory). To acclimatise, start with the nearby Süphan Dağı (4434m; p644). Also in eastern Anatolia, the Kaçkars (p563 and p579) are increasingly popular with Europeans. They offer lakes, forests and varied flora, at altitudes ranging from 2000m to 3937m. The Trans-Kaçkar Trek can be tackled in four to five days and connects the north slopes of the Kaçkars with Barhal Valley, near Yusufeli.

Cappadocia also has a few good mountain walks, including Mt Hasan (3268m; see boxed text, p530) and the Taurus Mountains in the Ala Dağlar National Park (p525).

WATER SPORTS

Forget lounging on a white-sand beach – there are too many opportunities to dip your toes in the sea.

Scuba Diving

OK, the Red Sea it ain't, but where else in the world can you swim over amphoras and broken pottery from ancient shipwrecks? Turkey also offers a wide choice of reefs, drop-offs and caves. The waters are generally calm, with no tides or currents, and visibility averages 20m (not too bad by Mediterranean standards). Pelagics are rare, but small reef species are prolific. Here you can mingle with groupers, dentex, moray eels, sea breams, octopus, parrot fish, as well as the occasional amberjack, barracuda and ray. You don't need to be a strong diver; there are sites for all levels of proficiency. For experienced divers, there are superb expanses of red coral to explore (usually under 30m of water).

There are four major spots in Turkey that have a deserved reputation for fine scuba diving: Bodrum (p269), Marmaris (p336), Ayvalık (p210) and Kaş (p381). The standard of diving facilities is high, and you'll find professional dive centres staffed with qualified instructors who speak English. Most dive centres are affiliated with internationally recognised dive organisations.

Compared to other destinations in the world, diving in Turkey is pretty cheap, and it's also a great place to learn. Most dive companies offer introductory dives for beginners and reasonably priced open-water certification courses.

While it is possible to dive all year, the best time is May to October, when the water is at its warmest (you can expect up to 25°C in September).

Sea Kayaking & Canoeing

Look at the map of Turkey. See the tortuous coastline in the western Mediterranean part of the country? So many secluded coves, deep blue bays, pine-clad mountains, islands shimmering in the distance, laid-back villages… Paddling is the best way to experience the

Canoe in the paradise that is Butterfly Valley (p368)

GEOGPHOTOS / ALAMY

PARAGLIDING

Picture yourself, comfortably seated, gracefully drifting over the velvety indigo of the sea, feeling the caress of the breeze on your face... Paragliding from the slopes of the Baba Dağ (1960m) in Ölüdeniz (p365), which has consistently excellent uplifting thermals from late April to early November, is top notch. For beginners, local operators offer tandem flights, for which no training or experience is required. You just have to run a few steps and the rest is entirely controlled by the pilot, to whom you're attached with a harness. Though less charismatic than Ölüdeniz, Kaş (p381) is another mecca for paragliders, who take off from the 1000m-high Mt Assas.

breathtaking scenery of the aptly named Turquoise Coast and to comfortably access pristine terrain. Take the Sunken City in Kekova (p385): this magical spot – think Byzantine ruins partly submerged 6m below the sea – perfectly lends itself to a sea-kayaking tour from Kaş (p381). This superb day excursion, suitable for all fitness levels, allows you to glide over underwater walls, foundations and mosaics dating back to the 2nd century, clearly visible through crystal-clear waters.

Another draw is that you can disembark at places that are not accessible by road – ideal if you need to find your own slice of paradise. Adding excitement to the journey, you might see flying fish and turtles and, if you're really lucky, you might even come across dolphins frolicking around your kayak.

Day trips are the norm, but longer tours can be organised with overnight camping under the stars on deserted beaches. They include transfers, guides, gear and meals.

You could also try canoeing in Patara (p373). Canoeing trips on the Patara River offer the unique opportunity to row past jungle-like river banks and discover a rich ecosystem, with birds, crabs and turtles. The fact that you end your journey on splendid Patara beach adds to the appeal.

Canyoning

Canyoning is a mix of climbing, hiking, rappelling, swimming and some serious jumping or plunging down water-polished chutes in natural pools, down river gorges and waterfalls. Experience is not usually necessary. Water confidence and reasonable fitness are an advantage. Adventure centres that offer canyoning provide wetsuits, helmets and harnesses, and all canyoning outings are led by a qualified instructor. The top spot for canyoning in Turkey is the 18km-long Saklıkent Gorge (p371), near Fethiye. It features jumps, leaps in natural pools, scrambling over rocks and rappelling.

White-Water Rafting

Come to Yusufeli in June or July for fantastic white-water rafting. Thanks to rugged topography and an abundance of snowmelt, the iconic Çoruh River offers world-class runs with powerful Class 2 to 5 rapids to really get the blood racing. An added thrill is the breathtaking scenery along the sheer walls of the Çoruh Gorge. The fainter of heart can take a mellow but equally scenic float trip on the upper Barhal River, which flows into the Çoruh. Trips can last from three hours to a week.

Although they can't compare with the Çoruh River, other prime spots include gentler rapids near Çamlıhemşin (p565) and the Zamantı River in Cappadocia's Ala Dağlar National Park (p525). If you're in the western Med, try Saklıkent Gorge (p371) near Fethiye or the Köprülü Kanyon (p404) near Antalya.

It's particularly important to choose an operator that has the experience, skills and equipment to run a safe and exciting expedition. Stick to the more reputable ones. Your guide should give you a comprehensive safety talk and paddle training before you launch off downstream.

Windsurfing & Kitesurfing

The sixth leg of windsurfing's 2008 world cup was held in Alaçatı (p235) on the Çeşme peninsula, and it's no wonder. The combination of constant, strong breezes (around 16 to 17 knots) and a protected, 500m-long and 400m-wide shallow area with calm water conditions from mid-May to early November make this place a world-class destination for windsurfers. It's also an ideal place to learn the sport, with a wide array of classes available. The bay is a prime spot for kitesurfing, too.

For more information check out www .alacati.de.

WINTER SPORTS

Turkey is not just a summer destination. Winter sports are also widely available (bet you didn't know that), with excellent skiing

DO YOU WANNA GÜLET?

How about a boat trip along the Aegean or Mediterranean coast? There are endless possibilities – ranging from day trips out of Kuşadası, Bodrum, Marmaris, Fethiye, Antalya and all the smaller places in between – for chartering a graceful *gület* (wooden yacht) for a week-long tour of the coastline. The most popular option is probably the four-day, three-night boat trip from Kale (near Olympos) to Fethiye or vice versa (p354).

Gülets moored in Kuşadası (p253)

WAYNE WALTON

(*kayak* in Turkish). Don't get us wrong; it ain't the Alps, but powder junkies will be genuinely surprised at the quality of the infrastructure and the great snow conditions from December to April. Whether you're a seasoned skier or an utter novice standing in snow for the first time, there are options galore. Most ski resorts have been upgraded in recent years and now feature good facilities, including hotels equipped with saunas, hamams and even indoor pools. Best of all, prices are considerably lower than in any resort in Western Europe and the vibe is more unpretentious and family-oriented. Locals form a significant portion of the clientele, though Russians, people from the Middle East as well as Germans account for a growing share of the skiing crowd. Off the slopes there's a thriving nightlife. Ski resorts in Turkey are probably the most liberal spots in the country, with clubs and licensed bars in the resorts (steaming mulled wine!).

The biggest and most renowned ski resort is Palandöken (p575), on the outskirts of Erzurum. Shadowed by Palandöken's popularity, the low-key resort of Sarıkamış (p592), near Kars, is the most scenic of the lot, surrounded by vast expanses of conifers. It's famous for its reliable snow pack and sunny skies. Snowboarders are also catered for.

Other places to consider include Tatvan, on the slopes of Nemrut Dağı (the one near Van; p642), Uludağ (p300, near Bursa), Davraz Dağı (p315, near Eğirdir), and Erciyes Dağı (above Kayseri), though they're a bit more compact.

Most hotels offer daily or weekly packages that include lift passes and full board. Rental of skis, boots and poles is available, as is tuition, though English-speaking instructors are hard to find.

Cross-country skiing is also popular in Sarıkamış, with a network of groomed tracks that snake around the forest. Snowshoeing is available in Cappadocia, Sarıkamış and Mt Ararat.

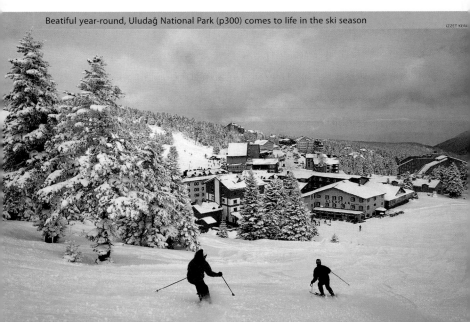

Beatiful year-round, Uludağ National Park (p300) comes to life in the ski season

IZZET KERI

(Continued from page 356)

Olympos (TL15, five hours, 219km). The inland road to Antalya (TL16, four hours, 222km) is much quicker.

For intermediate destinations, go to the minibus station near the mosque. Here you'll find rides to Faralya, Göcek, Hisarönü, Kabak, Kayaköy (Kaya), Kemer, Kumluova, Ovacık, Ölüdeniz (stops at main otogar as well), Saklıkent and Tlos.

Getting Around

Minibuses ply the one-way system along Atatürk Caddesi and up Çarşı Caddesi to the otogar. There's a fixed charge of TL1.50 no matter how far you go. A taxi from the otogar to the pensions east of the centre costs about TL10.

A couple of agencies along Atatürk Caddesi hire out scooters for TL25 per day.

ÖLÜDENİZ

☎ 0252

About 15km southeast of Fethiye is Ölüdeniz (Dead Sea), the once cherished paradise of the western Mediterranean. With its sheltered blue-ish lagoon beside a lush national park, a long spit of sandy beach, and Baba Dağ (Mt Baba) casting its shadow across the sea, Ölüdeniz is still a naturally stunning place. Sadly, however, package tourism has spoiled much of the Dead Sea's motionless charms, and those in search of quiet will be shocked.

Today, bawdy hotel operators jostle for your custom with faux-fancy restaurants and parasailing salesmen. The beachcombing bohemians of yesteryear have been replaced, en masse, by short-breakers out for 15 minutes of fun.

Still, on the upside, Ölüdeniz is a good place to party hearty before the mellows of Butterfly Valley or Kabak. Plus it's the stepping off point for the wonderful Lycian Way, which starts from near the nicer hotels, high above the madness below.

Note that the name of the lagoon (Ölüdeniz) is becoming synonymous with the town and that asking for Belcekız may draw a blank.

Orientation & Information

The beach is very much the centre of things – pass through the package-tour colonies of Ovacık and Hisarönü till you reach it. Near the junction of the roads to Fethiye, Belcekız and to Ölüdeniz, you will find a *jandarma* post, a PTT and the entrance to the lagoon.

The road continues behind the park to several camping grounds.

To your left as you arrive, the beach promenade is closed to traffic and backed with restaurants and a tight cluster of hotels.

The wistful **Ölüdeniz Tourism Development Cooperative** (Ölüdeniz Turizm Geliştirme Kooperatifi; ☎ 617 0438; Ölüdeniz Caddesi; 8am-8pm) has an information booth on the access road just inland from the beach.

Sights & Activities
LAGOON

The **Ölüdeniz Tabiat Parkı** (Ölüdeniz Caddesi; TL2; 8am-8pm) is still a lovely place to while away a few hours on the beach with mountains soaring above you. It has been laid out with paths, showers, toilets and makeshift cafés.

BOAT TRIPS

Throughout summer, boats set out to explore the coast, charging about TL30 for a day trip (including lunch). A typical cruise might take in Gemile Beach, the Blue Cave, Butterfly Valley (see p368) and St Nicholas Island, with time for swimming. Boats to Butterfly Valley leave from the beach around 11am and return around 5pm.

PARAGLIDING

If ever you wanted to jump off a 1960m-high cliff, Ölüdeniz is the place to do it. The imposing Baba Dağ is the perfect place for paragliding. Indeed it now hosts the International Air Games each October.

The descent from the mountain can take up to 45 minutes, with amazing views over the Blue Lagoon, Butterfly Valley and, on a clear day, out to Rhodes.

Various companies offer tandem paragliding flights, but prices vary greatly according to the reputation of the company and the experience of the pilot (usually around TL150 to TL200). Don't be a cheapskate – ensure the company has insurance and the pilot has appropriate qualifications and experience. Parasailing is also possible (TL100), but is infinitely less cool.

Sleeping
BUDGET

Camping grounds are the only budget options currently in Ölüdeniz, but some offer bungalows or cabins too.

Sugar Beach Club (☎ 617 0048; www.thesugarbeach club.com; Ölüdeniz Caddesi 20; camp site per person TL10, car

ÖLÜDENİZ & BELCEKIZ

0 — 500 m
0 — 0.3 miles

To Kayaköy (15km) **A**

B

To Paradise Garden (2km); Sultan Motel (Lycian Lodge) (2.5km); Hisarönü (3km); Ovacık (4.5km); Fethiye (15km) **C**

D

Mosque

Ölüdeniz

ÖLÜDENİZ KÖRFEZİ (ÖLÜDENİZ BAY)

Ölüdeniz Tabiat Parkı

Ölüdeniz Cad

MEDITERRANEAN SEA (AKDENIZ)

Jandarma Post

Belcekız

Mimar Sinan Cad

To Beyaz Yunus Lokantası (400m); Kıdrak Faralya (6km); Kabak (14km)

To Butterfly Valley (10km)

Belcekız Beach (Belcekız Plajı)

1 Sokak

INFORMATION
Ölüdeniz Tourism Development Co-operative.................1 C3

SIGHTS & ACTIVITIES
Boat Trips.........................2 C3
Entrance to Ölüdeniz Tabiat Parkı...........................3 B2
Paragliding Companies.....4 C3

SLEEPING
Blue Star Hotel................5 C3
Hotel Mellis Hill...............6 D1
Jade Residence................7 C3
Nicholas Genç Beach........8 A1
Seahorse Beach Club.......9 B1
Sugar Beach Club...........10 B1

EATING
Buzz Beach Bar & Seafood Grill...........................11 C3
Oba Restaurant.............12 C3

ENTERTAINMENT
Beach Bar.....................13 D3
Help Beach Lounge........14 C3

TRANSPORT
Dolmuş Stand................15 C3

& caravan TL10, bungalows per person TL70, without bathroom TL35-45; Apr-Oct;) About 600m to the right of the main drag, Sugar Beach is a well-run theme park for beach party backpackers. The redesign is first class – a private strip of beach shaded by palms, shaded lounging areas, a beach bar and café. The bungalows range from basic to air-conditioned and comfortable but they're all spotless. Bikes can be hired, small shops are on site. If you're not staying here but want to hang out, it costs TL5 to use the sun lounges, parasols and showers. Dolmuşes pass along the road beside the camping.

Seahorse Beach Club (617 0123; www.seahorse beachclub.com; Ölüdeniz Caddesi; camp site per person TL10, caravan TL100-140) An excellent new boutique caravan park in fierce competition with the Sugar next door. The restaurant is superbly set in a lofted cabin, and the beach is a very short stroll away. The blue-and-white caravans are barely scratched and come with all the mod-cons. The manager will consider discounts.

Nicholas Genç Beach (617 0088; www.nicholas -hotels.com; Ölüdeniz Caddesi; s/d TL40/70) If you've ever wondered what it was like to be a caravanner,

here's your chance. This place rents out 10 small but comfortable air-conditioned caravans with fridge, satellite TV, private bathroom and even a table and chairs. It's a well run, well maintained place with a pleasant beach, though most visitors come through agencies. It lies around 1km from the town centre, past the Sugar Beach Club.

MIDRANGE & TOP END
Sultan Motel (Lycian Lodge; 616 6139; www.sultanmotel .com; s/d TL40/80;) Just off the road down to Ölüdeniz, on the left as you descend from Hisarönü (2.5km from Ölüdeniz), the Sultan acts as a starting point for the Lycian Way and rooms are in simple but spotless stone chalets, some with good views.

Blue Star Hotel (617 0069; www.hotelbluestar oludeniz.com; Mimar Sınan Caddesi 8; s/d TL50/100;) Quite attractively designed and well maintained, this two-star place is 60m from the beach. Though they're not large, the rooms are light, bright and airy and have balconies overlooking the pool.

Hotel Mellis Hill (617 0690; Belcekız Mevkii; s/d TL50/100;) This much-loved place has a large swimming pool set against a mountain, a restaurant that heats up at night and a garden with all manner of furry, sometimes shelled, friends. Rooms are well presented and very clean. The beach is a 10-minute stroll down a dirt track.

Jade Residence (☎ 617 0124; Belcekiz Mevkii; s/d TL100/200; ❲ ❑ ❳) The diminutive Jade Residence, with its eight delicately presented rooms, feels a world away from the cackle of Ölüdeniz. Its intimacy is rare, while the rooms are fitted with French doors and filled with designer decor. The pool and garden layout is an oasis of good taste – surely the best small hotel in town.

Paradise Garden (☎ 617 0545; www.paradisegarden hotel.com; Ölüdeniz Yolu; s/d TL120/200; ❲ ❳) Situated up the hill to the right just before you enter Ölüdeniz village, around 2.5km from the centre, this Eden-like place is well named. Set in a 6-hectare garden, it boasts spectacular views, three pools, a menagerie and a gourmet restaurant. Rooms are attractively furnished with authentic arts and crafts.

Eating & Drinking

Buzz Beach Bar & Seafood Grill (☎ 617 0526; 1 Sokak 1; beer TL4; mains TL10-30; ❲ restaurant 8am-midnight, bar noon-2am mid-Apr-Oct) With a nice situation on the waterfront, this place offers a wide menu from pizza and pasta to kebabs, fillet steak and seafood. At lunch time you can watch the paragliders plop down on the landing point outside. It's also a very popular nightspot.

Oba Restaurant (☎ 617 0158; Mimar Sınan Caddesi; mains TL15-25; ❲ 8am-midnight) Built like a log cabin, the restaurant of the Oba Hostel has a great reputation for home-style food at a palatable price. It also does great Turkish/European breakfasts (TL10/12) including homemade muesli with mountain yoghurt and local pine honey. Ranging from snacks to full-on mains, the menu also offers 12 veggie dishes.

Beyaz Yunus Lokantası (White Dolphin; ☎ 617 0068; Likya Yolu; beer TL6; fish per 450g TL40; ❲ 11am-midnight May–mid-Oct) Set on a stunning terrace overlooking the bay, the Beyaz is famous for its fresh fish and seafood. Sample some of the exquisite seafood mezes (TL15) such as calamari stuffed with feta, or octopus slow-cooked in red wine. Down some steps is a delightful 'Sunset Bar' – perfect for a pre-dinner aperitif. It's on the Faralya road about 1km from the town centre.

Entertainment

Help Beach Lounge (Sugar Shack; ☎ 617 0650; 1 Sokak; beer TL5; ❲ 9am-4am May-Oct) The most happening place in town, this funky joint has a large terrace with a beach bar right on the seafront with comfy cushioned benches. Happy 'hour' (cocktails TL12) is from 6pm to 8pm.

Getting There & Away

In high season, minibuses leave Fethiye for Ölüdeniz roughly every 10 minutes during the day (TL3, 25 minutes, 15km), passing through Ovacık and Hisarönü; in low season they go every 30 to 45 minutes.

KAYAKÖY (KARMYLASSOS)

☎ 0252

About 5km west of Hisarönü is Kayaköy, a beautifully eerie town of 2000 **stone houses** (admission TL8; ❲ 9am-7pm) and a ghost-filled modern past. Recently it provided the inspiration for Eskibahçe, the village in Louis de Bernieres' novel, *Birds Without Wings*, but the town's history needs no fictional embellishment.

Long known as Levissi, Kayaköy (Karmylassos) was deserted by its mostly Ottoman-Greek inhabitants after WWI and the Turkish War of Independence. The League of Nations supervised an exchange of populations between Turkey and Greece (see p40), with most Greek Muslims coming from Greece to Turkey and most Ottoman Christians moving to Greece. The people of Levissi, most of whom were Orthodox Christians, moved to the outskirts of Athens and founded Nea Levissi there.

As there were far more Ottoman Greeks than Greek Muslims, many of the Turkish towns were left unoccupied after the exchange of populations. Kayaköy, as it is called now, has only a handful of long-term Turkish inhabitants.

With the tourism boom of the 1980s, a development company wanted to restore Kayaköy's stone houses and turn the town into a holiday village. Scenting money, the local inhabitants were delighted, but Turkish artists and architects were alarmed and saw to it that the Ministry of Culture declared Kayaköy (or Kaya as it's called locally) a historic monument, safe from unregulated development. What remains is a gorgeous, timeless village set in a lush valley with some fine vineyards nearby. In the evening, when the stone houses are spotlit for visitors, Kayaköy is truly surreal.

Two **churches** are still prominent: the Kataponagia in the lower part of the town and the Taxiarkis further up the slope. Both retain some of their painted decoration and black-and-white pebble mosaic floors.

Sleeping & Eating

Selçuk Pension (☎ 618 0075; enginselcuk48@hotmail.com; s/d TL20/40) Set in flower and veg gardens, the Selçuk has rooms that are spotless, quite spacious and homely; four have lovely views of Kaya. Guests can use the swimming pool of the restaurant next door.

Villa Rhapsody (☎ 618 0042; www.villarhapsody.com; s/d TL50/80; ✪ mid-Apr–Oct; ✪) With a swimming pool set in a rather grand walled garden, this place is friendly and welcoming. Comfortable rooms have balconies overlooking the garden. Atilla and Jeanne, the Dutch-Turkish owners, can also offer advice and sketch maps on walking in the area, as well as organising bike hire. Out of season, call first.

Sarniç Café & Restaurant (☎ 618 0118; large meze plate TL4, mains TL15-20; ✪ 10am-midnight) At the foot of the ruins off the main road about 100m beyond the Selçuk Pension, this is a real find. Located in a characterful 300-year-old stone house, its menu is select, more interesting than most and superb, offering regional dishes made with the freshest local ingredients. Prices are extremely reasonable.

Levissi Garden (☎ 618 0108; www.levissigarden.com; meals TL15-25) This 400-year-old stone building has been a horse stable and mayoral residence, and is now a stunning wine house and restaurant, with a cellar that stocks over 400 of Turkey's finest drops. Spotlighting the ghostly ruins, the Levissi's kitchen stars a stone oven that ekes out slow-cooked lamb stew (TL25) and mouth-watering *klevliko* (leg of lamb cooked in red wine, garlic and herbs, TL25). The English-speaking owner is charismatic and cool, and happy to retell the history of the enchanting premises.

Kaya Wine House (☎ 618 0454; www.kayawinehouse.com; Keçiler Mahallesi; meals around TL30; ✪ 11am-midnight) Set in a shaded courtyard within a beautiful old stone house, this is a delightful place for dinner, and the traditional Turkish dishes are delicious.

Getting There & Away

Minibuses run to Fethiye (TL2.50, 20 to 30 minutes) every half-hour from mid-June to September, every hour in low season. A taxi costs TL30.

To Ölüdeniz, two to three minibuses run daily in high season, or you can go to Hisarönü (TL2.50, 20 minutes) from where minibuses go every 10 minutes to Ölüdeniz. A taxi there costs around TL30.

You can also walk here from Fethiye in 1½ to 2½ hours, depending on your route. The simplest is to follow the road that winds up behind Fethiye's fortress.

Alternatively it's about a one-hour walk downhill through pine forest from Hisarönü. Or we recommend the very pretty trail to Ölüdeniz that takes two to 2½ hours (8km).

BUTTERFLY VALLEY & FARALYA

Tucked around the coast from Ölüdeniz is the paradise-found of Butterfly Valley, where mellow young Turks doss about in hammocks and curious day trippers wish they'd packed an overnight bag. As well as being home to the unique Jersey tiger butterfly, beautiful **Butterfly Valley** (☎ 614 2619; www.butterflyvalley.com) also boasts a 60m-high waterfall (admission TL5 for nonguests), a fine beach, and some lovely walks through a lush gorge. Almost the moment the last tour boat turns back for Ölüdeniz, Butterfly Valley turns on its beguiling, neo-hippy smile.

A rocky path that's steep in places winds up a cliff to the village of Faralya, on a terrace above the canyon on the right-hand (south) side of the valley. If you take this, be sure to wear proper shoes and keep to the marked trail (indicated with painted red dots) – an Australian backpacker died here after taking a wrong turn. It usually takes an hour to ascend from the valley; 30 to 40 minutes to descend. There are fixed ropes along the path in the steepest or most dangerous parts. Faralya is on a stage of the Lycian Way walk (p359).

Faralya is the first village south of Ölüdeniz (12km away) on the Yedi Burun (Seven Capes) coast, one of the last undeveloped stretches of the Turkish Mediterranean. Until a road was bulldozed along the steep side of Baba Dağ, the village was largely cut off from the world and the residents had to be self-sufficient. The views, as you'd imagine, are unforgettable.

Sleeping

If you decide to stay in Butterfly Valley itself, you'll be getting back to nature in the aptly named **Butterfly Valley** (☎ 0538 511 6454; tent with half-board per person TL34, bungalow with half-board per person TL42). There are 16 clean, simple stilted bungalows, with thin mattresses on the floor. Be warned that these rooms bake during the summer.

For those who prefer a little new-fashioned civilisation at the end of a hard day on the chill, the following places are all above the valley in Faralya.

Gül Pansiyon (☎ 642 1145; s/d TL30/50) With its firm family feel, here you can join the old ladies for a gossip on the attractive terrace, knitting and podding peas. Though the eight rooms are simple, they're very clean and some share a veranda overlooking the valley. A bubbling pond contains trout which can be cooked up for your feast (TL15). It's the first pension you come to on the road from Ölüdeniz.

George House (☎ 642 1102; www.georgehouse.net; s/d TL30/50; 💻) Run by a charming family, the George offers mattresses in the family house, in tree houses (tented platforms) or in basic bungalows (at the same price). The home cooking is delicious and ingredients come fresh from the family's organic garden, cow or hives! It has a spring water source and a natural pool and the views are ethereal.

Melisa Pansiyon (☎ 642 1012; melisapan@hotmail .com; s/d TL40/60) Next door to the Gül, the Melisa has four well-maintained and cheerful rooms, and a pretty terrace overlooking the valley. The owner, Mehmet, speaks English and is a good source of information. Home-cooked set menus are available for TL10 to TL15.

Die Wassermühle (The Watermill; ☎ 642 1245; www .natur-reisen.de; d per person with half-board TL80, ste TL120; 🍴) This beautiful 150-year-old former wheat mill boasts a hillside setting that commands gorgeous views from its restaurant and pool terraces. The seven 'suites' are spacious and have kitchenettes. The gourmet kitchen serves six courses for dinner. To find it, take the small road heading uphill to the left immediately before the Gül Pansiyon.

Getting There & Away

You can either take a tour to Butterfly Valley from Fethiye (see p353) or Ölüdeniz (p365) or – and particularly if you want to spend the night – you can take the 'water dolmuş' (TL6.25 each way), which departs daily from Ölüdeniz May to September at 11am, 2pm and 6pm. From Butterfly Valley to Ölüdeniz, they leave at 10am, 1pm and 5pm.

Besides the rocky path connecting Faralya to Butterfly Valley, there are six minibuses

daily (TL4, 25 minutes, 8km) in summer (three in spring and two in winter) between Faralya and Fethiye. Coming from Fethiye, they call in at the minibus stand in Ölüdeniz 30 minutes later.

If you miss the bus, you can take a taxi from either Ölüdeniz or Faralya (TL25). You can also get to Faralya by scooter, though the road is steep, twisting and not quite fully asphalted yet.

KABAK
☎ 0252

The startlingly remote beach community of Kabak is slowly becoming the solitude searchers' end point. Regardless of how you make the steep, downward 40-minute trek – by tractor, trek or mule – you'll be rewarded with spectacular and empty Gemile beach flanked by two long cliffs. Eight kilometres south of Faralya – and worlds away from everywhere else – Kabak is for the camping and trekking enthusiast, yoga devotee or any doyen of quiet, untapped beauty.

The beach and almost all of the accommodation is a 25-minute walk from Faralya, which begins about 30m down from the minibus stop.

Kabak is on a section of the Lycian Way walk, described on p359.

Sleeping

Accommodation in Kabak consists of camping or tented platforms (translated from the Turkish 'wood house'). All include half-board in the price, and most open only from May to October.

Reflections (☎ 642 1020; www.reflectionscamp.com; own tent/camp tent/platform per person TL25/30/40) Built from scratch and an 'ongoing project' for American Chris and his Turkish girlfriend, this characterful place has views of the surrounding forest. The toilet, with ferns and ginger plants for decoration, boast the best views in Turkey!

Full Moon (☎ 642 1081; platform per person TL30; 🍴) The Full Moon boasts a natural swimming pool (fed with mountain spring water) and pleasant platforms that have delightful little cushioned 'verandas' that give glorious views over the bay below. They're also nicely spread out from one another and there's a platformed *köşk* (chill-out area). Take the second road down – it's the first camp you cross.

Turan Camping (☎ 642 1227; www.turancamping .com; platform with/without balcony TL50/40; 🍴) Run

---

TOP SIX SPOTS SANS SUNBED

If you prefer your beach bumming without the crowds, the following will give you both privacy and the perfect tan:

- **Selimiye** (p340) A few boats, the odd goat and a promenade – heaven is such a simple place.

- **Patara Beach** (p373) With 20km of gorgeous white sand to lie on, you can pack a hundred oversized umbrellas for all we care.

- **Kabak** (p369) Are we there yet? Are we there yet? Are we there... Wow.

- **Kaleköy** (p385) Undersea ruins to dive for (or at least paddle over). And not *quite* an island, but island-ish?

- **Kaputaş** For those who like a beach on the rocks, no people, then dinner till two in Kalkan (p374).

- **Çıralı** (p387) Up-scale and down beach from Olympos, the Baby Boomers return (near) to where it all began.

---

by the dynamic Ece and Ahmet, a young Turkish couple who fell for the place following a holiday here, the Turan has platforms with individuality (one with a tree growing inside!), lovely views and lots of mellow lounging areas. Three-week yoga courses are regularly held here, which guests are welcome to join. Meals (mainly vegetarian) are good too.

our pick **Shambala** (☎ 642 1147; www.theshambala .com; Indian tent TL40, tree house TL45, bungalow TL70-100; 🆇 🖳 🐾) On occasions you come across a place that reminds you why you love travelling. Halfway down the Kabak Valley, this newly consecrated 'sacred ground' consists of bungalows, spacious tree houses and breezy Indian tents with the ultimate sea view. There's also a beautiful swimming pool, hip bar, chilled-out hammock seats, and Shamanic healing therapy. It's greater than the sum of its parts. Call ahead to arrange pick-up, or just to thank them with all your beating heart.

Eating

Lying at the top of the valley, near the dolmuş stop (and the end of the main road) are a couple of simple restaurants.

Mamma's Restaurant (☎ 642 1071; mains TL7) Mamma's offers a couple of simple but hearty dishes as well as *gözleme* (TL3) and its own deliciously refreshing home-brewed *ayran* (yoghurt drink, TL2).

Olive Garden (☎ 642 1083; mezes TL5-10, mains TL12-15; 🕐 mid-Apr-Oct) You'll find it down a side road 100m beyond Mamma's (though she may swear it's closed!). With a heavenly and

peaceful setting and gorgeous views from the cosy hillside platforms, it's a wonderful place for a meal. It's run by the friendly Fatih, an ex-chef, and many ingredients come from his family's 15 hectares of fruit trees, olive groves and vegetable gardens. If you can't tear yourself away, it has four wooden cabins (TL40 per person with half-board).

Getting There & Away

The twisting road from Faralya is as memorable for its views as for its knuckle-whitening corners. There are minibuses from Fethiye to Kabak. For more information see p369.

TLOS
☎ 0252

On a rocky outcrop high above a pastoral plain sits one of the oldest and most important cities of ancient Lycia. Tlos' prominence was matched only by its promontory; its elevated position so effective, in fact, that the city remained inhabited until the early 19th century.

There's plenty to see here. As you climb the winding road to the **ruins** (admission TL8; 🕐 8am-6pm), look for the fortress-topped **acropolis** on the right. What you see is Ottoman-era work but the Lycians once had a fort in the same place. Beneath it, reached by narrow paths, are the familiar **rock-cut tombs**, including that of Bellerophon, a pseudo-temple facade carved into the rock face that has a fine bas-relief of the hero riding Pegasus, the winged horse. You can reach the tomb by walking along a stream bed, then turning left and climbing a crude ladder.

The **theatre** is 100m further up the road from the ticket kiosk. It's in excellent condition, with most of its marble seating intact, although the stage wall is gone. There's a fine view of the acropolis from here. Off to the right of the theatre (as you sit in the centre rows) is an ancient **Lycian sarcophagus** in a farmer's field. The **necropolis** on the path up to the fortress has many stone sarcophagi.

One of the men at the ticket kiosk will offer to guide you (for a tip) – a good idea if you want to see all the rock-cut tombs.

Set in a pretty garden with a stream, a pool, lots of shade, seating areas and birdsong, **Mountain Lodge** (☎ 638 2515; www.themountainlodge.co.uk; r per person €20-31; ☺ Feb-Dec; ⊠ 🞅) is a peaceful and attractive place designed like an old stone house. Rooms are comfy and homely (rates vary according to size) and there is a pool set on a terrace with views. Melahat (Mel) offers home-cooked set menus (€11). From the theatre, it lies 2km back down the road to the highway and another 2km up a side road; coming by minibus, get off at the village of Güneşli, and walk or hitch the 2km up the road to Yaka Köyü.

Getting There & Away

From Fethiye, minibuses travel to Saklıkent (TL4.50, 45 minutes) every 20 minutes via Güneşli (Tlos). If you are driving, follow the signs to Saklıkent from Kayadibi and watch for the yellow ancient monument sign on the left.

SAKLIKENT GORGE

The spectacular **Saklıkent Gorge** (adult/student high season TL8/4, low season free; ☺ 8am-8pm) is literally a crack in the Akdağlar Mountains. This 18km gorge, found 12km after the turn-off to Tlos, is too narrow for even sunlight to squeeze through. Luckily you can, but prep yourself for some very cold water, all year round.

You approach the gorge along a wooden boardwalk above the river that opens out into a series of wooden platforms suspended above the water. Here you can buy and eat slippery fresh trout, and watch other tourists slip and slide their way across the river, hanging onto a rope, and then slop into the gorge proper. Good footwear is essential, though plastic shoes can be hired (TL2). Guides can also be hired and it's a good place to try tubing (TL15 per person).

Sleeping

Across the river from the car park is **Saklıkent Gorge Camp** (☎ 659 0074; www.saklikentgorge.net; camp site TL10, dm on platform by river half-board TL20, tree house without bathroom s/d TL35/60; ☺ Jan-Nov; 🖳 🞅), a rustic backpacker-oriented camp with basic but clean tree houses (all have little fridges), a natural pool, bar and restaurant (fresh trout TL10, *köfte* TL12).

The camp can organise various activities (which include transport and drinks), including tubing (TL25 per person, 45 to 60 minutes), rafting (TL25/50 for 45 to 60 minutes/three hours), canyoning (TL40/100/200 for trips of six hours/one day/two days and one night, minimum four people), fishing (TL20 including guide and equipment, half a day), and trekking (TL25, five hours). Also offered are jeep safaris (TL60 including lunch and guide) and tours of Tlos (TL20) and Patara (TL20).

Getting There & Away

Minibuses run every 15 minutes between Fethiye and Saklıkent (TL4.50, 45 minutes).

PINARA

Some 46km southeast of Fethiye, near the village of Eşen, is a turn-off (to the right) for the **Pınara ruins** (admission TL3), which lie another 6km up in the mountains.

Pınara was among the most important cities in ancient Lycia, but although the site is vast the actual ruins are not Turkey's most impressive. Instead it's the sheer splendour and isolation that makes the journey so worthwhile.

Rising high above the site is a sheer column of rock honeycombed with **rock-cut tombs**. Other **tombs** are within the ruined city itself. The one called the Royal (or King's) Tomb has particularly fine reliefs, including several showing walled cities. Pınara's **theatre** is in good condition, but its **odeum** and **temples** of Apollo, Aphrodite and Athena (with heart-shaped columns) are badly ruined.

The road winds through tobacco and corn fields and across irrigation channels for more than 3km to the village of Minare, then takes a sharp left turn to climb the slope. The last 2km or so are extremely steep. If you decide to walk make sure you stock up on water first. There's a café at the foot of the slope and nothing after that.

At the top of the slope is an open parking area and near it a cool, shady, refreshing spring. The guardian will probably appear and offer to show you around the ruins – a good idea as the path around the site (which is always open) is not easy to follow. You should probably tip the guardian (about TL10).

Infrequent minibuses from Fethiye (TL3, one hour) drop you at the start of the Pınara road and you can walk to the site or plead with the driver to take you all the way. The village at Eşen, 3km southeast of the Pınara turn-off, has a few basic restaurants.

SİDYMA

About 4km south of Eşen, a rough dirt road to the left goes 12km to Sidyma, where there are some minor Lycian ruins. The village of Dodurga sits in the centre of the site, with the **acropolis** and a badly damaged **theatre** above it. Many of the old stone houses in the village incorporate building materials from the ancient city. In the village outskirts you'll find the **necropolis**, which has an interesting collection of tombs from the Roman era.

LETOÖN

The Unesco-designated World Heritage site of Letoön is home to some of the finest **ruins** (admission TL8; 8.30am-5pm) on the Lycian Way. Located 17km south of the Pınara turn-off, Letoön is often considered a double-site with the all-conquering, nearby Xanthos (right). However, with its near-permanently saturated **nymphaeum**, Letoön carries its own, somewhat soppy, romantic charm.

Letoön takes its name and importance from a large shrine to Leto, who, according to legend, was loved by Zeus and became the mother of Apollo and Artemis. Unimpressed, Zeus's wife Hera commanded that Leto spend an eternity wandering from country to country. According to local folklore she spent much of this time in Lycia, becoming the Lycian national deity. The federation of Lycian cities then built this very impressive religious sanctuary to worship her. It's possible that the shrine was originally dedicated to the Anatolian Mother Goddess.

The site consists of three **temples** side by side: to Apollo (on the left), Artemis (in the middle) and Leto (on the right). The Temple of Apollo has a fine mosaic showing a lyre and a bow and arrow. The **nymphaeum**, inhabited by frogs in ponds, is appropriate as worship of Leto was associated with water. Nearby is a large Hellenistic **theatre** in excellent condition.

Getting There & Away

Driving from Patara, the turn-off is on the right-hand (southwest) side near the village of Kumluova. Turn right off the highway, go 3.2km to a T-junction, turn left, then right after 100m (this turn-off is easy to miss) and proceed 1km to the site through fertile fields and orchards, and past greenhouses full of tomato plants. If you miss the second turn you'll end up in the village's main square.

Minibuses run from Fethiye via Eşen to Kumluova (TL5.25, 60km, 65 minutes). Get out at the Letoön turn-off and walk with your thumb (or tongue, depending on the time of day) hanging out in hope.

XANTHOS

At Kınık, 63km from Fethiye, the road crosses a river. Up to the left on a rock outcrop is the ruined city of **Xanthos** (admission TL5; 8.30am-5pm), once the capital and grandest city of Lycia, with a fine **Roman theatre** and pillar **tombs** with Lycian inscriptions.

It's a short uphill walk to the site. For all its grandeur, Xanthos had a chequered history of wars and destruction. Several times, when besieged by clearly superior enemy forces, the city was destroyed by its own inhabitants. You'll see the theatre with the **agora** opposite but the **acropolis** is badly ruined. As many of the finest sculptures and inscriptions were carted off to the British Museum in 1842, most of the inscriptions and decorations you see today are copies of the originals. However, French excavations in the 1950s have made Xanthos well worth seeing.

Follow the road round to the right to find more attractive **Lycian tombs** cut into the rock face.

Minibuses run to Xanthos from Fethiye and Kaş, and some long-distance buses will stop here if you ask.

PATARA
☎ 0242

Scruffy little Patara (Gelemiş) is the perfect spot to mix your ruin-rambling with some dedicated sand-shuffling on 20-odd kilometres of wide, golden beach. The town is not at all inundated with travellers – a miracle given its obvious attractions – and traditional village life still goes on here. The friendly locals mix easily with a small community of eccentric foreigners, all pinched pink that Patara is still largely their own.

But perhaps it's all just seasonal good fortune, for Patara was once the birthplace of St Nicholas, the 4th-century Byzantine bishop who later passed into legend as Santa Claus. Before that though, Patara was famous for its temple and oracle of Apollo, of which little remains. It was once the major port for eastern Lycia and the Eşen valley – St Paul and St Luke had to change boats here – but the harbour silted up in medieval times and became a reedy wetland.

Orientation

The Patara turn-off is just east of the village of Ovaköy; from here it's 2km to the village and another 1.5km to the Patara ruins. The beach is a further 1km past the ruins. Between June and October local minibuses trundle down to the beach from the village. In the height of summer, it's well worth swallowing your pride and grabbing a lift.

As you come into the village, on your left is a hillside holding various hotels and pensions. A turn to the right at Golden Pension takes you to the village centre, across the valley and up the other side to more pensions; go straight on for the beach and ruins.

Sights & Activities

RUINS

Admission to the **ruins** and **beach** costs TL5. Patara's ruins include a triple-arched triumphal arch at the entrance to the site with a necropolis containing several Lycian tombs nearby. Next are the baths and, much further, a basilica.

You can climb to the top of the theatre, which backs onto a small hill, for a view of the whole site. On top of the hill are the foundations of a Temple of Athena and an unusual circular cistern, cut into the rock with a pillar in the middle.

Squelch to the lake to see several other baths, two temples and a Corinthian temple. Across the lake is a granary.

Cars must be parked in either the village or beach car park as hungry bulldozers often ply the entry roads.

PATARA BEACH

Backed by fluffy sand dunes (and not a pebble between toes), this splendid beach is quite unique for the region. You can get there by following the road past the ruins, or by turning right at Golden Pension and following the

track, which heads for the sand dunes and mimosa bushes along the western side of the archaeological zone. It's about a 30-minute walk, or minibuses run to the beach from the village dolmuş stop (TL1).

If you've walked this far barefoot, now's the time to run – the sand is hot and there are few places to escape the sun. You can rent an umbrella on the beach for TL6.

To the left as you approach, **Patara Restaurant** (grilled fish TL12) provides shade and sustenance. The beach closes at dusk as it's a nesting ground for sea turtles. Camping is prohibited.

ÇAYAĞZI BEACH

On the western side of the stream by the access road from the highway to Patara, a sign points the way to Çayağzı Beach 5km away. There are basic beach services and camping facilities.

Tours

Dardanos Travel (☎ 843 5151; ⏰ 9am-6pm) offers three-hour horse-riding trips through the Patara dunes (TL80) and excellent full-day canoeing trips (with BBQ lunch TL50) along the Eşen stream, ending at Patara Beach.

Sleeping

Rose Pension (☎ 843 5165; www.rosepensionpatara.com; s/d TL20/35; ✷) This large sand-coloured pension is favoured by shrewd travellers who can spot genuine hospitality from the ass-end of a dolmuş. The 16 double rooms are cosy and clean, but it's the extra efforts such as garden fresh produce and stylish lounge that make this an appealing place to stay.

Akay Pension (☎ 843 5055; www.pataraakaypension .com; s/d/t TL25/35/45; ✷ 🖳) Run by super-keen-to-please Kazım and family, the pension has well-maintained little rooms and comfortable beds with balconies overlooking orange trees. You pay an extra TL5 per room for air-con. Mrs Akay does a good breakfast.

Flower Pension (☎ 843 5164; www.pataraflower pension.com; s/d TL20/40, 2-/3-person apt TL50/60; ✷) On the road into town, the Flower has simple, sparkling and well-maintained rooms with balconies overlooking the garden. There's a free shuttle to the beach.

Sema Hotel (☎ 843 5114; www.semahotel.com; s/d TL25/40; ✷) The Sema is not the most luxurious hotel you will find in Turkey, but is ideal for those who prefer to share their travel experience with warm locals such as Ali and

Hanife, the proprietors. The large hotel sits 60 steep steps above the town where rooms are basic but spotless and cool (and pretty much mosquito-free!). Meals are served in the family kitchen.

St Nicholas Pension (☎ 843 5154; www.stnicholas pension.com; s/d TL25/40; ✖) This fine pension sports a lush terrace covered in grapevines and sleeping pets. Rooms are small but have recently been redecorated in a beach motif.

Golden Pension (☎ 843 5162; www.goldenpension .com; s/d TL30/40; ✖ 🖳) With homely rooms with balconies, a pretty shaded terrace and a friendly family that's not overeager to please, it's peaceful and private. There are also plans for a pool. Arif, the village mayor and owner, can take guests canoeing (TL30 per day) or on boat trips (TL40) including lunch, and also owns a travel agency.

Delfin Hotel (☎ 843 5154; s/d TL30/50; ✖ 🖳 🖳) The same folk who run St Nicholas are also in charge of this neighbouring, smart top-end alternative, befit with exquisite swimming pool and palm trees.

Zeybek 2 Pension (☎ 843 5086; www.zeybek2pension .com; s/d TL30/50; ✖ 🖳) Rooms are clean, homely and hung with traditional rugs, and have lovely views from their balcony – as does the attractive roof terrace that boasts 360-degree vistas of the hills. To get here, follow the road past Dardanos Travel up the hill.

Zeybek 1 Pension (☎ 843 5072; www.zeybek1pen sion.com; s/d TL30/50; ✖ 🖳) Near the Zeybek 2 Pension – and equally as good – is Zeybek 1. It's a touch older (as you'd expect), but still a relaxing option set back from the village.

Patara View Point Hotel (☎ 843 5184; www.patara viewpoint.com; s/d TL60/90; ✖ Apr-Oct; ✖ 🖳 🖳) Off the main road, it has a nice swimming pool, an Ottoman-style cushioned terrace and rooms with balconies that have views over the valley. The interior is hung with old farm implements – heirlooms from the owner's grandmother. There's a tractor-shuttle twice a day to and from the beach.

Eating

Lazy Frog (☎ 843 5160; mains €6-9; ✖ 8am-midnight) With its own kitchen garden, this place offers various vegetarian options, as well as *gözleme* on its relaxing terrace. 'Frog' steaks cost TL16.

Golden Terrace (☎ 843 5162; www.goldenpension .com; mains TL10-20) The restaurant at the Golden Pension enjoys good foot traffic thanks to

a comprehensive menu of meat, fish and vegetarian dishes.

Tlos Restaurant (☎ 843 5135; mezes €2, mains €4.50-10; ✖ 8am-midnight Apr-Oct) The Tlos is run by the moustached and smiling Osman, the chef-owner of proud culinary stock. The Turkish goulash (TL10) is particularly recommended. About 50m north of the Golden Pension on the main road into the village. Bring your own booze.

Drinking

Medusa Bar (☎ 843 5193; beer TL4; ✖ 9am-3am Apr-Sep) Styled like an old pub with cushioned benches and walls hung with old photos and posters, it has a fairly eclectic CD collection.

Gypsy Bar (beer TL4; ✖ 9am-3am) Tiny but traditional and much loved locally, the Gypsy has live Turkish music from 10pm to 3am every Monday, Wednesday and Saturday.

Getting There & Away

Buses on the Fethiye–Kaş route drop you on the highway 4km from the village. From here dolmuşes run to the village every 45 minutes.

Minibuses run from the beach through the village to Fethiye (TL6, six daily) and regularly to Kalkan (TL5, 20 minutes, 15km) and Kaş (TL8, 45 mins, 41km).

KALKAN
☎ 0242

Kalkan is a stylish hillside harbour town that slides steeply into a sparkling blue bay. It's as rightly famous for its restaurants as its sublimely pretty beach, and makes a smart alternative to the better-known, neighbouring Kaş.

Although Kalkan was once an Ottoman-Greek fishing village called Kalamaki, the town is now devoted to upscale tourism. Development continues unchecked on the outskirts of town (see boxed text, p378), but thankfully Kalkan's charms are found right in the middle. Spend a night or two in one of many great value pensions, and you'll quickly see why foreign investors have driven up property prices faster than the new Turkish lira can shed zeroes.

Orientation & Information

Coming in from the highway the road zigzags down past a taxi rank, the PTT, municipality building and banks to a central car park. It then enters the main commercial area and

Book your stay at lonelyplanet.com/hotels

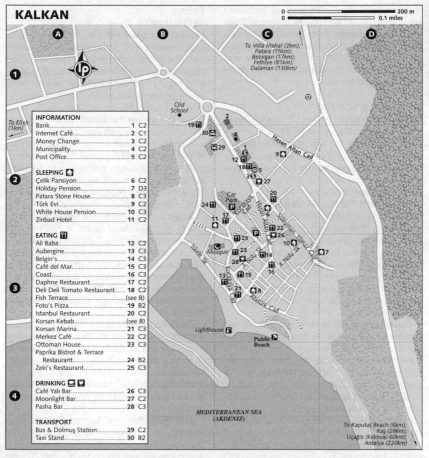

KALKAN

0   200 m
0   0.1 miles

To Villa Mahal (2km);
Patara (15km);
Bezirgan (17km);
Fethiye (81km);
Dalaman (130km)

To Elixir
(1km)

Old
School

INFORMATION
Bank... 1 C2
Internet Café............................... 2 C1
Money Change........................... 3 C2
Municipality................................ 4 C2
Post Office.................................. 5 C2

SLEEPING
Çelik Pansiyon............................ 6 C2
Holiday Pension......................... 7 D3
Patara Stone House.................... 8 C3
Türk Evi..................................... 9 C2
White House Pension................. 10 C3
Zinbad Hotel.............................. 11 C2

EATING
All Baba..................................... 12 C2
Aubergine.................................. 13 C3
Belgin's..................................... 14 C3
Café del Mar............................. 15 C3
Coast... 16 C3
Daphne Restaurant.................... 17 C2
Deli Deli Tomato Restaurant..... 18 C2
Fish Terrace..........................(see 8)
Foto's Pizza............................... 19 B2
Istanbul Restaurant................... 20 C2
Korsan Kebab.......................(see 8)
Korsan Marina............................ 21 C3
Merkez Café............................... 22 C2
Ottoman House.......................... 23 C3
Paprika Bistrot & Terrace
    Restaurant............................. 24 B2
Zeki's Restaurant....................... 25 C3

DRINKING
Café Yalı Bar............................. 26 C3
Moonlight Bar............................ 27 C3
Pasha Bar................................... 28 C3

TRANSPORT
Bus & Dolmuş Station................ 29 C2
Taxi Stand.................................. 30 B2

Hasan Altan Cad

Car
Park

İskele Sk

Mosque

Kocakoya Cad

Süleyman Yılmaz Cad

4 Nolu Sk

Atatürk Cad

Lighthouse

Public
Beach

*MEDITERRANEAN SEA
(AKDENIZ)*

To Kaputaş Beach (6km);
Kaş (28km);
Uçağız (Kekova) 60km);
Antalya (220km)

descends the hill as Hasan Altan Caddesi (also called 6 Sokak).

There are several places to go online in Kalkan. The most established **internet café** (☎ 844 1670; Hasan Altan Caddesi; ⌚ 9am-5pm), opposite the dolmuş stand, is really just a stationery shop with two computer terminals perched outside. Kalkan has a **website** (www .kalkan.org.tr) instead of a tourist office.

Sleeping
BUDGET
Çelik Pansiyon (☎ 844 2126; Süleyman Yılmaz Caddesi 9; s/d TL30/40; 😺) One of the few cheap guest houses open year-round, the Çelik has simple and rather spartan rooms, though they're spotless and quite spacious. Two, attic-like,

have a balcony overlooking the rooftops and marina, as does the roof terrace.

Holiday Pension (☎ 844 3777; Süleyman Yılmaz Caddesi; d without/with breakfast TL35/50) Though rooms are simple, they're spotless and charming, some with old wooden beams, antique lace curtains and delightful balconies with good views. It's run by the charming Ahmet and Şefıka, who make delicious breakfast jams.

our pick Türk Evi (☎ 844 3129; www.kalkanturkevi .com; Hasan Altan Caddesi; d TL60-80; 😺) Multilingual and multitalented Önder and Selma Elitez lay claim to the finest small hotel in Kalkan. In fact, this beautifully restored stone house is considered among the more endearing places to stay on the western Mediterranean. The eight rooms (some with original bathtubs) are filled with rare antique furniture and huge beds, while the downstairs 'family' room feels lifted from an interiors magazine. Breakfast on the terrace draped in bougainvillea and oleander trees is enough to make you campaign for the good life.

MIDRANGE & TOP END

White House Pension (☎ 844 3738; www.kalkanwhitehouse.co.uk; Yalıboyu Mah; s/d TL40/80; ✖) Situated on a quiet corner at the top of the hill, this attentively-run place has 10 compact, breezy rooms in a spotless family home. The real winner here though is the view from the terrace, worth the price alone.

Zinbad Hotel (☎ 844 3404; www.zinbadhotel.com; Yalıboyu Mah 18; s/d TL60/80; ✖ mid-Apr-Nov; ✖) The Zinbad has cheerful and comfortable rooms sponged Mediterranean blue, some with balconies and sea views. Close to the beach, central and with a large terrace, it's a good choice. Prices rise by €8 per person in high season. Renate, the German manager, offers guests archaeological tours (you pay just for the petrol).

Patara Stone House (☎ 844 3622; www.korsankalkan.com; Atatürk Caddesi; d TL80/110; ✖) Above the Fish Terrace restaurant, it offers just two rooms in a lovely old stone house. Spacious, elegantly decorated and right on the waterfront, they're a great choice.

our pick **Elixir** (☎ 843 5032; Kalamar Yolu 8; d €100-120; ✖ 🖳 ✖) It's always exciting to see a hotel attempt something new, even more so when it pulls it off. Part body-focused retreat, part designer hotel, the Elixir features two swimmingly handsome pools (one on the roof) and a smooth-edged Turkish bath. The rooms have a palpably modern, healthy feel, and all come with balcony. It's a short, appetising walk from town.

Villa Mahal (☎ 844 3268; www.villamahal.com; d €120-220; ✖ ✖) One of the most elegant hotels in Turkey lies on a steep hillside on the western side of Kalkan bay, about 2km from town. The 13 rooms, all individually designed in Mediterranean minimalist fashion, are unspeakably tasteful. All have superb views from the walls of windows that open onto private terraces. The pool suite has its own swimming pool, spectacularly suspended on the edge of the hill. There's a bathing platform by the sea. A taxi from Kalkan costs about TL8.

Eating
RESTAURANTS

Istanbul Restaurant (☎ 844 2282; Süleyman Yılmaz Caddesi; mains TL10-20) This understated classic Turkish, without the pretence fancier Kalkan restaurants, serves delicious *ali nazik* (aubergine, pepper and beef puree) and *ahtapot güveç* (octopus casserole). Its few white-clothed tables are usually filled with knowing diners.

Deli Deli Tomato Restaurant (☎ 844 2655; mains TL12-17) It may have a strange name, but there's a friendly buzz and an interesting international menu at this brand-new restaurant next to the PTT. Chicken is the go, in all its permutations: tarragon, sesame, Thai, Indian. It's popular for breakfast and can be found beside the post office.

Belgin's (☎ 844 3614; Hasan Altan Caddesi; mains TL12-20; ✖ 10am-midnight Apr-Oct) A 150-year-old former olive-oil press, Belgin's serves traditional Turkish food at very palatable prices. The speciality is *mantı* (TL14). Despite the faux Ottoman artefacts and stuffed sheep, the roof terrace is very pleasant. There's usually live Turkish music nightly from 8pm to 1am.

Zeki's Restaurant (☎ 844 3884; Kocakaya Caddesi; starters €3-5, mains €9-11; ✖ 10am-midnight May-Nov) Small but chicly decked out right down to the fresh oleander flowers and crisp linen tablecloths, Zeki's does excellent French-Turkish cuisine. It claims to serve 'the best steaks in Kalkan' and its *tarte au chocolat* is much sought-after.

Foto's Pizza (☎ 844 3464; large pizza TL15-25) Listing a pizza joint in a town of such culinary repute seems sacrilege, yet the views from Foto's deck – and the wonderful pizzas themselves (try the Turkish special!) – make it hard to overlook. It's next to the fish market.

Daphne Restaurant (☎ 844 3547; Kocakaya Caddesi; mains TL15-30; ✖ May-Oct) Owned by the same crowd as the heralded Aubergine, big things were expected of the former Daphne Hotel. Luckily, thanks largely to the uber cool cocktail bar, this place delivers. The food is also excellent, with an emphasis on wok-style dishes and seafood. Live music, sometimes jazz, is played on most nights. There's also a small gift shop selling lovely prints.

Ottoman House (☎ 844 3867; Kocakaya Caddesi 35; ✖ 9am-1am) Carpet- and cushion-clad *à l'Ottoman*, this traditional-style restaurant serves excellent Turkish classics such as *testi kebap* (Cappadocian pots containing beef or chicken, broken at your table, TL22). The attractive roof terrace has good views.

Coast (☎ 844 2971; Yalıboyu 3; 🕑 9am-midnight Apr-Oct) This modern and minimalist place offers superb Turkish dishes with a European twist. Try the speciality, the steak served flaming on a block of hot marble (€14).

Korsan Marina (☎ 844 3622; Kocakaya Caddesi; mezes €3-7, mains €9.50-14.50; 🕑 9.30am-midnight May-Oct) Neighbouring the town beach is one of the oldest (1979) and most consistent restaurants in Kalkan. Its mezes are a speciality (try the mouth-watering *mücver* – courgette fritters), as is the Korsan paella (€11.50), loaded with seafood and spices.

Aubergine (☎ 844 3332; İskele Sokak; mains €10-20; 🕑 9am-midnight) With tables right on the yacht marina, as well as cosy seats inside, the restaurant is famous for its slow-roasted wild boar (€13), as well as its swordfish fillet served in a creamy vegetable sauce (€13).

Paprika Bistrot & Terrace Restaurant (☎ 844 1136; Yalıboyu 12/B; mains €11-15) Lying opposite the municipal car park, Paprika specialises in meat dishes, which you can eat on its terraces. Try the sumptuous speciality, *incik* (€15) – roasted shank of lamb served with a wine and onion sauce – or the famous hot chocolate fondant (€5.50).

Fish Terrace (☎ 844 3076; Atatürk Caddesi; meals TL30-40; 🕑 9.30am-midnight) On the roof of Patara Stone House, this restaurant is the finest seafood experience in Kalkan. We suggest you linger over the meze. On Monday and Thursday from 8.30pm to 10pm there's live jazz. Its homemade lemonade (TL3.50) is legendary.

CAFÉS & QUICK EATS
Ali Baba (☎ 844 3627; Hasan Altan Caddesi; mains €2.75; 🕑 5am-midnight low season, 24 hr high season) With its long opening hours and rock-bottom prices, this is the local choice. It's a great place for breakfast (€3.50), and also does good veggie dishes (€1.75 to €2.50).

Café Del Mar (☎ 844 1068; Hasan Altan Caddesi; 🕑 8am-1am) A tiny but rather sweet place that claims to offer over 70 varieties of coffee (€1.70 to €2.80), as well as milkshakes and smoothies (€2.50).

Merkez Café (☎ 844 2823; Hasan Altan Caddesi 17; 🕑 8am-1am May-Oct) With its own bakery, this modest-looking café makes ethereal pastries and cakes, many of them its own inventions, such as the gorgeous chocolate baklava (€4

for four pieces) and the legendary coconut and almond macaroons (€1.50)! With fresh fruit juices (€2) and *pain au chocolat* (€0.75) too, it also makes a great choice for brekkie or a snack. The pizzas (€3.50 to €6) please even its Italian clientele.

Korsan Kebap (☎ 844 2116; Atatürk Caddesi; meals TL20) With tables on a terrace by the harbour, Korsan does delicious, upmarket kebaps (TL12) and pide (TL8 to TL10). Try the speciality, the *dürüm kebap* made with spicy tender steak.

Drinking
Moonlight Bar (☎ 844 3043; Süleyman Yılmaz Caddesi 17; beer €2; 🕑 10am-4am or later mid-Apr–Oct) Kalkan's oldest bar and still its most 'happening', though 95% of people sitting at the tables outside, or on the small dance floor inside, are tourists.

Pasha Bar (☎ 844 3256; Yalıboyu Mah; beer TL5) This hot new place sees Kalkan's young and mobile drink beers on the street level tables then fire up the tight dance floor inside – as is their wont.

Café Yalı Bar (☎ 844 2417; Hasan Altan Caddesi 19; beer TL4; 🕑 1pm-midnight May-Oct) Positioned as it is on a three-road junction, this is a popular place for getting drunk in public.

Getting There & Away
In high season, minibuses connect Kalkan with Fethiye (TL7, 1½ hours, 81km) and Kaş (TL2.50, 35 minutes, 29km). Around eight minibuses also run daily to Patara (TL3, 25 minutes, 15km).

AROUND KALKAN
Bezirgan
In a high-hanging valley roughly 17km behind Kalkan sits the beautiful village of Bezirgan and a delightful sample of Turkish rural life. Fields of plump fruit trees are ringed by golden shocks of sesame, and the unexplained cisterns and citadel of **Pirha**, another mystery site of the Lycian age.

If you decide to stay over, then by far the best choice is **Owlsland** (☎ 837 5214; www.owlsland .com; s/d €37/74, with half-board €57/114), a 150-year-old farmhouse run by a charming Turkish-Scottish couple. Erol, a trained chef, turns out traditional Turkish dishes made with the freshest village ingredients and Pauline makes her own breakfast jams. Rooms are simple but cosy and decorated with old farm implements,

WESTERN MEDITERRANEAN

THE GOOD FIGHT *Önder Elitez*

I was born in İstanbul in 1939. I always wanted to play football, but as a student I worked in the streets laying rainwater drain pipes. In the '50s and '60s there was no money in football and, although my skills gave me advantages during military service, I moved east to Lake Van to work on the railroad lines being built up to the Persian border. I earned enough money to travel to Croatia and Albania.

There I developed a taste for Europe and when, in the early '60s, workers were being asked to go to Germany a friend and I applied. Those days were chaos. We were driven to the factories at dusk and returned home on foot in darkness. Unable to find their hostels or speak the language, most workers spent their first nights in Germany in police stations. I persisted for two years, learning the language, though missing the pay in Turkey, and wondering what we were doing.

I went back to work in the east of Turkey at a time when everyone else was trying to go to Europe. There the villagers gave me a pet bear cub that I fed with milk, honey and biscuits until one day after a short wrestling match I thought I would never be able to walk again. He was getting strong. I took him to the forest where we parted ways, both of us with tears in our eyes.

I decided to go back to Germany. I worked various jobs and became a football trainer, coaching foreign youngsters to keep them off the streets. All my savings in the '70s went towards travelling – England, Sweden with jazz musicians, and France's Côte d'Azur. One evening a friend invited me to join him on his journey to Kathmandu. I asked him where that was, and the next day we bought two buses. Taking passengers on the way, we drove from Düsseldorf down to İstanbul to the infamous 'Pudding Shop' by the Blue Mosque. We moved according to the number of passengers: Iran, Afghanistan, Pakistan, India and finally Nepal where we sold our buses. Our passengers were hippies, from Japanese to Americans, getting on and off the bus with no sense of time, on the 'silk route'. We experienced the magic of Mt Ararat, caviar and ram's bollocks with Russian vodka by the Caspian Sea (try doing that now); the rough but peaceful highlands of Afghanistan; the dangerous mountain pass area crossing into Pakistan; and the smugglers' territory around Peshawar. When the Pakistanis saw my passport with a star and crescent they kissed and hugged me as their long lost brother.

I passed by Kalkan in the mid-'70s and decided to retire here to open a small hotel and meet people from all over the world. I wanted to swim in this sea exactly, which is refreshed by cold water springs during the hot summers. I finally came back in 1983 and bought an old village house which I restored and later enlarged as the Türk Evi hotel.

During my life I learned to fight. First as a footballer, then in military service guarding the President (and later the General) during the military coup of 1960. And then there was the fight to earn a living so I could travel.

Now, as a retired man still active in tourism, I am fighting to keep the sea clean in Kalkan. We live here to be able to swim in the sea, not in a swimming pool. And that's what I intend to do every day from now on. Kalkan is growing too big, too fast. I hope others will join me in this fight.

Önder Elitez is a seasoned traveller who runs Türk Evi in Kalkan with his wife, Selima.

heirlooms from Erol's grandfather. Walking tours (TL50 including lunch) are also offered. There's a free transfer to/from Kalkan.

GETTING THERE & AWAY

Unless you're staying at Owlsland, the easiest way to get to Bezirgan is by car or scooter from Kalkan or Kaş. From Kalkan head towards Fethiye, then take the turn-off to Elmalı. The road climbs steadily, with stunning views across the sea. Eventually you enter the gorge that runs down to the sea at Kaputaş, then at a T-junction turn left and head further up the mountain. Once the road crests the pass you can see Bezirgan below you. Where the road descends to the basin floor there is a turn-off to the left that leads into the village.

Otherwise, the one minibus (TL1.50) heads back to the village from Kalkan at around 3pm.

Kaputaş

About 7km east of Kalkan and 21km west of Kaş, Kaputaş is a striking mountain gorge crossed by a small highway bridge. Below the bridge is a perfect little sandy cove and often empty **beach**, accessible by a long flight of stairs. A dolmuş from Kalkan will take you there in high season for TL1.25, but the water here is so beautiful it's half-tempting to tip the driver.

KAŞ
☎ 0242 / pop 5990

The 500m-high mountain known as 'Sleeping Man' (Yatan Adam) has watched Kaş evolve from an incongruously beautiful place of exile for political dissidents, to a funky boutique shopping and café strip, to a seaside adventure playground. Its amused and charming local establishment, however, is borne mostly of proud fishing stock.

While Kaş proper may not sport the finest beach culture in the region, it's a yachties' haven and the atmosphere of the town is wonderfully mellow. The surrounding areas are ideal for day trips by sea or scooter, and a plethora of adventure sports are on offer, in particular some world-class diving.

A well-preserved ancient theatre is about all that's left of ancient Antiphellos, which was the Lycian town here. Above the town several Lycian rock tombs in the sheer rock mountain wall are illuminated at night.

Lying just offshore is the geopolitical oddity of the Greek island of Meis (Kastellorizo).

ORIENTATION

The otogar is a few hundred metres uphill north of the town centre; descend the hill along Atatürk Bulvarı to get into the town centre. Cheap pensions are mostly to your right (west), the more expensive hotels and restaurants to the left (east). At the Merkez Süleyman Çavuş Camii (mosque), turn left to reach the main square, Cumhuriyet Meydanı. İbrahim Serin Caddesi strikes north to the PTT and a bank with an ATM. From the mosque, Likya Caddesi cuts east past lovely shops and bars in restored wooden houses and on past some Lycian rock tombs. Beyond the main square over the hill are more hotels and a small pebble beach.

Turning right at the mosque onto Necip Bey Caddesi and Yaşar Yazici Caddesi takes you to the ancient theatre and a camping ground. Beyond lies the Çukurbağ Peninsula and the narrow stretch of sea to the island of Meis.

INFORMATION

There are several banks with ATMs along Atatürk Bulvarı.

Net-C@fé (☎ 836 4505; İbrahim Serin Caddesi 16/B; per hr TL2; ☾ 9am-1am)

Tourist office (☎ 836 1238; ☾ 8am-noon & 1-7pm Mon-Fri May-Oct, to 5pm Nov-Apr) On the main square.

SIGHTS & ACTIVITIES
Antiphellos Ruins

Walk up the hill on the street behind (to the east of) the tourist office to reach the **Monument Tomb**, a Lycian sarcophagus mounted on a high base. Kaş was once littered with such sarcophagi but over the years most were broken apart to provide building materials.

The **theatre**, 500m west of the main square, is in very good condition and was restored some time ago. You can walk to the rock tombs in the cliffs above the town. The walk is strenuous so go at a cool time of day.

Swimming

For swimming, head for pretty Büyük Çakıl beach – there's a scene among young Turks here in high season. It's clean and just 1.3km from the town centre. Although it's largely pebble-based, parasols and sun beds are free, and a few shaded cafés sell beer.

Hamam

It's small and part of a resort, but the mixed bath at the **Phellos Health Club** (☎ 836 1953; Doğrunyol Sokak 4; massage TL50) is well worth a visit.

TOURS

Most companies offer more or less the same journeys, but you can always tailor your own (for a negotiated price).

Among the stalwarts, the three-hour **boat trip** (TL25-30) to Kekova and Üçağız (see p385) is a fine day out, and includes time to see several interesting ruins as well as swimming stops.

Other standard tours go to the Mavi Mağara (Blue Cave), Patara and Kalkan or to Liman Ağzı, Longos and several small nearby islands. There are also overland excursions to Saklıkent Gorge.

A great idea is to charter a boat from the marina. A whole day spent around the islands of Kaş should cost between TL150 and TL200 for the entire boat (for up to eight people).

Good tour companies in Kaş include the following:

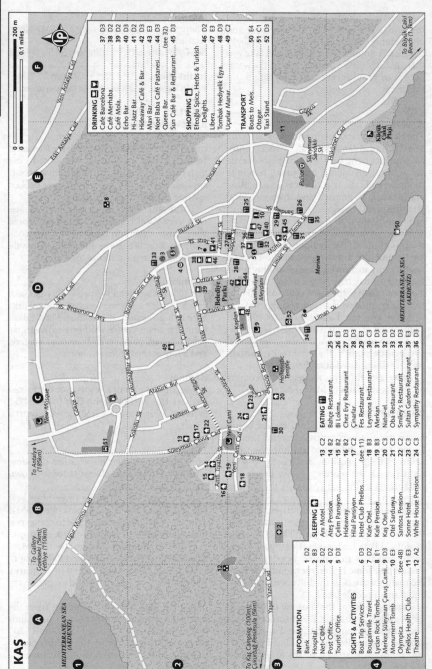

ALIVE & KAYAKING IN KAŞ

Kaş is a great place for adventure and activities. The listed agencies offer the following:
Canoeing TL60 per person for a full day on Patara River. Scheduled trips run three times a week.
Canyoning TL100 per person for a full day.
Mountain biking TL80 per person per full day.
Paragliding TL200 per person. Flights last 20 to 30 minutes, depending on weather.
Scuba diving For qualified divers, TL60 per dive including all equipment. For beginners keen to qualify, a three-day PADI open-water course costs €340 all-inclusive.
Sea kayaking TL50 per person for a full day all-inclusive.

Bougainville Travel also hires out mountain bikes for TL25 per day and canoes (though you'll need to be qualified) for TL25/35 for a single/double.

Amber Travel (☎ 836 1630; www.ambertravel.com) Run by a British couple, Amber specialises in country-wide itineraries with an intrepid focus. Good option for activities too.

Bougainville Travel (☎ 836 3737; www.bougainville -turkey.com; İbrahim Serin Caddesi 10) A long-established English-Turkish tour operator with a good reputation and much experience in organising activities for travellers; see above for what is on offer.

Olympica (☎ 836 2049; www.olympicatravel.com; Ortaokul Sokak 1; ⊙ 8.30am-5.30pm) Run by an Austrian-Turkish team who combine Teutonic efficiency with local know-how, it specialises in 'build your own activity packages' according to clients' time, interests and budget. The more activities you book, the cheaper the package.

FESTIVALS & EVENTS
The annual **Kaş Lycia Festival** runs for three days at the end of June. It features prominent folk-dancing troupes and musicians – and an international swimming race – and works to foster an improved relationship between Greece and Turkey.

SLEEPING
Budget
Kaş Camping (☎ 836 1050; Yaşar Yazici Caddesi; 2-person camp sites TL20) Situated on an attractive rocky site 800m west of town, this has long been the most popular place for camping. The main draw is the lovely swimming area and bar.

Santosa Pension (☎ 836 1714; Recep Bilgin Caddesi 4; s/d TL20/40; 🐱 🖳) Clean, quiet and cheap is how best to describe this backpacker hang-out. The rooms are bare and simple, but excellent for the price. The family who runs the show are fine hosts (and cooks!). There's also a handy book exchange.

Ateş Pension (☎ 836 1393; www.atespension.com; Amfi Tiyatro Sokak 3; s/d TL30/50; 🐱 🖳) Well run by

Ahmed and his family, this is a friendly place with a pleasant roof terrace where BBQs are sometimes held. Guests also have free use of the kitchen and internet.

Anı Motel (☎ 836 1791; www.motelani.com; Süleyman Çavuş Caddesi; dm/s/d TL15/30/50; 🐱 🖳) Though rooms are rather small and spartan, they're spotless and have been lent a little charm with personal touches such as towels folded to look like bows. All rooms have balconies, there's a book exchange and a relaxing roof terrace with DVD player. Guests can also use the kitchen.

Hilal Pansiyon (☎ 836 1207; www.korsan-kas.com; Süleyman Çavuş Caddesi; dm/s/d TL15/30/50; 🐱 🖳) Run by the friendly Süleyman and family, the Hilal offers similar rooms to the Anı. It also has a plant-potted terrace where BBQs (TL15) sometimes take place. The travel agency below it offers guests 10% discounts on activities including kayaking, diving and trips to Saklıkent.

Midrange
Hideaway (☎ 836 1887; www.kasturkey.com; Amfi Tiyatro Sokak; s TL50, d TL70-80; 🐱 🐱 🖳) Aptly named, the Hideaway is located at the far end of town and so is quieter than many. Rooms are simple but in good order and all have a balcony. There's a roof terrace with sea views over the water and amphitheatre, and a pool.

Otel Sardunya (☎ 836 3080; www.sardunyaotel.com; Necip Bey Caddesi 56; s/d 50/80; 🐱) Set in a modern white building, rooms are reasonably spacious and all have balconies; eight have direct sea views. The big boon is the verdant and peaceful seashell-clad restaurant across the road, where breakfast is served under mulberry and orange trees a few metres from the water. Just below, there's a sunbathing terrace and swimming platform.

Kaş Otel (☎ 836 1271; fax 836 2170; Necip Bey Caddesi 15; s/d TL50/80; ⊠) One of the best locations, right above the water: the sea's so close you can hear it lapping from the pleasant terrace or the balconies of the eight simple rooms. The sea views are great too and it's not as noisy as many.

White House Pension (☎ 836 1513; fazisevenz@hot mail.com; Yeni Cami Caddesi 16; s/d TL60/80) Decked out in wood, wrought iron, marble and terracotta paint, this is a stylish little gem with attractive rooms and a pretty little terrace. Ask for one of the attic rooms with a balcony.

Sonne Hotel (☎ 836 1528; www.sonneotel.com; Yeni Cami Yanı 6; s/d TL60/90; ⊠ 🖵) Located at the town-end of 'hotel hill', the Sonne is a tightly managed beauty that constantly attracts return visitors. The rooms are tasteful and quite spacious, all with LCD televisions and Ottoman-esque mirrors. The junior suite (TL100) is worth the minor splurge. The breakfast terrace and bar are brilliant, while the Turkish-German owners are super keen.

Kale Otel & Pension (☎ 836 4074; hotelkale@hotmail.com; Yeni Cami Caddesi 8; s/d pension TL90/110, s/d hotel TL120/150; ⊠) Close to the amphitheatre, this well-run hotel offers simple but pleasantly furnished rooms with balconies, many with gorgeous views over the water. Breakfast is an excellent open buffet (the chef cooks omelettes to order in front of you), and you can eat it in the garden overlooking the water. The rooms of the pension are more basic with views set back but are still good value.

Hotel Club Phellos (☎ 836 1953; Doğrunyol Sokak 4; s/d/tr TL100/130/170; ⊠ 🖳) Though something of an eyesore sprawling down the hillside, it's got a great pool overlooking the sea and three-star comfort.

EATING
Restaurants
Smiley's Restaurant (☎ 836 2812; Yat Limanı Girişi; mains TL20-30; ☯ 9am-midnight) Smiley's is a congenial dining experience, starting with the delicious complimentary homemade dips, and ending with Ismael, the hilarious owner, ensuring your satisfaction. In between can be a touch pricey, particularly fish dishes.

Leymona Restaurant (☎ 836 2647; Hastane Caddesi; ☯ 9am-11pm) Anatolian and fish specialities, such as rolled strips of salmon stuffed with spinach, are to be found in this lemon grove by the sea. The olive oil and pomegranate vinegar combination makes a great salad

dressing. The wine list is extensive and the service is sharp.

Bi Lokma (☎ 836 3942; Hukumet Caddesi 2; ☯ 9am-midnight) The Bi Lokama has tables meandering around a terraced garden overlooking the harbour. Sabo (Mama) turns out great traditional dishes including famous mantı (TL8 to TL12) and Mama's pastries (TL8). The wine list is also reasonably priced.

Sultan Garden Restaurant (☎ 836 3762; Hükümet Caddesi; mains TL15-25; ☯ 10am-midnight) This is a very pretty place complete with original Lycian tombs and a functional cistern. The staff have a wealth of restaurant experience, which feeds into their excellent meat and vegetarian dishes. The veggie burger (TL15) is awesome, and the hünkar beğendı (spiced lamb pieces on aubergine puree, TL18) is soft and flavoursome. The long wine list starts at around TL22.

Mercan (☎ 836 1209; Balıkçı Barınağı 2; mains TL15-30; ☯ 9am-midnight) Since 1956 – back when the owner's father was working the magic – the Mercan has been satisfying customers with fish and meat creations and confident, disarming service. The swordfish kebap (TL20) should win awards. Get there early to nab a table on the marina.

Natur-el (☎ 836 2834; Gürsöy Sokak 6; meals TL15-20) With its dishes cooked to old Ottoman recipes passed down from generation to generation, Natur-el and the family who runs it provide a chance to sample Turkish cuisine at its brilliant best. If you haven't yet eaten mantı, then chose from the three varieties (TL10) here.

Sympathy Restaurant (☎ 836 2418; Uzun Çarşı Gürsöy Sokak 11; meals TL10-20) Mrs Sevim's cooking is well known locally and attracts a loyal and regular following. Try the delicious aubergine fritters.

Fes Restaurant (☎ 836 3759; Sandıkçı Sokak 3; mezes TL5; ☯ 10am-midnight Apr-Oct) With tables on a peaceful terrace overlooking the harbour, steak (served with enticing sauces) is the speciality (TL20) but ask about the daily specials, which are usually superb.

Bahçe Restaurant (☎ 836 2370; Likya Caddesi 31; meals around TL25; ☯ dinner) Up behind the Lycian sarcophagus, this place has a pretty garden and serves excellent dishes at decent prices, including a terrific range of mezes (TL4). The fish in paper (TL16) has received rave reviews.

Chez Evy Restaurant (☎ 836 1253; Terzi Sokak 2; ☯ 7pm-midnight mid-Apr–Oct) Run by Evy, the restaurant's French namesake, and ex-head chef for a private yacht, this place is unabashedly French *haute cuisine*. It serves superb classics such as *gigot d'agneau* (TL35) or *filet de boeuf sauce Béarnaise* (TL40). If you can, opt to sit in the beautiful and verdant courtyard and listen out for Şahin the parrot, which can be heard whistling for Evy and usually makes a nightly appearance himself!

Cafés

Café Mola (☎ 836 7826; Halk Pazan Sokak; ☷ 8am-10pm) A great and inexpensive place for a Turkish breakfast (TL8) or a snack such as a crêpe or sandwich (TL4) with coffee or juice.

Noel Baba Café Pastanesi (☎ 836 1225; Cumhuriyet Meydanı 1; beer or cappuccino TL4, tea TL1.50; ☷ 7am-6pm low season, to midnight high season) On the main square yet not overpriced, this is a favourite local meeting point. With its shaded terrace it also makes a welcome escape from the midday sun.

Café Merhaba (☎ 836 1883; İbrahim Serin Caddesi 19; coffee TL3-5; ☷ 9.30am-midnight Mon-Sat mid-April–Oct) Claiming to make the 'best cakes in Kaş', the mellow Merhaba sells delicious confections cooked from natural products. It's not the cheapest place (slices TL5 to TL6) but it's the atmosphere you come for. It also stocks one-day-old European and American magazines.

Hideaway Café & Bar (☎ 836 3369; Cumhuriyet Caddesi 16/A; meals around TL15-20; ☷ 8.30am-3am Apr-Oct) Well named, this enchanting café-garden is hidden from the street and a whole world away from it. Charming owners, Nur and Erdem, are proud of their fresh fare all made with the highest quality local ingredients. On Sunday there's a fabulous eat-all-you-can buffet. At night, lit up with lanterns, it seems truly magical.

Quick Eats

Oba Restaurant (☎ 836 1687; İbrahim Serin Caddesi 26; mezes TL4, moussaka TL6) With a pleasant walled terrace under bitter orange trees, the Oba offers tasty Turkish dishes cooked daily by Nuran, the owner's mother. Hearty, tasty and great value, it's simple Turkish home cooking at its best. Try the speciality, *köfte* – oven-baked or sautéed – or chicken or beef *güveç*.

Çınarlar (☎ 836 2860; Mütfü Efendi Sokak 4; pide TL5-8, pizza TL8-15; ☷ 8am-1am) Perennially popular among Kaş' young, who come for the affordable pide and pop music, it also has a pleasant courtyard tucked away off the street.

DRINKING

Echo Bar (☎ 836 2047; www.echocafebar.com; Gürsoy Sokak; ☷ 9am-midnight) This hip new bar on the harbour makes classic fruit daiquiris (TL10) to acid-jazz soundtracks. The airy upstairs sections hosts regular video installations and artist exhibitions; downstairs is a gourmet sandwich shop. The owner Kemal is a prominent local artist who knows the Kaş cultural scene backwards. Check it out.

Hi-Jazz Bar (☎ 836 1165; Zümrüt Sokak 3; ☷ 5pm-3am May-Oct) Run by Yılmaz, a retired New York City taxi driver who has a story or two to tell, this is a mellow little bar with seating inside and out. From mid-June to the end of September there's live jazz daily from 10pm to 2am.

Mavi Bar (☎ 836 1834; Mütfü Efendi Sokak; ☷ 5pm-3am Apr-Oct) Seasonal hi-jinx are played out at the far end of the main square at the Mavi. Permanently packed with people, it plays a good mix of music and has tables outside.

Sun Café Bar Restaurant (☎ 836 1053; Hükümet Caddesi; ☷ 9am-3am) With its garden setting next to the Lycian sarcophagus, its decor and lighting, this is a civilised and rather glamorous place for a drink. There's live music nightly (9pm to midnight in low season, 11pm to 2am in high season).

Queen Bar (☎ 836 1403; Orta Sokak; ☷ 4pm-3am) Popular with travellers and locals alike, this place has a lively dance floor on the 1st floor and a more sedentary bar on the 2nd. The friendly DJ, Emin, encourages musical requests!

Café Barcelona (☎ 836 4490; Uzun Çarşı Gürsoy; ☷ 9am-midnight) Another hole-in-the-wall to give you holes in the head.

SHOPPING

Kaş has a great selection of little shops selling traditional wares that range from carpets and ceramics to wood-carved furniture and jewellery. Every Friday there's a market on the Kaş to Fethiye road opposite the marina.

Tombak Hediyelik Eşya (☎ 836 1820; Ortaokul Sokak 1; ☷ 8.30am-midnight Apr-Sep) Run by the charming İsmail, who will happily tell you about his wares, the shop sells high-quality Turkish artefacts including İstanbullu coloured-glass lanterns (TL25 to TL400), intricate inlay work, and good-quality backgammon sets (TL20 to TL550).

Efeoğlu Spice, Herbs & Turkish Delights (☎ 836 7429; İbrahim Serin Caddesi 16; ☷ 9am-8.30pm) If you're keen on culinary keepsakes or looking for a pressie for mamma, then this shop sells all sorts, from mountain tea and strings of dried chillies (so urban-chic) to wonderful spices and delicious Turkish delight (TL20 per kg).

Libera (☎ 836 4396; Uzançarşi Caddesi 14; ☼ 9am-6pm) A great little bookshop with local photography and English-language books, and a small CD collection. Upstairs is a café to browse through your purchase.

Gallery Göekseki (☎ 839 7078; www.gallerygoekseki .com; open Sundays 2-5pm) This German three-artist collective 5km west of Kaş holds regular exhibitions in town, and welcomes curious visitors every Sunday afternoon. Ceramic workshops are held every Monday, Tuesday and Thursday from 1pm to 4pm.

Uçarlar Manav (☎ 836 3096; ☼ 7am-midnight) Come to this place, about 100m northwest of the Belediye Parkı, for gorgeous local honey as well as high-quality fresh fruit.

GETTING THERE & AWAY
Boat
Kaş is not a serious ferry hub, though you can book tickets here for Marmaris then make your own way across.

Ferries from Kaş sail every weekday throughout the year for the tiny Greek island of Meis (Kastellorizo) at 10am (TL70 per person return, 30 minutes) and return at 3.30pm. Meis is a simple fishing village with a sprinkle of restaurants, which makes an expensive mission just to get your passport stamped. However you can now make it a one-way service by either staying overnight in Meis, or continuing onwards into Greece. There are five regular ferries (euros 18, 5 hours) and five fast ferries (36 euros, 21/2 hours) between Meis and Rhodes per week. Alternatively, flights between Meis and Rhodes (euros 28) go every day but Thursday.

Tickets can be bought from any travel agency. When booking you'll need to take your passport 24 hours prior to departure. If you charter your own boat (around TL50 per person), you can usually supply passports two hours before the trip. If you can muster up four or five people, it's worth a day trip with a local boat. Negotiate hard with the boat captains at the harbour.

If you don't have a multiple-entry visa, you'll need to renew your Turkish visa even for the day trip to Meis. You can usually pick these up at an immigration desk near Customs at Meis.

Note that you cannot currently travel to Rhodes from Meis.

Bus
There are daily buses from the Kaş otogar to İstanbul (TL65, 15 hours) at 6.30am, a nightly one to Ankara (TL50, 11 hours) at 8.30pm, and two a day to İzmir (TL25, 8½ hours), at 9.15am and 9pm.

There are also dolmuşes every half-hour to Kalkan (TL2.50, 30 minutes, 29km), Olympos (TL8, 2½ hours, 109km) and Antalya (TL9, 3½ hours, 185km) and every hour to Fethiye (TL7, two hours 50 minutes, 110km). Services to Patara (TL5, 45 minutes, 42km) run every half-hour in high season, hourly in low season.

ÜÇAĞIZ (KEKOVA)
☎ 0242
Declared off-limits to development, Üçağız (Three Mouths) is a Turkish fishing and farming village in an absolutely idyllic setting on a bay amid islands and peninsulas. Little has changed here (locals say otherwise!) aside from the steady trickle of high-end visitors, some choosing to stay long-term. There's not a lot to do – the water isn't especially good for swimming – but it's a regular stop on the *gület* junket, and a final taste of the mainland before the sunken city at Kekova or secluded Kaleköy (Kale). Here and there are remnants of ancient Lycian tombs.

Orientation & Information
The village you enter is Üçağız, the ancient Teimiussa. Continue through to the harbour car park, where you'll find fishermen, restaurants and tour buses. Across the water to the east is Kaleköy (Kale) – a village on the site of the ancient city of Simena – which is accessible only by boat, or a much longer walk.

South of the villages is a harbour (called Ölüdeniz) and south of that is the channel entrance, shielded from the Mediterranean's occasional fury by a long island named Kekova.

There's a small shop selling groceries in the village centre, opposite an information booth that is open in high summer. If it's closed, ask the Onur Pension for advice.

Sleeping & Eating
Ekin Hotel Pension (☎ 874 2064; www.ekinhotel.com; s €11-22, d €19.50-28; ☒) Run by two busy brothers, the Ekin's attractive rooms have balco-

UNRAVELLING ÜÇAĞIZ (KEKOVA) & KALEKÖY

Given the difficulty of getting to Üçağız (Kekova) and Kaleköy/Simena by public transport, most people end up taking a boat tour of the area from Kaş or Kalkan. A standard boat excursion might start by passing Kekova Island (Kekova Adası).

Along the shore of the island are Byzantine ruins, partly submerged 6m below the sea and called the Sunken City (Batık Şehir). The result of a series of terrible earthquakes during the 2nd century AD, most of what you can still see is said to be the residential part of ancient Simena. Foundations of buildings, staircases and the old harbour can be viewed. Some tour operators have become slack in recent years and cruise rather fast over the most interesting parts. Note, however, that it is now forbidden to stop, photograph or swim around or near the Sunken City (though you can swim around Kekova Island).

Afterwards you have lunch on the boat and then head on to Kaleköy, passing sunken Lycian tombs just offshore. There's usually about an hour to explore Kaleköy and climb up to the eponymous castle. On the way back to Kaş there should be time for another swim. Tours generally leave at 10am and charge around TL40 to TL50 per person.

The closest you can get to the underwater walls and mosaics is to take a sea-kayaking tour run by one of the travel agencies in Kaş (p379). This superb day excursion, suitable for all fitness levels, also ensures you beat the rush of large tour cruises. A sea-kayaking tour including transfers from Kaş and lunch in Üçağız is TL60 per person.

nies and sea views. Try to get a room in the new block.

Telemenin Evi (☎ 874 2076; s/d TL20/40; 😢) Telemen has opened his cute house to a maximum of 10 guests, but is most happy in the kitchen preparing your evening meal. Rooms are fairly simple but everything's in its right place.

Onur Pension (☎ 874 2071; www.onurpension.com; s/d TL40/60; 😢 💻) With a picturesque setting right above the sea, this well-run pension combines charm with attentive service. It offers free internet access, a free boat service to reach the beaches and a book exchange. Locally born Onur can give great trekking advice and also act as guide. Four of the rooms, kept shipshape by Onur's Dutch wife, Jacqueline, have full sea views.

Kekova Pension (☎ 874 2259; kekovatour@hotmail.com; d TL60-80; 😢) Set on the far end of the waterfront, this is a peaceful and handsome old stone building with a terrace dotted with flowerpots. Rooms are comfortable and share a lovely veranda with views over the water and comfy cushioned benches. There's a free boat service to beaches. Louise is the helpful English manager.

Kordon Restaurant (☎ 874 2067; Üçağız Köyü; mixed plate mezes TL10, fish per 500g TL25; 😋 9am-midnight 20 Apr-25 Oct) With an attractive and cool terrace overlooking the marina and fresh fish served daily, the Kordon is considered the best restaurant in town and its prices are reasonable.

Getting There & Away

Unless you can arrange pick-up in Demre, Kekova is a tricky place to get to. One dolmuş leaves Antalya for Üçağız daily at 2pm (TL10), and returns at 8am. Dolmuşes also run every 40 minutes from Antalya to Demre (TL6, three hours), from where you can get a taxi (TL40) to Üçağız.

From Kaş, no dolmuşes run to Üçağız. A taxi (TL70) is the only option. However, in summer, you can hitch a lift (TL20 one way, two hours) with one of the boat companies making daily tours to Üçağız.

From Kale (Demre), one dolmuş runs daily to Üçağız at 5pm (TL4, 30 minutes). From Üçağız, dolmuşes leave at 8am.

After all this, perhaps the most adventurous – and the simplest – way to get here is by hired scooter from Kaş.

KALEKÖY
☎ 0242

Kaleköy is one of the western Mediterranean's truly delightful outposts. This tiny inhabited rock is also home to the ruins of ancient **Simena** and a Crusader **fortress** perched above a lovely hamlet facing flat out to sea. Within the fortress a little theatre is cut into the rock and nearby you'll find ruins of several temples and public baths, several sarcophagi and Lycian tombs; the **city walls** are visible on the outskirts. There are also several sandy spots from where you can splash about.

Be prepared for peace and quiet – Kaleköy is accessible only from Üçağız by motorboat (10 minutes) or on foot (45 minutes) along a rough track.

Kaleköy has a couple of pensions, including the well-run **Kale Pansiyon** (☎ 874 2111; kale pansiyon@superonline.com; s/d TL60/90; ❄), closest to the harbour, which has eight homely little rooms all with balconies (with direct views) that are so close to the sea you can hear the water lapping, as well as a nice swimming area. The family also owns the restaurant (set menu with meze, main and beer TL25) next door with tables sitting prettily on the pier.

The family dynasty spreads to the **Olive Grove** (☎ 874 2234; kalepansiyon@superonline.com; s/d TL70/100), which is set back from the harbour. It's a gorgeous 150-year-old Greek stone house (look out for the lovely mosaic on the veranda). The four rooms are simple but elegant and share a large veranda with sea views. Amid the cooing doves and ancient olive trees, it's a blissfully peaceful place.

The premier choice is the **Mehtap Pansiyon** (☎ 874 2146; www.mehtappansiyon.com; camp site TL20, s/d TL90/110; ❄), with spectacular views over the harbour and the Lycian tombs below. The 200-year-old stone house is so quiet and tranquil you may start snoozing as you check in.

You can either eat at your pension or there are a couple of restaurants on the seafront, all offering similar fare for similar prices. Check out what's currently in favour when you get there.

KALE (DEMRE)
☎ 0242 / pop 14,600

The sprawling, dusty town of Kale was once the Roman city of Myra and by the 4th century was important enough to have its own bishop (including St Nicholas of Santa Claus fame). Several centuries before that, St Paul stopped here on his voyage to Rome.

Once situated by the sea, Kale slid inland in pursuit of precious alluvium from the Demre stream. That silting is the foundation of the town's wealth, but most visitors will only pass through here for the wonderful Myra ruins or the ancient stone church of St Nicholas.

Though Myra had a long history as a religious, commercial and administrative town, Arab raids in the 7th century and the silting of the harbour led to its decline. Today, as you pass by endless greenhouses, you'll see that Kale is all about vegetables.

Orientation & Information

Kale is spread out over an alluvial plain. The street going west from the square to the Church of St Nicholas is Müze Caddesi (aka St Nicholas Caddesi). Alakent Caddesi leads 2km north to the Lycian rock tombs of Myra (below). PTT Caddesi (or Ortaokul Caddesi) heads east to the PTT. The street going south from the square passes the otogar (100m).

Looming above the town on a hilltop to the north is the huge *kale* (castle).

Sights
CHURCH OF ST NICHOLAS

Not vast like Aya Sofya or brilliant with mosaics like İstanbul's Chora Church (Kariye Museum), the **Church of St Nicholas** (admission TL10; ☾ 8.30am-7pm May-Oct, to 5.30pm Nov-Apr) is nonetheless a star attraction for pilgrims and tourists alike. The remains of the eponymous saint were laid here upon his death in AD 343.

The bare earthen church features some interesting Byzantine frescoes and mosaic floors, though its dignity is often tainted by noisy, thinly-clad tour group. It became a Byzantine basilica when it was restored in 1043. Italian merchants smashed open the sarcophagus in 1087 and carted St Nicholas' bones off to Bari. Restorations sponsored by Tsar Nicholas I of Russia in 1862 changed the church by building a vaulted ceiling and a belfry. More recent work by Turkish archaeologists was designed to protect it from deterioration.

It's a block west of the main square.

MYRA

If you only have time to see one striking honeycomb of rock-hewn **Lycian tombs**, then choose the memorable ruins of **Myra** (admission TL10; ☾ 7.30am-7pm May-Oct, 8am-5.30pm Nov-Apr). Located about 2km inland from Kale's main square, they are among Turkey's finest and also feature a well-preserved **Greco-Roman theatre**, which includes several carved theatrical masks lying in the nearby area. St Nicholas was one of Myra's early bishops and after his death Myra became a popular place of pilgrimage.

A section of the Lycian Way (p359) begins at Myra.

A short taxi ride from the quare will cost TL5 – the site is fairly self-explanatory.

ÇAYAĞZI (ANDRIAKE)

About 5km west of Kale's centre is Çayağzı (Stream Mouth), called Andriake by the

Romans at a time when the port was an important entrepot for grain on the sea route between the eastern Mediterranean and Rome.

The **ruins** of the ancient town cover a wide area around the present settlement, which is little more than a dozen boat yards and a beachfront restaurant with decent food and sea views. Some of the land is swampy, so the great **granary** built by Hadrian (finished in AD 139), to the south of the beach access road, can be difficult to reach in wet weather. Boat builders are often at work here.

You can usually find an excursion boat or a taxi boat to Üçağız from here, too.

Dolmuşes sporadically run out to Çayağzı – your best bet is probably a taxi (TL10).

Sleeping & Eating

Most visitors visit the area on a day trip. Alas, sleeping options are limited.

Şahin Otel (☎ 871 5687; yusufkamilkolcu@hotmail .com; Müze Caddesi 2; s/d TL30/50; 🐾) Huge rooms like your grandpa used to doze in, featuring dusty armchairs and velvety drapes. Lying 20m from the clock tower off the main square, the hotel is conveniently located and has an enormous shaded terrace outside which regularly fills with day trippers.

Hotel Andriake (☎ 871 4640; antriakehotel@hotmail .com; Finike Caddesi 62; s/d €17/33; 🏊) On the main road at the junction into town stands this standard provincial three-star. It's rather '70s and impersonal but comfortable enough. The pool could do with some chlorine.

Akdeniz Restaurant (☎ 871 5466; Müze Caddesi; pide TL3, köfte TL5; 🕑 7am-midnight) On the main square in front of the clock tower, this simple but spotless place is a local favourite for its home-style dishes made daily.

Sabancı Pastaneleri (☎ 871 2188; PTT Caddesi 12; fresh orange juice TL2, pastries TL3; 🕑 7am-1am; 🐾) Down the road past the Şahin, this place is fabulous for breakfast or a snack. It also does ice cream (TL1 per scoop).

Getting There & Away

Buses and dolmuşes travel to Kaş (TL3, one hour, 45km) every hour, and to Antalya (TL9.25, 2½ to three hours).

FİNİKE TO OLYMPOS

East of Finike the highway skirts a sand and pebble **beach** that runs for about 15km. Once past the long beach, 19km east of Finike,

the road transits **Kumluca**, a farming town surrounded by citrus orchards and plastic-roofed greenhouses. The town is only worth visiting on Friday for its lively market or – as Olympos/Çıralı do not have banking facilities – for its ATMs.

After Kumluca the highway winds back up into the mountains for about 30km until you enter the **Beydağları Sahil National Park** (Beydağları Sahil Milli Parkı).

OLYMPOS, ÇIRALI & CHİMAERA
☎ 0242

Midway between Kumluca and Tekirova a road leads southeast from the main highway – veer to the right then follow the signs – to Çavuşköy, Olympos, Çıralı, and Adrasan beach.

Olympos

Olympos has long had an ethereal hold over its visitors. An important Lycian city in the 2nd century BC, the Olympians devoutly worshipped Hephaestus (Vulcan), the God of Fire. No doubt this veneration sprang from reverence for the mysterious Chimaera, an eternal flame that still springs from the earth not far from the city. Along with the other Lycian coastal cities, Olympos went into a decline in the 1st century BC. With the coming of the Romans in the 1st century AD, things improved, but in the 3rd century pirate attacks brought impoverishment. In the Middle Ages the Venetians, Genoese and Rhodeans built fortresses along the coast (bits of which still hang from the cliff tops) but by the 15th century the site had been abandoned.

Olympos (admission per day TL3) is fairy tale pretty. Set inside a deep shaded valley that runs directly to the sea, its enchanting ruins appear 'undiscovered' among wild grapevines, flowering oleander, bay trees, wild figs and pines. Rambling along the trickling stream that runs through a rocky gorge, listening to the wind in the trees and the songs of innumerable birds is a rare treat, with never a tour bus in sight.

The site is open all the time but during daylight hours a custodian (sporadically) collects the fee.

Çıralı

Çıralı is a relaxed, family-friendly township of upscale pensions on a long, empty beach. It's a near shout from Olympos – or a pleasant trudge through shifting pebbles – and makes an excellent alternative from the backpacking set down beach. It's also the nearest bed to mystical Chimaera.

Chimaera

Also known as Yanartaş or Burning Rock, the Chimaera is a cluster of flames that blaze spontaneously from crevices on the rocky slopes of Mt Olympos. This site is the stuff of legend and it's not difficult to see why ancient peoples attributed these extraordinary flames to the breath of a monster – part lion, part goat and part dragon.

In mythology, Chimaera was the son of Typhon, himself the fierce and monstrous son of Gaia, the earth goddess; he was so frightening that Zeus set him on fire and buried him alive under Mt Etna, thereby creating the volcano. Chimaera was killed by the hero Bellerophon on the orders of King Iobates of Lycia. Bellerophon killed the monster by aerial bombardment – mounting Pegasus, the winged horse, and pouring molten lead into Chimaera's mouth.

Today gas still seeps from the earth and bursts into flame upon contact with the air. The exact composition of the gas is unknown, though it is thought to contain some methane. Although the flames can be extinguished by covering them, they will reignite when uncovered again. In ancient times they were much more vigorous and easily recognised at night by coastal mariners.

These days there are 20 or 30 flames in the main area and a less impressive collection at the top of the hill. By far the best time to visit is after dark, and preferably in a small group to better appreciate their gaseous intrigue.

From Çıralı, follow the road along the hillside marked for the Chimaera until you reach a valley and walk up to a car park. From there it's another 20- to 30-minute climb up a dirt track through the forest (bring a torch) to the site. It's about a 7km walk from Olympos, but most pensions will run you there for around TL10.

Sleeping & Eating

OLYMPOS

Much like its colourful though largely unrecorded history, staying in an Olympos treehouse has long been the stuff of travel legend. The former Med hippie hot spot has gentrified considerably over the past decade but, love it or hate it, Olympos still offers fabulous value

and community-minded accommodation in a stunning natural setting.

The tree-house dream is fading to modern convenience, but all camps include breakfast and dinner in the price (drinks are extra). Bathrooms are generally shared, but many bungalows have their own bathroom and some have air-conditioning. Not all tree houses have reliable locks, so store valuables at reception.

Note that it's worth being extra attentive with personal hygiene while staying here. Every year some travellers wind up ill. Unfortunately the huge numbers of visitors, over the summer in particular, can overwhelm the camps' capacity for proper waste disposal, so be vigilant in particular about when, what, where and how you eat. And don't swim around the point area.

A dozen or so camps line the track along the valley down to the ruins.

Kadir's Yörük Top Treehouse (☎ 892 1250; www .kadirstreehouses.com; dm TL20, bungalows TL40; 😵 💻) Kadir's started it all back before people lived in trees. For the first time in many years, however, this quirky place has grown smaller due to a recent fire damaging a large section of the property. But the fun has resurfaced with even greater irony. There are three bars (including the time-honoured Bull Bar) and, if you please, a rock-climbing wall. It veritably buzzes with backpackers but is well managed. The on-site Adventure Centre (p390) offers a range of activities.

Şaban (☎ 892 1265; www.sabanpansion.com; dm/tree house TL20/30, bungalows TL35-40; 😵) The sight of travellers laid out in hammocks snoozing in the shade soon confirms the local lore: that you come here to chill. In the words of the charming manager Meral, 'It's not a party place' and instead sells itself on tranquillity, space, a family feel and great home cooking. It's an excellent choice for single women.

Caretta Caretta (☎ 892 1292; carettaolympos@hot mail.com; dm/tree house TL20/30, bungalow with bathroom TL40) Pretty and peaceful with wooden benches under shady orange trees, it also prides itself on its food, which is home-cooked by the family's mother.

Bayram's (☎ 892 1243; www.bayrams.com; tree house TL30, bungalow with/without air-con TL50/40; 😵 💻) Here chilled-out 20-somethings sit on cushioned benches in post-party states. Backgammon, books and orange-tree serenading are Bayram's activities of choice, except for the odd swim in the sea.

Orange Pension (☎ 892 1317; www.olympos orangepension.com; bungalow with/without bathroom TL40/35; 🅿) A long-standing favourite that's especially big with Turkish university students and, oddly enough, Japanese guests, the Orange has morphed in size in recent years, but Yusuf and friend still run a good show. The wooden en-suite rooms upstairs feel like a Swiss Family Robinson future, while the concrete rooms downstairs are perhaps the future of Olympos. It's got a great communal dining area and the same guys run a nightclub hidden in the valley.

Türkmen Tree Houses (☎ 892 1249; www.olympos turkmentreehouses.com; tree house TL20, bungalow with/without bathroom TL40/35; 🅿 💻) With the capacity to sleep over 400 guests, the Turkmen is pretty much a village within a village, and the biggest party rival to Kadir's. It's no longer all wilderness either, with small convenience store located on site. The comfy bungalows are made from the pine trees in the orange garden. The dinner is allegedly the best in Olympos. Yacht trips to Kaş can also be arranged.

Pirate's Camp (☎ 892 1265; www.pirates-camp.com; s/d/t bungalows TL55/80/100; 🅿 💻) This newcomer to the wilds of Olympos has unwrapped 24 pretty, ready-made bungalows and plonked them on the road to the beach. Aside from the gaudy sign, however, it's a sympathetic site with a developing sense of balance.

Varuna (☎ 892 1347; beer TL3, mains TL10-15; ⌚ 8am-2.30am) Next to Bayram's, this popular restaurant serves a fair range of snacks and mains including fresh trout (TL10), *gözleme* (TL4) and *şiş* kebaps (roast skewered meat, TL8 to TL10) in some attractive open cabins.

ÇIRALI

Çiralı, to put it crudely, is just two dirt roads lined with pensions. To put it another way, it's a delightful beach community for nature lovers and post-backpackers. Driving in, you cross a small bridge where a few taxis wait to run people back up to the main road. Continue across the bridge and you'll come to a junction in the road disfigured with innumerable signboards – there are about 60 pensions here. Go straight on for the pensions nearest to the path up to the Chimaera. Turn right for the pensions closest to the beach and the Olympos ruins.

Olympia Treehouse & Camping (☎ 825 7311; camp site/tree house per person TL10/20) Copying the tree house experience of its namesake, Olympia, but lacking the party atmosphere, this is a pleasant, peaceful place set by the beach amid fruit trees. Boat and snorkelling excursions can be organised.

Orange Motel (☎ 825 7327; www.orangemotel.net; s/d TL50/90; 🅿 💻) Another smart and affordable choice right on the beach. The garden is hung with hammocks and the stairs leading to the agreeable rooms are wrought in iron design. The evening meal is about as wild as it gets at the Orange – indeed, in all Çiralı – though nonguests often drop by for a taste of what's cooking.

Myland Nature (☎ 825 7044; www.mylandnature.com; s/d/tr TL80/110/140; 🅿 💻) This is an arty, holistic and laid-back place that has a vibe to rub you the right way. The spotless bungalows are set around a pretty garden and the food garners high praise. Bikes are available and there are daily boat trips.

Hotel Canada (☎ 825 7233; www.hotelcanada.com; s/d TL80/100; 🅿 💻 🅿) This is a beautiful place to stay offering pretty much the quintessential Çiralı experience; warmth, friendliness and steady relaxation. The garden is filled with hammocks, citrus trees, and the odd chicken and rabbit. It's ideal for families and children. Carrie and Saban are impeccable hosts.

Odile Hotel (☎ 825 7163; www.hotelodile.com; s/d TL70/100; 🅿 🅿) This unassuming hotel is set on a large garden property with the best mountain backdrop in Çiralı. The rooms are spacious, the pool spectacular, though the service is a little detached. It's opposite the beach opening.

Arcadia Hotel (☎ 825 7340; www.arcadiaholiday.com; d with half-board TL200; 🅿) Escaping over-developing Ölüdeniz, the Canadian-Turkish owners of these four luxury bungalows have established a lovely escape amid verdant gardens at the northern end of the beach, across the road from Myland Nature. The place is well laid out and well managed, and the friendly owners are keen to please. The food at the restaurant is also of a high standard.

Olympos Lodge (☎ 825 7171; www.olymposlodge .com.tr; s/d with half-board TL280/350; 🅿 💻) Not only situated right on the beach, it also boasts over 1.5 hectares of cool citrus orchards and verdant, manicured gardens. It's professionally managed and the private villas are very peaceful and comfortable. Find it by walking along the beach towards the Olympos ruins.

ACTIVE IN OLYMPOS

If you're chilled-out to the bone, Kadir's Yörük Top Treehouse (p388) has an **Adventure Centre** (☎ 892 1316; ✆ 8.30am-7pm), which offers the following activities (prices are per person):

Boat cruises Full-day trip TL40 (minimum eight to 10 people); includes snorkelling gear and lunch.
Canyoning Full-day trip TL60; includes lunch at trout farm in mountains.
Chimaera Flame Tours TL20 for three hours; departures after dinner at 9pm.
Jeep safaris Full-day trip for TL50 includes lunch and transport.
Mountain biking TL40 for four hours.
Rock climbing On a natural wall; TL25 for two climbs.
Scuba diving TL60 for two dives (qualified divers only); the full-day trip includes all equipment and lunch.
Sea-kayaking Half-day trip (noon to 4pm) TL40; includes lunch on beach.
Trekking TL35, five hours; lunch included.

Getting There & Away

Generally any bus taking the coast road between Antalya and Fethiye will drop you or pick you up from the roadside restaurant at the top of the hill – just look for the travellers lying about. From there, minibuses leave for Çıralı and Olympos.

From May to October, the first minibus (TL2.75, 20 minutes) leaves the restaurant at 8.30am, then they depart every hour on the half-hour until 6.30pm. Returning, minibuses leave Olympos at 9am, then every hour until 7pm. They pick up all along the road, so just stick out your hand to hail one.

After October they will wait until enough passengers arrive, which can sometimes take quite a while. Assuming enough people show up, the dolmuş then passes all the camps until it reaches the one the driver is paid to stop at.

To Çıralı there are six daily minibuses (TL2.25) from May to November, leaving at 9am, 11am, 1pm, 3pm, 5pm and 6pm. Minibuses do a loop along the beach road, then pass the turn-off to the Chimaera and head back along the edge of the hillside.

On Friday there are dolmuşes from Çıralı to Kumluca market.

ADRASAN

☎ 0242

Attached to the farming village of Çavuşköy – about 10km south along the coast from Olympos – is the expatriate corner of Adrasan. Especially popular with older British expats, this tiny place is often overlooked by the younger crowd, even though it consists of a mile of pebbly beach – with some non-native litter – a sheltered bay, and another sublime mountain backdrop. An unpaved road skirting the beach has a few nice pensions and restaurants.

Eviniz Pension (☎ 883 1110; www.eviniz.de; r per person TL60; ✆ May-Nov; ✖ ✆) About 1km back from the beach on the road between Adrasan and Çavuşköy, this is a boutique hotel that boasts a beautiful pool on a terrace. The comfortable, attractive rooms have balconies and distant sea views.

Grand Çengis Kaan (☎ 883 1012; www.cengizkaan hotel.com; s/d with half-board TL80/140; ✖ ▢ ✆) The newest hotel in Adrasan comes courtesy of the Pinar family, who efficiently manage these better-than-average premises. The spacious rooms which surround an attractive pool are replicas of resort chic.

Ön Otel (☎ 883 1099; www.onotel.com; s/d TL40/60; ✖ ✆) An attractive whitewashed building with a lovely pool and a tennis court set amid gorgeous grounds, the Ön is a family-run and friendly sort of place. Rooms are simple but spacious and attractive, and all have balcony. There's also a good book collection and bikes are available.

North of the beach along the delightful tree-lined river is a string of restaurants where you eat on wooden platforms set in the water. **Paradise Café** (☎ 883 1267; meals TL20-30; ✖), run by Nikret and Jill, has a pleasant atmosphere and exquisitely prepared trout.

Getting There & Away

To Antalya (TL8, two hours) three buses leave daily in high season at 7.30am, 11am and 5pm; and in low season at 7.30am only. From Antalya two buses leave daily at 9am and 3.30pm in high season; in low season they go at 3.30pm only.

In high season, boats run from Adrasan beach to Kale and Kaş.

PHASELİS

About 3km north of the Tekirova turn-off (56km from Antalya) is the incomparably romantic and ruined Lycian city of Phaselis. Apparently founded by Greek colonists on the border between Lycia and Pamphylia around 334 BC, its wealth came from being a port for the shipment of timber, rose oil and perfume. These days it's just another unforgettable holiday hideaway.

Shaded by pines, the **ruins of Phaselis** (admission TL8; 🕗 8am-7pm May-Oct, 9am-5.30pm Nov-Apr) are arranged around three small, perfect bays, each with its own diminutive beach. The ruins are not particularly exciting, and are all from Roman and Byzantine times, but the setting is divine.

About 1km from the highway is the site entrance, with a small building where you can buy soft drinks, snacks and souvenirs, use the toilet and visit a one-room museum. The ruins and the shore are another 1km further on.

The aptly named **Sundance Nature Village** (Sundance Camp; ☎ 821 4165; www.sundancecamp.com; camp site/s/d/tr tree houses per person TL15/22/27/35, bungalows TL40/60) is a lifestyle you'll most likely embrace in Phaselis. It's sublimely peaceful with charming bungalows and tree houses shaded under fragrant pine trees. The restaurant offers excellent organic food. BBQs and camp fires are often set up for guests and horses are available for rides (TL40 per person for up to three hours).

Getting There & Away

Frequent buses between Kaş and Antalya pass the Phaselis turn-off. To get to Sundance Camp from Antalya, alight at the Tekirova junction, turn left and follow the signs. It's a 20-minute walk from the junction or – if you're lucky/lazy – you can get a taxi.

ANTALYA

☎ 0242 / pop 798,500

Once seen by travellers as the gateway to the 'Turkish Riviera', Antalya quickly became a bona fide international travel destination unto itself. Situated directly on the Gulf of Antalya (Antalya Körfezi), the largest Turkish city on the Mediterranean is both stylishly modern and classically beautiful. It also boasts the creatively preserved Roman-Ottoman quarter of Kaleiçi, a splendid and pristine Roman harbour, plus stirring ruins in the surrounding Beydağları (Bey Mountains).

Antalya is generating a buzz among culture-vultures. The city's restaurants rival those throughout the country, many of its boutique hotels are of tremendous quality and value, and the archaeological museum is world-class. For nightlife lovers, there are a number of chic Med-carpet clubs, while the opera and ballet season at the Aspendos amphitheatre continues to draw critical attention.

Kaleiçi is also a boon for architecture buffs, with some of Turkey's best preserved Ottoman houses – many with *Satilik* ('For Sale') signs disappearing overnight. And with the town council effortlessly rebranding Antalya as a luxury yachting must-moor, its future is crystal blue.

History

This area has been inhabited since the earliest times. The oldest artefacts, found in the Karain Cave (Karain Mağarası; p402) 2km inland from Antalya, date back to the Palaeolithic period. As a city, Antalya is not as old as many others that once lined this coast, but it is still prospering while the older ones are dead.

Founded by Attalus II of Pergamum in the 1st century BC, the city was named Attaleia after its founder. When the Pergamene kingdom was bequeathed to Rome, Attaleia became a Roman city. Emperor Hadrian visited here in AD 130 and a triumphal arch (now known as Hadrian's Gate) was built in his honour.

The Byzantines took over from the Romans but in 1207 the Seljuk Turks based in Konya snatched the city from them and gave Antalya a new version of its name, and also its symbol, the Yivle Minare (Grooved Minaret). After the Mongols broke the Seljuk grip on power, Antalya was held for a while by the Turkish Hamidoğulları emirs. It was taken by the Ottomans in 1391.

After WWI the Allies divided up the Ottoman Empire. Italy got Antalya in 1918 but by 1921 Atatürk's armies had put an end to all such foreign holdings.

Orientation

At the centre of the historic city is the Roman harbour, which is set to undergo a many-million-lira makeover (not that you really need it, dear). Around it is the old-stone historic district called Kaleiçi, which features fine Ottoman houses and remnants of the Roman Empire. Around Kaleiçi, beyond the ivy-decked Roman walls, is the commercial centre of the city.

ANTALYA

0 — 1 km
0 — 0.6 miles

To Otogar (2km);
Termessos (34km);
Karian Cave (45km);
Isparta (175km);
Ankara (550km);
İstanbul (725km)

To Antalya Kültür
Merkezi (400km)

To Konyaaltı (200m);
Hillside (200m);
Aqualand (200m);
Olympos (86km)

To Airport (10km);
Perge (15km);
Side (65km);
Alaniya (115km)

To Dedeman Aquapark (5km);
Lara Plajı (10km)

Antalya Bay
(Antalya
Körfezi)

See Kaleiçi Map (p395)

INFORMATION
Banks and Exchange Offices........ 1 C3
Central Post Office...................... 2 B3
Post Office.................................. 3 C3
Post Office.................................. 4 B2
Tourist Office.............................. 5 B3

SIGHTS & ACTIVITIES
Antalya Museum........................ 6 A3

EATING 🍴
7 Mehmet.................................. 7 A3
Can Can Pide Yemek Salonu....... 8 C3
Güneyliler................................... 9 C3

ENTERTAINMENT 🎭
Aspendos Opera & Ballet Festival Ticket
  Office.................................... 10 B3
Plaza Cinemas.......................... 11 D3

TRANSPORT
Atlasjet................................... 12 B3
Dolmuşes to Otogar.................. 13 C3
Turkish Airlines........................ 14 B3

Antalya's central landmark and symbol is the Yivli Minare. It stands near the main square, called Kale Kapısı (Fortress Gate), which is marked by an old stone *saat kalesi* (clock tower). The broad plaza with the bombastic equestrian statue of Atatürk is Cumhuriyet Meydanı (Republic Sq).

From Kale Kapısı, Cumhuriyet Caddesi goes west past the tourist office and Turkish Airlines office, then becomes Kenan Evren Bulvarı, which continues for several kilometres to the Antalya Museum and Konyaaltı Plajı, a 10km-long pebble beach.

Northwest from Kale Kapısı, Kazım Özalp Caddesi (formerly Şarampol Caddesi), is a pedestrian way. Antalya's small bazaar is east of Kazım Özalp Caddesi. East from Kale

Kapısı, Ali Çetinkaya Caddesi goes to the airport (10km).

The Gazi Bulvarı *çevreyolu* (ring road) carries long-distance traffic around the city centre. Antalya otogar (Yeni Garaj) is 4km north of the centre on the D650 Hwy.

Information
BOOKSHOPS
Owl Bookshop (Map p395; ☎ 243 2944; owlbook shop@yahoo.com; Barbaros mah, Kocatepe sok9, kapısı; ☻ 10am-7pm Mon-Sat) The best secondhand bookshop on the Turkish Mediterranean has moved around the corner. Owl Bookshop is very well edited and pretty well stocked, care of literary larrikin, Kemal Özkurt. The owner's booming voice gives heartfelt reading advice. Shout out if unattended.

SIX QUESTIONS ABOUT BOOKS

Sharing stories is half the fun of travel – Kemal from Owl Books has the finest in town.

When, where and why did you first start selling secondhand books? I grew up in Antalya where 25 years ago I started selling books. During the early days I sold books to backpackers at a local hotel. Before that I sold lemon juice to passengers boarding buses to İstanbul.

Which writers best describe Turkey? For the Turkish mentality, Kurban Said's *The Girl from Golden Horn;* for the landscape, *The Towers of Trebizond* by Rose Macaulay.

Which five books could you not live without? *Portnoy's Complaint* by Philip Roth (this is more than enough).

How has the traveller to Turkey changed over the years? The traveller now has more money.

Is there one book you would never sell? I never sell holy books.

What's the best deal you've ever made with a traveller? I once exchanged a book for a kiss.

INTERNET ACCESS

There are numerous internet cafés in the alleys and arcades off Atatürk Caddesi, most within easy walking distance of Hadrian's Gate.

Cevher Internet (Map p395; ⏰ 9am-midnight) This tiny café offers high-speed access in an alley across the street from Hadrian's Gate.

Natural Internet Café (Map p395; ⏰ 8am-11pm) The city's most atmospheric internet café, located within the maze of eateries down the steps behind the Atatürk statue. Next door is the Natural Nargile Café, a cosy spot offering decent food and nargilehs.

INTERNET RESOURCES

About Antalya (www.aboutantalya.net) Historical information about the region and its preserved ancient cities.

Antalya Guide (www.antalyaguide.org) A comprehensive site with info on everything from climate to TV channels.

MONEY

A number of banks are located on Kazım Özalp Caddesi (Map p392) as are several *döviz* (currency exchange) offices.

POST

There are several post offices within walking distance of Kaleiçi.

Central Post office (Map p392; Kenan Evren Bulvarı) A few hundred metres past the tourist office and across the street. Use the Seleker tram stop.

TELEPHONES

Turk Telecom (Map p395; Recep Peker Caddesi 4; ⏰ 8.30am-10.30pm) Call centre near Hadrian's Gate. International calls placed here are generally cheaper than those made with a Turkish calling card.

TOURIST INFORMATION

Tourist office (Map p392; ☎ 241 1747; Yavuz Ozcan Parkı; ⏰ 8am-7pm) In a small wooden shack tucked behind the souvenir vendors of Yavuz Ozcan Parkı. Employees speak English, French and German, depending on the shift.

Sights & Activities

YIVLI MINARE & THE BAZAAR

The Yivli Minare (Map p395), downhill from the **clock tower**, is a handsome and distinctive minaret erected by the Seljuk sultan Alaeddin Keykubad I in the early 13th century, next to a church that the sultan had converted to a mosque. It is now the **Güzel Sanatlar Galerisi** (Fine Arts Gallery) with changing exhibits. To its northwest is a **Mevlevi tekke** (whirling dervish monastery), which probably dates from the 13th century; nearby are two **tombs**, those of Zincirkıran Mehmet Bey (built 1377) and the lady Nigar Hatun.

KALEİÇİ (OLD ANTALYA)

Go down Uzun Çarşi Sokak, the street opposite the clock tower. On the left is the **Tekeli Mehmet Paşa Camii** (Map p395), built by the Beylerbey (Governor of Governors) Tekeli Mehmet Paşa. The building was repaired extensively in 1886 and 1926. Note the beautiful Arabic inscriptions in the coloured tiles above the windows.

Wander further into Kaleiçi, now a historical zone protected from modern development. Many of the gracious old **Ottoman houses** have been restored then converted to pensions, hotels or, inevitably, carpet and souvenir shops. The northern part of Kaleiçi is the most touristy; persevere and explore the quieter backstreets abutting Karaalioğlu Parkı.

The **Roman harbour** at the base of the slope was restored during the 1980s and is now a marina for yachts and excursion boats. It was Antalya's lifeline from the 2nd century BC until late in the 20th century, when a new port was constructed about 12km west of the city, at the far end of Konyaaltı Plajı.

In the southern reaches of Kaleiçi is the **Kesik Minare** (Cut Minaret; Map p395; Hesapçı Sokak), a stump of a minaret which marks the ruins of a substantial building. Built originally as a 2nd-century Roman temple, it was converted in the 6th century to the Byzantine Church of the Virgin Mary.

Korkut Camii (Map p395) nearby served the neighbourhood's Muslim population until 1896, when it was mostly destroyed by fire. Gates and walls prevent fire now, but it's possible to see bits of Roman and Byzantine marble from outside.

At the southwestern edge of Kaleiçi, on the corner with Karaalioğlu Parkı, rises the **Hıdırlık Kalesi** (Map p395), a 14m-high tower in the ancient walls, which dates from the 1st century AD.

Down Atatürk Caddesi is the monumental marble **Hadriyanüs Kapısı** (Hadrian's Gate, Üçkapılar or the Three Gates, Map p395), erected during the Roman emperor Hadrian's reign (AD 117–38). It leads into Kaleiçi.

Further along Atatürk Caddesi towards the sea is **Karaalioğlu Parkı** (Map p395), a large, attractive, flower-filled park good for a stroll, particularly at sunset.

SUNA & İNAN KIRAÇ KALEIÇI MUSEUM

In the heart of Kaleiçi, just off Hesapçı Sokak, you'll find a **museum** (Map p395; Kocatepe Sokak 25; admission €0.85; 9am-noon & 1-6pm Thu-Tue). The main building is a lovingly restored Antalya mansion; the 2nd floor contains a very well done but still somewhat hokey series of life-size dioramas depicting some of the most important rituals and milestones in typical Ottoman lives.

Much more impressive is the collection of Turkish ceramics found in the museum's next building – the former Greek Orthodox church of Aya Yorgo (St George) – which has been so well restored that it's worth seeing in itself.

ANTALYA MUSEUM

Comprehensive, inspired and thoroughly entertaining is how best to describe the **Antalya Museum** (Map p392; Cumhuriyet Caddesi; admission TL15; 9am-7.30pm Tue-Sun), roughly 2km west of the centre and easily reachable by tram. Beginning your leisurely, measured walk through time is a collection of small works, including finely detailed figurines, which are arranged chrono-

logically from the Stone and Bronze Ages, and then through to the Mycenaean, Classical and Hellenistic periods. It's tempting to yield and hurry through to the Hall of Gods and the museum's simply phenomenal collection of priceless treasures. We forgive you.

Even those not particularly fascinated by Greek mythology will be moved by this collection, which includes numerous representations of 16 gods, some in near-perfect condition. The curatorial artistry is again on display as a motion detection system that casts a dramatic light upon each statue as a visitor approaches. The vast majority of the statues were found during excavations of the nearby city of Perge in the 1970s; some were uncovered at Aspendos. Viewing the gods either before or after a visit to Perge will certainly enhance your experience.

Other exhibitions include an ancient piggybank in the Hall of Coins, and a curious collection of stone legs and feet in the shaded back garden.

BEACHES & WATER PARK

Lara Plajı is your best bet for swimming; it's about 12km southeast of the centre, and plays host to a hot new summer rock festival, Rock'n Antalya. The alternative is **Konyaaltı Plajı**, a name synonymous with mega beach culture; it can be accessed by taking the tram to its final stop (Müze), and then walking further west and down the snaking road.

Continue west and you'll come to the **Aqualand** (249 0900; www.beachpark.com.tr) water park, complete with slides and, yes, live dolphins. Also 6km south of Antalya is the **Dedeman Aquapark** (316 4400; Dedeman Hotel; Lara Yolu; admission TL25; 10am-6pm), said to be the largest water park in the Middle East. The latest addition is a giant half-pipe.

Dolmuşes run from Fevzi Çakmak Caddesi to Lara Plajı, passing the aquapark (TL1).

HAMAMS

Kaleiçi is a great place to start your massage fetish, most notably at the 700-year-old **Balık Pazarı Hamam** (Map p395; 243 6175; cnr Balık Pazarı Sokak & Paşa Camii Sokak; 8am-midnight for men, 8am-9pm for women) where a bath, a peeling, and a soap and oil massage cost TL30, or it's TL10 for a bath only. More of the good oil is found at the atmospheric **Sefa Hamam** (Map p395; www.sefahamam.com; Kocatepe Sokak 32; 9am-11pm), which retains much of its 13th-century Seljuk

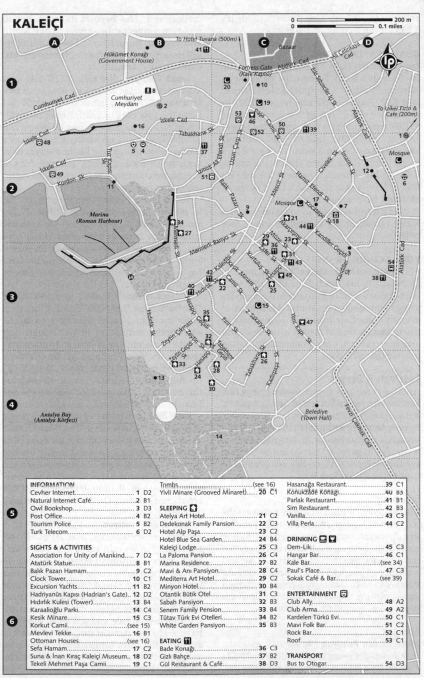

KALEİÇİ

architecture. A bath here costs TL15, or it's TL35 for the recommended works.

BOAT & RAFTING TRIPS

Excursion yachts (Map p395) tie up in the Roman harbour in Kaleiçi. Some trips go as far as Kemer, Phaselis, Olympos, Kale (Demre) and Kaş. You can take one-hour (TL20) or two-hour (TL35) trips or a six-hour voyage (TL80 with lunch) which visits the Lower Düden Falls (p401), Gulf of Antalya islands and some beaches for a swim. It's a good idea to ask about lunch when comparing prices; there's a big difference between a sandwich and a three-course seafood feast. Ask also if alcoholic beverages are included.

Many travel agencies in town offer white-water rafting in the Köprülü Kanyon (see p404).

YOGA SCHOOLS & INSTRUCTION

The **Association for the Unity of Mankind** (Map p395; ☎ 244 5807; Hesapçı Sokak 7) is an all-encompassing socio-spiritual organisation that includes a yoga and meditation studio. Morning and evening classes are held daily in a variety of disciplines, as well as classes in aerobics and arts and crafts. A weekly schedule is posted outside the front door.

Festivals & Events

Antalya is famous for its **Golden Orange Film Festival** (Altın Portakal Film Festivali; http://altinportakal .tursak.org.tr/indexen.php), held in late September or early October. **Rock'n Antalya** (Lara Plajı) should become a regular fixture on the Antalya music scene, as a huge crowd turned out in late June for this inaugural three-day celebration of contemporary Turkish rock.

Sleeping

Undoubtedly the place to stay in Antalya is the old town of Kaleiçi. In this virtually vehicle-free district is everything you need, including some of the better guest houses in Turkey. To reach Kaleiçi, pass through Hadrian's Gate and walk along Hesapçı Sokak. Kaleiçi's winding streets can be confusing to navigate, although signs pointing the way to most pensions are posted in alleys and on street corners.

BUDGET

White Garden Pansiyon (☎ 248 9115; www.xhost .co.uk/whitegarden; Hesapçı Geçidi 9; s/d TL30/40; �にか 🖳) The White Garden combines tidiness, dis-

cretion and class beyond its price, not to mention impeccable service from Metin and co, the proprietors. The building itself is a fine restoration – the courtyard particularly charming.

Sabah Pansiyon (Map p395; ☎ 247 5345; www .sabahpansiyon.8m.com; Hesapçı Sokak 60/A; dm/s/d without shower TL20/30/40, s/d with shower TL30/40; 🌔 🖳) Long the first port of call for budget travellers to Kaleiçi, rooms vary greatly in size and standard, so insist on seeing a few. Service can be aloof, though the kitchen serves delicious home-cooked meals. The real draw is the shaded courtyard, perfect for hooking up with other travellers.

Senem Family Pension (Map p395; ☎ 247 1752; fax 247 0615; Zeytin Geçidi Sokak 9; s/d TL40/50; 🌔) Homesick backpackers will feel immediately comfortable here, as Mrs Seval Ünsal (call her 'Mama') clearly enjoys doting on guests. Some of the spotless but simple rooms have bay views; rooms without air-conditioning or a view are cheaper.

Dedekonak Family Pansion (Map p395; ☎ 248 5264; Hıdırlık Sokak 13; s/d TL30/50) An affordable, super-clean and more upscale alternative. The rooms, with retro French advertising on the walls and satellite television, aren't terribly impressive, although the outdoor patio with built-in bar more than picks up the slack. Definitely stick around for the evening feast, created nightly by the French-Turkish owners.

Hotel Blue Sea Garden (☎ 248 8213; www.bluesea garden.com; Hesapçı Sokak 65; s/d with half-board TL40/60; 🌔 🌔) The two pluses here are the extra large swimming pool area – vital in the heat of summer – and the go-getting management team who works in happy droves. The rooms are nothing special, though the elevated ones are more peaceful. The restaurant prepares excellent meals.

Mavi & Ani Pansiyon (Map p395; ☎ 247 0056; www.maviani.com; Tabakhane Sokak 26; s/d TL40/60) Something of an odd cross between a lovingly restored Ottoman house and Japanese *ryokan* where some rooms sport a mattress laid directly atop raised wooden floors, and the common areas are decorated in Anatolian style. Ask for the single or double rooms with the attached terrace and sea view; they also have a shared refrigerator. Discounts are available for stays longer than three days, and guests can swim for free at the nearby Backside Hotel.

MIDRANGE

Kaleiçi Lodge (☎ 243 2270; www.kaleicilodge.com; Hesapçi Sokak 37; s/d TL50/80; ⬚ ▣) This stylish, small hotel is sparklingly new and very affordable. The stark white lobby and hallways reveal red-draped, sharp-lined rooms, with hard, clean surfaces.

Tütav Türk Evi Otelleri (Map p395; ☎ 248 6591; www .turkeviotelleri.com; Mermerli Sokak 2; s/d TL50/100; ⬚ ▣) Because it is comprised of three restored Ottoman guest houses, this is easily the largest hotel of its type in the area. The pool area, surrounded by the towering harbour wall, is especially charming. Don't be fooled by the rococo lobby; the 20 Turkish- and Ottoman-themed rooms are detailed with particularly impressive taste.

La Paloma Pansion (Map p395; ☎ 244 8497; www .lapalomapansion.com; Tabakhane Sokak 3; s/d TL80/100; ⬚ ▣ ▣) A change in ownership has not dented the condition of this excellent mid-range hotel. Despite being housed in a single Ottoman building, La Paloma has surprisingly large rooms – some with Jacuzzi, all with satellite TV – with the best facing inwards to the figure-eight–shaped swimming pool. Except to produce a reasonable breakfast spread, the kitchen does not open.

Atelya Art Hotel (☎ 241 6416; www.atelyahotel.com; Civelek Sokak 21; d TL120; ⬚ ▣) Timelessness is hard to pin down, but the Atelya makes a bold effort in this eccentric art-inspired hotel. The owner displays his diverse portfolio on the walls, but it's the sultanic splendour of richly coloured fabrics and beautiful furniture cast in beams of sunlight that best capture the spirit of the Ottomans. As you'd expect with such a breathy place, in winter it can get a little musty.

Otantik Butik Otel (☎ 244 8530; www.otantikbutik otel.com; Hesapçi Sokak 14; d TL120; ⬚ ▣) Six brand-new, intimate rooms, each with ample space and privacy, set above a well-stocked wine cellar on a main street of Kaleiçi – Otantik is off to a good start.

Tuvana (Map p395; ☎ 247 6015; www.tuvanahotel.com; Tuzcular Mah, Karanlık Sokak 7; s/d TL100/150; ⬚ ▣ ▣) This hidden once-royal compound of six Ottoman houses has been converted into a fine inner-old city inn. The Tuvana is refinement personified by its hosts, Aziz and Nermins who prepare this 'Special Class' hotel (and dreamy breakfast table) with precision and grace. Rooms are suitably plush, with kilims, linen and light fittings emitting soft

oranges and yellows; the small swimming pool tops it off.

TOP END

Mediterra Art Hotel (☎ 244 8624; www.mediterraart .com; Zafer Sokak 5; d TL160, ste TL200; ⬚ ⬚ ▣ ▣) The sign of things to come in Antalya, perhaps, is this brand-new up-scale masterpiece of wood and stone that immediately impresses in both service and design. The Mediterra offers sanctuary by a cutting-edge pool and has a marvellous winter dining room. Space is harnessed to maximum effect, especially in the small though modestly luxurious rooms, all with LCD TVs.

Minyon Hotel (Map p395; ☎ 247 1147; www.minyon hotel.com; Tabakhane Sokak 31; s/d TL150/200; ⬚ ▣) Seven artfully decorated rooms send the Minyon beyond boutique hotel to a private townhouse for the wealthy and cultured. Critically acclaimed for its attention to detail (imagine laying the tiles on the pool deck), the Minyon is attentively priced to match. For all that it's worth, request a sea view.

Hotel Alp Paşa (Map p395; ☎ 247 5676; www.alppasa .com; Hesapçi Sokak 30-32; s/d €65/85, with jacuzzi €70/95; ⬚ ▣ ▣) The most effectively signposted hotel in the Kaleiçi labyrinth has 60 individually designed rooms fitted out with tasteful Ottoman detail. The outdoor courtyard, where swimming and dining takes place, displays Roman columns and other artefacts unearthed during the hotel's construction. There's an on-site hamam and an atmospheric stone-walled restaurant featuring an impressive list of French and Turkish wines – the evening set menu (TL40) is open to nonguests. A remarkable drop in prices will make booking essential.

Marina Residence (Map p395; ☎ 247 5490; www.mar inaresidence.net; Mermerli Sokak 15; s/d €110/130; ⬚ ▣) Located away from the hubbub, the Marina is known as one of Antalya's signature top-end hotels. The rooms, however, are starting to show their 18 years, despite the efforts of the smiling and efficient staff. The Marina's oddest touch is its outdoor pool; a glass wall on one side allows café patrons a view of the underwater goings-on.

Hillside Su (☎ 249 0700; www.hillsidesu.com; s/d €160/240; ⬚ ▣) Architect Eren Talu's jaw-dropping peon to 1960s minimalism is a blinding wash of clean white. The rooms themselves have sleek low-level plinths as beds, lava lamps and goldfish bowls, and a disco choice of lighting – red, pink or, you guessed it, white. Sadly, however, the service got a little mixed up in the wash. The pool deck, where celeb-spotting is in season, is made from criss-crossed Icoco wood. There's a very good sushi bar, but general bar prices (TL25 for a whisky!) will get lodged firmly in your throat.

Eating

A nearly endless assortment of cafés and eateries are tucked in and around the harbour area; those perched over the bay command the highest prices. For cheap eating, cross over Atatürk Caddesi and poke around deep in the commercial district.

Ulker Fırın & Café (Map p395; ☎ 247 0324; Recep Perker Caddesi 21A; baklava TL3) Take care not to over-order at this thoroughly modern bakery, which is packed with both traditional and non-traditional Turkish sweets – the tiny pieces of *şöbiyet* (walnut curd) and *fıstıklı* (pistachio) baklava are significantly more filling than they first appear. It's close to Plaza Cinemas.

Can Can Pide Yemek Salonu (Map p392; ☎ 243 2548; Hasim Iscan Mahallesi, Arik Caddesi 4A; Adana durum TL6; ⓧ 9am-11pm Mon-Sat) Looking for very cheap and cheerful? The Can Can most certainly can! Fantastically prepared *çorba* (soup), pide and Adana *durum* at bargain prices. It's elbow room only, so go ahead and nudge right in. It's located diagonally across the street from Plaza Cinemas.

Konukzade Konağı (Map p395; ☎ 244 7456; Hıdırlık Sokak 20; mains TL10-15) This lovely living-room restaurant, with couches and paintings in the style of Australian Aboriginal art, is overseen by a friendly Dutch woman and long-term expat. The busy kitchen makes reasonably priced and quickly prepared Turkish dishes, plus a gorge-worthy *appeltaart* (apple pie). There's a lovely alfresco garden at the front.

Bade Konaği (Map p395; ☎ 248 0185; Zafer Sokak 7; mains TL10-20) This stylish and friendly two-storey restaurant – popular in winter for its warm interiors – doubles as a jumping live music bar on weekends. The grills are delicious, but the sides are the stars here, such as *siyah pirinçli pilav* (wild black rice) and the dill and mint salad served in a fruit bowl.

Hasanağa Restaurant (Map p395; ☎ 242 8105; Mescit Sokak 15; meals TL10-20) Expect to find the garden dining area here absolutely packed on Friday and Saturday nights, when traditional Turkish musicians and folk dancers entertain. Entrées are predictable – *köfte* and mixed grills and such – although the chefs seem to regularly

work wonders and all veggie dishes clock in at around TL10.

Gül Restaurant & Café (Map p395; ☎ 247 5126; Kocatepe Sokak 1; meals TL10-20) On the cusp of Atatürk Caddesi is the backyard garden at this intimate eatery, popular with German couples. It's shaded by a crop of Antalya's famous orange trees. Small but affordable portions include octopus with baked veggies and cheese (TL12), and an entrée of mushrooms and veggies for TL8.

Sim Restaurant (Map p395; ☎ 248 0107; Kaledibi Sokak 7; meals TL10-20) A choice of seated areas make this simple, charming restaurant an experience worthy of return. When the weather's balmy, dine underneath the canopy in the narrow passageway at the front – the Byzantine walls will keep your secrets. Inside, global graffiti gives it a youthful pulse, while upstairs, eclectic antiques complement *köfte*, white bean salads and glorious *çorba*.

Güneyliler (Map p392; ☎ 241 1117; Elmali Mahallesi 4 No 12; meals TL12) With its spare, cafeteria-style interior, this *very* reasonably priced locals-only joint isn't much to look at. But the wood-fired *lahmacun* (Arabic-style pizza) and expertly grilled kebaps are served with so many complimentary extras, you'll likely find yourself returning again and again. If you get lost on the way, ask for directions at the Best Western on Kazım Özlap Caddesi.

Parlak Restaurant (Map p395; ☎ 241 6553; Kazım Özlap Qvenue Zincirlihan 7; meals TL12-25) Behind the jewellery bazaar is this sprawling open-air patio favoured by locals and legendary for its slow-roasted chicken. The service is theatrical and exact, as waiters shuffle mezes and seafood off white table cloths, while cute kittens keep you company. A good choice if you're looking to relax for a while, and just steps away from Kale Kapısı.

Vanilla (Map p395; ☎ 247 6013; Zafer Sokak 13; mains TL20-30) Another indicator of Antalya's rising stock is this outstanding, ultra-modern restaurant led by English chef Wayne and his brilliant host and wife, Emel. Glass surfaces and creamy vanilla leather seating let in an attractive mid-summer cool. The evolving menu is a Western European blend of steaks, pasta and reinvigorated Turkish dishes. Presentation and service are first-class.

Villa Perla (Map p395; ☎ 248 9793; Hesapçı Sokak 26; meals TL20-30) A small garden restaurant attached to a pension, this relaxing spot has a locally renowned meze plate (TL15).

Gizlı Bahçe (Map p395; ☎ 244 8010; Dizdar Hasan Bey Sokak 1; meals TL25-35) The location atop the harbour is the reason to visit this pseudo-Italian restaurant. The pasta and grills are fairly standard, though the fish – lemon sole, TL30 – are beautifully prepared. Smart dress is encouraged, but the service isn't worthy of the price.

7 Mehmet Restaurant (Map p392; ☎ 238 5200; www.7mehmet.com; Atatürk Kültür Parkı 333; meals TL25; ⊗ 11am-midnight) One of Antalya's most legendary and highly regarded eateries, 7 Mehmet's spacious indoor and outdoor dining areas sit on the hillside overlooking Konyaaltı Plajı, the city and the bay. The menu of mostly standard grilled entrées and mezes contains some of the most creatively prepared and toothsome food you're likely to encounter anywhere in Turkey.

Drinking

Kaleiçi after dark is getting cooler by the season. The café and cocktail cultures are merging as venues jostle for harbour views. There are also pretty beer gardens humming with rhetoric; live music venues brimming with discord; and raunchy discotheques where drinks are outrageously expensive and Russian and Turkish prostitutes are in full effect. Choose wisely.

Kale Bar (Map p395; ☎ 248 6591; beer TL6; ⊗ 11am-2am) Attached to the Tütav Turk Evi Hotel and artfully constructed around the old city wall, this is a wonderful choice for quiet evening conversation. But much better is the rooftop patio bar, which may very well own the most spectacular harbour and sea view in all of Antalya. Cocktails (TL15 to TL20) are accordingly charged for the pleasure.

Dom-Lik (Map p395; ☎ 247 1920; Zafor Sokak 16; boor TL4, coffee TL3.50; ⊗ noon-midnight) Hidden behind high stone walls, Antalya's university crowd reshapes the world between ice-cold beers, while watching rock and blues bands perform on weekends. Meals are about TL10.

Hangar Bar (Map p395; Uzun Çarşi Sokak; beer TL7) The new bar in town is very loud and very proud. Set back from the street, there's a feeling of quiet opulence as you enter the all-purpose grounds. Yes, you may come inside.

Paul's Place (Map p395; ☎ 244 6894; www.stpaulcc-turkey.com; Yeni kapı Sokak 24; latte TL5, smoothie TL6; ⊗ 10am-5pm Mon-Fri) The good word comes in coffee cups at this informal expat 'club' on the 2nd-floor of St Paul Cultural Center.

Regardless of faith, enjoy the espresso coffee, real filter coffee and home-baked pastries on offer to the genuinely needy. There's a fairly well-stocked lending library, and Turkish language classes and conversation groups happen weekly.

Entertainment

NIGHTCLUBS

Club Ally (Map p395; ☎ 244 3000; Selçuk Mahallesi, Musalla Sokak; admission TL20) A massive outdoor discotheque complete with seven bars, laser lights, and an eardrum-shattering sound system featuring Top 40 and hip-hop. Club Ally is best experienced late at night, when a sea of beautiful bodies can be found dramatically gyrating around the dance floor's circular bar. An onsite restaurant offers seafood and meat entrées (TL16 to TL20) with a gorgeous sea view.

Club Arma (Map p395; ☎ 244 9710; www.clubarma.com; Yatlimani 42; admission TL15) Formerly known as Club 29, this fantastically garish outdoor disco is built right into the cliff-side above the harbour. This may in fact be Antalya's sexiest club in which to watch *gülets* float by while sipping a gin and tonic, but do take care not to fall over the railing or you'll literally end up in the drink.

Mavi Folk Bar (Map p395; ☎ 244 2825; Uzun Çarşi Sokak 58) A laid-back audience of mostly young Turks gathers around the candle-lit tables here – a multitiered, outdoor bar where Turkish folk musicians take to the stage nightly. The vibe is decidedly low-key and the bands set up on a stage cut right out of the old stone wall.

Rock Bar (Map p395; Uzun Çarşi) Something of a non-ironic throwback to the grunge era, this dark and slightly seedy tavern features local guitar bands playing covers of alt-rock classics. Located down the long alley directly across the street from Mevlana Tours on Uzun Çarşi Sokak; look for the ad-hoc motorcycle parking lot.

Roof (Map p395; Uzun Çarşi Sokak 36; admission TL6) The strobe lights inside this cramped 2nd-floor dance club are enough to give you a brain aneurism, but the music – banging techno and jungle – more than makes up for it. The crowds here are generally small and, although the music is played at a ridiculously high volume, there's an outdoor balcony well suited to conversation.

Sokak Café & Bar (Map p395; ☎ 243 8041; Mescit Sokak 17; beer TL5) Over a low stone wall from Hasanağa Restaurant is this canopy-covered beer (Efes, TL5) garden that plays loud music to light drinkers.

Kardelen Türkü Evi (☎ 244 6962; Cami Sokak 9, beer TL5) An interesting mix of indie singer-songwriters and classical folk groups perform in this small, sweaty live venue.

CINEMA
Plaza Cinemas (Map p392; ☎ 312 6296; Sinan Quarter, Recep Peker Caddesi 22; admission TL10) First-run Hollywood blockbusters and the occasional Turkish film are shown at this four-screen cinema, located on the ground floor of a modest shopping centre. Exit Kaleiçi from Hadrian's Gate, walk straight ahead and look for the large building with 'Antalya 2000' posted across the facade.

THEATRE
Antalya Kültür Merkezi (☎ 238 5444; www.altimportakal.org.tr; 100 Yil Bulvarı Atatürk Kültür Parkı İci) West of the city centre by the Sheraton Hotel, this theatre has an interesting program of cultural events, from opera and ballet to folk dancing and performances by the university choir. Tickets are cheap – never more than €5.

Getting There & Away
AIR
Antalya's small but busy airport is 10km east of the city centre on the Alanya highway. A helpful tourist information desk is located in the lobby; a number of car-hire agencies have counters here as well. **Turkish Airlines** (Map p392; ☎ 243 4383; Cumhuriyet Caddesi 91) has at least eight nonstop daily flights in high season to/from İstanbul and at least two from Ankara. Its office is across the street and two blocks west from the recently relocated tourist office. Across the street is the office of the more affordable **Atlasjet** (Map p392; ☎ 330 3900; Cumhuriyet Caddesi), which also has daily nonstop flights to/from İstanbul.

BUS
Antalya's otogar (Yeni Garaj), about 4km north of the city centre, consists of two large terminals fronted by a park. Looking at the otogar from the main highway or its parking lot, the Şehirlerarası Terminalı (Intercity Terminal), which serves long-distance destinations, is on the right. The Provincial Terminal, serving nearby destinations such as Side and Alanya, is on the left. Buses heading to Olympos and Kaş depart from a stop directly across the street from the Sheraton Voyager Hotel.

Getting Around
Antalya's *tramvay* (TL1) has 10 stops and provides the simplest way of crossing town. You pay as you board and exit through the rear door. The tram runs from the Antalya Museum (the stop nearest to Konyaaltı Plajı) along Cumhuriyet Caddesi, Atatürk Caddesi and Isiklar Caddesi.

TO/FROM THE AIRPORT
Havas buses (TL10) depart from the Antalya airport every 30 minutes or so. Passengers

SERVICES FROM ANTALYA'S OTOGAR

Destination	Fare (TL)	Duration (hr)	Distance (km)	Frequency (per day)
Adana	35	11	555	several buses
Alanya	10	2	115	every 20 min
Ankara	30	8	550	frequent
Bodrum	38	11	600	once
Denizli (Pamukkale)	20	4½	300	several
Eğirdir	15	2½	186	every hr
Fethiye (coastal)	30	7½	295	several
Fethiye (inland)	16	4	222	several
Göreme/Ürgüp	38	10	485	frequent
İzmir	28	9	550	several
Kaş	14	4	185	frequent in high season
Kemer	5	1½	35	every 10 min
Konya (via Isparta)	18	6	365	several
Konya (via Akseki)	15	5	349	several
Marmaris	35	7	590	a few
Olympos/Çıralı	8	1½	79	several minibuses & buses
Side/Manavgat	8	1½	65	every 20 min in high season

are conveniently dropped off at Kale Kapısı, just outside Kaleiçi. But to return to the airport, you'll have to get the shuttle outside the Turkish Airlines office on Cumhuriyet Caddesi (take the tram to the Selekler stop).

TO/FROM THE BUS STATION

The blue-and-white Terminal Otobusu 93 (TL1) heads for Atatürk Caddesi in the town centre every 20 minutes or so from the bus shelter near the taxi stand. To get from Kaleiçi to the otogar, go out of Hadrian's Gate, turn right and wait at any of the bus stops along Atatürk Caddesi. Look for 'No 93' on the bus stop's marker.

If you're in a hurry, take a dolmuş: go out of Hadrian's Gate, cross Atatürk Caddesi and walk one block towards the large Antalya 2000 building. Follow the constant stream of dolmuş traffic to the nearby glass shelter; most drivers pass the otogar on the highway (just ask). Be sure the driver knows to let you off at the otogar, and be forewarned that you'll need to dart across a wide and busy highway to reach your destination.

Too complicated? A taxi between the otogar and Kaleiçi should cost approximately TL15 during the day and TL20 at night.

AROUND ANTALYA

Antalya is regularly used as a base for excursions to Phaselis Termessos, Perge, Aspendos and Selge. If you're travelling strictly along the coast, however, substantial time can be saved by visiting Phaselis on your way to or from Olympos or Kaş. Likewise, visiting Perge and Aspendos is easiest when travelling to or from Side or Alanya.

There's a huge array of travel agencies in Antalya's Kaleiçi area, although it's often simpler to book tours at your pension or guest house; the vast majority of sleeping options also have agencies attached. A half-day tour to the Düden Selalesi (Düden Falls) and Termessos costs TL60 per carload. A full-day tour to Perge and Aspendos with side trips to Side and the Manavgat waterfall costs TL80. There are plenty of agencies in Antalya hiring out cars for TL50 to TL70 per day.

Düden Şelalesi (Düden Falls)

Less than 10km north of the city centre, the **Yukari Düden Selalesi** (Upper Düden Falls) can be reached by dolmuş from the Antalya dolmuş stand. Within view of the falls is a

pleasant park and teahouse. This can be a relaxing spot on a hot summer afternoon, but avoid it on summer weekends when the park is crowded.

Asagi Düden Şelalesi (Lower Düden Falls) are down where the Düden Creek meets the Mediterranean at Lara Plajı, southeast of Antalya. Excursion yachts (p396) include a visit to the Lower Düden Falls on their rounds of the Gulf of Antalya.

Termessos

Hidden high and deep in a rugged mountain valley, 34km inland from Antalya, lies the ruined but still massive city of **Termessos** (admission TL8; �} 8am-5.30pm). It is believed that the Termessians, a Pisidian people, were fierce and prone to battling. It's known that they successfully fought off Alexander the Great in 333 BC; and that the Romans (perhaps wisely) accepted the Termessos' wishes to remain an independent ally in 70 BC.

Certainly one of the best preserved archaeological sites in Turkey, Termessos is also magnificently situated: the backdrop of forested mountains against bits and pieces of the ruined city, especially the somewhat difficult-to-reach theatre, is absolutely majestic. Yet to reach many parts of the city requires much scrambling over loose rocks and up steep paths. Do allow a minimum of two hours to explore; you need closer to four hours if you plan to see everything. Also keep in mind that, on a hot day, Termessos boils over. There's nowhere to buy refreshments, so pack your own water.

The first remains you'll come across are, conveniently enough, located within the car park. The portal on the elevated surface was once the entrance to the **Artemis-Hadrian Temple** and **Hadrian Propyleum**. Next, follow the steep path and glance occasionally to your left, where you see remains of the lower city walls and the city gate before reaching the **lower gymnasium** and **colonnaded street**, which leads to the **quarry** and some **sarcophagi**. It's a full hour's walk all the way to the southern necropolis with a detour to the **upper agora** and its five large partitions. The upper agora is an ideal spot to explore slowly and in which to catch a bit of shade. Next, push on to the nearby **theatre**, which sits in an absolutely jaw-dropping locale atop a peak, surrounded by a mountain range that seems remarkably closer than it actually is. Return from the temple to view the cut-limestone

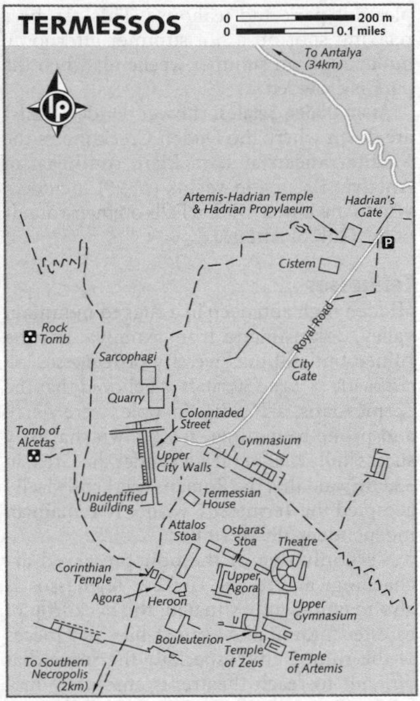
TERMESSOS
0 200 m
0 0.1 miles
To Antalya (34km)
Artemis-Hadrian Temple & Hadrian Propylaeum
Hadrian's Gate
Cistern
Royal Road
Rock Tomb
Sarcophagi
City Gate
Quarry
Colonnaded Street
Tomb of Alcetas
Gymnasium
Upper City Walls
Unidentified Building
Termessian House
Attalos Stoa
Osbaras Stoa
Theatre
Corinthian Temple
Upper Agora
Agora
Heroon
Upper Gymnasium
Bouleuterion
Temple of Zeus
Temple of Artemis
To Southern Necropolis (2km)

bouleuterion, but use caution when scrambling across the crumbled **Temple of Artemis** and **Temple of Zeus** south of it. Both are in a fairly sorry state of disrepair, although the Temple of Zeus does offer a rather pleasant view.

The **southern necropolis** *(mezarlik)* is at the very top of the valley, 3km up from the car park. Viewed from afar, it's a rather disturbing scene of still-intact sarcophagi that seem to have been tossed intermittently from the mountainside by angry gods. In reality, earthquakes and grave robbers created the mess. There isn't much to see at the nearby **tomb of Alcetas** (head back to the main path, take a left and follow the signs), but continue on to encounter a magnificent set of **rock-hewn tombs** before returning to the car park. Free Termessos city plan maps are available for the asking at the ticket booth.

Güllük Dağı National Park has mountain goats, fallow deer, golden eagles and other wild and endangered animals. You'll need to pay a separate park admission fee (TL8) at the entrance, which is also where you'll find the **Flora and Fauna Museum**, which contains a bit of information about the ruined city, as well as about the botany and zoology of the immediate area.

GETTING THERE & AWAY

Taxi tours from Antalya cost around TL80. A cheaper option is to catch a Korkuteli-bound bus to the entrance of Güllük Dağı National Park where, in summer, taxis wait about an hour to run you up the Termessos road and back for TL25.

If you're driving, leave Antalya by the highway towards Burdur and Isparta, turning left after about 11km onto E87/D350, the road marked for Korkuteli, Denizli and Muğla. About 25km from Antalya, look for a road on the right marked for Karian.

Just after the Karian road, look on the left for the entrance to the national park.

Karain Cave

A simply astounding site and one of the more unusual locales in this region of the Turkish Mediterranean, the Karain Mağarası (Karain Cave) is believed by archaeologists (who first excavated the site between 1946 and 1973) to have been continuously occupied for 25,000 years. Much of what was discovered, including stone hand-axes and arrowheads, now resides in Antalya's archaeology museum and in the Museum of Anatolian Civilizations in Ankara. Bone fragments of Neanderthal man were also found. The largest fragment found belonged to the skull of a child. An on-site **museum** (admission TL3; 8am-6pm) has an interesting collection of animal bones and teeth that were found in the cave.

Expect to spend about 15 minutes trekking from the museum to the cave. Once you've arrived, look for the somewhat disturbing relief mask of a human face, which is carved on the central pillar of the main inner room.

GETTING THERE & AWAY

With your own car you can visit Termessos and Karain in the same day; a taxi tour combining the two costs around TL100. Descending from Termessos, take the Karain road just outside the national park then follow the signs. Coming from Antalya it's the next left after the road to Muğla.

Perge

Now little more than a ruined site that can easily be explored in an hour, **Perge** (admission TL15; 9am-7.30pm), 15km east of Antalya

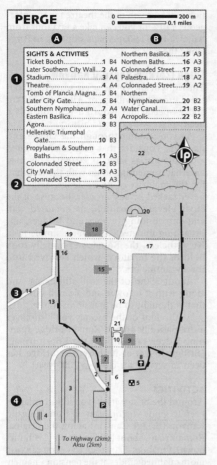

PERGE

SIGHTS & ACTIVITIES	
Ticket Booth...................1 B4	Northern Basilica......15 A3
Later Southern City Wall...2 A4	Northern Baths..........16 A3
Stadium.........................3 A4	Colonnaded Street....17 B3
Theatre.........................4 A4	Palaestra...................18 A2
Tomb of Plancia Magna...5 B4	Colonnaded Street....19 A2
Later City Gate..............6 B4	Northern
Southern Nymphaeum....7 A4	Nymphaeum..........20 B2
Eastern Basilica.............8 B4	Water Canal...............21 B3
Agora............................9 B3	Acropolis...................22 B2
Hellenistic Triumphal	
Gate.........................10 B4	
Propylaeum & Southern	
Baths.......................11 A3	
Colonnaded Street........12 B3	
City Wall.....................13 A3	
Colonnaded Street........14 A3	

To Highway (2km);
Aksu (2km)

riously off axis, to reach the **colonnaded street**, where an impressive collection of columns still stands erect.

Stroll the length of the street, which ends at the fantastic northern **nymphaeum**; it was responsible for supplying water to the colonnaded street. Look closely at the street and notice the narrow concave channel running down the centre. From the nymphaeum, which dates to the 2nd century AD, it's possible to follow a path through the brush to the ridge of the acropolis hill. The ruins in this part of the city date from the Byzantine era, when many of the city's inhabitants relocated here after attacks from invaders on the flat land below.

GETTING THERE & AWAY
A visit to Perge can be included in the trip eastwards to Aspendos and Side, doing it all in a very long day.

Dolmuşes leave for Aksu from the Antalya otogar. Ride the 13km east from Antalya to Aksu and the turn-off for Perge, then walk (20 to 25 minutes) or hitch the remaining 2km to the ruins. You can include Perge in a taxi tour to Aspendos for roughly TL110.

Silyon
About 7km east of Perge are the remains of Silyon, a thriving city when Alexander the Great came through in the 4th century BC. Unable to take the city, the conqueror left it and passed on. The greatest curiosity here is an inscription in the Pamphylian dialect of ancient Greek, a unique example of this little-seen language.

The ruins are difficult to reach without your own vehicle. Despite the sign saying 'Silyon 8km' on the highway, it is further 7.2km to another right turn (unmarked); go 900m and bear left, then another 100m and turn left at a farm. The ruins are visible 1km further along.

Aspendos
They come to **Aspendos** (Belkis; admission TL15, parking TL5; ☼ 8am-7pm) with one solitary objective in mind: to view the ancient city's awe-inspiring **theatre**, generally agreed to be the finest structure of its type in all of Anatolia, and the best preserved Roman theatre of the ancient world.

The structure was constructed by the Romans during the reign of Emperor Marcus

and 2km north of Aksu, was one of the most important towns of ancient Pamphylia. Perge experienced its golden age during the 2nd and 3rd centuries BC under the Romans; the town surrendered to Alexander the Great in 334 BC. Turkish archaeologists first began a series of excavations here in 1947 and a selection of the statues uncovered – many in magnificent condition – can be seen at the Antalya Museum.

Before approaching the site proper, the **theatre** (capacity 15,000) and **stadium** (capacity 12,000) appear along the access road. Both have been closed for some time due to unsafe conditions. The massive **Roman and Hellenistic gates** are found just inside the site. Walk through the Roman Gate, which is cu-

Aurelius (AD 161–80), and restored during the 13th century. Yet while the golden age of Aspendos stretched only from the 2nd to 3rd centuries AD, the history of the city goes all the way back to the Hittite Empire (800 BC). In 486 BC a battle took place here between the Greeks and the Persians in which the Greeks were victorious.

After a tour of the region in the early 1930s, Atatürk declared Aspendos too fine an example of historical architecture to not be in use. Following a restoration that many purists weren't entirely pleased with (some questioned the authenticity of the project) the theatre continues to stage operas, concerts and folklore festivals even today.

Should your schedule allow a visit to any event happening at Aspendos, take advantage. The acoustics and lighting radically changes the atmosphere of the stadium once night falls, and the experience is 2000-year dreamy.

When leaving the theatre, follow the path on the left marked for Theatre Hill. Hack through overgrown thornbushes for a phenomenal view of the theatre, the surrounding farm land and the Taurus Mountains. Follow the 'Aqueduct' fork in the trail for a good look at the remains of the city's **aqueduct** and of the modern village to its left. You can also follow the unpaved road north for 1km for fine views of the aqueduct.

The ruins of the ancient city are extensive and include a stadium, *agora* and basilica, but they offer little to look at. Follow the aqueduct trail along the ridge to reach them.

FESTIVALS & EVENTS
The internationally regarded **Aspendos Opera & Ballet Festival** is held in the Roman theatre from mid-June to early July. Tickets are TL20 (travel agencies charge a lot more) and can be bought at the office near to the tourist office in Antalya, from the office at the theatre in Side and from the Side museum (see p407).

GETTING THERE & AWAY
Aspendos lies 47km east of Antalya. If you are driving, go as far as the Köprü Creek, and notice the old Seljuk humpback bridge. Turn left (north) along the western bank of the creek, following the signs to Aspendos.

Minibuses to Manavgat drop you at the Aspendos turn-off, from where you can walk (45 minutes) or hitch the remaining 4km to the site. Taxis waiting at the highway junc-

tion will take you to the theatre for an outrageous TL12, or you can take a taxi tour from Antalya for TL90, perhaps stopping in Perge along the way.

Selge (Zerk) & Köprülü Kanyon
The ruins of ancient Selge are scattered about the Taurus-top village of Altınkaya, 12km above spectacular Köprülü Kanyon. It's a heady place with a proud history.

As you wander through the village and its ruins, consider that Selge once boasted a population as large as 20,000. This may have had something to do with the fact that, for the majority of its existence, Selge was never sacked by any invader. Because of the city's elevated position, its enclosed wall and surrounding ravines and bridges, approaching undetected wasn't a simple task. Nevertheless, the Romans eventually took hold of the territory, which survived into the Byzantine era.

About 350m of the wall still exists, and along with it a tower and a small building that is thought to be a customs house.

At the foot of the ascent, you'll discover a dramatically arched Roman bridge spanning a deep canyon with the Köprü Irmağı (Bridge River) at its base; the bridge has been in service for close to 2000 years.

ACTIVITIES
Around the bridge itself, you'll find villagers keen to guide you on **hikes** up from Köprülü Kanyon (Bridge Canyon) along the original Roman road, about two hours up (1½ hours down), for about TL20 each way. You can find more qualified guides at the pensions, namely Adem at Perge Pansiyon (opposite).

You can also arrange mountain treks for groups to Mt Bozburun (2504m) and other points in the Kuyucuk Dağları (Kuyucuk Range), with a guide, *katırcı* (muleteer) and *yemekçi* (cook) for about TL120 per day. There is a three-day walk through the Köprülü Kanyon on the St Paul's Trail (p359).

Numerous agencies in Antalya offer **rafting trips** in the canyon, but there are also a few sleeping options if you want to do it independently. The best rafting company is certainly **Medraft Outdoor Camp** (☎ 312 6296; www.medraft.com), a large Turkish adventure company, with fit, young staff. A day on the excellent intermediate rapids is about TL80 which includes a lesson and a four-hour trip, including a break for lunch. Other operators charge less, but be wary of compromise.

SLEEPING & EATING

A string of riverside pensions with excellent restaurants and a couple of good camping grounds are situated about 2km past Medraft, on the Selge side of the river. The best is **Perge Pansiyon** (☎ 765 3074; bungalow with half-board s/d TL30/50), which has brand new stylish timber bungalows, with good bathrooms, and is right on the water's flowing edge. Camping is around TL15 per person. **Selge Pansiyon** (☎ 765 3244; TL30/50) is also good value.

GETTING THERE & AWAY

Köprülü Kanyon Milli Parkı and Selge are included in tours from Antalya, Side and Alanya for about TL70 per person. If you'd rather do it independently, the one daily minibus departs from Antalya's otogar in the morning for Altınkaya (TL15, two hours), returning to Antalya in the evening.

If you have your own vehicle, you can visit in half a day, though it deserves a lot more time. The turn-off to Selge and Köprülü Kanyon is about 5km east of the Aspendos road (48km east of Antalya) along the main highway.

The road is paved for the first 33km. Then, about 4km before the town of Beşkonak, the road divides, with the left fork marked for Altınkaya, the right for Beşkonak. If you take the Altınkaya road along the river's western bank, you'll pass Medraft Outdoor Camp, then a few lodgings at the river's edge. About 11km from the turn-off is the graceful old Ottoman Oluk bridge.

If instead you follow the road through Beşkonak, it is 6.5km from that village to the canyon and the bridge. The unpaved road on the western bank of the river marked for Altınkaya or Zerk (the Turkish name for Selge) climbs some 12km from the bridge to the village through increasingly dramatic scenery.

Eastern Mediterranean

Turkey's eastern Mediterranean has long lived in the shadow of its more fashionable neighbour to the west. But with the requisite sites, scenes, sounds and pristine beaches, this Arab-spiced peninsula is due its place in the year-round sun.

While Alanya and Side possess the razzle-dazzle trimmings of a package-tour playground, it's the region beyond the red pines of the Toros that holds a more timeless Turkish life. Here you'll find an equally stunning coastline, dotted by hillside villages, unexplored ancient ruins and – as you round the Hatay peninsula – a certain Middle Eastern air.

Many Turks spend summer holidays here, in the low-key beach resorts of Anamur – a banana-rich town of clean beaches and remnants of the Roman Empire – and quirky Kızkalesi, famed for its floating Maiden Castle and the deep, dark chasms of 'Heaven and Hell'. The surrounding Olbian Plateau is an archaeological heaven where aimless wandering leads to genuine discovery.

Continuing east through the wide-open Çukurova Plain, the industrial cities of Mersin and Adana swell on the horizon, the heat rises and the tourists all but disappear. Yet these are youthful, modern and thoroughly secular parts where a stopover is rewarded with friendly, unaffected locals, and rarely seen sites including the Roman fortress city of Anazarbus, the Armenian retreat of Yılankale, and important Hittite and Christian sites.

The energy of the eastern Med turns south of İskenderun, due to the area's proximity to the Syrian border. Here is one of Turkey's most fascinating mixes of cultures, religions and languages. In the buzzing, prosperous city of Antakya – formerly fabled Antioch – you'll find a bazaar-ful of Sunnis, Alevis and Orthodox Christians, a world-class museum and Arabic spoken on the streets.

HIGHLIGHTS

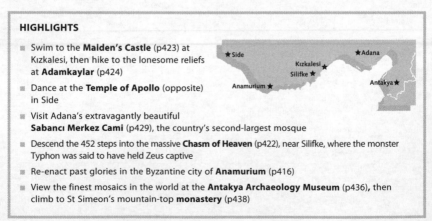

- Swim to the **Maiden's Castle** (p423) at Kızkalesi, then hike to the lonesome reliefs at **Adamkaylar** (p424)
- Dance at the **Temple of Apollo** (opposite) in Side
- Visit Adana's extravagantly beautiful **Sabancı Merkez Cami** (p429), the country's second-largest mosque
- Descend the 452 steps into the massive **Chasm of Heaven** (p422), near Silifke, where the monster Typhon was said to have held Zeus captive
- Re-enact past glories in the Byzantine city of **Anamurium** (p416)
- View the finest mosaics in the world at the **Antakya Archaeology Museum** (p436), then climb to St Simeon's mountain-top **monastery** (p438)

SİDE

☎ 0242 / pop 18,000

The seasonal village of Side (*see*-duh) is the Turkish version of a carnival by the sea. With its souvenir peddlers, quaint beaches, family-friendliness and peculiar slapstick charm, this once docile fishing town is now a firmly established high season playground.

Entering the town is like entering a film set; glorious Roman and Hellenistic ruins mark out the road, and an evening performance at the ancient amphitheatre is spectacularly showbiz. Adding to Side's appeal (and keeping its postcard industry firmly afloat) is the heart-warming Temple of Apollo – step from beach bar to bar until you gaze through this impossible arch to a horizon free from Ferris wheels.

Of course there is a very loud downside. The local operators have a natural appetite for foreign currency, and the do-anything-to-please customer service of endless back alley tack-shops and tourist restaurants can fall away soon after a sale. But visitors to Side often return despite themselves, happy to get fleeced now and then by the same 2000-year-old tricks, happy to swim in the sea and sip tonics on the rocks, happy to unwind in Side.

History

Side, meaning 'pomegranate', is one of the oldest Anatolian settlements. The Aeolians lived here around 600 BC, but by the time Alexander the Great swept through the inhabitants had abandoned much of their Greek culture and language. Since then it moved through various hands and prospered as a major port in the Hittite era.

Piracy and slavery kept it buoyant, and many of Side's great buildings were financed by such pursuits under the Greeks, only to be stopped when the city came under Roman control. After that, Side managed to prosper from legitimate commerce; under the Byzantines it was still large enough to rate a bishop. The 7th-century Arab raids diminished the town, which was dead within two centuries. During the late 19th century it had a brief flowering under Ottoman rule when it was settled by Muslims from Crete.

Orientation

Side juts out on a promontory, 3km south of the coastal highway. Vehicular access is tightly

controlled, so if you're driving, use the car park outside the village.

Liman Caddesi, leading through the village to the harbour, is considered the main street. The main beach is in the north of town.

The otogar (bus station) is east of the archaeological zone. To get to town, follow signs for the main road then turn left if you want to walk, or board the incongruous toy train that rolls in every 15 minutes in high season.

Information

The **tourist office** (☎ 753 1265; ⏰ 8am-noon & 1-5pm Mon-Fri) is about 800m from the village centre, on the road in from Manavgat. Internet cafés abound around Nergis Caddesi – the best is **Side Internet C@fe** (per ½hr TL5) and there are ATMs on Liman Caddesi.

Sights

Although the site is relatively small, the **Temples of Apollo and Athena** are among the most romantic and moving sites you're likely to encounter in Turkey. These ruins, which date from the 2nd century BC, are at the southwestern tip of Side harbour. A number of columns from the Temple of Apollo have been preserved and placed upright in their original locations, and after dark a spotlight outlines their form dramatically against the night sky.

The spectacular **theatre** (admission TL10; ⏰ 8am-7pm), built in the 2nd century AD, rivals nearby Aspendos for sheer drama. In fact it's one of the largest Greco-Roman ruins in Asia Minor and can seat well over 15,000 spectators. If the opportunity allows, an evening performance here is a truly special occasion.

Next to the theatre and across the road from the museum are the remains of an **agora**. You'll find a good number of columns, although a chain-link fence restricts access. The delightful **museum** (admission TL10; ⏰ 9am-7pm) is a ruin itself; its rather impressive, if small, collection of statues and sarcophagi resides inside the old Roman baths.

Take a left as you exit the museum for Side's spectacular field of ruins, among them a **library**, an **agora** and a **Byzantine basilica**.

Festivals & Events

Tickets for the **Aspendos Opera & Ballet Festival** (☎ 753 4061) can be bought at the Side museum or at the **ticket office** (☎ 753 4061) outside the Roman theatre. For more information see p404.

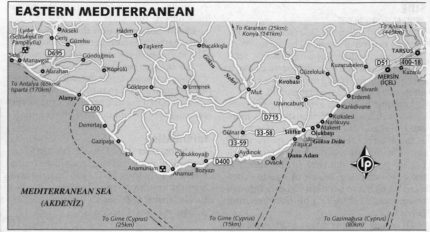

Sleeping

As many of the pensions in Side are sublet for the summer, customer service can be compromised. Try to find a place where employees don't change with the seasons.

Yıldırım Pansiyon (☎ 753 2010; www.yukser-pansiyon .com; Sümbül Sokak 8; s/d TL40/50; ☒) Located just steps from the theatre, this exceptionally laid-back pension is conveniently located across the street from a car park. Expect shipshape rooms and a beautiful silence after dark.

Yükser Pansiyon (☎ 753 2010; www.yukser-pansiyon .com; Sümbül Sokak 8; s/d TL40/50; ☒) Tucked away from the noise of the main drag but still just steps from the beach, this traditional stone-and-timber house offers average but well-maintained rooms and a rather large back patio and garden.

Onur Pansiyon (☎ 753 2328; www.onur-pansiyon.com; Sümbül Sokak 3; s/d TL30/60; ☒ ☒) This excellent family-run option has regular guests year-round who return for the bright, cosy rooms – and the cocktails by the fireplace. The young manager has a London accent. It's down the road from Uğur Lokantası

Chillout Side (☎ 753 2041; www.chilloutside .com; Zambak Sokak 32; dm TL25, s/d TL40/60; ☒ ☒) The backpacker scene is primed to return to Side with the opening of this keenly run new premises. Set around a pretty garden of mulberry trees, palms and roses, the up-scale hostel features a smart little bar and a genuine travel vibe. Rooms are new, though heavy on the wood panelling. Those upstairs have balconies.

Beach House Hotel (☎ 753 1607; www.beachhouse -hotel.com; Barbaros Caddesi; s/d TL35/70; ☒ ☒) Run by a long-term Australian expat, this is a justifiably popular choice. It has the prime beachside locale, yet still promotes restfulness, and the steady flow of tour groups and regulars merely add to the warmth of the place. Most rooms face the sea and all have spacious balconies. Sunbeds are free for guests.

Hotel Lale Park (☎ 753 1131; www.hotellalepark.com; Lale Caddesi 17; s/d TL60/90; ☒ ☒) One of Side's largest gardens acts as a sort of commons area here. Roman columns and stone walkways are scattered about; there's also an abundance of conversation areas and an outdoor bar.

Yali Hotel (☎ 753 1011; www.yalihotel.com; Barbaros Caddesi 50; s/d TL70/90; ☒ ☒) With redecorated rooms – all with TV and minibar – hanging over the ocean's edge, it's a mystery why this place isn't constantly packed. Management tends to take things pretty easy though, so perhaps the view to die for is killing business. The swimming pool is a welcome addition.

Eating

While the number of restaurants may increase every season, the menus tend to repeat. Fresh fish (TL15 to TL25) is usually the way forward here – check what's included in the price.

Uğur Lokantası (☎ 753 3654; Orkide Sokak; meze TL5) The best local restaurant in town, the Uğur has been serving up the workers' trade for 13 years. Service is smooth and unhurried, and the selections – including delicious lentil *çorba* (soup) – turn over regularly.

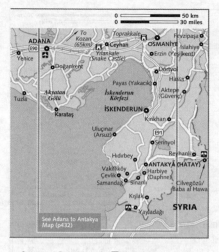

See Adana to Antakya Map (p432)

Ottoman Restaurant (☎ 753 1434; Liman Caddesi; meals TL20) Rasim is half the reason to dine at this excellent, good-value restaurant. There's no harbour view, but this is compensated by a relatively diverse menu, including some fine Indian dishes. If you're staying out of town, a courtesy bus can be arranged.

Soundwaves Restaurant (☎ 753 1059; Barbaros Caddesi; meals about TL20) This ship-shaped institution is managed by the same crew from Beach House next door, so the vibe is expectedly friendly, relaxed and professional. The menu doesn't stray far from the traditional tourist Turkish, though the casseroles are most hearty.

Paradise Restaurant (☎ 753 2080; Barbaros Caddesi 56; meals about TL25) This family-first restaurant has a large play area for the little ones, a substantial kids menu, and very accommodating staff. The adults can enjoy a fine sea view and good seafood and international staples.

Aphrodite Restaurant (☎ 753 1171; İskele Caddesi; meals about TL25) This place wins the prize for 'closest table to the sea'. Not only is it an ideal spot to soak up the harbourside drama at eye level, it's also good for seafood, grills and *köfte* (meatballs).

Paşaköy Bar & Restaurant (☎ 753 3622; Liman Caddesi 98; meals TL25) More theme park than theme restaurant, the infamous Paşaköy is well worth an evening of absurdist dining. Giant plastic plants fight for space with stuffed buffalo and some nondescript mammals. But the stream is a lovely touch, and the bar decor grows weirdly familiar by each drink. Luckily the standard Turkish food is pretty reliable.

Moonlight Restaurant (☎ 753 1400; Barbaros Caddesi 49; meals around TL25) Probably the classiest joint in town, with an extensive Turkish wine list and unfussy service. The mostly seafood offerings are well presented and very fresh. The biggest drawcard, however, is the romantic back patio, which is regularly filled with happy couples feeding (on) each other.

Drinking
For a town that more or less promotes binge drinking, the patrons in Side are remarkably well behaved. There are plenty of opportunities to do otherwise.

Kiss Bar (☎ 753 3182; Barbaros Caddesi 64) Like Romper Room for adults, it's fun watching people being forced to dance – until you get asked yourself, that is.

Stones Dance Bar (☎ 512 1498; Barbaros Caddesi 67) Watch pints of lager flow to the crooning sounds of 'new' England (of the mid-1990s). This excellent pre-club venue can easily become all you need to reach the tiles safely.

Jungle Bar (☎ 753 2235; Liman Caddesi 37) Hidden upstairs above busy Liman Caddesi, this hip new bar is understated by Side standards. The staff is formal and funky, and the music is set at a modest volume. It's good for a drink post-dinner while you plan your next move.

Café Dreams (☎ 753 1023; Barbaros Caddesi) Daggy acoustic covers somehow fit the bill in this shiny new, open-air lounge bar. If it wasn't for the seaside setting, you could be in a 1980s hotel foyer having a few 'in-betweeners'. If the night gets away, there's a pension upstairs.

Royal Castle Pub (☎ 753 4373; Reis Caddesi) This bizarre and busy place feels like Sherwood Forest on week-old shrimp. Staff dressed like Robin Hood in the navy bounce quality cocktails (TL15) to giggling tourists. Big screens show all manner of sports, and the faux-Britishness extends to a menu of greasy pub snacks. You've got to love it.

Mehmet's Bar (Barbaros Caddesi) This lovely booze shack is better suited to a tropical island than a Turkish promontory. Still, it's decidedly chilled, and ideal for sipping a quiet beer (TL4) while listening to the waves and reggae music.

Entertainment
Oxyd (☎ 753 4040; Denizbuku Mevkii; cover charge €10-15) If your clubbing experience has lost its sheen lately, you'll find reinvention and decadence at Oxyd, a super-duper club 3km outside

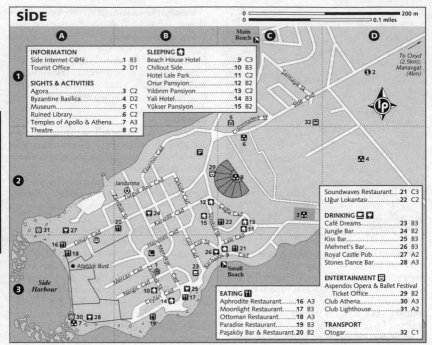

SIDE

INFORMATION
Side Internet C@fé........................1 B3
Tourist Office..............................2 D1

SIGHTS & ACTIVITIES
Agora..3 C2
Byzantine Basilica.......................4 D2
Museum..5 C1
Ruined Library.............................6 C2
Temples of Apollo & Athena......7 A3
Theatre...8 C2

SLEEPING 🛏
Beach House Hotel......................9 C3
Chillout Side..............................10 B3
Hotel Lale Park..........................11 C2
Onur Pansiyon...........................12 B2
Yıldırım Pansiyon......................13 C2
Yali Hotel...................................14 B3
Yükser Pansiyon.......................15 B2

EATING 🍴
Aphrodite Restaurant.......16 A3
Moonlight Restaurant.......17 B3
Ottoman Restaurant.........18 A3
Paradise Restaurant..........19 B3
Paşaköy Bar & Restaurant.20 B2

Soundwaves Restaurant....21 C3
Uğur Lokantası...................22 C2

DRINKING 🍸 🍷
Café Dreams.......................23 B3
Jungle Bar...........................24 B2
Kiss Bar...............................25 B3
Mehmet's Bar......................26 B3
Royal Castle Pub................27 A2
Stones Dance Bar................28 A3

ENTERTAINMENT 🎭
Aspendos Opera & Ballet Festival
Ticket Office.......................29 B2
Club Athena........................30 A3
Club Lighthouse.................31 A2

TRANSPORT
Otogar.................................32 C1

---

the city. Like a sci-fi sandcastle inhabited by beautiful scene-stealers, this love-it-or-leave-it extravagance is up there with Turkey's best. Pack a swimming costume for a really wild night out. Best get there by taxi (TL15).

Club Athena (☎ 753 1637; Apollo Temple) The only changes here are nominal, as the former Club Apollo continues to set the pace for raving in ruins. Some big name Euro-trash DJs are making their way here of late. Entry is free, but the drink prices are steep. If you can't find it, follow the green lasers in the night sky – or get yourself home!

Club Lighthouse (☎ 753 3588; Liman Caddesi) Italian restaurant by day, cheese music factory by night, the Lighthouse has the advantage of a makeshift marina where fishing boats docked alongside the outdoor patio lend a much-needed aura of elegance. It's techno pop on most nights, and the odd bubble 'n' trouble party.

Getting There & Away

Frequent minibuses connect Side otogar with the Manavgat otogar (TL8), 4km away, from where buses go to Antalya (TL8, 1¼ hours, 65km), Alanya (TL8, 1¼ hours, 63km) and

Konya (TL25, 5½ hours, 296km). Coming into Side, most buses either drop you at the Manavgat otogar, or stop on the highway so you can transfer onto a free *servis* (shuttle bus) into Side.

In summer Side has direct bus services to Ankara, İzmir and İstanbul.

AROUND SİDE

About 12km east of Manavgat (50km west of Alanya) the excellent D695 highway heads northwest up to the Anatolian plateau and Konya (280km) via Akseki, curving through some beautiful mountain scenery. The road is the preferred route to Konya from this part of the coast. Along the coastal road it's a seven-hour drive from Side to Isparta (via Antalya).

Manavgat

If your beach holiday in Side has you suspecting you're not getting a taste of the 'real' Turkey, consider hopping on a dolmuş (minibus) to Manavgat (TL1.50), a commercial town with a large covered bazaar. It sits about 4km to the north and east of Side.

The otogar is on the outskirts of town, on the bypass. Except at the height of summer, you'll have to come here from Side to connect with bus services to Antalya, Alanya, Konya and the lakes.

GETTING THERE & AWAY

Frequent *servises* connect Side with Manavgat otogar (TL1), where there are onward buses to Antalya (TL7, 1¾ hours, 65km) and Alanya (TL6, one hour, 63km). 'Şehiriçi' dolmuşes from outside the otogar will run you into the town centre (TL1.50). A taxi from Side to Manavgat otogar costs TL15.

Manavgat Waterfall

About 4km north of Manavgat on the Manavgat River is the appropriately named **Manavgat Waterfall** (Manavgat Şelalesi; admission TL2), a colossally popular tourist attraction filled with souvenir vendors and restaurants, some of which sit mere metres from the falls. Manavgat is well known for its trout, which is on the menu at some of the eateries here.

GETTING THERE & AWAY

A dolmuş from Manavgat costs TL1.60. In the town centre you'll find boats waiting to run you upriver to the waterfalls. An 80-minute round trip costs TL20 per person, providing there are at least four people.

Lyrbe (Seleukeia in Pamphylia)

These interesting **ruins,** 23km northeast of Side, are particularly appealing due to their location atop three vertical cliffs. Situated among an expanse of pine trees, the site is shaded and somewhat forested, and can be cool even on hot summer days. Many of the buildings are difficult to identify, although you can clearly make out a bathhouse, an *agora* and a necropolis.

For years, archaeologists believed this site to be the Seleukeia in Pamphylia, founded by Seleucus I Nicator, a presumably egocentric officer of Alexander the Great who founded a total of nine cities in his own honour. However, a fairly recent discovery of an inscription found in the city, written in the language of ancient Side, has convinced researchers that this site is more likely the ruined city of Lyrbe.

Shortly after passing the Roman aqueduct, look for a sign on the left marked Lyrbe (Seleukeia; 7km). Continue on through the village of Şıhlar, and note the small bits of columns built into the walls of the village's stone houses. Take the road to the right opposite the minaret, which winds another 3km uphill to the ruins.

GETTING THERE & AWAY

If you don't have your own transport, taxi drivers wait across the bridge in Manavgat to run you to Seleukeia, with a stop at Manavgat waterfall thrown in (TL40 return).

ALANYA

☎ 0242 / pop 110,100

In just a few short decades, Alanya has mushroomed from a sparsely populated highway town on a silky sand beach to a densely populated tourist haven for northern Europeans who prefer to pay upfront. Aside from the odd boat cruise or beach stroll, many visitors to Alanya move only from the airport shuttle to the hotel pool, and in the evening frequent restaurants and banging nightclubs.

But like little Side to the west, Alanya has something special up its ancient dusty sleeve. Looming high above the newly modern centre is a brilliant fortress district, with trappings of a fine Seljuk castle, a wonderful mess of ruins, active remnants of village life and a touch of revamped 'Ottomania'. Sipping a beer in one of the many hillside cafés affords a stunning view of the marina and, perhaps, a requisite break from the party below.

There's a growing concern in the local media about female tourists dressing inappropriately around town. Please remember to be considerate, especially during Ramazan.

Orientation

Having gone from a small town to a 20km long city almost overnight, Alanya has no real main square or civic centre. The centre lies inland (north) from the promontory on which the fortress walls sit. The closest thing to a main square is Hürriyet Meydanı, a nondescript traffic junction at the northern end of İskele Caddesi.

About 23km west of Alanya are **İncekum** and **Avsallar**, these days virtual extensions of Alanya.

Information

The **tourist office** (☎ 513 1240; Kalearkası Caddesi; ☒ 8.30am-5.30pm) is opposite the Alanya Museum. There's also a small information

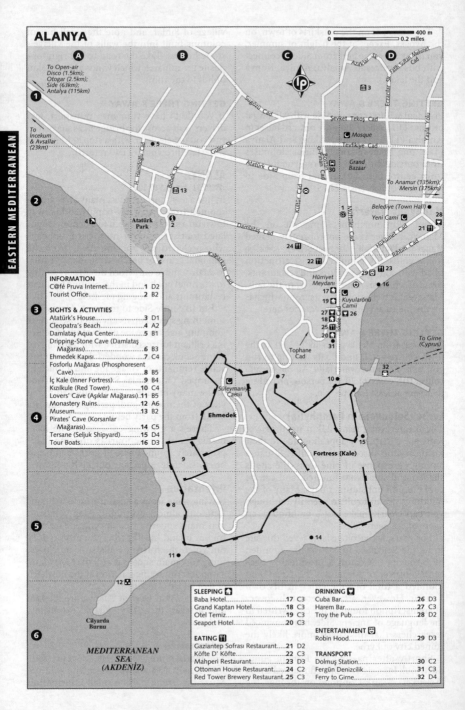

ALANYA

INFORMATION
C@fé Pruva Internet.....................1 D2
Tourist Office..............................2 B2

SIGHTS & ACTIVITIES
Atatürk's House..........................3 D1
Cleopatra's Beach.......................4 A2
Damlataş Aqua Center................5 B1
Dripping-Stone Cave (Damlataş
  Mağarası)................................6 B3
Ehmedek Kapısı..........................7 C4
Fosforlu Mağarası (Phosphoresent
  Cave).......................................8 B5
İç Kale (Inner Fortress)................9 B4
Kızılkule (Red Tower).................10 C4
Lovers' Cave (Aşıklar Mağarası)..11 B5
Monastery Ruins........................12 A6
Museum....................................13 B2
Pirates' Cave (Korsanlar
  Mağarası)................................14 C5
Tersane (Seljuk Shipyard)..........15 D4
Tour Boats................................16 D3

SLEEPING
Baba Hotel...............................17 C3
Grand Kaptan Hotel..................18 C3
Otel Temiz...............................19 C3
Seaport Hotel...........................20 C3

EATING
Gaziantep Sofrası Restaurant.....21 D2
Köfte D' Köfte...........................22 C3
Mahperi Restaurant...................23 D3
Ottoman House Restaurant........24 C2
Red Tower Brewery Restaurant..25 C3

DRINKING
Cuba Bar..................................26 D3
Harem Bar................................27 C3
Troy the Pub............................28 D2

ENTERTAINMENT
Robin Hood..............................29 D3

TRANSPORT
Dolmuş Station.........................30 C2
Fergün Denizcilik......................31 C3
Ferry to Girne..........................32 D4

booth near the police station. **C@fé Pruva Internet** (☎ 519 2306; ☽ 8am-midnight) is off Müftüler Caddesi, just south of Atatürk Caddesi.

The Alanya Tourism and Cultural Festival runs every May.

Sights
FORTRESS
The only 'must-see' site in Alanya is its awesome Seljuk **kale**, which overlooks the city as well as the Pamphylian plain and the Cilician mountains.

Before reaching the entrance to the fort, the road passes through the old inner citadel; this was the Turkish quarter during Ottoman and Seljuk times, and a number of old wooden houses are still standing. At the top is the **Ehmedek Kapısı**, the gateway to the fort. Enter the **İç Kale** (Inner Fortress; admission TL10; ☽ 9am-7.15pm), where you'll find poorly preserved ruins including cisterns and an 11th-century Byzantine church. It's worth walking down to explore the village of **Ehmedek**, which includes a former Ottoman **bedesten** (vaulted market enclosure), some deluxe holiday houses, a fine mosque and a pretty wooded cemetery. Continue walking down the hill to reach the rows of requisite cafés.

The winding road to the fortress is 3km. If you don't want to walk, catch a city bus from Hürriyet Meydanı (TL1.25, hourly from 9am to 7pm) or opposite the tourist office (10 minutes past the hour). Taxis wait at the bottom of the hill (TL15).

KIZILKULE & TERSANE
Kızılkule (Red Tower; admission TL2; ☽ 9am-7.30pm Tue-Sun) is a five-storey octagonal structure measuring nearly 30m in diameter and more than 30m high. Constructed in 1226 by Seljuk Sultan Alaettin Keykubat I (who was also responsible for the fortress), it was very likely the first structure erected after the then-Armenian controlled town surrendered to the sultan. You can work the calves by climbing 85 steep steps to the top floor.

Kızılkule looms over the harbour at the far lower end of İskele Caddesi. Across the harbour from the tower are the remains of the only Seljuk-built **tersane** (shipyard) remaining in Turkey.

ATATÜRK'S HOUSE
When Atatürk visited Alanya on 18 February 1935, he slept in a house on Azaklar Sokak,

off Fatih Sultan Mehmet Caddesi. The owner of the house left it to the Ministry of Culture, which has turned it into a small **museum** (admission free; ☽ 8.30am-noon & 1-5pm Tue-Sun).

MUSEUM
Alanya's small **museum** (☎ 513 1228; Bebek Sokak; admission TL3; ☽ 9am-noon & 1.30-7.30pm) is worth a visit. Artefacts from various regions of Anatolia include tools, jugs and jewellery. Also on display is a life-sized re-creation of a traditional 19th-century Alanya home.

DRIPPING-STONE CAVE (DAMLATAŞ MAĞARASI)
About 100m towards the sea from the tourist office and near the souvenir booths of Cleopatra's Beach is the entrance to this **cave** (admission TL4; ☽ 10am-7pm). Filled with hanging stalactites and heavy with 95% humidity, it is said to cure asthma sufferers.

Activities
BEACHES & WATERPARKS
Cleopatra's Beach (Kleopatra Plajı) is the city's best. Sandy and quite secluded in low season, it has fine views of the fortress. At the start of July, a popular beach handball tournament takes place here. Alanya's main beaches are also decent, although east of the centre they're fronted by a busy main road.

Alanya also boasts an impressive waterslide park. **Damlataş Aqua Centre** (☎ 512 5944; İsmet Hilmi Balcı Caddesi 62; adult/child TL20/15; ☽ 9am-6pm) is packed with tube slides, pools and lots and lots of floaties.

TOURS
Every day at around 10.30am **boats** (per person TL35, incl lunch) leave from near Ganipaşa Caddesi for a six-hour voyage around the promontory, visiting several caves and Cleopatra's Beach.

Many local operators organise tours to the ruins along the coast west of Alanya and to Anamur. A typical tour to Aspendos, Side and Manavgat will cost around TL55 per person, while a village-visiting 4WD safari into the Taurus Mountains will cost about TL40 per person.

Sleeping
Alanya has hundreds of hotels and pensions, almost all of them designed for groups and those in search of *apart-otels* (self-catering

THE ASTHMA-CURING CAVES OF TURKEY

Sufferers of asthma have good reason to holiday in the eastern Mediterranean. Two caves in the area are said to produce a certain kind of air that, if inhaled and exhaled for long enough stretches of time, has the ability to relieve the afflicted of their ailment.

The more famous of the two is Alanya's Dripping-Stone Cave (Damlataş Mağarası; p413), where the 95% humidity is believed to have something to do with the cave's impressive powers. Many locals are confident the caves actually work, and in the area doctors have even been known to send patients there.

North of Narlıkuyu, at the Caves of Heaven and Hell, is the site known as Astım Mağarası (Asthma Cave; p422). This cave is much less touristy, although the jury remains out as to whether you get a better cure in heaven or in hell.

flats). The following individual options are close to the main drag.

Baba Hotel (☎ 513 1032; İskele Caddesi 6; s/d TL35/45) Baba still offers the cheapest sleep on İskele Caddesi, but you pay for what you get (which is not much). The front entrance is located on the left side of a cement stairway just off the street.

Otel Temiz (☎ 513 1016; fax 519 1560; İskele Caddesi 12; s/d TL50/100; 🏠) A great choice, Hotel 'Clean' is just that. Plus the rooms are spacious, and the balconies offer a bird's-eye view of the thumping club and bar action down below.

Grand Kaptan Hotel (☎ 513 4900; www.kaptanhotels.com; İskele Caddesi 70; s/d TL80/140; 🏠 🏊) This three-star hotel has a large and somewhat opulent lobby with a nautical theme and a bar. The perfectly clean and tidy rooms have all mod cons but are rather characterless.

Seaport Hotel (☎ 513 6487; fax 519 4320; www.hotelseaport.com; İskele Caddesi 12; s/d TL80/150; 🏠) This brand new business-type hotel on the İskele strip offers slick service and brilliant sea views. Rooms are not huge but are still very well drawn. It's particularly popular with upmarket tourists who prefer to do it their own way.

Eating

Cheap restaurants are being eaten by rising rents, so if you're tired of the tourist traps, look for a *köfte* joint (TL10 a meal), or any *lokantası* (ready-food eateries) popular with workers.

Köfte D' Köfte (☎ 512 1270; Kale Caddesi; meals around TL12) A flashy yellow-and-red sign greets diners at this new 'boutique' fast-food joint. Clean lines, attentive service and generous meat, rice and salad combinations are all part of the deal.

Gaziantep Sofrası Restaurant (☎ 513 4570; İzzet Azakoğlu Caddesi; meals TL15) For something more adventurous than the standard grills and seafood,

this is one of central Alanya's best options. Traditional food from Gaziantep is on offer; try the *patlıcan* kebap (fried eggplants) or the *beyti sarma* (spicy meatballs and flat bread).

Red Tower Brewery Restaurant (☎ 513 6664; info@redtowerbrewery.com; İskele Caddesi 80; meals TL20-25) If EU membership were dependent on a good brewpub, then the Red Tower would be Turkey's sole delegate. Not only is this place rare, it also makes staggeringly good Pilsen. Still, perhaps mistakenly, it's a restaurant first and foremost, and upstairs on the 1st floor you can eat fairly standard international fare (with great potato wedges – presumably to accompany the beer!). There's also seating across the street that overlooks the harbour.

Ottoman House Restaurant (☎ 511 1421; Damlataş Caddesi 31; meals TL25-30) An internationally reputed eatery in the heart of Alanya might be hard to swallow, metaphorically, but after so many unimaginative menus, it's a dream. Set inside a 100-year-old former hotel made from stone and timber, the Ottoman House is a revelation. The *beğendili* kebap, a traditional Ottoman dish of lamb and aubergine puree, is testament to the creativity of the kitchen staff. Likewise the fresh tuna barbeque (TL30 per person) is a spectacle of swordsmanship as much as culinary skill. Quality live music (not muzak!) is performed most evenings in summer and a free shuttle can be arranged from your hotel.

Mahperi Restaurant (☎ 512 5491; www.mahperi.com; Rıhtım Caddesi; meals €15-25) A much-loved fish and steak restaurant that's been in operation since 1947 (a fairly astonishing feat in Alanya), this place is quite the class act, offering a good selection of international dishes. If you're feeling the need to escape the tourism glitz, this is certainly your best choice in the town centre.

Entertainment

Alanya's postcards should undoubtedly feature its nightclubs, some of the most bawdy, bright and banging in the land. It's all good fun though, so long as you don't have to sleep within a kilometre or three of the blistering tech stompers.

Cuba Bar (☎ 511 8745; İskele Caddesi) The newest addition to the Alanya party junket, this stylish and relatively small club is a (slightly) less manic alternative. Girls dressed in white get a free mojito. It's near Otel Temiz.

Harem Bar (☎ 511 9225; İskele Caddesi) A great little live Turkish music venue, filled with young locals chain-smoking around small tables. Drinks are cheaper than elsewhere (beer TL5) and the vibe far more relaxed.

Robin Hood (☎ 535 7923; Rihtım Caddesi 24; ☺ 9pm-3am) Supposedly the biggest club in Alanya, the first two floors of this monstrosity are decked out in (you guessed it) a Sherwood Forest theme. The Hawaiian Beach Club is on the 3rd floor and above that is the Latino Club. Beers are around TL10.

Troy the Pub (☎ 511 4718; Ziraat Bankaşi Karşişi 67; ☺ 24hr) A restaurant during the day and a bar at night, this pub changes its attitude drastically as the clock slowly turns. Breakfasts here are quiet and relaxing; show up in the afternoon or evening to hear reggae, jazz and hip-hop.

During the summer, free buses drive along İskele Caddesi about every half-hour. A taxi will cost about TL20.

Getting There & Away
BOAT

There are services to Girne (Kyrenia) in Northern Cyprus from Alanya harbour, operated by **Fergun Denizcilik** (☎ 511 5565, 511 5358; www.fergun.net; İskele Caddesi 84). Boats leave at noon on Mondays and Thursdays. In June they also leave on Tuesdays at noon and Mondays at 6am. Boats return to Alanya at 11am on Wednesdays and Sundays.

You must buy a ticket and present your passport a day before departure for immigration formalities. Not included in the TL68/118 one-way/return ticket prices is a TL12 Alanya harbour tax. Returning from Girne there is a TL18 departure tax.

BUS

The otogar is on the coastal highway (Atatürk Caddesi), 3km west of the centre. It is served by city buses (TL0.50, every half-hour). Most services are less frequent outside summer, but buses generally leave hourly for Antalya (TL10, two hours, 115km) and eight times daily to Adana (TL25, 10 hours, 440km), stopping at a number of towns along the way. Buses to Konya (TL20, 6½ hours, 320km) take the Akseki–Beyşehir route.

Getting Around

Frequent dolmuşes shuttle along the coast, transporting passengers from the outlying hotel areas to the centre.

Dolmuşes to the otogar (TL1.30) can be picked up in the bazaar, north of Atatürk Caddesi. From the otogar, you walk out towards the coast road and the dolmuş stand is on the right.

AROUND ALANYA

Some 23km to the west, the **İncekum Orman İçi Dinlenme Yeri** (Fine Sand Forest Rest Area; ☎ 345 1448) has a camping ground (no facilities) in a pine grove near the beach.

About 13km west of Alanya, notice the **Şarapsa Hanı**, a Seljuk *han* (caravanserai) built in the mid-12th century, which is occasionally reinvented as a function centre. Further west towards Side, there's another *han*, the **Alarahan**, accessible by a side road heading north for 9km.

Heading east towards Silifke (275km), the twisting road is cut into the cliffs. Every now and then it passes through the fertile delta of a stream, planted with bananas (as at Demirtaş) or crowded with greenhouses. It's a long drive with few places to stop until you get to Anamur, but the sea views and the cool pine forests are extremely beautiful. On a clear day you can see the mountains of Cyprus across the sea.

This region was ancient Cilicia Tracheia ('Rough' Cilicia), a somewhat forbidding part of the world because of the mountains. Pirates preyed on ships from the hidden coves along this stretch of the coast. In the late 1960s the government completed the good road running east from Alanya and since then tourism has grown rapidly.

ANAMUR
☎ 0324 / pop 50,000

Easygoing Anamur has a horticultural industry that far outweighs its tourism. As the closest town to the massive Byzantine city of

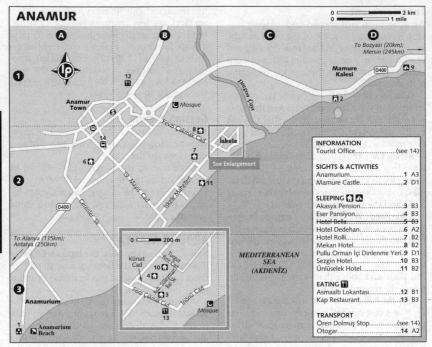

ANAMUR

INFORMATION	
Tourist Office....................(see 14)	

SIGHTS & ACTIVITIES	
Anamurium........................1 A3	
Mamure Castle....................2 D1	

SLEEPING	
Akasya Pension....................3 B3	
Eser Pansiyon.....................4 B3	
Hotel Bella.......................5 B3	
Hotel Dedehan....................6 A2	
Hotel Rolli.......................7 B2	
Mekan Hotel......................8 B2	
Pullu Orman İçi Dinlenme Yeri.9 D1	
Sezgin Hotel.....................10 B3	
Ünlüselek Hotel..................11 B2	

EATING	
Asmaaltı Lokantası...............12 B1	
Kap Restaurant...................13 B3	

TRANSPORT	
Ören Dolmuş Stop..............(see 14)	
Otogar..........................14 A2	

Anamurium (below) – and with a very pretty beach and waterfront – there's good reason to hang around. Anamur is also close to the impressive Mamure Castle (opposite) that sits directly on the highway to the east.

Orientation & Information

Anamur lies to the north of the highway, 1km from the main square. Mamure Kalesi is 7km east of the town centre, the ruins of Anamurium 8.5km west. The otogar is on the intersection of the highway and Anamur's main street (see p418 for information about getting around). The **tourist office** (☎ 814 3529; ⏰ 8am-noon & 1-5pm Mon-Fri) is in the otogar complex behind the police station.

Around 2.5km from the otogar is İskele, a popular waterfront district.

Sights

ANAMURIUM

On the isolated lovely stone beach is Anamurium, founded by the Phoenicians, toyed with by the Romans and sympathetic to the Byzantines. The site is both sprawling and inspiring, with ruins stretching from the beach

to the peak of the mountainside. It's primarily the sheer size of the city that impresses.

Historians and archaeologists are still debating how Anamurium fell. The city suffered a number of devastating setbacks throughout its active existence, including an attack in AD 52 by a Cilician tribe known as the Cetae. However, it was long believed that corsairs from Arabia plundered and pillaged themselves silly in the mid-7th century. More recently, however, archaeologists working at Anamurium claim to have uncovered evidence suggesting that a massive earthquake destroyed the city sometime in the late 6th century.

The best-preserved structure here is the **public bath**; look for the coloured mosaic tiles that still decorate portions of the floor. Other ruins of interest include a 900-seat **theatre** dating from the 2nd century AD, a **stadium** and a rather large **necropolis**. There are also the remains of numerous private houses.

Approaching Anamur from the west or down from the Cilician mountains, a sign on the right points south towards the **ruins** (admission TL3; ⏰ 8am-8pm). This road bumps 3km past fields and through the ruins to a dead end at

BEHOLD THE ANAMUR BANANA

Nearly every city and town along Turkey's eastern Mediterranean coast seems to be known for growing a certain type of fruit, and Anamur is no different. Here, the banana reigns supreme.

Until the mid-1980s, Anamur bananas were the only sort of banana available in Turkey. That certainly wasn't a bad thing. It's true the bananas are small, but their smell and taste are outstanding. Anamur bananas are much sweeter and more tasty than those common in Europe and North America. Unfortunately for local growers though, Turkey began importing cheaper (but less tasty) bananas from other countries; large numbers of Anamur banana growers were driven out of business.

Happily, if you're in Anamur the local bananas can still be bought more cheaply than imported varieties. Keep your eyes peeled when driving through the mountainous regions surrounding town, where you're certain to spot dozens of farmers along the highway hawking great bunches of bananas from wooden fruit stands.

the beach. A good way of exploring the area is on bicycle, which can be arranged at Hotel Dedehan (below).

MAMURE CASTLE (MAMURE KALESI)

This tremendous roadside **castle** (admission TL3; 8am-6pm) – with its original 36 towers still intact – is by far the biggest and best-preserved fortification on either Mediterranean coast. As if attempting to mimic Maiden's Castle to the east, the rear end of Mamure sits directly on the beach, while its front end almost reaches the highway.

Mamure dates from the 12th century – it was constructed by the Christian leaders of the Armenian kingdom of Cilicia – although it could date as far back as the 3rd century BC. It's known that a Roman castle was built here in the 3rd century AD, although no remains of that structure exist. Mamure was briefly held by the Ottomans in the middle of the 14th century.

Climbing to the castle's peak is something of an adventure, although some stairs are a bit crumbled so use extreme caution. Your reward is an astounding view of the sea.

Sleeping

ANAMUR

Pullu Orman İçi Dinlenme Yeri (827 1151; camp sites or caravans TL10) This government-run camping ground in a cool forest is especially popular with Turkish families and school groups who arrive for picnics by the sea (where pious Muslim women swim fully clothed). It's just under 2km east of Mamure Castle.

Hotel Dedehan (814 7522; D400 Hwy; d TL30;) Conveniently located next to the otogar, this is a good choice if you're stuck in town overnight. Rooms are cheap, clean and quite large. It's also a good base for excursions to Anamurium or Mamure Castle, as the friendly owner allows guests free use of a bicycle. Motorbikes can be rented for about TL25 a day.

İSKELE

The popular İskele (harbour) district is where most visitors to Anamur end up. Numerous pensions and hotels run along İnönü Caddesi, the main waterfront street. The dolmuş drops you off at the main intersection.

Pensions & Hotels

There are several hotels in the Yalıevleri district, a treeless expanse of apartment blocks about 2km along the coast towards Anamurium from İskele. Catch the local bus that passes every 20 minutes through the main intersection.

Eser Pansiyon (814 2322, 814 9130; www.eser pansiyon.com; İnönü Caddesi 6; s/d/tr TL25/40/50, 5-person flat TL70;) By far the best value in town, this well-run pension includes satellite TV in every room, a self-catering kitchen and a barbeque pit in the shaded back garden. The owner, energetic and accommodating Tayfun, is a real character. The spacious flats and suites come complete with real bathtubs.

Akasya Pansiyon (814 5272; Kursat Caddesi; s/d 35/60;) In a bright orange building, the Akasya is a family-run pension with light-filled, comfy rooms and a young manager who is eager to please.

Ünlüselek Hotel (☎ 814 1973; www.unluselekotel.com; Fahri Görülü Caddesi; s/d TL40/70; ✷ ▯) This sprawling, family-oriented hotel is more like a low-budget resort. Along with live music at night, films are occasionally screened on a projector outside, where there's also a playground area for kids. Located just steps from the sea, a beach-volleyball court is usually set up in the summer. The owner loans his small boat to guests.

Mekan Hotel (☎ 816 4300; Fevzi Çakmak Caddesi; s/d TL50/100; ✷) The Mekan is a brand new hotel on the road back to town. It's very neat and business-like, but lacks the character and convenience of other hotels in İskele. The owner will give discounts.

Hotel Rolli (☎ 814 4978; www.hotel-rolli.de; Yahvleri Mahallesi; s or d TL90; ✷ ▯ ✷) A niche hotel specially designed for wheelchair-bound tourists, the Rolli does what it does well. The majority of guests here are German and the polite staff all speak the language. Airport transfers are available from as far away as Antalya (TL120).

Sezgin Hotel (☎ 814 9421; İskele Mahallesi 11; s/d/tr €35/60/75; ✷) Rooms at the Sezgin are simple but tidy; 10 out of the 24 have sea views and all have TV. The lobby walls feature an interesting collection of kilims (pileless woven rugs).

Eating

In the warmer months the İskele waterfront is filled with large open-air cafés serving kebaps, gözleme (savoury pancake) and other snacks. Most guest houses prepare evening meals.

Asmaaltı Lokantası (☎ 814 8040; Solyu Caddesi; meals TL10) Situated in the city centre, this busy restaurant is a hit with the locals for its cheap stews. It makes an ideal lunch spot between buses, or if you're staying at the Hotel Dedehan.

Kap Restaurant (☎ 814 2374; İskele Meydanı; meals around TL15) On the prime corner in town, and with the best contacts down at the harbour, Kap is the fish restaurant of choice. The mezes are also delicious, but service can be sloppy.

Getting There & Away

There are several buses daily to Alanya (YT15, three hours, 135km) and Silifke (TL18, 3½ hours, 160km).

Getting Around

Anamur is quite spread out, but easy to get around on public transport. Buses and dolmuşes to İskele depart from a small stand behind the otogar (TL1, every 30 minutes). A taxi between İskele and the otogar costs about TL15.

Dolmuşes to Ören also leave from next to the mosque, over the road from the otogar, and can drop you off at the Anamurium turn-off on the main highway. Alternatively, you'll need to take a taxi from Anamur otogar or from İskele. Expect to pay about TL40 to go there and back, with an hour's waiting time – but this is barely enough time to see the highlights.

Frequent dolmuşes to Bozyazı (TL1) travel past Mamure Kalesi.

AROUND ANAMUR

About 20km east of Anamur, you'll come to the town of **Bozyazı**, spread across a fertile plain. East across the plain, and clearly visible for miles around, is **Softa Castle** (Softa Kalesi), impossibly perched on the rocks above the hamlet of Çubukköyağı. Like Mamure Castle (p417) to the west, Softa was built by the Armenian kings who ruled Cilicia for a short while during the Crusades. It is now pretty ruined, but the walls and location are mightily impressive. As you leave Bozyazı, a sign on the left points inland to the castle, but the road doesn't go all the way to the top.

If you'd like to climb into the mountains and see yet another medieval castle, turn left at Sipahili 3km southwest of Aydıncık and head up towards Gülnar (25km) for **Meydancık Castle** (Meydancık Kalesi), which has stood here in one form or another since Hittite times.

TAŞUCU
☎ 0324

Taşucu is best known as the working port of Silifke, but this quaint, low-key tourist resort has a fine city beach filled with friendly locals. The town lives for the ferries to Girne (Kyrenia) in Northern Cyprus. Car ferries and hydrofoils take travellers across the sea.

Orientation & Information

The main square by the ferry dock, one block south of the highway, has a PTT, banks, a customs house, assorted shipping offices and several restaurants. The beach is fronted by Sahil Yolu, which stretches out east of the docks and has several good pensions. There is an internet café in the plaza opposite the pier.

Sleeping

Meltem Pansiyon (☎ 741 4391; Sahil Caddesi 75; s/d TL25/40; ✷) This fulfils the proper criteria of a pension – intimate, affordable and friendly. Sitting just a few steps from the small, sandy beach, this family-run place has a few sea-facing rooms; breakfast is served on the back patio. Rooms are modest but squeaky clean.

Holmi Pansiyon (☎ 741 5378; holmi.pansiyon.kafe terya@hotmail.com; Sahil Caddesi 23; s/d €16/21; ❸) The covered front porch here is particularly nice for relaxing on a hot day. The rooms have small desks and balconies, although not much of a sea view. It's a short walk to the beach.

Dilara Pansiyon (☎ 741 5378; dilarapansiyontasucu@ hotmail.com; Sahil Caddesi 25; s/d TL30/50; ❸ 🖳) This delightful little two-storey pension, right next door to Holmi, has cheap but stylish rooms, all with spacious bathrooms. It's run by two keen young sisters who speak good English.

Olba Otel (☎ 741 4222; Sahil Caddesi; s/d TL50/80; ❸) Next door to Meltem Pansiyon and directly on the sea, Olba is tidy and well run. The 2nd-floor balcony (where breakfast is served) offers wonderful sea views. The rooms are clad in cosy, kitsch wood-panelling. The couple who manages is very professional and discounts are negotiable.

Lades Motel (☎ 741 4008; www.ladesmotel.com; Atatürk Caddesi 89; s/d €37/51; ❸ 🖳) This hotel is a favourite of birdwatchers who come to visit nearby Göksu Delta (p421). The rooms, set around a big pool, are a touch disappointing. But there are wonderful harbour views from the balconies. The lobby and sitting areas are well designed for comparing 'twitching' notes.

Taşucu Best Resort Hotel (☎ 741 6300; www.best -resorthotel.com; Atatürk Caddesi 97; s/d €60/90, f €120; ❸ 🖳) A five-star hotel that suits a family vacation, this massive place has two restaurants, four bars, a hairdresser and hamam all on site, and a shell-shaped pool featuring a bridge and waterslide. Some of the technicolour rooms even come with portholes, while the family rooms have connecting (or separating) doors.

Eating & Drinking

Alo Dürüm (☎ 741 2464, 741 2463; Atatürk Caddesi 17; meals about €3) In the middle of the main drag and close to the ferry terminal, this is an open-air döner (spit roast) and pide (Turkish pizza) place popular with locals and travellers. A 24-hour delivery service is available, should you get a hankering for *lahmacun* (Arabic pizza) at 3am.

Denizkizi Restaurant (☎ 741 4194; Atatürk Caddesi; meals TL10-20) Opposite the Atatürk statue and ferry terminal, this classy, quiet place is good for fish, meze and general wellbeing. The shaded outdoor seating is perfect on a hot afternoon.

Baba Restaurant (☎ 741 5991; Atatürk Caddesi 87; meals TL10-20) Next to the Lades Motel, locals regard Baba as Silifke's best eatery. The terrace is a beautiful place to sip a cold beer, but it's the food that brings in the punters. Portions are generous and artfully prepared, as is the meze cart, which will tempt you all evening long. Don't miss the updated selection of fresh fish on the chalkboard.

Getting There & Away

Akgünler Denizcilik (☎ 741 4033; fax 741 4324; www .akgunler.com.tr; Taşucu Atatürk Caddesi) runs *feribotlar* (car ferries) and/or *ekspresler* (hydrofoils) between Taşucu and Girne (Kyrenia) in Northern Cyprus. It has a daily hydrofoil at 10am (one way TL72, return TL110) and a car ferry (one way TL55, return TL90; car one way/return TL150/300) leaving at midnight (although they don't actually sail until 2am), from Sunday to Thursday. The hydrofoil leaves Girne at 9.30am daily while the car ferry leaves at 11.30am Monday to Friday.

Hydrofoils are faster (two hours) but the ride can be stomach-churning on choppy seas. Passenger tickets cost less on the car ferry, but the trip is longer (anything from four to 10 hours depending on the weather). Provided your visa allows for multiple entries within its period of validity, you shouldn't have to pay for a new one when you come back into Turkey.

Dolmuşes drop you at the petrol station to the north of town – it's a five-minute walk to the beach. There are frequent dolmuşes between Taşucu and Silifke (TL1.50), where you can connect with long-distance services to major destinations.

SİLİFKE

🕾 0324 / pop 65,000

Silifke is a lush riverside country town of historic significance and contemporary charm. There's a striking castle above – and handsome park along – the gushing Göksu River. Plus in the vicinity lie some fascinating archaeological relics and serene mountain villages.

Seleucia, as it was known, was founded by Seleucus I Nicator in the 3rd century BC. Seleucus was one of Alexander the Great's most able generals and founder of the Seleucid dynasty that ruled Syria after Alexander's death.

The town's other claim to fame is that Emperor Frederick Barbarossa (r 1152–90) drowned in the river near here while leading his troops on the Third Crusade.

Orientation & Information

The otogar is near the junction of the highways to Alanya, Mersin and Konya, 800m along İnönü Caddesi from the town centre. Halfway between the otogar and the town centre you pass the ruins of the Temple of Jupiter.

The town is split by the Göksu River, called the Calycadnus in ancient times. Most of the services, including the otogar, are on the southern bank of the river. Exceptions are the tourist office and the dolmuş stop for Uzuncaburç.

The **tourist office** (☎ 714 1151; Veli Gürten Bozbey Caddesi 6; ⏰ 8am-noon & 1-5pm Mon-Fri) is just north of Atatürk Caddesi. The excellent book *Silifke (Seleucia on Calycadnus) and Environs*, is available across the road at **Bilgen Kirtasiye** (☎ 714 1367; Ilhan Akgün Caddesi) for TL20.

Sights & Activities

The Byzantine hilltop **fortress** was once Silifke's command centre. Today it's just a wonderful place to visit. The castle itself has 23 towers and underground storage rooms that can still be seen. From the fortress it's possible to see the **Tekir Ambarı**, an ancient cistern carved from rock. To reach the cistern, first head to the

junction of İnönü and Menderes Caddesis, then walk up the steep road to the left of the Küçük Hacı Kaşaplar supermarket. Providing a very pleasant alternative to a dreadful walk up the hill to the castle are the motorcycle drivers who wait at this corner. Expect to pay around TL12 per person for a round-trip journey; you'll be riding in the small wooden box up front.

The Roman **Temple of Jupiter** is especially striking if you're not expecting to see it; it literally sits right along the side of the very busy İnönü Caddesi. The temple dates from the 2nd century AD, but was turned into a Christian Basilica sometime in the 5th century.

The **Archaeological Museum** (Arkeoloji Müzesi; İnönü Caddesi; admission TL3; ⏰ 8am-noon & 1-5pm Tue-Sun), located about halfway between the otogar and Taşucu proper, has a decent collection of Roman statues and busts, coins and jewellery, as well as an archaeological hall filled with pottery, tools and weapons from the Roman and Hellenistic eras.

The **Ulu Cami** (Great Mosque; Fevzi Çakmak Caddesi) is a Seljuk-built mosque, although it's seen renovations over the years. At the **Reşadiye Camii** (İnönü Caddesi), take note of the Roman

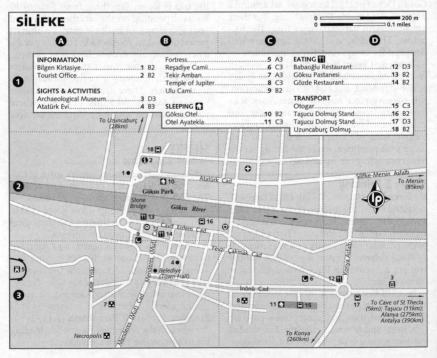

SİLİFKE

0 — 200 m
0 — 0.1 miles

INFORMATION		
Bilgen Kirtasiye	1	B2
Tourist Office	2	B2

SIGHTS & ACTIVITIES		
Archaeological Museum	3	D3
Atatürk Evi	4	B3

Fortress	5	A3
Reşadiye Camii	6	C3
Tekir Amban	7	A3
Temple of Jupiter	8	C3
Ulu Cami	9	B2

SLEEPING		
Göksu Otel	10	B2
Otel Ayatekla	11	C3

EATING		
Babaoğlu Restaurant	12	D3
Göksu Pastanesi	13	B2
Gözde Restaurant	14	B2

TRANSPORT		
Otogar	15	C3
Taşucu Dolmuş Stand	16	B2
Taşucu Dolmuş Stand	17	D3
Uzuncaburç Dolmuş	18	B2

To Uzuncaburç (28km)

Atatürk Cad

Silifke-Mersin Asfaltı
To Mersin (85km)

Göksu Park

Stone Bridge

Göksu River

Cavit Erdem Cad

Fevzi Çakmak Cad

Kale Yolu

Belediye (Town Hall)

İnönü Cad

Necropolis

To Cave of St Thecla (5km); Taşucu (11km); Alanya (275km); Antalya (390km)

Konya Asfaltı

To Konya (260km)

columns standing on the back porch and at the entrance.

The **Atatürk Evi** (admission free; 9am-noon & 1-4.30pm) is an old Silifke house with an interesting photo gallery of Mustafa Kemal. Be prepared to show your passport at the door.

The **stone bridge** over the Göksu dates back to AD 78 and has been restored many times.

Sleeping

Otel Ayatekla (715 1081; fax 715 1085; Otogar Civari; s/d TL30/50;) A quite nice two-star hotel next to the otogar with a large restaurant on the ground floor. Some rooms come with decent views of the city and mountains, and all have TV. A suite with balcony is available.

Göksu Otel (712 1021; fax 712 1024; Atatürk Caddesi 20; s/d TL35/60;) As pretty much the only midrange option in town, the Göksu has the market well in hand. Luckily it's also a very relaxing place to stay on the northern bank of its namesake. Business in style and decor, its provincial sensibility gives it more warmth than you might expect in the bigger cities. The ground-floor restaurant is excellent.

Eating

Göksu Pastanesi (Cavit Erdem Caddesi; pastries from TL1) A large and shaded terrace perched atop the rumbling river below. Close to the stone bridge, this modest eatery sells çay (tea) and snacks.

Gözde Restaurant (714 2764; Menderes (Mut) Caddesi; meals TL8) This döner kebap and *lahmacun* joint also serves up delicious soups in a shaded outdoor dining area. The English-speaking wait staff make it a fine – if rather casual – evening outing.

Babaoğlu Restaurant (714 2041; meals TL10) It's an unlikely location near the otogar for Silifke's most upscale restaurant. The fish, lamb and chicken dishes are particularly well prepared. And if you've got a bus to catch it also makes a mean pide.

Getting There & Away

Located at the junction of the coastal highway and the road into the mountains, Silifke is an important transit point with good bus services.

Buses depart for Adana along the highway east of Silifke (TL15, two hours, 155km, hourly) throughout the day and will stop to pick up ruin ramblers.

Dolmuşes to Taşucu (TL1) depart every 20 minutes from opposite Babaoğlu Restaurant –

across the highway from the otogar – or from a stand on the south bank of the Göksu.

Other services from Silifke include to Antalya (TL35, nine hours, 390km, 10 per day) and to Mersin (TL6, two hours, 85km, three per hour).

AROUND SİLİFKE
Cave of St Thecla

This area is rich in Christian pilgrimage sites, such as the **Cave of St Thecla** (Ayatekla; admission TL2; 9am-noon & 1.30-6pm Mon-Fri), a small rock shelter hidden underneath the remains of a Byzantine church. St Thecla (Ayatekla in Turkish) was the first person to be converted by St Paul. A religious outcast, Thecla spent her last few years in the cave living a pious life. The church was built in her honour in AD 480.

To reach the cave when driving from Taşucu to Silifke, look for the Alpet petrol station on your left. Next to it is Ayatekla Sokak, which leads directly up a hill and to the site. The entrance to the cave is directly behind the basilica ruins.

GETTING THERE & AWAY

To get to the cave from Silifke take a Taşucu dolmuş (TL1) and ask to be dropped off at the Ayatekla junction, 1km from the site.

Göksu Delta & Around

Some 334 species of bird nest in the lush salt marshes, lakes and sand dunes of the Göksu Delta, a renowned wetland area immediately south of Silifke.

East of Silifke, the slopes of the maquis-covered Olbian Plateau, one of Turkey's richest areas for archaeological sites, stretch along the coast for about 60km before the Cilician Plain opens into an ever-widening swathe of fertile land.

Narlıkuyu

Tiny, beautiful Narlıkuyu village is more than just a cove on a bend in the highway. It's got justifiably famous fish restaurants and refreshing harbour currents, a singular mosaic and some hellish mountain caves nearby.

Inside the village's tiny **museum** (admission TL3), which is actually a 4th-century Roman bath, you'll find a wonderful mosaic of the goddesses of fertility, also known as the Three Graces – Aglaia, Thalia and Euphrosyne.

You won't go far wrong at any restaurant here, but **Kerim** (723 3295; meals about TL20), and

Narlıkuyu Balık (☎ 723 3286; meals about TL20) are both worth a shot.

Frequent dolmuşes run between Narlıkuyu, Ertur, Kızkalesi and Silifke (TL1).

Caves of Heaven & Hell (Cennet ve Cehennum)

As you wind 2km up the road behind Narlıkuyu, the last thing you'd expect to find is a geological netherworld. An area of great mythological significance, these creepy, gargantuan **caves** (admission TL3; ☑ 8am-5pm) are famed above Earth for their descent into a beautiful abyss.

For those expecting an easy ticket to hereafter, the 250m-wide **Chasm of Heaven** (Cennet Cöküğü) is reached via 452 steps through a gorgeous leafy expanse. When you reach a landing, check out the 5th-century Byzantine **Chapel of Virgin Mary**, which for a short time in the 19th century was used as a mosque.

Continue following the path down and into the cave itself, where you'll find the **Cave-Gorge to Hell** (Cehennem Çukuru), a damp, jagged-edged, devilish theatre – indeed locals believe this cave to be a gateway to the eternal furnace. Should you hear a certain roaring sound, though, fear not: it's simply the sound of an underground stream (which can be seen in the winter but not summer). Legend had it that the roaring stream connects at some point with Styx, the river which in Greek mythology is the border between our world and the underworld.

You'll need a separate ticket to view the nearby **Pit of Hell** (Cehennem Çukuru; TL2), which can only be seen from a small viewing platform above. This deep charred hole is allegorically where Zeus imprisoned the 100-headed monster Typhon after defeating him in battle.

Near the car park is the **Astim Mağarası** (Asthma Cave), which is said to relieve the affliction.

Uzuncaburç

The mountain village of **Uzuncaburç** (admission TL2; ☑ 8am-noon & 1-5pm Mon-Fri) thoroughly rewards the short 30km trip north from Silifke. It sits within the ancient Roman city of Diocaesarea, originally a Hellenistic city known as Olbia. This area is thought to have been home to a zealous cult that worshipped Zeus Olbius.

The **Temple of Zeus Olbius** is just inside the site and on the left, but first visit the Roman **theatre** which can be found before the car park, also on the left. The theatre is easy to miss; it's half-sunken into the ground, and is covered with a

beautiful bed of wildflowers. Some of the sight's most important structures were Roman-built, including the **fountain** (2nd or 3rd century), the **Temple of Tyche** (1st century), and the **city gate**.

To view a Hellenistic structure built before the Romans sacked Olbia, leave the site and turn left through the village. On the right a road leads to a massive *burç* (tower), which seems to pop out of the roadside. Continue on and you'll discover a path to the left that winds down 500m to a **necropolis**.

GETTING THERE & AWAY

Minibuses to Uzuncaburç (TL4) leave from a side street near the tourist office in Silifke at 9am, 11am, 1pm and 3pm, and return an hour later.

Hiring a taxi costs about TL50 return, waiting time included, which would allow you to inspect some tombs along the way.

Göksu Valley

From Uzuncaburç the road continues via Kırobası to Mut and then to Karaman and Konya. Winding up into the forests you may pass huge stacks of logs cut by the Tahtacılar, the Alevi mountain woodcutters who live a secluded life in the forest.

About 40km before Mut the road skirts a fantastic limestone **canyon** that extends for several kilometres. High above in the limestone cliffs are **caves**, which were probably once inhabited. The land in the valleys is rich and well watered. About 20km north of Mut a turn-off on the right leads 5km to the ruins of another **medieval castle** at Alahan. Continuing further west the road runs through spectacular mountain scenery towards **Ermenek**, a pretty Anatolian village where a large dam is set to alter the landscape.

KIZKALESİ
☎ 0324

Wonderful Kızkalesi, bang up against the D400, is not your typical highway town. It not only fronts one of the region's loveliest sand beaches, but is also the jumping off point for the Olbian Plateau, a virtual open-air museum of rocky hill ruins and unrecorded history.

Kızkalesi's whacky tack of tourism is sedated by the relaxed vibe of its locals. The foreshore is graced by a fine promenade filled with holidaying Turks, and within swimming distance is the mesmerising Maiden's Castle.

For a visitor, the scene here is more inclusive and relaxed than you'd expect of a typical

Turkish village of this size – perhaps thanks to the regularity of archaeology buffs from America and Europe kicking off their shoes here. And while the evening music may have deepened its bass lines of late, Kızkalesi still feels like old-school fun in the sun.

Information

There is an ATM in the municipality building, and several internet cafés.

Sights & Activities

A castle floating in the sea is the stuff of fairy tales and Turkish coastlines. **Kızkalesi** (Maiden's Castle; admission TL3), which lies 200m from the shore, is a suspended dream of impossible beauty. However, it is possible to swim to the castle; though most people choose to pay around TL5 for a lift on a boat.

To its left and on the shore is **Korykos Castle** (admission TL3), an antiquated fortress that was either built or rebuilt by the Byzantines, and was briefly occupied by the kings of Lesser Armenia. It's a bit of a rough-and-ready site, so be sure to wear proper footwear.

Across the highway from Korykos Castle is a **necropolis** that's well worth exploring. There are sarcophagi and rock carvings scattered about as well.

Sleeping

Hotel Hantur (☎ 523 2367; hotelhantur@tnn.net.tr; s/d TL40/60; 🕸) The Hantur has long had the front row view of the sea (guests need do little else but watch the tides roll in). The sterile white rooms are cool, comfortable and all have balconies, but try to grab one facing the sea (hint: Room 201!) The breezy front garden is another bonus, as is the helpful management.

Baytan Hotel (☎ 523 2095; www.baytanotel.com; s/d TL40/70; 🕸 💻) Granted it's a touch tacky and faded, but it's right on the beach, rooms are spacious (though could do with a coat of paint) and the hilarious manager will ensure your stay is memorable. The rooftop terrace is great viewing at 'beer' o'clock.

Hotel Korykos (☎ 523 2212; www.korykoshotel.com; s/d TL40/70; 🕸 💻) A complete makeover has done wonders for this smart hotel near the Yaka. Staff is attentive and professional, while the lobby space is particularly welcoming. Rooms have TV and firm, big beds. The bathrooms are newly fitted.

Hotel Rain (☎ 523 2782; www.rainhotel.com; s/d TL50/80; 🕸 💻) With its youthful vibe suited to meeting fellow travellers, Hotel Rain has blossomed on the grapevine. Run by the same crowd as Café Rain, it's got a similar anything-is-possible ethos, including scuba diving trips, thanks largely to its attached travel agency. The spotless, spacious rooms are sparingly decorated and conducive to long stays.

Yaka Hotel (☎ 523 2444; yakahotel@yakahotel.com; s/d TL60/90; 🕸 💻) Yakup Kahveci, the Yaka Hotel's multilingual and quick-witted owner, runs the smartest hotel in Kızkalesi. Lodgers can dine in the attractive garden area, rooms are impeccably tidy and local knowledge abounds. The Yaka is also a great place to meet budding archaeologists in the midst of great discovery.

Club Hotel Barbarossa (☎ 523 2364; www.barbarossa hotel.com; s/d with half-board TL105/140; 🕸 💻 🍴) With the addition of your evening meals, the Barbarossa is a surprisingly good value choice. The finer touches are impressive too. The back garden – scattered with bits of Roman columns – provides welcome relief from the exposed beach, and the choice of two swimming pools means you can usually splash about in private. Even if you're not a guest, book yourself a massage (TL40).

Eating & Drinking

Kızkalesi has yet to develop the restaurant scene to match its hungry crowd, due in part to the fine kitchens of the pensions. It's worth paying a TL1.25 bus fare for the 10-minute hop to Narlıkuyu (p421) to dine at the higher end.

Honey Restaurant & Bar (☎ 523 2430; Inci Plaj Yolu 1; meals around TL6) Unimpressive on the exterior, Honey is nonetheless a cosy and pleasantly palatable surprise. Try the *saç kavurma* (TL5), an Anatolian speciality of meat and veggies, or the *patlıcan kebap* (TL5), which is meat wrapped in eggplant. It's right on the highway, and features retro posters and a thirst-inducing mirrored bar.

Café Rain (☎ 523 2234; meals around TL10) The colourful decor compliments the cheery menu of tasty, good-value meals and, perhaps, the finest *börek* (pastry filled with cheese or meat) on the eastern Mediterranean. In the evenings, travellers transform it into a happening cocktail bar.

Titanic (☎ 523 2669; Cetin Ozvaran Caddesi; meals TL10) Near Café Rain, this new lounge bar has ample couches, pop posters, good indie music and a genuine gallivanting spirit. It's perhaps preferable to the nascent club scene.

Paşa Restaurant (☎ 523 1389; İnci Plaj Yolu; meals around TL10) A large open-air spot for grills, mezes and light Turkish snacks with agreeable prices.

At the time of writing, the Kızkalesi club scene was starting to make noise, albeit at a reasonable volume.

Getting There & Away

There are frequent buses to Silifke (TL2, 30 minutes) and to Mersin.

AROUND KIZKALESI

The limestone-filled Olbian Plateau is a veritable adventure park of great ruins, many with little or no explanation. If short of time, head straight for ethereal **Adamkayalar** (Men's Rocks). These 17 reliefs from the Roman era immortalise warriors wielding axes, swords and lances, sometimes accompanied by their wives and children. There are more ruins and tombs scattered around at the top of the cliff. It's about a 1.5km walk from the main road, but the once-rugged track has recently been cleared. Follow the painted arrows down a tricky incline – best not to go it alone.

About 25km further along the road are the ruins of **Çambazlı**, which feature a necropolis and a Byzantine-era church in remarkably good condition.

About 3km east of Kızkalesi are the extensive but badly ruined remains of ancient **Elaiussa-Sebaste**, a city with foundations dating back to at least the early Roman period and perhaps even to the Hittite era.

About 8.5km east of Kızkalesi at Kumkuyu is the road to **Kanlıdivane** (admission TL3; ☒ 8am-7pm), the ancient city of Kanytelis. The site lies about 4km north of Kumkuyu. The first structure to come into view upon entering the car park is a **Hellenistic Tower**, which was built by the son of a priest-king in Olba (today known as Uzuncaburç; p422) to honour Zeus. It became the location of an ancient Zeus-worshipping cult.

The name Kanlıdivane means 'Bloodstained Place of Madness'. Take a stroll around the 90m-deep chasm where criminals were said to have been tossed to their deaths. Various ruins dramatically ring the pit – most from the Roman and Byzantine eras. Kanlıdivane's morbid past and isolated present probably give it the nod of Narlıkuyu (p421) as the creepiest depiction of the bowels of 'hell'.

Follow the footpath behind the Roman road to discover the splendidly preserved mausoleum perched atop the hill.

MERSİN (İÇEL)

☎ 0324 / pop 1.06 million

Mersin's bustling port – one of Turkey's largest – recently underwent a fine facelift. Capital of the province of İçel, the site was earmarked 50 years earlier as a way to give Anatolia a port close to Adana and its rich agricultural hinterland. Until the 1991 Gulf War, the city was a major port for goods going to and from Iraq. Today the city is home to a number of underrated arts festivals and several good hotels.

Mersin has been renamed İçel, but everyone seems to be sticking with the former.

Orientation

The town centre is Gümrük Meydanı, the plaza occupied by the Ulu Cami. On the western side is Atatürk Caddesi, a pedestrians-only shopping street, while two blocks north is İstiklal Caddesi, the main thoroughfare and a pedestrian mall.

To get to the centre from the otogar, leave by the main exit, turn right and walk up to the main road (Gazi Mustafa Kemal Bulvarı). Cross to the far side and catch a bus travelling west (TL1).

Information

INTERNET ACCESS

Bilgi Internet (Soğuksu Caddesi 30; TL2 per hr)

MONEY

Exchange offices and ATMs are clustered around Gümrük Meydanı and the Ulu Cami. Many ATMs run out of money on weekends, so you may be forced to try several before securing your cash.

POST

PTT (☎ 237 3237; İsmet İnönü Bulvarı)

TOURIST INFORMATION

Tourist office (☎ 238 3271; fax 238 3272; İsmet İnönü Bulvarı; ☒ 8am-noon & 1-5pm)

Sights

A stroll along the harbour is one way to get an idea of what Mersin is all about. Another is to wander through the pedestrian streets between Uray Caddesi and İstiklal Caddesi. There is a small fish market and a covered bazaar with stores selling dried goods and piles of spices. At the eastern end of Atatürk Caddesi is the fine stone **Atatürk Evi** (admission free; ☒ 9am-noon & 1-4.30pm Mon-Sat), a museum in a house where Atatürk once stayed.

A little further west, beside the Kültür Merkezi (Cultural Centre; not open for tourists), is Mersin's small **museum** (admission TL3; 🕒 8am–noon & 1–5pm). This has a reasonably good archaeological collection with many Roman artefacts on the ground floor, including a small, headless statue of Eros, and the usual ethnographical bibs and bobs on the 1st floor.

Next to the museum, the modest **Orthodox church** has some fine icons. To gain entry, go to the left side of the church, on 4302 Sokak and look for the entry door. You may have to shout for the caretaker (who will expect a tip to show you around) if no-one is in sight.

For active souls there's a 12km-long **pathway** that runs parallel to the sea. The path starts behind the Mersin Hilton and continues west.

Or, to discover a working-class neighbourhood where döner kebaps can be had for TL1 and vendors sell strawberries and nuts from wooden carts, leave the guidebook at your hotel and stroll the length of **Çakmak Caddesi**.

Archaeology buffs might want to check out **Viranşehir** (TL4), the ancient Soles or Pompeiopolis. Buses depart from outside the tourist office.

Sleeping

Mersin specialises in business hotels, most of them good value. If you're on the move early, there are some decent hotels facing the otogar.

Hotel Savran (☎ 232 4472; Soğuksu Caddesi 14; s/d TL25/45; ☒) The hotel might not be pretty,

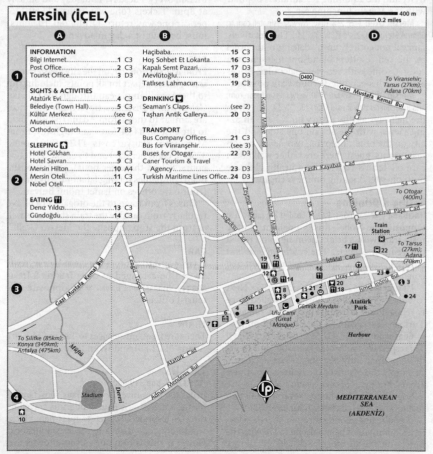

MERSİN (İÇEL)

0   400 m
0   0.2 miles

INFORMATION
Bilgi Internet...........................1 C3
Post Office.............................2 C3
Tourist Office........................3 D3

SIGHTS & ACTIVITIES
Atatürk Evi............................4 C3
Belediye (Town Hall)...............5 C3
Kültür Merkezi.....................(see 6)
Museum..................................6 C3
Orthodox Church...................7 B3

SLEEPING 🏠
Hotel Gökhan........................8 C3
Hotel Savran.........................9 C3
Mersin Hilton.......................10 A4
Mersin Oteli..........................11 C3
Nobel Oteli...........................12 C3

EATING 🍴
Deniz Yıldızı.........................13 C3
Gündoğdu.............................14 C3

Haçibaba................................15 C3
Hoş Sohbet Et Lokanta.........16 C3
Kapalı Semt Pazarı.................17 D3
Mevlütoğlu............................18 C3
Tatlıses Lahmacun.................19 C3

DRINKING 🍸
Seaman's Claps....................(see 2)
Taşhan Antik Galleryra...........20 D3

TRANSPORT
Bus Company Offices............21 C3
Bus for Vinranşehir..............(see 3)
Buses for Otogar...................22 D3
Caner Tourism & Travel
      Agency.............................23 D3
Turkish Maritime Lines Office..24 D3

but management at the Savran gives a lot more than one-star service. The rooms are unexpectedly large, though your sleep may be interrupted by dreams of a firm mattress. Still, it's a popular budget choice.

Hotel Gökhan (☎ 232 4665; fax 237 4462; Soğuksu Caddesi 22; s/d TL40/65; ☒) The interior decorator of this two-star hotel has been inspired by the Roaring Twenties – either that or a great aunt just passed away. The airy rooms include satellite TV and minibar – opt for a balcony at no extra cost. There's ample free parking.

Nobel Oteli (☎ 237 2210; www.nobelotel.com; Istiklal Caddesi; s/d TL65/90) A very smart choice in the heart of the city, the Nobel has big, bargain rooms with some deft design touches and satellite TV. The foyer is a hive of business activity and the adjoining restaurant is popular with the Mersin lunching set.

Mersin Oteli (☎ 238 1040; www.mersinoteli.com.tr; Gümruk Meydanı 112; s/d TL80/130; ☒) This relatively fancy if not entirely up-to-date four-star hotel in the centre offers bland but nice-enough rooms, some with sea-view balconies. Prices are a touch steep but discounts are possible.

Mersin Hilton (☎ 326 5000; www.mersin.hilton.com; Adnan Menderes Bulvarı; s/d €95/120; ☒ ☐ ☒) Even the hallways at this luxury hotel have amazing views, with the sea on one side and the city on the other. Enjoying two Asian-fusion restaurants, guests here are rather well taken care of. Tennis courts and a health club are both on-site. Booking online is cheaper.

Eating & Drinking

Hacıbaba (☎ 238 0023; Istiklal Caddesi 82; meals TL8) Opposite the Nobel, this is a delightful little restaurant with a bright neon sign and rolled out reddish carpets. The *zeytinyagli dolma* (stuffed pepper) is up there with the best of a constantly rotating menu.

Mevlütoğlu (☎ 237 7024; Uray Caddesi 22; TL10) Next to Yoncas supermarket, this glass-walled place is relaxed and efficient. It serves a range of Turkish stews, with all the usual trimmings.

Gündoğdu (☎ 231 9677; Silifke Caddesi 22; meals €3) This especially toothsome fast-food joint seems to be permanently heaving. It has no menu, so simply order one of the house specialities: İskender döner, *börek* or *salata* (salad).

Soğuksu Caddesi boasts several small fish restaurants, such as **Deniz Yıldızı** (meals TL8).

If you're just passing through, there are lots of restaurants and beer halls mixed in with the hotels outside the otogar. Self-caterers can try

Kapalı Semt Pazarı (Çakmak Caddesi), a small fruit and vegetable market.

Taşhan Antik Gallerya is a collection of humming little working-class bars and cafés, popular with locals and Greek sailors – it's a great entry point into Turkish social life. The area around the Hilton has a few new clubs.

Getting There & Away
BOAT

The **Turkish Maritime Lines** (☎ 231 2536, 237 0726) ticket office is on the 2nd floor, right next to the dock entrance where the ferries depart. Ferries travel from Mersin to Gazimağusa (Famagusta) on the east coast of Northern Cyprus every Monday, Wednesday and Friday at 8pm. The ferry travels from Gazimağusa to Mersin every Tuesday, Thursday and Sunday at 8pm. Tickets (one way/return TL60/115, per car one way/return TL140/280, 10 hours) must be bought a day in advance.

BUS

From Mersin's otogar, on the city's eastern outskirts, buses depart for all points, including up to the Anatolian plateau through the Cilician Gates (p429). Distances, travel times and prices are similar to those from Adana (p430), 70km to the east on a fast, four-lane highway. From Mersin to Alanya costs TL22 (8½ hours, 375km, eight per day) and to Silifke TL8 (two hours, 85km, three per hour). Several of the main companies serving İstanbul, Ankara and İzmir have offices on İsmet İnönü Bulvarı.

Buses from town to the otogar (TL1) leave regularly from outside the train station, as well as from the stop opposite the Mersin Oteli.

CAR

If you want to explore the coast by car, rentals can be arranged at **Caner Tourism & Travel Agency** (Ismet İnönü Bulvarı 88A), opposite the tourist office.

TRAIN

There are frequent services to Tarsus (TL1.80), Adana (TL2.80) and İskenderun (TL5).

TARSUS
☎ 0324 / pop 319,000
In the 2000th anniversary of Tarsus' most famous former citizen – St Paul – pilgrims travelling through a sprawl of concrete apartment blocks would concede its beauty as largely historic. However this is also one of those towns that

repays some perseverance, and a stroll through the Old City, or along Tarsus Nehri (Cydnus River), can be reason enough to linger.

Information

The otogar is some way out of town. A taxi from there will cost you TL8 to the city centre; or you can walk out the front exit and hop on a bus (TL1) on the same side of the street. Detailed maps of Tarsus and its attractions are available at the tourist information booth in the town centre.

Sights & Activities

Buses drop you off beside **Cleopatra's Gate**, a Roman city gate that has little to do with the famous lady, although she is thought to have met Mark Antony in Tarsus. In any case, restoration carried out in 1994 has robbed it of any sense of antiquity.

Walk straight ahead, and just before the *hükümet konağı* (government house) is a sign pointing left to **St Paul's Well** (Senpol Kuyusu; see boxed text right). The ruins of Paul's house can be viewed underneath plates of glass.

At the same road junction a second sign to the left points to the **Old City** (Antik Şehir). Follow it and you'll come to Cumhuriyet Alanı, where excavations have uncovered a wonderful stretch of **Roman road**, with heavy basalt paving slabs covering a lengthy drain.

Return to the *hükümet konağı* and continue northwards until you come to the 19th-century **Makam Camii** on the right. Directly across the street is **Eski Cami** (Old Mosque), a medieval structure which may originally have been a church dedicated to St Paul. Right beside it looms the barely recognisable brickwork of a huge old **Roman bath**.

Beside the Eski Cami you can catch a dolmuş (TL1) to Tarsus' other main sight, the **waterfall** (*şelale*) on the Tarsus Nehri (Cydnus River) which cascades over the rocks right inside the town, providing the perfect setting for tea gardens and restaurants.

To reach the 16th-century **Ulu Cami** (Great Mosque), which sports a curious 19th-century clock tower, turn right beside the Makam Camii and continue along the side street. Behind it and one street over on the right are the ruins of **St Paul's Church**.

The **Tarsus Museum** (Tarsus Müzesi; admission TL3; 8am-noon & 1-5pm Mon-Fri) is located near the corner of Muvaffak Uygur and Cumhuriyet Caddesis, close to the stadium.

> ### BIRTHPLACE OF ST PAUL
>
> Jewish by birth, Paul (born Saul) was one of Christianity's most zealous proselytisers; during his lifetime he converted scores of pagans and Jews to Christianity throughout much of the ancient world. After dying in Rome, sometime after AD 60, the location of his birthplace became sacred to his followers. Today pilgrims still flock to the site of his ruined house in Tarsus to take a small drink from the well (note that we can't vouch for its cleanliness!).

Sleeping & Eating

Cihan Palas Oteli (☎ 624 1623; fax 624 7334; Mersin Caddesi 21; s/d TL20/35; 😤) Acceptable only in a pinch; best save up your pennies for Mersin.

Tarsus Mersin Oteli (☎ 614 0600; fax 614 0033; Şelale Mevkii; s/d TL60/100; 😤) This four-star hotel looms above the waterfall, and although the rooms are rather lovely and most conveniences are available, the decor and interior design could have used an update some 30 years ago.

Getting There & Away

There are plenty of buses and dolmuşes connecting Tarsus with Mersin (TL2, 27km) and Adana (TL3, 43km), so you could take a break here while travelling between the two.

ADANA

☎ 0322 / pop 1.2 million

The huge, steaming city of Adana – Turkey's fourth largest – has a habit of jolting those who approach with sand still between their toes. Split down the middle by the D400, it's a thoroughly modern and secular affair with some good nightlife and an old-fashioned working class grit.

North of the city's main road (Turan Cemal Beriker Bulvarı) is leafy and slick, a symptom of strong local industry led by the Sabancı Conglomerate – Turkey's second-largest – and the fertile Çukurova, the ancient Cilician plain deposited as silt by the Seyhan and Ceyhan rivers. But south of the trendy high-rise apartments, the mood deepens and the houses start to sprawl. Adana is in part a victim of Turkey's rising middle class, as the have-nots jostle for space on the fringes, and the *simit* (circular bread with sesame seeds) sellers are forced to re-bake their bread.

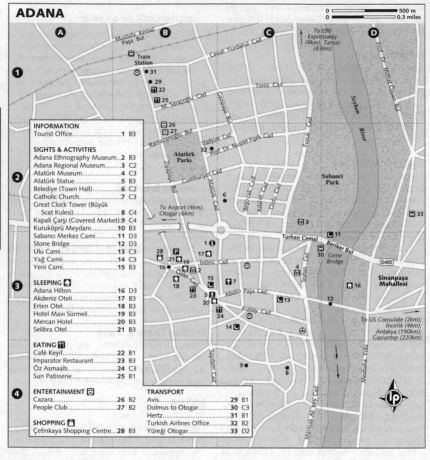

ADANA

INFORMATION
Tourist Office..........................1 B3

SIGHTS & ACTIVITIES
Adana Ethnography Museum..2 B3
Adana Regional Museum.........3 C2
Atatürk Museum.....................4 C3
Atatürk Statue.......................5 B3
Belediye (Town Hall)..............6 C2
Catholic Church.....................7 C3
Great Clock Tower (Büyük
    Saat Kulesi)......................8 C4
Kapali Çarşi (Covered Market).9 C4
Kuruköprü Meydanı...............10 B3
Sabancı Merkez Cami.............11 D3
Stone Bridge.........................12 D3
Ulu Cami..............................13 C3
Yağ Camii.............................14 C3
Yeni Cami.............................15 B3

SLEEPING
Adana Hilton.........................16 D3
Akdeniz Oteli........................17 B3
Erten Otel.............................18 B3
Hotel Mavı Sürmeli.................19 B3
Mercan Hotel.........................20 B3
Selibra Otel...........................21 B3

EATING
Café Keyif.............................22 B1
Imparator Restaurant.............23 B3
Öz Asmaaltı...........................24 C3
Sun Patisserie.......................25 B1

ENTERTAINMENT
Cazara..................................26 B2
People Club...........................27 B2

SHOPPING
Çetinkaya Shopping Centre...28 B3

TRANSPORT
Avis.....................................29 B1
Dolmus to Otogar.................30 C3
Hertz...................................31 B1
Turkish Airlines Office............32 B2
Yüreği Otogar.......................33 D2

Adana is, expectedly, a major transport hub, with bus, train and plane connections. It's also home to a large American military base. While not blessed with the must-see tourist sites of the region, Adana's fast pace and thoroughly secular outlook is perhaps the most Turkish of all.

Orientation

The Seyhan River skirts the city centre to the east. Adana's airport (Şakirpaşa Havaalanı) is 4km west of the centre on the D400. The otogar is 2km further west on the north side of the D400. The train station is at the northern end of Ziyapaşa Bulvarı, 1.5km north of İnönü Caddesi, the main commercial and hotel street.

The E90 expressway skirts the city to the north. If you approach by car from the north or west, take the Adana Küzey (Adana North) exit to reach the city centre.

At the western end of İnönü Caddesi is Kuruköprü Meydanı, marked by the highrise Çetinkaya shopping centre. There are several hotels on Özler Caddesi between Kuruköprü Meydanı and Küçüksaat Meydanı to the southeast.

Information

There's a **tourist office** (☎ 359 1994; Atatürk Caddesi 13; 8am-noon & 1-5pm) one block north of İnönü Caddesi, in the town centre, and a smaller **office** (☎ 436 9214) at the airport. Internet cafés are on İnönü Caddesi north of the hotels.

Sights
MOSQUES

The attractive 16th-century **Ulu Cami** (Great Mosque; Abidin Paşa Caddesi) is reminiscent of the Mamluk mosques of Cairo, with black-and-white banded marble and elaborate window surrounds. The tiles in the *mihrab* (niche indicating the direction of Mecca) came from Kütahya and İznik.

The 1724 **Yeni Cami** (New Mosque) follows the general square plan of the Ulu Cami, with 10 domes, while the **Yağ Camii** (1501), with its imposing portal, started life as the church of St James. Both are on Özler Caddesi.

More conspicuous than either of these is the six-minaret **Sabancı Merkez Cami**, right beside the Girne Bridge and the bank of the Ceyhan River. The biggest mosque between İstanbul and Saudi Arabia, it was built by the late industrial magnate Sakıp Sabancı, a wildly successful businessman, generous philanthropist and, when he passed away in 2004 at the age of 71, the richest man in all of Turkey. Take one look at the mosque he left behind and it's very obvious that Sabancı was also a devoutly religious man. Which isn't to say he was unapproachable: having grown up in the central Anatolian village of Akcakaya, it's said he purposely spoke in a country accent so as to assure his fellow Turks – and certainly his shareholders – that big business hadn't ruined him. Nonetheless, the Sabancı Merkez Cami is certainly a conspicuous monument. Roughly 20,000 worshippers can fit inside, and one of the minarets even conceals a small elevator. Fittingly, the marble and gold-leaf inlaid mosque has quite an influence in the surrounding areas: prayers originating here are broadcast to nearly 300 other mosques within a 60km radius.

MUSEUMS

The excellent **Adana Ethnography Museum** (Adana Etnografya Müzesi; admission TL3; ☯ 8.30am-noon & 1-4.30pm Tue-Sun), on a side street off İnönü Caddesi, is housed in a nicely restored Crusader church. It now holds a display of carpets and kilims, weapons, manuscripts and funeral monuments.

Scheduled to re-open in mid-2009, the **Adana Regional Museum** (Adana Bölge Müze; admission TL5; ☯ 8.30am-noon & 1-4.30pm Tue-Sun) is rich in Roman statuary from the **Cilician Gates**, north of Tarsus. The 'Gates', the main passage through the Taurus Mountains, were an important transit point as far back as Roman times. Note especially the 2nd-century Achilles sarcophagus, decorated with scenes from the *Iliad*. Hittite and Urartian artefacts are also on display.

The small **Atatürk Museum** (Atatürk Müze; Seyhan Caddesi; admission free; ☯ 8am-noon & 1.30-5pm), on a riverside street, is one of the city's few remaining traditional houses. It is a mansion that once belonged to the Ramazanoğulları family. Atatürk stayed here for a few nights in 1923.

OTHER SIGHTS

Have a look at the 16-arched Roman **stone bridge** *(taş köprü)* over the Seyhan, at the eastern end of Abidin Paşa Caddesi. Built by Hadrian (r 117–138), repaired by Justinian (r 527–565), and now sullied by modern traffic, it's still an impressive sight.

The **Great Clock Tower** (Büyük Saat Kulesi) dates back to 1881. Around it you'll find Adana's **kapalı çarşı** (covered market).

Sleeping

Though Adana has lodgings in all price ranges, there are no hotels near the airport, otogar or train station. All but the cheapest places post high prices as required by the city council and slash them to far more manageable levels at the first sign of interest.

Selibra Otel (☎ 363 3676; fax 363 4283; İnönü Caddesi 50; s/d TL 35/60; ☒) This perennial two-star favourite has left its 1970s mojo in the decor, but it's certainly decent enough for the price. The reception is vintage Bond, and the rooms are quite, well, roomy. Should you need to call home during your morning constitutional, there's even a phone next to the toilet.

Mercan Hotel (☎ 351 2603; fax 459 7710; Ocak Meydanı; s/d TL35/70; ☒) Set amid cheap fabric and fashion dens, the Mercan is a bona fide budget winner. It's a boutique oasis in a desert of bland. Think we like it? It's got well-appointed, comfortable rooms, a quaint breakfast area and a stylish lounge with unusual art.

Akdeniz Oteli (☎ 363 1510; fax 363 0905; İnönü Caddesi 14/1; s/d TL60/100; ☒) This is a clean and smartly-decorated two-star place with glassed-in shower stalls. Don't miss the psychedelic mirrored staircase leading from the lobby to the 2nd-floor bar, which we don't recommend for a nightcap, as prostitutes generally outnumber actual guests by a ratio of two-to-one.

Erten Otel (☎ 359 5399; www.adanaertenotel.com .tr; Özler Caddesi 53; s/d TL90/120; ☒) A great addition to Adana's four-star hotel bracket, the

EASTERN MEDITERRANEAN

Erten is deep downtown and stars the city's friendliest reception. In each room, you can pen your memoirs at a sturdy desk, put your feet up in the small sitting area and pace the oval shower.

Hotel Mavı Sürmeli (☎ 363 3437; www.mavisurmeli .com.tr; İnönü Caddesi 109; s/d TL100/150; 🛜) The best value high-end hotel in Adana, the Mavı is centrally located and a truly luxurious four-star choice. Rooms are spacious enough for contact sports, while the bar is all orange-and-red armchair brilliance.

Adana Hilton (☎ 355 5000; www.adana.hilton.com; 1 Sokak; Sinanpaşa Mahallesi; s/d €110/185; 🛜 🖵 🐾) Imagine a riverside location with an unreal view of the Sabancı Mosque, out-of-this-world dining options, a fitness centre, and rock-star sized rooms. A little FYI: you'd be wise not to let inquiring locals on the opposite side of the river know that you're staying here.

Eating & Drinking

Adana is famous Turkey-wide for its kebap: minced lamb mixed with hot pepper, squeezed on a flat skewer then charcoal-grilled. It's served with sliced purple onions dusted with fiery paprika, handfuls of parsley, a lemon wedge and flat bread.

Sun Patisserie (☎ 458 2134; Ziyapaşa Bulvarı 15a; cake TL3-TL10; 🕔 9am-midnight) Cakes, puddings and a delightfully delicious assortments of chocolates and ice cream have been served up at this Adana standby for over three decades. Don't have a sweet tooth? Come anyway, and join the city's trendiest sidewalk seating scene.

Café Keyif (☎ 457 7820; Ziyapaşa Bulvarı 17/A; meals €5) You might think Turkey had finally joined the EU after spending an hour or two at this wood-panelled, faux-British pub, where nine-to-fivers politely munch on the chef's salads and quietly sip glasses of Efes Pilsen. Sidewalk booths are available for prime people-watching.

Imparator (☎ 352 3062; Ozler Caddesi 43; meals TL10) There's a lot to like about this busy restaurant covered in posters of Turkish folk heroes. The chunky Adana kebaps come with all manner of sides and the English-speaking manager knows everyone's name.

Öz Asmaaltı (☎ 351 4028; Pazarlar Caddesi 9; meals TL15) Near the Mercan, this local favourite is also the finest restaurant in Adana. It's a fairly spartan place, but the mains and mezes are delightful – the hummus is pure creamy goodness.

Entertainment

Cazara (☎ 459 3305; Ziyapaşa Bulvarı 27/B; 🕔 11am-3am Mon-Sat) The late-eighties metal craze didn't fade away; it just moved to the Middle East. Guitar bands jam every Saturday night; Whitesnake burnouts pound Efes.

A new salsa club called People was scheduled to open next door.

Getting There & Away

AIR

Turkish Airlines (☎ 457 0222; Prof Dr Nusret Fisek Caddesi 22) has daily nonstop flights between Adana and Ankara (one hour), İzmir (1½ hours) and İstanbul (1½ hours). **Onur Air** (☎ 456 0607; Atatürk Caddesi 11) flies between Adana and İstanbul.

BUS

Adana's large otogar offers direct buses or dolmuşes to anywhere. Some useful daily services are listed in the table (opposite). Dolmuşes to Kadirli (TL6, one hour, 75km) and Kozan (TL6, one hour, 72km) leave from the Yüreğı otogar, on the east bank of the Seyhan River.

CAR

Avis city (☎ 453 3045; Ziyapaşa Bulvarı); airport (☎ 453 0476)

Hertz (☎ 458 5062; Ziyapaşa Bulvarı 9)

TURNIP JUICE, ANYONE?

A once-tried, never-forgotten local drink made by boiling turnips and carrots and adding vinegar, is the crimson-coloured şalgam, sold at stalls around town. It's often drunk with a kebap meal or as an accompaniment to rakı (aniseed-flavoured grape brandy). The juice carries an especially strong tang and tastes as if it were freshly squeezed. You'll probably do a good bit of puckering and funny-face making while you drink your first glass – as with coffee, cigarettes and beer, şalgam is an acquired taste. However, you may find yourself hankering for more after the initial shock has worn off. Locals drink the juice to relieve an upset stomach, so you might give it a shot the next time you experience a particularly painful dose of Traveller's D.

SERVICES FROM ADANA'S OTOGAR

Destination	Fare (TL)	Duration (hr)	Distance (km)	Frequency (per day)
Adıyaman (for Nemrut Dağı)	35	6	370	7 buses
Alanya	35	10	440	8 buses (in summer)
Ankara	35	10	490	hourly
Antakya	18	3½	190	hourly
Antalya	45	10	555	2 or 3
Diyarbakır	25	10	550	several
Gaziantep	18	4	220	several
İstanbul	50	16	940	hourly
Kayseri	30	6½	335	several
Konya	35	6½	350	frequent
Şanlıurfa	25	6	365	several
Silifke	18	2	155	14 buses
Van	55	18	950	at least one

EASTERN MEDITERRANEAN

TRAIN
The facade of the Adana **train station** (☎ 453 3172), at the northern end of Ziyapaşa Bulvarı, is decorated with lovely tiles. The *Toros Ekspres* and the *İçanadolu Mavi* train both travel to İstanbul's Haydarpaşa Station (TL32, 19 hours) via Konya (TL14.50, seven hours). Departures are at 2.10pm daily and at 9.10pm on Tuesday, Thursday and Sunday. The *Toros Ekspres* departs for Gaziantep (TL9, 5½ hours) at 5.05am every Wednesday, Friday and Monday. There are many trains to Mersin via Taurus, and to İskenderun.

Getting Around
A taxi from the airport into town costs about TL10; it's about TL15 to the main otogar. Make sure the meter is switched on. A taxi from the city centre to the Yüreği otogar will cost TL8.

AROUND ADANA
Tucked around the southeast corner of the coast are the plentiful Bay of İskenderun (İskenderun Körfezi) and the province of Hatay. Inland from the bay are ruins (p433) of an ancient Hittite city at Karatepe, and of a later Roman one, Anazarbus (Anavarza; right). Along the road stand assorted medieval fortresses. The cotton-growing Çukurova plain south of Adana is the landscape used by Turkey's famous author Yaşar Kemal (p56) in his powerful novels about working-class and rural people.

Yılankale
Yılankale (Snake Castle) was built when this area was part of the Armenian kingdom of Cilicia. It's said to have taken its name from a serpent that was once entwined in the coat of arms above the main entrance. It's 35km east of Adana and 2.5km south of the highway – then a 10-minute climb over the rocks to the fort's highest point.

To continue on to Anazarbus (Anavarza) and Karatepe, head north and east just after the Yılankale turn-off. About 37km east of Adana an intersection is signed on the left (north) for Kozan and Kadirli, on the right (south) for Ceyhan. Take the Kozan–Kadirli road.

Anazarbus (Anavarza)
When the Romans moved into this area in 19 BC they built this fortress city on top of a hill dominating the fertile plain and called it Caesarea-ad-Anazarbus. Later, when Cilicia was divided in two, Tarsus remained the capital of the west and Anazarbus became capital of the east. In the 3rd century AD, Persian invaders destroyed the city. The Byzantine emperors rebuilt it, as they were to do over and over again when later earthquakes destroyed it.

The Arab raids of the 8th century gave Anazarbus new rulers and a new Arabic name, Ain Zarba. The Byzantines reconquered and held it for a brief period, but Anazarbus was an important city at a strategic nexus, and other armies came and snatched it away, including those of the Hamdanid princes of Aleppo, the Crusaders, a local Armenian king, the Byzantines again, the Turks and the Mamluks. The last owners didn't care about it much and it fell into decline in the 15th century. Today it's called Anavarza.

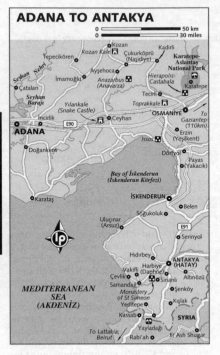

ADANA TO ANTAKYA

After 5km you reach a road junction and a large **gateway** set in the city walls. Through this gate was the ancient city, now given over to crops and pasture but strewn with ancient stones. Turn left through a village where every other gatepost reuses a Roman column and, after walking 650m, you'll reach the remains of an **aqueduct** with several arches that are still standing.

The village of Anavarza has a couple of simple tea houses and a shop with cold drinks, but that's it.

GETTING THERE & AWAY

From the D400 highway follow the Kozan/Kadirli road north to the village of Ayşehoca, where a road on the right is marked for Anavarza/Anazarbus, 5km to the east. If you're in a dolmuş or bus you can get out here and hitch a ride pretty easily in the morning. Heading on towards Kadirli, hitch back the 5km to Ayşehoca and take the 817 road north to Naşidiye/Çukurköprü, where the road divides. The left fork is marked for Kozan and Feke, the right for Kadirli.

Kozan

This transcendent little citrus and market town – within easy reach of Adana – was once the capital of the kingdom of Cilicia, and the lynchpin of a series of castles overlooking the Çukurova plain. Formerly Sis, the town features a stunning **fortress** built by Leo II (r 1187–1219) which stretches along a narrow ridge 300m above the town – it's a view nearing heaven.

Climbing up the road to the castle you pass a pair of towers and then the main gate itself. Inside is a mess of ruined buildings, but if you climb up a narrow ridge (not good if you don't like heights) you can see a many-towered keep on your right, and on your left a massive tower, which once held the royal apartments.

Between the first set of towers and the main gates are the ruins of a church, locally called the *manastir* (monastery). Up until 1921 this was the cathedral of the Catholics of Sis, one of the two senior patriarchs of the Armenian Church.

Kozan itself has some fine old houses and several cheap eateries and tea houses, and makes a good day trip. There are frequent buses between it and Adana (TL3.30, one hour).

OSMANIYE
☎ 0322

Osmaniye is a dusty hot highway town that makes a useful base for getting to Hierapolis-Castabala and Karatepe-Aslantaş National Park. It lies on the E90, linking Adana and Gaziantep.

Sleeping & Eating

Şahin Otel (☎ 812 4444; Dr Ahmet Alkan Caddesi 27; s/d TL40/60) Opposite the park on the main street, this is easily the best place to stay in town. The rooms are large and inviting with everything you would expect in a three-star hotel.

This is a town where people eat early. **Uğrak Lokantası** (☎ 813 4990; meals around TL5), a few doors down from the Şahin Otel, is a bustling joint serving up delicious *pilav* (rice) meals as well as hearty *şiş* (spit roast) for around TL2.

Getting There & Away

Without your own transport your best bet for seeing Hierapolis-Castabala and Karatepe in one day is to organise a taxi. There's a handy taxi rank beside the otogar; to go to Hierapolis

ARMENIAN CILICIA

During the early 11th century the Seljuk Turks swept westwards from Iran wresting control of much of Anatolia from a weakened Byzantium and pushing into the Armenian highlands. Thousands of Armenians fled south, taking refuge in the rugged Taurus Mountains and along the Mediterranean coast, where in 1080 they founded the kingdom of Cilicia (or Lesser Armenia) under the young Prince Reuben. The town of Sis (now Kozan; opposite) became their capital.

While Greater Armenia struggled against foreign invaders and the subsequent loss of their statehood, the Cilician Armenians lived in wealth and prosperity. Geographically, they were in the ideal place for trade and they quickly embraced Western European ideas, including its feudal class structure. Cilicia became a country of barons, knights and serfs, the court at Sis even adopting European clothes. Latin and French became the national languages. During the Crusades the Christian armies used the kingdom as a safe haven on their way to Jerusalem.

This period of Armenian history is regarded as the most exciting for science and culture, as schools and monasteries flourished, teaching theology, philosophy, medicine and mathematics. It was also the golden age of Armenian ecclesiastical manuscript painting, noted for its lavish decoration and Western influences.

The Cicilian kingdom thrived for nearly 300 years before if fell to the Mamluks of Egypt. The last Armenian ruler, Leo IV, spent his final years wandering Europe trying to raise support to recapture his kingdom, before dying in Paris in 1393.

for an hour, then to Karatepe for two hours, and either on to Kadirli or back to Osmaniye, should cost about TL60.

From the centre of Osmaniye, road 01-08 is signposted northwest for Hierapolis-Castabala and the Karatepe-Aslantaş Museum. Follow the road until you come to a sign on the right for Hierapolis-Castabala which is 6km along a bumpy road. About 10km beyond Hierapolis-Castabala a road on the left is marked for Karatepe (9km).

Heading south, there are dolmuşes from Osmaniye to İskenderun (TL3, one hour). There are also frequent connections west to Adana (1½ hours) and east to Gaziantep.

AROUND OSMANİYE
Karatepe-Aslantaş National Park

The **Karatepe-Aslantaş National Park** (Karatepe-Aslantaş Milli Parkı; admission per person/car TL3/6) incorporates the open-air **Karatepe-Aslantaş Museum**, a site which has been inhabited for almost 4000 years. The ruins date from the 13th century BC, when this was a summer retreat for the neo-Hittite kings of Kizzuwatna (Cilicia), the greatest of whom was named Azitawatas.

From its beautiful, forested hilltop site, the park overlooks **Lake Ceyhan** (Ceyhan Gölü), an artificial lake used for hydroelectric power and recreation.

There is a charge for entrance to the **Hittite ruins** (admission TL3; ☯ 8am-noon & 1-5pm) in addition to the park admission fee. Be warned that on top of the difficulty of getting to Karatepe without your own transport, the opening hours are rigorously adhered to, and the custodians will only take you around in a group, which can involve hanging about waiting for other people to arrive. Nor are you allowed to take any photographs.

The Hittite remains here are certainly significant, although you shouldn't come expecting something on the scale of Hattuşa (p465). The city was defended by 1km-long **walls**, traces of which are still evident. Its **southern entrance** is protected by four lions and two sphinxes, and lined with fine reliefs showing a coronation or feast complete with sacrificial bull, musicians and chariots.

Hierapolis-Castabala

Set in the midst of cotton fields about 19km south of Karatepe and 15km north of Osmaniye are the ruins of **Hierapolis-Castabala** (admission TL3; ☯ 8am-7pm). A *kale* tops a rocky outcrop above the plain about 1km east of the road. The ticket seller will lend you a leaflet in English and you can see everything in about an hour.

From the ticket-seller's shed, walk along a **colonnaded street** that once boasted 78 paired columns; some still bear their fine Corinthian capitals. You pass a badly ruined **temple** and **baths** on the right. Keeping the castle on your left, walk past the rock outcrop to the theatre, also badly ruined. Beyond it to the south in the fields is a ruined Byzantine **basilica**. Further along the same path is a *çeşme* (spring) and, in the ridge of rocks further on, some **rock-cut tombs**.

For information on getting to Hierapolis-Castabala, see p432.

İSKENDERUN

☎ 0326 / pop 300,000

İskenderun – a translation of Alexandretta – is a modern industrial town with a working port and a naval sense of order.

Strategically located, the town has more than once changed ruling hands. Alexander the Great took charge in 333 BC, and it was occupied by the British in 1918, turned over to the French in 1919 and incorporated into the French Protectorate of Syria as the Sanjak of Alexandretta. In 1938 Atatürk reclaimed it for the Turkish Republic – and so it sits today.

İskenderun is a handy stopover between Adana and Antakya on the soon-to-be-extended coastal highway, but it's got little of Hatay's energy. Still, there are several places to stay and eat near the attractive waterfront.

Orientation & Information

To find the sea you'll need to cross the highway and take a right turn headed south towards Şehit Pamir Caddesi. Once on this road, head north until you come to Atatürk Bulvarı. The main square at the top of Şehit Pamir Caddesi is marked by a huge monument on the waterfront. Most hotels are within a few blocks of this monument.

At the time of writing, the **tourist office** (☎ 614 1620; 49 Atatürk Bulvarı; � 8am-noon & 1.30-5pm Mon-Fri) was closed for renovations. In the meantime, try Hataylı Oteli (right) or Hasan Baba (right) for maps and good advice.

Sleeping

Hotel Altındişler (☎ 617 1011; www.altindisler.com; Şehir Pamir Caddesi 11; s/d TL40/50; ☒) In the wake of welcome renovations, the Altındişler got its groove back. The kitsch element is still strong – abstract Polish prints, plastic plants and wild splashings of paint – but the rooms are now spotless and shiny to ensure a good night's rest. The mood in the huge 2nd-floor lobby is unashamedly voyeuristic.

Hotel İmrenay (☎ 613 2117; fax 613 5984; Şehir Pamir Caddesi 5; s/d TL40/60; ☒) A pinch rugged and run-down, although the lobby is rather classy and

complete with a flat-screen TV. The owner and his father enjoy having a chat with guests.

Hataylı Oteli (☎ 614 1590; Osman Grazi Caddesi 2; s/d TL85/125; ☒) Three-star travellers unite! İskenderun has a new first-rate midrange hotel, ideally located near the water. The excellent lobby bar has a mild equine theme, and the rooms are huge and handsome. The terrace restaurant offers a glorious breakfast vista.

Grand Hotel Ontur (☎ 616 2400; Dr Muammer Aksoy Caddesi 8; s/d €76/97; ☒) İskenderun's poshest hotel has spacious if somewhat dully decorated rooms. Bathrooms are spotless, but considering the outdated state of the place, discounts are definitely in order.

Eating

The waterside area has some lovely tea gardens, plus a couple of long-standing fish restaurants and bars, especially popular on weekends.

Hasan Kolcuoğlu (☎ 614 7333; Ziya Gökalp Caddesi; meals TL7) By far the busiest restaurant in town, the double-storey 'HK' has been pumping out delicious, wholesome kebaps for decades. It's got an American diner feel but a truly Turkish clientele, and warm, casual service.

Hasan Baba (☎ 613 2725; Ulucami Caddesi 35; meals around TL10) This pide and *lahmacun* joint is sprawling and consistently packed with satisfied diners. Sit in the backyard and enjoy the fountain. City maps are generally available at the front counter.

Getting There & Away

There are frequent minibus and dolmuş connections to Adana (TL5, 2½ hours, 135km), Antakya (TL2, one hour, 58km) and Osmaniye (TL2.30, one hour, 63km). Regular dolmuşes scoot down the coast to Uluçınar (Arsuz; TL2, 30 minutes, 33km).

ANTAKYA (HATAY)

☎ 0326 / pop 681,700

Antakya (Hatay) is a prosperous and bustling near-Syrian-border city of modern convenience and ancient glory. Formerly Christianity's great Antioch, today it holds a mixture of Sunni, Alevi and Orthodox Christian faiths, 'the world's first cathedral' (the cave-church of St Peter), and a noticeably cultured air.

Antakya's wealth comes mostly from cotton farming and cross-border trade. Luxury car companies test the Turkish market here,

ANTAKYA (HATAY)

INFORMATION
Ferah Kırtasiye ve Kitabevi........1 C3
Oasis Internet Café.....................2 C3
Tourist Office..............................3 B1
Türk Telecom Phone & Internet..4 C2
Yapı Kredi ATM...........................5 C2

SIGHTS & ACTIVITIES
Antakya Archaeology Museum..6 B3
Bazaar..7 C3
Belediye (Town Hall)..................8 B3
Catholic Church..........................9 C4
Habibi Naccar Camii.................10 C3
Orthodox Church......................11 B4
Sermaye Cami...........................12 C3
Synagogue................................13 C4
Ulu Cami..................................14 C3

SLEEPING
Antik Beyazıt Otel.....................15 B4
Antik Grand Hotel....................16 B3
Büyük Antakya Oteli.................17 B2
Catholic Church Guesthouse....(see 9)
Divan Oteli...............................18 C3
Hotel Orontes...........................19 C2
Hotel Saray...............................20 C3
Mozaik Otel..............................21 C3
Narin Hotel...............................22 B3

EATING
Anadolu Restaurant..................23 B4
Antakya Evi...............................24 B4
Antik Han Restaurant................25 B4
Kral Künefe...............................26 C3
Sultan Sofrası...........................27 C3
Vitamin Shop Centre.................28 C3

DRINKING
Antioch Pub..............................29 B4
Sarmaşık Çay Bahçesi...............30 A4

ENTERTAINMENT
Konak Sinema...........................31 B3

TRANSPORT
İskenderun Dolmuş Stand........32 D2
Otogar......................................33 C2
Reyhanli Dolmuş Stand............34 D1
Samandağ Dolmuş Stand.........35 D1
Taxi Stand...........................(see 37)
Turkish Airlines Office..............36 B4
Yayladağı Dolmuş Stand..........37 D2

To İskenderun (58km); Adana (190km)
To Cave-Church of St Peter (St Pierre Kilisesi 1km); Syrian Frontier (60km)
To St Pierre Kilisesi (Cave-Church of St Peter, 1km); Syrian Frontier (60km)
To Samandağ (29km)
To Harbiye (9km); Syrian Frontier (60km)

Antakya Belediyesi Park

Vali Ürgen Alanı
Asi (Orontes) River
Ata Köprüsü

EASTERN MEDITERRANEAN

so expect to see some hot rides. The Asi Mountains form a fine backdrop and even siphon in cool evening breezes.

The Arab influence permeates local life, food and language, and indeed the city was only officially deemed part of Turkey in 1939. Most visitors to Antakya rush straight for the museum, and rightly so – the mosaics are unforgettable. And despite regular earthquakes – most shatteringly in AD 526 – the old city is still charming for a wander.

History

Antakya is the ancient Antioch-ad-Orontes, which was founded by Seleucus I Nicator in 300 BC and soon became a city of half a million people. Under the Romans an important Christian community developed out of the already large Jewish one. At one time this was headed by St Paul.

Persians, Byzantines, Arabs, Armenians and Seljuks all fought over Antioch, as did the Crusaders and Saracens. In 1268 the Mamluks of Egypt sacked the city. The Ottomans held onto it until Mohammed Ali of Egypt captured it in 1831, but with European help they eventually drove their rebellious vassal back.

Antakya was part of the French protectorate of Syria until 1938, after which it enjoyed a brief existence as the independent Republic of Hatay. But when Atatürk saw WWII approaching, he wanted the city rejoined to the republic as a defensive measure. Parliament voted for union with Turkey, and on 23 July

1939 Hatay became Turkish. The Syrian government never accepted this and some Syrian maps still show it as part of Syria.

The city is still the titular seat of five Christian patriarchs – three Catholic (Syrian Catholic, Maronite and Greco-Melchite), one Greek Orthodox and one Syrian-Tacobite – although none are based here any longer.

Orientation

The Asi (Orontes) River divides the town. The modern district is on the west bank, with the PTT, government buildings and museum circling the Cumhuriyet Alanı roundabout.

The older Ottoman town on the east bank is the commercial centre, with most of the hotels, restaurants and services, especially along Hürriyet Caddesi. The otogar is a few blocks northeast of the centre. Continue northeast along İstiklal Caddesi for dolmuşes to Samandağ.

Information

The **tourist office** (☎ 216 6098; ⏱ 8am-noon & 1-5pm) is on a roundabout on Atatürk Caddesi, a good 10-minute walk from town.

There are several ATMs close to the otogar as well as on the west bank of the Asi River next to the Büyük Antakya Oteli. The **Ferah Kırtasiye ve Kitabevi** (Hürriyet Caddesi 17/D) stocks English-language newspapers and current affairs magazines.

The ultra-stylish **Oasis Internet Café** (☎ 216 5697; off Hürriyet Caddesi) is behind Ferah Kırtasiye ve Kitabevi.

Sights

ANTAKYA ARCHAEOLOGY MUSEUM

At the Antakya **museum** (Antakya Arkeoloji Muzesi; ☎ 214 6168; Gündüz Caddesi; admission TL8; ⏱ 8.30am-noon & 1.30-5pm Tue-Sun), you'll see as fine a collection of Roman/Byzantine mosaics as graces any museum in the world, covering a period from the 1st century AD to the 5th century. While some are inevitably fragmentary, others were recovered almost intact. Most labels are in English and Turkish.

Salons I to IV are tall, naturally lit rooms, perfect for displaying mosaics so fine that at first glance you may mistake some of them for paintings. Be sure to see the **Oceanus and Thetis mosaic** (2nd century) and the **Buffet Mosaic** (3rd century). As well as the standard scenes of hunting and fishing there are stories from mythology. Other mosaics have quirkier subjects: don't miss the happy hunchback, the black fisherman or the mysterious portrayal of a raven, a scorpion and a pitchfork attacking the 'evil eye'. Many of the mosaics came from Roman seaside villas or from the suburban resort of Daphne (Harbiye), although some are from Tarsus.

BAZAAR DISTRICT

A sprawling **bazaar** fills the back streets between the otogar, Kemal Paşa Caddesi and Kurtulus Caddesi. Around Habibi Naccar Camii you'll find most of Antakya's remaining **old houses**, with carved stone lintels or wooden overhangs. It's one of the most interesting old neighbourhoods in Turkey to wander around; you might catch a glimpse of the courtyards within the compounds. The Italian priests at the Catholic Church believe St Peter would have lived in this area between 42 and 48 AD, as it was then the Jewish neighbourhood.

CAVE-CHURCH OF ST PETER

Recently reopened and rejuvenated, this beloved Christian **cave-church** (St Pierre Kilisesi; admission TL8; ⏱ 8.30am-noon & 1.30-4.30pm Tue-Sun) is cut into the slopes of Mt Staurin (Mountain of the Cross). It's said to be the earliest place where Christians met and prayed secretly. Tradition has it that this cave was the property of St Luke the Evangelist, who was from Antioch, and that he donated it to the burgeoning Christian congregation as a place of worship. Peter and Paul lived in Antioch for a few years and are thought to have preached here. When the Crusaders marched through in 1098, they constructed the wall at the front and a narthex.

To the right of the altar faint traces of fresco can still be seen, and some of the simple mosaic floor survives. The water dripping in the corner is said to cure sickness.

Three kilometres northeast of town, you can easily walk to the church in about half an hour, heading along Kurtuluş Caddesi.

RELIGIOUS BUILDINGS

Most of Antakya's 1200-odd Christians worship at the fine **Orthodox Church** (Hürriyet Caddesi; ⏱ prayers 8.15am & 6pm). Rebuilt in the 19th century with Russian assistance, the church contains some beautiful icons.

The **Catholic Church** (Kurtuluş Caddesi, Kutlu Sokak 6; ⏱ mass 8.30am daily & 6pm Sun) occupies two houses in the city's old quarter, with the chapel in the former living room of one house. Next door is the **Sermaye Cami**, with a wonderfully ornate minaret (you'll see it on posters of Antakya), and nearby at Kurtuluş 56 is a **synagogue**.

Sleeping

BUDGET

Divan Oteli (☎ 215 1518; İstiklal Caddesi 62; s/d TL20/40; ✷) Certainly the best of Antakya's budget options, some rooms here have balconies and small desks. There's also a quite comfortable lobby.

Hotel Saray (☎ 214 9001; fax 214 9002; Hürriyet Caddesi; s/d TL25/40; ✷) Definitely a little rugged and musty, although the rooms (with TV included) are certainly large enough and some have decent mountain views.

The Catholic Church's **guesthouse** (domenico bertoglio@hotmail.com; Kurtuluş Caddesi; Kutlu Sokak 6; per person TL20) has eight neat rooms around a suitably pensive courtyard. Tour groups often fill it up and guests are expected to attend daily mass.

MIDRANGE

Hotel Orontes (☎ 214 5931; fax 214 5933; www.orontes hotel.com; İstiklal Caddesi 58; s/d TL50/80; ✷) This two-star hotel near the otogar is somewhat plainly decorated, although rooms are quite large and satellite TV is included.

Mozaik Otel (☎ 215 5020; www.mosaikotel.com; İstiklal Caddesi 18; s/d TL50/80) This is an excellent mid-range choice near the Orontes. Rooms are decorated with multicoloured bedspreads and pretty mosaics, and some bathrooms are aqua blue. The restaurant is excellent.

Antik Grand Hotel (☎ 215 7575; www.antikgrand.com; Hürriyet Caddesi 18; s/d TL60/90; ✷) This well-placed hotel offers large, tasteful rooms in a beautiful faux-antique style. All rooms have TV and minibar. Long-stay discounts are available. The excellent Antik Grand Restaurant next door has a five-course set menu special for TL12.

Antik Beyazıt Otel (☎ 216 2900; beyazit@antikbeyazit oteli.com; Hükümet Caddesi 4; s/d TL85/110; ✷) One of the finest colonial dwellings in Hatay, this charming French period structure is filled with antique furniture and details. Expect Turkish carpets on the floors, European paintings and prints in the rooms, and an elegant lobby complete with drapery and an ornate chandelier. It's an excellent choice.

Narin Hotel (☎ 216 7500; www.narinhotel.com; Atatürk Caddesi 11; s/d TL80/120) Red-and-gold ornate

design – and a keen eye for detail – are the hallmarks of this refreshing business-minded hotel. The beds are soft and luxurious, and the bathrooms are decked in sleek white-and-grey tile. The restaurant upstairs looks the part, but the advertised menu is misleading.

Büyük Antakya Oteli (☎ 213 5858; fax 213 5869; www .buyukantakyaoteli.com; Atatürk Caddesi 8; s/d TL90/130; ✷) Stepping into the lobby of the 'Big Antakya' is like entering a department store. This aptly named four-star giant, with on-site hairdresser and travel agent, offers huge rooms, though prices are cheeky. Morning breakfast spreads are lavish, and some rooms have decent city and river views. It also has a deluxe sister 'spa' hotel on the road to the airport.

Eating & Drinking

Syrian influences permeate Antakya's cuisine. Handfuls of mint and wedges of lemon accompany many kebaps. Hummus, rare elsewhere in Turkey, is readily available here. Many main courses and salads are dusted with fiery pepper; if this isn't to your taste, ask for yours *acısız* (without hot pepper).

For dessert, try the local speciality, *künefe*, a cake of fine shredded wheat laid over a dollop of fresh, mild cheese, on a layer of sugar syrup, topped with chopped walnuts and baked. **Kral Künefe** near the Ulu Cami makes a mean one.

Another good place to hang out is the riverside Antakya Belediyesi Park, a few blocks southwest of the museum. Here you'll find tea gardens, such as the **Sarmaşık Çay Bahçesi**, as well as shady promenades.

Sultan Sofrası (☎ 213 8759; İstiklal Caddesi 20; meals around TL12) Antakya's premier cheap eatery, this place is spotless and turns over the food at a rapid pace. The articulate manager loves to guide diners through the menu. Try the *İskender* döner or the vegetable soup. The *sütlaç* (rice pudding) is also quite good. It's next door to the Mosaik Otel.

Antik Han Restaurant (☎ 215 8538; Hürriyet Caddesi 17/1; meals TL12) The Han has been doing its thing for some time now and it's still one of the city's most enjoyable eateries. The breezy outdoor terrace is tucked up a narrow staircase, past the spinning chicken. The limited menu is satisfying enough – round it off with the wonderful *künefe*.

Anadolu Restaurant (☎ 215 3335; Hürriyet Caddesi 30; meals TL15) Antakya's newest culinary hotspot serves up a long list of fine meat dishes (Anadolu kebap TL12 on white tablecloths in

EASTERN MEDITERRANEAN

a splendid alfresco garden. The local glitterati (and a few humble loners) sip beer by the fountain and scoff first-class meze (TL5), including silken *acili ezme* (hot pepper paste with walnuts) and hummus. It's near Antik Beyazit.

Antakya Evi (☎ 214 1350; Silahlı Kuvvetler Caddesi 3; meals TL12-15) With a name like Antakya Evi (*evi* means home), it's little wonder that dining here feels much like eating at a friend's place. It's tastefully decorated with photos and antique furniture, and serves toothsome kebaps and standard grills.

Vitamin Shop Center (☎ 216 3858; Hürriyet Caddesi 7) The juice bar to the stars judging by the photo gallery, this is the place for your Atom shake (TL5), a regional speciality of banana, pistachio, honey, apricot, sultanas and milk.

Antioch Pub (Hurriyet Caddesi 25; beer TL3.50) Antakya's only strictly drinking hole is a friendly, though mostly male domain, where patrons lean on wooden barrels and strike Irish poses.

Entertainment

Konak Sinema (Karaoğlanoğlu Caddesi; admission TL5) English-language blockbusters subtitled in Turkish are screened here.

Getting There & Around

Antakya is a small enough place to negotiate on foot.

BUS
To & From Syria

Everyone needs a visa to enter Syria (see the boxed text p681).

The Jet bus company at Antakya otogar has direct buses to Aleppo (TL6, four hours, 105km) at 9am and noon daily, and to Damascus (TL11, eight hours) at noon daily. These buses follow the route that all cross-border buses and trucks take, the Reyhanlı-Bab al-Hawa border, so you'll need to brace yourself for waits of two to four hours. To avoid hanging about at the border, ensure you are passing through before 8am or take a shared or private taxi, which can negotiate a path through the stationary buses and trucks. A taxi from Antakya (Turkey) to Aleppo (Syria) costs around TL60.

If you want to tackle the border in stages, local buses to Reyhanlı (TL2, 45 minutes) leave from in front of the petrol station on the corner of Yavuz Sultan Selim and İstiklal Caddesis. From Reyhanlı you can catch a dolmuş to the Turkish border. Then you

have to walk a couple of kilometres to the Syrian border.

Alternatively, catch a dolmuş south to Yayladağı (from behind the taxi rank across the road from the entrance to the otogar), from where you pick up a taxi or hitch a few kilometres further to the border. Once across (and crossing takes all of 15 minutes here), you're just 2km from the Syrian mountain village of Kassab, from where regular microbuses make the 45-minute run to Lattakia (S£25).

Within Turkey

The otogar has direct buses to most western and northern points (Ankara, Antalya, İstanbul, İzmir, Kayseri and Konya), usually travelling via Adana (TL10, 3½ hours) and through the Cilician Gates (p429). There are frequent services to Gaziantep (TL18, four hours) and Şanlıurfa (TL24, seven hours, 345km), either direct or via Gaziantep. Minibuses and dolmuşes for İskenderun (TL3, one hour) leave from a stand just north of the otogar.

AROUND ANTAKYA
Harbiye (Daphne)

The hill suburb of Harbiye, 9km to the south of Antakya, is the ancient Daphne where, according to classical mythology, the virgin Daphne prayed to be rescued from the attentions of the god Apollo and was turned into a laurel tree. There are no laurels to be seen nowadays, although pine trees ring a large pool of water, very popular as a picnic place. The best approach is to get off the dolmuş opposite Hotel Çağlayan and walk down into the wooded valley on the left, which is usually full of Antakyalı holiday-makers drinking beer beneath rivulets of cooling water.

GETTING THERE & AWAY

From Antakya, frequent dolmuşes and city buses run along Kurtuluş Caddesi to Harbiye (TL1, 15 minutes), where they stop (briefly) to pick up passengers.

Monastery of St Simeon

The remains of this 6th-century monastery sit on a mountain 7km from the village of Karaçay, about 18km from Antakya, on the way to Samandağ. There was no ticket office when we visited.

The cross-shaped monastery contains the ruins of three churches. The remains of mosaics can be seen in the first, but the central church is the most beautiful, with rich carvings. The third church is more austere and was probably once used by the monks. The monastery and pillar were carved out of the mountain with an octagonal area around the pillar (the base of it remains) where pilgrims could listen to St Simeon preaching against the iniquities of Antioch. There are also the remains of a stepped structure next to the pillar, which pilgrims might have been able to climb to address the saint personally.

GETTING THERE & AWAY

The turn-off to the monastery is just past the village of Karaçay, reachable by a Samandağ dolmuş (TL1, 20 minutes) from Antakya. The dolmuş stand is on İstiklal Caddesi at the junction with Yavuz Sultan Selim Caddesi.

You can take a taxi from the monastery for about €17 return, plus an hour at the site, or you could walk. A sign points up a road just past Karaçay. After 4km the road branches. The monastery lies about 2.5km down the track leading to the right.

Vakıflı

The last ethnic Armenian village in Turkey is beautifully set among orange orchards on the slopes of Mt Musa. There's little to hold the visitor, other than the local church (if it's open). Thirty-five households remain from the resettlement of five neighbouring Armenian villages in Lebanon in 1939 when Hatay returned to the Turks. Economics, it seems, is stronger than geo-politics, and Vakıflı survived thanks to its prosperous farming. Many Turkish Armenians from İstanbul visit in summer.

It's 35km west of Antakya.

GETTING THERE & AWAY

Dolmuşes from Antakya to Samandağ (TL1, 35 minutes, 29km) leave from an unmarked stand on Yavuz Sultan Selim Caddesi, near the corner with İstiklal Caddesi. From Samandağ

a few dolmuşes journey to Vakıflı every day, but you might have better luck hitching.

Çevlik

Çevlik feels like a run-down city at the end of the sea, and is oddly bewitching for it. Locals meander about for afternoon picnics and overnight booze-ups. The coastal highway from İskenderun is due to be completed in 2009 and with it should follow a welcome revamp. The scant ruins of **Seleuceia-in-Pieria** are hardly impressive, but this was the port of Antioch in ancient times.

Nearby, however, is the mighty **Titus & Vespasian Tunnel** (Titüs ve Vespasiyanüs Tüneli; admission TL3), an astonishing feat of Roman engineering. During its heyday, Seleucia lived under the constant threat of inundation from a stream that descended from the mountains and flowed through the town. To counter this threat, the Roman emperors Titus and Vespasian ordered their engineers to dig a diversion channel leading the water around the town.

There are two ways to see the tunnel; naturally the harder way is more fun. The easy way is to ascend the steps form the car park. A guide is optional, but good footwear is essential.

The alternative is to follow the channel until you come to a metal arch on the right. Then take the path behind the arch (right fork) which follows an irrigation canal past some rock-cut shelters, finally arriving at a humpback Roman bridge across the gorge. Here, steps lead down to the tunnel. Bring a torch (flashlight) since the path is still pretty treacherous. At the far end of the channel an inscription provides a date for the work.

The slopes above the Roman bridge provide a perfect picnic spot.

GETTING THERE & AWAY

Dolmuşes run between Samandağ and Çevlik (TL1) every 30 minutes or so during daylight hours.

Central Anatolia

Visitors to central Turkey's hazy plains occasionally suffer an affliction known as 'Hittite hip hopping' or 'Roman rhyming'. The patient, overwhelmed by ancient sites such as the Hittite capital Hattuşa, begins composing endless ditties to simplify the region's complex legacy of battling regimes.

The prognosis is grim. Luckily, the sense of history here is so pervasive that the average kebap chef can remind you that the Romans preceded the Seljuks. This is, after all, the region where the whirling dervishes first swirled, Atatürk began his revolution, Alexander the Great cut the Gordion knot and King Midas turned everything he touched to gold. Julius Caesar uttered his famous line, *'Veni, vidi, vici'* ('I came, I saw, I conquered'), near Tokat; the sentiment is shared by diners who devour a hefty Tokat kebap.

In Safranbolu and Amasya, drinking in the history involves nothing more than sipping a çay (tea) and gazing at the half-timbered Ottoman houses. These are two of Turkey's most beautiful towns, offering Ottoman digs with cupboard-bathrooms. Other spots are so seldom visited that foreigners may find themselves entered as just *turist* (tourist) in hotel guest books. This offers the opportunity to get to grips with everyday Anatolian life in a coach party–free environment – where the Hittites, the Phrygians, the Pontics, the Romans, the Seljuks, a mysterious neolithic society and Atatürk established major capitals.

If you can't stop rhyming about how the Hattis came before the Hittites as you examine Phrygian tumuli (burial mounds), Pontic tombs and Seljuk caravanserais, there may be an antidote. The incredible 'doctor fish' at Balıklı Kaplıca cure many ills…

HIGHLIGHTS

- Say hello to the Hittite storm god at Ankara's **Museum of Anatolian Civilisations** (p444), then beam back to the 21st century in **Kızılay** (p450)
- Feel like an intrepid archaeologist discovering a lost civilisation in atmospheric **Hattuşa** (p465)
- Stay in an Ottoman mansion among rocky bluffs in **Safranbolu** (p455) and **Amasya** (p469)
- Step beneath the turquoise dome of Konya's **Mevlâna Museum** (p485) to learn about the whirling dervishes' inspiration
- Head east to the exfoliating fish at **Balıklı Kaplıca** (p482) and the divine doors in **Divriği** (p482)

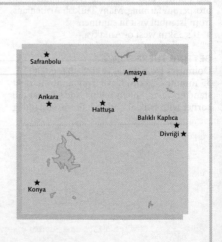

★ Safranbolu

★ Amasya

★ Ankara

★ Hattuşa

★ Balıklı Kaplıca

★ Divriği

★ Konya

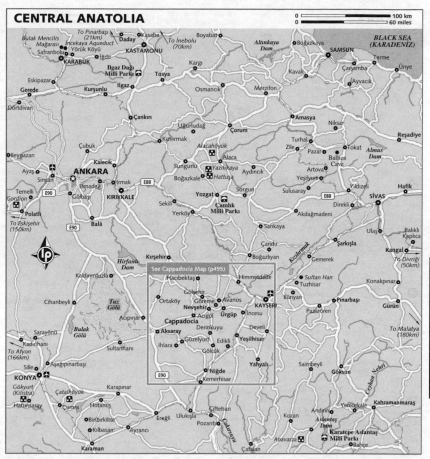

ANKARA

☎ 0312 / pop 4.5 million

İstanbullus may quip that the best view in Ankara is the train home, but the Turkish capital has more substance than its reputation as a staid administrative centre suggests. Catching the clean, efficient subway from the monolithic AŞTİ otogar (bus station) is the perfect introduction to a city that offers a mellower, more manageable vignette of urban Turkey than İstanbul. The capital established by Atatürk boasts two of the country's most important sights: the Anıt Kabir, the big man's mausoleum, and the Museum of Anatolian Civilisations, which will help you solve clues at ancient sites on the surrounding plains.

Having expanded from being an Anatolian nonentity to Turkey's second most-populous city in the 85 years since independence, Ankara can be a disjointed place. You don't have to walk far before you come to a few lanes of yellow taxis. However, a few areas have some charm: the historic streets in the citadel and, near the chic Kavaklıdere neighbourhood, vibrant Kızılay. One of Turkey's hippest urban quarters, Kızılay is enlivened by the student community, found strolling its boulevards and crowding its nightspots. Wandering the area, among crazy haircuts, revealing dresses and other fashion statements, looking at stalls selling everything from replica Ottoman daggers to flashing toy robots, is an excellent way to spend a warm Anatolian evening.

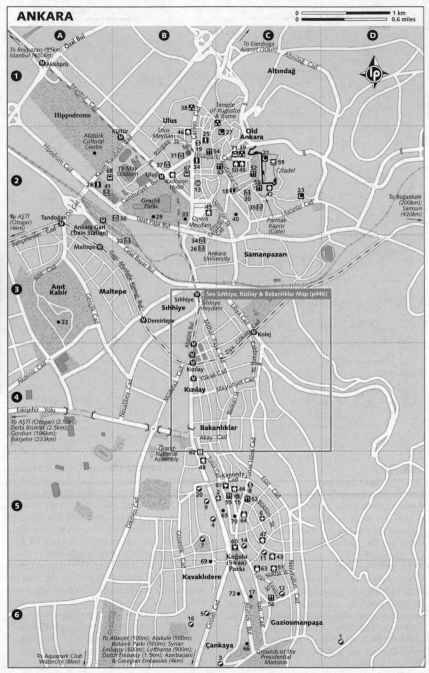

History

Although Hittite remains dating back to before 1200 BC have been found in Ankara, the town really prospered as a Phrygian settlement on the north–south and east–west trade routes. Later it was taken by Alexander the Great, claimed by the Seleucids and finally occupied by the Galatians around 250 BC. Augustus Caesar annexed it to Rome as Ankyra.

The Byzantines held the town for centuries, with intermittent raids by the Persians and Arabs. When the Seljuk Turks came to Anatolia, they grabbed the city but held it with difficulty. Later, the Ottoman sultan Yıldırım Beyazıt was captured by Tamerlane near here, and subsequently died in captivity. Spurned as a jinxed endeavour, the city slowly slumped into a backwater, prized for nothing but its goats.

That all changed when Atatürk chose Angora, as the city was known until 1930, to be his base in the struggle for independence. When he set up his provisional government here in 1920, the city was just a small, dusty settlement of some 30,000 people. After his victory in the War of Independence, Atatürk declared it the new Turkish capital (October 1923), and set about developing it. European urban planners were consulted, resulting in long, wide boulevards, a forested park with an artificial lake, and numerous residential and diplomatic neighbourhoods. The city's position in the centre of Turkey made it more suitable than İstanbul as a capital for the new republic. From 1919 to 1927, Atatürk never set foot in İstanbul, preferring to work at making Ankara top dog.

Orientation

The main street is Atatürk Bulvarı, which runs 5.5km south from the old part of town, Ulus, through Kızılay and Kavaklıdere, to Çankaya.

Ulus centres on the large equestrian statue of Atatürk in Ulus Meydanı. Some of the area's museums and sights are nearby, although the most interesting attractions, the Museum of Anatolian Civilisations and the citadel, are at the top of Hisarparkı Caddesi. Likewise, there are many budget and midrange hotels and restaurants around Ulus Meydanı, but the best options are mostly on the citadel hill.

The train station, near the terminus for the Havaş airport buses, is just over 1km southwest of Ulus Meydanı along Cumhuriyet Bulvarı.

Kızılay, the area around the intersection of Atatürk Bulvarı and Gazi Mustafa Kemal Bulvarı/Ziya Gökalp Caddesi, is the centre of buzzy 'new' Ankara, with midrange and top-end hotels, eateries and hang-outs of all descriptions.

Kavaklıdere, 2km south along Atatürk Bulvarı, is a fashionable district with embassies, airline and car-rental offices, trendy bars, smart shops, and the Hilton and Sheraton hotels.

In the hills south of Kavaklıdere is Çankaya, the residential neighbourhood that hosts the presidential mansion and many of the ambassadorial residences. Its most prominent landmark is the Atakule, a tower with a revolving restaurant, visible throughout the city.

The AŞTİ, Ankara's otogar, is 5.5km southwest of Ulus and 4.5km west of Kızılay.

Information

BOOKSHOPS

Dost Kitabevi (Map p446; ☎ 418 8327; Konur Sokak 4, Kızılay) In a good area for bookshops; stocks some foreign-language novels and local-interest titles.

Turhan Kitabevi (Map p446; ☎ 418 8259; Yüksel Caddesi 8/32, Kızılay) Stocks coffee-table books, guidebooks, English novels, Turkish dictionaries and phrasebooks, and periodicals.

INTERNET ACCESS

There are many internet cafés in Ulus and Kızılay, particularly around Ulus Meydanı and Karanfil Sokak, but they are scarcer in Kavaklıdere. Wi-fi access is widely available in hotels, cafés and bars.

İntek Internet Club (Map p446; Karanfil Sokak 47a, Kızılay; per hr €1.75; ☻ 7am-midnight) Expensive but reliable.

Redline (Map p442; off Tunalı Hilmi Caddesi, Kavaklıdere; per hr TL1.50; ☻ 10am-11pm) Near Kebap 49; has a variable connection.

MEDICAL SERVICES

Pharmacists take it in turns to open around the clock; look out for the *nobetçi* (24 hour) sign.

Bayındır Hospital (Map p442; ☎ 428 0808; Atatürk Bulvarı 201, Kavaklıdere) An up-to-date private hospital.

City Hospital (Map p442; ☎ 466 3838; Büklüm Sokak 72, Kavaklıdere) Near Tunalı Hilmi Caddesi, with a Women's Health Centre (Kadın Sağlığı Merkezi).

Hospital Information Hotline (☎ 444 0911)

MONEY

There are lots of banks with ATMs in Ulus, Kızılay and Kavaklıdere. To change money, *döviz bürosu* (currency-exchange offices) generally offer the best rates, often without commission.

Genel Döviz (Map p442; ☎ 468 1332; Tunalı Hilmi Caddesi 65, Kavaklıdere; ☻ 9am-6pm Mon-Sat)

POST & TELEPHONE

There are PTT branches in the train station, at the AŞTİ otogar and on Atatürk Bulvarı in Ulus. All have public phone booths nearby.

TOURIST INFORMATION

The Guide, available at the Rahmi M Koç Industrial Museum and Turhan Kitabevi bookshop, has listings for Ankara.

Tourist office (Map p442; ☎ 310 8789/231 5572; Anafartalar Caddesi 67, Ulus; ☻ 9am-5pm Mon-Fri, 10am-5pm Sat) Reasonably helpful and has lots of brochures available. Plans to move to a new office at the train station.

TRAVEL AGENCIES

Raytur (Map p446; ☎ 417 0021; www.raytur.com.tr; Karanfil Sokak 12/12, Kızılay) Operated by Turkish Railways. Sells train and air tickets, jeep safaris, domestic and outbound tours.

Saltur (Map p442; ☎ 425 1333; www.saltur.com.tr; Atatürk Bulvarı 175/4, Kavaklıdere) Airline and international tour agent.

Sights & Activities

MUSEUM OF ANATOLIAN CIVILISATIONS

The superb **Museum of Anatolian Civilisations** (Anadolu Medeniyetleri Müzesi; Map p442; ☎ 324 3160; Gözcü Sokak 2; admission TL15; ☻ 8.30am-5pm) is the perfect introduction to the complex weave of Turkey's chequered ancient past, housing artefacts cherry-picked from just about every significant archaeological site in Anatolia.

The museum is housed in a beautifully restored 15th-century *bedesten* (market vault). The 10-domed central marketplace houses reliefs and statues, while the surrounding hall displays exhibits from the earlier Anatolian civilisations: Palaeolithic, neolithic, chalcolithic, Bronze Age, Assyrian, Hittite, Phrygian, Urartian and Lydian. The downstairs sections hold classical Greek and Roman artefacts and a display on Ankara's history.

Get there early to avoid the flood of tour groups and school parties. If it's not too hot, you can climb the hill from Ulus to the museum (1km); from Ulus head east up

Hisarparkı Caddesi and follow the road along the hillside, then turn left. A taxi from Ulus should cost about TL3.

Touring the Museum

The exhibits are chronologically arranged in a spiral: start at the Palaeolithic displays to the right of the entrance, then continue in an anticlockwise direction, visiting the central room last.

Most of the Palaeolithic finds were found in the Karain Cave (p402), near Antalya, and suggest a nomadic hunter-gatherer lifestyle and the development of stone and, later, bone tools. Also here are finds from the neolithic era, when people started settling in villages, cultivating crops, raising livestock, and producing storage and cooking vessels. Çatalhöyük (p491), southeast of Konya, is one of the most important neolithic sites in the world. Here you can see a mock-up of the inside of a dwelling typical of those uncovered at the site; the clay bull-head icons were a feature of the cult of the time.

In the chalcolithic age copper and tin were used in addition to stone, leading to refinement of pottery and statues, as well as in painted decoration. The proficiency of metalwork took another leap forward with the introduction of bronze in the early Bronze Age. Many exhibits in this section of the museum come from the important archaeological site at Hacılar, southwest of Burdur, and many of the Bronze Age artefacts are from the ancient site of Alacahöyük (p468), east of Ankara. The gold jewellery, bronze standards and idols such as the mother goddess figurines would have been used for cult worship and were often buried with the dead.

Also on show are many finds from the Assyrian trading colony Kültepe, one of the world's oldest and wealthiest bazaars. These include baked-clay tablets found at the site, which dates to the beginning of the second millennium before Christ.

One of the striking Hittite figures of bulls and stags in the next room used to be the emblem of Ankara. The Hittites were known for their relief work, and some mighty slabs representing the best pieces found in the country, generally from around Hattuşa (p465), are on display in the museum's central room.

Most of the finds from the Phrygian capital Gordion (p454), including incredible inlaid wooden furniture, are on display in the museum's last rooms. The exhibits also include limestone blocks with a still-undecipherable inscription, in text resembling the Greek alphabet, and lion- and ram-head ritual vessels, which show the high quality of Phrygian metalwork.

The best artefacts left by the Urartians, the Phrygians' east Anatolian contemporaries, are on display in the Van and Elazığ museums, but Ankara has a good collection of works from this lesser-known civilisation. Spurred by rich metal deposits, the Urartians were Anatolia's foremost metalworkers, as the knives, horse-bit, votive plates and shields demonstrate. There are also terracotta figures of gods in human form, some revealing their divine powers by growing scorpion tails, and neo-Hittite artefacts.

Downstairs, the classical-period finds and regional history displays give the local picture. Excavations have unearthed a Roman road near the Column of Julian, and Ankara has its own 'missing link', the 9.8-million-year-old *Ankarapithecus*.

CITADEL

When you're done with the museum, make the most of its location by wandering to the imposing **hisar** (citadel or Ankara Kalesi; Map p442) just up the hill. The most interesting part of Ankara to poke about in, this well-preserved quarter of thick walls and intriguing winding streets took its present shape in the 9th century AD, when the Byzantine emperor Michael II constructed the outer ramparts. The inner walls, which the local authority is slowly rebuilding, date from the 7th century.

To find it, head around the back of the museum up Gözcü Sokak, past the octagonal tower, to the **Parmak Kapısı** (Finger Gate), also called the Saatli Kapı (Clock Gate).

Opposite the gate, in the beautifully restored Çengelhan, the **Rahmi M Koç Industrial Museum** (Rahmi M Koç Müzesi; ☎ 309 6800; Depo Sokak 1; www.rmk-museum.org.tr; adult/child €1.70/0.70; ☑ 10am-5pm Tue-Fri, 10am-7pm Sat & Sun) has three floors of rooms covering subjects as diverse as transport, science, music, computing, Atatürk and carpets, some with interactive features.

Walking straight ahead once you've entered Parmak Kapısı, through a gate on your left and past And Evi café, you'll see **Alaettin Camii** on the left. The citadel mosque dates from the 12th century but has been extensively rebuilt. To your right a steep road leads to a flight of stairs taking you up to the **Şark Kulesi**

CENTRAL ANATOLIA

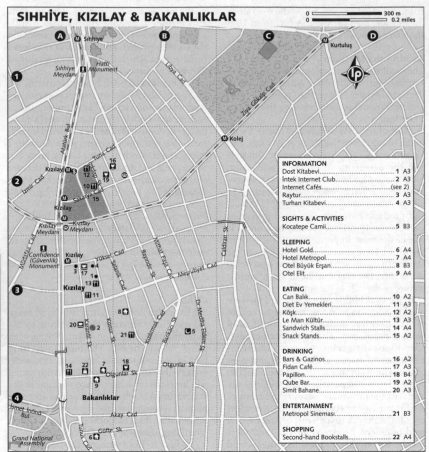

SIHHİYE, KIZILAY & BAKANLIKLAR

INFORMATION	
Dost Kitabevi	1 A3
İntek Internet Club	2 A3
Internet Cafés	(see 2)
Raytur	3 A3
Turhan Kitabevi	4 A3

SIGHTS & ACTIVITIES	
Kocatepe Camii	5 B3

SLEEPING	
Hotel Gold	6 A4
Hotel Metropol	7 A4
Otel Büyük Erşan	8 B3
Otel Elit	9 A4

EATING	
Can Balık	10 A2
Diet Ev Yemekleri	11 A3
Köşk	12 A3
Le Man Kültür	13 A3
Sandwich Stalls	14 A4
Snack Stands	15 A2

DRINKING	
Bars & Gazinos	16 A2
Fidan Café	17 A3
Papillon	18 B4
Qube Bar	19 A2
Simit Bahane	20 A3

ENTERTAINMENT	
Metropol Sineması	21 B3

SHOPPING	
Second-hand Bookstalls	22 A4

(Eastern Tower), with panoramic city views. Although it's much harder to find, a tower to the north, **Ak Kale** (White Fort), also offers fine views. If you're coming up to the citadel along Hisarparkı Caddesi, look left about halfway up to see the remains of a **Roman theatre** from around 200 to 100 BC.

Inside the citadel local people still live as in a traditional Turkish village, and you'll see women beating and sorting skeins of wool. Broken column drums, bits of marble statuary and inscribed lintels are incorporated into the walls.

ANIT KABİR

The monumental mausoleum of Mustafa Kemal Atatürk (1881–1938), the founder of modern Turkey, is worth a visit to see how much sway he still holds over the Turkish people. Located high above the city, with an abundance of marble and an air of veneration, the **Anıt Kabir** (Monumental Tomb; Map p442; admission free; [9am-5pm mid-May–Oct, to 4pm Nov-Jan, to 4.30pm Feb–mid-May) is one of Ankara's more relaxing areas.

As you approach the tomb, the **Hürriyet Kulesi** (Tower of Liberty) has interpretive panels and photos covering Atatürk's funeral, the construction of the tomb and the iconography of the site. Facing it, the **İstiklal Kulesi** (Tower of Independence) gives more detail, with models recreating scenes.

Continue along the **Lion Road**, a 262m walkway lined with 24 lion statues; Hittite symbols of power used to represent the strength of the Turkish nation. The path leads to a massive courtyard, framed by colonnaded walkways, with steps leading up to the huge tomb on the left.

Entered to the right of the tomb, the extensive **museum** displays Atatürk memorabilia, personal effects, gifts from famous admirers, recreations of his childhood home and school, and his favourite dog, Fox (stuffed). Just as revealing as all the rich artefacts are his simple rowing machine and huge multilingual library, which includes tomes he wrote.

Downstairs, extensive exhibits about the War of Independence and the formation of the republic move from battlefield murals with sound effects to overdetailed explanations of post-1923 reforms. At the end, a gift shop sells Atatürk items of all shapes and sizes, including key rings, jigsaw puzzles, cufflinks, clocks, ties and even height charts.

As you approach the tomb itself, look left and right at the gilded inscriptions, which are quotations from Atatürk's speech celebrating the republic's 10th anniversary in 1932. Remove your hat as you enter, and bend your neck to view the ceiling of the lofty hall, lined in marble and sparingly decorated with 15th- and 16th-century Ottoman mosaics. At the northern end stands an immense marble **cenotaph**, cut from a single piece of stone weighing 40 tons. The actual tomb is in a chamber beneath it.

It should take around two hours to see the whole site. It is virtually a pilgrimage site, so arrive early to beat the crowds; school groups frequently drop by midweek, especially in May, June and September.

The memorial straddles a hill in a park about 2km west of Kızılay and 1.2km south of Tandoğan, the closest Ankaray station to the entrance. A free shuttle regularly zips up and down the hill; alternatively, it's a pleasant walk to the mausoleum (about 20 minutes) or you can take a taxi (TL3). Note that security checks, including a bag scan, are carried out on entry; taxi drivers should turn off the meter while the guards go through the formalities.

OTHER MUSEUMS
Ethnography Museum
The **Ethnography Museum** (Etnografya Müzesi; Map p442; Talat Paşa Bulvarı; admission TL3; 8.30am-12.30pm & 1.30-5.30pm) is housed inside a white marble post-Ottoman building (1927) that served as

Atatürk's mausoleum until 1953. To get there, go to Ulus metro station and follow Talat Paşa Bulvarı until you see the 'Etnografya Müzesi' sign (*not* the 'Resim ve Heykel Müzesi' sign).

Past the equestrian statue out front, the mausoleum is preserved in the entrance hall. Around the walls are photographs of Atatürk's funeral. The collection is superb, with displays covering henna ceremonies, Anatolian jewellery, rug-making, Seljuk ceramics, early-15th-century doors and (opposite the anxious-looking mannequins in the circumcision display) coffee. Also of interest are the calligraphy and manuscript collection of Besim Atalay, who translated the Quran into Kurdish.

Next door, the **Painting & Sculpture Museum** (Resim ve Heykel Müzesi; admission free; 9am-noon & 1-5pm) occupies an equally elaborate building. Ranging from angular war scenes to society portraits, the pieces demonstrate that 19th- and 20th-century artistic developments in Turkey parallelled those in Europe, with Atatürk appearing in increasingly abstract form.

Museum of the War of Independence & Republic Museum
Both these **museums** (Cumhuriyet Bulvarı) were closed for renovation at the time of research, but are worth a look if they have reopened when you visit. The former has a collection of military photographs and documents, housed in Turkey's first parliament (the republican grand national assembly held early sessions here). The latter was the assembly's second headquarters, and features exhibits on the republic's beginnings.

Transport Museums
While waiting for a train at Ankara station you may want to take a look at the **Railway Museum & Art Gallery** (Demiryolları Müzesi ve Sanat Galerisi; Map p442; admission free; 9am-noon & 1-5pm), a small building on platform 1 that served as Atatürk's residence for 1½ years during the War of Independence. Right beside it is Atatürk's private 1930s rail coach.

The **Open-Air Steam Locomotive Museum** (Açık Hava Buharlı Lokomotif Müzesi; Map p442; Celal Bayar Bulvarı; admission free) is a collection of slowly rusting vintage engines. To find it, descend the underpass as though you were going to the train platforms, but keep walking straight on. Just before entering the Tandoğan Kapalı Çarşı shopping area, climb the steps to your left, then turn right and continue for around 800m. The museum may relocate when fast trains to Konya become operational in 2010.

The **Turkish Aeronautical Association Museum** (Türk Hava Kurumu Müzesi; Hipodrom Caddesi 2; Map p442; admission free) has a collection of old planes and some aviation displays in the shadow of its landmark parachute tower.

ATAKULE

Ankara's landmark tower, the **Atakule** (admission TL2.50; 11am-3am) has a revolving restaurant (mains TL16 to TL26) for 360-degree views; making a reservation exempts you from the admission fee. Shooting to the top in the glass lift is the hairiest part of the experience. There is a cinema in the mall at the bottom. Get here on Atakule- and Çankaya-bound buses down Atatürk Bulvarı.

MOSQUES

The huge outline of **Kocatepe Camii** (Map p446) in Kızılay is the symbol of Ankara. It is one of the world's largest mosques but is also very new (built between 1967 and 1987). However, there are one or two older mosques, and religious relics in the Ethnography Museum.

Ankara's most revered mosque is the **Hacı Bayram Camii** (Map p442), near the Temple of Augustus and Rome. Hacı Bayram Veli was a Muslim 'saint' who founded the Bayramiye dervish order in about 1400. Ankara was the order's centre, and Hacı Bayram Veli is still revered by pious Muslims. The mosque was built in the 15th century, with tiling added in the 18th century. Surrounding shops sell religious paraphernalia (including wooden toothbrushes as used, supposedly, by the Prophet Mohammed).

If you turn left on leaving the *hisar* and walk downhill past the antique shops you will come to the 13th-century **Arslanhane Camii** (Map p442), with pieces of Roman masonry in its walls.

HAMAMS

There are several hamams east of Opera Meydanı, including **Şengül Merkez Hamamı** (Map p442; Acıçeşme Sokak 3; wash & massage TL10; 5am-11pm for men, 7am-7pm for women), which has separate sections for men and women.

PARKS

Walk south of Ulus Meydanı along Atatürk Bulvarı and you'll reach the entrance to **Gençlik** **Parkı** (Youth Park; Map p442), where Atatürk had a swamp converted into an artificial lake. The park gets going during summer, but at other times the park appears to be returning to swampland. The Luna Park funfair overlooks the slow decay, and there are *çay bahçesi* (tea gardens) by the lake; single women should go for those with *aile* (family) in their name.

Other oases in the city are **Kuğulu Parkı** (Swan Park; Map p442), at the southern end of Tunalı Hilmi Caddesi, and the **Botanik Parkı** (Botanical Park), spilling into a valley beneath the Atakule.

Further out of town in Gölbaşı, **Aquapark Club Watercity** (498 2100; www.clubwatercity.com, in Turkish; Haymana Yolu 6km, Gölbaşı; adult/under 4yr/4-12yr/ TL20-30/free/15; 10am-7pm) has outdoor, indoor and children's pools, water slides, sports facilities and restaurants. Dolmuşes (shared taxis; can be a minibus or sedan) run here from Opera Meydanı.

OTHER SIGHTS

The sprawling ruins of the 3rd-century **Roman Baths** (Roma Hamaları; Map p442; admission TL3; 8.30am-12.30pm & 1.30-5.30pm) are 400m north of Ulus Meydanı. The layout of the baths is clearly visible; look for the standard Roman *apoditerium* (dressing room), *frigidarium* (cold room), *tepidarium* (warm room) and *caldarium* (hot room). A Byzantine tomb and Phrygian remains have also been found here.

The **Column of Julian** (Jülyanus Sütunu; Map p442; off Ulus Meydani) was erected in honour of the Roman Emperor Julian the Apostate's visit to Ankara. In a square ringed by government buildings, it is usually topped by a stork's nest.

Festivals & Events

Ankara offers festivals to satisfy music buffs of diverse leanings. The **Ankara Music Festival** (www.ankarafestival.com) provides three weeks of classical performances in April, and the three-day **Anki Rock Fest** (www.ankirockfest.com) takes place in late June.

The **Flying Broom** (www.ucansupurge.org) women's film festival takes place in May.

Folk dances and classical music can be seen at venues including the Atatürk Cultural Centre and the Painting and Sculpture Museum; ask at the tourist office for more details.

Sleeping

Ankara hotels are numerous, but very rarely exciting. Book ahead, as rooms are snapped up by businesspeople and bureaucrats. On a tight budget you will have to stick with Ulus, which is convenient for the main attractions but not the safest or most pleasant area. Most of the good midrange hotels are in Kızılay, while the top-end roosts are in Kavaklıdere.

ULUS

Ulus is handy for visiting the Museum of Anatolian Civilisations. There are cheap hotels around Ulus Meydanı, Opera Meydanı and on the streets below the citadel, south of Hisarparkı Caddesi. The latter area is smarter than central Ulus and ideally positioned for the museum.

Locals recommend that you do not wander Ulus' seedy streets after about 9pm. If you want to go out for the evening, given that most of the restaurants and nightlife are in Kızılay and you will probably catch public transport and/or a taxi back to Ulus, it may cost the same overall to upgrade to a room in Kızılay.

Otel Mithat (Map p442; ☎ 311 5410; www.otelmithat .com.tr; Tavus Sokak 2; s/d/tr TL23/33/43) Near Opera Meydanı, the Mithat's spartan rooms have tatty lino and small beds. On the plus side, there are TVs, phones, private bathrooms and wi-fi.

Kale Otel (Map p442; ☎ 311 3393; Şan Sokak 13; s/d TL30/50) One of the closest hotels to the museum, the Kale's yellow-and-red facade is rather off-putting but its pink-and-red interior is more palatable. One of Ulus' more pleasant budget options.

Otel Pınar (Map p442; ☎ 311 8951; Hisarparkı Caddesi 14; s/d TL32/62) Up towards the citadel, the Pınar supplies just the right kind of simple budget accommodation you need for a short stay. The breakfast, which costs extra, is terrible.

Hitit Oteli (Map p442; ☎ 310 8617; www.otelhitit.com; Hisarparkı Caddesi 12; s/d TL75/100) This is a small but noticeable step up from the nearby budget places. The rooms are not as smart as the reception, with its fish tank and budgie, but it is a reasonable option on the citadel ascent.

Şahinbey Hotel (Map p442; ☎ 310 4955; www.sahin beyhotel.com; Alataş Sokak 5; s/d €35/55; 🔀) The two-star Şahinbey is not as pleasant as the nearby Hitit and Kale hotels, but the rooms have mod cons such as fridges, digital TV and wi-fi.

ourpick Angora House Hotel (Map p442; ☎ 309 8380; angorahouse@gmail.com; Kalekapısı Sokak 16-18; s/ d/tr €45/60/75; 🕙 Mar-Oct; 🖳) Run by a friendly Turkish couple, Ankara's original boutique hotel has a great location inside the

citadel and offers six beautiful, individually decorated rooms in a restored house, benefiting from some fine half-timbering and a walled courtyard.

Hotel Oğultürk (Map p442; ☎ 309 2900; www.ogulturk .com; Rüzgarlı Eşdost Sokak 6; s/d/tr/ste €55/75/100/130; 🔀) Just off Rüzgarlı Sokak, the Oğultürk is one of central Ulus' smarter options, and on a par with many hotels in Kızılay. It's professionally managed and good for lone women.

KIZILAY & BAKANLIKLAR

The tree-shaded avenues of Kızılay and Bakanlıklar, close to some vibrant pedestrianised areas for shopping, dining and going out, are pleasanter than Ulus. Do ask for a discount from advertised rates if you are not offered one, as there are many hotels competing here.

Otel Elit (Map p446; ☎ 417 5001; elitotel@superonline .com; Olgunlar Sokak 10; s/d €40/55) Elit's decor may be stuck in a time warp, but the family hotel is conveniently located and the management runs a tight '70s ship.

Otel Büyük Erşan (Map p446; ☎ 417 6045; www.otel buyukersan.com; Selanik Caddesi 74; s/d/tr TL55/90/120) Past this 23-year-old hotel's brutal exterior, the lobby has a feeling of decayed grandeur. The cramped rooms have worn carpets, brown bedspreads and a smell of decay without the grandeur.

Hotel Metropol (Map p446; ☎ 417 3060; www.hotel metropol.com.tr; Olgunlar Sokak 5; s/d TL70/100; 🔀) A snip at these prices, the three-star Metropol provides comfort and quality across the board. The breakfast is excellent, but laundry rates are high.

Hotel Gold (Map p446; ☎ 419 4868; www.ankara goldhotel.com; Güfte Sokak 4; s/d/tr TL80/120/140; 🔀 🖳) Bling bling! Gold lives up to its name with its opulent reception and marbled lifts. The red-and-gold decor continues in the rooms, which have minibars and TVs.

Midas Hotel (Map p442; ☎ 424 0110; www.hotelmidas .com; Tunus Caddesi 20; s/d/tr from €80/100/130; 🔀 🖳) The luxury four-star Midas lives up to its kingly moniker with beautiful interiors, a spa and fitness centre, refreshingly professional staff and a restaurant with panoramic views.

KAVAKLIDERE

Gordion Hotel (Map p442; ☎ 427 8080; www.gordionhotel .com; Büklüm Sokak 59; d from €120; 🔀 🖳 🔀) This place is the epitome of a refined town house hotel, revelling quietly in deep-red fabrics, silver teasets, a conservatory restaurant and full set of spa facilities.

Mega Residence (Map p442; ☎ 468 5400; www .megaresidence.com; Tahran Caddesi 5; s/d from €200/225, ste €280; 😫) Targeting the German market, the pine facade of this smart establishment evokes the Austrian Alps. Apart from the schnitzel restaurant, there's not much Tyrolean flavour inside, but the rooms are good, especially the Jacuzzi doubles and kitchenette suite.

Also recommended are the **Ankara Hilton** (Map p442; ☎ 455 0000; www.hilton.com; Tahran Caddesi 12; s/d from €280/300, ste €445-820; 😫 💻 🏊) and, less welcoming but occupying a landmark cylindrical high-rise, the **Sheraton Hotel Ankara** (Map p442; ☎ 457 6000; www.sheraton.com/ankara; Noktalı Sokak; d €157-432; 😫 💻 🏊).

Eating

ULUS

Most Ulus options are cheap and basic. If self-catering suddenly seems like a good option, Ulus Hali food market (Map p442) is the place to pick up provisions from oversized chilli peppers to jars of honey.

In and around the citadel, a dozen old wood-and-stone houses have been converted into inviting, atmospheric licensed restaurants. Summer opening hours are around noon to midnight; most places are better visited in the evening, when live music creates more atmosphere, although they reduce their hours in winter.

Kubaşik Piknik (Map p442; ☎ 309 7274; Hükümet Caddesi; kebaps TL2.50-4) This hole in the wall is actually part of a chain. *Köfte* (meatballs), döner kebaps and chicken alternatives are available to eat in or take away.

Zenger Paşa Konağı (Map p442; ☎ 311 7070; www.zengerpasa.com; Doyran Sokak 13; mains TL12-17; 🕒 noon-12.30am; 😫) Crammed with Ottoman ephemera, the Zenger Paşa looks at first like a deserted ethnographic museum, but wealthy Ankaralıs love the pide, meze and grills, still cooked in the original Ottoman oven.

Kale Washington (Map p442; ☎ 311 4344; Doyran Sokak 5-7; mains TL15-20; 🕒 noon-midnight) Occupying a 17th-century mansion, the Washington is a favourite with visiting dignitaries (Hillary Clinton reportedly ate here). The service and the Turkish-international cuisine are not the best in town, and vegetarians who don't eat fish are not well catered for, but the views are impressive.

Boyacızâde Konağı (Map p442; ☎ 310 1515; Berrak Sokak 7/9; mains TL16-20; 🕒 from noon) Entered via a cluttered courtyard, this wonderfully converted mansion-restaurant offers great views and typical Ottoman-stalgic decor, as well as good fish dishes. Turkish classical, or *fasıl*, music provides the entertainment.

Çengelhan (Map p442; ☎ 309 6800; Depo Sokak 1; mains TL16-25) The Rahmi M Koç Industrial Museum restaurant nestles between vintage cars and a reconstructed Ottoman house. Well-to-do families tuck into dishes including aubergine kebap, pan-roasted sea bass and marinated lamb.

KIZILAY

This is undoubtedly the best area for a casual meal, particularly in the pedestrian zone north of Ziya Gökalp Caddesi, where pavement eateries and stalls serve everything from döner to corn on the cob. Ogunlar Sokak is good for an alfresco sandwich.

Can Balık (Map p446; ☎ 431 7870; Sakarya Caddesi 13; sandwiches TL4; 🕒 10am-10pm) A popular alternative to pricey Piscean restaurants, Can Balık offers fried fish, served with salad or in a sandwich.

Diet Ev Yemekleri (Map p446; ☎ 418 5683; Karanfil Sokak; mains TL5) Chow down with the students on cheap, filling food. Grub includes burgers, *köfte*, pizza, döner and İskender kebaps and all the classics.

our pick Le Man Kültür (Map p446; ☎ 310 8617; Konur Sokak 8a-b; mains TL6-11; 🕒 10am-11pm) One of Kızılay's coolest hang-outs, this restaurant packs in the ripped denim and Amy Winehouse haircuts between walls decorated with subversive cartoons. The menu features crêpes, Chinese, Mexican and even Argentinean dishes.

Köşk (Map p446; ☎ 432 1300; İnkılap Sokak 2; mains TL15-30; 🕒 9am-midnight) Ankara's best fish restaurant offers a glass-fronted dining room and live music. Meze such as fresh calamari with peppers, and simple but effective grills and fish mains, are just as alluring.

KAVAKLIDERE

The scene here is more European and sophisticated, catering primarily to the embassy set.

Laterna (Map p442; ☎ 468 5851; Tunus Caddesi 50b; mains TL11; 🕒 noon-10pm) Choose between rakı (aniseed brandy) and ouzo at this popular Aegean restaurant. Mains include papalina fish and salmon on herbs, and the good range of meze includes the recommended Ayvalık cold platter (TL9). There's live music most nights.

Café des Cafés (Map p442; ☎ 428 0176; Tunalı Hilmi Caddesi 83; mains TL14-21; 🕑 8.30am-11pm) Sit on red and white sofas between wood-lined walls to enjoy bistro flair from foreign Mediterranean shores. Dishes range across crêpes, Greek salad, sautéed steak with ginger sauce, and pasta.

Mezzaluna (Map p442; ☎ 467 5818; Turan Emeksiz Sokak 1; mains TL21-37; 🕑 noon-11pm) The capital's classiest Italian restaurant is busy busy busy, with chefs slapping pizzas on the counter for apron-clad waiters. The choice includes antipasti, risotto, wood-fire pizzas and seafood (a better bet than the steaks).

Drinking
CAFÉS
Kızılay is Ankara's café central, with terraces lining virtually every inch of space south of Ziya Gökalp Caddesi.

And Evi (Map p442; ☎ 312 7978; İçkale Kapısı, Ulus) Sit on the citadel walls and enjoy fabulous views at this Ottoman-styled café, near Angora House Hotel.

Fidan Café (Map p446; ☎ 425 8326; Karanfil Sokak 15, Kızılay) This smoky first-floor café is run by an amicable couple, with paintings by their grandchildren on the wall.

Simit Bahane (Map p446; Karanfil Sokak 36a, Kızılay) An antidote to Kızılay's smoother establishments, with backgammon, newspapers and nargilehs (traditional water pipes) providing entertainment.

BARS
Qube Bar (Map p446; ☎ 432 3079; Bayındır Sokak 16b, Kızılay) Slightly more sophisticated than the neighbouring pubs, Qube has a removable glass roof. Food is available.

Papillon (Map p442; ☎ 419 7303; Olgunlar Sokak 9, Kızılay) This neighbourhood bar has rock on the stereo and brick walls decorated with number plates and Hollywood posters.

Locus Solus (Map p442; ☎ 468 6788; Bestekar Sokak 60, Kavaklıdere) Locus Solus draws a sophisticated crowd to its terrace and beer garden. Seating is on beanbags and curvy sofas at low tables.

Golden Pub (Map p442; ☎ 427 8095; Tunalı Hilmi Caddesi 112d, Kavaklıdere) This basement pub has dartboards and music TV playing high on the walls.

Entertainment
CINEMAS
Some of Ankara's cinemas occasionally show Western films in the original language; check the *Hürriyet Daily News* or www.askfest.org. Screens include **Metropol Sineması** (☎ 425 7478; Selanik Caddesi 76, Kızılay; adult/student TL10/9), which costs TL6 on Thursdays.

NIGHTCLUBS & LIVE MUSIC
Ankara has a spectrum of venues from student dives to recherché nightspots. Consult fellow drinkers, bar staff, flyers or local listings to get the latest tips.

For a night out with Ankara's student population, head to Kızılay – particularly Bayındır Sokak between Sakarya and Tuna Caddesis. The tall, thin buildings pack in up to five floors of bars, cafés and *gazinos* (nightclubs). Many of the clubs offer live Turkish pop music, and women travellers should feel OK in most.

IF Performance Hall (Map p442; ☎ 418 9506; Tunus Caddesi 14a, Kavaklıdere) The grandly named basement venue stages cover bands such as Effecto Placebo and Achtung Babies, as well as bigger acts.

Shopping
It's cheapest to shop in Ulus, but to see what fashionable Turkey spends its money on, head south. Tunalı Hilmi Caddesi has lots of local stores alongside more-familiar names such as the British department store **Marks & Spencer** (Map p442). Nearby, just below the Sheraton Hotel, is **Karum** (Map p442; İran Caddesi), a glass-and-marble mall with branches of

---

RIGHTEOUS ANGORA
Can you tell the difference between a goat and a rabbit? It's not as easy as you think – or at least not if all you have to go on is the wool. One of the most popular misconceptions about Ankara's famous angora wool is that it comes from angora goats, a hardy breed believed to be descended from wild Himalayan ancestors. Not so: the soft, fluffy fabric produced from these goats is correctly known as mohair. Angora wool in the strictest sense comes from angora rabbits, also local but much cuter critters whose fur, weight for weight, could traditionally fetch as much as gold.

Swarovski, Body Shop, Swatch, Accessorize and Artemis.

Behind the Ulus Hali food market, on Konya Caddesi, is the **Vakıf Suluhan Çarşısı** (Map p442), a restored *han* (caravanserai) with clothes shops, a leafy café, toilets and a small free-standing mosque in its courtyard. With its stone balconies and low arches, the building itself is more inspiring than its shops.

The area around the Parmak Kapısı entrance to the citadel was traditionally a centre for trading in angora wool. Walking downhill towards Arslanhane Cami from the dried-fruit stalls in front of the gate, there are some carpet and antique shops. You'll come across copper-beaters and other assorted craftsworkers carrying on their age-old trades.

On tree- and café-lined Olgunlar Sokak is a row of **secondhand bookstalls** (Map p446).

Getting There & Away

AIR

Ankara's Esenboğa airport, 33km north of the city centre, is the hub for Turkish Airlines' domestic-flight network. Although many domestic and international budget carriers serve Ankara, İstanbul's airports offer more choice. Even flying domestically, it may save you time and money to travel via İstanbul.

Turkish Airlines and Atlasjet offer direct flights between Ankara and destinations including Adana, Antalya, Bodrum, Cyprus, Diyabakır, Erzurum, Gaziantep, İstanbul (IST and SAW), İzmir, Kars, Malatya, Trabzon and Van.

International airlines offer both direct services to/from Ankara and flights with connections in İstanbul.

Airline Offices

Atlasjet airport (☎ 398 0201); Kavaklıdere (Map p442; ☎ 440 6070; Cinnah Caddesi 43/1, Kızılay)

British Airways (Map p442; ☎ 467 5557; Atatürk Bulvarı 237/2, Kavaklıdere)

Japan Airlines & KLM (Map p442; ☎ 466 5640; Şili Meydani, Kavaklıdere Sokak 23/5, Kavaklıdere)

Lufthansa (Map p442; ☎ 442 0580; Cinnah Caddesi 102/5, Çankaya)

Turkish Airlines airport (☎ 398 0100); Kavaklıdere (Map p442; ☎ 428 0200; Atatürk Bulvarı 154)

BUS

Every Turkish city or town of any size has direct buses to Ankara. The gigantic otogar or AŞTİ (Ankara Şehirlerarası Terminali İşletmesi) is at the western end of the Ankaray underground train line, 4.5km west of Kızılay.

The terminal has departure gates on the upper level and arrivals on the lower. There are restaurants, internet cafés, ATMs, phones and newsstands. The *emanet* (left-luggage room) on the lower level charges

SERVICES FROM ANKARA'S OTOGAR					
Destination	Fare (TL)	Duration (hr)	Distance (km)	Frequency (per day)	Counter
Adana	30	6	490	seven	52
Amasya	30	5	335	four	31, 37
Antalya	30	8	550	four	32
Bodrum	45	13	785	two (evening)	41
Bursa	28	6	400	hourly	71
Denizli (for Pamukkale)	34	7	480	frequent	58
Diyarbakır	50	14	945	three (evening)	34
Erzurum	50	13	925	four (evening)	36
Gaziantep	45	10	705	frequent	43
İstanbul	25-33	5-6½	450	every 30 min	27, 29, 41
İzmir	35	8	600	every two hours	43
Kayseri	17.50	5	330	six	46
Konya	23	3	260	hourly	42
Marmaris	45	10½	780	frequent	41
Nevşehir (for Cappadocia)	25	5	285	seven	50
Samsun	30	7	420	five	52
Sivas	10	6	450	six	28
Sungurlu (for Boğazkale)	12	3	177	hourly	23
Trabzon	35	13	780	four (evening)	31, 32

EXPRESS SERVICES FROM ANKARA'S TRAIN STATION

Destination	Fare (TL)	Via	Duration (hr)	Frequency
Adana	20, sleeper 65	Niğde	12	daily
Diyarbakır	23, sleeper 61	Kayseri, Sivas, Malatya	35	4 weekly
İstanbul	23, sleeper 80	Eskişehir, İzmit	7-10	8 daily
İzmir	23-26.50	Kütahya, Balıkesir	14	3 daily
Kars	29-35	Kayseri, Sivas, Erzurum	28	2 daily
Tatvan	29	Kayseri, Sivas, Malatya	41	2 weekly
Zonguldak	12	Karabük	9½	3 weekly

TL4 per item stored; you'll need to show your passport.

As Ankara has many buses to all parts of the country, you can often turn up, buy a ticket and be on your way in less than an hour. Don't try this during public holidays, though.

AŞTİ has 80 gişe (ticket counters) and a central information booth where the surly staff will, in theory, point you in the right direction.

TRAIN

Train services between İstanbul and Ankara are the best in the country, and work is under way to develop an even faster rail link. **Ankara Garı** (Map p442; ☎ 311 0620) has a PTT, a restaurant, snack shops, kiosks, ATMs, telephones and a left-luggage room.

The table above summarises the main express routes out of Ankara; returning, most trains continue on to İstanbul. Slower standard trains serve many intermediate destinations.

Getting Around
TO/FROM THE AIRPORT

Esenboğa airport is 33km north of the city. **Havaş** (Map p442; ☎ 444 0487; Kazım Karabekir Caddesi) buses depart from Gate B at 19 May Stadium every half-hour between 4.30am and midnight daily (TL10, 45 minutes). They may leave sooner if they fill up, so get there early to claim your seat.

The same buses link the airport and the AŞTİ otogar (TL10 to TL12.50, 60 minutes), leaving the station every half-hour between 4.30am and 11.30pm from in front of the passenger arrival lounge.

Buses from the airport are scheduled according to flight arrivals. Don't pay more than TL50 for a taxi between the airport and the city.

TO/FROM THE BUS STATION

The easiest way to get into town is on the Ankaray metro line, which has a station at the AŞTİ otogar. Go to Maltepe station for the train station (a 10-minute walk), or to Kızılay for midrange hotels. Change at Kızılay (to the Metro line) for Ulus and cheaper hotels.

A taxi costs about TL15 to the city centre.

TO/FROM THE TRAIN STATION

The train station (see above) is about 1km southwest of Ulus Meydanı and 2km northwest of Kızılay. Many dolmuşes head northeast along Cumhuriyet Bulvarı to Ulus, and east on Talat Paşa Bulvarı to Kızılay.

It's just over 1km from the station to Opera Meydanı; any bus heading east along Talat Paşa Bulvarı will drop you within a few hundred metres if you ask for Gazi Lisesi.

To go from the train station to Maltepe subway stop (on the Ankaray line to AŞTİ otogar), follow the underpass in the train station through a subterranean shopping area, mostly populated by military stores. Turn left at the top of the steps at the far end. In the other direction, follow the TCDD signs out of Maltepe, turn right at the top of the steps and, after about 100m, you will see the stairs to the underpass.

BUS

Ankara has a good bus, dolmuş and minibus network. Signs on the front and side of the vehicles are better guides than route numbers. Buses marked 'Ulus' and 'Çankaya' run the length of Atatürk Bulvarı. Those marked 'Gar' go to the train station, those marked 'AŞTİ' to the otogar.

Standard TL3 tokens, available at subway stations and major bus stops or anywhere displaying an EGO Bilet sign, are valid for 45 minutes on multiple journeys. They work on most buses as well as the subway, and a 10-token pass costs TL12.

These tokens are not valid on express buses, which are the longer buses with ticket counters halfway down the vehicle.

CAR

Driving within Ankara is chaotic and signs are inadequate; it's easier to ditch your car and use public transport.

If you plan to hire a car to drive out of Ankara, there are many small local companies alongside the major international firms; most have offices in Kavaklıdere along Tunus Caddesi, and/or at Esenboğa airport. Some reliable operators:

Avis (Map p442; ☎ 467 2313; Tunus Caddesi 68/2)
Budget (Map p442; ☎ 468 0336; Tunus Caddesi 68/2)
National (Map p442; ☎ 426 4565; Tunus Caddesi 73/1)

METRO

Ankara's underground train network currently has two lines: the Ankaray line running between AŞTİ otogar in the west through Maltepe and Kızılay to Dikimevi in the east; and the Metro line running from Kızılay northwest via Sıhhiye and Ulus to Batıkent. The two lines interconnect at Kızılay. Trains run from 6.15am to 11.45pm daily.

Standard tokens cost TL3 and a 10-token pass is TL12 (see p453). Note that there are separate barriers for adult and child/student tokens at some subway stations, so if your token doesn't seem to work, check that you're using the right lane.

TAXI

Taxis are everywhere and they all have meters, with a TL1.70 base rate. It costs about TL6 to cross the centre; charges rise at night and the same trip will cost well over TL10. In Kızılay, beware the one-way roads, as the taxi may have to backtrack (without switching off the meter) to access a road going in the right direction.

AROUND ANKARA

You don't have to go far from Ankara to hit some major pieces of Anatolian history, but if it's a leisurely day trip you're after rather than an overnight, consider the Phrygian archaeological site at Gordion or the small Ottoman town of Beypazarı.

Gordion

The capital of ancient Phrygia, with some 3000 years of settlement behind it, Gordion lies 106km west of Ankara in the village of Yassıhöyük.

Gordion was occupied by the Phrygians as early as the 9th century BC, and soon afterwards became their capital. Although destroyed during the Cimmerian invasion, it was rebuilt before being conquered by the Lydians and then the Persians. Alexander the Great came through and famously cut the Gordian knot in 333 BC, but by 278 BC the Galatian occupation had effectively destroyed the city.

The moonscape-like terrain around Yassıhöyük is dotted with tumuli (burial mounds) marking the graves of the Phrygian kings. Of some 90 identified tumuli, 35 have been excavated; you can enter the largest tomb, and also view the site of the Gordion acropolis, where digs revealed five main levels of civilisation, from the Bronze Age to Galatian times.

MIDAS TUMULUS & GORDION MUSEUM

In 1957 the Austrian archaeologist Alfred Koerte discovered Gordion, and with it the intact **tomb** (admission incl museum TL3; ☼ 8.30am-5.30pm) of a Phrygian king, probably buried some time between 740 and 718 BC. The tomb is actually a gabled 'cottage' of cedar surrounded by juniper logs, buried inside a tumulus 53m high and 300m in diameter. It's the oldest wooden structure ever found in Anatolia, and perhaps even in the world. The tunnel leading into the depths of the tumulus is a modern addition, allowing you to glimpse some of the interior of the fenced-off tomb.

Inside the tomb archaeologists found the body of a man between 61 and 65 years of age, 1.59m tall, surrounded by burial objects, including tables, bronze *situlas* (containers) and bowls said to be part of the funerary burial feast. The occupant's name remains unknown (although Gordius and Midas were popular names for Phrygian kings).

In the **museum** opposite, Macedonian and Babylonian coins show Gordion's position at the centre of Anatolian trade, communications and military activities, as do the bronze figurines and glass-bead jewellery from the Syro-Levantine region of Mesopotamia. There is a good collection of Phrygian art, although the finest examples, including the intricate inlaid wooden tables found in the tomb, were removed to Ankara's Museum of Anatolian Civilisations.

In the grounds are displays on Phrygian architecture, terracotta work and mosaics from the acropolis (some of the oldest in Anatolia), and a reconstructed Galatian tomb.

ACROPOLIS

Excavations at the 8th-century-BC acropolis yielded a wealth of data on Gordion's many civilisations.

The lofty main gate on the city's western side was approached by a 6m-wide ramp. Within the fortified enclosure were four *megara* (square halls) from which the king and his priests and ministers ruled the empire. The mosaics found in one of these halls, the so-called Citadel of Midas, are on display outside the museum.

Today the site is a fenced-off collection of foundations with explanatory signs, which are of small appeal to the casual visitor. From the museum, continue along the main road through the village and it's the mound on your left just before the bridge.

GETTING THERE & AWAY

Baysal Turizm buses connect Ankara's otogar (ticket counter 28) with Polatlı every half-hour (TL5, one hour). Once in Polatlı, you can travel the last 18km to Yassıhöyük in a minibus (TL3), but this involves a 1.5km walk across town to the minibus stand and services depart sporadically. A taxi will charge about TL40 to drive you to the main sites and back to Polatlı otogar.

Beypazarı

☎ 0312 / pop 34,500

This picturesque Ottoman town is set high above the İnönü Vadisi. More than 3000 Ottoman houses line the narrow streets in the hilltop old quarter, where 500-plus buildings and some 30 streets have been restored. Coppersmiths and carpenters beaver away, shopkeepers flog model Ottoman houses in little bags to Ankaralı day trippers, and the 200-year-old market recalls Beypazarı's position on the Silk Rd.

Occupying a sizeable Ottoman mansion, the **museum** (Beypazarı Tarih ve Kültür Evi; admission TL1.50; ☉ 10am-6pm Tue-Sun) is good for nosing around to a classical music soundtrack. Exhibits range from Roman and Byzantine pillars to an Ottoman depiction of an elephant, and the characteristic cupboard-bathrooms are still intact.

On the first weekend in June, the **Havuç Guveç** (Traditional Dish Festival) celebrates the humble carrot (the area grows more than half of the carrots consumed in Turkey). Additional attractions, if any are needed, include craftwork markets and Ottoman house tours.

While you're here try the local delicacies, which include *havuç lokum* (carrot-flavoured Turkish delight), clumpy *cevizli sucuğu* (walnuts coated in grape jelly) and Beypazarı mineral water, bottled here and swigged throughout the country.

Me'vaların Konağı (☎ 762 3698; Köstyolu Sokak Müzeyanı 31; r with/without bathroom TL70/60), one of a few Ottoman house hotels on the square near the museum, has beautiful bedcovers and cupboard-bathrooms.

Occupying one of the town's most noted Ottoman piles, **Tarihi Taş Mektep** (☎ 762 7606; Alaaddin Sokak 4; mains TL6.50-9; ☉ 8am-10pm) is popular for dishes such as the surprisingly spicy salad, *yaprak sarma* (stuffed vine leaves) and grilled trout.

GETTING THERE & AWAY

From Ankara, take a Metro train to Akkoprü and cross the motorway, heading away from the Ankamall. Walk to your left, away from the flyover, until you reach the area between the M Oil garage and the pedestrian bridge, where you can hail passing Beytaş Turizm minibuses to Beypazarı (TL6, 1½ hours). In the Beytaş Turizm office across the road from the town centre bus stop (decorated with the Ottoman mural), you can check the time of the last bus back to Ankara.

SAFRANBOLU

☎ 0370 / pop 38,300

Every town in Turkey has its old Ottoman houses, but Safranbolu, the valley town at the heart of the new restoration movement, takes it to a different level: virtually the entire old Ottoman town has been preserved and now spruced up to such good effect that it made it onto the Unesco World Heritage list. This is as close as you'll ever come to historical Turkey, and the town's popularity with domestic tourists reinforces just what a rare treat this is.

The weather, too, can play a part in this unique experience. Summer thunderstorms periodically close over the sunken valley like a heavy black lid, and you can watch the lightning-pierced darkness drawing on

SAFRANBOLU

0   200 m
0   0.1 miles

INFORMATION
Batuta Turizm.....................1 C2
Paşa Internet.......................2 C3
TC Ziraat Bankası................3 C1
Tourist Office.......................4 B2

To Havuzlu Asmazlar
Konağı (400m);
Kıranköy:(1.7km);
Zalifre Otel (1.7km);
Savaş Turizm (1.7km);
Metro Doğuş (1.7km);
Havuzlu Köşk (3km);
Bağlar (3km);
Tokatlı Gorge (3km);
İncekaya Aqueduct (7.5km)

To Bulak Mencilis
Mağarası (10km)

To Yörük
Köyü (15km)

Kazdağlıoğlu Meydanı

Kazdağlı oğlu Camii

Çarşı

SIGHTS & ACTIVITIES
Çarşı Taksi............................5 C1
Cinci Hamam........................6 C2
Clock Tower..........................7 A2
Eski Hükümet Konağı............8 A2
İzzet Paşa Camii....................9 C4
Kaymakamlar Müze Evi.......10 D3
Kileciler Evi.........................11 C4
Köprülü Mehmet Paşa
  Camii................................12 C3
Mümtazlar Konağı...............13 A2

SLEEPING
Arpacıoğlu Otel...................14 C1
Ağa Çeşmesi Evi..................15 B2
Backpackers Pension...........16 D2
Bastoncu Pansiyon..............17 D3
Cinci Hanı...........................18 C3
Ebrulu Konağı......................19 D3
Gül Evi................................20 B2
Otel Hatice Hanım Konağı
  III......................................21 D2
Paşa Konağı........................22 A2
Paşa Mustafa Konağı...........23 D3
Selvili Köşk..........................24 B1
Turgut Reis Konağı..............25 C4

EATING
Çevrikköprü 2......................26 C2
Kadioğlu Şehzade Sofrası.....27 B2
Merkez Lokantası.................28 C2
Saranbolu Sofrası................29 D3

DRINKING
Arasna Pension....................30 C2
Arasta Lonca Kahvesi..........31 B2
Meydan...............................32 C2

SHOPPING
Safrantat..............................33 C2
Yemeniciler Arastası............34 B2

TRANSPORT
Karabük Minibus Stop.........35 C2
Kıranköy Bus Stop...............36 C2
Konan (Yörük Köyü) Minibus
  Stop..................................37 D2
Taxis....................................38 C2

Belediye (Town Hall)

Pazar Yeri

Cinci Hanı

Akçasu Canyon

Hıdırlık Parkı

inch by inch until finally the light is gone and the rain bursts down onto the tiled roofs. Simply magic.

History

During the 17th century, the main Ottoman trade route between Gerede and the Black Sea coast passed through Safranbolu, bringing commerce, prominence and money to the town. During the 18th and 19th centuries Safranbolu's wealthy inhabitants built mansions of sun-dried mudbricks, wood and stucco, while the larger population of prosperous artisans built less impressive but similarly sturdy homes. Safranbolu owes its fame to the large numbers of these dwellings that have survived.

The most prosperous Safranbolulus maintained two households. In winter they occupied town houses in the Çarşı (Market) district, which is situated at the meeting point of three valleys and so protected from the winter winds. During the warm months they moved to summer houses in the garden suburb of Bağlar (Vineyards). When the iron- and steelworks at Karabük were established in 1938, modern factory houses started to encroach on Bağlar, but Çarşı has remained virtually untouched.

During the 19th century about 20% of Safranbolu's inhabitants were Ottoman Greeks, but most of their descendants moved to Greece during the population exchange after WWI. Their principal church, dedicated to St Stephen, was converted into Kıranköy's Ulu Cami (Great Mosque).

Orientation

Safranbolu falls into three distinct parts: Kıranköy, Bağlar and Çarşı. Approaching from the steel town of Karabük, you arrive first in Kıranköy, the former Greek quarter and now the most modern part of Safranbolu, with plenty of banks, shops and bus offices. Continuing uphill (northwest) along Sadrı Artunç Caddesi, you'll reach Bağlar, with its centre at Köyiçi, which has many fine old houses.

However, most of what you've come to see lies downhill in Çarşı. To get there from Kıranköy, take Kaya Erdem Caddesi at the roundabout, and go 1.7km southeast, down the hill and over the next one. Buses ply this route roughly every half-hour.

Information

Paşa Internet (per hr TL1; ☺ 10am-11pm) Slow access near the İzzet Paşa Camii.
TC Ziraat Bankası (Kazdağlıoğlu Meydanı) Has an ATM; there is also one on Kapucuoğlu Sokak.
Tourist office (☎ 712 3863; www.safranbolu.gov.tr; ☺ 9am-12.30pm & 1.30-6pm) Off the main square; gives out a helpful *rehberi* (map).

Sights

OTTOMAN HOUSES

Just walking through Çarşı is a feast for the eyes. Virtually every house in the district is an original, and what little modern development there is has been held in check. Many of the finest historic houses have been restored, and as time goes on, more and more are being saved from deterioration and turned into hotels, shops or museums.

Kaymakamlar Müze Evi, the most interesting of three old houses that have been turned into museums, has all the typical features of Ottoman homes (see boxed text, p458). It was owned by a lieutenant colonel and still feels like an address of note as you climb the stairs towards the wooden ceiling decoration. Tableaux recreate everyday scenes such as bathing in the cupboard, and the wedding feast, when the women served the men using the *dönme dolaplar* (revolving cupboard).

The tall, thin **Mümtazlar Konağı** (1893), former home of the head mufti at Safranbolu's *medrese* (seminary), is bare inside and unenlightening without a guide. The dusty exhib-its are more evocative of the 1950s than the 19th century.

Kileciler Evi (1884) also has 1950s period pieces among the family heirlooms in its cupboards. However, the whitewashed interior has been attractively renovated, with exhibits including family photos, carpets and mannequins clad in traditional clothes. As the information sheet explains, the 99 cupboards symbolise the 99 names of God.

The exhibition rooms in the houses are generally open daily from 9am to 7pm and charge TL2 to TL2.50 for adult admission (TL1 for children). Tea is served in their gardens and the properties open more sporadically during winter.

Some of the largest houses had indoor pools, which, although big enough for swimming, were used instead to cool the rooms with running water, which also provided pleasing background noise. The best and most accessible example in Çarşı is the **Havuzlu Asmazlar Konağı** (Mansion with Pool; Çelik Gülersoy Caddesi 18, Çarşı), now run as a hotel (p459).

KENT TARIHI MÜZESİ

Safranbolu's hilltop castle was demolished early in the last century to make way for the yellow Eski Hükümet Konağı (old government building), which was restored following a fire in 1976. English interpretive panels are scarce in the **museum** (☎ 712 1314; Çeşme Mahallesi Hükümet Sokak; admission TL3; ☺ 9am-7pm Apr-Oct, 9am-5pm Nov-Mar) inside, but the exhibits are a decent introduction to local life. The reconstructions of old shops in the marble-floored basement include a chemist's store with the inevitable saffron teinture among the elixirs.

The ticket to the museum also covers the neighbouring **clock tower** (1797), built by grand vizier (prime minister) İzzet Mehmet Paşa. Climb the tower on the hour to see its clockwork hammer strike and hear the chimes ring around the surrounding hills.

OTHER HISTORIC BUILDINGS

Çarşı's most famous and imposing structure is the brooding **Cinci Hanı** (Eski Çarşı Çeşme Mahalessi; adult/student TL2/1), a 17th-century caravanserai, which is now an upmarket hotel (p460). On Saturday a market takes place in the square behind it.

Nearby, the contemporaneous **Cinci Hamam**, with separate baths for men and women, was closed for renovation at the time of research, set to reopen in autumn 2009.

CENTRAL ANATOLIA

OTTOMAN STYLE

Looking at the concrete cityscapes synonymous with Turkish modernity, it's hard to imagine being back in the 19th century, when fine wooden houses were the rule. Luckily, growing tourism has encouraged an Ottoman revival, and restoration has become a boom trade. Excellent examples can be found in Afyon, Amasya and Tokat, but Safranbolu is universally acknowledged to contain the country's single finest collection of pre-independence domestic architecture.

Ottoman wooden houses generally had two or three storeys, the upper storeys jutting out over the lower ones on carved corbels (brackets). Their timber frames were filled with adobe and then plastered with a mixture of mud and straw. Sometimes the houses were left unsealed, but in towns they were usually given a finish of plaster or whitewash, with decorative flourishes in plaster or wood. The wealthier the owner, the fancier the decoration.

Inside, the larger houses had 10 to 12 rooms, divided into *selamlık* (men's quarters) and *haremlik* (women's quarters). Rooms were often decorated with built-in niches and cupboards, and had fine plaster fireplaces with *yaşmaks* (conical hoods). Sometimes the ceilings were very elaborate; that of the Paşa Odası of Tokat's Latifoğlu Konağı, for example, is thought to emulate a chandelier in wood.

Details to look out for inside the Safranbolu houses include their *hayats* (courtyard areas where the animals lived and tools were stored); ingenious *dönme dolaplar* (revolving cupboards that made it possible to prepare food in one room and pass it to another without being seen); bathrooms hidden inside cupboards; and central heating systems that relied on huge fireplaces. *Sedirs* (bench seating that ran round the walls) doubled up as beds, with the bedding being stored in the bathrooms, which converted neatly into cupboards during the day. Space-efficient, certainly, but sometimes you wonder how anyone ever found anything!

The beefy, helmet-roofed **Köprülü Mehmet Paşa Camii**, beside the *arasta* (row of shops beside a mosque), dates to 1661. The metal sundial in the courtyard was added in the mid-19th century.

The **İzzet Paşa Camii** is one of the largest mosques built during the Ottoman Empire. It was built by the grand vizier in 1796 and restored in 1903, and shows European architectural influence.

Uphill past the Kaymakamlar Müze Evi, there are panoramic views from **Hıdırlık Parkı** (admission TL3). Peek through the windows of the locked mausoleum of 19th-century politician Hasan Paşa and you'll see a heap of coins left by visitors.

Tours

A couple of tours allow you to look around Safranbolu and the surrounding sights (p461) in a day. **Batuta Turizm** (☎ 725 4533; www.batuta .com.tr; Çeşme Mahallesi Hükümet Sokak) offers buggy tours, with circuits lasting from 40 minutes to three hours (TL8.50 to TL22.50). The short tour is a reasonable introduction to Safranbolu, but spending any longer in the company of the cheesy voiceover (available in English and Japanese) may be detrimental to your mental health.

More recommended is the excellent half-day tour of Bağlar and the three sights listed under Around Safranbolu (p461). It leaves at 1.30pm and costs TL40 including entrance fees. **Çarşı Taksi** (☎ 725 2595; Hilmi Bayramgil Caddesi) offers a longer tour of these sights and two others for TL65.

Festivals & Events

September is a great time to visit Safranbolu, with two festivals, the **Golden Saffron Documentary Film Festival** and the **Safranbolu Architectural Treasures & Folklore Week**, taking place in the same month. Be sure to book accommodation in advance. At the **Geleneksel Sezzetler Şenliği**, a food festival organised in May by the Association of Anatolian Cuisine, you can try specialities from across the region.

Sleeping

Safranbolu is very popular with Turkish tourists at weekends and over holidays. Prices may rise at particularly busy times, and it can be worth booking ahead.

Splashing out a bit is virtually an obligation, as you may never get another chance to sleep anywhere so authentically restored. Look out for places that have been sympathetically renovated, so you can appreciate some of the building's original character.

BUDGET

Backpackers Pension (☎ 725 2688; www.backpackers pension.com; Kayadibi Sokak; dm/s/d/tr TL15/25/45/55; 🖳) Run by the couple behind Bastoncu Pansiyon, this hostel is a solid budget choice, with eight rooms containing up to four beds each and a shared bathroom on each of the three floors. There are good views from the terrace and it offers the same services as its older sibling.

Bastoncu Pansiyon (☎ 712 3411; www.bastoncu pension.com; Hıdırlık Yokuşu Sokak; dm/s/d/tr TL20/35/50/70; 🖳) In a 300-year-old building, Bastoncu is an institution for both backpackers and folks who choose it over more-expensive options for its unrivalled sense of history. The rooms and three-bed dorms have all their original wood, tiled bathrooms, jars of dried flowers, and some closet toilets. It's run by a friendly Turkish couple who speak English and Japanese and appreciate travellers' needs, offering a laundry service, lifts from the otogar, tours and traditional, two-course dinners (TL10).

Turgut Reis Konağı (☎ 725 1301; www.turgut reiskonak.com, in Turkish; Akpınar Sokak 27; s/d/tr TL30/70/100) Boasting a quiet position and some of Safranbolu's best views, this friendly hotel is one of the best deals around. The 200-year-old building has been sensitively restored, with stylish furnishings and touches such as steps leading to the beds in room 106.

Paşa Mustafa Konağı (☎ 725 1748; pasamustafa konagi@hotmail.com; Massalla Mahallesi Hıdırlık Yokuşu Sokak 2; s/d/tr TL35/50/70) The three modern rooms in this intimate pension are not Safranbolu's most atmospheric, but the dapper, English-speaking owner is friendly to a fault. It's a pleasure to sit in the lounge at night, gazing between the kerosene lamps and an unbeatable view of the Cinci Hanı.

If you'd rather stay in a family home than a hotel, the tourist office has a list of 25 basic pensions (the *Safranbolu'daki Ev Pansiyonları Listesi*). They are cheaper than hotels, though often of lower quality, and generally cost TL20 to TL25 per person. One example is the **Ağa Çeşmesi Evi** (☎ 725 1717; Hükümet Sokak; s/d TL25/50).

MIDRANGE

Otel Hatice Hanım Konağı III (☎ 712 7545; info@hotel haticehanim.com; Baba Sultan Mahallesi Naiptarla Sokak 4; s/d

TL35/70) Part of a network of hotels in Ottoman buildings, this atmospheric establishment is excellent value for money. The terrace café and the windows between the wooden beams offer views of the *pazar yeri* (market square). Nearby Otel Hatice Hanım Konağı I, in the former governor's residence, has marble basins, original fittings and plenty of quirks.

Arpacıoğlu Otel (☎ 725 4340; www.arpacioglu otel.com; Kazdağlıoğulu Meydanı 1; s/d TL45/80, half-board TL60/90) Set back from the main square, this hotel occupies a cluster of 200-year-old buildings. The sparse but spacious rooms have satellite TV, room service and a car park.

Selvili Köşk (☎ 712 8646; fax 725 2294; Mescit Sokak 23; s/d/tr TL70/100/130) The most charming hotel in yet another Ottoman network, the blue Selvili overlooks a pretty garden. One of our favourites for authentic 19th-century character, it has a high-ceilinged salon and big, cool rooms with steps leading to cupboard-bathrooms, one with a bathtub.

Ebrulu Konağı (☎ 712 0714; www.ebrulukonak.com; Hıdırlık Yokuşu Sokak 13; s/d/tr TL75/145/180) Modern fittings don't dispel the sense of history, created by low ceilings and broad stone window sills, in this hillside mansion. There are great views of Safranbolu and a pleasant courtyard restaurant.

Paşa Konağı (☎ 725 3572; www.safranbolupasa.com; Kalealtı Sokak 1-7; s/d TL80/120) Two hundred years after Izzet Mehmet Paşa (p457) occupied his mansion, the spacious rooms and secluded garden foster a romantic nostalgia. Certain bathrooms are inside cupboards with high steps, which might be tricky for some guests.

Zalifre Otel (☎ 725 4718; www.zalifreotel.com; Barış Mahallesi, Kıranköy; s/d/tr TL110/150/200) This faux Ottoman hotel opposite some bus company offices feels older than its tender years, thanks to its wood-panelled reception and marble courtyard with a fountain. Rooms are less impressive, with small bathrooms and grilles on the windows.

Havuzlu Asmazlar Konağı (☎ 725 2883; www.safran bolukonak.com; Çelik Gülersoy Caddesi 18, Çarşı; r week/weekend from TL140/180) On the way to Kiranköy, the HAK is worth a stop just to glimpse the fine pool that gives the house its name. The rooms are beautifully furnished with brass beds, *sedirs* and kilims (pileless woven rugs), and the restaurant comes recommended. Bathrooms are minuscule and soundproofing minimal, but these are minor inconveniences. Two annexes provide less -atmospheric digs.

TOP END

`our pick` **Gül Evi** (☎ 725 4645; www.booking.com; Hükümet Sokak 46; s €60-83, d €80-110, ste €165-330) This recent arrival should give Cinci Hanı a run for its caravanserai gold. Set in two 150-year-old houses, the hotel perfectly balances stylish, minimalist decor with the Ottoman architecture. The 65-sq-metre suite, occupying the former *selamlık*, is the largest in Safranbolu and the restaurant will be serving Anatolian cuisine by the time you read this.

Cinci Hanı (☎ 712 0680; www.cincihan.com; Eski Çarşı Çeşme Mahalessi; s/d/tr from TL90/140/190) Safranbolu's stone caravanserai has a couple of centuries over most of the Ottoman houses, though rooms are comparatively limited on space and decor. The huge Han Ağası Odası suite is a gem, with kitchen, sitting room, and bathroom with old stone hamam basin.

Eating

As food is available at most hotels, Safranbolu is not overly endowed with great places to eat.

Just off the main square in Çarşı, the two branches of Çevrikköprü are neat old-style restaurants with plenty on the menu and views of the lower part of town. Gül Evi (see Sleeping) was opening a restaurant at the time of research.

`our pick` **Safranbolu Sofrası** (☎ 712 1451; Hıdırlık Yokuşu Sokak 28a; mains TL4; ☯ 9am-9pm) This friendly café offers an authentic local experience – in the sense that Turkish soap operas and music videos accompany dining. The delicious dishes include *dolma* with yoghurt and tomato sauce and *cevizli yayım* (macaroni topped with walnuts). If you like the saffron tea, buy a jar of the yellow powder.

Merkez Lokantası (☎ 725 1478; Yukarı Çarşı 1; mains TL4-5; ☯ 10am-10pm) This quaint, clean and friendly place still uses a real wood fire to cook its tasty basic staples.

Kadıoğlu Şehzade Sofrası (☎ 712 5657; Arasta Sokak 8; mains TL6-9.50; ☯ 11.30am-10.30pm) Pide is the speciality here, served in as many different ways as the kitchen has ingredients; even the bread that accompanies the *çorba* (soup) is superb. Grills and *zerde* (saffron dessert) are also available.

Cinci Hanı (☎ 712 0680; Eski Çarşı Çeşme Mahalessi; mains TL10-15) If you can't afford to stay in the 17th-century caravanserai (above), you could eat in the courtyard (the dining room is not as pleasant). The menu features healthy selections of pide, grills and Western favourites. There is also a café-bar.

Havuzlu Köşk (☎ 725 2168; Dibekönü Caddesi 32, Bağlar; mains TL10-20; ☯ 1pm-1am) At this historic house in the hills you can dine at tables set around an upstairs pool or in a pleasant garden. The menu runs the gamut of Turkish standards: kebaps, grills, vegetarian meze and that time-honoured hangover cure, tripe soup.

Drinking

Meydan (Arasta Arkası Sokak; snacks TL2.50-6) This central hang-out is popular with young guys who sit outside playing backgammon. The menu features *gözleme* (savoury pancake), *çeşiterli* (Turkish pancake) and *çorba*, with English translations.

Arasta Lonca Kahvesi (Boncuk Café; Yemeniciler Arastası) This is one of the town's most congenial places for a coffee, but it's in the thick of the *arasta* action, so you pay for the atmosphere (çay TL2.50); head to the backstreets for a quieter, cheaper cuppa.

Arasna Pension (☎ 712 4170; Arasta Arkası Sokak 5, Çarşı) This pension below the main mosque and tourist office has a bar with regular live music. Its atmospheric stone walls are illuminated by electric candles.

Shopping

Safranbolu is a great place to pick up handicrafts – especially textiles, metalwork, shoes and wooden artefacts – whether locally made or shipped in from elsewhere to supply coach tourists. The restored Yemeniciler Arastası (Peasant Shoe-Makers' Bazaar) is the best place to start looking, although the makers of the light, flat-heeled shoes have long since moved out. The further you go from the *arasta* the more likely you are to come across shops occupied by authentic saddle-makers, feltmakers and other artisans.

Safranbolu derived its name from saffron, the precious spice used to flavour the local *lokum* (Turkish delight), and the town is so packed with sweet shops that you half expect the houses to be made out of gingerbread. One regional speciality is *yaprak helvası*, delicious chewy layers of white *helva* (halva) spotted with ground walnuts. Pick it up at the sweet shops on the north side of Çarşı's main square and at Safrantat outlets. You can also visit the Safrantat factory behind the petrol station in Kıranköy to see how *lokum* is made.

Getting There & Away

The coach companies generally lay on *servis* buses to transport passengers between Karabük, on the main highway, and Kıranköy, Safranbolu's new town. If your ticket only takes you to Karabük, you can catch a minibus straight to Çarşı (TL1.40), Safranbolu's old town, 10km away.

From İstanbul, Ulusoy (p159) and the less reliable İzmir Turizm, which both have offices in Taksim, have a couple of daily services to Safranbolu. The journey takes about seven hours and costs TL30. There are also daily services from Ankara's AŞTİ otogar.

There are several bus company offices along Sadrı Artunç Caddesi and just off Adnan Menderes Caddesi in Kıranköy, where you can buy tickets to destinations including Ankara (TL20, three hours), İstanbul (TL35, seven hours) and Kastamonu (TL11, two hours). You will probably be taken by *servis* bus to meet the coach at Karabük otogar.

Metro Doğuş (☎ 712 1966) and **Şavaş Turizm** (☎ 712 7480) each have five daily services to Bartın (TL10, 1½ hours), where you change for Amasra; start early in the day to make the onward connection. During summer, Şavaş Turizm has three direct daily services to Amasra (TL11, two hours).

Driving, exit the Ankara–İstanbul highway at Gerede and head north, following the signs for Karabük/Safranbolu.

There is a direct train from Karabük to Ankara, but the bus is a better option.

Getting Around

Every 30 minutes or so until 10pm, local buses (TL1) ply the route from Çarşı's main square over the hills past the main roundabout at Kıranköy and up to the Köyiçi stop in Bağlar. A taxi from Çarşı to Kiranköy will cost you TL7.

AROUND SAFRANBOLU
Yörük Köyü

Along the Kastamonu road, 15km east of Safranbolu, Yörük Köyü (Nomad Village) is a beautiful settlement of crumbling old houses once inhabited by the dervish Bektaşi sect (see p516). The government forced the nomads to settle here so it could tax them, and the villagers grew rich from their baking prowess.

Sipahioğlu Konağı Gezi Evi (admission TL4; ☉ 8.30am-sunset) is one of the village's enormous Ottoman houses. The builder's warring sons divided the mansion in two, and you tour the *selamlık* and *haremlik* separately. Look out for the incredible early central heating system that used the fire to heat running water and behind-the-wall heating; painted clocks showing the time the painters finished their job; and the top-floor gazebo with its stand for the owner's fez.

Nearby in Cemil İpekçi Sokağı is the 300-year-old *çamaşırhane* (laundry), with arched hearths where the water was heated in cauldrons. Taller women scrubbed at one end of the tilted stone table, shorter ones at the other; the dirty water drained to the centre. The table's 12 sides are a clue to the village's Bektaşi origins (like modern Shi'a Muslims, the Bektaşis believed in 12 imams, the last of whom had been hidden by Allah). Older women would sit at the edges sizing up the grandchildren-producing potential of their younger counterparts, whose bodies would be revealed by their wet clothes. Ask at Sipahioğlu Konağı Gezi Evi for the key.

SLEEPING & EATING
Tarihi Yörük Pansiyon (☎ 737 2153; s/d without bathroom TL30/60) A lovely old wood-and-stone house with an inviting garden. Accommodation is simple but comfortable, although there is just one squat toilet between the four rooms. In one room you sleep on the *sedir,* Ottoman-style.

Yörük Sofrası serves traditional Anatolian dishes, *ayran* (yoghurt drink), baklava and *gözleme* at indoor and outdoor tables. There's also a **kahvehane** (coffeehouse) near the mosque.

GETTING THERE & AWAY
There is no direct bus service from Safranbolu to Yörük Köyü, but there are a few dolmuşes a day to the nearby village of Konarı. If you ask the driver he may drop you at Yörük Köyü (TL1.50). Getting back, you'll have to walk the 1km to the main road and hitchhike (for information on hitchhiking, see p689).

It's much less hassle to go there from Safranbolu on a tour (see p458) or by taxi, which costs TL25 return.

Bulak Mencilis Mağarası
Deep in the Gürleyik hills 10km northwest of Safranbolu, this impressive cave network opened to the public a decade ago, although troglodytes may have lived here many millennia before that. You can walk through 400m of

the 6km-long network, enough to reveal a fine array of stalactites and stalagmites with inevitable anthropomorphic nicknames. There are steps up to the **cave** (adult/child TL4/2; 9am-7.30pm) and you should wear sturdy shoes as the metal walkway inside can be slippery and wet. A taxi from Safranbolu costs TL30 return.

İncekaya Aqueduct

Just over 7km north of Safranbolu you can visit this **aqueduct** (Su Kemeri), which was originally built in Byzantine times but restored in the 1790s by İzzet Mehmet Paşa (see p457). Its name means 'thin rock' and the walk across it, high above the beautiful **Tokatlı Gorge**, would not suit vertigo sufferers. A taxi from Safranbolu costs TL20 return, but the walk there is recommended, following the steep gorge through lovely, unspoilt countryside.

KASTAMONU

☎ 0366 / pop 80,600

A town where the shops are full of chainsaws and milking machines doesn't seem immediately promising, but Kastamonu makes a reasonable stopover between central Anatolia and the Black Sea. Potential distractions include two museums, a castle, some old mosques, Ottoman houses and, further afield, Kasaba's wooden mosque and Pınarbaşı's 37,000-hectare national park.

History

Kastamonu's history has been as chequered as that of most central-Turkish towns. Archaeological evidence suggests there was a settlement here as far back as 2000 BC, but the Hittites, Persians, Macedonians and Pontic (Black Sea) kings all left their mark. In the 11th century the Seljuks descended, then the Danişmends. The 13th-century Byzantine emperor John Comnenus tried to hold out here, but the Mongols soon swept in, followed by the Ottomans.

Bizarrely, Kastamonu's modern history is inextricably linked to headgear: Atatürk launched his hat reforms here in 1925, banning the fez due to its religious connotations and insisting on the adoption of European-style titfers.

Orientation & Information

Kastamonu's otogar is 7km north of the city centre, reachable by dolmuş or taxi (TL10). If you're coming in from Ankara get the bus to drop you in the centre near the old Nasrullah Köprüsü (Nasrullah Bridge).

The centre of town is Cumhuriyet Meydanı, with an imposing *valilik* (government building), a statue of Atatürk, the PTT and local bus stops. Another public square, Nasrullah Meydanı, lies to the north, on the other side of Cumhuriyet Caddesi.

Also to the north of Cumhuriyet Meydanı, most of the new hotels are clustered around Nasrullah Bridge. The bus companies' offices and, opposite, web café **Bil & Ken Net** (İzbeli Sokak; per hr TL1; 9am-11pm) are in the same area. Despite the signs, there's no tourist office.

Sights

MUSEUMS

About 50m south of Cumhuriyet Meydanı, the **Archaeology Museum** (☎ 214 1070; Cumhuriyet Caddesi; admission TL3; 8.30am-noon & 1-5pm Tue-Sun) has introductions to Atatürk's sartorial revolution and Anatolian archaeology, with predominantly Hellenic and Roman finds from the area.

Heading south of Nasrullah Meydanı on the main drag, turn right at the Akbank ATM to reach the excellent **Ethnography Museum** (☎ 214 0149; off Cumhuriyet Caddesi; admission TL3; 9am-5pm Tue-Sun). Occupying the restored 1870 Liva Paşa Konağı, it's fully furnished as it would have been in Ottoman times.

HISTORIC BUILDINGS

Kastamonu's **castle** (kale; admission free; 9am-5pm), built on a tall rock behind the town, is a steep 1km climb through the streets of the old town. Parts of the building date from Byzantine times, but most belong to Seljuk and Ottoman reconstructions. Follow the walls round and admire the views before descending the spiral stairs to the portcullis (you have to jump the last metre).

Nasrullah Meydanı centres on the Ottoman **Nasrullah Camii** (1506) and the double fountain where men wash their feet. Poet Mehmet Akif Ersoy delivered speeches in the mosque during the War of Independence. The former **Munire Medresesi** at the rear houses some craft shops. The area immediately west of Nasrullah Meydanı is filled with old market buildings, including the **Aşirefendi Hanı** and the 15th-century **İsmail Bey Hanı**. Wander down any of the side streets in this area and you'll come across hamams, fountains and other historic structures. Look out in particular for the gateway from the Seljuk mosque complex, **Yılanlı Külliye**.

Sleeping

Otel Kale (☎ 214 2416; Cumhuriyet Caddesi; s/d TL20/40) Kale's rooms are worn and bathrooms shared. Staff are friendly, but spend some extra lira elsewhere if you can afford it.

Otel İdrisoğlu (☎ 214 1757; Cumhuriyet Caddesi 21; s/tw/d TL40/45/50) Right on the main road, the İdrisoğlu is geared towards businesspeople rather than tourists, but is adequate for an overnighter.

Otel Mütevelli (☎ 212 2018; www.mutevelli.com.tr; Cumhuriyet Caddesi 10; s/d TL50/75) Kastamonu's best business hotel, near Cumhuriyet Meydanı, has drab but well-serviced rooms beyond its gaudy reception.

Osmanlı Sarayı (Ottoman Palace; ☎ 214 8408; www.osmanlisarayi.tr.cx; Belediye Caddesi 81; s/d TL60/80) Atatürk once visited this former town hall, built between 1898 and 1915. The beautifully restored rooms have wooden ceilings and authentic but newly fitted cupboard-bathrooms. There is a basic restaurant in the basement.

Toprakçılar Konakları (☎ 212 1812; www.toprakcilar.com; Alemdar Sokak 2; s/d/ste TL70/120/220) More restored Ottoman splendour, this time in two town houses across the road from İsfendiyarbey Parkı. The rooms have been faithfully restored and the courtyard restaurant (mains TL6 to TL10) sometimes hosts live music, when you'd be better off in the second building.

Eating & Drinking

Eflanili Konağı (☎ 214 1118; Gazipaşa İlköğr Yanı; mains TL5-8) This restaurant in a restored Ottoman house has beautiful upstairs dining rooms and tables among fountains in the courtyard. Staff will happily recommend local specialities.

Divan Pide (☎ 214 2424; Simsar Sokak 28a; mains TL6-7) This clean and welcoming fast-food restaurant behind Otel Kale is recommended for its meal deals and dishes such as *ezo gelin* (bulgur and red lentil soup).

Canoğlu (☎ 213 9090; Cumhuriyet Caddesi; ☱ 6am-8pm) Near Nasrullah Bridge, this *pastane* (patisserie) with floor-to-ceiling windows on its second level is Kastamonu's premier catch-up spot. Goodies such as pizzas and burgers are available.

The winding streets to the west of Nasrullah Meydanı are great for a wander and a çay.

There used to be a café in a beautiful building in Kastamonu's first Seljuk hamam (1262) on Nasrullah Meydanı, but it was for sale when we visited.

Getting There & Away

Kastamonu's otogar offers regular departures for Ankara (TL25, 4½ hours), İstanbul (TL40, nine hours) and Samsun (TL25, six hours). There are direct services to Sinop (TL20, three hours), but it may be quicker to change in Boyabat (TL10, two hours). There are hourly departures for Karabük (TL10, two hours), with some buses continuing to Safranbolu.

Minibuses for İnebolu (TL10, two hours) also leave from the otogar.

AROUND KASTAMONU
Kasaba

The tiny village of Kasaba, 17km northwest of Kastamonu, is a pretty but unlikely place to find one of Turkey's finest surviving wooden mosques. The minaret of **Mahmud Bey Camii** (1366) stands out from miles away. The restored interior has four painted wooden columns, a wooden gallery and fine painted ceiling rafters. You can climb some rough ladders to the third storey of the gallery and look at the ornate beam-ends and interlocking motifs topping the pillars.

A return taxi from Kastamonu, with waiting time, costs TL35, and the driver should know where the imam lives if the mosque is locked. A cheaper option is to take the Pınarbaşı bus and jump off at the Kasaba turn-off, but it is a 4km walk to the village from there and you will have to ask around for the imam if Mahmud Bey Camii is shut.

Pınarbaşı

Pınarbaşı, a little hill town 97km northwest of Kastamonu, is the main access point for the 37,000-hectare **Küre Dağları National Park** (Küre Dağları Milli Parkı; www.ked.org.tr/empty.html; ☎ 0366-771 2465), which was gazetted in 2000. Despite some marketing efforts made by the local government, the Küre Mountains are still largely undiscovered and you will likely have the park to yourself. With gouged cliff faces towering above forests, this is a great place for outdoor types who can take the time to explore under their own steam. Spots worth seeking out include the Ilgarini 'Inn' and Ilıca 'Hamam' caves, Ilıca waterfall and Horma Canyon. There is a spectacular viewpoint overlooking

CENTRAL ANATOLIA

THE HITTITES

While the name may evoke images of skin-clad barbarians, the Hittites were a sophisticated people who commanded a vast Middle Eastern empire, conquered Babylon and challenged the Egyptian pharaohs more than 3000 years ago. Apart from a few written references in the Bible and Babylonian tablets, there were few clues to their existence until 1834 when a French traveller, Charles Texier, stumbled on the ruins of the Hittite capital of Hattuşa.

In 1905 excavations turned up notable works of art, most of them now in Ankara's Museum of Anatolian Civilisations. Also brought to light were the Hittite state archives, written in cuneiform on thousands of clay tablets. From these tablets, historians and archaeologists were able to construct a history of the Hittite empire.

The original Indo-European Hittites swept into Anatolia around 2000 BC, conquering the local Hatti, from whom they borrowed their culture and name. They established themselves at Hattuşa, the Hatti capital, and in the course of a millennium enlarged and beautified the city. From about 1375 to 1200 BC Hattuşa was the capital of a Hittite empire that, at its height, shared Syria with Egypt and extended as far as Europe.

The Hittites worshipped over a thousand different deities; the most important were Teshub, the storm or weather god, and Hepatu, the sun goddess. The cuneiform tablets revealed a well-ordered society with more than 200 laws. The death sentence was prescribed for bestiality, while thieves got off more lightly provided they paid their victims compensation.

Although it defeated Egypt in 1298 BC, the empire declined in the following centuries, undone by internal squabbles and new threats such as the Greek 'sea peoples'. Hattuşa was torched and its inhabitants dispersed. Only the city states of Syria survived until they, too, were swallowed by the Assyrians.

Valla Canyon, but you will need local help to find it and a head for heights to climb the rusty steps to the platform.

On the way into Pınarbaşı is an uninformative **information centre** (☎ 0366-771 3375; www.pinar basim.com, in Turkish).

You can stay at a basic ecolodge in the park, near the Ilıca waterfall. The dinky five-person cabins and smarter four-person cabin at **Park Ilıca Turizm Tesisi** (☎ 0366-771 2046; www.parkilica.com; per person TL45) have single beds on two floors. With nearby thermal springs, the cabins make a great base for looking around the park.

There are a couple of midibuses a day from Kastamonu to Pınarbaşı, but you really need your own transport to move around the park. A taxi will take you there and spend the afternoon touring the park before returning to Kastamonu for €80.

BOĞAZKALE, HATTUŞA & YAZILIKAYA

Out in the centre of the Anatolian plains, two Unesco World Heritage sites evoke a vital historical moment at the height of Hittite civilisation (above). Hattuşa was the Hittite capital, while Yazılıkaya was a religious sanctuary with fine rock carvings.

The best base for visiting the sites around here is Boğazkale, a farming village 200km east of Ankara. Boğazkale has simple traveller services; if you want or need something fancier you'll need to stay in Çorum (p468) or, if you get going early enough in the morning, Ankara.

Boğazkale

☎ 0364 / pop 1600

The village of Boğazkale has ducks, cows and wheelbarrow-racing children wandering its cobbled streets, farmyards with Hittite and Byzantine gates, and a constant sense that a once-great city is just over the brow. Most visitors come solely to visit Hattuşa and Yazılıkaya, which can be accessed on foot if it's not too hot, but there is more to explore. Hattuşa is surrounded by **valleys** with Hittite caves, eagles' nests, butterflies and a neo-lithic fort. Head 4km east of Yazılıkaya and climb the **Yıldız Dağı** (Star Mountains), as they are known locally, to watch the sun set on the sites.

Late in the day, the silence is broken only by the occasional car kicking up dust on the main street, and the rural solitude may tempt you to stay an extra night. Apart from the accommodation options, the village's only facilities are some small shops, a post office and bank with an ATM.

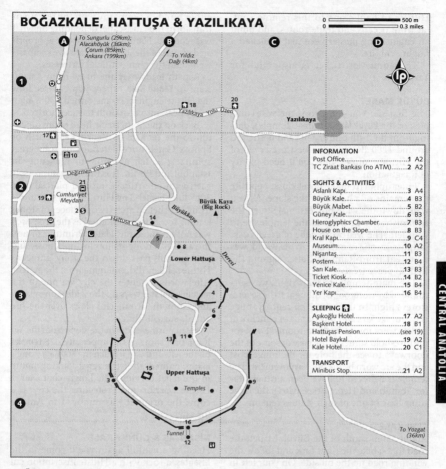

BOĞAZKALE, HATTUŞA & YAZILIKAYA

0 _____ 500 m
0 _____ 0.3 miles

To Sungurlu (29km);
Alacahöyük (36km);
Çorum (85km);
Ankara (199km)

To Yıldız
Dağı (4km)

Yazılıkaya Yolu Üzeri

Yazılıkaya

Degirmen Yolu SK

Cumhuriyet
Meydanı

Hattuşa Cad

Büyük Kaya
(Big Rock) ▲

Büyükkaya

Deresi

Lower Hattuşa

Upper Hattuşa

● Temples

Tunnel

To Yozgat
(36km)

INFORMATION	
Post Office.......................................**1** A2	
TC Ziraat Bankası (no ATM).........**2** A2	
SIGHTS & ACTIVITIES	
Aslanlı Kapı....................................**3** A4	
Büyük Kale.....................................**4** B3	
Büyük Mabet..................................**5** B2	
Güney Kale.....................................**6** B3	
Hieroglyphics Chamber...............**7** B3	
House on the Slope.......................**8** B3	
Kral Kapı..**9** C4	
Museum..**10** A2	
Nişantaş..**11** B3	
Postern..**12** B4	
Sarı Kale..**13** B3	
Ticket Kiosk..................................**14** B2	
Yenice Kale...................................**15** B4	
Yer Kapı..**16** B4	
SLEEPING 🏠	
Aşıkoğlu Hotel..............................**17** A2	
Başkent Hotel................................**18** B1	
Hattuşaş Pension.....................(see **19**)	
Hotel Baykal.................................**19** A2	
Kale Hotel.....................................**20** C1	
TRANSPORT	
Minibus Stop.................................**21** A2	

CENTRAL ANATOLIA

BOĞAZKALE MUSEUM

Unsurprisingly, Hittite artefacts dominate the small **museum** (admission TL3; ⏰ 8am-5pm, closed Mon afternoon). Its disappointing collection includes examples of cuneiform tablets (including a state treaty between kings), signature seals, whimsically shaped vessels, arrow and axe heads, and a series of weathered black-and-white photographic displays. If you look closely at the Turkish/German labels you'll find that some items are copies, the originals having been taken to Ankara.

Hattuşa

Hattuşa (adult/student TL4.50/free; ⏰ 9am-5pm) was the capital of an ancient kingdom that stretched from Syria to Europe, and squared up to the Egyptian, Babylonian and Assyrian empires. The mountainous, isolated site was a busy and impressive city, with 50,000 inhabitants, a 100-step pyramid and seven ponds that each stored enough water for 10,000 people. Its defences included stone walls over 6km in length, some of the thickest in the ancient world, with watchtowers and secret tunnels.

The best way to tour the atmospheric ruins is to get up early and walk the 5km circuit; before the 21st century intrudes in the form of coaches and souvenir sellers (better quality serpentine statues are available at the Yazılıkaya stands). As you climb out of the village to the site, an evocative reconstruction of a section of city wall comes into view. Imagine the sense of purpose that drove the

Hittites to haul stone to this remote spot, far from oceans and trade routes, and build an engineering masterpiece that launched a mighty empire.

The admission ticket is also valid for Yazılıkaya.

BÜYÜK MABET

The first site you come to is the vast complex of the **Büyük Mabet** (Great Temple), dating from the 14th century BC and destroyed around 1200 BC. It is the best preserved of the Hittite temples, but you'll need plenty of imagination.

Enter uphill from the ticket kiosk, opposite the remains of a house on the slope. As you walk down the wide processional street, the administrative quarters of the temple are to your left. The well-worn cube of green rock, supposedly one of only two in the world, was a present from Ramses II after signing the Kadesh peace treaty.

The main temple, to your right, was surrounded by storerooms, thought to be several storeys high. In the early 20th century, huge clay storage jars and thousands of cuneiform tablets were found in these rooms. Look for the threshold stones at the base of some of the doorways to see the hole for the hinge-post and the arc worn by the door's movement. The temple is believed to have been a ritual altar for Teshub and Hepatu (see p464); the large stone base of one of their statues remains.

SARI KALE

About 250m south of the Büyük Mabet, the road forks; take the right fork and follow the winding road up the hillside. On your left in the midst of the old city you can see several ruined structures fenced off from the road, including the **Sarı Kale** (Yellow Castle), which may be a Phrygian fort on Hittite foundations.

CASTLE WALLS & GATES

From the fork in the road it's about 750m uphill to the **Aslanlı Kapı** (Lion Gate), where two stone lions (one badly defaced) protect the city from evil spirits. This is one of at least six gates in the city's defensive walls, though it may never have been completed. You can see the best-preserved parts of the fortifications from here, stretching up the ridge southeast to Yer Kapı and from there to Kral Kapı. These 4000-year-old walls illustrate the Hittites' engineering ingenuity, which enabled them to

either build in sympathy with the terrain or transform the landscape, depending on what was required. Natural outcrops were appropriated as part of the walls, and massive ramparts were built to create artificial fortresses.

A path leads over the brow from Aslanlı Kapı to **Yenice Kale**, where you can see how the Hittite engineers transformed a 30m-high rocky peak into a smooth terraced fortress.

Back on the main track, head 600m downhill to the **Yer Kapı** or **Sfenksli Kapı** (Earth or Sphinx Gate), once defended by four great sphinxes, which are now in museums in İstanbul and Berlin. It is the most impressive gate, with an artificial mound pierced by a 70m-long **tunnel**. The Hittites built the tunnel using a corbelled arch (two flat faces of stones leaning towards one another) as the 'true' arch was not invented until later. Primitive or not, the arch has done its job for millennia, and you can still pass down the stony tunnel as Hittite soldiers did, emerging from the **postern**. Afterwards, re-enter the city via one of the **monumental stairways** up the wide stone glacis, and enjoy the wonderful views over the site and its surroundings.

Head northeast down the slope from the Yer Kapı, past some of the upper city's 28 **temples** on the left, and you'll reach the **Kral Kapı** (King's Gate), named after the regal-looking figure in the relief carving. The kingly character, a Hittite warrior god protecting the city, is a copy; the original was removed to Ankara for safekeeping.

NİŞANTAŞ & GÜNEY KALE

Heading downhill again you'll come to the **Nişantaş**, a rock with a Hittite inscription cut into it. The lengthy inscription dates to the time of Suppiluliuma II (1215–1200 BC), the final Hittite king, and narrates his deeds.

Immediately opposite, a path leads up to the excavated **Güney Kale** (Southern Fortress) and to what may have been a royal tomb, with a fine (fenced-off) **hieroglyphics chamber** with human figure reliefs.

BÜYÜK KALE

The ruins of the **Büyük Kale** (Great Fortress) are 200m downhill from the Nişantaş. Although most of the site has been excavated, many of the older layers of development have been re-covered to protect them, so what you see today can be hard to decipher. This fortress held the royal palace and the Hittite state archives. The archives, discovered in 1906, contained about 2500 pieces, including the Hittite-Egyptian Kadesh peace treaty, written in cuneiform on a clay tablet. Five such collections were unearthed at Hattuşa; one of the largest and oldest libraries ever discovered.

From the fortress it's about 1km back to the ticket kiosk.

Yazılıkaya

Yazılıkaya means 'Inscribed Rock', and that's exactly what you'll find in these outdoor **rock galleries**, just under 3km from Hattuşa. There are two galleries: the larger one, to the left, was the Hittite empire's holiest religious sanctuary; the narrower one, to the right, has the best-preserved carvings. Together they form the largest known Hittite rock sanctuary anywhere, sufficiently preserved to make you wish you could have seen the carvings when they were new.

In the larger gallery, Chamber A, the fast-fading reliefs show numerous goddesses and pointy-hatted gods marching in procession. Heads and feet are shown in profile but the torso is shown front on, a common feature of Hittite relief art. The lines of men and women lead to some large reliefs depicting a godly meeting. Teshub stands on two deified mountains (depicted as men) alongside his Hepatu, who is standing on the back of a panther. Behind her, their son and (possibly) two daughters are respectively carried by a smaller panther and a double-headed eagle. The largest relief, on the opposite wall, depicts the complex's bearded founder, King Tudhaliya IV, standing on two mountains. The rock ledges were probably used for offerings or sacrifices and the basins for libations.

On the way into Chamber B, you should supposedly ask permission of the winged, lion-headed guard depicted by the entrance before entering. The narrow gallery is thought to be a memorial chapel for Tudhaliya IV, dedicated by his son Suppiluliuma II. The large limestone block could have been the base of a statue of the king. Buried until a century ago and better protected from the elements, the carvings include a procession of 12 scimitar-wielding underworld gods. On the opposite wall, the detailed relief of Nergal depicts the underworld deity as a sword; the four lion heads on the handle (two pointing towards the blade, one to the left and the other to the right) double as the deity's knees

and shoulders. Nearby, Teshub's son Sarruma is shown with his arm protectively around Tudhaliya IV. The rock-cut ledges presumably held crematory urns.

Sleeping & Eating

The following generally offer camping for about TL5 to TL8 per site.

Hotel Baykal/Hattuşas Pension (☎ 452 2013; www.hattusha.com; Cumhuriyet Meydanı 22; pension s/d/tr TL15/25/35, hotel s/d/tr TL35/50/75). Behind its floor-to-ceiling downstairs windows, overlooking the square, this friendly establishment is dotted with artefacts, maps of Hattuşa, coffee-table books and a TV for Hittite documentaries. Entered via a tiled courtyard, the neat, compact hotel rooms have TVs and bar heaters. Ask to see a few as there is some difference between those on the ground floor and the second floor. The pension rooms are more basic affairs with a squat toilet. English and German are spoken. Main meals cost TL10.

Aşıkoğlu Hotel (☎ 452 2004; www.hattusas.com; Sungurlu Asfalt Caddesi; s/d/tr €20/40/50) Just walking around the Aşıkoğlu is educational: the modern rooms, which have bright bedspreads and all amenities, are named after Hittite figures, with potted biographies. There is a restaurant (mains TL10) with a terrace, patio and cinevision screen for documentaries, and an Ottoman-style café with a fireplace. In summer, the hotel often fills up with tour groups.

Başkent Hotel (☎ 452 2037; www.baskenthattusa.com; Yazılıkaya Yolu Üzeri 45; s/d/tr TL25/40/60; ☼ Apr-Oct) The rooms at Boğazkale's most basic option have narrow bathrooms but are decent enough. The long porch and upstairs balcony boast the best views of the four hotels, but the restaurant is unlikely to win any awards.

Kale Hotel (☎ 452 3126; www.bogazkoyhattusa.com; Yazılıkaya Yolu Üzeri; s/d/tr TL30/45/60; ☼ Apr-Oct) Kale's light, good-value rooms have cheery floral linen and bathrooms; the top ones at the front have good views and some have balconies. The restaurant, with its adjoining terrace, mostly caters to groups.

Getting There & Away

To get to Boğazkale by public transport, you'll need to go via Sungurlu. Many of the buses from Ankara to Sungurlu (TL12, three hours, hourly) are run by Mis Amasya (counter 23 at Ankara's otogar). Passengers are sometimes dropped off on the highway outside Sungurlu, but even if you are dropped at the otogar, the rapacious taxi drivers will be quick to deny the existence of any dolmuşes to Boğazkale. Make your way to the Boğazkale dolmuş stand, 1km from the otogar near the soccer stadium; buses may drop you there if you ask. There are more dolmuşes (TL3) in the morning, but they run until about 5.30pm. Taking a taxi may be your only resort at the weekend; don't pay more than TL30.

Travellers coming from Cappadocia should note that dolmuşes between Boğazkale and Yozgat, 41km southeast, are thin on the ground. You're probably better off going via Kırıkkale and Sungurlu.

Getting Around

To get around Hattuşa and Yazılıkaya without your own transport you'll need to walk or hire a taxi. It's 1km from the Aşıkoğlu Hotel to the Hattuşa ticket kiosk. From there the road looping around the site from the ticket kiosk (not including Yazılıkaya) is another 5km. The walk itself takes at least an hour, plus time spent exploring the ruins, so figure on spending a good three hours here. There is no shop on the site so take a bottle of water, and start early in the day before the sun is too hot, as there's little shade.

You could tour Hattuşa in a taxi or haggle for a day trip also taking in Yazılıkaya (just under 3km from both Hattuşa and Boğazkale) and Alacahöyük. As Alacahöyük is closer to the main highway, another option is to tour Hattuşa on foot and catch a taxi to the highway (where you can pick up dolmuşes in either direction) via Yazılıkaya and Alacahöyük; this can be accomplished in a day and costs about TL70. In all cases, negotiating a price should be cheaper than using the meter.

ALACAHÖYÜK

The tiny farming hamlet of Alacahöyük is 36km north of Boğazkale and 52km south of Çorum. It's a very old site, settled from about 4000 BC, but so little remains that it's really only worth the effort if you've got your own transport and have some time spare after Hattuşa. As at the other Hittite sites, movable monuments have been taken to the museum in Ankara, although there is a small museum and a few worn sphinxes at the entrance to the complex.

The **museum** (admission TL4; ⏰ 8am-noon & 1.30-5.30pm) is right by the ruins, displaying artists' impressions of the site at various points in its history and finds dating back to the chalcolithic and Old Bronze ages. A glass case shows the 15 layers of Alacahöyük's buried history, from 5500 to 600 BC.

At the ruins, the **monumental gate** has two eyeless sphinxes guarding the door. The detailed reliefs (copies, of course) show musicians, a sword swallower, animals for sacrifice and the Hittite king and queen – all part of festivities and ceremonies dedicated to Teshub, shown here as a bull. The extensive site also includes the foundations of a granary, up the wooden planks on the right, and of a temple, where some rocks have holes for sacrificial offerings. On the far left is an underground tunnel. Walk through it and look down at the fields to see how the site was built up over the millennia.

The clay-and-stone Hittite **dam** 1km east of the village, discovered in 2002, is one of 10 built in Anatolia during a drought as an offering to the sun goddess Hepatu. The mound and rock overlooking Alacahöyük are the remains of a **Phrygian castle**.

There's a small **café** at the museum entrance, perfect for a post-ruins drink or snack.

Getting There & Away

There's no public transport between Alacahöyük and Boğazkale. If you're really keen, you could take a bus or dolmuş from Çorum to Aloca and another from Aloca to Alacahöyük (one or two services per day, none at weekends). Taxis can take you from Boğazkale to Alacahöyük, wait for an hour and then run you to Aloca or the busy Sungurlu–Çorum highway.

ÇORUM

☎ 0364 / pop 178,500

Set on an alluvial plain on a branch of the Çorum River, Çorum is an unremarkable provincial capital, resting on its modest fame as the chickpea capital of Turkey. The town is full of *leblebiciler* (chickpea roasters) and sacks upon sacks of the chalky little pulses, all sorted according to fine distinctions obvious only to a chickpea dealer.

If you're travelling north or east from Boğazkale you may have to change buses in Çorum. Its museum is excellent preparation for Hattuşa and the other Hittite sites to the southeast, and the town can be a handy base for visiting them. It is a friendly place and offers some glimpses of provincial Turkish life.

Orientation & Information

The clock tower (1894) marks the centre of Çorum, with the PTT and *belediye* (town hall) close by. The otogar is 1km southwest of the clock tower along the main drag, İnönü Caddesi, where there are a few internet cafés and banks with ATMs, mostly at the northeast end.

Sights

On the far side of Anitta Otel from the otogar, the excellent **Çorum Museum** (admission TL3; ☺8am-noon & 1-7pm Tue-Sun) is well worth a visit before heading to Hattuşa et al. Major improvements were under way when we visited, but the exhibits on display traced Anatolian history from the Bronze Age to the Roman period. The centrepiece is a reconstruction of the royal tomb at Alacahöyük, with bull skulls and a crumpled skeleton clad in a crown, and there are some incredible artefacts such as a Hittite ceremonial jug with water-spouting bulls around its rim.

Sleeping & Eating

Atak Hotel (☎ 225 6500; hotelatak@hotmail.com; İnönü Caddesi 38; s/d/tr TL30/45/60) Between the otogar and the clock tower, Atak's rooms have bathrooms and are a reasonable choice for one night.

Hotel Sarıgül (☎ 224 2012; Azap Ahmet Sokak 18; s/d/tr TL45/60/70; 🖳) On a side street near the clock tower, this is a hotel befitting a provincial capital, with kitschy decor throughout the bar, basement disco, first-floor restaurant (mains TL7 to TL12), backgammon room and dingy internet area.

Anitta Otel (☎ 213 8515; www.anittahotel.com, in Turkish; İnönü Caddesi 80; s/d/tr TL70/120/160; 🕱 🖳) Çorum might be the place to splurge on a good hotel, as the city's grandest digs are good value for money, with prices including access to the swimming pool and hamam. Rooms have glass-fronted minibars, plasma TVs and profuse mirrors.

Katipler Konağı (☎ 224 9651; Karakeçili Mahallesi, 2 Sokak 20; mains TL6-11; ☺11am-9pm) This restaurant is spread across two floors of a restored Ottoman house. Highlights include the mulberry juice and filling local starters (TL3 to TL7) such as *çatal asi* (lentil and wheat soup) and *keşkek* (roasted wheat, chicken, red pepper and butter). To find it from Hotel Sarıgül, turn left, cross the road and turn right; turn right on to the side street behind the mosque, turn left and it's on the right.

Getting There & Away

Being on the main Ankara–Samsun highway, Çorum has good bus connections. Regular buses go to Alaca (TL4, 45 minutes), Amasya (TL7, two hours), Ankara (TL15, four hours), Kayseri (TL20, 4¾ hours), Samsun (TL15, three hours) and Sungurlu (TL5, 1¼ hours).

AMASYA

☎ 0358 / pop 74,400

Amasya is certainly not the only Turkish town to have realised the value of its Ottoman houses, but not even Safranbolu can rival its eastern counterpart's location. The half-timbered mansions line the Yeşilırmak River, their balconies bulging over the brown water and gazing across at the whippersnappers in the new town. There is as much to gawp at above Amasya's minarets and *medreses,* with Pontic tombs carved into the wrinkly cliff faces below the citadel's lofty perch. A tunnel worms between two of the tombs, looking like a Pontic log flume, and the valley feels like a fairy-tale Ottoman kingdom. Wandering a narrow valley where a succession of empires left their marks, the historical fantasies that fill your head are interrupted only when a train chugs between the old town and the castle rock.

History

Called Hakmış by the Hittites, the Amasya area has been inhabited continuously since around 5500 BC. Alexander the Great conquered Amasya in the 4th century BC, then it became the capital of a successor kingdom ruled by a family of Persian satraps (provincial governors). By the time of King Mithridates II (281 BC), the Kingdom of Pontus entered a golden age and dominated a large part of Anatolia from its HQ in Amasya.

During the latter part of Pontus' flowering, Amasya was the birthplace of Strabo (c 63 BC to AD 25), the world's first geographer. Having travelled in Europe, west Asia and North Africa, Strabo wrote 47 history and 17 geography books. Though most of his history books have been lost, we know something of their content because many other classical writers quoted him. He left an account of Amasya under Roman rule, which began here in 70 BC.

Amasya's golden age continued under the Romans, who named it a 'first city' and used it as an administrative centre for rulers such

AMASYA

INFORMATION	
Doğan Bilgisayar Internet Café....**1** D3	
Proposed Site of Tourist Office....**2** C3	
SIGHTS & ACTIVITIES	
Amasya Museum.........................**3** B4	
Atatürk Monument.....................**4** D3	
Baths of the Maidens Palace.......**5** C3	
Beyazıt Paşa Camii....................**6** D1	
Burmalı Minare Camii.................**7** C4	
Büyük Ağa Medresesi..................**8** D1	
Citadel......................................**9** B2	
Darüşşifa..................................**10** D3	
Gök Medrese Camii...................**11** A4	
Gümüşlü Camii..........................**12** D3	
Hazeranlar Konağı....................**13** C3	
Kumacık Hamamı.......................**14** D2	
Mehmet Paşa Camii...................**15** D2	
Mustafa Bey Hamamı................**16** D2	
Palace of the Maidens.............(see 19)	
Proposed Site of Ottoman Architecture	
Interpretive Centre.............(see 2)	
Sultan Beyazıt II Camii..............**17** B4	
Taş Han...................................**18** C4	
Tombs of Pontic Kings..............**19** C2	
Tombs of Pontic Kings Ticket	
Office..................................**20** C3	

Vakıf Bedesten Kapalı Çarşı........**21** C3	
Yıldız Hamamı.........................**22** B3	
SLEEPING	
Grand Pasha Hotel...................**23** C3	
Harşena Otel.............................**24** C3	
İlk Pansiyon..............................**25** D3	
Konfor Palas Hotel....................**26** C3	
Taha Hotel...............................**27** B3	
Şükrübey Konağı........................**28** B3	

EATING	
Amasya Şehir Kulübü......**29** C3	
Bahçeli Ocakbaşı.............**30** C3	
Subaşı Çay Bahçesi.........**31** C3	
Tea Gardens...................**32** D3	
Yimpaş Supermarket.......**33** D3	
DRINKING	
Tea Garden.....................**34** B3	

as Pompey. It was Julius Caesar's conquest of a local town that prompted his immortal words '*Veni, vidi, vici*' – 'I came, I saw, I conquered'. After Rome came the Byzantines, the Danışmend Turks, the Seljuks, the Mongols and the national republic of Abazhistan. In Ottoman times, Amasya was an important military base and testing ground for the sultans' heirs; it also became a centre of Islamic study, with as many as 18 *medreses* and 2000 theological students by the 19th century.

After WWI, Atatürk met his supporters here and hammered out the basic principles of the Turkish struggle for independence, which were published in the Amasya Circular. The monument in the main square commemorates the meeting and depicts the unhappy state of

Anatolian Turks before the revolution. Each year, Amasyalıs mark the revolutionary rendezvous with a week-long art and culture festival.

Orientation & Information

The otogar is at the northeastern edge of town and the train station at the northwestern edge. It's 2km from either to the main square, marked by the statue of Atatürk and a bridge across the river. The majority of everyday amenities are on the south bank of the river, but the north bank is the prettiest part of town, with the tombs of the Pontic kings, most of the Ottoman half-timbered houses and the castle. You may want to take a dolmuş or taxi to and from the otogar and train station; otherwise everything is within walking distance.

Despite the signs, there's no tourist office, but there are plans to open one near Hazeranlar Konağı. **Doğan Bilgisayar Internet Café** (Mustafa Kemal Bulvarı 10; per hr TL1; ☺ 7.30am-2am) is just north of the main square.

Sights & Activities

PONTIC TOMBS

Looming above the northern bank of the river is a sheer rock face with the conspicuous rock-cut **Tombs of the Pontic Kings** (Kral Kaya Mezarları; admission TL3; ☺ 9am-noon & 1-6.30pm). The tombs, cut deep into the limestone as early as the 4th century BC, were used for cult worship of the deified rulers. There are more than 20 (empty) tombs in the valley (nicknamed Kings' Valley).

Climb the steps from the souvenir stalls to the ticket office. Just past the office the path divides: turn left to find the **Baths of the Maidens Palace**, built in the 14th century and used until the 19th century, and, through a rock-hewn tunnel, a couple of tombs. Turn right to find more tombs and the remnants of the **Palace of the Maidens** (Kızlar Sarayı). In the cliff behind the terrace are several more tombs. You'll have to tackle an assault course of disintegrating rock-cut stairs and ledges to get to them, but the views over the town make the effort worthwhile. You can walk around the tombs to see how they have been cut away from the rock face, but beware of couples in dark corners!

Another Pontic tomb, the **Mirror Cave** (Aynalı Mağara), sits apart from the others, northeast of Amasya. One of the finest tombs, its name derives from the glaring effect produced by the sun on its pale facade. Although built during Pontic times, it's likely the cave was later used as a chapel by the Byzantines, who painted the fast-fading frescoes. With a Greek inscription high on the facade, this is one of the few tombs with any type of adornment.

The cave is 4km from the main square (TL10 return in a taxi). Follow the Yeşilırmak north and cross it on Künç Köprüsü, then look for the signpost on your right after a few hundred metres; Mirror Cave is 3km before Ziyaret.

CITADEL

Above the tombs is the *kale* (citadel) or Harşena castle, perched precariously atop rocky Mt Harşena and offering magnificent views down the valley. The remnants of the walls date from Pontic times, perhaps around King Mithridates' reign, but a fort stood here from the early Bronze Age. The castle was destroyed and repaired by several empires, including the Danışmend Turks. It had eight defensive layers, descending 300m to the Yeşilırmak, and a tunnel with 150 steps cut into the mountain. On a ledge just below the citadel is an old Russian cannon, fired during Ramazan to mark the end of the daily fast.

The castle is being renovated and is popular for a family day out, but travellers of either sex are advised not to go up unaccompanied later in the day. To reach the citadel, cross Künç Köprüsü and follow the Samsun road for about 1km to a street on the left marked 'Kale'. It's 1.7km up the mountainside to a small car park, then another steep 15-minute climb to the summit, marked by a flagpole.

AMASYA MUSEUM

Amasya's **museum** (☎ 218 4513; Atatürk Caddesi; admission TL3; ☺ 8.15am-noon & 1-4.45pm Tue-Sun) packs in Ottoman artefacts including vibrant banners, unwieldy manuscripts, and an armoury of flintlock guns, gunpowder flasks and inscribed daggers. Displays cover crafts such as rope-making, and wooden doors from Amasya's Gök Medrese Camii show the progression between Seljuk and Ottoman carving. The extensive collection also covers earlier periods; look out for the famous Statuette of Amasya, a bronze figure of the Hittite storm god Teshub, with conical hat and almond-shaped eyes.

Outside, a tiled Seljuk tomb in the garden contains a unique collection of mummies dating from the 14th-century İlkhan period. The bodies, mummified without removing the organs, were discovered beneath the Burmalı Minare Cami. None of it's for squeamish or young eyes, although, touchingly, one ruler is accompanied by his son, daughter and concubine.

HATUNIYE MAHALLESİ

Immediately north of the river, the Hatuniye Mahallesi is Amasya's wonderful neighbourhood of restored old Ottoman houses, interspersed with good modern reproductions to make a harmonious whole.

Just past the steps up to the Pontic Tombs is the **Hazeranlar Konağı** (admission TL3; ☺ 8.15am-noon & 1-4.45pm Tue-Sun), constructed in 1865 and restored in 1979. Hasan Talat, the

THE LEGEND OF FERHAT & ŞİRİN

Amasya is the setting for one of Turkey's best-loved folk tales, the tragic love story of Ferhat and Şirin.

In its simplest form, it's the Eastern equivalent of Romeo and Juliet. The young *nakıs* (wall painting) craftsman Ferhat falls in love with Şirin, the sister of sultan-queen Mehmene Banu, but the sultana disapproves of the match, so she demands that the young suitor carve a channel through the mountains to bring water to her drought-struck city. In the course of his Herculean labours, Ferhat hears that his beloved has died and kills himself in grief; Şirin, very much alive, finds his body and commits suicide in her turn. When they're buried together, tears flow from the graves and bring Amasya the water it so desperately needs.

Of course, as with all legends, there's no definitive telling of the story; all kinds of interpretations of the myth have been offered over the years, in print and on stage or screen. Celebrated playwright Nazım Hikmet offers a more complex reading, in which the lovers are undone by Ferhat's stubborn refusal to abandon his ill-fated project, turning it from a superhuman feat of love into an all-consuming act of pride and folly.

Elsewhere, you might come across the much-performed Karagöz puppet rendition, where the lovers achieve a happy ending by killing a wicked witch. Jale Karabekir's 2001 feminist stage version removes Ferhat entirely, defining him through absence in the fears and desires shaping the two sisters at the heart of the story.

Whichever reading you prefer, Amasya is the place to come to ponder the poignant lessons of the story amid the epic scenery that inspired it. A statue of the two lovers can be seen on the south bank of the river in town, and the Ferhat Su Kanalı, a late-Hellenic water channel, feeds the imagination perfectly. It runs through the Ferhatarası area alongside Atatürk Caddesi, beginning some 2km southwest of town.

accountant of governor-poet Ziya Paşa, built the mansion for his sister, Hazeran Hanım. The restored rooms are beautifully furnished in period style, with a refined feel to their chandeliers and carved wood, and have models to illustrate their use. The Directorate of Fine Arts gallery in the basement has changing exhibitions and there are plans to open an Ottoman architecture interpretive centre nearby.

HAMAMS

Amasya has several venerable hamams that are still in operation. Attached to Hatunıye Camii, the **Yıldız Hamamı** (Star Hamam; wash & massage TL13) was built by a Seljuk commander in the 13th century and restored in the 16th century. On the northern side of the Darüşşifa is the 1436 Ottoman **Mustafa Bey Hamamı** (wash & massage TL6), while not far away is the 1495 **Kumacık Hamamı** (wash & massage TL13). All are open from about 6am to 10am and 4pm to 11pm for men; from 10am to 4pm for women.

OTHER SIGHTS

You could spend a very pleasant couple of hours exploring Amasya's minor sights on both banks of the river. The advantage of the south bank is that you can see the scenic north bank from it, especially at night, when the castle and rock tombs are artily lit in neon. The bulk of Amasya's old religious buildings are also on this side of the river.

South of the River

At the northeastern end of the south bank, near Künç Köprüsü, is the **Beyazıt Paşa Camii** (1419). The early-Ottoman mosque follows a twin-domed plan that was a forebear in style to Bursa's famous Yeşil Cami.

Follow the river southwest and you'll come to the pretty **Mehmet Paşa Camii**, built in 1486 by Lala Mehmet Paşa, one of Sultan Beyazıt II's viziers (ministers). Don't miss the embroidered marble *mimber* (pulpit). The complex originally included the builder's tomb, an *imaret* (soup kitchen), *tabhane* (hospital), hamam and *handan* (inn).

Continue along the river and on the left you'll see the **Darüşşifa** (Mustafa Kemal Bulvarı; 1309) or Bimarhane. With its intricately carved portal, it was built as a mental hospital by Ilduş Hatun, wife of the İlkhanid Sultan Olcaytu, and may have been the first place to try to treat mental disorders with music. The İlkhans were the successors to Genghis Khan's

Mongols, who had defeated the Anatolian Seljuks. Their architecture reflects motifs borrowed from many conquered peoples, and the building is based on the plan of a Seljuk *medrese*. Today the building is often used for exhibitions, concerts and events.

A bit further along the river is Amasya's main square with its imposing memorial to the War of Independence. Perched on a rise to the east of the square, the boxy mosque with a wooden dome is the **Gümüşlü Cami** (Silvery Mosque; 1326). The town's earliest Ottoman mosque, it was rebuilt in 1491 after an earthquake, in 1612 after a fire, and again in 1688, then added to in 1903 and restored yet again in 1988.

If you keep walking west and head inland from the river you'll come to the 15th-century **Vakıf Bedesten Kapalı Çarşı** (Covered Market), still in use today. Keep heading west along Atatürk Caddesi and on the left you'll see the partly ruined **Taş Han** (1758), an Ottoman caravanserai. Behind it is the Seljuk **Burmalı Minare Camii** (Spiral Minaret Mosque). It was rebuilt in 1590 after an earthquake, and following a fire in 1602, when its wooden minaret was superseded by the current stone structure with elegant spiral carving.

Keep walking west and you'll come to the graceful **Sultan Beyazıt II Camii** (1486), Amasya's largest *külliye* (mosque complex), with a *medrese,* fountain, *imaret* and *muvakkithane* (astronomer's house). The mosque's main door, mihrab (niche indicating the direction of Mecca and pulpit are made of white marble and its windows feature *kündekari* (interlocking wooden carving).

Finally, you'll reach the 13th-century **Gök Medrese Camii** (Mosque of the Sky-Blue Seminary), built for Seljuk governor Seyfettin Torumtay. The *eyvan* (vaulted hall) serving as its main portal is unique in Anatolia, while the *kümbet* (domed tomb) was once covered in *gök* (sky-blue) tiles.

North of the River

Across Künç Köprüsü is the impressive **Büyük Ağa Medresesi** (1488). With an octagonal layout, rarely seen in Ottoman *medrese* architecture, it was built by Sultan Beyazıt II's chief white eunuch Hüseyin Ağa, or Grandagha. It still serves as a seminary for boys who are training to be *hafız* (theologians who have memorised the entire Quran) and is not open to the public.

Sleeping
BUDGET
Like Safranbolu, Amasya is one of those places where it's worth paying a bit more to stay in a real Ottoman house, but at least one budget option is far from terrible.

Taha Hotel (☎ 218 2675; Hazeranlar Sokak; s/d/tr TL25/50/75) This tidy hotel is friendly enough, though no English is spoken, and it offers a budget way to stay in the old town.

Konfor Palas Hotel (☎ 218 1260; www.konforpalas .com in Turkish; Ziyapaşa Bulvarı 2c; s/d/tr TL40/65/85) This enthusiastically titled hotel's rooms are comfortable enough if you overlook the stained carpets and minor design flaws. It has a central location, right next to the cafés; choose a back or side room to avoid ambient noise.

İlk Pansiyon (☎ 218 1689; ilkpansiyon@hotmail.com; Hitit Sokak 1; s/d/tr TL40/65/85) An oasis of history in Amasya's new town, this restored Ottoman mansion has authentic-feeling, characterful rooms. The airy, spacious salons have low-lying beds and simple bathrooms. The rickety box room off the leafy courtyard is fine in summer but draughty in winter.

MIDRANGE
Grand Pasha Hotel (☎ 212 4158; www.grandpashahotel .com; Tevfik Hafız Çıkmazı 5; s/d TL50/100) This hotel in a 140-year-old riverside mansion is one of the best deals in town, with bright white beds on colourful rugs. There are plenty of Ottoman quirks beneath the high ceilings and a tempting bar-restaurant in the green courtyard.

Şükrübey Konağı (☎ 212 6285; www.sukrubeykonagi .com.tr; Hazeranlar Sokak 55; s/d/tr TL55/100/150) Another good-value option, Şükrübey has pleasantly simple rooms with bathrooms and TVs perched on wooden stands or tables. The real highlight is the balconies with wooden stools and views of the tombs or the river below. The restaurant also has views across the Yeşilırmak and the friendly manager speaks good English.

Harşena Otel (☎ 218 3979; info@harsenaotel.com; PTT Karşısı; s/d/tr TL75/120/150; 🖂) Some choices are harder than others. Will you go for the smart but unexceptional modern building, or a mellow, yellow room in the creakingly authentic old house overhanging the river? Well, duh. In case you're undecided, there's a courtyard and café-bar-restaurant in the old part, too.

TOP END
Apple Palace Hotel (☎ 219 0019; www.applegrup.com; Vermiş Sokak 7; s/d/tr TL110/210/280; 🖂 🖵 🛜) On

the hillside south of the river, Amasya's four-star hotel overlooks the town and the Pontic tombs. The building is in need of a paintbrush in places, but the rooms are comfortable and there are spectacular views from the balconies. Facilities range from a billiards room to an outdoor pool, and buses shuttle up and down the hill.

Eating & Drinking

As well as the hotels listed above, there are a few reasonable cafés and restaurants in Hatuniye Mahallesi and a smattering of more basic options around town. Amasya is famed for its apples, which give autumn visitors one more thing to sink their teeth into.

Bahçeli Ocakbaşı (☎ 218 5692; Ziyapaşa Bulvarı; mains TL4-5) You can gaze up at the tombs from this café, one of half a dozen *lokantas* competing amiably for business in a lively, crowded courtyard.

Yimpaş Supermarket (☎ 212 7184; Ziyapaşa Bulvarı 16; mains TL6) More than just a place to buy groceries, the big new Yimpaş has a rooftop café for light meals and ravine views.

Amasya Şehir Kulübü (☎ 218 1013; mains TL10; ☽ 11am-11pm) Downstairs from the smarter Amasya Şehir Derneği, this restaurant is popular for its food and balconies, which overlook the river next to the Hükümet Köprüsü. The menu includes meze, pizza, pide, Tokat kebap and the onion-laden Izgara *köfte*, which is recommended unless you are a Ferhat trying to woo his Şirin (or visa versa).

Ali Kaya Restaurant (☎ 218 1505; Çakallar Mevkii; mains TL12; ☽ 12-11pm) The best time to visit this simple licensed restaurant above Amasya is at sunset, when you can recharge after the steep climb with meze while taking in views of town and the tombs. Taxis will ferry you up for TL8.

The riverside **Subaşı Çay Bahçesi** (Tevfik Hafız Çıkmazı), opposite the Grand Pasha Hotel, is a popular tea garden. Several pleasant tea gardens also line the Yeşilırmak around Belediye Parkı and Sultan Beyazıt II Camii.

Getting There & Away

Amasya is not far south of the busy Ankara–Samsun highway, so buses are frequent. You should be able to jump off buses when they pass through – or just to the northeast of – the town centre en route to the otogar. Leaving, some bus companies have ticket offices on the main square and they provide *servis* buses from there to the otogar.

A number of companies have daily services to locations including Ankara (TL30, five hours), Çorum (TL10, two hours), İstanbul (TL40, 10 hours), Kayseri (TL35, eight hours), Malatya (TL35, eight hours), Nevşehir (TL50, nine hours), Samsun (TL10, two hours), Sivas (TL25, 3½ hours) and Tokat (TL10, two hours).

To get to Safranbolu, the cheapest option is to take an early-morning minibus to Gerede, alight at the Karabük junction and flag down a bus to Safranbolu, probably via Karabük. It's a long day; travelling via Ankara is easier.

Amasya **train station** (☎ 218 1239; ☽ 4am-10pm) is served by daily trains between Samsun (4.53am and 2.09pm, three hours, TL6) and Sivas (11.27am, 5½ hours, TL11).

TOKAT

☎ 0356 / pop 128,000

Like Amasya, Tokat has a riverside location and mosques, mansions, hamams and *hans* built under various rulers, all overlooked by rocky promontories and an ancient fort. Unfortunately, it lacks Amasya's charm, but you can console yourself by tucking into a Tokat kebap, the succulent feast of lamb, aubergine, tomato, peppers and garlic. This is the best place in the world to try the dish; if you are a carnivore, you should be very excited.

The whole town is thought to have risen by up to 5m between the 13th and 20th centuries, as rain and floods washed silt and debris into the valley, but architectural treats such as Gök Medrese and Alı Paşa Hamam are thankfully above ground. It is worth spending a night here, to see the citadel disappearing into the dark sky above the illuminated dome of Ali Paşa Camii.

History

Tokat's history features an inevitable roll-call of Anatolian conquerors. The Hittites and Phrygians, the Medes and the Persians, the empire of Alexander the Great, the Kingdom of Pontus, the Romans, the Byzantines, the Danışmend Turks, the Seljuks and the Mongol İlkhanids all marched through here.

By the time of the Seljuk Sultanate of Rum, Tokat was Anatolia's sixth-largest city and on important trade routes; the approach roads are littered with Seljuk bridges and caravanserais. However, the Mongols and their subordinates the İlkhanids reversed the trend

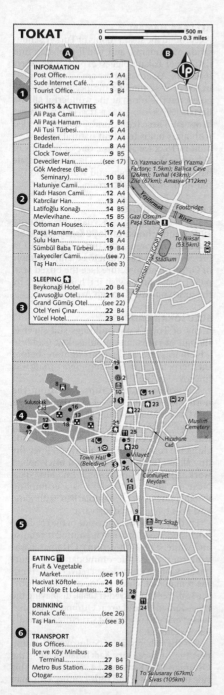

TOKAT

0 ____ 500 m
0 ____ 0.3 miles

INFORMATION
Post Office.....................1 A4
Sude Internet Café...........2 B4
Tourist Office..................3 B4

SIGHTS & ACTIVITIES
Ali Paşa Camii.................4 A4
Ali Paşa Hamam...............5 B4
Ali Tusi Türbesi................6 A4
Bedesten.......................7 A4
Citadel..........................8 A4
Clock Tower....................9 B5
Deveciler Hanı.............(see 17)
Gök Medrese (Blue
   Seminary)..................10 B4
Hatuniye Camii...............11 B4
Kadı Hason Camii...........12 A4
Katırcılar Han.................13 A4
Latifoğlu Konağı..............14 B5
Mevlevihane..................15 B5
Ottoman Houses.............16 A4
Paşa Hamamı................17 A4
Sulu Han......................18 A4
Sümbül Baba Türbesi........19 B4
Takyeciler Camii............(see 7)
Taş Han......................(see 3)

SLEEPING
Beykonağı Hotel.............20 B4
Çavuşoğlu Otel..............21 B4
Grand Gümüş Otel.......(see 22)
Otel Yeni Çınar..............22 B4
Yücel Hotel...................23 B4

EATING
Fruit & Vegetable
   Market......................(see 11)
Hacivat Köftole...............24 B6
Yeşil Köşe Et Lokantası.....25 B4

DRINKING
Konak Café..................(see 26)
Taş Han......................(see 3)

TRANSPORT
Bus Offices...................26 B4
İlçe ve Köy Minibus
   Terminal...................27 B4
Metro Bus Station...........28 B6
Otogar........................29 B2

To Yazmacılar Sitesi (Yazma Factory; 1.5km); Ballıca Cave (26km); Turhal (43km); Zile (67km); Amasya (112km)

Yeşilırmak River
Footbridge
Gazi Osman Paşa Statue
To Niksar (53.5km)
Gazi Osman Paşa (GOP) Bul
Stadium
Sulusokak Cad
Muslim Cemetery
Hızarhane Cad
Town Hall (Belediye)
Vilayet
Cumhuriyet Meydanı
Bey Sokağı
To Sulusaray (67km); Sivas (105km)

---

around the mid-13th century, leaving the city disinherited.

Only in 1402, under the Ottomans, did Tokat resume its role as an important trading entrepot, agricultural town and copper-mining centre. Gazi Osman Paşa even rose from a poor Tokat background to become one of the empire's greatest generals, and the main street here bears his name.

Significant non-Muslim populations (Armenian, Greek, Jewish) were in charge of Tokat's commerce until the cataclysm of WWI, and there's still a small but active Jewish community.

Orientation

The town centre is Cumhuriyet Meydanı, a large square where you'll find the *vilayet konağı* (provincial government headquarters), *belediye*, PTT and Ali Paşa Hamam. There is a cluster of ATMs around Çavusoğlu Otel nearby.

Looming above the town is a rocky outcrop crowned by the obligatory ancient fortress. Beneath it, many of the town's Seljuk and Ottoman relics dot the area around Sulusokak Caddesi, which used to be the main street.

The main street, Gazi Osman Paşa (universally abbreviated to GOP) Bulvarı, runs north from the main square past the Gök Medrese to a traffic roundabout. The otogar is 1.7km from Cumhuriyet Meydanı. Local minibuses leave from the İlçe ve Köy minibus terminal a few blocks east of GOP Bulvarı; across the canal from Hatuniye Camii and the fruit and vegetable market.

Information

Sude Internet Café (Yazıcık Sokak 4; per hr TL1; ◷ 8am-11pm)

Tourist office (☎ 211 8252; Taş Han, GOP Bulvarı 138/I; ◷ 8am-5pm) An informative Tokat brochure is available and an English-speaking Fenerbahçe fan may be on hand to help out.

Sights & Activities
GÖK MEDRESE
Constructed by Pervane Muhinedin Süleyman, a local potentate, after the fall of the Seljuks and the coming of the Mongols, the 13th-century **Gök Medrese** (Blue Seminary; GOP Bulvarı; admission TL3; ◷ 8am-noon & 1-5pm Tue-Sun) has also served as a hospital, a school and, today, Tokat's museum.

Very few of the building's *gök* (sky-blue) tiles are left on the facade, but there are enough on the interior courtyard walls to give an idea of what it must have looked like in its glory days.

Although the courtyard is the highlight of the museum, the collection packs in Roman tombs, Seljuk carpets, Hellenic jewellery and local folkloric dresses, with informative signs in English. Look out for Bronze Age and Hittite artefacts, icons and relics from Tokat's churches (including a Greek Orthodox representation of John the Baptist with his head on a platter) and dervish ceremonial tools and weapons (fancy a 'mystic awl' or 'stones of submission'?). An ethnographic section on costume and textiles explains the local art of *yazma* (headscarf) making.

The seminary contains the **Tomb of 40 Maidens** (Kırkkızlar Türbesi; 1275), actually an assembly of 20 tombs, possibly of the seminary's founders, though another theory has it that they are the tombs of 40 nurses who worked here.

The grounds also contain Ottoman and Seljuk tombstones and some statues, including one of an unnamed 19th-century chaplain of the East India Company, 'known as a man of god'.

TAŞ HAN & AROUND

Virtually next door to the Gök Medrese is the 17th-century **Taş Han** (GOP Bulvarı; 8am-8pm), an Ottoman caravanserai and workshop with a café in the courtyard. Two floors of shops sell a mixture of local garb and copperware, and paintings of sailboats and doe-eyed puppies.

Behind the Taş Han are streets lined with old half-timbered **Ottoman houses**. There are more shops in this area; some of the designs you see on *yazmas*, kilims and carpets were assimilated from Afghan refugees who settled here during the Soviet invasion of Afghanistan in the 1980s.

In the fruit and vegetable market, across GOP Bulvarı from the Taş Han, stand the **Hatuniye Camii** and ruined *medrese*, dating from 1485 and the reign of Sultan Beyazıt II.

A few hundred metres north of the Taş Han, behind some plastic sandal stands on the same side of the street, look out for **Sümbül Baba Türbesi** (1291), an octagonal Seljuk tomb. Beside it a road leads up around 1km to the **citadel**, built in the 5th century and restored during the Seljuk and Ottoman eras. Little remains but the fine view, and women travellers should not go up alone.

ALİ PAŞA HAMAM

Ask around the steam rooms of Turkey's thousands of hamams, and you'll probably find that one of Tokat's biggest exports is its expert masseurs. Assuming there are actually any left in town, it seems like the perfect excuse to go for a scrub'n'rub at the wonderful **Ali Paşa Hamam** (GOP Bulvarı; 5am-11pm for men, 9am-5pm for women). These baths, under domes studded with glass bulbs to admit natural light, were built in 1572 for Ali Paşa, one of the sons of Süleyman the Magnificent. They have separate bathing areas for men and women, and the full works should cost around TL15.

LATİFOĞLU KONAĞI

South of Cumhuriyet Meydanı, the splendid 19th-century house **Latifoğlu Konağı** (GOP Bulvarı) was being restored at the time of research. On previous visits we found it to be a fine example of Ottoman architecture (see the boxed text, p458), well worth a visit if it has reopened by the time you pass through Amasya.

SULUSOKAK CADDESİ

Many of Tokat's old buildings still survive, though in ruins, along Sulusokak Caddesi, which was the main thoroughfare before the perpendicular Samsun–Sivas road was improved in the 1960s.

Sulusokak Caddesi runs west from the north side of Cumhuriyet Meydanı, past **Ali Paşa Camii**, which was built at the same time as the nearby hamam and has classical Ottoman features on its grand central dome. Continue along the road and on the right you'll see the tiny **Ali Tusi Türbesi** (631–1233), a brick Seljuk work that incorporates some fine blue tiles. Next up, also on the right, is a crumbling wooden caravanserai, **Katırcılar Han**, with some vast pots lying in its courtyard.

Further on, on the same side of the road, the brick-and-wood **Sulu Han** is painted turquoise and white. The 17th-century Ottoman caravanserai provided accommodation for merchants visiting the *bedesten* (covered market), the remains of which are next door. Nearby, the 16th-century **Takyeciler Camii**, displaying the nine-domed style of great Ottoman mosques, is as at one end of a line of structures currently being restored.

On the other side of Sulusokak Caddesi, past the 14th-century **Kadı Hasan Camii**, is the Ottoman **Paşa Hamamı** (1434). Also on this side of the street is the 16th-century Ottoman

Deveciler Hanı, one of Tokat's finest caravanserais. The two-storey structure had a covered barn and a residential section with a porch and a courtyard.

OTHER SIGHTS

To the south of the centre don't miss the 19th-century **clock tower** with the numerals on its faces still in Arabic, and a watch-repair shop (what else?) at the bottom.

Just across the canal, among Ottoman houses and cobbled lanes, is the **Mevlevihane** (Bey Sokağı; ☼ 9am-6pm), a 19th-century building built as a dervish lodge and dancing hall, before serving as a women's prison in the 20th century. The exhibits include carpets and prayer rugs, Ottoman perfume bottles and candlesticks, and Qurans from down the centuries. However, the real action is upstairs, where the mechanical whirring dervishes are made slightly less laughable by the explanatory displays. With its reddish wood exterior, the house itself is stunning.

Sleeping

Yücel Hotel (☎ 212 5235; Çekenli Caddesi 20; s/d/tr TL35/70/105; ▯ ▭) Still cheap, but with some major plusses – the fifth-floor restaurant and the hamam (included in the price). Rooms have minibars, TVs and cheap furniture, and there's a digital TV and internet area in the lobby. Prices can be haggled down.

Çavuşoğlu Otel (☎ 213 0908; GOP Bulvarı 168; s/d/tr TL45/65/80) This smart, central bargain has pistachio bathrooms, TVs, hairdryers and a breakfast buffet.

Otel Yeni Çınar (☎ 214 0066; GOP Bulvarı 167; s/d/tr TL45/70/90) A good range of rooms with nice bathrooms and vistas over the hills from the back. The first-floor restaurant does a good line in grills, including one of the best Tokat kebaps in town (TL12.50).

Grand Gümüş Otel (☎ 214 1331; GOP Bulvarı; s/d/tr TL45/70/115; ▨) Virtually opposite the Taş

Han, this good-value option offers comfortable rooms with stripy duvets and excellent facilities, including minibars and TVs. The bar-restaurant has violet tablecloths and a series of meal deals (TL5 to TL10).

Beykonaği Hotel (☎ 214 3399; www.otelbeykonagi.com; Cumhuriyet Meydanı; s/d TL55/85; ▨) A relative newcomer, this 40-room three-star curries favour with compact but smart rooms in light shades and orchid art, plus bar and restaurant.

Eating & Drinking

Kebaps and *köfte* are the usual fare here, with eateries clustered around the fruit and vegetable market near the Hatuniye Camii. More upmarket restaurants and *pastanes* are found around Cumhuriyet Meydanı.

Hacivat Köftole (☎ 212 9418; GOP Bulvarı 275; set menus TL4-5; ☼ 9am-11pm) Opposite the Metro bus office, Hacivat is popular with a young crowd. Magazine cuttings and photos decorate the stone walls, allowing you to swot up on modern Turkish culture as you wait for one of the top-value daily set menus.

Yeşil Köşe Et Lokantası (GOP Bulvarı 1; mains TL5-6; ☼ 6.30am-10pm) This takeaway joint and café, popular at lunchtime for kebaps, moussaka and *çorba*, is one of the best places in town to try a Tokat kebap (TL12). There is quieter seating upstairs.

Konak Café (☎ 214 4146; GOP Bulvarı; ☼ 9am-11pm) At the rear of a restored Ottoman building, this friendly café has multilevel outdoor seating.

Taş Han (GOP Bulvarı) The café in the caravanserai's courtyard is a popular spot for a nargileh, although we can't recommend the cappuccino.

Shopping

At one time Tokat had a monopoly on the right to make *yazmas*, the richly colourful

---

AUBERGINE DREAM

The Tokat kebap is made up of skewers of lamb and sliced eggplant (aubergine) hung vertically, then baked in a wood-fired oven. Tomatoes and peppers, which take less time to cook, are baked on separate skewers. As the lamb cooks, it releases juices that baste the aubergine. All these goodies are then served together with a huge fist of roasted garlic, adding an extra punch to the mix.

It's almost worth coming to Tokat just to sample the dish, and in fact you might have to; it's inexplicably failed to catch on in menus much further afield than Sivas or Amasya, and Tokat's chefs do it best anyway. Standard aubergine döners that crop up are a far cry from the glorious blow-out of the original.

block-printed headscarves traditionally worn by many Turkish women, and it's still a good place to buy souvenir scarves or printed tablecloths. For years the Gazioğlu Han (block-printers' *han*) near the Gök Medrese was the centre of the trade. However, these days the materials are prepared in a modern **factory** (Yazmacılar Sitesi; Rodi Halısaha), opposite the Küçük Sanayi Sitesi 4km northwest of the town centre; you can visit to see the cloths being made.

Getting There & Away

Tokat's small otogar is about 1.7km northeast of the main square. Bus companies should provide a *servis* to ferry you to/from town; otherwise, if you don't want to wait for a dolmuş, a taxi will cost about TL10. A ride across town in one of the dolmuşes that regularly trundle along GOP Bulvarı costs about TL0.70.

The otogar is not as busy as some, especially in the morning (there are, for example, fewer buses to Sivas than you might expect), so it's a good idea to book ongoing tickets well ahead, especially on Friday. Several bus companies have ticket offices around Cumhuriyet Meydanı.

There are regular buses to Amasya (TL10, two hours), Ankara (TL30, 6½ hours), Erzurum (TL40, 8½ hours), İstanbul (TL50, 12 hours), Samsun (TL20, four hours) and Sivas (TL12, 1¾ hours).

Local minibuses leave from the separate İlçe ve Köy terminal.

AROUND TOKAT
Ballıca Cave

The **Ballıca Cave** (Ballıca Mağarası; ☎ 0356-261 4236; adult/child TL4/2; ☉ daylight hr), 26km west of Tokat, is one of Turkey's most famous caves. The limestone labyrinth, 3.4 million years old and 8km long (680m is open to the public), bristles with rock formations such as onion-shaped stalactites and mushroom-like stalagmites. Smugglers used to live here and the squeaks of the current residents, dwarf bats, add to the atmosphere created by dripping water.

Unfortunately, the ambience is quickly lost if you share the metal walkways with many others. With its copious lighting and signposts, the cave can feel like an underground theme park; exploring Safranbolu's less-visited Bulak Mencilis Mağarası (p461) is more rewarding.

There are a lot of steps both inside and outside the cave, although many schoolchildren manage it without snapping their pencils. The views from the café at the entrance are stunning, but its toilets are not the cleanest in Anatolia.

Returning, pause in Pazar to inspect the beautiful remains of a Seljuk *han* on the way out of town on the Tokat road. You can wait outside it for minibuses to Tokat.

GETTING THERE & AWAY

To get to Ballıca, take a minibus from Tokat's İlçe ve Köy minibus terminal to Pazar (TL2.50, 40 minutes), where a taxi will be waiting to run you up the winding country road to the cave (8km). Drivers exploit their captive audience and you may have to pay as much as TL20 return (including an hour's waiting time). If you are driving from Amasya, Pazar is signposted 14km south of the main road to Tokat.

SİVAS
☎ 0346 / pop 294,000

Sivas lies at the heart of Turkey politically as well as geographically, thanks to its role in the run-up to the War of Independence. The Congress building resounded with plans, strategies and principles as Atatürk and his adherents discussed their great goal of liberation. The Turkish hero commented: 'Here is where we laid the foundations of our republic'.

The city was a sometime capital under the Seljuks and the centre of the Ottomans' vast province of Rum. They were just two of the empires that left stately piles in and around the park near Hükümet Meydanı. At night, as the red flags on the *meydanı* compete for attention with the spotlit minarets nearby, İnönü Bulvarı might be Central Anatolia's slickest thoroughfare outside Ankara. The occasional horse and cart gallops down the boulevard, past the plasma screens, clothes emporiums and neon, like a ghost of Anatolia past.

With a colourful, sometimes tragic history and some of the finest Seljuk buildings ever erected, Sivas is a good stopover en route to the wild east and the best base for visiting the diverse attractions to the southeast.

History

The tumulus at nearby Maltepe shows evidence of settlement as early as 2600 BC, but

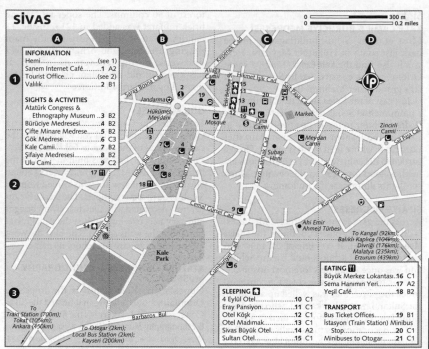

SİVAS

INFORMATION
Hemi............................(see 1)
Sanem Internet Café........**1** A2
Tourist Office...............(see 2)
Valılık............................**2** B1

SIGHTS & ACTIVITIES
Atatürk Congress &
  Ethnography Museum ..**3** B2
Bürüciye Medresesi.........**4** B2
Çifte Minare Medrese......**5** B2
Gök Medrese..................**6** C3
Kale Camii....................**7** B2
Şifaiye Medresesi.............**8** B2
Ulu Cami......................**9** C2

SLEEPING
4 Eylül Otel....................**10** C1
Eray Pansiyon.................**11** C1
Otel Köşk **12** C1
Otel Madımak.................**13** C1
Sivas Büyük Otel.............**14** A2
Sultan Otel....................**15** C1

EATING
Büyük Merkez Lokantası..**16** C1
Sema Hanımın Yeri.........**17** A2
Yeşil Café.....................**18** B2

TRANSPORT
Bus Ticket Offices...........**19** B1
İstasyon (Train Station) Minibus
  Stop.........................**20** C1
Minibuses to Otogar.......**21** C1

CENTRAL ANATOLIA

Sivas itself was probably founded by the Hittite king Hattushilish I in around 1500 BC. It was ruled in turn by the Assyrians, Medes and Persians, before coming under the sway of the kings of Cappadocia and Pontus. Eventually the city fell to the Romans, who called it Megalopolis; this was later changed to Sebastea, then shortened to Sivas by the Turks.

Byzantine rule lasted from AD 395 to 1075, when the city was seized by the Danişmend emirs. The Seljuks and the Danişmends slogged it out for supremacy between 1152 and 1175 until the Seljuks finally prevailed, only to be dispossessed by the Mongol invasion of 1243. The İlkhanids succeeded the Mongols, and the city was then grabbed by the Ottomans (1398), Tamerlane (1400) and the Ottomans again (1408).

More recently Sivas was the location for the famous Sivas Congress in September 1919. Seeking to consolidate Turkish resistance to the Allied occupation and partition of his country, Atatürk arrived here from Samsun and Amasya, and gathered delegates to confirm decisions made at the Erzurum Congress. The two congresses heralded the War of Independence.

Orientation

The centre of town is Hükümet Meydanı (or Konak Meydanı), just in front of the attractive *valilik* (government building). The main sights, hotels and restaurants are all within walking distance.

The train station, Sivas Garı, is about 1.5km southwest of Hükümet Meydanı along İnönü Bulvarı/İstasyon Caddesi. The otogar and local bus station are 2km south of the centre. Bus offices and banks with ATMs are just east of Hükümet Meydanı, along Atatürk Caddesi.

Information

Hemi (☎ 0506-273 4662; Tekel Sokak) This local sports association, which has English-speaking members, can give advice about local skiing, scuba diving, rafting, canoeing, climbing and paragliding; the latter is popular on the hills above the city's university.

Sanem Internet Café (Tekel Sokak; per hr TL1; ✹ 8.30am-midnight)

Tourist office (☎ 222 2252; ✹ 9am-5pm Mon-Fri) In the European Union office on the first floor of the *valilik*; the helpful representatives give out brochures.

Sights

KALE CAMİİ & BÜRÜCİYE MEDRESESİ

Most of Sivas' Seljuk buildings are in the park just south of Hükümet Meydanı. Here you'll also find the **Kale Camii** (1580), a squat Ottoman work constructed by Sultan Murat III's grand vizier Mahmut Paşa.

Just east of the Kale Camii, reached through a monumental Seljuk gateway, is the **Bürüciye Medresesi**, built to teach 'positive sciences' in 1271 by the Iranian businessman Muzaffer Bürücerdi, whose tiled tomb is inside. The tea garden in the courtyard, where exhibitions are held, is good for a çay in the evening, when spotlights illuminate the building.

ŞİFAİYE MEDRESESİ

Across the park from the Bürüciye Medresesi is one of the city's oldest buildings, the **Şifaiye Medresesi** (1218). It was one of the most important medical schools built by the Seljuks and was once Anatolia's foremost hospital.

Look to the right as you enter the courtyard to see the porch that was walled up as a tomb for Sultan İzzettin Keykavus I, who commissioned the building before he died of TB.

The decoration features stylised sun/lion and moon/bull motifs, beautiful blue Azeri tile work and a poem in Arabic, composed by the sultan. The main courtyard has four *eyvans*, with sun and moon symbols on either side of the eastern one.

ÇİFTE MİNARE MEDRESE

Commissioned by the Mongol-İlkhanid vizier Şemsettin Güveyni after defeating the Seljuks at the battle of Kösedağ, the **Çifte Minare Medrese** (Seminary of the Twin Minarets; 1271) has a *çifte* (pair) of mighty minarets. In fact, that's about all that is left, along with the elaborate portal and facade. Stand on the path between the Çifte and Şifaiye *medreses* to see the difference made by half a century and a shift in power.

ULU CAMİ

The town's other sights are southeast of Hükümet Meydanı along Cemal Gürsel and Cumhuriyet Caddesi; walk just past the southern end of the park and turn left onto Cemal Gürsel Caddesi.

The **Ulu Cami** (Great Mosque; 1197) is Sivas' oldest significant building, and one of Anatolia's oldest mosques. Built by the Danışmends, it's a large, low room with a forest of 50 columns. The super-fat leaning brick minaret was added in 1213. Inside, 11 handmade stone bands surround the main praying area and the ornate *mihrab* was discovered during renovations in 1955. It has a certain old-Anatolian charm, slightly marred by modern additions.

GÖK MEDRESE

From the Ulu Cami, turn right (south) on Cumhuriyet Caddesi and you will soon see the twin minarets of the glorious **Gök Medrese** (Sky-Blue Seminary). This was built in 1271 at the behest of Sahib-i Ata, the grand vizier of Sultan Gıyasettin Keyhüsrev III, who funded Konya's Sahib-i Ata mosque complex. The facade is exuberantly decorated with tiles, brickwork designs and carving, covering not just the usual inlaid portal but the walls as well. The blue tile work on the minarets gave the school its name.

ATATÜRK CONGRESS & ETHNOGRAPHY MUSEUM

Opposite the Kale Camii is the imposing Ottoman school building that hosted the Sivas Congress in 1919. Today it's the **Atatürk Congress & Ethnography Museum** (Atatürk Kongre ve Etnografya Müzesi; İnönü Bulvarı; admission TL3; ⏰ 8.30am-noon & 1.30-5pm Tue-Sun), entered around the back.

The extensive Ottoman ethnographical collection, displayed on the ground floor, features a fine selection of kilims and carpets, including some impressive examples showing local weaving style; a pillowcase-making demonstrating (another local craft), a 12th-century wooden *mimber* from Divriği's Ulu Cami (see p483); and dervish ceremonial beads, weapons and mystics' caps.

Upstairs, the Congress Hall is preserved as it was when the Sivas Congress met, with photos of the delegates displayed on old school desks. You can see Atatürk's bedroom and the cable room that played an important role in developments, with replicas of missives laying out the principles of the Turkish Republic. The hallway is lined with pictures of Atatürk and his cohorts and a photocopy of his passport.

Sleeping

Most hotels are within a few minutes' walk of the junction of Atatürk Caddesi and Eski Belediye Sokak.

Eray Pansiyon (☎ 223 1647; Eski Belediye Sokak 12; www.eraypansiyon.com; dm per person TL20) German is spoken at this friendly pension, where smart marble stairs and sturdy brown doors lead to clean six-bed dorms.

Otel Madımak (☎ 221 8027; Eski Belediye Sokak 2; s/d/tr TL60/90/115) This rebuilt 1st-floor hotel has comfortable digs with a burgundy theme, right down to the chairs and tiled bathrooms. Be aware, however, that the name has sad resonances (see boxed text, below).

4 Eylül Otel (☎ 222 3799; www.dorteylulotel.com; Atatürk Caddesi 15; s/d/tr TL70/120/150; 🖳) The discreet entrance next to the Akbank ATM sets the tone for this low-key hotel, where rooms have dark wood, minibars concealed in tables and paintings of Ottoman mansions. There is a rooftop restaurant and the popular hotel offers a similar experience to the Sultan for less money. Breakfast is TL17.50.

Sultan Otel (☎ 221 2986; www.sultanotel.com.tr; Eski Belediye Sokak 18; s/d/tr TL90/140/170) The perfect mix of quality and price, with ample extras including a roof bar-restaurant with live music, safes built into the TV cabinets, extensive breakfast buffets and free hot drinks. Oh, and the bathrooms are virtually as big as the rooms themselves. Popular with business travellers midweek.

Sivas Büyük Otel (☎ 225 4763; www.sivasbuyukotel .com; İstasyon Caddesi; s/d/tr TL120/190/225; 🖳) Plain corridors and stately rooms characterise the city's original luxury hotel, a chunky seven-storey block laced with marble and mosaics. Refreshingly, one thing it's not short on is space. Breakfast is TL15.

Otel Köşk (☎ 225 1724; www.koskotel.com; Atatürk Caddesi 7; s/d/tr TL130/180/220; 🖳) You can't get

much more modern than this towering glass block. From the fire-engine-red seats in reception to the laminate floors, glass washbasins and curvy showers in the rooms, slick design rules. Even the views of the dive bar across Atatürk Caddesi manage to be cool thanks to the neon Efes sign.

Eating

On summer evenings everyone promenades along İnönü Bulvarı and Atatürk Caddesi, where stalls sell everything from *gözleme* to corn on the cob. There is a fruit and vegetable market around Subaşı Hanı.

our pick **Sema Hanımın Yeri** (☎ 223 9496; İstasyon Caddesi Öncü Market; mains TL2.50-5; 🕐 8am-midnight) In this rustic, wood-panelled restaurant, the welcoming Madame Sema serves home-cooked food such as *içli köfte* (meatballs stuffed with spices and nuts). Watch *gözleme* being made while trying three dishes for TL3.

Yeşil Café (☎ 222 2638; Selçuklu Sokak; mains TL4-8; 🕐 7.30am-11pm) This friendly café-restaurant might not look like much, but the tiny balcony upstairs has amazing views of spotlit twin minarets. What's more, the menu's enough to distract you from them, with schnitzel, grills, spaghetti, macaroni and milkshakes.

Büyük Merkez Lokantası (☎ 223 6434; Atatürk Caddesi 13; mains TL7; 🕐 4am-midnight) This *lokanta* is popular at lunchtime, when you may find yourself sharing a table with an office clerk. The menu includes döners and the house speciality *sebzeli Sivas kebapı* (TL14.50), a local take on the Tokat kebap.

MADIMAK MEMORIAL

The original Madımak Hotel was the site of one of modern Turkey's worst hate crimes, on 2 July 1993, when 37 Alevi intellectuals and artists were burned alive in a mob arson attack. The victims, who had come for a cultural festival, included Aziz Nesin, the Turkish publisher of Salman Rushdie's *Satanic Verses*. A crowd of 1000 extreme Islamist demonstrators gathered outside the hotel after Friday prayers to protest about the book's publication, and in the ensuing chaos the hotel was set alight and burned to the ground.

The Madımak has since reopened (with a kebap shop in the foyer!), although many human rights groups are calling for the site to be turned into a memorial and museum. The government has already rejected this plan once, sparking accusations that some ministers were directly involved or at least sympathetic to the arsonists.

As well as a memorial, many protesters want to see the trial of the Madımak suspects reopened, believing they were let off too lightly. Thirty-one death sentences, upheld in a 2001 appeal, were commuted to life in prison when Turkey abolished the death sentence the following year.

The scars from the tragedy show no signs of fading, and Sivas' name has become synonymous with the incident. Demonstrations and vigils take place in Sivas on the anniversary of the attack; in 2008, tens of thousands of people attended a service to mark the 15th anniversary.

CENTRAL ANATOLIA

Getting There & Away

BUS

Bus services from Sivas aren't all that frequent, so you may want to book ahead at one of the ticket offices in town. From the otogar, TL8 from the city centre by taxi, there are fairly regular services to Amasya (TL20, 3½ hours), Ankara (TL30, six hours), Diyarbakır (TL35, eight hours), Erzurum (TL30, seven hours), İstanbul (TL50, 13 hours), Kayseri (TL16, three hours), Malatya (TL20, four hours), Samsun (TL30, six hours) and Tokat (TL12, 1½ hours).

'Yenişehir-Terminal' dolmuşes (TL0.70) pass the otogar and end their run just uphill from the Paşa Camii, a five-minute walk from the hotels on Atatürk Caddesi and Eski Belediye Sokak.

TRAIN

Sivas **station** (☎ 221 7000) is a major rail junction for both east–west and north–south lines. The main daily east–west expresses, the *Doğu Ekspresi* and the *Erzurum Ekspresi,* go through Sivas to Erzurum and Kars (16 hours) or back to Ankara and İstanbul (22 hours); the *Güney Ekspresi* (from İstanbul to Kurtalan) runs four times a week in either direction and the *Vangölü Ekspresi* (between İstanbul and Tatvan) runs twice in either direction. There are also local services to Kangal, Divriği and Amasya (five hours).

'İstasyon' dolmuşes run from the station to Hükümet Meydanı and the Paşa Camii.

AROUND SİVAS
Balıklı Kaplıca

Visiting the health spa at **Balıklı Kaplıca** (Hot Spring with Fish; ☎ 469 1151; www.balikli.org, in Turkish; visitor/patient TL5/30; ⏰ 8am-noon & 2-6pm) is a satisfyingly unusual experience from the moment you enter Kangal, 12km southwest of the resort. The tiny service town gave its name to the black-faced, pale-bodied Kangal dogs (see p74) seen throughout Turkey and a statue of a spiky-collared mutt guards the approach from Sivas.

A shepherd boy is said to have discovered the healing qualities of the local mineral water, which is high in the dermatologically curative element selenium. Amazingly, the warm water is inhabited by **'doctor fish'**, which not only live at a higher temperature than most fish can survive at, but nibble fingers, toes and any other body part you offer

them. The fish supposedly favour psoriasis-inflicted skin and the spa attracts patients from all over the world, but the swarming school happily gets stuck into any patch of flesh. It is wonderfully therapeutic to dangle your feet in the water and feel nature giving you a thorough pedicure, with the nippers tickling and then soothing like tiny vacuum cleaners.

The spa complex has six sex-segregated pools set amid trees, and a **hotel** (r & ste TL80-125; 🖥) with a buffet restaurant, a café above the mineral water, a weighing machine and some massage chairs. Rates depend on whether you define yourself as 'normal' or 'ill'; the recommended course for genuine patients is eight hours a day in the pool for three weeks! If you are staying over, full board costs TL35 extra; half-board TL20.

GETTING THERE & AWAY

Minibuses from the terminal beside Sivas' otogar run to Kangal (TL5, one hour), from where you can take a taxi to the resort (TL20). Balıklı Kaplıca offers group transfers from Sivas.

Kangal train station is served by three daily services to/from Sivas (TL2.50, 4¼ hours) and the daily *Doğu Ekspresi* and *Erzurum Ekspresi* to/from Erzurum (TL10, 11 hours).

DİVRİĞİ
☎ 0346 / pop 14,500

Arriving in Divriği from the west, the village has an edgy feel, perhaps because it lies on the edge of Anatolia's distinct eastern region. It is also a dead end, in a valley between 2000m-plus mountains, and you must detour 100km to the northwest to continue into eastern Anatolia by car or bus. But there are three good reasons to come here: a trio of 780-year-old stone doorways, which are so intricately carved that some say their craftsmanship proves the existence of god. The doors belong to one of Turkey's finest old religious structures, Divriği's mosque-*medrese* complex, which is remarkably undervisited despite its inclusion on the Unesco World Heritage list.

Divriği village occupies a fertile valley and still has an agricultural economy. Its population is mostly made up of Alevis (see p55). The narrow streets conceal a busy market, PTT, internet café, some simple restaurants and a couple of banks with ATMs; there are petrol stations on the main road.

Sights

ULU CAMİ & DARÜŞŞİFA

Uphill from the town centre stands the beautifully restored **Ulu Cami and Darüşşifa** (Grand Mosque & Mental Hospital; admission free; ☺ 8am-5pm), adjoining institutions founded in 1228 by the local emir Ahmet Şah and his wife, the lady Fatma Turan Melik.

It's the ornamental gateways overlooking the village that put Divriği on the map (and the World Heritage list). The entrances to both the Ulu Cami and the Darüşşifa are truly stupendous, their reliefs densely carved with a wealth of geometric patterns, stars, medallions, textured effects and intricate Arabic inscriptions, all rendered in such minute detail that it's hard to imagine the stone ever started out flat. It's the tasteful Ottoman equivalent of having a cinema in your house, the sort of thing only a provincial emir with more money than sense could have dreamt of building.

Inside the hospital, built on an asymmetrical floor plan, the stone walls and uneven columns are completely unadorned. The octagonal pool in the court has a spiral runoff, similar to the one in Konya's Karatay Medresesi (see p487), which allowed the tinkle of running water to break the silence of the room and soothe patients' nerves. A platform raised above the main floor may have been for musicians who likewise soothed the patients. The building was used as a *medrese* from the 18th century.

The mosque is also very simple inside, with 16 columns, carpets, some fresco fragments and a plain *mihrab*. The valley views from the terrace outside are equally impressive, as is the entrance facing the clifftop castle, with more detailed stonework.

The complex is generally open during the listed hours, but if you find it locked, ask around and someone will probably find the key. Friday afternoon is a good time to come, as you should be able to visit following noon prayers. Wear trousers or similar rather than shorts and refrain from photographing Muslims during prayer.

OTHER ATTRACTIONS

As this was once an important provincial capital you will notice several **kümbets** (Seljuk tombs) scattered about town, including Ahmet Şah's tomb, near the Ulu Cami.

Trailing down the sides of the hill above the Ulu Cami are the ruined walls of a 9th-century **castle**, crowned by the crumbling *aslanı burç* (lion bastion). The road heading behind the Ulu Cami and Darüşşifa leads up to the castle.

Getting There & Away

Minibuses from Sivas to Divriği (TL10, three hours), 176km southeast, depart from the minibus terminal. Services are infrequent and you may speed up your journey by changing in Kangal. It is possible to get there and back in a day from Sivas, but if you do not start early, you may have to stay the night at Balıklı Kaplıca (opposite).

A return taxi ride from Sivas, stopping in Balıklı Kaplıca and Divriği, costs about TL170. Take some ID as there is sometimes a police checkpoint between Kangal and Divriği.

The train station is about 1.5km north of the Ulu Cami, served by trains including the daily *Doğu Ekspresi* and *Erzurum Ekspresi* between Sivas (TL5, 4¼ hours) and Erzurum (TL10, 7½ hours).

Both trains and Nazar Turizm buses serve İstanbul and Ankara, though it's a long way to come for a day trip!

Drivers should note that there's no through road to Erzincan from Divriği, forcing you to head northwest to Zara and the highway before you can start driving east.

KONYA

☎ 0332 / pop 762,000

Turkey's equivalent of the 'Bible Belt', Konya treads a delicate path between its historical significance as the home town of the whirling dervish orders and a bastion of Seljuk culture on the one hand, and its modern importance as an economic boom town on the other.

The city derives considerable charm from this juxtaposition of old and new. Ancient mosques and the mazey market district rub up against contemporary Konya around Alaaddin Tepesi, where hip-looking university students talk religion and politics in the tea gardens.

If you are passing through this region, say from the coast to Cappadocia, bear in mind that the wonderful shrine of the Mevlâna is one of Turkey's finest and most characteristic sights.

History

Almost 4000 years ago the Hittites called this city 'Kuwanna'. It was Kowania to the

CENTRAL ANATOLIA

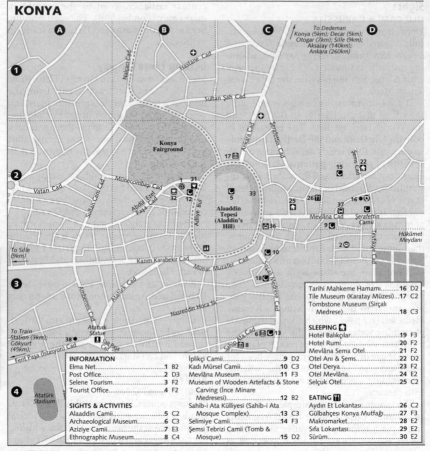

KONYA

To:Dedeman
Konya (5km); Decar (5km);
Otogar (7km); Sille (9km);
Aksaray (140km);
Ankara (260km)

Konya
Fairground

Alaaddin
Tepesi
(Aladdin's
Hill)

Mevlâna Cad

Şerafettin
Camii

Hükümet
Meydanı

To Sille
(9km)

To Train
Station (3km);
Gökyurt
(45km);

Atatürk
Statue

Atatürk
Stadium

Tarihi Mahkeme Hamamı	16	D2
Tile Museum (Karatay Müzesi)	17	C2
Tombstone Museum (Sırçalı Medrese)	18	C3
SLEEPING		
Hotel Balıkçılar	19	F3
Hotel Rumi	20	F2
Mevlâna Sema Otel	21	F2
Otel Anı & Şems	22	F2
Otel Derya	23	F2
Otel Mevlâna	24	E2
Selçuk Otel	25	C2
EATING		
Aydın Et Lokantası	26	C2
Gülbahçesi Konya Mutfağı	27	F3
Makromarket	28	E2
Sıfa Lokantası	29	E2
Sürüm	30	E2

INFORMATION		
Elma Net	1	B2
Post Office	2	D3
Selene Tourism	3	F2
Tourist Office	4	F2
SIGHTS & ACTIVITIES		
Alaaddin Camii	5	C2
Archaeological Museum	6	C3
Aziziye Camii	7	E3
Ethnographic Museum	8	C4

İplikçi Camii	9	D2
Kadı Mürsel Camii	10	C3
Mevlâna Museum	11	F3
Museum of Wooden Artefacts & Stone Carving (İnce Minare Medresesi)	12	B2
Sahib-i Ata Külliyesi (Sahib-i Ata Mosque Complex)	13	C3
Selimiye Camii	14	F3
Şemsi Tebrizi Camii (Tomb & Mosque)	15	D2

Phrygians, Iconium to the Romans and then
Konya to the Turks. Iconium was an important provincial town visited several times by
Sts Paul and Barnabas. There are few remains
of its early Christian community, but Sille
(p492) has several ruined churches.

From about 1150 to 1300 Konya was capital of the Seljuk Sultanate of Rum, which
encompassed most of Anatolia. The Seljuk
sultans endowed Konya with dozens of fine
buildings in an architectural style that was
decidedly Turkish, but had its roots in Persia
and Byzantium.

Traditionally Konya lay at the heart of
Turkey's rich farming 'bread basket', but these
days light industry and pilgrimage tourism are
at least as important.

Orientation

The city centre is Alaaddin Tepesi (Aladdin's
Hill), encircled by a ring road. From the hill,
Mevlâna Caddesi goes east 700m to Hükümet
Meydanı (Government Plaza) – where you'll
find the provincial and city government
buildings, the main PTT, several banks
with ATMs and a jewellery black market –
then continues to the tourist office and the
Mevlâna Museum.

The otogar, connected by regular trams,
is 7km due north of the centre; the local bus
terminal (Eski Garaj) is 1km to the south.

Information

Elma Net (Çinili Sokak 14; per hr TL1; 🕙 10am-11pm)
Internet café.

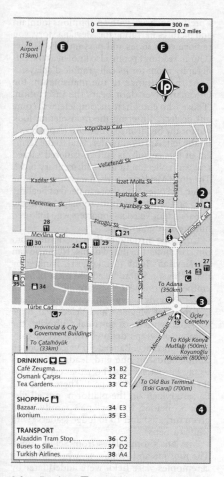

DRINKING
Café Zeugma.....................**31** B2
Osmanlı Çarşısı.................**32** B2
Tea Gardens.....................**33** C2

SHOPPING
Bazaar............................**34** E3
Ikonium..........................**35** E3

TRANSPORT
Alaaddin Tram Stop...........**36** C2
Buses to Sille....................**37** D2
Turkish Airlines.................**38** A4

Selene Tourism (☎ 353 6745; www.selene.com.tr;
Ayanbey Sokak 22b) Organises tours and, during summer,
dervish performances for groups.
Tourist office (☎ 353 4020; Mevlâna Caddesi 21;
⏱ 8.30am-5.30pm Mon-Sat) Gives out a city map and a
leaflet covering the Mevlâna Museum; can also organise
guides for the museum.

Dangers & Annoyances

Konya has a long-standing reputation for religious conservatism; you'll see more women in religious headscarves here than in many other towns, and you'll find Friday observed as a day of rest in a way it rarely is elsewhere. None of this should inconvenience you, but take special care not to upset the pious and make sure *you're* not an annoyance! If you

visit during Ramazan (see p664) don't eat or drink in public during the day, as a courtesy to those who are fasting.

Ironically, non-Muslim women seem to encounter more hassle in this bastion of propriety than in many other Turkish cities, and dressing conservatively will help you avoid problems. Men can wander around in shorts without encountering any tension, but you may prefer to wear something longer to fit in with local customs.

If you want a guide for the Mevlâna Museum, try to arrange it through the tourist office rather than hiring one of the carpet salesmen who loiter at the museum entrance.

Male travellers have reported being propositioned in the Tarihi Mahkeme Hamamı.

Sights & Activities
MEVLÂNA MUSEUM

For Muslims and non-Muslims alike, the main reason to come to Konya is to visit the **Mevlâna Museum** (☎ 351 1215; admission TL2; ⏱ 9am-6.30pm Tue-Sun, 10am-6pm Mon), the former lodge of the whirling dervishes. On religious holidays the museum (really a shrine) may keep longer hours.

In Celaleddin Rumi, the Seljuk Sultanate of Rum produced one of the world's great mystic philosophers. His poetry and religious writings, mostly in Persian, the literary language of the day, are among the most beloved and respected in the Islamic world. Rumi later became known as Mevlâna (Our Guide) to his followers.

Rumi was born in 1207 in Balkh (Afghanistan). His family fled the impending Mongol invasion by moving to Mecca and then to the Sultanate of Rum, reaching Konya by 1228. His father, Bahaeddin Veled, was a noted preacher, known as the Sultan of Scholars, and Rumi became a brilliant student of Islamic theology. After his father's death in 1231, he studied in Aleppo and Damascus, returning to live in Konya by 1240.

In 1244 he met Mehmet Şemseddin Tebrizi (Şemsi Tebrizi or Şems of Tabriz), one of his father's Sufi (Muslim mystic) disciples. Tebrizi had a profound influence on Rumi but, jealous of his overwhelming influence on their master, an angry crowd of Rumi's disciples put Tebrizi to death in 1247. Stunned by the loss, Rumi withdrew from the world to meditate, and wrote his greatest poetic work, the 25,000-verse *Mathnawi* (*Mesnevi* in Turkish).

CENTRAL ANATOLIA

He also wrote many aphorisms, *ruba'i* and *ghazal* poems, collected into his 'Great Opus', the *Divan-i Kebir*.

Tolerance is central to Mevlâna's teachings, as in this famous verse:

Come, whoever you may be,
Even if you may be
An infidel, a pagan, or a fire-worshipper, come.
Ours is not a brotherhood of despair.
Even if you have broken
Your vows of repentance a hundred times, come.

Rumi died on 17 December 1273, the date now known as his 'wedding night' with Allah. His son, Sultan Veled, organised his followers into the brotherhood called the Mevlevi, or whirling dervishes.

In the centuries following Mevlâna's death, over 100 dervish lodges were founded throughout the Ottoman domains. Dervish orders exerted considerable conservative influence on the country's political, social and economic life, and numerous Ottoman sultans were Mevlevi Sufis (mystics). Atatürk saw the dervishes as an obstacle to advancement for the Turkish people and banned them in 1925, but several orders survived on a technicality as religious fraternities. The Konya lodge was revived in 1957 as a 'cultural association' intended to preserve a historical tradition.

For Muslims, this is a very holy place, and more than 1.5 million people visit it a year, most of them Turkish. You will see many people praying for Rumi's help. When entering, women should cover their heads and shoulders, and no one should wear shorts.

A guide is not essential, but if you want to hire one, recruit a professional through the tourist office rather than engaging one of the carpet salesmen at the entrance. Guides are available in many languages; when we visited, English speakers were scarce, but it is worth checking at the tourist office to see if this has changed. You can avoid the worst of the crowds by visiting during the week and getting there first thing in the morning.

Visiting the Museum

The lodge is visible from some distance, its fluted dome of turquoise tiles one of Turkey's most distinctive sights. After walking through a pretty courtyard with an ablutions fountain and pictures narrating the Mevlâna story, you remove your shoes and pass into the Tilavet (Quran reading) room, also known as the calligraphy room for its calligraphic displays.

At the entrance to the mausoleum, the Ottoman silver door bears the inscription, 'Those who enter here incomplete, will come out perfect'. Entering the mausoleum, look out for the big bronze *Nisan tası* (April bowl) on the left. April rainwater, vital to the farmers of this region, is still considered sacred and was collected in this 13th-century bowl. The tip of Mevlâna's turban was dipped in the water and offered to those in need of healing. Also on the left are six sarcophagi belonging to Bahaeddin Veled's supporters who followed him from Afghanistan.

Continue through to the part of the room directly under the fluted dome. Here you can see **Mevlâna's Tomb** (the largest), flanked by that of his son Sultan Veled and those of other eminent dervishes. They are all covered in velvet shrouds heavy with gold embroidery, but those of Mevlâna and Veled bear huge turbans, symbols of spiritual authority; the number of wraps denotes the level of spiritual importance. Bahaeddin Veled's wooden tomb stands on one end, leading devotees to say Mevlâna was so holy that even his father stands to show respect. There are some 65 sarcophagi on the platform, not all visible; 55 belong to Mevlâna's family (with green turbans) and 10 to lodge leaders (with white turbans).

Mevlâna's tomb dates from Seljuk times. The mosque and *semahane,* where whirling ceremonies were held, were added later by Ottoman sultans (Mehmet the Conqueror was a Mevlevi adherent and Süleyman the Magnificent made charitable donations to the order). Selim I, conqueror of Egypt, donated the Mamluk crystal lamps.

The small mosque and *semahane* to the left of the sepulchral chamber contain exhibits such as musical instruments, the original copy of the *Mathnawi*, Mevlâna's prayer rug, and a 9th-century gazelle-skin Christian manuscript. There is a casket containing strands of Mohammed's beard, with holes in the display case to smell the hair's scent of roses, and a copy of the Quran so tiny that its author went blind writing it. This was actually a mark of honour in the Ottoman Empire, which prized miniature art; grains of rice inscribed with prayers are also on display. Look to the left of the *mihrab* for a *seccade* (prayer carpet) bearing a picture of the Kaaba at Mecca. Made in Iran of silk and wool, it's extremely fine, with some three million knots (144 per square centimetre).

The rooms surrounding the courtyard were once the dervishes' offices and quarters – one near the entrance is decorated as it would have been in Mevlâna's day, with mannequins dressed as dervishes. Look out for the wooden practice board, used by novice dervishes to learn to whirl.

Across from the museum entrance is the **Selimiye Camii**, built between 1566 and 1574 when Sultan Selim II was the governor of Konya.

OTHER MUSEUMS
Museum of Wooden Artefacts & Stone Carving

On the western side of Alaaddin Tepesi is the İnce Minare Medresesi (Seminary of the Slender Minaret), now the **Museum of Wooden Artefacts and Stone Carving** (Tas ve Ahsap Eserler Müzesi; ☎ 351 3204; Adliye Bulvarı; admission TL3; 🕑 9am-noon & 1.30-5.30pm). It was built in 1264 for Seljuk vizier Sahip Ata, who may have been trying to outdo the patron of the contemporaneous Karatay Medresesi (see below).

The extraordinarily elaborate doorway, with bands of Arabic inscription, is more impressive than the small building behind it. The octagonal minaret in turquoise relief is over 600 years old and gave the seminary its popular name. If it looks short, this is because the top was sliced off by lightning.

Inside, many of the carvings feature motifs similar to those used in tiles and ceramics. The Seljuks didn't heed Islam's traditional prohibition of human and animal images: there are images of birds (the Seljuk double-headed eagle, for example), humans, lions and leopards. The *eyvan* in particular contains two delightful carvings of Seljuk angels. The Ahşap Eserler Bölümü (Carved Wood Section) contains some intricately worked wooden doors.

Tile Museum (Karatay Müzesi)

Housed in a former Seljuk theological school, this **museum** (☎ 351 1914; Alaaddin Meydanı; admission TL3; 🕑 9am-noon & 1.30-5.30pm) was closed for restoration when we visited. The building was constructed in 1251–52 by Emir Celaleddin Karatay, a Seljuk general, vizier and statesman

who is buried in one of the corner rooms. The museum is well worth a look if it reopens before your visit; the outstanding collection of ceramics includes interesting octagonal Seljuk tiles.

Tombstone Museum (Sırçalı Medrese)

Several other Seljuk monuments lurk in the narrow warren of streets to the south of Alaaddin Tepesi. Look for the pint-sized Kadı Mürsel Camii, then turn down the side of it, opposite the brown school building with the blue sign. After a few minutes you'll come to another Seljuk seminary, the Sırçalı Medrese (Glass Seminary), named after its tiled exterior. Sponsored by the Seljuk vizier Bedreddin Muhlis, the 13th-century building houses a small **Tombstone Museum** (Mezar Anıtlar Müzesi; ☎ 353 4031; Sırçalı Caddesi; admission free; 🕑 8.30am-5.30pm), with a collection of tombstones featuring finely carved inscriptions. The *eyvan* on the western side of the courtyard was used for classes; it is decorated with blue tiles and its arch has a band of particularly fine calligraphic tile work.

Archaeological & Ethnographic Museums

Beside the Sahib-i Ata Külliyesi, the **Archaeological Museum** (☎ 351 3207; Larende Caddesi; admission TL3; 🕑 9am-12.30pm & 1.30-5pm Tue-Sun) is like a continuation of the museum at Çatalhöyük, with neolithic finds including the skeleton of a baby girl, clutching jewellery made of stone and bone. Artefacts range across the millennia, from chalcolithic terracotta jars to Hittite hieroglyphs, an Assyrian oil lamp shaped like a bunch of grapes, and bronze and stone Roman sarcophagi, one narrating the labours of Hercules in high-relief carvings.

Nearby, the dusty **Ethnographic Museum** (Larende Caddesi; admission TL3; 🕑 8.30am-noon & 1.30-5.30pm Tue-Sun) has a good collection of Ottoman craftwork, including some keys the size of 21st-century doors.

Koyunoğlu Museum

This little-visited **museum** (Kerimler Caddesi 25; admission free; 🕑 8.30am-5.30pm Tue-Sun) contains the legacy of Izzet Koyunoğlu. The railway inspector built up his collection on his travels through Turkey.

Our heart goes out to the tired-looking stuffed pelican, but there is a wonderful variety of exhibits, encompassing prehistoric bones, rhino-horn rosaries, boxwood spoons bearing words of wisdom about food, 19th-century carriage clocks, and old photos of Konya and whirling dervishes.

Ask the guards to unlock the recreated **Koyunoğlu Konya Evi**, which shows how a well-heeled Konyalı family lived a century ago. Izzet lived in the original building with US$3 million of art around him.

The quickest way to the museum lies alongside the **Üçler Cemetery**. Carry straight on at the roundabout at the end of the cemetery, taking the road just to the left of the garage. If you decide to walk through the graveyard, only do so during the day when other people are about; women are advised not to walk through alone.

MOSQUES
Alaaddin Camii
Konya's most important religious building after the Mevlâna shrine, this Seljuk **mosque** (☿ 8.30am-5.30pm) bestrides Alaaddin Tepesi. You may be able to wander in outside the listed opening hours. Built for Alaeddin Keykubad I, Sultan of Rum from 1219 to 1231, the rambling 13th-century building was designed by a Damascene architect in Arab style. Over the centuries it was embellished, refurbished, ruined and restored.

Today, the mosque is entered from the east. The grand original entrance on the northern side incorporates decoration from earlier Byzantine and Roman buildings. The courtyard here features two huge Seljuk *türbes* (tombs), the left of which is the most impressive part of the complex, containing the blue-tiled tombs of 12th- and 13th-century notables.

The mosque's exterior is otherwise plain, but the interior has old marble columns surmounted with recycled Roman and Byzantine capitals. There's also a fine wooden *mimber* and an old marble *mihrab* framed by modern Seljuk-style blue-and-black calligraphy.

Other Mosques
A few blocks south of the Tombstone Museum, along Sırçalı Medrese Caddesi, is the **Sahib-i Ata Külliyesi** (Sahib-i Ata Mosque Complex; ☿ 9am-noon & 1-5pm). Behind its requisite grand entrance with built-in minaret is the Sahib-i Ata Camii, originally constructed during the reign of Alaaddin Keykavus. Destroyed by fire in 1871, it was rebuilt in 13th-century style. The *mihrab* is a fine example of blue Seljuk tile

work. Alongside the mosque another grand gateway once led to a dervish lodge.

Dotted about town are other interesting mosques. The **Şemsi Tebrizi Camii**, containing the elegant 14th-century tomb of Rumi's spiritual mentor, is in a park just northwest of Hükümet Meydanı.

Originally built in the 1670s and destroyed in a fire, the **Aziziye Camii** was rebuilt in 1875 in late-Ottoman, baroque and rococo styles. Located in the bazaar, it has twin minarets with sheltered balconies, and a sign pointing out its interesting features.

On Mevlâna Caddesi, the **İplikçi Camii**, perhaps Konya's oldest mosque (1202), was built for the Seljuk vizier Şemseddin Altun-Aba. It is currently being restored and you can only see its plain brick exterior.

Festivals & Events
The annual **Mevlâna Festival** (☎ 353 4020) runs for a fortnight, culminating on 17 December, the anniversary of Mevlâna's 'wedding night' with Allah. Tickets (and accommodation) should be booked well in advance; contact the tourist office or Selene Tourism for assistance. If you can't get a ticket, other venues around town host dancers during the festival, although they are not of the same quality.

At other times of year, **semas** (☎ 352 8111; Aslanı Kışla; ☿ 8pm Sat) take place behind the Mevlâna Museum. Tickets to the one-hour performances are free and can be organised through travel agencies, hotels or the tourist office.

Sleeping
There's certainly no shortage of hotels in Konya, but the steady throughput of pilgrims can lead to high prices, and alcohol-stocked minibars are obviously not a common feature.

BUDGET
Otel Mevlâna (☎ 352 0029; Cengaver Sokak 2; s/d/tr from TL40/60/85) Across Mevlâna Caddesi from Otel Bera Mevlâna, this friendly central option is a good choice for backpackers of both sexes. Rooms have firm beds, fridges, bathrooms and kitschy paintings.

MIDRANGE
Mevlâna Sema Otel (☎ 350 4623; www.semaotel.com; Mevlâna Caddesi 67; s/d/tr TL50/75/100; ☒) With a great position, some swanky decor and comfort-

DANCING WITH DERVISHES

The Mevlevi worship ceremony, or *sema,* is a ritual dance representing union with God; it's what gives the dervishes their famous whirl, and appears on Unesco's third Proclamation of Masterpieces of the Oral and Intangible Heritage of Humanity. Watching a *sema* can be an evocative, romantic, unforgettable experience. There are many dervish orders worldwide that perform similar rituals, but the original Turkish version is the smoothest and purest, more of an elegant, trancelike dance than the raw energy seen elsewhere.

The dervishes dress in long white robes with full skirts that represent their shrouds. Their voluminous black cloaks symbolise their worldly tombs, their conical felt hats their tombstones.

The ceremony begins when the *hafız,* a scholar who has committed the entire Quran to memory, intones a prayer for Mevlâna and a verse from the Quran. A kettledrum booms out, followed by the plaintive sound of the *ney* (reed flute). Then the *şeyh* (master) bows and leads the dervishes in a circle around the hall. After three circuits, the dervishes drop their black cloaks to symbolise their deliverance from worldly attachments. Then one by one, arms folded on their breasts, they spin out onto the floor as they relinquish the earthly life to be reborn in mystical union with God.

By holding their right arms up, they receive the blessings of heaven, which are communicated to earth by holding their left arms turned down. As they whirl, they form a 'constellation' of revolving bodies, which itself slowly rotates. The *şeyh* walks among them to check that each dervish is performing the ritual properly.

The dance is repeated over and over again. Finally, the *hafız* again chants passages from the Quran, thus sealing the mystical union with God.

able, beige rooms, the Mevlâna Sema has a lot going for it. Ask for a room at the rear, away from noisy Mevlâna Caddesi.

Otel Derya (☎ 352 0154; Ayanbey Sokak 18; s/d/tr TL50/80/100; ⛨) Quiet and spotless, the Derya is a good choice for families and female travellers. Rooms are slightly bland, with pink bathrooms, TVs and minibars, but the management is friendly and efficient and overall it's recommended.

Otel Anı & Şems (☎ 353 8080; www.hotelani.com; Şems Caddesi 6; s/d/tr €30/45/60; ⛨) The mosque-side location may not look promising, but the interiors have a distinct charm. The rooms are worn but serviceable, with minibars and TVs, and there's an in-house travel agent.

Hotel Rumi (☎ 353 1121; www.rumihotel.com; Durakfakih Sokak 5; s/d/tr/ste €50/75/100/125; ⛨ 💻) Boasting a killer position near the Mevlâna Museum, the stylish Rumi's rooms and suites have an abundance of curvy chairs, slender lamps and mirrors. The palatial breakfast room with views of the museum, the friendly staff and the hamam make this an oasis of calm in central Konya.

TOP END

Selçuk Otel (☎ 353 2525; www.otelselcuk.com.tr; Babalık Sokak 4; s/d/tr €60/100/125; ⛨) Both comfort and character are on offer at the Selçuk, where fish tanks part a sea of beige seats in the lobby.

Prices are high, but the facilities, decor and professional service are worth it.

Hotel Balıkçılar (☎ 350 9470; www.balikcilar.com; Mevlâna Karşısı 2; s/d/tr/ste €89/120/140/157; ⛨) The reception's Ottoman theme (it's styled as a cobbled street) doesn't continue in the rooms, but there are nice wooden touches. Facilities include a large lobby bar, restaurant, sauna, hamam and *sema* performances. Breakfast costs €12.

Dedeman Konya (☎ 221 6600; www.dedeman .com; Özalan Mahallesi, Selçuklu; s/d from €160/180; ⛨ 💻 ⛨) Opposite the Kipa mall, the 18-floor Dedeman is impressive from the moment you step beneath the chandeliers in its reception. Attractions include a health club, live music in the top-deck bar-restaurant, and a patisserie and snack bar. The standard rooms are stronger on comfort than character, featuring plasma screens with pay TV, safes and minibars.

Eating

Konya's speciality is *fırın* kebap, slices of (hopefully) tender, fairly greasy oven-roasted mutton served on puffy bread. The city bakers also make excellent fresh pide topped with minced lamb, cheese or eggs, but in Konya pide is called *etli ekmek* (bread with meat).

Be careful what you eat; if you ask a local to recommend a restaurant, they may mumble darkly about food poisoning. Some restaurants around the Mevlâna Museum and tourist office have great views, but their food is not recommended.

The fast-food restaurants on Adilye Bulvarı, competing with the golden arches, are lively places for a snack, but check that the swift grub is thoroughly cooked.

RESTAURANTS

Gülbahçesi Konya Mutfağı (☎ 351 0768; Gülbahçe Sokak 3; mains TL4-8; ♥ 8am-10pm) One of Konya's best restaurants, mostly because of its upstairs terrace with views of the Mevlâna Museum. Dishes include *yaprak sarma*, Adana kebap and *etli ekmek*. There are occasional *sema* performances.

Aydın Et Lokantası (☎ 351 9183; Şeyh Ziya Sokak 5e; mains TL4.50-7) This *lokanta's* decor centres on a fake green oak tree with an ailing goldfish in the pool at its base, but the open kitchen is reassuring. You can try *etli ekmek* here and the menu has English translations.

Şifa Lokantası (☎ 352 0519; Mevlâna Caddesi 29; mains TL5-8) *Tandır kebap* tops Şifa's bill of standards. Service can be pretty rushed when it's busy, but at least there's a good view of the main drag.

Köşk Konya Mutfağı (☎ 352 8547; Mengüç Caddesi 66; mains TL8; ♥ 11am-10pm) Southeast of the centre, this excellent traditional restaurant is run by the well-known food writer Nevin Halıcı, who puts her personal twist on Turkish classics. The service is excellent and the outside tables rub shoulders with vine-draped pillars and a fragrant rose garden. The menu features some unusual dishes like the mouth-clogging dessert *höşmerim*.

For self-caterers, the **bazaar** (right) is the most exciting place to buy produce. Alternatively, there's a supermarket, **Makromarket** (Mevlâna Caddesi), and sugar addicts can satisfy their cravings at **Sürüm** (İstanbul Caddesi), a chocolate shop established in 1926.

Drinking

In summer few things could be more pleasurable than relaxing in one of the innumerable tea gardens dotting the slopes of Alaaddin Tepesi.

Osmanlı Çarşısı (☎ 353 3257; İnce Minare Sokak) Looking like an apple-smoke-spewing pirate ship, this early-20th-century house has terraces and seats on the street, where students talk politics or just inhale a lungful.

Café Zeugma (☎ 350 9474; Adliye Bulvarı 33; cover charge weekend TL3) With its backlit carvings and strobes, this cavernous cultural centre is popular with students for its live music.

Shopping

Konya's **bazaar** sprawls back from the modern PTT building virtually all the way to the Mevlâna Museum, cramming the narrow streets with stalls, roving vendors and the occasional horse-drawn cart. There's a concentration of shops selling religious paraphernalia and tacky souvenirs at the Mevlâna Museum end.

Ikonium (☎ 350 2895; www.thefeltmaker.net; Bostan Çelebi Sokak 12a) Konya was traditionally a felt-making centre but the art is fast dying out in Turkey. Passionate *keçeki* (felt-maker) Mehmet and his Argentinean wife Silvia offer treats including op-art-style patterns and what might be the world's largest hand-decorated piece of felt.

Getting There & Away

AIR

There are three flights every day to and from İstanbul with **Turkish Airlines** (☎ 321 2100; Ferit Paşa Caddesi; ♥ 8.30am-5.30pm Mon-Fri, 8.30am-1.30pm Sat).

The airport is about 13km northeast of the city centre; TL30 by taxi. Havaş was setting up a shuttle-bus service at the time of research; enquire at the tourist office.

BUS

Konya's otogar is about 7km north of Alaaddin Tepesi, accessible by tram from town (see opposite). Regular buses serve all major destinations, including Afyon (TL25, 3¾ hours), Ankara (TL20, four hours), İstanbul (TL45, 11½ hours), Kayseri (TL25, four hours) and Sivas (TL30, seven hours). There are lots of ticket offices on Mevlâna Caddesi and around Alaaddin Tepesi.

The *Eski Garaj* (Old Bus Terminal or Karatay Terminal), 1km southwest of the Mevlâna Museum, has services to local villages.

TRAIN

The **train station** (☎ 332 3670) is about 3km southwest of the centre. You can get to Konya by train from İstanbul Haydarpaşa (13½ hours) on the *Meram Ekspresi*, the *Toros Ekspresi* (İstanbul to Gaziantep) or the *İç Anadolu Mavi* (İstanbul to Adana), all via

Afyon. A new direct, high-speed train link between Konya and Ankara, scheduled to open in 2010, will trim the journey time from 10½ hours to 1¼ hours.

Getting Around

As most of the city centre sights are easily reached on foot, you need public transport only for the otogar or train station. To get to the city centre from the otogar take any tram from the east side of the station to Alaaddin Tepesi (30 minutes); tickets, which cover two people, cost TL2.20. Trams run 24 hours, with one per hour after midnight. A taxi costs around TL25.

There are half-hourly minibuses from the train station to the centre (TL1.25). A taxi from the station to Hükümet Meydanı costs about TL15.

Innumerable minibuses ply Mevlâna Caddesi if you're heading to the far end (TL1).

Cars can be rented from **Decar** (☎ 247 2343; Özalan Mahallesi, Selçuklu), based at the Dedeman Konya (see p489).

AROUND KONYA
Çatalhöyük

No, this isn't a hallucination brought on by the parched Konya plain. Rising 20m above the flatlands, the East Mound at **Çatalhöyük** (admission TL3; ☻ 8am-5pm) is left over from one of the largest neolithic settlements on earth. Up to 8000 people lived here at Çatalhöyük's peak, about 9000 years ago, and the mound comprises 13 levels of buildings, each containing around 1000 structures.

Little remains of the ancient centre other than five excavation areas, which draw archaeologists from all over the world. If you visit between June and September, when the digs mostly take place, you might find an expert to chat to. At other times, the **museum** does a good job of explaining the site and the excavations, which began in 1961 under British archaeologist James Mellaart and have continued with the involvement of the local community. The museum's eight-minute video is worth watching before looking at the exhibits, which are mostly reproductions of finds now in Ankara's Museum of Anatolian Civilisations; including some of Anatolia's oldest pottery vessels, the world's oldest ceramic shaker and man-made mirror, and a representation of the mother goddess. Mellaart's controversial theories about mother goddess worship here caused the Turkish government to close the site for 30 years.

Near the museum entrance stands the **experimental house**, a reconstructed mud-brick hut used to test various theories about neolithic culture. People at Çatalhöyük lived in tightly packed dwellings that were connected by ladders between the roofs instead of streets, and were filled in and built over when they started to wear out. Skeletons were found buried under the floors and most of the houses may have doubled as shrines. The settlement was highly organised, but there are no obvious signs of any central government system.

The guardian will happily show you the marquee-covered **south area**; a tip would probably be appreciated. With 21m of archaeological deposits, many of the site's most famous discoveries were made here. The lowest level of excavation, begun by Mellaart, is the deepest at Çatalhöyük and holds deposits left more than 9000 years ago. If you come during summer, you may be able to visit other excavation areas.

Çatalhöyük is one of the world's most famous archaeological sites, and one of the oldest town settlements ever discovered, but don't expect any towering monuments. However, you don't have to be an archaeologist to appreciate the romance and mystery of a site where, c 6000 BC, an egalitarian society lived, apparently without fighting a battle during its 1400-year lifespan.

GETTING THERE & AWAY

To get here by public transport from Konya, 33km northwest, get the Karkın minibus, which leaves the *Eski Garaj* at 9am, noon and 3pm. Get off at Kük Koy (TL2.50, 45 minutes) and walk 1km to the site, or you may be able to persuade the driver to take you the whole way. Going back, minibuses leave Kük Koy at noon, 3pm and 5pm.

Alternatively, take a minibus from *Eski Garaj* to Çumra (TL3, 45 minutes) and then hire a taxi from beside the otogar for the last 11km (TL35 return).

You should get going early on both routes to give yourself time to tour Çatalhöyük and catch the last minibus back to Konya. A taxi from Konya to the site and back will cost about TL70.

Gökyurt (Kilistra, Lystra)

A little piece of Cappadocia to the southwest of Konya, the landscape at Gökyurt is reminiscent of what you'll see in Güzelyurt or the Ihlara Valley: a gorge with dwellings and medieval churches cut into the rock face, but without the crowds.

St Paul is thought to have stayed here on his three Anatolian expeditions and the area has long been a Christian pilgrimage site; especially for 12 months from June 2008, declared by Pope Benedict XVI as 'the year of St Paul' to celebrate the 2000th anniversary of the saint's birth.

There's one particularly fine church cut completely out of the rock, but no frescoes. A trip out here makes a lovely half-day excursion, and the surrounding landscape is simply stunning.

GETTING THERE & AWAY

The easiest way to get here from Konya, 45km away, is by car or taxi; the latter will charge TL100 return (including waiting time). There are several daily buses from Konya's *Eski Garaj* to Hatunsaray, 18km from Gökyurt, but taxis there are actually more expensive than from Konya as the drivers make the most of their captive audience. If enough Gökyurt villagers want to visit Konya, a minibus will travel to the city, and you can jump on the bus on its return journey.

Driving, you should take the Antalya road, then follow signs to Akören. After about 34km, and a few kilometres before Hatunsaray, look for a tiny brown-and-white sign on the right (marked 'Kilistra-Gökyurt, 16km'). Cyclists need to watch out for sheepdogs roaming about.

Sille

☎ 0332 / pop 2000

If you're looking for an excursion from Konya, head past the 'turtle crossing' road signs to the pretty village of Sille, a patch of green surrounded by sharp rocky hills. A rock face full of cave dwellings and chapels overlooks bendy-beamed village houses in several states of decay and a few bridges across the dry river.

The domed Byzantine **St Helen's Church** (Ayaelena Kilisesi), near the last bus stop, was reputedly founded by Empress Helena, mother of Constantine the Great. It was completely restored in 1833; the vandalised and fast-fading frescoes date from 1880. Despite its later use as a WWI military depot and a clinic where a German doctor attached artificial limbs, the church retains some of its old woodwork, including a broken pulpit and an iconostasis stripped of its icons. If you find it closed, ask at Sille Konak restaurant for the key.

On the hill to the north stands a small ruined chapel, the **Küçük Kilese**; it's worth the scramble up for the views over the village.

At **Sille Konak** (☎ 244 9260; mains TL5-9), a restored Greek house lovingly decorated by the family who run it, a team of headscarf-clad cooks rustles up home-cooked food. The owner will happily recommend dishes such as Konak kebap and *düğün* (soup with yoghurt, mint and rice, often served at weddings); order a selection, as portions are small. The restaurant is popular with coach parties, which can destroy the atmosphere.

There are a couple of cafés and a family restaurant at the entrance to the village, overlooking the glass-studded hamam.

GETTING THERE & AWAY

Bus 64 from Mevlâna Caddesi (near the post office) leaves every half-hour or so (less often on Sunday) for Sille (TL1.10, 25 minutes).

KARAMAN

☎ 0338

After the fall of the Seljuk Empire, central Anatolia was split into several different provinces with different governments, and for some time Karaman served as a regional capital. Although little visited these days, it boasts a selection of fine 13th- and 14th-century buildings and makes a base for excursions to Binbirkilise (opposite).

The **Hacıbeyler Camii** (1358) has a magnificent squared-off entrance, with decoration that looks like a baroque variant on Seljuk art. The **Mader-i Mevlâna (Aktepe) Cami** (1370) is the burial place of the great Mevlâna's mother and has a dervish-style felt hat carved above its entrance. The adjacent **hamam** is still in use.

The tomb of the great Turkish poet Yunus Emre is beside the **Yunus Emre Camii** (1349). Extracts from his verses are carved into the walls of a poetry garden to the rear of the mosque.

Later buildings include the hilltop **castle**, which dates to 1471 in its present incarnation, and the **Imaret Cami** (1417), which is under restoration but remains a superb example of pre-Ottoman mosque architecture.

The slightly disorganised **Karaman Museum** (Turgut Özal Bulvarı; admission TL3; ⏰ 8am-noon & 1-5pm

Tue-Sun) contains cave finds from nearby Taşkale and Canhasan and has a fine ethnography section. Next door, the magnificent **Hatuniye Medresesi** (1382), whose ornate portal is one of the finest examples of Karaman art, now houses a restaurant.

If you get caught in Karaman overnight, the two-star **Nas Hotel** (☎ 214 4848; İsmetpaşa Caddesi 30; r TL50) is low on luxury but comfortable, welcoming to travellers of both sexes and close to the sights.

Getting There & Away

Regular buses link Karaman with Konya (TL20, two hours) and Ereğli (TL20, two hours). Getting to Karaman from Nevsehir (Cappadocia) is more time-consuming, as you must change in Nigde and Ereğli. The *Toros Ekspresi* and *İç Anadolu Mavi* trains (see p490) stop here between Konya and Adana.

BİNBİRKİLİSE

Just before WWI, the great British traveller Gertrude Bell travelled 42km northwest of Karaman and recorded the existence of a cluster of Byzantine churches set high on a lonely hillside and rather generously known as Binbirkilise (One Thousand and One Churches). Later Irfan Orga came here in search of the last remaining nomads, a journey recorded in his book *The Caravan Moves On*. You won't see any nomads around these days, or indeed much to mark the ruins out as churches, but half a dozen families live

---

HAN SWEET HAN

The Seljuks built a string of *hans* (caravanserais) along the route of the 13th-century Silk Rd through Anatolia. These camel-caravan staging posts were built roughly a day's travel apart (about 15km to 30km), to facilitate trade. Expenses for construction and maintenance of the *hans* were borne by the sultan, and paid for by the taxes levied on the rich trade in goods.

As well as the Sultanhanı, fine specimens include the Sarıhan (p513), 6km east of Avanos, and the Karatay Han, 48km east of Kayseri. Many other *hans* dot the Anatolian landscape, including the Ağzıkara Hanı (p534), 16km northeast of Aksaray on the Nevşehir highway, and the Sultan Han (p538), 45km northeast of Kayseri off the Sivas highway.

---

around the ruins (and in them, in the case of some of their animals) and the site is a rural alternative to busier attractions.

It's easiest to reach the churches with your own transport. Drive out of Karaman on the Karapınar road and follow the yellow signs. The first sizeable ruin pops up in the village of Madenşehir, 36km north, after which the road becomes increasingly rough. There are fantastic views all along the road, which is just as well, as you'll have to come back the same way.

A taxi from Karaman's otogar should cost around €45 for the return trip; the drivers know where the churches are.

SULTANHANI
☎ 0382

The highway between Konya and Aksaray crosses quintessential Anatolian steppe: flat grasslands as far as the eye can see, with only the occasional tumbleweed and a fist of mountains in the distance breaking the monotony. Along the way, 110km from Konya and 42km from Aksaray, is the dreary village of Sultanhanı, its only redeeming feature being one of several Seljuk *han* bearing that name. This stunning **Sultanhanı** (admission TL3; ☉ 7am-7pm), 200m from the highway, is the largest in Anatolia.

The site is a popular stop for tour groups, and you may field invitations to visit the nearby carpet-repair workshop. If you resist such offers, you could easily explore Sultanhanı in half an hour.

The building was constructed in 1229, during the reign of the Seljuk sultan Alaaddin Keykubad I and restored in 1278 after a fire (when it became Turkey's largest *han*). Through the wonderful carved entrance in the 50m-long east wall, there is a raised *mescit* (prayer room) in the middle of the open courtyard, which is ringed with rooms used for sleeping, dining and cooking. A small, simple doorway leads to the atmospheric *ahır* (stable), with arches, domes and pillars in the pigeon-soundtracked gloom.

Getting There & Away

Regular buses run from Aksaray's otogar Monday to Friday (TL5, 45 minutes); there are fewer services at weekends. Leaving Sultanhanı, flag down a bus or village minibus heading to Aksaray or Konya on the main highway. If you start out early you can hop off the bus, see the *han* and be on your way again an hour or so later.

CENTRAL ANATOLIA

494

Cappadocia

Between Kayseri and Nevşehir, Central Anatolia's mountain-fringed plains give way to a land of fairy chimneys and underground cities. The fairy chimneys – rock columns, pyramids, mushrooms and a few camels – and the valleys of cascading cliffs were formed when Erciyes Dağı erupted. The intervening millennia added to the remarkable Cappadocian canvas, with Byzantines carving cave churches and subterranean complexes to house thousands of people.

You could spend days touring the rock-cut churches and admiring their frescoes (technically seccos, actually). Alternatively, view the troglodyte architecture from far above on a dawn hot-air balloon ride or from a panoramic hotel terrace.

Whether it's a pension or a boutique hideaway with as few rooms as it has fairy chimneys, Cappadocia's accommodation rates as some of Turkey's best and allows guests to experience cave dwelling firsthand. The restaurants in dreamy spots such as Göreme and Ürgüp are equally alluring, with yet more terraces offering sweeping views of the knobbly landscape. Staying in villages where eroding castles overlook small communities of very laid-back people, you might just become a world expert on the aesthetic qualities of rocky valleys at sunset. It will require evenings of study on the terrace, but you will get there with a good supply of çay (tea) or Efes.

However, between lingering looks at the rocky remains of Cappadocia's unique history, it is worth checking out some further-flung spots. Caravanserais dot the roads to the seemingly lost valleys of Ihlara and Soğanlı, and former Greek settlements such as Mustafapaşa.

HIGHLIGHTS

- Explore Byzantine tunnels at Kaymaklı and Derinkuyu **underground cities** (p524)
- Examine fresco-covered churches in the **Göreme Open-Air Museum** (p499)
- Gaze at the pigeon houses riddling cliffs and fairy chimneys in Göreme's labyrinthine **valleys** (p502)
- Gasp at the outcrops doubling as castles in **Uçhisar** (p507) and **Ortahisar** (p516)
- Take the trip of a lifetime in a **hot-air balloon** (p510)
- Drink in the views over multiple mezes in chic **Ürgüp** (p517)
- Part the vines and peer into a tumbledown Greek mansion in **Mustafapaşa** (p522)
- Trek through secluded monastic settlements in **Soğanlı** (p523), **Ihlara Valley** (p528) and **Güzelyurt** (p531)

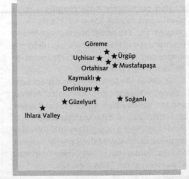

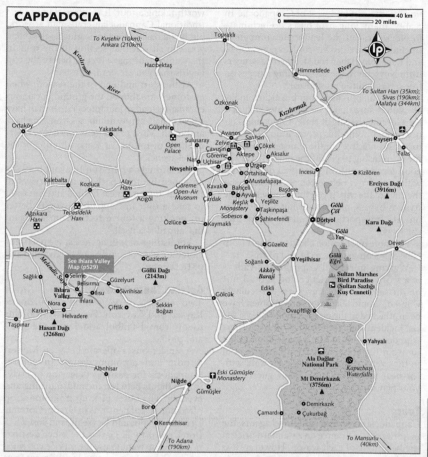

History

The Hittites settled Cappadocia (Kapadokya) from 1800 BC to 1200 BC, after which smaller kingdoms held power. Then came the Persians, followed by the Romans, who established the capital of Caesarea (today's Kayseri). During the Roman and Byzantine periods, Cappadocia became a refuge for early Christians and, from the 4th to the 11th century, Christianity flourished here; most churches, monasteries and underground cities date from this period. Later, under Seljuk and Ottoman rule, Christians were treated with tolerance.

Cappadocia progressively lost its importance in Anatolia. Its rich past was all but forgotten until a French priest rediscovered the rock-hewn churches in 1907. The tourist boom in the 1980s kick-started a new era, and now Cappadocia is one of Turkey's most famous and popular destinations.

Dangers & Annoyances

A warning is needed about bus services to Cappadocia from other parts of Turkey. Many readers have complained that although they purchased tickets to Göreme, they found themselves instead deposited at Nevşehir's otogar (bus station), or even outside it, and were left with no alternative except to catch an overpriced taxi to Göreme. We've even heard of some unscrupulous bus companies abandoning travellers on the highway outside Avanos. Problems most frequently occur on buses travelling between destinations to the east and west of Cappadocia. In reality, many long-haul buses do terminate in Nevşehir, but the legitimate companies (including Göreme, Metro, Nevşehir, Öncü and Kapadokya) then transfer their passengers from Nevşehir to the surrounding villages on free *servis* (shuttle minibuses).

When you purchase your bus ticket, make absolutely sure that it clearly states that it is for Göreme; having it state 'Cappadocia' is not enough. With this proof, you will be able to insist on a free shuttle transfer (even if it means refusing to get off the bus!). It's also a good idea to confirm your final destination with your driver before you get on the bus at the start of the trip. If you find yourself on the Avanos bypass, phone your hotel to arrange onward transport or walk to the garage and call a taxi.

For more information about transport from Nevşehir's otogar, see p514 and p515.

Walking in central Cappadocia's valleys is a wonderful experience and should not be missed, but lone travellers, particularly women, should take care there. Women have been attacked in the often-remote valleys; the last incident happened in 2008. Solo travellers who do not want to hire a guide are advised to avoid the areas away from Göreme et al in the evening and, if possible, to walk with (or near to) a worker or fellow guest from your pension.

Tours

Cappadocia is overrun with travel agents, the majority of which agree on a standard price at the beginning of each season. However, it is worth shopping around as tours vary in terms of value for money – the quality of the guide or the number of sights covered.

Most tour companies offer the following:

Full-day tours Similarly priced, these packages often take in one of the underground cities, a stretch of the Ihlara Valley and one of the caravanserais, but others go to Soğanlı and Mustafapaşa.

Guided day hikes Usually in the Rose, Sun, Red or Pigeon Valleys. Costs vary according to the destination, degree of difficulty and length, but should not exceed the above prices as less motor transport and pricey petrol are involved.

Ihlara Valley trip A full day, including a guided hike and lunch; most operators charge TL50 to TL60, but prices go up to TL80.

Most itineraries finish at a carpet shop, onyx factory or pottery workshop, but it is still worth taking a tour. It is interesting to see a traditional Cappadocian craftsman at work, but if you really object to hearing a sales pitch, you can sit out that section of the tour in the minibus, or make it clear before the trip begins that you are not interested.

At the start and end of the season, when customers are thin on the ground, local tour companies tend to join forces rather than have a fleet of half-empty minibuses trundling back and forth. Most of the pensions either operate their own tours or work with one of the travel agencies.

We strongly advise you to avoid booking an expensive tour package upon arrival in İstanbul. If your time is limited and you want to take a tour in Cappadicia, you're better off booking a tour directly from an agent in Cappadocia itself.

For listings of tour agencies, see p500 (for Göreme), p509 (Çavuşin), p512 (Avanos) and p518 (Ürgüp).

Getting There & Away

Two airports serve central Cappadocia: Kayseri and Nevşehir. For details of flights to or from İstanbul and İzmir see p537 and p515.

Transfer buses operate between Kayseri airport and accommodation in central Cappadocia for passengers leaving or arriving on flights between the mid-morning and evening. The buses pick up from and drop off to hotels and pensions in Ürgüp, Göreme, Uçhisar, Avanos and Nevşehir, and cost TL15 (for Ürgüp) to TL17 (for the other destinations). If you want to use the service you *must* pre-book by phone or email with **Argeus Tours** (p518) in Ürgüp if you fly Turkish Airlines; or through **Peerless Travel Services** (p518), also in Ürgüp, if you fly Onur Air or Sun Express. Alternatively, you can easily request your hotel or pension in Cappadocia to book a seat for you. If you don't pre-book, you may be able to jump on a bus at the airport if it is picking up other passengers on your flight. However, you will more likely have to make your way to Kayseri's otogar to catch a bus to your final destination (note that this is not an option in the evening) or catch a taxi there – an expensive proposition.

It's easy to get to Cappadocia by bus from İstanbul or Ankara. Buses from İstanbul to Cappadocia travel overnight (in high summer there may also be day buses) and bring you to Nevşehir, where there should be a *servis* to take you to Uçhisar, Göreme, Avanos or Ürgüp (see p515). From Ankara you can travel more comfortably during the day. It's easy enough to travel back from Cappadocia to İstanbul by day bus via Ankara because there are so many buses between these two cities.

The nearest train stations are at Niğde and Kayseri. See p528 and p538 for information about services.

Getting Around

The most-convenient bases for exploring central Cappadocia are Göreme, Ürgüp and Avanos. In summer, travelling between these places by bus and dolmuş (minibus) is relatively easy, although on Sunday the transport slows right down. In winter, public transport is less frequent.

Belediye Bus Corp dolmuşes (TL1.75 to TL2 depending on where you get on and off) travel between Ürgüp and Avanos via Ortahisar, the Göreme Open-Air Museum, Göreme village, Çavuşin and (on request) Paşabağı and Zelve. The services leave Ürgüp every two hours between 8am and 4pm (6pm in summer) and Avanos between 9am and 5pm (7pm in summer). You can hop on and off anywhere around the loop.

There's also an hourly *belediye* (municipal council) bus running from Avanos to Nevşehir (TL3) via Çavuşin (10 minutes), Göreme (15 minutes) and Uçhisar (30 minutes). It leaves Avanos from 7am to 6pm.

The Ihlara Valley in southwest Cappadocia can be visited on a tour from Göreme; it is difficult to visit in a day by bus, as you must change in Nevşehir and Aksaray.

GÖREME

☎ 0384 / pop 2250

Göreme is the archetypal travellers' utopia: a beatific village where the surreal surroundings spread a fat smile on everyone's face. Beneath the honeycomb cliffs, the locals live in fairy chimneys – or increasingly, run hotels in them. The wavy white valleys in the distance, with their hiking trails, panoramic viewpoints and rock-cut churches, look like giant tubs of vanilla ice cream. Rose Valley, meanwhile, lives up to its name; watching its pink rock slowly change colour at sunset is best accompanied by meze in one of the excellent eateries. Tourism is having an impact on a place where you can start the day

in a hot-air balloon, before touring a valley of rockcut Byzantine churches at the Göreme Open-Air Museum. Young locals are less interested in agriculture in the face of relatively rich tourist pickings. The pigeon houses peppering cliffs and fairy chimneys, traditionally used to collect the birds' droppings for use as fertiliser, increasingly lie empty. The village's permanent population has slipped below 2500, meaning it might lose its *belediye*. Nonetheless, you can still see rural life continuing in a place where, once upon a time, if a man didn't own a pigeon house, he would struggle to woo a wife.

Orientation & Information

Most of Göreme's shops and restaurants are in the streets surrounding the otogar. The Open-Air Museum is an easy walk 1km to the east of town.

BOOKSHOPS

1001 Books (☎ 271 2767; Müze Caddesi 35; ☼ 8am-8pm) One of Turkey's best bookshops for English reads, with guidebooks and a pile of free magazines. English-speaking staff work in the afternoon and some of the profits are donated to local causes.

INTERNET ACCESS

Flintstones Internet Centre (Belediye Caddesi; per hr TL2; ☼ 10am-midnight) Get an hour free for donating a tome to the book swap.

Mor-tel Telekom Call Shop/Internet Café (Roma Kalesi Arkası; per hr TL2; ☼ 9am-midnight) Also offers cheap international calls.

MONEY

There are four ATMs in booths at the otogar (Vakif Bank, Türkiye Bankası, HSBC and Garantı Bankası). The one at Deniz Bank on Müze Caddesi dispenses lira, euros and US dollars. Some of the town's travel agencies will exchange money, although you're probably better off going to the PTT.

POST

Post office (off Bilal Eroğlu Caddesi) Phone, fax and money-changing services.

TOURIST INFORMATION

Despite being the centre of the Cappadocian tourist industry, Göreme has no real tourist office. There's an information booth at the otogar that is open when most long-distance buses arrive, but it's run by the **Göreme**

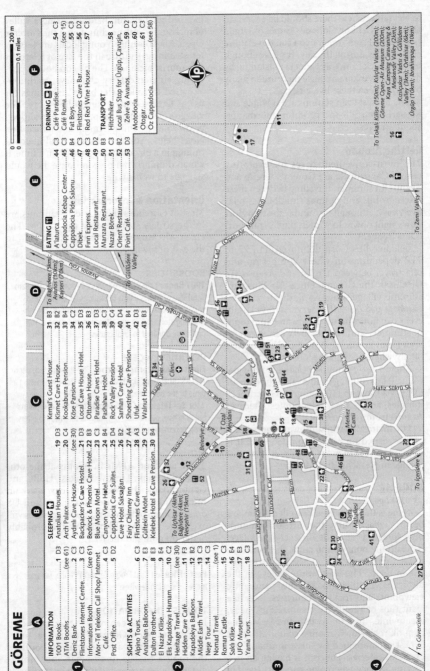

GÖREME

Turizmciler Derneği (Göreme Tourism Society; ☎ 271 2558; www.goreme.org). This coalition of hotel and restaurant owners is solely aimed at directing travellers to accommodation in the village and staff can't supply any meaningful information. They give out free maps and sell one for TL5.

Sights & Activities
GÖREME OPEN-AIR MUSEUM
One of Turkey's World Heritage sites, the **Göreme Open-Air Museum** (Göreme Açık Hava Müzesi; admission TL15; ☉ 8am-5pm) is an essential stop on any Cappadocian itinerary and deserves a two-hour visit. First an important Byzantine monastic settlement that housed some 20 monks, then a pilgrimage site from the 17th century, the cluster of rock-cut churches, chapels and monasteries is 1km uphill from the centre of the village.

Try to arrive early in the morning in summer and space yourself between tour groups – when lots of people crowd into one of the little churches they block the doorway, which is often the only source of light. Alternatively, go at midday, when the tour parties stop for lunch. If possible, avoid weekends, when domestic tourists descend.

Follow the cobbled path until you reach **Aziz Basil Şapeli**, the chapel dedicated to Kayseri-born St Basil, one of Cappadocia's most important saints. The grate-covered holes in the floor were the graves of the chapel's architects and financiers; the small boxes contained less-affluent folks' bones. In the main room, St Basil is pictured on the left; a Maltese cross is on the right, along with St George and St Theodore slaying a (faded) dragon, symbolising paganism. On the right of the apse, Mary holds baby Jesus, with a cross in his halo.

Above Aziz Basil Şapeli, bow down to enter the 12th-century **Elmalı Kilise** (Apple Church), overlooking a valley of poplars. Relatively well preserved, it contains both simple, red-ochre daubs and professionally painted frescoes of biblical scenes. The Ascension is pictured above the door. The church's name is thought to derive from an apple tree that grew nearby or from a misinterpretation of the globe held by the Archangel Gabriel, in the third dome.

Byzantine soldiers carved the **Azize Barbara Şapeli** (Chapel of St Barbara), dedicated to their patron saint, who is depicted on the left as you enter. They also painted the mysterious scenes on the roof – the middle one could represent the Ascension; above the St

George representation on the far wall, the strange creature could be a dragon, and the two crosses, the beast's usual slayers. The decoration is typical of the iconoclastic period, when images were outlawed – red ochre painted on the stone without any images of people or animals.

Uphill, in the **Yılanlı Kilise** (Snake Church or Church of St Onuphrius), the dragon is still having a bad day. To add insult to its fatal injuries, it was mistaken for a snake when the church was named. The hermetic hermaphrodite St Onuphrius is pictured on the right, holding a genitalia-covering palm leaf. Straight ahead, the small figure next to Jesus is one of the church's financiers.

A few steps away, hundreds of students chowed down in the **refectory**, with its long dining table with rock-cut benches and holes for candles. The trough in the floor was probably used for pressing grapes. In the attached larder, you can see storage shelves carved into the walls, and a kitchen. Another smaller, nameless church here retains a rock-cut iconostasis.

The museum's most famous church, the stunning, fresco-filled **Karanlık Kilise** (Dark Church; admission TL8), is definitely worth the extra outlay. The supplementary fee is due to its costly renovation, and an attempt to keep numbers down and preserve the frescoes. One of Turkey's finest surviving churches, it took its name from the fact that it originally had very few windows. The lack of light preserved the frescoes' vivid colour, particularly the upper examples, which were also spared by the iconoclastic Muslim vandals. On the right of the entrance, you can see two of the church's founders wearing curved ceremonial hats; in the main room, five more are visible, one reduced to a disembodied head. The copious biblical scenes include the birth of Jesus, on the left, with an ox and ass poking their noses into the manger.

Just past the Karanlık Kilise, the small **Azize Katarina Şapeli** (Chapel of St Catherine) has frescoes of St George, St Catherine and the Deesis.

The relatively recent, 13th-century **Çarıklı Kilise** (Sandal Church) is named for the footprints marked in the floor, representing the last imprints left by Jesus before he ascended to heaven. The four gospel writers are depicted below the central dome; in the arch over the door to the left is the Betrayal by Judas.

Downhill, the cordoned-off **Rahibeler Manastırı** (Nun's Convent) was originally several storeys high; all that remains are a large plain dining hall and, up some steps, a small chapel with unremarkable frescoes.

When you exit the museum, don't forget to cross the road and visit the **Tokalı Kilise** (Buckle Church), 50m down the hill towards Göreme. Covered by the same ticket, it is one of Göreme's biggest and finest churches, with an underground chapel and fabulous frescoes painted in a narrative (rather than liturgical) cycle. Entry is via the 10th-century 'old' Tokalı Kilise, through the barrel-vaulted chamber with frescoes portraying the life of Christ. Upstairs, the 'new' church, built less than a hundred years later, is also alive with frescoes on a similar theme. The holes in the floor once contained tombs, taken by departing Christians during the population exchange (p40).

CHURCHES

On the road between Göreme and the Open-Air Museum, a sign points to the 10th-century **El Nazar Kilise** (Church of the Evil Eye; admission TL8; ☻ 8am-5pm). Carved out of a fairy chimney, the church has been restored and is considerably quieter than the Open-Air Museum, although its frescoes are in worse condition. It's a pretty 10-minute walk from the main road.

Back towards the Open-Air Museum, a yellow sign points to the **Saklı Kilise** (Hidden Church), up the path to the right of the Hidden Cave Café. When you reach the top of the hill, follow the track to the left and look out for steps leading downhill to the right.

GÖREME VILLAGE

Göreme village, set amid cones and pinnacles of volcanic tuff, is its own biggest attraction. Just wandering its windy streets, glimpsing Cappadocia's undulating valleys between stone houses, is an experience that will stay with you for as long as it takes a fairy chimney to erode. Calls to prayer, apricots drying on flat roofs and vine cuttings protecting the tops of walls are reminders that, despite the fantastical setting, everyday rural life takes place here.

At Göreme's centre is the so-called **Roman Castle** (Roma Kalesi), a fairy chimney with a rock-cut Roman tomb; you can see the re-mains of column tops on its facade. Göreme may have been a burial ground for the Romans of Venasa (now Avanos).

UFO MUSEUM

ET says *hoş geldiniz* (welcome) at the world's fifth **UFO Museum** (admission TL3; ☻ 9am-7pm). Mostly consisting of magazine cuttings displayed haphazardly on cave walls, the exhibition ends with video footage of a possible seven-UFO sighting in Göreme.

ELİS KAPADOKYA HAMAM

Unwind after the chimney-spotting and treat yourself to a thorough massage at the beautiful **Elis Kapadokya Hamam** (☎ 271 2974; Adnan Menderes Caddesi; admission TL35, massage TL10; ☻ 10am-midnight), which has women-only and mixed areas.

Tours

See p496 for details of the types of tours offered by all of these agencies.

The following businesses have been recommended by readers or can be vouched for by us. However, the list is by no means exhaustive.

Alpino Tours (☎ 271 2727; www.alpino.com.tr; Müze Caddesi 5)

Heritage Travel (☎ 271 2687; www.turkishheritage travel.com; Yavuz Sokak 31) Local tours with the knowledgeable Mustafa are highly recommended (TL60 for four people minimum and €100 for a private tour). Based at the Kelebek Hotel & Cave Pension (p504), the company also offers traditional Turkish weddings and longer packages such as two-week cuisine tours (€2800).

Middle Earth Travel (☎ 271 2559; www.middle earthtravel.com; Cevizler Sokak 20) The adventure-travel specialist offers climbing and treks ranging from local, one-day expeditions (€30 to €40) to one-week missions along the Lycian Way or St Paul's Trail, through the Kaçkar Mountains or up Mt Ararat.

Neşe Tour (☎ 271 2525; www.nesetour.com; Avanos Yolu 54) Also offers trips to Nemrut Dağı (Mt Dağı) lasting between two and four days.

Nomad Travel (☎ 271 2767; www.nomadtravel.com.tr; Müze Caddesi 35) Offers an excellent Soğanlı tour.

Yama Tours (☎ 271 2508; www.yamatours.com; Müze Caddesi 2) Also offers three-day trips to Nemrut Dağı (€150), leaving on Monday and Thursday.

Sleeping

With about 100 hostels, pensions and hotels in Göreme, competition keeps prices low.

If you're visiting between October and May, pack warm clothes as it gets very cold at night

EKREM ILHAN

When Persia ruled Turkey (see p29), Katpatuka (Cappadocia) was famous throughout the empire for its beautiful horses. In Iran's Persepolis palace, among the reliefs depicting delegates from Persia's subject states, visitors from Katpatuka are pictured with equine offerings.

It seems appropriate, then, that present-day Göreme has a horse whisperer. Ekrem Ilhan brings wild horses to Göreme from Erciyes Dağı (Mt Erciyes), where a tribe of 400 has grown as local farmers have replaced them with machinery.

'They are in shock when they arrive here, but when their eyes open they see me, talking and giving them sweet things,' he says. 'People teach animals to bite and kick, because they are angry with them. But when you're friends, and you talk to them and give them some carrot and cucumber, you don't have any problems.'

Looking like a Cappadocian Clint Eastwood in a hat brought from America by a carpet-dealing friend, Ilhan tells a story about two pregnant mares he returned to Mt Erciyes to give birth. 'One year later, I went into the mountains, among the 400 horses, and called their names and they came directly to me.'

Ilhan treats the 11 horses in his cave stable using homemade remedies, such as grape water to extract parasites, and olive oil, mint and egg for indigestion. He is starting a trekking company, called **Dalton Brothers** (☎ 0532-275 6869; 2hr TL50) at the suggestion of a Canadian traveller and *Lucky Luke* fan. 'People like wild horses because it's difficult riding in the mountains, it's rocky, and the horses are used to it,' he says.

Göreme-born Ekrem Ilhan and Dalton Brothers are based at the stables behind the Anatolian Balloons office in Göreme.

and pension owners may delay putting the heating on. Ring ahead, too, to check that your choice is open. Those that do open in winter sometimes offer a low-season discount, but the prohibitive cost of heating means that this is relatively unusual.

BUDGET
Camping
Kaya Camping Caravaning (☎ 343 3100; kayacamping@www.com; camp sites per adult/child TL13/8.50; 🖵 🐾) This impressive camping ground is 2.5km from the centre of Göreme town, uphill from the Göreme Open-Air Museum. Set among fields of vines and a good sprinkling of trees, it has magnificent views and top-notch facilities such as clean bathrooms, plentiful hot water, a restaurant, supermarket, communal kitchen and washing machines. It's an excellent place for a family holiday, particularly as it has a large swimming pool complete with kiddie pool and sun lounges.

Pensions
Backpacker's Cave Hostel (☎ 271 2258; info@cappadocia-backpackers.com; Cevizler Sokak 13; dm TL12, s TL20-35, d TL30-45, tr TL45-60; 🖵) The hostel also known as 'Yasin's place' is a mixed bag. You're better off with an arch room, as their musty cave counterparts have low ceilings and narrow

beds. Room 5 is a triple-arch room with a small balcony, and the dorm has 13 beds.

Shoestring Cave Pension (☎ 271 2450; www.shoestringcave.com; Aydınlı Mahallesi; dm €6, r per person with/without bathroom €9/8; 🖵 🐾) One of Göreme's longest-running pensions, the Shoestring Cave has a swimming pool on the roof terrace and some attractive double rooms with marble bathrooms. The rock-cut rooms and dorm are not as appealing, but are set in a wonderfully organic chunk of rock with mushrooming walls. Tasty breakfasts and snacks are served in the courtyard restaurant.

Ufuk (☎ 271 2157; www.ufukpension.com.tr; off Müze Caddesi; dm/s/d/tr TL10/25/40/55, breakfast TL5; 🖵) Popular with Japanese and Korean travellers, Ufuk has a five-bed cave dorm and rooms with cramped bathrooms and satellite TV, all ranged around a scruffy courtyard with fruit trees. Visitors rate the owner Hasan, who ensures there's some conversation on the terrace among guests gazing at the *ufuk* (horizon).

Flintstones Cave (☎ 271 2555; www.theflintstonescavehotel.com; dm incl/excl breakfast TL15/10, s/d TL20/40, with jacuzzi TL40/60; 🖵 🐾) Among fields on the edge of the village, Flintstones is a lively hostel where the pool has hosted a barbecue party for every fairy chimney in Cappadocia. Manager Fatih, who claims to be Fred Flintstone's nephew, advertises heaps of activities in the

WALKS AROUND GÖREME

Göreme village is surrounded by the magnificent Göreme National Park. Valleys with gorgeous scenery and a mixture of ancient pigeon houses and even older rock-cut churches fan out from all around the village.

A handful of valleys are easily explored on foot; each needs about one to three hours. Most are interconnected, so you could easily combine several in a day, especially with the help of the area's many dolmuşes.

For example, you can walk to the Göreme Open-Air Museum and have a look around, then catch a Belediye Bus Corp otobus to Ürgüp, which stops outside the museum at 10 minutes past every even hour, to Zelve (TL2). Ask the driver to stop there or he may head straight to Avanos on the main road. It may be possible to get off further on at Aktepe (for Devrent Valley). Walk back to Göreme from Zelve via Paşabağı, Çavuşin and Meskendir Valley, Rose Valley and Red Valley. Don't forget a bottle of water!

These are some of the most interesting and accessible valleys:

Bağlıdere (White Valley) From Uçhisar to Çavuşin.

Güllüdere (Rose Valley) Connecting Çavuşin and Kızılçukur viewpoint.

Güvercinlik (Pigeon Valley) Connecting Göreme and Uçhisar; colourful dovecotes.

İçeridere (Long Valley) Running south from Rock Valley Pension.

Kılıçlar Vadısı (Swords Valley) Running off the Göreme Open-Air Museum road.

Kızılçukur Vadısı (Red Valley) Superb dovecotes, churches with frescoes.

Meskendir Valley Trail head next to Kaya Camping; tunnels and dovecotes.

Zemi Valley (Love Valley) West of the Göreme Open-Air Museum, with some particularly spectacular rock formations.

A word of warning: most of the valleys have signposts directing you to them, but nothing to keep you on the straight and narrow once you get there. Nor are they all particularly easy to walk, and there's no detailed map available – you'll have to rely on basic printouts. If you are exploring the Meskendir Valley area, it is easier to get lost if you climb out of the valleys.

Mehmet Güngör (☎ 0532-382 2069) is one local guide with an encyclopedic knowledge of Göreme's highways and byways. Most pension owners will also happily guide you for a minimal fee (it may even be complimentary).

bar-restaurant, a cavernous hang-out with a pool table. Ask to see a few rooms because there is a range of choices in the 20 cave, 'semi-cave' and modern rooms. If you're dorm-bound, shoot for the five-bedder with two adjoining rooms and a private bathroom.

Kookaburra Pension (☎ 271 2549; kookagoreme@hotmail.com; Konak Sokak 10; dm excl breakfast TL10, s/d TL20/40; 🖳) This small pension, with agricultural tools and pot plants decorating its stone passages, has tidy, spacious rooms with private bathrooms. The roof terrace is a knockout. If you can tear yourself away from the view, there's internet access in the bar-restaurant.

Walnut House (☎ 271 2235; www.cevizliev.com; Karşıbucak Caddesi; s/d/tr TL20/40/60; 🖳) This Ottoman mansion by the otogar offers one of the best deals in this price range. It's plain and low on atmosphere but popular with older and solo travellers. The main building has upstairs rooms with arched stone ceilings,

hard beds and small but clean bathrooms, and there's a new extension. In the attractive, kilim (pileless woven rug)-filled lobby-lounge, the views of the rose garden are some compensation for the odour of cigarette smoke.

Rock Valley Pension (☎ 271 2153; www.rockvalleycappadocia.com; Iceri Dere Sokak; dm/s/d TL10/40/50, tr & q per person TL15-20; 🖳 🐾) At the mouth of a valley on the edge of the village, Rock Valley's backpacker credentials are obvious from the Ireland T-shirt decorating its pavilion restaurant, which is the perfect place to get acquainted with a Cappadocian cushion. The five- and six-bed dorms are pleasant, with blue sheets and vines painted on the walls. Unfortunately, guests have complained about the hot-water supply and standards of cleanliness. Camping is also available.

Paradise Caves Hotel (☎ 271 2248; www.paradisecaveshotel.com; off Müze Caddesi; dm excl breakfast TL10, s/d incl breakfast TL30/50; 🖳) It's smarter than neighbouring Ufuk, but its name is a generous description of the rooms with old carpets and purple bedclothes. Positive features include fairy-chimney rooms, a functioning fireplace in the three-bed dorm, and a pirate-ship-like, multitiered terrace that winds around the cliff.

Bedrock & Phoenix Cave Hotel (☎ 271 2604; www.bedrockcavehotel.com; Cami Sokak; dm/s/d/tr TL10/30/50/75; 🖳) This central option has a leafy upstairs terrace and clean, spacious rooms, including an eight-bed dorm. Rooms have private bathrooms and beds tucked under arches, but are unlikely to inspire much purple prose in emails home.

Sarıhan Cave Hotel (☎ 271 2216; www.sarihancave hotel.com; Ünlü Sokak; s TL40-50, d TL50-70, tr TL60-80, ste TL100-150; 🖳) Fifteen of the 20 rooms in this decades-old hotel occupy caves and offer stunning views across the village. All are a little characterless but clean and comfortable, with access to the obligatory terrace.

Kemal's Guest House (☎ 271 2234; www.kemals guesthouse.com; Karşıbucak Caddesi; dm incl/excl breakfast €9/6, s/d/tr/q €24/30/42/52) Entered via a flowery garden and a laid-back reception with big bookshelves and comfy chairs, popular Kemal's is run by a genial Turkish-Dutch couple. Barbara offers guided hikes (€7 including a picnic) and her beau Kemal rustles up four-course Turkish feasts (€10). There are cave, Ottoman and modern rooms, with cheaper double and triple options with shared bathrooms available, and two six-bed, single-sex cave dorms with private bathrooms.

Köse Pension (☎ 271 2294; www.kosepension.com; Ragıp Üner Caddesi; dm TL12, s without bathroom TL20, tw hut TL40, d & tw with bathroom TL60, tr with/without bathroom TL75/60; ✗ 🖳) Like all youth hostels, Köse Pension has some rough edges, but unlike most, it has a swimming pool in the garden and a terrace where communal meals are served. Breakfast costs TL3.50; for dinner, choose between Western meals (TL10) and the three-course Turkish extravaganza (TL15), washed down with a drink from the self-service fridge. Run by Edinburgh-born Dawn and family, the backpacker institution is cheerily painted with grinning spiders and winding creepers. Many rooms have balconies and, on the roof, there are wooden huts and a 20-bed dorm with mattresses on the floor (sheet sleeping bags can be rented).

Gültekin Motel (☎ 271 2584; www.gultekin-motel .com; Roma Kalesi Arkası; s/d/tr TL35/60/85, without bath-

room TL25/50/75; 🖳) Up the hill from the Roman Castle, the Gültekin is popular for the excellent views from its roof terrace, the hearty breakfasts and its friendly owner. The cave and arch rooms, on a couple of levels, are not very atmospheric, but are clean with cheery bedspreads.

Cave Hotel Saksağan (☎ 271 2165; www.cavehotel saksagan.com; Adnan Menderes Caddesi; s/d/tr TL45/65/100) This pyramidal fairy chimney boasts a walled garden, a terrace, and proximity to one of the balloon companies for that early-morning start. In the tastefully restored rooms, rugs hang between photos of yet more fairy chimneys and there are few modern additions beyond the private bathrooms and satellite TVs. The newer arch rooms (they are only 200 years old) are in a former stable and farmer's cottage.

Canyon View Hotel (☎ 271 2333; www.canyonview hotel.com; Yavuz Sokak; s/d/tr TL50/65/75, with jacuzzi TL60/85/100; ✗ 🖳) As well one of Göreme's best roof terraces, with views of Çavuşin, Canyon View offers rooms in a converted 9th-century church and Byzantine house. Decorated with local pottery, the rooms, which include a former winery, pigeon house and stable, retain features from their original incarnations. The family offers free tours to new arrivals, but readers have advised against accepting the offer.

MIDRANGE

There is a cluster of rock-cut retreats on Aydınlı Hill (around Orta Mahallesi Camii), gazing across the fairy-chimney-punctured village.

Arch Palace (☎ 271 2575; www.archpalace.com; Ünlü Sokak 14; s/d TL30/70; ✗ 🖳) The Arch Palace inspires fierce loyalty, largely because owner Mustafa Yelkalan is a helpful and knowledgeable host, everything is squeaky clean and the rooftop terrace restaurant has sensational views. The simple, peaceful rooms are decorated with local pottery and carpets.

Blue Moon Motel (☎ 271 2433; www.bluemoonmotel .net; Müze Caddesi; s/d/tr/q from TL40/70/90/110; 🖳 🖳) A 150-year-old village house is the setting for this central hotel's sunny rooms with flowery bedspreads. The rooftop 'architectural' rooms have arched ceilings and little windows opening on to the terrace, which has a front-row view of the main drag. Breakfast takes place here or, during the winter, in a cave room downstairs.

Ottoman House (☎ 271 2616; www.ottomanhouse .com.tr; Orta Mahalle 25; s/d TL45/70; ☑) With its indoor swimming pool, this restored building is certainly no fairy chimney, but the professional management has attempted to create a local ambience. Candelabras stand in reception and rugs adorn the white walls. The rooftop restaurant is pleasant and it's a reasonable option if there's no room at more-traditional inns.

our pick Kelebek Hotel & Cave Pension (☎ 271 2531; www.kelebekhotel.com; Yavuz Sokak 31; s/d €28/35, deluxe €36/45, ste €65-220; ☑ ☑) In 1993, pioneering Ali Yavuz became Göreme's first hotelier to step above the backpacker sector. Not just because he had to climb Aydınlı Hill to reach his family home, which now boasts the village's best terrace for surveying the Cappadocian dreamscape, but because he converted it into Göreme's first boutique hotel. Divided into the modestly named Kelebek Pension and the newer Kelebek Suites, the 32-room complex ranges across stone houses and two fairy chimneys, once used as chapels by hermits. The sympathetically restored rooms and suites mix Anatolian decoration and handmade furniture with modern luxuries. The 10 newer suites have their own dining terrace, and traditional Cappadocian wedding ceremonies are available. As much as the hamam, garden and small swimming pool, it's the helpful staff and Yavuz' passion for village life that make this a magical spot.

Pashahan Hotel (☎ 271 2283; www.pashahan.com; Roma Kalesi Arkası 7; s/d/tr TL45/85/100; ☒ ☑) The Pashahan promises to makes guests 'feel like a Pasha' and the double beds in its cave rooms are certainly kingly. Although they are slightly gloomy at the bottom of the hotel, the eight rooms have TVs, minibars, polished floor-boards and excellent bathrooms. The Roman Castle virtually explodes through the roof terrace, with its indoor and outside sections, and carpets and textiles are piled throughout the building.

Local Cave House Hotel (☎ 271 2171; www.local cavehouse.com; Cevizler Sokak 11; s/d €30/50; ☒ ☑ ☑) The Local's attractive cave rooms have features such as big beds, local artwork, antique furniture and wooden ceilings, although the bathrooms are not a highlight. There are two terraces with wonderful views and a glass-fronted lounge-restaurant overlooking the swimming pool among the fairy chimneys.

Fairy Chimney Inn (☎ 271 2655; www.fairychimney .com; Güvercinlik Sokak 5-7; s/d/tr from €44/55/66, students €22; ☒ ☑) This fairy chimney high on Aydınlı Hill has been wonderfully converted by its owner, a German anthropologist who has ensured the conversion is as respectful of the original fabric as possible. With his Turkish wife, he has created a tranquil retreat at the village's highest point, with some of the best views around. Rooms are beautifully decorated, with simple furniture, cushions and carpets everywhere and a refreshing lack of TVs and jacuzzis. The palatial Byzantine family suite is one of the most alluring in town, spread across four floors with peephole windows. Other treats include the cave hamam, communal lounge, home-cooked meals and glorious garden terrace.

Aydınlı Cave House (☎ 271 2263; www.thecave hotel.com; Aydınlı Sokak 12; standard s/d/tr €45/60/75, deluxe €55/85/100) This recent addition to the hilltop posse of midrange cave abodes has six immaculately presented rooms. With features such as hamam taps and stone fireplaces, the decor never sacrifices tradition and taste in the pursuit of comfort. The deluxe rooms have jacuzzis and show-stealing touches such as an old illuminated winery, while the standard rooms are more minimal.

Kismet Cave House (☎ 271 2416; www.kismetcave house.com; Kağnı Yolu 9; d €60-80) Opened in 2007, this eight-room guest house has quickly built a strong reputation; one reader told us it was the best-value accommodation they found in Turkey. The arched rooms up top have the edge on the chimney chambers, but Afghani bedspreads, jacuzzis and views of Rose Valley are common features. If you check into the deluxe Tulip Room, you will be loath to drag yourself away from its open fire, with logs at the ready. Knowledgeable owner Faruk encourages communal Anatolian living at the long dining tables.

TOP END

Cappadocia Cave Suites (☎ 271 2800; www.cappadocia cavesuites.com; Ünlü Sokak 19; s/d/ste from €103.50/115/300; ☑) Göreme's long-established top-end favourite consistently bags awards for its boutique appeal, although it's not in the same league as Anatolian Houses. As well as satellite TV, minibar and a promised fitness centre, rooms have decor such as the Turkmenistan-meets-Cappadocia bedspread in suite 2. The suites are not the best in town but fairy chimney rooms such as 109, with its low archway leading to the bedroom and lounge in a former stable, are sure winners.

Anatolian Houses (☎ 271 2463; www.anatolian houses.com.tr; Gaferli Mahallesi, Ünlü Sokak; r €195-290, ste €420-610; ☐ ⚓ 🐾) It took six years to build this swish boutique hotel occupying a group of fairy chimneys, and no wonder. If you're not bowled over by features such as the spa, with its indoor/outdoor swimming pool, hamam, sauna and wellness centre, you certainly will be by the hotel's sleek restaurant (mains TL20) and extensive wine cellar. With rooms exquisitely decorated with objets d'art and handmade textiles, this is as luxurious as Cappadocia gets.

Eating

There is a strip of good eateries on the quiet side of the dry canal, away from the busy Bilal Eroğlu Caddesi.

Cappadocia Kebap Center (☎ 271 2682; Müze Caddesi; mains TL3.50) This tiny, friendly joint is a great place for a fast feed. You can enjoy a chicken döner kebap sandwich for a mere TL3 or a spicy *acılı* kebap sandwich for TL4, accompanied by chips (TL3.50) and a beer (TL3.50) or fresh orange juice (TL3).

Fırın Express (☎ 271 2266; Eski Belediye Yanı Sokak; pide & pizza TL4-8, mains TL8-13; ☽ 11am-11pm) Set slightly back from the main strip, this wood-cabinlike eatery is praised by carnivores and vegetarians alike for the pide (Turkish pizza) and pizza produced in its large wood oven. More-substantial claypot dishes such as *tavuk güveç* (chicken stew, TL6) are also available.

Nazar Börek (☎ 271 2441; Müze Caddesi; mains TL5) If you're after a cheap and filling meal, sample this simple place's *börek* (filled pastries), *gözleme* (savoury pancakes) and *sosyete böregi* (stuffed spiral pastries served with yoghurt and tomato sauce). Friendly staff and a pleasant outdoor eating area on the canal make it perennially popular. There's often a tasty daily special, and the baklava and generous glasses of orange juice (TL4.50) are also recommended.

Cappadocia Pide Salonu (☎ 271 2858; Hakki Paşa Meydanı; pide TL5-9) Göreme's pide hot spot has a more local feel than most of the village's eateries, created by the uncontrived decor of rugs and Coke posters. Sitting under the canalside umbrellas, you can tuck into 12 types of pide, as well as spaghetti, grills, pottery kebaps, beer and rakı (aniseed brandy).

Point Café (Müze Caddesi; mains TL10) Missing your favourite comfort foods? Cenap and Anniesa, a Turkish-South African couple, dish up curries, burgers, fruit smoothies, filter coffee and home-baked cakes. Sit on the balcony above the canal or in the cabinlike restaurant.

Dibek (☎ 271 2209; Hakkı Paşa Meydanı 1; mains TL10; ☽ 9am-11pm) Dibek is one of Göreme's best and most original restaurants. You pass a winery on the way into the 475-year-old building, before reclining at low circular tables in alcoves decorated with hoes and scythes. Although many local eateries offer *testi kebap* (pottery kebap, with meat or mushrooms and vegetables cooked in a sealed terracotta pot, which is broken at the table; TL15), this is the only place where you must give three hours' notice before eating, so the dish can be slow cooked in an oven in the stone floor. Other offerings include homemade wine, *saç tava* (cubed lamb with tomatoes, peppers and garlic, TL13) and the less-exciting *kurufasulye* (white beans with tomato sauce and optional sundried lamb, TL6).

our pick A'laturca (☎ 271 2882; Müze Caddesi; mains TL10-25) Style meets substance at this elegant eatery. Offering Anatolian cuisine as well as the odd T-bone, the menu has been thoughtfully and creatively designed and the food is exceptionally well prepared. Pick one of the many seating areas, such as the upstairs terrace or the garden with its bright beanbag seating, and tuck into some of the best mezes we tasted in Turkey. Recommended mains include the succulent Erciyes kebap, served on a bed of thinly sliced fried potatoes and garlic yoghurt; and Ali Nazik, a *şiş* kebap with an aubergine, garlic and yoghurt puree.

Local Restaurant (☎ 271 2629; Müze Caddesi 38; mains TL11) At the start of the road to the Open-Air Museum, the Local is one of Göreme's best eateries. There's an outdoor terrace and an elegant, stone-walled dining room with an open fire and candles flickering in alcoves. The service is attentive, ingredients are fresh, and prices are reasonable for scrumptious dishes such as lamb shanks and *tavuklu mantarli krep* (chicken and mushroom pancake).

Manzara Restaurant (☎ 271 2712; Harım Sokak 14; mains TL12) With its bird's-eye view of Göreme's flat roofs and less-flat rock formations, Manzara is a prime spot to spend a meze-and-rakı evening. Choose between two terraces and an indoor dining room with a fireplace. Classics such as aubergine kebap are on offer and staff are considerate enough to consult diners about the background music.

Orient Restaurant (☎ 271 2346; Adnan Menderes Caddesi; mezes TL8, mains TL12-40, 4-course set menus TL20) Göreme's smartest restaurant is light on views but heavy on ambience in its stylish ground-floor dining room. This is the place to spend a leisurely evening savouring good food. Dishes include chicken cordon bleu, pasta and grills, and the restaurant has a good reputation for meat dishes such as the tender marble steak, served on a sizzling marble slab. Vegetarians, less well catered for, can opt for the assorted meze plate.

Drinking

Most of the village's watering holes open from noon till late.

Fat Boys (☎ 0535-386 4484; Belediye Caddesi; mains TL7; ☺ 24hr) Head to this happening, rock-soundtracked hang-out, run by an Australian-Turkish couple, to shoot some pool, dig into burgers, pies and vegemite, and lounge outside with a nargileh (traditional water pipe).

Red Red Wine House (☎ 271 2183; Müze Caddesi) The two tiny tables outside Göreme's most atmospheric bar are hot property for people-watching. The candle-lit cave inside is an intimate setting for a nargileh and a beer or a glass of Cappadocian wine, available hot.

Café Roma (Müze Caddesi; mains TL9) With a prime spot overlooking four floors of rugs hanging from a carpet shop, this lantern-lit garden is a good place to chill out to Pink Floyd records or the long-haired troubadour, who strums the *saz* (long-necked lute) most nights.

Café Paradise (☎ 271 2545; El Sanatları Çarşısı 13) Hiding in the centre of town, this secluded tea garden is entered by a dinky bridge over a moat. The shaded sofas are the ideal accompaniment to a nargileh.

Flintstones Cave Bar (Müze Caddesi) This long-time backpacker favourite, cut right into the rock face, mixes a roaring fire and rugs on the walls with a dance floor and satellite TV.

Getting There & Away

For details of shuttle-bus services between Kayseri airport and Göreme see p496. See p495 for extra information about bus services to Göreme.

There are daily long-distance buses to all sorts of places from Göreme's otogar, although normally you're ferried to Nevşehir's otogar to pick up the main service (which can add nearly an hour to your travelling time). See p497 for the bus services that connect Göreme with nearby villages.

Details of some useful long-distance daily services from Göreme are listed in the table (above). Note that the morning bus to İstanbul goes via Ankara, so takes one hour longer than the evening bus. For Aksaray, change in Nevşehir.

Getting Around

There are several places to hire mountain bikes, scooters, cars and the objectionable quads, including **Hitchhiker** (☎ 271 2169; www .cappadociahitchhiker.com; T Ozal Meydanı), **Oz Cappadocia** (☎ 271 2159; www.ozcappadocia.com; T Ozal Meydanı) and **Motodocia** (☎ 271 2517; Uzundere Caddesi), all located near the otogar. It pays to shop around, as prices vary dramatically.

As a rule, mountain bikes cost between TL10 and TL15 for a day; TL3 to TL5 for an

SERVICES FROM GÖREME'S OTOGAR			
Destination	Fare (TL)	Duration (hr)	Frequency (per day)
Adana	30	5	3
Ankara	25	4½	6
Antalya	35	9	2 evening
Çanakkale	60	16	1 evening
Denizli (for Pamukkale)	35	11	2 evening
Fethiye	55	14	1 evening
İstanbul	40	11-12	1 morning & 2 evening
İzmir	40	11½	1 evening
Kayseri	10	1½	hourly morning, afternoon & evening
Konya	20	3	2 morning
Marmaris/Bodrum	55	13	2 evening
Selçuk	50	11½	1 evening

hour. Mopeds and scooters go for TL25 to TL40 for a day; TL20 to TL25 for half a day. A small Renault or Fiat car costs TL35 to TL90 for a day, with features such as air-con, automatic gears and a diesel engine available.

You'll need to leave some ID as a security deposit. Since there are no petrol stations in Göreme and the rental companies will hike petrol prices, refill your tank in Nevşehir, Avanos or Ürgüp, or at one of the garages on the main road near Ortahisar and Ibrahimpaşa. The companies may let you off if you have been on a small journey to, say, Çavuşin and used a minimal amount of fuel.

UÇHİSAR

☎ 0384 / pop 6350

Welcome to *Cappadoce*, as the French call Cappadocia. At times, pretty Uçhisar is like a 'Petite France', having been the local 'kilometre zero' for Gallic gallivanters since Club Med revived the village's fortunes in the 1960s.

Spotted from Göreme, Uçhisar Castle is a distinctive blip on the horizon, adding yet another dollop of character to the landscape. It is equally impressive up close, its jumble of rock faces gazing across the valleys at **Erciyes Dağı** (Mt Erciyes; 3916m). The mountain's snow-capped summit provides a fantastic backdrop for old Uçhisar, which is quieter than Göreme and worth considering as a base for exploring Cappadocia.

There are Vakif Bank and Garanti Bankası ATMs on the main square, and an **internet café** (per hr TL1; ☺ 9am-midnight) and a PTT nearby.

Watching the sun set over the Rose and Pigeon Valleys from the wonderful vantage point of **Uçhisar Castle** (Uçhisar Kalesi; admission TL3; ☺ 8am-8.15pm) is a popular activity. A tall volcanic-rock outcrop riddled with tunnels and windows, the castle is visible for miles around. Now a tourist attraction complete with terrace cafés at its entrance, it provides panoramic views of the Cappadocian countryside. Unfortunately, many of the bus groups that visit leave rubbish, which diminishes the experience. The lack of barriers means you should be very careful – one photographer died when he fell over the edge after stepping back to get a good shot.

There are some excellent **hiking** possibilities around Uçhisar; see the boxed text, p502, for more information.

Sleeping

BUDGET

Uçhisar Pension (☎ 219 2662; www.uchisarpension.com; Kale Yani 5; s/d TL30/60) The blue-and-white bedspreads give the eight clean, simple rooms, including three cave rooms, the feel of a breezy country escape. Rooms have private bathrooms and the terraces may be small but there's nothing modest about their views.

Anatolia Pension (☎ 219 2339; www.anatoliapension .com; Hacialibey Caddesi; d €25-30; ☒ ☐) Occupying a sturdy stone house on the main street, this pension has 15 vaulted, light-filled rooms with comfortable beds, clean linen and sparkling bathrooms. Traditional Turkish meals are available.

La Maison du Rève (☎ 219 2199; www.lamaison dureve.com; Tekelli Mahallesi 32; s/d/tr €20/30/40; ☐) Teetering on the edge of a cliff and enjoying spectacular views from the large terrace, 'Dream House' is an ant colony of a hotel. Rambling over three floors, the 30 compact rooms include 20 with attached balconies. There's a ramshackle restaurant (five-course menu TL15) and the owners rent out scooters (TL40 per day).

Kilim Pension (☎ 219 2774; www.sisik.com; Tekelli Mahallesi; s/d/tr €25/35/52) Roomy Kilim's spectacular views are the closest you'll get to the view from a hot-air balloon basket without leaving the ground. The nine beautifully decorated rooms, including one cave room, overlook a vine-shaded courtyard. Ask for one upstairs, as they have more light. There's also a relaxing rooftop terrace and an atmospheric restaurant.

MIDRANGE

Les Terrasses d'Uçhisar (☎ 219 2792; www.terrassespen sion.com; Eski Göreme Yolu; s/d/tr/ste €38/38/46/80; ☐) The splendid location of this relaxed French-owned place is its best asset. Rooms are arched or in caves and all feature simple but stylish decoration; those upstairs have absolutely fabulous views. There's a great terrace for soaking up the views, and a well-regarded restaurant.

Lale Saray (☎ 219 2333; www.lalesaray.com; Göreme Caddesi; s €45-80, d €50-85, tr €60-95; ☒ ☐ ☒) Inspiring love hearts in its guest book for its service, Lale Saray has a large restaurant and a terrace splashed with cushions. The sweet-smelling cave and arch rooms have features such as massage showers, heated towel rails, minibars, and terraces with wicker furniture.

TOP END

Villa Cappadocia (☎ 219 3133; www.villacappadocia .com; Kayabaşı Sokak 18; r TL150; ✗) This small and immensely comfortable hotel takes good advantage of its spectacular views of Rose Valley. With just 12 rooms, it has a tranquil atmosphere and is designed to give guests as relaxed a holiday as possible. The pick of the rooms is the Honeymoon Room, which has a jacuzzi and a private terrace. Steps lead through a rose garden to the small cave restaurant (mains TL7 to TL10), and the two terraces are perfect spots for a sunset drink.

Karlık Evi (☎ 219 2995; www.karlikevi.com; Karlık Mahallesi; s/d from €120/140; ☻) A former hospital, this retreat offers 20 spacious rooms, some with private balcony or terrace. The atmosphere is one of discreet elegance, and the overall style is best described as 'rustic chic'. The excellent facilities include a restaurant, a hamam, a garden, a roof terrace and a massage service.

Les Maisons de Cappadoce (☎ 219 2813; www .cappadoce.com; Belediye Meydanı 28; studios €130-180, villas €240-980) French architect Jacques Avizou's 15-year-old empire now numbers 16 rental properties. Located above Pigeon Valley in Uçhisar's old quarter, the properties offer stylish and supremely comfortable accommodation, which allows maximum independence and privacy alongside services such as daily cleaning. A breakfast basket is left hanging at your door every morning. Six of the properties are studios perfect for a romantic getaway, the others are well-equipped houses that can accommodate up to seven people. Reception is in a first-floor office in the main square.

Museum Hotel (☎ 219 2220; www.museum-hotel .com; Tekeli Mahallesi 1; d from €130-195, ste €250-1650; ▣ ☻) This exquisitely decorated boutique hotel is one of Cappadocia's best, featuring magnificent common areas and luxe rooms and suites. Standard rooms come complete with brass beds, rich rugs and attractive textiles, and the opulent suites (some in caves) have to be seen to be believed. The mosaic-adorned infinity pool, stylish Lil'a restaurant (mains TL20) and panoramic rooftop terrace are equally impressive.

Eating

Kandil House (☎ 219 3191; Göreme Caddesi; snacks TL4) With its spot-on views of Rose Valley, randomly painted furniture and backgam-mon board, the café under the arches makes a pleasant hideout on a hot day.

Le Mouton Rouge (☎ 219 3000; Belediye Meydanı; mains TL10) The Red Sheep has a bistro ambience, created by orange tablecloths, French TV, jolly *mouton* motifs and a large courtyard. The menu, however, is not particularly Gallic, featuring salads and meat dishes such as *saç tava*. Better for a *bière* and a bite than a meal.

House of Memories (☎ 219 2947; Göreme Caddesi 41; mains TL10-12) Despite the name, the food here isn't particularly memorable. Seating is in the kilim-strewn downstairs dining room or on the ramshackle but undeniably welcoming upstairs terrace, which enjoys a good view. The menu features mezes and other Turkish staples, a beer costs TL5.50 and the service is friendly.

Center Café & Restaurant (☎ 219 3117; Belediye Meydanı; mains TL10-15) This outdoor eatery on the main square has tables dotted around a shady but slightly scruffy garden. Locals enjoy the kebaps and swear by the *patlican salatası* (eggplant salad, TL7.50). A good pit stop for *gözleme* (TL5) and a beer (TL5).

Les Terrasses d'Uçhisar (☎ 219 2792; www.terrasses pension.com; Eski Göreme Yolu; dinner €5-8) With its yellow tablecloths, candelabras and small French menu, the cosy bar-restaurant in the pension of the same name has the air of a Provençal bistro. The home-cooked food includes Turkish classics such as *saç tava* (€5), French alternatives such as *filet de boeuf avec sauce poivre* (beef fillet with pepper sauce, €8) and a nine-course menu (from €5). Nonguests are welcome, but should book ahead.

Elai (☎ 219 3181; www.elairestaurant.com; Eski Göreme Yolu; mains TL24-45; ⏱ 10.30am-2.30pm & 6.30-11pm) This stylish place is in a converted café, where the gossiping old men have been replaced by a sharp dining room with velvety curtains and exposed beams. Guests can kick off with a drink on the terrace, with its magnificent view, before moving inside to sample dishes ranging from duck confit to grilled jumbo. Dishes travel around the world but really shine when they are Turkish in inspiration.

Getting There & Away

Dolmuşes and midibuses leave from outside the *belediye* for Göreme, Çavuşin and Avanos (TL1.50 to TL2.50, every half-hour from 7am to 7.30pm, to 6pm in winter). Similarly priced and timed buses to Ortahisar and Ürgüp

---

RUDE BOYS

The *peribacalar* (fairy chimneys) that have made Cappadocia so famous were formed when erosion wiped out the lava covering the tuff (consolidated volcanic ash), leaving behind isolated pinnacles. They can reach a height of up to 40m, have conical shapes and are topped by caps of harder rock resting on pillars of softer rock. Depending on your perspective, they look like giant phalluses or outsized mushrooms. The villagers call them simply *kalelar* (castles).

---

depart from near Chez Kemal on the main square. Both services stop at Nevşehir after Uçhisar on their return journeys.

A taxi to Göreme costs TL10 and to Ürgüp TL25.

You can book longer bus journeys at Chez Kemal. You'll probably be taken to Göreme in a *servis* to pick up onward connections to destinations throughout Turkey; see p506 for details.

For details of shuttle buses between Kayseri airport and Uçhisar see p496.

ÇAVUŞIN
☎ 0384

Midway between Göreme and Avanos is sleepy little Çavuşin, where the main activity is at the souvenir stands beneath the cliff houses. It has some sterling accommodation options and offers an authentic village experience.

On the highway you'll find the **Çavuşin Church** (Big Pigeon House Church; admission TL8; � 8am-5pm, last admission 4.30pm), accessed from the pottery shop via a steep and rickety iron stairway. Cappadocia's first post-iconoclastic church, it served as a pigeon house for many years and is home to some fine frescoes.

Walk up the hill through the new part of the village and continue past the main square to find the old part of Çavuşin. Here you can explore a steep and labyrinthine complex of abandoned houses cut into a rock face, as well as one of the oldest churches in Cappadocia, the **Church of John the Baptist**, which is located towards the top of the cliff.

Çavuşin is the starting point for scenic **hikes** to the southeast, through Güllüdere (Rose Valley), Kızılçukur Vadisi (Red Valley) and Meskendir Valley. You can even go as far as the Zindanönü viewpoint (6.5km), then walk

out to the Ürgüp–Ortahisar road and catch a dolmuş back to your base.

There is no bank or ATM in the village, but there are three internet cafés, including **MustiNet** (per hr TL1; � 4pm-midnight) near İn Pension.

Tours
Mephisto Voyage (☎ 532 7070; www.mephistovoyage .com) is based at the İn Pension and has a very good reputation. It's been operating for over a decade and offers trekking and camping packages ranging from a two-day local wander to a 14-day trip around Cappadocia and the Taurus Mountains (€500). It also rents out bicycles and offers tours by bike, horse cart and, for mobility-impaired people, the Joelette system.

Sleeping & Eating
Camping Cappadocia (☎ 532 7070; 2 people incl tent & breakfast €10, sleeping bag €2) Being set up by Mephisto Voyage at the time of writing, this network of camping grounds in scenic spots such as Red Valley will allow trekkers to camp out without having to lug their own equipment.

Green Motel (☎ 532 7050; www.motelgreen.com; camp sites TL7, r TL30-50; 🖳) Our favourite Çavuşin accommodation option, this friendly place is set in a lush garden where owner Mehmet's father kept horses. The simple, spacious rooms in the 80-year-old family house and newer extension have rugs on the walls and bathrooms of varying sophistication. At the top end, you can step out on to a balcony with views of Red Valley. The Ottoman-style restaurant churns out pide and the atmosphere could not be more relaxing.

İn Pension (☎ 532 7070; www.pensionincappadocia .com; s/d/tr TL35/70/80, s/d without bathroom TL15/30; 🖳) Right on the main square, this converted village house is nothing flash but it's worth considering due to its knowledgeable owners, Ahmet and son Ali, who run Mephisto Voyage. With their whitewashed walls, blue doors and red curtains, the rooms are being restored and a rooftop café and children's swimming pool added.

Turbel Motel (☎ 532 7084; www.turbelhotel.com; s/d TL40/80, cave TL125/150) A good choice, Turbel has commanding views from its restaurant and rooms, which have basic private bathrooms and rugs, folkloric dolls and kitschy paintings for decor. Owner Mustafa, who spent 15 years

CAPPADOCIA FROM ABOVE

If you've never taken a flight in a hot-air balloon, Cappadocia is one of the best places in the world to try it. Flight conditions are especially favourable here, with balloons operating most mornings from the beginning of April to the end of November. It's a truly magical experience and many travellers judge it to be the highlight of their trip; see the boxed text, p656, for a first-hand account of a flight.

Flights take place at dawn. The reputable companies have an unwritten agreement that they will only offer one early flight per day due to the fact that the winds can become unreliable and potentially dangerous later in the morning. Transport between your hotel and the balloon launch site is included in the hefty price, as is a champagne toast.

Despite the fact that there is an ever-increasing number of ballooning companies in Cappadocia, increased competition hasn't led to price discounting. This is because the balloon companies offer large commissions to the hotels and tour agencies who sell their flights, and don't want to further erode their profits by discounting flights sold direct to customers. Some companies will give a discount for cash payments or direct online bookings, but that's about as far as the reputable outfits will go.

You'll quickly realise that there's a fair amount of hot air between the operators about who is and isn't inexperienced, ill-equipped, underinsured and unlicensed. Be aware that hot-air ballooning is potentially dangerous. It's your responsibility to check the credentials of your chosen tour operator carefully and make sure that your pilot is experienced and savvy – even if it means asking to see their licences and logbooks. And don't pick the cheapest operator if it means they might be taking short cuts with safety (eg operating two flights per day).

It's important to note that the balloons travel with the wind, and that the companies can't ensure a particular flight path on a particular day. All companies try to fly over the fairy chimneys, but sometimes – albeit rarely – the wind doesn't allow this. Occasionally, unfavourable weather conditions mean that the pilot will cancel the flight for the day for safety reasons; if this happens you'll be offered a flight on the next day or will have your payment refunded. All passengers should take a warm jumper or jacket and women should wear flat shoes and pants. Children under seven and adults over 70 will not be taken up by most companies.

The following agencies have good credentials:

Ez-Air Balloons (☎ 0384-341 7096; www.ezairballoons.com; Kavaklionu Mahallesi 8a, Ürgüp) Running since 1991, and offering the services of veteran pilot Hasan Ezel, Ez-Air charges €160 for a one-hour-minimum flight. Its two balloons have capacities of eight and 20 passengers.

Kapadokya Balloons (Map p498; ☎ 0384-271 2442; www.kapadokyaballoons.com; Adnan Menderes Caddesi, Göreme) The premium balloon airline, partly because it is the only operator to change its launch site based on wind direction, ensuring the most scenic flight path. Run by Kaili and Lars, who kicked off Göreme's ballooning industry 20 years ago, and their team of four multilingual pilots, the company offers an exclusive deluxe flight (€250, children aged 6 to 12 €125, at least 1½ hours, 10 passengers) and a sponsored flight (€175, one hour, up to 20 passengers).

Sultan Balloons (☎ 0384-353 5249; www.sultanballoons.com; Kaktus Sokak 21, Mustafapaşa Kasabası, Ürgüp) Established in 2005 by long-time chief pilot Ismail Keremoglu, the company offers a standard flight (€155, one hour) in its 12- and 20-passenger balloons. It is the only operator to offer VIP flights for two passengers in a small balloon (€600 for two, 1¼ hours).

in Strasbourg and resembles the French actor Roger Hanin, attracts many French travellers. A new underground cave section has five rooms with jacuzzis and a disco-bar.

Ayse & Mustafa's Place (☎ 0535-947 8649; snacks TL3-4; ☺ 9am-5pm) Sitting under the plum trees, sample Ayse's home cooked *gözleme*, *menemen* (Turkish omelette) and bigger meals on reservation. Fresh fruit juice, beer and nargilehs are also available.

Getting There & Away

See p497 for info about the bus services that connect Çavuşin with nearby villages.

ZELVE

The road between Çavuşin and Avanos passes a turn-off to the **Zelve Open-Air Museum** (admission incl Paşabağı TL8, parking TL2; ☺ 8am-5pm, last admission 4.15pm), where three valleys of abandoned homes and churches converge.

Zelve was a monastic retreat from the 9th to the 13th century. It doesn't have as many impressive painted churches as the Göreme Open-Air Museum, but its sinewy valley walls with rock antennae could have been made for poking around.

The valleys were inhabited until 1952, when they were deemed too dangerous to live in and the villagers were resettled a few kilometres away in Aktepe, also known as Yeni Zelve (New Zelve). Remnants of village life include the small, unadorned, rock-cut **mosque** in Valley Three and the old *değirmen* (mill), with a grindstone and graffitied wooden beam, in Valley One.

Beyond the mill, the **Balıklı Kilise** (Fish Church) has fish figuring in one of the primitive paintings. Adjoining it is the more impressive **Üzümlü Kilise** (Grape Church), with obvious bunches of grapes.

Unfortunately, erosion continues to eat into the valley structures and parts may be closed because of the danger of collapse, while others require scrambling and ladders. If Valley Two is open, what's left of the **Geyikli Kilise** (Church with Deer) is worth seeing.

There are cafés and *çay bahçesi* (tea gardens) in the car park outside.

Paşabağı, a valley halfway along the turn-off road to Zelve near a fairy-chimney *jandarma* (police station), has a three-headed formation and some of Cappadocia's best examples of mushroom-shaped fairy chimneys. Monks inhabited the valley and you can climb up inside one chimney to a monk's quarters, decorated with Hellenic crosses. Wooden steps lead to a chapel where three iconoclastic paintings escaped the Islamic vandals; the central one depicts the Virgin holding baby Jesus.

Getting There & Away

The hourly buses running between Ürgüp, Göreme, Çavuşin and Avanos (see p497) will stop at Paşabağı and Zelve on request. If you're coming from Ürgüp, Göreme or Çavuşin and tell the driver that you want to go to Paşabağı or Zelve, the bus will turn off the highway past Çavuşin, let you off and then go up to Aktepe and on to Avanos. If no one wants Paşabağı or Zelve, the bus will not make this detour. Getting a bus from Zelve is more difficult; you may have to walk the 3.5km from the site to the main highway, from where you can flag down a bus going towards either Göreme or Avanos.

DEVRENT VALLEY

Look, it's a camel! Stunning Devrent Valley's volcanic cones are some of the best-formed and most thickly clustered in Cappadocia, and looking at their fantastic shapes is like gazing at the clouds as a child. See if you can spot the dolphin, seals, Napoleon's hat, kissing birds, Virgin Mary and various reptilian forms.

Most of the rosy rock cones are topped by flattish, darker stones of harder rock that sheltered the cones from the rain until all the surrounding rock was eaten away, a process known as differential erosion.

To get to Devrent Valley (also known as Imagination Valley) from Zelve, go about 200m back down the access road to where the road forks and take the right road, marked for Ürgüp. After about 2km you'll come to the village of Aktepe (Yeni Zelve). Bear right and follow the Ürgüp road uphill for less than 2km.

AVANOS

☎ 0384 / pop 11,800 / elevation 910m

In Avanos' main square, the usual Atatürk monument is joined by a statue of a potter. The town is famous for pottery – made with red clay from the Kızılırmak (Red River), which runs through its centre, and white clay from the mountains. Typically painted in turquoise or the earthy browns and yellows favoured by the Hittites, the beautiful pieces are traditionally thrown by men and painted by women. As for Avanos itself, its old town is run-down and its riverside setting does not match the other Cappadocian centres. However, it boasts some superb views of Zelve and, when the tour groups have moved on, it's an appealingly mellow country town.

Orientation & Information

Most of the town is on the northern bank of the river, with Atatürk Caddesi providing the main thoroughfare. Although there is an otogar south of the river, all dolmuşes for the local area stop outside the PTT, on Atatürk Caddesi near the main square. The **tourist office** (☎ 511 4360; Atatürk Caddesi; ☼ 8.30am-5pm), which doesn't always stick to its opening hours, is on the main street. You'll find several banks with ATMs on or around the main square.

To check your email or surf the net, head to the **Hemi Internet Café** (Uğur Mumcu Caddesi; per hr TL1; ☼ 9am-midnight).

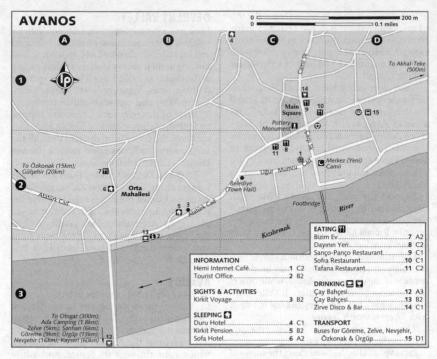

AVANOS

0 — 200 m
0 — 0.1 miles

Sights & Activities

Tour groups tend to find themselves shopping for pots in vast warehouses on the outskirts of town. It's much more enjoyable (and infinitely cheaper) to patronise one of the smaller **pottery workshops** right in town, most of which will happily show you how to throw a pot or two. These are located in the small streets around the main square and in the group of shops opposite the PTT.

If you fancy horse riding, **Akhal-Teke** (☎ 511 5171; www.akhal-tekehorsecenter.com; Camikebir Mahallesi, Kadı Sokak 1) and **Kirkit Voyage** (☎ 511 3148; www.kirkit.com; Atatürk Caddesi 50) organise guided treks in the area. Prices range from TL60 for two hours to TL150 for a full day; it's worth shopping around.

Tours

Kirkit Voyage (above) has an excellent reputation. As well as the usual guided tours, it can arrange walking, biking, canoeing, horseriding and snowshoe trips. It's an agency for Onur Air, Pegasus Airlines, Turkish Airlines and Atlasjet, and runs a shuttle between Avanos and Kayseri airport (€15, reservation essential).

Sleeping

Ada Camping (☎ 511 2429; www.adacampingavanos.com; Jan Zakari Caddesi 20; camp sites per person TL10 incl electricity; ☑) Take the Nevşehir road and bear right to reach this large, family-run camping ground, in a superb setting near the river. The toilet block could be cleaner but there's lots of shade and grass, a restaurant and a cold but inviting swimming pool.

Kirkit Pension (☎ 511 3148; www.kirkit.com; Atatürk Caddesi; s/d/tr €30/40/55; ☑) Set in converted old stone houses, this long-running pension is known throughout Cappadocia for its congenial, laid-back atmosphere. The simple rooms are decorated with kilims, historical photographs of the region and *suzani* (Uzbek bedspreads) – some are a bit cramped, so ask to see a few before checking in. Guests can enjoy a home-cooked local meal (TL13 for dinner) in the vaulted restaurant or pleasant courtyard. Recommended.

Duru Hotel (☎ 511 2404; www.hotelduru.com; Yukarı Mahallesi; s €20-25, d €30-35, tr €45-50; ☑) Perched high above the town (it's one hell of a walk), this slightly run-down place offers two types of rooms. It's worth spending €5 more to stay in the newer rooms, with arches and origami towels. The dingy older rooms have brown doors that look like they would shatter if you leant against them. The real drawcards here are the grassy terrace and the exceptional views over Avanos.

Sofa Hotel (☎ 511 5186; www.sofa-hotel.com; Orta Mahallesi, Baklacı Sokak 13; s/d TL60/100; ⊠) Lots of Cappadocian cave establishments have their idiosyncrasies, but this hotel is downright bonkers. With sofas and dining tables in the central courtyard, indoor and outdoor spaces organically merge in the 15-house complex. Staircases, bridges and terraces lead you up the hill, past eyes suddenly staring out from a mosaic fragment or a pottery face, to 33 rooms crammed with knick-knacks. No prizes for guessing the owner's an artist.

Eating

Sanço-Panço Restaurant (☎ 511 4184; Çarşı Sokak; mains TL6) This basic but welcoming eatery on the main square is a great spot to have a beer (TL4) and people-watch. Given Avanos' pottery trade, it's hardly surprising that the speciality is *güveç* (beef stew with potatoes, tomatoes, garlic, paprika and cumin, baked in a clay pot; TL7).

Sofra Restaurant (☎ 511 4324; Hükümet Konağı Karşısı; mains TL7-8) In a line of restaurants catering to the tour groups visiting the nearby pottery shops, Sofra has a wide-ranging meze menu, pottery dishes and a small terrace.

Tafana Restaurant (☎ 511 4862; Atatürk Caddesi 31; mains TL8) Decorated with plates in earthy Hittite style, this reasonably attractive eatery is not as popular as nearby Dayının Yeri, but is a decent fall-back option if one is needed. It specialises in pide (TL6), cooked in a wood-fired oven, and the beer is cheap (TL2).

Dayının Yeri (☎ 511 6840; Atatürk Caddesi 23; mains TL10) This shiny, modern *ocakbaşıs* (grill restaurant) is one of Cappadocia's best, and is an essential stop on any visit to Avanos. The kebaps are sensational and the pide is just as good. Don't even *think* of leaving without sampling the freshly prepared *künefe* (strands of cooked batter over a creamy sweet cheese base baked in syrup; TL4), cooked on little hobs near the tables. No alcohol is served.

Bizim Ev (Our House; ☎ 511 5525; Orta Mahallesi, Baklacı Sokak 1; mezes TL6, mains TL11) This welcoming family-run restaurant is about as swish as dining gets in Avanos, with an air-conditioned, stone-walled dining room and a rooftop terrace. Try local specialities such as trout cooked in a clay pot and optionally topped with melted cheese (TL11), catfish skewers (TL12) and *mantı* (Turkish ravioli, TL9).

Drinking

If you're keen to linger over a tea and nargileh, try the *çay bahçesi* adjoining the tourist office, which is as welcoming to women as it is to men, or the large riverside *çay bahçesi* on the southwestern side of the bridge.

There are a few bars on Atatürk Caddesi and around the main square, but most are local hang-outs where visitors (particularly females) may not feel welcome. The only one we'd recommend is **Zirve Disco & Bar** (Yukarı Mahallesi), which hosts live music.

Getting There & Around

For details of shuttle-bus services between Kayseri airport and Avanos see opposite.

There are two bus routes from Avanos to Nevşehir: one leaves every 30 minutes and goes direct and the other leaves every hour and travels via Çavuşin and Göreme. Both services operate from 7am to 7pm and charge TL2.50 per ticket. There's also an hourly *belediye* bus running from Avanos to Nevşehir via Çavuşin (10 minutes), Göreme (15 minutes) and Uçhisar (30 minutes). It departs from Avanos from 7am to 6pm and costs between TL1.50 and TL3 depending on where you get on and off.

Dolmuşes to Ürgüp (TL2) pass through town at 9am, 11am, 1pm, 3pm and 5pm.

Kirkit Voyage (opposite) hires out mountain bikes for TL20 per day or TL10 for half a day.

AROUND AVANOS
Sarıhan

Built in 1249, the **Sarıhan** (Yellow Caravanserai; admission TL3; ☉ 9am-midnight) has an elaborate gateway with a small mosque above it. Having been restored in the late 1980s, it's one of the best remaining Seljuk caravanserais. Gunning down the highway towards it makes you feel like a 13th-century trader, ready to rest his camels and catch up with his fellow dealers.

Inside, you also have to use your imagination in the bare stone courtyard. Visitors are allowed on the roof, but the main reason to come here is the 45-minute **whirling dervish ceremony** (☎ 511 3795; admission €25; ☉ 9.30pm Apr-Oct, 9pm Nov-Mar). You must book ahead – most pensions in Göreme, Ürgüp, Avanos and Uçhisar will arrange it for you. The price may vary according to how much commission your tour agent or pension is skimming off the top.

Though the setting is extremely atmospheric, the *sema* (ceremony) is nowhere near as impressive as those staged at the Mevlevi Monastery in İstanbul's Beyoğlu (see p116). If you've seen one of those you should probably give this a miss.

GETTING THERE & AWAY

Getting to the Sarıhan, 6km east of Avanos, without your own transport is difficult, as there are no dolmuşes and few vehicles with which to hitch a ride. An Avanos taxi driver will probably want around TL25 to take you there and back, including waiting time.

Özkonak Underground City

About 15km north of Avanos, the village of Özkonak hosts a smaller version of the underground cities of Kaymaklı and Derinkuyu (see boxed text, p524), with the same wine reservoirs, rolling stone doors etc. **Özkonak underground city** (admission TL8; ⏱ 8.30am-5.30pm) is neither as dramatic nor as impressive as the larger ones, but is much less crowded.

The easiest way to get there is by dolmuş from Avanos (TL1.50, 30 minutes), but there are few services on weekends. Ask to be let off for the *yeraltı şehri* (underground city); the bus stops at the petrol station, a 500m stroll from the entrance.

NEVŞEHİR
☎ 0384 / pop 81,700 / elevation 1260m

According to local lore, if you set eyes on the beautiful view from Nevşehir's hilltop castle, you will be compelled to stay here for seven years. The legend must be very old, because the provincial capital is an ugly modern town that offers travellers little incentive to linger.

Orientation & Information

The main otogar is behind the Total garage, across thoroughfare Atatürk Bulvarı from the museum. Dolmuşes to Göreme, Uçhisar, Avanos and Ürgüp also stop on the main road outside the museum (on the same side of the road, but a bit further towards Göreme).

Nevşehir's **tourist office** (☎ 214 4062; Atatürk Bulvarı; ⏱ 8am-5pm) is in a large government building on the town's main road. Staff here can supply a basic map of Nevşehir, but not much else. There are also a number of banks with ATMs along here.

Dangers & Annoyances

The tour companies and taxi drivers based at Nevşehir's otogar have a formidable reputation for pouncing on travellers who arrive from long-distance destinations as soon as they get off the bus. If you are seeking a *servis* to your final Cappadocian destination, you may be led to a travel agent's office on the pretence that it is the place to arrange your transfer. Once cornered, unsuspecting and tired victims are often conned into signing up for overpriced tours or agreeing to ridiculously overinflated prices for a taxi trip (be it to Göreme, Ürgüp, Uçhisar or any of the nearby villages).

We suggest that you avoid any dealings with the tour agents here and follow the advice outlined on p495 to ensure that your bus ticket includes a shuttle-bus transfer to your final destination from Nevşehir. Unfortunately, malpractice is so institutionalised at the otogar that even people at the bus companies' counters may take you to the travel agents. If you do find yourself in need of a *servis* or a taxi and you have booked a hotel, it is worth phoning it for assistance; Nevşehir's otogar has long been problematic for travellers and the tourist industry in the rest of Cappadocia is well aware of it.

Sights

Nevşehir Museum (☎ 213 1447; Türbe Sokak 1; admission TL3; ⏱ 8am-5pm Tue-Sun) is housed in an ugly building 1km from the centre and 400m east of the tourist office. The collection includes an archaeological room with Phrygian, Hittite and Bronze Age pots and implements, as well as Roman, Byzantine and Ottoman articles. Upstairs, the dusty ethnographic section is less interesting.

The statue in the small park in front of the cultural centre is of Nevşehir'li Damat İbrahim Paşa (1662–1730), the Ottoman grand vizier after whom the town is named. The local luminary endowed the town's grand mosque complex, which is clearly visible on the hill to the south of Atatürk Caddesi and still has a functioning mosque, a *medrese* (seminary – now a library), a hamam and a teahouse.

CAPPADOCIA

Sleeping & Eating

Nevşehir's accommodation falls into two categories: bland four- and five-star resorts on the city fringe that are geared mainly towards package groups, and dingy places in the city centre where Russian prostitutes ply their trade. Even if you arrive here in the middle of the night, we recommend that you make your way to nearby Göreme, where the accommodation is cheaper and infinitely superior.

Nevşehir Konağı (☎ 213 6183; Aksaray Caddesi 46; 🕑 9am-9.30pm; mezes TL2.50, mains TL7) There is one good reason to visit Nevşehir. This municipal restaurant, set up to serve local cuisine, serves Cappadocian specialities such as *bamya çorba* (ochre soup) and *dolma mantı* (ravioli). The location – an Ottoman-style building with Greek-style pillars in the park at the Kültür Merkezi (City Cultural Centre), 1.5km southwest of the centre – is the perfect place to tuck into scrumptious dishes such as *yoğurtlu beyti* (Adana kebap with yoghurt).

Getting There & Away

Turkish Airlines (www.thy.com) has a returning flight from İstanbul to Nevşehir on Wednesday, Friday, Saturday and Sunday (TL69 to TL199 one way).

Nevşehir is the main regional transport hub. There are services to surrounding towns and villages from the otogar and other stops (see opposite). These go to Göreme (TL1.75, every 30 minutes from 8am to 6pm Monday to Friday, every hour on weekends); Uçhisar (TL1, every 30 minutes from 7.30am to 6pm Monday to Friday, every hour on weekends); Niğde (TL7, every two hours from 7.30am to 6pm) via Kaymaklı and Derinkuyu; and Ürgüp (TL3.50, every 15 minutes from 7.30am to 10pm). Some Ürgüp buses go via Ortahisar and all can drop you at the turn-off on the main highway, a 1km walk from the town centre. There are two services to Avanos: one leaves every hour and goes direct and the other leaves every 30 minutes and travels via Göreme and Çavuşin. Both operate from 7am to 7pm and charge TL2 per ticket. The otogar is set to move by the end of 2010 to a new position on the Gülşehir road.

A taxi to Göreme should cost around TL35.

AROUND NEVŞEHİR

If you're heading for Ankara, consider stopping off to see Gülşehir and Hacıbektaş along the way. While this is easily done if you have your own vehicle, it's not too hard by public transport either.

Gülşehir
☎ 0384 / pop 9800

This small town 19km north of Nevşehir has two rocky attractions on its outskirts that are worth visiting if you're passing through.

Four kilometres before Gülşehir's town centre you'll find the **Open Palace** (Açık Saray; admission free; 🕑 8am-5pm), a fine rock-cut monastery dating from the 6th and 7th centuries. It includes churches, refectories, dormitories and a kitchen, all of which are cut into fairy chimneys.

Two kilometres closer to town, just before the turning to the centre, is the rock-cut **Church of St John** (admission TL8; 🕑 8am-5pm). A five-minute walk down a signed road on the left of the highway, it's signposted 'Church of St Jean/Karşı Kilise'. The 13th-century church on two levels has marvellous frescoes, including scenes depicting the Annunciation, the Descent from the Cross, the Last Supper, the Betrayal by Judas, and the Last Judgment (rarely depicted in Cappadocian churches). The frescoes are particularly well preserved due to the fact that until restoration in 1995 they were covered in a layer of black soot.

Buses and dolmuşes to Gülşehir (TL1.50, 15 minutes) depart from the dolmuş and bus stop in the centre of Nevşehir (see left). Ask to be let off at the Açık Saray or Karşı Kilise to save a walk back from town. Returning, just flag the bus down from the side of the highway. Onward buses to Hacıbektaş leave from Gülşehir's small otogar opposite the Kurşunlu Camii (TL2, 30 minutes).

Hacıbektaş
☎ 0384 / pop 4900

Other than the municipal announcements ringing across town, the main activity in tiny Hacıbektaş, 46km from Nevşehir, takes place at the museum. Inside, pilgrims queue to pay their respects at the tomb of Hacı Bektaş Veli, the founder and spiritual leader of the Bektaşi dervishes. The visitors' numbers swell to 10,000 during the festival dedicated to the Muslim saint – held from 16 to 18 August.

You'll find a Vakıf Bank ATM in a booth in front of the PTT on the main street, and TC Ziraat Bankası and Turkiye Bankası ATMs near the Ethnographic Museum.

HACI BEKTAŞ VELİ & THE BEKTAŞI SECT

Born in Nishapur in Iran in the 13th century, Hacı Bektaş Veli inspired a religious and political following that blended aspects of Islam (both Sunni and Shi'ite) with Orthodox Christianity. During his life he is known to have travelled around Anatolia and to have lived in Kayseri, Sivas and Kırşehir, but eventually he settled in the hamlet that is now the small town of Hacıbektaş.

Although not much is known about Hacı Bektaş himself, the book he wrote, the *Makalât*, describes a mystical philosophy less austere than mainstream Islam. In it he laid out a four-stage path to enlightenment (the Four Doors). Though often scorned by mainstream Islamic clerics, Bektaşı dervishes attained considerable political and religious influence in Ottoman times. Along with all the other dervishes, they were outlawed by Atatürk in 1925.

The annual pilgrimage of Bektaşı dervishes is an extremely important event for the modern Alevi community. Politicians tend to hijack the first day's proceedings, but days two and three are given over to music and dance.

Not to be confused with the town's normally closed Ethnographic Museum, the **Hacıbektaş Museum** (admission TL3; 8am-noon & 1-5pm Tue-Sun) contains the tombs of Hacı Bektaş Veli (see box, above) and his followers. Pilgrims carry out superstitious activities such as hugging a pillar, kissing door frames and tying ribbons around a mulberry bush known as *dilek ağacı* (wish tree). Several rooms are arranged as they might have been when the Bektaşı order lived here, with exhibits such as photos of the dervishes and earrings worn by celibate members of the sect.

Hacıbektaş has limited hotel options. The unremarkable **Hünkar Otel** (441 3344; s/d TL25/50), on the *meydanı* (town square) between the shrine and the otogar, offers basic rooms with blue and yellow furniture and reasonable bathrooms. Prices should be negotiable except in August, when it's booked solid. Eating options are limited to the basic *lokantas* (eateries serving ready-made food), *pastanes* (patisseries) and *kebapçıs* (kebap eateries) on the main street.

Buses from the centre of Nevşehir to Hacıbektaş (TL3, 45 minutes, 11 daily between 7.30am and 6.15pm on weekdays, fewer services on weekends) depart from the 'Has Hacıbektaş' bus office, just down from the Alibey Camii on the road to Gülşehir. The last bus from Hacıbektaş' otogar to Nevşehir leaves at 5pm (4.45pm on weekends).

ORTAHİSAR

☎ 0384 / pop 4800

Apart from the groups visiting the Culture Folk Museum, mainstream tourism has bypassed this farming village, leaving it to survive on its traditional trade of storing citrus fruit in underground caves. Ortahisar may lack its neighbours' buzz, but this is the place to slow to the pace of old men whose lined faces resemble the surrounding canyons. Its castle is a crazy crag even by local standards. In the gorge, cobbled streets wind past houses that look ready to lie down for a snooze.

Staff at the small **tourist office** (☎ 343 3071; Tepebaşı Meydanı; 8am-5pm) near the castle are friendly, but don't speak English. They will probably take you to 'Crazy Ali', who runs the neighbouring antique shop and speaks some English, French and German. The loquacious poet, who says he was given his nickname when he drove an ox cart to the moon, offers guided walks to spots such as Pancarlık Valley.

You can check emails at **Antiknet** (Huseyin Galif Efendi Caddesi; per hr TL1; 8am-midnight), downhill from the PTT.

Sights

There are no monuments in the village other than the **castle**, an 18m-high rock used as a fortress in Byzantine times and now undergoing a seemingly interminable restoration.

On the main square near the castle, the **Culture Folk Museum** (Kültür Müzesi; Cumhuriyet Meydanı 15; admission TL5; 9am-7pm) gets bombarded with tour groups but is a good place to get to grips with the basics of local culture. In the dioramas, with their multilingual interpretive panels, mannequins in headscarves and old men's *şapkas* (hats) make *yufka* (thinly rolled, unleavened bread), *pekmez* (syrup made from grape juice) and kilims.

On the road to the AlkaBris hotel, the municipal park **Manzara ve Kültür Parkı**, is slightly dishevelled but its grassed areas are good picnic spots. Near some holes in the cliff big enough to accommodate Volvo-driving pigeons, the café has views down the gorge to the castle.

From Ortahisar you can hike to little-known churches in the nearby countryside, especially in the Pancarlık Valley.

Sleeping & Eating

Kapadokya Otel (☎ 343 2221; Ulus Meydanı; s/d/tr TL25/50/75) Up a psychedelically carpeted staircase with a colourful painting of the castle on the wall, the reasonably clean rooms have blankets on the beds. Although the beds look like they would collapse if you snored too loudly, they are comfortable enough and benefit from a terrace with views across the countryside.

Burcu Kaya Hotel (☎ 343 3200; www.burcukayaotel .com.tr; s/d/tr/ste €60/90/105/120; 🏊) Uphill from the centre, this quiet hotel's swimming pool has a view of rock formations and pigeon houses. The rooms have arched ceilings and, upstairs, small balconies overlooking the leafy central courtyard. Rooms are comfortable but a little bare and hardly offer Cappadocian cave character.

AlkaBris (☎ 343 3433; www.alkabris.com; Cedid Mahallesi, Ali Reis Sokak 23; r €100-125, ste €140; 🖳) An oasis of calm and luxury, this lovingly restored Cappadocian house offers five tastefully furnished rooms and suites. Four are in caves and the fifth, Gılgamış, beguiled us with its double-whammy view of the castle and Erciyes Dağı. Jacuzzis in the suites, homemade bread and jam for breakfast, two magnificent terraces, a rock-hewn restaurant (dinner €25) and mosaic decorations by hostess Sait all justify the 1.5km climb from the centre of town.

Park Restaurant (☎ 343 3361; Tepebaşı Meydanı; pides TL6-9, mains TL9-15) Overlooking the main square, with the castle as a backdrop, this attractive garden is a perfect spot to recharge with a meat pide and green salad, accompanied by a beer (TL5) or glass of 'energy drink' (fresh orange juice, TL3).

Cultural Museum Restaurant (☎ 343 3344; set menus TL20; ☷ lunch & dinner) The museum's attractive upstairs restaurant mainly caters to groups, but it is possible for individuals to dine here, particularly if you phone ahead. Dishes on offer include meatballs and *testi kebap* (pottery kebap). The English-speaking manager Cenk, a good source of local information, has proudly served Fenerbahçe players, Hungarian politicians and the Queen of Spain.

Getting There & Away

For details of shuttle-bus services between Kayseri airport and Ortahisar see p496.

Dolmuşes make the 5km run between Ortahisar and Ürgüp every 30 minutes from 8am to 5pm Monday to Saturday (TL1.50). See p497 for details of the Belediye Bus Corp dolmuşes between Ortahisar and Avanos via Göreme and Çavuşin. All services stop next to the museum. There are buses to Nevşehir, but it may be quicker to walk 1km to the Ortahisar turn-off on the main highway, as passing buses pick up passengers there.

Bus companies including Metro, Kent and Nevşehir have offices in the village.

ÜRGÜP

☎ 0384 / pop 15,500

If you have a soft spot for upmarket hotels and fine dining, you need look no further – Ürgüp is the place you're looking for. The ever-growing battalion of boutique hotels in the town's honey-coloured stone buildings (left over from the pre-1923 days when the town had a large Greek population) are proving very popular with travellers. With a spectacular natural setting and a wonderful location at the very heart of central Cappadocia, this is one of the most seductive holiday spots in the whole of Turkey.

Orientation & Information

Ürgüp is set within a steep valley about 18km east of Nevşehir and 9km east of Göreme. Most of the action occurs on or around Cumhuriyet Meydanı, the main square, 150m west of the otogar.

There are several **banks** with ATMs on or around the main square. The **post office** is northeast of Cumhuriyet Meydanı.

The helpful **tourist office** (☎ 0384-341 4059; Kayseri Caddesi 37; ☷ 8am-5pm Mon-Fri Oct-Apr, 8am-5.30pm Mon-Fri May-Sep) gives out a colour walking map and has a list of Ürgüp's hotels.

You can check your emails among pot plants and nargilehs at **Teras Internet Café** (3rd fl, Suat Hayri Caddesi 40; per hr TL1.25; ☷ 8am-1am), in the arcade next to Kardeşler Restaurant and Vodafone, and at **Eftelya** (Refik Basaran Heykeli; per hr TL1.50; ☷ 9.30am-11pm).

Sights & Activities

Northwest of the main square is the oldest part of town, with many fine **old houses**, reached through a stone arch. It's well worth a stroll, after which you can head up Ahmet Refik

ÜRGÜP

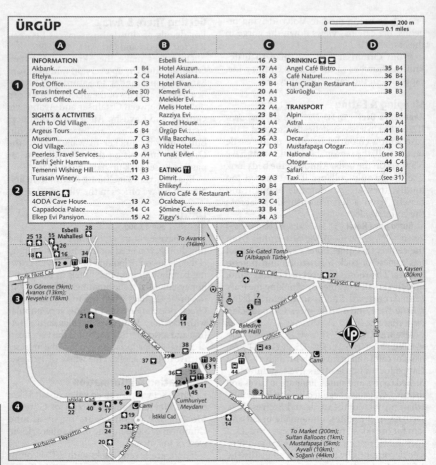

Caddesi and turn right to **Temenni Wishing Hill** (🕑 9am-11pm), home to a saint's tomb, a café and 360-degree views over the town. It doesn't always stick to its opening hours.

Right by the main square is the **Tarihi Şehir Hamamı** (admission TL15; 🕑 7am-11pm), the hamam. Partly housed in what was once a small church, it offers mixed but respectable bathing.

The **museum** (admission TL3; 🕑 8am-noon & 1-5pm Tue-Sun) features some 10-million-year-old teeth from a forerunner of the elephant, unearthed at Mustafapaşa, but the overall collection is uninspiring.

WINERIES
The abundant sunshine and fertile volcanic soil of Cappadocia produce delicious sweet grapes, and several wineries carry on the Ottoman Greek winemaking tradition. You can sample some of the local produce at the big **Turasan Winery** (☎ 341 4961; Çimenli Mevkii; 🕑 7.30am-8pm).

Tours
Several Ürgüp-based travel agents run tours around Cappadocia. Two recommended agents:

Argeus Tours (☎ 341 4688; www.argeus.com.tr, www .cappadociaexclusive.com; İstiklal Caddesi 7) Offers three-to nine-day packages, including an eight-day mountain-biking option, as well as day tours and flights. Ürgüp's Turkish Airlines representative.

Peerless Travel Services (☎ 341 6970; www .peerlessexcursions.com; İstiklal Caddesi 59a) Also Ürgüp's representative for Onur Air, Sun Express, Atlasjet and Pegasus Airlines.

Sleeping

Ürgüp has a glut of boutique hotels, mostly on Esbelli hill, and a couple more-central budget and midrange options worth considering. Many close down between November and March, when Ürgüp's weather keeps locals indoors and travellers elsewhere.

BUDGET

Hotel Elvan (☎ 341 4191; www.hotelelvan.com; Barbaros Hayrettin Sokak 11; s/d/tr TL35/60/80; 🖳) A friendly welcome and homely atmosphere await you at this unpretentious but immaculate guest house. The rooms are arranged around a small courtyard and have midrange amenities such as satellite TVs and hairdryers. There's also a small roof terrace and comfortable dining room. Excellent value.

Yıldız Hotel (☎ 341 4610; www.yildizhotel.com; Kayseri Caddesi; s TL30-60, d TL60-100) Nowhere near as impressive as the other budget options mentioned here, the Yıldız offers old-fashioned rooms that are clean but in need of a paint job and new carpet. The renovated bungalows in the flowery garden are much nicer, but carry a slightly ambitious price tag.

MIDRANGE

Cappadocia Palace (☎ 341 2510; www.hotel-cappadocia .com; Duayeri Mahallesi Mektep Sokak 2; s/d/tr TL35/70/85, cave TL60/120/140; 🖳) This large and comfortable hotel is housed in a converted Greek house that's conveniently located a stone's throw from Cumhuriyet Meydanı. It has 13 motel-style rooms with satellite TV and small bathrooms, as well as four impressive cave suites. There's a lovely arched restaurant-lounge and an attractive foyer area. Book ahead.

Razziya Evi (☎ 341 5089; www.razziyaevi.com; Cingilli Sokak 24; s/d/tr TL70/80/120) This lovingly restored *evi* (house) is one of Ürgüp's few decent midrange options. Its seven cheerful rooms (some in slightly musty caves) are comfortable and clean; they're not at all posh, but in a town where posh boutique hotels are a dime a dozen this almost comes as a welcome relief. There's a hamam, a salon with satellite TV, a pretty courtyard and a kitchen that guests can use.

Hotel Akuzun (☎ 341 3869; www.hotelakuzun.com; Yeni Cami Mahallesi 49; s/d/tr €40/55/65) This centrally located fall-back option has a boxy exterior and professional staff who make the most of the uninspiring interior. The water feature tries to compensate for the lack of cave character here, but a recent restoration has added little charm to the 20-year-old building. The staff and the bushy garden are Akuzun's main selling points.

Melis Hotel (☎ 341 2495; www.melishotel.com; İstiklal Caddesi 34; s/d/tr from €35/50/65; 🖳 🖳) On a main road right next to a mosque (pack those earplugs!), the Melis offers Ottoman-and Greek-style stone rooms and cave rooms with jacuzzis. The main building, a 300-year-old Greek house, stands at one end of a long swimming pool – the site is a picture when the floodlights come on. There's also a cave bar-restaurant.

TOP END

Ürgüp Evi (☎ 341 3173; www.urgupevi.com.tr; Esbelli Mahallesi Sokak 54; d €65-80, ste €110-140; 🖳) A chic makeover of this long-running favourite left its gorgeous stonework untouched, but installed extremely comfortable beds with luxe linen in the cave rooms. The hotel's strongest points are its location right at the top of the hill (the views are quite amazing), its attractive cave restaurant and its terrace garden, which is home to a scattering of brightly coloured beanbag seats.

Elkep Evi Pansiyon (☎ 341 6000; www.elkepevi.com; Esbelli Mahallesi Sokak; s/d €50/70, with jacuzzi from €80/100, with Turkish bath from €100/120; 🖾 🖳) The largest of the boutique hotels in Esbelli Mahallesi has 21 rooms in four former cave houses, sprawling across the cliff at Ürgüp's highest point. All rooms have their own terrace or alcove to take in the view and two even have hamams. There's plenty of space in the rooms and in public areas such as the rooftop terrace and the pillar-dotted garden, where fresh *gözleme* is one of the treats served for breakfast.

Kemerli Evi (☎ 341 5445; www.kemerliev.com; Dutlu Camii Mahallesi Çıkmaz Sokak 12; s/d €60/80; 🖾 🖳 🖳) Lost up backstreets inhabited by friendly locals, this converted 13th-century house straddles the divide between midrange and top end. In the eight rooms, antique chairs and carpets, nooks and crannies are everywhere and an air of calm hangs between the thick stone walls. The elevated terrace has a beautiful swimming pool and views of the main square and the hills beyond.

Villa Bacchus (☎ 341 6623; www.villabacchus.com; Esbelli Mahallesi Sokak 6; standard s/d €65/75, deluxe s/d €75/95, ste from €110, villas €255; 🖾 🖳) Standards on

CAPPADOCIA

Esbelli hill are high and Villa Bacchus, like the affiliated Kayadam Cave House, is falling behind the rest of the boutique pack. It could be cleaner and the garden gnomes don't exactly lend a touch of class. We mention it mainly as a possible option for groups. The open-plan Argeus suite has a kitchen and you can hire out all three rooms, which overlook a walled garden. Children under 10 can stay for free.

Hotel Assiana (☎ 341 4960; www.assianahouse.com; Esbelli Mahallesi Dolay Sokak 1; s/d/ste €65/85/100; 🖳) The youngest member of the boutique family on Esbelli hill has three cave rooms and two arched stone rooms. The interiors are simple but tasteful, with maroon bedding, rugs on the varnished wooden floors, the occasional pot on a clutter-free shelf and a tree carving in one wall. The stone rooms upstairs are our favourites – the suite has a living room with a small fireplace and a vintage radio.

40DA Cave House (☎ 341 6080; www.4oda.com; Esbelli Mahallesi Sokak 46; s/d €70/90; 🖳) It may only have five rooms, but this peaceful pension has more than its fair share of atmosphere and comfort. The infectiously cheerful and friendly owner goes out of her way to make guests feel at home, rustling up homemade pastries and jams for breakfast and sharing her personal library and lounge room. The sense of pride continues in the rooms, where everything is arranged around the original cave features. Highly recommended.

our pick Esbelli Evi (☎ 341 3395; www.esbelli.com; Esbelli Mahallesi Sokak 8; s/d/ste €80/90/200; ✕ 🐾 🖳) Süha Ersöz opened Cappadocia's first boutique hotel in 1990 and the consummate host is still at the head of the pack. Having bought surrounding properties to preserve Esbelli's atmosphere of hilltop serenity, his complex now has 15 rooms and suites in nine houses. However, it feels small and intimate, thanks to the welcoming atmosphere and the communal areas where guests are encouraged to congregate. The lounge is scattered with laptops, coffee-table books, CDs and DVDs, and a sense of culture pervades the hotel. We were impressed by the deep understanding of what appeals to guests; from Flintstones-like windows to amuse children in the family suite to a bottle of single malt next to the freestanding bath in the amazing honeymoon cave suite.

Melekler Evi (☎ 341 7131; www.meleklerevi.com.tr; Dereler Mahallesi Dere Sokak 59; d €90-145) This seven-room boutique hotel's name, House of Angels, could refer to its lofty position at the top of the old town, eye to eye with the pigeon houses and castle carved into the cliff. Restored by an architect and an interior designer from İstanbul, the cave and arch rooms are tastefully decorated in subtle shades. The modern sauna and massage systems are counterbalanced by wooden beams, flowery carvings above fireplaces and hi-fis in the place of TVs. A music-listening and wine-tasting area is on the way, in case guests tire of the beds under the fruit trees, the dining room in a former stable, and the nightly fires on the terraces.

Yunak Evleri (☎ 341 6920; www.yunak.com; Yunak Mahallesi; d €100-115, ste €145; ✕ 🖳) This swish hotel regularly appears in the 'best hotels in the world, ever' lists that travel magazines love to compile. Its 30 well-appointed rooms occupy six cave houses, their cliffside location giving them the feel of a secret kingdom. Housed in an attractive 19th-century Greek mansion, the main building boasts a state-of-the-art DVD room and music lounge, and the terrace restaurant has prime sunset-watching potential.

Sacred House (☎ 341 7102; www.sacred-house.com; Dutlu Cami Mahallesi, Barbaros Hayrettin Sokak 25; d €115-190; ✕ 🖳) This 12-room, uber-boutique hotel is set in a 250-year-old Greek mansion crammed with antiques. When we say 'crammed', we mean it – you'll either love the sumptuously decorated rooms or find them overcooked and pretentious. Objets d'art, antiquarian books and Ottoman swords are scattered throughout the building, but your eye may be drawn by sleek red and black walls or the hi-fi with more decks than an ocean liner. Sacred House wasn't our glass of Cristal, but it has certainly made more bold design decisions than any other Cappadocian hotel.

Eating

The range of restaurants in Ürgüp is more limited than in Göreme, but the overall standard is much higher. If you're passing through the otogar, there are plenty of *pastanes* and cafés right outside.

Micro Café & Restaurant (☎ 5341 5110; Cumhuriyet Meydanı; mains TL11) It's not the plaza's most popular restaurant, but Micro's diverse menu, ranging across Ottoman chicken, spinach crêpes and peppered T-bone steak, attracts some tourists and locals. Its outside seating has unlimited people-watching potential. The semolina with chocolate sauce and ice cream is recommended, but the spoon salad is not.

Şömine Cafe & Restaurant (☎ 341 8442; Cumhuriyet Meydanı; mezes TL5, salads TL5-7, mains TL9-15) This popular restaurant on the plaza has a roof terrace and an attractive indoor dining room. Start with a salad or a meze choice such as *sosyete mantısı* (one large ravioli, covered in yoghurt, tomatoes and mint), then attack a *kiremit* (meat or vegetable dish baked on a clay tile). There's a large menu of quality dishes, although they don't quite live up to the promise of the pristine napery and quality tableware.

Dimrit (☎ 341 8585; Yunak Mahallesi, Teyfik Fikret Caddesi 40; mains TL10-21) With mezes served in curvy dishes and three types of rakı, Dimrit's hillside terraces are top spots to spend a sunset. The extensive menu features salads, fish, classic grills such as *beyti* kebap (beef or lamb with tomato and yoghurt) and house specials such as *beğendili* kebap (beef or lamb with eggplant purée).

Ocakbaşı (☎ 341 3277; Güllüce Caddesi 44; mains TL13) This long-established place has a cavernous dining room and a terrace with an unbeatable view of the otogar. It's low on atmosphere but has a long list of meze and a good reputation for its grilled meats.

Ehlikeyf (☎ 341 6110; Cumhuriyet Meydanı; mains TL12-25) Competing with nearby Şömine in the sophistication stakes, and suffering from the same flaws, Ehlikeyf occupies a sleek dining room with a wavy ceiling. Dishes such as the fabulous Ehlikeyf kebap (steak served on slivered fried potatoes, garlic yoghurt and a demi-glace sauce; TL19) arrive on glass plates; a gloved waiter wielding a carving knife accompanies the *testi* kebap. The large, well-spaced tables with leather chairs are comfortable places to spend an evening, but the bill at the end of it will be as ambitious as the presentation.

our pick Ziggy's (☎ 341 7107; Yunak Mahallesi, Teyfik Fikret Caddesi 24; set menus TL30, mains TL13-16) Cool Ziggy's, named after the David Bowie song, has multilevel terraces where its logo, Snowy the dog from the *Tintin* books, decorates the lampshades. Whether you opt for a cocktail or the 12-course set menu, which features 10 meze plates such as the distinctive smoked aubergine, hosts Selim and Nuray add a sprinkling of İstanbul sophistication to the Cappadocian views. If you find it tough to tear yourself away from the stylish decor and jazz soundtrack, console yourself with a visit to the on-site shop where Nuray sells the jewellery she makes.

Drinking

The main square is the best place to grab an alcoholic or caffeinated beverage at an outside table and watch Cappadocia cruise by. *Pastanes* and cafés such as **Şükrüoğlu** and **Café Naturel** vie for attention with sweet eats and shiny window displays.

Bookended by carpet shops, the pedestrian walkway running northeast from Ehlikeyf restaurant is full of cafés, bars and old men playing backgammon.

Angel Café Bistro (☎ 341 6894; Cumhuriyet Meydanı) Readers rate this pointedly untraditional place, which provides a soundtrack of synth hits for the south side of the square. You may prefer to sit outside than in the red-and-black interior, and you can take a break from the Efes with Gusta, a Turkish wheat beer.

Han Çirağan Restaurant (☎ 341 2566; Cumhuriyet Meydanı) This local institution has a good terrace for a beer, but we wouldn't recommend eating here as the service is lacklustre and the food is bog-standard Turkish fare.

Getting There & Away

For details of shuttle-bus services between Kayseri airport and Ürgüp see p496.

Most buses leave from the main otogar. Dolmuşes travel to Nevşehir every 15 minutes from 6.55am to 11.30pm (TL2.50). A service runs between Ürgüp and Avanos (TL2) via Ortahisar, the Göreme Open-Air Museum, Göreme village and Çavuşin every two hours between 8am and 6pm.

Seven buses per day (fewer on Sunday) travel between Ürgüp and Mustafapaşa between 8.15am and 5.30pm (TL1). They leave from the Mustafapaşa otogar, next to the main otogar.

Details of some useful long-distance daily services from Göreme are listed in the table (p522).

Getting Around

The steep walk from the centre of town up to Esbelli Mahallesi is an absolute killer – many people instead opt to catch a taxi (TL5) from the rank next to Micro Café & Restaurant on the main square.

Ürgüp is a good base for hiring a car, with most agencies located on the main square or İstiklal Caddesi. Rates hover around TL70 to TL75 per day for a small manual sedan such as a Fiat Palio and climb to TL90 to TL120 for a larger automatic. **Decar** (☎ 341 6760) is more

SERVICES FROM ÜRGÜP'S OTOGAR

Destination	Fare (TL)	Duration (hr)	Frequency (per day)
Adana (via Nevşehir)	25	5	3 morning & afternoon
Aksaray	7	1½	hourly
Ankara	25	4½	7
Antalya	40	10	1 night (& 1 morning in summer)
Çanakkale	60	16	1 afternoon
İstanbul	40	11	1 morning, 2 evening
İzmir & Selçuk	40/50	11½	1 evening
Kayseri	6	1¼	hourly 7am to 7.30pm (to 5.30pm in winter)
Konya	20	4	5
Marmaris/Bodrum/Pamukkale	55	11-15	1 evening

expensive but provides the best service; you can also try **Astral** (☎ 341 3344), **National** (☎ 341 6541) and **Avis** (☎ 341 2177). If you plan to drop the car off in another part of Turkey, your best bet is Decar. If you book ahead, it does not charge the prohibitively large relocation fees (eg TL200 to drop off in Ankara) that other companies levy.

Several outlets in town rent mopeds and motorcycles from TL50 per day, and bicycles from TL25. Try Astral, **Safari** (☎ 341 6480) or **Alpin** (☎ 341 7522).

AYVALI
☎ 0384 / pop 500

Heading south from Ürgüp to Mustafapaşa look out for a turn-off to Ayvalı, a tiny unspoilt village where healthy bunches of onions and bags of footballs are sold on the main street. In this rural setting is a gorgeous 25-room boutique hotel, the **Gamırasu Hotel** (☎ 341 5825; www.gamirasu.com; d €90-140, ste €200-400). Occupying a 1000-year-old Byzantine monastery, it offers top-end comfort and style in a secluded gorge where the only noise at night is the frogs. It has an on-site restaurant reached by a bridge, a church with frescoes, and an ancient winery on the premises. A walking trail leads down the valley and horse riding and cycling can be organised.

MUSTAFAPAŞA
☎ 0384 / pop 1600

Until WWI, Mustafapaşa was called Sinasos and was a predominantly Ottoman Greek settlement. These days it greatly benefits from this Greek legacy, as its exquisitely decorated stone-carved houses and minor rock-cut churches attract the attention of a small but respectable number of foreign and domestic tourists. It's a wonderful spot to spend a day or two.

You enter Mustafapaşa at an enlarged intersection, the Sinasos Meydanı, where a signboard indicating the whereabouts of the local rock-cut churches is located. Follow the road downhill and you'll come to Cumhuriyet Meydanı, the centre of the village, which sports the ubiquitous bust of Atatürk and several teahouses.

There's no tourist office in town, and no ATMs; internet access is available on the main square and at **Monastery Hotel** (opposite; per hr TL1.50; ⏱ 8.30am-midnight).

Sights

A sign pointing off Sinasos Meydanı leads 1km to the 12th-century **Ayios Vasilios Kilise** (St Basil Church; admission TL5; ⏱ 9am-6pm), perched near the top of a ravine. Its interior features unimpressive 20th-century frescoes. There should be someone there with a key; if not, enquire at the *belediye*.

Between Sinasos Meydanı and Cumhuriyet Meydanı is a 19th-century **medrese** with a fine carved portal. The stone columns on either side of the doorway are supposed to swivel when there's movement in the foundations, thus warning of earthquake damage.

Cumhuriyet Meydanı is home to the imposing **Ayios Kostantinos-Eleni Kilise** (Church of SS Constantine & Helena; admission TL5; ⏱ 8.30am-noon & 1-5.30pm), erected in 1729 and restored in 1850. A fine stone grapevine runs around the door but the ruined interior with faded 19th-century frescoes is not worth the admission charge. If you are keen to see it, a uniformed council worker should be posted outside; if not, ask for the key at the nearby *belediye*.

There are also churches in **Monastery Valley**, but they're disappointing compared with others in Cappadocia. Nonetheless, it's a lovely walk. Also to the west of Mustafapaşa, there are 4km to 8km walks in **Gomeda Valley**, where there is a ruined 11th-century Greek town. Local guide Niyazi, who charges €25 for individuals and groups, can be contacted through Old Greek House.

Sleeping & Eating

Many of Mustafapaşa's accommodation options are closed from November to March.

Monastery Hotel (☎ 353 5005; www.monasteryhotel .com; Mehmet Şakirpaşa Caddesi; dm/s/d/tr TL20/30/60/70; 🖳) This rough hotel has been running since 1968 – and looks like it. The rooms could use a spring clean but have TVs, private bathrooms and all amenities. The four- to six-bed dorms have TVs and the bizarre cave disco-bar opens for groups. Take care of your valuables, as the courtyard is an insalubrious local hang-out.

Hotel Pacha (☎ 353 5331; www.pachahotel.com; Sinasos Meydanı; s/d €20/30) Hotel Pacha is the real thing: a family-run business that offers a warm welcome and home cooking by the lady of the house, Demra. The restored Ottoman Greek pile has a great feel about it from the moment you enter its pretty vine-trellised courtyard. Entered under painted archways, the rooms have a bright, modern appearance and are very clean. Guests spend most of their time relaxing in the simply wonderful upstairs restaurant-lounge, which overlooks the courtyard.

Hotel Natura (☎ 353 5030; www.clubnatura.com; Sümer Sokak 16; r incl dinner TL70) There is decayed elegance to this 19th-century Greek mansion, where a rusty banister climbs the stone staircase from the central courtyard. Carpets are everywhere in the 'antique' rooms, alongside lamps, pictures, hatstands and the occasional broken window. Smaller modern rooms lack the eclectic mishmash of decor.

Old Greek House (☎ 353 5306; www.oldgreekhouse .com; Şahin Caddesi; s TL60, d TL80-120) This hotel restaurant (mains TL6 to TL20, set menus TL22 to TL30) is about the best place to try Ottoman cuisine in Cappadocia. Prepared by half a dozen village women, the dishes include unusual choices such as *barbunya* (lima beans in tomato sauce), carrot salad and some of the best *baklava* we tasted. The hotel, occupying an Ottoman Greek house inhabited by the same family since 1938, is an excellent place to stay thanks to its historic

aura. The large rooms have polished floorboards covered in rugs and comfortable beds with embroidered bedspreads.

Ukabeyn Pansiyon (☎ 353 5533; www.ukabeyn.com; d/tr €55/75; 🖳) This boutique hotel high on the hill overlooking the town has six arched and cave rooms furnished in an attractive modern style. There's a swimming pool, a series of terraces and a fully equipped apartment (€75 to €95) that would make a fabulous base for an extended visit. From Cumhuriyet Meydanı, it's a stiff 1km up the hill.

Sinasos Gül Konaklari (Rose Mansions; ☎ 353 5486; www.rosemansions.com; Sümer Sokak; s/d incl dinner €100/150; 🖳) Occupying two heavily restored Greek mansions, this hotel is part of the Dinler chain. Rooms are luxurious but a little impersonal, with blue and yellow cushions scattered on the beds, which sit on raised platforms. There's a posh restaurant, a hamam and a strange 'Ottoman-meets-Holiday-Inn' lounge in a wooden pavilion in the rose garden.

Most of the hotels and pensions offer meals and this is fortunate, as the town's other eateries are dreadful. For lunch or dinner, we recommend Old Greek House and Hotel Pacha; set menu €8).

Getting There & Away

Nine buses a day (three on Sunday) travel the 5km between Ürgüp and Mustafapaşa (TL1, 10 minutes). The first leaves Mustafapaşa at 7.45am and the last leaves Ürgüp at 7pm. A taxi costs TL20.

SOĞANLI

☎ 0352 / pop 400

The twin valleys of Soğanlı, about 36km south of Mustafapaşa, look so magical that mischievous guides have falsely claimed they featured in *Star Wars*. Yoda is not snoozing in any of the rock-cut churches, but they are much less visited than those at Göreme or Zelve. Soğanlı is a magnificent place to explore, and unless your visit coincides with a day tour from Göreme, you may well have the valleys to yourself.

To reach Soğanlı turn off the main road from Mustafapaşa to Yeşilhisar and proceed 4km to the village. Buy your ticket for the **churches** (adult/child TL2/free; ☼ 8am-8.30pm, to 5pm in winter) near the Kapadokya Restaurant (p525). In the village square, local women sell the dolls for which Soğanlı is supposedly famous.

GOING UNDERGROUND

During the 6th and 7th centuries, when Persian and Arabic armies set off to vanquish the Christians, beacons were lit and the warning could travel from Jerusalem to Constantinople in hours. When the message reached Cappadocia, the Byzantine Christians would escape into secret tunnels leading to vast underground cities.

Some 37 cities have been opened, and there at least 100 more. Excavations have not proceeded further because they have uncovered little more than graves and pottery pieces, as the cities' inhabitants took their possessions with them when they returned to the surface.

Some 10,000 people lived at **Derinkuyu** and 3000 at **Kaymaklı**, spending months at a time down there. They cunningly disguised the air shafts as wells. The Persian horsemen might throw some poison into the 'wells', thinking they were contaminating the water supply. They would not notice any smoke from the fires burning beneath their feet, as the soft tuff rock absorbed most of it and the remaining fumes dispersed in the shafts.

The shafts, which descend almost 100m in some of the cities, also served a construction purpose. As rooms were made, debris would be excavated into the shaft, which would then be cleared and deepened so work could begin on the next floor.

Touring the underground cities, mentioned by the ancient Greek historian Xenophon in his *Anabasis*, is like tackling an assault course for history buffs. Narrow walkways lead you into the depths of the earth, through stables with handles used to tether animals, churches with altars and baptism pools, walls with air circulation holes, granaries with grindstones, and blackened kitchens with ovens.

As on an ocean liner, the poshest families lived closest to the surface, where the air supply was better. In the dwellings, you can see holes used for wooden doors, for holding candles and for hanging hammocks. Huge rolling stone doors would have served as last lines of defence if the Muslim soldiers had discovered the hideout.

Some archaeologists date the earliest portions of the underground cities back 4000 years to Hittite times, and they were certainly used to make and store wine before they were inhabited. All year round, the underground chambers remain at the optimum temperature for making and ageing wine.

Visiting the cities is fascinating, but be prepared for unpleasantly crowded and sometimes claustrophobic passages. Avoid visiting on weekends, when busloads of domestic tourists descend. Even if you don't normally like having a guide, it's worth having one when you tour an underground city, since they can conjure up the details of life below ground better than you can on your own.

Kaymaklı underground city (yeraltı şehri; admission TL15; 8am-5pm, last admission 4.30pm) features a maze of tunnels and rooms carved eight levels deep into the earth (only four are open). As this is the most convenient and popular of the underground cities, you should get here early in July and August to beat the tour groups, or from about 12.30pm to 1.30pm when they break for lunch.

To reach **Özlüce underground city** (admission free), turn right as you enter Kaymaklı from the north and you'll be heading for the small village of Özlüce, 7km further away. More modest than Kaymaklı or Derinkuyu, this underground city is also less developed and less crowded.

Derinkuyu underground city (Deep Well; admission TL15; 8am-5pm, last admission 4.30pm), 10km south of Kaymaklı, has larger rooms arrayed on seven levels. When you get all the way down, look up the ventilation shaft to see just how far down you are – claustrophobics beware!

There are also underground cities at Güzelyurt (p531) and Özkonak (p514), near Avanos.

Getting There & Away

Although you can visit one of the cities on a day tour from Göreme, Avanos or Ürgüp, it's also easy to see them on your own. The half-hourly Nevşehir–Niğde bus stops in both Kaymaklı (TL2, 30 minutes) and Derinkuyu (TL3, 40 minutes). You could easily visit Kaymaklı and Derinkuyu and then continue onto Niğde the same day using the local buses.

You'll need a taxi to take you to Özlüce from Kaymaklı.

Sights

The valleys of **Aşağı Soğanlı** and **Yukarı Soğanlı** were first used by the Romans as necropolises and later by the Byzantines for monastic purposes (similar to Göreme and Zelve), with ancient **rock-cut churches**.

Most of the interesting churches are in the right-hand valley (to the north), easily circuited on foot in about two hours. All are signposted, but be careful as many are in a state of disrepair.

Coming from the main road, about 800m before the ticket office, signs point to the **Tokalı Kilise** (Buckle Church), on the right, reached by a steep flight of worn steps; and the **Gök Kilise** (Sky Church), to the left across the valley floor. The Gök has twin naves separated by columns and ending in apses. The double frieze of saints is badly worn.

The first church on the right after the ticket booth, the **Karabaş** (Black Hat), is one of the most interesting. It is covered in paintings showing the life of Christ, with Gabriel and various saints. A pigeon in the fresco reflects the importance of pigeons to the monks, who wooed them with dovecotes cut into the rock.

Furthest up the right-hand valley is the **Yılanlı Kilise** (Church of St George or Snake Church), its frescoes deliberately painted over with black paint, probably to protect them. See p499 for an explanation of its name. The hole in the roof of one chamber, surrounded by blackened rock, shows fires were lit there.

Turn left at the Yılanlı Kilise, cross the valley floor and climb the far hillside to find the **Kubbeli** and **Saklı Kilisesi** (Domed and Hidden Churches). The Kubbeli is unusual because of its Eastern-style cupola cut clean out of the rock. Nestling in the hillside, the Hidden Church is indeed hidden from view – until you get close.

In the left-hand valley, accessed from the village, you'll first come across the **Geyikli Kilise**, where the monks' refectory is still clearly visible. The **Tahtalı Kilise** (Church of Santa Barbara), 200m further on, has well-preserved Byzantine and Seljuk decorative patterns.

Sleeping & Eating

Kapadokya Restaurant (☎ 0352-653 1045; set menus TL6; ☻ lunch) boasts tables set under shady trees and serves stodgy but acceptable omelettes, casseroles and *çorba*. Modest **Soğanlı Restaurant** (☎ 653 1016; ☻ lunch only) has a good, shady garden for sipping *çay*. Nearby, the village's only pension, the family-run **Emek** (☎ /fax 653 1029; dm with half board €16), is a picture of rural simplicity, with clean cave dorms. Meals are cooked by the owner's wife and served on a pleasant upstairs terrace overlooking the square.

Getting There & Away

It's basically impossible to get to Soğanlı by public transport. Your best bet is to make your way to Yeşilhisar from Kayseri (TL2.50, every 30 minutes from 7am to 9pm) and then negotiate for a taxi to take you the rest of the way. Alternatively you can rent a car (see boxed text, p526) or sign up for a day tour in Ürgüp or Göreme.

ALA DAĞLAR NATIONAL PARK

The Ala Dağlar National Park (Ala Dağlar Milli Parkı) protects the rugged middle range of the Taurus Mountains between Kayseri, Niğde and Adana. It's famous throughout the country for its extraordinary trekking routes, which make their way through craggy limestone ranges dotted with waterfalls. It's best to trek here between mid-June and late September; at other times weather conditions can be particularly hazardous, especially since there are few villages and little support other than some mountaineers' huts. Bring warm gear and be prepared for extreme conditions.

The most popular walks start at the small villages of **Çukurbağ** and **Demirkazık**, which lie beneath Demirkazık Dağı (Mt Demirkazık, 3756m), some 40km east of Niğde.

You can also reach the mountains via Yahyalı, 70km due south of Kayseri, a short drive away from the impressive **Kapuzbaşı Waterfalls** on the Zamantı River.

Although there are a variety of walks in the mountains, many people opt for the two-day minimum walk to the beautiful **Yedigöller** (Seven Lakes, 3500m), which starts and finishes at Demirkazık. An easier three- to four-day walk begins at Çukurbağ and leads through the forested Emli Valley, before finishing at Demirkazık.

Although solo trekkers do sometimes venture into the mountains, unless you're experienced and well prepared you should consider paying for a guide or joining a tour. A guide should cost around €50 per day; a horse, which can carry up to four people's luggage, about €30. If you want to do a full trek in the

CAPPADOCIA

SOĞANLI ROADTRIP

If you only rent a car once on your trip, the day you visit Soğanli could be the time to do it. Not only are the valleys tricky to reach by public transport, but the drive there is beautiful. The open countryside makes a change from central Cappadocia's canyons and you can stop in sleepy country villages that give an idea of what Göreme was like 30 years ago.

Signposted from the main road, some 10km south of Mustafapaşa, the rock-cut Byzantine complex at **Keşlik Monastery** includes vandalised frescoes and 16 houses where hundreds of monks lived. Inside the dwellings, you can see chimneys, fireplaces, bookshelves and grey nicks left on the rock by metal chisels. The kitchen features a hatch for passing meals to the refectory, which has seats at the far end for the teachers.

Some 7km further south, tractors bounce along hilly, cobbled streets in **Taşkınpaşa**, which is named after its 600-year-old Seljuk **mosque**. Photos near the entrance to the mosque show its original, 14th-century pulpit, now in Ankara's Museum of Anatolian Civilisations (p444). Outside, Taşkın Paşa himself is buried in one of the two Seljuk tombs; traders stayed under the arches during the caravanserai days. On the way back to the main road you will see a *medrese* with an ornate door frame.

At the ancient city of **Sobesos** (admission free; 🕑 8.30am-5.30pm), signposted from Şahinefendi, the various sections of the Roman baths can easily be distinguished. There are also some fine Roman mosaics, a mummy and a Byzantine church, built during renovations of the Roman city in the late 4th century.

Some day tours also stop at these sights.

range (about €200 for a week, all inclusive), Middle Earth Travel (p500) is a good first port of call in Göreme. The agency offers a five-day program for €280, for a minimum of six people. **Osman Üçer** (☎ 0536-813 6032) and **Ahmet Üçer** (☎ 0536-712 0728) are two guides based in the park, and there are agencies in Niğde:

Demavend Travel (Map p527; ☎ 0388-232 7363; www.demavendtravel.com; 5th fl, Esenbey Mahallesi Bahadir Is Merkezi 15, Niğde)

Sobek Travel (☎ 0388-232 1507; www.trekkingin turkeys.com; Avanoğlu Apt 70/17, Bor Caddesi, Niğde)

Sleeping & Eating

Şafak Pension & Camping (☎ 0388-724 7039; www .safaktravel.com; Çukurbağ; camp sites per person €10, d per person with half-board €25; ☒ 🖳) This is run by the friendly, English-speaking walking and climbing guide Hassan. Rooms are simple but clean, with plentiful hot water, heating and comfortable beds. Camp sites have electricity and their own bathroom facilities. The terrace and garden command magnificent views of Mt Demirkazık.

On the other side of the road, the same family has recently opened another, similar pension, **Öz Şafak**, which charges the same rates. You'll find both pensions near the main road, about 1.5km from the bridge and the signpost marked 'Demirkazık 4, Pinarbaşı 8'.

Çukurbağ has basic shops for supplies.

Getting There & Away

From Niğde, take a Çamardı-bound minibus (TL5, 90 minutes, every hour between 7am and 5.30pm) and ask to be let off at the Şafak Pension (it's 5km before Çamardı).

NIĞDE

☎ 0388 / pop 331,677

Backed by the snowcapped Ala Dağlar range, Niğde, 85km south of Nevşehir, was founded by the Seljuks. It's an agricultural centre with a clutch of historic buildings. You won't want to stay, but may have to if you want to visit the fabulous Eski Gümüşler Monastery, 10km to the northeast. You may also pass through en route to the base-camp villages for trekking in the Ala Dağlar National Park (p525).

French is spoken in the helpful **tourist office** (☎ 232 3393; Belediye Sarayı 38/39; 🕑 8am-noon & 1-5pm Mon-Fri), located on the 1st floor of the ugly Kültür Merkezi (City Cultural Centre) on Bor Caddesi. There are plenty of internet cafés on the main street, including **Cafe In** (Bor Caddesi; per hr TL1; 🕑 9am-midnight), opposite the tourist office. ATMs are dotted along Bankalar/İstiklal/Bor Caddesi.

Sights

Niğde Museum (Niğde Müzesi; admission TL3; 🕑 8am-noon & 1-5pm Tue-Sun) houses a well-presented selection of finds from the Assyrian city of Acemhöyük near Aksaray, through the Hittite and Phrygian ages to sculptures from Tyana (now Kemerhisar), the former Roman centre and Hittite capital 19km southwest of Niğde. Several mummies are exhibited too, including the 11th-century mummy of a blonde nun discovered in the 1960s in the Ihlara Valley.

The Seljuk **Alaeddin Camii** (1223), on the hill crowned with the fortress, is the town's grandest mosque but the **Süngür Bey Camii**, on a terrace at the end of the marketplace, is more interesting. Built by the Seljuks and restored by the Mongols in 1335, it is a curious blend of architectural styles.

The attractive **Ak Medrese** (1409) houses a cultural centre that may – or may not – be open.

Also in the centre are the **Hüdavend Hatun Türbesi** (1312), a fine Seljuk tomb, and the Ottoman **Dış Cami**.

Sleeping & Eating

Niğde has several drab concrete hotels and numerous cheap and cheerful *lokantas* and *pastanes* on its thoroughfares.

Hotel Nahita (☎ 232 3536; fax 232 1526; Emin Erişingil Caddesi 19; s/d/tr TL45/60/70) On the main road into town and close to the otogar, this three-star block lacks character but is clean and comfortable and has a large green-and-orange restaurant.

Saruhan (☎ 232 2172; Bor Caddesi 13; mains TL6-10) Occupying a restored *han* (caravanserai) dating from 1357, Saruhan is heavy on atmosphere and no lightweight when it comes to its food. It serves delicious kebaps as well as rustic dishes such as *işkembe çorba* (tripe soup). We enjoyed the Adana kebap and were blown away by how cheap everything was. No alcohol is served and beware the toilet: it was out of order when we visited, and previous patrons advise that you give it a wide berth.

Arısoylar Restaurant (☎ 232 5035; Bor Caddesi 8; mains TL7-9) This sleek modern eatery offers classics such as İskender kebap, *çiğ köfte* (patties of raw spiced lamb) and *beyti sarma* (wrapped lamb with garlic, TL9). Its air-conditioned dining room with pink and white tablecloths is a perfect place to escape the heat and noise of Niğde.

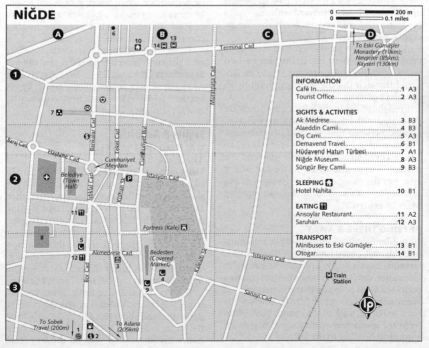

NİĞDE

INFORMATION
Café In...1 A3
Tourist Office................................2 A3

SIGHTS & ACTIVITIES
Ak Medrese...................................3 B3
Alaeddin Camii.............................4 B3
Dış Cami.......................................5 A3
Demavend Travel.........................6 B1
Hüdavend Hatun Türbesi............7 A1
Niğde Museum.............................8 A3
Süngür Bey Camii........................9 B3

SLEEPING
Hotel Nahita...............................10 B1

EATING
Arısoylar Restaurant..................11 A2
Saruhan......................................12 A3

TRANSPORT
Minibuses to Eski Gümüşler.......13 B1
Otogar..14 B1

To Eski Gümüşler Monastery (10km); Nevşehir (85km); Kayseri (130km)

Terminal Cad

Baraj Cad
Hastane Cad
Cumhuriyet Meydanı
Belediye (Town Hall)
İstasyon Cad
Fortress (Kale)
Akmedrese Cad
Bedesten (Covered Market)
İstasyon Cad
Sanayi Cad
Train Station
To Sobek Travel (200m)
To Adana (205km)

CAPPADOCIA

Getting There & Away

Minibuses to and from the otogar trundle along Bankalar/İstiklal/Bor and Terminal Caddesis; it costs TL1 from the otogar to the tourist office. There are buses to Adana (TL15, 3½ hours, five daily), Aksaray (TL10, 1½ hours, hourly between 7am and 9pm), Ankara (TL25, five hours, five daily), İstanbul (TL50, 11 hours, five daily), Kayseri (TL10, 1½ hours, hourly between 7am and 9pm), Konya (TL20, 3½ hours, 10 daily) and Nevşehir (TL10, one hour, hourly from 7am to 6pm).

Niğde is on the Ankara–Adana train line. A daily service leaves for Adana at 6am (TL15, four hours) and for Ankara at 11.30pm (TL25, 9¼ hours).

AROUND NİĞDE
Eski Gümüşler Monastery

The ancient rock-hewn **Eski Gümüşler Monastery** (admission TL3; ⏱ 8.30am-noon & 1-5pm), sprawling along the base of a cliff about 10km northeast of Niğde, has some of Cappadocia's best-preserved frescoes.

The monastery was only rediscovered in 1963. You enter via a rock-cut passage, which opens onto a large courtyard with reservoirs for wine and oil, and rock-cut dwellings, crypts, a kitchen and a refectory.

A small hole in the ground acts as a vent for a 9m-deep shaft leading to two levels of subterranean rooms. You can descend through the chambers or climb to an upstairs bedroom.

Even the pillars in the lofty main church are decorated with colourful Byzantine frescoes, painted between the 7th and 11th centuries. The charming Nativity looks as if it is set in a rock-caved structure like this one, and the striking Virgin and Child to the left of the apse has the elongated Mary giving a *Mona Lisa* smile – it's said to be the only smiling Mary in existence.

GETTING THERE & AWAY

Gümüşler Belediyesi minibuses (TL1, 15 minutes) depart every hour from the minibus terminal beside Niğde's otogar. As you enter Gümüşler, don't worry when the bus passes a couple of signs pointing to the monastery – it eventually passes right by it. To catch a bus back to Niğde, walk to the roundabout 500m from the monastery entrance and flag down a minibus heading to the left.

IHLARA VALLEY (IHLARA VADİSİ)
☎ 0382

Southeast of Aksaray, Ihlara Valley scythes through the stubbly fields. Once called Peristrema, the valley was a favourite retreat of Byzantine monks, who cut churches into the base of its towering cliffs. Following the river (Melendiz Suyu), which snakes between painted churches, piles of boulders and a sea of greenery ringing with birdsong, is an unforgettable experience. In the words of one Slovakian traveller, Radovan: 'The deep canyon with lots of churches and trees opens up as you approach Selime. After that you're in a sleepy valley with the river flowing, big mountains typical of Cappadocia in the distance, and a gorgeous monastery in Selime.'

Like Soğanlı, Ihlara Valley looks worthy of *Star Wars* but did not actually feature in the films. Nonetheless, walking the 13km between Ihlara village and Selime is likely to be a highlight of your trip. Given the tricky public-transport situation, many people visit on day tours from Göreme, although these allow only a few hours to explore the central part of the gorge. Good times to visit are midweek in May or September when fewer people are about. Midway along the valley, at Belisırma, a swath of riverside restaurants means you needn't come weighed down with provisions.

There are no ATMs in Ihlara village, Selime or Belisırma. Internet access is available at **Kappadokya Café** (per hr TL1; ⏱ 9am-midnight), near Akar Pansion in Ihlara village, and at **Derren Net** (per hr TL1.50; ⏱ 8am-10pm), next to the supermarket and the PTT in Selime.

Sights & Activities
WALKING IHLARA VALLEY

There are four entrances along the **Ihlara Valley** (admission TL5, parking TL2; ⏱ 8am-6.30pm). If, like most people, you only want to walk the short stretch with most of the churches, then enter via the 360 knee-jarring steps leading down from the Ihlara Vadisi Turistik Tesisleri (Ihlara Valley Tourist Facility), perched on the rim of the gorge 2km from Ihlara village. Alternatively there are entrances near the derelict Star Otel in Ihlara village (follow the path uphill to the left), at Belisırma and at Selime.

It takes about 2½ to three hours to walk from the Ihlara Vadisi Turistik Tesisleri to Belisırma, and about three hours to walk from Belisırma to Selime. You'll need seven to eight hours if you want to walk all the way from

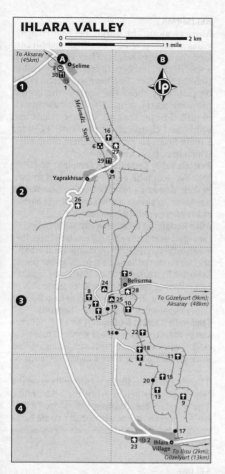

IHLARA VALLEY

CAPPADOCIA

Ihlara village to Selime, stopping in Belisırma for lunch along the way.

If you're planning to walk all the way, it's best to start early in the day, particularly in summer, when you'll need to take shelter from the fierce sun.

The ticket for the valley should also cover Selime Monastery (p530) and Güzelyurt's Monastery Valley & Antique City (p531).

CHURCHES

Along the valley floor, signs mark the different churches. Although they're all worth visiting if you have the time, the following list includes the real must-sees:

Kokar (Fragrant) Kilise This church has some fabulous frescoes – the Nativity and the Crucifixion for starters – and tombs buried in the floors.

Sümbüllü (Hyacinth) Kilise Some frescoes remain, but the church is mostly noteworthy for its well-preserved, simple but elegant facade.

Yılanlı (Serpent) Kilise Many of the frescoes are badly damaged, but it's still possible to make out the one outlining the punishments doled out to sinners; especially the three-headed snake with a sinner in each mouth and the nipple-clamped women (ouch!) who didn't breastfeed their young.

Kırk Dam Altı (St George) Kilise It's a scramble to get to, but the views of the valley make all the puffing worthwhile. The frescoes are badly graffitied, but above the entrance you can see St George on a white horse, slaying a three-headed snake.

Bahattın'ın Samanlığı (Bahattın's Granary) Kilise With some of the valley's best-preserved frescoes, the church is named after a local who used to store grain here. Frescoes show scenes from the life of Christ, including the Crucifixion, Massacre of the Innocents and Baptism scenes.

Direkli (Columned) Kilise This cross-shaped church has six columns, hence the name. The large adjoining chamber originally had two storeys, as you can see from what's left of the steps and the holes in the walls from the supporting beams. There are burial chambers in the floor.

SELİME MONASTERY

The **monastery** (dawn-dusk) at Selime is an astonishing rock-cut structure incorporating a vast kitchen with soaring chimney, a church with a gallery around it, stables with rock-carved feed troughs and other evidence of the troglodyte lifestyle. The admission price is included in the Ihlara Valley ticket. The entrance is just opposite the Ali Paşa Tomb (1317).

Tours

Travel agencies in Göreme (p500), Avanos (p512) and Ürgüp (p518) offer full-day tours to Ihlara for TL50 to TL60 per day, including lunch.

Sleeping & Eating

If you want to walk all the way along the gorge there are modest pensions handily placed at both ends (in Ihlara village and Selime). You can also break your journey into two parts with an overnight stay in Belisırma's camping grounds or pension. Note that all accommodation is closed out of season (December to March).

IHLARA VILLAGE

Akar Pansion & Restaurant (453 7018; fax 453 7511; s/d/tr TL20/40/55) One of the only places in town, Akar's 18 motel-style rooms are simple but clean with private bathrooms. The restaurant (mains TL6 to TL7) serves saç tava, grilled local trout, fried chicken and omelettes, and a small shop sells picnic ingredients. Owner Cengiz shuttles people to Selime (TL20), Belisırma (TL15) and the Ihlara Vadisi Turistik Tesisleri (free).

BELİSIRMA

Midway along the gorge, below Belisırma village, four low-key licensed restaurants feed the hungry hikers. They are not worth a special trip, but benefit from their position right by the river. Two have wonderful tables on platforms above the water – the hottest property on the strip. All serve basic meals of grilled trout, saç tava, kebaps, salads and soups, and charge about the same: TL10 for a main and TL5 per site in their camp sites, which have basic ablution blocks.

Anatolia Valley Restaurant & Camping (457 3040) This good site has a couple of vine-covered pergolas for shade, although the toilet block isn't too clean. Wooden 'tree houses' are planned and the owner will drive hikers back to Ihlara car park if they are tired (TL15).

Aslan Restaurant & Camping (457 3033) The camp site is set at the base of a cliff with lots of trees. The waiters in the busy restaurant are brusque and objectionable, and the river platforms are generally held for groups.

Belisırma Restaurant (457 3057) On the opposite bank of the river, Belisırma's balconies are popular with groups. The camp site at the rear makes up for its lack of shade with respectable toilets and some hammocks.

Tandırcı Restaurant & Camping (457 3110) Camp sites are dotted among vegetable gardens and a small orchard. Groups often bypass the restaurant, leaving a mellow, shady spot and a sporting chance of scoring a river platform.

There's a pension in the scruffy village on the hill, across the bridge from the restaurants. The spartan **Vadi Pansiyon** (457 3067; d TL50) has four green rooms with small private bathrooms, and a terrace café with views across the fields.

SELİME

The cheapest and most pleasant accommodation option at the northern end of the gorge is the worn but clean **Piri Pension** (454 5114;

BIG HASAN

If a stroll through Ihlara Valley gets you salivating for more walking, the area around Cappadocia's second-highest mountain, Hasan Dağı (Mt Hasan), is good for trekking. The closest village to the 3268m inactive volcano is **Helvadere**, about 10km southwest of Ihlara village and 20km east of Taşpınar. Helvadere is the site of the ancient city of Nora, the architecturally unique remains of which can be seen 1km east of the village. From the mountain hut, 8km southwest of Helvadere, it takes eight hours to hike to and from the summit, where the basement of what was once Turkey's highest church remains. There are views of the Ala Dağlar and Bolkar ranges and Tuz Gölü, the country's second-largest salt lake. The challenging trek requires some mountaineering experience during the winter. You can get more information in Göreme at Middle Earth Travel (p500), which offers a two-day trip incorporating Kaymaklı and Ihlara Valley from €150.

carpet_Mustafa@gmail.com; s/d TL20/40), a tranquil, friendly place overlooking some fairy chimneys. Owner Mustafa guides around the valley and the nearby monastery (TL15).

In an olive-green block 2km outside the village on the road to Belisırma, the bare, clean rooms at **Kayabaşi Motel** (☎ 454 5565; s/d TL25/50) are chiefly notable for their views of the yawning mouth of the gorge.

There is a ramshackle eatery, **Çatlak Restaurant**, on a muddy riverbank a few steps from the start of the walk.

Getting There & Away

Ten dolmuşes a day travel down the valley from Aksaray, stopping in Selime, Belisırma, Ihlara village and Ilısu en route to Güzelyurt (p533). In Belisırma, dolmuşes stop in the new part of the village, up on the plateau, and you have to hike a few hundred metres down into the valley. To travel in the opposite direction, you have to catch a taxi. A taxi between Ihlara village and Selime should cost about TL25; from Selime to Aksaray, about TL45. See p532 for taxi fares from Güzelyurt.

GÜZELYURT
☎ 0382 / pop 3735 / elevation 1485m

According to signposts on the deserted roads east of Ihlara Valley, 'a trip without Güzelyurt is not a Cappadocia trip'. It may seem an optimistic slogan, but Güzelyurt both ticks all the important Cappadocian sightseeing boxes and receives a refreshing lack of visitors. A scree slope with Hollywood-style letters spelling out the town's old name, Gelveri, overlooks underground cities, rock-cut churches, stone houses and a lakeside monastery.

In Ottoman times Karballa (Gelveri) was inhabited by 1000 Ottoman Greek families and 50 Turkish Muslim families. In the population exchanges between Turkey and Greece in 1924, the Greeks of Gelveri went to Nea Karvali in Greece, while Turkish families from Kozan and Kastoria in Greece moved here. The relationship between the two countries is now celebrated in an annual **Turks & Greeks Friendship Festival** held in July.

Güzelyurt has a PTT, a branch of the TC Ziraat Bankası (but no ATM) and several shops. English-speaking staff at the helpful **tourist office** (☎ 451 2498; ⏰ 8.30am-7pm) in the main street can supply information about both the town and the Ihlara Valley. The poorly signed **Arikan Internet Café** (per hr TL1;

⏰ 8am-11pm) is on the 1st floor of a *pastane* in a small square behind the bank.

Sights
MONASTERY VALLEY & ANTIQUE CITY

Walk downhill from the main square following the signs to the Monastery Valley and Antique City. About 300m from the square, a sign points left to a small, uninteresting satellite of the **underground city** (yeraltı şehri; admission TL5; ⏰ 8am-6.30pm). Next stop is the ticket booth; admission should be free with an Ihlara Valley ticket. The restored complex ranges across several levels and includes one hair-raising section where you descend through a hole in the floor.

The valley is also home to several churches, most impressive of which is the **Aşağı** or **Büyük Kilise Camii** (Lower or Big Mosque). Built as the Church of St Gregory of Nazianzus in AD 385, it was restored in 1835 and turned into a mosque following the population exchange in 1924. St Gregory (330–90) grew up locally and went on to become a theologian, patriarch and one of the four Fathers of the Greek Church. The building was being restored at the time of research, but if you can get into its wrecked interior, you can see the wooden sermon desk that was reputedly a gift from a Russian tsar. There are plans to uncover the whitewashed frescoes.

Signposted up some steps on the left after the Büyük Kilise Camii, the **Sivişli Kilise** (Anargyros Church) is a much later rock-hewn church with square pillars and an impressive cupola sporting some weathered frescoes. Climb the steps behind it for fabulous valley views.

Further on are the **Koç** (Ram) church and the neighbouring **Cafarlar** (Rivulets), with its interesting frescoes.

Afterwards you can continue through the 4.5km **Monastery Valley**, a sort of Ihlara in miniature. Panoramic viewpoints abound and just walking through it is pleasant, but there are more rock-cut churches and dwellings to explore. Some 2km after the previous group, the **Kalburlu Kilisesi** (Church with a Screen) has a superb entrance. The almost adjoining **Kömürlü Kilisesi** (Coal Church) has carvings including an elaborate lintel above the entrance and some Maltese crosses.

YÜKSEK KİLİSE & MANASTIR

Perched high on a rock overlooking Güzelyurt lake is the **Yüksek Kilise and Manastır** (High

Church and Monastery), some 2km south of a signposted turn-off on the Ihlara road 1km west of Güzelyurt. The road there creeps between huge boulders balancing on other rocks like outsized sculptures in a gallery. The walled compound containing the plain church and monastery is graffitied inside and looks more impressive from afar, but has sweeping views of the lake and mountains.

KIZIL KİLİSE

Set in farmland surrounded by rugged mountains, the **Kızıl Kilise** (Red Church) is about 6km southeast of Güzelyurt, off the road to Çiftlik and Niğde, just past the village of Sivrihisar. Named for the rusty colour of its stone, the dilapidated building is not worth a visit unless you have your own transport or a penchant for windy taxi journeys. The road wiggles uphill and through some boulder fields. A taxi from Güzelyurt costs about TL15, including waiting time.

GAZİEMİR

Some 18km east of Güzelyurt, just off the road to Derinkuyu, Gaziemir's **underground city** (yeraltı şehri; admission TL3; ☉ 8am-6pm) opened in 2007. Churches, a winery with wine barrels, food depots, hamams and tandoor fireplaces can be seen. Camel bones and loopholes in the rock for tethering animals suggest that it also served as a subterranean caravanserai.

Sleeping & Eating

Asrav Konak (☎ 451 2501; asravpansiyon@asrav.com.tr; s/d €17/32) Housed in an imposing building, Asrav's simple rooms and bare wooden floors are not as grand as its exterior. However, it is comfortable and stylish enough, and the balcony is a perfect place to start the day.

Kadir's Houses (☎ 451 2166; www.kadirshouses.com; s/d/tr/q TL50/80/100/120) A budget version of Hotel Karballa, Kadir's occupies a 120-year-old Ottoman house entered through an antique carved wooden door. The three rooms have modern bathrooms, subtle lighting, mezzanines and beds with natural, woollen duvets. Homemade wine is served in the small outdoor bar and village tucker is available for dinner (TL15).

Halil Pension (☎ 451 2707; www.halilpension .com; Yukarı Mahallesi Amaç Sokak; s/d/tr with half-board TL80/120/150; 🖳) This family home would make a great base for those intending to explore the area for a few days. The meals, packed

with goodies from the garden and served at a table fashioned from an antique door, could be the culinary highlight of your trip. In a modern extension to the original 140-year-old Greek house, the rooms have loads of natural light, small but spotlessly clean bathrooms and cheerful modern decor. The roof terrace has magnificent views of Yüksel Kilise and one room has a private balcony. As you enter town from the west, it's signposted off to the right, a short walk downhill from the centre.

Hotel Karballa (☎ 451 2103; www.karballahotel .com; standard s/d/tr/q €40/55/75/100, deluxe €50/65/85/110; 🏊 🖳) We bet the monks enjoyed living in this 19th-century Greek monastery above the town centre. The hotel has retained a contemplative atmosphere and you feel like a father breaking his fast in the arched former refectory, now the restaurant (dinner €10). The rooms, named after the holy one-time inhabitants, have cross-shaped windows, bright Uzbeki bedspreads and mezzanines. Some of the standard rooms, reached by spiral staircases, snuggle into their vaulted ceilings. There is even a pensive atmosphere in the pool, which overlooks the town's Gelveri sign.

There are three similar *lokantas* on and around the main square, serving cheap beer and rakı and dishes such as pide, *köfte* (meatballs) and kebaps for TL4 to TL7.

Getting There & Away

Returning buses travel from Güzelyurt to Aksaray (TL5, one hour) every two hours between 6.30am and 5.30pm. On Sundays there are fewer buses.

You'll have to catch a taxi to get to Selime (TL25), Ihlara village (TL35) and Hasan Dağı (Mt Hasan; TL60). A taxi to Aksaray costs TL60.

AKSARAY
☎ 0382 / pop 152,000

Like Nevşehir, Aksaray is an ugly modern town with a sprinkling of old buildings and very little to attract the traveller. You may need to transit through here on your way to the Ihlara Valley, but otherwise you're best off avoiding it.

Orientation & Information

Aksaray's main otogar is about 3km west of town. A free *servis* shuttles between it and the small *eski* otogar (old otogar), from where it's a 200m walk to the *vilayet* (provincial government building) in the centre of town. You'll find banks with ATMs along Bankalar Caddesi, a main thoroughfare running past the *vilayet*, which overlooks the pedestrianised main square. Continue straight along Bankalar Caddesi to find the Ulu Cami.

French is spoken in the helpful **tourist office** (☎ 213 2474; Taşpazar Mahallesi; ☼ 8.30am-noon & 1.30-5pm Mon-Fri). To find it, walk along Ankara Caddesi (which runs west off Bankalar Caddesi near the *vilayet*), walk past the Zafer Okulu (school) and take the first left. You can check your emails near Harman (right) at **VIP Net** (Hükümet Sokak 10; per hr TL1; ☼ 9am-10pm), where fish tanks glow alongside six flat screens.

Sights

The **Ulu Cami** (Bankalar Caddesi) has decoration characteristic of the post–Seljuk Beylik period and a little of the original yellow stone remains in the grand doorway.

The **Aksaray Museum** (Aksaray Müzesi; admission TL3; ☼ 8.30am-noon & 1-5pm), in a new building en route from the otogar to the centre, covers both ethnography and archaeology. Exhibits include neolithic beads, a Hellenic child's sarcophagus, Roman perfume bottles, carpets from the Ulu Cami and, in the hall of mummies, a mummified cat.

The older part of town, along Nevşehir Caddesi, has the curious **Eğri Minare** (Crooked Minaret), built in 1236 and leaning at an angle of 27 degrees. Inevitably, the locals know it as the 'Turkish Tower of Pisa'.

Sleeping & Eating

All of the following are on, or within walking distance of, the main square.

Otel Yuvam (☎ 212 0024; fax 213 2875; Eski Sanayi Caddesi Kavşağı; s/d/tr TL25/40/60) This budget option is located on the main square next to the Kurşunlu Cami. The overwhelming feel is old-fashioned, with rooms sporting lino floor coverings and solid wooden furniture. Bathrooms are spotless and beds are hard but have crisp, clean linen. The small lounge with satellite TV is a good retreat from central Aksaray – until the call to prayer intrudes.

Otel Vadim (☎ 212 8200; fax 212 8232; 818 Vadi Sokak 13; s/d/tr TL30/50/60; ▢) It is certainly worth paying a few extra lira to upgrade from Otel Yuvam to this excellent midrange choice. Located in a quiet side street off Büyük Kergi

Caddesi, the southern extension of Bankalar Caddesi, it has a green-tiled facade and large, comfortable rooms with wi-fi.

Grand Saatçioğlu Otel (☎ 214 2020; www.saatci oglu otel.com; Turizm Caddesi 3; s/d/tr/ste TL80/110/140/225; ▩ ▢) This stripy grey building with smoked windows has comfortable rooms with mini-bar, TV and attractive green bedspreads. It's about the smartest accommodation you'll find in Aksaray and has a hamam.

Yeni Merkez Lokantası (☎ 213 1076; Bankalar Caddesi Valilik Karsısı 8d; mains TL4-7) A local favourite, this friendly place facing the *vilayet* has an array of daily specials on display in the bains marie, or you can order specialities such as the İskender kebaps. Takeaway döner sandwiches are available here and at the street vendors nearby.

Harman (☎ 212 3311; Bankalar Caddesi 16a; mains TL7) Aksaray's best restaurant, a few doors from Yeni Merkez Lokantası, is adorned with photos of visiting celebrities posing with the star-struck waiters. It offers a great selection of *ızgara* (grills, TL6.50), döner kebaps (TL7), pide and soups (TL2). Those who enjoy a sweet at the end of the meal will be impressed by the excellent homemade baklava and *künefe* (TL4).

Melisa Pastanesi (☎ 212 3134; Eski Sanayi Caddesi 11) This patisserie near Otel Yuvam serves the usual range of sweet treats and the friendly staff speak some English; particularly Tariq, who worked in a kebap shop in Stoke-on-Trent, England.

Getting There & Away

From Aksaray, direct buses go to Ankara (TL18, 3½ hours, 230km), Konya (TL14, two hours, 140km) via Sultanhanı (TL5, 45 minutes, 50km), Nevşehir (TL10, one hour, 65km) and Niğde (TL10, 1½ hours, 115km).

Dolmuşes run between the old otogar and Güzelyurt (TL5, one hour, 45km, six daily) every two hours between 7.30am and 6pm, stopping in Selime, Belisırma, Ihlara village and Ilısu. Between 9am and 2pm, there are also four dolmuşes for Ihlara Valley alone. Sultanhanı (TL5, 45 minutes, 50km, 10 daily) is also served; there are few Sunday services.

AROUND AKSARAY

The road between Aksaray and Nevşehir follows one of the oldest trade routes in the world, the Uzun Yol (Long Rd). The route linked Konya, the Seljuk capital, with its other great cities (Kayseri, Sivas and Erzurum) and ultimately with Persia (Iran).

The Long Rd was formerly dotted with *hans* where the traders would stop for accommodation and business. The remains of three caravanserais can be visited from Aksaray, the best preserved being the impressive **Ağzıkara Hanı** (admission TL3; ☺ 7.30am-8pm), 16km northeast of Aksaray, which was built between 1231 and 1239. From Aksaray a taxi will charge about TL50 for the run there and back. If you'd prefer to go by bus, catch one heading to Nevşehir and jump off at the Ağzıkara Hanı. Day tours from Göreme and Ürgüp also call in on the caravanserai.

Further towards Nevşehir you'll pass the scant remains of the 13th-century **Tepesidelik Hanı**, 23km northeast of Aksaray, and the 12th-century **Alay Hanı**, another 10km on.

KAYSERİ

☎ 0352 / pop 1.2 million / elevation 1067m

Mixing Seljuk tombs, mosques and modern developments, Kayseri is both Turkey's most Islamic city after Konya and one of the economic powerhouses nicknamed the 'Anatolian tigers'. Colourful silk headscarfs are piled in the bazaar, one of the country's biggest, and businesses shut down at noon on Friday, but Kayseri's religious leanings are less prominent than its manufacturing prowess. The city is overlooked by Erciyes Dağı and the Hilton may not boast central Cappadocia's charms, but its residents are both confident of their city's future and proud of its past. With no need to rely on the tourism game for their income, Kayseri's people are often less approachable than folk in Göreme et al, and this can be frustrating and jarring if you arrive fresh from the fairy chimneys. However, if you are passing through this transport hub, it's worth taking a look at a Turkish boom town with a strong sense of its own history.

History

Under the Roman emperor Tiberius (r AD 14–37), Eusebia (as the settlement at Kayseri was known) was renamed Caesarea. The Arabs renamed it Kaisariyah and the Seljuks gave it its current name.

Kayseri became famous as the birthplace of St Basil the Great, who was responsible for organising the monastic life of Cappadocia. Its early Christian history was interrupted by Arab invasions from the 7th century. The

Seljuks took over in 1084 and held the city until the Mongols' arrival in 1243, except for a brief period when the Crusaders captured it on their way to the Holy Land.

When Kayseri had been part of the Mongol empire for almost 100 years, its governor set up his own emirate (1335). This lasted just 45 years and was succeeded by another emirate, before being conquered by the Ottomans, captured by the Mamluks, and finally retaken by the Ottomans in 1515 – all in just over a century.

Orientation & Information

The basalt-walled citadel at the centre of the old town, just south of Cumhuriyet Meydanı, the huge main square, is a good landmark. Another convenient point of reference is Düvenönü Meydanı, 350m west of the citadel along Park Caddesi.

The train station is at the northern end of Atatürk Bulvarı, over 500m north of Düvenönü Meydanı. Kayseri's otogar is about 3km northwest of Düvenönü Meydanı, along Osman Kavuncu Caddesi and Çevre Yol.

English and German are spoken at the helpful **tourist office** (☎ 222 3903; Cumhuriyet Meydanı; ☺ 8am-5pm Mon-Fri), which gives out maps and brochures.

You'll find numerous banks with ATMs in the centre. To collect your email, head to **Soner Internet Café** (Düvenönü Meydanı; per hr TL1.50; ☺ 8am-midnight).

Sights

Now acting as an overflow valve for the nearby bazaar, the monumental, black volcanic-stone walls of the **citadel** (*hisar* or *kale*) were constructed in the early 13th century, during the Seljuk sultan Alaattin Keykubat's reign. Kayseri saw its first castle in the 3rd century, under the Roman emperor Gordian III, and the Byzantine emperor Justinian made alterations 300 years later. The present building has been restored over the years – twice in the 15th century.

Among Kayseri's distinctive features are several important building complexes that were founded by Seljuk queens and princesses, including the austere-looking **Mahperi Hunat Hatun Complex** (Seyyid Burhaneddin (Talas) Caddesi), east of the citadel. It comprises the Mahperi Hunat Hatun Camii (1238), built by the wife of Alaattin Keykubad; the Hunat Hatun Medresesi (1237); and a hamam, which is still in use.

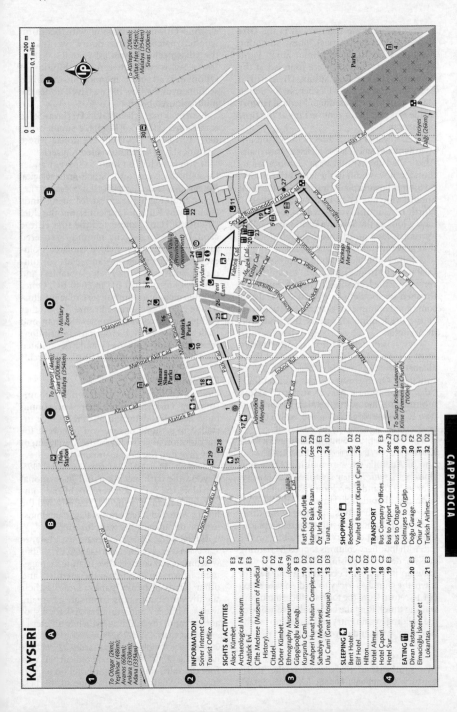

KAYSERİ

To Ötögar (2km);
Yeşilhisar (48km);
Avanos (60km);
Ankara (330km);
Adana (335km)

To Military
Zone

To Airport (4km);
Sivas (200km);
Malatya (354km)

To Ötögar (2km);
Yeşilhisar (48km);
Avanos (60km);
Ankara (330km);
Adana (335km)

To Kültepe (20km);
Sultan Han (45km);
Malatya (354km);
Sivas (200km)

To Erciyes (26km)

To Erciyes
Dağı (26km)

To Sırup Krikoi Lusavoric
Kilise (Aremenian Church)
(100m)

Train
Station

200 m
0.1 miles

CAPPADOCIA

Another striking monument is the **Çifte Medrese** (Twin Seminaries). These adjoining religious schools, set in Mimar Sinan Parkı north of Park Caddesi, were founded at the bequest of the Seljuk sultan Gıyasettin I Keyhüsrev and his sister Gevher Nesibe Sultan (1165–1204). The Museum of Medical History inside was closed for renovations at the time of research.

Back towards the citadel is the Ottoman-style **Kurşunlu Cami** (Lead-Domed Mosque; Atatürk Parkı). Also called the Ahmet Paşa Camii after its founder, it was built in the late 16th century, possibly following plans drawn up by the great Sinan (who was born in a nearby village). North of Cumhuriyet Meydanı, be sure to have a look at the **Sahabiye Medresesi** (from 1267; Ahmetpaşa Caddesi), an Islamic theological school that now functions as a book bazaar.

Another notable mosque is Kayseri's **Ulu Cami** (Great Mosque), begun in the mid-12th century by the Danışmend Turkish emirs and finished by the Seljuks in 1205. It features some good examples of early Seljuk style, such as the brick minaret, one of the first built in Anatolia.

Kayseri is dotted with conical **Seljuk tombs**, most famous of which is the so-called **Döner Kümbet** (Revolving Tomb; Talas Caddesi) at Kartal Junction. On the way to the archaeological museum, you'll pass a cluster of Seljuk monuments, including the **Alaca Kümbet** (Alaca Tomb; Seyyid Burhaneddin (Talas) Caddesi), with a typical quadratic design and pyramidal roof.

The 19th-century **Surup Krikor Lusavoriç Kilise** (Church of St Gregory the Illuminator; off Nazım Bey Bulvarı) is one of Anatolia's few remaining Armenian churches. *Asiatic Review* described it as 'tawdry' back in 1937, and the seldom-used building is certainly dilapidated. However, the domed interior is worth a look, mostly for the three gilded altars, containing paintings that replaced the originals last century. The painting on the left, with four fiery columns topped by flaming crosses, depicts the vision of St Gregory, who grew up in Kayseri. Located in a bad part of town, the church is tricky to find, so take a taxi (TL15 return from the tourist office, including waiting time). Ring the bell on the west side of the building to gain entry and leave a tip for the caretaker at the end of your visit.

MUSEUMS

Just southeast of the citadel is the 18th-century **Güpgüpoğlu Konağı** (off Tennuri Sokak),

a stone Ottoman mansion with beautiful wooden balconies and doorways. Inside, the **Ethnography Museum** (admission TL3; 8am-5pm Tue-Sun) is split between an exhibition of Ottoman craft and a mannequin-inhabited section, evoking how life was lived under the multicoloured beams.

Nearby is the stylish **Atatürk Evi** (Tennuri Sokak; admission free; 8am-5pm Mon-Fri), a small, originally furnished Ottoman-era house where Atatürk stayed when he visited Kayseri.

If you have half an hour to spare, wander through the park to the small **Archaeological Museum** (Kışla Caddesi 2; admission TL3; 8am-5pm Tue-Sun), a minor magpie's nest featuring finds from nearby Kültepe (ancient Kaniş, the chief city of the Hatti people and the first Hittite capital). The largest city mound discovered in Anatolia, Kültepe yielded the area's oldest written documents. Many relate to commerce, such as the Assyrian clay tablets and envelopes from 1920 BC to 1840 BC. Other exhibits include a stunning sarcophagus illustrating Hercules' chores, a Bronze Age mother goddess idol, child mummies, Roman and Hellenistic jewellery, hieroglyphic inscriptions relating to King Tuthalia IV and a decapitated but imposing statue of the Hittite monarch.

Sleeping

Due to Kayseri's cult status among chain-smoking Turkish businessmen, you should book accommodation in advance. Once installed in a room, ensure you reserve it for the duration of your stay or the management may give it to the next claimant.

Hotel Sur (222 4367; Talas Caddesi 12; s/d/tr TL40/60/75) Beyond the dark reception and institutional corridors, the Sur's rooms are bright and comfortable. The management is friendly and the hotel's withered international flags can almost lean on the ancient city walls for support.

Elif Hotel (336 1826; elifotelkayseri@elifotelkayseri .com; Osman Kavuncu Caddesi 2; s/d/tr TL40/70/90) The Elif's welcoming but conservative Islamic management frowns on alcohol on the premises and other forms of hanky-panky. Despite their slightly worn bathrooms, rooms are a bargain, with satellite TV and minibars. Ask for a spot at the rear of the building, which is quieter.

Hotel Çapari (222 5278; www.hotelcapari.com; Gevher Nesibe Mahellesi Donanma Caddesi 12; s/d/tr/ste TL60/90/110/120;) With thick red carpets and friendly staff, this three-star hotel on a quiet street off Atatürk Bulvarı is one of the best deals in town. The well-equipped rooms have satellite TV, wi-fi and massive minibars.

Bent Hotel (☎ 221 2400; www.benthotel.com; Atatürk Bulvarı 40; s/d/tr TL75/100/120) Its name may not inspire confidence, but the Bent is a good midrange choice overlooking the pedal boats in Mimar Sinan Parkı. The small but comfortable rooms have TVs, Efes-stocked minibars and 24-hour room service.

Hotel Almer (☎ 320 7970; www.almer.com.tr; Osman Kavuncu Caddesi 15; s/d/tr TL75/120/150; 🏖 🖳) Kayseri's top sub-Hilton establishment is smoothly professional from the moment you reel through the revolving door. The relaxing reception has a backlit bar and little alcoves for working your way through the magazine rack. Mirrored pillars glint between pink tablecloths in the restaurant, and the wi-fi-enabled rooms are surprisingly quiet despite the busy road.

Hilton (☎ 207 5000; www.hilton.com; İstasyon Caddesi 1; s €120-135, d €140-155; 🏖 🖳) Slap bang in the town centre, this is Kayseri's only five-star hotel. Its futuristic design is a striking contrast to the surrounding mosques and historical buildings. Inside it's swanky, with an atrium as vast as a station, luxurious rooms and all the requisite amenities, including a fitness centre. The views from the upper floors are great.

Eating

Kayseri boasts a few special dishes, among them *pastırma* (salted, sun-dried veal coated with *çemen*, a spicy concoction of garlic, red peppers, parsley and water), the original pastrami.

Few restaurants serve alcohol – if you want a tipple with your tucker, try Hotel Almer (above, mains TL12, open 7pm to 11.30pm) or the Hilton (above).

The western end of Sivas Caddesi has a strip of fast-food joints that still seem to be pumping when everything else in town is quiet.

Divan Pastanesi (☎ 222 3974; Millet Caddesi) Across Millet Caddesi from the Elmacioğlu İskender et Lokantası, this modern pastry shop is a favourite among Kayseri's sweet tooths.

İstanbul Balık Pazarı (☎ 231 8973; Sivas Caddesi; mains TL3; 🕙 8am-11pm) Choose between the fish frying at the door, then head past the glistening catches in the fishmongers to the small dining room, with its mishmash of nautical and historical paintings.

Tuana (☎ 222 0565; 2nd fl, Sivas Caddesi; mains TL7) Entered from the lane leading from the PTT

to Sivas Caddesi, the smart Tuana offers a rollcall of classics such as kebaps and Kayseri *mantı*. When it's quiet, the ocean of red tables and chairs adorned with golden ribbons have the air of an out-of-season seaside resort, but it's easy to distract yourself with the views of the citadel and Erciyes Dağı.

Öz Urfa Sofrası (☎ 232 7777; 1st fl, Millet Caddesi 11; mains TL8; 🕙 10am-10pm) This busy place overlooking the billboard-flanked LC Waikiki store is a little expensive, but its Urfa specialities are popular nonetheless. In addition to the usual pide and meat on sticks, the *künefe* is a winner and the *ayran* (a yoghurt drink) presentation is certainly novel.

Elmacioğlu İskender et Lokantası (☎ 222 6965; 1st & 2nd fl, Millet Caddesi 5; mains TL8-10; 🕙 9am-10.30pm) Ascend in a lift to Kayseri's best restaurant, with waiters sporting bow ties and big windows overlooking the citadel. İskender kebaps are the house speciality, available with *köfte* or in 'double' form (TL13), and other dishes include *pastırma* pide (TL8.5). Recommended.

Shopping

Set at the intersection of age-old trade routes, Kayseri has been an important commercial centre for millennia and its *kapalı çarşı* (vaulted bazaar) was one of the largest built by the Ottomans. Restored in the 1870s and again in the 1980s, it remains the heart of the city and is well worth a wander. The adjoining *bedesten* (covered market), built in 1497, was first dedicated to the sale of textiles and is still a good place to pick up carpets and kilims. An antique carpet auction takes place here on Monday and Thursday.

Getting There & Away

AIR

Turkish Airlines (☎ 222 3858; Tekin Sokak Hukuk Plaza 6c) has three daily flights to and from İstanbul (TL69 to TL169 one way, 1½ hours) and one Sun Express flight to and from İzmir (TL74 one way, 1½ hours) on Wednesday and Saturday mornings.

Onur Air (☎ 231 5551; Ahmetpaşa Caddesi 7) has a daily flight to and from İstanbul (TL54 to TL174 one way).

A taxi between the city centre and the *havaalanı* (airport) costs TL15 and a dolmuş is TL1.25. There are shuttle buses between the airport and hotels in central Cappadocia (see p496).

SERVICES FROM KAYSERİ'S OTOGAR

Destination	Fare (TL)	Duration (hr)	Frequency (per day)
Adana	22	5	frequent
Ankara	25	5	hourly
Erzurum	40	10	frequent
Gaziantep	25	6	six a day
Göreme	10	1½	hourly
Kahramanmaraş	20	4	hourly
Malatya	25	5	frequent
Nevşehir via Ürgüp	12/6	1½/1¼	hourly
Sivas	18	3	frequent
Van	50	13	frequent

BUS

On an important north–south and east–west crossroads, Kayseri has lots of bus services – see the table (above).

The otogar has an internet café, luggage storage (TL6 for 24 hours), a barber, car rental and a café with an *ayran* fountain. If there's no *servis* from there to the *merkez* (centre), grab a taxi (TL15) or catch a local bus (TL1.25).

Dolmuşes run to Ürgüp (TL5, 1¾ hours) from the west garage.

TRAIN

Kayseri is served by the *Vangölü Ekspresi* (between İstanbul and Tatvan), the *Güney Ekspresi* (between İstanbul and Kurtalan), the *Doğu Ekspresi* (between İstanbul and Kars), the *Erzurum Ekspresi* (between Ankara and Kars), the *Çukurova Mavi* (between Ankara and Adana) and the *4 Eylül Mavi Train* (between Ankara and Malatya). The RAJA Passenger Trains İstanbul–Tehran service (see p682) stops in Kayseri en route to Iran.

To reach the centre from the train station, walk out of the station, cross the big avenue (Çevre Yol) and board any bus heading down Atatürk Bulvarı to Düvenönü Meydanı. Alternatively you could walk along Altan Caddesi, which isn't as busy as Atatürk Bulvarı.

AROUND KAYSERİ
Sultan Han

Built in the 1230s, the **Sultan Han** (admission TL3; ☯ daylight) is a striking old Seljuk caravanserai on the old Kayseri–Sivas highway, 45km northeast of Kayseri. It is a fine, restored example of a Seljuk royal caravan lodging – the largest in Anatolia after the Sultanhanı, near Aksaray.

Locals should unlock the door and issue tickets, but visitors have reported frustrated attempts to gain access. If you are coming from Kayseri, enquire at the Kayseri's Archaeological Museum (p536).

Sultan Han is southeast of the Kayseri–Sivas road, near Tuzhisar. To get there from Kayseri, take a Sivas-bound bus (TL5), or a dolmuş (TL2.50) heading to Sarioğlan or Akkişla from the *doğu* (east) garage.

TRAINS FROM KAYSERİ

Trains depart daily unless otherwise stated.

Destination	Fare (TL)	Duration (hr)	Departures
Adana	14	6	2.15am & 7.40am
Ankara	13	8	midnight, 12.55am, 2.51am (not Sun), 4am & 4.19am
İstanbul	22	18	2.51am (not Sun) & 4am
Kars	26	20½	1.30am & 10.17pm
Kurtalan	21	20	11.50am (Mon, Wed, Fri & Sat)
Malatya	15	9	2.52am & 11.50am (not Thu)
Tatvan	22	24	11.50am (Tue & Sun)

Black Sea Coast & the Kaçkar Mountains

Quick. Turn around. There's an entire travel experience over your shoulder that you probably haven't even considered. While you've been planning your Turkish sojourn south to the Med or west to the Aegean, to the north and east the Black Sea (Karadeniz) is equally deserving. Leave the sunbathing and swimming until you head west or south, and expect a more distinctive experience on the country's often overlooked northern coast.

It's only travellers who have been slow to catch on to the appeal of the Black Sea. The craggy and spectacular coastline is scattered with the legacy of the civilisations and empires that have dramatically ebbed and flowed in this historic region. Often bereft of other travellers, castles, churches and monasteries as important as the must-see sights in other parts of Turkey recall the days of the kings of Pontus, the Genoese and the Ottomans. Even earlier times are marked by myths of Amazon warriors and Jason and his Argonauts. The very existence of modern Turkey owes a massive debt to the passionate local support thrown behind Atatürk's republican revolution.

With the region's best views looking north out to sea, the people of the Black Sea really don't think too much about distant İstanbul or Ankara. They're too busy enjoying a relaxed, but cosmopolitan, lifestyle. When you tire of Sinop's laid-back Mediterranean-style vibe, or Trabzon's modern Turkey buzz, head further east to explore the isolated mountain villages and alpine lakes and valleys of the Kaçkar Mountains.

It's often quite surprising what's hidden behind you, isn't it?

HIGHLIGHTS

- Absorb the beauty of centuries-old Byzantine frescoes in the improbable cliff-face setting of the **Sumela Monastery** (p559)

- Walk off tasty home-cooked food amidst the stunning lakes, valleys and peaks of the **Kaçkar Mountains** (p563)

- Take to the back roads to discover **Perşembe** and **Çaka beach** (p550) on the old coastal route from Bolaman to Ordu

- Count the glorious, vertigo-inducing curves on the drop-dead-scenic coastal road from **Amasra** to **Sinop** (p543)

- Fulfil your cosmopolitan urges in the busy streets and bustling big smoke of **Trabzon** (p552)

History

The coast was colonised in the 8th century BC by Milesians and Arcadians, who founded the towns at Sinop, Samsun and Trabzon. Later it became the Kingdom of Pontus. The Pontic king, Mithridates VI Eupator, waged war against the Romans from 88 to 84 BC. He conquered Cappadocia and other Anatolian kingdoms, but had to settle peace based on pre-war borders.

From 74 to 64 BC he was at it again, this time encouraging his son-in-law, Tigranes I of Armenia, to seize Cappadocia from the Romans. The Roman response was to conquer Pontus, forcing Mithridates to flee. He later committed suicide. The Romans left a small kingdom of Pontus based in Trebizond (Trabzon).

The coast was subsequently ruled by Byzantium. Alexius Comnenus, son of Emperor Manuel I, proclaimed himself emperor of Pontus when the Crusaders sacked Constantinople in AD 1204. His descendants ruled until 1461, when Pontus was captured by the Ottomans under Mehmet the Conqueror.

While Alexius remained in Trabzon, Samsun was under Seljuk rule and the Genoese had trading privileges. But when the Ottomans came, the Genoese burned Samsun to the ground and sailed away.

After WWI the region's Ottoman Greek citizens attempted to form a new Pontic state with Allied support. Disarmed by the Allied occupation authorities, Turkish inhabitants were persecuted by ethnic Greek guerrillas who still had weapons. Under these circumstances, local Turks proved responsive to calls for revolution. Mustafa Kemal (later named Atatürk) escaped the sultan's control in İstanbul and landed at Samsun on 19 May 1919. He soon moved inland to Amasya to organise Turkey's battle for independence.

Climate

The Black Sea coast receives the heaviest rainfall in Turkey with warm, showery summers and mild, rainy and foggy winters. Spring and autumn bring changeable conditions. In the Kaçkar Mountains winters are long, harsh and snowy. Be prepared for unpredictable weather because of the altitude.

BLACK SEA COAST

AMASRA

☎ 0378 / pop 7000

From İstanbul to Amasra is a fair journey, but your first glimpse from the hills above Amasra will make it worthwhile. The first substantial town along the Black Sea coast, Amasra effortlessly assumes the mantle of the region's prettiest port.

It's a popular tourist centre, but is lowkey in contrast to the resorts of the Aegean coast. International visitors are still relatively uncommon, and the welcome from

BLACK SEA COAST & THE KAÇKAR MOUNTAINS

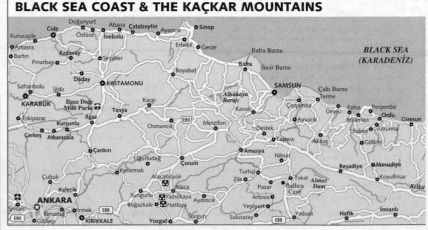

locals and Turkish visitors will be warm and unaffected.

The Byzantines held Amasra as part of the Pontic kingdom, but rented the port to the Genoese as a trading station from 1270 until 1460, when Mehmet the Conqueror waltzed in without a fight. Under Ottoman rule, Amasra lost its commercial importance to other Black Sea ports, and today it's a laid-back spot to relax, dine on excellent seafood, and plan your impending journey along the Black Sea coast.

Orientation

Entering Amasra, on your left is the museum in an old stone building. Most buses stop at an intersection near the post office (PTT). Follow the sign to 'Şehir Merkezi' (north) for the Küçük Liman (Small Harbour) with restaurants and pensions. Walk straight (east) to hit the sandy strip of the Büyük Liman (Large Harbour).

The entrance to the citadel lurks around souvenir shops in the Küçük Liman.

Information

The **tourist office** adjacent to the Can Internet Café was closed at the time of writing. A cluster of **ATMs** is on Küçük Liman.

Amasra Turizm (☎ 315 1978; www.amasraturizm .com; Cumhuriyet Caddesi 13) Hotel bookings, car hire and tourist services.

Can Internet Café (Atatürk Kültür Parkı; per hr TL1.50; ❂ 9am- 10pm) Near the statue of Atatürk.

Sights & Activities

North of the two harbours, three massive gateways lead to Amasra's **kale** (citadel). It encompasses the promontory fortified by the Byzantines when the port was known as Sesamos Amastris.

Inside the citadel is now mainly residential. The original walls survive and contain relics including the 15th-century **Eski Chapel** (Old Chapel).

The excellent **Amasra Museum** (Amasra Müzesi; ☎ 315 1006; Dereoğlu Sokak 4; admission TL3; ❂ 9am-5.30pm Tue-Sun), overlooking Küçük Liman, contains Roman, Byzantine and Hellenistic finds showcasing Amasra's many-mastered history.

Amasra's location is best admired from the sea. Operators in Büyük Liman offer **boat trips** around the harbour and along the coastline. Expect to pay about TL5 for a short tour (45 minutes) and TL30 for a longer tour (six hours) including swimming stops and lunch on a nearby island.

Sleeping

Rates in Amasra can rise by 10% to 40% on busy summer weekends. Prices quoted here are for midweek.

Amasra is a good spot for *ev pansiyons* (pensions in private homes). Look for 'Pansiyon' notices along the seafront and in the *kale.*

All *pansiyons* close from November to April, and most hotels will only be open on weekends during these months.

Balkaya Pansiyon (☎ 315 1434; İskele Caddesi 35; s/d TL30/60) The cheapest formal pension in town, offering small, basic rooms on a side street between the harbours.

Çarşı Pansiyon Evi (☎ 315 1146; carsipansiyon@ amasra.net; Zeki Çakan Caddesi 23; s/d TL30/60) In the market near the castle entrance, this new place has private patios decorated with comfy cushions. The wood-trimmed rooms somehow manage to be modern and rustic at the same time.

Pansiyon Evi (☎ 661 6337; Küçük Liman 33a; s/d TL30/60) Just inside the castle gates, this rambling three-storey wooden house has tidy rooms and breakfast on a breezy terrace overlooking Küçük Liman. Amasra's postage-stamp-sized pub district is nearby.

Şahil Otel (☎ 315 2211; Turgut Işık Caddesi 82; s/d TL35/70) Opposite the sailing club on the Büyük Liman, this compact but modern option has sea-facing balconies. Good waterfront eating and drinking is just a stroll away.

Kuşna Pansiyon (☎ 315 1033; kusnapansiyon@mynet .com; Kurşuna Sokak 36; s/d TL40/80; 🖳) Bright and modern rooms overlooking a verdant (read: 'pleasantly overgrown') garden feature at this castle *ev pansiyon* looking out onto a private, rocky cove.

Timur Otel (☎ 315 2589; www.oteltimur.com; Çekiciler Caddesi 27; s/d/tr TL45/80/110) Good English is spoken at this central option with spotless, pretty-in-pink rooms overlooking a quiet square. Double-glazing on the windows ensures a good night's kip.

Büyük Liman Otel (☎ 315 3900; Turgut Işık Caddesi; s/d TL55/90; 🍴) In an excellent location on the harbour road, look forward to spacious rooms, some with beachfront balconies. A lick of paint wouldn't go amiss though.

Hotel Türkili (☎ 315 3750; www.turkili.com.tr; Özdemirhan Sokak 6; s/d TL60/100; 🍴) The wrought-iron balconies and pink facade add a European tinge to this Amasra favourite. Wi-fi, satellite TV and good English skills at reception add up to one of Amasra's best. Türkili's 5th-floor restaurant offers views over both harbours.

Işıkaltın Otel (☎ 315 3951; www.isikaltinotel.com, in Turkish; Çamlık Sokak; s/d TL60/100; 🍴) An imposing structure overlooking Küçük Liman, the Işıkaltın has slightly characterless, but very comfortable rooms, with the added attraction of an excellent fish restaurant. We just wish the folk in reception would smile.

Eating

Amasra has licensed seafront restaurants serving *canlı balık* (fresh fish) by the portion. Cheaper seafood stalls huddle at the castle end of Büyük Liman.

Hamam Café (☎ 378 3878; Tarihi Sağır Osmanlar Hamamı; mains TL2-10) In an old hamam (bathhouse), this reader-recommended spot has an easygoing ambience perfect for sipping tea, eating pizza or challenging the locals to a game of backgammon.

Amasra Sofrası (☎ 315 2483; G Mithat Ceylan Caddesi; mains TL4-10) On a quiet square midway between the two harbours, this is Amasra's prime grill house, with plenty of chicken dishes and a pretty garden.

Karadeniz Aile Pide Salonu (☎ 315 1543; Mustafa Cengiz Caddesi 9; mains TL5-8) Also known as Hayder's Place, this streetside spot just off Küçük Liman does great pide (Turkish-style

pizza). Try the 'Amasra Special' (TL6) with a dash of zingy chilli.

Çesmi Cihan Restaurant (☎ 315 1062; Büyük Liman; mains TL10-20; 🕚 11am-11pm) This is the locals' pick for a splurge, with top-of-the-line harbour views, cold beer and three floors of seafood-loving diners. *Levrek* (bass) and *istavrit* (mackerel) are regulars on the menu, and the excellent salads will convert the staunchest of carnivores.

Mustafa Amca'nın Yeri (☎ 315 2606; Küçük Liman Caddesi 8; mains TL10-20; 🕚 11am-11pm) This sea-shell-clad fish restaurant is popular both with tour groups and locals. They were building a huge new deck when we were there so they must be doing something right. Go early to grab a waterfront table for a chilled twilight beer.

Drinking

Ağlayan Ağaç Çay Bahçesi (Nöbethane Sokak; 🕚 8am-8pm) Head up through the *kale* to this cliff-top kiosk with views of squawking seagulls a few hundred metres offshore. Signs point the way.

Atafirin (cnr Cumhuriyet Caddesi & Mustafa Cengiz Caddesi; 🕚 8am-10pm) Amasra's bright young things crowd this corner spot for coffee, smoothies and a tempting array of sweet-tooth nibbles.

Han Kir Çay Bahçesi (Küçük Liman; 🕚 8am-10pm) Sip away and see how many different plant species you can spy in this leafy tea garden.

Na Bar (Büyük Liman 50b) Tucked between beachfront apartments on Büyük Liman, this friendly pub with rustic decor is less rowdy than Amasra's other bars.

Han Bar (Küçük Liman Caddesi 17) The most popular of Amasra's small cluster of pubs, Han Bar is sandwiched between houses opposite the castle walls. There's usually *canlı musik* (live music) at night.

Everyone needs good neighbours and the friendly **Kupu Bar** (complete with an Astroturf deck) is right next door.

Getting There & Away

If you're travelling east from Amasra, get an early start. Dolmuşes (minibuses) become increasingly scarce later in the day.

Intercity bus companies don't operate to Amasra. Instead, minibuses to Bartın (TL2, 30 minutes) leave every 40 minutes from near the PTT. From Bartın there are buses to Safranbolu (TL12, two hours), Ankara (TL30, five hours) and İstanbul (TL45, seven hours).

AMASRA TO SİNOP

Winding sinuously around rugged hills hugging the Black Sea, the road from Amasra east to Sinop (312km) is wonderfully scenic, and has echoes of California's Hwy 1 or New Zealand's West Coast. Expect minimal traffic and stunning views at every turn. Expect narrow roads and slow going, though (average speed is 40km/h to 50km/h, taking seven or eight hours to Sinop), with the road surface often broken and the occasional *heyelan* (landslide). By public transport, you'll need to use local services between the settlements along the way. Get an early start, and if you're lucky you might nab one of the daily bus services from İstanbul.

A few villages have camping grounds, and with your own wheels you can stop where and when the vista is most appealing. From west to east, have a swim at **Bozköy beach**, west of **Çakraz**, or visit the boat-builders in **Kurucaşile**, 45km east of Amasra. Both towns have modest hotels and pensions.

Consider also the picturesque two-beach village of **Kapısuyu**, or the tiny harbour at **Gideros**, the perfectly idyllic cove of your dreams. A couple of fish restaurants keep the dream alive.

About 63km east of Amasra, the road descends to a sand-and-pebble beach stretching several kilometres to the aptly named **Kumluca** (Sandy). The beach continues 8km eastward to **Cide**, a small town where many dolmuş services terminate. The **Yalı Otel** (☎ 0366-866 2087; www.yaliotel.com; Liman Yolu; s/d TL25/50) is a good overnight option with an on-site restaurant.

Leaving Cide, there's a panoramic viewpoint by the flagpole above town. Around 12km on is **Kuscu Köyü**, a small village with access to the **Aydos Canyon**, a steep river ravine.

Doğanyurt, 31km before İnebolu, is yet another pleasant harbour town, while further east from İnebolu, **Abana** has a decent beach.

Over halfway to Sinop, **İnebolu** is another handy stopping point, especially as onward transport by late afternoon may be hard to find. The **Yakamoz Tatıl Köyü** (☎ 0366-811 3100; www.yakamoztatilkoyu.com, in Turkish; İsmetpaşa Caddesi; bungalow s/d TL45/65, s/d/tr TL55/80/120;) is a beachside resort 800m west of the centre with a restaurant (mains TL6 to TL15), bar and café. In the town centre are old Ottoman houses, and a restored mansion where Atatürk stayed in 1925.

About 41km east of İnebolu, near **Çatalzeytin**, is a long pebble beach surrounded by beautiful scenery. At **Ayancık** the road divides, with the left (northern) fork offering the more scenic route to Sinop, about 2½ hours from İnebolu.

SİNOP

☎ 0368 / pop 101,000

Wrapped around a rocky promontory, Sinop is the only southern facing town along the Black Sea. Maybe that's why the town feels more Akdeniz (Mediterranean) than Karadeniz (Black Sea). Sinop has been a trading port for over a thousand years, and still retains a bustling, cosmopolitan air. The town's heritage is also reflected in the many shops selling model ships. Today's visitors are more likely to be holidaying Turks, and for international travellers Sinop is a welcoming Black Sea base tinged with the ambience of the Med.

History

Colonised from Miletus in the 8th century BC, Sinop's trade grew, and successive rulers – including the Pontic kings (who made it their capital), Romans and Byzantines – turned it into a busy trading centre.

The Seljuks used Sinop as a port after taking it in 1214, but the Ottomans preferred to develop Samsun, which had better land communications.

On 30 November 1853, a Russian armada attacked Sinop without any warning, overwhelming the local garrison and inflicting great loss of life. The battle hastened the beginning of the Crimean War, in which the Ottomans allied with the British and French to fight Russian ambitions in the Near East.

Orientation

Sinop is at the narrow point of the peninsula, with the road continuing east beyond the town to beaches and land's end. From the western entrance of the fortified walls, the main street, Sakarya Caddesi, cuts east through the centre 800m to the Sinop *vilayet konağı* (provincial government headquarters). Sinop's new otogar (bus station) is 5km northwest of town on the main road to Kastamonu.

Information

Furkan Temilik Laundry (Derinboğazağzı Sokak 5; per kg TL3.50; 8.30am-6pm)
Hit Café Internet (Gazi Caddesi; per hr TL1.25; 10am-midnight)

SINOP

0 _____ 200 m
0 _____ 0.1 miles

INFORMATION
Furkan Temilik Laundry...............1 B3
Hit Cafe Internet.....................2 D3
Tourist Information..................3 D3
Tourist Information Booth......4 A3

SIGHTS & ACTIVITIES
Alaadin Camii..........................5 B2
Archaeological Museum..........6 C2
Kumkapı (Sand Gate).............7 A3
Pervane Medresesi..................8 B2
Sinope Tours..........................9 C2
Tarihi Cezaevi.......................10 A3
Tersane Hacı Ömer Camii....11 C3

SLEEPING
Denizci Otel...........................12 C3
Otel 57..................................13 C3
Otel Gönül............................14 C2
Otel Mola..............................15 B3
Otel Sarı Kadır......................16 C3
Yılmaz Aile Pansiyonu...........17 C3

EATING
Diyarbakır.............................18 C2
Dolunay Pastanesi.................19 C3

Gaziantep Sofrası..................20 C2
Mangal................................(see 12)
Saray Restaurant...................21 C3
Sinop Sofrası........................22 C3

DRINKING
Burç Café..............................23 C3
Karainçl Kahve......................24 C3
Liman...................................25 C3
Pub....................................(see 21)
Yalı Kahvesi...........................26 C3

ENTERTAINMENT
Deniz Sinema Café.................27 C3

TRANSPORT
Dolmuş to Otogar..................28 C2

BLACK SEA
(KARADENİZ)

To Otogar (5km);
Akliman (12km);
Türkelii (12km);
Ayancık (62km);
Samsun
(169km)

To Zinos Country
Hotel (2km);
Karakum
Beach (3km);
Erfelek (28km);
Gerze (40km)

BLACK SEA
(KARADENİZ)

Tourist information (☎ 261 5298; Gazi Caddesi;
🕑 8.30am-5pm mid-Jun–mid-Sep) Helpful with English-
speaking staff.
Tourist information booth Near the Tarihi Cezaevi (right)

Sights & Activities

Sinop's prime attraction are the relatively
well-preserved **fortifications**. Open to attack
from the sea, Sinop has been fortified since
2000 BC, but the existing walls are developments of those originally erected in 72 BC by
Pontic king Mithridates VI. At one time the
walls, some 3m thick, were more than 2km
long, with seven gates, and towers 25m high.
Walk along the ramparts for sea views.

On the northern side is an ancient bastion
called the **Kumkapı** (Sand Gate). On the south-

ern side is the **Tarihi Cezaevi** (Old Jail; admission TL3;
🕑 9am-6pm), a hulking former prison. Inside is
a modest selection of craft shops.

Sinop's excellent **Archaeological Museum**
(☎ 261 1975; Okullar Caddesi; admission TL3; 🕑 8am-
noon & 1-5pm Tue-Sun) has a collection of poignant Roman stele, Byzantine icons, and an
Ottoman tomb in the cool and shady garden. We just wish they'd fix the annoying on
again/off again automatic lighting.

In the town centre on Sakarya Caddesi
stands the **Alaadin Camii** (1267), also called the
Ulu Cami, a mosque set in an expansive walled
courtyard. It was constructed for Muinettin
Süleyman Pervane, a powerful Seljuk grand
vizier. The mosque has been repaired many
times; its marble *mihrab* (the niche indicating

BLACK SEA COAST & THE
KAÇKAR MOUNTAINS

THE SİNOP RUMOUR FACTORY *Brett Atkinson*

'So, do you work for the CIA?' It was a question I'd never heard before, but the conversation was about to get even more interesting. My new drinking buddy began to tell me fantastic stories of a lost city beneath the waters around Sinop. Apparently it was immersed in water when the Mediterranean broke through a narrow land bridge almost 8000 years ago to turn a small lake into what we know now as the Black Sea. And on the hill above our simple clifftop bar at Sinop's Karakum beach, Noah's Ark was apparently buried.

Other rumours circulating in Sinop are more contemporary and tangible. In 2006 the region was earmarked as the site of one of Turkey's first nuclear power plants. Resistance in normally reticent Turkey has been well organised and robust (see www.sinopbizim.org), but in mid-2008, Sinop was reconfirmed as the site of Turkey's second nuclear plant, with the first confirmed near the southern city of Mersin.

And do I work for the CIA? Well, according to other rumours I've heard, I wouldn't be the first guidebook writer to lead such a double life.

---

the direction of Mecca) and *mimber* (pulpit) were added by the local Candaroğlu emir. At the time of research, further careful restoration was being undertaken.

Adjacent is the **Pervane Medresesi** (Pervane Seminary), built by Süleyman Pervane in 1262 to commemorate the second conquest of Sinop. It's now full of shops selling crafts and local products.

Near the harbour is the **Tersane Hacı Ömer Camii** (1903) with the poignant Şehitler Çeşmesi (Martyrs' Fountain), built in memory of the Turkish soldiers who died in the surprise Russian attack of 1853. The fountain was built using the money recovered from the soldiers' pockets.

Sinope Tours (☎ 261 7900; www.sinopetours.com; Kibris Caddesi 3) runs daily city and local tours. Ask here if the catamaran is running to Yalta in Ukraine.

Sleeping

Yılmaz Alle Pansiyonu (☎ 261 5752; Tersane Çarşısı 11; s/d/tr TL20/40/60) Great value, these plain but neat rooms have TV and individual gas showers. Homely touches abound at this friendly spot near the harbour. A few rooms have sea views.

Otel 57 (☎ 261 5462; www.otel57.com; Kurtuluş Caddesi 29; s/d TL35/50; ✿ ▣) Spic-and-span leather chairs in reception give way to comfortable rooms with bright duvets and crisp wooden floors. The whole place has recently been refurbished for even better value.

Otel Sarı Kadır (☎ 260 1544; Derinboğazağzı Sokak 22; s/d TL35/50) Plain but spacious rooms with TV, sofa and fridge make this waterfront establishment a good-value choice. There are sea

views from the balconies, and a tea garden right opposite.

Otel Gönül (☎ 261 1829; www.sinopotelgonul.com; Meydankapı Mahallesi 11; s/d/tr TL40/60/70; ✿ ▣) The promise of a big screen telly in reception dissolves in the compact but kitschy rooms upstairs. A reliable backup, but the in-town location negates sea views.

Otel Mola (☎ 261 1814; Derinboğazağzı Sokak 34; www.sinopmolaotel.com.tr; s/d/tr TL50/80/100; ✿ ▣) A lovely garden and sea views give this new spot near the harbour high marks. Rooms are comfortable, but the carpet should come with a volume knob.

Denizci Otel (☎ 260 5934; Kurtuluş Caddesi 13; www.denizciotel.com; s/d/tr TL50/80/110; ✿ ▣) The flashest spot in town with a maritime-themed restaurant and spacious rooms with heritage decor. The friendly staff gamely summons up every word of English they know.

Zinos Country Hotel (☎ 260 5600; Enver Bahadır Yolu 75; www.zinoshotel.com; s/d TL85/145; ✿ ▣) Around 2km from town en route to Karakum beach, the Zinos is hardly in the country. But despite the geographical confusion, this is a splurge-worthy spot with romantic Ottoman-styled rooms with rug-trimmed wooden floors and sea views. Across the road, there's a hilltop bar, and a trail leads to a private swimming platform.

Eating

Sinop's waterfront is lined with licensed open-air restaurants.

Dolunay Pastanesi (☎ 261 8688; Kurtuluş Caddesi 14; desserts from TL2) This modern take on the pastry shop serves up ice-cream and baklava. Both are perfect for a stroll along the nearby harbour.

Mangal (Kurtuluş Caddesi 15; crêpes TL2-4) Delicious *gözleme* (savoury crêpes) are served up by an older lady with just maybe Sinop's biggest smile.

Diyarbakır (☎ 260 0833; Nalbank Sokak 1; mains TL3-5) Diyarbakır may be slightly rough and ready, but this popular spot provides top-notch versions of kebaps from Adana to Bursa. The *paket serviş* (takeout) option is good for bus journeys.

Sinop Sofrası (☎ 260 0915; Kurtuluş Caddesi 28; mains TL3-5) Hugely popular, this humble spot has a wide array of goodies including stuffed eggplant, *köfte* (meatballs) and rice. Pide and kebaps also fuel loyal locals.

Gaziantep Sofrası (Atatürk Caddesi; mains TL4-6) Families and dating couples crowd the upstairs salon for foot-long eggplant kebaps and excellent *lahmacun* (Arabic-style pizza). It's a welcoming place that's good for women travellers.

Saray Restaurant (☎ 261 1729; İskele Caddesi 18; fish mains TL10-15; ☒ 11am-11pm) Excellent salads and continuously sipped rakı (aniseed brandy) make this the preferred spot for local fans of caught-this-morning seafood. Grab a spot on the floating pontoon and begin your meal with Saray's excellent mezes.

Drinking & Entertainment

Yalı Kahvesi (Derinboğazağı Sokak 14; ☒ 8am-10pm) Harbourside tables and shady umbrellas combine at this popular tea garden.

Burç Café (☎ 260 0420; Sinop Kalesi, Tersane Caddesi) In the tower of the fortifications, this atmospheric spot attracts a young crowd for live music, ocean views and cold beer. Bring a sweatshirt as it can get chilly.

Liman (İskele Caddesi 20; ☒ noon-10pm) Bring your backgammon A-game to this harbourside bar. If you're a novice maybe just settle for a sunset beer.

Pub (İskele Caddesi 19; ☒ noon-10pm) How about a cold 0.7L beer outside beside colourful fishing boats? Sometimes life's simple pleasures are the best.

Karainçı Kahve (Derinbogazazgi Sokak 9; coffee TL3-5; ☒ noon-10pm) This coolly minimalist café has a wide range of tea and coffee. There are muffins and cookies galore, and laptop travellers can hop aboard the wi-fi network.

Deniz Sinema Café (☎ 261 0643; Ergül Sokak; ☒ 2pm-midnight) Coffee, tea and beers feature at this movie-themed café with an arty, student vibe. The attached cinema shows mainly Turkish flicks but you might get lucky. It's down a lane near Karainçı Kahve.

Getting There & Away

The table, below, lists daily services from Sinop. There are no direct services to Amasra, 312km to the west. Take point-to-point minibuses or change at İnebolu or Cide. Catch a dolmuş (TL1.50) to Sinop's otogar from the corner northwest of Sinop's *vilayet konağı*.

In recent years a catamaran service ran from Sinop to Yalta in Ukraine, but it was suspended at the time of writing. Ask at Sinope Tours (p545) for the latest information.

AROUND SİNOP

Consult Sinop's tourist office or Sinope Tours (p545) for suggestions for local tours. The most common excursions are to **Erfelek**, famed for its 28 waterfalls, the historic fishing town of **Gerze**, and the area around **Ayancık**. Walking and canoeing are popular pastimes for the more energetic visitor.

To swim in the Black Sea, the blacksand **Karakum beach** (admission TL1) with a restaurant and camping site, is 3km east of Sinop harbour.

SAMSUN
☎ 0362 / pop 504,000

Sprawling Samsun is the Black Sea's biggest port. Few travellers stop for more than a

SERVICES FROM SİNOP'S OTOGAR				
Destination	**Fare (TL)**	**Duration (hr)**	**Distance (km)**	**Frequency (per day)**
Ankara	40	9	443	3
İnebolu	20	3	156	1 at 8am
İstanbul	50	10½	700	5
Karabük (for Safranbolu)	30	6	340	5
Samsun	20	3½	168	roughly hourly
Trabzon	50	9	533	1 at 8pm

ARE WE THERE YET?

For multiple editions of the Turkey guidebook, we've commented on the road works blighting the Black Sea coast east from Samsun. Across 20 years bulldozers and road-compactors have been rumbling away to build the Black Sea Coastal Highway. Since construction began, Turkey has experienced 14 different governments, and at the time of writing, the four- to six-lane highway linking Samsun to the Turkey–Georgia border at Sarp was *still* being completed, despite an 'official' opening date almost 18 months earlier.

The road provides an essential trade link for Turkey with the world to the east, especially to Central Asia and former Soviet states like Russia and Georgia. And while Turkey's potential membership of the EU is endlessly discussed, the country's traditional cultural and linguistic links are already forging a trade bonanza to the east.

The economic benefits of the road are undeniable, but a significant cost has been a cutting off of many Black Sea settlements from the sea, and a cavalcade of goods-laden TIR trucks rushing through coastal towns like Ünye and Ordu. Environmentalists also contend that many ecologically valuable areas were destroyed during the road's construction.

The Black Sea Coastal Highway doesn't follow the coast all the way though, and a sleepy stretch of the old coast road from Bolaman to Ordu (p550) still affords a glimpse into a quieter yesteryear.

---

change of bus. Even the enterprising Genoese only paused long enough to burn the city to the ground in the 15th century. With accommodation and eateries handily crammed around the centre, it's a convenient stop on your journey east or west. Samsun also marks the beginning of the Black Sea Coastal Highway (see boxed text, above).

Orientation & Information

The city centre is Cumhuriyet Meydanı (Republic Sq), inland, and just west of Atatürk Park, which lies on the coastal highway. The Samsun *valiliği* (provincial government headquarters) is slightly to the north. Cumhuriyet Caddesi runs along the south side of the park.

The **tourist office** (☎ 431 1228; Atatürk Bulvan 179; ☺ 9am-noon & 1-6pm daily Jun-Aug, Mon-Fri Sep-May), across the coastal road from Cumhuriyet Meydanı, has decent maps and brochures.

The train station is 550m southeast of Atatürk Park on the coastal road, Atatürk Bulvarı. Samsun's new otogar is 3km inland. Bus companies run *servis* (shuttle) buses from Cumhuriyet Meydanı to the otogar. There are also frequent dolmuşes (TL1.50) from the otogar to Cumhuriyet Meydanı, and left luggage facilities at the otogar if you've got time to kill between buses.

Sights

With an hour to spare it's worth visiting the **Archaeology & Ethnography Museum** (Arkeoloji ve Etnoğrafya Müzesi; ☎ 431 6828; Fuar Caddesi; admission TL3; ☺ 8.30am-noon & 1-5pm Tue-Sun), west of the big pink Samsun *valiliği* building. Most striking is a huge Romano-Byzantine mosaic depicting Thetis, Achilles and the Four Seasons, found nearby at Karasamsun (Amissos). Other highlights include the elegant gold jewellery thought to date from the time of the legendary Mithridates (VI Eupator, 120 to 130 BC), and a scary display on ancient skull surgery.

Adjacent is the **Atatürk Museum** (Atatürk Müzesi; Fuar Caddesi; admission TL2; ☺ 8.30am-1pm & 2-5pm), commemorating the start of the War of Independence here on 19 May 1919.

Sleeping & Eating

Explore the clothing bazaar location for budget accommodation.

Hotel Necmi (☎ 432 7164; www.otelnecmi .com.tr; Bedestan Sokak 6; s/d/tr without bathroom TL40/55/70) Downstairs is a pot plant–filled lounge, while the rooms upstairs are compact with mushroom-coloured carpet and shared bathrooms.

Samsun Park Otel (☎ 435 0095; www.samsunpark otel.com; Cumhuriyet Caddesi 38; s/d/tr TL60/70/100; ❄ 🖳) A hieroglyphic lift whisks you to compact but comfortable rooms just south of the city centre. The attached restaurant and several nearby patisseries are all good.

Vidinli Oteli (☎ 431 6050; Kazımpaşa Caddesi 4; s/d TL70/140; ❄ 🖳) The Vidinli plays the business traveller card a little too strongly, with the comfortable rooms veering towards bland-ness. Plus points are the tiled bathrooms and an expense-account-friendly bar/restaurant.

Hotel Amisos (☎ 435 9400; www.hotelamisos.com; Cumhuriyet Caddesi 18; s/d TL150/200; ⊠ ⊡) Samsun's flashest address offers rooms with a classic combination of red and gold decor, minibars and satellite TV. Cheap eateries nearby will counterbalance the room prices.

Sıla Restaurant (☎ 432 9515; Vilayet Karşısı 36; mains TL4-10) All the usual kebap and pide favourites await at this reliable central eatery.

Samsun Balık Restaurant (☎ 435 7550; Kazımpaşa Caddesi 20; mains TL8-15; ✆ 11am-10pm) Samsun's number-one fish eatery is in a quaint brick house. A glistening array of piscine beauties awaits your choice, and upstairs is a flower-trimmed dining room.

Getting There & Away

AIR

Turkish Airlines (☎ 444 0849; www.thy.com; Havaalani Samsun) flies direct to İstanbul's Havaalani Samsun (Samsun Airport) up to five times daily. There are also four flights per week to Ankara. **Onur Air** (☎ 844 8808; www.onurair.com; Havaalani Samsun) has two flights per day to İstanbul. **Pegasus Airlines** (☎ 444 0737; www.flypgs.com) flies to İzmir on Mondays and Saturdays. **SunExpress** (☎ 444 0797; www.sunexpress.com.tr) and **Izair** (☎ 444 4499; www.izair .com) link Samsun and İzmir during summer.

BUS

Most major bus companies have offices at the Cumhuriyet Meydanı end of Cumhuriyet Caddesi. Services to major destinations are listed in the table (below).

CAR & MOTORCYCLE

Samsun has car-rental agencies around Lise Caddesi including **Avis** (☎ 231 6750; Ümraniye Sokak

2) and **Eleni** (☎ 230 0091; Ümraniye Sokak 6). Head southeast for 700m from Atatürk Park along Cumhuriyet Caddesi to Lise Caddesi. After 150m veer right into Ümraniye Sokak.

TRAIN

Two daily trains run from Samsun **station** (☎ 233 5002) to Sivas (TL15.75, 8½ hours) and Amasya (TL5.25, three hours).

ÜNYE
☎ 0452 / pop 72,800

Today's Ünye is popular with holidaying Turks, but this bustling spot 95km east of Samsun also has one of the longest settlement histories in Anatolia. There is evidence of civilisation during the Palaeolithic period, and Ünye was an important port at the junction of the Silk Rd and the coastal highway during the Ottoman period. Former residents include the 14th-century Turkish mystical poet Yunus Emre, and St Nicholas before his life morphed into the legend of Santa Claus. Today it's a modern city combining a coastal promenade and a labyrinth of well-kept winding streets and lanes.

The friendly **tourist office** (☎ 323 2569; ✆ 8am-noon & 1-5pm Mon-Fri) is in the pink government Kaymakamliği building on the main square.

Sights & Activities

About 7km inland stands **Ünye Castle**, a ruined fortress founded by the Pontics and rebuilt by the Byzantines, with an ancient tomb cut into the rock face below. Catch a minibus heading to Kaleköy or Akkuş (TL1) from the Niksar road, and ask to be dropped off at the road to the castle. It's a further half-hour trek to the top.

Another excursion is the **Tozkoparan Kay Mezarı** (Tozkoparan Rock Tomb), off the

SERVICES FROM SAMSUN'S OTOGAR				
Destination	Fare (TL)	Duration (hr)	Distance (km)	Frequency (per day)
Amasya	10	2½	130	frequent
Ankara	49	7	420	frequent
Artvin	40	8	577	4
Giresun	20	3½	220	5
İstanbul	79	11	750	several
Kayseri	45	9	530	a few
Sinop	20	3	168	several
Trabzon	30	6	355	several
Ünye	8	1½	95	every 30 minutes

THE AMAZIN' RACE

The Samsun-Ünye region is often associated with the Amazons, one of the most enduring Greek myths. This race of warrior women, famed for cutting off one breast to aid their archery skills, were said to have ruled the coast in pre-Pontic times. Homer, Herodotus and Amasya's own Strabo all relate tales of strapping female soldiers. Reputedly their reproductive habits involved annual coitus with a neighbouring tribe, or 'breeding colonies' of captive male sex slaves. Some early biographers even claim Alexander the Great fathered a child with the Amazonian queen Thalestris.

Historically speaking, there is little evidence to support any Amazonian presence in the Black Sea area around the purported 1200 BC timeframe. One theory is that the myth evolved from the role of high priestesses in mother-goddess cults. Other historians believe that it arose from travellers encountering Anatolian tribes with matriarchal systems or greater gender equality, both contrary to their own ingrained societal values.

This enduring classical myth continued to capture public imagination across following centuries, and eventually provided the name for the world's largest river.

Trabzon road 5km from the centre. Any eastbound minibus can drop you by the cement factory at the turn for the cave.

Back in town, just east of the square is the **Ali-Namık Soysal Eski Hamam**. It was once a church, but now it's open for bathing to men from early morning to noon and all day Sunday, and for women from noon until 4pm.

Sleeping

Otel Çınar (☎ 323 1148; Hükümet Caddesi 18; s/d TL15/30) This central budget option has shared bathrooms and no breakfast is provided. From the tourist office turn left and head one block inland.

Otel Lider (☎ 324 9250; Hükümet Caddesi 36; s/d TL20/40) Centrally located, the Lider has a rooftop terrace. No breakfast is served but there's a good kebap place nearby that can rustle up *kahvalti* (breakfast).

Hotel Grand Kuşçalı (☎ 324 5200; Devlet Sahilyolu Şehir Merkezi 42; s/d/tr TL70/80/120; 🍴 🖳) That's 'grand' with a small 'g', but the 1970s-tinged rooms are still the most comfortable in town with minibars and satellite TV. The sea-view restaurant and sauna/hamam complex keep the tour groups happy.

Ünye has an array of camping grounds and a handful of beach pensions, mostly spread out along the Samsun road west of town. **Cafe Gülen Plaj Camping** (☎ 324 7368; Devlet Sahil Yolu; camp sites per 2 people TL20, bungalows TL60) has an excellent setting and cute wooden bungalows. The adjacent **Uzunkum Restaurant Plaj & Camping** (☎ 323 2022; Devlet Sahil Yolu; camp sites per 2 people TL20) is another welcoming spot graced

with a beachfront setting, loads of shade and a good restaurant. Green-and-white minibuses regularly ply the coastal route between these places and the centre of town from early in the morning until around 11pm.

Eating

Café Vanilya (☎ 324 4106; Cumhuriyet Meydanı 3; snacks TL2-5; 🕙 10am-8pm) Set in a restored villa-style townhouse on the southwest edge of the main square, the Vanilya is a chic but unpretentious terrace café serving Ünye's would-be bright young things. Backgammon and Turkish pop videos provide a mix of old and new.

Evim (☎ 324 3341; Hacı Emin Caddesi; mains TL2-6) Just off the main square, and dishing up baklava, *börek* (filled pastries) and *mantı* (Turkish ravioli) to regulars. Look for the faded *gözleme* sign.

Çakırtepe (☎ 323 2568; Çakırtepe; mains TL5-10; 🕙 11am-10pm) Atop the hill west of town, this picnic site and café is a local favourite for long summer lunches. Tuck into excellent pide or *güveç* (stew in a clay pot). Minibuses leave from the west side of Cumhuriyet Meydanı and pass close to the restaurant.

Çamlık Restaurant (☎ 323 1175; Çamlık İçi; mains TL5-12; 🕙 11am-10pm) This picnic place and recreation area also includes an excellent grill restaurant which cascades over several levels to the ocean. The fish and the *köfte* are excellent. Kick off with a cold beer and Çamlık's mezes.

Yunus Emre Çay Bahçesı (☎ 323 3068; Yunus Emre Parkı; mains TL5-12) This well-frequented tea garden beside the pier serves substantial pides and stews as well as the usual drinks.

DETOUR: THE OLD COAST ROAD

Around 25km east of Ünye just after the town of Bolaman, the Black Sea Coastal Highway veers inland and doesn't touch the coast again until just before Ordu. It's a spectacular stretch traversing Turkey's longest road tunnel (3.28km), but the diversion inland has created a lovely alternative route on the old coast road.

A winding few kilometres east from Bolaman is rugged **Cape Yason**, where a tiny medieval chapel marks the spot where sailors used to pray at a temple remembering Jason and his Argonauts. Further east is the surprising **Çaka beach**, a 400m strip of white sand regarded as the Black Sea's best beach. A grill restaurant and beer garden makes it easy to enjoy.

Further on, 15km west of Ordu, **Perşembe** is a fishing port framed by two lighthouses. The rooms at the two-star **Dede Evi** (☎ 0452-517 3802; Atatürk Bulvarı; s/d TL35/70; ✖ ☐) have parquet floors and sea views. Later at night locals fish from the slender pier and fish restaurants prepare the day's catch.

This meandering detour is best achieved with your own transport, but there is also relatively frequent dolmuş traffic to Perşembe from Fatsa to the west and Ordu to the east.

Sofra (☎ 323 4083; Belediye Caddesi 25; mains TL6-12) Sofra is a square stone house with pide, kebaps and Ottoman dishes. It's a tad pricey, but the faded elegance makes it worth the premium. It's a couple of blocks east of the main square.

Getting There & Away

Bus companies have offices on the coastal road. Minibuses and midibuses travel to Samsun (TL8, 1½ hours) and Ordu (TL8, 1¾ hours).

ORDU

☎ 0452 / pop 124,000

Ordu is 80km east of Ünye, with a well-kept centre around a palm tree–lined seafront boulevard. The city sprawls in both directions, but winding narrow lanes give central Ordu a village-like ambience.

At the time of writing the tourist office was closed due to local funding issues. Ask at the Karlıbel Atlıhan Hotel if it's reopened. The hotel can supply a good map in the interim.

Check your email at **Ordu Net** (Fidangör Sokak; per hr TL1.25; ☒ 10am-midnight).

Sights

The interesting **Pasha's Palace & Ethnography Museum** (Paşaoğlu Konağı ve Etnoğrafya Müzesi; Taşocak Caddesi; admission TL3; ☒ 9am-noon & 1.30-5pm Tue-Sun) occupies a late-19th-century house 500m uphill from Cumhuriyet Meydanı. Signs reading 'Müze – Museum' direct you here past a handicrafts bazaar. The re-created rooms on the 1st floor are telling reminders that upper-class Ottomans enjoyed a sophisticated and cosmopolitan life. There's also a chair where

Atatürk supposedly had a rest in 1924. We hope he also enjoyed pide from the wood-fired oven in the peaceful garden.

A few other scraps of Ordu's old town survive, centred around the **Tasbaşı Cultural Centre**, an old Greek church with magnificent coastal views about 800m west from the main square.

Catch a dolmuş west to **Boztepe** (TL3, 6.5km) for more breathtaking views and good restaurants.

Sleeping & Eating

The accommodation and eating scene features a couple of good-value splurges.

Hotel Turist (☎ 225 3140; Atatürk Bulvarı 134; s/d/tr TL45/60/80; ✖) That's definitely 'turist' with a small 't', but a recent paint job and good English at reception redeems this place with seafront balconies and a sunny breakfast conservatory.

Karlıbel Atlıhan Hotel (☎ 225 0565; www.karlibel hotel.com.tr; Kazım Karabekir Caddesi 7; s/d/tr TL60/90/120; ✖) A professional establishment with spacious rooms in subdued colours and a horsey predilection for equine art. It's one block back from the seafront behind the *belediye* (town hall). The same company also runs two nearby boutique hotels, the seafront Atherina, and the hilltop İkizevler.

our pick **İkizevler Hotel** (☎ 225 0081; www.karlibel hotel.com.tr; Kazım Karabekir Caddesi 7; s/d TL60/90; ✖) The name may mean 'Two Houses', but this hilltop boutique hotel is unified in delivering 17 rooms of gracious Ottoman style. The property was originally two stately homes, and it now dominates a hilltop in Ordu's southwest. Wooden floors, antique rugs and a view-worthy garden café all support the relaxed heritage ambience. Ask for directions at the Karlıbel Atlıhan Hotel in town.

Jazz Café (☎ 214 6778; Sımpasa Caddesi 28; mains TL3-10) A modern eatery on Ordu's pedestrian shopping drag, offering everything from pizza and omelettes to *gözleme* and *kumpir* (baked potatoes). Grab an upstairs table for great people-watching below.

Ayışığı (☎ 223 2870; Atatürk Bulvarı; mains TL4-10; ✆ from 11am) Occupying a whitewashed concrete structure on the beach, the 'Moonlight' combines a terrace café, restaurant and *meyhane* (Turkish pub) to good effect. Next door is a pleasant Mondrian-styled tea garden.

Mıdı Restaurant (☎ 214 0340; İskele Üstü 55; mains TL7-15; ✆ 11am-11pm) Ordu's best eating combines with Ordu's best seafront ambience at this long and classy pontoon restaurant that's good for equally long and classy lunches. Local seafood provides the culinary highlights, beer and wine are available, and black-and-white pictures of old Ordu turn the heritage charm up to 11.

Getting There & Around

Ordu's otogar is 5km east on the coastal road. Buses depart regularly to Giresun (TL4, one hour) and Ünye (TL8, 1¾ hours). You can also usually flag down buses along the coastal road.

Local dolmuşes regularly loop through the city centre. Line 2 goes from the centre of town past the Karlıbel İkizevler Hotel in one direction, and near the otogar in the other.

GİRESUN

☎ 0454 / pop 84,000

The historic town of Giresun, 46km east of Ordu, was founded around 3000 years ago. The city is credited with introducing cherries to Italy, and from there to the rest of the world. The name Giresun comes from the Greek for cherry.

Now the humble hazelnut (*fındık*) drives Giresun's economy, and the area has Turkey's finest plantations. Enjoy the edible treats and fabulous views from the hillside park near the centre.

Orientation & Information

Giresun's centre is Atapark on the coastal road. The town hall is just inland from the park. The main commercial street is Gazi Caddesi, climbing uphill from the town hall.

At the time of writing, the local tourist information was closed. Ask at the Otel Başar for a good map and brochure. The post office and internet cafés are a few hundred metres uphill from the town hall.

Sights & Activities

After your fill of hazelnuts and cherries, burn off the calories by walking 2km to the **Kalepark** (Castle Park), perched on the steep hillside above the town. This shady park has panoramic views, beer gardens and barbecues. Weekends are very busy. No public transport serves the park, so you'll need to walk (about 2km) inland and uphill from Atapark on Gazi Caddesi and turn left onto Bekirpaşa Caddesi. A taxi costs around TL3.

The **City Museum** (Şehir Müzesi; ☎ 212 1322; Atatürk Bulvarı 62; admission TL2; ✆ 8am-5pm) occupies the 18th-century Gogora church, 1.5km around the promontory east of Atapark on the coastal road. The well-preserved building outshines the usual archaeological and ethnographic exhibits.

If you've got time, head to the **alpine plateaus** about 40km inland, which offer opportunities for walking and winter sports.

Festivals & Events

The four-day **International Giresun Aksu Festival**, starting annually on May 20, hails fecundity and the new growing season with concerts, traditional dance performances and other open-air events. A highlight is boat trips out to Giresun Island (p552).

Sleeping & Eating

Er-Tur Oteli (☎ 216 1026; otelertur@mynet.com; Çapulacılar Sokak 8; s/d/tr TL50/70/90) International flags hint at something flasher, but the two-star standards are entirely acceptable at this welcoming spot on a side street east of Atapark. The staff will even squeeze a fourth traveller into a three-bed 'family' room.

Otel Çarıkçı (☎ 216 1026; Osmanağa Caddesi 6; s/d/tr TL65/100/130; ✆) More excellent value in this price range with laminate floors, tiled bathrooms and wi-fi access. It's down the first street east off Gazi Caddesi. Look for the sign featuring a curly-toed shoe.

Otel Başar (☎ 212 9920; www.hotelbasar.com.tr; Atatürk Bulvarı; s/d/tr TL75/125/150; ✆) Scratch the surface of this eight-storey blue and yellow eyesore overlooking the coastal road, and you'll find a surprisingly comfortable hotel

AMAZON ISLAND

Just 1.5km off the eastern end of Giresun Bay, the tiny Giresun Aksu is actually the biggest island on the Black Sea.

As many as 50,000 visitors a year make the short hop to the island, most during the International Giresun Aksu Festival (p551) in late May. At other times, local fishermen seem reticent to provide transport, but a cable car has been rumoured.

Visitors during the festival pay homage to the Hamza Taşl (Hamza Stone), an ancient stone up to 4000 years old said to contain magical powers enhancing fertility. Local myths claim the island's temple was first built by the Amazons (p549) and that Jason and his Argonauts stopped off to dine on local birdlife during their quest for the Golden Fleece.

Now the island's 14 different species of birds are protected, and Giresun Aksu has been declared an Important Bird Area by the International Bird Protection Council.

with English-speaking staff, a cosy brick-lined bar and a rooftop restaurant.

Deniz Lokantası (☎ 216 1158; Alpaslan Caddesi 3; mains TL3-8; ☑ 10am-10pm) Next to the town hall, this modernised cafeteria has been churning out good-value meals since 1953. Expect a short wait at lunchtime, but it's worth it.

Ellez (☎ 216 1491; Fatih Caddesi 9; TL4-12; ☑ 10am-11pm) One block north of Atapark, this compact pide-and-pizza joint attracts a younger crowd with top food and Turkish flags protruding from a tiny balcony.

Piccolo Café & Bistro (Gazi Caddesi 47; TL6-10; ☑ 9am-11pm) On the left going uphill on Giresun's main drag, the cute Piccolo does omelettes, crêpes, salads, and a wider range of java for when you're tired of Nescafe or Turkish coffee. Wi-fi's a bonus for laptop travellers.

Getting There & Away

The bus station is 4km west of the centre, but buses usually drop people at Atapark too. Minibuses shuttle from Giresun to Trabzon (TL10, two hours) and to Ordu (TL5, one hour). Trabzon services leave from the bus offices near Atapark. Buses to Ordu stop across the road outside the sprawling car park.

GİRESUN TO TRABZON

From Giresun it's another 150km to Trabzon, but the Black Sea Coastal Highway has diminished the coastal vistas. The road passes through several small towns, including the attractive town of **Tirebolu**, with a compact harbour and two castles (St Jean Kalesi and Bedrama Kalesi). The Çaykur tea-processing plant signals your arrival in Turkey's tea country.

Görele is the next town eastward, famous for big round loaves of bread. Next is **Akçakale**

with the ruins of a 13th-century Byzantine castle on a little peninsula. Shortly before reaching Trabzon is **Akçaabat**, famous for its *köfte* restaurants. The Korfez and Cemilusta are two worth trying.

TRABZON

☎ 0462 / pop 400,000

Trabzon's one of those 'love it or hate it' kind of places. Some are polarised by its slightly seedy port town character, while others appreciate the city's cosmopolitan buzz. Arguably the Black Sea coast's most sophisticated city – sorry Samsun – Trabzon is too caught up in its own whirl of activity to worry about what's happening in far-off İstanbul or Ankara.

The Black Sea's past is displayed in the gracious medieval church of Aya Sofya and the Byzantine monastery at Sumela, but in Atatürk Alanı, Trabzon's crazily busy main square, it's a thoroughly modern mix. Beeping dolmuş traffic hurtles anti-clockwise like a modern chariot race, while local students team headscarves with Converse All Stars beneath a giant screen showcasing the city's beloved Trabzonspor football team. It's infectious after take-it-easy times in the Black Sea's smaller centres.

Trabzon is the eastern Black Sea's busiest port, handling and dispatching goods for Georgia, Armenia, Azerbaijan and Iran. Expect to also see a few bleach-blonde 'natashas' (prostitutes) from former Soviet states offering their own spin on international trade.

Trabzon definitely makes an impression, and it's as quintessential a Black Sea experience as Amasra's laid-back castle ambience, or the Kaçkars' lakes and mountains.

History

Trabzon's recorded history begins around 746 BC, when Miletus colonists came from Sinop and founded a settlement, Trapezus, with an acropolis on the *trápeza* (table) of land above the harbour.

The busy port town did reasonably well for 2000 years, until the Christian soldiers of the Fourth Crusade seized and sacked Constantinople in 1204, forcing its noble families to seek refuge in Anatolia. The Comneni imperial family established an empire along the Black Sea coast in 1204, with Alexius Comnenus I reigning as the emperor of Trebizond.

The Trapezuntine rulers skilfully balanced alliances with the Seljuks, the Mongols and the Genoese. Prospering through trade with eastern Anatolia and Persia, the empire peaked during the reign of Alexius II (1297–1330), before declining in factional disputes. The Empire of Trebizond eventually survived until the Ottoman conquest in 1461, eight years longer than Constantinople.

When the Ottoman Empire was defeated after WWI, Trabzon's Greek residents sought to establish a Republic of Trebizond echoing the old Comneni Empire. The Turks were ultimately victorious, and Atatürk declared Trabzon 'one of the richest, strongest and most sensitive sources of trust for the Turkish Republic'.

Trabzon is now a stronghold of ultranationalist Turkish politics, but this is unlikely to affect travellers.

The idolised local football (soccer) team Trabzonspor is the only team outside of İstanbul to ever have won the Turkish national league.

Orientation & Information

Trabzon's heart is the Atatürk Alanı district, also known as Meydan Parkı. The port is east of Atatürk Alanı, down a steep hill.

There are cafés and restaurants west of Atatürk Alanı along Uzun Sokak (Long Lane) and Kahramanmaraş Caddesi (Maraş Caddesi for short). West of the centre past the bazaar is Ortahisar, a picturesque old neighbourhood straddling a ravine. Trabzon's otogar is 3km east of the port.

Banks, ATMs, exchange offices and the PTT are along or around Maraş Caddesi.

Atlas Laundry (Map p555; ☎ 322 4475; Deniz Sokak; per 5kg load TL8; ☻ 10am-4pm)

Çağri Internet (Map p555; Atatürk Alanı; per hr TL1.25; ☻ 10am-11pm)

Tourist office (Map p555; ☎ 326 4760; Camii Sokak; ☻ 8am-5.30pm daily Jun-Sep, 8am-5pm Mon-Fri Oct-May) This helpful place is used to travellers' needs and English is usually spoken.

Tourist Police (Map p555; ☎ 326 3077; Atatürk Alanı)

Ustatour (Map p555; ☎ 326 9545; İskenderpaşa Mahallesi 3) Domestic airline agent in the Usta Park Hotel.

VIP Internet (Map p555; Gazıpaşa Caddesi 6; per hr TL1.25; ☻ 9am-midnight)

Sights & Activities
TRABZON MUSEUM

Just south of Uzun Sokak, this Italian-designed mansion was built for a Russian merchant in 1912 and inhabited briefly by Atatürk. It now houses the **Trabzon Museum** (Trabzon Müzesi; Map p554; Zeytinlik Caddesi 10; admission TL3; ☻ 9am-noon & 1-6pm Tue-Sun). The fantastic interiors and original furnishings put most Ottoman re-creations to shame, with a series of impressive high-ceilinged rooms displaying ethnographic and Islamic artefacts, mostly labelled in English. The basement archaeological section also has significant pieces, including a flattened bronze statue of Hermes from local excavations at Tabakhane and Byzantine finds from near Sumela.

AYA SOFYA MUSEUM

Originally called Hagia Sophia (Church of the Divine Wisdom), the **Aya Sofya Museum** (Aya Sofya Müzesi; ☎ 223 3033; admission TL3; ☻ 9am-6pm Tue-Sun Apr-Oct, 9am-5pm Tue-Sun Nov-Mar) is located 4km west of Trabzon's centre on a terrace that once held a pagan temple. Built in the late Byzantine period, between 1238 and 1263, the church has clearly been influenced by Georgian and Seljuk design, although the wall paintings and mosaic floors follow the prevailing Constantinople style of the time. It was converted to a mosque after the Ottoman conquest in 1461, and later used as an ammunition storage depot and hospital by the Russians, before being fully restored in the 1960s.

Enter the Aya Sofya through the western entrance into the vaulted narthex to view the best-preserved frescoes of various biblical themes. Entering the church, its design becomes immediately obvious. A cross-in-square plan is topped by a single dome showing Georgian influence. A fresco in the southern portico depicts Adam and Eve's expulsion. Look for a relief of an eagle, the

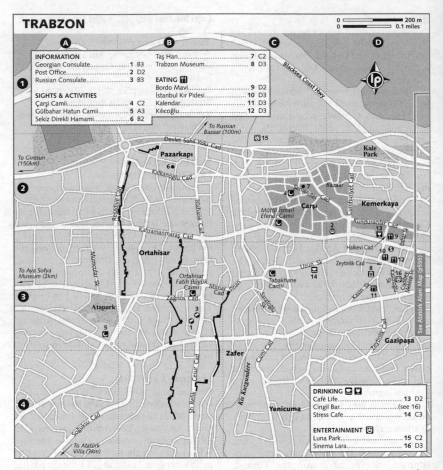

TRABZON

symbol of the founders, the Comnenus family. Unfortunately most of the frescoes within arm's reach have been heavily defaced. Flash photography is prohibited to preserve the remaining painted fragments.

Beside the museum is a square bell tower, a reconstructed farmhouse, and a *serander* (granary) from Of county, set on tall posts to combat vermin.

The site is above the coastal highway, reachable by dolmuş (TL1.25) from the northern side of Atatürk Alanı.

ATATÜRK VILLA

Escape busy Trabzon at the **Atatürk Villa** (Atatürk Köşkü; ☎ 231 0028; admission TL2; ☺ 8am-7pm May-Sep, 8am-5pm Oct-Apr), 5km southwest of

Atatürk Alanı. Set above Trabzon in a forested neighbourhood, it has fine views and lovely gardens. The three-storey white villa, designed in a Black Sea–style popular in the Crimea, was built between 1890 and 1903 for a wealthy Trabzon banking family, and given to Atatürk when he visited in 1924. It's now a museum of Atatürk memorabilia. Don't miss the simple table in the study with a map of the WWI Dardanelles campaign scratched into the wood.

City buses labelled 'Köşk', leaving from the northern side of Atatürk Alanı, drop you outside the villa (TL1.20). Don't get out at the stop that says 'Atatürk Köşk 200m'. The actual stop is a steep 1km trek further up the hill.

BAZAAR DISTRICT

Trabzon's bazaar is west of Atatürk Alanı in the Çarşı (Market) quarter, accessible by the pedestrianised Kunduracılar Caddesi from Atatürk Alanı. After the touristy vibe of İstanbul's Grand Bazaar, it's down to earth and proudly local. Close to the restored **Çarşı Camii** (Market Mosque; Map p554), is the **Taş Han** (or Vakıf Han; Map p554), a single-domed *han* (caravanserai) constructed around 1647, and the oldest marketplace in Trabzon. It's now full of workshops and stores.

MOSQUE OF THE OTTOMANS

West of the centre, **Gülbahar Hatun Camii** (Map p554) is another interesting mosque. It was built in 1514 by Selim the Grim, the great Ottoman conqueror of Syria and Egypt, in honour of his mother, Gülbahar Hatun. Next to it, the **Atapark** (Map p554) has a tea garden and a reconstructed wooden *serander*.

BOZTEPE PICNIC PLACE

On the hillside 2km southeast of Atatürk Alanı is the **Boztepe Picnic Place** (Boztepe Piknik Alanı), with fine views of the city and the sea, tea gardens and restaurants. In ancient times, Boztepe harboured temples to the Persian sun god Mithra. Later the Byzantines built churches and monasteries here. Now it's a top place for a sunset beer.

From Atatürk Alanı, take a frequent Boztepe dolmuş (TL1.25), from near the southern end

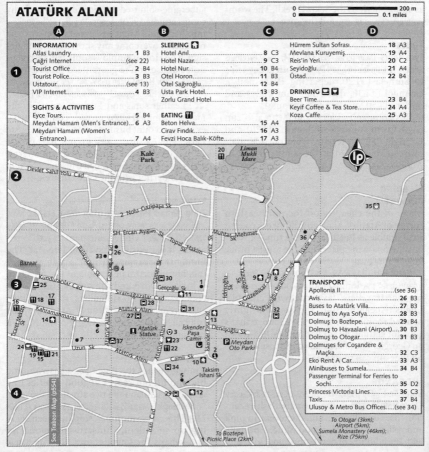

ATATÜRK ALANI

0 — 200 m
0 — 0.1 miles

INFORMATION		
Atlas Laundry	1	B3
Çağrı Internet	(see 22)	
Tourist Office	2	B4
Tourist Police	3	B3
Ustatour	(see 13)	
VIP Internet	4	B3

SIGHTS & ACTIVITIES		
Eyce Tours	5	B4
Meydan Hamam (Men's Entrance)	6	A3
Meydan Hamam (Women's Entrance)	7	A4

SLEEPING		
Hotel Anıl	8	C3
Hotel Nazar	9	C3
Hotel Nur	10	B4
Otel Horon	11	B3
Otel Sağıroğlu	12	B4
Usta Park Hotel	13	B3
Zorlu Grand Hotel	14	A3

EATING		
Beton Helva	15	A4
Cirav Fındık	16	A3
Fevzi Hoca Balık-Köfte	17	A3

Hürrem Sultan Sofrası	18	A3
Mevlana Kuruyemiş	19	A4
Reis'in Yeri	20	C2
Seyidoğlu	21	A4
Üstad	22	B4

DRINKING		
Beer Time	23	B4
Keyif Coffee & Tea Store	24	A4
Koza Caffe	25	A3

TRANSPORT		
Apollonia II	(see 36)	
Avis	26	B3
Buses to Atatürk Villa	27	B3
Dolmuş to Aya Sofya	28	B3
Dolmuş to Boztepe	29	B4
Dolmuş to Havaalani (Airport)	30	B3
Dolmuş to Otogar	31	B3
Dolmuşes for Coşandere & Maçka	32	C3
Eko Rent A Car	33	A3
Minibuses to Sumela	34	B4
Passenger Terminal for Ferries to Sochi	35	D2
Princess Victoria Lines	36	C3
Taxis	37	B4
Ulusoy & Metro Bus Offices	(see 34)	

BLACK SEA COAST & THE KAÇKAR MOUNTAINS

of Atatürk Alanı. The route goes uphill 2.2km to Boztepe park.

HAMAMS

The **Sekiz Direkli Hamamı** (Map p554; Direkli Hamami Sokak; sauna & massage TL25; ☼ men 7am-5pm Fri-Wed, women 8am-5pm Thu), 600m west of the Çarşı Camii, is Trabzon's best Turkish bath. The rough-hewn pillars – 'Sekiz Direkli' translates to 'Eight Columns' – date from Seljuk times, although the rest of the building has been modernised. A few of the creaking old-timers who work there appear to be only slightly younger. They're damn strong though. Expect a very robust massage.

The **Meydan Hamam** (Map p555; Maraş Caddesi; sauna TL12; ☼ men 6am-11pm, women 9am-6pm), in central Trabzon, is clean and efficiently run, but not as atmospheric as the Sekiz Direkli. The women's entrance is around the corner.

Tours

Eyce Tours (Map p555; ☎ 326 7174; www.eycetours .com, in Turkish; Taksim İşhanı Sokak 11) offers day trips to Sumela (TL20, departing 10am daily), Uzungöl (TL30, departing 9am daily) and Ayder (TL50, minimum six people).

Bus companies **Ulusoy** and **Metro** also run day trips in summer to Sumela (TL20) and Uzungöl (TL30), leaving from outside their offices (Map p555) at the southern end of Atatürk Alanı.

Sleeping

BUDGET

Many of the cheapies off the northeastern corner of Atatürk Alanı and along the coastal road double as brothels. At the time of writing, the following places had the tourist office tick of approval.

Hotel Nur (Map p555; ☎ 323 0445; Camii Sokak 15; s/d 40/60; ❄) A long-standing, but often over-popular travellers' favourite, with amiable, English-speaking staff and small, brightly painted rooms. Downstairs is a lounge that's good for getting the latest travellers' low-down on Georgia. The nearby mosque doesn't skimp on the 5am call to prayer.

MIDRANGE

Hotel Anıl (Map p555; ☎ 326 7282; Güzelhisar Caddesi 12; s/d TL50/80; ❄) A promisingly flash reception lures travellers in, and the rooms in pink and yellow are actually good value, especially with the addition of new bathrooms, wi-fi and aircon. It's built into the side of a hill, so even the downstairs rooms have views.

Hotel Nazar (Map p555; ☎ 323 0081; www.nazarhotel .net; Güzelhisar Caddesi 5; s/d TL70/100; ❄) Look beyond the flagrant photoshopping in the brochure (flower gardens in central Trabzon? Yeah right), and the Nazar is a smart business-class option. There's usually someone on board who speaks English.

Otel Sağıroğlu (Map p555; ☎ 3323 2899; www .sagirogluotel.com, in Turkish; Taksim İşhanı Sokak 1; s/d/tr TL70/100/120; ❄) This large yellow block calls itself a 'Butik Otel'. Er…not quite. How about a solid midranger with a few rooms featuring heritage wooden floors and a faux gentlemen's club ambience?

Otel Horon (Map p555; ☎ 326 6455; www.otelhoron .com; Sıramağazalar Caddesi 125; s/d TL90/125; ❄) The aubergine-coloured exterior conceals unflashy rooms amidst 1970s decor. Wi-fi, well-stocked minibars and city views from the rooftop bar/restaurant overcome any shortcomings in design. The Horon employs some female reception staff, so you're guaranteed propriety.

Usta Park Hotel (Map p555; ☎ 326 5700; www.usta parkhotel.com; İskenderpaşa Mahallesi 3; s/d/tr €115/140/170; ❄) Leather sofas and Turkish muzak in the marble-trimmed lobby provide comfort to the expense-account business travellers at the Usta Park. There's also a restaurant, bar, fitness centre, travel agency and hamam on offer. A wall clock shows the time in Moscow if you're still wondering who the core clientele are.

TOP END

Zorlu Grand Hotel (Map p555; ☎ 326 8400; www .zorlugrand.com; Maraş Caddesi 9; s/d €300/350, ste €400-950; ❄ ▯ ▨) Understatement is jettisoned at this ludicrously extravagant five-star. The immense mezzanine atrium is quite staggering, but unfortunately some of the furniture is looking worn and the carpet grubby. The rack rates are also ridiculous, so negotiate a substantial discount if you want to enjoy the roll call of amenities including restaurants, a pub and a hamam.

Eating

Trabzon is not the Black Sea's gastronomic high point, but scores of good eateries line Atatürk Alanı and the two streets to the west.

Seyidoğlu (Map p555; Uzun Sokak 15a; dishes TL1.50-2.50) This compact snack stop has been serving up succulent, thin-crusted *lahmacun* and kebaps for four decades. Roll up a few *lahmacun* with fresh salad and you can't go wrong.

İstanbul Kır Pidesi (Map p554; ☎ 321 2212; Uzun Sokak 48; mains TL3-5) Three floors of wood-fired goodness for the pide and *börek* (filled pastries) aficionado within. C'mon, pide is *almost* good for you.

Kalendar (Map p554; Zeytinlik Caddesi 10; mains TL3.50) Low tables and mood lighting give this place near the Trabzon Museum a cosmopolitan vibe. It's perfect for a post-museum coffee or brunch of *menemen* (eggs scrambled with tomatoes, onions, peppers and white cheese) and toast (TL3.50), if you're getting tired of cucumbers, tomatoes and cheese.

Hürrem Sultan Sofrası (Map p555; ☎ 321 8651; Maraş Caddesi 30; mains TL4-10) This popular lunch spot sometimes includes regional dishes like *muhlama* and *kuymak* (both melted cheese dishes; see p561) in their daily offerings. Businessmen, students and the local cops; no-one's safe from becoming a regular at this friendly spot where 'Where are you from?' will probably be asked in the very first minute.

Üstad (Map p555; ☎ 326 5406; Atatürk Alanı 18b; meals TL5-8) Locals squeeze into this compact *lokanta* right on Trabzon's main square. We can thoroughly recommend the *biber dolması* (stuffed peppers) that come with a surprisingly robust pinch of chilli reinforcing how far east you've travelled.

Bordo Mavi (Map p554; ☎ 326 2077; Halkevi Caddesi 12; meals TL6-10; ⏱ 11am-10pm) This cosmopolitan garden café adjoins the clubhouse of Trabzonspor, the local football team. It's not at all boozy and noisy though. The strongest drink you'll get is a Coke, and the excellent pizzas and pasta have an authentic tinge of Italy. Next door is a shop selling Trabzonspor merchandise. Don't you know New York Yankees caps are passé?

Reis'in Yeri (Map p554; Liman Mukli İdare; meals TL8-14; Liman Mukli İdare; ⏱ 11am-11pm) Surrounded by traffic around Atatürk Alanı, it's easy to forget Trabzon is a coastal city. Head down the hill and across the pedestrian overbridge to this sprawling fish/chicken/*köfte* grill place that also doubles as a beer garden. It's guaranteed dolmuş-free, and you can even hire rowboats to steer around the tiny cove.

Fevzi Hoca Balık-Köfte (Map p555; ☎ 326 5444; İpekyolu İş Merkezi, Maraş Caddesi; meals TL12-25; ⏱ noon-9.30pm) There are no menus at this fish restaurant. Just choose your glistening beastie and it comes in a meal deal with salads,

pickles and dessert. The hushed ambience resembles somewhere you'd go with your parents for a birthday dinner. Cheaper *köfte* meals (TL5) are available if you're a bargain-seeking fish phobic. It's on the 1st floor of a shopping arcade.

Trabzon's sweetest street is represented by **Kılıçoğlu** (Map p554; ☎ 321 4525; Uzun Sokak 42; desserts from TL3) with an irresistible array of ice cream and pastries. Across the way, **Mevlana Kuruyemiş** (Map p555; ☎ 321 9622; Uzun Sokak 31) is a renowned *kuruyemiş* (dried fruit) vendor, and also sells *lokum* (Turkish delight), *helva* (a traditional sweet made from sesame seeds), *pestil* (sheets of dried fruit) and excellent *kestane balı* (chestnut honey). Nearby, old-fashioned **Beton Helva** (Map p555; ☎ 321 2550; Uzun Sokak 15b) sells sweet slabs of *helva* that look like loaves of bread. Down a nearby lane is **Cirav Fındık** (Map p555; ☎ 322 2050; Ticaret Mektep Sokak 8c), off Maraş Caddesi, a tiny shop that's supplied Trabzon folk with hazelnuts and confectionery since 1940.

Drinking & Entertainment

Trabzon has a small drinking scene, but most places close by midnight.

Keyif Coffee & Tea Store (Map p555; ☎ 326 8026; Canbakkal İş Merkezi, Uzun Sokak 37; ⏱ 8am-10pm) Trabzon's studenty types gather amidst Anglophile vintage sporting gear and leather armchairs to enjoy more than 200 varieties of hot beverage.

Koza Caffe (Map p555; ☎ 321 0225; cnr Kunduracılar Caddesi & Sanat Sokak 1; ⏱ 10am-11pm) Ignore the incongruous medieval decor and settle in for coffee, beer and wine with a soundtrack of bouncy Turkish pop. Get lucky and grab a seat at the tiny outdoor balcony.

Stress Café (Map p554; ☎ 321 3044; Uzun Sokak) Stress? You must be joking. One of Trabzon's best live music and nargileh spots, the Stress Café is so laid-back it's almost horizontal. The Ottomans-R-Us decor is a bit naff, but it's an undeniably relaxing haven. Look for the backgammon-playing mannequins out front.

Beer Time (Map p555; Atatürk Alanı; ⏱ noon-11pm) Definitely does what it says on the tin. Downstairs it's a rough and ready pub with 0.7L handles of Efes, while upstairs it's a little quieter and a good spot for drinkers of either gender to watch the nightly dolmuş races around Atatürk Alanı. On your marks, get set...

Café Life (Map p554; ☎ 321 2955; Halkevi Caddesi 15) Two floors up past wildlife pics from National Geographic, this is one of Trabzon's more vibrant nightlife venues with live music, fast food and free-flowing booze.

Cingil Bar (Map p554; 1st fl Gazipaşa Mahallesi Saray Çarşisi, Kasimoğlu Sokak) Hidden in a shopping arcade, this cosy music bar with a collage of your favourite musos (c 1975) is a good spot for a quiet drink away from the blokey beer halls. There's occasional live music at weekends. From Sinema Lara head upstairs to the opposite end of the arcade.

Sinema Lara (Map p554; ☎ 321 0006; Gazipaşa Mahallesi Saray Çarşisi 5, Kasimoğlu Sokak; admission TL8) Hollywood blockbusters show just days after their international release. How's that for globalisation?

Head to **Luna Park** between the old and new coastal roads for Black Sea fairground action.

Shopping

Thanks to the influx of cheap goods from former Soviet territories, Trabzon is a good place for cheap clothes, especially from the stalls along Karaoğlanoğlu Caddesi (Map p555). If you're lucky you might even find a few correctly spelt Western logos on the T-shirts, sweatshirts and sports shoes.

This is the former location of the **Russian Bazaar**, now relocated to a purpose-built hall in grassy wasteland near the Black Sea Coastal Highway. It's a shadow of its former self with only a few stalls run by émigrés from the former Soviet states. The bazaar also has clothing with lookalike labels you've nearly heard of, and martial arts DVDs starring Jackie Van Damme and Jean-Claude Chan. Or is that…

Leather shops along Sıramağazalar Caddesi (Map p555) sell jackets, bags and other garments, with alterations and made-to-measure fittings available. Expect to pay around half as much as in İstanbul's Grand Bazaar.

Getting There & Away

AIR

Turkish Airlines (☎ 444 0849; www.thy.com) has daily flights to Ankara, İstanbul (both airports) and İzmir. There are also flights to Bursa (Wednesday and Saturday) and Antalya (Thursday and Sunday).

Pegasus Airlines (☎ 444 0737; www.flypgs.com) has two daily direct flights to İstanbul (Sabiha Gökçen airport) and one to Ankara. **Onur Air** (☎ 444 6687; www.onurair.com.tr) has three daily direct flights to İstanbul Atatürk, and during summer **SunExpress** (☎ 444 0797; www.sunexpress.com.tr) flies to İstanbul five times a week, Sivas and Bursa twice a week, and Adana and Antalya once a week.

At the time of writing **Azerbaijan Airways** (www.azal.az) was trialling a Tuesday flight (30 minutes; €155) from Trabzon to Baku. Check with Ustatour (p553) for the latest.

BOAT

Timetables for ferries to Sochi in Russia change with alarming regularity, but at the time of writing the following was correct. Check the latest situation at the following shipping offices. Both are down the hill from Atatürk Alanı on İskele Caddesi. The sailing takes around 12 hours.

Princess Victoria Lines (Map p555; ☎ 326 6674; İskele Caddesi 53a) sail Monday and Thursday evening, departing Trabzon at 10pm (one way US$90).

Apollonia II (Map p555; ☎ 326 484; İskele Caddesi) sails at 5pm on Fridays (US$75).

When you book your ticket ask when you'll need to report to the port police as it's usually several hours before the departure time. For visa information see p680.

BUS

Trabzon's otogar is 3km east of the port, on the landward side of the coastal road. It is served by dolmuşes to Atatürk Alanı.

There are no direct buses to Ayder and the Kaçkar Mountains. Catch a bus heading to Hopa and change at Pazar or Ardeşsen.

CAR

Car rental agencies include **Avis** (Map p555; ☎ 322 3740; Gazipaşa Caddesi 20) and **Eko Rent A Car** (Map p555; ☎ 322 2575; Gazipaşa Caddesi 3/53).

Getting Around

TO/FROM THE AIRPORT

The *havaalanı* (airport) is 5.5km east of Atatürk Alanı. Dolmuşes to the airport (TL2) leave from a side street on the northern side of Atatürk Alanı, but drop you on the opposite side of the coastal road, 500m from the terminal entrance. Alternatively, pay TL8 extra to be dropped at the door. A taxi costs about TL20. Buses bearing the legend 'Park' or 'Meydan' go to Atatürk Alanı from the airport.

SERVICES FROM TRABZON'S OTOGAR

Destination	Fare	Duration (hr)	Distance (km)	Frequency
Ankara	TL45	12	780	several per day
Artvin	TL22	4½	255	frequent
Baku, Azerbaijan	US$50	30		1 weekly
Erzurum	TL25	6	325	several per day
Hopa	TL15	3½	165	half-hourly
İstanbul	TL60	24	1110	several per day
Kars	TL35	10	525	1 nightly or change at Erzurum or Artvin
Kayseri	TL45	12	686	several per day
Rize	TL6	1	75	half-hourly
Samsun	TL25	6	355	frequent
Sinop	TL38	9	533	1 at 8pm
Tbilisi, Georgia	US$30	20		several per day
Erivan	US$60	25		8am Thu & Sun

BUS & DOLMUŞ

To reach Atatürk Alanı from the otogar, cross the shore road in front of the terminal, turn left, walk to the bus stop and catch any bus with 'Park' or 'Meydan' in its name. The dolmuş for Atatürk Alanı is marked 'Garajlar-Meydan'. A taxi between the otogar and Atatürk Alanı costs around TL10.

To get to Trabzon's otogar catch a dolmuş marked 'Garajlar' or 'KTÜ' from the north-eastern side of Atatürk Alanı.

Dolmuşes mainly leave from Atatürk Alanı, although you can flag them down along their routes. Whatever your destination, the fare should be TL1.50.

TAXI

Trabzon's main taxi stand is on Atatürk Alanı.

SUMELA MONASTERY

The Greek Orthodox **Monastery of the Virgin Mary** (admission TL8; 9am-6pm) at Sumela, 46km south of Trabzon, is an undeniable highlight of the Black Sea coast. The monastery was founded in Byzantine times and abandoned in 1923 after the creation of the Turkish Republic quashed local Greek aspirations for a new state.

Sumela clings improbably to a sheer rock wall high above evergreen forests and a rushing mountain stream. It's a mysterious place, especially when mists swirl in the tree-lined valley below and the call of a hidden mosque drifts ethereally through the forest.

To get to Sumela, take the Erzurum road and turn left at Maçka, 29km south of Trabzon. It's also signposted as Meryemana (Virgin Mary), to whom the monastery was dedicated. The road then winds into dense evergreen forests, following the course of a rushing mountain stream punctuated by commercial trout pools and fish restaurants.

At the entrance to the **Altındere Vadısı Milli Parkı** (Altındere Valley National Park) there's an TL8 charge for private vehicles and a TL3 per person entry fee. If you're visiting by public transport, try and catch a dolmuş from Trabzon at around 8am to avoid the mid-morning flow of tour groups.

At the end of the road from the entrance you'll find a shady riverside park with picnic tables, a post office, restaurant and several bungalows for rent (no camping is allowed).

The main trail to the monastery begins by the restaurant and is steep but easy to follow. A second trail begins further up the valley. Follow the concreted road 1km uphill and across two bridges until you come to a wooden footbridge over the stream on the right. This trail cuts straight up through the trees, past the shell of the Ayavarvara chapel. It's usually much quieter than the main route.

If you drive further up the road from the restaurant, you'll reach a small car park, from which it's only a 10-minute walk to the monastery. A few kilometres before the car park is a lookout point with the monastery suspended on a cliff face high above the forest.

From the restaurant to the monastery, you'll ascend 250m in about 30 to 45 minutes, and the air gets noticeably cooler as you climb through forests and alpine meadows. After the ticket office, a steep flight of steps leads to the monastery complex sheltered underneath a hefty outcrop. The main chapel, cut into the rock, is the indisputable highlight, covered both inside and outside with colourful frescoes. The earliest examples date from the 9th century, but most of them are actually 19th-century work. Sadly, bored shepherd boys used the paintings as targets for their catapults, and later heedless visitors – from Russian tourists to US Air Force grunts (1965 vintage) – scratched their names into them, proving that idiocy is indeed international. Even in a new century Turkish visitors sadly feel the need to validate their visit with the scrawl of a marker pen.

In recent years the monastery has been substantially restored to showcase the various chapels and rooms used by pious types in earlier centuries. Restoration continues, but in no way detracts from this essential Black Sea experience.

Sleeping & Eating

Most travellers visit Sumela as a day trip from Trabzon, but the following are good bases for exploring the surrounding area on a self-drive basis.

Coşandere Tesisleri Restaurant & Pansiyon (☎ 0462-531 1190; www.cosandere.com, in Turkish; Sümela Yolu; r from TL40) Located in Coşandere, a sleepy stream-fed village 5km out of Maçka, this place has three converted, pine-clad *seranders* sleeping up to six, and a huge motel-like building favoured by tour groups. The owners organise various tours, treks and day trips. Anyone for a *yayla* (villages) safari or a 4WD truck trip? It's a handy way to get out and about in the mountains if you don't have your own transport.

Sümela Sosyal Tesisleri (☎ 0462-531 1207; www.sumelaotel.com; bungalows from TL100) Right by the car park at Sumela itself, these comfortable A-frame bungalows have full amenities, including kitchenettes. Despite the wooden floors and Turkish rugs, the bungalows are a bit overpriced, but you're really paying for the attractive setting.

Getting There & Away

From May to the end of August, Ulusoy and Metro (p556) run buses from Trabzon to Sumela, departing at 10am and returning at 3pm.

Dolmuşes for Maçka and Coşandere village depart all day from the minibus ranks down the hill from Atatürk Alanı on Karaoğlanoğlu

Caddesi (Map p555). It'll cost you around TL15 return to Sumela, but you may have to wait until the driver decides enough people are coming. For an extra TL5 you'll know exactly when you're leaving with Ulusoy or Metro.

TRABZON TO ERZURUM

Heading south into the mountains, you're in for a long (325km) but scenic ride. Along the highway south, **Maçka** is 29km inland from Trabzon. About 1.5km north of Maçka, look out for basaltic rock columns resembling California's Devil's Postpile or Northern Ireland's Giant's Causeway. From Maçka, the mountain road ascends through active landslide zones towards the **Zigana Geçidi** (Zigana Pass; 2030m).

The dense, humid air of the coast disappears as you rise and becomes light and dry as you reach the southern side of the eastern Black Sea mountains. Snow can be seen in all months except perhaps July, August and September.

Gümüşhane, about 145km south of Trabzon, is a small town in a mountain valley with a few simple travellers' services.

At the provincial capital of **Bayburt**, 195km from Trabzon, you reach the rolling steppe and low mountains of the high Anatolian plateau. A dry, desolate place, Bayburt has a big medieval fortress.

The road from Bayburt passes through rolling green farm country with poplar trees and flocks of brown-fleeced sheep. In early summer wild flowers dominate.

Exactly 33km past Bayburt is the **Kop Geçidi** (Kop Pass; 2370m), with excellent views. From Kop Geçidi, the open road to Erzurum offers fast, easy travelling.

UZUNGÖL
☎ 0462 / pop 2800

With its lakeside mosque and Swiss-style forested mountains, Uzungöl is another Turkish scene that's on display in tourist offices around the country. The idyllic scenery still exists, but be prepared for an overlay of a few tacky hotels and a growing number of visitors from the Gulf States. You'll even see a few menus in Arabic dotted around town. Uzungöl is a worthwhile day trip or overnight stop, and a good base for day hikes in the Soğanlı Mountains to the lakes around Demirkapı (Holdizen). Note that summer weekends get very busy, so try and visit during the week.

GOOD-TASTING CABBAGE? SURELY NOT

The eastern Black Sea has a unique culture, and chances are you'll first experience the region's uncommon character through your stomach. Local cuisine provides a few taste sensations you won't find anywhere else.

The people of the Black Sea have a reverence for cabbage only surpassed by certain Eastern Europeans, and no trip would be complete without sampling *labana sarması* (stuffed cabbage rolls) or *labana lobia* (cabbage and beans). Even if you're not a cabbage fan, these fibre-rich dishes are both healthy and tasty.

Also very popular are *muhlama* (or *mıhlama*) and *kuymak*, both types of thick molten cheese served in a metal dish, much like a fondue or raclette, but without the fiddly carrot and celery sticks. Scooped up with bread for breakfast, it can sit heavily in your stomach, especially if it's followed by a long bus ride. Try it instead in the mountain villages of the Kaçkars, where it's cooked with egg for a lighter effect. It will set you up for a long day's trekking.

If your taste buds aren't reacting to these savoury treats, consider *laz böreği*, a delicious flaky pastry layered with custard. Like most Turkish desserts, a few bites can easily become a daily addiction. And when you consider that many of Turkey's pastry chefs are from the Black Sea, you just know it's going to be good.

A good place to try Laz food is the Sevimli Konak (p562) in Rize.

Ensar Otel (☎ 656 6321; www.ensarotel.com; Fatih Caddesi 18; r TL150-200) is an attractive resort with comfortable bungalows. Everything is wood panelled except the roof, and there's traditional decoration throughout. The bungalows sleep up to four, and the restaurant has live music on summer weekends. It's at the opposite end of the lake to the mosque amidst a clutch of wood-trimmed pansiyons (around TL 40/80 for a single/double). Nearby you can rent **mountain bikes** (per hour TL2) to circumnavigate the lake.

On the main road into Uzungöl are cheaper and simpler pansiyons (around TL30/60 for a single/double), and in the centre of the village opposite the mosque, the **Euxinus Café & Motel** (☎ 0532 622 0652; ekrmtgn@hotmail.com; r TL80) has comfortable rooms accommodating up to three people, and a popular **café** that doubles as a hang out for Uzungöl's internet-literati (TL1.50 per hour).

A couple of **minibuses** travel daily between Trabzon and Uzungöl; Ulusoy (p556) has a daily service at 9am in summer (TL30). Alternatively, take a Rize-bound dolmuş to Of (TL5) and then wait for another heading inland. Eyce Tours (p556) runs regular day trips (TL30) from Trabzon.

RİZE

☎ 0464 / pop 78,000
Around 75km east of Trabzon, in the heart of Turkey's tea-plantation area, Rize is a modern city centred on a bustling main square.

The hillsides above town are thickly planted with tea, which is dried, blended, and shipped throughout Turkey. There are a couple of excellent eating options, and Rize is a good spot for a refreshing cuppa as you break your journey east or west.

Orientation & Information

The main square, Atatürk Anıtı with a beautifully reconstructed PTT and the Şeyh Camii, is 200m inland from the coastal road, Menderes Bulvarı. The hotels are east of the main square along or just off Cumhuriyet Caddesi, one block inland and parallel to Menderes Bulvarı. The otogar is along Cumhuriyet Caddesi, 1km northwest of the main square.

The friendly **tourist office** (☎ 213 0408; ☺ 9am-5pm Mon-Fri mid-May–mid-Sep) is on the main square next to the PTT. Ask for the handy guide, 'Rize – From Now Every Season'.

Sahra Internet Café (Atatürk Caddesi; per hr TL1; ☺ 10am-11pm) is one block back from the main square.

Sights

Up the hill behind the tourist office you'll find the **Rize museum** (☎ 214 0235; Ulubatlı Sokak; admission TL3; ☺ 9am-noon & 1-4pm Tue-Sun), a fine reconstructed Ottoman house with a lovely *serander*. The rooms upstairs have been decorated in traditional style, with artefacts and an old radio to remind you that the later Ottomans were part of the modern age. Mannequins model traditional Laz costumes

---

ONE OF THE LAZ

Rize is the last major centre of the Laz people (see p49), a loose community numbered at around 250,000, of which 150,000 still speak the Caucasian-based Lazuri language. Known for their colourful traditional costumes and *lazeburi* folk music, you can see Laz cultural performances at any major local festival in the Rize region.

However, calling someone Laz is not that straightforward. The Turkish Laz strenuously dispute any kind of categorisation that would lump them in with their Georgian counterparts. Local folk of non-Laz backgrounds call themselves 'Karadenizli' (from the Black Sea), and many Turks use Laz as a lazy (or should that be Lazy?) catch-all term for anyone living east of Samsun.

The majority population in towns like Pazar and Ardeşsen, the Laz are just as keen to distance themselves from other coastal citizens, and dismiss the stereotype of the simple anchovy-munching 'Laz fisherman' that is the butt of countless Turkish jokes.

The Laz are actually having the last laugh because many of Turkey's shipping lines are owned by wealthy Laz families. They routinely resource their boats with Laz sailors, so don't be surprised if a few retired maritime types regale you in pretty good English with their memories of San Francisco, Sri Lanka or Singapore.

---

from central Rize and Hemşin costumes from the Ayder region.

Don't miss Rize's fragrant and floral **tea garden**, 900m above town via the steep road behind the Şeyh Camii (it's signposted in English 'Çaykur Tea and Botany Garden'). Enjoy the superb views with a fresh brew of the local leaves (TL1) – a typical Rizeli experience. A taxi from outside the mosque is around TL5.

The town's ancient **castle** was built by the Genoese on the steep hill at the back of town. Signs point the way up Kale Sokak from Atatürk Caddesi.

Sleeping

Hotel Milano (☎ 213 0028; www.hotelmilanorize.com, in Turkish; Cumhuriyet Caddesi 169; s/d/tr TL40/60/110; 🗙 🖳) Newly painted in yellow tones and with Ezy-Kleen tile floors, this friendly spot has maybe the best shower pressure in all of Rize. Wi-fi and a central location do the trick too.

Otel Kaçkar (☎ 213 1490; www.otelkackar.com, in Turkish; Cumhuriyet Caddesi 101; s/d/tr TL60/90/120; 🗙 🖳) Just off the main square, look out for the Kaçkar's mosaic facade, which conceals the neat and simple rooms. There's a hamam round the back. It's favoured by tour groups so you might want to phone ahead.

Eating & Drinking

Deragh Pastaneleri (☎ 532 1704; Deniz Caddesi 19; mains TL4-7; 🕚 7am-10pm) This gleaming modern *pastane* (patisserie) has been luring fans of sweet and savoury flavours since 1985. There's also wi-fi access, so come early for breakfast and

check your email. There's a smaller second branch at Atatürk Caddesi 356.

ourpick **Bekiroğlu** (☎ 217 1380; Cumhuriyet Caddesi 161; mains TL5-8; 🕚 9am-10pm) A cut above most Turkish *lokantas*, Bekiroğlu has a modern interior, and the busy, bustling waiters summon up all their limited knowledge of English to treat you like a regular. Inside the huge display cases are 1001 variations on salads and kebaps, but there's also top-notch pide on offer. Come hungry – the meals are huge – and leave wishing this place would open up in your hometown. Leave room for dessert with Bekiroğlu's superb *fırın sütlaç* (baked rice pudding). One of the best eateries on the coast, and the only reason you need to rest up in Rize.

Sevimli Konak (☎ 217 0895; Cumhuriyet Caddesi; mains TL5-10) This restored Ottoman house with a garden setting is a good spot to try local Laz food like *muhlama* and *labana sarması* (p561). You'll find the Sevimli Konak around 300m northwest of the main square en route to the otogar.

Nat's Cocktails & Bar (Deniz Caddesi 3) OK, you might struggle to get a perfectly prepared Cosmopolitan, but this cosy spot opposite the Deragh Pastaneleri is a top spot for an Efes at the end of the day.

Getting There & Away

From Rize's otogar, frequent minibuses run to Hopa (TL9, 1½ hours) and Trabzon (TL6, one hour). In summer there are daily direct services to Ayder (TL12, 1¾ hours). Otherwise take an eastbound minibus to Pazar (TL5) or Ardeşsen (TL5.50) and change for Ayder. A few local minibuses also travel to

Hopa and Trabzon from a mini-otogar 150m northeast of Rize's main square on the old coastal road. From the Deragh Pastaneleri turn east (right).

HOPA

☎ 0466 / pop 24,000

Hopa is the archetypal border town with cheap hotels, traders markets, and a depressingly functional vibe. Just 30km southwest of the Georgian border and 165km east of Trabzon, it's best appreciated on a grey day with a bad rakı hangover. It'll probably feel like that anyway. Even when the Black Sea shimmers blue, Hopa can feel mighty gloomy. Stay here only if you're heading to or arriving from Georgia and have arrived too late to move on. There's a PTT, a couple of banks with ATMs, and internet cafés. Note that Hopa's exchange offices give lousy rates for Georgian lari, knowing that you won't be able to change them anywhere else.

Sleeping

Otel İmren (☎ 351 4069; Cumhuriyet Caddesi; s/d TL15/25) Here's one for the budget-conscious Georgian traveller. Spearmint decor and relatively clean rooms provide cheap digs before or after the border crossing. Downstairs cards are played in a smoky and very masculine atmosphere. It's on the main drag in the centre of town.

Otel Ustabaş (☎ 351 4507; Ortahopa Caddesi; s/d TL30/50; 🛢) An OK budget deal, with blinding carpets and optional shower heads offset by simple comforts and a café downstairs. Only in Hopa would this place be dubbed 'three star'.

Otel Huzur (☎ 351 4095; Cumhuriyet Caddesi 25; s/d TL35/55) Newish rooms, some with sea views, and wi-fi feature at this friendly spot used to travellers doing the Black Sea shuffle to Georgia. It's on the main road opposite the truck park.

Otel Cihan (☎ 351 4897; www.hotelcihan.com; Ortahopa Caddesi 36; s/d TL50/70; 🛢 🖳) This yellow tower offers a bar and rooftop restaurant along with small, well-equipped rooms with satellite TV, wi-fi and minibars. It's 300m along the coast road, next to a petrol station.

Eating & Drinking

Green Kebap (☎ 351 4277; Cumhuriyet Caddesi; mains TL3-6; 🕙 9am-10pm) Does exactly what it says on the tin, with two terraces and a brick dining room dishing up pide and kebaps in a shady park.

There's a nearby *tekel bayii* (off licence) to score a cold beer after a dusty bus journey.

Down a narrow lane off Cumhuriyet Caddesi the **Hayde Café** is a rooftop bar with occasional live music.

Getting There & Away

The otogar is on the western side of the Sundura Çayı, on the road to Artvin. Direct buses from Hopa to Erzurum (TL30, six hours) leave at 9am, 4pm and 7pm. There are also regular buses or minibuses to Artvin (TL12, 1½ hours), Rize (TL8, 1½ hours) and Trabzon (TL15, 3½ hours). For Kars (TL18, 11 hours), there's one direct bus at 10.30am.

Minibuses for Sarp (TL8) and the Georgian border leave from the petrol station beside the Otel Cihan and the stand at the Sundura Çayı junction north of the otogar. Trabzon–Tbilisi buses also pass through Hopa, some going via the Posof border crossing (Türkgözü, TL40, 10 hours). For more details on crossing to Georgia, see p679.

KAÇKAR MOUNTAINS

The Kaçkar Mountains (Kaçkar Dağları) form a rugged range bordered by the Black Sea coast to the north and the Çoruh River to the south. The range stretches for about 30km, from south of Rize almost to Artvin at its northeastern end. Dense forest covers the lower valleys, but above 2100m grasslands carpet the passes and plateaus, and the jagged ranges are studded with lakes and alpine summer *yayla*.

The Kaçkars are popular for their trekking opportunities. Popular locations include the highest point, **Mt Kaçkar** (Kaçkar Dağı; 3937m), with a glacier on its northern face, and the northeastern ranges around the peak of **Altıparmak** (3310m). Visiting the Kaçkars on a day trip is possible, but a longer stay of at least three days will uncover the best of this beautiful region.

Activities
TREKKING

Trekking is why most travellers come to the Kaçkars, and there are innumerable walks. Talk to locals and the trekking guides.

The Kaçkars' trekking season is very short, and you can only trek the higher mountain routes between mid-July and mid-August,

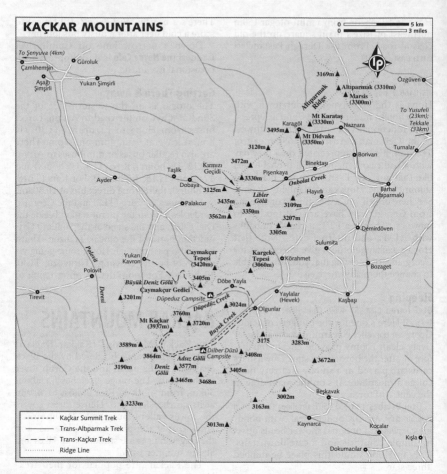

KAÇKAR MOUNTAINS

Legend:
- - - - - - - Kaçkar Summit Trek
———— Trans-Altıparmak Trek
— — — Trans-Kaçkar Trek
·········· Ridge Line

when the snowline is highest. From mid-May to mid-September there are plenty of walks on the lower slopes, and many mountain villages to experience authentic Kaçkar life.

One of the most popular multiday trips is the **Trans-Kaçkar Trek** (p360). The trek to the **Kaçkar Summit** by its southern face takes an easy three days, but may require specialist snow equipment. The three- to four-day **Trans-Altıparmak** route is similar to the Trans-Kaçkar, except that it crosses the Altıparmak range and doesn't climb the summit. If you stay in **Barhal (Altıparmak)** you could trek for four to five sweaty hours up to **Karagöl**, camp overnight, and return the next day.

Most people base themselves in Ayder or Çamlıhemşin, and start treks from the east-

ern flanks of the range at Barhal, Yaylalar (Hevek) or Olgunlar. **Day walks** around the slopes and lakes are possible from Yukarı Kavron, Caymakçur and Avusor, all served by dolmuş from Ayder.

See www.kackarmountains.com for more information or pick up a copy of the 2008 book, *The Kaçkar – Trekking in Turkey's Black Sea Mountains*. The book details 30 different Kaçkar routes. See www.lycianway.com for purchase details.

Trekking Guides

In the Kaçkars it's a good idea to hire a local who knows the tracks. The walks are mostly unsigned, and misty weather conditions can make orientation difficult. Ask at the pensions and you should be able to find a guide for around TL75 per day.

A good tent, stove and sleeping bag is necessary, but you could get away with walking boots and warm clothes if you're trekking with an all-inclusive operator.

For fully guided tours, including guide fee, tents, bedding, and all transport and food, expect to pay between TL100 and TL120 per day from Ayder, depending on group size (a minimum number often applies). A one-week trek should cost around TL800.

Reliable English-speaking guides include **Mehmet Demirci** (p566; ☎ 0464-651 7787, 0533-341 3430), a friendly local entrepreneur offering day walks, longer treks, 4WD safaris, biking trips and rafting. Seven-day, six-night treks cost TL840 to TL890. Ask at Türkü Tourism (right) in Çamlıhemşin or the Fora Pansiyon (p567) in Ayder. If he's busy, Mehmet will be able to arrange another local guide.

Most pension owners will also happily help you organise a trek. There are also mountain guides in Yusufeli, Tekkale and Barhal, on the southern side of the range (see p579). Another option is to join a tour led by **Middle Earth Travel** (www.middleearthtravel.com; 1-week Kaçkars trek €460). Several treks are on offer.

OTHER ACTIVITIES

White-water rafting is possible in July and August on the rapids west of Çamlıhemşin. Ask at the hotels or at **Dağraft** (☎ 752 4070; www.dagraft.com.tr; per person TL40-70). You'll find them 9km from the coast on the Ayder to Çamlıhemşin road. Their 'Amateur Course' is a 9km Grade 1 to 2 scenic spin, but Dağraft's 'Professional Course' is an 18km Grade 3 to 4 journey all the way from Çamlıhemşin.

Rafting around Çamlıhemşin is smaller compared to the more exciting waters near Yusufeli (p578), but the Black Sea region has arguably the more impressive scenery.

Some **winter sports** such as cross-country skiing are also possible in the region, but as there are few people around outside the trekking season, this is best organised in advance. Contact Mehmet Demirci (above) for more information.

ÇAMLIHEMŞİN
☎ 0464 / pop 2400

At an altitude of 300m, 20km off the coastal road, Çamlıhemşin is definitely a climatic transition point. Mist and drizzle will flag

you've left the coastal zone, and once you start heading up the valleys towards Ayder, expect a stronger alpine influence in the climate, terrain and vegetation.

You'll pass several ancient **humpback bridges** across the Fırtına Çayı (Storm Stream) which were restored for the 75th anniversary of the Turkish Republic in 1998. There are a couple of camping spots and Dağraft's (left) rafting base between here and the coast.

Çamlıhemşin is a functional village with the only **ATM** in the Kaçkars. Stock up on provisions or refuel in cheap eateries. For information and trekking arrangements, see **Türkü Tourism** (☎ 651 7230; www.turkutour.com; İnönü Caddesi 47). Ask the guys at Türkü about joining a trek to their rustic Kotençur Mountain House (2300m).

Çamlıhemşin offers basic cafés as well as **Yeşilvadi** (☎ 651 7282; İnönü Caddesi; meals TL10-14), by the Ayder bridge. It serves excellent trout dinners and mezes in its conservatory. Situated 1km along the road from Çamlıhemşin to Ayder, **Dağdibinde** (meals TL4-10) has alfresco eating beside the graceful arch of a centuries-old stone bridge. It's a top spot for a riverside beer.

Just beyond Çamlıhemşin the road forks. Straight ahead (signposted 'Zil Kale & Çat') follows the river to Şenyuva, and left (signposted 'Ayder Kaplıcaları') heads uphill to Ayder (17km).

Accommodation-wise you're best to push on to Ayder, except for one hidden gem. **Ekodanitap** (☎ 651 7230; www.turkutour.com) is a series of four cabins concealed up a steep hill on the main road coming into Çamlıhemşin. With an organic garden and solar power, the cabins harness sustainability, but still incorporate modern features like fridges and solar showers. Meals are served in a shared pavilion overlooking a river valley. The cabins are used for week-long trekking and jeep safaris (TL960 per person) run by Türkü Tourism (above), but it's also worth phoning them to see if there's room for independent travellers.

There is no direct dolmuş from Trabzon – you'll need to go from Pazar or Ardeşşen.

ŞENYUVA
☎ 0464

Şenyuva is beautiful and atmospheric. Even getting there is special, negotiating verdant valleys crisscrossed with winch wires for hoisting goods up to the remote mountain houses.

Look for the hilltop mansions built in the early 20th century when locals returned flush with cash after working as chefs and bakers in pre-Revolutionary Russia. Pension owners can organise hikes in the surrounding area.

ourpick Otel Doğa (☎ 651 7455; www.hoteldogafirtina.com; half board per person TL45) is a friendly base about 4km from Çamlıhemşin. The owner İdris Duman speaks French and English, and is a passionate champion of his home region. After 25 years travelling the world as an engineer for France Telecom, he returned to build this rustic, but very comfortable, hotel on a gentle bend in the river. Most rooms have private bathrooms and balconies, and the home-cooked food is the ideal pick-me-up after a long day of walking. The hotel is popular so booking ahead is recommended. Look forward to İdris' conversational skills honed during a life well lived. During summer, dolmuşes pass by the front door heading for the villages in the Kaçkars' high meadows.

Around 2km further, in Şenyuva village, is leafy **Fırtına Pansiyon** (☎ 653 3111; pansiyon@firtinavadisi.com; half-board per person TL50; ☾ Apr–Sep), with two cute bungalows near the river and cheerful rooms in former school buildings. All accommodation has shared bathrooms.

A few hundred metres north is the graceful arch of the **Şenyuva Köprüsü** (Şenyuva Bridge,

1696). From here the road continues for 9km to the spectacularly situated ruins of **Zil Castle** (Zil Kale), a round stone tower on a stark rock base, surrounded by lush rhododendron forests. It's a superb walk, but tough-going for cars. Another 15km will lead you to **Çat** (1250m), a mountain hamlet used as a trekking base, where you'll find a shop, a couple of seasonal pensions and the start of the even rougher roads into the heart of the mountains.

Only one minibus a day runs between Şenyuva and Çamlıhemşin, so you may have to walk (6km) or take a taxi for about TL15 each way.

AYDER
☎ 0464

Ayder is the hub of tourism in the Kaçkars. This high-pasture village revels amidst a valley perched at 1300m, with snow-capped mountains above and waterfalls cascading to the river below. Earlier unregulated development saw ugly concrete buildings encroach on the glorious setting, but now charming alpine-chalet structures predominate, and new buildings must be in 'traditional style' (ie sheathed in wood).

Ayder's firmly on the agenda for Turkish tourists, and is now also becoming increasingly popular with walking groups from

---

MOUNTAIN MAN MEHMET

How long have you lived in the Kaçkar Mountains? I was born here and lived with my grandfather in a village 1800m up in the mountains. When I was older I went to university and then to İstanbul.

These mountains are very different from İstanbul. How did you like living in the big city? I soon realised that I had a more natural approach to life, and that I just had to come back to the Kaçkars. I came back in 1993 and was a trekking guide for five years. I then set up an eco-farm which was one the first in Turkey. In 1998 I set up Türkü Tourism (p565), and now the company's also moving into alternative tourism like our cabins at Ekodanitap (p565).

Tell more about Ekodanitap. It's got four cabins in a quiet spot near the village in Çamlıhemşin. There's solar power and an organic farm. When we're not here in Ayder during the trekking season, I stay there with my family. There are no people and I just love looking up at the solar system.

What's your favourite trek in the Kaçkar Mountains? My favourite is a week-long trek beginning in Çamlıhemşin and going up the Firtina Valley to Çat. It carries on to an altitude of 2650m, and then we descend slightly to spend three nights using the Kotençur Mountain House at 2300m as a base. Then we carry on back down to the hot springs at Ayder before returning to Çamlıhemşin.

Your son's very active. How long before he's also a trekking guide? He's only four years old, but he already comes with me sometimes. His name is Dağlar, which means 'mountain', so maybe he'll be ready next year.

Because he's so young, will trekkers get a good discount? (Laughter…)

Mehmet Demirci (46) is a trekking guide based in Ayder

HEMŞİN CULTURE

If you visit Ayder over a summer weekend you may get the chance to witness some of the last surviving Hemşin culture (see p49). In the meadows of the village, groups of Hemşin holidaymakers often gather to dance the *horon*, a cross between the conga and the hokey-cokey set to the distinctive whining skirl of the *tulum*, a type of goatskin bagpipe. Even if you don't run into one of these parties, you'll see women all around the mountains wearing splendid head-dresses, often incongruously matched with cardigans, long skirts and running shoes or woollen boots. In the second week of June many Hemşin émigrés return from overseas for the annual Çamlıhemşin Ayder Festival. Accommodation can be almost impossible to secure at this time.

Western countries, and Israel especially. As a result, Ayder's previous budget traveller ethos is creeping upmarket, eventuating in a better standard of accommodation but also slightly higher prices.

It's still really only busy during the trekking season (mid-May to mid-September) and at other times there may only be a few local families living here. But if you come in the second week of June for the annual **Çamlıhemşin Ayder Festival** (see above), or during weekends in July and August, Turkish tourists fill most accommodation by midafternoon.

Orientation & Information

About 4.5km below Ayder is the gate marking the entrance to the Kaçkar Dağları Milli Parkı (Kaçkar Mountains National Park), with an admission fee of TL8 per vehicle.

The nominal centre of the village has a few restaurants, a supermarket, an off-licence (liquor store), an internet café, the minibus office and bus stop, and several gift shops. Other accommodation, restaurants and souvenir shops are scattered for about 1km along the road uphill either side of the centre. There is nowhere to change money and the nearest ATM is in Çamlıhemşin.

Activities

Most people use Ayder as a base for **trekking** in the mountains, but even if you don't have time to do that it's still worth popping up

for an overnight stay to experience the glorious scenery. Wildlife enthusiasts should note that rare Caucasian black grouse, salamanders and brown bears all live in the national park, though it'd be a miracle to see them anywhere near the village.

Post-trek muscle relief can be had at the spotless **kaplıca** (hot springs; ☎ 657 2102; admission TL6, private cabin TL25; ☉ 8am-8pm), where the water reaches temperatures of 56°C. The springs are said to be good for ulcers, skin complaints, cuts and allergies.

Sleeping

Many of Ayder's pensions are set halfway up the hill next to the road, reached by narrow, slanting paths. Getting up to them can be tricky when the mist rolls in. Usually your bags will be dragged up the hill on nifty winch arrangements.

Zirve Ahşap Pansiyon (☎ 657 2162; s/d without bathroom TL20/40) One for the budget crowd, this hillside house is pretty rustic, but there's a kitchen for guests, it's friendly and English is spoken. Breakfast costs TL6.

Otel Çağlayan (☎ 657 2073; s/d without bathroom TL20/40) Wrapped in rustic wood, this welcoming place has been around for yonks and keeps up the old Ayder tradition of good-value budget accommodation while other places in the village creep upmarket. It's around 300m uphill on your right.

Vesile Otel (☎ 657 2110; koksacolak@hotmail.com; s/d TL40/80) Marble and pine (trust us, it works) combine with a job lot of colourful kilims at this rustic spot with a few modern touches like wi-fi. Some of the rooms are a bit small and awkwardly shaped, but the terrace restaurant is a tasty bonus.

Fora Pansiyon (☎ 657 2153; www.forapansiyon .com; half-board s/d without bathroom TL45/90) Türkü Tourism's original hillside pension provides a cosy sitting room, pine-clad bedrooms with shared bathrooms, balconies and a laundry. The Demirci family are very welcoming, and dinner on the view-laden terrace with the kids shouldn't be missed. Just don't blame us if you get homesick all of a sudden. Ask here about treks, activities and visits to Türkü Tourism's Ekodanitap cabins (p565) and Kotençur Mountain House.

Yeşil Vadi Otel (☎ 657 2050; www.ayderyesilvadi.com, in Turkish; s/d TL50/100) Clad in more pine than a Swedish sauna, this is a good central option by the main road with rustic timber rooms, heavy duvets and impeccable bathrooms. Many rooms boast valley views, and the restaurant out the front does a great *menemen* if you want something different for breakfast. The 'Green Valley' is also open year-round if you're planning on getting active during winter.

Kuşpuni Pansiyon (☎ 657 2052; www.kuspuni .com; s/d TL60/120) Another very appealing family-run chalet-pension, Kuşpuni revels in a stove-heated lounge with decent views and hearty meals, including a mean *muhlama*. In fact visitors rave about the food, often served on a pleasant terrace overlooking the valley. Adjacent is a pleasingly rustic *serander*.

Otel Ayder Haşimoğlu (☎ 657 2037; www.hasimoglu otel.com; s/d/tr TL65/130/195) Run by Ayder Turizm, which also operates the hot springs and the Ayder Sofrası restaurant up the hill, this flash pine-clad place is absolute riverside, and 100m downhill from the centre (follow the path by the town mosque). With facilities including a fitness centre and spa, you're losing the personal, family touch available at other smaller places around town, but these are Ayder's best digs.

Ayder Turizm also rents **villas** (half-board from TL200) next to the hot springs, sleeping at least four people.

Eating & Drinking

Many people go for the half-board option at their pensions, but there are other options.

Nazlı Çiçek (☎ 657 2130; mains TL4-8) Right in the centre of the village, this charming old house specialises in freshly caught trout, but also whips up a limited range of standards and Black Sea specialities such as *muhlama*.

Çise Restaurant (☎ 657 2171; mains TL4-8) Next door to the Nazlı Çiçek, it plagiarises its rival's menu shamelessly, but adds live music in place of traditional decor.

Dört Mevsim (mains TL5-10) With reach-and-touch-it waterfall views straight from an advertisement for mineral water, the 'Four Seasons' is your best bet for a cold beer. The food's pretty good too, and there's a jukebox packed with Turkish pop you've probably never heard of. Turn it up loud and you might attract the *horon* dancers (see boxed text, p567) that gather occasionally in the meadow across the road. The Dört Mevsim is around 400m uphill on your right from the centre of the village.

Getting There & Away

From mid-June to mid-September frequent dolmuşes run between Pazar on the coast to Ayder (TL6, one hour) via Ardeşsen and Çamlıhemşin. There are also daily direct services from Rize (TL10). On summer Sundays the trickle of minibuses up to Ayder turns into a flood. Otherwise, passengers are mostly shoppers from the villages, so dolmuşes descend in the morning and return from Pazar in the early afternoon.

In season, morning dolmuşes also run from Ayder to other mountain villages, including Galer Düzü, Avusor, Yukarı Kavron and Caymakçur. Check with locals for exact schedules.

Even in the low season there are still four minibus services daily between Pazar and Çamlıhemşin. A taxi between Ayder and Çamlıhemşin costs around TL50.

Northeastern Anatolia

Two words: *saklı cennet* (secret paradise). These pretty much sum up northeastern Anatolia. Almost a void on the tourist radar due to its remoteness, this far-flung outpost is a red flag to those hungry for the unknown, and one of nature's most perfect playgrounds. You can pant up Turkey's highest summit (Mt Ararat) or ramble through the delightful Kaçkar Mountains in summer; swoosh down superb ski runs in Palandöken or Sarıkamış in winter; or whip down the rapids through spectacular canyons on the foaming Çoruh, one of the world's top 10 white-water runs. For such a tiny territory (by Turkish standards), the palette of landscapes is astonishing: precipitous gorges, unending steppes, refreshing *yaylalar* (highland pastures) and pine tree–clad mountains.

Travelling in northeastern Anatolia is like falling into a time warp. You'll find a bonanza of palaces, castles, mosques and churches dotted around the steppe, with not another traveller in sight. While the astonishing İshak Paşa Sarayı and the ruins of Ani are the stand-out highlights, for those with their own wheels there's nothing quite like the thrill of shifting gears on scenic byways and backways and stumbling across fairytale Georgian or Armenian monuments in splendid isolation, all testifying to Turkey's once flourishing ancient civilisations. Need to catch some urban vibes? Erzurum, with its portfolio of Seljuk buildings, and Kars, renowned for its Russian architecture (not to mention its delicious honey and cheese), will deliver. Best of all, the people are among the country's most hospitable. Shhh, that's just between you and us.

HIGHLIGHTS

- Cut the fresh powdery snow at the **Palandöken** (p575) or **Sarıkamış** ski resorts (p592) or test your mettle on a white-water run through the **Çoruh Gorge** (p578)

- Lose yourself in the former glories of **Ani** (p587), once a thriving Armenian capital

- Leap off the map into the **Karagöl Sahara National Park** (p583) and wander around its quaint villages and gorgeous alpine forests

- Measure how far your jaw drops in front of **İshak Paşa Palace** (p593) in Doğubayazıt or **Çifte Minareli Medre** (p571) in Erzurum

- Soak up the fabulous location and spectacular architecture of **Beşkilise** (p592), **Magazbert Fortress** (p591) and **Şeytan Kalesi** (p590)

- Let time pass you by in the oh-so-serene hamlets of **Barhal** (p580) and **Olgunlar** (p580)

- Hit the summit of the iconic **Mt Ararat** (p595), Turkey's highest mountain

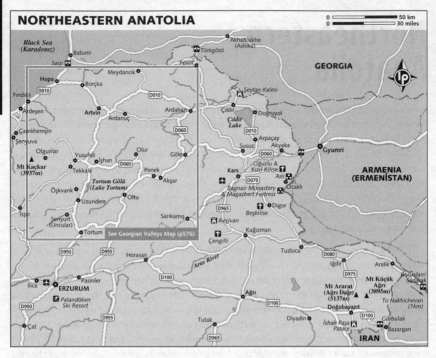

ERZURUM

☎ 0442 / pop 402,000 / elevation 1853m

Who said Erzurum was a cold and conservative city? Strolling down Cumhuriyet Caddesi, the main artery, on a sunny day and sampling a *tatlı* (dessert) in one of its hip pastry shops, you'll find Erzurum appealing and relaxed. Truth is, it is a contradictory place; it's Islamic to its core and with deep roots in tradition, but adapted to Western consumerism. Here you can shop till you drop and quaff an incendiary *rakı* (aniseed brandy) – all while the *müezzins* call the faithful to prayer. A gregarious student population adds a liberal buzz to the air.

Erzurum promotes itself as the architectural capital of eastern Anatolia. Its impressive array of Seljuk monuments makes this tag well deserved and you'll oohhh and aahh over the wonderful *medreses* (seminaries) and mosques that line the main drag. Then sweat it up to the citadel, where you can check out the entire city before you, with the steppe forming a heavenly backdrop.

Still too tame for you? Come in winter and enjoy the nearby high-octane Palandöken ski resort.

History

Being in a strategic position at the confluence of roads to Constantinople, Russia and Persia, Erzurum was conquered and lost by armies of Armenians, Persians, Romans, Byzantines, Arabs, Saltuk Turks, Seljuk Turks, Mongols and Russians. As for the Ottomans, it was Selim the Grim who conquered the city in 1515. It was captured by Russian troops in 1882 and again in 1916.

In July 1919 Atatürk came to Erzurum to attend the congress that provided the rallying cry for the Turkish independence struggle. The Erzurum Congress is most famous for determining the boundaries of what became known as the territories of the National Pact, the lands that became part of the Turkish Republic.

Orientation

Cumhuriyet Caddesi, which becomes Cemal Gürsel Caddesi along its western reaches, is Erzurum's most sizzling eat-drink-shop-bank street. These streets are divided by the Havuzbaşı traffic roundabout. Most of the city's blockbuster sights and hotels are in this vicinity.

Information

Most banks have branches with ATMs on or around Cumhuriyet Caddesi. There are also a few moneychangers, including **Cihan Döviz** (☎ 234 9488; Çaykara Caddesi; ☼ 8am-7pm Mon-Fri, 10am-5pm Sat & Sun). There are internet cafés everywhere. The **tourist office** (☎ 235 0925; Cemal Gürsel Caddesi; ☼ 8am-5pm Mon-Fri) has some brochures and, if you're lucky, a city map. The **Iranian consulate** (☎ 316 2285; fax 316 1182; Atatürk Bulvarı; ☼ 8.30am-noon & 2.30-4.30pm Mon-Thu & Sat) is about 2km south of the centre, towards Palandöken ski resort (also see boxed text, p680).

Sights & Activities

The single most definitive image of Erzurum is the magnificent **Çifte Minareli Medrese** (Twin Minaret Seminary; Cumhuriyet Caddesi), east of the centre of town. It dates from the 1200s when Erzurum was a wealthy Seljuk city before it suffered attack and devastation by the Mongols in 1242. The facade is an example of the way the Seljuks liked to try out variation even while aiming for symmetry: the panels on either side of the entrance are identical in size and position but different in motif. The panel to the right bears the Seljuk eagle; to the left the motif is unfinished.

The twin brick minarets are decorated with eye-catching small blue tiles. Don't look for the tops of the minarets – they are gone, having succumbed to the vagaries of Erzurum's violent history even before the Ottomans claimed the town.

The main courtyard has four large niches and a double colonnade on the eastern and western sides. At the far end of the courtyard is the grand, 12-sided, domed hall that served as the Hatuniye Türbesi, or Tomb of Huand Hatun, the founder of the *medrese*.

Equally attention-seeking is the **Ulu Cami** (Great Mosque; Cumhuriyet Caddesi), next to the Çifte Minareli. Unlike the elaborately decorated Çifte Minareli, the Ulu Cami, built in 1179 by the Saltuk Turkish emir of Erzurum, is restrained but elegant, with seven aisles running north to south and six running east to west, resulting in a forest of columns. You enter from the north along the central aisle. Above the third east–west aisle a striking stalactite dome opens to the heavens. At the southern end of the central aisle are a curious wooden dome and a pair of bull's-eye windows.

A short hop from the Ulu Cami, you'll notice the small Ottoman **Caferiye Camii** (Caferiye Mosque; Cumhuriyet Caddesi), constructed in 1645.

Walk south between the Çifte Minareli and the Ulu Cami until you come to a T-junction. Turn left then immediately right and walk a short block up the hill to the **Üç Kümbetler** (Three Tombs) in a fenced enclosure to the right. Note the near-conical roofs and the elaborately decorated side panels.

Back on Cumhuriyet Caddesi proceed further west until you reach the **Yakutiye Medrese** (Yakutiye Seminary; Cumhuriyet Caddesi), a Mongol theological seminary dating from 1310. The Mongol governors borrowed the basics of Seljuk architecture and developed their own variations, as is evident in the entrance to the *medrese*. Of the two original minarets, only the base of one and the lower part of the other have survived; the one sporting superb mosaic tile work wouldn't be out of place in Central Asia. The *medrese* now serves as Erzurum's **Turkish-Islamic Arts & Ethnography Museum** (Türk-İslam Eserleri ve Etnoğrafya Müzesi; admission TL3; ☼ 8am-noon & 1-5pm Tue & Thu-Sun). Inside, the striking central dome is lined with faceted stalactite work that catches light from the central opening to make a delightful pattern. It's surrounded by leafy gardens – the perfect place for a tea break.

Right next to the Yakutiye Medrese is the classical **Lala Mustafa Paşa Camii** (1562).

If you haven't run out of stamina, you can climb to the **kale** (citadel; admission TL3; ☼ 8am-5pm), perched on the hilltop to the north of the Çifte Minareli, and savour the views over the city and the steppe. It was erected by the emperor Theodosius around the 5th century.

Archaeology buffs will make a beeline for the **Erzurum Museum** (Erzurum Müzesi; Yenişehir Caddesi; admission TL3; ☼ 8am-5pm Tue-Sun), several long blocks southwest of the Yakutiye Seminary. It houses finds from nearby digs.

Sleeping

Despite a relative dearth of tourists, the accommodation scene in Erzurum is surprisingly varied.

BUDGET

Otel Çınar (☎ 213 2055; Ayazpaşa Caddesi; s without bathroom TL13, s/d TL20/30) If the Yeni Çınar Oteli is full, the adjoining Çınar is a tolerable runner-up. Some travellers might have a heart attack when they see the diminutive singles,

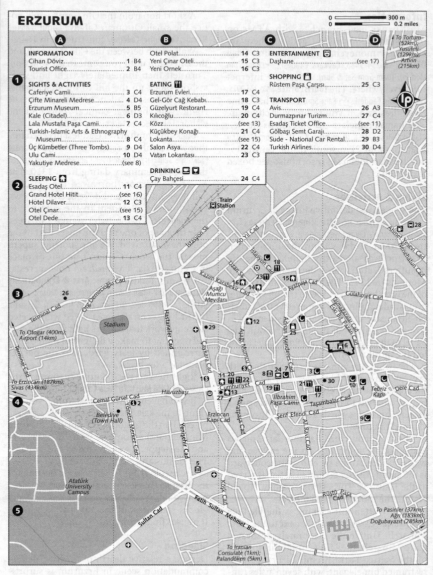

ERZURUM

0 _____ 300 m
0 _____ 0.2 miles

INFORMATION
Cihan Döviz...........................**1** B4
Tourist Office.........................**2** B4

SIGHTS & ACTIVITIES
Caferiye Camii........................**3** C4
Çifte Minareli Medrese.............**4** D4
Erzurum Museum....................**5** B5
Kale (Citadel).........................**6** D3
Lala Mustafa Paşa Camii...........**7** C4
Turkish-Islamic Arts & Ethnography
Museum.............................**8** C4
Üç Kümbetler (Three Tombs)....**9** D4
Ulu Cami.............................**10** D4
Yakutiye Medrese...............(see 8)

SLEEPING
Esadaş Otel..........................**11** C4
Grand Hotel Hitit...............(see 16)
Hotel Dilaver........................**12** C3
Otel Çınar........................(see 15)
Otel Dede...........................**13** C4

Otel Polat...........................**14** C3
Yeni Çınar Oteli...................**15** C3
Yeni Örnek..........................**16** C3

EATING
Erzurum Evleri......................**17** C4
Gel-Gör Cağ Kebabı...............**18** C3
Güzelyurt Restorant................**19** C4
Kılıcoğlu.............................**20** C4
Közz..............................(see 13)
Küçükbey Konağı...................**21** C4
Lokanta..........................(see 15)
Salon Asya...........................**22** C4
Vatan Lokantası.....................**23** C3

DRINKING
Çay Bahçesi..........................**24** C4

ENTERTAINMENT
Daşhane..........................(see 17)

SHOPPING
Rüstem Paşa Çarşısı................**25** C3

TRANSPORT
Avis..................................**26** A3
Durmazpınar Turizm................**27** C4
Esadaş Ticket Office..............(see 11)
Gölbaşı Semt Garajı................**28** D2
Sude - National Car Rental.......**29** B3
Turkish Airlines.....................**30** D4

but apart from that the Çınar will do the trick for unfussy backpackers, with rooms daubed a gaudy shade of green and well-scrubbed bathrooms. No breakfast is served.

Yeni Çınar Oteli (☎ 213 6690; Ayazpaşa Caddesi; s/d TL25/35) This place may not look like much, but has a lot of virtues for true budget-seekers. It's clean, safe, quiet and within walk-

ing distance of everything you might need. Avoid the rooms at the rear, which have obstructed views. Breakfast is not included. Hungry? There's a *lokanta* (eatery serving ready-made food) next door. It's in the market, a short bag-haul from İstasyon Caddesi. The only flaw is the deserted, dimly lit street at night.

Yeni Ornek (☎ 233 0053; Kazım Karakebir Caddesi; s/d TL30/40) Style? Er, no. Despite a canary-yellow facade, the Yeni Ornek is as no-frills as it gets but the rooms are well kept and the staff pleasing, making it a reliable lower-midrange option. After a long day's turf pounding, sink into the comfy leather armchairs in the lobby while marvelling at the ancient switchboard.

Otel Dede (☎ 233 1191; Cumhuriyet Caddesi; s/d TL30/50) If you want to be right on the main drag and not pay through the nose, this is the place. Room design is in a generic hotel style, with tiled floors, a pinkish colour scheme, unfortunate frumpy bedding and less-than-perky mattresses. Bathrooms could do with a touch up. Közz (see right) is just behind the reception.

Otel Polat (☎ 235 0363; fax 234 4598; Kazım Karabekir Caddesi; s/d TL35/60) Don't judge a book by its cover. The greyish facade is off-putting, but it's much more appealing inside, with prim bathrooms and fresh rooms, as well as a bright rooftop breakfast room boasting smashing views of the city. Some rooms are darker than others, so ask to see a few before committing.

MIDRANGE

Erzurum also has a couple of comfortable midrange options, but top-end ventures are as scarce as hen's teeth in the centre. If you want full-on luxury you'll need to stay at the Palandöken Ski Resort (p575), 5km southwest of Erzurum.

Grand Hotel Hitit (☎ 233 5001; fax 233 2350; Kazım Karabekir Caddesi; s/d TL40/70) A good lair in this price bracket, with rooms that seemingly get plenty of TLC. Convenient location and good views from the rooftop breakfast room.

our pick **Esadaş Otel** (☎ 233 5425; www.erzurumesadas.com.tr, in Turkish; Cumhuriyet Caddesi; s/d TL45/80) Pros: right on the main thoroughfare, close to everything, including our beloved Kılıçoğlu. Cons: right on the main thoroughfare, dangerously close to Kılıçoğlu, and a bit noisy (traffic ceases around 11pm). Very well maintained and efficiently run. Terrific breakfast, with five varieties of local cheese, sausages and yoghurt. Bargain down the prices a bit if it's slack.

Hotel Dilaver (☎ 235 0068; www.dilaverhotel.com.tr; Aşağı Mumcu Caddesi; s/d TL60/90; 🐾) A bit overpriced, but first let's talk location. It's within spitting distance of the main sights but in a tranquil street. Then there are the rooms. Here the mattresses are springy, the carpets

have no stains and the tiles in the bathrooms are unchipped. From the rooftop breakfast room, check out the entire city spread out below you.

Eating & Drinking

You'll find plenty of eateries sprinkled around Cumhuriyet Caddesi.

Çay Bahçesi (Cumhuriyet Caddesi) This lovely leaf-dappled tea garden, just off the Turkish-Islamic Arts & Ethnography Museum, is a godsend if you need a cool place to rest your weary feet.

Közz (☎ 235 1516; Cumhuriyet Caddesi; mains TL2) We'd say three things about this fast-food joint on the main street; it's enormously popular, the staff is efficient and the *tavuk* (chicken) sandwiches will keep you coming back for more.

Kılıçoğlu (☎ 235 3233; Cumhuriyet Caddesi; snacks & pastries from TL2) With 27 kinds of baklava and 23 ice-cream flavours, this slick pastry shop is the place to head in case of hypoglycaemia. The playful picture-book format menu will help you navigate between the treats on offer. How could you resist such poetic names as *fıstıklı kıvrım, beyaz saray, prenses* or *dilber dudağı*? Snacks are also available.

Salon Asya (☎ 234 9222; Cumhuriyet Caddesi; mains TL4-8) Buzzing and packed, come here for satisfying kebaps and heaving ready-made meals in rosy surrounds. The food is fresh and hygienically prepared.

Küçükbey Konağı (☎ 214 0381; Cumhuriyet Caddesi, Erzurum Düğün Salonu Karşısı; mains TL4-8) Ah, oh-so-mellow Küçükbey. Set in a rambling old mansion-turned-café, this welcoming oasis is popular with students of both sexes, here to enjoy the atmosphere, gossip, flirt and puff a nargileh (traditional water pipe for smoking). Food-wise, it features textbook meat dishes, *mantı* (Turkish-style ravioli) and snacks, but it's the atmosphere that most come to ingest. It's tucked away in a side street off the main drag.

Vatan Lokantası (☎ 234 8191; İstasyon Caddesi; mains TL5-8) This snappy joint cranks out above-average kebaps and döner, along with not-too-greasy *sulu yemekler* (ready-made meals), but no pide (Turkish-style pizza).

Gel-Gör Cağ Kebabı (☎ 213 3253; İstasyon Caddesi; mains TL5-8) This charismatic Erzurum eatery specialises in *cağ* kebap (mutton grilled on a horizontal spit) served with small plates of salad, onions and yoghurt. It's a concept that's

SERVICES FROM ERZURUM'S OTOGAR

Destination	Fare (TL)	Duration (hr)	Distance (km)	Frequency (per day)
Ankara	50	13	925	about 10
Diyarbakır	30	8	485	5
Doğubayazıt	20	4½	285	5
İstanbul	60	19	1275	7
Kars	15	3	205	frequent
Kayseri	40	10	628	several
Trabzon	20	6	325	several
Van	25	6½	410	about 3

been a cult since 1975, so dedicated carnivores can't go wrong here.

our pick Güzelyurt Restorant (☎ 234 5001; Cumhuriyet Caddesi; mains TL5-13) This iconic restaurant, in business since 1928, is so adorable because it feels so anachronistic, with shrouded windows, old-fashioned charm and thick carpets. It's also a great place to spill money on a great meal. The mezes are a headliner, with about 20 different specialities (from inoffensive eggplant to, ahem, brains), but the menu also features a smattering of mains, including 'Bof Straganof' (no typo), all handled with apt deftness and served by old-school, bow-tied waiters. It's licensed – yeah!

our pick Erzurum Evleri (☎ 212 8372; Cumhuriyet Caddesi, Yüzbaşı Sokak; mains TL7-12) Yes, two 'our pick' restaurants in this city. Push the door of the Erzurum Evleri and you'll immediately see why. It feels like half the paraphernalia from six centuries of the Ottoman Empire has ended up here, with an onslaught of kilims (pileless woven rugs), pictures, weapons, farming tools and other collectibles from floor to ceiling. Surrender to the languor of the private alcoves with cushions and low tables and treat yourself to a soup, a *börek* (filled pastry) or a *tandır* kebap (stew). The nearby Dashane (☎ 213 7080), which has the same management, features live music on Friday and Saturday evenings. If only it was licensed!

Shopping

Erzurum is known for the manufacture of jewellery and other items from *oltutaşı*, the local black amber.

Rüstem Paşa Çarşısı (Adnan Menderes Caddesi) Built between 1540 and 1550 by Süleyman the Magnificent's grand vizier, this two-storey covered *han* (Ottoman tavern), north of Cumhuriyet Caddesi, now serves as a centre for the manufacture and sale of items made from *oltutaşı*.

Getting There & Away

AIR

Durmazpınar Turizm (☎ 233 3690; Cumhuriyet Caddesi; ⌚ 8am-8pm) An agent for Sun Express and Onur Air. Sun Express has two weekly flights to Antalya and Bursa (from TL119), three weekly flights to İstanbul (from TL119) and four weekly flights to İzmir (from TL119). Onur Air has one daily flight to İstanbul (from TL112, two hours). Also sells tickets on behalf of Turkish Airlines.

Turkish Airlines (☎ 213 6717; www.thy.com; Cumhuriyet Caddesi; ⌚ 9am-6pm Mon-Fri, 9am-2pm Sat) One to two daily flights to İstanbul (from TL112, 1¾ hours) and a daily flight to Ankara (from TL59, 90 minutes).

BUS

The otogar (bus station), 2km from the centre along the airport road, handles most of Erzurum's intercity traffic.

If you're heading to Ankara or İstanbul, Esadaş buses have the best reputation. For Iran (if you already have your visa; see the boxed text on p680), take a bus to Doğubayazıt from where you can catch a minibus to the Iranian frontier.

Details of some daily services from Erzurum's otogar are listed in the table (above).

The Gölbaşı Semt Garajı, about 1km northeast of Adnan Menderes Caddesi through the back streets, handles minibuses to towns to the north and east of Erzurum, including Artvin, Hopa, Rize and Yusufeli. Minibuses to Yusufeli leave at 9am, 1.30pm and 4pm daily (TL15, three hours, 129km); minibuses to Artvin (TL20, four hours, 215km), Hopa and Rize leave at 7.30am, 11.30am, 2pm, 4.30pm and 6pm.

TRAIN

The train station is about 1km north of Cumhuriyet Caddesi. The *Doğu Ekspresi* leaves daily at noon for İstanbul via Sivas, Kayseri and Ankara (TL40); for Kars, it departs at 5.20pm (TL10). The *Erzurum Ekspresi* leaves for Ankara, via Sivas and Kayseri, daily at 1.30pm (TL35, 24 hours); for Kars, it departs at 11am (TL10, 4½ hours).

Getting Around

A taxi to/from the airport, about 15km from town, costs around TL30.

Minibuses and city buses pass the otogar and will take you into town for TL1; a taxi costs about TL7.

Car rental is available through **Avis** (☎ 233 8088; www.avis.com.tr; Terminal Caddesi, Mavi Site 1 Blok 5; ☽ 8am-7pm) and **Sude – National Car Rental** (☎ 234 3025; fax 234 3024; Milletbahçe Caddesi; ☽ 8am-7pm), off Çaykara Caddesi.

AROUND ERZURUM
Palandöken Ski Resort
☎ 0442

Did you know this? A mere 5km south of Erzurum, Palandöken is regarded as the best ski resort in the country, with 10 ski lifts, including one telecabin, 28km of ski runs on three levels (seven beginner runs, six intermediate and two advanced) and an excellent après-ski scene. At weekends from December to April, be prepared to jostle with other snowlovers for a spot on the slopes and a place in the ski-lift queues. Rental equipment is available at the hotels (about TL35 per day).

SLEEPING & EATING

With the exception of the Dedeman, the following places to stay are open all year. All hotels have their own restaurants, bars and discos. The prices quoted here are high-season winter rates (expect discounts of up to 30% in low season).

Palan Otel (☎ 317 0707; www.palanotel.com; s/d with half-board TL170/240; ✖ ▣ ✿) Reliable. That's code for 'utilitarian and unexciting'. This pretty much sums up the Palan, where the rooms are reliably clean, the service is reliably well disposed and amenities reliably comprehensive.

Polat Renaissance (☎ 232 0010; www.polatrenaissance.com; s/d with half-board TL220/300; ✖ ▣ ✿) Gloating over its five-star rating, the pyramid-shaped Polat is a very impressive option, gigantic in scale, with the feel of a mini-city, but rates zero on the charm meter.

Dedeman (☎ 316 2414; www.dedeman.com; s/d with half-board TL250/400; ✿) This Dedeman is older than the Ski Lodge but it's right at the foot of the ski runs, at 2450m.

ourpick Ski Lodge Dedeman (☎ 317 0500; www.dedeman.com; s/d with half-board TL350/450; ✖ ▣) A pleasing alternative to the pomp of the larger ventures in Palandöken, the smaller but more stylish Ski Lodge Dedeman boasts appealing rooms that are tastefully decked out with king-size beds and chocolate-brown and white furnishings, as well as a few historic Erzurum sketches hung on the walls. Don't scream at the posted rates – they're negotiable.

Another massive hotel, the Astrila Kayak Oteli, was under construction at the time of writing.

GETTING THERE & AWAY

From central Erzurum, a taxi will set you back about TL15.

GEORGIAN VALLEYS

Don't miss the mountainous country north of Erzurum towards Artvin because, in addition to being spectacular, it's also one of northeastern Anatolia's most culturally peculiar areas. It was once part of the medieval kingdom of Georgia, and has numerous churches and castles to show for it. The trouble you take to see this region will be amply rewarded. The mountain scenery is awesome, and the churches, which mix characteristics of Armenian, Seljuk and Persian styles, are eyecatching and seldom visited. If you happen to be passing in mid-June, the orchards of cherries and apricots should be in bloom – a special treat.

For a vivid account of this little corner of Turkey, look no further than Tony Anderson's *Bread and Ashes: A Walk Through the Mountains of Georgia*, which includes a chapter about the Georgian Valleys.

HISTORY

The Persians and Byzantines squabbled over this region from the 4th century AD. Then it was conquered by the Arabs in the 7th century, recovered by the Byzantines, lost again and so on. It was part of the medieval Georgian kingdom in the 10th century, governed by the Bagratids, from the same lineage as the Armenian Bagratids ruling over the Kars region. A mixture of isolation brought about by the rugged terrain, piety and the support of Byzantium all fostered a flourishing culture that produced the churches you see today.

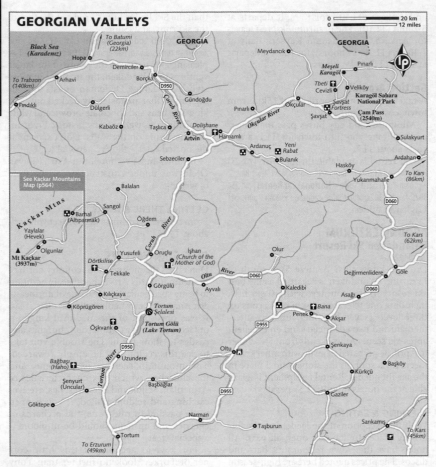

GEORGIAN VALLEYS

However, it was the ambitious King Bagrat III who looked outside the sheltered valleys and unified Georgia's warring kingdoms in 1008. Bagrat III shifted the focus of the newly formed kingdom by moving the capital from Tbilisi, nominally under the control of the Arabs, to Kutaisi, and by gradually disengaging from the southwest valleys that had been under the sway of the Byzantines since 1001.

The southwest provinces had been coexisting relatively harmoniously between the Byzantines and Georgians, but the arrival of the Seljuk Turks in 1064 dashed hopes of real stability. King David IV ('The Builder'; 1089–1125) defeated the Seljuks in 1122, and took up where King Bagrat III had left off by

reunifying Georgia with Tbilisi and the southwest provinces. So began the 'golden age' for Georgian culture, which reached its peak during the rule of Queen Tamar (1184–1213).

Alas, stability was relatively short-lived. With the arrival of the Mongol conqueror Tamerlane in 1386, the kingdom was dealt its most savage blow by the Ottoman capture of Constantinople in 1453 and the ending of the protection the Georgians had enjoyed under quasi-Byzantine rule. The kingdom went into decline, the Ottomans annexed the Georgian Valleys and, later, imperial Russia took care of the rest.

Today many locals have Georgian heritage, but most converted to Islam or left after the troubles in the early 20th century.

GETTING THERE & AWAY

The small mountain villages in the valleys are a delight to explore, but public transport to and from most of them consists of one minibus that heads between Erzurum and Artvin early in the morning, returning in the afternoon. Buses run between Erzurum and Yusufeli, though these allow little opportunity for exploration. It's best to hire a car in Erzurum or a taxi in Yusufeli (about TL250 for a day).

The following itinerary starts from Yusufeli.

İşhan

From Yusufeli, drive to the petrol station along the Artvin–Erzurum road (9km) and go another 8km until you reach the junction with the D060. Take the road on the left marked for Olur and Ardahan. You'll reach İşhan after 6km. Turn left at a junction marked by a sign reading 'İşhan Kilisesi'. The upper village is spectacularly situated, 6km up a steep, paved road carved out of the mountainside.

Located past the modern white mosque, the wonderful **Church of the Mother of God** (admission TL2) was built in the 8th century and enlarged in the 11th. There are traces of blue frescoes in the near-conical dome (vanishing fast – 25 years ago whole walls were covered in them), and a superb arcade of horseshoe-shaped arches in the apse, all with different capitals. The four pillars are impressive, as in Öşkvank (right). Unfortunately, a huge dividing wall was built in the nave – half of this church functioned as a mosque until the replacement mosque was built in 1984. The most detailed of the many fine reliefs – above the portal of the small chapel next door – ascribes the founding of the church to King Bagrat III. Also worth admiring are the inscriptions above the bricked-up portal of the main building and an elaborate fretwork around the windows. The drum also sports some fine blind arcades and elegantly carved colonnades.

Tortum Gölü & Tortum Şelalesi

Back at the junction with the D060, take Hwy 950 in the Erzurum direction (south). You'll reach the impressive **Tortum Şelalesi** (Tortum Waterfalls) after about 16km, signposted 700m off the main road. Continuing south, Hwy 950 skirts the western shore of **Tortum Gölü** (Lake Tortum), which was formed by a landslide about three centuries ago. You can break your journey at the **İskele Alabalık Tesisleri**

(☎ 0442-792 2022; fish dishes TL6), about 4km south of the waterfalls, and enjoy well-prepared fish dishes right by the lake. The setting is awesome and boats are available for rent (TL5).

Öşkvank

Continuing 8km south on Hwy 950, you'll reach the turn-off to Öşkvank, which is 7km off the highway. Keep on the main road winding up the valley to the village, where you can't miss the impressive **cathedral**, built in the late 10th century. It's the grandest of the Georgian cathedrals in this region with a three-aisled basilica (as in the earlier churches of Dörtkilise or Barhal) topped off by a dome. Keep an eye out for the blind arcades and the reliefs of the archangels.

The central nave has two walled-off aisles on either side. The southwest aisle, like the triple-arched narthex, is still in relatively good shape – notice the intricate carvings on the capitals, with elaborate geometric designs, typical of Georgian church decoration. There are other fine relief carvings, both on the massive capitals that supported the equally majestic dome (it has fallen in) and on the exterior walls. Look for the fine relief of the three wise men and Mary and Joseph, to the right (northeast) of the main entrance.

Much of the roof has fallen in, but there are still well-preserved fragments of frescoes; look in the half-dome on the inside of the main porched portal.

Bağbaşı (Haho)

About 15km south of the turn-off to Öşkvank is another turn-off on the right (west), over a humpbacked bridge, to the village called Haho by the Georgians. It's signposted 'Taş Camii, Meryemana Kilisesi'. Go 7km up the partly paved road through orchards and fields to the village. The **monastery complex** is about 800m further up the road. It dates from the late 10th century and is in good condition. Don't miss the conical-topped dome, with its multicoloured tiles, or the fine reliefs, including a stone eagle grasping a doe in its claws. The use of alternating light and dark stones adds to the elegance of the building.

The church is used as a mosque, so some restoration work has taken place here.

Oltu

Continue south along Hwy 950 until you reach the turn-off to Narman. Drive past

Narman. When the road meets the D955, turn left (north). Along the D955, the peaceful town of Oltu is huddled beneath a startling **kalesi** (citadel), painstakingly restored in 2002. Little is known about its history, but it is supposed to have been built by Urartus in 1000 BC. The castle was probably used by Genoese colonies and was of some importance during the Roman and Byzantine periods, before being occupied by the Seljuks and then by the Ottomans in the 16th century.

Bana & Penek

Continuing a further 18km north along the D955 brings you to the junction with the D060. Turn left and drive for about 4km and you'll see a **castle** on a mound. It's an eerie sight, in keeping with the surreal landscape, where craggy gorges alternate with reddish bluffs. About 400m further on you'll see a second crumbling **castle** on the left, built on a rocky outcrop and overlooking a river lined with poplars.

Backtrack to the junction with Highway 955. From the junction, turn left onto the D060 towards Kars. A further 14.2km will lead you past a bridge crossing the Penek Çayı (it's signposted). About 100m past the bridge, take the side track on the left. It goes uphill for 2km to the village of **Penek**. Continue through the village. The awesome Armenian **church of Bana** soon comes into view, standing on a hill with the mountains forming a fantastic backdrop – an unforgettable vision. Its most distinctive architectural feature is its rotunda shape. You can approach the church by following a dirt road that branches off to the left about 600m after leaving the village (don't brave it in wet weather with an ordinary car).

YUSUFELİ
☎ 0466 / pop 6400 / elevation 560m

Be sure to squeeze Yusufeli into your itinerary because work on the foundations of a nearby dam is scheduled to be carried out in the forthcoming years and the whole valley will vanish underwater. Nobody knows exactly when it's going to happen, which makes matters even more painful. People will be relocated higher in the mountains, and Turkish officials have guaranteed that no church will be submerged. The good news is that before this happens there's a lot to do here if you're an adrenaline junkie. The swift Barhal Çayı (Barhal River) rushes noisily through Yusufeli on its way to the nearby Çoruh River, and the town is a popular base for white-water rafting and trekking groups from Europe, Israel, Turkey and America.

Yusufeli is also a good base for culture vultures. The churches at nearby Barhal and Dörtkilise are definitely worth the trip. Yusufeli is also a kicking-off point for the Georgian Valleys (p575).

Orientation & Information

A short stroll reveals everything Yusufeli has to offer: Halit Paşa Caddesi and İnönü Caddesi, joining to form the main street; the banks with ATMs; a couple of internet cafés; the post office behind the school in the eastern part of town; and the **tourist office** (☎ 811 4008; İnönü Caddesi; ☿ 8am-6pm Mon-Sat), near the otogar. In principle, it's staffed by English-speaking students.

Activities

WHITE-WATER RAFTING

The Çoruh River is one of the world's best rafting rivers, with superb rapids and brilliant playholes around Yusufeli and Barhal. The river offers a wide range of rafting options for all skill levels, from II to V depending on the stretches and the levels of water. Beginners will tackle more forgiving sections on the nearby Barhal River. Bobbing down the river you can also enjoy a taste of traditional eastern Anatolian village life and admire the tall craggy gorges. Rafting is best in May, June and July; early August the volume of water is usually insufficient.

Various local operators run day trips out of Yusufeli for about TL50 per person (minimum four people) for about 3½ hours of rafting; ask at Hotel Barhal, Otel Barcelona, Greenpiece Camping or at the tourist office. Be sure to choose an outfitter with bilingual guides. Other companies run longer trips with three nights' camping and four days' rafting culminating at Yusufeli Gorge. Prices start at around €1200 for one week, including food and camping. **Water by Nature** (☎ in the UK 0148-872 293; www .waterbynature.com), based in the UK, comes recommended. This company uses Cemil's Pension in Tekkale as a base. Another reputable outfit is **Alternatif Outdoor** (☎ 0252-417 2720; www.alternatifraft.com), which operates out of Marmaris.

TREKKING

From Yusufeli, a few guides can lead you on customised treks up into the Kaçkar Mountains; see p563. The tourist office, Otel Barcelona or Greenpiece Camping can help with organising such trips. Pension owners in Barhal (p580) and Olgunlar (p580) also arrange treks.

Sleeping

Unfortunately, Yusufeli doesn't have a lot of good accommodation, and it's no wonder – the dam project has blighted tourism development.

YUSUFELİ

Greenpiece Camping (☎ 811 3620; www.raftingyusuf eli.com, in Turkish; camping per person TL8, tree house TL30, s/d TL20/40; 🖳) Greenpiece boasts an excellent setting and has various types of accommodation. For budget travellers, the ultra-basic tree houses hiding in the leaves of an orchard can do the trick, or you can pitch your tent in the grassy grounds. The three rooms by the river are the best ones; the other rooms, in a building in the orchard, feel more cramped. There's a pleasant restaurant by the riverside (dinner is about TL12) and, yes, it's licensed. Add another TL7 for breakfast. Rafting and trekking trips can be organised here. Cross the bouncing suspension footbridge beside Hotel Barhal & Restaurant, and follow the signs to find this place about 700m from the bridge.

Hotel Barhal & Restaurant (☎ 811 3151; Enver Paşa Caddesi; s/d TL20/30) Scraping funds together for your sojourn in Yusufeli? Consider staying at this well-run cheapie conveniently located by the suspension bridge. The dark carpets are permanently stained from who knows what but the bathrooms get all the proper scrubbing. Some rooms open onto the river, and there's an on-site restaurant with a terrace overlooking the gushing river. The owners can organise various trips in the area, including trekking and rafting. Breakfast is extra.

our pick **Otel Barcelona** (☎ 811 2627; www.hotelbar celona.com.tr; Arikli Mahallesi; s/d TL80/120; 🏠 🖳) The pièce de résistance of accommodation options, this upmarket resort-style abode, under Turkish-Spanish (well, Catalan) management, flaunts excellent amenities, bright rooms with scrupulously clean bathrooms, pleasing colourful tones and an attached quality restaurant. Post-rafting you can bask lizard-like by

the big pool – utter bliss. The owners are very well clued up and can organise various trips in the area, including 4WD tours, as well as hiking and rafting trips. Oh, and staff speak good English. Warmly recommended.

BETWEEN YUSUFELİ & BARHAL

The following ventures are on the road to Barhal, right by the Barhal River, and easily accessible by minibus from Yusufeli (TL4).

Hotel River (☎ 824 4345; Bostancı; s/d with half-board TL60/95; 🖳) This family-run pension is about 12km from Yusufeli. Rooms are neat and cosy, with pine cladding, TV, well-sprung mattresses and private bathrooms, though prices are somewhat inflated. Meals are served on a breezy terrace, and the gushing river provides a soothing soundtrack. Rafting and trekking trips can be organised.

İhtiyaroğlu (☎ 824 4086; www.apartagara.com; Sarıgöl Yolu; camping per person TL8, s/d with half-board TL40/80) Almost a carbon copy of the Hotel River, with three chalet-like buildings overlooking the river. You can also pitch your tent in a grassy area. It's 1.5km further on from its competitor.

Eating

Most places to stay have attached restaurants, but there are a few independent restaurants worthy of note.

Çoruh Pide ve Lahmacun Salonu (☎ 811 2870; Ersis Caddesi; mains TL4-7) You wouldn't guess it from the humble surrounds, but this place does excellent Turkish and Arabic pizzas, served freshly baked from the oven.

Hacıoğlu Cağ Döner (☎ 811 3009; İnönü Caddesi; mains TL5-8) Close to the tourist office. Energy-boosting servings of meat (including *cağ* döner) and fish dishes, as well as *sulu yemekler*. Avoid the latter – too much gravy – and go for the fresh trout, best enjoyed on the terrace overlooking the river.

Arzet Lokantasi (☎ 811 2181; İnönü Caddesi; mains TL5-8) Arzet keeps things plain and simple: ordinary decor, neon lighting, brisk service and a good range of kebaps and other standard fare.

Getting There & Away

From Yusufeli there are at least three buses in the morning for Erzurum (TL15, three hours), a 9am service to Trabzon (TL35) and several minibuses to Artvin (TL13). For Kars, you'll have to take a taxi out to the petrol station (TL20) along the Artvin–Erzurum road and catch the bus from there, at about 1pm (TL15).

AROUND YUSUFELİ
Barhal (Altıparmak)
☎ 0466 / pop 1000 / elevation 1300m

In Barhal (officially called Altıparmak), about 27km northwest of Yusufeli, '*Hayat çok güzel*' ('It's a nice life'). Imagine a *köy* (village) nestled in a verdant valley, a rippling stream running through its heart, a lovely mountainscape and a handful of cosy pensions. It can't get more bucolic than that – you feel you've stumbled onto the set of *Little House on the Prairie*. Once you've had your fill of playing the roles of the Ingalls, look for the well-preserved, 10th-century **Georgian church** that stands besides Karahan Pension. You can also take the walk up to the small ruined **chapel** in a meadowed ridge above the town – it's worth the 45 minutes' pant for the bird's-eye views over the town and the jagged, snow-capped peaks beyond. The (unsigned) walk starts over a plank footbridge near Karahan Pension.

Pension owners also arrange two- to four-day treks across the mountains to Çamlıhemşin with horses to carry your baggage. One horse, costing TL60, can porter for two trekkers. Add another TL80 per day for a guide (flat fee). Other costs are negotiable.

SLEEPING

Once you arrive in Barhal you won't want to leave, especially since the handful of pensions here are far more inviting than those in Yusufeli. No glitz or pomp, just friendly ambience and cosy rooms equipped with pine cladding. And the soothing soundtrack of the river.

Barhal Pansiyon (☎ 0535-264 6765; www.barhal pansiyon.com, in Turkish; half-board per person TL35-50) The first place you'll pass on the road into town. The seven rooms (with shared bathroom) in the main house are hanky-sized yet well tended, with pine cladding. For more privacy, it's worth shelling out for the newer rooms with private facilities (but no views to speak of) in a separate building. The copious dinner includes six *çeşit* (dishes).

Marsis Village House (☎ 826 2002; www.marsisotel .com; half-board per person TL35) A few steps further up, just back from the river. It feels like a cosy doll's house, with 16 rooms, an agreeable terrace and amiable staff. Three rooms come

with private bathrooms. If you're travelling solo, aim for rooms 106 and 107, which feature river views. The wholesome dinners come in for warm praise.

Karahan Pension (☎ 826 2071; half-board per person TL40) This pension is as cosy as a bird's nest and boasts an adorable setting on a hillside on the outskirts of the village. The main house is full of nooks and crannies and harbours 17 smallish rooms. Tip: angle for a room with a bathroom and a view over the valley. Food here is a definite plus; owner Mehmet Karahan does wonders with simple ingredients. And Barhal's Georgian church is almost on your doorstep. Amen.

GETTING THERE & AWAY

A couple of minibuses make the run from Yusufeli (TL10, two hours), usually at 2pm and 4pm or 5pm. If you have your own vehicle, note that only the first 18km (until Sarıgöl) are surfaced. From Sarıgöl to Barhal (9km), only 6km of road is surfaced. If it's dry, the winding, narrow road can be braved in an ordinary car, but it's wise to seek local advice before setting off.

Yaylalar (Hevek) & Olgunlar
☎ 0466 / pop 500

It's a darn tiring ride to get to **Yaylalar**, about 22km further from Barhal, but this is an ideal retreat to rejuvenate mind and body, with a glorious setting, jagged peaks, babbling brooks, traditional farmhouses and the purest air we've ever breathed in Turkey – not to mention the superb hikes that await you. Recharge the batteries, feast on organic food, explore the surrounding *yaylalar* (highland pastures) and you'll be happy with life. A hint: don't forget your Turkish phrasebook as nobody speaks a single word of English.

Yaylalar boasts an excellent place to stay, **Altunay Pension** (☎ 832 2001; www.kackar3937.com; half-board per person TL45, bungalow TL100), with a variety of sleeping options. You can bunk down either in the plain rooms with shared bathrooms in the first building or, if you seek more privacy and comfort, in one of the four adjoining cabins, which are called, with some exaggeration, bungalows (up to four persons). A second building resembling a big Swiss chalet features spotless rooms with bathrooms. Your friendly hosts, İsmail and Naim, also run a food shop and a bakery. İsmail is the minibus driver to Yusufeli and can drive you to Olgunlar.

RAFTING & TREKKING IN THE KAÇKARS

A rafting and trekking guide based in Yusufeli, Cumhur Bayrak can't gush enough superlatives about his playground.

'Here in Yusufeli we're lucky enough to have both rafting and hiking possibilities. People come from all over Europe and Israel to enjoy them. The rafting season begins in June. For beginners, it's best to come in July or August, because the level of water is lower and the rapids less challenging.

'We begin with a practice session and a briefing on a calm section of the river, usually on the Barhal River, before tackling more thrilling sections. There's always a guide on the boat, who gives the instructions to the team, and a minibus follows along the road and picks us up at the end of the ride.

'What makes rafting so special here is that the scenery is awesome, with gorges and castles, so you have history and adventure all in one trip! I also guide tourists in the Kaçkar Mountains, which is gaining in popularity among the trekking community. Here again, the scenery is terrific; in just a few days, you can enjoy alpine lakes, awesome summits, a plethora of wild flowers and, if you're lucky, you might come across ibex and bears. It's very photogenic, and it offers more diversity than, say, Mt Ararat.'

So will Yusufeli remain a rafting mecca once the dam is completed? 'If not, we'll find other places on the river'. Cumhur Bayrak is a lesson in optimism!

The village of **Olgunlar** is about 3km further up in the mountains. Here you'll find the **Denizgölü Pansion** (☎ 832 2105; half-board per person TL45), with salubrious rooms and private bathrooms, overlooking the river, and the 15-room **Kaçkar Pansion** (☎ 832 2047; www.kackar.net; half-board per person TL45), another haven of peace complete with pine cladding and similar in standard to the Denizgölü.

Both these villages can be used as bases for **hikes** (p563) over the Kaçkar Mountains. From Olgunlar, it takes about two to three days to reach Ayder, through the Çaymakçur Pass (approximately 3100m). The pension owners will be happy to help you organise a trek. They can provide mules, horses, a guide and camping equipment.

GETTING THERE & AWAY

Minibuses to Barhal usually travel a further 22km to the end of the line at Yaylalar (TL20 from Yusufeli). There are no services for Olgunlar, about 3km from Yaylalar.

Tekkale & Dörtkilise

☎ 0466 / pop 2000

Peaceful Tekkale lies 7km southwest of Yusufeli. It's an ideal jumping-off point for exploring **Dörtkilise** (Four Churches), another ruined 10th-century Georgian church and monastery lying about 6km further upstream, on a hillside (there's no sign). The building is domeless, with a gabled roof and very few

frescoes. It's similar to, but older and larger than, the one at Barhal. It's a perfect picturesque ruin, with weeds and vines springing from mossy stones.

On the way to Tekkale you'll pass the ruins of a **castle** almost hanging above the road.

The term 'cheap and cheerful' could have been written for **Cemil's Pension** (☎ 811 2908, 0536-988 5829; cemil_pansion@hotmail.com; Tekkale; half-board per person TL35). So could 'you get what you pay for'. This budget stalwart has lots of nooks and crannies as well as a convivial terrace right beside the river and a tank full of trout. Aim for a room in the new building, which won't cost you any more and is much, much friendlier on the eyes. Note that bathrooms are shared. Evening meals are available by arrangement. Cemil Albayrak, the chirpy owner, can arrange treks into the surrounding countryside, as well as rafting trips. He may also play *saz* (guitar) for his guests in the evening.

GETTING THERE & AWAY

To get to Tekkale take a minibus from the south side of the bridge (along Mustafa Kemal Paşa Caddesi) in Yusufeli towards Kılıçkaya or Köprügören; there are about three services per day (TL2). A taxi costs about TL20. From Tekkale you can hike to Dörtkilise (6km), bearing in mind that there is no sign for the church, which is high up amid the vegetation on the left-hand side of the road. If you have a car, the road is partly surfaced but pretty

---

GEORGIA, ANYONE?

Wanna make your friends jealous? Consider a nice little foray into neighbouring Georgia. It's all the more tempting now that visas (p680) are no longer necessary for most Western nations (but it's still wise to check beforehand). From Kars, you can take a minibus to Posof (TL15), then ask the driver to continue to the border, a further 16km ride (TL20). Cross the border (no hassles), then take a taxi to Akhaltsikhe, the nearest substantial town. From there, there are buses to Borjomi, where you can find accommodation and, most importantly, some good Georgian wines to sluice. The next morning, you could forge west to Batumi, get an eyeful of the Black Sea and take a minibus to the Turkish border at Sarpi. A more direct option consists of taking a minibus to Ardahan (TL10 from Kars), where you can hop on the daily bus proceeding from İstanbul and heading to Tbilisi, which leaves from Ardahan at around 10am (TL35). It stops in front of the office of the **Özlem Ardahan** (☎ 0478-211 3568) bus company, on the main drag, and also uses the Posof border crossing.

Despite a military confrontation with Russia in 2008, Georgia is a safe place to visit. For Ossetia and Abkhazia, check out the situation while in Georgia.

---

rough from Tekkale and shouldn't be braved if it's wet.

ARTVİN

☎ 0466 / pop 21,000 / elevation 600m

Artvin's main claim to fame is its spectacular mountain setting – it's precariously perched on a steep hill above the road linking Hopa (on the Black Sea coast) and Kars. Sadly, in the last few years this has turned into a spectacularly scarred setting, thanks to kilometres of dam and road works. Apart from a couple of ancient houses, the city itself does not have much to captivate you, but it's the best launching pad for exploring the mystifying *yaylalar*. And if you plan a visit in summer, try to make it coincide with the **Kafkasör Kültür ve Sanat Festivalı** (Caucasus Culture & Arts Festival; ☎ 212 3711), which takes place over the last weekend of June in the Kafkasör Yaylası, a pasture 7km southwest of Artvin, with *boğa güreşleri* (bloodless bull-wrestling matches) as the main attraction.

Up the main drag is a roundabout overlooked by the **tourist office** (☎ 212 3071; artvin@ ttmail.com; İnönü Caddesi; ☻ 8am-5pm Mon-Fri), where you can pick up a couple of brochures and a useful map of the area.

Most hotels are within a block of the *valiliği* (provincial government building). Many hotels double as brothels, but you should do fine if you stick to the **Otel Kaçkar** (☎ 212 9009; Hamam Sokak; s/d TL25/40), tucked away in a quiet lane off the main drag, or the more upmarket **Karahan Otel** (☎ 212 1800; fax 212 2420; İnönü Caddesi; s/d TL55/80; ☒), which is a good deal if you can ignore the grotty entrance on the main drag (the second entrance at the back is much more appealing).

For cheap fare, stroll along İnönü Caddesi and size up the small eateries and pastry shops.

The otogar lies further down the valley, about 500m from the town centre, off a hairpin bend. There's one morning bus a day to Kars (TL25, five hours, 270km) and regular buses to Trabzon (TL20, 4½ hours, 255km). For Erzurum there are several daily buses and minibuses (TL25, five hours, 215km). Some buses coming from Erzurum or Ardahan and heading on to Hopa don't go into the otogar but drop you at the roadside at the bottom of the hill.

There are also frequent minibuses to Hopa (TL15, 1½ hours, 70km), about two minibuses to Ardahan (TL20, 2½ hours, 115km), and at least six minibuses to Yusufeli (TL13, 2¼ hours, 75km). There are also regular services to Ardanuç (TL8, one hour, 30km) and to Şavşat (TL12, 1½ hours, 60km).

KARS

☎ 0474 / pop 78,500 / elevation 1768m

What a quirky city. 'Where am I?', is probably what you'll find yourself wondering on arrival. With its stately, pastel-coloured stone buildings dating from the Russian occupation and its well-organised grid plan, Kars looks like a slice of Russia teleported to northeastern Anatolia. And the mix of influences – Azeri, Turkmen, Kurdish, Turkish and Russian – adds to the feeling of surprise.

It won't be love at first sight (especially on a rainy day), but Kars is high on personality and atmosphere. No wonder it provided the setting for Orhan Pamuk's prize-winning novel *Kar (Snow)*.

Kars is usually regarded as a base for excursions to Ani (p587) and other hidden treasures in the surrounding steppe, but it would be a shame not to take time exploring its excellent sights and soaking up the eclectic vibe. And don't leave Kars without sampling the delicious local *bal* (honey) and *peynir* (cheese).

The border with nearby Armenia was still closed at the time of writing, but when it's reopened, it should foster a thriving business be-

tween the two countries – not to mention an exhilarating overland route to the Caucasus.

History

Dominated by a stark medieval fortress, Kars was once an Armenian stronghold, capital of the Armenian Bagratid kingdom (before Ani) and later a pawn in the imperial land-grabbing tussle played out by Turkey and Russia during the 19th century. The Russians captured Kars in 1878, installed a garrison, and held it until 1920 and the Turkish War of Independence when the republican forces retook it. Many of the sturdier stone

---

A MAGICAL TRIP IN THE BACKCOUNTRY

In summer, the area that extends to the northeast of Artvin is simply stunning. There's a tapestry of bucolic ambience, with lakes, rivers, mountains and forests straight out of a Brothers Grimm fairy tale, *yaylalar* (high-altitude pastures), traditional wooden houses and villages…with the added appeal of a distinctly Caucasian flavour, courtesy of the proximity of Georgia. Amid this setting reminiscent of *Heidi*, stand the ruins of several churches and castles as well as off-the-beaten track towns that are definitely worth a look. From west to east:

Church of Dolişhane About 17km east of Artvin, on the road to Kars and Ardanuç, a signposted turn-off ('Dolişhane Kilisesi 3km') leads to this beautiful 10th-century church, blessed with a few reliefs.

Georgian Monastery and Church of Porta This 10th-century church is accessed by a path off the Artvin–Şavşat road (look for the brown metal sign), about 10km before the turn-off to Meydancık.

Meydancık The quintessential *yaylalar* settlement, near the Georgian border, is accessed by a good tarred road that branches off the Artvin–Şavşat road.

Ardanuç Coming from Artvin, you'll first drive past the Ferhatlı castle (look up on your right, it's perched on a rocky outcrop) and, another 8.5km further east, the Gevernik castle, before entering Ardanuç set in a dramatic canyon guarded by an impregnable fortress.

Church of Yeni Rabat About 17km past Ardanuç, near the village of Bulanık, this church is a bit hard to reach because the road is in bad shape a few kilometres past Ardanuç, but was being widened and upgraded when we visited.

Şavşat This old Georgian town is worth a peek for its fairy-tale castle standing sentinel on the western outskirts of town.

Church of Tbeti Easily accessed from the Artvin–Şavşat road, on the way to Karagöl Sahara National Park, this 10th-century church is in ruins but in a beautiful setting. Look for the elaborately carved windows.

Karagöl Sahara National Park A national park blessed with spectacular mountain scenery and a lovely lake called Meşeli Karagöl.

Ardahan From Şavşat, a wonderfully scenic road leaves the lush, wooded valleys behind and snakes steeply around numerous twists and turns to the Çam Pass (2540m) before reaching Ardahan, the typical steppe town, with a citadel and an old bridge.

This territory lends itself perfectly to a DIY approach, preferably with your own wheels as public transport is unreliable. All you need is a map (the *Artvin İli Şehir Planı ve İl Haritası*, which is available at the tourist office in Artvin, and any good touring map of the country should suffice). Of course, some words in Turkish for directions always help.

Should you fall under the spell of this lovely area (no doubt you will!), you can bunk down at the **Laşet Tesisleri** (☎ 0535-734 6711; Şavşat Ardahan Karayolu; s/d TL35/50), an adorable little hotel nestled in lush vegetation on the Şavşat–Ardahan road, about 8km east of Şavşat. There's also the **Karagöl Pansiyon** (☎ 0466-531 2137; Meşeli Karagöl; r per person TL40), just by the shore of the Meşeli Lake. It's open from mid-June to August only.

KARS

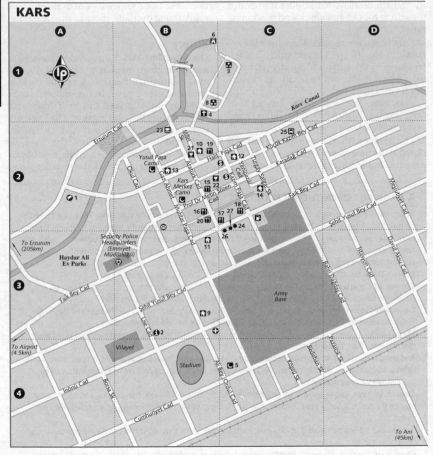

buildings along the main streets date back to the Russian occupation.

The locals are said to be descended from the Karsaks, a Turkic tribe that came from the Caucasus in the 2nd century BC and gave their name to the town.

Orientation & Information

Most banks (and ATMs), internet cafés, hotels and restaurants are in or close to Atatürk Caddesi, the main drag. Although the otogar is 2km southeast of the centre, off the Artvin–Ardahan road, almost everything else (except the train station and the museum) is within walking distance.

Limited tourist information is available at the **tourist office** (☎ 212 6817; Lise Caddesi; ⏰ 8am-

noon & 1-5pm Mon-Fri), west of the centre. To organise transport to Ani, a good bet is to contact **Celil Ersoğlu** (☎ 212 6543, 0532-226 3966; celilani@hotmail.com), who acts as a private guide and speaks good English. He'll probably meet you at your hotel's reception.

The **Azerbaijani consulate** (☎ 223 6475, 223 1361; fax 223 8741; Erzurum Caddesi; ⏰ 9.30am-12.30pm Mon-Fri) is northwest of the centre (also see boxed text, p680).

Sights & Activities

The prominent **Kars Castle** (Kars Kalesi; admission free; ⏰ 8am-5pm), north of the river in the older part of the city, is worth the knee-jarring climb, if only for the smashing views over the town and the steppe in fine weather. Records show

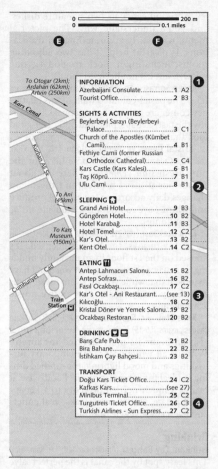

that Saltuk Turks built a fortress here in 1153. It was torn down by the Mongol conqueror, Tamerlane, in 1386 and rebuilt for the Ottoman sultan Murat III by his grand vizier Lala Mustafa Paşa in 1579. The entire complex was rebuilt yet again in 1855. The castle was the scene of bitter fighting during and after WWI. When the Russian armies withdrew in 1920, control of Kars was left in the hands of the Armenian forces, until the republican armies took the *kalesi*.

On the way to the castle, along the riverbanks huddle assorted crumbling reminders of Kars' ancient past, including the **Church of the Apostles** (Kümbet Camii). Built between 932 and 937 for the Bagratid King Abas, it was repaired extensively and turned into a mosque

in 1579 when the Ottomans rebuilt much of the city; the Russians added the porches in the 19th century. The 12 relief carvings on the drum are of the apostles. Near the church you'll see the ruins of the **Ulu Cami** and the **Beylerbeyi Sarayı** (Beylerbeyi Palace) nestling beneath the castle.

One of the more attractive – and intact – structures in the area is the 15th-century **Taş Köprü** (Stone Bridge), ruined by an earthquake and rebuilt in 1725.

Kars' beguiling résumé also features clusters of Russian belle époque mansions and other buildings sprinkled around the city centre, including the **Fethiye Camii**, a converted 19th-century Russian Orthodox church. It's easy to take a self-guided walking tour with the booklet *Kars*, available from most hotels.

The **Kars Museum** (Kars Müzesi; Cumhuriyet Caddesi; admission TL3; 8am-5pm Tue-Sun), on the eastern fringes of the town, has exhibits from the Old Bronze Age, the Urartian, Roman and Greek periods, and the Seljuk and Ottoman times. Photographs show excavations at Ani and the ruins of some of the Armenian churches in Kars province.

Sleeping

Kent Otel (223 1929; Hapan Mevkii; s/d TL15/30) Rooms are what you'd expect: the beds are kind of lumpy, decor is plain, the facilities are a little outdated and the shared bathrooms have seen their fair share of bodies and odours. But it's well taken care of and secure, and the great central location and economical rates keep it popular with travellers who have one eye on the bank balance. Breakfast is not included but the affable owner will point you to a *kahvaltı salonu* (breakfast restaurant) nearby.

Güngören Hotel (212 5630; fax 223 4821; Millet Sokak; s/d TL30/50) If you're seeking a billet in Kars with attentive staff, good-sized rooms with modern furniture and a handy location, this fine pile is your answer. The most colourful rooms are on the 1st and 2nd floors. Perks include a satisfying breakfast, a restaurant and a men-only hamam (TL15). It's popular with savings-minded European groups, and it's also a good choice for solo women travellers. One grumble: there's no lift.

Hotel Temel (223 1376; fax 223 1323; Yenipazar Caddesi; s/d TL30/45) Value for money, the Güngören's main competitor offers neat rooms with immaculate sheets and a soothing blue and yellow colour scheme. Unlike the Güngören, there's a lift. The management here gets mixed reviews.

Hotel Karabağ (☎ 212 9304; www.hotel-karabag .com; Faik Bey Caddesi; s/d TL85/130; 🗙) After a much-needed refurbishment, the Karabağ now suffers from excessive self-esteem and charges exorbitant rates for rooms that can't quite shake that just-a-motel feeling. Its trump card is its ace location, right on the main drag, and its wide array of facilities, including a restaurant. Bargaining wouldn't hurt.

our pick Kar's Otel (☎ 212 1616; www.karsotel.com; Halit Paşa Caddesi; s/d TL190/260; 🗙 🖳) Seeking a luxurious cocoon in Kars with homely qualities, efficient hosts and a big dollop of atmosphere? Look no further than this savvy boutique hotel, housed in an old Russian mansion. A cool exercise in interior loveliness, it breathes an air of repose, though some might find the white colour scheme a bit too clinical. It has just eight rooms, so you can expect personalised service. Added bonuses include free wi-fi, flat screen TVs and the Ani Restaurant (right). Well worth the splurge.

A new hotel, the Grand Ani Hotel (Ali Bey Caddesi), was under construction when we visited and should play in the same league as the Karabağ.

Eating

Kars is noted for its excellent honey. It's on sale in several shops along Kazım Paşa Caddesi, which also sell the local *kaşar peyniri* (a mild yellow cheese), *kuruyemiş* (dried fruits) and other sweet treats – the perfect ingredients for a picnic in the steppe.

Kılıçoğlu (☎ 212 6039; Faik Bey Caddesi; pastries & snacks from TL2) *Dondurma-* (ice cream) and baklava-holics rave about this slick venture smack dab in the centre, which presents its treats almost as beautifully as a jewellery store. We surrendered to a couple of *vezir parmağı*, filled with Antep pistachios, and to an excellent *kazandibi* (caramelised rice pudding).

Antep Lahmacun Salonu (☎ 223 0741; Atatürk Caddesi; mains TL2-4) Pide and *lahmacun* (Arabic pizza) aficionados head straight to this humble joint to gobble a flavoursome local-style pizza at paupers' prices.

our pick Ocakbaşı Restoran (☎ 212 0056; Atatürk Caddesi; mains TL5-8) This well-established restaurant is at the pinnacle of Kars' eating scene. One mouthful of its *ali nazık* (eggplant puree with yoghurt and meat) or its Anteplim pide (sesame bread stuffed with meat, cheese, pars-ley, nuts and eggs), its two signature dishes, and you'll understand why. The pictorial menu, with fairly accurate English translations, is of great help. It has two adjoining rooms, including a mock troglodytic one (wow!), but it's not licensed (boo!).

Antep Sofrası (☎ 212 9093; Atatürk Caddesi; mains TL5-8) The pastel-coloured walls of this relative newcomer are only part of its appeal. It's usually the tasty kebaps, pide and other feel-good food that keep the cash register ringing.

Kristal Döner ve Yemek Salonu (☎ 212 5100; Halit Paşa Caddesi; mains TL4-9) Come here for the ultra fresh *sulu yemekler*. There are about 10 various dishes on offer, and the menu changes daily according to seasonal produce and whim. Save room for the exquisite *sütlaç* (rice pudding).

Fasıl Ocakbaşı (☎ 212 1714; Faik Bey Caddesi; mains TL6-10) Joy of joys, the Fasıl is licensed. It's housed on the 1st floor in an unsightly building, at a major intersection, but you don't have to look at that while you tuck into meze, grills and ready-made meals. There's live music at weekends.

Kar's Otel – Ani Restaurant (☎ 212 1616; Halit Paşa Caddesi; mains TL6-15) Kars' most luxurious hotel also harbours its most civilised restaurant. With its all-white decor, contemporary furnishings and mood lighting, the rarefied dining is ideal for romantic meals. Food-wise, it brings a much-needed diversity to a kebap-jaded palate, with sirloin steaks, veal cutlets and even a few veggie options.

Drinking

İstihkam Çay Bahçesi (Atatürk Caddesi; ⏰ 8am-9pm) This leafy spot by the canal is the perfect salve after trudging up to the castle. Sip a glass of tea in the shade.

Barış Cafe Pub (☎ 212 8281; Atatürk Caddesi) Housed in a historic mansion, this atmosphere-laden café-bar-disco-restaurant has a happening buzz and is a magnet for students of both sexes who come here to gossip, puff a nargileh, dance and listen to live bands (three times a week). If hunger beckons, snacks are available. The disco in the basement is something to behold – headscarved women tear it up on the dance floor!

Bira Bahane (☎ 212 5389; Küçük Kazım Bey Caddesi) Amazing how first impressions can be deceptive. Seen from the outside, you wouldn't guess that this recent venture boasts a rather atmospheric setting (think sturdy furniture

SERVICES FROM KARS' OTOGAR

Destination	Fare (TL)	Duration (hr)	Distance (km) (per day)	Frequency
Ankara	50	16	1100	a few
Ardahan	10	1	80	frequent minibuses
Artvin	25	6	270	1 in the morning
Erzurum	15	3	205	frequent minibuses
Iğdır	15	3	132	several
Posof	15	2	142	2 in the morning
Trabzon	40	9-10	525 Erzurum or Artvin	1 direct, or change at
Van	30	6	370	1 in the morning

and fake brick walls) and a well-stocked bar. Homesick? A cold Foster's (yeah, mate) will keep your spirits high. On the ground floor, you can sample excellent grills served on huge *mangals* (barbecues). Good mezes too.

Getting There & Around

AIR

A *servis* (TL3) runs from the agencies to the airport, 6km from town.

Turkish Airlines – Sun Express (☎ 212 4747; Faik Bey Caddesi; ❂ 8am-8pm) One daily flight to/from Ankara (from TL114, 1¾ hours) and to/from İstanbul (from TL114, two hours). Also an agent for Sun Express.

Sun Express (www.sunexpress.com.tr) Has two weekly flights to İzmir (from TL144).

BUS

Kars' otogar, for long-distance services, is 2km southeast of the centre, although *servises* ferry people to/from the town centre. The major local bus companies, **Doğu Kars** (Faik Bey Caddesi) and **Kafkas Kars** (Faik Bey Caddesi), have a ticket office in the centre. **Turgutreis** (cnr Faik Bey & Atatürk Caddesis), a few doors away from Doğu Kars, has a daily bus to Van. The table (above) lists some useful daily services.

Minibuses to local towns (including Iğdır, Erzurum, Sarıkamış, Ardahan and Posof) leave from the **minibus terminal** (Küçük Kazım Bey Caddesi). If you're heading for Doğubayazıt be warned that there are no direct services. The usual way to get there is to take a minibus to Iğdır, then another to Doğubayazıt. For Georgia (see p582), take a minibus to Posof or take the first minibus to Ardahan at 8am to hop on the bus to Tbilisi at around 10am. Should the border with Armenia eventually reopen to travellers, you'll need to get a minibus to Akyaka. For Yusufeli, take a

bus to Artvin and ask to be dropped at the nearest junction (about 10km to Yusufeli) along the Artvin–Erzurum road, from where you'll have to hitch a ride to Yusufeli. For more information on the dangers of hitching see p689.

For details of transport to Ani, see p590.

CAR

Steer clear of the car-selling companies in the centre – they claim they can rent cars but we're told that they don't provide proper insurance.

TRAIN

The *Doğu Ekspresi* leaves for İstanbul (TL40), via Erzurum, Kayseri and Ankara, at 7.10am daily. The *Erzurum Ekspresi* (TL35) leaves for Ankara, via Erzurum and Kayseri, at 9am daily. It's worth considering these trains for the relatively short hop to Erzurum (TL10, about four hours).

ANI

The ruins of Ani, 45km east of Kars, are an absolute must-see, even if you're not an architecture buff. Set amid spectacular scenery, the site exudes an eerie ambience that is unique and unforgettable.

Once the stately Armenian capital, Ani is now little more than ruins dotting a windswept plateau overlooking the Turkish–Armenian border. Come here to ponder what went before: the thriving kingdom; the solemn ceremony of the Armenian liturgy; and the travellers, merchants and nobles bustling about their business in this Silk Rd entrepot. There's a mystique here that transcends its abandonment and leaves you with a mix of wonderment and melancholy at Ani's fate.

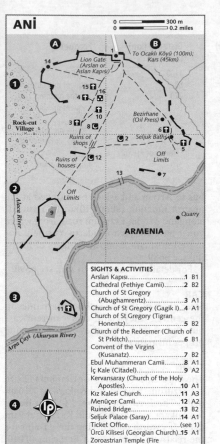

ANİ

Given the proximity of the border, the area is still under military control, but it's hassle-free and no permit is required.

History

On an important east–west trade route and well served by its natural defences, Ani was selected by the Bagratid king Ashot III (r 952–77) as the site of his new capital in 961, when he moved here from Kars. His successors Smbat II (r 977–89) and Gagik I (r 990–1020) presided over Ani's continued prosperity, but after Gagik, internecine feuds and Byzantine encroachment weakened the Armenian state.

The Byzantines took over the city in 1045, then in 1064 came the Great Seljuks from

Persia, then the Kingdom of Georgia and, for a time, local Kurdish emirs. The struggle for the city went on until the Mongols arrived in 1239 and cleared everybody else out. The nomadic Mongols had no use for city life, so they cared little when the great earthquake of 1319 toppled much of Ani. The depredations of Tamerlane soon afterwards were the last blow: trade routes shifted, Ani lost what revenues it had managed to retain and the city died. The earthquake-damaged hulks of its great buildings have been slowly crumbling away ever since.

Information

Not all the site is open to visitors; some parts are still off-limits. Allow at least 2½ hours at the site, and preferably three or four.

There are no facilities at the site.

Sights

Enter the **ruins of Ani** (admission TL5; 8.30am-5pm) through the sturdy **Arslan Kapısı** (also called Aslan Kapısı), a gate that was supposedly named after Alp Arslan, the Seljuk sultan who conquered Ani in 1064, but probably also suggested by the *aslan* (lion) in relief on the inner wall.

Your first view of Ani is stunning: wrecks of great stone buildings adrift on a sea of undulating grass, landmarks in a ghost city that was once home to nearly 100,000 people, rivalling Constantinople in power and glory.

Follow the path to the left and tour the churches in clockwise order.

CHURCH OF THE REDEEMER

Just past the remains of an **oil press**, the Church of the Redeemer (Church of St Prkitch) soon comes into view. It's a startling vision – only half of the ruined structure remains, the other half having been destroyed by lightning in 1957. This church dates from 1034–36 and was supposedly built to house a portion of the True Cross brought here from Constantinople; Armenian inscriptions on the facade relay the history. The facade also sports a superb *khatchkar* (cross stone) designed on an elaborate rectangular background, about 3m above ground.

The architecture is typical of the circular-planned, multi-apsed Armenian churches built in this era. The round porthole window above the ornamental portal is one of the few windows the church could withstand.

CHURCH OF ST GREGORY (TIGRAN HONENTZ)

Beyond the Church of the Redeemer, down by the walls separating Ani from the gorge of the Arpa Çayı and easy to miss, is the Church of St Gregory the Illuminator (in Turkish, Resimli Kilise – Church with Pictures). Named after the apostle to the Armenians, it was built by a pious nobleman named Tigran Honentz in 1215, and although exposure and vandalism have done great damage to the interior, it is still in better condition than most other buildings here. Look for the long Armenian inscription carved on the exterior walls, as well as the colourful and lively frescoes depicting scenes from the Bible and Armenian church history. It also features well-preserved relief work, with floral, avian and sinuous geometric designs, as well as a small sundial.

CONVENT OF THE VIRGINS (KUSANATZ)

Dramatically perched on the edge of the Arpa Çayı gorge, the Convent of the Virgins is off-limits but is clearly visible from the Menüçer Camii (right). Its distinctive, serrated-domed chapel is enclosed by a defensive wall. Scant ruins of a **bridge** across the river lie to the west in an area that is also off-limits.

CATHEDRAL

Up on the plateau again, the cathedral, renamed the Fethiye Camii (Victory Mosque) by the Seljuk conquerors, is the largest and most impressive of the buildings. Ani cathedral was begun by King Smbat II in 987 and finished under Gagik I in 1010.

Ani was once the seat of the Armenian Orthodox Patriarchate; the three doorways served as separate entrances for the patriarch, the king and the people. As the grandest religious edifice in the city, it was transformed into a mosque whenever Muslims held Ani, but reverted to a church when the Christians took it back again. Unfortunately, the spacious dome, once supported by four massive columns, fell down centuries ago.

Seen from a distance, the building looks quite featureless, but a closer inspection reveals eye-catching decorative elements, including several porthole windows, slender windows surrounded by elegant fretwork, several triangular niches, inscriptions in Armenian near the main entrance and a blind arcade with slim columns running around the structure.

Walking towards the Menüçer Camii to the west, you'll go past an **excavated area**, supposed to be a former street lined with shops. Further north the ruins of a toppled minaret, which is supposed to have belonged to the **Ebul Muhammeran Camii**, have been exposed.

MENÜÇER CAMII

The rectangular building with the tall octagonal, truncated minaret, the Menüçer Camii is said to have been the first mosque built by the Seljuk Turks in Anatolia (1072). Six vaults remain, each of them different, as was the Seljuk style, but several others have fallen into ruin. This odd but interesting blend of Armenian and Seljuk design probably resulted from the Seljuks employing Armenian architects, engineers and stonemasons. The alternating red-and-black stonework is a distinctive feature. Look also for the polychrome stone inlays that adorn the ceilings. The structure next to the mosque may have been a Seljuk *medrese* or palace.

The minaret sports an inscription in Arabic, which is *bismillah* ('in the name of Allah'). Climbing up the minaret is forbidden – the spiral staircase is steep and narrow, and there's no parapet at the top. It's much safer to enjoy the view over the canyon, the Convent of the Virgins, the ruined bridge and the cathedral from the main gallery.

Nearby is a recently excavated area, which contains remains of **houses**, with ovens, a granary and bathrooms.

İÇ KALE

Across the rolling grass, southwest of the mosque, rises the monumental İç Kale (the Keep), which holds within its extensive ruins half a ruined church. Beyond İç Kale on a pinnacle of rock in a bend of the Arpa Çayı is the small church called the **Kız Kalesi** (Maiden's Castle). You'll have to look from a distance – both these sites are out of bounds.

CHURCH OF ST GREGORY (ABUGHAMRENTZ)

On the western side of the city, this rotunda-shaped church topped by a conical roof dates from the late 900s. It was built for the wealthy Pahlavuni family by the same architect of the Church of the Redeemer. On the 12-sided exterior you'll see a series of deep niches topped by scallop-shell carvings. Then look up to see the windows of the drum, framed by a double set of blind arcades.

From the church you can savour the view of a rock-cut village beyond the river escarpment, on the Armenian side.

KERVANSARAY (CHURCH OF THE HOLY APOSTLES)

The Church of the Holy Apostles (Arak Elots Kilisesi) dates from 1031, but after their conquest of the city in 1064 the Seljuks added a gateway with a fine dome and used the building as a caravanserai, hence its name.

Seen from a distance you could think it's in ruins, but in fact it's fairly well preserved. Taking a closer look, you'll notice decorative carvings, porthole windows, diagonally intersecting arches in the nave, and ceilings dynamically decorated with geometric patterns made of polychromatic stone inlays, as well as various Armenian inscriptions and a *khatchkar* carved on a rectangular background.

CHURCH OF ST GREGORY (GAGIK I)

Northwest from the Kervansaray, the gigantic Church of St Gregory was begun in 998 to plans by the same architect as Ani's cathedral. Its ambitious dome collapsed shortly after being finished, and the rest of the building is now also badly ruined. You can still see the outer walls and a jumble of columns.

ZOROASTRIAN TEMPLE (FIRE TEMPLE)

North of the Church of the Holy Apostles are the remains of a Zoroastrian temple, thought to have been built between the early 1st century and the first half of the 4th century AD – therefore the oldest structure in Ani. It might have been converted into a Christian chapel afterwards. The only remains consist of four circular columns, not exceeding 1.5m in height – it's not easy to spot them in the undulating steppe. They lie between the Church of the Holy Apostles and the Georgian Church – proceed about 100m due north from the Church of the Holy Apostles and you should come across the temple.

GEORGIAN CHURCH (ÜRCÜ KILISESI)

You can't miss the only surviving wall of the Georgian Church, north of the Zoroastrian temple, which was probably erected in the 11th century. It used to be a large building, but most of the south wall collapsed around 1840. Of the three arcades left, two sport bas-reliefs, one representing the Annunciation, the other the Visitation.

SELJUK PALACE (SARAY)

To the northwest of the Church of St Gregory (Gagik I) is a Seljuk palace built into the city's defensive walls and painstakingly over-restored so that it looks quite out of place.

Getting There & Away

Transport to Ani has always been a problem. Most people opt for the taxi minibuses to the site organised by Kars' tourist office or Celil Ersoğlu (see p584), for about TL30 per person, provided there's a minimum of six persons. If there are no other tourists around, you'll have to pay the full fare of TL100 return plus waiting time; the drive takes around 50 minutes. You can also hire a taxi (from TL70). Make sure that your driver understands that you want a minimum of 2½ hours and preferably three hours at the site.

NORTH OF KARS

Very few tourists even suspect **Çıldır Gölü**'s existence. Far less talismanic than Lake Van, this loch-like expanse of water about 60km north of Kars is worth the detour nonetheless, if only for the complete peace and quiet. It's also an important breeding ground for various species of birds, best observed at **Akçekale Island**. **Doğruyol**, the only significant town on the eastern shore, has an eye-catching hilltop church.

From the town of **Çıldır**, on the northern shore, continue 3.5km until you reach the village of Yıldırımtepe. From there, a path snakes into a gorge and leads up to **Şeytan Kalesi** (Devil's Castle). Standing sentinel on a rocky bluff over a bend of the river, it boasts a sensational setting that will make even the most panorama-weary traveller dewy-eyed.

You'll need your own transport to reach these places.

SOUTH OF KARS

While you're in Kars, you should definitely take a trip to the Kurdish village of **Çengilli**. It is home to a superb 13th-century **Georgian monastery**, which jabs the skyline. It's similar in many respects to the Armenian churches near Ani, but the views over the Aras mountains are unforgettable. Çengilli is about 20km off the D965-04 (the road that connects Kars with Kağızman). The road that leads up from the D965-04 to Çengilli is not tarred, and some sections are very steep – don't brave it in wet weather.

HIDDEN GEMS – ARMENIAN CHURCHES AROUND ANİ

So you loved Ani and want more? No problem, there are other impressive Armenian churches and castles in the vicinity. These sites usually boast awesome settings (the steppe, my friend, the steppe), and part of the pleasure lies in getting to them. To reach these sites, you'll have to rely on your own wheels or hire a taxi for the day (it shouldn't cost more than TL150). Although the area is still under military control, tourists won't be hassled. There are no tourist facilities, so stock up on food and water.

A word of warning: village sheepdogs can be seriously nasty; it's best to be accompanied by locals when arriving in a village. If it's wet, the gravel roads may be impassable without 4WD.

Oğuzlu Church

From Kars, take the road to Ani. In Subatan, about 27km from Kars, take the asphalted road marked for Başgedikler, 11km to the northeast. There's a right-angle intersection at the entrance to the village; bear left onto the gravel road for 3km and you'll arrive in Oğuzlu. The monumental 10th-century church rises up from the steppe and dominates the surrounding houses. Unfortunately, it's in a bad state of preservation. An earthquake in 1936 caused the dome and other structures to collapse.

Kızıl Kilise (Karmir Vank)

From Oğuzlu, a further 2km brings you to Hamzagerek. In Hamzagerek, ignore the turn-off marked for Akyaka and bear left when at a little fork just past the turn-off to Akyaka. As you come out of the village, you'll be overwhelmed by the eerie sight of the church standing on a small mound, in the distance. It's the sole towering element in an otherwise flat, treeless grassland. If you're lucky, you'll see Mt Ararat in the distance. Go 4km further and you'll be close to Yağkesen, with the church clearly visible on your right. It's the best-preserved structure in the area. Outstanding features include a conical roof, V-shaped niches on the exterior and slender windows, an inscription in Armenian above the portal and some handsome carvings. To approach the church, you'll have to enter the village; follow the road for another 1.5km and turn right at a junction (you can't miss the church as it's a landmark). Backtrack at the junction and bear right. About 3km from the junction, you'll cross Bayraktar (no sign). Around 3km from Bayraktar, you'll skirt Ayakgedik (no sign). It's another 1.5km to Başgedikler.

Bagnair Monastery

Back on the main road linking Kars with Ani, drive east until the village of Esenkent comes into view. About 600m from the sign marked 'Esenkent's Hoşgeldiniz', take the gravel road on the right. Drive 4.5km until you reach a first junction; continue straight ahead for about 1.5km and you'll arrive at a second intersection. Bear right at a sign marked 'Kozluca' and after 1.5km uphill you'll enter the Kurdish village of Kozluca, where you can admire two Armenian monuments. The larger church, thought to have been constructed in the 11th century, is badly damaged, whereas the minor one, 200m across a small ravine easily negotiated on foot, is still in good shape, with a nice, 12-sided dome-drum adorned with blind arcades. Both are used as cattle pens.

Magazbert Fortress

From Bagnair Monastery, return to the junction, 1.5km downhill. Turn right (south) and carry on a further 3km to another right-angle intersection. Bear left for 1.3km and you'll reach Üçölük village. Continue through the village and stop at the *jandarma* (police) barracks. From here you can see a Turkish flag flying about 1km to the south on a mound. Try to persuade the *jandarma* to escort you to this vantage point and you'll be rewarded by an achingly beautiful view over this pearl of an Armeno-Byzantine fortress standing atop a rock spur and overlooking a bend in the river. It's said to date from the early 11th century and was captured by the Ottomans in 1579. Unfortunately, at the time of writing you were not allowed to walk down into the valley and approach this superb fortress. Even from a distance, you can easily see a row of three semicircular bastions.

From Çengilli, backtrack to the main road and drive to the north (towards Kars), until you see a turn-off on the left for Ortaköy. This secondary road leads to the village of Keçivan, which boasts superb ruins of a castle, precariously perched on a ridge – another dazzling sight.

Still not enough for you? Make a beeline for Beşkilise (Five Churches), which must rank as one of Turkey's most dramatically situated religious buildings. This Armenian church is about 35km south of Kars, off the road to Digor and Iğdır, in the Digor River gorge. Access is hard to find; coming from Kars, it's about 4km before Digor and 600m before a dirt track leading to a white-pumice quarry, on the right. From the main road, you'll have to walk across pastures to find the entrance of the gorge, then follow the valley upstream staying on a vague path on the hillside, midway between the valley floor and clifftop above. After about 30 minutes, the church appears like a mirage, perched on a ledge overlooking the valley floor. There were initially five churches (hence the name) here. The one you see, dating from the 11th century, is the only survivor. Despite some names scratched into the walls, it's still in good shape, with an intact dome and elaborate Armenian inscriptions.

These sights are difficult to reach without your own transport. Your best bet is to rent a car in Erzurum, or to hire a taxi and a cooperative driver for a day in Kars. Celil Ersoğlu (see p584) in Kars can also drive you to these sights.

SARIKAMIŞ

Innsbruck? St-Moritz? No, Sarıkamış. Snow bunnies, take note: the town and ski resort of Sarıkamış, 55km southwest of Kars, has deep, dry powder combined with terrain that pleases both skier and snowboarder. There's also interesting cross-country options. How does it compare with Palandöken (p575)? We're told that the vibe is more down-to-earth and family-oriented, and the area much less windy. We also found the slopes more scenic, with vast expanses of Scotch pines that make for a magnificent background. The ski season generally lasts from December to April, but Sarıkamış can also be enjoyed in summer, with a good network of hiking trails.

The infrastructure is surprisingly state-of-the-art, with two computerised *telesiej* (chair lifts) and nine ski runs (three beginner runs, three intermediate and three advanced), at an altitude ranging from 2200m to 2634m. Rental equipment is available at the hotels (about TL25 per day).

The ski resort proper is 3km away from the town centre. The welcoming Çamkar Hotel (☎ 0474-413 6565; www.camkar.com; s/d with full board winter TL190/250, summer TL55/110; 🖳 🎿) and the massive Toprak Hotel (☎ 0474-413 411; www.sarika mistoprakhotels.com; s/d with full board in winter TL290/390, in summer TL150/190; 🖳 🎿) are just at the foot of the ski runs and offer excellent amenities, including a kids' club, sauna, bar, disco, shops and licensed restaurants. Prices include ski passes. A third establishment, the Ce-Mar, was under construction when we visited.

Regular minibuses ply the route between Kars and Sarıkamış (TL5, 45 minutes). From Sarıkamış, take a taxi to the resort (TL7).

KARS TO DOĞUBAYAZIT

To reach Doğubayazıt and Mt Ararat, head south from Kars via Digor, Tuzluca and Iğdır, a distance of 240km. From Tuzluca the road follows the Armenian frontier. The army patrols the area to prevent border violations and smuggling, and if you're on the road at night expect a couple of checkpoints.

You can break your journey in Iğdır, which has a good choice of accommodation, though most establishments double as brothels. Try the Grand Derya, on the main drag, not far from the minibus stop for Kars.

From Iğdır it's possible to take a bus east to the Azerbaijani enclave of Nakhichevan (TL15, 2½ hours, at least five daily buses), provided you have already obtained a visa (there's an Azerbaijani consulate in Kars). The bus leaves from near Otel Aşar, on the main drag. This enclave is cut off from the rest of Azerbaijan by Armenia, and you'll have to take one of the few daily flights to get to Baku.

Minibuses for Kars (TL15, three hours, about seven daily services) also leave from near Otel Aşar; cross the street and head to Impaş store. The last minibus departs at 5pm. If you come from Kars and want to go to Doğubayazıt, the minibus stop is a few minutes' walk from Otel Aşar, near a mosque (ask for directions).

DOĞUBAYAZIT

☎ 0472 / pop 36,000 / elevation 1950m

Gosh, what an awesome backdrop. On one side, the talismanic Mt Ararat (Ağrı Dağı,

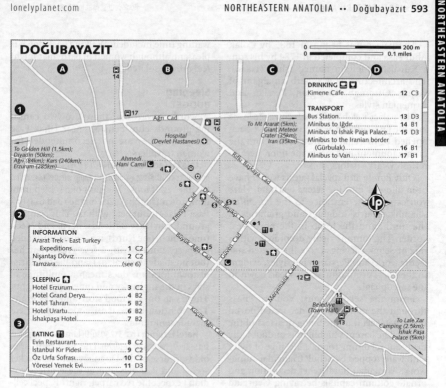

DOĞUBAYAZIT

0   200 m
0   0.1 miles

To Golden Hill (1.5km);
Diyadin (50km);
Ağrı (84km); Kars (240km);
Erzurum (285km)

Ağrı Cad

Hospital
(Devlet Hastanesi)

To Mt Ararat (5km);
Giant Meteor
Crater (35km);
Iran (35km)

Ahmedi
Hani Camii

Rıfkı Başkaya Cad

Dr İsmail Beşikçi Cad

Emniyet Cad

Büyük Ağrı Cad

Güven Cad

Meryemana Cad

Küçük Ağrı Cad

Belediye
(Town Hall)

To Lale Zar
Camping (2.5km);
İshak Paşa
Palace (5km)

DRINKING

Kimene Cafe.................... 12 C3

TRANSPORT

Bus Station.................... 13 D3
Minibus to Iğdır.................... 14 B1
Minibus to İshak Paşa Palace....... 15 D3
Minibus to the Iranian border
(Gürbulak).................... 16 B1
Minibus to Van.................... 17 B1

INFORMATION

Ararat Trek - East Turkey
Expeditions.................... 1 C2
Nişantaş Döviz.................... 2 C2
Tamzara.................... (see 6)

SLEEPING

Hotel Erzurum.................... 3 C2
Hotel Grand Derya.................... 4 B2
Hotel Tahran.................... 5 B2
Hotel Urartu.................... 6 B2
İshakpaşa Hotel.................... 7 B2

EATING

Evin Restaurant.................... 8 C2
İstanbul Kır Pidesi.................... 9 C2
Öz Urfa Sofrası.................... 10 C2
Yöresel Yemek Evi.................... 11 D3

5137m), Turkey's highest mountain, hovers majestically over the horizon. On the other side, İshak Paşa Palace, a breathtakingly beautiful fortress-palace-mosque complex deploys itself 6km southeast of town. Not too bad for such a charmless frontier town high on testosterone (read: lots of soldiers, policemen, moustached men and the occasional touts, but, alas, very few women on the streets). A lack in charm doesn't however mean a lack in character; this is a quintessentially Kurdish town that prides itself on its strong Kurdish heritage, which it celebrates each year during the **Kültür Sanat ve Turizm Festival** (Culture and Arts Festival), over the last weekend of June. This is a great occasion to immerse yourself in Kurdish culture, with singing, dancing and theatre.

Doğubayazıt is also the main kicking-off point for the overland trail through Iran (the border is a mere 35km away).

Orientation & Information

Doğubayazıt is small and easily negotiated on foot. For tourist information, various travel agencies, including **Ararat Trek – Eastern Turkey**

Expeditions (☎ 0535-616 0267; www.ararattrek.com; Dr İsmail Beşikçi Caddesi; ☼ 8am-8pm), run by knowledgeable Zafer Onay, and **Tamzara** (☎ 0544-555 3582; Emniyet Caddesi; ☼ 8am-8pm), in Hotel Urartu, will be able to help with your queries. Staff speak English.

Most banks have ATMs. There are also several money changers, including **Nişantaş Döviz** (Dr İsmail Beşikçi Caddesi; ☼ 7am-7pm Mon-Sat, 7am-noon Sun), which keeps longer hours and happily changes cash. It sometimes has Iranian rials.

There are several outlets on the main drag where you can check your emails.

Sights

İSHAK PAŞA PALACE & ESKI BEYAZIT

One of eastern Turkey's star attractions, the stalwart and (over)restored **İshak Paşa Palace** (İshak Paşa Sarayı; admission TL2; ☼ 8.30am-5.30pm Tue-Sun Apr-Oct, 8.30am-5pm Nov-Mar), 6km uphill southeast of town, is the epitome of the *Thousand and One Nights* castle. Part of its magic derives from its setting – it's perched on a small plateau abutting stark cliffs and overlooking a plain, framed by Mt Ararat.

The palace was begun in 1685 by Çolak Abdi Paşa and completed in 1784 by his son, a Kurdish chieftain named İshak (Isaac). The architecture is a superb amalgam of Seljuk, Ottoman, Georgian, Persian and Armenian styles.

The palace's elaborate main entrance leads into the **first courtyard**, which would have been opened to merchants and guests. Note the ornate fountain just inside the door, here to refresh weary visitors.

Only family and special guests would have been allowed into the **second courtyard**. Here you can see the entrance to the *haremlik*, selamlık, guards' lodgings and granaries to the south, and the tomb in the northwest corner. The tomb is richly decorated with a mix of Seljuk carvings (note the faceted stalactite work) and Persian relief styles, evident in the floral decorations. Steps lead down to the sarcophagi.

From the second court you can pass through the marvellously decorated portal of the **haremlik** into the living quarters of the palace. The harem's highlight is undoubtedly the beautiful dining room, a melange of styles with walls topped by Seljuk triangular stonework, Armenian floral-relief decoration and ornate column capitals betraying Georgian influence. It also contains a kitchen and a colonnaded dining hall.

You'll have to return to the second courtyard to enter the **selamlık** from the northern side. Entry is via the stately hall where guests would have been greeted before being entertained in the ceremonial hall-courtyard to the right. The selamlık also has a library and a lovely mosque, which has kept much of its original relief decoration (note the life tree) and ceiling frescoes.

Across the valley from the palace are the ruined foundations of **Eski Beyazıt** (Old Beyazıt), which was probably founded in Urartian times c 800 BC. Modern Doğubayazıt is a relative newcomer, the villagers having moved from the hills to the plain only in 1937. You can also spot a well-worn mosque, a tomb and the ruins of a fortress, which may date from Urartian times (13th to 7th centuries BC).

For that perfect picture, head to the teahouse on the hill above the palace.

Minibuses (TL1) rattle between the otogar and the palace, but there's no fixed schedule – they leave when they are full; otherwise a taxi driver will want about TL20 for a return trip,

waiting time included. Walking back down is pleasant, although women in particular might feel rather isolated.

Sleeping
BUDGET
A word of warning: there are two camping grounds-cum-pension, near İshak Paşa Palace but they are not recommended for women travellers.

Lale Zar Camping (☎ 0544-269 1960; lalezarcamping@ hotmail.com; İshakpaşa Yolu Üzeri; camp site per person incl tent TL8) Yes, it looks like a bit of a schlep from downtown Doğubayazıt (on the road to İshak Paşa Palace). But bear with us. This camping ground, run by two friends, Bertil and Mecit (one Dutch, one Kurd), is set in a well-tended property dotted with a few grassy patches (but no shade to speak of), and the outskirts-of-town location does mean a multitude of stars in the night sky and quiet, quiet nights. There's an on-site food store and restaurant. The ablution block is in good nick. Prices include tent rental.

Hotel Erzurum (☎ 312 5080; Dr İsmail Beşikçi Caddesi; s/d without bathroom TL10/20) The Erzurum is an old warhorse of the Doğubayazıt backpacker scene, and it shows. But at these prices you didn't expect the red carpet, right? Expect cell-like, threadbare rooms and saggy mattresses. It's conveniently located and the shared bathrooms won't have you squirming. No breakfast is served.

Hotel Tahran (☎ 312 0195; www.hoteltahran.com; Büyük Ağrı Caddesi 124; s/d TL20/36; 🖳) The Tahran's recipe for success has served it well over the years: keep your prices low, your standards high and employ attentive (in a good way) staff. Although on the small side, the rooms come equipped with crisp sheets and the views of the Ararat might provide some diversion. Same verdict for the private bathrooms: tiny but salubrious, with hygienic red floor tiles. The rooftop terrace, with an internet terminal (free access), is a good place to relive your Ararat expedition over a beer. Going to Iran? Bilal, the affable manager, is well clued up on the subject. A safe bet for solo women travellers, too. Breakfast is extra.

İshakpaşa Hotel (☎ 312 7036; fax 312 7644; Emniyet Caddesi; s/d TL25/45) Most rooms have been equipped with new mattresses and the old carpets have been dumped (we saw them piled on the pavement), which is a good sign. Some bathrooms are in better shape than others, though, so ask to see a few rooms before settling in.

Hotel Urartu (☎ 312 7295; fax 312 2450; Dr İsmail Beşikçi Caddesi; s/d TL30/60) Reliable and central, the Urartu is not a bad place to start your Ararat adventure but it has one problem: it's fully booked by *öğretmen* (teachers) and other civil servants during the school year. From mid-June to September, though, it welcomes travellers. No breakfast is served.

MIDRANGE
Hotel Grand Derya (☎ 312 7531; fax 312 7833; Dr İsmail Beşikçi Caddesi; s/d TL50/90) An ideal retreat after a few days' clambering in knee breeches and hiking boots. This excellent venue has benefited from an overhaul and now offers comfortable rooms with all mod cons. Top tip: for Ararat views, request a room ending with 01 or 12 and avoid the ones ending in 02 (they look onto the facade of the building next door). Bring earplugs or the call to prayer at 5am emanating from the nearby mosque will be etched forever on your mind.

Golden Hill (☎ 312 8717; fax 312 5865; Çevreyolu Üzeri; s/d TL70/90; 🖳) This recent venture on the road to Ağrı, about 2km from the centre, doesn't have a whit of soul or character but it boasts sparkling rooms decorated with a liberal use of cream and chocolate-brown. Some rooms have Ararat views. Other features include a sauna, hamam, bar and restaurant. It's popular with tour groups. Surprisingly, there's no air-con.

Eating & Drinking
İstanbul Kır Pidesi (☎ 312 8352; Dr İsmail Beşikçi Caddesi; pide TL1) No typo – this modest eatery serves up the best value pide this side of the Ararat. Choose between the cheese, potato or meat pide (and that's about it).

our pick Yöresel Yemek Evi (☎ 312 4026; Dr İsmail Beşikçi Caddesi; mains TL3-5) Hooray! Some feminine touches in this male-dominated city! This establishment is run by an association of Kurdish women whose husbands are imprisoned. They prepare lip-smacking *yöresel* (traditional) meals at bargain-basement prices. Servers speak minimal English but do their best to explain the contents of their stainless steel trays to the clueless bulging-eye. If you want to give your tastebuds something new to sing about, try the *keşke* (good-bye figure!). The döner kebap is also worth every bite.

Kimene Cafe (Dr İsmail Beşikçi Caddesi; snacks TL3-5) The closest thing the town has to a 'smart' café, with a chilled-out vibe. The Turkish coffee is jaw-clenchingly strong, and snacks are available. Though it's not licensed, it may serve beer to foreigners (but that's between you and us). There's live music in the evening.

Other options:

Öz Urfa Sofrası (☎ 312 2673; Dr İsmail Beşikçi Caddesi; mains TL5-8) The all-wood, barnlike surrounds boast a kind of ramshackle charm. Pide, grills and ready-made meals.

Evin Restaurant (☎ 312 6073; Dr İsmail Beşikçi Caddesi; mains TL5-8) This modest number was recommended to us by trekking guides who fill their belly here after completing a Mt Ararat expedition. It serves all the usual suspects.

Getting There & Away
Minibuses (TL4) to the Iranian border (Gürbulak) leave from near the junction of Ağrı and Rıfkı Başkaya Caddesis, just past the *petrol ofisi* (petrol station), approximately every hour. The last one departs around 5pm. See also the boxed text, p680.

There are no buses to Van, only minibuses that leave at *approximately* 7.30am, 9am, noon and 2pm daily (TL10, three hours, 185km). Getting to Kars, you'll have to catch a minibus to Iğdır (TL5, 45 minutes, 51km, every hour) and change there. From Iğdır to Kars should cost TL15.

Go to the main otogar for services to other long-distance destinations; often you'll have to travel via Erzurum (TL20, four hours, 285km).

AROUND DOĞUBAYAZIT
The travel agencies and most hotels in Doğubayazıt can help you organise a daily excursion to sights around the town. Half-day tours (about TL50 per person) take in İshak Paşa Palace, 'Noah's Ark' (an elongated oval shape in stone that is supposed to be Noah's boat), the over-rated 'Meteor Crater' (most probably a geological aberration) at the Iranian border and a village at the base of Mt Ararat. Full-day tours cover the same sites plus a visit to the Diyadin Hot Springs, 51km west of Doğubayazıt.

MT ARARAT (AĞRI DAĞI)
A highlight of any trip to eastern Turkey, the twin peaks of Mt Ararat have figured in legends since time began, most notably as the supposed resting place of Noah's Ark.

The left-hand peak, called Büyük Ağrı (Great Ararat), is 5137m high, while Küçük Ağrı (Little Ararat) rises to about 3895m.

Climbing Mt Ararat

For many years permission to climb Ararat was routinely refused because of security concerns, but this fantastic summit is now back on the trekking map, albeit with restrictions. A permit and a guide are mandatory. At the time of research you needed to apply at least 45 days in advance, your application had to be endorsed by a Turkish travel agency and you had to include a passport photocopy and a letter requesting permission and stating the dates you wish to climb. You can apply through any reputable agency in Turkey, including Ararat Trek – Eastern Turkey Expeditions and Tamzara (p593) in Doğubayazıt.

Several guides, hotel staff and touts in Doğubayazıt claim they can get the permit in a couple of days. *Don't* believe them. There's probably some bribery involved or, even worse, a scam, whereby they take your passport and let you think they'd obtained the permit but in reality would be taking you up Ararat unofficially. Follow the official procedure, even if you have to endure the slow-turning wheels of bureaucracy.

And now, the costs. Whatever agency you use, expect to cough up at least TL700 per person for the trek (three days, including guides, camping and food) from Doğubayazıt (a bit less if you're a group). Most reputable agencies recommend four-day treks in order to facilitate acclimatisation before tackling the summit.

Despite the extortionate fare, climbing Ararat is a fantastic experience. Expect stupendous views and stunning landscapes. The best months for climbing are July, August and September. You'll need to be comfortable with snow-climbing techniques using crampons past 4800m even in the height of summer.

The usual route is the southern one, starting from Eliköyü, an abandoned village in the foothills, at about 2500m. There's another route starting from the village of Çevirme, but it's seldom used. The first camp site is at 3200m, and the second one at 4200m.

You can also do daily treks around the mountain. Provided you stay under 2500m you won't have to go through so much official hoo-ha, but you still need permission from the local *jandarma* – it's best to go with a local agent. Expect to pay around TL300 per person.

Southeastern Anatolia

Turkey's wild child – southeastern Anatolia does feel different from the rest of the country, and that's part of its appeal. Apart from a few Arabic and Christian pockets, this huge chunk of territory is predominantly Kurdish.

What does it have on its menu? For starters, you can choose from a wealth of historical cities, such as Mardin, the region's trophy piece, perched on a hill dominating Mesopotamia; Şanlıurfa, swathed in historical mystique; the old city of Diyarbakır, ensnared in mighty basalt walls; Bitlis, brimming with Islamic architecture; and the honey-coloured town of Hasankeyf. For main course, adjust your camera setting to 'panoramic' and shoot life-enhancing images of enigmatic Nemrut Dağı, topped with colossal ancient statues; shimmering Lake Van; or the water-filled crater of the second Nemrut Dağı, near Tatvan. And for dessert there's an array of off-the-beaten track cachet destinations, including Bahçesaray, possibly Turkey's most secluded village; Darende, a hideaway near Malatya; and a string of lovely churches around Midyat. Best of all, you can savour these sights without any tourist hustle and bustle. Oh, and southeastern Anatolia has its fair share of earthly pleasures (hmmm, pistachio baklavas…).

With all the negative coverage this area gets in the media, you are probably worried about security. Rest easy: apart from a few spots that are off-limits to foreigners (mainly along the border with Iraq), southeastern Anatolia poses very few travel challenges and most of its attractions are perfectly accessible to independent travellers. Here what will linger longest in your memory is a warm-hearted *hoş geldiniz* (welcome). So clear the slate and plunge in.

HIGHLIGHTS

- ■ Feel elation while watching the sun set (or rise) from **Nemrut Dağı** (Mt Nemrut; p616), the 'thrones of gods'

- ■ Go heritage-hunting among the historic buildings of **Bitlis** (p641), **Hasankeyf** (p639) and **Mardin** (p633)

- ■ Swap stress for bliss in the perfect valley-village seclusion of **Darende** (see boxed text, p627) and **Savur** (p637)

- ■ Fall in love with the *Gipsy Girl* and feast on culinary delights in hedonistic **Gaziantep** (p598)

- ■ Nourish your soul in the great pilgrimage city of **Şanlıurfa** (Urfa; p607) and confess your sins in a Syriac church around **Midyat** (p638)

- ■ Scramble all over **Van's castle** (p646) and get a rush from its lively atmosphere before touring the shores of **Lake Van** (p642)

- ■ Catch the daily minibus to the mountain village of **Bahçesaray** (p650) – a white-knuckle ride you're unlikely to forget

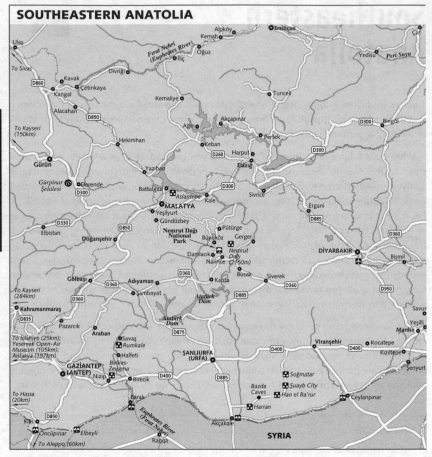

KAHRAMANMARAŞ (MARAŞ)
☎ 0344 / pop 543,900

If you're heading to this neck of the woods from Cappadocia or the Mediterranean coast, a stop in Kahramanmaraş is mandatory for all ice-cream lovers. This town produces an insanely good *dövme dondurma* (beaten ice cream), which is justly revered throughout Turkey. If you find that's not reason enough to stop here, there are a handful of cultural treasures that will keep you busy for at least a day, including the **Ulu Cami** (Atatürk Bulvarı), built in Syrian style in 1502, the hilltop **kale** (fortress) and the lively **bazaar**.

The **Hotel Belli** (☎ 223 4900; fax 214 8282; Trabzon Caddesi; s/d TL45/80; ✕) has been refurbished and features spruce rooms and prim bathrooms.

From the otogar (bus station) there are hourly minibuses to Gaziantep (TL12, two hours, 80km), while five daily buses ply the stunning route to Kayseri (TL20, 5½ hours, 291km).

GAZİANTEP (ANTEP)
☎ 0342 / pop 1,100,000

There's one Turkish word you should learn before visiting Gaziantep: *fıstık* (pistachio). This fast-paced and epicurean city is reckoned to harbour more than 180 pastry shops and to produce the best pistachio baklavas you can gobble down in Turkey, if not the world.

Antep is a greatly underrated city that proclaims a modern, laissez-faire attitude while thumbing its nose at Urfa's piety. One of the

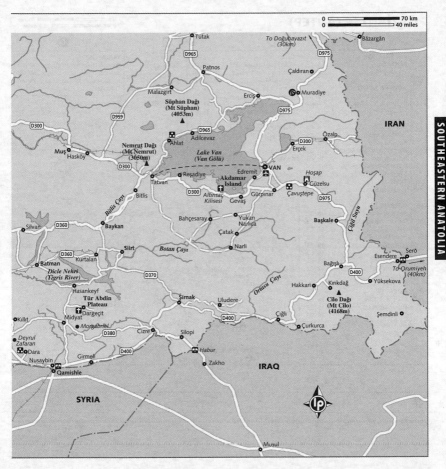

SOUTHEASTERN ANATOLIA

most desirable places to live in southeastern Anatolia, it's high on ambitions, and not only in the gastronomic domain. With the biggest city park this side of the Euphrates and a buzzing café culture, Antep has lots of panache and thinks the time has come to share it with the outside world. And it also has one attraction that alone makes the trip across Turkey worth the fare: the Gaziantep Museum. Even if you've never had any enthusiasm for Roman mosaics you'll soon be a convert the minute you cast your eyes upon the *Gipsy Girl*.

The physical fabric of the city is being reinvigorated. Great monuments such as the fortress, the bazaars and a smattering of old stone houses and caravanserai are being given the loving restorations they so richly deserve. One of southeastern Anatolia's gateways, Gaziantep has rarely been as full of confidence and hope for the future as it is today. Urfa, watch your back!

History

Before the Arabs conquered the town in AD 638, the Persians, Alexander the Great, the Romans and the Byzantines all left their imprints on the region. Proceeding from the east, the Seljuk Turks strolled into the picture around 1070.

Aintab (the former name of Gaziantep) remained a city of Seljuk culture, ruled by petty Turkish lords until the coming of the Ottomans under Selim the Grim in 1516.

SOUTHEASTERN ANATOLIA

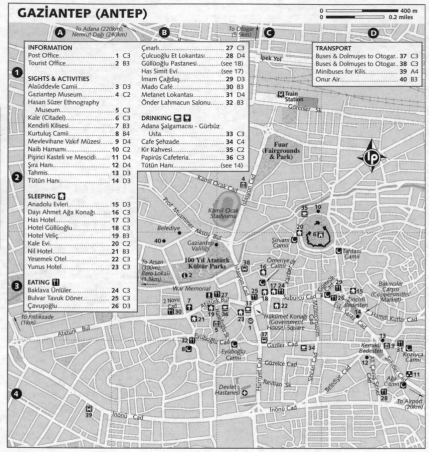

GAZIANTEP (ANTEP)

0 ___ 400 m
0 ___ 0.2 miles

INFORMATION	
Post Office	1 C3
Tourist Office	2 B3

SIGHTS & ACTIVITIES	
Alaüddevle Camii	3 D3
Gaziantep Museum	4 C2
Hasan Süzer Ethnography Museum	5 C3
Kale (Citadel)	6 C3
Kendirli Kilisesi	7 B3
Kurtuluş Camii	8 B4
Mevlevihane Vakıf Müzesi	9 C4
Naib Hamamı	10 C2
Pişirici Kasteli ve Mescidi	11 D4
Şıra Hanı	12 D4
Tahmis	13 D3
Tütün Hanı	14 D3

SLEEPING	
Anadolu Evleri	15 D3
Dayı Ahmet Ağa Konağı	16 C3
Has Hotel	17 C3
Hotel Güllüoğlu	18 C3
Hotel Veliç	19 B3
Kale Evi	20 C2
Nil Hotel	21 B3
Yesemek Otel	22 C3
Yunus Hotel	23 C3

EATING	
Baklava Ünlüler	24 C3
Bulvar Tavuk Döner	25 C3
Çavuşoğlu	26 D3

Çınarlı	27 C3
Çulcuoğlu Et Lokantası	28 D4
Güllüoğlu Pastanesi	(see 18)
Has Simit Evi	(see 17)
İmam Çağdaş	29 D3
Mado Café	30 B3
Metanet Lokantası	31 D4
Önder Lahmacun Salonu	32 B3

DRINKING	
Adana Şalgamacısı - Gürbüz Usta	33 C3
Cafe Şehzade	34 C4
Kir Kahvesi	35 C2
Papirüs Cafeteria	36 C3
Tütün Hanı	(see 14)

TRANSPORT	
Buses & Dolmuşes to Otogar	37 C3
Buses & Dolmuşes to Otogar	38 C3
Minibuses for Kilis	39 A4
Onur Air	40 B3

During the Ottoman period, Aintab had a sizable Christian population, especially Armenians. You'll see Armenian churches, community buildings and mansions scattered throughout the city's historical core.

In 1920, as the victorious Allies sought to carve up the Ottoman territories, Aintab was besieged by French forces intent on adding Turkish lands to their holdings in Syria and Lebanon. Aintab's fierce nationalist defenders surrendered on 8 February 1921. The epithet 'Gazi' (War Hero) was added to Antep in 1973 to pay homage to their tenacious defence.

Orientation

The centre of this fast-growing city is the intersection of Atatürk Bulvarı and Suburcu, Hürriyet and İstasyon Caddesis, marked by a large equestrian statue of Atatürk and still called *hükümet konağı* (government house) square.

Most essentials are within walking distance of the main intersection, including hotels, banks with ATMs, *bureaus de change*, restaurants and sights; the train station is 800m north. The otogar is about 6km from the town centre.

Information

The post office, internet cafés, most banks with ATMs and exchange offices are on or around the main square.

Arsan (☎ 220 6464; www.arsan.com.tr; Nolu Sokak; ⏰ 8am-7pm) This reputable travel agency sells tickets for domestic and international companies and can arrange various tours (from TL90 per person), including the 'Magical Triangle' (Birecik, Halfeti-Rumkale, Belkıs-Zeugma), Yesemek and even Aleppo (Syria). Ayşe, the helpful manager, speaks good English.

Tourist office (☎ 230 5969; 100 Yıl Atatürk Kültür Parkı İçi; ☻ 8am-noon & 1-5pm Mon-Fri) In a pinkish building standing in the city park, it has well-informed staff who speaks English and German. A few brochures and maps are available.

Sights

KALE DISTRICT

Get your bearings of the urban sprawl you're going to embrace by climbing up the unmissable **kale** (admission free; ☻ 8.30am-4.30pm Tue-Sun). The citadel is thought to have been constructed by the Romans. It was restored by Emperor Justinian in the 6th century AD, and rebuilt extensively by the Seljuks in the 12th and 13th centuries.

Restoration, restoration, restoration. The quarter at the foot of the citadel has been entirely revamped over the last few years, and old shops and workshops have been modernised. Needless to say, they have lost much of their character in the process. Immediately north of the citadel, check out the elegant proportions of the **Naib Hamamı** (Kale Arası) before heading south to the partially covered **bazaar** area, which includes Zincirli Bedesten. Much of it has been recently restored, too. Continuing south, make a beeline for the well-organised **Mevlevihane Vakıf Müzesi** (☎ 232 9797; Tekke Camii Yanı; admission free; ☻ 9am-5pm Tue-Sun), which focuses on the Mevlevi Sufis (a dervish order), with various artworks, kilims (pileless woven rugs), manuscripts, clothing worn by Mevlevi and other dervish paraphernalia. Panels are in English. Also worth a peek are the **Şıra Hanı**, another restored caravanserai, and the **Pişirici Kasteli ve Mescidi** (Şehitler Caddesi), which harbours ancient underground ablutions blocks.

If you need a coffee break, try to find **Tahmis** (Buğdaypazarı Sokak), possibly the most atmospheric *kahvehane* (coffeehouse) in Gaziantep, and on a par with the more institutionalised **Tütün Hanı** (Eski Saray Caddesi Yanı), set in a restored caravanserai right in the heart of the bazaar.

GAZİANTEP MUSEUM & ZEUGMA KÜLTÜR VE MÜZE MERKEZI

Even if the idea of an archaeology museum would usually send you off to sleep, the **Gaziantep Museum** (☎ 324 8809; İstasyon Caddesi; admission TL2; ☻ 8.30am-noon & 1-5pm Tue-Sun) will amaze you with its collection of the many mosaics unearthed at the rich Roman site of Belkıs-Zeugma, just before the new Birecik Dam flooded some of the site forever. It's impossible not to fall in love with the *Gipsy Girl*, from the 2nd century AD, the museum's highlight. Also make a beeline for the famous *Scene of Achilles being sent to the Trojan War*.

All the mosaics are due to be transferred to a new museum called Zeugma Kültür ve Müze Merkezi, which should have opened by the time you read this. The current museum will focus on archaeology only.

HASAN SÜZER ETHNOGRAPHY MUSEUM

Occupying a restored two-century-old Gaziantep stone house tucked away in a side street off Atatürk Caddesi, the **Hasan Süzer Ethnography Museum** (admission TL2; Hanefioğlu Sokak; ☻ 8.30am-5pm Tue-Sun) is well worth a visit. A central *hayat* (courtyard) patterned with light and dark stone provides light and access to the rooms. Those on the ground floor were for service; those on the 1st floor made up the selamlık (quarters for male family members and their visitors); and those on the 2nd floor made up the *haremlik* (for female family members and their visitors).

100 YIL ATATÜRK KÜLTÜR PARKI

If you're all market-ed and museum-ed out, the **100 Yıl Atatürk Kültür Parkı** (admission free), within spitting distance of Gaziantep's traffic-snarled main thoroughfares, is a lovely space in the middle of the city and provides a green haven for nature lovers, families and courting 20-somethings.

KENDİRLİ KİLİSESİ

Wedged between modern buildings smack in the centre, this **church** (Atatürk Bulvarı) is a startling vision. It was constructed by French priests with the help of Napoleon III in 1860. Seen from a distance, the building looks quite featureless, but a closer inspection reveals a number of eye-catching decorative elements, including black-and-white medallions.

MOSQUES

Of Gaziantep's many mosques, the most impressive is the **Kurtuluş Camii**, built on a small hill off the main drag. Initially constructed as a cathedral in 1892, it features alternating black-and-white stone banding. Another mosque worth admiring is the **Alaüddevle Camii**, near the Coppersmiths' Market.

Sleeping

Gaziantep is rolling in accommodation, much of it on or near Suburcu, Hürriyet and Atatürk Caddesis.

BUDGET

Yunus Hotel (☎ 221 1722; hotelyunus@hotel.com; Kayacık Sokak; s/d TL30/50; 🞅) As far as physical beauty goes, this a real plain Jane, but it's a secure spot to hang your rucksack, the rates are good and it's handily set in the centre of town. It features anodyne rooms with well-scrubbed bathrooms (but please, upgrade the boarding school-style furnishings). The breakfast room is windowless.

Hotel Veliç (☎ 221 2212; www.velicotel.com; Atatürk Bulvarı; s/d TL35/55; 🞅) A recent lick of paint (yellow and lilac) in the rooms and the communal areas has elevated this concrete lump on the main drag a couple of notches on the comfort ladder. The rooms are a bit on the small side, though (check out a few before committing). Top marks go to the bright top-floor breakfast area – the perfect spot to eye up the city.

Hotel Güllüoğlu (☎ 232 4636; fax 220 8689; Suburcu Caddesi; s/d TL40/60; 🞅) The decor's a bit blah and the carpets are tatty, but the bathrooms are kept in fine fettle and location is primo. Oh, and there's the Güllüoğlu pastry shop on the ground floor.

MIDRANGE

Has Hotel (☎ 232 8882; info@hotelhas.com; Suburcu Caddesi; s/d TL40/70; 🞅) If fancy decor is not the issue but hygiene, location and solid amenities are high on your list, then the newish Has could be worth it. It offers well-appointed rooms with TV, darkwood furnishings, minibar, prim bathrooms and well-sprung mattresses. As with nearby Güllüoğlu, there's a bit of street noise but nothing to lose sleep over. And as with the Güllüoğlu, you can sate a sweet tooth on the ground floor – at the Has Simit Evi.

Nil Hotel (☎ 220 9452; fax 220 9965; Atatürk Bulvarı; s/d TL40/70; 🞅) There's nothing overly adventurous in this small 'high-rise' hotel, but what do you want from a middle-of-the-road establishment? At least the bathrooms are sanitary and it's high on facilities, with satellite TV, air-con, lift and car park – not to mention a central location.

Yesemek Otel (☎ 220 8888; www.yesemekotel.com; İsmail Sokak; s/d TL50/70; 🞅) Come across the modern exterior and imposing lobby and you could easily mistake Yesemek for a bank. Bang in the thick of things, this well-regarded pile offers great service and facilities, including a restaurant and a private *otopark* (car park) just next door, although its executive look doesn't really scream holidays.

TOP END

Kale Evi (☎ 231 4142; www.kaleevi.com; Köprübaşı Sokak; s/d TL100/150; 🞅) This newish eight-room hotel aims to offer a boutique stay for less, but gets sidetracked by a few tacky touches – such as huge air-conditioners and cheesy bedspreads in the rooms, or a mock fresco of the *Gypsy Girl* in the restaurant. At least it's cosy and the location is ace – it clings like a limpet to a section of the citadel.

our pick **Anadolu Evleri** (☎ 220 9525, 0533-558 7996; www.anadoluevleri.com; Köroğlu Sokak; s/d TL105/135, 1-/2-person ste TL135/170; 🞅 🖳) A tastefully restored old stone house in a lovely position that provides the perfect soft landing into Gaziantep. This oasis celebrates local tradition: a beguiling courtyard, beamed or painted ceilings, mosaic floors, secret passageways, and antique furniture and artefacts. It's within spitting distance of the bustling bazaar, yet it feels quiet and restful. No two rooms are identical. Rooms 1 and 2, on the ground floor, are a tad sombre, but the other 11 rooms, including three gleaming suites, get plenty of natural light. Your host, Timur Schindel, rules his kingdom with relaxed bonhomie and will give you the lowdown on all that's worth seeing in the city, in perfect English.

Dayı Ahmet Ağa Konağı (☎ 232 1626; www.dayi ahmetagakonagi.com; Eski Postane Sokak; s/d TL110/150; 🞅) An air of mystery and romance lingers around this historic *konak* (mansion) refurbished in 2008. The eight rooms feel like cocoons, with rugs, wood panels and parquet flooring (pity about the bulky air-conditioners, though), and there's an on-site restaurant (yes, it's licensed). It's incredibly central, but still feels like a personal sanctuary.

Eating

Food, glorious food! Gaziantep is a nirvana for gourmands, with a prodigious selection of eateries and pastry shops to suit all palates and budgets. For a cheap meal on the go at lunchtime, try one of the numerous *dönerci* on Suburcu Caddesi or Gaziler Caddesi.

Çavuşoğlu (☎ 231 3069; Eski Saray Caddesi; mains TL4-8) Partly *baklavaci* (see boxed text, below), partly *kebapci*, this sprightly outfit rustles up dishes that will fill your tummy without emptying your wallet. Portions are copious, the meat is perfectly slivered and the salads are fresh.

our pick **İmam Çağdaş** (☎ 231 2678; Kale Civarı Uzun Çarşı; mains TL4-10) This talismanic pastry shop and restaurant is run by Imam Çağdaş, our culinary guru, who concocts wicked pistachio baklava that are delivered daily to customers throughout Turkey. If there were a kebap Oscar, this place would be a serious contender. The secret? Fresh, carefully chosen ingredients and the inimitable 'Çağdaş touch' (see boxed text, below). If you want to whet your appetite before your trip, check out www.imamcagdas.com.

Çınarlı (☎ 221 2155; Çınarlı Sokak; mains TL4-11) Resisting the passage of time, the Çınarlı still enjoys a great reputation for its *yöresel yemeks* (traditional dishes), a perfect excuse to experiment with lesser-known dishes such as *ekşili ufak köfte, yuvarlama* or *kuruluk dolma*. The decor works a treat, with three small rooms decorated with rugs, weapons and other collectibles, as well as a bigger dining room upstairs where you can enjoy live music in the afternoon. It's a pistachio's toss from the war memorial (walk down the stairs).

Çulcuoğlu Et Lokantası (☎ 231 0241; Kalender Sokak; mains TL5-10; ☾ 11.30am-10pm Mon-Sat) Surrender helplessly to your inner carnivore at this Gaziantep institution. The yummy kebaps are the way to go, but grilled chicken also puts in menu appearances. Don't be fooled by the unremarkable entrance; there's a vast, neat dining area at the back. It's tucked away down a narrow side street across the *otopark* from the Şıra Hanı, about 20m from a little mosque called Nur Ali.

Metanet Lokantası (Kozluca Camii Yanı; mains TL6-8; ☾ lunch) Left, right, left again. That's it, over there. The sort of place you only find if you go looking for it. Tucked away in a side street near Kozluca Camii, the Metanet has always been part of the local knowledge. The moustached waiters, who seem to have been a fixture here for decades, conscientiously mince the meat around noon in front of a big grill. *Ayran* (yoghurt drink) is served in a tin bowl, and the atmosphere is convivial. Much less institutionalised than İmam Çağdaş.

Mado Café (☎ 221 1500; Atatürk Bulvarı; mains TL7-9) Young couples... Ladies with bare arms (almost an anomaly in eastern Turkey)... Young businessmen working on their computers... The super-slick Mado is *the* place to meet Gaziantep's movers and shakers in a smart

SOUTHEASTERN ANATOLIA

GAZİANTEP FOR THE SWEET TOOTH

For any baklava (layered filo pastries with honey and nuts) devotee, Gaziantep is a Shangri-la. The city is reckoned to produce the best *fıstıklı* (pistachio) baklavas in Turkey, if not in the world. When they are served ultrafresh, you'll lose all self-control (trust us). With more than 180 pastry shops scattered around the city, it's hard to determine which is the best, but some baklava shops have reached cult status, such as **Güllüoğlu** (☎ 231 2282; Suburcu Caddesi), **Çavuşoğlu** (☎ 231 3069; Eski Saray Caddesi), **Baklava Ünlüler** (☎ 232 2043; Suburcu Caddesi), **Fıstıkzade** (☎ 336 0020; Fevzi Çakmak Bulvarı) and the talismanic **İmam Çağdaş** (☎ 231 2678; Kale Civarı Uzun Çarşı). Baklava purists swear İmam Çağdaş is the ultimate, but on our last trip we also made ourselves a nuisance at Güllüoğlu. If you find other treasure troves, we'll be happy to learn about your experience.

We asked Burhan Çağdaş the owner of the eponymous İmam Çağdaş, which has been tormenting carb-lovers since 1887, what the qualities of a perfectly crafted baklava are. 'I carefully choose the freshest ingredients imaginable. Everything is organic. I know the best oil and pistachio producers in the Gaziantep area. The nature of the soil here gives a special aroma to pistachio. And we don't go into mass production.' We also asked another expert, Sedat Kirişci, the owner of Fıstıkzade and a former *usta* (master) at Güllüoğlu, how long it takes to become a baklava chef. *'Yirmi yıl'* (20 years) – you get the picture. To get addicted, it takes just a moment on the lips...

How can one judge whether a baklava is fresh? 'It's simple: when it's in your mouth, it should make like a *kshhhh* sound,' says Burhan Çağdaş. He's right. You'll never forget the typical ksshhh that characterises a fresh baklava when it titillates your taste buds. Stop, we're drooling over the keyboard!

setting (contemporary furnishings, muted lighting, comfortable seating, big-screen TV). You can nosh on snacks and sip fruity cocktails, but the pastries and the ice creams are what make the place tick.

Baro Lokali (☎ 339 4140; 100 Yıl Atatürk Kültür Parkı; mains TL7-10) It's the setting that's the pull here, with an enchanting leaf-dappled outdoor terrace, at the western end of the 100 Yıl Atatürk Kültür Parkı (about TL6 by taxi) – perfect for escaping sticky Gaziantep on a hot summer day. Good choice of mezes and meat dishes. You can order beer, rakı (aniseed brandy) or wine with your meal.

Other temptations in the centre:

Bulvar Tavuk Döner (İstasyon Caddesi; mains TL2-4) If money matters, this sprightly little joint is the ideal pit stop (only TL2 for a chicken sandwich).

Has Simit Evi (Suburcu Caddesi; simits from TL2) This humming venue adjoining the Has Hotel churns out *simits* (bread rings sprinkled with sesame seeds) that will leave you a drooling mess.

Önder Lahmacun Salonu (☎ 231 6455; Eyüboğlu Caddesi; pide from TL4) Turkish pizzas never tasted so good in this modern eatery situated a short bag-haul from Kurtuluş Camii.

Drinking

Cafe Şehzade (☎ 231 0350; Gaziler Caddesi; snacks TL2-4; ⏰ 8.30am-8pm) The decor alone is worth a gander: the atmospheric Şehzade is housed in an 800-year-old converted hamam (bathhouse). The food, mostly snacks, is so-so, but it's a good place to meet students and sip a cup of tea. Drop by late afternoon, when there's live music.

Adana Şalgamacısı – Gürbüz Usta (Hürriyet Caddesi; juices from TL2) See the heaps of grapefruit, banana and orange on the counter at this buzzing hole-in-the-wall? They're just waiting to be squeezed. Try the delicious *atom* (an explosive mixture of milk, honey, banana, hazelnuts and pistachio).

Kir Kahvesi (Köprübaşı Sokak; Turkish coffee TL4) This newish café in an overrestored historic building at the foot of the citadel lacks the patina and atmosphere of the Papirüs, but it's still a good place to recuperate after visiting the area.

Tütün Hanı (Eski Saray Caddesi Yanı) Set in the picturesque courtyard of the recently restored Tütün Hanı, this teahouse is a great place to enjoy a cheap tea and nargileh (traditional water pipe). It has bags of character, featuring rugs, low wooden tables and cushions.

our pick **Papirüs Cafeteria** (☎ 230 3279; Noter Sokak) What a find! A student crowd (male *and* female, we promise) gathers here to take advantage of the delightfully authentic setting – it's housed in a historic mansion off Atatürk Caddesi – and swap numbers in the leafy courtyard. Don't miss the ancient frescoes in the upstairs rooms.

Getting There & Away

AIR

Gaziantep's Oğuzeli airport is 20km from the centre. An airport bus departs from outside each airline office 1½ hours before flights (TL5).

Cyprus Turkish Airlines (www.kthy.net) Four weekly flights to Ercan (Northern Cyprus), from TL275 return (one hour). Has also a weekly flight to London-Stansted.

Onur Air (www.onurair.com.tr) Daily flight to/from İstanbul (from TL59, 1¾ hours).

Pegasus (www.flypgs.com) Four weekly flights to/from İstanbul (from TL59).

Sun Express (www.sunexpress.com.tr) Four weekly flights to/from İzmir (from TL59, 1¾ hours).

Turkish Airlines (www.thy.com) Three to four daily flights to/from İstanbul (from TL100, 1¾ hours) and to/from Ankara (from TL59).

Any travel agency in Gaziantep, including Arsan (see p600), can issue tickets on behalf of these companies.

BUS

The otogar is 6km from the town centre. Frequent city buses (TL1) rattle between the otogar and the centre. To get to the otogar, catch a bus or minibus in Hürriyet Caddesi, north of Gaziler Caddesi, or in İstasyon Caddesi, about 400m further north. A taxi costs about TL13.

There's no direct bus to Syria; you'll have to go to Kilis first, then take a taxi to the border or to Aleppo. Minibuses to Kilis (TL6, 65km) leave every 20 minutes or so from a separate *garaj* (minibus terminal) on İnönü Caddesi. Minibuses to Birecik (TL7, 46km) leave from the otogar.

Details of some daily services are listed in the table, opposite.

CAR

You may need a car to see the surrounding sights, especially Yesemek Open-Air Museum (opposite). Arsan (p600) can arrange car rental at no extra cost. Plan on TL80 a day.

SERVICES FROM GAZİANTEP'S OTOGAR

Destination	Fare (TL)	Duration (hr)	Distance (km)	Frequency (per day)
Adana	12	4	220	frequent buses
Adıyaman	12	3	162	frequent minibuses
Ankara	40	10	705	frequent buses
Antakya	12	4	200	frequent minibuses
Diyarbakır	20	5	330	frequent buses
İstanbul	50	15	1136	several buses
Kahramanmaraş	12	1½	80	frequent buses & minibuses
Mardin	25	6	330	several buses
Şanlıurfa	12	2½	145	frequent buses
Van	30	12	740	several buses

TRAIN

The comfortable *Toros Ekspresi* leaves for İstanbul via Adana and Konya at 2.30pm on Tuesday, Thursday and Sunday (TL40, 27 hours). To get to Aleppo and Damascus by train, you'll need to go to İslahiye to catch the twice-weekly train to Syria.

AROUND GAZİANTEP

Kilis

☎ 0348 / pop 70,700

Architecture buffs should not miss Kilis, which is easily accessible from Gaziantep. Kilis bristles with lovely ancient buildings scattered around the city centre, including mausoleums, caravanserais, hamams, mosques, fountains, *konaks*... Mosey around the narrow streets off the main drag and you'll find them all, some recently restored. On or around the main square, look for the superb Adliye, the Mevlevi Hane, the Tekye Camii, the Paşa Hamamı and the Kadı Camii. The Cuneyne Camii and the Çalik Camii are a bit more difficult to find (ask around).

Take a minibus from Gaziantep and allow a day in this surprising city to do it justice. Should you want to stay overnight here, the **Mer-Tur Otel** (☎ 814 0834; mer-turotel@hotmail.com; Zekerya Korkmaz Bulvarı; s/d TL55/80; 🖭) is a commendable haunt, although it won't knock your socks off. If you need to sate a sweet tooth, there's an ice-cream parlour on the ground floor.

There are frequent minibus services to Gaziantep (TL6, 65km, one hour). For Aleppo in Syria, take a taxi to Öncüpınar at the border (TL10, 7km). From the Syrian side of the border, you can pick up a taxi for Aleppo.

Yesemek Open-Air Museum

One of the star attractions in the Gaziantep area is the **Yesemek Open-Air Museum** (Yesemek Açık Hava Müzesi; admission TL2; 🖭 dawn-dusk), a vast hillside studded with some 300 Hittite stones and statues. Even if you're not a fan of the Hittites, you will find a visit rewarding, if only for the picturesque setting.

The use of the site is intriguing. From around 1375 BC this hillside was a Hittite quarry and sculpture workshop. For over 600 years it churned out basalt blocks, weighing anywhere from 1.5 to 8 tonnes, that were carved into lions, sphinxes and other designs. Today, the pieces are left in various states of completion, abandoned at the end of the Hittite era.

Yesemek is a long 113km haul from Gaziantep. Getting there by public transport is a chore, because there's no direct service. It's easier to hire a car in Gaziantep. You could do a scenic loop, taking in Kilis, Yesemek and İslahiye. From Kilis, follow the D410 to Hassa/Antakya, then bear right onto the gravel road marked for Yesemek.

Belkıs-Zeugma

The city of Belkıs-Zeugma was once an important city. Founded by one of Alexander the Great's generals around 300 BC, it had its golden age with the Romans, and later became a major trading station along the Silk Road. Unfortunately, it has lost much of its appeal since most of the site disappeared beneath the waters of the Birecik Dam. Most interesting mosaics and finds have been transferred to Gaziantep Museum (p601), where some are on display. All that is left of the city's former grandeur is a pile of rubble and a couple of dilapidated pillars. Nor are there any explanatory signs. There are plans for an open-air museum to give the site a bit more lustre – stay tuned.

The site is about 50km from Gaziantep and 10km from Nizip, off the main road to Şanlıurfa (it's signposted from Nizip), but there's no minibus service. If you don't have your own vehicle, you may think it's too much effort getting there for too little reward.

Birecik

If birdwatching gets you chirpy, make a beeline for Birecik, about 46km east of Gaziantep, right by the Euphrates River (Fırat Nehri). This unintimidating town harbours a breeding station for the eastern bald ibis (Geronticus eremita), a bird species that, sadly, hovers on the brink of extinction. The birds are tagged, released into the wild, and are only supposed to be here during the breeding season (February to July), but you can usually see at least a few of them all year-round. Photographers take note: you'll need a 400mm lens – the nest boxes are set up in the cliff.

Birecik is also the main launching pad for Halfeti (see right).

With your own vehicle, getting to the breeding station is reasonably simple. From the main bridge, follow the riverbank north for about 2km looking out on the right for the signs marked Kelaynak Parkı and **Birecik Kelaynak Üretme İstasyonu** (Birecik Ibis Breeding Station; 7am-7pm).

If feathered creatures are not your thing, you can visit the ruins of the **fortress** perched on the hill.

If you get stuck in Birecik, **Hotel Acar** (0414-652 8885; İskele Çarşısı; s/d TL45/80;) is the best shut-eye option. It's conveniently located near the vegetable market and the Halfeti minibus stop. The 15 rooms are fresh, clean and serviceable, and some have views of the Euphrates. If hunger beckons, the welcoming and immaculate **Altın Sofra** (0414-652 6476; İskele Çarşısı; mains TL5-10) is on the ground floor (same management). Its çiğ köfte (raw minced mutton) and kaşarli pide (pide with cheese) are flavoursome.

Any of the buses travelling between Şanlıurfa and Gaziantep can drop you at Birecik. At Birecik ask to be let off at the köprü (bridge), by the river. Then you'll have to walk 2km to the breeding station or hire a taxi.

The small otogar near the vegetable market, by the river, at the foot of the fortress, handles minibuses to Gaziantep (TL7, one hour). Minibuses for Halfeti (TL3, 45km) leave from near the Hotel Acar, on the other side of the vegetable market. There are regular minibuses on weekdays, but very few services at weekends. A taxi ride to Halfeti costs about TL50. Minibuses to Şanlıurfa (TL10, 1½ hours) leave from a durak (bus stop) that is under the bridge, on the road that skirts the river. Or you can go to the main otogar, which is inconveniently positioned at the eastern fringe of Birecik, on the road to Şanlıurfa.

Halfeti & Rumkale

If you need a break in a more secluded place, then Halfeti is for you. This peaceful village lies about 40km north of Birecik, right on the bank of the Euphrates. It's the perfect spot to unwind before tackling the busy cities of Şanlıurfa to the east or Gaziantep to the west. The setting couldn't be more appealing, with attractive houses that trip down the hillside above the river. Sadly, construction of the Birecik Dam meant that half of the city, including several archaeological sites, was inundated and part of the population had to be resettled.

There are several places to soak up the atmosphere along the river while noshing on fresh fish. The leafy **Siyah Gül Restaurant** (0414-751 5235; mains TL6-9), overlooking the river, is a sound option and alcohol is served. The licensed **Duba Restaurant** (0414-751 5704; mains TL6-10), at the end of the village (just go along the road that follows the river), is also worth considering, with a purpose-built pontoon on the water and a teensy bahçe (garden). Other eateries have recently opened up but their locations are not that fantastic. Should you decide to stay overnight, the welcoming **Şelaleli Konak** (0414-751 5500; d per person TL20) fits the bill, but there are only three rooms (one with private bathroom). The owner of the Siyah Gül Restaurant has a room for rent in his house.

From Halfeti, boat trips to **Rumkale** can easily be organised (about TL40 for the whole boat) – a definite must-do. The boat putt-putts along the river for about 20 minutes until it reaches the base of the rocky bluff on top of which sits this ruined fortress. The fortress is accessible by a short but steep path (be careful if you are with children). It features a mosque, a church, a monastery, a well and other remains, all in a relatively good state of preservation. And, man-oh-man, the views of the Euphrates valley are just wonderful. Back at your boat, ask the driver to continue until **Savaş**, another partly inundated village, a mere 10 minutes' boat ride from Rumkale. There's

---

GAP – THE SOUTHEASTERN ANATOLIA PROJECT

The character of the landscape in southeastern Anatolia is changing as the Southeast Anatolia Project (Güneydoğu Anadolu Projesi), better known as GAP or Güneydoğu, comes online, bringing irrigation waters to large arid regions and generating enormous amounts of hydroelectricity for industry. Parched valleys have become fish-filled lakes, and dusty villages are becoming booming market towns and factory cities.

The scale of the project is awe-inspiring, affecting eight provinces and two huge rivers (the Tigris and the Euphrates). In 2008, 17 dams (out of a planned total of 22) had been completed.

Such a huge, hope-generating project can also generate sizable problems, especially ecological and sanitary ones, due to the change from dry to wet agriculture. According to data from the Malaria Division of the Turkish Health Ministry, the reported cases of malaria rose from 8680 in 1990 to 18,676 in 1992.

The project has also generated political problems, as Syria and Iraq, the countries downriver for whom the waters of the Tigris and Euphrates are also vital, complain bitterly that Turkey is using or keeping a larger share of the water than it should. Innumerable archaeological sites have also disappeared under dam water, or are slated to do so.

---

limited infrastructure in Savaş but nothing beats a cup of *çay* (tea) in one of the little tea gardens by the river.

Halfeti is relatively easily accessible by public transport on weekdays. Hourly minibuses ply the route between Birecik and Halfeti (TL3).

ŞANLIURFA (URFA)

☎ 0414 / pop 463,800 / elevation 518m

After the secular pleasures of Antep (and the subsequent crisis of faith), it's time to exercise your soul in mystical and pious Şanlıurfa (the Prophets' City; also known as Urfa), a spiritual centre par excellence and great pilgrimage town. This is where the prophets Job and Abraham left their marks. As has been the case with centuries of pilgrims before you, the first sight of the Dergah complex of mosques and the holy Gölbaşı area (with the call to prayer as a soundtrack) will be a magical moment that you will remember for a long time to come.

It's also in Urfa that you begin to feel you've reached the Middle East, courtesy of its proximity to Syria. Women cloaked in black chadors elbow their way through the odorous crush of the bazaar streets; moustached gents in *şalvar* (traditional baggy Arabic pants) swill tea and click-clack backgammon pieces in shady courtyards; pilgrims feed sacred carp in the shadows of a medieval fortress… If you're after touches of exoticism, you'll be amply rewarded here.

Sadly, the modern town is a fairly utilitarian collection of apartment blocks and concrete eyesores, and out on the highway the traffic is noisy. Despite its few shortcomings, Urfa is a place to lock onto your travel radar and deserves at least a couple of days to see all the sights and soak up the atmosphere of the back streets.

History

The Hittites imposed their rule over the area around 1370 BC. After a period of Assyrian rule, Alexander the Great hit Urfa. He and his Macedonian mates named the town Edessa, after a former capital of Macedonia, and it remained the capital of a Seleucid province until 132 BC, when the local Aramaean population set up an independent kingdom and renamed the town Orhai. Orhai finally succumbed to the Romans, as did everywhere hereabouts.

Edessa pursued its contrary history by speedily adopting Christianity (c 200) before it became the official religion of the conquerors.

Astride the fault line between the Persian and Roman empires, control of Edessa was batted back and forth from one to the other. In 533 the two empires signed a Treaty of Endless Peace – that lasted seven years. The Romans and Persians kept at it until the Arabs swept in and cleared them all out in 637. Edessa enjoyed three centuries of peace under the Arabs, after which everything went to blazes again.

Turks, Arabs, Armenians and Byzantines battled for the city from 944 until 1098, when the First Crusade under Count Baldwin of Boulogne arrived to set up the Latin County of

SOUTHEASTERN ANATOLIA

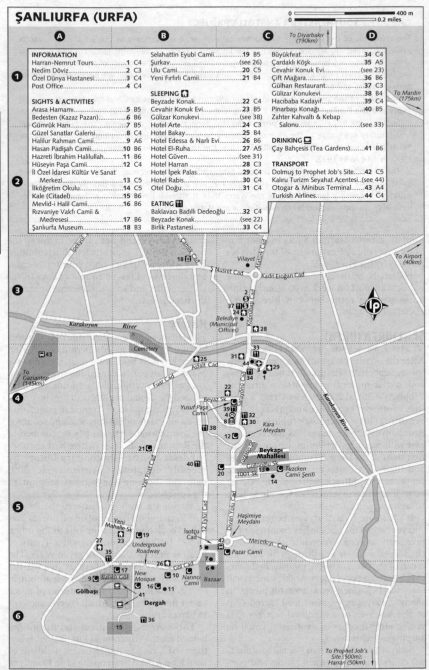

ŞANLIURFA (URFA)

0 — 400 m
0 — 0.2 miles

INFORMATION
Harran-Nemrut Tours................1 C4
Nedim Döviz.............................2 C3
Özel Dünya Hastanesi...............3 C4
Post Office...............................4 C4

SIGHTS & ACTIVITIES
Arasa Hamamı..........................5 B5
Bedesten (Kazaz Pazarı)............6 B6
Gümrük Hanı............................7 B5
Güzel Sanatlar Galerisi..............8 C4
Halilur Rahman Camii................9 A6
Hasan Padişah Camii................10 B6
Hazreti İbrahim Halilullah.........11 B6
Hüseyin Paşa Camii.................12 C4
İl Özel İdaresi Kültür Ve Sanat
  Merkezi...............................13 C5
İlköğretim Okulu.....................14 C5
Kale (Citadel)..........................15 B6
Mevlid-i Halil Camii.................16 B6
Rızvaniye Vakfı Camii &
  Medresesi.............................17 B6
Şanlıurfa Museum....................18 B3

Selahattin Eyubi Camii..............19 B5
Şurkav................................(see 26)
Ulu Cami................................20 C5
Yeni Fırfırlı Camii.....................21 B4

SLEEPING
Beyzade Konak........................22 C4
Cevahir Konuk Evi....................23 B5
Gülizar Konukevi..................(see 38)
Hotel Arte...............................24 C3
Hotel Bakay............................25 B4
Hotel Edessa & Narlı Evi............26 B6
Hotel El-Ruha..........................27 A5
Hotel Güven........................(see 31)
Hotel Harran...........................28 C4
Hotel İpek Palas.......................29 C4
Hotel Rabis.............................30 C4
Otel Doğu...............................31 C4

EATING
Baklavacı Badıllı Dedeoğlu 32 C4
Beyzade Konak....................(see 22)
Birlik Pastanesi........................33 C4

Büyükfırat...............................34 C4
Çardaklı Köşk..........................35 A5
Cevahir Konuk Evi................(see 23)
Çift Mağara............................36 B6
Gülhan Restaurant....................37 C3
Gülizar Konukevi......................38 B4
Hacıbaba Kadayıf.....................39 C4
Pınarbaşı Konağı......................40 B5
Zahter Kahvaltı & Kebap
  Salonu..............................(see 33)

DRINKING
Çay Bahçesis (Tea Gardens).......41 B6

TRANSPORT
Dolmuş to Prophet Job's Site.....42 C5
Kalıru Turizm Seyahat Acentesi..(see 44)
Otogar & Minibus Terminal........43 A4
Turkish Airlines.......................44 C4

To Diyarbakır (190km)
To Mardin (175km)
To Airport (40km)

Çamlık Cad
Atatürk Cad
18 Vilayet
Nusret Cad
Kadri Eroğan Cad
İpekyol

Karakoyun River
Köprübaşı Cad
37
2
S
24
Belediye (Municipal Offices)
28

Cemetery
To Gaziantep (145km)
43
Asfalt Cad
Fuat Cad
25
31
33
44
3
29
34
1
22
Sarayönü Cad
Beyaz Sk
39
Yusuf Paşa Camii
8
32
30
12
Kara Meydanı

21
Vali Fuat Cad
40
Köprülü Cad
20
Beykapı Mahallesi
Gülinoğlu Sk
1001 Sk
14
Tüzcken Camii Şerifi
Karakoyun River

Yeni Mahalle Sk
23
27
35
19
Underground Roadway
12 Eylül Cad
Divan Yolu Cad
Haşimiye Meydanı
İsotçu Cad
5
42
Meserkyır Cad
Pazar Camii
New Mosque
26
Göl Cad
17
9 Balıklı Göl
16
10
Narıncı Camii
6
7
Bazaar
11
41
Gölbaşı
Dergah
15
36
To Prophet Job's Site (500m); Harran (50km)

Edessa. This odd European feudal state lasted until 1144 when it was conquered by a Seljuk Turkish *emir* (tribal leader).

The Seljuk Turkish *emir* was succeeded by Saladin, then by the Mamluks. The Ottomans, under Selim the Grim, conquered most of this region in the early 16th century, but Edessa did not become Urfa until 1637 when the Ottomans finally took over.

As for its modern sobriquet, Urfa became Şanlıurfa (Glorious Urfa) in 1984. Since 1973, when Heroic Antep (Gaziantep) was given its special name, the citizens of Urfa had been chafing under a relative loss of dignity. Now that their city is 'Glorious', the inhabitants can look the citizens of 'Heroic' Antep straight in the eye.

Orientation

Except for inside the bazaar, it's fairly easy to find your way around Urfa. You'll see the citadel to the right as you enter the town along the highway from Gaziantep. The otogar is about 1km from the centre (but probably will be relocated out of town in the near future).

Along different stretches the city's main thoroughfare is called Atatürk, Köprübaşı, Sarayönü and Divan Yolu Caddesis.

Information

The post office, internet cafés and most banks with ATMs are on or near the main drag.

Harran-Nemrut Tours (☎ 215 1575, 0542-761 3065; ozcan_aslan_teacher@hotmail.com; Köprübaşı Caddesi; ☯ 8.30am-6pm) In the absence of a tourist office, this small travel agency is the most reliable source of information. It's efficiently run by Özcan Aslan, a local teacher, who speaks very good English and is a mine of local information. He runs tours to nearby sites, including Harran, Şuayb City, Soğmatar, Mardin and Nemrut Dağı, sells bus and flight tickets (at no extra costs) and can arrange car rental. It's just behind the Özel Dünya Hastanesi.

Nedim Döviz (☎ 312 7070; Köprübaşı Caddesi; ☯ 8.30am-6.30pm Mon-Fri, 8.30am-1pm Sat) Private exchange office. Keeps longer hours than the banks. No queues.

Özel Dünya Hastanesi (☎ 216 2772; Köprübaşı Caddesi) A well-equipped private hospital.

Sights
CITADEL

With an astounding view, the **kale** (admission TL2; ☯ 8am-8pm) on Damlacık hill, from which Abraham was supposedly tossed (see right), is a defining city landmark and an absolute must-see. Depending upon where you go for your information, it was built during Hellenistic times or by the Byzantines or during the Crusades or by the Turks. In any case, it's vast, looks magnificent when floodlit and can be reached via a flight of stairs or a tunnel cut through the rock. On the top, the most interesting things are the pair of columns that local legend has dubbed the Throne of Nemrut after the supposed founder of Urfa, the biblical King Nimrod. But really, you come up here for the spectacular views over Urfa.

GÖLBAŞI

Legend had it that Abraham (İbrahim), who is a great Islamic prophet, was in old Urfa destroying pagan gods one day when Nimrod, the local Assyrian king, took offence at this rash behaviour. Nimrod had Abraham immolated on a funeral pyre, but God turned the fire into water and the burning coals into fish. Abraham himself was hurled into the air from the hill where the fortress stands, but landed safely in a bed of roses.

The picturesque Gölbaşı area of Urfa is a symbolic re-creation of this story. Two rectangular pools of water (Balıklı Göl and Ayn-i Zeliha) are filled with supposedly sacred carp, while the area west of the Hasan Padişah Camii is a gorgeous rose garden. Local legend has it that anyone catching the carp will go blind. Consequently, these appear to be the most pampered, portly fish in Turkey.

On the northern side of Balıklı Göl is the elegant **Rızvaniye Vakfı Camii & Medresesi**, with a much-photographed arcaded wall, while at the western end is the **Halilur Rahman Camii**. This 13th-century building, replacing an earlier Byzantine church, houses the site where Abraham fell to the ground. The two pools are fed by a spring at the base of Damlacık hill, on which the castle is built.

DERGAH

Immediately to the southeast of the pools and the park is the Dergah complex of mosques and parks surrounding the colonnaded courtyard of the **Hazreti İbrahim Halilullah** (Prophet Abraham's Birth Cave; admission TL1), built and rebuilt over the centuries as an active place of pilgrimage. Its western side is marked by the **Mevlid-i Halil Camii**, a large Ottoman-style mosque. At its southern side you'll see the entrance to the Hazreti İbrahim Halilullah in which legend has it that Abraham was born. He lived here in hiding for his first seven years – King Nimrod, responding to a prophecy he'd received in a dream, feared that a newly born would eventually steal his crown, so he had all babies killed. This is still a place of pilgrimage and prayer, with separate entrances for men and women.

To the north, on Göl Caddesi, is the **Hasan Padişah Camii** (1460), but it's of little interest inside. All of these buildings are open to visitors but, as they are important places of worship, you should be modestly dressed.

MOSQUES

Urfa's Syrian-style **Ulu Cami** (Divan Yolu Caddesi) dates from the period 1170–75. Its 13 *eyvans* (vaulted halls) open onto a spacious forecourt with a tall tower topped by a clock with Ottoman numerals.

At Kara Meydanı, the square midway between the *belediye* (town hall) and Dergah, is the **Hüseyin Paşa Camii**, a late-Ottoman work built in 1849.

On Vali Fuat Caddesi, which leads up from behind Gölbaşı to the Cevahir Konuk Evi (see boxed text, p612), is the enormous, beautifully restored **Selahattin Eyubi Camii**. It was once St John's Church, as you can see by the altar, and is adorned with carvings. Follow Vali Fuat Caddesi north and you'll notice the **Yeni Fırfırlı Camii**, another finely restored building, once the Armenian Church of the Twelve Apostles.

ŞANLIURFA MUSEUM

Up the hill to the west of the *vilayet* (provincial government headquarters) building, off Atatürk Caddesi, the **Şanlıurfa Museum** (Şanlıurfa Müzesi; admission TL2; 8am-5pm Tue-Sun) captivates visitors with a journey through eastern Turkey's archaeological evolution.

The gardens contain various sculptures, and on the porch as you enter are several mosaics, the most interesting showing assorted wild animals. Inside, noteworthy artefacts include Neolithic implements, Assyrian, Babylonian and Hittite relief stones and other objects from Byzantine, Seljuk and Ottoman times.

BAZAAR

After visiting the museum, ponder on your new-found knowledge with a wander through Urfa's **bazaar** (daylight Mon-Sat). Spreading east of the Narıncı Camii, it is a jumble of streets, some covered, some open, selling every-thing from sheepskins and pigeons to jeans and handmade shoes. It was largely built by Süleyman the Magnificent in the mid-16th century. The best idea is just to dive in and inevitably get lost. Women should be on guard for lustful hands.

One of the most interesting areas is the **bedesten** (covered market), an ancient caravanserai where silk goods were sold. Today you'll still find silk scarves here, as well as gaudy modern carpets and the lovely blue and red scarves worn by local women. Right by the *bedesten* is the **Gümrük Hanı** (customs depot), with a delightful courtyard that is always full of tea- or coffee-swilling moustached gents playing backgammon, providing an authentic ambience.

Buried in the lanes of the bazaar are several ancient and very cheap **hamams**, including **Arasa Hamamı**.

OLD HOUSES

Delve into Urfa's back streets and you'll find examples of the city's distinctive limestone houses with protruding bays supported on stone corbels. Although many of these houses are falling into decay (and some are far too large for modern families), a few have been restored, most notably the house of Hacı Hafızlar, near the PTT, which has been turned into an art gallery, the **Güzel Sanatlar Galerisi** (8am-5.30pm Mon-Fri, noon-4pm Sat). The courtyards and fine carved stonework are a joy to behold and the custodians don't mind you wandering through.

You can also pop into the **Şurkav** (Balıklı Göl Mevkii), a local government building near the entrance to Hotel Edessa, where the courtyard is draped with greenery.

In the market area, in the neighbourhood called Beykapı Mahallesi (take 1001 Sokak), try to find the **İl Özel İdaresi Kültür Ve Sanat Merkezi**, another splendid house restored in 2002. It was once a church. Nearby, a stately building now houses a school, the **İlköğretim Okulu**. Look for the elaborate lintels and the colonnades that adorn the facade.

PROPHET JOB'S SITE

Although it's not the highlight of a trip, Prophet Job's Site is worth the bus ride for its historic significance. It's about 1km southeast of the Gölbaşı district. Legend holds that Eyyüp (Job) was a prosperous and devout man, thus despised by İblis (Satan). İblis took away Job's health, wealth and family, to force him into a crisis of faith. Instead, Job retreated to the **cave** (Eyyüp Peygamber Makamı) you see here, where he waited patiently in devotion to God. After seven years, God restored his possessions and health, the latter by means of a freshwater spring that Job unleashed by thumping the ground with his heel. Pilgrims come here to wish for the patience of Job and to restore their health with the spring water collected from a **well**.

Entrance is free but a small donation is expected. The nearby mosque features exquisitely tiled archways.

Regular 'Eyyüp Pey' minibuses departing from outside the Urfa bazaar will drop you right by the gate to the compound.

Sleeping

BUDGET

The Hotel Bakay is often recommended as a comfortable place for solo women; unmarried couples should feel welcome at Hotel İpek Palas. Ignore the touts for the pensions who may accost you at the bus station or in the centre – we've had some bad reports about these pensions especially from women.

Otel Doğu (☎ 215 1228; Sarayönü Caddesi; s/d TL15/25) We can't remember a more minimalist 'reception': one stool and one counter attended by a moustached man. Try to resist the temptation to run away, because the rooms are fine for the price you pay, with clean-smelling bathrooms (well, cubicles), bare floors, a super central location and double-glazing. Some rooms have shared bathrooms. The catch? No air-con and no fan equals Dante's inferno in summer.

Hotel Bakay (☎ 215 8975; fax 215 4007; Asfalt Caddesi; s/d TL30/50; ❄ 🖳) The Bakay is a safe bet that won't hurt the hip pocket, and is remarkably clean, but be prepared to trip over your backpack in the tiny rooms. Some are brighter than others, so ask to ogle a few before settling in. Standout features include crisp sheets, a pretty good location, pathogen-free bathrooms and a satisfying *kahvaltı* (breakfast). It's popular with Turkish families – a good sign for female travellers.

Hotel İpek Palas (☎ 215 1546; Köprübaşı Dünya Hastanesi Arkası; s/d TL30/50, without bathroom TL20/30; ❄) The slightly peeling walls and the tatty carpets will give you a rude awakening, but otherwise the İpek delivers the goods perfectly adequately, with friendly staff, functional bathrooms and an excellent location. And

yes, there's air-con. It's worth shelling out for the more expensive rooms with private facilities. Breakfast is skimpy, but Zahter Kahvaltı (see p612) is an egg's toss away.

Hotel Güven (☎ 215 1700; www.hotelguven.com; Sarayönü Caddesi; s/d TL40/60; ❄) The whiff of hospital-strength disinfectant when we checked in is testament to the place's spotlessness. Pity about the neon-lit corridors, though, which are as sexy as a dentist's waiting room. It's super central, and the rooms are well insulated from the hubbub of the main drag. The views from the rooftop breakfast room are particularly lovely.

MIDRANGE

Hotel Rabis (☎ 216 9595; www.hotelrabis.com, in Turkish; Sarayönü Caddesi; s/d TL60/80; ❄) Urfa's latest arrival is a model of shiny midrange quality; the decor is light brown and beige, with thick carpets, flat-screen TVs and double-glazing. Good views from the rooftop terrace, too. One of the best deals in town.

Hotel Arte (☎ 314 7060; www.otel-arte.com.tr; Köprübaşı Caddesi; s/d TL60/90; ❄) Style and sleekness in Urfa? Yes, it's possible at the Arte. The design-led interior, with Barbie-esque plastic chairs in the lobby, laminated floors and contemporary furniture in the rooms, is appealing, and the floor-to-ceiling windows afford superb views of the main drag.

Hotel Harran (☎ 313 2860; www.hotelharran.com; Köprübaşı Caddesi; s/d TL60/95; ❄ 🖳 ⛲) A longtime favourite, this hulking tower lording it over the main drag seems unfazed by its upstart new rival, the Rabis. It has the full complement of services and can't be faulted for cleanliness, but it scores nil in the charm department. Plus points include an on-site restaurant (with a good choice of Turkish tipples), a hamam (men only), a sauna and a swimming-pool.

Hotel Edessa & Narlı Evi (☎ 215 9911; fax 215 5030; Balıklı Göl Mevkii; s/d TL75/120; ❄) This venture has a split personality. The old wing (the Edessa) features bland rooms that don't even register a blip on the charm radar, while the new wing (the Narlı Evi) has a boutique feel and consists of 12 vaulted rooms that are tastefully decorated. Be sure to book one room in the Narlı Evi.

Hotel El-Ruha (☎ 215 4411; www.hotelelruha.com, in Turkish; Balıklı Göl; s/d TL100/135; ❄ 🖳 ⛲) No-one could accuse the El-Ruha management of a lack of ambition – the list of facilities is prolific, with a sauna, a hamam, a pool, two huge caves dedicated for those oh-so-popular *sıra geceleri* ('traditional nights' – live music evenings), a restaurant and a fitness centre. It pulls in pious yet wealthy pilgrims interested in unmonastic, fairly chintzy rooms with thick carpets and mahogany-like furniture. Alcohol is forbidden on the premises but you're here to repent your sins in the nearby Dergah complex, right?

Eating & Drinking

Urfa's culinary specialities include: Urfa kebap (skewered chunks of lamb served with tomatoes, sliced onions and hot peppers); *çiğ köfte*; *içli köfte* (deep-fried mutton-filled meatballs covered with bulgur); and *şıllık*, a type of walnut pancake. It pays to be a bit careful what you eat in Urfa, especially in summer, because the heat makes food poisoning more likely. Alcohol is not usually served.

Baklavacı Badıllı Dedeoğlu (☎ 215 3737; Sarayönü Caddesi; pastries TL1-2) Death by pistachio baklavas, pistachio *sarması* ('vine leaves') and other suave stuff – pick your sweet poison and thicken your arteries.

Birlik Pastanesi (☎ 313 1823; Köprübaşı Caddesi; pastries TL2) This pastry shop has a tantalising array of cakes and other goodies.

Hacıbaba Kadayıf (Sarayönü Caddesi; pastries TL2) Back home, don't tell your dietician that you couldn't resist the *peynirli kadayıf* (cheese-filled shredded wheat doused in honey) at this little den near the Yusuf Paşa Camii.

Zahter Kahvaltı & Kebap Salonu (Köprübaşı Caddesi; mains TL2-5) Skip your hotel's breakfast and instead wolf down gooey honey, *pekmez* (grape syrup), jam and cream on flat bread at this cute little place on the main drag. Wash it all down with a large glass of *çay* or *ayran* – all for around TL4.

Büyükfırat (☎ 215 8552; Sarayönü Caddesi; mains TL4-9) With its fountain and breezy outdoor seating, this restaurant-café-fast-food joint is the perfect salve after a day's sightseeing. Here you can nosh on burgers, pizzas, stews and kebaps or slug down a freshly squeezed orange juice.

our pick Çift Mağara (☎ 215 9757; Çift Kubbe Altı Balıklıgöl; mains TL4-9) The dining room is directly carved into the rocky bluff that overlooks the Gölbaşı, but the lovely terrace for dining alfresco beats the cavernous interior (views!). It's famed for its delicious *içli köfte*. If only it served alcohol, life would be perfect.

Gülhan Restaurant (☎ 313 3318; Atatürk Bulvarı; mains TL6-11) Razor-sharp waiters (wearing ties); well-presented food that impresses rather than threatens; the right mood; slick and salubrious surrounds; a pictorial menu with English translations to help you choose – all good ingredients. Everything's pretty good, but if you want a recommendation, go for the Bursa İskender kebap.

Be sure to try one of the restaurants set in atmospheric *konuk* (mansions); see boxed text, below.

URFA'S SPECIAL PLACES

Urfa's famed for its atmospheric *konuk evi* – charming 19th-century stone mansions that have been converted into restaurants and, to a lesser extent, hotels. They usually feature a courtyard around which are arranged several comfy *şark odası* (Ottoman-style lounges), as well as a few rooms upstairs. They are smart places to rest your head and get a typical Urfa experience but bear in mind that they can be noisy at weekends when they host *sıra geceleri* (live music evenings). Also note that not all rooms have private facilities. Consider the following options:

Beyzade Konak (☎ 216 3535; www.beyzadekonak.com, in Turkish; Sarayönü Caddesi, Beyaz Sokak; s/d TL30/60, mains TL4-9; ▓) Good food and comfy lounges but the rooms don't quite live up to the atmospheric surrounds.

Çardaklı Köşk (☎ 217 1080; Vali Fuat Caddesi, Tünel Çıkışı; mains TL6-10) This old house has been so restored it feels almost new. Food is only so-so – the real wow is the view over Gölbaşı from the upstairs terrace. No accommodation.

Cevahir Konuk Evi (☎ 215 4678; www.cevahirkonukevi.com; Yeni Mahalle Sokak; s/d TL70/130, mains TL6-10; ▓) Excellent *tebbule* (tabouleh) and faultlessly cooked *tavuk şiş* (roast chicken kebap). Accommodation-wise, the six rooms are a bit disappointing, with mismatched furniture and brownish carpets.

Gülizar Konukevi (☎ 215 0505; Karameydanı Camii Yanı; s/d TL30/55, mains TL7-12; ▓) Good food and traditional surrounds. The six rooms in the mansion across the street were being given the final touches when we visited.

Pınarbaşı Konağı (☎ 215 3919; 12 Eylül Caddesi; mains TL8-10) Offers an eclectic menu, with kebaps, grills and stews. No accommodation.

SERVICES FROM ŞANLIURFA'S OTOGAR

Destination	Fare (TL)	Duration (hr)	Distance (km)	Frequency (per day)
Adana	25	6	365	frequent
Ankara	40	13	850	5-6
Diyarbakır	15	3	190	frequent
Erzurum	35	12	665	1
Gaziantep	15	2½	145	frequent
İstanbul	50	20	1290	a few
Kayseri	30	9	515	2
Malatya	20	7	395	1
Mardin	15	3	175	a few
Van	35	9	585	2

If all you want is to relax over a cup of tea in leafy surrounds, head for the various *çay bahçesi* (tea gardens) in the Gölbaşı park – a great experience any time of the day.

Entertainment

Urfa is an equivocal city: pious during the day, wild in the evening. What makes the city tick is the *sıra geceleri* that are held in the *konuk* (see boxed text, opposite), usually at weekends. Guests sit, eat, sing and dance in *şark odası* (lounges) and, after the meal, a live band plays old favourites that keep revellers rocking and dancing. Foreigners are welcome to join the party and showcase their dance repertoire.

Getting There & Away

AIR

The airport is 40km from the centre. **Turkish Airlines** (☎ 215 3344; www.thy.com; Kaliru Turizm Seyahat Acentesi, Sarayönü Caddesi; ☽ 8.30am-6.30pm) has daily flights to/from Ankara (from TL99, 1½ hours) and İstanbul (TL114). A bus service leaves from outside the office for the airport, 1½ hours before check-in (TL15).

BUS

The otogar, on the main highway serving the southeast, receives plenty of traffic, but most buses are passing through, so you must take whatever seats are available. Buses to the otogar can be caught on Atatürk Bulvarı (TL1). Taxis usually ask TL10 for the short hop between the otogar and the main drag. Details of some daily services are listed in the table, above. There are plans to relocate the otogar outside the city in 2010.

Minibuses to Akçakale (TL5), Harran (5TL), Birecik (TL10), Kahta (TL15) and Adıyaman (TL8, two hours) leave from the minibus terminal beside the otogar. If you're travelling to Syria, you'll need to catch a minibus to Akçakale, then catch a taxi over the border to Talabiyya. Take note that the border is open from 11am to 3pm on the Syrian side (closed on Friday). For Harran, Harran-Nemrut Tours (p609) can organise pick-ups in the centre at no extra cost, even for one traveller.

CAR

For car hire try **Kaliru Turizm Seyahat Acentesi** (☎ 215 3344; fax 216 3245; Sarayönü Caddesi, Köprübaşı; ☽ 8.30am-6.30pm), the Turkish Airlines agency. Harran-Nemrut Tours (p609) can also arrange car rental for about TL80 per day.

HARRAN

☎ 0414 / pop 6900

Don't skip Harran. It seems certain that this settlement is one of the oldest continuously inhabited spots on Earth. The Book of Genesis mentions Harran and its most famous resident, Abraham, who stayed here for a few years back in 1900 BC. Its ruined walls and Ulu Cami, crumbling fortress and beehive houses are powerful, evocative sights and give the city a feeling of deep antiquity. Traditionally, locals lived by farming and smuggling, but the coming of the Atatürk Dam looks set to change that as cotton fields sprout over what was once desert. Many seemingly poor villagers are actually quite comfortably off, with huge TVs and ghetto blasters in their houses.

On arrival in Harran you are officially expected to buy a ticket (TL2), but there may not be anyone in the booth to collect the money. If anyone in the castle tries to charge you, insist on being given the official ticket.

History

Besides being the place of Abraham's sojourn, Harran is famous as a centre of worship of Sin, god of the moon. Worship of the sun, moon and planets was popular in Harran, and at neighbouring Soğmatar, from about 800 BC until AD 830, although Harran's temple to the moon god was destroyed by the Byzantine emperor Theodosius in AD 382. Battles between Arabs and Byzantines occupied the townsfolk until the coming of the Crusaders. The fortress, which some say was built on the ruins of the moon god's temple, was restored when the Crusaders approached. The Crusaders won and maintained it for a while before they, too, moved on.

Sights

BEEHIVE HOUSES

Harran is famous for its beehive houses, the design of which may date back to the 3rd century BC, although the present examples were mostly constructed within the last 200 years. It's thought that the design evolved partly in response to lack of wood for making roofs and partly because the ruins provided a ready source of reusable bricks. Although the Harran houses are unique in Turkey, similar buildings can be found in northern Syria.

The **Harran Kültür Evi**, within walking distance of the castle, is set up to allow visitors to see inside one of the houses and then sip cold drinks in the walled courtyard afterwards. The **Harran Evi** is similar.

KALE

On the far (east) side of the hill, the crumbling *kale* stands right by some beehive houses. Although a castle probably already existed on the site from Hittite times, what you see now dates mainly from after 1059 when the Fatimids took over and restored it. Originally, there were four multi-angular corner towers, but only two remain. Once there were also 150 rooms here, but many of these have caved in or are slowly filling up with silt.

WALLS & MOSQUE

The crumbling stone **city walls** were once 4km long and studded with 187 towers and four gates; of these only the overly restored **Aleppo Gate**, near the new part of town, remains.

Of the ruins inside the village other than the *kale,* the **Ulu Cami**, built in the 8th century by Marwan II, last of the Umayyad caliphs, is most prominent. You'll recognise it by its tall, square and very un-Turkish minaret. It's said to be the oldest mosque in Anatolia. Near here stood the first Islamic university, and on the hillside above it you'll see the low-level ruins of ancient Harran dating back some 5000 years.

Sleeping

Most people visit from Urfa on a day trip.

Bazda Motel (☎ 441 3590; bazda1@ttnet; s/d/ste TL35/50/80; 🖾) On the road as you come into town, you can't miss this motel – it's been designed to mimic the beehive houses. This is a nice surprise, with modern and serviceable rooms, prim bathrooms, colourful bed linen, a recent lick of paint on the walls, satellite TVs and a grassy area. One problem, though: it's occupied by teachers most times of the year (but welcomes travellers if it's slack).

Harran Evi (☎ 441 2020; bed with full board TL40) This is the place to choose if you want to text your friends 'I've slept in a beehive'. Truth is, it will probably be too hot to do so and you'll end up sleeping under the stars on raised *tahts* (sleeping thrones). A bit folksy (tour groups stop here for souvenirs when they visit Harran), but quirky and atmospheric, top marks go to the ablutions blocks, with their mix of functioning flush and squat toilets, all kept *temiz* (clean).

Harran Kültür Evi (☎ 441 2477; beds with full board TL40) Same concept as the Harran Evi.

Getting There & Away

Getting to Harran is straightforward and you don't really need to take a tour. Minibuses (TL5, one hour) leave from Urfa's otogar approximately every hour and will drop you at the new part of Harran near the *belediye* and PTT – it's a 10-minute walk to the old part.

If you're driving to Harran, leave Urfa by the Akçakale road at the southeastern end of town and go 40km to a turn-off to the left (east). From there, it's another 10km to Harran.

AROUND HARRAN

Although the sites beyond Harran are missable if you're pushed for time, it would be a shame not to see the astonishing transformation wrought on the local scenery by the GAP project (see boxed text, p607) – field upon field of cotton and barley where once there was just desert.

To get around the sites without your own transport is virtually impossible unless you have limitless time. The roads have been upgraded over the last few years but signage is insufficient, so the tours offered by Harran-Nemrut Tours (see p609) are certainly worth considering. For TL15 per person for four or more people you visit Harran, Han el Ba'rur, Şuayb City and Soğmatar, with a chance to take tea with villagers. Expect a simple taxi service. You may need to take a picnic lunch, or you might have a village lunch stop. It's useful to have a pocketful of change for the tips you'll be expected to give.

Bazda Caves

About 20km east of Harran you can visit the impressive Bazda Caves (signed 'Bazda Mağaları'), which are supposed to have been used to build the walls of Harran.

Han el Ba'rur

A further 6km east are the remains of the Seljuk Han el Ba'rur, a caravanserai built in 1128 to service the local trade caravans. Although some restoration work has been done here, there are not enough visitors to justify any services (or tickets for that matter).

Şuayb City

Another 12km northeast of Han el Ba'rur are the extensive remains of Şuayb City, where hefty stone walls and lintels survive above a network of subterranean rooms. One of these contains a mosque on the site of the supposed home of the prophet Jethro. Once again, don't expect to find any services, but it's a good idea to bring a torch (flashlight) and to wear sturdy shoes.

Soğmatar

About 18km north of Şuayb, the isolated village of Soğmatar is a very atmospheric, eerie place, surrounded by a barren landscape with bare rocks and ledges. On one of the ledges there was once an open-air temple, where sacrifices were made to the sun and moon gods, whose effigies can be seen carved into the side of the ledge. Like Harran, Soğmatar was a centre for the cult worship of Sin, the moon god, from about AD 150 to AD 200. This open-air altar was the central, main temple. In a cave near the centre of the village you'll find 12 carved statues as well as Assyrian inscriptions.

Standing on the summit of the structure, you can see remains of other temples on the surrounding hills. There were apparently seven in all.

Once again there are no services at Soğmatar, although villagers will no doubt be happy to point out the sites.

KAHTA

☎ 0416 / pop 60,700

Dusty Kahta isn't the most atmospheric place to spend a holiday, but it's well set up for visits to Nemrut Dağı, with plenty of tours on offer and a decent selection of hotels. If you'd prefer somewhere more inspiring head straight to Karadut Pension (see p621).

A good time to visit would be 25 June when the three-day **International Kahta Kommagene Festival** starts, with music, folk dancing and all sorts of fun and games. All the hotels will be filled with tour groups, so it's wise to book ahead at this time.

You'll find several internet cafés on the main drag.

Sleeping

Pension Kommagene (☎ 725 9726; fax 725 5548; Mustafa Kemal Caddesi; camp sites per person TL7, s/d TL35/50; 🖭) The most obvious choice for budget-minded travellers, not so much because of its inherent merits, but because of the lack of competitors in this price bracket. Rooms are unflashy but clean, secure and well organised. Campers can pitch their tent on the parking lot, and the ablutions block is shipshape. Add TL6 for breakfast and TL12 for dinner. Expect some hard selling with tours to Nemrut at some point.

Hotel Nemrut (☎ 725 6881; www.hotelnemrut.net; Mustafa Kemal Caddesi; s/d TL45/70; 🖭) There's nothing distinctive about this stolid lump with a glass-fronted facade. It's just your run-of-the-mill motel, with uninspiring yet well-maintained rooms and excellent bathrooms. Tour groups stop here on their way to Nemrut. A few smiles at the reception would sweeten the deal.

Zeus Hotel (☎ 725 5694; www.zeushotel.com .tr; Mustafa Kemal Caddesi; camp sites per person TL20, s/d TL80/100; 🖭 🛋) Another group-friendly stalwart, opposite the Hotel Nemrut. This solid three-star option gets an A+ for its swimming pool in the manicured garden – blissful after a long day's travelling by bus. Angle for the renovated rooms, which feature top-notch bathrooms and flat-screen TVs. Campers can pitch tents on the parking lot and have their own ablutions block.

Eating

All accommodation options have restaurants but if you want to dine out there are a couple of eateries on the main drag.

Papatya Restaurant (☎ 726 2989; Mustafa Kemal Caddesi; mains TL4-7) This snappy joint next to Hotel Nemrut whips up all the usual suspects. There's no menu – just point at what you want.

Kahta Sofrası (☎ 726 2055; Mustafa Kemal Caddesi; mains TL4-8) Off the main intersection, this is the most obvious place to line the stomach without breaking the bank. Tasty kebaps and melt-in-your-mouth pide.

For something different take a taxi (about TL8) to the vast lake formed by the Atatürk Dam, about 4km east of Kahta. The lure is the two licensed restaurants serving fresh fish, with lovely views over the lake. It's well worth the detour.

Akropalian (☎ 725 5132; Baraj Yolu; mains TL5-9) Perched on a hillside, about 1km from the lakeshore. Bag a seat in the verdant *bahçe* and drink in the views.

Neşetin Yeri (☎ 725 7675; Baraj Yolu; mains TL5-9) The leafy garden is soothingly positioned right by the lakeside (avoid the hospital-like dining room). Tuck into a faultless grilled *alabalık* (trout), served in a *kiremit* (clay pot), with a background symphony of frogs; come just before sunset. It can't get more atmospheric than this.

Getting There & Away

Kahta's small otogar is in the town centre with the minibus and taxi stands right beside it. There are regular buses to Adıyaman (TL1, 30 minutes, 32km), Ankara (TL40, 12 hours, 807km), İstanbul (TL60, 20 hours, 1352km), Kayseri (TL35, seven hours, 487km), Malatya (TL10, 3½ hours, 225km) and Şanlıurfa (TL10, 2½ hours, 106km).

There are three daily services (except Sunday) to Karadut (TL5), usually at 1.30pm, 3pm and 4.30pm. Minibuses return from Karadut between 7.30am and 8.30am the next day.

The road east to Diyarbakır was flooded by the lake formed behind the Atatürk Dam, and buses from Kahta now travel to Diyarbakır north of the lake (TL20, five hours, 174km). A more interesting way to travel is via one of

the six daily minibuses to Siverek, which are timed to meet the ferries across the lake. In Siverek you may have to wait half an hour or so for a connection to Diyarbakır.

NEMRUT DAĞI NATIONAL PARK

Mt Nemrut National Park (Nemrut Dağı Milli Parkı) is probably the star attraction of eastern Turkey, and rightly so. The enigmatic statues sitting atop the summit have become a symbol of Turkey. The stunning scenery and historical sights and the undeniable sense of mystique and folly that emanates from the site make a visit here essential.

The spellbinding peak of **Nemrut Dağı** (*nehm-root dah-uh*) rises to a height of 2150m in the Anti-Taurus Range between the provincial capital of Malatya to the north and Kahta in Adıyaman province to the south. It is not to be confused with the less visited Nemrut Dağı (3050m, p642) near Lake Van.

Nobody knew anything about Nemrut Dağı until 1881, when a German engineer, employed by the Ottomans to assess transport routes, was astounded to come across the statues covering this remote mountaintop. Archaeological work didn't begin until 1953, when the American School of Oriental Research undertook the project.

The summit was created when a megalomaniac pre-Roman local king cut two ledges in the rock, filled them with colossal statues of himself and the gods (his relatives – or so he thought), then ordered an artificial mountain peak of crushed rock 50m high to be piled between them. The king's tomb and those of three female relatives may well lie beneath those tonnes of rock. Nobody knows for sure.

Earthquakes have toppled the heads from most of the statues, and now many of the colossal bodies sit silently in rows with the 2m-high heads watching from the ground.

Although it's relatively easy to get to the summit with your own vehicle, most people take tours, organised in either Kahta or Malatya or, increasingly, from Şanlıurfa or Cappadocia (see boxed text, p620).

Plan to visit Nemrut between late May and mid-October, and preferably in July or August; the road to the summit becomes impassable with snow at other times. Remember that at any time of year, even in high summer, it will be chilly and windy on top of the mountain. This is especially true at sunrise, the coldest

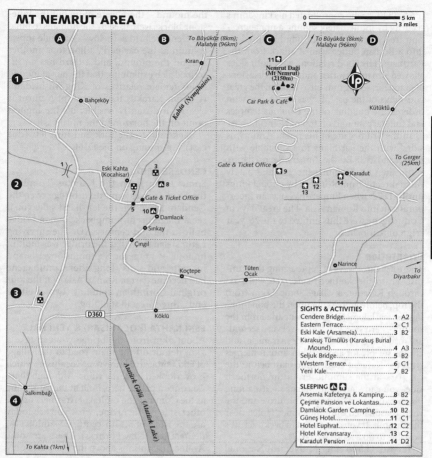

MT NEMRUT AREA

SIGHTS & ACTIVITIES
Cendere Bridge	1 A2
Eastern Terrace	2 C1
Eski Kale (Arsameia)	3 B2
Karakuş Tümülüs (Karakuş Burial Mound)	4 A3
Seljuk Bridge	5 B2
Western Terrace	6 C1
Yeni Kale	7 B2

SLEEPING
Arsemia Kafeterya & Kamping	8 B2
Çeşme Pansion ve Lokantası	9 C2
Damlacık Garden Camping	10 B2
Güneş Hotel	11 C1
Hotel Euphrat	12 C2
Hotel Kervansaray	13 C2
Karadut Pension	14 D2

time of the day. Take warm clothing on your trek to the top, no matter when you go.

There are various accommodation options on the mountain, and it's well worth taking advantage of them since the stunning views and peaceful setting make up for any lack of mod cons. Be sure to check that adequate blankets are provided.

History

From 250 BC onwards, this region straddled the border between the Seleucid Empire (which followed the empire of Alexander the Great in Anatolia) and the Parthian Empire to the east, also occupying a part of Alexander's lands. A small but strategic area, rich, fertile and covered in forests, it had a history of independent thinking ever since the time of King Samos (c 163 BC).

Under the Seleucid Empire, the governor of Commagene declared his kingdom's independence. In 80 BC, with the Seleucids in disarray and Roman power spreading into Anatolia, a Roman ally named Mithridates I Callinicus proclaimed himself king and set up his capital at Arsameia, near the modern village of Eski Kahta. Mithridates prided himself on his royal ancestry, tracing his forebears back to Seleucus I Nicator, founder of the Seleucid Empire to the west, and to Darius the Great, king of ancient Persia to the east. Thus he saw himself as heir to both glorious traditions.

Mithridates died in 64 BC and was succeeded by his son Antiochus I Epiphanes (r 64–38 BC), who consolidated his kingdom's security by immediately signing a nonaggression treaty with Rome, turning his kingdom into a Roman buffer against attack from the Parthians. His good relations with both sides allowed him to grow rich and revel in delusions of grandeur, seeing himself as equal to the great god-kings of the past. It was Antiochus who ordered the building of the fabulous temples and funerary mound on top of Nemrut.

In the 3rd decade of his reign, Antiochus sided with the Parthians in a squabble with Rome, and in 38 BC the Romans deposed him. From then on, Commagene was alternately ruled directly from Rome or by puppet kings until AD 72, when Emperor Vespasian incorporated it into Roman Asia. The great days of Commagene were thus limited to the 26-year reign of Antiochus.

Orientation

There are three ways of approaching the summit. From the southern side, you will pass through Karadut, a village some 12km from the top, before embarking upon the bone-jolting last few kilometres to the car park. From the southwestern side, you will travel via a secondary road that goes past Eski Kale (Arsameia) and climbs steeply for about 10km until it merges with the Karadut road, some 6km before the car park at the summit. From the northern side, you can start from Malatya – it's a long 98km haul, but it's a very scenic drive and the road is asphalted until the Güneş Hotel, near the summit. If you don't want to backtrack, it's possible to do a loop (see p622).

It costs TL5 to enter Mt Nemrut National Park. Coming from the southwest, the entrance gate is at the turn-off to Eski Kale (Arsameia); from the south, the gate is just past Çeşme Pansion; from the north, the gate is at the Güneş Hotel.

At the car park just below the summit are a café and toilets. To reach the ruins themselves, you'll have to walk for about 600m.

Sights & Activities
KARAKUŞ TÜMÜLÜS

Highway D360, marked for Nemrut Dağı Milli Parkı (9km), starts in Kahta next to the Pension Kommagene. After a few kilometres, you'll reach a fork; the road to the left takes you 1.5km to **Karakuş Tümülüs**. Like the Nemrut mound, the Karakuş burial mound, built in 36 BC, is artificial. A handful of columns ring

the mound – there were more but the limestone blocks were used by the Romans to build the Cendere bridge (below). An eagle tops a column at the car park, a lion tops another around the mound, and a third has an inscribed slab explaining that the burial mound holds female relatives of King Mithridates II. From Karakuş the summit of Nemrut is clearly, if distantly, visible; it's the highest point on the horizon to the northeast.

Backtrack to the fork and turn left (due east), continuing on the D360.

CENDERE BRIDGE

Some 10km from the Karakuş Tümülüs, the road crosses a modern bridge over the Cendere River. On the left-hand side, you'll see a magnificent humpback Roman bridge built in the 2nd century AD. The surviving Latin stelae state that the bridge was built in honour of Emperor Septimius Severus and his wife and sons (long after Commagene had become part of Roman Asia). Of the four original Corinthian columns (two at either end), three are still standing.

ESKİ KAHTA (KOCAHİSAR) & YENİ KALE

About 5km from the bridge you can take a 1km detour off the main road to the village of **Eski Kahta**, also known as Kocahisar, which is overlooked by castle ruins. Although there was once a palace here, built at the same time as the Commagene capital of Arsameia on the other side of the ravine, what you see today are the ruins of a 13th-century Mamluk castle, **Yeni Kale** (New Fortress). There are some Arabic inscriptions above the main and only gateway. You can climb up to look at the castle, but make sure you're wearing appropriate shoes, and watch your step.

At the base of the path up to the castle is the **Kocahisar Halı Kursu** (Kocahisar Carpet Course), a rudimentary workshop where local women learn carpet-weaving techniques to keep the tradition alive. They don't sell the carpets here but usually won't mind if you poke your head in to have a look.

After Yeni Kale you'll cross the Kahta (Nymphaios) River, where you can see the old road that crossed the river at a graceful **Seljuk Bridge**.

ESKİ KALE (ARSAMEİA)

About 1.5km further along the main road, a road to the left takes you 2km to Eski Kale, the ancient Commagene capital of Arsameia, founded by Mithridates I Callinicus in around 80 BC and added to by his son Antiochus I. Just after the turn-off, you stop at the **park entrance**, where you'll be asked to pay for both the Arsameia site and access to the summit (TL5).

At Eski Kale, walk up the path from the car park. Just off to the left you'll come to a large **stele** depicting Mithras (or Apollo), the sun god, wearing a cap with sunrays radiating from it. Further along are two more **stelae**. Only the bases have survived, but they were thought to depict Mithridates I Callinicus, with Antiochus I, the taller stele, holding a sceptre. Behind them is a cave entrance leading down to an underground room. These cave-temple structures were thought to have been built for Mithras-worshipping rites.

Continue on the path uphill to the striking and virtually undamaged stone relief that portrays Mithridates I shaking hands with the god Heracles. Next to it is another cave-temple that descends 158m through the rock. Don't attempt to go down the steps as they are said to be perilous. The long Greek inscription above the cave describes the founding of Arsameia; the water trough beside it may have been used for religious ablutions.

Above the relief on the level top of the hill are what are left of the foundations of Mithridates' capital city, and a spectacular view – the perfect spot for a picnic.

ARSAMEIA TO THE SUMMIT

From Arsameia you can take the 16km partly surfaced short cut to the summit or backtrack to the main road, which is a longer route but less steep and fully surfaced. The short cut leaves from beside the entrance to Arsameia and slogs up the mountain for about 8km to join the main route about 6km before the summit car park. It's passable only during daytime and in dry weather, and it has precipitous hairpin bends, so drive slowly and very carefully. The last 2km before the junction are unpaved and can be muddy if it's wet.

Most tours combine the two routes, thus making a loop. Sunrise tours take the longer route (via Narince and Karadut) on the way up and take the short cut to descend back to Kahta. Sunset tours take the short cut on the way up and the longer route to get back to Kahta.

If you take the longer route from Arsameia, return to the main road and turn left. About 3km further is the sleepy village of **Damlacık**. Then you'll pass through various little stone-housed settlements until you reach larger **Narince**, where a turn-off to the left is marked for Nemrut. North of Karadut, the last half-hour's travel (12km) to the summit is along a steep, bumpy road mostly paved with basalt blocks. The last 3km are particularly horrendous – you'll have to drive in first gear.

Hiking

Travellers staying in Karadut can walk the 12km to the summit. It's a clearly marked road with a steady gradient.

THE SUMMIT

By the time you arrive at the car park and café you're well above the tree line. The **Nemrut Dağı park entrance** (admission TL5; ☑ dawn-dusk) is 200m up from Çeşme Pansion and 2.5km before the junction with the short cut to Arsameia.

Beyond the building, hike 600m (about 20 minutes) over the broken rock of the stone pyramid to the **western terrace**. Antiochus I Epiphanes ordered the construction of a combined tomb and temple here. The site was to be approached by a ceremonial road and was to incorporate what Antiochus termed 'the thrones of the gods', which would be based 'on a foundation that will never be demolished'. Antiochus planned this construction to prove his faith in the gods, and in so doing assumed that upon his death his spirit would join that of Zeus-Ahura Mazda in heaven.

As you approach, the first thing you see is the western temple with the conical funerary mound of fist-sized stones behind it. At the western temple, Antiochus and his fellow gods sit in state, although their bodies have partly tumbled down, along with their heads.

From the western terrace it's five minutes' walk to the **eastern terrace**. Here the bodies are largely intact except for the fallen heads, which seem more badly weathered than the western heads. On the backs of the eastern statues are inscriptions in Greek.

Both terraces have similar plans, with the syncretistic gods, the 'ancestors' of Antiochus, seated. From left to right they are Apollo, the sun god (Mithra to the Persians; Helios or Hermes to the Greeks); Fortuna, or Tyche; in the centre Zeus-Ahura Mazda; then King Antiochus; and on the far right Heracles, also

ORGANISED TOURS TO NEMRUT DAĞI (MT NEMRUT)

The main tour centres are Kahta and Malatya, but there are also tours from Karadut, Şanlıurfa and Cappadocia.

From Karadut

Several pensions in Karadut offer return trips to the summit, with one hour at the top for about TL40 per vehicle (Karadut Pension) or TL75 (hotels Euphrat or Kervansaray).

From Kahta

Kahta has always had a reputation as a rip-off town so you will need to be wary of what's on offer. Always check exactly what you will be seeing during the tour in addition to the heads themselves, and how long you'll be away for. The hotels and guesthouses in Kahta run most of the tours to Nemrut Dağı.

The majority of tours are timed to capture a dramatic sunrise or sunset. If you opt for the 'sunrise tours', you'll leave Kahta at about 2am via Narince and Karadut, arriving at Nemrut Dağı for sunrise. After an hour or so, you'll go down again following the upgraded direct road to Arsameia. Then you'll stop at Eski Kahta, Yeni Kale, Cendere Bridge and Karakuş Tümülüs. Expect to be back in Kahta at about 10am. If you sign up for the 'sunset tour', you'll do the same loop but in the reverse direction – in other words, you'll leave at 1.30pm and start with the sights around Arsameia, then go up to the summit, before descending via Karadut and Narince. You'll be back in Kahta at 9.30pm.

A third option is the 'small tour', which lasts about three hours. It zips you from Kahta to the summit and back again, allowing about an hour for sightseeing. It's a bit less expensive (a taxi would charge about TL70), but it's much less interesting.

Although Kahta hotels and guest houses advertise these services as 'tours', you'll quickly catch on that they're only taxi services when your driver proffers comments like 'that's an old bridge'. If you want an informative English-speaking guide, go with **Mehmet Akbaba** (☎ 0535-295 4445; akbabamehmet@hotmail.com) or **Nemrut Tours** (☎ 0416-725 6881; Mustafa Kemal Caddesi), based in Hotel Nemrut. Expect to pay an additional TL100 per group.

---

known as Ares or Artagnes. The seated figures are several metres high, their heads alone about 2m tall.

Low walls at the sides of each temple once held carved reliefs showing processions of ancient Persian and Greek royalty, Antiochus' 'predecessors'. Statues of eagles represent Zeus.

Sleeping & Eating

There are several places to stay along the roads to the summit. The village of Karadut has a few small eateries. Places are listed in order of appearance, starting from the southwestern side (Eski Kale) up to the summit.

Damlacık Garden Camping (☎ 0416-741 2027; camp sites per person TL5; ▣) Call it simple but hospitable. At Damlacık, about 2km from the junction for the entrance gate, this camping ground features a rudimentary ablutions block but the host family is genuinely courteous and the grassed camping areas work a treat. There's also a secure parking lot for camper vans,

equipped with electricity. In summer you'll probably be offered apricots and prunes from the orchard. Just forget about the minuscule swimming pool. Meals are available (TL8). Transport to Nemrut is TL60 per vehicle.

Arsemia Kafeterya & Kamping (☎ 0416-741 2118, 0505-320 0882; arsemia_52@hotmail.com; camp sites per person TL5, d per person TL15) If you're looking to tune into nature and drop out for a while, this is the place. Pitch your tent or park your campervan on a well laid-out ridge (no grass, alas, and no shade) and enjoy the wicked views over the valleys. The ablutions block is in good nick and there's even a nicely landscaped garden. On a balmy summer's night you can also drag a mattress out on the rooftop and sleep beneath the star-studded skies. At the time of research, the owners, the Karakaş family, were in the process of building five rooms with bathrooms. Mamma-style meals are available (about TL8). Transport to Nemrut costs TL70 per vehicle. It's in Eski Kale, about 1km past the entrance gate.

From Malatya

Malatya offers an alternative way to approach Nemrut Dağı. However, visiting Nemrut from this northern side means you miss out on the other fascinating sights on the southern flanks (reached via Kahta). You can get the best of both worlds by traversing the top by foot and hitching a ride to Kahta; if you're travelling by car you'll have to take the long route via Adıyaman.

The Malatya tourist office organises hassle-free minibus tours to Nemrut Dağı from early May to the end of September, or to mid-October if the weather is still warm. Tours leave at noon from near the tourist information booth in the tea garden behind the *valiliği* (provincial government offices).

The three-hour ride through dramatic scenery to the summit is asphalted all the way up. After enjoying the sunset from the summit for two hours, you descend to the Güneş Hotel. Here you have dinner and stay the night before taking the minibus back up to the summit for sunrise. After breakfast at the Güneş you return to Malatya at around 10am.

The per person cost of TL80 (minimum two people) includes transport, dinner, bed and breakfast, and you pay for admission to the national park and the site. In theory, there are tours every day, but if you turn up alone you have to be prepared to pay substantially more. If you prefer to descend via Kahta, hike across the summit to the car park and café building (30 minutes), and ask around for a minibus with an empty seat; or hitch a ride with someone going down to Kahta.

From Şanlıurfa

Two-day tours (TL120, minimum four) or sunrise/sunset tours (TL80, minimum four) to Nemrut are also available from Harran-Nemrut Tours (p609) in Şanlıurfa. These tours usually take you to the Atatürk Dam along the way. They're relatively good value, but don't expect more than a driver.

From Cappadocia

Many companies in Cappadocia (p500) offer minibus tours to Nemrut from mid-April to mid-November, despite the distance of over 500km each way. Two-day tours cost about TL250 and involve many hours of breakneck driving. If you have enough time, it's better to opt for a three-day tour, which allows the journey to be broken into more manageable chunks. Three-day tours usually also include Harran, Şanlıurfa and Gaziantep. Check where you'll be stopping before committing.

Karadut Pension (☎ 0416-737 2169; www.karadut pansiyon.net; camp sites per person TL5, d per person TL20; 🔀 🖳) This pension-cum-hostel at the northern end of Karadut has 11 neat rooms (some with air-con), cleanish bathrooms and a kitchen you can use. Conditions are cramped; luggage usually occupies the last patch of floor space. Meals are available on request (about TL8). At the end of the day, treat yourself to a tipple (wine, beer or rakı) in the cute-as-a-button garden and you'll be in seventh heaven. Campers can pitch their tent in a partially shaded plot at the back, with good views over the mountains and a superclean ablutions block. Free internet at reception.

Çeşme Pansion ve Lokantası (☎ 0416-737 2032; camp sites per person TL5, s with half-board TL30) The closest shut-eye option to the summit (only 6km; the owners will drive you there for TL25). Depending on how you look at it, you'll find the rooms (all with private bathrooms) either bleak (greyish, stained carpets) or cheery (colourful linen). Campers will revel at the lovely

setting, in a shady garden, equipped with a well-scrubbed ablutions block.

Hotel Kervansaray (☎ 0416-737 2190; www.nemrut kervansaray.com; camp sites per person TL10, s/d with half-board TL60/90; 🐾) Same brick walls, same setting and same family, the neighbouring Kervansaray is a carbon copy of the Euphrat. What sets it apart, though, is the smaller number of rooms (21). The rooms are a bit more appealing than at the Euphrat – or perhaps it's just the colourful bed linen? It has a restaurant with a kitsch, rustic interior, a pleasant camping ground and – don't get too excited – a 'swimming pool' (with stagnant water). Again, the owners can drive you to the summit (TL75 per minibus).

Hotel Euphrat (☎ 0416-737 2175; 0416-fax 737 2179; camp sites per person TL12, s/d with half-board TL60/90; 🐾) With 52 rooms, the low-rise Euphrat has the largest capacity in the area and is popular with tour groups in peak season. It lacks atmosphere and rooms are a tad long in the tooth, but the views over the valley from the terrace are terrific. Yes, there's a 'pool', but the water looked murky when we visited. The owners can drive you to the summit (TL75 per minibus).

Güneş Hotel (☎ 0544-459 4144, 0542-2720 0130; half-board per person TL55) Standing in Gothic isolation about 2.5km from the eastern terrace, in the valley below, this place is of use mostly to those coming up from Malatya. The setting is dramatic (bordering on spooky on a cloudy day), amid rocky boulders, the hush enjoyable and the rooms ordinary yet clean. The meals are disappointing, though.

Getting There & Away

CAR

To ascend the southern slopes of Nemrut from Kahta, you can drive along the D360 via Narince, or take a longer but more scenic route that includes Karakuş, Cendere, Eski Kahta and Arsameia, then the 15km short cut to the summit. Make sure you have fuel for at least 250km of normal driving. Though the trip to the summit and back is at most 160km, you have to drive some of that in low gear, which uses more fuel. Be prepared for the rough, steep last 3km up to the summit.

You can also approach the summit from Malatya (98km one way) and drive up to the Güneş Hotel – the road is surfaced and it's a very scenic drive. From there, a rough road leads to the eastern terrace, a further 2.5km – it's OK with a normal car in dry weather.

The question on your lips is: is it possible to drive from the southern side (the Kahta side) to the northern side (the Malatya side), or vice versa, which would avoid backtracking and the long detour via Adıyaman to travel between the two cities? The answer is yes, but don't get too excited, because it's a rough ride. From Kocahisar, a road skirts the base of Nemrut Dağı and goes 21km to the village of Büyüköz. The first 7km, up to the village of Kıran, are surfaced. The next 6km, on to the hamlet of Taşkale, deteriorate markedly and gradually become gravel; the last 8km, up to Büyüköz, are unsurfaced and the road is narrow and very steep (expect nerve-racking twists and turns). Don't brave it in wet weather and seek local advice at Kocahisar (if you're coming from Kahta and going to Malatya) or at Büyüköz (if you're doing Malatya–Kahta) before setting off.

TAXI & MINIBUS

There are three daily minibuses between Kahta and the Çeşme Pansion, about 6km

from the summit. They stop at Karadut village (TL5) on the way. Pension owners can also pick you up at Kahta's otogar (but set the price beforehand).

All pensions and hotels can run you up to the summit and back, but don't expect anything in the way of guidance. The closer to the summit, the cheaper it will be. Hotels in Kahta charge about TL150 for a whole minibus (up to eight people), while Çeşme Pension charges only TL25.

MALATYA

☎ 0422 / pop 455,000 / elevation 964m

What percentage of *yabanci* (foreigners) that traverse central Anatolia en route to the eastern reaches of the country actually stop in Malatya? Definitely not enough.

Sure, it's rarely love at first sight – the architecture wins no prizes and sights are sparse. But look beneath the city's skin and the place will start to grow on you. Among Malatya's rewards are a bevy of verdant parks, tree-lined boulevards, chaotic bazaars, a studentlike atmosphere and the smug feeling that you're the only tourist for miles around. For cultural sustenance, you can head to the nearby historic site of Battalgazi.

Oh, and there's the *kayısı* (apricot). Malatya is Turkey's apricot capital. After the late-June harvest thousands of tonnes of the luscious fruit are shipped from here throughout the world.

Malatya is also the optimal launching pad for exploring the heart of Anatolia and the upper Euphrates, with a smattering of sights and villages that are easily accessible on a half-day or day trip, including Darende. Ah, Darende…

History

The Assyrians and Persians alternately conquered the city, and later the kings of Cappadocia and Pontus did the same. In 66 BC Pompey defeated Mithridates and took the town, then known as Melita. The Byzantines, Sassanids, Arabs and Danışmend *emirs* held it for a time until the coming of the Seljuks in 1105. Then came the Ottomans (1399), the armies of Tamerlane (1401), Mamluks, Dülkadır *emirs* and the Ottomans again (1515).

When the forces of Egypt's Mohammed Ali invaded Anatolia in 1839, the Ottoman forces garrisoned Malatya, leaving much of it in ruins on their departure. Later the resi-

SOUTHEASTERN ANATOLIA

dents returned and established a new city on the present site. You can visit the remains of old Malatya (Eski Malatya), now called Battalgazi, nearby.

Orientation

Malatya stretches for many kilometres along İnönü/Atatürk Caddesi, the main drag, but hotels, restaurants, banks and other services are clustered near the main square with its massive statue of İnönü.

The otogar is 4km west of the centre, just off the main highway, Turgut Özal Bulvarı. The train station is also on the outskirts, 2km west of the centre. City buses and minibuses marked 'Vilayet' operate between the station and the centre.

Information

There are branches of the main banks with ATMs on the main street. Internet outlets are plentiful in the centre.

Information booth (☎ 0535-760 5080; Atatürk Caddesi; ☼ 8am-7pm May-Sep) In the tea garden behind the tourist office – ask for Kemal – and managed by the Güneş Hotel (opposite). Good English is spoken.

Öz Murat Döviz (Atatürk Caddesi; ☼ 7.30am-7pm Mon-Sat) A private exchange office right in the centre, keeps longer hours than banks.

Tourist office (☎ 323 2942; malatyakt@gmail.com; Atatürk Caddesi; ☼ 9am-5pm Mon-Fri) This helpful office is on the ground floor of the valiliği (provincial government headquarters) in the heart of town. Ask for Bülent. It distributes a good town map and a useful brochure on the Malatya area. Good English is spoken.

Sights & Activities

No trip to Malatya would be complete without a stroll through the particularly vibrant **bazaar** that sprawls north from PTT Caddesi and the Malatya Büyük Otel. It's a great place to ramble through and get lost – which you will certainly do at least once. The large covered area is fascinating, especially the lively metalworking area, where the air is filled with hammering, sawing and welding. You'll probably be invited for a tea in the workshop in exchange for a few words. Want to buy a bag of apricots? Brush up your Turkish and wind your way to the kayısı pazarı or the şire pazarı (apricot market). Good luck!

BACKROADS: UPPER EUPHRATES

If you really want to get off the beaten track, you could venture into the upper valley of the Euphrates, from **Elazığ** to **Erzincan**. For adventurous types with plenty of time and their own wheels, this region offers an insight into a fascinating world that few Westerners have seen. You could start your trip with a visit to **Harput**, about 6km from Elazığ. The main attraction there is the huge but badly ruined castle astride a rocky outcrop. Other assorted historic buildings are scattered about, including the Ulu Cami, sporting a crooked minaret, and several mausoleums. Then you could head north to **Pertek** and follow the shores of the Keban Barajı via **Kemaliye** or **Tunceli**. It's a wonderful scenic drive; there are no primary roads, only secondary roads that serve intriguing towns and villages amid the undulating steppe, with mountain ranges as a backdrop. Allow two to three days to cover this suggested route.

Malatya's **museum** (Fuzuli Caddesi; admission TL2; ☾ 8am-5pm Tue-Sun), about 750m from the town centre, has finds from the excavations at Aslantepe (p626).

It's worth taking a stroll along Sinema Caddesi, which features a string of **old Malatyan houses**, five of which have recently been (over)restored.

Malatya also offers tours with an alternative way to approach Nemrut Dağı (p616).

Sleeping

Malatya has a smattering of good-value options, conveniently located in the bazaar and the centre. They are suitable for female travellers.

Malatya Büyük Otel (☎ 325 2828; fax 323 2828; Halep Caddesi, Yeni Cami Karşısı; s/d TL35/60; ☒) This sharp-edged monolith behind the Yeni Cami wins no awards for character but sports serviceable (if a tad smallish) rooms with salubrious bathrooms and dashing views of the huge mosque across the street. The location is very handy – the bazaar is just one block behind – and the staff obliging. It's very quiet at night but due to the proximity of the mosque, be prepared for an early morning wake-up call.

Yeni Hotel (☎ 323 1423; yenihotel@turk.net; Yeni Cami Karşısı Zafer İşhanı; s/d TL35/60; ☒) Quite transparently intended to rival the Malatya Büyük Otel just next door, this well-run establishment makes a pretty good fist of its attempt at competition, enlivening its rooms with pastel hues and electric blue bedspreads. Some rooms have laminated floors too. Keen shoppers should relish the location, right on the edge of the market area. It shares the same morning soundtrack as the Malatya Büyük – the strident call to prayer.

Hotel Yeni Sinan (☎ 321 2907; Atatürk Caddesi; s/d TL50/70) 'Soviet tenement' springs to mind upon first sight of the greyish, peeling facade, but give this central abode a chance for it was undergoing a much-needed freshening up at the time of writing. When we checked in, brand-new mattresses were stacked next to the reception, which bodes well. The breakfast room boasts contemporary furnishings and a flat-screen TV.

Grand Akkoza Hotel (☎ 326 2727; www.grand akkozahotel.com; Çevre Yolu Üzeri Adliye Kavşağı; s/d TL75/110; ☒ ☐) This glass-fronted three-star venture provides a good level of comfort and service, and the sun-filled, capacious rooms boast pristine bathrooms, laminated floors, firm mattresses and a canary yellow colour scheme. There's also a hamam, sauna and gym. It's awkwardly placed (not so much if you're driving) on the busy ring road, but within easy access of the city centre.

Eating

Atatürk Caddesi is awash with inexpensive eateries, but there are funkier, more attractive options around. Kanal Boyu is a tree-lined boulevard divided by a canal and is the closest thing Malatya has to a hip area.

Serhent Simit Sarayı (İnönü Caddesi; simits from TL1) *Simit* aficionados, your search is over. This modern venture makes the best *simits* in the city. The *peynirli* (*simit* with cheese) melts in the mouth.

Sevinç (☎ 321 5188; Atatürk Caddesi; pastries from TL2) This pastry shop features a sleek, modern interior and a batch of mouth-watering desserts, including baklava and cakes. There's a welcoming *aile salonu* (family dining room) upstairs.

Mado (☎ 323 2346; Kanal Boyu; ice creams from TL3) The best outfit for enjoying an ice cream or a pastry in civilised surrounds. Also very central.

Mangal Vadisi (☎ 326 2200; Kışla Caddesi; mains TL4-10) Vegetarians, don't bother reading this review: the huge *mangals* (barbecues) that take centre stage on the ground floor set the tone. This well-regarded restaurant is a beacon for bona fide carnivores, with a wide choice of grilled meat (chicken, lamb, liver and more). Great stuff. It's in a little street off Atatürk Caddesi.

Şelale Kernek Restaurant (☎ 323 9313; Kernek Meydanı; mains TL6-9) In summer the open-air rooftop overlooking verdant gardens is a winner. Otherwise the dining room is dull. The menu focuses on pide and grills, as well as trout in summer.

Sarı Kurdela Restaurant & Cafe (☎ 324 7724; İnönü Caddesi; mains TL6-10) This supertrendy joint ticks all the right boxes, with contemporary decor, efficient waiters (and waitresses) and an eclectic menu, including excellent ready-made meals, vegetarian dishes and a wide choice of sweets that will have you moaning for more. Don't miss it.

Hacıbey Lahmacun (☎ 324 9798; Kışla Caddesi; mains TL6-10) Hands down the best joint for a hearty pide or a *lahmacun (*pizza with a thin, crispy base topped with chopped lamb, onion and tomato), washed down with a refreshing *ayran*. The menu is translated into English, and there are photos of each kind of pide. The wood-panelled facade of the building looks like a Swiss chalet – very exotic for Malatya.

Drinking

Vilayet Çay Bahçesi – VIP Cafe (Vilayet Tea Garden; İnönü Caddesi; tea TL1, snacks TL3-7) This unexpected oasis of calm, behind the *valiliği*, is a good place to recharge the batteries. Nab a table at VIP Cafe and chow down on burgers or *gözleme* (thin savoury crêpes cooked with cheese, spinach or potato), or linger over a cuppa. No doubt you'll be approached by friendly Kemal, who runs the information booth nearby.

Semerkant (☎ 325 6031; Kanal Boyu; coffee TL2, mains TL3-7) Hmm! We can still smell the sweet aroma of nargileh wafting from the door. This relaxed café with a few amusing rustic touches (think fake stone walls and small wooden chairs) is a good place to imbibe the atmosphere of Kanal Boyu.

ourpick Nostalji (☎ 323 4208; Müçelli Caddesi; coffee TL2, snacks TL4-7) No matter how hectic your day, as soon as you step inside this squeaky-boarded, old Malatya mansion complete with memorabilia, stress evaporates as fast as light drizzle on asphalt in summer. Soak up the cool karma in the light-filled main lounge while listening to the mellow music and sipping a cup of Turkish coffee. Simple dishes are also available. It's also a good place to meet students of both sexes.

Shopping

You won't leave Malatya without filling your bags with apricots, the city's delight. There's a handful of dried-fruit shops specialising in apricot baskets, jams and pickles on Atatürk Caddesi but nothing beats a shopping session in the *şire pazarı* (see p623).

Getting There & Away

AIR

The airport is 35km northwest of the centre. All companies operate an airport bus (TL7).

Onur Air (☎ 326 5050; www.onurair.com.tr; İnönü Caddesi; ☯ 8am-8pm) One daily flight to/from İstanbul (from TL112, 1½ hours). Also an agent for Sun Express.

Sun Express (www.sunexpress.com.tr) Has three weekly flights to/from İzmir (from TL109, 1½ hours).

Turkish Airlines (☎ 324 8001; www.thy.com; Kanal Boyu; ☯ 8.30am-5.30pm Mon-Fri, 8.30am-1.30pm Sat) Two daily flights to/from İstanbul (from TL114), and a daily flight to/from Ankara (from TL59, one hour).

BUS

Malatya's enormous otogar, MAŞTİ, is 4km out on the western outskirts. Most bus companies operate *servises* (shuttle minibuses) there from the town centre. If not, minibuses from the otogar travel along Turgut Özal Bulvarı/ Buhara Bulvarı (aka Çevre Yol). However, they aren't allowed into the town centre. Ask to be let off at the corner of Turan Temelli and Buhara Caddesis and walk from there. City buses to the otogar leave from near the *vilayet*. A taxi to the otogar costs about TL15.

Some daily bus services to major destinations are listed in the table, p626.

CAR

Car-hire agencies are clustered just west of the Tekel Factory on İnönü Caddesi. **Meydan Rent a Car** (☎ 325 3434; www.meydanoto.com.tr, in Turkish; İnönü Caddesi, Sıtmapınarı Ziraat Bankası Bitişiği; ☯ 8am-7pm) is a reliable outlet. The tourist office can also arrange car rental.

TRAIN

Right in the middle of Turkey, Malatya is a major railway hub and is well connected by train to the east of the country (Elazığ, Tatvan, Diyarbakır), the west (İstanbul, Ankara, Sivas,

SERVICES FROM MALATYA'S OTOGAR

Destination	Fare (TL)	Duration (hr)	Distance (km)	Frequency (per day)
Adana	25	8	425	a few
Adıyaman	15	2½	144	frequent
Ankara	45	11	685	frequent
Diyarbakır	20	4	260	a few
Elazığ	8	1¾	101	hourly
Gaziantep	20	4	250	a few
İstanbul	50	18	1130	a few
Kayseri	25	4	354	several
Sivas	20	5	235	several

Kayseri) and the south (Adana). A train via here can be a good alternative to tiring bus trips.

The *Vangölü Ekspresi* leaves for İstanbul via Sivas, Kayseri and Ankara on Tuesday and Sunday (TL25); for Elazığ and Tatvan (TL11), it leaves on Wednesday and Sunday.

The *Güney Ekspresi* leaves for İstanbul via Sivas, Kayseri and Ankara on Monday, Wednesday, Friday and Sunday (TL25); for Elazığ and Diyarbakır (TL12), it departs on Tuesday, Thursday, Saturday and Sunday.

The *4 Eylül Ekspresi* leaves daily for Ankara via Sivas and Kayseri (TL25).

The *Firat Ekspresi* leaves daily for Adana (TL16) and for Elazığ (TL6).

Check at the train station for exact departure times of all trains.

Malatya's train station can be reached by minibus (TL1) or by 'İstasyon' city buses from near the *valiliği*.

AROUND MALATYA
Aslantepe
The scant finds of this archaeological site, about 6km from Malatya, are not exactly gripping, but if you have an interest in Anatolian archaeology you'll enjoy **Aslantepe** (⏰ 8am-5pm) and its pretty village setting.

When the Phrygians invaded the Hittite kingdom at Boğazkale, around 1200 BC, many Hittites fled southeast over the Taurus Mountains to resettle and build walled cities. The city of Milidia, now known as Aslantepe, was one of these neo-Hittite city-states (for more information about the Hittites, see boxed text, p464).

On-off excavations since the 1930s have so far uncovered seven layers of remains.

To get to Aslantepe from Malatya, catch a bus marked 'Orduzu' (TL1, 15 minutes) from the southern side of Buhara Bulvarı near the junction with Akpınar Caddesi. Buy an extra ticket for the return trip, and tell the driver where you want to get off; the site is a pleasant 500m stroll from the bus stop.

Battalgazi (Old Malatya)
You don't need to be an archaeology buff to be captivated by the remains of old Malatya, the walled city settled alongside Aslantepe, about 11km north of Malatya at Battalgazi.

As you come into the village you'll see the ruins of the old **city walls** with their 95 towers, built during Roman times and completed in the 6th century. They've lost all their facing stone to other building projects, and apricot orchards now fill what were once city blocks. The village of Battalgazi has grown in and around the ruins.

The bus from Malatya terminates in the main square. Just off here, beside the mosque boasting the smooth-topped minaret, is the **Silahtar Mustafa Paşa Hanı**, an Ottoman caravanserai dating from the 17th century. Although restored, it's virtually abandoned.

When you've finished at the caravanserai, turn right and follow Osman Ateş Caddesi for about 600m until you see the broken brick minaret of the finely restored 13th-century **Ulu Cami** on the left. This is what you've really come to see. This stunning, if fast-fading, Seljuk building dates from the reign of Alaettin Keykubad I. Note the remaining Seljuk tiles lining the dome over the *mimber* (pulpit) and worked into Arabic inscriptions on the *eyvan* and *medrese* (seminary) walls. Also worthy of interest is the **Ak Minare Camii** (White Minaret Mosque), about 50m from the Ulu Cami. This also dates from the 13th century.

Close by is the 13th-century **Halfetih Minaret**, made completely of bricks, and the **Nezir Gazi Tomb**.

Buses to Battalgazi (TL1, 15 minutes) leave every 15 minutes or so from the same bus stop in Malatya as those for Aslantepe.

Yeşilyurt & Gündüzbey

In summer, it's a true pleasure to enjoy the refreshingly peaceful atmosphere of Yeşilyurt and Gündüzbey, respectively 9km and 11km from Malatya. Old houses, lots of greenery, pleasing tea gardens, picnic areas…so cool! Take a minibus from Milli Eğemenlik Caddesi in Malatya (TL1, 20 minutes) and enjoy the hush.

DİYARBAKIR

☎ 0412 / pop 665,400 / elevation 660m

Filled with heart, soul and character, Diyar has recently realised that its tourism potential is fantastic and it's time to tap into it. While it's proud of remaining the symbol of Kurdish identity and tenacity, these days the city also wants to grab a piece of the tourism pie. Thanks to increasing promotion and restoration programs, Turkish and foreign tourists are streaming back, lured by the city's architectural mix. Behind the grim basalt walls, the old city is crammed full of historical buildings and Arab-style mosques. Stroll along the narrow, twisting alleyways and soak up the uniquely unforgettable ambience.

Speak to Turks from western Turkey and they will recoil in fear if you mention Diyarbakır because, since the 1980s, this animated city has been the centre of the Kurdish resistance movement and violent street demonstrations still occur from time to time. And yes, nowhere else in eastern Turkey will you hear people priding themselves so much on being Kurdish.

Banned until a few years ago, the Nevruz festival takes place on 21 March and is a great occasion to immerse yourself in Kurdish culture. For more details, see p662.

Apart from a few street kids, some of whom might harass foreigners, Diyarbakır is as safe as any other city in the region. You only need a little common sense and street savvy to enjoy yourself without any problems.

History

Mesopotamia, the land between the Tigris and Euphrates Valleys, saw the dawn of the world's

---

DETOUR TO DARENDE – THE FORGOTTEN OASIS

Who knows if the utterly mellow town of Darende, about 110km west of Malatya, will be able to handle all this publicity, but it can't go without mention because it's a terrific place to kick off your shoes for a day or two in a fabulous setting. Darende itself won't knock your socks off but it has a splendid canyon right on its doorstep as well as a smattering of well-preserved architectural treasures, including the **Somuncu Baba Camii ve Külliyesi** (with a museum), the **Kudret Havuzu**, a purpose-built rock pool set in the **Tohma Canyon**, near the Sumuncu Baba Camii, and the **Zengibar Kalesi**, perched on a rocky outcrop.

Few things could be more pleasurable than tucking into a fresh trout in one of the few restaurants that have been set up along the riverbank in the canyon. **Hasbahçe** (☎ 0422-615 2215; Somuncu Baba Camii Civarı; mains TL5-10) is a firm favourite – the fish is so fresh it could jump off your plate. Or you could picnic in one of the numerous sheltered *köşk* (picnic areas). In summer, you can dunk yourself in the Kudret Havuzu – just blissful. Action seekers, rejoice: **rafting** is also available in the Tohma Canyon in summer.

The brilliant-value **Tiryandafil Otel** (☎ 0422-615 3095; s/d TL40/70; ✂ ▯) is conveniently located on the outskirts of Darende, about 1km before the canyon and monuments. It has impeccable, commodious rooms with the requisite mod cons. The on-site restaurant is a winner, with excellent local specialities – try the *şelale sızdırma* (meat with melted cheese, mushrooms and butter) – but it's not licensed. Ask for Hassan, who speaks good English and will help you with any queries.

With your own wheels, you can easily reach the **Gürpinar Şelalesi** (waterfalls), about 7km from Darende (from the hotel, follow the road to Ankara for 6km; then it's signposted). Don't expect Niagara-like falls, but it's an excellent picnic spot.

Regular buses (TL10) and minibuses (TL7) ply the route between Malatya and Darende. In Malatya, they depart from the minibus terminal (also known as 'Eski Otogar') on Çevre Yol.

Darende is popular with Turkish families at weekends, and one thing is sure: you'll be the only *yabanci* (foreigner) for miles around. Enjoy!

first great empires. So it's no surprise that Diyarbakır's history begins with the Hurrian kingdom of Mitanni around 1500 BC and proceeds through domination by the civilisations of Urartu (900 BC), Assyria (1356–612 BC), Persia (600–330 BC) and Alexander the Great and his successors, the Seleucids.

The Romans took over in AD 115, but because of its strategic position the city changed hands numerous times until it was conquered by the Arabs in 639. The Arab tribe of Beni Bakr that settled here named their new home Diyar Bakr, which means the Realm of Bakr.

For the next few centuries the city was occupied by various tribes, until 1497 when the Safavid dynasty founded by Shah İsmail took over Iran, putting an end to more than a century of Turkoman rule in this area. The Ottomans came and conquered in 1515, but even then, Diyarbakır was not to know lasting peace. Because it stood right in the way of invading armies originating from Anatolia, Persia and Syria, it suffered many more tribulations.

Orientation & Information

Old Diyarbakır is encircled by walls pierced by several main gates. Within the walls the city is a maze of narrow, twisting, mostly unmarked alleys. New Diyarbakır sprawls to the northwest of the old city, but you'll have no reason to go there, as most services useful to travellers are in Old Diyarbakır, on or around Gazi Caddesi, including the PTT, internet cafés and banks with ATMs.

Nazlı Saray Döviz (Gazi Caddesi; ☼ 8am-7pm Mon-Sat) Private exchange office that keeps longer hours than banks.

Tourism information bureau (☼ 9am-noon & 1-6pm Tue-Sat) Municipal office, off Kıbrıs Caddesi. Has brochures and can help with simple queries.

Tourist office (☎ 228 1706; Kapısı; ☼ 8am-5pm Mon-Fri) Provincial office housed in a tower of the wall. Also has brochures and can help with simple queries.

Sights

CITY WALLS & GATES

Diyarbakır's single most conspicuous feature is its great circuit of basalt walls, probably dating from Roman times, although the present walls date from early Byzantine times (AD 330–500). At almost 6km in length these walls are said to be second in extent only to the Great Wall of China. They make a striking sight whether you're walking along the top or the bottom.

Numerous bastions and towers stand sentinel over the massive black walls. There were originally four main gates: **Harput Kapısı** (north), **Mardin Kapısı** (south), **Yenikapı** (east) and **Urfa Kapısı** (west).

Fortunately, the most easily accessible stretch of walls is also the most interesting in terms of inscriptions and decoration. Start near the Mardin Kapısı close to the Deliller Han, a stone caravanserai now home to the Otel Büyük Kervansaray. Be sure not to miss **Nur Burcu** (Tower Nur), the **Yedi Kardeş Burcu** (Tower of Seven Brothers), with two Seljuk lion bas-reliefs, which you can see only from outside the walls, and the **Malikşah Burcu** (Tower of Malik Şah, also called Ulu Badan), which has some bas-reliefs too.

You can also ascend the walls of the **İç Kale** (keep) to enjoy the fine views of the Tigris, flanked by a patchwork of market gardens. The İç Kale was being restored at the time of writing and should be one of the most attractive parts of the city walls when it's completed.

At various spots inside the base of the walls you can see brightly painted, open-air **Sufi sarcophagi**, notable for their turbans – their size is a symbol of spiritual authority. There's a cluster a few hundred metres northeast of the Urfa Kapısı.

Unfortunately, you must be careful when walking on and along the walls as there have been reports of attempted robberies. Try to go in a group.

MOSQUES

Of Diyarbakır's many mosques, the most impressive is the **Ulu Cami**, built in 1091 by Malik Şah, an early Seljuk sultan. Incorporating elements from an earlier Byzantine church on the site, it was extensively restored in 1155 after a fire. It's rectangular in plan – Arab style, rather than Ottoman. The entrance portal, adorned with two medallions figuring a lion and a bull, leads to a huge courtyard. This is the most elegant section of the building, with two-storey arcades, two cone-shaped *şadırvans* (ritual ablutions fountains), elaborate pillars, and friezes featuring fruits and vegetables – a real feast for the eyes.

Across Gazi Caddesi is the **Hasan Paşa Hanı**, a 16th-century caravanserai occupied by carpet shops and souvenir sellers. It was extensively restored in 2006.

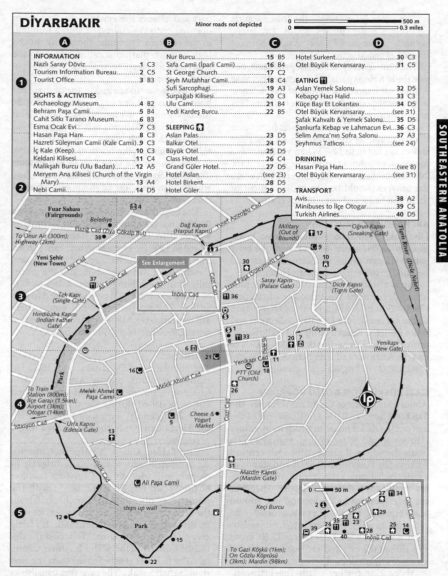

DİYARBAKIR

Minor roads not depicted

Alternating black-and-white stone banding is a characteristic of Diyarbakır's mosques, many of which date from the time of the Akkoyunlu dynasty. One of these is the **Nebi Camii** (1530) at the main intersection of Gazi and İzzet Paşa/İnönü Caddesis, which has a detached minaret sporting a stunning combination of black-and-white stone.

The **Behram Paşa Camii** (1572), in a residential area deep in the maze of narrow streets, is Diyarbakır's largest mosque. More Persian in style, the **Safa Camii** (1532) has a highly decorated minaret with blue tiles incorporated in its design.

The **Şeyh Mutahhar Camii** (1512) is also famous for its detached minaret, but its engineering is even more interesting – the tower stands on four slender pillars about 2m high, earning it the name Dört Ayaklı Minare (Four-Legged Minaret).

The 12th-century **Hazreti Süleyman Camii**, beside the İç Kale, is particularly revered because it houses the tombs of heroes of past Islamic wars. Local people flock here on Thursdays to pay their respects.

Note that most of these mosques have more than one name; the alternative names are shown on the map key. When visiting these mosques, you should try to time your visit for 20 to 25 minutes after the call to prayer (when the prayers should be finished), as most of them will be locked outside prayer times.

ARCHAEOLOGY MUSEUM

Diyarbakır's **Archaeology Museum** (Arkeoloji Müzesi; admission TL2; ☉ 8am-5pm Tue-Sun) is near the Fuar Sahası (Fairgrounds), off Elazığ Caddesi and behind the towering Dedeman Hotel.

It has a well-presented collection including finds from the Neolithic site of Çayönü (7500–6500 BC), 65km north of Diyarbakır. There's also a decent Urartian collection and relics from the Karakoyunlu and Akkoyunlu, powerful tribal dynasties that ruled much of eastern Anatolia and Iran between 1378 and 1502. Labels in English are a great help.

GAZİ KÖŞKÜ & ON GÖZLU KÖPRÜSÜ

About 1km south of the Mardin Kapısı, the **Gazi Köşkü** (admission TL1) is a fine example of the sort of Diyarbakır house to which its wealthier citizens would retire in high summer. The house dates from the time of the 15th-century Akkoyunlu Turkoman dynasty and stands in a well-tended park, very popular with picnicking families at weekends. It's open whenever the caretaker can be found, and you should leave him a tip for showing you around.

To get there, it's a pleasant, if rather isolated, downhill walk. Taxis charge TL10. From this side of the city you get fine, unimpeded views of Diyarbakır's dramatic walls.

About 2km further south, the 11th-century **On Gözlu Köprüsü** (Ten-Eyed Bridge) is also worth a look.

DİYARBAKIR HOUSE MUSEUMS

Old Diyarbakır houses were made of black basalt and decorated with stone stencilling. They were divided into summer and winter quarters, and the centre of the summer part was always the *eyvan*, a vaulted room opening onto the courtyard with a fountain in the centre. In summer, the family moved high wooden platforms called *tahts* into the courtyard for sleeping, making it possible to catch any breeze.

The best way to see inside one of these old houses is to visit one of the museums inside the city walls. For example, the poet Cahit Sıtkı Tarancı (1910–56) was born in a two-storey black basalt house built in 1820, in a side street about 50m north of the Ulu Cami. It now houses the **Cahit Sıtkı Tarancı Museum** (Ziya Gökalp Sokak; admission free; ☉ 8am-5pm Tue-Sun), which contains some of the poet's personal effects and furnishings.

The beautiful grey-and-white-striped **Esma Ocak Evi**, not far from the Dört Ayaklı Minare, was built in 1899 by an Armenian and restored in 1996 by a female writer, Esma Ocak. You'll need to bang hard on the door to alert the caretaker, who will show you the gracefully furnished living rooms. Admission is by donation, but you'll be encouraged to give at least TL2 per person. While you're there ask the caretaker to show you the Armenian Surpağab Kilisesi opposite (see below).

CHURCHES

The population of Diyarbakır once included many Christians, mainly Armenians and Chaldeans, but most of them were pushed out or perished during the troubles in the early 20th century or, more recently, with the Hezbollah. Only their churches linger as reminders.

The **Keldani Kilisesi** (Chaldean Church), off Yenikapı Caddesi, is a plain, brightly lit church, still used by 30 Christian families of the Syrian rite (in communion with the Roman Catholic Church). The chaplain from the Meryem Ana Kilisesi holds a service here on the second Sunday of the month. It's fairly easy to find on your own. Walk past the detached minaret of the Şeyh Mutahhar Camii, take the first left (Dicle Sokak) then the first right (Şeftali Sokak). The caretaker usually sits outside the Nebi Camii.

The Armenian **Surpağab Kilisesi**, also just off Yenikapı Caddesi, has long been grass-infested since the roof caved in, but it's well worth visiting. Bang on the blue doors if it's closed.

The wonderful **Meryem Ana Kilisesi** (Church of the Virgin Mary) is still used by Orthodox Syrian Christians; they are Jacobites, or

Monophysites, who refused to accept the doctrine laid down at the Council of Chalcedon in 451. This stated that Jesus had two natures, being simultaneously fully divine and fully human – the Monophysites insisted he had only one divine nature. The church is beautifully maintained, although only about seven families still attend services. You will have to hammer on the door as the custodian lives two courtyards away and may not hear you.

Inside the İç Kale, the **St George Church** was being restored at the time of writing.

Other churches have found new uses, including the **old church** near the Dört Ayaklı Camii, now a PTT.

Sleeping

Most accommodation options are conveniently located on Kıbrıs Caddesi and the nearby İnönü Caddesi, where there's a range of hotels in all price brackets interspersed with restaurants. In summer it's scorching hot here, something to bear in mind when choosing a room. The best accommodation choices for lone female guests are Hotel Birkent, the Balkar Otel and the top-end options.

BUDGET

Aslan Palas (☎ 228 9224; fax 223 9880; Kıbrıs Caddesi; s/d TL20/30; 🅿) A worthwhile back-up for cash-strapped (male) travellers. A few broken tiles in the bathrooms and ageing plumbing may raise a few eyebrows, but that's about the worst surprise you'll get. Air-con is in all the rooms. Prices don't include breakfast, but you'll find several *kahvaltı salonu* (eateries specialising in full Turkish breakfasts) on the street.

Hotel Surkent (☎ 228 1014; İzzet Paşa Caddesi; s/d TL30/45; 🅿) Tangerine frames and aluminium plates on the facade, flamingo-pink walls, technicolour bed linen and flashy orange curtains: the owners of the Surkent certainly like your life to be colourful. The top-floor rooms boast good views (for singles, rooms 501, 502 and 503 are the best). It's in a peaceful street, close to everything. One downside: there's no lift – good to know if your backpack weighs a tonne.

Hotel Güler (☎ /fax 224 0294; Yoğurtçu Sokak; s/d TL30/45; 🅿) Tucked in an alleyway off Kıbrıs Caddesi, this two-star outfit has impersonal yet well-looked-after rooms, good mattresses and prim, if pint-sized, bathrooms.

Hotel Aslan (☎ 224 7096; fax 224 1179; Kıbrıs Caddesi; s/ d TL35/50; 🅿) *'Her gün temizlik yapıyoruz'* ('We

do the cleaning everyday'), staff told us. And it shows. Next door to the Palas, the Aslan stands its ground with bright rooms, clean linen and bathrooms you won't dread using.

Hotel Birkent (☎ 228 7131; fax 228 7145; İnönü Caddesi; s/d TL40/60; 🅿 🖥) We saw a few female travellers at this hotel, which is a good sign. With its neat bathrooms, spotless rooms, turquoise bedspreads, convenient location and copious breakfast, the Birkent makes for a cost-effective base from which to explore Diyar.

Grand Güler Hotel (☎ 229 2221; fax 224 4509; Kıbrıs Caddesi; s/d TL40/60) The billet of choice for tour groups, the Güler is not *that* grand but its blue mosaic facade brings a touch of fancy to an otherwise dull street. A recent coat of (baby-pink) paint has spruced-up the rooms, which are well equipped and serviceable. The front rooms have double-glazing so it shouldn't be too noisy.

MIDRANGE

Balkar Otel (☎ 228 6306; fax 224 6936; Kıbrıs Caddesi 38; s/d TL50/80; 🅿) This typical middling three-star boasts well-appointed rooms with TV and minibar. Bathroom-wise, don't even think of gesticulating in the cramped cubicles in the single rooms. Added bonuses include a lift, a hearty breakfast and a rooftop terrace that proffers stunning views over the walls.

Büyük Otel (☎ 228 1295; fax 221 2444; İnönü Caddesi; TL60/80; 🅿) If you want no surprises and no hassles, you'll strike gold at the Büyük. Service is everything it should be – no more, no less – while the unadventurous, motel-style rooms are exactly what you'd expect. A reliable option for women travellers.

our pick Otel Büyük Kervansaray (☎ 228 9606; fax 228 7145; Gazi Caddesi; s/d/ste TL80/120/250; 🅿 🖥) This is your chance to sleep in the 16th-century Deliller Han, a converted caravanserai. This is not the height of luxury, but it scores high on amenities, with a restaurant, a bar, a hamam and a nifty pool in which to cool off. The standard rooms are itty-bitty, but how much time are you going to spend in your room when the inner courtyard is so agreeable?

TOP END

Class Hotel (☎ 229 5000; www.diyarbakirclasshotel .com, in Turkish; Gazi Caddesi; s/d TL220/320; 🅿 🖥) Tired and jaded from so much travelling? Or just overweight from all those squishy baklava? Work it off at this five-star bigwig that comes with a fully equipped gym, a sauna, a hamam and even a swimming pool. You'd never guess it from the outside, but this Manhattan-esque building in the heart of the old town has a well-kept secret: the Çizmeci Köşkü, a traditional house that's been renovated and integrated into the hotel's premises, with several small Ottoman-style lounges where guests can relax. A neat surprise.

Eating

A stroll along Kıbrıs Caddesi reveals plenty of informal places to eat. They're nothing fancy, but they offer authentic fare at very moderate prices.

Şafak Kahvaltı & Yemek Salonu (Kıbrıs Caddesi; mains TL5-8) Nosh on freshly prepared meat dishes and expertly cooked pide in this brisk Diyarbakır institution, ideally positioned on Kıbrıs Caddesi. It's also a good place to partake in a restorative morning breakfast.

Şanlıurfa Kebap ve Lahmacun Evi (☎ 228 2312; İzzet Paşa Caddesi; mains TL5-10; ☼ 7am-8pm Mon-Sat) Slip into this neat restaurant and hoe into well-executed kebaps and pide.

Otel Büyük Kervansaray (☎ 228 7131; Gazi Caddesi; mains TL5-10) Even if you're not staying in this historic hotel it's worth popping in for a meal in the restaurant, which is a converted camel stable. There's live music here most nights and, joy of joys, it's licensed.

Küçe Başı Et Lokantası (☎ 229 5661; Kıbrıs Caddesi; mains TL6-10) A few doors away from most hotels, this outfit gets kudos for its wide-ranging menu and original setting – the room at the back is designed like a rustic barn. Try innovative dishes like *tavuk tava* (deep-fried chicken meat in a flat-bottomed pan). There's a picture menu to facilitate your choice.

ourpick Selim Amca'nın Sofra Salonu (☎ 224 4447; Ali Emiri Caddesi; mains TL6-12, set menu TL19) This bright eatery outside the city walls is famous for its *kaburga dolması* (lamb or chicken stuffed with rice and almonds). Round it off with a devilish *İrmik helvası* (a gooey dessert). Hardly the foodstuff of Heart Foundation ticks but undeniably delicious. If only alcohol was served!

Other recommendations:

Aslan Yemek Salonu (Kıbrıs Caddesi; mains TL4-9) An excellent-value stomach-filler, with a wide selection of meat dishes.

Kebapçı Hacı Halid (Borsahan Sokak; mains TL5-10) The ideal pit stop if money matters. Tasty kebaps and ready-made meals served in bright surroundings. Look for the black-and-white pictures of old Diyarbakır on the 1st floor. It's in a small pedestrianised side street off Gazi Caddesi.

Şeyhmus Tatlıcısı (Kıbrıs Caddesi; ☼ 7am-8pm) Keep up your strength with a delectable baklava or a sticky *kadayıf* (dough soaked in syrup).

Drinking

The delightful courtyard of the **Otel Büyük Kervansaray** (☎ 228 7131; Gazi Caddesi) is a great place to unwind over a cup of tea and take in the atmosphere. There's also a smattering of appealing teahouses in the recently restored Hasan Paşa Hanı (see p628).

Getting There & Away

AIR

There is no airport service; a taxi from the town centre to the airport will cost about TL15.

Onur Air (☎ 223 5312; www.onurair.com.tr; Gevran Caddesi, Rızvan Ağa Sokak; ☼ 8am-7pm) Has two daily flights to/from İstanbul (from TL110).

Pegasus Airlines (www.flypgs.com) Has four weekly flights to/from İzmir (from TL100), six weekly flights to/from Ankara (from TL100) and a daily flight to/from İstanbul (from TL100).

Sun Express (www.sunexpress.com.tr) Has five weekly flights to İzmir (from TL100, two hours), three weekly flights to Antalya (from TL100), two weekly flights to Bursa (from TL110) and four weekly flights to İstanbul (from TL100).

Turkish Airlines (☎ 228 8393; www.thy.com; İnönü Caddesi; ☼ 8am-7pm) Has two daily flights to/from İstanbul (from TL114) and two daily flights to/from Ankara (from TL109). Also represents Sun Express and Pegasus Airlines.

BUS

Many bus companies have ticket offices on İnönü Caddesi or along Gazi Caddesi near the Dağ Kapısı. The otogar is about 14km from the centre, on the road to Urfa (about TL20 by taxi).

There's a separate minibus terminal (İlçe Garajı) about 1.5km southwest of the city walls, with services to Batman (TL7, 1½ hours), Elazığ (TL10, two hours), Mardin (TL7, 1¼ hours), Malatya (TL15, five hours), Midyat (TL10) and Siverek (to get to Kahta without going right round the lake via Adıyaman). For Hasankeyf, change in Batman. To get to the minibus terminal, take a bus from near the Balkar Otel, across the street, and ask for 'İlçe Garajı' (TL1), or take a taxi (TL10).

SERVICES FROM DİYARBAKIR'S OTOGAR

Destination	Fare (TL)	Duration (hr)	Distance (km)	Frequency (per day)
Adana	35	8	550	several
Ankara	55	13	945	several
Batman	7	1½	85	frequent minibuses
Erzurum	30	8	485	several
Malatya	20	5	260	frequent
Mardin	7	1½	95	hourly
Şanlıurfa	15	3	190	frequent
Sivas	30	10	500	several
Tatvan	20	4	264	several
Van	30	7	410	several

For Iraq, take a bus to Cizre (TL17, four hours) or Silopi (TL20, five hours) from the main otogar. There are about four services per day. See boxed text, p635, for more details.

Details of some daily services on the main routes are listed in the table, above.

CAR
There is an Avis (☎ 236 1324, 229 0275; www.avis .com.tr; Elazığ Caddesi; ⏰ 8am-7pm) office across the street from the *belediye* and at the airport.

TRAIN
The train station is about 1.5km from the centre, at the western end of İstasyon Caddesi. The *Güney Ekspresi* leaves for İstanbul via Malatya, Sivas and Kayseri at 11.36am on Monday, Wednesday, Friday and Sunday.

MARDİN
☎ 0482 / pop 55,000 / elevation 1325m

Pretty-as-a-picture Mardin is a highly addictive, unmissable spot to slap your backpack down. No doubt you'll ooohh and aaahh over its fabulous setting, breathtaking layout and wealth of architectural treasures. With its minarets poking out of a baked brown labyrinth of lanes, its old castle dominating the old city and the honey-coloured stone houses that cling to the hillside, Mardin emerges like a phoenix from the roasted Mesopotamian plains.

Another draw is the mosaic of people. As a melting pot of Kurdish, Yezidi, Christian and Syrian cultures, among others, it has a fascinating social mix.

Don't expect to have the whole place to yourself, though. With daily flights from İstanbul and lots of positive coverage in the Turkish media over the last few years, Mardin is no longer a sleeping beauty. You will come across lots of Turkish tour groups in summer.

If you really want something extra special, take a little detour to Dara or, better still, Savur (but you didn't hear it from us…).

History
As with Diyarbakır, Mardin's history is one of disputes between rival armies over millennia, though in recent years the only dispute that anyone has really cared about was the one between the PKK (Kurdistan Workers Party) and the government. A castle has stood on this hill from time immemorial, and the Turkish army still finds the site useful.

Assyrian Christians settled here during the 5th century, and the Arabs occupied Mardin between 640 and 1104. After that, it had a succession of Seljuk Turkish, Kurdish, Mongol and Persian overlords, until the Ottomans under Sultan Selim the Grim took it in 1517. In the early 20th century many of the Assyrian Christians were pushed out or perished during the troubles, and in the last few decades many have emigrated. An estimated 600 Christians remain, with 11 churches still in use on a rotational basis.

Orientation & Information
Coming from Diyarbakır, you first pass through the new part of Mardin, where you'll find the Otel Bilen. From here the main road winds up a hill. Continue up the hill to the roundabout where the road forks. Go uphill to the main drag, Cumhuriyet Caddesi (still called by its former name, Birinci Caddesi), to find the hotels and the main square, Cumhuriyet Meydanı, with the statue of Atatürk. The right-hand road from the roundabout, Yeni Yol, curves round the hillside on a

SOUTHEASTERN ANATOLIA

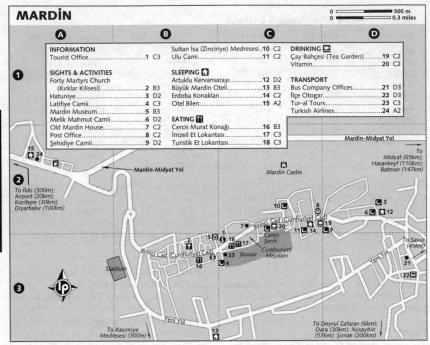

MARDİN

INFORMATION
Tourist Office.............................1 C3

SIGHTS & ACTIVITIES
Forty Martyrs Church
(Kırklar Kilisesi)........................2 B3
Hatuniye....................................3 D2
Latifiye Camii.............................4 C3
Mardin Museum.........................5 B3
Melik Mahmut Camii..................6 D2
Old Mardin House......................7 C2
Post Office.................................8 C2
Şehidiye Camii...........................9 D2

Sultan İsa (Zinciriye) Medresesi..10 C2
Ulu Cami..................................11 C2

SLEEPING
Artuklu Kervansarayı.................12 D2
Büyük Mardin Oteli...................13 B3
Erdoba Konakları.......................14 C2
Otel Bilen.................................15 A2

EATING
Cercis Murat Konağı..................16 B3
İmzeil Et Lokantası....................17 C3
Turistik Et Lokantası..................18 C3

DRINKING
Çay Bahçesi (Tea Garden)..........19 C2
Vitamin....................................20 C2

TRANSPORT
Bus Company Offices................21 D3
İlçe Otogar...............................22 D3
Tur-al Tours..............................23 C3
Turkish Airlines.........................24 A2

Sights

Mardin's most obvious attraction is the rambling **bazaar** that parallels Cumhuriyet Caddesi one block down the hill. Here donkeys are still the main form of transport, and are decked out in all the finery you sometimes see on sale in carpet shops. Look out also for saddle repairers who seem to be able to restore even the shabbiest examples.

Strolling through the bazaar, keep your eyes open for the secluded **Ulu Cami**, a 12th-century Iraqi Seljuk structure that suffered badly during the Kurdish rebellion of 1832. Inside it's fairly plain, but the delicate reliefs adorning the minaret make a visit worthwhile.

lower latitude to rejoin Cumhuriyet Caddesi, just north of the İlçe Otogar.

Everything you'll need, including banks with ATMs and internet cafés, is along or just off Cumhuriyet Caddesi, a one-way street with minibuses running along it.

The **tourist office** (Cumhuriyet Caddesi; 8.30am-5.30pm), right in the centre of town, has a few brochures.

Mardin Museum (Mardin Müzesi; Cumhuriyet Caddesi; admission TL2; 8am-5pm), prominently positioned on the main drag, is worth visiting for the late-19th-century building alone. This superbly restored mansion sports carved pillars and elegant arcades on the upper floor. Inside, it has a small but well-displayed collection including a finely detailed 7th-century BC Assyrian vase and finds from Girnavaz, a Bronze Age site 4km north of Nusaybin. Afterwards, head east along Cumhuriyet Caddesi, keeping your eye out for a fabulous example of Mardin's domestic architecture on your left – the three-arched facade of an ornately carved **house**.

Continue east, looking for steps on the left (north) that lead to the **Sultan İsa (Zinciriye) Medresesi** (daylight hours), dating from 1385 and the town's prime architectural attraction. The highlight is the imposing recessed doorway, but make sure you wander through the pretty courtyards, lovingly tended by the caretaker, and onto the roof to enjoy the cityscape.

Further east is what surely must be Turkey's most gorgeous **post office**, housed in a 17th-century caravanserai with carvings such as frills around the windows and teardrops in stone dripping down the walls – shame they added the clunky staircase! Across the street you can't miss the elegant, slender minaret of the 14th-century **Şehidiye Camii**. It's superbly carved, with colonnades all around, and three small bulbs superimposed at the summit. The base of the minaret sports a series of pillars.

Also worth visiting is the 14th-century **Latifiye Camii**, behind the Akbank, where a shady courtyard has a *şadırvan* in the middle. The 15th-century **Forty Martyrs Church** (Kırklar Kilisesi; Sağlık Sokak) is to the west, with the martyrs depicted above the doorway of the church as you enter. If it's closed, bang hard on the door to alert the caretaker. Services are held here each Sunday. In the vicinity of the Artuklu Kervansarayı, the eye-catching **Hatuniye** and nearby **Melik Mahmut Camii** have been recently restored.

Another striking sight, the **Kasımiye Medresesi**, 800m south of Yeni Yol, was built in 1469. Two domes stand over the tombs of Kasım Paşa and his sister, but the highlights are the sublime courtyard walled with arched colonnades and the magnificent, carved doorway. Upstairs, you can see the students' quar-ters, before ascending the stairs to the rooftop for another great Mardin panorama.

Sleeping

You're dead right: for such a tourist hot spot, there aren't many options, especially if you're on a budget.

Otel Bilem (☎ 213 0315; fax 212 2575; Yenişehir; s/d TL60/120; 🖭) The Bilem is a safe albeit unsexy choice in the new part of Mardin (Yenişehir), 2km northwest of Cumhuriyet Meydanı. Although the facade and the lobby were reno-vated (the rooms also were to be refurbished), there's no disguising the fact that, architectur-ally speaking, this is no beauty queen – its boxy concrete frame boasts comfortable mod-ern facilities but little personality. Still, it's often full to the brim with tour groups.

Artuklu Kervansarayı (☎ 213 7353; www.artuklu .com; Cumhuriyet Caddesi; s/d TL90/140; 🖭) Quirky, there's no doubt about it: dark floorboards and furniture, stone walls, sturdy wooden doors…you'll feel like you're in a castle. We're not quite sure how to take the Artuklu (which bills itself as a 'boutique hotel'), but at least it broke the mould when it conceived the 'me-dieval' interior of this venture. It sports a wide

---

GETTING TO KURDISH IRAQ

Yes, it's possible, but don't tell your family – they'd be worried sick, even though the crossing of the Turkish–Iraqi border at Habur, 15km southeast of Silopi (reached by bus from Mardin or Diyarbakır via Cizre), is pretty straightforward, and safe. At Silopi's otogar, you'll soon realise that crossing the border is a well-organised business that's in the hands of the local taxi mafia. For TL60 (or the equivalent in euros or US dollars), a taxi driver will handle all formalities up to the Iraqi border post. Going through Turkish immigration and customs is quick (no queues), and few questions are asked. Then the taxi drives you to the Ibrahim Halil border post (the Iraqi side), over the bridge on the Tigris. Here too, we found the border crossing process fairly harmless. You might be asked for a place to stay in Iraq; just mention any hotel in Zakho or Dohuk (such as the Birjin). Then you just have to take one of the Iraqi (well, Kurdish) taxis that wait in a car park just outside customs. In total, it took us less than an hour.

It had to be too good to be true. The next day, after having spent the night in Dohuk, we crossed the border in the reverse direction. And this was not quite the same story. One of the Turkish taxi drivers, who was waiting on the Iraqi side (they are allowed to), offered to drive us back to Silopi for the usual amount (TL60). Here comes the glitch: while we were standing with him at the immigration counter, he got back to his car for a few minutes, only to stuff our backpack (which we had left in the car) with smuggled cigarettes… Aaargh! We quickly unpacked everything to check if other forbidden stuff (remember *Midnight Express*?) had been placed in the bag. Smuggling is taken very seriously at the Turkish customs, as we realised. Customs offic-ers dutifully searched all cars, removing bumpers, upholstery etc. Luggage was scanned. There was palpable tension in the air. After two hours (queues are common in this direction), we were off to Silopi. Phew! The moral of the story: never leave your luggage unattended at the border.

If you want to know more about travelling in Kurdish Iraq, get a copy of Lonely Planet's *Middle East*, which has a chapter on Iraq.

SOUTHEASTERN ANATOLIA

A SUCCESS STORY

Ebru Baydemir is what you would call a 'local character'. Aged 33, she is the dynamic owner of Cercis Murat Konağı (below) in Mardin. A rare example of a female entrepreneur in eastern Anatolia, she has managed to foster a new mindset among many Mardin women. 'When I opened my restaurant in 2001, I wanted to offer jobs to women but this was difficult because of the prevailing women-should-stay-at-home mentality. I started with a few female cooks who knew tried-and-true recipes, but I was obliged to set up partition walls so that they could not be visible in the kitchen. Little by little, I gained the confidence of their husbands. At present 15 female employees work here and they don't have to conceal themselves any longer. In Mardin it's now accepted that women can work outside.' Any other achievement, Mrs Ebru? 'Cercis is the first licensed restaurant in southeastern Anatolia', something for which travellers will be eternally grateful.

Best of all, cooking courses are available for tourists. Check out www.cercismurat.com for more details.

---

range of amenities but there are no views of which to speak.

ourpick Erdoba Konakları (☎ 212 7677; www .erdoba.com.tr; Cumhuriyet Caddesi; s/d TL100/160; ☒) Such serenity after the clamour of the main drag. Right in the heart of the old town, this boutique hotel – the first of its kind in Mardin – comprises four finely restored mansions, with lots of period charm. Rooms 101, 102, 201, 202, 203 and 402 all have vaulted ceilings and feel like cocoons. Feeling romantic? Room 301, with parquet flooring and a four-poster bed, will wow you. The downside: only five rooms come with a view (although a few terraces at the back look onto the Mesopotamia plain). There's a high-quality on-site restaurant.

Büyük Mardin Oteli (☎ 213 1047; www.buyuk mardinoteli.com, in Turkish; Yeni Yol Caddesi; s/d TL110/140; ☒ ▯) The Büyük is an eyesore and shelters generic rooms, so don't say you weren't warned, but the views over old Mardin or the Mesopotamia plain (depending on the orientation of the room) are sensational – you'll be glued to the window (sadly, there's no balcony). It caters predominantly for groups and is often booked solid, so reservations are advised.

Eating & Drinking

İmzeil Et Lokantası (☎ 212 1062; Cumhuriyet Meydanı; mains TL5-9; ☺ 10am-7pm) This bright little spot on the main square is not breaking much new ground but it's popular for cheap hot lunches. And it's much less touristy than the Turistik Et Lokantası next door.

Turistik Et Lokantası (☎ 212 1647; Cumhuriyet Meydanı; mains TL6-12) The supercentral Turistik is firmly on the package-tour itinerary, and

yabanci are usually greeted with a 'Hello'. With its wide-ranging menu, the Turistik can plug the empty spaces in any stomach, but, judging by the *tavuk şiş*, the food is just OK, and the terrace overlooking the main square is charmless.

ourpick Cercis Murat Konağı (☎ 213 6841; Cumhuriyet Caddesi; mains TL10-18) There's certainly wow-factor in the setting and decor here: the Cercis occupies a traditional Syrian Christian home with two finely decorated rooms and a terrace affording simply stunning views. Treat yourself to a series of dainty dishes thoughtfully crafted by women from Mardin, with recipes from the days of yore and a creative twist (not a kebap in sight). There's a TV screen where you can watch them working their magic in the kitchen. *Mekbuss* (eggplant pickles with walnut), *kitel raha* (Syrian-style meatballs) and *dobo* (lamb with garlic, spices and black pepper) rank among the highlights. Service is exemplary and a well-considered wine list yields a varied selection of Turkish tipples. Don't miss it.

Other choices:

İldo (☎ 213 7288; Hükümet Konağü Arkası; pastries from TL2) This trendy hang-out has a mouth-watering array of pastries and ice creams. The *fıstıklı dondurma* (pistachio ice cream) is addictive (and we know what we're talking about). It's in the new town, but well worth the minibus ride.

Vitamin (Cumhuriyet Caddesi; juices from TL2; ☺ 8am-7pm) With its dramatic bright orange walls adorned with musical instruments, this pea-sized joint on the main drag has to be Mardin's kookiest spot. Freshly squeezed juices are served in glasses filled to the brim.

Çay Bahçesi (Cumhuriyet Caddesi) The perfect place to scribble a few postcards: 'The views over old Mardin and Mesopotamia are phenomenal…'

Getting There & Away

AIR

Mardin airport is 20km south of Mardin. There's no airport shuttle, but any minibus to Kızıltepe can drop you at the entrance (TL2). **Tur-al Tours** (☎ 212 4141; Cumhuriyet Meydanı; 🕑 8am-7pm) Agent for Pegasus Airlines (www.izair.com .tr) and Turkish Airlines. Pegasus Airlines has two weekly flights to/from İzmir (from TL118).

Turkish Airlines (Bilem Turizm ve Seyahat Acentası; ☎ 213 3773; www.thy.com; Karayolları Karşısı Yenişehir; 🕑 8am-6pm) Next door to the Otel Bilen. One daily flight to/from İstanbul (from TL134).

BUS

Most buses leave from the İlçe Otogar east of the centre. For long-distance destinations, buses stop in front of the bus company offices in the old town and in new Mardin. From around 4pm services start to dry up so it's best to make an early start. Minibuses depart every hour or so for Diyarbakır (TL7, 1¼ hours), and for Midyat (TL6, 1¼ hours) and Nusaybin (the Syrian border; TL6, one hour). There are also five to six daily minibuses to Savur (TL5, one hour). Other useful regular services for travellers include to Urfa (TL15, three hours); to Cizre and Silopi (TL15, three hours), the major hub for northern Iraq (see boxed text, p635); to Şirnak (TL15, 3½ hours); and to Batman (TL8).

AROUND MARDİN

Deyrul Zafaran

The magnificent **Deyrul Zafaran** (monastery of Mar Hanania; admission TL3; 🕑 8.30am-noon & 1-5pm) stands about 6km along a good but narrow road in the rocky hills east of Mardin. The monastery was once the seat of the Syrian Orthodox patriarchate and, although this has now moved to Damascus, the site continues to act as a local boarding school.

In AD 495 the first monastery was built on a site previously dedicated to the worship of the sun. Destroyed by the Persians in 607, it was rebuilt, only to be looted by Tamerlane six centuries later.

Shortly after you enter the walled enclosure via a portal bearing a Syriac (a dialect of Aramaic) inscription, one of the school kids will volunteer their services as a guide. First they'll show you the **original sanctuary**, an eerie underground chamber with a ceiling of huge, closely fitted stones held up as if by magic, without the aid of mortar. This room was allegedly used by sun worshippers, who viewed their god rising through a window at the eastern end. A niche on the southern wall is said to have been for sacrifices.

The guide then leads you through a pair of 300-year-old doors to the **tombs** of the patriarchs and metropolitans who have served here.

In the chapel, the **patriarch's throne** to the left of the altar bears the names of all the patriarchs who have served the monastery since it was refounded in 792. To the right of the altar is the **throne of the metropolitan**. The present **stone altar** replaces a wooden one that burnt down about half a century ago. The walls are adorned with wonderful paintings and wall hangings. Services in Aramaic are held here.

In the next rooms you'll see **litters** used to transport the church dignitaries, and a **baptismal font**. In a small side room is a 300-year-old **wooden throne**. The floor **mosaic** is about 1500 years old.

A flight of stairs leads to very simple guest rooms for travellers and those coming for worship. The patriarch's small, simple bedroom and parlour are also up here.

There's no public transport here so you must take a taxi or walk. Hopeful drivers wait outside the bus company offices in Mardin and will ask TL25 to run you there and back and to wait while you look round.

Dara

About 30km southeast of Mardin, this magnificent ancient Roman city that has been forgotten in time will impress you. Dating back to the 6th century, Dara is the town where Mesopotamia's first dam and irrigation canals were built. You can see the ruins of the aqueducts and cisterns, as well as cave dwellings and rock-cut tombs.

Bar a couple of teahouses, there are no facilities in Dara. From Mardin, there are three daily services (TL3).

Savur

If you need an escape hatch, Savur is the one. This diamond of a town appears like a mirage in the countryside, just an hour's minibus ride (60km) from Mardin. Savur is a miniature Mardin, without the crowds. The atmosphere is wonderfully laid-back and the setting enchanting, with a weighty citadel surrounded by a honey-coloured crinoline of old houses, lots of greenery and a gushing river running

SOUTHEASTERN ANATOLIA

HIDDEN GEMS AROUND THE TÜR ABDİN PLATEAU

Culture vultures and independent travellers, provided you have your own wheels or you're OK with arranging a taxi for a day in Midyat (as there's no public transport), we've got something for you: the plateau of Tür Abdin, a traditional homeland of the Syrian Orthodox Church, just east of Midyat (towards Dargeçit). Dotted around the plateau is a smorgasbord of historic village churches and monasteries awaiting discovery. Some of them have been recently restored. A few not-to-be-missed places include **Mor Yakup**, near Barıştepe, **Mor Izozoal**, perched on a knoll in Altıntaş, **Mor Kyriakos** in Bağlarbaşı, **Mor Dimet** in İzbarak, the thoughtfully restored **Meryemana** in Anıtli, and **Mor Eliyo** in Alagöz (about 3km from Anıtli), which was being restored when we dropped by.

All you need is a good road map. Roads are asphalted, villages are signposted and villagers will be happy to point you in the right direction. Here's the starting point of this trip: from Midyat, take the road to Hasankeyf (due north); after about 7km you'll reach the turn-off to Mor Yakup, on your right. *İyi yolculuklar* (have a good trip)!

in the valley. Go now, before this haven of serenity is let out of the bag, but promise you won't tell *too* many people!

With your own wheels, you can drive to **Dereiçi**, also known as Kıllıt, about 7km east of Savur. This Syrian Orthodox village has two restored churches and is famous for its wine.

SLEEPING & EATING

our pick **Hacı Abdullah Bey Konağu** (☎ 0535-275 2569, 0482-571 2127, 0533-239 7807; r per person half-board & without bathroom TL70) The moment you step through the door into this sturdy *konak* perched on the hilltop, you know you're in for something special. Could this be the *Thousand and One Nights* experience you thought you couldn't afford? The seven cocoonlike rooms are cosily outfitted with kilims, comfortable furnishings, brass beds, antiques and old fabrics. Bathrooms are shared, but that's a minor inconvenience when you factor in all the positives. Another pull is the friendly welcome of the Öztürk family. They don't speak much English, but they create a convivial atmosphere. Enjoy *yöresel yemeks* grandmama-style prepared from simple fresh ingredients. The rooftop terrace view will keep you intrigued for hours.

You'll find several simple *lokantas* (eateries serving ready-made food) in town, but for something special head to the **Uğur Alabalık Tesisleri & Perili Bahçe** (☎ 0482-571 2832; Gazi Mahallesi; mains TL5-9; ☺ 8am-9pm), which features a shady garden by the gushing river. Relish fresh trout, salads, potatoes or *içli köfte* and sluice it all down with a glass of *kıllıt* (local wine) or rakı. So cool!

GETTING THERE & AWAY

From Mardin there are about eight daily minibus services to Savur (TL5, one hour).

MİDYAT
☎ 0482 / pop 61,600

About 65km east of Mardin lies sprawling Midyat, with a drab new section, Estel, linked by 3km of potholed Hükümet Caddesi to the inviting old town. Midyat has lots of potential but is not as touristy as Mardin, mostly because it lacks Mardin's hillside setting. It's definitely worth a visit, nonetheless.

The centrepiece of the old part of town is merely a traffic roundabout. Close by, **honey-coloured houses** are tucked away behind a row of jewellery shops. Here, the alleyways are lined with houses whose demure doorways open onto huge courtyards surrounded by intricately carved walls, windows and recesses.

Like that of Mardin, Midyat's Christian population suffered in the early 20th century and during the last few decades, and much of the community has emigrated. There are nine Syrian Orthodox **churches** still in use in the town, though only four regularly hold services. Although you can see the steeples, it's hard to find the churches in the maze of streets so the best option is to accept one of the local guides, who are likely to be hot on your heels.

Midyat's range of accommodation is disappointingly slim. Most travellers (and the occasional tour group) bunk down at the **Hotel Demirdağ** (☎ 462 2000; www.hoteldemirdag.com, in Turkish; Mardin Caddesi; s/d TL35/60; ☒ 🖵), in new Midyat, where you don't have to pay a king's ransom to enjoy the well-equipped rooms, colourful as a box of Smarties (but avoid rooms 107 and 109, which are windowless). Its location is handy – the otogar is just one block behind. **Saray Lokantası** (☎ 462 3436; Mardin Caddesi; mains TL6-8), on the same street, whips up good-value kebaps at criminally low prices.

Rattly minibuses regularly ply the bumpy route from outside the Saray Lokantası to old Midyat to save you the charmless walk. Midyat has two otogars, one in new Midyat (one block behind Hotel Demirdağ) and one in old Midyat, some 200m south of the roundabout along the road to Cizre. There are frequent services for Hasankeyf (TL5, 45 minutes), Batman (TL7, 1½ hours, 82km) and Mardin (TL6, 1¼ hours). Minibuses for Cizre (TL10, 1½ hours) and Silopi (for Iraq; TL12, two hours) leave from the otogar in old Midyat.

Minibuses from Mardin will pass through the new town, then drop you off at the roundabout in the old town. You could easily base yourself in Midyat and make a day trip to Mardin or Hasankeyf.

AROUND MİDYAT
Morgabriel

About 18km east of Midyat, **Morgabriel (Deyrul Umur) Monastery** (◷ 9-11.30am & 1-4.30pm) rises like a mirage from its desertlike surroundings. Though much restored, the monastery dates back to AD 397. St Gabriel, the namesake of the monastery, is buried here – the sand beside his tomb is said to cure illness. You'll see various frescoes and the immense ancient dome built by Theodora, wife of Byzantine emperor Justinian, and a more recent bell tower.

Morgabriel is home to the archbishop of Tür Abdin (Mountain of the Servants of God), the surrounding plateau. These days he presides over a much diminished flock of around 80 people, the majority students. Fortunately, life for the residents seems to be looking up after the recent troubles, and there should be no problem about visiting.

You could ask here about visiting some of the other churches in the region, such as the **Meryem Ana Kilisesi** at **Anıttepe** (Hah).

To get to the monastery from Midyat take a minibus (TL4) heading along the Cizre road and ask to be dropped at the signposted road junction, from where it's a 2.5km walk uphill to the gate. Start early in the morning as minibuses become increasingly difficult to find as the day wears on. If you don't feel like walking you can hire a taxi for about TL50 return, including waiting time.

Hasankeyf
☎ 0488 / pop 5500

Hasankeyf is a heartbreaker. This gorgeous honey-coloured village clinging to the rocks of a gorge above the Tigris River is a sort of Cappadocia in miniature and a definite must-see, but it's slated to vanish underwater (see boxed text, p640). Nobody knows exactly when this will happen because the Turkish authorities keep silence on the issue. Meanwhile, don't miss Hasankeyf, which has become a popular tourist destination.

SIGHTS

On the main road towards Batman, on the right-hand side of the road you'll see the conical **Zeynel Bey Türbesi**, isolated in a field near the river. This turquoise-tiled tomb was built in the mid-15th century for Zeynel, son of the Akkoyunlu governor, and it's a rare survivor from this period.

A modern bridge now spans the Tigris, but as you cross you'll see, to the right, the broken arches and pylons of the **Eski Köprüsü** (Old Bridge), their size giving some idea of the importance of Hasankeyf in the period immediately before the arrival of the Ottomans.

Across the bridge a sign to the right points to the **kale** and **mağaras** (caves). As you walk along the road you'll see the **El-Rizk Cami** (1409), sporting a beautiful, slender minaret similar to those in Mardin and topped with a stork's nest. Just past the mosque, the road forks. The right fork leads down to the banks of the river with a great wall of rock soaring up on the left. The left fork cuts through a rocky defile, the rock faces pitted with caves. Take the slippery stone steps leading up on the right to the *kale*.

You quickly come to the finely decorated main gate to the *kale* where you'll pay TL2. This strategic site has been occupied since Byzantine times, but most of the relics you see today were built during the reign of the 14th-century Ayyubids. Beyond the gate are caves, which youthful guides will describe as shops and houses. At the top of the rock you face the ruins of the 14th-century **Küçük Saray** (Small Palace), with pots built into the ceiling and walls for sound insulation and superb views over the river.

HASANKEYF UNDER THREAT

Hasankeyf is a gem of a place, but has the cloud of a giant engineering project hanging over it. Despite its beauty and history, the town is destined to vanish beneath the waters of the Ilisu Dam, part of the GAP project – see boxed text, p607. The proposed dam will flood a region from Batman to Midyat, drowning this historic site and several other archaeological treasures, and displacing over 37 villages. In 2002, several foreign investors pulled out amid the controversy provoked by the dam, but it seems that construction won't be delayed indefinitely, in spite of local resistance. The mayor of Hasankeyf has tried to gain international support to protect the sites, but the battle is virtually almost lost. With all this publicity, the town has become quite an attraction and draws hordes of Turkish tourists in summer. So join the visitors before it's too late.

You will then be led past a small **mosque**, which was obviously once a Byzantine church, to the **Büyük Saray** (Big Palace), with a creepy jail underneath, right by a tower teetering on the edge of the cliff. It was probably built as a watchtower. The 14th-century **Ulu Cami** was built on the site of a church.

SLEEPING & EATING
There is only one accommodation option in Hasankeyf. If it's full, you can base yourself in Batman, a charmless modern town about 37km to the north, which is well connected to Hasankeyf.

Hasankeyf Motel (☎ 381 2005; Dicle Sokak; s/d TL20/40) This modest 'motel' takes advantage of its spiffing location, right by the Tigris bridge. Keep your expectations in check, though. Rooms are no-frills, carpets are battered and bathrooms are shared (Turkish toilets). The only touch of fancy is the colourful bed linen. Aim for one of the rooms at the back, with a balcony that overlooks the river. Hot water and towels are available on request. No breakfast is served, but there are a few eateries nearby. It has only seven rooms, so it's not a bad idea to book ahead. The owner's sons speak good English.

Has Bahçe (☎ 381 2609; Dicle Sokak; mains TL5-10) This eatery occupies a shady garden and serves up fresh fish from the Tigris (look for the trouts in the pools) and meat dishes. It's down the road from the Hasankeyf Motel.

Few things could be more pleasurable than lunching where a series of çardaks (leafy-roofed shelters) have been set up along the riverbank. A normal meal of grilled meat or fish with salad and a cold drink is unlikely to come to more than TL8. There's also the **Yolgeçen Hanı** (☎ 381 2287; Dicle Kıyısı; mains TL5-10), which boasts a series of rock-hewn dining rooms overlooking the river. Sit on lumpy cushions,

hoe into a kebap or a grilled fish, knock it all down with a glass of rakı (yes, it's licensed!) and you should depart happy and buzzing.

GETTING THERE & AWAY
Frequent minibuses run from Batman to Midyat, transiting Hasankeyf (TL3, 40 minutes, 37km). To Midyat, it costs TL5. There are also two daily services to Van (TL30, six hours), both at around 10.30am.

ŞIRNAK
Şirnak boasts a stunning location, with jagged mountains as a backdrop. There's not much to do, but it's a convenient staging post if you plan to reach Van on an alternative route. From there, you can take the long but highly scenic haul to Hakkari in the one daily minibus. The landscape is sublime, with a mix of canyons, passes, gorges and mountains; at times the road skirts the border with neighbouring Iraq. There's a high military presence in the area, and a passport control at a checkpoint is the worst you'll get.

There's one catch, though; the accommodation scene is pretty dismal. After a ruthless inspection of all hotels in town, we were left with only one acceptable option, the **Otel Murat** (☎ 0486-216 2857; Uludere Caddesi; s without bathroom TL15, d TL30; 🖾), which fits the bill for a night's kip. Mattresses sink like hammocks and the shared bathrooms (for the singles) are a tad dank but it has air-con, clean sheets, wi-fi, and it's a wee walk from the minibus stop to Hakkari.

If your stomach is in knots, **Özlem Fırınlı Et Lokantası** (☎ 216 3492; Cumhuriyet Meydanı; mains TL4-8), on the main square, is a winner. It tosses up a competently cooked tavuk şiş accompanied with bulgur. There's no menu – just point at what you want. Pides are also available. Also worth considering is the **Diyarbakır Faysal**

Ustanin Evi (Cumhuriyet Caddesi; mains TL5-7), down the road to Otel Murat, and serving up a wicked *döner tavuk*, with just enough chilli to send your taste buds into a tailspin. The outdoor tables work a treat on a balmy evening. Right on the main square, the **Aile Çay Bahçesi** (Aile Tea Garden; Cumhuriyet Caddesi; ☾ dawn-dusk) is a great place for plotting out your next itinerary ('Am I going to Cizre and on to Iraq or not?') while absorbing the magical mountain views.

From Şirnak onwards to the west, there is at least one daily minibus to Siirt (TL10, two hours, 96km), where you'll find connections to Bitlis and Tatvan, and five bus services to Diyarbakır (TL20, five hours, 340km). There are also frequent services to Cizre (TL4, one hour), from where you'll easily reach Silopi and the border with Iraq. There's a daily minibus to Hakkari (TL20, five to six hours depending on waits at checkpoints), leaving at about 9am from near Otel Murat, but at the time of writing foreigners were not allowed on board because of military activity in the area (for more details see p652). Şirnak is also connected to Mardin (TL15, three hours, four daily).

BİTLİS
☎ 0434 / pop 44,000

Bet you didn't know, but underrated Bitlis has one of the highest concentrations of historic buildings in eastern Anatolia, and thanks to a few EU-sponsored projects, has received a bit more attention over the last few years. For culture vultures, this is a great surprise, with a smorgasbord of monuments that testify to rich ancient origins. The contrast with neighbouring Tatvan is striking. While modern Tatvan boasts an orderly street plan, Bitlis is a somewhat chaotic old town squeezed into the narrow valley of a stream.

A **castle** dominates the town, and two ancient bridges span the stream. Make a beeline for the **Ulu Cami**, which was built in 1126, while the **Şerefiye Camii** dates from the 16th century. Other must-sees include the splendid **İhlasiye Medrese** (Quranic school), the most significant building in Bitlis, and the **Gökmeydan Camii**, which has a detached minaret.

The **İl Kültür Merkez** (Cumhuriyet Caddesi; ☾ 8am-5pm Mon-Fri) has good maps of the city and brochures covering the area. It's housed inside the İhlasiye Medrese.

Opened in 2008, the **Dideban Hotel** (☎ 226 2820; Nur Caddesi; s/d TL30/50) features spruce rooms

and has an excellent on-site restaurant. It's conveniently located about 100m from the minibus stand for Tatvan and within easy reach of most monuments.

Regular minibuses travel from Tatvan to Bitlis (TL3, 30 minutes).

TATVAN
☎ 0434 / pop 54,000

While Tatvan doesn't set the heart aflutter, it's ideally positioned if you plan a trip to spectacular Nemrut Dağı (Mt Nemrut, p642; not to be confused with the higher-profile Nemrut Dağı, p616, south of Malatya), Ahlat (p644) and Bitlis (left). Several kilometres long and just a few blocks wide, Tatvan is not much to look at, but its setting on the shores of Lake Van (backed by bare mountains streaked with snow) is magnificent. It is also the western port for Lake Van steamers.

Information

Everything you'll need (hotels, restaurants, banks, internet outlets, the PTT and the bus company offices) huddles together in the town centre.

Sleeping & Eating

Tatvan has a handful of hotels that are well used to housing tourists.

Hotel Üstün (☎ 827 9014; Hal Caddesi; s/d TL25/40) Ignore the atrocious carpets and depressing couches in the reception – most rooms in the family-run Üstün have been spruced up and given a lick of fresh *boya* (paint) so they look clean and neat. Some rooms share toilets, but prices are the same – it's well worth getting in early and requesting room 205, 206, 207, 211 or 212, which come with private bathrooms.

Hotel Dilek (☎ 827 1516; Yeni Çarşı; s/d TL35/60) The Dilek gets good marks for its spruce, colourful rooms with tiled bathrooms. Some have balconies. Singles are tiny – just enough room to scoot past a full-sized bed. Angle for room 201, 202, 301 or 302, which are more spacious and get more natural light. It's in a street running parallel to the main drag.

Tatvan Kardelen (☎ 827 9500; Belediye Yanı; s/d TL50/80) This is usually where tour groups bunk down when in town, which is enough to recommend this high-rise in a quiet location next to the *belediye*. It sports spacious and well-equipped rooms, but the furnishings are dated and the neon-lit corridors as sexy as a hospital's.

Şimşek Lokantası (☎ 827 1513; Cumhuriyet Caddesi; mains TL5-10) This Tatvan stalwart on the main drag has all the usual kebaps as well as ready-made meals that will have you walking out belly-first. With its wood-panelled interior, it feels surprisingly cosy.

Kaşı Beyaz İzgara Salonu (☎ 827 6996; PTT Yanı; mains TL6-9) Locals flood here for supertasty kebaps, cooked to perfection on a big *ocak* (grill) on the ground floor. Choose your victim from the display case (will it be an Adana or a *yoğurtlu*?), then snap up a table upstairs. Excellent pide, too. On the same street as Hotel Dilek.

Eyvan Pide Lahmacun ve Melemen Salonu (☎ 827 6579; 1 Sokak; mains TL6-10) This discreet joint is heralded as the best place in town to enjoy a thin-crust pide or a *lahmacun*. After having vacuumed up a flavoursome *kaşarli pide*, faultlessly cooked in the *fırın* (wood-fired oven) on the ground floor, we won't argue. It's one block behind the Şimşek Lokantası.

Getting There & Away

If you're heading to Van, you can take the ferry that crosses the lake twice a day (TL6 per person, about four hours). It doesn't have a fixed schedule, though. Buses to Van run round the southern shore of the lake (TL10, 2½ to three hours, 156km).

Minibuses to Ahlat (TL3, 30 minutes) leave every hour or so from PTT Caddesi, beside Türk Telekom and the PTT. The minibus stand for Bitlis (TL3, 30 minutes) is a bit further up the street. Direct minibuses to Adilcevaz are infrequent; you'll have to change in Ahlat.

AROUND TATVAN
Nemrut Dağı (Mt Nemrut)

This Nemrut Dağı (3050m) rising to the north of Tatvan is an inactive volcano with several crater lakes – not to be confused with the more famous Nemrut Dağı (Mt Nemrut, topped with the giant heads; see p616) near Kahta.

A trip up this Nemrut Dağı is also an unforgettable experience. Once you've reached the crater rim (13km from the main road), you'll be awed by the sensational views back over Lake Van and Tatvan, and forth over the water-filled craters. From the crater rim, you can **hike** to the summit, reached after 30 to 45 minutes – just follow the lip of the crater (the last stretch is a bit of a scramble). The scenery is almost completely unspoilt. In spring and early summer the lower slopes of the mountain are a sea of sweet-smelling wildflowers. Midweek, the only company you're likely to have is the shepherds with their flocks (and dogs) and the hoopoes, nuthatches, skylarks and other birds. Once you've had your fill of vistas, follow the dirt road that leads down to the lake from the crater rim and find your own picnic area. Memorable!

You can visit Nemrut only from around mid-May to the end of October. At other times the summit is under metres of snow. **Skiing** is available in winter, on the outside slopes of Nemrut Dağı, and there's a state-of-the-art chairlift.

GETTING THERE & AWAY

It's not easy to get to Nemrut, as there are no regular services from Tatvan. In high season, you could try to hitch a ride. Your best bet is to ask the staff at your hotel in Tatvan for advice or hire a taxi. Expect to pay about TL100 return.

With your own transport, leave Tatvan by the road around the lake and then turn left towards Bitlis; about 300m further, turn right following a sign saying 'Nemrut 13km'. The road is rough but passable in an ordinary car except in wet weather. You'll reach the crater rim, from which a dirt road winds down into the crater and connects with other dirt roads that snake around the crater – this is your chance to make your own 'caldera tour' (fear not, you can't really get lost).

AROUND LAKE VAN (VAN GÖLÜ)
☎ 0432

Lake Van (Van Gölü) is eastern Anatolia's pièce de résistance. After the rigours of central Anatolia, this vast expanse of water surrounded by snowcapped mountains sounds deceptively like a holy grail for those in search of beaches and water sports. Lake Van has great potential for activities, but nothing has been really developed yet and infrastructure is lacking. Water sports? Lakeside resorts? Dream on! But at least this means it's scenic and virtually untouched. A circumnavigation around its shores reveals plenty of surprises.

By far the most conspicuous feature on the map of southeastern Turkey, this 3750-sq-km lake was formed when a volcano (Nemrut Dağı) north of Tatvan blocked its natural outflow.

South Shore

Travelling south around the lake between Van and Tatvan the scenery is beautiful, but there's little reason to stop except at a point 5km west of Gevaş, where the 10th-century Church of the Holy Cross at Akdamar is a glorious must.

Sleeping & Eating
You can pitch your tent at the **Akdamar Camping ve Restaurant** (☎ 216 1505; camp sites per person TL2-5; mains TL10-12; ☒ Apr-Sep). It's basic – just a few patches of grass behind the restaurant, and no showers – but it's immediately opposite the ferry departure point for Akdamar island. The restaurant has a terrace with lake views and an indoor area in case of bad weather; the fish is fresh. Another speciality is the *kürt tavası* (meat, tomato and peppers cooked in a clay pot). It's licensed, but an Efes costs a whopping TL5.

Closer to Van, just east of Edremit, along the main road, you'll find a couple of midrange hotels by the water, including the bland but well-equipped **Merit Şahmaran** (☎ 214 3479; fax 612 2420; s/d TL80/120; ☐ ☒), 12km from Van.

Getting There & Away
Minibuses run the 44km from near Beş Yol in Van to Akdamar harbour for TL3 during high season. At other times, there's an hourly minibus to Gevaş (TL3). If you want to be dropped at the boat dock 5km further on, negotiate the price with the driver. Alternatively, catch a minibus heading to Tatvan and ask to be let off at Akdamar harbour. Make sure you're out on the highway flagging a bus back to Van by 4pm, as soon afterwards the traffic dries up and buses may be full.

Boats to the island run as and when traffic warrants it (minimum 10 people). Provided others are there to share the cost, a return ticket for the 20-minute voyage and admission to the island costs TL5. Getting to Çarpanak is harder. The boatmen are likely to want TL400 before they'll consider the 2½-hour voyage.

EDREMİT
About 15km west of Van you'll pass through Edremit, a small lakeside settlement with the feel of a seaside resort: all lilos, beach balls and ice cream.

GEVAŞ
Like Ahlat on the north shore, Gevaş has a cemetery full of tombstones dating from the 14th to 17th centuries. Notable is the polygonal **Halime Hatun Türbesi**, built in 1358 for a female member of the Karakoyunlu dynasty.

AKDAMAR
One of the marvels of Armenian architecture is the recently restored **Akdamar Kilisesi** (Church of the Holy Cross). It's perched on an island 3km out in the lake, and motorboats ferry sightseers back and forth.

In 921 Gagik Artzruni, King of Vaspurkan, built a palace, church and monastery on the island. Little remains of the palace and monastery, but the church walls are in superb condition and the wonderful relief carvings are among the masterworks of Armenian art. If you're familiar with biblical stories, you'll immediately recognise Adam and Eve, Jonah and the whale (with the head of a dog), David and Goliath, Abraham about to sacrifice Isaac, Daniel in the lions' den, Samson etc. There are some frescoes inside the church.

Akdamar island is also an ideal spot for a picnic.

North of Akdamar even more isolated and forgotten 11th-century Armenian church stands on the island of **Çarpanak**, popular with birdwatchers.

ALTINSAÇ KILISESI
Not surprisingly, the well-publicised, easily accessible Akdamar Kilisesi has overshadowed the southern shore's other highlights, and Altınsaç Kilisesi is no exception. Another relatively well-preserved Armenian church, it's perched on a mound overlooking the lake. This is a pearl of a site; if you have your own wheels, be sure to squeeze it into your itinerary. The word is not out, and you'll have the whole place to yourself.

From Akdamar, drive about 12km towards Tatvan until you reach a junction. Turn right onto the road marked for Altınsaç. After 3km the asphalt road ends and becomes a gravel road. The road skirts the shore of the lake for another 14km, until you reach the village of Altınsaç. On a clear day this is a wonderfully scenic drive, with breathtaking views over the shimmering waters of the lake and the undulating hills of the steppe. From the village it's another 2km to the church, which is visible from some distance – an awesome vision.

North Shore
If anything the journey around the north shore of Lake Van from Tatvan to Van, with first Nemrut Dağı (Mt Nemrut, opposite) and then Süphan Dağı (Mt Süphan, p644) looming

beside the road, is more beautiful than going around the south shore.

The major bus companies take the shortest route around the south of the lake from Tatvan to Van. If you want to travel around the north shore you'll have to take a minibus to Ahlat from Tatvan, then hop on another minibus to Adilcevaz, where you'll have to break your journey. The next morning you'll take a bus to Van.

AHLAT

A further 42km along the lakeshore is the small town of Ahlat, famous for its splendid Seljuk Turkish tombs and graveyard. Don't overlook this largely underrated site, and allow at least one hour to visit the sights.

Founded during the reign of Caliph Omar (AD 581–644), Ahlat became a Seljuk stronghold in the 1060s. When the Seljuk sultan Alp Arslan rode out to meet the Byzantine emperor Romanus Diogenes in battle on the field of Manzikert, Ahlat was his base. Later, Ahlat had an extraordinarily eventful history even for Anatolia, with *emir* defeating prince and king driving out *emir;* hence, perhaps, the fame of its cemeteries.

Just west of Ahlat you'll see the overgrown polygonal 13th-century tomb, **Usta Şağirt Kümbeti** (Ulu Kümbeti), 300m off the highway and set in the midst of a field near some houses and a new mosque. It's the largest Seljuk tomb in the area.

A bit further along the highway on the left is a little museum, and behind it a vast unique **Selçuk Mezarlığı** (Seljuk cemetery), with stele-like headstones of lichen-covered grey or red volcanic tuff with intricate web patterns and bands of Kufic lettering. It's thought that Ahlat stonemasons were employed on other great stoneworking projects, such as the decoration of the great mosque at Divriği, near Sivas.

Over the centuries earthquakes, wind and water have set the stones at all angles, so they stand out like broken teeth – a striking sight with spectacular Nemrut Dağı as a backdrop. Most stones have a crow as sentinel, and tortoises cruise the ruins.

On the northeastern side of the graveyard is the beautiful and unusual **Bayındır Kümbeti ve Camii** (Bayındır Tomb & Mosque; 1477), with a colonnaded porch and its own *mihrab* (niche indicating the direction of Mecca).

The small **museum** (admission TL2; ◷ 8am-noon & 1-5pm) has a reasonable collection including

Urartian bronze belts and needles as well as some Byzantine glass-bead necklaces.

Other sites in Ahlat worth exploring if you have the time include the **Çifte Kümbet** (Twin Tombs), about 2km from the museum towards the town centre, and the **Ahlat Sahil Kalesi** (Ahlat Lakeside Fortress), south of the Çifte Kümbet, built during the reign of Süleyman the Magnificent. The poplars here are knotted with crows' nests.

From Tatvan, minibuses leave for Ahlat (TL3, 30 minutes) from beside Türk Telekom and the PTT. Make sure you ask to be let off at the museum on the western outskirts of Ahlat, or you'll have to leg it back from the town centre. From Ahlat, there are regular minibuses to Adilcevaz (TL3, 20 minutes).

ADILCEVAZ

About 25km east of Ahlat is the town of Adilcevaz, once a Urartian town but now dominated by a great Seljuk Turkish **fortress** (1571).

Snowmelt from the year-round snowfields on Süphan Dağı flows down to Adilcevaz, making its surroundings lush and fertile. As you enter the town along the shore, the highway passes the nice little **Ulu Camii**, built in the 13th century and still used for daily prayer.

From the centre of town, you can take a taxi to the **Kef Kalesi**, another Urartian citadel perched higher up in the valley (about TL20 return).

If you want to pause here, you can bunk down in the **Hotel Kent** (☎ 0434-311 3231; s/d without bathroom TL15/25), in the centre. The place is pervaded by a somewhat musty fug (those greyish carpets…) but the sheets are immaculate and the shared bathrooms (squat toilets) won't make you squirm.

From Adilcevaz, there are five direct buses to Van (TL10, 2½ hours), but the last one departs around 2pm – make sure you start out early in the day.

SÜPHAN DAĞI (MT SÜPHAN)

The Kilimanjaro-esque bulk that frames the horizon is **Süphan Dağı** (4053m), Turkey's second-highest mountain after Mt Ararat (Ağrı Dağı; p595). Though much less advertised than Mt Ararat, it offers excellent **hiking** options and is a good way to prep yourself for the more challenging climb to Mt Ararat. Contact one of the travel agencies in Doğubayazıt (see p593).

SOUTHEASTERN ANATOLIA

VAN

☎ 0432 / pop 391,000 / elevation 1727m

Frontier towns never looked so liberal. Young couples walking hand in hand on the main drag, students flirting in the pastry shops, live bands knocking out Kurdish tunes in pubs (nightlife, at last!), unscarved girls sampling an ice cream on a terrace and daring eye contact with foreigners... Van is different in spirit from the rest of southeastern Anatolia – more urban, more casual, less rigorous – but don't get too excited because you're not in Marmaris, darling.

Good news: Van boasts a brilliant location, near the eponymous lake. Bad news: forget about water sports and beaches – it's slim pickings in these departments. Instead, focus on the striking monuments, including Van Kalesi (Van Castle or the Rock of Van), spend a few days journeying around the lake, and explore the nearby historic sites of Çavuştepe, Hoşap and Yedi Kilise. But if all you need is to get away from it all, ditch your guidebook and take the daily minibus to the remote village of Bahçesaray and forget about everything.

History

The kingdom of Urartu, the biblical Ararat, flourished from the 13th to the 7th centuries BC. Its capital was on the outskirts of present-day Van. The Urartians borrowed much of their culture, including cuneiform writing, from the neighbouring Assyrians with whom they were more or less permanently at war. The powerful Assyrians never subdued the Urartians, but when several waves of Cimmerians, Scythians and Medes swept into Urartu and joined in the battle, the kingdom met its downfall.

Later the region was resettled by a people whom the Persians called Armenians. By the 6th century BC it was governed by Persian and Median satraps.

In the 8th century AD, Arab armies flooded through from the south, forcing the Armenian prince to take refuge on Akdamar island. Unable to fend off the Arabs, he agreed to pay tribute to the caliph. When the Arabs retreated, the Byzantines and Persians took their place, and overlordship of Armenia seesawed between them as one or the other gained military advantage.

After defeating the Byzantines in 1071 at Manzikert, north of Lake Van, the Seljuk Turks marched on, with a flood of Turkoman nomads in tow, to found the sultanate of Rum, based in

---

KURDISH WAY WITH WORDS

Southeastern Anatolia is predominantly Kurdish territory. Most Kurds speak Turkish, but in remote places you'll hear Kurmancı and Zazakı, the two Kurdish dialects spoken in Turkey. Surprisingly, those who speak Kurmancı won't understand those who speak Zazakı. Kurdish languages don't share any linguistic features with Turkish, but are related to Persian and other Indo-European languages. Instead of the ubiquitous *teşekkür ederim* ('thanks' in Turkish), you'll hear the much more straightforward *spas* in Kurmancı and instead of *merhaba* (hello), you'll hear *rojbas*.

Konya. The domination of eastern Anatolia by Turkish *emirs* followed and continued until the coming of the Ottomans in 1468.

During WWI, Armenian guerrilla bands intent on founding an independent Armenian state collaborated with the Russians to defeat the Ottoman armies in Turkey's east. From then on the Armenians, formerly loyal subjects of the sultan, were viewed by the Turks as traitors. Bitter fighting between Turkish and Kurdish forces on the one side and Armenian and Russian forces on the other brought devastation to the entire region and to Van. For more, see boxed text, p38.

The Ottomans destroyed the old city of Van (near Van Kalesi) before the Russians occupied it in 1915. Ottoman forces counterattacked but were unable to drive the invaders out, and Van remained under Russian occupation until the armistice of 1917. After the founding of the Turkish Republic, a new planned city of Van was built 4km east of the old site.

Orientation

Everything you'll need (such as hotels, restaurants, banks, internet cafés, the PTT and the bus company offices) lies on or around Cumhuriyet Caddesi, the main commercial street.

The city's otogar is on the northwestern outskirts, and most bus companies operate *servises* there from the town centre. The main train station is northwest of the centre near the otogar, with another station, İskele İstasyonu, several kilometres to the northwest on the lakeshore.

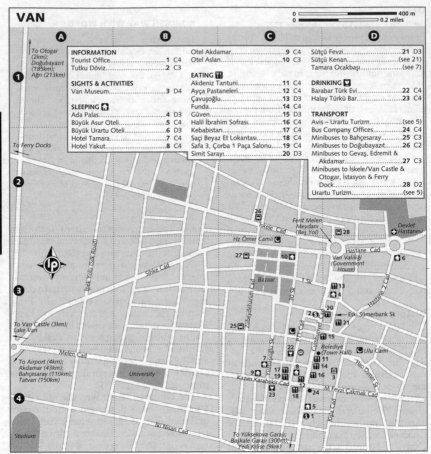

VAN

0 — 400 m
0 — 0.2 miles

INFORMATION
Tourist Office..........................1 C4
Tutku Döviz............................2 C3

SIGHTS & ACTIVITIES
Van Museum...........................3 D4

SLEEPING
Ada Palas...............................4 D3
Büyük Asur Oteli.....................5 C4
Büyük Urartu Oteli..................6 D3
Hotel Tamara.........................7 C4
Hotel Yakut............................8 C4

Otel Akdamar.........................9 C4
Otel Aslan.............................10 C3

EATING
Akdeniz Tantuni....................11 C4
Ayça Pastaneleri...................12 C4
Çavuşoğlu............................13 D3
Funda..................................14 C4
Güven.................................15 D3
Halil İbrahim Sofrası..............16 C4
Kebabistan..........................17 C4
Saçı Beyaz Et Lokantası.........18 C4
Safa 3, Çorba 1 Paça Salonu...19 D3
Simit Sarayı.........................20 D3

Sütçü Fevzi..........................21 D3
Sütçü Kenan......................(see 21)
Tamara Ocakbaşı.................(see 7)

DRINKING
Barabar Türk Evi...................22 C4
Halay Türkü Bar....................23 C4

TRANSPORT
Avis – Urartu Turizm.............(see 5)
Bus Company Offices............24 C4
Minibuses to Bahçesaray.......25 C3
Minibuses to Doğubayazıt......26 C2
Minibuses to Gevaş, Edremit &
    Akdamar...........................27 C3
Minibuses to İskele/Van Castle &
    Otogar, İstasyon & Ferry
    Dock................................28 D2
Urartu Turizm.....................(see 5)

Information
Banks with ATMs are easily found on Cumhuriyet Caddesi, as are internet cafés. Tours to nearby areas can be organised by Büyük Asur Oteli (see opposite).

Tourist office (☎ 216 2530; Cumhuriyet Caddesi; ⏱ 8.30am-noon & 1-5.30pm Mon-Fri) Hands out some brochures on the Van area.

Tutku Döviz (☎ 214 1847; Cumhuriyet Caddesi; ⏱ 8am-6.30pm Mon-Sat) Exchange office.

Sights
VAN CASTLE (VAN KALESİ) & ESKİ VAN
Nothing is quite so impressive in Van as the **Van Castle** (Rock of Van; admission TL2; ⏱ 9am-dusk), which dominates the view of the city, about 3km west of the centre.

The site is fairly spread out – something to bear in mind when it's scorching hot. The bus will drop you at the northwestern corner of the rock, where there's the ticket office and a tea garden.

Just past the ticket office, you'll see an old **stone bridge** and some willows. To the left, a stairway leads up the rock. On your way up you'll notice a ruined **mosque** with a minaret, as well as an arched-roof building, which used to be a Quranic school.

Once you've reached the summit, the foundations of **Eski Van** (the old city) reveal themselves like Pandora's box, immediately on the southern side of the rock. You'll see a flat space broken up by the grass-covered foundations of numerous buildings. This was the site of the old city, destroyed during the upheavals of WWI. A few buildings have survived and are clearly visible from the top of the rock: the **Hüsrev Paşa Külliyesi**, dating back to 1567, which has been restored and has a *kümbet* (tomb) attached; the nearby **Kaya Çelebi Camii** (1662), with a similarly striped minaret; the brick minaret of the Seljuk **Ulu Cami**; and the **Kızıl Camii** (Red Mosque).

After soaking up the views, go down to the ticket office and ask the custodian (he'll expect a tip) to show you the huge cuneiform inscriptions (ask for the *tabela*) as well as the numerous *khachkars* (Armenian crosses) that are carved into the southern side of the rock. After skirting the western tip of the rock and crossing over a fence, you'll walk along the southern side of the rock, and you will be shown the most prominent features. You'll also walk past a water reservoir, an ancient hamam and a ruined palace (not visible from the top of the rock). The Kızıl Cami and the Ulu Cami can also easily be approached, further south. Taking some distance from the rock to get a wider perspective, the custodian will point out various rock-cut **funeral chambers** (not visible from the base of the rock), including that of King Argishti.

On the way back to the ticket office, ask the custodian to show you the **Sardur Burcu** (Sardur Tower; 840–830 BC), in the little willow forest (as there's no sign, it's not easy to find). It's a large black stone rectangle sporting cuneiform inscriptions in Assyrian praising the Urartian King Sardur I.

If you still have the stamina, get to the northeastern side of the rock, about 900m from the ticket office. There's a modern mosque and the **tomb** of Abdurrahman Gazi, a Muslim holy man. It's frequently visited by pilgrims including infertile women who are thought to be helped by coming here.

To get to Van Kalesi take a 'Kale' minibus from the minibus terminal that's just off Beş Yol (Ferit Melen Meydani; TL1), which will drop you at the ticket office.

VAN MUSEUM

The small **Van Museum** (Van Müzesi; Kişla Caddesi; admission TL2; ☯ 8am–noon & 1-5pm Tue-Sun) boasts an outstanding collection of Urartian exhibits. The Urartian gold jewellery is the highlight, but the bronze belts, helmets, horse armour and terracotta figures are also well worth seeing.

The ethnographic exhibits upstairs include local Kurdish and Turkoman kilims and a carpeted sitting area, such as is found in village houses. The Genocide Section is a piece of one-sided propaganda displaying the contents of graves left from the massacres of Turks and Kurds by Armenians at Çavuşoğlu and Zeve.

The museum has a good bookshop with plenty of foreign-language titles about the region.

Sleeping

Van has a decent range of accommodation, though inspiration can be hard to find (please someone – open a boutique hotel!) and it's a wee bit more expensive than elsewhere in eastern Turkey. Most hotels are on or around the main drag, making comparisons relatively easy.

BUDGET

Otel Aslan (☎ 216 2469; Özel İdare İş Merkezi Karşısı; s TL15-20, d TL20-35) The great central location and budget rates keep this hotel-cum-hostel popular with travellers who have an eye on the bank balance. They've opted for tiled floors and bright colours here, and nobody's complaining. Rooms are shoebox-sized but light-filled and well maintained. Cheaper rooms share bathrooms – pray you're not the last in line to shower. No breakfast is served. Don't leave valuables in your room.

MIDRANGE

Büyük Asur Oteli (☎ 216 8792; asur_asur2008@hotmail .com; Cumhuriyet Caddesi, Turizm Sokak; s/d TL45/75) Even if you're on a tight budget, consider spending a little more to enjoy the comforts of this reliable midrange venture. The Soviet-style facade is off-putting, but the rooms are more colourful and come complete with fresh linen, back-friendly beds, TV and well-scrubbed bathrooms. It's also noteworthy for its ultracentral location and its vast lobby where you can unwind over a beer. English is spoken and the hotel can organise tours to Akdamar island, Hoşap Castle and other local attractions.

Hotel Yakut (☎ 214 2832; fax 216 6351; PTT Caddesi; s/d TL45/80) The interior and exterior looks of the Yakut aren't going to inflame the passions of many architects or interior designers, but the renovated rooms, laminated floors, pristine (yet pokey) bathrooms and attentive service make this one of the more solid midrange options in the centre.

Ada Palas (☎ 216 2716; Cumhuriyet Caddesi; s/d TL50/80) The 2nd floor is *yeşil* (green), the 3rd floor canary yellow and the 4th floor electric *mavi* (blue). The rooftop breakfast room is awash with pastel hues. The owners of the recent Ada Palas certainly like to add colour to life. It's well organised and bank-manager-friendly, and its very central location is a gem, with all the restaurants and pastry shops within easy reach.

Otel Akdamar (☎ 214 9923; www.otelakdamar.com; Kazım Karabekir Caddesi; s/d TL60/90) The Akdamar has long been a key player in Van's accommodation scene. These days, it's looking rather worn, like a grand old dame past her prime but not yet ready to retire from public appearances. The location is excellent, it's well organised and amenities are solid, but this place needs to move with the times if it's not to be left resting on its former glories.

Büyük Urartu Oteli (☎ 212 0660; www.buyukurartuotel .com; Hastane 2 Caddesi; s/d TL70/100; ☒ ☒) This reassuring choice gives off a serious hotel vibe, with professional staff and an impressive lobby. The motel-like rooms are nothing to write home about but the full array of amenities, including a sauna, a pool and rooftop restaurant, offers ample compensation. The Urartu's primary clientele are business travellers and tour groups.

Hotel Tamara (☎ 214 3295; Yüzbaşıoğlu Sokak; s/d TL100/140) For classic comfort and convenient location, this solid, wedge-shaped option is a real steal, although its executive look doesn't really scream vacation. Highlights include cosy rooms with the requisite mod cons, a hamam, unflappable staff and the impressive hotel restaurant's *mangals*. It caters mainly for businesspeople.

Eating

Safa 3, Çorba 1 Paça Salonu (☎ 215 8121; Kazım Karabekir Caddesi; soups TL2; ☽ 24hr) If you're a gastronomic adventurer, head to this quirky little restaurant. Regulars swear by the *kelle* (mutton's head), and we're more than happy for them to be the judge! The lentil soup, though a bit spicy for the uninitiated, takes you into more traditional culinary territory.

Ayça Pastaneleri (☎ 216 0081; Kazım Karabekir Caddesi; snacks TL2-4) With its see-and-be-seen glass front on the 1st floor and modern furnishings, this place lures in students in search of a pleasant spot to flirt and relax over toothsome baklavas and decent snacks. Nab a table out front, allowing premium views of the people parade filing past. So cute.

Funda (☎ 216 7498; Cumhuriyet Caddesi; mains TL2-6) This elegant café has been spoiling customers and waistlines for several years with its irresistible cakes, ice creams and pastries. It's on the main thoroughfare.

Akdeniz Tantuni (☎ 216 9010; Cumhuriyet Caddesi; sandwiches TL3) This delightful little den on the main drag features colourful surrounds and low tables. It prepares devilish chicken sandwiches at paupers' prices.

Saçı Beyaz Et Lokantası (☎ 214 4016; Kazım Karabekir Caddesi; mains TL4-13) With an appetising selection of pastries and other delicacies, carb lovers should make this pastry shop their first port of call. The vast, vivacious terrace is usually packed to bursting with Van's movers and shakers in the late afternoon. Snacks, pasta and grills available at the restaurant section upstairs will quell greater hunger pangs.

Kebabistan (☎ 214 2273; Sinemalar Sokak; mains TL5-10) You're within safe boundaries here: the kitchen turns out expertly cooked kebaps (go for the *kuşbaşsı*, with little morsels of beef). One grumble: no side salad is served with your meat dish. Its second branch, across the street, specialises in pide. Getting there is half the fun: it's in a side street where men can be seen sitting on low chairs, playing backgammon and drinking tea.

Halil İbrahim Sofrası (☎ 210 0070; Cumhuriyet Caddesi; mains TL6-12) One word describes this downtown hot spot: yum. The eclectic food is well presented and of high quality, with service to match, and served in sleek surrounds. Ah, the İskender kebap…so rich, so tender. Pide aficionados will go for the generous 'pide special', with a bit of everything – it melts in the mouth. If only alcohol was available…

Tamara Ocakbaşı (☎ 214 3295; Yüzbaşıoğlu Sokak; mains TL6-13) A meal here is dizzying, especially for carnivores. In the Hotel Tamara, the dining room eatery features 40 *ocak* – each table has its own grill. Mood lighting adds a touch of atmosphere in the evening, something that's in short supply in this part of Turkey! High-quality meat and fish dishes feature prominently, but the list of meze is equally impressive.

Other temptations in the centre:
Çavuşoğlu (☎ 214 2669; Cumhuriyet Caddesi; pastries from TL2) Luscious ice creams and dangerously good baklavas

---

YUMMY BREAKFASTS

Van is famed for its tasty *kahvaltı* (breakfast). Skip the usually bland breakfast that is served in your hotel and head straight to Eski Sümerbank Sokak, also called 'Kahvaltı Sokak' (Breakfast St), a pedestrianised side street running parallel to Cumhuriyet Caddesi. Here you'll find a row of ea-teries specialising in complete Turkish breakfasts, including the buzzing **Sütçü Fevzi** (☎ 216 6618; Eski Sümerbank Sokak; ☺ 7am-noon) and **Sütçü Kenan** (☎ 216 8499; Eski Sümerbank Sokak; ☺ 7am-noon), which have tables set up outside. The other restaurants on the street are equally good. On summer mornings the street literally heaves with punters sampling *otlu peynir* (cheese mixed with a tangy herb, Van's speciality), *beyaz peynir* (a mild yellow cheese), honey from the highlands (mmm!), olives, *kaymak* (clotted cream), butter, tomatoes, cucumbers, and *sucuklu yumurta* (omelette with sausage). Whet your appetite by checking out the pictures on www.vandakahvalti.com (in Turkish). A full breakfast will set you back around TL8. A typical Van experience.

Güven (☎ 214 0300; Cumhuriyet Caddesi; pastries from TL2) Van's prime pastry peddler will leave you a drooling mess.

Simit Sarayı (Cumhuriyet Caddesi; simits TL1.50; ☺ 8am-8pm) If you can't find this bustling *simit* shop on the main drag you've lost either your eyesight or your sense of smell.

Drinking & Entertainment

While Van can't be mistaken for Ibiza, there are a couple of lively hang-outs that can be recommended. They are resoundingly popular among students of both sexes and make for a great evening out.

Barabar Türk Evi (☎ 214 9866; Sanat Sokak) The closest thing Van has to a pub, the Barabar is a definite rare breed in eastern Turkey. It may be lodged on the 1st floor of an un-prepossessing building, but there is a fever-pitch energy with its mainly student crowd of both sexes gulping down pints of frothy draught beer (about TL5). It gets frantic here at weekends, with a live band knocking out Kurdish tunes.

Halay Türkü Bar (☎ 214 8233; Kazım Karabekir Caddesi) Almost a carbon copy of the Barabar, the Halay also features *canli müzik* (live bands). Although it's trying hard and is a great place, the Halay lacks the charisma of the Barabar.

Getting There & Away

AIR

A taxi to the airport costs about TL20.

Pegasus Airlines (www.flypgs.com) Has six weekly flights to/from Ankara (from TL108).

Sun Express (www.sunexpress.com.tr) Has six weekly flights to/from İzmir (from TL148, two hours) and three weekly flights to/from Antalya (from TL148, 1¼ hours).

Turkish Airlines (www.thy.com) Has one to two daily flights to/from İstanbul (from TL128) and one daily flight to/from Ankara (from TL128).

Urartu Turizm (☎ 214 2020; Cumhuriyet Caddesi; ☺ 8am-8pm) An agent for Pegasus, Sun Express and Turkish Airlines.

BOAT

A ferry crosses Lake Van between Tatvan and Van twice daily. There's no fixed schedule. The trip costs TL6 per passenger and takes about four hours. 'İskele' dolmuşes ply İskele Caddesi to the harbour (TL1).

BUS

Many bus companies have ticket offices at the intersection of Cumhuriyet and Kazım Karabekir Caddesis. They provide *servises* to shuttle passengers to and from the otogar.

Minibuses to Doğubayazıt leave from a small bus stand off İskele Caddesi, a few blocks west of Beş Yol. Minibuses to Bahçesaray (TL15, three hours, one morning service) leave from near a teahouse called Bahçesaray Çay Evi, south of the bazaar. For Hoşap and Çavuştepe (TL5, 45 minutes), you can take a minibus that leaves from the Yüksekova Garajı or the Başkale Garajı, both on Cumhuriyet Caddesi, a few hundred metres south of the Büyük Asur Oteli. Minibuses to Gevaş and Akdamar (TL3, about 45 minutes) depart from a small bus stand in a side street off Zübeydehanım Caddesi, near the Otel Aslan. For Hoşap, Çavuştepe and Akdamar, there are regular services and you shouldn't wait more than an hour.

To get to Iran, there are direct buses to Orumiyeh (in Iran).

Details of some services are listed in the table, p650.

CAR

Consider renting a car to journey around Lake Van. **Avis – Urartu Turizm** (☎ 214 2020; Cumhuriyet

SOUTHEASTERN ANATOLIA

SERVICES FROM VAN'S OTOGAR

Destination	Fare (TL)	Duration (hr)	Distance (km)	Frequency (per day)
Ağrı	20	3	213	frequent buses
Ankara	40	22	1250	frequent buses
Diyarbakır	25	7	410	frequent buses
Doğubayazıt (via Çaldıran)	10	3	185	several morning minibuses
Erciş	5	1¼	95	several buses
Erzurum	25	6	410	several buses
Hakkari	15	4	205	a few buses
Malatya	35	9-10	500	frequent buses
Orumiyeh (Iran)	20	6	311	2
Şanlıurfa	30	9	585	a few buses
Tatvan	10	2½	156	frequent buses
Trabzon	40	12	733	a few direct buses, most via Erzurum

Caddesi), next door to Büyük Asur Oteli, rents cars for about TL90 per day.

TRAIN
The twice-weekly *Vangölü Ekspresi* from İstanbul and Ankara terminates at Tatvan; from Tatvan, the ferry will bring you to the dock at Van. The weekly *Trans Asya Ekspresi* connects İstanbul to Tehran and stops at Van. It leaves for Tehran (TL45) on Tuesday and Friday any time between 9pm and midnight; for İstanbul (TL60), it also leaves on Tuesday and Friday. Confirm exact times at the train station.

You can get to the station İstasyon by minibus from near Beş Yol (TL1).

Getting Around
For minibuses to Van Kalesi and the *iskele* (ferry dock), go to the minibus terminal near Beş Yol at the northern end of Cumhuriyet Caddesi.

AROUND VAN
Yedi Kilise
The poignant, crumbling Yedi Kilise (Seven Churches) is about 9km southeast of Van, in a typical Kurdish village. It used to be a large monastery. The arched portal sports elaborate stone carvings, and you can also see various Armenian inscriptions above it. Inside, there are some well-preserved frescoes. There's no admission fee but a small donation is expected. If you want to buy souvenirs, women selling knitted gloves and socks usually wait near the building and will be happy to show their handicrafts. After visiting the church,

you can mosey around the muddy streets of the village.

There's no reliable public transport to Yedi Kilise. The most practical way to get there is by taxi (about TL30 including waiting time), or you could walk back to Van and enjoy the scenery.

Bahçesaray
From Van, the 110km ride to reach this town in the middle of nowhere, set deep in the mountains, is exhilarating – be prepared to run out of superlatives. Bahçesaray's main claim to fame is its isolation: because of the snow it's cut off from the outside world at least six months of the year. 'Half the year we belong to God,' say the locals. From Van, the highly scenic road crosses the steppe before gradually ascending to the Karabel Geçiti, at 2985m dizzying. On your way look for *zoma* (encampments), with Kurdish shepherds, their flocks and their damn dogs (beware!). The scenery is captivating on a clear day – the air is intoxicatingly crisp and the surrounding mountains make a perfect backdrop.

Bahçesaray is a place to get away from it all, but there are also a few nearby monuments that are worth a visit, including a couple of Armenian churches and an ancient bridge. You could also play chess with the locals, who are reputedly the best players in eastern Anatolia. Those with a sweet tooth won't leave without sampling the delicious local *bal* (honey).

Bahçesaray has a little **guesthouse** (per person TL10) that overlooks the river. Standards are modest but you're not really here to pamper yourself, right?

In summer, you could reach Bahçesaray with a normal vehicle, but you should know that the road is tarred only up to Yukarı Narlıca and deteriorates markedly near the pass – a 4WD or a high-clearance vehicle would be more appropriate. If it's wet, this part of the road is impassable with a normal vehicle. Take note also that this ride is not for the faint-hearted; expect lots of twists and turns, steep gradients and precipitous ravines. There is sometimes a *jandarma* (police) checkpoint at Yukarı Narlıca.

One or two minibuses leave daily except Sunday from a small minibus stand in Van (ask for Bahçesaray Çay Evi, off Zübeydehanım Caddesi). The bumpy ride takes about three hours and costs TL15.

Hoşap & Çavuştepe

A day excursion southeast of Van along the road to Başkale and Hakkari takes you to the Urartian site at Çavuştepe (25km from Van) and the spectacular Kurdish castle at Hoşap (Güzelsu; 33km further along). Both sites amply reward the effort of visiting them.

Hoşap Castle (admission TL2) perches photogenically on top of a rocky outcrop alongside Güzelsu, a hicksville truck-stop village. Cross one of the two bridges (the one with alternate dark and light stones dates from the 17th century) and follow the signs around the far side of the hill to reach the castle entrance, above which are superb lion reliefs. You might not be allowed to enter the fortress because some parts are crumbling. Looking east from the castle you can see a row of mud defensive walls that once encircled the village.

Built in 1643 by a local Kurdish chieftain, Mahmudi Süleyman, the castle has a very impressive entrance gateway in a round tower. The guardian will quickly spot you and rush to sell you a ticket.

The narrow hill on the left side of the highway at Çavuştepe was once crowned by the fortress-palace **Sarduri-Hinili** (admission TL2), home of the kings of Urartu and built between 764 and 735 BC by King Sardur II, son of Argishti. These are the best-preserved foundations of any Urartian palace.

From the car park, the **yukarı kale** (upper fortress) is up to the left, and the vast **aşağı kale** (lower fortress) to the right. At the upper fortress there is little to see except a platform, possibly used for religious rites, and the ruins of a temple to Haldi, the national god of the

ancient kingdom of Urartu, but from here you can see the layout of the lower fortress.

Climb the rocky hill to the lower fortress temple ruins (Mabet), marked by a gate of black basalt blocks polished to a high gloss; a few blocks on the left side are inscribed in cuneiform. As you walk around, notice other illustrations of Urartian engineering ingenuity: the cisterns under the pathways, the storage vessels, the kitchen and the palace. Down on the plains to the south you'll see canals also created by the Urartians.

To get to the Hoşap and Çavuştepe sites, catch a minibus (on Cumhuriyet Caddesi in Van) heading to Başkale or Yüksekova and say you want to get out at Hoşap (TL5). After seeing the castle, flag down a bus back to Çavuştepe, 500m off the highway, and then catch a third bus back to Van. It's pretty easy to do this trip on your own as frequent minibuses and buses ply the route.

HAKKARİ

☎ 0438 / pop 236,000 / elevation 1720m

Hakkari has one problem: it's a bit too close to the Qandil mountains in Iraq, where PKK rebels are supposed to be based. In other words, the Turkish army is seriously active in the area and, at the time of writing, Hakkari was the only city in southeastern Anatolia that was a bit tricky to access for foreigners. We tried to get to Hakkari from Şırnak, but we weren't allowed on the daily minibus that plies the route between the two cities. The only option is to take a bus from Van, and go back to Van the same way.

Hakkari is ragged around the edges, as befits a city that was at the epicentre of the Kurdish rebellion during the 1980s and '90s and that is tucked away in Turkey's far southeastern corner, at 1700m, far from any other major urban centre. The ongoing conflict with the PKK in the area reinforces this impression. It's not all that grim, though. The setting is truly sensational. The city is ringed by the jagged **Cilo Dağı** mountains, which have fabulous trekking potential. No doubt Hakkari will be back on the trekking map when the situation improves.

Dangers & Annoyances

Women travellers should expect to be the main focus of attention. The area is overwhelmingly male-oriented, and female travellers can be made to feel unwelcome. It's wise to dress modestly.

VISITING TURKEY'S DEEP SOUTHEAST

The southeastern corner of Turkey (east of Siirt and Midyat) still carries a fearsome reputation among travellers and among Turks from western Anatolia (who usually know nothing about the area). The southeast was at the epicentre of the Kurdish rebellion during the 1980s and '90s and for a long time was off limits to travellers. At the time of writing, there was military activity against the PKK (Kurdistan Workers Party, or PKK/Kongra-Gel) rebels in the mountains along the border between Turkey and Iraq. Truth is, very few areas are off limits to travellers. The whole area is under heavy military control and there are checkpoints, but no hassles to speak of – just have your passport on hand and don't deviate from the main road.

It might be a bit intimidating for first-timers, especially women travellers, but you shouldn't believe all the scare stories. While a few pockets of the region remain problematic, the vast majority of people are as warm and welcoming to visitors as anywhere in Turkey. At the time of research, we were able to travel without problem (and using public transport) as far as Şırnak, Siirt, Cizre and Silopi, as well as Hakkari (from Van; see p651). The only road that was closed to foreigners was the long stretch from Şırnak to Hakkari, and it's easy to understand why – the road goes along the border with Iraq.

The only thing you need to do is to be more vigilant and seek local advice before setting off. Anyway, the military will simply not allow you to get too close to trouble – if any. Whatever the situation, you'll probably be the only travellers for miles around.

Check the situation out. If it looks OK, jump right in. You won't regret it.

Sleeping & Eating

Hotel Şenler (☎ 211 5512; Bulvar Caddesi; s/d TL60/90) Hakkari's best-value and most reassuring hotel, by far. Staff are professional and eager to help (ask for Turan Şimşek), bathrooms are kept in top nick and you won't be tripping over your backpack in the generous-sized rooms. It's also very central.

Hacibaba Kebap Salonu (☎ 211 3003; Cumhuriyet Caddesi; mains TL4-9) One of the best restaurants in town. As well as the usual kebaps, the Hacibaba turns out satisfying *tavuk şiş* served with salad and fresh bread. The big grill at the back is impressive. It's just off the main square.

Getting There & Away

From Van to Hakkari, there are regular bus services (TL15, four hours). There are also several daily minibuses to Yüksekova

(TL7, 78km), from where you can cross the border at Esendere-Sero and journey on to Iran. Westwards you can take the long but highly scenic haul to Şırnak in the one daily minibus (TL20, five to six hours depending on waits at checkpoints) but, at the time of research, foreigners were not allowed on this road because of military activity in the nearby mountains.

NORTH OF VAN

If you're bound for Doğubayazıt from Van, the most direct way is to take one of the minibuses that travel via Muradiye, Çaldıran and Ortadirek. This 185km run is worth taking for the magnificent pastoral scenery along the way, especially if you can pause at the spectacular **Muradiye Waterfalls**. Keep your passport handy for any army checkpoints you may encounter.

Directory

CONTENTS

ACCOMMODATION

Turkey has accommodation options to suit all budgets, with concentrations of good, value-for-money pensions and hotels in all the places most visited by independent travellers – such as İstanbul, Çanakkale, Selçuk, Fethiye and Göreme.

The rates quoted in this book are for high season (May to September) and include tax (KDV); room prices can be discounted by up to 20% during the low season (October to April, but not during the Christmas period and major Islamic holidays; see p664). Places within easy reach of İstanbul and Ankara (eg Safranbolu) may hike their prices during summer weekends.

In general, you can expect to spend up to TL70 for a double room in places we list as budget options, from TL70 to TL150 for a double room in those we list as midrange, and from TL150 to a couple of hundred euros in places we list as top end. Prices in İstanbul (generally quoted in euros) are considerably higher, and you should expect to pay up to €70 for budget accommodation, €71 to €200 for midrange, and more than €200 at the top end. Out east, prices are lower than elsewhere in the country.

Breakfast is included in the price of all accommodation unless otherwise mentioned.

Turkish hotels quote tariffs in Turkish lira or euros, sometimes both, and we've used the currency quoted by the business being reviewed. In general, you will find that more-Westernised spots such as İstanbul quote in euros, while less-touristy locations use lira; most hotels happily accept either currency.

If you are planning a stay of a week or more in a coastal resort, check the prices in package-holiday brochures before leaving home. British, French and German tour companies in particular often offer flight-and-accommodation packages to places such as Kuşadası, Bodrum, Marmaris, Dalyan, Fethiye, Antalya, Side and Alanya for much less than you would pay if you made your own bookings.

These days, most hotels have websites for making advance reservations. Once on the travellers' circuit you will find that many pensions operate in informal chains, referring you from one to another. If you've enjoyed staying in one place you will probably enjoy its owner's recommendations, but of course you should hold hard to your right not to sign up to anything sight unseen.

Note that along the Aegean, Mediterranean and Black Sea coasts, and in some parts of Cappadocia, the majority of hotels, pensions and camping grounds close from mid-October to late April. These dates are variable, though; see p18 for more information.

Apartments

Apartments for holiday rentals are usually thin on the ground. Wherever possible we have listed them in this book; otherwise your best bet is to try www.ownersdirect.co.uk or www.holidaylettings.co.uk. If you're interested in hiring an apartment along the coast (eg Kaş, Antalya, Bodrum), your best bet is to contact local real estate agents (emlakci), who hold lists of available holiday rentals and are used to dealing with foreigners.

Camping

Most camping facilities are along the coasts and are usually privately run. Inland, camping facilities are fairly rare – with the exception of Cappadocia and a few places in eastern Anatolia, notably Nemrut Dağı National Park – and are likely to be on Orman Dinlenme Yeri (Forestry Department land). You usually need your own transport to reach these. Other facilities inland tend to be barren, overcrowded options on the outskirts of towns and cities.

If there are no designated camping grounds, ask about at hotels and pensions. Often they will let you camp in their grounds and use their facilities for a fee (TL5 to TL15 per person). Otherwise, camping outside official camping grounds is often more hassle than it's worth; the police may drop by to check you out and possibly move you on. Out east, there are wolves living in the wild, so be wary of them; don't leave food and rubbish lying outside your tent, to avoid attracting unwanted attention. Also look out for Kangal dogs (p74). We recommend female travellers always stick to official camp sites and camp where there are plenty of people around – especially out east.

Hostels

Given that pensions are so cheap, Turkey has no official hostel network, although İstanbul and Pamukkale have a few Hostelling International members. There are plenty of hostels offering dormitories in touristy destinations, where dorm beds usually cost about TL10 to TL15 per night.

Hotels

Hotels range from dirt-cheap to boutique. The cheapest hotels (around TL20 for a single room) are mostly used by working-class Turkish men on business and are not suitable for solo women. While we don't want to restrict women's freedom of choice, if you're greeted by silence and stony stares in a hotel reception, it may be better to move on.

Not surprisingly, the most difficult places to find really good cheap rooms are İstanbul, Ankara, İzmir and package-holiday resort towns such as Alanya. In most other cities and resorts, good, inexpensive beds are readily available.

Moving up a price bracket, one- and two-star hotels, which cost around TL70 to TL120 for a double room with shower, are less oppressively masculine in atmosphere, even when the clientele is mainly male. Three-star hotels are usually used to catering for female travellers.

Hotels in more-traditional Turkish towns, however clean and comfortable, normally offer only Turkish TV, Turkish breakfast and

---

PRACTICALITIES

- Turkey uses the metric system for weights and measures. Basic conversion charts appear on the inside front cover of this book.

- Electrical current is 220V AC, 50Hz. Wall sockets are the round, two-pin European type. You can buy adaptors at most electrical shops for around TL3.50. Take a surge protector to guard against power cuts.

- For the news in English, pick up the *Hürriyet Daily News* (formerly *Turkish Daily News*) or the *New Anatolian*. The Turkish Airlines in-flight magazine, *Skylife,* is an excellent glossy magazine, as is *Cornucopia*, published three times per year and full of excellent articles on Turkish life and culture. The APA Group's guides to İstanbul, Ankara, Bodrum and Antalya, which retail at tourist gathering points, feature listings and articles.

- TRT3 (Türkiye Radyo ve Televizyon) provides short news broadcasts in English, French and German, and can be found on 88.2MHz, 91.6MHZ, 92.8MHz, 94MHz or 99MHz depending on where you are in the country. BBC World Service broadcasts on 12095kHz in İstanbul.

- Digiturk offers hundreds of Turkish and international TV channels, including CNN International and BBC World.

> **BOOK YOUR STAY ONLINE**
>
> For more accommodation reviews and recommendations by Lonely Planet authors, check out the online booking service at www.lonelyplanet.com/hotels. You'll find the true, insider lowdown on the best places to stay. Reviews are thorough and independent. Best of all, you can book online.

none of the 'extras' that are commonplace in pensions.

Prices should be displayed at the reception desk. You should never pay more than these official prices; often you will be able to haggle for a lower (sometimes much lower) price.

Unmarried foreign couples don't usually have any problems sharing rooms, although out east you'll often be given a twin room even if you asked for a double. However, some establishments still refuse to accept an unmarried couple when one of the parties is Turkish. The cheaper the hotel, and the more remote the location, the more conservative its management tends to be.

BOUTIQUE HOTELS

Increasingly, old Ottoman mansions, caravanserais and other historic buildings are being refurbished or completely rebuilt as hotels equipped with all mod cons and bags of character. Most of these options are in the mid-to-upper price range. Some are described in this guide; many more are in the excellent *Little Hotel Book,* by Sevan and Müjde Nişanyan, available in bookshops in İstanbul or through www.nisa nyan.net.

There are now also a few boutique hotels in southeastern Anatolia, and one in Kars (northeastern Anatolia).

Pensions & Guest Houses

In all of the destinations popular with travellers you'll be able to find simple family-run pensions and guest houses (they are one of a kind) where you can get a good, clean single or double for around TL30 or TL50. Many also have larger, triple and quadruple rooms and dorms. These places usually offer a choice of simple meals, book exchanges, laundry services, international TV services etc, and it's these facilities that really distinguish them from traditional small, cheap

hotels. Most pensions also have staff who speak at least one foreign language.

In a few places, such as Safranbolu, a handful of old-style *ev pansiyonu* (pensions in a private home) survive. These are simply rooms in a family house that are let to visitors at busy times of the year and won't normally offer extra facilities, let alone anyone who speaks English. Often they do not advertise their existence in a formal way: ask locals where to find them and look out for *kıralık oda* (room for rent) in the windows.

In smaller tourist towns such as Fethiye, Pamukkale and Selçuk, touts for the pensions may approach you as you step from your bus and offer you accommodation. Some may string you a line about the pension you're looking for (it's burnt down; was destroyed by earthquake; the owner died) in the hope of getting you to their lair, where they extract a commission from the hotelier. Taxi drivers sometimes like to play this game as well. Most people like to politely decline these offers and go to the pension of their choice; however, sometimes it's worth taking them up – especially if you're on a budget – as these touts often work for newly opened pensions offering cheap rates. Before you let them take you to the pension, make it known you're only looking and are under no obligation to stay.

Tree Houses

Olympos, on the western Mediterranean coast near Antalya, is famous for its 'tree houses' (p388) – rough-and-ready permanent shelters of minimal comfort in forested settings near the beach. A few of these places are real tree houses, but many are just tented platforms. They're fun, backpacker hang outs, with bars, communal dining and internet connections. Although the hippie hot spot has gentrified in the last decade, there's little security and there have been instances of guests falling ill as a result of what they've eaten or drunk. Sewage treatment is an ongoing problem, so consider swimming well away from the camps and check for odours before you check in. There have also been some isolated cases of drugged beverages.

The success of Olympos has started to spawn tree houses elsewhere in Turkey (eg at nearby Çıralı and at Saklıkent, near Fethiye). More will probably have appeared by the time you read this.

ABOVE THE FAIRY CHIMNEYS *James Bainbridge*

Morning! For the first time in my life, I was happy to get up at 5am. We were taking a hot-air balloon flight over Cappadocia's unique landscape of fairy chimneys (p509). With 10 other passengers, I clambered into the basket and took a deep breath of crisp country air as we left the ground crew far below.

The valleys housing the chimneys looked as remarkable, if not as snigger-inducing, as the often-phallic rock formations; the wavy tuff (compressed volcanic ash) resembled a mound of wobbly blancmange. With the balloon's bulbous shadow falling on the curvy cliff faces, it was a symphony of surreal shapes.

Some 28 balloons fly most mornings and the multicoloured crafts dotted the bright blue sky. The pilot could control the balloon's height to within a few centimetres, allowing us to descend into a valley to pinch some breakfast from an apricot tree in a secret garden. Around us, the rock was riddled with pigeon houses, traditionally used to collect the birds' droppings for fertilising the fields. As we used the katabatic currents of cool air to surf down the valleys, or rose on a warm anabatic wind, the only sound was the flame shooting into the balloon.

Leaving the fairy chimneys, we climbed almost 1000m upwards and admired Erciyes Dağı (Mt Erciyes), which formed Cappadocia when it erupted. I had to pinch myself to check I hadn't overslept: moving effortlessly through the air above those flowing valleys was just like dreaming.

For more information about hot-air ballooning in Cappadocia, see p510.

ACTIVITIES

For more detailed information about the many activities on offer in Turkey, see p357. Popular activities include hiking and trekking in the Kaçkar Mountains and southern Cappadocia's Ala Dağlar National Park. Another popular stroll is the 509km Lycian Way (p359), starting at Fethiye and finishing near Antalya. The spectacular valleys of central Cappadocia are also excellent, and if you're a serious hiker, you could consider conquering Turkey's highest mountain, Mt Ararat (5137m).

All sorts of water sports, including diving, waterskiing, rafting and kayaking, are available on the Aegean and Mediterranean coasts. The best diving is offered off Kaş, Bodrum and Marmaris. You can also try tandem paragliding at Ölüdeniz.

Skiing is becoming more popular, with the best facilities at Palandöken, near Erzurum and the most scenic runs at conifer-studded Sarıkamış, near Kars. However, their facilities do not meet the standards of the better European resorts.

If you fancy getting airborne, Cappadocia is one of the best places in the world to try hot-air ballooning, mixing a fairy-tale landscape with favourable weather conditions; see the boxed text (above).

There's also plenty of airborne action in the form of birds travelling north to south and vice versa. Turkey is on an important migration route, and spring and autumn are particularly good times to see feathered commuters in the sky. There are several bird sanctuaries (*kuş cennetler*, bird paradises) dotted about the country, although unfortunately they are often popular with noisy, picnicking Turks who frighten the birds away. See p75 for more on birds and conservation issues in Turkey. East of Gaziantep it's possible to visit one of the last nesting sites of the eastern bald ibis (*Geronticus eremita*) at Birecik (p606).

Those of a lazier disposition may want to take a *gület* (wooden yacht) trip along the coast, stopping off to swim in bays along the way. The laziest 'activity' of all consists of paying a visit to a hamam, where you can get yourself scrubbed and massaged for a fraction of what it would cost in most Western countries.

BUSINESS HOURS

Government departments, offices and banks usually open from 8.30am to noon and 1.30pm to 5pm Monday to Friday. During the summer the working day in some cities, including the Aegean and Mediterranean regions, begins at 7am or 8am and finishes at 2pm.

The working day gets shortened during the holy month of Ramazan, and more-Islamic cities such as Konya and Kayseri virtually shut down during noon prayers on Friday (the Muslim sabbath). Apart from that, Friday is a normal working day in Turkey.

In tourist areas food, souvenir and carpet shops are usually open from around 8am to 11pm or later if it's very busy. Elsewhere, grocery shops are usually open from 9am to 6pm Monday to Friday, and shops are usually closed on Sunday, the secular day of rest.

Many museums close on Monday, especially in İstanbul. From April to October museums usually open half an hour earlier and close 1½ to two hours later.

Internet cafés are usually open from around 9am until late at night, or until the last customer has left.

CHILDREN
Practicalities

Çocuklar (children) may not be well catered for in Turkey, but they are the beloved centrepiece of family life and your children will be welcomed wherever they go. Your baby or young child's journey through the streets will be peppered with *Maşallah* (glory be to God) and your child clutched into the adoring arms of strangers, sometimes even against their will. You might want to learn your child's age and sex in Turkish – *ay* (month), *yil* (year), *erkek* (boy) and *kız* (girl). You might also want to make polite inquiries about the other person's children, present or absent: *kaç tane çocuklariniz varmı?* (how many children do you have?).

Pasteurised UHT milk is sold in cartons everywhere, but fresh milk is harder to find. Also hard to find is baby food and what you do find, your baby will understandably find inedible; or it will be mashed banana, which you could easily prepare yourself. Consider bringing a supply with you. Migros supermarkets have the best range of baby food in the country. Alternatively you could rely on hotel and restaurant staff to prepare special dishes for your children. Most Turkish women breastfeed their babies (discreetly) in public and no one is likely to mind you doing the same. You can buy formula and vitaminfortified rice cereal in all supermarkets. High chairs in restaurants are the exception, not the rule.

Disposable *bebek bezi* (nappies or diapers) are readily available. The best brands are Prima or Huggies, sold in pharmacies and supermarkets – don't bother with the cheaper local brands. Oh, and if you find a public baby-changing facility in the country please let us know!

Most hotels can arrange some sort of babysitting service if you ask, but kids' clubs are few and far between and agencies are nonexistent. Many of the seaside towns have children's play equipment, but elsewhere, including İstanbul, the situation is grim. Check the equipment for safety before letting your child use it.

It's important to remember that bus journeys can be very long and that buses do not have toilets on board. They generally stop every few hours, but trains, planes or automobiles might be the best option. Most carrental companies provide child-safety seats for a small extra charge. In Turkey, traffic and treacherous road surfaces make travelling by stroller an extreme sport.

Always double-check the suitability of prescriptions you may be given for children while in Turkey – see p696 for more information.

Check out Lonely Planet's *Travel with Children*, which has lots of practical information and advice on how to make travel with children as stress-free as possible.

Sights & Activities

Beaches aside, in terms of things to see and do Turkey doesn't have a lot of attractions that have been designed with children in mind. With the exception of the Rahmi M Koç museum (p125) in İstanbul, most Turkish museums would leave them bored to tears, and there are no zoos or activity centres easily accessible and worthy of mention. For other ideas on how to keep your kids entertained in İstanbul, see p128.

Activity options are a better bet, with boating, ballooning and, depending on their age, horse riding, snorkelling and white-water rafting all great options.

Apart from the coasts, the area of the country most likely to appeal to older children is Cappadocia, with its underground cities, cave dwellings and kooky landscapes.

Safety

Parents need to remember that in Turkey ideas of safety consciousness rarely meet the norms of countries such as the UK or the USA. Traffic must be at the forefront of parents' minds constantly, and we've already mentioned the broken-down and poorly designed play equipment. Watch out for open power points in hotels, crudely covered electric mains and open stairwells on the streets.

Serious potholes, open drainage and carelessly secured building sites are also a fact of life in Turkey.

If you are looking for childcare while in Turkey, you may want to get some tips from **Child Wise** (www.child wise.net).

CLIMATE CHARTS

For meteorologists, Turkey has seven distinct climatic regions, but from the point of view of most casual visitors, the most important distinctions are between the coast, with its moderate winter temperatures and hot, humid summers, and the inland areas, which have extremely cold winters and excessively hot summers. The further east you travel, the more pronounced these climatic extremes become, so that much of eastern Turkey is unpassable with snow from December to April, with temperatures sometimes falling to around -12°C. In July and August temperatures rise rapidly

and can exceed 45°C, making travel in the east very uncomfortable.

The Black Sea coast gets two to three times the national average rainfall, along with more-moderate temperatures, making it rather like Central Europe but pleasantly warmer. See p17 for more information.

COURSES
Cooking

Many small but established restaurants now offer Turkish cookery courses for foreigners, such as **Guru's Place** (☎ 0242-844 3848; www.kalkan guru.com; 2½hr course €33) near the Mediterranean epicurean centre Kalkan.

Dynamic Ebru Baydemir runs cookery courses in her restaurant, **Cercis Murat Konağı** (p636; www.cercismurat.com, in Turkish), in gorgeous Mardin, southeastern Anatolia. Come here for lessons by female chefs – a rarity anywhere in the country, let alone out east!

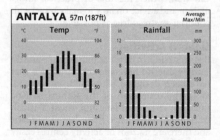

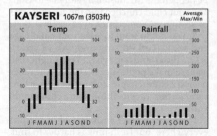

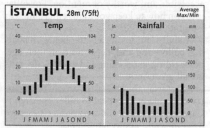

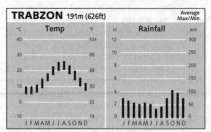

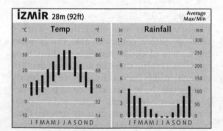

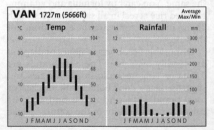

Gökpinar Retreat (☎ 0252-313 1896; www.caravan turkey.com), run by Caravan Travel, offers an all-inclusive seven-day cooking retreat in a small village out of Bodrum for €500. There are sometimes other low-key courses running simultaneously at the retreat, such as carpet weaving or belly dancing. Jiggling the waistline may be the perfect antidote to a day's taste-testing.

See p71 for information about four-day residential courses run 135km from Bodrum in Ula.

Heritage Travel (p500) runs two-week cuisine tours (€2800).

If you're more interested in a no-fuss introduction to whipping up a few tasty Turkish specialities, you're probably better off with the classes at the **Sarnıç Hotel** (☎ 0212-518 2323; www .sarnichotel.com; Küçük Ayasofya Caddesi 26, Sultanahmet, İstanbul). After the four-hour introductory lesson, you adjourn to the rooftop to polish off the results, and you can keep the recipes. Group sizes range from four to 10, and work better when there are a few less attendees.

See p128 for more information about cooking courses in İstanbul.

Belly-dancing
Gökpinar Retreat (☎ 0252-313 1896; www.caravanturkey .com) runs seven-day belly-dancing courses from June to December at its retreat near Bodrum from €650, including accommodation, meals, transfers and 12 hours of lessons. A great option in İstanbul is the artistic collective **Les Arts Turcs** (p128), which also organises trips to dervish ceremonies.

Language
İstanbul is the most popular place to learn Turkish, though there are also courses in Ankara, İzmir and a few other spots around the country. Tömer and Taksim Dilmer (see right) are the most popular schools, but both have their fans and detractors. To lessen the risk of disappointment, ask to sit in on a class before you commit, as the quality of your experience definitely depends on the teacher and your classmates. Prices start at about €230 for 80 hours of teaching spread over four weeks.

Private tuition is more expensive, costing more than €300 per week or from €100 for a two- to three-hour crash course; tutors often advertise in the *Hürriyet Daily News* and on the expat website www.mymerhaba.com.

Teach Yourself Turkish by David and Asuman Çelen Pollard is the best of the many books on teaching yourself Turkish.

Schools to learn Turkish include the following:

EF Language School (☎ 0212-282 9064; www.turkish lesson.com; Aydin Sokak F Block 12, 1 Levent, İstanbul) From €264 for an intensive two-week course; private tuition available from €42 per lesson.

Les Arts Turcs (p128) Two to three hours of private tuition available for €100 to €150.

Spoken Turkish (☎ 0212-244 9000; www.spokeneng lishtr.com; 7th fl, İstiklal Caddesi 212, Beyoğlu, İstanbul) A relative newcomer, offering less-intensive courses than its competitors, but relatively untested.

Taksim Dilmer (p128)

Tömer (☎ 0212-230 7083; www.tomer.com.tr; Abide-i Hürriyet Sokak 43, Şişli, İstanbul) Affiliated with Ankara University, and with branches throughout the country, Tömer offers four- and eight-week courses from €232 and €278 (more expensive in İstanbul and Antalya).

Handicrafts
If you're interested in making pottery, you might like to head to Avanos, the small Cappadocian town famous for its ceramics. So many workshops there offer informal short courses that it's best to just go and see what suits; try **Chez Galip** (☎ 0384-511 5758; www.chez-galip.com).

Travellers interested in learning weaving can also contact Chez Galip or **Gökpinar Retreat** (☎ 0252-313 1896; www.caravanturkey.com). Cappadocia-based Heritage Travel (p500) runs 10- to 15-day kilim-weaving tours where you stay in a nomad village and learn all about carpet making. In İstanbul, the **Turkish Cultural Services Foundation** (p128), based in the gorgeous Caferağa Medresesi, offers courses in calligraphy, miniature painting, *ebru* (traditional Turkish marbling), binding and glass painting.

CUSTOMS
Goods including one carton of (200) cigarettes and 50 cigars or 200g of tobacco, 1.5kg of coffee, five 1L or seven 700mL bottles of wine or spirits, five 120mL bottles of perfume and one camera with five rolls of film can be imported duty-free. There's no limit to the amount of Turkish liras or foreign currency you can bring into the country.

Items valued over US$15,000 must be declared and may be entered in your passport to guarantee that you take the goods out of the country when you leave. It's strictly illegal to export genuine antiquities. Customs officers spot-check luggage and will want proof that you have permission from a museum before letting you leave with an antique carpet. Ask for advice from vendors you buy items from and keep receipts and all paperwork relating to your purchases.

DANGERS & ANNOYANCES

Although Turkey is by no means a dangerous country to visit, it's always wise to be a little cautious, especially if you're travelling alone. Be wary of pickpockets in buses, markets and other crowded places. Keep an eye out for anyone lurking near ATMs.

In Turkey safety seems a low priority. Holes in pavements go unmended and unlit at night; precipitous drops go unguarded; safety belts are worn only as long as it takes to drive past a police officer before being released; lifeguards on beaches are conspicuous by their absence. Don't even ask yourself how safe it is for a dolmuş (minibus) driver to negotiate a bend while simultaneously counting out change! Things are changing slowly, but parents of young children in particular need to be on their guard at all times.

At the time of writing, travelling in the southeast is safe as the unrest there appears to have largely subsided. However, the Kurdish issue is far from resolved, so be sure to check the situation before setting out; see p652 for more information.

There are occasionally terrorist bombings in Turkey, generally taking place in İstanbul near political buildings (occupied by the Turkish government or foreign diplomatic missions) or in wealthy suburbs. They are often linked to Islamic extremists or the PKK (Kurdistan Workers Party) separatist group. In İstanbul in 2008, six people died in a gun battle outside the US consulate and two bombs killed 17 and wounded 150.

Flies & Mosquitoes

In high summer, mosquitoes can make a stay along the coast a nightmare. Some hotel rooms come equipped with nets and/or plug-in bugbusters, but it's a good idea to bring your own mosquito coils to burn as well. As dusk falls, remember to cover your arms and legs or at least to slather yourself with insect repellent.

TRAVEL ADVISORIES

For the latest travel information log on to the following websites:

www.fco.gov.uk/travel UK Foreign & Commonwealth Office

www.smartraveller.gov.au Australian Government's Travel Advisory & Consular Assistance Service

www.travel.state.gov US Department of State's Bureau of Consular Affairs

In some towns the authorities try to combat the more general problem of insects by sending out vans that belch repellent into the sky, usually at about the time in the evening when everyone has just sat down on a terrace for dinner. Some people might consider these dubious clouds of noxious fumes to be as alarming as the insects they're supposed to be eradicating.

Lese-Majesty

The laws against insulting, defaming or making light of Atatürk, the Turkish flag, the Turkish people, the Turkish Republic etc are taken very seriously. Be warned that even if such remarks were never made, Turks have been known to claim they were in the heat of a quarrel, which is enough to get the foreigner carted off to jail.

Traffic

Unfortunately Turkey has a terrible record when it comes to road safety, which means you must drive defensively at all times. It's particularly unwise to drive in the dark on country roads where tractors may be ambling along with unlit trailers. See p686 for more information. When travelling long distances, it's worth paying slightly more to use a bus company with relief drivers, rather than risk being driven by someone who may be at the wheel for a straight 18 hours.

As a pedestrian, note that there is no such thing as right of way, despite the little green man. Give way to cars and trucks in all situations, even if you have to jump out of the way.

Scams & Druggings

Turkey is one of the friendliest and most welcoming countries on the planet, but there will always be a few sharks in the mix. Although it wouldn't do to be paranoid about potential scams, it does pay to be careful, especially in İstanbul.

One of the most popular scams targeted at single men is the nightclub-bar shakedown, which mostly happens in İstanbul. You may know the initial scene: you're strolling through Sultanahmet, when you're approached by a dapper young man who starts up a conversation. After your initial hesitation, and once you realise he's not affiliated with a carpet shop, you start chatting away. He's says he's off to meet friends for a drink in Beyoğlu, as there's nowhere to party in Sultanahmet. Would you like to go along? Woohoo! You go into a bar and are approached by some girls, by which time it's way too late to back out. When the bill arrives, lo and behold the girls' outrageously expensive drinks appear on it. When you complain, the scammers may even be able to produce a menu with the gutting prices printed on it. It's no good claiming you have no cash on you – you'll be frogmarched to the nearest ATM and 'persuaded' to cough up. If this happens to you, make sure you report it to the tourist police; some travellers have taken the policeman back to the bar and received some or all of their money back.

Drugging isn't a common problem, but it's worth mentioning nonetheless. In this situation a single guy is approached by two or three so-called friends, often claiming to be from Egypt, Lebanon or Romania and often accompanied by the fig leaf of a woman. Fall for this one and you risk finding your drink spiked and waking up in some unexpected location with all your belongings, right down to your shoes, missing – or worse. In 2005 when the missing person billboards went up for a Korean tourist, most locals knew the fate of this unlucky young man – a month later his body was found on the outskirts of İstanbul. Most likely he was a victim of a drugging gone wrong.

The moral of these stories? Single men should not accept invitations from unknown folk in large cities without sizing the situation up very carefully. You could also invite your new-found friends to a bar of *your* choice; if they're not keen to go, chances are they are shady characters.

We've also heard reports of two female travellers claiming to have had their drinks spiked in Olympos.

Smoking

Turks smoke here, there and everywhere. One extreme example was a driver holding a newborn with his left hand and a cigarette, the gear stick and the steering wheel with his right! There's even a joke about the country's propensity for puffing: Who smokes more than a Turk? Two Turks.

Prime Minister Recep Tayyip Erdoğan is against the habit and a ban on smoking in enclosed public spaces is set to start in mid-to late 2009, though its proponents have the tobacco lobby to contend with. Existing bans, which cover public buildings such as hospitals and schools, are widely disregarded; you'll also have to endure smoking in restaurants, cafés, bars and hotel lobbies.

In İstanbul, many cafés and restaurants are introducing nonsmoking sections or floors and most of the city's hotels say their rooms are smoke-free. This is certainly not the case in the rest of Turkey, and we've used the nonsmoking icon in reviews to indicate businesses where you can escape the fumes.

Public transport is usually smoke-free and taxi drivers will generally butt out if you ask them to.

DISCOUNT CARDS

Currently the only really useful cards to lay your hands on are the International Student Identity Card (ISIC) and International Youth Travel Card (IYTC). To get the former, you'll need a letter from your college or university stating that you are a student, a student ID card or similar; to get an IYTC card, you need a passport or similar showing you are aged between 12 and 26. With an ISIC card you should be able to get discounts of up to 60% on accommodation in Turkey, and smaller reductions on eating, entertainment, shopping and transport. Get the cards before you go to Turkey.

EMBASSIES & CONSULATES

Most embassies and consulates in Turkey are open from 8am or 9am to noon Monday to Friday, then in the afternoon until 5pm or 6pm for people to pick up visas. Exceptions to these opening hours are noted below. The embassies of some Muslim countries may be open Sunday to Thursday. If you need to ask the way to an embassy say: '[Country] başkonsolosluğu nerede?'

For details on getting visas to neighbouring countries, see p680.

Armenia Contact Russian embassy.

Australia embassy in Ankara (Map p442; ☎ 0312-459 9521; www.embaustralia.org.tr; 7th fl, Uğur Mumcu Caddesi 88, Gaziosmanpaşa); İstanbul (☎ 0212-243 1333; 2nd fl, Suzer Plaza, Asker Ocağı Caddesi 15, Elmadağ)

Azerbaijan embassy in Ankara (☎ 0312-491 1681; Diplomatik Site, Baku Sokak 1, Oran); İstanbul (☎ 0212-325 8042; Sümbül Sokak 17, Levent 1); Kars (Map pp584-5; ☎ 0474-223 6475/1361; fax 223 8741; Eski Erzurum Caddesi; ☑ 9am-6pm Mon-Fri)

Bulgaria embassy in Ankara (Map p442; ☎ 0312-467 2071; Atatürk Bulvarı 124, Kavaklıdere); Edirne (Map p170; ☎ /fax 0284-214 8481; Talat Paşa Caddesi 31; ☑ 9am-6pm Mon-Fri); İstanbul (☎ 0212-281 0115; www.bulgarianconsulate-ist.org; Ahmet Adnan Saygun Caddesi 44, Levent 2)

Canada embassy in Ankara (Map p442; ☎ 0312-409 2700; Cinnah Caddesi 58, Çankaya; ☑ 8.30am-5.45pm Mon-Thu, to 1pm Fri); İstanbul (Map pp94-5; ☎ 0212-251 9838; 5th fl, İstiklal Caddesi 373, Beyoğlu)

France embassy in Ankara (Map p442; ☎ 0312-455 4545; www.ambafrance-tr.org; Paris Caddesi 70, Kavaklıdere; ☑ 8.30am-6pm Mon-Fri); İstanbul (Map pp94-5; ☎ 0212-334 8730; fax 334 8727; İstiklal Caddesi 8, Taksim)

Georgia (☑ 9am-6pm Mon-Fri) embassy in Ankara (☎ 0312- 491 8030; Diplomatik Site, Kılıç Ali Sokak 12, Oran); İstanbul (Map pp86-7; ☎ 0212-343 9257; Cumhuriyet Caddesi 169, Şişli); Trabzon (Map p554; ☎ 0462-326 2226; trabzoncons@gul.net; Pertev Paşa Sokak 10)

Germany embassy in Ankara (Map p442; ☎ 0312-455 5100; Atatürk Bulvarı 114, Kavaklıdere); İstanbul (Map pp94-5; ☎ 0212-334 6100; İnönü Caddesi 16-18, Taksim)

Iran embassy in Ankara (Map p442; ☎ 0312-427 4320; Tahran Caddesi 10, Kavaklıdere; ☑ 8am-1.30pm & 3-5pm Mon-Thu & Sat, 8am-1.30pm Sun); Erzurum (Map p572; ☎ 0442-315 9983; fax 0442-316 1182; Alparslan Bulvarı, 201 Sokak); İstanbul (Map pp92-3; ☎ 0212-513 8230; 2nd fl, Ankara Caddesi 1, Cağaloğlu; ☑ 8am-4pm Mon-Fri)

Iraq (☑ 9am-3pm Mon-Fri) embassy in Ankara (Map p442; ☎ 0312-468 7421; fax 0312-468 4832; Turan Emeksiz Sokak 11, Gaziosmanpaşa); İstanbul (☎ 0212-299 0120; Köybaşı Caddesi 3, Yeniköy)

Netherlands embassy in Ankara (☎ 0312-409 1800; Hollanda Caddesi 3, Yıldız); İstanbul (Map pp94-5; ☎ 0212-393 2121; fax 0212-292 5031; İstiklal Caddesi 393, Tünel)

New Zealand (☑ closes 1pm Fri May-Oct & 4.30pm Fri Nov-Apr) embassy in Ankara (Map p442; ☎ 0312-467 9054; www.nzembassy.com/turkey; 4th fl, İran Caddesi 13, Kavaklıdere); İstanbul (☎ 0212-244 0272; nzhconist@hatem-law.com.tr; 3rd fl, İnönü Caddesi 48, Taksim)

Russia embassy in Ankara (Map p442; ☎ 0312-439 2122; www.turkey.mid.ru; Karyağdi Sokak 5, Çankaya); İstanbul (Map pp94-5; ☎ 0212-292 5101; visavi@turk.net; İstiklal Caddesi 443, Beyoğlu); Trabzon (Map p554; ☎ 0462-326

2728; rusconsultrb@ttnet.net.tr; Şh Refik Cesur Caddesi 6, Ortahisar)

Syria embassy in Ankara (☎ 0312-440 9657; fax 438 5609; Abdullah Cevdet Sokak 7, Çankaya); Gaziantep (☎ 0342-232 6047; fax 232 3938; Kemal Köker Caddesi 16); İstanbul (Map pp86-7; ☎ 0212-232 6721; Maçka Caddesi 59, Ralli Apt 3, Nişantaşı)

UK embassy in Ankara (Map p442; ☎ 0312-455 3344; fax 0312-455 3320; Şehit Ersan Caddesi 46a, Çankaya; ☑ closes 4.15pm Mon-Fri); İstanbul (Map pp94-5; ☎ 0212-334 6400; fax 0212-334 6401; Meşrutiyet Caddesi 34, Tepebaşi; ☑ closes 4.45pm Mon-Fri); İzmir (☎ 0232-463 5151; bcizmir@fco.gov.uk; 1442 Sokak 49, Alsancak); Marmaris (☎ 0252-412 6486; fax 412 4565; Barbados Caddesi 118)

USA embassy in Ankara (Map p442; ☎ 0312-455 5555; fax 467 0019; Atatürk Bulvarı 110, Kavaklıdere); Adana (☎ 0322-346 6262; fax 0322-346 7916; Girne Bulvarı 212, Guzelevler Mahallesi); İstanbul (☎ 0212-335 9000; fax 0212-335 9102; Kaplıcalar Mevkii 2, İstinye; ☑ closes 4.30pm Mon-Fri)

FESTIVALS & EVENTS

Turkey has loads of festivals – İstanbul seems to have something on almost every week! (See p129 for details of some of these.) The following are some of the national standouts.

January

New Year's Day A surrogate Christmas on 1 January, with the usual decorations, exchange of gifts and greeting cards.

Camel Wrestling On the last Sunday in January, hoof it to Selçuk for the camel wrestle of a lifetime. Be a savvy spectator with our wrestling low-down on p51.

March

Nevruz Kurds and Alevis celebrate the ancient Middle Eastern spring festival on 21 March with much jumping over bonfires and general jollity. Banned until a few years ago, Nevruz is now an official holiday with huge parties, particularly in Diyarbakır, that last well into the morning.

April

Children's Day Every 23 April is celebrated with an international children's festival, with kids invited to countrywide events.

Anzac Day The WWI battles for the Dardanelles are commemorated with dawn services at Gallipoli on 25 April.

June & July

International İstanbul Music Festival (p129) Held from early June to early July.

Tarihi Kırkpınar Yağlı Güreş Festivali (p172) Every June or July, Turkey's greatest oil wrestlers slug it out for supremacy in Edirne.

MAJOR ISLAMIC HOLIDAYS					
Islamic year	New Year	Prophet's Birthday	Start of Ramazan	Şeker Bayramı	Kurban Bayramı
1430	29 Dec '08	9 Mar '09	22 Aug '09	21 Sep '09	28 Nov '09
1431	18 Dec '09	26 Feb '10	11 Aug '10	10 Sep '10	17 Nov '10
1432	7 Dec '10	15 Feb '11	1 Aug '11	30 Aug '11	6 Nov '11

Uluslararasi Bursa Festival (p296) Taking place in June and July, this three-week festival can be a mixed bag (Kim Wilde and Julio Iglesias?), but it features some great stuff such as Roma bands and Portugese *fado*.

Aspendos Opera & Ballet Festival (p404) From mid-June to early July this festival is an excellent excuse to enjoy a performance in one of the finest Roman theatres in the world.

International İzmir Festival (p225) Mid-June to mid-July, İzmir, Çeşme and Ephesus host opera, classical and dance.

Kiraz Festivali (Cherry Festival; p176) Tekirdağ's week-long homage to the fruit that Turkey introduced to the world takes place in mid-June.

Kafkasör Kültür ve Sanat Festivalı (p582) In the last weekend of June join the crush at the bull-wrestling matches at Artvin.

Rock'n Antalya (Lara Plajı; p396) Antalya's first festival of Turkish rock music was a big success in late June 2008, and is set to be repeated.

Kültür Sanat ve Turizm Festival (p593) During the last weekend of July Doğubayazıt hosts a culture and arts festival celebrating Kurdish music, dance and theatre.

August
Hacı Bektaş Veli Festival (p516) From 16 to 18 August, sleepy little Hacıbektaş comes alive for the annual pilgrimage for followers of the Bektaşi order of dervishes.

International Ballet Festival (p272) Can you think of a more atmospheric location than the Castle of St Peter in Bodrum for this annual festival?

September
International İstanbul Biennial (p129) Fills the city with culture during the autumn in odd-numbered years.

December
Mevlâna Festival (p488) This Konya festival, honouring Celaleddin Rumi, the great poet and mystic who founded the Mevlevi order of whirling dervishes, usually lasts from 10 to 17 December.

FOOD

For information about what you'll find on Turkish menus, see p65.

Eateries generally open daily from 8am to 10pm; exceptions to this are noted in listings.

Prices vary greatly between Istanbul (at the top end of the spectrum) and eastern Anatolia. However, as a general rule, a main course in eateries we list as 'budget' shouldn't cost more than TL8, while prices for mains in midrange and top-end restaurants are respectively about TL8 to TL15 and TL15-plus.

In the Eating sections of this guide, we often subdivide eating establishments into restaurants, places for quick, cheap feeds, and cafés. Restaurants are the smarter places where you can expect to find tablecloths and alcoholic drinks. You'll pay between TL10 and TL30 for a main course in most parts of Turkey (sometimes more in İstanbul, and less out east).

Quick eats include the many *lokantas* (eateries serving ready-made food) that dish up soups, stews and grills – they rarely serve alcohol. A snack or meal is likely to cost as little as TL3, even in the big cities.

Cafés fall somewhere between the two categories. They are usually much smarter than *lokantas* but not as formal as restaurants. Most offer a selection of pastas, sandwiches and salads – you'll pay between TL5 and TL10 for a main. There will probably be alcohol available and there may well be music in the evening.

GAY & LESBIAN TRAVELLERS

Homosexuality is legal in Turkey and attitudes are changing thanks to the hard work of groups such as **Kaos GL** (www.kaosgl.com), but prejudice remains strong and there are sporadic reports of violence towards gays – the message is discretion. İstanbul has a flourishing gay scene (see p152), as does Ankara. In other cities there may only be a bar or two.

For more information, contact Turkey's gay and lesbian support group, **Lambda İstanbul** (www.lambdaistanbul.org), and Kaos GL, based in Ankara, which publishes the country's only gay-and-lesbian magazine (in Turkish only).

Gay-friendly travel agents include **Pride Travel** (www.turkey-gay-travel.com) and **Absolute Sultans** (www.absolute sultans.com).

HOLIDAYS

When you're planning your trip, it's worth noting the dates of Turkish holidays. You should book accommodation and transport ahead of time wherever possible if you're planning to travel during a holiday or a few days either side of one. The biggest Islamic holiday, Kurban Bayramı, sees locals travel all over the country: for those working in the big cities it may be the only time of the year they get to see their families.

All banks, businesses and most shops are closed on public holidays; however, most restaurants, grocery shops, supermarkets and businesses catering for foreign tourists will remain open. Note that just prior to and after the holidays banks will be extremely busy and ATMs may run out of cash during the holiday period. It's well worth planning ahead so you don't end up having to change money at inflated rates.

Islamic Holidays

The official Turkish calendar is the Gregorian one used in Europe, but religious festivals are celebrated according to the Islamic lunar calendar. Dates in the table (p663) are estimates; exact dates are not confirmed until the moon is sighted.

Turkey celebrates all the main Islamic holidays, of which the most important are the month-long Ramazan and, two months later, Kurban Bayramı. Since these holidays are celebrated according to the Muslim lunar calendar, they take place around 11 days earlier each year.

An unofficial half-day holiday for 'preparation' precedes the start of major public and religious holidays; shops and offices close about noon, and the eve of the festival is celebrated from sunset. Of the religious festivals, only Şeker Bayramı and Kurban Bayramı are also public holidays.

RAMAZAN

The Holy Month of Ramazan (Ramadan in other Muslim countries) is similar in some ways to Lent. Fasting during Ramazan is one of the five pillars of Islam, and for 30 days devout Muslims let *nothing* pass their lips during daylight hours: no eating, drinking, smoking or even downing an Aspirin. Pregnant or nursing women, young children, the infirm and aged, and travellers are not obliged to fast.

Before dawn, drummers wake the faithful so they can eat before sunrise. Traditionally, a cannon shot signals the end of the fast at sunset, whereupon everyone sits down to an *iftar* (the break-of-fast meal).

During Ramazan, some restaurants may be closed from dawn to nightfall, but most eateries catering to tourists remain open. As a non-Muslim you're allowed to eat and drink when you like – and in the big cities you'll find lots of nonfasting Muslims beside you – but it's best to be discreet, especially in conservative towns.

Ramazan is not an official public holiday, although many businesses operate in a half-hearted manner, opening late and closing early. Unsurprisingly, tempers can fray faster than usual at this time, and driving can be even more erratic.

ŞEKER BAYRAMI

A three-day festival that celebrates the end of Ramazan, Şeker Bayramı (Sweets Holiday; Ramazan Bayramı) takes its name from the children who go from door to door asking for sweet treats. Their elders go visiting, and everybody drinks lots of tea in broad daylight after the long fast. Banks and offices close; hotels, buses, trains and planes are booked solid.

KURBAN BAYRAMI

The most important religious and secular holiday of the year, Kurban Bayramı (Festival of the Sacrifice) is as important to Muslims as Christmas is to Christians. The festival commemorates İbrahim's near-sacrifice of İsmael on Mt Moriah (Quran, Sura 37; Genesis 22), the same story as the biblical tale about Abraham and Isaac.

Every year around four million cows and sheep are sacrificed for Kurban Bayramı. Traditionally, every head of household who can afford to buys a beast to sacrifice. Immediately after early-morning prayers on the first day of the holiday the animal's throat is slit. It's then flayed and butchered, and family and friends prepare a feast. Part of the meat is given to the needy; the skin is donated to a charity, which then sells it to a leather products company. These days you won't see the sacrifices in the cities, but out in the countryside it's a different story.

Kurban Bayramı is a four- or five-day holiday, and banks usually close for a full week. Transport is packed, and hotel rooms, particularly along the coasts, become scarce and expensive.

For more about the part played by food in these festivals, see p69.

Public Holidays
New Year's Day (Yılbaşı; 1 January)
National Sovereignty & Children's Day (Ulusal Egemenlik ve Çocuk Günü; 23 April) Commemorates the first meeting of the Turkish Grand National Assembly in 1920.
Youth & Sports Day (Gençlik ve Spor Günü; 19 May) Dedicated to Atatürk and the youth of the republic.
Victory Day (Zafer Bayramı; 30 August) Commemorates the republican army's victory over the invading Greek army at Dumlupınar during the War of Independence.
Republic Day (Cumhuriyet Bayramı; 29 October) Commemorates the proclamation of the republic by Atatürk in 1923 (p39).

School Holidays
You need to take Turkish school holidays into account when planning your trip. Along with increasing affluence has come a swelling domestic tourism market that gets into its stride in mid-June and continues until mid-September. During those months many coastal towns, especially along the north Aegean coast north of İzmir, get very busy and transport can become very crowded.

INSURANCE
A travel insurance policy to cover theft, loss and medical expenses is a very good idea. A huge variety of policies is available, so check the small print.

Some policies specifically exclude 'dangerous activities', which can include scuba diving, motorcycling and even trekking. Some policies don't recognise locally obtained motorcycle licences.

Some policies will pay your medical expenses directly, while others will reimburse you later. For more on health insurance, see p692.

Note that some insurance policies may not cover you if you travel to regions of the country where your government warns against travel (see p660). Similarly, if you decide to cancel your trip on the advice of an official warning against travel your insurer may not cover you.

See p688 for information about motor insurance.

INTERNET ACCESS
Laptops
If you plan to carry your notebook or palmtop with you, remember that the power supply voltage in Turkey may differ from that at home, which entails the risk of damage to your equipment. The best investment is a universal AC adaptor that will enable you to plug your appliance in anywhere without frying the innards. See www.kropla.com for more information.

In four- and five-star hotels, most phone connections are made using the American-style clear-plastic RJ11 plug, so it's easy to plug in a laptop. Many of these hotels also have WLANs. In cheaper and older hotels, the phones often use a larger white or beige three-prong Turkish plug. In such cases you'll need to find an electrical shop and buy a cable with one of these plugs on one end and an RJ11 plug on the other.

You'll find wi-fi in the majority of hotels of all standards, and many restaurants, cafés and airports throughout the country. In accommodation listings, we have used the internet icon where the hotel provides a computer with internet access for guest use. See http://tinyurl.com/6jm3hb for wi-fi hot spots.

Internet Cafés
Turks took to the internet like ducks to water. Wherever you go, you'll be two steps from an internet café, and most have ADSL connections. Most hotels, pensions, travel agencies and carpet shops are also hooked up, with many offering wi-fi access. Fees are generally TL1 to TL2 for an hour. Internet cafés are usually open from about 9am until 11pm or midnight – or when the last customer leaves.

The best internet cafés have English keyboards. Others will have Turkish keyboards, in which case you need to be aware that Turkish has two 'i's: the familiar dotted 'i', and the less-familiar, dotless 'ı'. Unfortunately the one in the usual place on a Turkish keyboard is the dotless 'ı'; ensure you are using the correct dotted 'i' when typing in email addresses.

Likewise, on a Turkish keyboard you will have to create the '@' symbol by holding down the 'q' and ALT keys at the same time.

LEGAL MATTERS
It's important to remember that when you are in Turkey you are subject to Turkish law, *not* the law of your home country. Beyond

urging the Turkish authorities to treat you fairly, your embassy won't be able to help you if you break the law.

For most travellers driving is the only thing likely to land them in trouble with the law. You may be stopped by blue-uniformed *trafik polis*. You can be fined on the spot for speeding. However, if you know you have done nothing wrong and the police appear to be asking for money, play dumb. You'll probably have to pay up if they persist, but insisting on some proof of payment may dissuade them from extracting a fine destined only for their top pocket.

If you have an accident, don't move the car before finding a police officer and asking for a *kaza raporu* (accident report). The officer may ask you to do an alcohol breath-test. Contact your car-rental company within 48 hours.

You could also fall foul of the laws on lese-majesty (p660), antiquities smuggling (p660) or illegal drugs. Turkish jails are not places where you want to spend any time.

MAPS
Street Maps
Turkish tourist offices stock OK-quality local street maps in major cities such as Adana, Ankara, Antalya, İstanbul and İzmir. Of the local privately produced street maps, Map Medya's are recommended. Its proper street maps of many western Turkish cities start at a few euros. You can pick them up in İstanbul at Türkiye Diyanet Vakfı or İstanbul Kitapçısı (see p83), or in the good bookshops on and around İstiklal Caddesi (see p83).

Touring Maps
Turkish tourist offices stock a free sheet *Tourist Map* (1:1,850,000) – it's OK at a pinch, but it's usually out of date. The best sheet map of the whole country you can buy is the *Türkiye Karayolları Haritası* (1:1,000,000), by Map Medya, updated twice a year.

For detailed touring, the *Köy Köy Türkiye* (Turkey Village by Village; 1:400,000) atlas is the best. The *Oto Atlas Türkiye* (Road Atlas Turkey) at 1:600,000 is another good option. Map Medya also produces excellent regional maps. You can buy these in İstanbul.

MONEY
Turkey's currency is the Türk Lirası (Turkish lira; TL). The lira comes in notes of five, 10, 20, 50 and 100, and coins of 1, 5, 10, 25 and 50 kuruş and one lira.

Prices in this book are quoted in euros or lira, depending on which currency is used by the business being reviewed. For exchange rates, see the Quick Reference on the inside front cover of this book. For details on costs in Turkey, see p17.

After decades of rampant inflation – as high as 70% – the Turkish lira started to stabilise in 2003; by 2004 inflation was down to around 12%. The Yeni Türk Lirası (YTL) was introduced in 2005. At the time of writing, the 'Yeni' (New) prefix was set to be dropped in January 2009, with the currency's name returning to plain old Türk Lirası.

Inflation is an ongoing problem and it makes sense to wait until you arrive in Turkey to change your money into lira since you will probably get a better exchange rate inside the country than outside. (It can be good to have some Turkish lira upon arrival, though; see p675.) Turkish lira are virtually worthless outside Turkey, so make sure you spend them all before leaving.

Restaurateurs and shop owners don't often carry large-denomination notes on them, so try to keep a supply of small money on you for small payments.

ATMs
ATMs dispense Turkish lira to Visa, MasterCard, Cirrus and Maestro card holders. Look for these logos on the machines; they are found in most towns. Virtually all the machines offer instructions in English, French and German. It's possible to get around Turkey using only ATMs, provided you remember to draw out money in the towns to tide you through the villages that don't have them, and keep some cash in reserve for the inevitable day when the machine throws a wobbly, or it's a holiday. You can usually draw out about TL700 per day.

Note that if your card is swallowed by a stand-alone ATM booth, it may be tricky getting it back in a hurry. The booths are often run by franchisees rather than by the banks themselves.

Cash
US dollars and euros are the easiest currencies to change, although many banks and exchange offices will change other major currencies such as UK pounds and Japanese yen. You may find it difficult to exchange Australian or Canadian currency except at banks and offices in major cities.

Credit Cards

Visa and MasterCard/Access are widely accepted by hotels, shops and restaurants, although often not by pensions and local restaurants outside main tourist areas. You can also get cash advances on these cards. Amex cards are not accepted as often.

Moneychangers

It's easy to change major currencies in exchange offices, some post offices (PTTs), shops and hotels, although banks tend to make heavy weather of it. Places that don't charge a commission usually offer a worse exchange rate instead.

Although Turkey has no black market, foreign currencies are readily accepted in shops, hotels and restaurants in many tourist areas. Taxi drivers accept foreign currencies for big journeys, which may drive down the price if the exchange rate is working in your favour.

Exchange rates for several major currencies are listed on the inside front cover of this book.

Tipping

Turkey is fairly European in its approach to tipping and you won't be pestered with demands for baksheesh as elsewhere in the Middle East.

In the cheapest restaurants locals leave a few coins in the change tray. Elsewhere you should tip about 10% to 15% of the bill. Some more-expensive restaurants automatically add a 10% or 15% *servis ücreti* (service charge) to your bill, but there's no guarantee this goes to the staff directly, so you may want to tip the staff directly.

Tips are not expected in cheaper hotels. In more-expensive places a porter will carry your luggage and show you to your room. For doing this (and showing you how to turn on the lights and the TV) he'll expect about 3% of the room price.

It's usual to round up metered taxi fares to the nearest 50 kuruş, so round up TL4.70 to TL5. Dolmuş drivers never expect a tip.

In Turkish baths you should tip around 10% to 20% to the masseur. In the tourist-oriented hamams the fixed price may be so high that you may assume that service is included, but it usually isn't and a tip is appreciated.

If you are shown around a site that is not normally open to the public or are given a guided tour by the custodian, you should certainly tip them for their trouble. A few lira for 10 or so minutes is usually fine.

Travellers Cheques

Banks, shops and hotels usually see it as a burden to change travellers cheques, and will either try to get you to go elsewhere or charge you a premium for the service. If you do have to change them, try Akbank.

POST

The base rate to send postcards and letters to the UK and Europe is TL0.85; to Australia, New Zealand and the USA it's TL0.90. Post your letters in the post office: the *yurtdışı* slot is for mail to foreign countries, the *yurtiçi* for mail to other Turkish cities; the *şehiriçi* for local mail. See www.ptt.gov.tr for information on post offices and rates.

Turkish *postanes* (post offices) are indicated by black-on-yellow 'PTT' signs. Main post offices in large cities are open from 8am to 8pm daily. Smaller post offices keep more-limited hours (8.30am to 12.30pm and 1.30pm to 5.30pm) and may be closed on Saturday afternoon and Sunday.

Most central post offices in tourist areas offer poste-restante services, generally from 8.30am to noon and 1.30pm to 4pm. To collect your mail, go to the *merkez postane* (main post office) with your passport. Letters should be addressed as follows: Name, Poste Restante, Merkez Postahane, District, Postcode, City, Province, Turkey. There are no guarantees you will receive mail, so never have anything valuable or important sent to you.

Letters sometimes take several weeks to arrive (parcels even longer), so plan ahead accordingly.

Parcels

If you decide to ship something home from Turkey, don't close your parcel before it has been inspected by a customs official. Take packing and wrapping materials with you to the post office. Parcels sent by surface mail to Europe cost around TL40 for the first 1kg, then TL12 per kilogram thereon; to North America, Australia and New Zealand, TL58 for the first 1kg, then TL17 per kilogram thereon.

If you'd prefer the security of an international courier, DHL, for example, charges about €90 for a 2kg parcel to Europe, €110 for the USA and €145 to Australia.

We receive occasional complaints from readers who have bought a beautiful kilim and agreed to have the shopkeeper ship it out, only to find a much cheaper item arriving. This is only likely to happen if the shop is a fly-by-night operation. Shops that have been in business a long time have no vested interest in ripping off their customers and are usually used to shipping parcels worldwide.

SHOPPING

Travellers are usually surprised and delighted by the range and quality of things to buy in Turkey. Sure, there are plenty of chintzy souvenirs, but most of what you buy here won't end up in the cupboard within a week of returning. Goodies here are increasingly being exported to designer boutiques round the world.

If you're wondering about the meaning behind the ubiquitous blue-glass eyes, see p228.

Note that most shops close on Sunday except in prime tourist locations.

Carpets & Kilims

Turkey is famous for its beautiful carpets and kilims (pileless woven rugs). Most carpet shops have a range of pieces made using a variety of techniques. Besides the traditional pile carpets, they usually offer double-sided flat-woven mats such as kilims. Most feature beautiful traditional designs and techniques, but many are patchwork or other contemporary designs.

As well as Turkish carpets, most carpet shops sell pieces from other countries, in particular from Iran, Pakistan, Afghanistan and the ex-Soviet republics of Azerbaijan, Turkmenistan and Uzbekistan. If it matters that your carpet is actually from Turkey, bear in mind that Iran favours the single knot and Turkey the double knot. Turkish carpets also tend to have a higher pile, more dramatic designs and more-varied colours than their Iranian cousins.

The carpet market is lucrative and the hard-sell antics of some dealers have tended to bring the trade into disrepute, putting off some potential purchasers. To ensure you get a good buy, spend time visiting shops and comparing prices and quality. It's also worth taking a look in the shops at home before you leave so that you'll know

what's available and for what prices at home. When deciding whether to buy a particular carpet it might help to follow some of these guidelines:

- A good-quality, long-lasting carpet or kilim should be 100% wool (*yüz de yüz yün*). Is the wool fine and shiny, with signs of its natural oil? Recycled or cheap wool feels scratchy and has no sheen, and the cheapest carpets may be made from mercerised cotton or 'flosh'. Another way to identify the material is to turn the carpet over and look for the fine, frizzy fibres common to wool. But bear in mind that just being made of wool doesn't guarantee a kilim or carpet's quality. If the dyes and design are ugly, even a 100% woollen piece can be a bad buy.
- Check the closeness of the weave by turning the carpet or kilim over and inspecting the back. In general, the tighter the weave and the smaller the knots, the higher the quality and durability of the piece.
- Beware the salesman who asserts that all his range is coloured with natural dyes. Chemical dyes have been the main method of colouring in the country for the last 50 years. There is nothing wrong with chemical dyes, but natural dyes and colours tend to be preferred and therefore fetch higher prices. Spread the nap with your fingers and look at the bottom of the pile. Both natural and chemical dyes fade (despite what the salesman might tell you). If you see the colours are lighter on the surface than deep in the pile, it's often an indication that the surface has faded in the sun, but not necessarily that it is an antique.
- Unless you know something about antique carpets and kilims, which are always more expensive, it's probably best to stick with new productions. New carpets can be made to look old, and damaged or worn carpets can be rewoven (good work, but expensive), patched or even painted. There's nothing wrong with a dealer offering you a patched or repainted carpet provided they point out these defects and price the piece accordingly.
- If you are buying a carpet that could be considered an antique, check with the seller that Turkish customs will allow you to export it (see p660).

THE ART OF BARGAINING

Traditionally, when customers enter a Turkish shop to make a significant purchase, they're offered a comfortable seat and a drink (çay tea, coffee or a soft drink). There is some general chitchat, then discussion of the shop's goods in general, then of the customer's tastes, preferences and requirements. Finally, a number of items in the shop are displayed for the customer's inspection.

The customer asks the price; the shop owner gives it; the customer looks doubtful and makes a counteroffer 25% to 50% lower. This procedure goes back and forth several times before a price acceptable to both parties is arrived at. It's considered very bad form to haggle over a price, come to an agreement, and then change your mind.

If you can't agree on a price it's perfectly OK to say goodbye and walk out of the shop. In fact, walking out is one of the best ways to test the authenticity of the last offer. If shopkeepers know you can find the item elsewhere for less, they'll probably call out, 'OK, it's yours for what you offered'. Even if they don't stop you, there's nothing to prevent you from returning later and buying the item for what they quoted.

To bargain effectively you must be prepared to take your time, and you must know something about the items in question, not to mention their market price. The best way to do this is to look at similar goods in several shops, asking prices but not making counteroffers. Always stay good-humoured and polite when you are bargaining – if you do this the shopkeeper will too. When bargaining you can often get a discount by offering to buy several items at once, by paying in a strong major currency, or by paying cash.

If you don't have sufficient time to shop around, follow the age-old rule: find something you like at a price you're willing to pay, buy it, enjoy it, and don't worry about whether or not you received the world's lowest price.

In general, you shouldn't bargain in food shops or over transport costs. Outside tourist areas, hotels may expect to 'negotiate' the room price with you. In tourist areas pension owners are usually fairly clear about their prices, although if you're travelling in winter or staying a long time it's worth asking about *indirim* (discounts).

Ceramics

After carpets and kilims, Turkey's beautiful ceramics would have to be the most successful souvenir industry. Many of the tiles you see in shops have been painted using a silkscreen printing method and this is why they're cheap. One step up are the ubiquitous hand-painted bowls, plates and other pieces; these are made by rubbing a patterned carbon paper on the raw ceramic, tracing the black outline, and filling in the holes with colour. The most-expensive pieces are hand-painted by master craftspeople, without the use of patterns.

Note that many ceramics have been covered in lead-based glaze so it's probably safest to use them as ornaments.

Copper

Gleaming copper vessels will greet you in every souvenir shop. Some are old, most are handsome and some are still eminently useful. New copperware tends to be of lighter gauge, but will still have been made by hand.

Copper vessels should not be used for cooking or eating unless they have been tinned inside: that is, washed with molten tin that covers the toxic copper. If you intend to use a copper vessel, make sure the interior layer of tin is intact or negotiate to have it *kalaylı* (tinned). Be sure to ask about the price of the tinning in advance as *teneke* (tin) is expensive.

Inlaid Wood

You'll find cigarette boxes, chess and *tavla* (backgammon) boards and all sorts of items inlaid with different coloured woods, silver or mother-of-pearl on sale all over Turkey. Make sure what you're buying actually is inlay – these days, there are alarmingly accurate imitations (for instance with paint effects or plastic mother-of-pearl). Also, check whether the 'silver' is not actually aluminium or pewter.

Jewellery

Turkey is a wonderful place to buy jewellery, whether new or old. Jewellers' Row in any market is a dazzling strip of glittering shop windows filled with gold for brides-to-be. Serious gold-buyers should check the daily price for unworked gold in the daily papers – it changes according to carat. Watch carefully as the jeweller weighs the piece in question, and then calculate what part of the price is for gold and what part for labour.

Silver is another matter. You can certainly find sterling silver jewellery (look for the hallmark) but beware of nickel silver and pewterlike imitations. Silver, too, is sold by weight as well as labour.

Leather

On any given Kurban Bayramı (p664), more than 2.5 million sheep get the axe in Turkey. Add to that the normal day-to-day needs of a cuisine based on mutton and lamb, and you have a huge amount of raw material to be made into leather; hence the country's thriving leather industry.

Jackets are one of the most popular purchases. To be sure of a good buy, examine the piece thoroughly. Try it on just as carefully and check whether the sleeves are full enough, the buttonholes are positioned well and the collar rubs.

Meerschaum

If you smoke a pipe, you know about meerschaum (lületaşı). The world's largest and finest beds of this hydrous magnesium silicate, a soft, white stone, are found near the city of Eskişehir (p301). This porous but heat-resistant material is used most famously to make pipes. Artful carving of the stone produces pipes portraying anything from turbaned paşas (Ottoman lords) to mythological beasts.

SOLO TRAVELLERS

Turkey is a great country for solo travellers since most hotels and pensions have a per-head charge or offer discounts for lone travellers; only rarely will you have to pay the full price of a double (except at the Hilton, Sheraton and their ilk). However, single travellers do need to develop a thick skin as most Turks couldn't conceive of going anywhere alone (except, perhaps, on business). People will sometimes double-check with you that you're really alone, and even ask you to explain your solitary status.

If you, too, are having doubts about solitude then Turkey's many small pensions are great places to meet potential travelling companions, as are the hostels in İstanbul.

Lone women inevitably have a harder time of it, although the problems rarely go much further than the occasional unsolicited knock on the hotel door at midnight; see p673 for more information.

TELEPHONE

Türk Telekom (www.telekom.gov.tr) has a monopoly on phone services, and service is efficient if costly. You can direct-dial within Turkey and overseas with little difficulty. When calling Turkey from overseas the country code is ☎ 90, and you drop the 0 on the area codes. The international access code to call abroad from Turkey is ☎ 00. Numbers starting with 444 don't require area codes and, wherever you call from, are charged at the local rate.

Kontörlü Telefon

If you're only going to make one call, it's best to look for a booth with a sign saying kontörlü telefon (metered telephone); you make your call and the owner reads the meter and charges you accordingly. The cost of a local call depends on what the phone's owner charges for each kontör (unit). In touristy areas you can get rates as low as TL0.50 per minute to Europe, the UK, the US and Australia. These rates are, however, significantly higher than using international phonecards (see opposite), but may be the best option if you're only making a quick call.

Mobile Phones

Turks adore mobile (cep, pocket) phones, and reception is excellent throughout nearly all of the country. Mobile phone numbers start with a four-figure code beginning with ☎ 05.

If you want to use your mobile phone in Turkey, note that Turkey uses the standard GSM network operating on 900MHz or 1800MHz. Most phones are GSM so they should be fine, but some US-, Canadian- and Scandinavian-bought mobiles phones are not compatible. You should set up an international roaming facility with your home phone provider before you leave home. Mobiles can connect with Turkey's **Turkcell** (www.turkcell.com.tr), **Vodafone** (www.vodafone.com.tr) or **Avea** (www.avea.com.tr) networks.

If you want to buy a SIM card while you're in Turkey, it's a good idea to stick to the big networks, as you'll get good coverage over the country as well as competitive rates. A SIM card with Turkcell, the most comprehensive network, costs around TL35, including some free credit. You'll need to show your passport and ensure the seller sends your details through to Turkcell to activate your account. You can buy prepaid phonecards at streetside booths and shops displaying the yellow-and-blue logo, which pop up on every street corner throughout the country.

If you buy a Turkcell SIM card and use it in your home mobile, the network detects and bars foreign phones within a fortnight. Removing your phone from the blacklist requires a convoluted bureaucratic process. You can pick up a basic mobile phone for about TL50, or get one thrown in with the SIM card for a little extra.

Payphones & Phonecards

Türk Telekom payphones can be found in most major public buildings and facilities, public squares and transportation termini. International calls can be made from all payphones. All payphones require cards that can be bought at telephone centres or, for a small mark-up, at some shops. There are two sets of cards in use: magnetic strip floppy cards and ones with chips on them called Smart cards.

In general, both cards cost about the same. A 50-unit card (TL3.75) is sufficient for local calls and short domestic intercity calls, 100 units (TL7.50) for longer domestic intercity calls or short international chats. The newer phones also accept major credit cards.

INTERNATIONAL PHONECARDS

The cheapest option for international calls is with phonecards that you use with a landline (ie the phone in your hotel room), public phone or mobile. You call the national toll-free number, key in the PIN number on the card and dial away. Companies such as Bigalo offer the best rates (note, these are *not* the cards with the Türk Telecom logo). For a 100-*kontör* Bigalo card (about TL15) you can speak for 23 minutes to the USA and Europe, and six minutes to Japan. It's worthwhile sticking to a reputable phonecard company, as with other companies' cards credit has been known to disappear or calls won't go through. These cards are widely available in the streetside booths in tourist areas of İstanbul and Ankara but can be difficult to find elsewhere.

TIME

Turkish time is two hours ahead of GMT/UTC. Daylight saving (summer time) runs from the last Sunday in March until the last Sunday in October. During daylight saving time, when it's noon in İstanbul it's 2am in Los Angeles and Vancouver, 5am in New York, 10am in London, 6pm in Tokyo, 7pm in Sydney and 9pm in Auckland. See www.timeanddate.com to calculate other time differences.

Turks use the 24-hour clock.

TOILETS

Although most hotels and public facilities have sit-down toilets, you'll also see hole-in-the-ground models in Turkey. The custom is to wash yourself with your left hand using water from a jug, or to use the little copper tube in the toilet, which spurts water where needed. You then dry yourself with tissues, which you usually provide yourself. In most slick, modern bathrooms you can flush paper directly down the toilet, but in many places if you do this you may flood the premises. If you're not sure, play it safe and put it in the bin provided.

Fairly clean public toilets can usually be found at major attractions and transport hubs. In an emergency it's worth remembering that every mosque has a basic toilet (for both men and women). It's also worth keeping a stash of toilet roll as many places do not provide it, or are slow at replacing it when it runs out. Most public toilets require payment of around 50 kuruş.

TOURIST INFORMATION

Every Turkish town of any size has an official tourist office run by the Ministry of Tourism. They're usually open from about 8.30am to noon or 12.30pm, and from 1.30pm to 5.30pm Monday to Friday, with longer hours and at weekends during the summer in popular tourist locations. Staff are often enthusiastic and helpful, particularly when it comes to supplying brochures, but may have sketchy knowledge of the area, and English speakers are rare. If the information you need is not already in this book, you are more likely to find it by seeking out a sympathetic tour operator or pension owner.

Following is a select list of Turkish tourist offices outside Turkey:

France (☎ 01 45 62 78 68; info@infoturquie.com; 102 Ave des Champs-Élysées, 75008 Paris)

Germany Berlin (☎ 030-214 3752; info@turkei-kultur -info.de; Tauentzien Str 9-12, 10789 Berlin); Frankfurt (☎ 069-23 3081; info@reiseland-tuerke-info.de; Baseler Str 37, 60329 Frankfurt)

UK (☎ 0207-839 7778; www.gototurkey.co.uk; 4th fl, 29-30 St James's St, London SW1A 1HB)

USA New York (☎ 212-687 2194; www.tourismturkey .org; 821 UN Plaza, New York, NY 10017); Los Angeles (☎ 323-937 8066; 5055 Wilshire Blvd, Suite 850, Los Angeles, CA 90036); Washington DC (☎ 202-612 6800; 2525 Massachusetts Ave, Washington, DC 20008)

TRAVELLERS WITH DISABILITIES

On the whole, Turkey is a challenging destination for disabled (engelli or özürlü) travellers. Ramps, wide doorways and properly equipped toilets are extremely rare, and Braille and audio information at sights nonexistent. Crossing most streets is particularly challenging; everyone does so at their peril.

Airlines and the top hotels and resorts have some provision for wheelchair access, and ramps are beginning to appear in a few other places, but very slowly. Hotel Rolli (p418) in Anamur is that rare thing – a hotel specially designed for wheelchair-users. **Mephisto Voyage** (p509) offers special tours in Cappadocia for mobility-impaired people, utilising the Joelette system.

Increasingly, dropped kerb edges are being introduced to cities, especially in western Turkey – in cities such as Edirne, Bursa and İzmir they seem to have been sensibly designed. Selçuk, Bodrum and Fethiye have been identified as relatively user-friendly towns for people with mobility problems because their pavements and roads are fairly level. Some towns – and even a few service stations – now have toilets adapted for disabled access, but these are the exception rather than the rule.

Check out www.everybody.co.uk for information on the facilities for disabled travellers offered by various airlines. Turkish Airlines offers 25% discounts to travellers with minimum 40% disability and their companions. In İstanbul, disabled people are eligible for free bus travel. However, to qualify for these discounts you may have to show an identity card and/or a doctor's letter as 'proof' of your disability, however obvious it may seem to you. Trams are wheelchair-accessible too.

Organisations

Information resources dedicated to travellers with disabilities include the following:

Access-Able (www.access-able.com) Includes a small list of tour and transport operators in Turkey.

Accessibility (☎ 1300-222 377; www.accessibility.com .au; Suite 105, 56 Bowman St, Pyrmont NSW 2009, Australia)

Radar (☎ 020-7250 3222; www.radar.org.uk; 12 City Forum, 250 City Rd, London EC1V 8AF, UK)

Society for Accessible Travel and Hospitality (SATH; ☎ 212-447 7284; www.sath.org; Suite 605, 347 Fifth Ave, New York, NY 10016, USA)

The website of the İstanbul- and Antalya-based **Physically Disabled Support Association** (Bedensel Engellilerle Dayanışma Derneği; www.bedd.org .tr) has helpful information for visitors to Turkey, but is unfortunately only in Turkish. The site has contact details if you want to get in touch.

VISAS

Nationals of the following countries (among others) don't need a visa to visit Turkey for up to three months: Denmark, Finland, France, Germany, Ireland, Israel, Italy, Japan, New Zealand, Sweden and Switzerland. Although nationals of Australia, Austria, Belgium, Canada, the Netherlands, Norway (one month only), Portugal, Spain, the UK and the USA do need a visa, this is just a sticker bought on arrival at the airport or border post rather than at an embassy in advance. Make sure to join the queue to buy your visa before the queuing for immigration.

How much you pay for your visa (essentially a tourist tax) varies; at the time of writing, Australians and Americans paid US$20 (or €15), Canadians US$60 (or €45), and British citizens UK£10 (or €15 or US$20). You *must* pay in hard-currency cash. The customs officers expect to be paid in one of these currencies and may not accept lira; they also don't give any change. No photos are required.

The standard visa is valid for three months and, depending on your nationality, usually allows for multiple entries. See the **Ministry of Foreign Affairs** (www.mfa.gov.tr) for the latest information.

For details on getting visas to neighbouring countries, see p680.

Residency Permits

If you plan to stay in Turkey for more than six months, you can apply for an *ikamet tezkeresi* (residence permit), which is usually valid for a year. You'll need to get a provisional permit from a local Turkish embassy or consulate by showing that you have some means of supporting yourself (savings, a steady income from outside the country) or legal work within the country, then swap your provisional paperwork for a 'blue book' at the *emniyet müdürlüğü* (security police). As the permit costs TL500-plus for a year, and it rises every January, many expats find it more convenient and cheaper to cross the border every three months.

Pat Yale's *A Handbook for Living in Turkey* (2006) is a comprehensive source of info for people planning to settle in Turkey.

Visa Extensions

In theory a Turkish visa can be renewed once after three months at the nearest branch of the *emniyet müdürlüğü*, but the bureaucracy and costs involved mean that it's easier to leave the country (usually to a Greek island) and then come back in again on a cheaper new visa. Unless you speak Turkish, dealing with the security police is complicated.

Working Visas

It's best to obtain a *çalışma izni* (working permit) from the Turkish embassy or consulate in your country before you leave home. As long as possible before your departure date (at least two months), submit paperwork including the completed visa form, your passport and a notarised copy of it, a photo of yourself, your proof of employment (a contract or letter from your employer) and the required fee (€150 to €200, depending on your nationality). After six to eight weeks (*Inşallah*, God willing), your passport will be returned with the visa stamped inside.

In Turkey, you can apply through the security police. If you have a job set up in Turkey, your employer should take care of the paperwork for you. The permit is initially valid for one year, then for three as long as you can prove you're still working.

Most people who are working in Turkey illegally (as private English tutors, for example) cross the border into Greece, Northern Cyprus or Bulgaria every three months rather than bother with the cost and hassle of trying to extend their visa or get residency. In theory an immigration officer could query a passport full of recent Turkish stamps. However, in our experience most of them happily turn a blind eye to this bending of the rules.

Note that rules seem to change regularly, so see www.e-konsolosluk.net and the Turkish embassy or consulate in your home country for the latest information about visa requirements. It's getting tougher to apply for work permits. Within Turkey, even applying for a renewal has been known to take up to six months.

WOMEN TRAVELLERS

Travelling Turkey as a female traveller is easy and enjoyable, provided you follow some simple guidelines. Tailor your behaviour and your clothing to your surrounds. Look at what local women are wearing. On the streets of Beyoğlu in İstanbul you'll see skimpy tops and tight jeans, but cleavage and short skirts without leggings are a no-no everywhere except nightclubs in İstanbul and in heavily touristed destinations along the coast. Having a banter with men in restaurants and shops in western Turkey can be great fun, especially since most won't necessarily think anything of it. Out east it's a different story. Passing through some towns you can count the number of women you see on one hand, and those you do see will be headscarved and wearing long coats. Life here for women is largely restricted to the home. This is not the place to practise your Turkish (or Kurdish) for hours on end with the local *kebapci* and expect him not to get the wrong idea. Keep your dealings with men formal and polite, not friendly. You don't need to don a headscarf, but long sleeves and baggy long pants should attract the least attention.

It is not unheard of, particularly in romantic spots such as Cappadocia, for women to have holiday romances with local men. We only mention this because it has some influence on the perception of foreign women, and because there have been occasional cases of men exploiting such relationships. Some men, for example, develop close friendships with visiting women, then invent sob stories, such as their mother has fallen ill, and ask them to help out financially.

Men and unrelated women are not expected to sit beside each other in long-distance buses, and lone women are often assigned seats at the front of the bus near the driver. If you're not told where to sit, avoid sitting at the back as this has 'back-of-the-cinema' connotations for some men. We've received reports of some conductors on night buses harassing their female customers. If this happens to you, complain loudly, making sure that others on the bus hear, and repeat your complaint on arrival at your destination – you have a right to be treated with respect. When travelling by taxi avoid getting into the seat beside the driver.

When looking for a hotel, you may have to accept that the cheapest fleapits are not suitable for lone women and stick with family-oriented midrange hotels. If conversation in the lobby invariably grinds to a halt as you cross the threshold it might suggest that this is not really a great place for a woman. If there is a knock on your hotel door late at night, don't open it; in the morning, complain to the manager.

We recommend female travellers always stick to official camp sites and camp where there are plenty of people around – especially out east. A female traveller was raped in mid-2006 while camping beside a waterfall near Van with her male companion and, while this is a very rare occurrence, it's a risk you need to weigh up nonetheless. We've heard reports about two female travellers claiming to have been drugged with drinks at a camp in Olympos.

Restaurants that aim to attract women usually set aside a special room (or part of one) for family groups. Look for the term *aile salonu* (family dining room).

WORK

Some travellers come to Turkey for a week and end up staying for months, or even a lifetime. However, jobs aren't all that easy to find (Turkey has a high unemployment level) and most people end up teaching English, though there are other opportunities of course. Job hunters may have luck with the *Hürriyet Daily News* and the expat websites www.mymerhaba.com, www.expatinturkey .com and http://istanbul.craigslist.org.

Nannying

One of the most lucrative nonspecialist jobs available to foreigners involves nannying for the wealthy city elite (from €300 to €650 per week, including accommodation with the family). The work is mainly restricted to English-speaking women who must be prepared for long hours and demanding employers. Contact **Anglo Nannies** (☎ 0212-287 6898; www.anglonannies.com; Bebek Yolu Sokak, Ebru Apt 25/2, Etiler, İstanbul, 80630), the main agency dealing with placements.

Teaching English

You can earn a decent living as an English teacher, either privately, for a university, a *der-shane* (private school), or for one of the many private language schools around the country.

If you don't have any teaching qualifications, you can usually still find a job, though it'll be private tuition (which pays from €17 to €30 per hour) or at a private language school (where you can expect around €11 an hour). If you have teaching qualifications (at least a Bachelor of Education, majoring in English) you should arm yourself with a TEFL certificate as well to place yourself within reach of the best jobs. Universities will not hire without teaching qualifications, nor will most *dershanes,* and the best private language schools expect at least a TEFL. Pay can be from €1000 to €2000 per month, often with accommodation, flights home and a work permit thrown in. The best time of the year to job hunt is near the end of the summer school break, around mid- to late August, when schools are desperate for teachers to replace those who found a spot on a beautiful beach and decided to stay.

As well as those job-hunting resources listed in the introduction to this section, you may also want to log onto www.eslcafe.com and www.te fl.com.

Tourism

Many travellers also find work illegally for room and board in pensions, bars and carpet shops, leaving the country every three months to renew their visas. This sort of work has the advantage that you can take it or leave it at will. But be warned that the authorities take a dim view of foreigners 'stealing' local jobs and that there are occasional shake-outs when they rush around threatening people with prosecution (it rarely actually happens).

Volunteer Work

There is a slowly growing number of volunteering opportunities in Turkey, offering everything from working on an organic farm to helping out on an archaeological dig. **Volunteer Abroad** (www.volunteerabroad.com) is a UK-based company listing volunteering opportunities through international organisations in Turkey. Local operators:

Alternative Camp (www.alternativecamp.org) A fully volunteer-based organisation running camps for disabled people around the country.

Genctur (www.genctur.com) A portal for various volunteering schemes throughout the country, and a good first port of call to see what's on offer in Turkey.

Ta Tu Ta (www.bugday.org/tatuta) Organises work on some 60-odd organic farms around the country, where you can stay for free or for a small donation to cover costs.

Transport

GETTING THERE & AWAY

ENTERING THE COUNTRY

Generally speaking, entering Turkey by air is pretty painless. The only snag to be aware of is that most people need a 'visa' which is really just a sticker and a stamp in their passport issued at the point of entry. If you fly into the country you must *first* join the queue to pay for the stamp in your passport before joining the queue for immigration. See p672 for more details on visas. Rarely do customs officers stop you to check your bags at airports.

Entering the country by land can be more trying. As at the airports, sometimes you can pay for the visa only in pounds sterling, euros or US dollars, and at many of the land border crossings there are no facilities for changing money or ATMs; make sure you bring enough to pay for your visa. You may also want to consider having some Turkish lira (TL) on you before you get to the border.

Security on borders with countries to the east and southeast (Georgia, Iran, Iraq and Syria) is generally tight, so customs officers may want to see what you are bringing in; see p635 for a cautionary tale about crossing the Iraqi border. If you're travelling by train or bus

expect to be held up at the border for two to three hours – or even longer if your fellow passengers don't have their paperwork in order.

Passport

Make sure your passport will still have at least six months' life in it after you enter Turkey.

AIR

Airports & Airlines

Turkey's busiest international airport is İstanbul's **Atatürk International Airport** (IST; p157; Atatürk Hava Limanı; ☎ 0212-465 5555; www.ataturkairport.com), 23km west of Sultanahmet (the heart of Old İstanbul). The international terminal (*dış hatlar*) and domestic terminal (*iç hatlar*) are side by side. İstanbul also has the smaller **Sabiha Gökçen International Airport** (SAW; p158; ☎ 0216-585 5000; www.sgairport.com), some 50km east of Sultanahmet on the Asian side of the city. Sabiha Gökçen mainly services cheap flights from Europe, particularly Germany, and some domestic routes.

Throughout the year, but especially during the busy summer months, you can also catch international flights to and from **Antalya** (AYT; p400; ☎ 0242-330 3221; www.aytport.com), **Bodrum** (BJV; p276; ☎ 0252-523 0080), **Dalaman** (DLM; p350; ☎ 0252-692 5899) and İzmir's rapidly expanding **Adnan Menderes Airport** (ADB; p228; ☎ 0232-455 0000, www.adnanmenderesairport.com). From Turkey's other airports, including Ankara, you usually have to transit İstanbul.

Turkey's national carrier is Turkish Airlines (Türk Hava Yolları), which has direct flights from İstanbul to most capital cities around the

THINGS CHANGE...

The information in this chapter is particularly vulnerable to change. Check directly with the airline or a travel agent to make sure you understand how a fare (and ticket you may buy) works and be aware of the security requirements for international travel. Shop carefully. The details given in this chapter should be regarded as pointers and are not a substitute for your own careful, up-to-date research.

TRANSPORT

world. It has a reasonable safety record, and service is usually pretty good too.

AIRLINES FLYING TO & FROM TURKEY

For contact details for many of these airlines in İstanbul, see p159.

Aeroflot (AFL; www.aeroflot.com)
Air France (AF; www.airfrance.com)
Alitalia (AZ; www.alitalia.com)
Atlasjet (KK; www.atlasjet.com)
American Airlines (AA; www.aa.com)
Armavia Airlines (U8; www.u8.am)
Azerbaijan Airlines (AHY; www.azal.az)
Blue Wings (BWG; www.bluewings.com)
BMI (BMI; www.flybmi.com)
British Airways (BA; www.britishairways.com)
Condor (DE; www.condor.de)
Corendon Airlines (CAI; www.corendon.com)
Cyprus Turkish Airlines (KTHY; www.kthy.net)
Delta Airlines (DL; www.delta.com)
EasyJet (EZY; www.easyjet.com)
Emirates Airlines (EK; www.emirates.com)
First Choice Airways (FCA; www.firstchoice.co.uk)
German Wings (GWI; www.germanwings.com)
Iberia (IB; www.iberia.com)
Iran Air (IR; www.iranair.com)
Japan Airlines (JL; www.jal.co.jp)
KLM-Royal Dutch Airlines (KL; www.klm.com)
Lufthansa (LH; www.lufthansa.com)
Malaysia Airlines (MAS; www.malaysiaairlines.com)
Olympic Airways (OA; www.olympicairlines.com)
Onur Air (OHY; www.onurair.com.tr)
Pegasus Airlines (PGT; www.flypgs.com)
Singapore Airlines (SIA; www.singaporeair.com)
Sun Express Airlines (XQ; www.sunexpress.com.tr)
Thomas Cook Airlines (TCX; www.thomascookairlines.co.uk)
Turkish Airlines (THY; www.thy.com)

Tickets

If you're after cheap flights, the cheapest routes between Europe and İstanbul are flying through Germany, and with EasyJet, which flies between London Luton and İstanbul, London Gatwick and Dalaman, and Switzerland (Basel) and İstanbul. Sometimes you can also find cheap flights by booking on less usual airlines such as Cyprus Turkish Airlines and Azerbaijan Airlines. Some airlines offer student fares too. Otherwise Turkey is not the best destination for special deals.

It's a good idea to book at least two months in advance for flights to Turkey if you plan to arrive in the country any time from early April until late August.

Flights quoted in this chapter are for peak season and include airport taxes.

Australia

You can fly to İstanbul with airlines including Emirates Airlines (via Dubai), Singapore Airlines (via Singapore and Dubai) and Malaysia Airlines (via Kuala Lumpur) from around A$1899 return from Sydney or Melbourne. You can often get cheaper flights with European airlines such as Lufthansa, but you'll have to transit in a European city first (eg in Frankfurt for Lufthansa), before catching a flight back to İstanbul – very frustrating!

Three well-known agencies for cheap fares are **STA Travel** (☎ 134 782; www.statravel.com.au), **Flight Centre** (☎ 133 133; www.flightcentre.com.au) and **Best Flights** (☎ 1300 767 757; www.bestflights.com.au).

Canada

Most flights from Toronto, Ottawa and Vancouver connect with İstanbul-bound flights in the UK and continental Europe. One-way/return fares from İstanbul start at around C$950/1550 with Lufthansa and Air Canada. Try **Travelcuts** (☎ 1866-246 9762; www.travelcuts.com), Canada's national student travel agency, or **Airlineticketsdirect.com** (☎ 1877-679 8500; www.airlineticketsdirect.com).

Continental Europe

Generally, there's not much variation in fares to Turkey from one European city or another. Most European national carriers fly direct to İstanbul for around €200 return. Cheaper return flights can be found for around €150 but usually involve changing planes en route, so if you travelled from Paris to İstanbul with Lufthansa, you'd fly via Frankfurt or Munich. **STA Travel** (www.statravel.com/worldwide.htm) has offices throughout Europe. If you plan to visit a resort, check with your local travel agents for flight and accommodation deals.

Germany has the biggest Turkish community outside Turkey, which has enabled some great deals between the two countries. Lufthansa has direct flights to İstanbul, Ankara and İzmir from €150. There are also a number of charter airlines offering flights between several German cities and İstanbul, Antalya, Bodrum, Dalaman and İzmir. Try Condor, German Wings or Corendon Airlines (see left for contact details).

In France, travel agents **Voyageurs du Monde** (☎ 08 92 23 56 56; www.vdm.com), **Nouvelles Frontières**

(☎ 08 25 00 07 47; www.nouvelles-frontieres.fr) and **Voyages Wasteels** (☎ 08 92 05 11 55; www.wasteels.fr) are recommended.

In Italy, **CTS Viaggi** (☎ 199 501150; www.cts.it) is one of the major travel agencies. In Spain, we recommend **Barcelo Viajes** (☎ 902 11 62 26; www.barceloviajes.com).

Turkish Airlines, Cyprus Turkish Airlines, Atlasjet and Pegasus Airlines have daily direct services between Ercan Airport at Lefkoşa (Nicosia) in Northern Cyprus and locations across Turkey.

Middle East & Asia

If you want to fly to Turkey from any of the Central Asian countries, you can usually pick up a flight with Turkish Airlines or the country's national carrier. Turkish Airlines flies İstanbul–Tbilisi (Georgia) and İstanbul–Baku (Azerbaijan) for around TL550 each way. Azerbaijan Airlines also offers direct flights between Baku and İstanbul or Ankara, and these are generally much cheaper. Because the border between Turkey and Armenia is closed, you can't travel overland between the two countries, but you can fly. Armavia Airlines has weekly flights (sometimes daily) between İstanbul and Yerevan. Turkish Airlines has daily flights to Tehran and Tabriz (Iran) for about TL530.

One of the cheapest ways to get between northeast or southeast Asia and Turkey is to fly via Dubai. Emirates Airlines flies to İstanbul and to cities throughout India, to Pakistan and further afield to Hong Kong and Bangkok. Singapore Airlines often has good deals on its website between Asia and İstanbul, with return flights between Dubai and İstanbul going for €380, and between Hong Kong and İstanbul for €695.

New Zealand

Air New Zealand serves İstanbul, but it involves flying to Frankfurt and then flying back to Turkey with Lufthansa. It's better to use one of the airlines listed under Australia (see opposite), which follow the same routes through Asia.

Flight Centre (☎ 0800 243 544; www.flightcentre .co.nz) and **STA Travel** (☎ 0800-474 400; www.statravel .co.nz) are recommended travel agencies.

UK & Ireland

British Airways, Turkish Airlines and EasyJet offer direct flights between London and Turkey. British Airways flies to İstanbul (from UK£105 return), Ankara, Antalya and İzmir. Turkish Airlines usually has direct flights only between İstanbul and London (from UK£145 return). EasyJet flies direct between London (Luton) and İstanbul from UK£60 return.

For most cheap flights you can generally expect to fly to Turkey with a transit in a European city (though EasyJet flies direct). Or you could look into charter flights, which are usually cheaper at the beginning and end of the season. Typical return charter fares, bought in advance, are UK£109 to UK£220 for a five-to-10-night stay on the Turkish coast. Charter flights to Turkey go from Birmingham, Bristol, Gatwick, London, Manchester, Nottingham and Newcastle. Try online charter flight agents **Just the Flight** (☎ 08718-551 551; www.just theflight.co.uk) and **Thomsonfly.com** (☎ 0871-231 4691; www.thomsonfly.com).

Other recommended travel agencies in the UK and Ireland:

STA Travel (☎ 0870-230 0040; www.statravel.co.uk)
Student Flights (☎ 0870-499 4004; www.student flight.co.uk)
Trailfinders (☎ 0845-058 5858; www.trailfinders.co.uk)

USA

Turkish Airlines offers flights to İstanbul from New York from about US$1200 return. From Los Angeles, you can get some good deals with American Airlines, Delta Airlines, Northwest Airlines/KLM-Royal Dutch Airlines and Lufthansa, via New York or Europe, for less than US$1000 return.

Some leading US travel agencies:

Expedia (☎ 800-397 3342; www.expedia.com)
STA Travel (☎ 800-781 4040; www.statravel.com)
Travelocity (☎ 888-872 8356; www.travelocity.com)

LAND

If you are planning to travel overland, you'll be spoilt for choice since Turkey has land borders with eight countries. Bear in mind, however, that Turkey's relationships with most of its neighbours tend to be tense, which can affect the availability of visas and when and where you can cross. Always check with the Turkish embassy in your country for the most up-to-date information before leaving home.

Border Crossings

Crossing land borders by bus and train is fairly straightforward, but expect delays of between one and three hours. You'll usually have to get

TRANSPORT

CLIMATE CHANGE & TRAVEL

Climate change is a serious threat to the ecosystems that humans rely upon, and air travel is the fastest-growing contributor to the problem. Lonely Planet regards travel, overall, as a global benefit, but believes we all have a responsibility to limit our personal impact on global warming.

Flying & Climate Change

Pretty much every form of motor travel generates CO_2 (the main cause of human-induced climate change) but planes are far and away the worst offenders, not just because of the sheer distances they allow us to travel, but because they release greenhouse gases high into the atmosphere. The statistics are frightening: two people taking a return flight between Europe and the US will contribute as much to climate change as an average household's gas and electricity consumption over a whole year.

Carbon Offset Schemes

Climatecare.org and other websites use 'carbon calculators' that allow jetsetters to offset the greenhouse gases they are responsible for with contributions to energy-saving projects and other climate-friendly initiatives in the developing world – including projects in India, Honduras, Kazakhstan and Uganda.

Lonely Planet, together with Rough Guides and other concerned partners in the travel industry, supports the carbon offset scheme run by climatecare.org. Lonely Planet offsets all of its staff and author travel.

For more information check out our website: lonelyplanet.com.

---

off the bus or train and endure a paperwork and baggage check of all travellers – on both sides of the border. This is a relatively quick process if you're on a bus, but naturally takes longer when there's a trainload of passengers. Before you ditch the idea of trains, however, be aware that delays can be caused by the long line of trucks and cars banked up at some borders – especially at the Reyhanlı–Bab al-Hawa border between Turkey and Syria – not by the number of fellow passengers.

Crossing the border into Turkey with your own vehicle should be fairly straightforward. No special documents are required to import a car for up to six months, but be sure to take it out again before the six months is up. If you overstay your permit, you may have to pay customs duty equal to the full retail value of the car! If you want to leave your car in Turkey and return to collect it later, the car must be put under a customs seal, which is a tedious process.

For more on each country's border crossings, see the relevant country headings following.

Armenia

At the time of writing, the Turkey–Armenia border was closed to travellers. The situation could always change, particularly with the recent thawing in relations between the two countries (see p16), so it's worth checking (the Russian embassy handles Armenian diplomatic interests in Turkey).

If you want to travel from Turkey to Armenia (or vice versa) you can fly (see p677) or travel by bus via Georgia (see p582).

Azerbaijan (Nakhichevan)

Several daily buses depart from Trabzon's otogar (bus station; p559) heading for Tbilisi, where you can change for a bus to Baku.

You can also cross from Turkey to the Azerbaijani enclave of Nakhichevan (p592) via the remote Borualan–Sadarak border post, east of Iğdır. From there you'll need to fly across Armenian-occupied Nagorno-Karabakh to reach Baku and the rest of Azerbaijan.

Bulgaria & Eastern Europe

It's fairly easy to get to İstanbul by direct train or bus from many points in Europe via Bulgaria. There are three border crossings between Bulgaria and Turkey. The main border crossing is the busy Kapitan-Andreevo–Kapıkule one, 18km northwest of Edirne on the E80, used by most buses and motorists travelling to and from the Balkans and Eastern Europe. The closest town on the Bulgarian side is Svilengrad, some 9km from the border. Petrol, foreign-exchange facilities, restaurants and accommodation are available at this crossing, which is open 24 hours a day. For more details, see p174. A second crossing at Lesovo-Hamzabeyli, some 25km northeast of Edirne, is favoured by big trucks and lorries and should be avoided. In any case it takes a little longer to get to and there's no public transport. The third crossing, at Malko Tărnovo-Aziziye, some 70km northeast of Edirne via Kırklareli and 92km south of Burgas in Bulgaria, is only useful for those heading to Bulgaria's Black Sea resorts.

Note that while Turkish border guards will allow pedestrians to cross the frontier, the Bulgarians only occasionally do. Play it safe and either take the bus from Edirne or hitch a lift with a cooperative motorist.

BUS

There are several departures daily to Sofia and to the coastal cities of Varna and Burgas in Bulgaria from İstanbul's otogar – at least six companies offer services. There are also daily departures to Skopje, Tetovo and Gostivar in Macedonia, and to Constanta and Bucharest in Romania. The following companies run serves from İstanbul's otogar (p158):

Drina Trans (☎ 0212-658 1851; ticket office 88) Daily departures for Skopje, Macedonia (€30, 14 hours).
Metro Turizm (☎ 0212-658 3232; www.metroturizm
.com.tr; ticket office 107) Daily departures to Sofia (TL45, nine hours), Varna and Burgas in Bulgaria.
Öz Batu (☎ 0212-658 0255; ticket office 149) Daily departures for Bulgarian destinations including Sofia (TL40, nine hours).
Özlem (☎ 0212-658 0522; ticket office 97) Daily departures for Constanta (TL75, eight hours) and Bucharest (TL75, eight hours) in Romania.

TRAIN

The *Bosphorus Express* leaves İstanbul daily and runs to Bucharest, from where you can travel onwards by train to Chişinău (Moldova) and Budapest (Hungary). You can also catch the *Bosphorus Express* to Dimitrovgrad (Bulgaria), from where you can travel to Sofia (Bulgaria) and on to Belgrade (Serbia).

Essentially the *Bosphorus Express* leaves İstanbul with a line of carriages. There are separate carriages for passengers heading to Budapest, to Sofia and Belgrade, and to Chişinău. The carriages are switched to local trains at either Bucharest or Dimitrovgrad, depending on where you're heading. Confused?

Don't worry; bookings are simply from A to B, though there will be some delay as carriages are transferred.

You'll need to take your own food and drinks as there are no restaurant cars on these trains. Note also that the Turkey–Bulgaria border crossing is in the early hours of the morning and you need to leave the train to get your passport stamped – the hold-up takes about two hours. We've heard stories of harassment, especially of women, at the border, so lone women may be best taking an alternative route. Travelling in the sleeper cars is the safest and most comfortable option.

A suggested train route from London to İstanbul is via Paris and Munich to Zagreb, Croatia, where you can catch trains to Belgrade to join the *Bosphorus Express*. For more information, see http://tinyurl.com/6ne478; there are other suggested train routes from London at http://tinyurl.com/25h54t.

Georgia

The main border crossing is at Sarp on the Black Sea coast, between Hopa (Turkey) and Batumi (Georgia). You can also cross inland at the Türkgözü border crossing near Posof, north of Kars (Turkey) and southwest of Akhaltsikhe (Georgia). The Sarp border crossing is open 24 hours a day; Türkgözü is open from 8am to 8pm, though in winter you might want to double-check it's open at all.

Göktaş Ardahan (☎ 0212-658 3476; İstanbul otogar, ticket office 7) runs direct buses between İstanbul otogar and Tbilisi (Tiflis) for TL90. The journey takes around 26 hours. Several daily buses head for Tbilisi from Trabzon's otogar (p559).

If you're heading to the Türkgözü border from the Turkish side, a convenient starting point is Kars. You need to get to Posof first, then hire a taxi or minibus to take you to the border post (16km, TL20). From the border, hire another taxi to take you to Akhaltsikhe (€15; two hours), from where regular buses head to Tbilisi (which can take up to seven hours). There is also a better, more direct route from Kars to Tbilisi via Ardahan (see p582).

Greece & Western Europe

One option to get to Turkey from Western Europe is to make your way via Alexandroupolis in Greece and cross at Kipi–İpsala, 29km to the northeast. The closest Turkish centre with major transport links is Keşan, 35km to the

TRANSPORT

TRANSPORT

VISAS FOR NEIGHBOURING COUNTRIES

Armenia

Most nationalities can get visitor visas online or on arrival at the border (including the airport) for US$44 (valid for 120 days); or a three-day transit visa for US$29. Note that Armenia's border with Turkey is closed (see p678). See www.armeniaforeignministry.com for more information.

Azerbaijan

The visa conditions for Azerbaijan can be a little tricky to pin down. The republic's website (http://tinyurl.com/6emed9) does not list prices, but it does state that visitors can obtain a three-month visa at embassies; you need a letter of invitation and two passport photos. You can also obtain a visa at Baku's Heydar Aliyer International Airport. We have heard of European travellers applying at the consulate in Kars, paying only US$40 (valid 15 days), with two photos, and having their visa issued in three days.

Bulgaria

Citizens of nations including Australia, Canada, Israel, Japan, New Zealand, the US and most EU countries can obtain a free 90-day tourist visa at any Bulgarian border post. See www.mfa.bg/en.

Georgia

Most people (including from Canada, Israel, Japan, Switzerland, EU countries and the US) can obtain a 90-day tourist visa upon arrival at any Georgian border. Single-entry visas cost US$30; double-entry visas are US$45. See www.mfa.gov.ge.

Greece

Nationals of Australia, Canada, all EU countries, New Zealand and the USA can enter Greece for up to three months without a visa. See www.mfa.gr.

Iran

All visitors to Iran need to get a visa in advance. There is an embassy in Ankara and consulates are located in İstanbul and Erzurum. Your passport must be valid for at least another six months and you will need a passport photo. Some people wait 10 days to hear whether their application has been granted, others weeks. American and British applicants aren't too popular, but the Dutch can often get them virtually straight away. You can organise one through the consulate in Erzurum or İstanbul, but it's better to arrange it in advance. There is an electronic visa service at

---

east. You can also cross at Kastanies–Pazarkule, which is just 13km south of the Turkish city of Edirne. Both borders are open 24 hours.

To cross at Kipi–İpsala take a bus from Alexandroupolis to the Greek border point of Kipi, then hitch to the border. From there you can get a taxi (TL20) to the bus station in İpsala and an onward bus to İstanbul. Greek and Turkish border guards always allow you to cross the frontier on foot.

If you're crossing from Turkey into Greece, do so as soon after 9am as possible in order to catch one of the few trains or buses from Kastanies south to Alexandroupolis, where there are better connections. Alternatively, take a bus from Edirne to Keşan, then to İpsala and cross to Kipi.

BUS

Germany, Italy, Austria and Greece have most direct buses to İstanbul, so if you're travelling from other European countries, you'll likely have to catch a connecting bus. Two of the best Turkish companies – **Ulusoy** (☎ 444 1888; www.ulusoy.com.tr) and **Varan Turizm** (☎ 444 8999; www.varan.com.tr) – operate big Mercedes buses on these routes. Sample one-way fares to İstanbul are Athens €68 (20 hours) and Vienna €110 (27 hours).

CAR & MOTORCYCLE

The E80 highway makes its way through the Balkans to Edirne and İstanbul, then on to Ankara. Using the car ferries from Italy and Greece can shorten driving time from

www.mfa.gov.ir and it is also possible to pick up a 48-hour transit on arrival at the airport; you need at least two blank pages in your passport and a ticket for onward travel from Iran. New Zealanders can get a one-week tourist visa at the airport. Women must be wearing hijab (full body cover), the rules for which are more relaxed nowadays so that you can show your fringe, wear make-up and jewellery, and brave colours other than black (although never red).

Iraq

The Republic of Iraq issues visas for Arab regions of the country such as Baghdad and Basra, but they are only available to people with official business in the country such as journalists, diplomats, contractors and aid workers. Visas must be obtained prior to departing your home country and cost US$20 to US$50.

The Kurdish Regional Government issues its own tourist visa, which is good for travelling within Kurdish Iraq only. Citizens of most countries, including Australia, New Zealand and the USA as well as the European Union, are automatically issued a free, 10-day tourist visa at the point of entry. Travellers of Arab descent need prior permission to enter Kurdish Iraq. Thirty-day visa extensions can be obtained at the Directorate of Residency in Erbil (Arbil).

See www.mofa.gov.iq for more information.

Northern Cyprus

Visas for the Turkish Republic of Northern Cyprus (TRNC) are available on arrival, on similar conditions to those for Turkey. If you're planning to visit Greece or the Greek islands as well, remember that relations between the Greek Cypriot–administered Republic of Cyprus (in the south) and Northern Cyprus remain chilly. Also, if you enter the TRNC and have your passport stamped you may later be denied entry to Greece. The Greeks will only reject a stamp from the TRNC, *not* a stamp from Turkey proper, so have the Turkish Cypriot official stamp a piece of paper instead of your passport, a procedure with which they are familiar. See www.mfa.gov .cy and www.mfa.gov.tr.

Syria

All foreigners need a visa to enter Syria, which has an embassy in Ankara and consulates in İstanbul and Gaziantep. Getting visitor visas is a straightforward process in Ankara, where a single-entry visa costs €20. You need two passport photos and you can pick up the visa on the same day as you lodge your application. Do not leave the application until Gaziantep (as there have been reports that it only processes applications for Turkish nationals) or until the border, as travellers have been knocked back.

Western Europe considerably, but at a price (see p682).

From Alexandroupolis in Greece, the main road goes to the most convenient crossing (Kipi–İpsala) then to Keşan and east to İstanbul or south to Gallipoli, Çanakkale and the Aegean.

TRAIN

From Western European cities (apart from those in Greece) you will come via Eastern Europe; see p678.

The best option for travelling between Greece and Turkey is the overnight train between Thessaloniki and İstanbul called the *Filia-Dostluk Express*. The journey takes 12 to 14 hours, including an hour or two's delay at the border, and accommodation is in comfy, air-conditioned sleeper cars. Good-value one-way rates are TL46 for 2nd-class between İstanbul and Thessaloniki; or TL93 if you take a connecting Greek intercity train to Athens.

You can buy tickets at the train stations but not online. For more information see the websites of **Turkish State Railways** (TCDD; www.tcdd.gov.tr) or the **Hellenic Railways Organisation** (www.ose.gr).

Iran

There are two border crossings between Iran and Turkey, the busier Gürbulak–Bazargan, near Doğubayazıt (Turkey) and Şahabat (Iran); and the Esendere–Sero border crossing, southeast of Van (Turkey). Gürbulak–Bazargan is open 24 hours. Esendere–Sero is

TRANSPORT

open from 8am until midnight, but double-check in winter as the border might be closed. Travellers are increasingly using this second crossing into Iran, which has the added bonus of taking you through the breathtaking scenery of far southeastern Anatolia. And to make things easy, there is a direct bus running between Van (Turkey) and Orumiyeh (Iran). See p650 for departure information.

BUS

There are regular buses from İstanbul and Ankara to Tabriz and Tehran. From İstanbul otogar, try **Best Van Tur** (☎ 0212-444 0065; otogar ticket office 147) with daily departures (TL120, 35 hours). From Ankara, they leave from the AŞTİ bus terminal.

You may also want to consider taking a dolmuş from Doğubayazıt 35km east to the border at Gürbulak, for about TL4, and then walking across the border. The crossing might take up to an hour. From Bazargan there are onward buses to Tabriz; from Sero there are buses to Orumiyeh. You can catch buses to Iran from Van.

TRAIN

The *Trans-Asya Espresi* leaves İstanbul every Wednesday and arrives two nights later in Tehran (TL111), travelling via Ankara, Kayseri and Van before crossing the border at Kapikoi/Razi and stopping in Salmas, Tabriz and Zanjan. The journey involves a five-hour ferry crossing of Lake Van. See the Iranian Railways site, **RAJA Passenger Train Co** (www.rajatrains.com) for more information about this service and the train from Tehran to Damascus (Syria), which passes through Van and across the lake.

Iraq

Although we obviously don't suggest that travelling to wider Iraq is at all advisable, a handful of hardy travellers have been travelling into northern Iraq via the Habur–Ibrahim al-Khalil border post. It's near Cizre and Silopi, on the Turkish side; Zakho is the closest town to the border on the Iraqi side. There's no town or village at the border crossing and you can't walk across it. A taxi from Silopi to Zakho costs US$50; to the Ibrahim al-Khalil post costs TL60 and you can pick up a taxi there to Zakho or Dohuk.

Either way, your driver will manoeuvre through a maze of checkpoints and handle the paperwork. Bring 10 photocopies of your passport's photograph page. You may be searched and interviewed by Turkish border guards. As the Kurdish issue is a sensitive topic in Turkey, never refer to your destination as 'Kurdistan', and don't carry patriotic Kurdish items. When you reach the big 'Welcome to Iraqi Kurdistan Region' sign, you'll be led into a small office, offered tea and interviewed by one or more Kurdish Peshmerga (military) officials. Be honest. It helps to have the name and phone number of an Iraqi Kurdish contact.

Think you've got it covered? Wait until you cross the border in the opposite direction… See boxed text, p635.

Syria

There are eight border posts between Syria and Turkey, but the border at Reyhanlı–Bab al-Hawa is by far the most convenient, and therefore the busiest. Daily buses link Antakya in Turkey with the Syrian cities of Aleppo (Halab; TL6, four hours, 105km) and Damascus (Şam; TL11, eight hours, 465km). Also close to Antakya is the border post at Yayladağı. For both these crossings see p438. Other popular crossings to Syria include via Kilis, 65km south of Gaziantep (p604), the Akçakale border, 54km south of Şanlıurfa (p613), and the Nusaybin-Qamishle border, 75km southeast of Mardin (p637).

It's possible to buy bus tickets direct from İstanbul to Aleppo or Damascus. **Hatay Pan Turizm** (☎ 0212-658 3911; İstanbul otogar, ticket office 23) has a daily service from İstanbul otogar, arriving in Damascus (TL60) the following day. **Urfa Seyahat** (☎ 0212-444 6363; otogar ticket office 9) has daily departures for Aleppo.

The very comfortable *Toros Ekspresi* train runs between İstanbul and Aleppo (and not all the way to Damascus as it says in the official timetables) – see the table, p161, for details. Bring your own food and drinks as there is no restaurant car. Several comfortable trains link Aleppo and Damascus daily.

There's a weekly train service between Tehran (Iran) and Damascus, running through the Turkish cities of Van and Malatya. See www.tcdd.gov.tr for more information.

SEA

Car ferry services operate between Italian and Greek ports and several Turkish ports, but not to İstanbul. There are also a handful of routes over the Black Sea. **Ferrylines** (www

FERRIES BETWEEN TURKEY & GREECE

Route	Frequency	Fare (one way/return)	More details
Ayvalık-Lesvos	daily Jun-Sep; twice weekly Oct-May	€40/50	(p211)
Bodrum-Kos	daily	hydrofoil €30/35, open return €60; ferry €25/25, open return €50	(p276)
Bodrum-Rhodes	twice weekly Jun-Sep	€50/60, open return €100	(p276)
Çeşme-Chios	5 times a week Jun-Sep; twice weekly in winter	€40/65	(p234)
Datça-Rhodes	Sat May-Sep	TL90/180	(p343)
Datça-Simi	hydrofoil Sat May-Sep, *gület* on demand	hydrofoil TL60/120, *gület* TL120	(p343)
Kaş-Kastellorizo (Meis)	daily	TL70 return	(p384)

TRANSPORT

.ferrylines.com) is a good starting point for information about ferry travel in the region.

Greece

Private ferries link Turkey's Aegean coast and the Greek islands, which are in turn linked by air or boat to Athens. Services are generally daily in summer, and are operating with increasing frequency at other times of year, but bad sailing conditions mean they often run on a weekly basis during the winter. The table, above, summarises the services between the Greek islands and Turkey.

Italy

Marmara Lines (www.marmaralines.com) ferries connect Brindisi and Ancona in Italy with Çeşme. **Turkish Maritime Lines** (www.tdi.com.tr in Turkish) also operates twice-weekly ferries between Brindisi and Çeşme. For more details on these services, see p234.

Northern Cyprus

The main crossing point between Northern Cyprus and Turkey is between Taşucu (near Silifke) and Girne on the north coast of Northern Cyprus. **Akgünler Denizcilik** (p419; www.akgunler.com.tr) makes this journey. You can also travel between Alanya and Girne with **Fergün Denizcilik** (p415; www.fergun.net). Finally, you can travel between Mersin and Gazimağusa (Famagusta) on the east coast of Northern Cyprus, with **Turkish Maritime Lines** (p426; ☎ 0324-231 2536, 237 0726).

Russia

Ferries travel between Trabzon and Sochi in Russia three times a week; see p558 for more details.

Russia has an embassy in Ankara and consulates in İstanbul and Trabzon. To get a 29-day tourist visa, you need to go through a travel agency to get the required documentation; the three missions will recommend agents. In the past the consulate in Trabzon has referred applicants to nearby Burcu Turizm.

Ukraine

UKR Ferry (www.ukrferry.com) has a comfortable 36-odd-hour weekly service crossing the Black Sea between Odessa and İstanbul from €130 per person (one way).

Another weekly service runs between Sevastopol and İstanbul, departing Sevastopol at 6pm Sunday (arriving at İstanbul 9am Monday). Prices start at €175 return and range up to €235 for a two-room luxury cabin. Departures from İstanbul are on Thursday nights at 10pm (arriving 9am Saturday). Ferries travel between İstanbul and Yalta too. For more information email the folk at www.aroundcrimea.com.

TOURS

The following are international tour companies whose trips to Turkey generally receive good reports:

Backroads (☎ 800 462 2848; www.backroads.com) US-based company offering combined bike and sailing tours of western Turkey.

Cultural Folk Tours of Turkey (☎ 800 935 8875; www.boraozkok.com) US-based company offering group and private cultural and history tours.

Exodus (☎ 0845 863 9600; www.exodus.co.uk) UK-based adventure company offering a wide range of tours including diving, walking the Lycian Way and sea kayaking.

Imaginative Traveller (☎ 0845 077 8802; www
.imaginative-traveller.com) UK-based company offering a
variety of overland adventures through Turkey, including
one following the footsteps of Alexander the Great to Cairo.
Intrepid Travel (☎ 1300 364 512; www.intrepidtravel
.com.au) Australia-based company with a variety of small-
group, good-value tours for travellers who like the philosophy of independent travel, but prefer to travel with others.
Pasha Tours (☎ 800 722 4288; www.pachatours
.com) US-based company offering general tours as well as
special-interest packages such as Jewish heritage, 'Seven
churches of Asia Minor', 'In the steps of St Paul' etc.

See p689 for details of some Turkey-based
tour operators.

GETTING AROUND

Many countries could learn a thing or two
from Turkey about how to run an effective
and affordable transport system. Turkey's
intercity bus system is as good as any you'll
find, with modern coaches crossing the
country at all hours and with very reasonable prices. The railway network is useful
on a few major routes, and becoming an
increasingly popular choice as improvements
are made. And finally, flying is an excellent
option for such a large country, and fierce
competition between the many domestic airlines keeps tickets affordable.

AIR
Airlines in Turkey
Domestic airlines fly to some 30 cities
throughout the country. Many flights, for
instance from Dalaman to Van, go via
the hubs of İstanbul or Ankara. Atlasjet
is one of the few airlines offering direct
flights between west coast and central and
eastern destinations.

You can book flights on most airlines'
websites. You'll get cheaper seats and more-
convenient departure times if you book a
couple of months ahead.

Domestic flights are available with the following airlines:
Atlasjet (KK; ☎ 0216-444 3387; www.atlasjet.com) A
growing network, with flights from İstanbul, Çanakkale,
İzmir and Antalya to cities throughout the country.
Onur Air (OHY; ☎ 0212-444 6687; www.onurair.com
.tr) Flies from Antalya, Bodrum, Dalaman, Diyarbakır,
Erzurum, Gaziantep, İstanbul, İzmir, Kayseri and Trabzon,
among others.

Pegasus Airlines (PGT; www.pegasusairlines.com) Flies
between İstanbul and locations from Antalya to Van.
Sun Express Airlines (XQ; www.sunexpress.com.tr) A
Turkish Airlines subsidiary.
Turkish Airlines (THY; ☎ 0212-252 1106; www.thy
.com) State-owned Turkish Airlines provides the main
domestic network, and you can book and pay for tickets
online. One-way fares from TL105.

BICYCLE
Like bike touring anywhere else, riding in
Turkey can be a wonderful adventure, full
of surprises, challenges and a whole lotta
grunt. Highlights are the spectacular scenery, the easy access to archaeological sites,
which you might have all to yourself, and
the curiosity and hospitality of locals, especially out east. You will have to take the
road-hog drivers, rotten road edges and, out
east, stone-throwing children, wolves and
ferocious Kangal dogs (p74) in your stride.
To give yourself the best chance of an enjoyable and safe trip, plan to avoid main roads
wherever possible.

You'll be able to find excellent-quality
spare parts in İstanbul and Ankara, but
bring whatever you think you might need
elsewhere. The best bike brand in Turkey is
Bisan, with decent models starting at around
TL350, but you can find leading international brands in bike shops in İstanbul such
as **Pedal Sportif** (☎ 0212-511 0654; www.pedalbisiklet
.com in Turkish; Mimar Kemalettin Caddesi 29, Sirkeci), or
in Ankara at **Delta Bisiklet** (☎ 0312-223 6027; www
.deltabisiklet.com; Bosna Hersek Caddesi 21, Emek). Both
these shops have English-speaking staff and
come highly recommended by tourers. They
service bikes and can send parts throughout
the country.

The best map for touring by bike is the *Köy
Köy Türkiye Yol Atlası* (TL45) available in
bookshops in İstanbul; for other map recommendations see p666. You can usually transport your bike by air, bus, train or ferry free
of charge, although mini- and midibuses will
charge for the space it takes up. You can hire
bikes for short rides in tourist towns along the
coast and in Cappadocia.

BOAT
Sea of Marmara Ferries
İstanbul Deniz Otobüsleri (p158; İstanbul Fast Ferries, İDO;
☎ 444 4436; www.ido.com.tr) operates high-speed
car ferry services crossing the Sea of Marmara.
There are services from İstanbul (Yenikapı

FEZ BUS

A hop-on, hop-off bus service, the **Fez Bus** (Map pp92-3; ☎ 0212-516 9024; www.feztravel.com; Akbıyık Caddesi 15, Sultanahmet, İstanbul) links the main tourist resorts of the Aegean and the Mediterranean with İstanbul and Cappadocia. The big bonuses of using the Fez Bus are convenience (you never have to carry your bags), flexibility (the passes are valid from June to October and you can start anywhere on the circuit) and atmosphere (it's fun and energetic, with a strong party vibe). The downsides? You spend most of your time with other travellers rather than with locals, and it can rapidly become boring once you've had your fill of the backpacker fraternity. And it doesn't work out to be cheaper than doing it yourself with point-to-point buses.

A Turkish Delight bus pass (adult/student €176/164) allows you to travel from İstanbul to Çanakkale, Ephesus, Köyceğiz, Fethiye, Olympos, Cappadocia and then back to İstanbul via Ankara.

---

terminal) to Bandırma (for İzmir; p197) and Yalova (for Bursa; p283).

BUS

Buses form Turkey's most widespread and popular means of transport. Virtually every first-time traveller to the country comments on the excellence of the bus system compared with that in their home country. The buses are well kept and comfortable too, and you'll be treated to snacks and tea along the journey, plus liberal sprinklings of the Turks' beloved *kolonya* (lemon cologne).

Most Turkish cities and towns have a central bus station generally called the otogar, *garaj* or *terminal*. Besides intercity buses, the otogar often handles dolmuşes (minibuses that follow prescribed routes) to outlying districts or villages. Most bus stations have an *emanetçi* (left luggage) room, which you can use for a nominal fee.

These are some of the best companies, with extensive route networks:

Boss Turizm (☎ 444 0880; www.bosturizm.com, in Turkish) Specialises in superdeluxe İstanbul–Ankara services.

Kamil Koç (☎ 444 0562; www.kamilkoc.com.tr, in Turkish)

Ulusoy (☎ 444 1888; www.ulusoy.com.tr)

Varan Turizm (☎ 444 8999, 0212-251 7474; www.varan.com.tr)

Costs

Bus fares are subject to fierce competition between companies, and sometimes you can bargain them down by claiming a student discount etc. Some companies, such as Varan Turizm, are nominally part of the ISIC scheme (see p661), but this doesn't guarantee you a saving. Prices reflect what the market will bear, so the fare from Rich City X to Poor Village Y may not always be the same as from Poor Village Y to Rich City X.

We give sample fares from all Turkey's main bus stations under Getting There & Away in the individual towns. Typically, a bus ticket from İstanbul to Çanakkale costs TL30 to TL35, from İstanbul to Ankara TL25 to TL44, and from İstanbul to Göreme TL40.

Reservations

Although you can usually walk into an otogar and buy a ticket for the next bus, it's wise to plan ahead for public holidays, at weekends and during the school-holiday period from mid-June to early September. You can reserve seats over the web with most of the bus companies listed here (left).

When you enter the bigger otogars prepare for a few touts, all offering buses to the destination of your choice. How do you choose which company to go with? It's usually a good idea to stick to the reputable big-name companies we've listed. You may pay a bit more, but at least you can be more confident the bus has been well maintained, will run on time, and that there will be a relief driver on really long hauls. For shorter trips, you'll find other bus companies have big localised city networks; for example Truva serves the area around Çanakkale, and Uludağ covers destinations around Bursa. We've mentioned names to look out for under Getting There & Away.

After buying a ticket, getting a refund can be difficult; exchanging it for another ticket with the same company is easier.

All seats can be reserved, and your ticket will bear a specific seat number. The ticket agent will have a chart of the seats with those already sold crossed off. They will often assign you a seat, but if you ask to look at the chart and choose a place, you can avoid sitting right at the back of the bus (which can get stuffy) and immediately above the wheels (which can get bumpy). On night buses you may also want to avoid the front row of seats behind the driver, which have little legroom (you may also have to inhale the driver's cigarette smoke and listen to him chatting to his conductor into the early hours). The seats immediately in front of and behind the middle door are also a bad choice; those in front don't recline, and those behind have no legroom.

Servis

While it obviously makes sense from a town-planning point of view to move the otogars out of the town centres, it means that journey times are becoming longer and vaguer. The timings we give are from otogar to otogar, but you may need to add up to an hour in either direction for getting to and from the otogars. This is especially true if you're using a *servis* (shuttle minibus) to get there. As otogars move further out of town, so most bus companies provide a *servis* to take passengers to and from the city centre. When buying a ticket ask whether there's a *servis* and when it leaves for the otogar. On arrival, say 'Servis var mı?' to find out whether there's a *servis* into town. Rare cities where there are no *servis* include Ankara, Bursa, Konya and Safranbolu.

Servis drivers like to allow plenty of time for getting to the otogar, which means that in Göreme, for example, you must usually be at the otogar for transfer to Nevşehir a good 45 minutes before the bus is scheduled to leave even though it's just a 15-minute drive.

While these services are free, they do have some snags. You may find yourself waiting around interminably for another busload of passengers to arrive or for your driver to be dragged away from the TV to run his *servis*. Journeys starting at the otogar tend to get going quicker, but can be protracted as the driver drops each and every passenger off at their doorstep (or at least near it). If time is more important than money, then forget it and jump into a taxi.

Also, beware of pension owners who lead you to believe that the private minibus to their pension is the bus company *servis*. This certainly happens at Nevşehir otogar, where there are all sorts of scams to steer clear of (see p514).

CAR & MOTORCYCLE

Driving around Turkey gives you unparalleled freedom to enjoy the marvellous countryside and coastline. You can stop at the teeny roadside stalls selling local specialities, explore back roads leading to hidden villages, and picnic at every opportunity, just like the locals. Road surfaces and signage are generally good on the main roads at least – the most popular route with travellers, along the Aegean and Mediterranean coast, offers excellent driving conditions. Hiring a scooter to explore the rugged Hisarönü Peninsula (p341) is a day out you'll cherish long after you've recovered from the knuckle-whitening corners.

The bad news is that Turkey has one of the world's highest motor-vehicle accident rates. Turkish drivers are not particularly discourteous, but they are impatient and incautious. They like to drive at high speed and have an irrepressible urge to overtake. To survive on Turkey's highways, drive cautiously and very defensively, and *never* let emotions affect what you do. Avoid driving at night, when you won't be able to see potholes, animals, or even vehicles driving with their lights off.

When you're planning your trip, be mindful that Turkey is a huge country and spending time in the car travelling huge distances will eat up your travel time. Consider planes, trains or buses to cover long distances and hiring a car for localised travel. Public transport is a less stressful way of getting around the traffic-clogged big cities.

Automobile Associations

Turkey's main motoring organisation is the **Türkiye Turing ve Otomobil Kurumu** (Turkish Touring & Automobile Association; ☎ 0212-282 8140; www.turing.org .tr; Oto Sanayi Sitesi Yanı 1, Levent 4, İstanbul).

Motorcyclists may want to check out **One More Mile Riders İstanbul** (www.ommriders.com), a community resource for riding in Turkey, and the Turkey-related information on **Horizons Unlimited** (www.horizonsunlimited.com/country/turkey).

Bring Your Own Vehicle

You can bring your vehicle into Turkey for six months without charge. However, the fact that you brought one in with you will be marked in your passport to ensure you take it back out again. Don't plan on selling it here, and be prepared to be charged a hefty fine for any time over the six months. Ensure you have your car registration and insurance policy on you. If you don't have insurance, buying it at the border is a straightforward process.

Driving Licence

Drivers must have a valid driving licence. Your own national licence should be sufficient, but an international driving permit (IDP) may be useful if your licence is from a country likely to seem obscure to a Turkish police officer.

Fuel & Spare Parts

In Turkey there is little difference in price between *süper benzin* (normal/leaded petrol) and *kurşunsuz* (unleaded); both cost around TL3.50 per litre. You can usually pay with credit cards at petrol stations. Diesel is cheaper.

There are petrol stations everywhere, at least in western Turkey, and many are mega enterprises. All the same, it's a good idea to have a full tank when you start out in the morning across the vast empty spaces of central and eastern Anatolia.

Yedek parçaları (spare parts) are readily available in the big cities, especially for European models such as Renaults, Fiats and Mercedes-Benz. Ingenious Turkish mechanics can also contrive to keep some US models in service. Repairs are usually quick and cheap. Roadside repair shops can often provide excellent, virtually immediate service, although they (or you) may have to go somewhere else to get the parts. For tyre repairs find an *oto lastikçi* (tyre repairer). The *sanayi bölgesi* (industrial zone) on the outskirts of every town will have repair shops.

It's always wise to get an estimate of the repair cost in advance. Repair shops are usually closed on Sunday.

If you bring your motorcycle to Turkey you're bound to have a fine time. Spare parts may be hard to come by everywhere except the big cities, so bring what you might need, or rely on the boundless ingenuity of Turkish mechanics to find, adapt or make you a part. If you do get stuck for a part you could also ring an İstanbul or Ankara repair centre and get the part delivered by bus. **Horizons Unlimited** (www.horizonsunlimited.com/country/turkey) has a list of repair centres in İstanbul.

Hire

You need to be at least 21 years old, with a year's driving experience, to be able to hire a car. If you don't pay with a major credit card you will have to leave around €500 (or the equivalent in TL or US$) cash deposit. Most hire cars have standard (manual) transmission; you'll pay more for automatic transmission. Note that most of the big-name companies charge a hefty drop-off fee starting at TL200 (eg pick up in Ürgüp, and drop off in Ankara).

You can hire a car from the big international companies (Avis, Budget, Europcar, Hertz and National) in all main cities, towns and most airport. **Avis** (www.avis.com.tr/english) has the most extensive network of agencies, but **Europcar** (www.europcar.com) often offers the best value for money. Recommended local companies include **Decar** (www.decar.com.tr), with no drop-off fee, İstanbul-based **Car Rental Turkey** (☎ 0533-467 0724; www.carrentalturkey.info) and **Green Car** (www.greenautorent.com), the largest operator in the Aegean region. The recommended **Economy Car Rentals** (www.economycarrentals.com) undercuts the other companies without scrimping on good service, and **Turkey Car Hire Express** (http://turkey.carhireexpress.co.uk) is also a good place to start your search.

If your car incurs any accident damage, or if you cause any, do not move the car before finding a police officer and asking for a *kaza raporu* (accident report). The officer may ask you to take a breath-alcohol test. Contact your car-hire company within 48 hours. Your insurance may be void if it can be shown that you were operating under the influence of alcohol or other drugs, were speeding, or if you did not submit the required accident report within 48 hours.

The total cost of a standard hire vehicle arranged during the summer months (for a week with unlimited kilometres, including tax and insurance) ranges from TL400 to TL800. Daily hire is from TL70 to TL120, depending on the size and type of car and the hire location. You will generally save money by booking ahead, and you run the risk of there not being any cars available if you leave it until the last minute. Baby-seat hire is usually available for between TL5 and TL10 per day. At the lower end, these prices may seem cheap, but bear in mind that Turkey has some of the highest fuel prices in the world.

This has led in turn to an irritating local practice. Some budget and local agencies are delivering cars with virtually no fuel; about 1/8 of a tank is normal. If challenged, many agencies will point out that it clearly states on the back of the contract that you could request (and pay for at inflated prices) a full tank. The practice is both annoying and dangerous – particularly if it tempts you into the risky game of getting your own back by returning the vehicle with an empty tank...

Insurance

You *must* have third-party insurance, valid for the entire country (not just for Thrace or European Turkey), or a Turkish policy purchased at the border.

If you hire a car there will be two types of mandatory insurance included in the fee, the Collision Damage Waiver (CDW), which covers damage to the vehicle or another, and the Theft Protection (TP) insurance. Personal accident insurance is usually optional; you may not need it if your travel insurance from home covers the costs of an accident.

Parking

Parking around the country is fairly easy to find. You can find parking even in the largest cities – İstanbul, Ankara, İzmir, Antalya and so on – though in some cases it may be a short walk from your accommodation.

Top-end and a handful of midrange hotels offer undercover parking for guests, and most midrange and budget options have a roadside parking place or two that is nominally theirs to use. If they don't, car parking will be close by in an empty block overseen by a caretaker, or on the road, in which case you may be required to pay an hourly rate to a fee collector. Your best bet is to set it up in advance when you book your room; otherwise, staff will be able to point out the nearest and/or cheapest option when you arrive.

Note that car clamping is a fact of life in Turkey. Park in the wrong place and you risk having your car towed away, with the ensuing costs and hassle.

Road Conditions

There are good *otoyols* (motorways) from the Bulgarian border near Edirne to İstanbul and Ankara, and from İzmir all the way around the coast to Antalya. Elsewhere, roads are being steadily upgraded, although they still tend to be worst in the east. Severe winters play havoc with the surfaces and it's hard for the highways department to keep up with the repairs.

If driving in winter be careful of icy roads. In bad winters you will need chains on your wheels almost everywhere except along the Aegean and Mediterranean coast; the police may stop you in more-remote areas to check that you're properly prepared for emergencies.

If driving from İstanbul to Ankara you should be aware of a nasty fog belt around Bolu that can seriously reduce visibility even in summer.

Road Rules

In theory, Turks drive on the right and yield to traffic approaching from the right. In practice, they often drive in the middle and yield to no one. Be prepared for drivers overtaking on blind curves. If a car approaches from the opposite direction, all three drivers slam on the brakes and pray.

The international driving signs are there but are rarely observed. Maximum speed limits, unless otherwise posted, are 50km/h in towns, 90km/h on highways and 120km/h (40km/h minimum) on *otoyols*.

As there are only a few divided highways and many two-lane roads are serpentine, you must reconcile yourself to spending hours crawling along behind slow, overladen trucks. Try to avoid driving at night, but if you do, expect to encounter cars without lights or with lights missing, vehicles stopped in the middle of the road and oncoming drivers flashing their lights just to announce their approach.

DOLMUŞES & MIDIBUSES

Dolmuşes started life as shared taxis that operated on set routes for flat fares, but these days they are very often intercity minibuses. (They also provide local transport within a city – see opposite.) Some wait until every seat is taken before starting out, others operate at set times. You'll usually use them to get between small towns and villages.

To let the driver know that you want to hop out, say *'inecek var'* (someone wants to get out).

Midibuses generally operate on routes that are too long for dolmuşes, yet not quite popular enough for full-size buses. They usually have narrow seats with rigid upright backs, not at all comfortable on long stretches. Try to avoid the midibuses that ply the long and winding road from Bodrum and Marmaris to Antalya via Fethiye.

HITCHING

Hitching is never entirely safe in any country, and we don't recommend it. Travellers who decide to hitch should understand that they are taking a potentially serious risk.

If you must *otostop* (hitch), you should probably offer to pay something towards the petrol, although most drivers pick up foreign hitchers for their curiosity value. Private cars are not as plentiful as in Europe, so you could be in for a long wait on some routes.

As the country is large and vehicles relatively scarce, short hitches are quite normal. If you need to get from the highway to an archaeological site, you hitch a ride with whatever comes along, be it a tractor, lorry or private car.

Instead of sticking out your thumb for a lift you should face the traffic, hold your arm out towards the road, and wave it up and down as if bouncing a basketball.

LOCAL TRANSPORT
Bus

For most city buses you must buy your *bilet* (ticket) in advance at a special ticket kiosk, found at major bus terminals and, less frequently, at transfer points. Some shops near bus stops also sell local bus tickets, which normally cost around TL1.50.

In some cities, notably İstanbul, private buses operate on the same routes as municipal buses. The private buses are usually older, accept either cash or tickets, and follow the same routes as municipal buses.

Local Dolmuş

Dolmuşes are minibuses that operate on set routes within a city. They're usually faster, more comfortable and only slightly more expensive than the bus. These days only a few cities still have old-fashioned, shared-taxi dolmuşes (Bursa, Trabzon and İzmir are examples).

Once you've got to grips with a few local routes, you'll feel confident about picking up a dolmuş at the kerb. In the larger cities, stopping places are marked by signs with a black 'D' on a blue-and-white background reading '*Dolmuş İndirme Bindirme Yeri*' (Dolmuş Boarding and Alighting Place). They're usually conveniently located near major squares, terminals or intersections, but you may need to ask: '[your destination] *dolmuş var mı?*' (Is there a dolmuş to [destination]?').

Metro

Several cities now have underground or partially underground metros, including İstanbul, İzmir, Bursa and Ankara. These are usually quick and simple to use, although you may have to go right through the ticket barriers before you find a route map. Most metros require you to buy a *jeton* (transport token) for around TL1.50 and insert it into the ticket barrier.

Taxi

All over Turkey taxis are fitted with digital meters, and most drivers routinely use them. If your driver doesn't, mention it right away by saying '*saatiniz*' (your meter). The starting rate is about the same as the local bus fare (around TL1.50). Check to see the driver is running the right rate: *gündüz* in the daytime, and *gece* at night (which costs 50% more).

Some taxi drivers – particularly in İstanbul – try to demand flat payment from foreigners. Sometimes they offer a decent fare and pocket the money instead of giving the cab owners their share. But most of the time they'll ask an exorbitant amount, give you grief, and refuse to run the meter. If this happens find another cab and, if convenient, complain to the police. Only when you are using a taxi for a private tour involving waiting time (eg to an archaeological site) should you agree on a set fare, which should work out cheaper than using the meter. Taxi companies normally have set fees for longer journeys written in a ledger at the rank – they can be haggled down a little. Always confirm such fares in advance to avoid argument later.

Tram

Several cities have *tramvays* (trams), which are a quick and efficient way of getting around; normally you pay around TL1.50 to use a tram.

TOURS

Every year we receive complaints from travellers who feel that they have been fleeced by local travel agents, especially some of those operating in İstanbul's Sultanahmet area. However, there are plenty of very good agents operating alongside the sharks, so try not to get too paranoid. Figure out a ballpark figure for doing the same trip yourself using the prices in this book and shop around before committing.

TRANSPORT

TRANSPORT

MAN IN SEAT 61 *Mark Smith*

According to an old Turkish joke, the Germans were paid by the kilometre to build most of Turkey's railways, and they never used a straight line where a dozen curves would do! You'll certainly come to believe this as your train snakes its way across Turkey, round deep valleys and arid mountains, with occasional glimpses of forts on distant hilltops. Turkish train travel is incredibly cheap, but the best trains are air-conditioned and as good as many in Western Europe. The scenery is often better! Chilling out over a meal and a beer in the restaurant car of an İstanbul–Ankara express is a great way to recover from trekking round the sights of İstanbul, and the night trains from İstanbul to Denizli (for Pamukkale) or Konya are a most romantic and time-effective way to go. Other trains are slower and older, but just put your feet up, open a bottle of wine, and let the scenery come to you!

Mark Smith, aka the Man in Seat 61, is a global rail travel authority and founder of the website www.seat61.com. If you're even remotely interested in travelling by train, check it out.

The list of agents we recommend in İstanbul is on p128. Others are named in the relevant destination chapters; Kaş Göreme and Ürgüp have many good operations. The following are some Turkish tour operators we believe offer a reliable service:

Amber Travel (p381) British-run adventure travel specialist based in Kaş.

Bougainville Travel (p381) Also based in Kaş, this adventure travel specialist offers a range of water- and bike-based activities.

Fez Travel (Map pp92-3; ☎ 0212-516 9024; www.feztravel.com; Akbıyık Caddesi 15, Sultanahmet, İstanbul) Backpacker tours around Turkey, including Gallipoli tours. Also operates the Fez Bus (p685).

Kirkit Voyage (p512) Customised tours around Turkey (Cappadocia specialists), including İstanbul city and Ephesus tours. French spoken too.

Olympica (p381) Kaş-based Olympica specialises in 'build your own' activity packages.

TRAIN

Turkish State Railways (Türkiye Cumhuriyeti Devlet Demiryolları, TCDD; ☎ 444 8233; www.tcdd.gov.tr) runs services across the country. Lines laid out during the late Ottoman era rarely follow the shortest route, though a few newer, more direct lines have since been laid, shortening travel times on the best express trains. There were three train crashes in the space of a few weeks in 2004, including one on the high-speed İstanbul–Ankara run, leading some to contest that the network needed a complete overhaul, but the TCDD is forging ahead with building zippy new rail links. The government is throwing money at the system, hoping to build a fast-rail network throughout the country. Rapid links between İstanbul and Ankara (a new line), Ankara and Konya

(scheduled to open in 2010), Sivas and Kars, and Edirne and Kars have started or are on the drawing board.

The train network covers central and eastern Turkey fairly well, but doesn't go along the coastlines at all, apart from a short stretch between İzmir and Selçuk. For the Aegean and Mediterranean coasts you could go by train to either İzmir or Konya, and take the bus from there.

In terms of what to expect, train travel through Turkey has a growing number of fans embracing the no-rush travel experience: stunning scenery rolling by picture windows, the rhythmic clickity-clacks through a comfy slumber and the immersion with friendly locals (see above). The occasional unannounced hold-up and public toilets gone feral by the end of the long journey are all part of the adventure. And if you're on a budget, an overnight train journey is a great way to save accommodation costs.

The key to enjoying train travel in Turkey is to plan stops en route for long-haul trips and to know what to expect in terms of how long a journey will take. For example, the *Vangölü Ekspresi* from İstanbul to Lake Van (Tatvan), a 1900km trip, takes almost two days – and that's an express! The bus takes less than 24 hours, the plane less than two hours. Popular train trips include İstanbul to Ankara, and the overnight trains between İstanbul and Konya, İstanbul and Tehran (Iran), and İstanbul and Aleppo (Syria). Make sure you double-check all train departure times. See p160 for details of trains to and from İstanbul.

Note that train schedules usually indicate stations rather than cities. So most schedules refer to Haydarpaşa and Sirkeci rather than İstanbul. For İzmir, you will probably see Basmane and Alsancak, the names of the two main stations.

Classes & Costs

Turkish trains have several seating and sleeping options. Most of the trains have comfortable reclining Pullman seat carriages. Some also have European-style compartments with six seats, usually divided into 1st- and 2nd-class coaches. Sometimes seats can be booked in these compartments, sometimes they're 'first come, best seated'.

There are three types of sleeper. A *küşetli* (couchette) wagon has shared four- or sometimes six-person compartments with seats that fold down into shelf-like beds. Bedding is not provided for these wagons unless it's an *örtülü küşetli* or 'covered' couchette. A *yataklı* wagon has private European-style sleeping compartments, with washbasin and all bedding provided, capable of sleeping one to three people; this is the best option for women travelling on their own on overnight trips.

There is usually a mix of these options on the same service. The *Doğu Ekspresi* from İstanbul to Kars, for example, typically has three Pullman carriages, a covered couchette, an unreserved seating compartment and a sleeper.

Train tickets are usually about half the price of bus tickets. Children, students, seniors, disabled travellers and return tickets get a 20% discount.

Inter-Rail, Balkan Flexipass and Eurodomino passes are valid on the Turkish railway network; Eurail passes are not.

Reservations

Most seats and all sleepers on the best trains must be reserved. As the *yataklı* (sleeping-car) wagons are very popular, you should make your reservation as far in advance as possible, especially if a religious or public holiday (p664) is looming. Weekend trains tend to be busiest.

You can book and pay for tickets online at www.tcdd.gov.tr.

Health

CONTENTS

Prevention is the key to staying healthy while travelling in Turkey. Infectious diseases can and do occur in Turkey, but they are usually associated with poor living conditions and poverty, and can be avoided with a few precautions. The most common reason for travellers needing medical help is as a result of accidents – cars are not always well maintained, and poorly lit roads are littered with potholes. Medical facilities can be excellent in large cities, but in remoter areas they may be more basic.

BEFORE YOU GO

A little planning before departure, particularly for pre-existing illnesses, will save you a lot of trouble later. See your dentist before a long trip; carry a spare pair of contact lenses and glasses (and take your optical prescription with you); and carry a first-aid kit with you.

It's tempting to leave it all to the last minute – don't! Many vaccines don't ensure immunity until two weeks after they are given, so visit a doctor four to eight weeks before departure. Ask your doctor for an International Certificate of Vaccination (otherwise known as the yellow booklet), which will list all the vaccinations you've received. This is mandatory for countries that require proof of yellow-fever vaccination upon entry, but it's a good idea to carry it wherever you travel.

Travellers can register for free with the **International Association for Medical Advice to Travellers** (IAMAT; www.iamat.org). Its website can help travellers to find a local doctor with recognised training.

Bring medications in their original, clearly labelled, containers. A signed and dated letter from your physician describing your medical conditions and medications, including generic names, is also a good idea. If carrying syringes or needles, be sure to have a physician's letter documenting their medical necessity.

INSURANCE

Find out in advance if your insurance plan will make payments directly to providers or reimburse you later for overseas health expenditures (in Turkey doctors generally expect payment in cash). If you are required to pay upfront, make sure you keep all documentation. Some policies ask you to call a centre in your home country (reverse charges) for an immediate assessment of your problem. It's also worth ensuring your travel insurance will cover ambulances or transport, either home or to better medical facilities elsewhere. Not all insurance covers emergency medical evacuation home by plane or to a hospital in a major city, which may be the only way to get medical attention in a serious emergency.

Your travel insurance will not usually cover you for dental treatment other than in an emergency.

RECOMMENDED VACCINATIONS

The World Health Organization recommends that all travellers, regardless of the region they are travelling in, should be covered for diphtheria, tetanus, measles, mumps, rubella and polio, as well as hepatitis B. While making preparations to travel, take the opportunity to ensure that all of your routine vaccination cover is complete. The consequences of these diseases can be severe, and outbreaks do occur in the Middle East. Rabies is also endemic in Turkey, so if you will be travelling off the beaten track you might want to consider an antirabies jab.

MEDICAL CHECKLIST

Here is a list of items you should consider packing in your medical kit:

- antibiotics (if travelling off the beaten track)
- antidiarrhoeal drugs (eg loperamide)
- acetaminophen/paracetamol (Tylenol) or aspirin
- anti-inflammatory drugs (eg ibuprofen)
- antihistamines (for hay fever and allergic reactions)
- antibacterial ointment (eg Bactroban) for cuts and abrasions
- steroid cream or cortisone (allergic rashes)
- bandages, gauze, gauze rolls
- adhesive or paper tape
- scissors, safety pins, tweezers
- thermometer
- pocket knife
- DEET-containing insect repellent for the skin
- permethrin-containing insect spray for clothing, tents and bed nets
- sun block (it's very expensive in Turkey)
- oral rehydration salts
- iodine tablets (for water purification)
- syringes and sterile needles (if travelling to remote areas)

INTERNET RESOURCES

There is a wealth of travel health advice on the internet. For further information, the Lonely Planet website (www.lonelyplanet .com) is a good place to start. The **World Health Organization** (www.who.int/ith/en) publishes a superb book, *International Travel and Health,* which is revised annually and is available online at no cost. Another website of general interest is **MD Travel Health** (www.mdtravelhealth.com), which provides complete travel health recommendations for every country, updated daily, also at no cost. The website for the **Centers for Disease Control & Prevention** (www.cdc.gov) is a very useful source of travellers' health information.

FURTHER READING

Recommended references include *Travellers' Health* by Dr Richard Dawood, *International Travel Health Guide* by Stuart R Rose MD and *The Travellers' Good Health Guide* by

Ted Lankester, an especially useful health guide for volunteers and long-term expats working in the Middle East.

Lonely Planet's *Travel With Children* is packed with useful information on topics such as pretrip planning, emergency first aid, immunisation and disease information and what to do if you get sick on the road.

IN TURKEY

AVAILABILITY & COST OF HEALTH CARE

The standard of the health care system in Turkey is very variable. Although the best private hospitals in İstanbul and Ankara offer world-class standards of care, they are expensive. Elsewhere, even private hospitals don't always offer particularly high standards and their state-run equivalents even less so.

For basic care for things such as cuts, bruises and jabs you could ask for the local *sağulık ocağıı* (health centre), but don't expect anyone to speak anything but Turkish. The travel assistance provided by your insurance may be able to locate the nearest source of medical help – otherwise, ask at your hotel. In an emergency, contact your embassy or consulate.

Medicine, and even sterile dressings or intravenous fluids, may need to be bought from a local pharmacy. Nursing care is often limited or rudimentary, the assumption being that family and friends will look after the patient.

Standards of dental care are variable and there is a risk of hepatitis B and HIV transmission via poorly sterilised equipment, so watch the tools in use carefully. Your travel insurance will not usually cover you for anything other than emergency dental treatment.

For minor illnesses, such as diarrhoea, pharmacists can often provide advice and sell over-the-counter medication, including drugs that would require a prescription in your home country. They can also advise when more-specialised help is needed.

INFECTIOUS DISEASES
Diphtheria
Diphtheria is spread through close respiratory contact. It causes a high temperature and severe sore throat. Sometimes a membrane forms across the throat requiring a tracheotomy to prevent suffocation. Vaccination is recommended for those likely to be in close contact with the local population in infected areas. The vaccine is given as an injection alone, or with tetanus, and lasts 10 years.

Hepatitis A
Hepatitis A is spread through contaminated food (particularly shellfish) and water. It causes jaundice, and although it is rarely fatal it can cause prolonged lethargy and delayed recovery. Symptoms include dark urine, a yellow colour to the whites of the eyes, fever and abdominal pain. Hepatitis A vaccine (Avaxim, VAQTA, Havrix) is given as an injection: a single dose will give protection for up to a year, while a booster 12 months later will provide a subsequent 10 years of protection. Hepatitis A and typhoid vaccines can also be given as a combined single-dose vaccine (hepatyrix or viatim).

Hepatitis B
Infected blood, contaminated needles and sexual intercourse can all transmit hepatitis B. It can cause jaundice and affects the liver, occasionally causing liver failure. All travellers should make this a routine vaccination, especially as the disease is endemic in Turkey. (Many countries now give hepatitis B vaccination as part of routine childhood vaccination.) The vaccine is given singly, or at the same time as the hepatitis A vaccine (hepatyrix). A course will give protection for at least five years. It can be given over four weeks or six months.

HIV
HIV is spread via infected blood and blood products, sexual intercourse with an infected partner and from an infected mother to her newborn child. It can be spread through 'blood to blood' contacts such as contaminated instruments during medical, dental,

> **AVIAN INFLUENZA**
>
> The H5N1 avian influenza virus was confirmed in Turkey in late 2005, and there were 12 cases and four fatalities reported in 2006. The fatalities were all linked with ongoing close contact with birds, and there were no cases reported in 2007 or 2008. The risk to humans is considered very low unless the virus develops the ability to spread sustainably and efficiently between humans. For the latest outbreak news and general information log on to the **World Health Organization** (www.who.int).

acupuncture and other body-piercing procedures and sharing used intravenous needles.

Leishmaniasis
Spread through the bite of an infected sandfly, leishmaniasis can cause a slowly growing skin lump or ulcer. It may develop into a serious, life-threatening fever usually accompanied by anaemia and weight loss. Infected dogs are also carriers. Sandfly bites should be avoided whenever possible.

Leptospirosis
Leptospirosis is spread through the excreta of infected rodents, especially rats. It can cause hepatitis and renal failure that may be fatal. It is unusual for travellers to be affected unless living in poor sanitary conditions. It causes a fever and jaundice.

Malaria
You stand the greatest chance of contracting malaria if you travel in southeastern Turkey. The risk of malaria is minimal in most cities, but you should check with your doctor if you are considering travelling to any rural areas. It is important to take antimalarial tablets if the risk is significant. For up-to-date information about the risk of contracting malaria in a specific country, contact your local travel-health clinic.

If you're travelling in southeastern Turkey it's important to be aware of the symptoms of malaria. It is possible to contract malaria from a single bite from an infected mosquito. Malaria almost always starts with marked shivering, fever and sweating. Muscle pain, headache and vomiting are common. Symptoms may occur anywhere from a few days to three weeks after a bite by an infected mosquito. The illness can start while you are taking preventative tablets if they are not fully effective, and may also occur after you have finished taking your tablets.

Poliomyelitis

Generally, poliomyelitis is spread through contaminated food and water. It is one of the vaccines given in childhood and should be boosted every 10 years, either orally (a drop on the tongue) or as an injection. Polio may be carried asymptomatically, although it can cause a transient fever and, in rare cases, potentially permanent muscle weakness or paralysis.

Rabies

Spread through bites or licks on broken skin from an infected animal, rabies is, if untreated, fatal. Animal handlers should be vaccinated, as should those travelling to remote areas where a reliable source of postbite vaccine is not available within 24 hours. Three injections are needed over a month. If you have not been vaccinated and you suffer a bite, you will need a course of five injections starting within 24 hours or as soon as possible after the injury. Vaccination does not provide you with immunity, it merely buys you more time to seek appropriate medical help.

Tuberculosis

Tuberculosis (TB) is spread through close respiratory contact and occasionally through infected milk or milk products. BCG vaccine is recommended for those likely to be mixing closely with the local population. It is more important for those visiting family or planning on a long stay, and those employed as teachers and health-care workers. TB can be asymptomatic, although symptoms can include a cough, weight loss or fever months or even years after exposure. An X-ray is the best way to confirm if you have TB. BCG gives a moderate degree of protection against TB. It causes a small permanent scar at the site of injection, and is usually only given in specialised chest clinics. As it's a live vaccine it should not be given to pregnant women or immunocompromised individuals. The BCG vaccine is not available in all countries.

Typhoid

Typhoid is spread through food or water that has been contaminated by infected human faeces. The first symptom is usually fever or a pink rash on the abdomen. Septicaemia (blood poisoning) may also occur. Typhoid vaccine (typhim Vi, typherix) will give protection for three years. In some countries, the oral vaccine Vivotif is also available.

Yellow Fever

Yellow fever vaccination is not required for any areas of the Middle East; however, any travellers coming from a yellow-fever-endemic area will need to show proof of vaccination against yellow fever before entry to the Middle East – this normally means if a traveller is arriving directly from an infected country, or has been in an infected country during the previous 10 days.

The yellow-fever vaccination must be given at a designated clinic, and lasts for 10 years. It is a live vaccine and must not be given to immunocompromised or pregnant travellers.

TRAVELLER'S DIARRHOEA

To prevent diarrhoea, avoid tap water unless it has been boiled, filtered or chemically disinfected (with iodine tablets). Eat fresh fruits or vegetables only if they're cooked or if you have peeled them yourself, and avoid dairy products that might contain unpasteurised milk. Buffet meals are risky since food may not be kept hot enough; meals freshly cooked in front of you in a busy restaurant are more likely to be safe.

If you develop diarrhoea, be sure to drink plenty of fluids, preferably an oral rehydration solution containing lots of salt and sugar. A few loose stools don't require treatment, but if you start having more than four or five motions a day, you should start taking an antibiotic (usually a quinolone drug) and an antidiarrhoeal agent (such as loperamide). If diarrhoea is bloody, persists for more than 72 hours or is accompanied by fever, shaking chills or severe abdominal pain, you should seek medical attention.

ENVIRONMENTAL HAZARDS
Heat Illness

Heat exhaustion occurs following heavy sweating and excessive fluid loss with inadequate replacement of fluids and salt. This is particularly common in hot climates when taking unaccustomed exercise before full acclimatisation. Symptoms include headache, dizziness and tiredness. Dehydration is already

HEALTH

happening by the time you feel thirsty – aim to drink sufficient water such that you produce pale, diluted urine. The treatment of heat exhaustion consists of fluid replacement with water, fruit juice, or both, and cooling by cold water and fans. The treatment of the salt-loss component consists of consuming salty fluids such as soup or broth, and adding a little more table salt to foods than usual.

Heatstroke is much more serious. This occurs when the body's heat-regulating mechanism breaks down. An excessive rise in body temperature leads to sweating ceasing, irrational and hyperactive behaviour, and eventually loss of consciousness and death. Rapid cooling by spraying the body with water and fanning is an ideal treatment. Emergency fluid and electrolyte replacement by intravenous drip is usually also required.

Insect Bites & Stings

Even if mosquitoes do not carry malaria, they can cause irritation and infected bites. Using DEET-based insect repellents will prevent bites. Mosquitoes also spread dengue fever.

There is a risk of bee stings along the Aegean and Mediterranean coastal areas. Bees and wasps only cause real problems for those with a severe allergy (anaphylaxis). If you have a severe allergy to bee or wasp stings, you should carry an adrenalin injection or something similar. There is a higher risk of bee stings in the area around Marmaris in southwest Turkey.

Sandflies are located around the Mediterranean beaches. They usually only cause a nasty, itchy bite, but can carry a rare skin disorder called cutaneous leishmaniasis (see p694); use a DEET-based repellent to avoid bites.

Scorpions are frequently found in arid or dry climates. Turkey's small white scorpions can give a painful bite that will bother you for up to 24 hours, but they won't kill you.

Snake Bites

Do not walk barefoot or stick your hand into holes or cracks. If bitten by a snake, do not panic. Half of those bitten by venomous snakes are not actually injected with poison (envenomed). Immobilise the bitten limb with a splint (eg a stick) and apply a bandage over the site, with firm pressure, similar to applying a bandage over a sprain. Do not apply a tourniquet, or cut or suck the bite. Get the

victim to medical help as soon as possible so that antivenene can be given if necessary.

Water

It's probably not wise to drink Turkey's tap water if you're only here on a short visit. Stick to bottled water, boil water for 10 minutes or use water-purification tablets or a filter. Do not drink water from rivers or lakes, since it may contain bacteria or viruses that can cause diarrhoea or vomiting.

TRAVELLING WITH CHILDREN

All travellers with children should know how to treat minor ailments and when to seek medical treatment. Make sure children are up to date with routine vaccinations, and discuss possible travel vaccines with your doctor or paediatrician well before departure as some vaccines are not suitable for children aged under one year. You may want to consider giving children the BCG vaccine for tuberculosis (TB) if they haven't already had it – see p695 for more information.

In hot, moist climates any wound or break in the skin may lead to infection. The area should be cleaned and then kept dry and clean. Remember to avoid contaminated food and water. If your child is vomiting or experiencing diarrhoea, lost fluid and salts must be replaced. It may be helpful to take rehydration powders for reconstituting with boiled water. Ask your doctor about this.

Children should be encouraged to avoid dogs or other mammals because of the risk of rabies and other diseases. Any bite, scratch or lick from a warm-blooded, furry animal should immediately be thoroughly cleaned. If there is any possibility that the animal is infected with rabies, seek immediate medical assistance.

It always pays to double-check the drug and dosage your child has been prescribed by doctors or pharmacists in Turkey as they may be unsuitable for children. Some information on the suitability of drugs and recommended dosage can be found on travel-health websites (see p693).

WOMEN'S HEALTH

Emotional stress, exhaustion and travelling through different time zones can all contribute to an upset in the menstrual pattern. If you're using oral contraceptives, remember that some antibiotics, diarrhoea and vomiting can stop the pill from working and lead to increased risk of pregnancy. Remember to take condoms with you just in case. Condoms should be kept in a cool, dry place or they may crack and perish.

Emergency contraception is most effective if taken within 24 hours after unprotected sex; ask at a pharmacy for the *ertesi gün hapı* (morning-after pill). The **International Planned Parent Federation** (www.ippf.org) can advise you about the availability of contraception in Turkey and other countries. Sanitary pads are fairly readily available, but tampons are not always available outside major cities and are expensive – bring your own from home.

Travelling during pregnancy is usually possible, but there are important things to consider. Have a medical check-up before embarking on your trip. The most risky times for travel are during the first 12 weeks of pregnancy, when miscarriage is most likely, and after 30 weeks, when complications such as high blood pressure and premature delivery can occur. Most airlines will not accept a traveller after 28 to 32 weeks of pregnancy,

and in the later stages long-haul flights can be very uncomfortable. Antenatal facilities vary greatly in Turkey and you should think carefully before travelling in out-of-the-way places, bearing in mind the cultural and linguistic difficulties, not to mention poor medical standards you might face if anything goes wrong. Take written records of the pregnancy, including details of your blood group, which is likely to be helpful if you need medical attention while away (in Turkey you have to pay for blood infusions unless a friend supplies the blood for you). Ensure your insurance policy covers birth and postnatal care, but remember that insurance policies are only as good as the facilities available.

If you are pregnant or breastfeeding, it always pays to double-check the drug and dosage you have been prescribed by doctors or pharmacists in Turkey. The appropriateness of some drugs and correct dosage for pregnant or lactating women is sometimes overlooked. You can use travel-health websites (see p693) to check the generic drug and its recommended dosage.

HEALTH

Language

CONTENTS

Turkish is the dominant language in the Turkic language group, which also includes lesser-known tongues such as Azeri, Kirghiz and Kazakh. Although distantly related to Finnish and Hungarian, the Turkic languages are now seen as comprising their own unique language group. You can find people who speak Turkish, in one form or another, from Belgrade all the way to Xinjiang in China.

In 1928, Atatürk did away with Arabic script and adopted a Latin-based alphabet that was better suited to easy learning and correct pronunciation. He also instituted a language reform process to purge Turkish of Arabic and Persian borrowings, returning it to its 'authentic' roots. The result is a logical, systematic and expressive language with only one irregular noun, *su* (water), one irregular verb, *olmek* (to be) and no genders. It's so logical, in fact, that Turkish grammar formed the basis for the development of Esperanto, an ill-fated artificial international language.

Word order and verb formation in Turkish are very different from what you'll find in Indo-European languages like English. Words are formed by agglutination, meaning affixes are joined to a root word – one scary example is *Avustralyalılaştıramadıklarımızdanmısınız?*, which means 'Are you

one of those whom we could not Australianise?' This makes it somewhat difficult to learn at first, despite its elegant logic.

In larger cities and tourist areas you'll usually have little trouble finding someone who speaks English, but a few hints will help you comprehend signs, schedules and menus. For more information on language courses, see p569, and for a comprehensive language guide get Lonely Planet's *Turkish Phrasebook*. You may also want to check out the excellent websites www.turkishclass.com and www.practicalturkish.com.

PRONUNCIATION

Pronouncing Turkish is pretty simple for English speakers as it uses sounds that are very similar to ones you already use. You'll hear some variation in pronunciation in different parts of Turkey, but this language chapter is based on standard pronunciation so you'll be understood wherever you go.

Vowels

Most Turkish vowel sounds can be found in English, although in Turkish they're generally shorter and slightly harsher. When you see a double vowel, such as *saat* (hour) you need to pronounce both syllables separately. Be careful of the symbols ı and i – the ı is undotted in both lower and upper case (like Iğridir), while the i has dots in both cases (like İzmir). It's easy to read both of these as an English 'i', but you can be misunderstood if you don't pronounce the two sounds distinctly – *sık* means 'dense', 'tight' or 'frequent' but *sik* is the Turkish equivalent of a certain 'f' word meaning 'to copulate'. The same care should be taken with o/ö and u/ü.

TURKISH	PRONUNCIATION GUIDE	
a	a	as in 'father'
ay	ai	as in 'aisle'
e	e	as in 'red'
ey	ay	as in 'say'
ı	uh	as the 'a' in 'ago'
i	ee	as in 'bee'
o	o	as in 'go'
ö	er	as in 'her' with no 'r' sound

| u | oo | as in 'moon' |
| ü | ew | like 'ee' with rounded lips |

Consonants

Most Turkish consonants sound the same as their English counterparts, but there are a couple of exceptions. The Turkish **c** is pronounced like English 'j', **ç** is like English 'ch' and **ş** is like English 'sh'. The letter **h** is never silent, so always pronounce it as in 'house'. The **ğ** is a silent letter that extends the vowel before it – it acts like the 'gh' combination in 'weigh', and is never pronounced. The letter **r** is always rolled and **v** is a little softer than the English sound.

TURKISH	PRONUNCIATION GUIDE	
b	b	as in 'big'
c	j	as in 'jam'
ç	ch	as in 'church'
d	d	in as 'day'
f	f	as in 'fun'
g	g	as in 'go'
h	h	as in 'house'
j	zh	as the 's' in 'pleasure'
k	k	as in 'kilo'
l	l	as in 'loud'
m	m	as in 'man'
n	n	as in 'no'
p	p	as in 'pig'
r	r	a strong, rolled 'r'
s	s	as in 'sea'
ş	sh	as in 'ship'
t	t	as in 'tin'
v	v	as in 'van' but softer
y	y	as in 'you'
z	z	as in 'zoo'

Word Stress

Word stress is quite light in Turkish, and generally falls on the last syllable of the word. Most two-syllable place names (eg Kıbrıs) are stressed on the first syllable, and in three-syllable names the stress is usually on the second syllable (eg İstanbul).

ACCOMMODATION

Where can I find a ...?
Nerede ... bulabilirim? ne·re·de ... boo·*la*·bee·lee·reem
  camping ground
  kamp yeri kamp ye·*ree*
  guest house
  misafirhane mee·*sa*·feer·ha·ne

MAKING A RESERVATION
(for written and phone inquiries)

To ...	*Alıcı ...*	a·luh·*juh* ...
From ...	*Gönderen ...*	gern·de·*ren* ...
Date	*Tarih*	ta·reeh
in the name of ...	*... adına*	... a·duh·*na*
credit card number	*kredi kartı numara*	kre·dee kar·tuh noo·ma·*ra*
expiry date	*son kullanma tarihi*	son kool·lan·*ma* ta·ree·*hee*

I'd like to book ...
  ... ayırtmak istiyorum lütfen.
  ... a·yurt·mak ees·tee·yo·room *lewt*·fen
From (2 July) to (6 July).
  (2 Temmuz'dan) (6 Temmuz'a) kadar.
  (ee·*kee* tem·mooz·*dan*) (al·*tuh* tem·moo·za) ka·*dar*
Please confirm availability and price.
  Lütfen fiyatı ve mal mevcudiyetini teyit eder misiniz?
  lewt·fen fee·ya·*tuh* ve mal mev·joo·dee·ye·tee·*nee* te·*yeet* e·*der* mee·see·neez

---

hotel
otel o·*tel*
youth hostel
gençlik hosteli gench·*leek* hos·te·*lee*
pension
pansiyon pan·see·*yon*
pension (in a private home)
ev pansiyonu ev pan·see·yo·*noo*

Can you recommend somewhere cheap?
Ucuz bir yer tavsiye edebilir misiniz?
oo·*jooz* beer yer tav·see·ye e·de·bee·leer mee·see·*neez*
What's the address?
Adresi nedir?
ad·re·see ne·deer
Could you write it down, please?
Lütfen yazar mısınız?
lewt·fen ya·*zar* muh·suh·*nuhz*

Do you have a ...?
... odanız var mı?
... o·da·*nuz* var muh
  single room
  Tek kişilik tek kee·shee·*leek*
  double room
  İki kişilik ee·*kee* kee·shee·*leek*
  twin room
  Çift yataklı cheeft ya·tak·*luh*
  dormitory room
  Yatakhane ya·tak·*ha*·ne

LANGUAGE

How much is it per night/person?
  Geceliği/Kişi başına   ge·je·lee·*ee*/kee·*shee* ba·shuh·*na*
  ne kadar?   ne ka·*dar*
May I see it?
  Görebilir miyim?   ger·re·bee·leer mee·yeem
Where's the bathroom/toilet?
  Banyo/Tuvalet nerede?   ban·yo/too·va·*let* ne·re·de
I'm leaving now.
  Şimdi ayrılıyorum.   *sheem*·dee ai·ruh·*luh*·yo·room

CONVERSATION & ESSENTIALS
Hello.
  Merhaba.   *mer*·ha·ba
Goodbye.
  Hoşçakal.   hosh·*cha*·kal (person leaving)
  Güle güle.   gew·*le* gew·*le* (person staying)
Yes.
  Evet.   e·*vet*
No.
  Hayır.   *ha*·yuhr
Please.
  Lütfen.   lewt·fen
Thank you.
  Teşekkür ederim.   te·shek·*kewr* e·*de*·reem
You're welcome.
  Birşey değil.   beer·*shay* de·*eel*
Excuse me.
  Bakar mısınız.   ba·*kar* muh·suh·*nuhz*
Sorry.
  Özür dilerim.   er·*zewr* dee·*le*·reem
What's your name?
  Adınız nedir?   a·duh·*nuhz* ne·deer
My name is ...
  Benim adım ...   be·*neem* a·*duhm* ...
Where are you from?
  Nerelisiniz?   ne·re·lee·see·neez
I'm from ...
  Ben ...   ben ...
I like ...
  ... seviyorum.   ... se·*vee*·yo·room
I don't like ...
  ... sevmiyorum.   ... sev·mee·yo·room

DIRECTIONS
Can you show me (on the map)?
  Bana (haritada)   ba·*na* (ha·ree·ta·*da*) gers·te·re·
    gösterebilir misin?   bee·leer mee·seen
Where is ...?
  ... nerede?   ... ne·re·de
It's straight ahead.
  Tam karşıda.   tam kar·shuh·*da*
Turn left.
  Sola dön.   so·*la* dern
Turn right.
  Sağa dön.   sa·*a* dern

SIGNS	
Ada	Island
Belediye	Town Hall
Cami	Mosque
Deniz	Sea
Göl	Lake
Harabeler	Ruins
Havaalanı	Airport
Kale	Castle/Fortress
Kilise	Church
Köprü	Bridge
Liman	Harbour/Port
Meydan	Town Square
Müze	Museum
Otogar	Bus Station
Plaj	Beach
Şehir Merkez	Town Centre
Giriş	Entrance
Çıkışı	Exit
Açık	Open
Kapalı	Closed
Yasak	Prohibited
Sigara İçilmez	No Smoking
Boş Oda	Rooms Available
Boş Yer Yok	Full (No Vacancies)
Tuvaletler	Toilets/WC
Bay	Male
Bayan	Female

at the corner
  köşeden   ker·she·*den*
at the traffic lights
  trafik ışıklarından   tra·*feek* uh·shuhk·la·ruhn·*dan*

behind   arkasında   ar·ka·suhn·*da*
in front of   önünde   er·newn·*de*
far (from)   uzak   oo·*zak*
near (to)   yakınında   ya·kuh·nuhn·*da*
opposite   karşısında   kar·shuh·suhn·*da*

HEALTH
I'm ill.
  Hastayım.   has·*ta*·yuhm
It hurts here.
  Burası ağrıyor.   boo·ra·*suh* a·*ruh*·yor
antiseptic
  antiseptik   an·tee·sep·*teek*
condoms
  kondom   kon·*dom*
contraceptives
  doğum kontrol ilaçları   do·*oom* kon·*trol* ee·lach·la·*ruh*
diarrhoea
  ishali   ees·ha·*lee*

EMERGENCIES

Help!
İmdat!   eem·dat
There's been an accident!
Bir kaza oldu.   beer ka·za ol·doo
I'm lost.
Kayboldum.   kai·bol·doom
Leave me alone!
Git başımdan!   geet ba·shuhm·dan
Call ...!
... çağırın!   ... cha·uh·ruhn
　a doctor
　Doktor   dok·tor
　the police
　Polis   po·lees
　an ambulance
　Ambulans   am·boo·lans

medicine
ilaç   ee·lach
nausea
mide bulantım   mee·de boo·lan·tuhm
sunblock cream
güneş kremi   gew·nesh kre·mee
tampons
tampon   tam·pon

I'm ...
... var.   ... var
　asthmatic
　Astımım   as·tuh·muhm
　diabetic
　Şeker hastalığı   she·ker has·ta·luh·uhm

I'm allergic to ...
... alerjim var.   ... a·ler·zheem var
　antibiotics
　Antibiyotiklere   an·tee·boo·yo·teek·le·re
　aspirin
　Aspirine   as·pee·ree·ne
　penicillin
　Penisiline   pe·nee·see·lee·ne
　bees
　Arılara   a·ruh·la·ra
　nuts
　Çerezlere   che·rez·le·re
　peanuts
　Fıstığa   fuhs·tuh·a

LANGUAGE DIFFICULTIES

Do you speak English?
İngilizce konuşuyor musunuz?
een·gee·leez·je ko·noo·shoo·yor moo·soo·nooz

Does anyone here speak English?
İngilizce bilen var mı?
een·gee·leez·je bee·len var muh
How do you say ...?
... nasıl söylüyorsuhn?
... na·seel say·lew·yor·soohn
Could you write it down, please?
Lütfen yazar mısınız?
lewt·fen ya·zar muh·suh·nuhz
I understand.
Anlıyorum.
an·luh·yo·room
I don't understand.
Anlamıyorum.
an·la·muh·yo·room

NUMBERS

0	*sıfır*	suh·fuhr
1	*bir*	beer
2	*iki*	ee·kee
3	*üç*	ewch
4	*dört*	dert
5	*beş*	besh
6	*altı*	al·tuh
7	*yedi*	ye·dee
8	*sekiz*	se·keez
9	*dokuz*	do·kooz
10	*on*	on
11	*on bir*	on beer
12	*on iki*	on ee·kee
13	*on üç*	on ewch
14	*on dört*	on derrt
15	*on beş*	on besh
16	*on altı*	on al·tuh
17	*on yedi*	on ye·dee
18	*on sekiz*	on se·keez
19	*on dokuz*	on do·kooz
20	*yirmi*	yeer·mee
21	*yirmi bir*	yeer·mee beer
22	*yirmi iki*	yeer·mee ee·kee
30	*otuz*	o·tuuz
40	*kırk*	kuhrk
50	*elli*	el·lee
60	*altmış*	alt·muhsh
70	*yetmiş*	yet·meesh
80	*seksen*	sek·sen
90	*doksan*	dok·san
100	*yüz*	yewz
200	*ikiyüz*	ee·kee·yewz
1000	*bin*	been
1,000,000	*bin milyon*	been meel·yon

PAPERWORK

name	*ad*	ad
nationality	*uyrukluk*	ooy·rook·look
date of birth	*doğum günü*	do·oom gew·new

place of birth	doğum yeri	do-oom ye-ree
sex/gender	cinsiyet	jeen-see-yet
passport	pasaport	pa-sa-port
surname	soyad	soy-ad
visa	vize	vee-ze

QUESTION WORDS

Who?	Kim?	keem
What?	Ne?	ne
When?	Ne zaman?	ne za-man
Where?	Nerede?	ne-re-de
Which?	Hangi?	han-gee
How?	Nasil?	na-seel

SHOPPING & SERVICES

I'd like to buy ...
... almak istiyorum.   al-mak ees-tee-yo-room
How much is it?
Ne kadar?   ne ka-dar
May I look at it?
Bakabilir miyim?   ba-ka-bee-leer mee-yeem
I'm just looking.
Sadece bakıyorum.   sa-de-je ba-kuh-yo-room
The quality isn't good.
Kalitesi iyi değil.   ka-lee-te-see ee-yee de-eel
It's too expensive.
Bu çok pahalı.   boo chok pa-ha-luh
I'll take it.
Tutuyorum.   too-too-yo-room

Do you accept ...?
... kabul ediyor musunuz?
... ka-bool e-dee-yor moo-soo-nooz
credit cards		
Kredi kartı		kre-dee kar-tuh
travellers cheques		
Seyahat çeki		se-ya-hat che-kee

more	daha fazla	da-ha faz-la
less	daha az	da-ha az
smaller	küçük	kew-chewk
bigger	büyük	bew-yewk

Where's   ... nerede?   ... ne-re-de
a/the ...?
bank	Banka	ban-ka
... embassy	... elçilik	... el-chee-leek
hospital	Hastane	has-ta-ne
market	Pazar yeri	pa-zar ye-ree
police	Polis	po-lees
post office	Postane	pos-ta-ne
public phone	Telefon	te-le-fon
	kulübesi	koo-lew-be-see
public toilet	Umumi	oo-moo-mee
	tuvalet	too-va-let

TIME & DATES

When?	Ne zaman?	ne za-man
What time is it?	Saat kaç?	sa-at kach
It's (10) o'clock.	Saat (on).	sa-at (on)
in the morning	öğleden evvel	er-le-den ev-vel
in the afternoon	öğleden sonra	er-le-den son-ra
week	hafta	haf-ta
year	yıl	yuhl
today	bugün	boo-gewn
tomorrow	yarın	ya-ruhn
yesterday	dün	dewn

Monday	Pazartesi	pa-zar-te-see
Tuesday	Salı	sa-luh
Wednesday	Çarşamba	char-sham-ba
Thursday	Perşembe	per-shem-be
Friday	Cuma	joo-ma
Saturday	Cumartesi	joo-mar-te-see
Sunday	Pazar	pa-zar

January	Ocak	o-jak
February	Şubat	shoo-bat
March	Mart	mart
April	Nisan	nee-san
May	Mayıs	ma-yuhs
June	Haziran	ha-zee-ran
July	Temmuz	tem-mooz
August	Ağustos	a-oos-tos
September	Eylül	ay-lewl
October	Ekim	e-keem
November	Kasım	ka-suhm
December	Aralık	a-ra-luhk

TRANSPORT
Public Transport

What time does the ... leave/arrive?
... ne zaman kalkacak/varır?
... ne za-man kal-ka-jak/va-ruhr
boat	Vapur	va-poor
bus	Otobüs	o-to-bews
plane	Uçak	oo-chak
train	Tren	tren

I'd like a ... ticket.
... bir bilet lütfen.
... beer bee-let lewt-fen
one-way		
Gidiş		gee-deesh
return		
Gidiş-dönüş		gee-deesh-der-newsh
1st-class		
Birinci mevki		bee-reen-jee mev-kee
2nd-class		
Ikinci mevki		ee-keen-jee mev-kee

ROAD SIGNS

Dur	Stop
Girilmez	No Entry
Park Etmek Yasaktir	No Parking
Yol Ver	Give Way
Ücret Ödenir	Toll
Tehlikeli	Danger
Yavaş	Slow Down
Çıkışı	Exit
Giriş	Entry
Otoyol	Freeway
Park Yeri	Parking Garage
Tek Yön	One Way

delayed	*ertelendi*	er·te·len·*dee*
cancelled	*iptal edildi*	eep·*tal* e·deel·*dee*
the first/the last	*ilk/son*	eelk/son
platform	*peron*	pe·*ron*
ticket office	*bilet gişesi*	bee·*let* gee·she·*see*
timetable	*tarife*	ta·ree·*fe*
train station	*istasyon*	ees·tas·*yon*

Private Transport

I'd like to hire a ...
Bir ... kiralamak istiyorum.
beer ... kee·ra·la·*mak* ees·*tee*·yo·room

car	*araba*	a·ra·*ba*
4WD	*dört çeker*	dert che·*ker*
motorbike	*motosiklet*	mo·to·seek·*let*
bicycle	*bisiklet*	bee·seek·*let*

Is this the road to ...?
... giden yol bu mu? ... gee·*den* yol boo moo
Where's a service station?
Benzin istasyonu ben·*zeen* ees·tas·yo·*noo* ne·re·de
nerede?
Please fill it up.
Lütfen depoyu doldurun. lewt·fen de·po·*yoo* dol·*doo*·roon
I'd like ... litres.
... litre istiyorum. ... leet·re ees·*tee*·yo·room

diesel	*dizel*	dee·zel
petrol	*benzin*	ben·*zeen*

(How long) Can I park here?
Buraya (ne kadar süre) park edebilirim?
boo·ra·ya (ne ka·dar sew·re) park e·de·bee·*lee*·reem
Do I have to pay?
Park ücreti ödemem gerekli mi?
park ewj·re·tee er·*de*·mem ge·rek·*lee* mee
I need a mechanic.
Tamirciye ihtiyacım var.
ta·meer·jee·ye eeh·tee·ya·*jum* var

The car/motorbike has broken down at ...
Arabam/motosikletim ...de bozuldu.
a·ra·*bam*/mo·to·seek·le·*teem* ...·de bo·zool·*doo*
I have a flat tyre.
Lastiğim patladı.
las·tee·*eem* pat·la·*duh*
I've run out of petrol.
Benzinim bitti.
ben·zee·*neem* beet·*tee*
I've had an accident.
Kaza yaptım.
ka·*za* yap·*tuhm*

TRAVEL WITH CHILDREN

Do you have a/an ...?
... var mı? ... var muh
  baby change room
  Alt değiştirme odası alt de·eesh·teer·*me* o·da·*suh*
  baby seat
  Bebek koltuğuna be·*bek* kol·too·oo·*na*
  child-minding service
  Çocuk bakım hizmeti cho·*jook* ba·*kuhm* heez·me·*tee*
  children's menu
  Çocuk menüsü cho·*jook* me·new·*sew*
  disposable nappies/diapers
  Bebek bezi be·*bek* be·zee
  highchair
  Mama sandalyesine ma·*ma* san·dal·ye·see·*ne*
  potty
  Oturağa o·too·ra·*a*
  pusher (stroller)
  Pusete/Bebek arabası poo·se·te/be·bek a·ra·ba·suh

Where's the nearest toy shop?
En yakın oyuncakçı nerede?
en ya·kuhn o·yoon·jak·*chuh* ne·re·de
Do you mind if I breast-feed here?
Burada çocuk emzirmemin bir sakıncası var mı?
boo·ra·*da* cho·*jook* em·zeer·me·meen beer sa·kuhn·ja·*suh*
var muh
Are children allowed?
Çocuklar girebilir mi?
cho·jook·*lar* gee·re·bee·leer mee

Also available from Lonely Planet:
Turkish Phrasebook

LANGUAGE

Glossary

See p71 in the Food & Drink chapter for useful words and phrases dealing with food and dining. See the Language chapter (p698) for other useful words and phrases.

acropolis – hilltop citadel and temples of a classical Hellenic city
ada(sı) – island
agora – open space for commerce and politics in a Graeco-Roman city
aile salonu – family dining room, for couples, families and single women in a Turkish restaurant
Anatolia – the Asian part of Turkey; also called Asia Minor
arabesk – Arabic-style Turkish music
arasta – row of shops near a mosque, the rent from which supports the mosque
Asia Minor – see Anatolia

bahçe(si) – garden
banliyö treni – suburban train lines
baraj – dam
baş oda – vacant room
bedesten – vaulted, fireproof market enclosure where valuable goods are kept
belediye (sarayı) – municipal council, town hall
bey – polite form of address for a man; follows the name
bilet – ticket
bouleuterion – place of assembly, council meeting place in a classical Hellenic city
büfe – snack bar
bulvar(ı) – boulevard or avenue; often abbreviated to 'bul'

cadde(si) – street; often abbreviated to 'cad'
cami(i) – mosque
caravanserai – large fortified way-station for (trade) caravans
çarşı(sı) – market, bazaar; sometimes town centre
çay bahçesi – tea garden
çayhane – teahouse
çayı – stream
çeşme – spring, fountain
Cilician Gates – a pass in the Taurus Mountains in southern Turkey

dağ(ı) – mountain
damsız girilmez – sign meaning that men unaccompanied by a woman will not be admitted
deniz – sea
deniz otobüsü – literally 'seabus'; hydrofoil or catamaran

dere(si) – stream
dervish – member of Mevlevi Muslim brotherhood
dolmuş – shared taxi; can be a minibus or sedan
döviz (burosu) – currency exchange (office)

emanet(çi) – left-luggage (baggage check) office
emir – Turkish tribal chieftain
eski – old (thing, not person)
ev pansiyonu – private home that rents rooms to travellers
eyvan – vaulted hall opening into a central court in a *medrese* or mosque; also balcony
ezan – the Muslim call to prayer

fasıl – Ottoman classical music, usually played by gypsies
feribot – ferry

GAP – Southeastern Anatolia Project, a mammoth hydro-electric and irrigation project
gazino – Turkish nightclub, not a gambling den
geçit, geçidi – (mountain) pass
gişe – ticket booth
göl(ü) – lake
gület – traditional Turkish wooden yacht

hamam(ı) – Turkish bathhouse
han(ı) – caravanserai
hanım – polite form of address for a woman
haremlik – family/women's quarters of a residence; see also *selamlık*
heykel – statue
hisar(ı) – fortress or citadel
Hittites – nation of people inhabiting Anatolia during 2nd millennium BC
hükümet konağı – government house, provincial government headquarters

imam – prayer leader, Muslim cleric
imaret(i) – soup kitchen for the poor, usually attached to a *medrese*
indirim – discount
İnşallah – God willing
iskele(si) – jetty, quay

jandarma – gendarme, paramilitary police force/officer
jeton – transport token

kahvaltı salonu – breakfast room
kale(si) – fortress, citadel

kapı(sı) – door, gate
kaplıca – thermal spring or baths
Karagöz – shadow-puppet theatre
kaya – cave
KDV – katma değer vergisi, Turkey's value-added tax
kebapçı – place selling kebaps
kervansaray(ı) – Turkish for *caravanserai*
keyif – relaxation, refined to a fine art in Turkey
kilim – flat-weave rug
kilise(si) – church
köfteci – *köfte* (meatballs) maker or seller
konak, konağı – mansion, government headquarters
köprü(sü) – bridge
köşk(ü) – pavilion, villa
köy(ü) – village
kule(si) – tower
külliye(si) – mosque complex including seminary, hospital and soup kitchen
kümbet – vault, cupola, dome; tomb topped by this
küşet(li) – couchette(s), or shelf-like beds, In a six-person train compartment

liman(ı) – harbour
lokanta – eatery serving ready-made food

mağara(sı) – cave
mahalle(si) – neighbourhood, district of a city
medrese(si) – Islamic theological seminary or school, attached to a mosque
mescit, mescidi – prayer room, small mosque
Mevlâna – also known as Celaleddin Rumi, a great mystic and poet (1207–73), founder of the Mevlevi whirling *dervish* order
meydan(ı) – public square, open place
meyhane – tavern, wine shop
mihrab – niche in a mosque indicating the direction of Mecca
milli parkı – national park
mimber – pulpit in a mosque
minare(si) – minaret, tower from which Muslims are called to prayer
MÖ – BC
MS – AD
müezzin – cantor who sings the *ezan*
müze(si) – museum

nargileh – traditional water pipe (for smoking); hookah
necropolis – city of the dead, cemetery

oda(sı) – room
odeon – odeum, small classical theatre for musical performances
otobus – bus
otogar – bus station

otoyol – motorway, limited-access divided highway
Ottoman – of or pertaining to the Ottoman Empire which lasted from the end of the 13th century to the end of WWI

pansiyon – pension, B&B, guesthouse
paşa – general, governor
pastane – pastry shop (patisserie); also *pastahane*
pazar(ı) – weekly market, bazaar
peribacalar – fairy chimneys
peron – gate (at the otogar); platform (train station)
peştimal – *hamam* cloth
petrol ofisi – petrol station
pideci – pide maker or seller
plaj – beach
PTT – Posta, Telefon, Telegraf; post, telephone and telegraph office

Ramazan – Islamic holy month of fasting

saat kulesi – clock tower
şadırvan – fountain where Muslims perform ritual ablutions
saray(ı) – palace
sedir – bench seating that doubled as a bed in Ottoman houses
şehir – city; municipality
şehir merkezi – city centre
selamlık – public/male quarters of a residence; see also *haremlik*
Seljuk – of or pertaining to the Seljuk Turks, the first Turkish state to rule Anatolia from the 11th to 13th centuries
sema – *dervish* ceremony
semahane – hall where whirling dervish ceremonies are held
serander – granary
servis – minibus shuttle service going to and from the otogar
sinema – cinema
sokak, sokağı – street or lane; often abbreviated to 'sk'
Sufi – Muslim mystic, member of a mystic *(dervish)* brotherhood

tabiat parkı – nature park
tavla – backgammon
TC – Türkiye Cumhuriyeti (Turkish Republic); designates an official office or organisation
TCDD – Turkish State Railways
Tekel – government alcoholic beverage and tobacco company
tekke(si) – *dervish* lodge
TEM – Trans-European Motorway
tersane – shipyard

THY – Türk Hava Yolları, Turkish Airlines
TML – Turkish Maritime Lines
tramvay – tram
TRT – Türkiye Radyo ve Televizyon, Turkish broadcasting corporation
tuff, tufa – soft stone laid down as volcanic ash
türbe(si) – tomb, grave, mausoleum

valide sultan – mother of the reigning sultan
vezir – vizier (minister) in the Ottoman government

vilayet, valilik, valiliği – provincial government headquarters

yalı – grand waterside residence
yarım pansiyon – half-pension, ie breakfast and dinner included
yatak(lı) – sleeping-compartment on train
yayla – highland pastures
yeni – new
yol(u) – road, way
yüzyıl – century

The Authors

JAMES BAINBRIDGE   Coordinating Author, Environment, Experience Turkey, Central Anatolia, Cappadocia

James first visited Turkey as a student, at the end of an eastern European trip. He lived on bread and cheese triangles for a week in İstanbul and the Princes' Islands, before using the last of his funds to get home to Britain. His latest Turkish trip was more successful: wandering Anatolia and making up for student starvation by spending his entire fee on kebaps. When he's not investigating various countries' national dishes, James lives in London's 'Little Turkey'. He has contributed to half a dozen Lonely Planet guidebooks, and coauthored *A Year of Festivals,* featuring Turkey's camel- and oil-wrestling festivals.

BRETT ATKINSON   Western Anatolia, Black Sea Coast & the Kaçkars

Brett first travelled to Turkey in 1985, 70 years after his paternal grandfather fought at Gallipoli as an Anzac soldier. Since then he's returned several times to go ballooning above Cappadocia, explored the ancient city of Ani and honeymooned with wife Carol in İstanbul. For this trip he negotiated the coastal roads of the Black Sea, was surprised by the buzz of Bursa and Trabzon, and reinstated memories of 1985 at Afrodisias and Pamukkale. When he's not on the road for Lonely Planet, Brett lives in Auckland, where a sizeable Turkish population means he's never far from a good kebap. His work on this book is dedicated to his late grandfather Albert Edward Atkinson.

JEAN-BERNARD CARILLET   Turkey's Outdoors, Northeastern Anatolia, Southeastern Anatolia

A Paris-based journalist and photographer, Jean-Bernard regularly needs his fix of adventures. Visiting remote Kurdish villages, seeking out churches and castles of yore lost in the steppe or perched on cliff tops, climbing majestic summits (including Mt Ararat), hiking in the Kaçkars, crossing the borders with Iraq and Georgia – for an adrenaline rush he can't think of a better playground than eastern Anatolia. But he also loves the region for its epicurean indulgences – after several sojourns in eastern Turkey, he is a now a certified baklava-holic.

LONELY PLANET AUTHORS

Why is our travel information the best in the world? It's simple: our authors are passionate, dedicated travellers. They don't take freebies in exchange for positive coverage so you can be sure the advice you're given is impartial. They travel widely to all the popular spots, and off the beaten track. They don't research using just the internet or phone. They discover new places not included in any other guidebook. They personally visit thousands of hotels, restaurants, palaces, trails, galleries, temples and more. They speak with dozens of locals every day to make sure you get the kind of insider knowledge only a local could tell you. They take pride in getting all the details right, and in telling it how it is. Think you can do it? Find out how at **lonelyplanet.com**.

THE AUTHORS

STEVE FALLON
Thrace & Marmara

Turkey came to Steve (or was it the other way round?) fairly late, beckoning for the first time just a decade ago. But never one to do things by halves, on a second visit five years later he bought with his partner what was purportedly a house in Kalkan. Slowly they started putting it together, brick by brick, learning words for things he doesn't even know in English. Steve spends a portion of every year in Turkey and although *Türkçe'yi hala mağara adamı gibi konuşuyor* (he still speaks Turkish like a caveman), no one has yet called him Tarzan.

JOE FULLMAN
North Aegean, South Aegean

Turkey represented Joe's first trip outside Europe, some five years into his travel-writing career, although, as the destination was İstanbul, he only had the chance to dip his toe into Asia. Still, the waters seemed warm. His next time out was more of a submersion as he travelled up and down the Aegean coast. The third opportunity came with the update of this guidebook and, by this stage, he feels he's beginning to get the hang of things, although his Turkish could use some work. When he's not being sent to Turkey, Joe is a writer and editor based in London, or, more precisely, its southern enclave of Croydon.

VIRGINIA MAXWELL
Food & Drink, İstanbul

After working for many years as a publishing manager at Lonely Planet's Melbourne headquarters, Virginia decided that she'd be happier writing guidebooks rather than commissioning them. Since making this decision she's authored Lonely Planet books to Turkey, Egypt, Spain, Italy, Lebanon, Morocco, Syria and the United Arab Emirates. Virginia knows Turkey well, and loves it to bits. She is the author of Lonely Planet's *İstanbul* city guide and *İstanbul Encounter* guide and has covered Cappadocia for a previous edition of the Turkey guide. She usually travels with partner Peter and young son Max, who have grown to love the country as much as she does.

TOM SPURLING
Western Mediterranean, Eastern Mediterranean

Tom's first experience of Turkey was to housesit for then Lonely Planet author, Pat Yale, in her cave house in Cappadocia. For a month he fought and fed 100 cats, and read all her Orhan Pamuk novels. His final experience on that trip was a 2am motorboat from a techno party on the Bosphorus. For this edition Tom moved from the Western to the Eastern Mediterranean smashing dolmuş-riding records in a midsummer blaze. Freakishly, all of Tom's highlights start with the letter 'K' – Kalkan, Kabak, Kaleiçi, Kızkalesi, Kaleköy and Kayaköy. But Antakya is also nice. When not travelling or writing, Tom teaches English (and various other things) in Melbourne.

CONTRIBUTING AUTHORS

Will Gourlay, a serial visitor to Turkey, first arrived in İstanbul in the early '90s intending to sit on a Mediterranean beach. However, Anatolia beckoned so he climbed Nemrut Dağı and wandered the southeast instead of working on his tan. He subsequently taught in İzmir for a year, learning the delights of İskender kebap and the perils of rakı. He still obsesses on all things Turkish/Turkic/Ottoman and recently took a second generation of Gourlays to Turkey. They loved the beach! Will updated the History and Culture chapters.

Behind the Scenes

THIS BOOK

This 11th edition of Turkey was researched and written by the estimable author team of James Bainbridge (coordinating author), Brett Atkinson, Jean-Bernard Carillet, Steve Fallon, Joe Fullman, Virginia Maxwell and Tom Spurling. Will Gourlay wrote the History chapter and updated the Culture chapter. The Health chapter is based on original research by Dr Caroline Evans. Tom Brosnahan researched and wrote the first five editions of Turkey. Pat Yale joined him in writing the 6th edition, and Richard Plunkett joined Pat and Tom for the 7th edition. Pat Yale, Richard Plunkett and Verity Campbell researched and wrote the 8th edition, the 9th edition saw Pat Yale teaming up with Jean-Bernard Carillet, Virginia Maxwell and Miriam Raphael. The 10th edition of Turkey was written by Verity Campbell (coordinating author), Jean-Bernard Carillet, Dan Eldridge, Frances Linzee Gordon, Virginia Maxwell and Tom Parkinson.

This guidebook was commissioned in Lonely Planet's London office, and produced by the following:

Commissioning Editors Fiona Buchan, Will Gourlay
Coordinating Editor Barbara Delissen
Coordinating Cartographer Amanda Sierp
Coordinating Layout Designer Jacqueline McLeod
Managing Editor Imogen Bannister
Managing Cartographer Adrian Persoglia
Managing Layout Designer Laura Jane
Assisting Editors David Andrew, Laura Crawford, Kim Hutchins, Anne Mulvaney, Diana Saad, Angela Tinson, Helen Yeates
Assisting Cartographers Jacqueline Nguyen, Julie Sheridan
Assisting Layout Designers Jessica Rose, Jacqui Saunders
Cover Designer James Hardy
Project Managers Rachel Imeson, Fabrice Rocher
Language Content Coordinator Quentin Frayne

Thanks to Shahara Ahmed, Adam Bextream, Yvonne Bischofberger, Sally Darmody, Alex Fenby, Jim Hsu, Lisa Knights, Erin McManus, Wayne Murphy, Lyahna Spencer, Celia Wood

THANKS
JAMES BAINBRIDGE

Teşekkür ederim to Padi and Hulya for the bed in İstanbul, and to Jahid, Aziz and the Hemi posse for the paragliding demo in Sivas; to Pat, Süha, Ali Mustafa, Maggie, Kaili and everyone who brought Cappadocia to life, and to Crazy Ali for giving a poem to the Queen of Spain; to Mustafa in Boğazkale and Nazlı in Konya (good luck in Ibiza); to Ollagh for the whisky and Reuters

---

THE LONELY PLANET STORY

Fresh from an epic journey across Europe, Asia and Australia in 1972, Tony and Maureen Wheeler sat at their kitchen table stapling together notes. The first Lonely Planet guidebook, *Across Asia on the Cheap*, was born.

Travellers snapped up the guides. Inspired by their success, the Wheelers began publishing books to Southeast Asia, India and beyond. Demand was prodigious, and the Wheelers expanded the business rapidly to keep up. Over the years, Lonely Planet extended its coverage to every country and into the virtual world via lonelyplanet.com and the Thorn Tree message board.

As Lonely Planet became a globally loved brand, Tony and Maureen received several offers for the company. But it wasn't until 2007 that they found a partner whom they trusted to remain true to the company's principles of travelling widely, treading lightly and giving sustainably. In October of that year, BBC Worldwide acquired a 75% share in the company, pledging to uphold Lonely Planet's commitment to independent travel, trustworthy advice and editorial independence.

Today, Lonely Planet has offices in Melbourne, London and Oakland, with over 500 staff members and 300 authors. Tony and Maureen are still actively involved with Lonely Planet. They're travelling more often than ever, and they're devoting their spare time to charitable projects. And the company is still driven by the philosophy of *Across Asia on the Cheap*: 'All you've got to do is decide to go and the hardest part is over. So go!'

anecdotes in Kayseri, and to the Kurds in Çorum for the beers and manly companionship. Şerefe (cheers)! Thanks to my Turkey 11 coauthors for all the help and pointers, and a special shout out to the book's commissioning editor Will Gourlay, a man with a deep knowledge of Anatolia and a damn fine editor to boot.

BRETT ATKINSON
Thanks to everyone who again demonstrated why Turkey is probably the most hospitable country in the world. In Pamukkale, thanks to Ibrahim and Karyn. Say hi to Fındık and Çilek for me. In Eğirdir thanks to another İbrahim and Kadir. To Birsen and family in Eğirdir, it's official: your sigara böreği are the best in all of Anatolia. In İznik, thanks to Ali for the good humour, and in Ayder cheers to Mehmet and the Demirci family for the forest views and great company. Teşekkür ederim to the staff at Turkey's tourist information offices, especially to Yahya Saka in Trabzon. In Lonely Planet–ville thanks to the passionate and well-informed Will Gourlay, to Shahara Ahmed and her carto team, and to my fellow scribes, especially coordinating author James Bainbridge. Back in Auckland, thanks and love to Carol for holding the fort and waiting so we could finally to go to Madagascar and Mozambique.

JEAN-BERNARD CARILLET
I'd like to give a bit shout out to the main man behind the Lonely Planet scenes, namely Will; it's been a pleasure working with you, and I wish our paths will cross somewhere in Eastern Anatolia. James, coordinating author extraordinaire, deserves a pat on the back for his efficient liaising and good cheer, as does the carto team. I'm also grateful to Steve and Tom for their input. On the road, a big teşekkür ederim to Cumhur Bayrak, the Diler family, Celil, Zafer, Remzi, Özcan, Ayşe, Timur and all the hospitable Turks and Kurds I met on the road for their support and tips. At home, a phenomenal gros bisou to my daughter Eva, who gives a direction to my otherwise gypsy life.

STEVE FALLON
A number of people assisted in the research of my (admittedly tiny) piece of Turkey, and I'd like to say çok teşekkürler to the boys at Crowded House in Eceabat, Ziya Artam and Polat Cenboz, Osman Akpınar at Hassle Free Travel Agency in Çanakkale, Eric and Özlem Goossens at Gallipoli Houses/Gelibolu Evleri in Kocadere on the Gallipoli peninsula and Mehmet Nurel and Ali İhsan Dağöttüren at Hotel Endorfina in Kıyıköy. As a prelude to hitting the road, nothing could beat a week on the Med in a 39-footer with Captain-Diva Sally Adamson Taylor, her First Mate Susan Troccolo and, of course, my partner Michael Rothschild, who kept us all well-fed. Rakı all around!

JOE FULLMAN
Many thanks to everyone in Turkey (and beyond) who took the time to talk to me, write back to me, sort things out for me, answer my queries, recommend things to me, point me in the right direction, show me a good time and generally help out as I made my convoluted way up and down the coast. These include, in no particular order, Nedim, Chris, Murat, Kadri and Deniz in Bodrum, Ali and Sezgin in Kuşadası, Nadir in İzmir, Zeynep in Alaçatı, Alamdar in Foça, Annette in Ayvalık and Lisa in Bozcaada. Big thanks also to Will for giving me the gig, to Greg for his supreme companionship and driving (and driving advice) and, of course, to Nicola for putting up with my incessant Turkey talk and forcing me to upgrade to a better standard of hotel.

VIRGINIA MAXWELL
Many thanks to Max, Peter, Pat Yale, René, Ames, Tahir Karabaş, Ercan Tanrıvermiş, Tina Nevens, Özlem Tuna, Shellie Corman, Saffet Tonguç, Barbara Nadel, Ünal Çakmak and the many locals who shared their knowledge and love of İstanbul with me. At Lonely Planet, thanks to Turcophile Will Gourlay for giving me this gig, to Mandy Sierp for steering the mapping so competently and to Barbara Delissen for doing the same with the editing. Thanks also to my fellow authors, particularly Steve and James.

TOM SPURLING
First up, a big shout out to Lucy for kicking off our first family holiday in style. To the friendly crowd at Villa Perla in Datça for easing me off the plane. To Matt and Emma for making the party, then steering it just the right amount off course. To Kemal at Owl Books for the fine food, company and literary friendship (and for answering my questions!). To Selma at Türk Evi for her grace and hospitality, and for promoting Kalkan's environmental cause with her wanderlusting husband. To Jayne Marshall for the heartful tour of Kızkalesi and for the old-school lesson in climbing. And to the crazy-arse Kurdish Red Bull rep for racing me hard along the Eastern Med. Finally, to all the Lonely Planet writing team for their generous advice and humour; and to Will Gourlay for his

BEHIND THE SCENES

astute editorial guidance and for giving me the chance to hit up Turkey one more time.

WILL GOURLAY

Thanks to James and the fantastic author team on this edition – great work *dostlar!* Thanks to Maureen Freely for following up for me. In Turkey, thanks to Pat in Göreme for years of gossip, advice and local updates; Ünal in İstanbul for minding the bags; Lisa in Bozcaada for island news and internet connections; Ercan in Hasankeyf; and Selma and Volkan on the train to Tehran. Finally, extra special thanks to Claire, Bridget and Tommy – the most fantastic Turkish travel companions I've ever had or could ever wish for. *Haydi gideliz!*

OUR READERS

Many thanks to the travellers who used the last edition and wrote to us with helpful hints, useful advice and interesting anecdotes:

A Yossef Aelony, Cristina Agdiniz, Rupal Agrawal, Sayim Ahin, Hylke B Akkerman, Catherine Allen, Laura Ambrey, Diana Amith, Yassine Amnay, Phillip Andre, Chris Andrews, Estela Aparisi, Kathy Arici, Mustafa Askin, Geoffroy Aubry, Ibrahim Aydemir **B** Howard Bade, Sandeep Bagchee, Charles Bagley, Olaf Ballnus, Christoph Balmert, Lee Banner, Susan Barlow, Jennie Barry, Rosa Barugh, Martin Baumann, Gary Beckman, Antonella Benvegna, Adam Berg, Douwe-Klaas Bijl, Richard Bloomsdale, Linda Bolt, Charlÿe Bosgra, Rosa Bosio, John Bosman, Flo Boyko, Alexander Brandt, Stella Brecknell, Jill Breeze, Andrea Brewer, Polly Briten, Christian Brockhaus, Daniel Broid, Amanda Brooks, Nina Broude, Sergey Broude, John Brozak, Chris Burns, Kent Buse, Graham Butterfield **C** Serena Cantoni, Ryan Cardno, Kim Carey, Martinez Carlos, Sarah Cartwright, Bee Castellano, Gilles Castonguay, Matej Cebohin, Marco Cencini, Yvonne Cheung, Ali Chunara, Huseyin Cicek, Lisa Cole, Angela Coleman, Heather Collins, Leela Corman, Cynthia Corrow, Paul Corvi, Jodie Costello, Alexandre Couture Gagnon, Anne & Philippe Croquet-Zouridakis, Sarah Cross, Melissa Crumpler, Majatta Cunynghame, Jo Curran **D** Karin de Boer, Bianca de Vos, Bert D'Hooghe, Chris Derosa, Paula Dickson, Alison Diskin, James Down, Michael Doyle, Erik Du Pon, D Dubbin, Julien Dumoulin-Smith, Heather Dutton **E** Gary Edwards, Alexander Eichholz, Katherine Ellis, Sara Emery, Izi Ersonmez, Jasmine Evans, Michael Evans **F** Jackie Farquhar, Rob Farrington, Sophie Feather-Garner, Adam Federman, Alberta Ferligo, Lee Ferron, Gianni Filippi, Laura Fine-Morrison, Brendan Finn, Christopher Fox, Dyanne Francis, Sandra Frank, Amber Franklin, Gerry Fuller, Thomas Furniss **G** Freek Geldof, Stephanie Geller, Sandy Gibbs, Carmelita Görg, David Graham, Stefano Grando, James Grieve, Maxmilian Grillo, Arnold Guinto, Leif Jr Gulddal **H** Rana Haddad, Spence Halperin, Jane Hamilton, Dik Sinclair Harris, Diana Hartshorn, Sarah Hawkes, Tom Haythornthwaite, Rachel Heatley, Karl-Wilhelm Heinle, Mike Hill, Adele Hogg, Jenny Hope, Sonya Hope, Joe Horacek, Kieren Howard, John Howell **I** Tolga Ilgar, Klaus Inhuelsen, Karina Ioffee **J** Terry Jack, Anthony Jenkins, Savin Ven Johnson, Craig Johnston **K** Orhan Kalender, Susan Kambouris, Geoff Kelsall, Malcolm Kent, Madaline Keros, Nader Khalil, Kevin Kingma, George Kingston, Cigdem Kiray, Alan Kirschbaum, Ashely Knight, Burakhan Kocaman, Diana Koether, Kristian Kofoed, Lauren Koopman, Allison Koslen, Regi Kozma, Martina Kyselova **L** Sukhjit Lalli, Tess Lambourne, Lorinda Lange, Ashley Lee, Mark Lee, Mike Lee, Lionel Leo, Allan Levenberg, Bev Lewis, Brian Lewis, Lorna Lewis, David Locke, Steve Locke, Paolo Lorenzoni, Sam Lovell **M** Josh Mackenzie, Eldar Mamedov, Andre Marion, Francesca Marini, Ah Mcadam, Pi Mcadam, Amber Mcclure, Warren Mcculloch, Ruth Mcdonald, Steven Meiers, Val Menenberg, Rod Mepham, Gerald Meral, Corrie Meus, Jason Milburn, Craig Miller, Monika Moesbauer, Dennis Mogerman, Caroline Moulton Ratzki, Rita Mushinsky **N** Holly Nazar, Andronikos Nedos, James Newman, Ngegerd Nilsson, Jessica Norcin, Anissa Norman, Aidan Norton **O** Oezen Odag, Nida Ogutveren, Funda Ozan, Kutay Ozay, Kemal Ozkurd **P** Denis Pacquelet, Rolf Palmberg, Vish Patel, David Pawley, Jo Peeters, A Penwala, Johan Petersman, Sonia Petrich, Megan Philpot, Susan Pike, Vivian Pisano, Boizen Platon, Jim Pleyte, Jeffrey Polovina, Ben Potter, Hélène Potvin **R** Boyden Ralph, Chas Rannells, Julie Reynolds, Claudio Riccio, Greg Ritchie, Narelle Ritchie, Katie Robinson, Gulsah Robertson, Gina Robinson, Carmen Rodriguez, Joshua Rogers, Xavier Roman, Rami Rosenbaum, Annie Rousseau **S** Maria Sachocos, Melih Saglambasoglu, Emilio Salami, Brianne Salmon, Olivier Savary, Max Scherberger, Lauren Schlanger, Manuela Schliessner, Claudia Schnellinger, Siegfried Schwab, Nicholas Scull, Paul Seaver, Ramazan Serbest, Lori Shapiro, Akbar Sharfi, Trish Shea, Jenny Sheat, Timothy Silvers, Paul Simon, Ellen Sitton, Ben Skinner, Tom Smallman, Christine Smith, Colleen

Smith, Richard Speer, Sabrina Spies, Branislav Srdanovic, Aarthi Srinath, Robert Stanton, Sandra Stanway, Sarah Steegar, Margaret Steel, Sam Steele, Clifford Stein, Jozef Steis, Joanne Steuer, Stan Steward, Taryn Stewart, Jody Steyls, George Stockton, Lei Sun, Monique Sweep, Patricia Szobar **T** Lindsay Tabas, Kristina Täht, Nes Tarjan, Robert Tattersall, Susan Taylor, Outger Teerhuis, Anne Thompson, Judith Thompson, Ted Todd, Cristian Tolhuijsen, Müjde Tosyali, Agnes Toth, Duncan Townend, Edward Trower **U** Jayda Uras, Cagri Uyarer **V** Jeannette van Eekelen, Anja van Heelsum, Hanny van den Bergh, Frederiek van der Sluijs, Wim van der Sluijs, Ronald van Velzen, Joachim Von Loeben, Beryl Voss, Simon Vuuregge, Wendy Walsh, Tom Weaver, Edward Wendt, Michael Wenham, Nancy Wigglesworth, Jo Williams, Sue Willingham, Brian Willis, Alison Willmott, Katarzyna Winiarska, Gordon Winocur, Sarah Wolbert, Celena Wong, Nicola Woodcock, Michael Woodley, Mirjam Wouters **Y** Mary Yang, Karen Yeung, Natalia Yialelis, Mehmet Yildirim **Z** Thelma Zarb, David Zaring, Manuele Zunelli

ACKNOWLEDGMENTS
Many thanks to the following for the use of their content:

Globe on title page ©Mountain High Maps 1993 Digital Wisdom, Inc.

Internal photographs: p142 (#1) Robert Harding Picture Library Ltd/Alamy; p148 Images&Stories/ Alamy. All other photographs by Lonely Planet Images, and by Greg Elms p146, p147 (#2); Jeff Greenberg p141; Izzet Keribar p142 (#2), p143 (#3), p144, p145 (#2 & #3); Chris Mellor 147 (#3).

All images are the copyright of the photographers unless otherwise indicated. Many of the images in this guide are available for licensing from Lonely Planet Images: www.lonelyplanetimages.com.

BEHIND THE SCENES

Index

INDEX

000 Map pages
000 Photograph pages

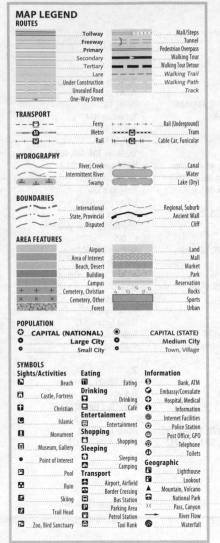

MAP LEGEND

ROUTES

Tollway	Mall/Steps
Freeway	Tunnel
Primary	Pedestrian Overpass
Secondary	Walking Tour
Tertiary	Walking Tour Detour
Lane	Walking Trail
Under Construction	Walking Path
Unsealed Road	Track
One-Way Street	

TRANSPORT

Ferry	Rail (Underground)
Metro	Tram
Rail	Cable Car, Funicular

HYDROGRAPHY

River, Creek	Canal
Intermittent River	Water
Swamp	Lake (Dry)

BOUNDARIES

International	Regional, Suburb
State, Provincial	Ancient Wall
Disputed	Cliff

AREA FEATURES

Airport	Land
Area of Interest	Mall
Beach, Desert	Market
Building	Park
Campus	Reservation
Cemetery, Christian	Rocks
Cemetery, Other	Sports
Forest	Urban

POPULATION

CAPITAL (NATIONAL)	CAPITAL (STATE)
Large City	Medium City
Small City	Town, Village

SYMBOLS

Sights/Activities	Eating	Information
Beach	Eating	Bank, ATM
Castle, Fortress	**Drinking**	Embassy/Consulate
Christian	Drinking	Hospital, Medical
Islamic	Café	Information
Monument	**Entertainment**	Internet Facilities
Museum, Gallery	Entertainment	Police Station
Point of Interest	**Shopping**	Post Office, GPO
Pool	Shopping	Telephone
Ruin	**Sleeping**	Toilets
Skiing	Sleeping	**Geographic**
Trail Head	Camping	Lighthouse
Zoo, Bird Sanctuary	**Transport**	Lookout
	Airport, Airfield	Mountain, Volcano
	Border Crossing	National Park
	Bus Station	Pass, Canyon
	Parking Area	River Flow
	Petrol Station	Waterfall
	Taxi Rank	

LONELY PLANET OFFICES

Australia
Head Office
Locked Bag 1, Footscray, Victoria 3011
☎ 03 8379 8000, fax 03 8379 8111
talk2us@lonelyplanet.com.au

USA
150 Linden St, Oakland, CA 94607
☎ 510 250 6400, toll free 800 275 8555
fax 510 893 8572
info@lonelyplanet.com

UK
2nd fl, 186 City Rd,
London EC1V 2NT
☎ 020 7106 2100, fax 020 7106 2101
go@lonelyplanet.co.uk

Published by Lonely Planet Publications Pty Ltd
ABN 36 005 607 983

© Lonely Planet Publications Pty Ltd 2009

© photographers as indicated 2009

Cover photograph: hot-air balloons over Göreme, Cappadocia, SIME/Schmid Reinhard/4Corners Images. Many of the images in this guide are available for licensing from Lonely Planet Images: www.lonelyplanetimages.com.

Printed by Hang Tai Printing Company.
Printed in China.

Mixed Sources
Product group from well-managed forests and other controlled sources
www.fsc.org Cert no. SGS-COC-005002
© 1996 Forest Stewardship Council

Although the authors and Lonely Planet have taken all reasonable care in preparing this book, we make no warranty about the accuracy or completeness of its content and, to the maximum extent permitted, disclaim all liability arising from its use.